CADOGAN

KT-166-944

Spain

Cadogan Guides
West End House, 11 Hills Place, London W1R 1AH, UK
guides@morrispub.co.uk

The Globe Pequot Press
6 Business Park Road, PO Box 833, Old Saybrook,
Connecticut 06475–0833

Copyright © Dana Facaros and Michael Pauls 1987, 1992, 1996, 1999
Illustrations © Alex Manolatos 1996

Design and cover illustration by Animage
Cover photographs (front and back) by Ellen Rooney
Maps © Cadogan Guides, drawn by Map Creation Ltd

Editorial Director: Vicki Ingle
Series Editor: Linda McQueen
Editor: Mary-Ann Gallagher
Updating: William Truini (Catalunya, Basque Lands, Navarra, La Rioja, Cantabria, Asturias, Galicia, Castilla y León, Barcelona); Alex Robinson (Andalucía and Extremadura); Nick Lyne (Madrid and Around Madrid, La Mancha); Annabel Skinner (Aragón and Valencia)
Proofreading: Mary Spicer Lambert
Indexing: Isobel McLean
Production: Book Production Services

A catalogue record for this book is available from the British Library
ISBN 1–86011–905–0

About the Authors

Dana Facaros and Michael Pauls have written over 20 books for Cadogan, including a guide to Northern Spain and one to Southern Spain. They have trailed an entourage of children, animals and assorted hangers-on all over Europe, but recently hung up their castanets in a shoreside cottage in southwest Ireland.

Acknowledgements

We would like to thank the many local, provincial and regional Spanish tourist offices who lent time and energy to this update. Also a big thanks to Kate and Victor for lending us their car, twice; to Carole and Bob for always being there; and to Mary-Ann for tying herself in knots to get this finished.

The publishers would like to thank all the updaters—Nick Lyne, Alex Robinson, Annabel Skinner, Willliam Truini (aided by Gloria Sallent, Gemma Ricona and Tom Randall)—for their cheerfulness, enthusiasm, patience and hard work.

Please help us to keep this guide up to date

We have done our best to ensure that the information in this guide is correct at the time of going to press. But places and facilities are constantly changing, and standards and prices in hotels and restaurants fluctuate. We would be delighted to receive any comments concerning existing entries or omissions. Authors of the best letters will receive a copy of the Cadogan Guide of their choice.

Contents

Maps

Introduction

Spain is a vivid country, one that catalyses the imagination. All of us, perhaps, carry around a certain picture of the particular Spain that once caught our fancy. It could be the Spain of blood and sand in the bullring, of medieval crusades and troubadours, or of Moorish gardens full of roses; the seed of it may have been planted by Cervantes or Hemingway, Gil Blas or Washington Irving. All of these Spains can be still be found if you seek them out, but they hardly exhaust the list of treasures and pleasures of this inexhaustible country. You must also see the lush valleys of the Atlantic coast, the snow-capped Pyrenees, the orange groves around Valencia, the weird dream landscapes of Old Castile. In between are 3000 castles, great cathedrals, gardens, villages, palaces, rare works of art, and cities so lively they bounce.

Another attraction is the Spaniards themselves. A remarkably lucid people, they are friendly, sane, enthusiastic, democratic in the widest sense of the word, and more awake than anyone in Europe—and not only because they regard going to bed before 3am as a kind of personal dishonour. They are in throes of creating something brand new, a novel kind of federal state—not a melting pot but a paella, in which each ingredient retains its integrity and flavour while enhancing the whole. To know Spain you must visit its seventeen autonomous regions, most of them born out of once independent kingdoms: the Galicians and Asturians, the Basques, Aragonese and Catalans, the Andalucíans and Riojans, and so on, all proud (and free now, since Franco) to express their differences in language, music, dance, cuisine, and traditions. Gone are the black and white, wrong and right days that lingered well past their sell-by date into the '70s. The Spain of the '90s comes in all hues. Paradoxes and contradictions abound and are not denied, but savoured like different plates of tapas.

Keep your eyes open. Spain is a subtler country than many people think, and reveals itself in surprising ways. You may see it in the moon reflected in a pool of the Alhambra, in the face of a Velázquez *infanta*, in a fond medieval jest like the cats and rats chiselled into the cloister in Tarragona, or in a lone eagle coasting over a strong castle in Extremadura. On a train travelling through a sparse Andalucían district in the spring, all at once your glance may take in more colour than you've ever seen: pink and white almond blossoms, oranges on the trees, red poppies and yellow daffodils along the track bed. In a second it will be gone, but you will have seen Spain.

We can't pretend to be opening up a new territory. Spain after all is Europe's biggest holiday playground, last year playing host to some 50 million foreign visitors. We suspect that many more who would like to go have been discouraged, thinking the tourist tide has spoiled it all. Nothing could be further from the truth. Spain is not the kind of place that would ever let such a trivial phenomenon make it change its ways.

Geography

Spain, by European standards, is an enormous chunk of territory, only marginally smaller than France and over twice the size of Great Britain. Americans may consider it as about four Pennsylvanias, with a basketful of Delawares thrown in. The 40 million Spaniards manage the world's 12th-biggest national economy, producing nearly as much as all of India.

The Pyrenees are not as lofty as most people think, but they are difficult to cross; there are only three reliable routes over. They divide the Iberian peninsula authoritatively from the rest of Europe, making it a kind of minor sub-continent, introverted and caught in its own strange destinies. To complete the isolation, more mountains hug the coast on three sides: the Cantabrian chain in the north, the Pénibetic chain in the south, including the Sierra Nevada with the highest peaks in Spain, and a string of low mountains in the regions of Catalunya and Valencia in the east. The ranges guard Spain like a castle wall; inside them is a high tableland, the *meseta*, broken by roughly parallel rivers and mountain ranges. The elevation of this plateau explains the difficult climate of the Spanish interior, chilly in winter and baked and bleached in summer. Madrid in the centre is one of the highest capitals in Europe.

Iberia naturally faces the Atlantic—a prime reason for its prominence in the Age of Discovery. Of its great rivers, only the Ebro (from which the Iberian peninsula takes its name) flows into the Mediterranean; the others meet the Atlantic, three of them through Portugal, the Duero, Tajo and Guadiana.

Spain is a harsh land. Nearly half its soil is unproductive or barren, and the brown, wrinkled hills of the central plateau in summer make a sight unique in Europe. Some parts of the south-east are nearly desert, while others, like the Huerta of Valencia and the Guadalquivir valley, are astoundingly fertile. Along the northern coast, Cantabria, Asturias, and Galicia display a well-tended countryside of forests and pasturelands as green as Ireland.

Travel

By Air

There is an astounding variety of flight options these days to Spain from the UK: **British Airways,** ✆ (0345) 222 111, operates direct services between Heathrow, Gatwick, Manchester Birmingham and Madrid, Barcelona, Bilbao (only Heathrow), Málaga, Murcia (only Gatwick), Valencia (only Gatwick) and Gibraltar. Spain's national airline, **Iberia,** ✆ (0171) 830 0011, operates on many of the same routes, and also offers direct services to Alicante, Santiago de Compostela, Jerez de la Frontera, Sevilla and the Canaries. Iberia's subsidiary **Aviaco,** ✆ (0171) 830 0011, flies non-stop to Oviedo from London Stanstead and also to San Sebastián, Pamplona, Vitoria, Santander, A Coruña and Vigo from Madrid and Barcelona. **Monarch Airlines,** ✆ (01582) 398333, flies from Luton to Alicante and Málaga, with increased frequency in summer. Málaga is also served by **British Midland Airways,** ✆ (0345) 554554, with a weekly service from East Midlands Airport.

A number of low-cost airlines have begun operating in the UK in recent years offering scheduled flights at near-charter prices. **Go,** ✆ 0345 605 4321 (*www.go-fly.com*), a subsidiary of British Airways, offers return flights from Stanstead to Madrid and Barcelona for as little as £80 and to Málaga for £120. Both **easyJet,** ✆ 0870 600 0000 (*www.easyjet.com*), and **Debonair,** ✆ 0541 500 300, fly from Luton to Barcelona and Madrid. Their starting prices are, respectively, £88 and £100. EasyJet also flies from Liverpool to Málaga. Note that the cheapest prices are only available if booked well in advance. Last minute fares are, in fact, not much cheaper than those of the major carriers.

charter flights

These can be incredibly cheap, and offer the added advantage of departing from local airports. Companies such as **Thomson, Airtours** and **Unijet** can offer return flights from as little £80. Check out your local economy agent, the Sunday papers and TV Teletext. In London, look in the *Evening Standard* and *Time Out.* Remember, there are no refunds for missed flights—most travel agencies sell insurance, so that you don't lose all your money if you become ill.

discount and youth travel specialists

Campus Travel, 52 Grosvenor Gardens, SW1, ✆ (0171) 730 3402 or find their web-site at *www.campustravel.co.uk.*

STA, 86 Old Brompton Rd, London SW7, or 117 Euston Rd, London NW1, ✆ (0171) 937 9921

By Sea

Brittany Ferries, ✆ (0990) 360360, operates between Plymouth and Santander (Portsmouth and Santander between November and March). Prices for vehicles vary according to size and season—it's most expensive from 28 June–1 September: an adult foot passenger fare costs £53–846 one way; one adult with a vehicle costs £162–279 depending on the length and type of vehicle; children from 4–13 go for half-price, under 4s free. These fares do not include on-board accommodation, which is strongly recommended; in the high season, this can cost anything from £6 for a simple Pullman seat to £120+ for a deluxe twin-berth cabin. The 24–27 hour crossing is made twice a week and can be rough.

P&O European Ferries, ✆ (0990) 980 980, operates the Portsmouth–Bilbao route with crossings twice weekly. Prices are somewhat variable: getting a car to Bilbao and back can cost anything from £160 to £525, with an additional £95–150 per person; children pay half fare. Cabins cost an additional £70–150. P&O offer a special discount rate for a one-week return trip, and 'Mini-Breaks' at £250–460 for a car and up to five passengers.

By Rail

London to Barcelona is a full day trip, changing trains in Paris and at Port Bou/San Sebastián/La Tour de Carol or Toulouse.

The TGV service from Paris to Bordeaux can cut some hours off the trip if the schedule works right for you. Time can also be saved by taking the Eurostar (✆ 0990 186186) through the Channel Tunnel to Paris. Services are frequent and take just under three hours from London (Waterloo) to Paris (Gare du Nord). Fares are lower if booked at least 14 days in advance.

If you've been resident in Europe for the past 6 months and are under 26, you might like to consider an **InterRail Pass**, available from most travel agents, which gives you a month of Europe-wide rail travel for £509, as well as half-price discounts on Channel crossings and ferries to Morocco, where the pass is also valid. Note that neither InterRail nor EurRail passes are valid on Spain's numerous narrow-gauge (FEVE) lines.

Bookings: Rail tickets to Spain from England or vice versa, can be obtained from **British Rail European Travel Centre**, Victoria Station, London SW1, ✆ (0990) 848 848 or **Rail Europe Travel Centre**, 179 Piccadilly, London W1A, ✆ (0990) 300 003. Take your passport. Tickets for local Spanish services can be obtained from certain UK travel agents.

By Bus or Coach

One major company, **Eurolines**, offers departures several times a week in the summer (once a week out of season) from London to Spain, along the east coast as far as Alicante, or to Algeciras via San Sebastián, Burgos, Madrid, Córdoba, Granada and Málaga. Journey times are 24 hours to Barcelona, 33 hours to Alicante, 27 to Madrid, 34 to Málaga and 37 to Algeciras. Single fares are about £79; return fares around £143. Peak season fares between 22 July and 4 September are slightly higher. There are discounts for anyone under 26, senior citizens and children under 12. In the summer, the coach is the best bargain for anyone over 26; off-season you'll probably find a cheaper charter flight.

Information and booking: Eurolines, 52 Grosvenor Gardens, London SW1, ✆ (0171) 730 8235; National Express, ✆ (0990) 808080.

By Car

From the UK via France you have a choice of routes. Ferries from Portsmouth cross to Cherbourg, Caen, Le Havre and St Malo. From any of these ports the most direct route takes you to Bordeaux, down the western coast of France to the border at Irún, and on to San Sebastián, Burgos and Madrid. An alternative route is Paris to Perpignan, crossing the border at the Mediterranean side of the Pyrenees, then along the coast to Barcelona. Both routes take an average of a 1½ days' steady driving. You may find it more convenient and less tiring to try the ferry from Plymouth to Santander (*see* above), which cuts out driving through France and saves expensive *autoroute* tolls.

By Air

There are numerous carriers that serve Spain. Most regular flights from the US or Canada are to Madrid or Barcelona. **Iberia**, the national airline, offers fly-drive deals and discounts. From anywhere in the US, you can use Iberia's toll-free line ✆ (800) 772 4642.

Iberia Offices in the USA and Canada

USA	655 Madison Avenue, New York, NY 10022, ✆ (212) 644 8797
	1725 K. Street NW, Washington DC 20006, ✆ (202) 293 6970
	4227 Wilshire Boulevard, 3209, Los Angeles, CA ✆ (323) 692 2965
Canada	102 Bloor Street West, Toronto, M5S 1M8, ✆ (416) 964 6625
	2020 University Street, Montreal, H3A 2A5, ✆ (514) 849 3352

Other Airlines with Direct Routes to Spain

American Airlines	toll-free ✆ (800) 433 7300
Continental Airlines	toll-free ✆ (800) 231 0856
Delta	toll free ✆ (800) 241 4141
United Airlines	toll-free ✆ (800) 538 2929
Air Canada	toll-free ✆ (800) 268 7240

Other Airlines with Routes via Europe

British Airways	toll-free ✆ (800) 247 9297
KLM	toll-free ✆ (800) 777 5553
Lufthansa	toll-free ✆ (800) 645 3880
TAP Air Portugal	toll-free ✆ (800) 221 7370
Virgin Atlantic	toll-free ✆ (800) 862 8621

charter flights

Currently a charter from New York to Madrid varies between $400–700 depending on the season. You may want to weigh this against the current transatlantic fares to London, where in most cases you can get a low-cost flight to Spain departing within a day or two of your arrival. The Sunday *New York Times* has the most listings.

Some Major Charter Companies and Consolidators

Council Charters: 205 East 42nd Street, New York, NY 10017, toll-free ✆ (800) 800 8222; uses Air Europa

Spanish Heritage Tours: 116–47 Queens Blvd, Forest Hills, NY 11375, ✆ (718) 520 1300; uses Air Europa

TFI: 34 West 32nd Street, New York, NY 10001, ✆ (212) 736 1140, toll-free ✆ (800) 745 8000

The American **EurRail Pass**, which must be purchased before you leave the States, is a good deal only if you plan to use the trains every day in Spain and elsewhere—though it's not valid in the UK, Morocco or countries outside the European Union. A month of travel is $623 for those under 26; those over 26 can get a 15-day pass for $554, a 21-day pass for $718 or a month for $890. **Contact**: CIT Tours, 342 Madison Avenue, Suite 207, New York 10173, ✆ (212) 697 2100, or toll-free ✆ (800) 248 7245. In Spain you'll have to pay supplements for any kind of express train and the EurRail pass is not valid on Spain's numerous narrow-gauge (FEVE) lines.

Specialist Tour Operators

The very helpful **Spanish Tourist Office** is located at 22–23 Manchester Square, London W1M 5AP, ✆ (0171) 486 8077, ✉ (0171) 486 8034. They stock brochures and leaflets on most main towns and cities in Spain as well as information on a variety of holiday options.

General

Cadogan Travel: Cadogan House, 9–10 Portland Street, Southampton SO14 7EB, ✆ (01703) 828300. Holidays in Gibraltar, Southern Spain and Morocco.

Kirker Holidays: 3 New Concordia Wharf, Mill Street, London SE1 2BB, ✆ (0171) 231 3333. Tailor-made itineraries in Madrid, Barcelona, Sevilla and rural Andalucía.

Palmer & Parker: The Beacon, Penn, Buckinghamshire HP10 8ND, ✆ (01494) 815411. Self-catering villa holidays to southern Spain.

Spanish Chapters: 102 St John's Wood Terrace, London NW8 6PL, ✆ (0171) 722 9560. Luxury villas in Andalucía and the Balearics.

Unicorn Holidays Ltd: 2 Place Farm, Wheathampstead, Hertfordshire AL4 8SB, ✆ (01582) 834400. Fly-drive and self-drive touring holidays featuring the *paradores* .

Cultural Tours

Martin Randall: 10 Barley Mow Passage, London W4 4PH, ✆ (0181) 742 3355. Lecturer-accompanied cultural tours throughout Spain.

Page & Moy Ltd: 136–140 London Road, Leicester LE2 1EN, ✆ (0116) 250 7000. Cultural guided tours throughout Spain.

Plantagenet Tours: 85 The Grove, Moordown, Bournemouth BH9 2TY, ✆ (01202) 521895. Historical tours of medieval Andalucía and of Castile, León, Asturias and Galicia.

Saga Holidays (Discover Europe): The Saga Building, Middelburg Square, Folkestone, Kent CT20 1AZ, ✆ (01303) 711111. Guided cultural coach tours for the over 50s.

Specialtours Ltd: 81a Elizabeth Street, London SW1W 9PG, ✆ (0171) 730 2297. Fully escorted cultural tours to major cities and sites throughout Spain.

Abercrombie & Kent Travel Ltd: Sloane Square House, Holbein Place, London SW1W 8NS, ✆ (0171) 730 9600. Walking tours in Andalucía.

Alternative Travel Group: 69–71 Banbury Road, Oxford OX2 6PE, ✆ (01865) 310399. Pilgrimage to Santiago de Compostela; walking tours of Andalucía, Catalunya, La Rioja.

Explore Worldwide Ltd: 1 Frederick Street, Aldershot, Hants GU11 1LQ, ✆ (01252) 344161. Small-group treks in the Picos de Europa, Sierra Nevada and Cazorla regions.

Ramblers Holidays: Box 43, Welwyn Garden City, Herts AL8 6PQ, ✆ (01707) 331133. Walking and trekking tours in rural Spain.

Waymark Holidays: 44 Windsor Road, Slough, SL1 2EJ, ✆ (01753) 516 477. Guided walks along the Camino de Santiago.

Special Interest Holidays

Andante Travel: Grange Cottage, Winterbourne Dauntsey, Salisbury SP4 6ER, ✆ (01980) 610555. Historical study tours of Roman Spain and Altamira cave paintings.

Arblaster & Clarke Wine Tours: Clarke House, The Green, West Liss, Hants GU33 6JQ, ✆ (01730) 893344. Wine tours to the Rioja, Navarra, Jerez and Penedes regions.

Bird Holidays: Mantra WGT Ltd, 115–117 Otley Road, Guiseley, Leeds LS20 8AF, ✆ (01943) 873465. Bird-watching holidays in the Coto Doñana National Park (Huelva).

Cox & Kings Travel Ltd: Gordon House, 10 Greencoat Place, London SW1P 1PH, ✆ (0171) 873 5005. Botanical tours in southern Spain; luxury train tour of Andalucía.

Dolphin Safari: Sheppard's Marina, Waterport, Gibraltar, ✆ from outside Spain (350) 71914, from Spain, ✆ (9567) 71914. Arranges dolphin-spotting trips May–October.

Safari Andalucia: Apartado 20, 29480 Gaucín (Málaga), ✆ 95 215 1148. Walking holidays in the Serranía de Ronda with tented camp and hunting lodge accommodation.

Entry Formalities

Passports and Visas

Visitors from the UK must present a valid passport. If you intend staying for more than 3 months, you must report to the Foreign Nationals Office (*Oficina de Extranjeros*) at the local police station and apply for a community resident's card (*tarjeta de residente comunitario*). If you fly to Gibraltar you'll have no trouble getting into Spain.

Holders of **US** or **Canadian** passports can enter Spain for up to 90 days without a visa; holders of **Australian** or **New Zealand** passports need a visa, available from any Spanish consulate. For **Gibraltar** there are no extra visa requirements for US citizens, and EU nationals have the same rights and status as in the UK.

Spanish Consulates

Canada:	1 West Mount Square, 1456 Montreal, H3Z 2P9, ✆ (514) 935 5235
	1200 Bay Street, Toronto, Ontario M5R 2A5, ✆ (416) 967 4949
Ireland:	17a Merlyn Park, Ballsbridge, Dublin 4, ✆ (1) 691 640
UK:	20 Draycott Place, London SW3 2RZ, ✆ (0171) 589 8989
	63 North Castle Street, Edinburgh EH2 3LJ, ✆ (0131) 220 1483
USA:	180 North Michigan Avenue, Chicago, IL 60601, ✆ (312) 782 4588
	6300 Wilshire Blvd, Los Angeles, CA 90048, ✆ (305) 446 5511
	150 East 58th Street, New York, NY 10155, ✆ (212) 355 4090
	2700 15th Street NW, Washington, DC 20009, ✆ (206) 265 0190

Customs

Customs are usually polite and easy to get through—unless you come through Morocco, when they'll search through everything you own. EU limits of duty free are 1 litre spirits or 2 litres liquors (port, sherry or champagne) plus 2 litres of wine and 200 cigarettes. Much larger quantities, bought locally and provided you are travelling between EU countries (up to 10 litres spirits, 90 litres wine, 110 litres beer), can be taken through customs if you can prove that they are for private consumption only. If coming from the UK or the USA, don't bother to pick up any duty-free alcohol—it's cheaper on the supermarket shelves in Spain.

Getting Around

By Air

Internal flights in Spain are on Iberia, Aviaco, Binter and Air Europa. These are nationally run and all operate under the Iberia Group umbrella, almost always sharing the same office in the cities. There are also several other carriers on national routes, such as the Alitalia service between Málaga and Barcelona. Prices are inexpensive compared to most of Europe, and if you shop around and are willing to travel at night on slow days you can pick up some bargains.

Iberia/Aviaco Offices in Spain

Barcelona:	Psg. de Gràcia 30, ✆ 93 301 6800 (domestic), ✆ 93 302 7656 (international)
Bilbao:	Calle Ercilla 20, ✆ 94 424 8639, Sondika Airport, ✆ 94 424 1935
A Coruña:	Calle Teresa Herrera 1, ✆ 981 22 5746
Madrid:	Velázquez 130, ✆ 91 411 1011 (domestic), ✆ 91 329 4553 (international)
Málaga:	Molina Larios 13, ✆ 95 213 6147
San Sebastián:	Bengoetxea 3, ✆ 94 342 3586
Sevilla:	Almirante Lobo 2, ✆ 95 422 8901
Valencia:	Paz 14, ✆ 96 352 7552

The *Trasmediterránea* line operates services from the Spanish mainland to the Balearic Islands, North Africa and the Canary Islands.

In **Málaga**, Estación Marítima, 29016, ✆ 95 222 4393. **UK Agents:** Southern Ferries, 179 Piccadilly, London W1V 9DB, ✆ (0171) 491 4968.

By Rail

If you're using public transport, there is usually an even choice between the bus and train. The slight difference in price usually favours the train, while buses are usually a bit faster. Democracy in Spain has made the trains run on time, but western Europe's most eccentric railway, **RENFE**, still has a way to go. The problem isn't the trains themselves—they're almost always clean and comfortable, and do their best to keep to schedule—but the new efficient RENFE remains so phenomenally complex it will foul up your plans at least once if you spend much time in Spain.

To start with there are no fewer than 13 varieties of train, from the luxury **TEE** (Trans-Europe Express) to the excruciating *semidirecto* and *ferrobús*. Watch out for these; they stop at every conceivable hamlet to deliver mail. The best are the **Talgo** trains, speedy and stylish beasts in gleaming stainless steel, designed and built entirely in Spain; the Spaniards are justifiably very proud of them. Every variety of train has different services and a different price. RENFE ticket people and conductors can't always get them straight, and confusion is rampant. Prices are never consistent. There are discounts for children (under 4 years old, free; 4–12 pay 50 per cent), large families, senior citizens (50 per cent) and regular travellers, and 25 per cent discounts on *Días Azules* ('blue days') for round trip tickets only. 'Blue days' are posted in the RENFE calendars in every station—really almost every day is a 'blue day'. Interpretations of the rules for these discounts differ from one ticket-window to the next, and you may care to undertake protracted negotiations like the Spaniards do. There is a discount pass for people under 26, the *tarjeta joven*, and BIGE or BIJ youth fares are available from TIVE offices in the large cities. There is also a *tarjeta turística*, similar to the EurRail pass, available to anyone resident outside Spain, with unlimited travel for periods of 8, 15 or 22 days (price depending on period), but again, it's not worth it unless you intend to do extensive travelling.

Every city has a **RENFE travel office** in the centre, and you can make good use of these for information and tickets. Always buy tickets in advance if you can. Don't rely on the list of trains posted; always ask at the station or travel office. Fares average 500 pts for every 100km (63 miles)—750 pts first class—but there are supplements on the faster trains that can raise the price by as much as 80 per cent.

RENFE has plenty of services you'll never hear about—like car transport to all parts of Spain. If you plan to do a lot of riding on the rails, buy the *Guía RENFE*, an indispensable government publication with all the schedules, tariffs, and information, available for a pittance from any station newsagent. It's heavy, but you can always tear out the pages you need. To add to the confusion Spain has two narrow-gauge railway lines which operate independently of RENFE: these are **FEVE**, which has tracks along the north coast of Spain connecting Bilbao to Oviedo via Santander, as well as a few lines on the east coast (FGV in Valencia); and in Euskadi, the **Eusko Trenbideak** (Basque Railways) connects Bilbao and San Sebastián by way of Zarautz and Zumaya. Both these lines show off rural Spanish life and scenery at their best, but are slow, stop everywhere and cost more than the bus.

You'll also come across *cercanías*, urban or suburban lines rather like the metro, linking places such as Barcelona with its outlying suburbs and beaches, and Málaga with its airport, Torremolinos and Fuengirola.

rail excursions

RENFE has inaugurated a series of special trains especially designed to attract tourists. The **Transcantábrica** takes in some of the loveliest parts of northern Spain, including the Picos de Europa (for more information contact RENFE direct) while in Southern Spain the **Al-Andalus Expreso** takes its passengers on a luxury tour from Sevilla to Córdoba, Granada, Málaga and Jerez. Although expensive, these trips are memorable experiences.

Contacts for Al-Andalus Expreso

Spain: Al-Andalus Iberrail, C/Capitán Haya 55, Madrid 28020, ✆ 91 571 5815
UK: Cox & King's Travel Ltd, Gordon House, 10 Green Coat Place, London SW1P 1PH, ✆ (0171) 873 5000.
USA: Marketing Ahead Inc, 433 Fifth Avenue, New York, NY 10016, ✆ (212) 686 9213.

By Bus

With literally hundreds of companies providing services over Spain, expect confusion. Not all cities have bus stations; in some, like Zaragoza or Bilbao, there may be a dozen little offices spread around town for each firm. Like the trains, buses are cheap by northern European standards but no memorable bargain; if you're travelling on the cheap you'll find that transportation is your biggest expense. Usually, whether you go by train or bus will depend on simple convenience: in some places the train station is far from the centre, in others the bus station is. Small towns and villages can normally be reached by bus only through their provincial capitals. And in the middle of Spain, it's almost impossible to get from one town to another without going through Madrid. Buses are usually clean and dependable. Tourist information offices are the best sources of information. They almost always know every route and schedule.

By City Bus and Taxi

Every Spanish city has a perfectly adequate system of public transportation. You won't need to make much use of it, though, for in almost every city except Madrid and Barcelona, all attractions are within walking distance of each other. City buses usually cost 120 pts, and if you intend to use them often there are books of tickets called *abonamientos* or *bono-Bus* or *tarjeta* cards to punch on entry, available at reduced rates from tobacco shops. Bus drivers will give change if you don't have the correct amount (within reason; don't give them a 1000-pts note). In many cities the bus's entire route will be displayed on the signs at each stop (*parada*). And don't take it for granted that the bus will stop just because you are waiting—nearly every stop apart from the terminus seems to be a request stop.

Taxis are still cheap enough for the Spaniards to use them regularly on their shopping trips. The average fare for a ride within a city will be 700–1000 pts. Taxis are metered, and the drivers are usually quite honest; they are entitled to certain surcharges (for luggage, night or holiday trips, to the train or airport, etc.) and if you cross the city limits they can usually charge double the fare shown. It's rarely hard to hail a cab from the street, and there will always be a few around the stations. If you get stuck where there are none, or in a small village, call information for the number of a radio taxi.

By Car

This is certainly the most convenient way of getting about, and often the most pleasurable. However, there are no petrol concessions or coupons for tourists. Another problem is that only a few hotels—the more expensive ones—have garages or any sort of parking. And in cities, parking is always difficult, although a useful tip to remember is that space which appears to be private—e.g. underground car parks of apartment blocks and offices—is often public, and rates are usually modest. Spain's highway network is adequate, usually in good repair, and sometimes impressive. The system of *autovías* (motorways) is constantly expanding. Spanish road building is remarkable for its speed if not always its durability. Be warned, the **tolls** on Spanish motorways are high.

To drive in Spain you'll need to pick up a pink EU driving licence or an **International Driver's Licence**, available through the AA or RAC in the UK, or any auto club in the USA, and a **Green Card** providing limited liability insurance. In some parts of Spain, particularly away from the centres, local police may not recognize the EU Driving licence so you are advised to take an IDP in any case. Though it's not compulsory, you are also advised to extend your motor insurance to include a **bail bond**. Should you be unfortunate enough to have an accident, without a bail bond your car will be impounded and you are likely to find yourself in jail for the night. Seat belts are mandatory. The speed limit is 100km (62 miles) per hour on national highways, unless otherwise marked, and 120km (75 miles) per hour on motorways. Drive with the utmost care at all times—having an accident will bring you untold headaches, and to make matters worse, many Spaniards drive without insurance

Hitchhiking is likely to involve a long, hot wait. Drivers in Spain are rarely inclined to give lifts and temperatures in midsummer can soar; few Spaniards ever hitchhike.

car rental

This is moderately cheaper than elsewhere in Europe. The big international companies are the most expensive but ATESA, the government-owned Spanish firm, is cheaper. Prices for the smallest cars begin at about £80 per week with unlimited mileage, but insurance adds considerably to the costs. Small local firms can sometimes offer a better deal, but these should be treated with some caution. If you want to book ahead from the **UK** or **Ireland**, contact your chosen airline or one of the following: **Avis**, ☎ (0181) 848 8733, **Hertz**, ☎ (0990) 996699, **Eurodollar**, ☎ (01895) 233 300, **Car Rental Direct**, ☎ (0171) 625 7766. From **North America**, try **Avis**, ☎ (1 800) 331 1084, **Hertz**, ☎ (1 800) 654 3001, Hertz (Canada) ☎ (1 800) 263 0600.

Local firms also rent **mopeds** and **bicycles**, especially in tourist areas.

Practical A–Z

Children

Spaniards love children, and they'll welcome yours almost everywhere. Baby foods, etc. are widely available, but don't expect to find babysitters except at the really smart hotels; Spaniards always take their children with them, even if they're up till 4am. Nor are there many special amusements for kids, though these are beginning to spring up with Spain's new prosperity, for better or worse; traditionally Spaniards never thought of their children as separate little creatures who ought to be amused. Ask at a local tourist office for a list of attractions in its area geared towards children.

Climate and When to Go

Spain is hot and sunny in the summer, brisk and sunny in the winter, with little variation among the regions except in the matter of rainfall. The northern coast, especially Euskadi and Galicia, fairly drowns all year—that's why it's so green. Rain is scarce nearly everywhere else, and every locality brags in its brochures about so many 'hours of guaranteed sunshine' each year. Statistically, the champion for the best holiday climate is Alicante, with Europe's warmest winter temperatures and hardly any rain, but most of the southern and eastern coasts are nearly as good.

Spring and autumn are the best times to visit, by far; the winter can be pleasant, though damp and chill in the north while Teruel and Soria provinces traditionally have the worst winter climate.

The chart below shows the highest and lowest temperatures in °C (°F) you're likely to encounter in each season.

Seasonal temperatures in °C (°F)

	Jan		April		July		Oct	
	max	min	max	min	max	min	max	min
Madrid	17 (63)	-8 (18)	27 (80)	10 (52)	39 (102)	12 (53)	29 (84)	0 (32)
Barcelona	17 (63)	-7 (19)	25 (77)	7 (44)	33 (91)	16 (61)	24 (75)	10 (50)
San Sebastián	15 (59)	-10 (14)	27 (80)	5 (41)	34 (93)	14 (57)	24 (75)	8 (46)
Alicante	21 (71)	-2 (36)	31 (88)	7 (44)	34 (93)	17 (63)	29 (84)	6 (42)
Sevilla	20 (68)	-4 (25)	31 (88)	4 (39)	35 (95)	21 (69)	31 (88)	8 (46)

Average monthly rainfall in mm (in.)

	Jan	April	July	Oct
Madrid	56 (2)	48 (2)	0 (0)	9 (0)
Barcelona	105 (4)	38 (2)	21 (1)	80 (3)
San Sebastián	142 (6)	84 (3)	92 (4)	142 (6)
A Coruña	125 (5)	78 (3)	35 (1)	135 (5)
Alicante	11 (0)	32 (1)	1 (0)	19 (1)
Sevilla	99 (4)	80 (3)	0 (0)	37 (2)

Disabled Travellers

Facilities for disabled travellers are limited within Spain and public transport is not particularly wheelchair-friendly, though RENFE usually provides wheelchairs at main city stations. You are advised to contact the Spanish Tourist Office, which has compiled a two-page fact sheet and can give general information on accessible accommodation, or any of the organizations that specifically provide services to people with disabilities.

Some Specialist Organizations in Spain

ONCE (Organización Nacional de Ciegos de España), Paseo de la Castellana 95, Planta 28, Madrid, ✆ 91 597 47 27, is the Spanish association for blind people.

ECOM, Gran Via de les Corts Catalanas 562 Principal, Barcelona, ✆ 934 51 55 50, the federation of private Spanish organizations offering services for disabled people.

Some Specialist Organizations in the UK

Holiday Care Service, 2nd Floor, Imperial Buildings, Victoria Road, Horley, Surrey RH6 9HW, ✆ (01293) 774 535, for travel information and details of accessible accommodation and care holidays. All sites have been visited and assessed by Holiday Care representatives.

RADAR (The Royal Association for Disability and Rehabilitation), Unit 12, City Forum, 250 City Road, London EC1V 8AF, ✆ (0171) 250 3222, has a wide range of travel information.

Royal National Institute for the Blind, 224 Great Portland Street, London W15 5TB, ✆ (0171) 388 1266. Its mobility unit offers a 'Plane Easy' audio-cassette which advises blind people on travelling by plane. It will also advise on accommodation.

Some Specialist Organizations in the USA

American Foundation for the Blind, 15 West 16th Street, New York, NY 10011, ✆ (212) 620 2000; toll free ✆ 800 232 5463.

Federation of the Handicapped, 211 West 14th Street, New York, NY 10011, ✆ (212) 747 4262. Organizes summer tours for members; there is a nominal annual fee.

Mobility International USA, PO Box 3551, Eugene, OR 97403, ✆ (503) 343 1248, offers a service similar to that of its sister organization in the UK.

SATD (Society for the Advancement of Travel for the Disabled), Suite 610, 347 5th Avenue, New York, NY 10016, ✆ (212) 447 7284, offers advice on all aspects of travel for the disabled.

Electricity

Current is 225 AC or 220 V, the same as most of Europe. Americans will need converters, and the British will need two-pin adapters for the different plugs. If you plan to stay in the less expensive *hostales*, it may be better to leave your gadgets at home. Some corners of Spain, even some big cities, have pockets of exotic voltage—150 V for example—guaranteeing a brief display of fireworks. Big hotels have the standard current.

Embassies and Consulates

Australia	Paseo de la Castellana 143, Madrid, ℂ 91 579 04 28.
	Gran Vía Carles III 98, Barcelona, ℂ 93 330 94 96.
Canada	Núñez de Balboa 35, Madrid, ℂ 91 431 43 00.
	Vía Augusta 125, Barcelona, ℂ 93 209 06 34.
Ireland	Claudio Coello 73, Madrid, ℂ 91 576 35 00.
	Gran Vía Carles III 94, Barcelona, ℂ 93 330 96 52.
New Zealand	Plaza de la Lealtad 2, Madrid, ℂ 91 523 02 26.
	Trav. de Gràcia 64, Barcelona, ℂ 93 209 03 99.
UK	Calle de Fernando el Santo 16, Madrid, ℂ 91 319 02 00.
	Avda. Diagonal 447, Barcelona, ℂ 93 419 90 44.
	Gibraltar: contact the Government Secretariat for consular enquiries at 6 Convent Place, ℂ (350) 70071.
USA	Calle Serrano 75, Madrid, ℂ 91 577 40 00.
	Passeig de la Reina Elisenda 23, Barcelona, ℂ 93 280 22 27.

Festivals

One of the most spiritually deadening aspects of Francoism was the banning of many local and regional fiestas. These are now celebrated with gusto, and if you can arrange your itinerary to include one or two you'll be guaranteeing an unforgettable holiday. Besides those listed below, there are literally thousands of others, and new ones spring up all the time.

The big holidays celebrated throughout Spain are *Corpus Cristi* in late May; Holy Week (*Semana Santa*), the week preceding Easter; 15 August, the Assumption of the Virgin and 25 July, the feast day of Spain's patron, Santiago. No matter where you are there are bound to be fireworks or processions on these dates. Do note, however, that dates for most festivals tend to be fluid, flowing towards the nearest weekend; if the actual date falls on a Thursday or a Tuesday, Spaniards 'bridge' the fiesta with the weekend to create a four-day whoopee. If there's a fiesta you want to attend, check the date at the tourist office in advance.

Many village patronal fiestas feature *romerías* (pilgrimages) up to a venerated shrine. Getting there is half the fun, with everyone in local costume, riding on horseback or driving covered wagons full of picnic supplies. Music, dancing, food, wine and fireworks are all necessary ingredients of a proper fiesta, while the bigger ones often include bullfights, funfairs, circuses and competitions. In Extremadura, and especially in the Basque lands and Navarra, summer fiestas often feature a loose bull or two stampeding through the streets—an *encierro*. 'Giants' (3.5m tall dummies of Ferdinand and Isabel and a Moor) and 'fat-heads' (comical or grotesque caricatures) pirouette through the throngs and tease the children.

January

First week	**Betanzos** (A Coruña): huge livestock fair.
	Granada: commemoration of the city's capture by the Catholic kings.
	Bainoa (Pontevedra) and **Malaga:** epiphany parade of *Los Reyes Magos* (Three Wise Men).
Third week	**Villanova de Arousa** (Pontevedra): San Mauro, big fiesta with fireworks. **San Sebastián**'s *Tamborrada*: marches of the Basque pipe-and-drum corps; **Igualada,** near Barcelona: Fiesta de San Antonio Abad.
End Jan	**Ituren** and **Zubieta** (Navarra): dances of the *ioaldunak* with pointed hats, fur vests and big bells. **Villafranca del Bierzo** (León): San Tirso, with dances and the burning of papier maché *falla.*

February

First weekend	**Bocairente** near Valencia: mock battles between Moors and Christians, and fireworks; **Almonacio del Marquesado** (Cuenca) celebrates *La Endiablada,* a religious rite of pre-Christian origin featuring day-long dances and processions of 'devils' wearing floral costumes and heavy metal bells; and **Zamarramala** outside Segovia: a very ancient custom where the 'mayoresses', the ladies of the village, take over for a day.
Mid-Feb	*Carnaval* is celebrated throughout Spain. **Cádiz** has perhaps the best in the country, and certainly the oldest: parades, masquerades, music and fireworks in abundance. Other lively celebrations are held at **Ciudad Rodrigo,** with lots of bull action on the nearby ranches, in the city streets and *plazas de toros,* and at **Solsona,** near Lleída, which features the explosive 'marriage of the mad giant'.
Lent	**Asturias** puts on the biggest show in the northwest in the week before Lent: at **Avilés** on Saturday and Tuesday, at **Gijón** on Monday; and in **Oviedo** on Tuesday, or Mardi Gras, the day before Ash Wednesday. During Lent there are Passion Play performances at **Ulldecona** (Tarragona), **Cervera** and **Esparraguera** (Barcelona). From the third Saturday in Lent until the fourth Sunday, **Castellón de la Plana** celebrates the *Fiestas de la Magdalena* with parades, night processions and pilgrimages.

March

15–19	**Valencia**'s *Las Fallas*: one of Spain's great fiestas, with the world's gaudiest bonfires and the best fireworks west of China (*see* p.162).
Sat before Palm Sunday	**Vic**'s *Mercat del Ram*: with palm fronds on sale, contests, demonstrations and the choosing of a palm queen.

Semana Santa	The most important celebrations are in **Sevilla**, with over 100 processions, broken by the singing of *saetas* (weird laments); **Cuenca**'s comes with a week-long festival of religious music; **Murcia** has the most charming *pasos*. On the Saturday of *Semana Santa*, **Chinchón** puts on a dramatic re-enactment of the Passion in the village's Plaza Mayor. Good Friday is celebrated with stark processions in **Bercianos de Aliste** (Zamora); Holy Thursday, by the medieval Dance of Death in **Verges**.
Easter week	Festivities continue in **Murcia** with Tuesday's *Bando de la Huerta* (a procession of floats dedicated to local agricultural products), jazz concerts, and on Saturday, the *Entierro de la Sardina* (the Burial of the Sardine) and great fireworks displays. In **Avilés** (Asturias), Easter and Easter Monday are celebrated with the **Fiesta del Bollo**, with folklore groups, cake eating and sailing regattas.

April

First Sun	**San Vicente de la Barquera**'s *La Folía*, where the sailors transport an after Easter image of the Virgin in an illuminated maritime procession.
23	**Barcelona**: St Jordi's day, exchange of books and roses. Around the same time **Alcoy** (Valencia) has the best of the 'battles' between Moors and Christians with pageantry, fireworks and great costumes.
Last week	**Sevilla**'s *Feria de Abril*: originally a horse-fair, now grown into the greatest festival of Andalucía. Costumed parades of the gentry in fine carriages, lots of flamenco, bullfights and drinking. **Andújar** (Jaén) hosts the *Romería de la Virgin de la Cabeza*, a pilgrimage from all over Andalucía which culminates in the procession to the sanctuary nearby in the Sierra Morena. **Ribadavia** (Ourense): Wine Festival.
End April/ early May	**Caravaca de la Cruz**: *Fiestas de la Santísima Vera-Cruz*, said to be a living memory of Templar rites.

May

First week	**Jerez de la Frontera**: much like the April Fair in Sevilla; first Friday, **Jaca** re-enacts victory over the Moors by local women; **Figueres**, **Badajoz** and **Granada** have *Fiestas de la Santa Cruz*. **Almeria**: Peña de Taranto Cultural Week. The foremost flamenco singers meet here every year for this prestigious contest. **Navas de San Juan** (north of Úbeda): in honour of *Nuestra Señora de la Estrella*, one of the most important pilgrimages in the province of Jaén.
Second Week	**Córdoba**: every third year the *Concurso Nacional de Arte Flamenco* takes place on the seventh Sun after *Pentecost*. **El Rocío** (Huelva): the biggest *romería* in Spain.
Mid-May	**St Feliu de Pallarols** (Girona): *Fiesta Mayor* with dances and giants.
23	Anniversary of battle of **Clavijo** (La Rioja).

Last 2 weeks	**Madrid:** *San Isidro,* with two weeks of entertainment, the best bullfights, parades and scores of free events, concerts and jazz.
End of May	*Corpus Cristi* initiates four days of festivities, especially at **Toledo, Sitges** (where the streets are covered with flower carpets), **Berga** (Barcelona), **Zahara de la Sierra** (Cádiz), **Zamora, Cáceres** and **Puenteareas.**

June

First Sunday	**Calella** (Barcelona): *Alpec de la Sardana,* Catalan dance and music contests.
Second week	**Mojácar:** Moorish and Christian troops re-enact the surrender of the town to the Christian army at Mojácar's annual two-day fiesta.
Mid-month	**Granada:** *Festival Internacional de Música y Danza* attracts famous names from around the world; classical music, jazz and ballet; also flamenco competitions in odd-numbered years.
21–24	**Alicante** celebrates St John's day (*San Juanes*) better than any with a huge *Fallas* bonfire similar to Valencia's; more celebrations at **Prats de Lluçanes** (Barcelona); **Coria** (Cáceres) with bulls in the streets; **Segovia**, with floats; **San Pedro Manrique** (Soria) with bonfires and walks on hot coals; **León** (with parties and bullfights).
End June	**Soria:** 13th-century, five-day celebration of St John, with bulls in the street; **Baños de Cerrato** (Palencia) celebrates a Mozarab-Visigothic mass with ancient music on Sunday after 24 June; **Haro** (La Rioja), pilgrimage and drunken 'wine battles'.
29	**Burgos,** *San Pedro:* beginning of two weeks of International Folklore Feria. **Haro** (La Rioja): wine battle.
30	**Hita,** near Guadalajara: Festival of Medieval Theatre; medieval food, dance, bullfights and falconry, all to the music of flutes and bagpipes.

July

All month	**Hecho** (Aragón): International Symposium of Contemporary Art and Sculpture, with art work all over the mountain sides; **Santander** holds its International Music Festival, jazz in August.
First weekend	**Vivero** (Lugo): *Rapa das Bestas,* Galician wild horses round-up; **Zumaya** (Euzkadi): Basque sports and dancing by the sea; **San Lorenzo de Sabucedo–La Estrada** (Pontevedra): another *Rapa das Bestas,* with big festivities from Saturday till Monday.
First 2 weeks	**Córdoba:** International Guitar Festival—classical, flamenco and Latino.
6–7	**Nava,** Asturias: cider festival.
6–14	**Pamplona:** the famous running of the bulls and party for San Fermín.
2nd Sun	**Olot,** near Girona: *Aplec de la Sardana,* big Catalan dance festival; **Teruel** begins 10-day *Fiesta de Vaquilla del Ángel,* with Aragonese *jotas,* other dances and more.

Second week	**Valencia,** *Feria:* lots of entertainment and the Valencian speciality, fireworks; **Segovia** has a Chamber Music festival; **Avilés** has dances, entertainment, and bullfights.
Mid-July–mid-Aug	**Cadaqués** (Girona): International Music and Art Festival.
15	**Comillas** (Cantabria): catch the goose and other country-fair festivities and humour.
16	**Sort** (Lleída): canoe races and festivities on the Río Noguera, Pallaresa; **San Pedro del Pinatar**: marine pilgrimage on the Mar Menor.
22	**Anguiano** (La Rioja): fiesta with the dance of the *Zancos*, down the streets and steps on stilts; **Bermeo** (Euskadi): boat races, Basque sports.
24	**Lloret de Mar** (Girona): the Costa Brava's biggest resort puts on a charming traditional fiesta, ancient Moorish dances.
25	**Santiago de Compostela**: great celebrations for Santiago—national offering to the saint, the swinging of the *Botafumeiro*, burning of a cardboard replica of Córdoba's Mezquita, great fireworks and more.
Last week	**San Sebastián**: International Jazz Festival, the biggest in Spain; **Tudela** (Navarra): music and dancing for Santa Ana; **Cangas de Onís** (Asturias): shepherds' festival; **Villajoyosa** (Alicante): mock battles between Christians and Moors.
29	**Luarca** (Asturias): Vaqueiro festival, mock wedding and dances; **Santa María de Ribarteme** (Pontevedra): pilgrimage made in coffins by people who narrowly escaped death the year before.
End July	**Jaca**, in odd-numbered years, celebrates the International Folklore festival of the Pyrenees; in even numbered years it takes place at Oloron-Ste Marie in France. **Almería**: festival, including jazz concerts.

August

3–9	**Estella** (Navarra): ancient fiesta, with giants and the only *encierro* where women can run with the bulls.
5	**Trevélez** (Granada) has a midnight pilgrimage up Mulhacén, Spain's highest mountain, so that pilgrims arrive exhausted for midday prayers.
First week	**Torrevieja** (Alicante): Habaneras International Music Festival.
	Daroca (Aragón): international Music Festival.
First Sat	**Arriondas-Ribadesella** (Asturias): great kayak race on the Río Sella.
First Sun	**Gijón**: Asturias Day celebrations, with lots of folklore.
4–9	**Vitoria**: giants, music, bonfires and more for the Virgen Blanca.
5	**Trevélez** (Granada): has a midnight pilgrimage up Mulhacén, Spain's highest mountain.

9–11	**Foz** (Lugo): San Lorenzo festivities, folklore and kayaking.
Second Sun	**Cabezón de la Sal** (Cantabria): Mountain Day folklore, song contests; **Carballino** (Ourense): octopus-eating festival and bagpipe music.
11–15	**Elche:** performances of 13th-century mystery play in the Basílica de Santa María, beautiful poetry and music.
11–18	**San Sebastián:** international fireworks contest.
15–16	Assumption of the Virgin and San Roque festivities at **La Alberca** (Salamanca), a very ancient festival; **Sada** (La Coruña): with a big sardine roast; **Amer** (Girona): with Sardana dancing; **Llanes** (Asturias): bagpipes and ancient dances; **Bilbao:** Basque sports and races; **Vejar** (Cádiz): with flamenco; **Chinchón:** with an *encierro*.
15–19	Battle of flowers at **Betanzos** (A Coruña).
Mid-month	**Málaga:** its *feria* is gaining a reputation as one of the best in Europe, with a week of concerts, bullfights dancing and singing in the old town.
Third week	**La Unión** (Murcia): festival of *Cante de Las Minas*, flamenco competition, specializing in miners' songs; **Jumilla** (Murcia), *La Vendimia* wine festival.
Last Sunday	**Cuéllar**, near Valladolid: music, dancing and an *encierro*; **Vivero** (Lugo): pilgrimage; **Ontentinete** (Valencia): four-day Christian and Moor battles.
Last week	**Sanlúcar de Barrameda** (Cádiz): exaltation of the Río Guadalquivir and major flamenco events; **Toro:** Fiesta de San Agustín, bulls and a 'fountain of wine'; **Medinaceli** (Soria): medieval music week.
30	**Villafranca del Penedés** (Tarragona): human towers, Sardana dances, etc.
31	**Loiola** (Euskadi): St Ignatius de Loiola Day.

September

First week	**Almagro** (Ciudad Real): Spanish Drama Festival in historic theatre; **Aranjuez** (Madrid): concerts and dancing; **San Sebastián:** Basque food festival; **Jerez** and **Valdepeñas:** *Vendimia* wine festivals; **Lekeitio** (Euskadi): Basque festival, including contest to pull the head off a goose with a greased neck.
8	Virgin's Birthday with celebrations in many places, especially **Salamanca, Algemesi** (Valencia), **Tordesillas. Ronda:** 18th-century-style bullfight in its historic ring; ceremonies at **Montserrat.**
11	**Sueca** (Valencia): festival of rice with *paella* contests.
12	**Graus** (Aragón): big folklore event, with dances and ancient songs; **Murcia:** International Mediterranean Music Festival; **Cardona** (Barcelona): dancing, bulls and Catalan fun and games
19	**Oviedo:** big *Americas Day* celebration, with floats and bands from all over Latin America; **Logroño** has the *Vendimia* wine festival of La Rioja.

| 19–28 | San Sebastián: International Film Festival. |
| 24 | Barcelona: music, human towers and tons of other entertainments for its patroness, the Virgen de la Merced. |

October

8–16	Zaragoza: festivities for the Virgen del Pilar, with huge floral offering.
Second week	Ávila has an equally big party for Santa Teresa.
Third week	Jaén: festival of San Lucás, bullfights, cultural and sporting events.
14 or so	O Grove (Pontevedra), shellfish festival.
18–20	Mondoñedo (Lugo), As San Lucas, a big horse fair dating from the Middle Ages.
Last weekend	Consuegra (Toledo), Fiesta of the Saffron Rose.
Last week	Girona, fireworks and more for San Narcís; Sitges has an International Festival of Vanguard Theatre and Fantasy and Terror Films, extending into November.

November

11	Fiesta de San Martin, Bueu (Galicia).
19	Fiesta de San Andrés, Estella (Navarra).
Last Sunday	Oyster Festival, Arcade (Pontevedra)

December

First Week	Martos (Jaén): Fiesta de la Aceituna. Annual four-day olive festival celebrating the olive in all its glory.
6	San Nicolás Obispillo, Segura (Guipúzcoa).
13	Santa Lucía fair, Zumárraga (Guipúzcoa).
21	Santo Tomás fair, with processions, San Sebastián, Bilbao, Azpeitia.
Last week	O Feitoman, handicrafts fair, Vigo (Pontevedra); Olentzero processions in many Basque villages.
31	The National Offering to the Apostle—a major religious ceremony with the Botafumeiro in Santiago de Compostela.

Food and Drink

Read an old guidebook to Spain, and when the author gets around to the local cooking, expressions like 'eggs in a sea of rancid oil' and 'mysterious pork parts' pop up with alarming frequency. One traveller in the 18th century fell ill from a local concoction and was given a purge 'known on the comic stage as angelic water. On top of that followed four hundred catholic pills, and a few days later...they gave me escordero water, whose efficacy or devilry is of such double effect that the doctors call it ambidexter. From this I suffered agony.'

You'll fare better; in fact the chances are you'll eat some of the tastiest food you've ever had at half the price you would have paid for it at home. The massive influx of tourists has had its effect on Spanish kitchens, but so has the Spaniards' own increased prosperity and, perhaps most significantly, the new federalism. Each region, each town even, has come to feel a new interest and pride in the things that set it apart, and food is definitely one of those. The best restaurants are almost always those specializing in regional cuisine. In Castile, where the cuisine is almost medieval, tureen-sized bowls of soup and roast suckling pig (*cochinillo*) or lamb have pride of place; in Valencia, the land of rice, you can order one of its famous *paellas* or a dozen other different rice dishes; in Andalucía, it's *gazpacho* (cold tomato, cucumber and onion soup) in several varieties, and *rabo de toro* (bull's tail cooked with sauce); in Asturias it's hake in *sidra* (the local cider) or *fabada*, an enchanting mess of pork and beans. And no regions pride themselves on their own cooking as much as the Basque lands, Catalunya, or Galicia—and rightfully.

Be careful, though. Spain still has plenty of bad restaurants. The worst offenders are often those with the little flags and ten-language menus in the most touristy areas, and in general you'd do better to buy some bread, *Manchego* cheese and a bottle of *Valdepeñas* red and have a picnic, than throw away your pesetas there. If you dine where the locals do you'll be assured of a good deal if not necessarily a good meal. Almost every restaurant offers a *menú del día*, or a *menú turístico*, featuring an appetizer, a main course, dessert, bread and drink at a set price, always a certain percentage lower than if you had ordered the items à la carte.

Tapas Bars

If you are travelling on a budget you may want to eat one of your meals a day at a **tapas bar** or **tasca**. Tapas means 'lids'. They started out as little saucers of goodies served on top of a drink and have evolved over the years to form a main part of the world's greatest snack culture. Bars that specialize in them have platter after platter of delectable titbits, from shellfish to slices of omelette or mushrooms baked in garlic or vegetables in vinaigrette or stews. All you have to do is pick out what looks best and order a *porción* (an hors d'oeuvre) or a *ración* (a big helping) if it looks really good. It's hard to generalize about prices, but on average 1000 pts of tapas and wine or beer really fill you up. You can always save money in bars by standing up; sit at that charming table on the terrace and prices can jump considerably. Another advantage of *tapas* is that they're available at what most Americans or Britons would consider normal dining hours. Spaniards are notoriously late diners; in the morning it's a coffee and roll grabbed at the bar, a huge meal at around 2pm, then after work at 8pm a few tapas at the bar to hold them over until supper at 10 or 11pm. After living in Spain for a few months this makes perfect sense, but it's exasperating to the average visitor. On the coasts, restaurants tend to open earlier to accommodate foreigners (some as early as 5pm) but you may as well do as the Spaniards do. Galicians are the early diners of Spain (8 or 9pm), while Madrileños might think of going for a bite at midnight or 1am.

Eating Out

Between restaurants and tascas are **comedores** (literally, dining-rooms) often tacked onto the backs of bars, where the food and decor are usually drab but cheap, and **cafeterías**, usually those places that feature photographs of their offerings of *platos combinados* (combination plates) to eliminate any language problem. Others are self-service, and most tend to be dreary bargains. **Asadores** specialize in roast meat or fish; **marisqueras** serve only fish and shellfish.

Keep an eye out for **ventas**, usually modest family-run establishments offering excellent *menús del día*. Try and visit one in the country on a Sunday lunchtime when all the Spanish families go out to eat and make merry. There are also many **Chinese restaurants** in Spain which are fairly good and often inexpensive, and **American fast-food outlets** in the big cities and resort areas; while Italian restaurants are 98 per cent dismal in Spain, you can get a good pizza in many places. Don't neglect the rapidly disappearing shacks on the beach—they often serve up roast sardines that are out of this world. Vegetarians are catered for in the cities, which always manage to come up with one or two veggie restaurants, usually good ones at that. In the countryside and away from the main resorts, proper vegetarians and vegans will find it harder going, though tapas make it easier to get your nutrition than in some other southern European countries. Fish eaters will manage just about everywhere. Menu and restaurant vocabulary are included in the 'language' section at the end of the book. Note that unless it's explicitly written on the bill (*la cuenta*), service is *not* included in the total, so tip accordingly.

Prices quoted in the 'Eating Out' sections throughout this book are for a three-course meal, including wine.

expensive	over 4500 pts
moderate	2500–4500 pts
cheap	under 2500 pts

Drink

No matter how much other costs have risen in Spain, **wine** has remained refreshingly inexpensive by northern European or American standards; what's more, it's very good and there's enough variety from the various regions of the country for you to try something different every day. There are 30 areas in Spain under the control of the *Instituto Nacional de Denominaciones de Origen (INDO)*, which acts as a guide to the consumer and keeps a strict eye on the quality of Spanish wine. Catalunya is best known for its wines from Penedés and Priorato, the former producing excellent whites and some fine reds (try *Gran Caus '87*). One of the most typical Catalunyan whites is *Blancs en Noirs* and, like the dry white wines of Tarragona, is excellent with fish, or as an *aperitivo*. Some of the best sparkling wines (*cava*) come from Sant Sadurni d'Anoia, near Barcelona; *Mestres Mas Vía* can rival any standard champagne. Navarra has some excellent reds (*Magaña Merlot '85*). Navarra's neighbour, La Rioja, is the best known and richest area for wine in Spain, producing a great range from young whites to heavy, fruity reds; its *vino de gran reserva* spends three years ageing in oak barrels, and another in bottles, before release to the public. In La Mancha, Valdepeñas is Spain's most prolific area; its young, inexpensive table wines are sold everywhere, and make even a potato tortilla something special. Valencia has some fresh, dry whites and an distinctive rosé (*Castillo de Liria*). Euskadi is known for its very palatable 'green' wine, *Txacoli*, while Galicia's excellent *Ribeiro* resembles the delicate *vinho verde* of neighbouring Portugal; other good wines from the region are *Rías Baixas* and *Valseorros*, pleasant light vintages that complement the regional dishes, seafood in particular. Andalucía is best known for Jerez, or what we in English call sherry. When a Spaniard invites you to have a *copa* (glass) it will nearly always be filled with this Andalucían sunshine. It comes in a wide range of varieties: *manzanillas* are very dry, *fino* is dry, light and young (the most famous is *Tío Pepe*); *amontillados* are a bit sweeter and rich; *olorosos* are very sweet dessert sherries, and can be either brown, cream or *amoroso*.

Spanish brandy is extremely palatable; the two most popular brands *103* (very light in colour) and *Soberano*, both drunk extensively by Spanish labourers and postmen at 7am. *Anís* (sweet or dry) is also quite popular. *Sangría* is the famous summertime punch of red wine, brandy, mineral water, orange and lemon with ice, but beware—it's rarely made very well, even when you can find it. Each region has its wine and liqueur specialities and nearly every monastery in Spain seems to make some kind of herbal potion. The north of Spain, where apples grow better than vines, produces cider, or *sidra*, which can come as a shock to the tastebuds. Ground almonds whipped to create *horchata de chufa* are refreshing in the summer.

Many Spaniards prefer **beer**, which is also good though dearer by degree than wine. The most popular brands are *San Miguel* and *Cruzcampo*—most bars sell it cold in bottles or on tap; try *Mahón* Five Star if you see it.

Health and Insurance

There is a standard EU agreement for citizens of EU countries, entitling you to a certain amount of free medical care, but it's not straightforward. You must complete all the necessary paperwork before you go to Spain, and allow a couple of months to make sure it comes through in time. Ask for a leaflet called *Before You Go* from the Department of Health and fill out form E111, which on arrival in Spain you must take to the local office of the *Instituto Nacional de Seguridad Social*, where you'll be issued with a Spanish medical card and some vouchers enabling you to claim free treatment from an INSS doctor. At time of writing the government is trying to implement a much easier system. In an emergency, ask to be taken to the nearest *hospital de la seguridad social*. Before resorting to a *médico* (doctor) and his £20 ($34) fee (ask at the tourist office for a list of English-speaking doctors), go to a pharmacy and tell them your woes. Spanish *farmacéuticos* are highly skilled and if there's a prescription medicine that you know will cure you, they'll often supply it without a doctor's note. (*El País* and the other national newspaper list *farmacías* in large cities that stay open all night.)

No inoculations are required to enter Spain, though it never hurts to check that your tetanus jab is up-to-date, as well as some of the more exotic inoculations (typhoid and cholera) if you want to venture on into Morocco. Tap water is safe to drink in Spain but, at the slightest twinge of queasiness, switch to the bottled stuff.

Insurance

You may want to consider travel insurance, available through most travel agents. For a small monthly charge, not only is your health insured, but your bags and money as well, and some will even refund a missed charter flight if you're too ill to catch it. Be sure to save all doctors' receipts (you'll have to pay cash on the spot), pharmacy receipts, and police documents (if you're reporting a theft).

Maps

Cartography has been an art in Spain since the 12th-century Catalans charted their Mediterranean Empire in Europe's first great school of map-making. The tourist offices hand out beautifully detailed maps of every town; ask for their *Mapa de Comunicaciones*, an excellent general map of the country. The best large-scale maps are produced by *Almax Editores*. If in London, visit Stanfords at 12 Long Acre, WC2.

The Socialist *El País* is Spain's biggest and best national **newspaper**, though circulation is painfully low. Most Spaniards just don't read newspapers (the little magazine *Teleprograma* with television listings and scandals is by far and away the best-selling periodical). *El País* has the best Madrid and regional **film** listings. Some films subtitled instead of dubbed, and English films are occasionally shown on the Costa del Sol and Costa Blanca in the expatriate communities. Films are cheap and the Spaniards are some of the world's most avid cinema-goers, and though half of the great movie palaces of Madrid have been converted into discos, others are still magnificent. There are also lots of cheap outdoor movie theatres in the summer. Look for films by Carlos Saura (*Carmen, Blood Wedding*), who is regarded as Buñuel's natural successor, or the poetic Victor Erice (*The Spirit of the Beehive, The Quince Tree Sun*), or Pedro Almodóvar (*Women on the Verge of a Nervous Breakdown, Tie Me Up! Tie Me Down!*) or new lights Fernando Trueba (*Belle Epoque*) and Pedro Olea.

The other big papers are *Diario 16* (centrist), *ABC* (conservative, in a bizarre '60s magazine format), and the *Alcázar* (neo-fascist). Major British newspapers are available in all tourist areas and big cities; the American *New York Herald Tribune*, the *Wall Street Journal*, and the awful *USA Today* are readily available where Americans go. Most hit the news stands a day late. There are also publications in English on the major costas—notably *Sur*, a translation of a Málaga paper with general items of news; *Lookout*, a glossy monthly general consumer maga-zine; *The Entertainer*, for local news, events and classified ads; the *Marbella Times*, another slick mag for the expats; and an English weekly in Madrid that features local events. All British newspapers are flown daily to Gibraltar.

Money

Spanish **currency** comes in notes of 1000, 2000, 5000 and 10,000 *pesetas* (pts), all in different colours, and coins of 1, 5, 10, 25, 50, 100, 200, and 500 pts. At street markets, and in out-of-the-way places, you may hear prices given in *duros* or *notas*. A *duro* is a 5 pts piece, and a *nota* is a 100 pts piece. On 1 January, 1999, the euro became the official currency of Spain, and the *peseta* a denomination of the euro. However, Spanish *peseta* notes and coins will continue to be used during the three-year transitional period. The introduction of euro bank notes is likely to start on 1 January 2002. Exchange rates vary of course, but unless any drastic changes occur, £1 is 200 pts, and $1 equivalent to 150 pts. Think of 100 pts as about 50p or 75 cents—so those green 1000 pta notes, the most common, are worth about £5 or $7.50. Spain's city centres seem to have a bank on every street corner, and most of them will exchange money; look for the *cambio* or *exchange* signs and the little flags. Beware of exchange offices, as they can charge a hefty commission on all transactions. You can sometimes change money at travel agencies, fancy hotels, restaurants and big department stores. Even the big supermarkets tend to have *telebancos* or automatic tellers. There are 24-hour *cambios* at the big train stations in Barcelona and Madrid. A Eurocheque card will be needed to support your British Eurocheques, and even then they may not be welcome.

Travellers' cheques, if they are from one of the major companies, will pass at most bank exchanges. Wiring money from overseas entails no special difficulties; just give yourself two weeks to be on the safe side, and work through one of the larger institutions (Banco Central, Banco de Bilbao, Banco Español de Crédito, Banco Hispano Americano, Banco de Santander, Banco de Vizcaya). All transactions have to go through Madrid.

Credit cards will always be helpful in town, rarely in the country. Perhaps the handiest way to keep yourself in cash is by using the automatic bank tellers that have appeared on the street-corners of almost every town—check with your bank before leaving to ensure your card can be used in Spain. But do not rely on hole-in-the-wall machines as your only source of cash; if, for whatever reason, the machine swallows your card, it usually take 10 days to retrieve it.

Opening Hours

Most **banks** are open Mon–Thurs 8.30–4.30, Fri 8.30–2 and Sat (sometimes) 8.30–1.

Most of the less important **churches** are always closed. Some cities probably have more churches than faithful communicants, and many are unused. If you're determined to see one, it will never be hard to find the *sacristán* or caretaker. Usually they live close by, and would be glad to show you around for a tip. Don't be surprised when cathedrals and famous churches charge for admission—just consider the cost of upkeep.

Shops usually open from 9.30am. Spaniards take their main meal at 2pm and, except in the larger cities, most shops close for 2–3 hours in the afternoon, usually from 1pm or 2pm. In the south, where it's hotter, the siesta can last from 1pm to 5pm. Most establishments stay open until 7pm or 8pm.

Museums and historical sites tend to follow shop opening hours too, though abbreviated in the winter months; nearly all close on Mondays. Seldom-visited ones have a raffish disregard for their official hours, or open only when the mood strikes them. Don't be discouraged: bang on doors and ask around.

Photography

Film is quite expensive everywhere; so is developing, but in any city there will be plenty of places—many in opticians' shops (*ópticas*) or big department stores—where you can get processing done in a hurry. Serious photographers must give some consideration to the strong sunlight and high reflectivity of surfaces (pavement and buildings) in towns. If you're there during the summer use ASA 100 film.

Police Business

Crime is not really a big problem in Spain and Spaniards talk about it perhaps more than is warranted. Pickpocketing and robbing parked cars are the specialities; in Sevilla they like to take the whole car. The big cities (Madrid, Barcelona and especially Málaga and Sevilla) are the places where you should be careful although, except for some quarters of the largest cities, walking around at night is not a problem—primarily because everybody does it. Crime is also spreading to the tourist areas, particularly the Costa del Sol. Even on the Costa, though, you're probably safer in Spain than you would be at home: the crime rate is roughly a quarter of that in Britain. Note that in Spain less than 8 grams of reefer is legal; anything else may easily earn you the traditional 'six years and a day'.

There are several species of **police**, and their authority varies with the area. Franco's old goon squads, the Policía Armada, have been reformed and relatively demilitarized into the *Policía Nacional,* whom the Spaniards call 'chocolate drops' for their brown uniforms; their duties largely consist of driving around in cars and drinking coffee.

The *Policía Municipal* are responsible for crime control in some cities, while in others they are limited to directing traffic. Mostly in rural areas, there's the *Guardia Civil,* with green uniforms, but minus the sinister black patent-leather tricorn hats of yesteryear. The 'poison dwarfs of Spain', as Laurie Lee called them, may well be one of the most efficient police forces in the world, but after a century and a half of upholding a sick social order in the volatile countryside, they have few friends. They too are being reformed; now they're most conspicuous as a highway patrol, assisting motorists and handing out tickets (ignoring 'no passing' zones is the best way to get one). Most traffic violations are payable on the spot; the traffic cops have a reputation for upright honesty. The Basques don't want anything to do with any of these. So far, they are the only community to take advantage of the new autonomy laws and set up their own police, the *Ertzantza.* You'll see them looking dapper in their red berets.

Post Offices

Every city, regardless of size, seems to have one post office (*correos*) and no more. It will always be crowded, but unless you have packages to mail, you may not need ever to visit one. Most tobacconists sell stamps (*sellos*) and they'll usually know the correct postage for whatever you're sending. The standard charge for sending a letter is 60 pts (European Union) and 87 pts (North America). Send everything air mail (*por avión*) and don't send postcards unless you don't care when they arrive. Mailboxes are bright yellow and scarce. The post offices also handle telegrams, which normally take 4 hours to arrive within Europe but are very expensive.

Public Holidays

The Spanish, like the Italians, try to have as many as possible. Everything closes on:

1 January:	Año Nuevo (New Year's Day)
6 January:	Epifanía (Epiphany)
March:	Viernes Santo (Good Friday)
1 May:	Día del Trabajo (Labour Day)
May/June:	Corpus Christi
25 July:	Santiago Apóstol (St James' Day)
15 August:	Asunción (Assumption)
12 October:	Día de la Hispanidad (Columbus Day)
1 November:	Todos los Santos (All Saints' Day)
6 December:	Día de la Constitución (Constitution Day)
8 December:	Inmaculada Concepción (Immaculate Conception)
25 December:	Navidad (Christmas Day)

Shopping

Notwithstanding the delightfully tacky tourist wares (Toledo 'daggers', plastic bulls and flamenco dolls ad nauseam) there are are some high quality items to be picked up in Spain, notably **leather** from Córdoba, **lace** from Galicia, **inlaid wood** *taracea* work from Granada (chests, chess boards and music boxes), **jewellery** from Toledo, **woven goods** and **rugs** from nearly every province of Spain and fine embroidered **linens** available everywhere. Good quality **antiques** can occasionally be picked up at a **rastro** (flea market), but there aren't the great finds there once were—Spaniards have learned what they're worth and charge accordingly. Guitars, mandolins and tapestries are some of the bulky, more expensive items you may want to ship home.

The major **department store** chains in Spain, El Corte Inglés and the Galerías Preciadas, often have good selections of crafts and will ship items home. You can also get some good buys at the **weekly markets** where Spaniards do a good deal of their shopping. Local tourist offices will have details. EU citizens are not entitled to tax refunds.

Sports and Activities

Bars and cafés collect much of the Spaniards' leisure time. They are wonderful institutions, where you can eat breakfast or linger over a glass of beer until 4 in the morning; in any of them you could see an old sailor delicately sipping his camomile tea next to a young mother, baby under her arm, stopping in for a beer break during her shopping. Some have music—jazz, rock or flamenco; some have great snacks, or tapas, some have games or pinball machines. Every bar has at least one slot machine, doling out electronic versions of *La Cucaracha* whenever it gets lonely.

Watch out for posters for **circuses**. The little travelling Spanish troupes with their family acts, tents, tinsel and names like 'The National Circus of Japan' will charm you; they often gravitate to the major fiestas throughout the summer.

cycling

Cycling is taken extremely seriously in Spain but you don't often see people using a bike as a form of transport. Instead, Lycra-clad enthusiasts pedal furiously up the steepest of hills, no doubt trying to reach the standards set by Miguel Indurain (of Navarra), the multi-winner of the *Tour de France*. If you do want to bring your own **bicycle** to Spain, you can make arrangements by ferry or train; by air, you'll almost always have to dismantle it and pack it in some kind of crate. Each airline seems to have its own policy.

fishing and hunting

Fishing and hunting are long-standing Spanish obsessions, and you'll need to get a licence for both. Freshwater fishing permits (*permiso de pesca*) are issued on a fortnightly basis from the municipal ICONA office, or from the Jefatura Provincial del ICONA, Licencia Nacional de Caza y Pesca, Jorge Juan 39, Madrid, © 91 225 59 85. **Information:** for a list of the best trout streams (there are many), write to the Spanish Fishing Federation, Navas de Tolosa 3, 28013 Madrid, ©/© 91 532 83 52. You can also get information from the Spanish Agricultural Office in London, © (0171) 235 5005.

You may bring sporting guns to Spain, but you must declare them on arrival and present a valid firearms certificate with a Spanish translation bearing a consulate stamp. Hunters (boar and deer are the big game, with quail, hare, ducks and geese in the winter) are obliged to get a licence as well (*permiso de caza*) from the local autonomous community, presenting their passports and record of insurance coverage.

Information: the Spanish Hunting Federation, Avenida Reina Victoria 72, 28003 Madrid, ✆ 91 253 90 17.

football

Soccer is the most popular sport throughout Spain, and the Spaniards play it well: FC Barcelona and Real Madrid are the best teams to watch. The season lasts from September to June, and matches are usually trouble free.

Information: Spanish Football Federation, Alberto Bosch 13, 28014 Madrid, ✆ 91 420 33 21; 🖷 91 420 20 94.

golf

Since the advent of Severiano Ballesteros and Jose Maria Olazabal Spaniards too have gone nuts for the game. The sunny warm winters, combined with greens of international tournament standard, attract golfing enthusiasts from all over the world throughout the year. Green fees have taken a leap in recent years, however and even the humblest clubs charge 3000 pts—most places hire out clubs. Many hotels cater specifically for the golfer and there are numerous specialist tour operators (some are listed on pp.5–6).

Information: the Royal Spanish Golf Federation, Capitán Haya 9–5, 28020 Madrid, ✆ 91 455 27 57.

hiking and mountaineering

Spain's sierras attract thousands of hikers and mountaineers. Los Picos de Europa and the Pyrenees are by far the most popular, though there are also some lovely hikes in the northern Cordillera Cantábrica mountains, in the Sierra Nevada above Granada and Las Hurdes of northern Extremadura. The tourist office or the Spanish Mountaineering Federation provide a list of *refugios*, which offer mountain shelter in many places. Some are well equipped and can supply food. Most, however, do not, so take your own sleeping bags, cooking equipment and food with you. Hiking boots are essential, as is a detailed map of the area.

Information: Spanish Mountaineering Federation, Alberto Aguilera 3, 28015 Madrid, ✆ 91 445 1382.

horse racing

Horse-racing is centred in Madrid, with a summer season at San Sebastián and winter season at the Pineda racecourse in Sevilla.

Information: Spanish Horse Racing Federation, Calle Montesquinza 8, 28006 Madrid, ✆ 912 577 78 92, 🖷 912 575 07 70.

pelota

Pelota, the Basque national sport, is a fast, thrilling game, where contestants wearing long basket-like gloves propel a hard ball with great force at high walls; rather like squash. The fast action on the *jai-alai* court is matched by the wagering frenzy of the spectators.

Information: Spanish Pelota Foundation, Los Madrazo 11, 28014 Madrid, ✆ 91 521 42 99, 🖷 91 532 38 79.

skiing

Spain's numerous ski resorts attract a sizeable number of foreign skiers who come to beat the high costs in France and Switzerland. In the south an hour from Granada you can be among the Iberian Peninsula's highest peaks and Europe's southernmost ski resorts, whose après-ski life can rival anything in the Alps. In Spain, it's easy to arrange all-inclusive ski packages through a travel agent. A typical deal would include six nights' accommodation in a three- or four-star hotel with half board, and unlimited use of ski lifts for the week, at a cost of just under 100,000 pts. With instruction fees, count on 10–15,000 pts extra per week.

Information: write to the Spanish Ski Federation, Claudio Coello 32, 28001 Madrid, ✆ 91 575 89 43.

tennis

There is equal fervour for tennis as for golf, inspired by international champion Arantxa Sánchez Vicario, and more recently by Conchita Martínez and Carlos Moya. Every resort hotel has its own courts; municipal ones are rare or hard to get to.

Information: Royal Spanish Tennis Federation, Avenida Diagonal 618, 08021 Barcelona, ✆ (93) 201 08 44.

water sports

Water sports are the most popular activities in the summer. You can rent a windsurf board and learn how to use it at almost any resort; *aficionados* head for Tarifa, the continent's southernmost tip and Europe's windsurfing mecca, while along the Atlantic coast of Euskadi and Cantabria there are several places where the waves are suitable for surfing.

Information: write to the Royal Spanish Sailing Federation, Luis de Salazar 12, 28002 Madrid, ✆ 91 519 5008, ✆ (91) 416 4504.

Underwater activists flock to the Almería coast in particular for its sparkling water and abundant marine life.

Information: write to the Spanish Sub-Aqua Federation, Santaló 15, 08021 Barcelona, ✆ (93) 200 6769; or contact the Federación Española de Esquí Náutico, Sabino de Arana 30, 08028 Barcelona, ✆ (93) 330 8903.

Telephones

Emergency Numbers

Spain:	*protección civil* ✆ 006	police ✆ 091	
Gibraltar:	ambulance and police ✆ 199	fire ✆ 190	

Spain has long had one of the best telephone systems in Europe. Calls within Spain are relatively cheap (25 pts for a short local call, remember all local telephone numbers in Spain are made up of seven digits plus a code which must be dialled even from within a province), and Spain is one of the few countries where you can make an international call conveniently from a phone booth—within Europe at least. Call boxes are blue and usually contain complete dialing instructions (in English) while the phone itself has a little slide on top that holds coins. This can be done to the US too, but take at least 3,000 pts in change with you. Overseas calls from Spain are among the most expensive in Europe: calls to the UK cost about 250—350 pts a minute, to the US substantially more. There are central telephone offices (*telefónicas*) in every big city, where you call from metered booths (and pay a fair percentage more for the comfort); they are indispensable, however, for reversed charge or collect calls (*cobro revertido*). *Telefónicas* are generally open from 9–1pm and 5–10pm and closed on Sundays. Expect to pay a big surcharge if you do any telephoning from your hotel or any public place that does not have a coin slot. Cheap rate is from 10pm–8am Monday–Saturday and all day Sunday and public holidays.

For calls to Spain from the UK, dial 00 followed by the country code (34), the area code (remember that if you are calling from outside Spain you drop the '9' in the area code) and the number. For international calls from Spain, dial 07, wait for the higher tone and then dial the country code, etc. Telephoning abroad from **Gibraltar**, dial 00 followed by country and area code. Spanish telephone codes have now been incorporated into the telephone numbers: all numbers in this guide are listed as they must be dialled.

Toilets

Outside bus and train stations, public facilities are rare in Spain. On the other hand, every bar on every corner has a toilet; don't feel uncomfortable using it without purchasing something—the Spaniards do it all the time. Just ask for *los servicios* and take your own paper.

Tourist Information

After receiving millions of tourists each year for the last two decades, no country has more information offices, or more helpful ones, or more intelligent brochures and detailed maps. Every city will have an office, and about two-thirds of the time you'll find someone who speaks English. Hours for most offices are Monday to Friday, 9.30–1.30 and 4–7, Saturday mornings and closed on Sundays.

Spanish National Tourist Offices

Australia   203 Castlereagh Street, Suite 21a, PO Box A-685,
Sydney South NSW 2000, © (2) 264 7966, @ (2) 267 5111.

Canada: 102 Bloor Street West, Toronto, Ontario, M5S 1M8, © (416) 961 3131,
@ (416) 961 1992

Japan: Daini Toranomon Denki Building, 4F, 3-1-10 Toranomon, Minato Ku,
Tokyo 105, © (813) 34326141, @ (813) 34326144.

UK: 22–23 Manchester Square, London, W1M 5AP, © (0171) 486 8077,
@ (0171) 629 4257

USA: 8383 Wilshire Boulevard, Suite 960, Beverly Hills, California, 90211,
© (213) 658 7188, @ (213) 658 1061

665 Fifth Avenue, New York, NY 10022, © (212) 759 8822,
@ (212) 980 1053

Gibraltar Information Bureau

UK: 179 The Strand, London WC2R 1EH, © (0171) 836 0777, @ 240 6612

Hotels in Spain are no longer the bargains they once were and have pretty much caught up with the rest of Europe. One thing you can still count on is a consistent level of quality and service; the Spanish government regulates hotels more intelligently, and more closely, than any other Mediterranean country. Room prices must be posted in the hotel lobbies and in the rooms, and if there's any problem you can ask for the complaints book, or *Libro de Reclamaciones*. No one ever writes anything in these; any written complaint must be passed on to the authorities immediately. Hotel keepers would always rather correct the problem for you.

The prices given in this guide are for double rooms with bath (unless stated otherwise) but do not include VAT (IVA) charged at 15 per cent on five-star *hoteles*, and 7 per cent on other *hoteles*. No VAT is charged on other categories of accommodation. On the whole, prices are surprisingly consistent. No government, however, could resist the chance to insert a little bureaucratic confusion, and the wide range of accommodation in Spain is classified in a complex system. Look for the little **blue plaques** next to the doors of all *hoteles*, *hostales*, etcetera which identify the classification and number of stars.

If you're travelling around a lot, a good investment would be the government publication *Guía de Hoteles*, a great fat book with every classified hotel and *hostal* in Spain, available for only 750 pts in many bookshops. The government also publishes similar guides to holiday flats (*apartamentos turísticos*) and campsites.

Price Ranges

price category	cities/tourist areas	everywhere else
luxury	top notch	top notch
expensive	over 16,000 pts	over 10,000 pts
moderate	6000–16,000 pts	4000–10,000
inexpensive	under 6000 pts	under 4000 pts
cheap	under 3000 pts	under 2500 pts

Paradores

The government, in its plan to develop tourism in the 1950s, started this nationwide chain of classy hotels to draw some attention to little-visited areas. They restored old palaces, castles and monasteries for the purpose, furnished them with antiques and installed fine restaurants featuring local specialities.

Paradores for many people are one of the best reasons for visiting Spain. Not all *paradores* are historical landmarks; in resort areas, they are as likely to be cleanly designed modern buildings, usually in a great location with a pool and some sports facilities. As their popularity has increased, so have their prices; in most cases both the rooms and the restaurant will be the most expensive in town. *Paradores* are classed as three- or four-star hotels, and their prices range from 8000 pts in remote provincial towns to 23,000 pts and upwards for the most popular. If you can afford a *parador*, there is no better place to stay.

Hoteles

Hoteles (H) are rated with from one to five stars, according to the services they offer. These are the most expensive places, and even a one-star hotel will be a comfortable, middle-range establishment. *Hotel Residencias* (HR) are the same, only without a restaurant. Many of the more expensive hotels have some rooms available at prices lower than those listed. They won't tell you, though; you'll have to ask.

You can often get discounts in the off season but will be charged higher rates during important festivals. These are supposedly regulated, but in practice hotel-keepers charge whatever they can get.

Hostales and Pensiones

Hostales (Hs) and *pensiones* (P) are rated with from one to three stars. These are usually more modest places, often a floor in an apartment block. *Pensiones* may require full- or half-board; there aren't many of these establishments, only a few in resort areas.

Hostal Residencias (HsR), like *hotel residencias*, do not offer meals except breakfast, and not always that. Of course, *hostales and pensiones* with one or two stars will often have rooms without private baths at considerable savings but be warned: small cheap *hostales* in ports and big cities can be crummy and noisy beyond belief.

Fondas, Casas de Huéspedes and Camas

The bottom of the scale is occupied by the *fonda* (F) and *casa de huéspedes* (CH), little different from a one-star *hostal*, though generally cheaper. Off the scale completely are hundreds of unclassified cheap places, usually rooms in an apartment or over a bar and identified only by a little sign reading *camas* (beds) or *habitaciones* (rooms). You can also ask in bars or at the tourist office for unidentified *casas particulares*, private houses with a room or two; in many villages these will be the best you can do, but they're usually clean—Spanish women are manic housekeepers. The best will be in small towns and villages, and around universities.

Occasionally you'll find a room over a bar, run by somebody's grandmother, that is nicer than a four-star hotel—complete with frilly pillows, old furnishings, and a shrine to the Virgin Mary. The worst are found in industrial cities or dull modern ones. Most inexpensive establishments will ask you to pay a day in advance.

Alternative Accommodation

Youth hostels exist in Spain, but they're usually not worth the trouble. Most are open only in the summer; there are the usual inconveniences and silly rules, and often hostels are in out-of-the-way locations. You'll be better off with the inexpensive *hostales* and *fondas*—sometimes these are even cheaper than youth hostels—or ask at the local tourist office for rooms that might be available in **university dormitories**.

If you fancy some peace and tranquillity, the national tourist office has a list of **monasteries** and **convents** that welcome guests (sometimes only in groups). Meals are simple and guests may usually take part in the religious ceremonies.

Campsites are rated with from one to three stars, depending on their facilities. On the whole, camping is a good deal, and facilities in most first-class sites include shops, restaurants, bars, laundries, hot showers, first aid, swimming pools and telephones. Caravans and trailers converge on all the more developed sites, but if you just want to pitch your little tent or sleep out in some quiet field, ask around in the bars or at likely farms. Camping is forbidden in many forest areas because of fears of fire, as well as on the beaches (though you can often get close to some quieter shores if you're discreet).

Price range (per day)

Adult	275–500pts
Caravan	300–600 pts
Child	200–350 pts
Tent	250–650 pts
Car	300–400 pts

Information: the government handbook *Guía de Campings* can be found in most bookstores and at the Spanish tourist office; further details can be obtained from the Federación Española de Campings, San Bernado 97–99, Edificio Colomina, 28015 Madrid, © 91 448 1234

resort accommodation

Almost everything along the coasts of Spain has been built in the last 25 years, and anonymous high-rise buildings abound. Lately the trend has turned towards low-rise 'villages' or *urbanizaciones* built around a pool, usually on or near the beach. We've tried to include places that stand out in some way, or which are good bargains for their rating. Most hotels in the big resorts cater for package tours, and may not even answer a request for an individual reservation during the peak season.

Resorts offer a choice of hotels in every price range, though the best bargains tend to be in the places where foreigners seldom tread—the Costa de la Luz west of Cádiz, or the small resorts west of Almería. If you intend to spend a couple of weeks on any of the costas, your best bet is to book an all-inclusive package deal from the UK or US. All beaches in Spain are public, which sounds extemely politically correct but in fact is a mixed blessing.

private homes and self-catering

With the rise in hotel prices, this has become an increasingly popular way of vacationing in Spain. Write ahead to any provincial tourist office (addresses in the various sections of this book) for the area you're interested in; most will send you complete listings, with detailed information and often photos. Self-catering is usually lumped together with what the Spanish call *Agriturismo*, or *Turismo Rural*, or in Basque (wait for it) *Nekazalturismoa*, because almost all the places are in rural areas.

On the whole, the horror stories of sexual harassment in Spain are a thing of the past—unless you dress provocatively and hang out by the bus station after dark. All Spaniards seem to melt when they see blondes, so if you're fair you're in for a tougher time. Even Spanish women sunbathe topless these days at the international *costa* resorts, but do be discreet elsewhere, especially near small villages. Apart from the coast, it often tends to be the older men who comment on your appearance as a matter of course. Whether you can understand what is being said or not, it is best to ignore them.

A Galician fresco depicting the Moors and Christians at war

History

Pre-history

Evidences of culture in Spain go back to remotest antiquity. Some 50,000 years ago, when Spain was a cooler, more forested place and glaciers coated the Pyrenees, Neanderthal man was minding his business in these mountains and in the caves around Gibraltar. Surprisingly, none of his low-brow skulls have been found anywhere in between. The next players on the Iberian stage arrive about 25,000 BC in the Palaeolithic age; at this time the peninsula's many caves began to fill up with Palaeospaniards, living well enough off herds of bison and deer to create impressive works of art on cave walls all across Spain and southern France. Scholars generally divide these people into the earlier Aurignacian and later Magdalenian cultures. The latter reached their height around 15,000 BC and created some of the Stone Age's finest art, notably in the caves of Altamira in Cantabria.

The Neolithic era, the age of settled agriculture, begins in the Iberian peninsula at an uncertain date. The people known as the Iberians may have arrived as early as 7000 BC. They are generally believed to have come from North Africa, and physical and linguistic clues lead to the possibility that they may be the precursors of the Basques, the oldest nation of western Europe. These people had little to show for themselves until around 2500 BC, and even then the anonymous culture that built the big dolmen burial chambers at Antequera, north of Málaga, are an exception to the rule. Indeed, so little is known about these millennia that speculation is useless. Many linguists believe the language of the Iberians to be related to modern Basque, though they learned letters later from the Phoenicians. Only 500 inscriptions have been found. Ancient Greek and Roman writers hint at close links between Iberia and Greece, and also the British Isles; Iberians at some time invaded and colonized parts of Ireland and southwest Britain, and the Irish bards claimed to have learned their alphabet by way of Spain. Surprisingly, while their cousins in the Balearic Islands were building *talayot* fortresses and trading across the Mediterranean, the Iberians of the mainland produced little in the way of architecture or art. About 800 BC the Iberians are joined by other peoples, notably the Celts from over the Pyrenees. These got along well enough with the Iberians; in many cases they gradually merged with some tribes, creating a new people, the Celtiberians, who occupied much of the centre of the country. We have little information on how these people lived. The great mystery of this era is the fabled kingdom of Tartessos, roughly modern Andalucía, the only place where the anarchistic Iberians ever founded a state. Archaeologists are still looking for the city of Tartessos; some place it near modern Cádiz, others somewhere on the coast further east.

1100 BC–AD 50: Phoenicians, Greeks and, Inevitably, Romans

If the Iberians, Celts and Basques were unwilling to coalesce into states and empires, others were happy to do it for them. In this period, when trade boomed all across the Mediterranean, we can think of Spain as, in modern terms, an 'undeveloped' country where foreigners with ambitions and superior technology came first as traders, then as conquerors. The Phoenician merchant capital of Tyre 'discovered' Spain about 1100 BC, founding Gades (Cádiz), perhaps the oldest city in western Europe. They were after Spain's mineral resources, and their successful exploitation of Spain made the Phoenicians the economic masters of the Mediterranean. Their rivals, the Greeks, arrived on the scene somewhat later; expanding from the colony of Massilia (Marseilles) they founded trading towns on Spain's eastern coast, notably Saguntum, Emporion, and Dianion (Denia), in the 7th and 6th centuries.

By this time Tyre was in decline, and Carthage, its western branch office, was building an empire out of their occupied coasts in Spain and North Africa. About 500 BC the Carthaginians gobbled up the remains of Tartessos (most of Andalucía) and stopped the Greek infiltration. Along the eastern coast, Iberian culture reaches its height in this period, developing a number of important towns, such as Ullastret, on the Costa Brava. The Carthaginians maintained the status quo on the peninsula until 264–241 BC when Rome drubbed them in the First Punic War. The loss of much of its commercial empire made Carthage heavily dependent on Spanish men and resources. The famous Carthaginian leaders, Hamilcar Barca, his son-in-law Hasdrubal, and his son Hannibal, spent most of their careers consolidating their Spanish lands, and when the Second Punic War came in 218 in a dispute over Saguntum, it was a largely Spanish army that Hannibal took over the Alps to ravage Italy. The Romans couldn't beat him, but they kept him at bay long enough for their legions to conquer Spain (210) in his absence. The total defeat of Carthage in 202 made Rome unquestioned master of Spain and all the western Mediterranean. Unlike their predecessors, the Romans were never content to hold just a part of Spain. Relentlessly, they slogged over the peninsula, subjugating one Celtic or Iberian tribe after another.

AD 50–406: Roman Hispania

For all the trouble they caused Rome at first, the inhabitants of Spain soon became some of the Empire's most useful citizens. Especially in the more civilized south, they assumed the Romans' language, religion and customs in short order. New cities grew up to join Cádiz, Saguntum and New Carthage (Cartagena). Of these the most important were Hispalis (Sevilla), Corduba (Córdoba), Tarraco (Tarragona), Augusta Emerita (Mérida) and Caesar Augusta (Zaragoza). The latter two were among the many towns founded specifically for the purpose of settling pensioned-off Roman veterans, an important part of the policy of Romanization. Another new element in the population was the Jews. Rome settled them here in numbers in the Diaspora, and they were to play a constructive rôle in Spanish life for the next 1500 years.

Roman Hispania, like Gaul, was divided into three parts: Lusitania included modern Portugal and Galicia, where the vanquished Celts lived quietly on; Baetica (named after the Baetis, or the Guadalquivir) occupied roughly all of Andalucía, the richest and most cultured Roman province west of Tunisia; all the rest was gathered into the big, sparsely settled province of Tarraconensis. Rome gave Spain bridges and aqueducts, roads and theatres, landlords and tax collectors, and Spain in turn contributed soldiers, metals, wheat and oil, Andalucían dancing girls and fish guts (don't laugh—we don't know exactly what fish *garum* was concocted from, but it was the most prized gourmet delicacy in the empire, and an important export for Baetica). Spain also gave Rome three of its best emperors: Trajan, Hadrian and Theodosius, as well as almost all of the great figures of the 'silver age' of Latin literature—Lucan, both Senecas, Martial and Quintilian. Spaniards today tend to wildly overestimate both the importance and prosperity of Roman Hispania, but there's no denying that while the peninsula lagged far behind the eastern half of the empire in both wealth and level of civilization, it outdistanced Gaul, Britain, Africa and eventually, in the last days of the empire, even Italy itself.

406–711: Roman Twilight and the Visigoths

Even before the western frontiers of the empire crumbled in the fatal year of 406, civilization in Spain and western Europe was in a bad way. In 264 Franks and Alemanni devastated the peninsula in a decade of raids. After their repulse, the crushing burden of maintaining the defence budget and the government bureaucracy sent Spain's economy into long-term regression. Cities declined, and in the countryside the great landowners of the senatorial class took advantage of the situation by squeezing the majority of the population into serfdom or outright slavery. Thus, when the bloody, anarchic Vandals arrived in the 5th century, they found plenty of bands of rural guerrillas, or *bagaudae*, to help them in smashing up the remnants of the Roman system. The Vandals moved on to Africa in 428, leaving nothing behind but the name Andalucía (originally *Vandalusia*) for their southern playground.

Here once more Spain's history becomes tremendously complicated. Up north, the Basques and Asturians achieved independence. The southern regions were occupied intermittently by imperial troops who took their orders from Byzantium. The Visigoths came down from Gaul in 412 to occupy the centre, a military aristocracy of semi-Romanized Teutons who claimed authority from a western Roman Empire that was by now little more than a name. Roving bands of Suebi, Alans, and Vandals marauded at will, not so much tribes as mobile protection rackets.

The Visigoths were illiterate, selfish and bloody-minded, but persistent enough to endure. There weren't many of them; probably only in the region between Burgos and Toledo did they form any substantial percentage of the population. For their support they depended on the landowners, who by now had made the slow but logical transition from Roman *senatores* to feudal lords. Visigothic princes were capable of knifing each other in the back at the slightest pretext, and when dynastic intrigue failed there was always the issue of religion to keep the pot boiling. The Visigoths were Arian Christians, while most of the old Roman elite were orthodox in the faith; as far as we can tell the vast majority of the population hadn't converted at all, and they probably looked on in bewildered amusement while the two factions anathematized and ambushed each other. The Visigoths ruled from Toledo, maintaining only a provisional authority in the rest of the peninsula. Despite all the troubles, Andalucía at least seems to have been doing well—probably better than anywhere else in western Europe—and there was even a modest revival of learning in the 6th century, the age of St Isidore, famous scholar of Sevilla. This helped to improve the manners of the Visigothic overlords somewhat. King Leovigild (573–86) was an able leader; his son Reccared converted to orthodox Christianity in 589; the two brought their state to the height of its power as much by internal reform as military victories. Allowing the Church a share of power, however, proved fatal to the Visigoths. As the clerics grew wealthy, they found it in their interest to join with the old Roman nobility in checking the power of the kings. Their depredations against the populace, and their persecutions of Jews and heretics, made the Visigoths as many enemies within as they ever had across their borders.

711–756: The Muslim Conquest

The great wave of Muslim Arab expansion that began in Muhammad's lifetime was bound to wash up on Spain's shores sooner or later. One of the unlikely protagonists of the Muslim conquest was a certain Count Julián of Ceuta, lonely ruler of the westernmost bastion of the Byzantine Empire, nominally cooperating with the Visigoths. Legend states that Julián's daughter had been violated by the last Visigothic king, Roderick; whatever his reasons, the Count ferried a small Arab force over to Spain in 710 led by a certain Tarif, who gave his name to today's Tarifa on the straits. Tarif came back to tell the tale of a rich land, in disarray and ripe for the plucking, and in the following year Julián assisted in taking over a larger army—

still only about 7000 men—under Tariq ibn-Ziyad, who quickly defeated the Visigoths near Zarbate. Within three years, the Arabs had conquered most of the peninsula, driving north-wards as far as Narbonne in France. The ease of the conquest is not difficult to explain. The majority of the population was delighted to welcome the Arabs and their Berber allies. The persecuted Jews supported them from the first, and for the country people, the final extinction of Roman law made free men of nearly all of them. Religious tolerance was guaranteed under the Muslims from the start; some historians have suggested that their campaign was more a financial speculation than a holy war, and since the largest share of taxes fell on non-believers, the Arabs were happy to refrain from seeking converts.

This conquest, however, was never completed. In 718, a legendary prince named Pelayo in the tiny kingdom of Asturias defeated the Muslims at an obscure skirmish the Spaniards call the Battle of Covadonga, opening the way for Alfonso I of Asturias to recover much of north-western Iberia. The Arabs barely noticed; they were busy elsewhere. By 732 their armies had penetrated as far as Poitou in northern France, where Charles Martel whipped them so soundly that their advance was halted permanently. Muslim control of most of Spain was solid, but hampered by dissension almost from the start between the haughty Arabs and the neglected Berbers, and between the various tribes of the Arabs themselves.

756–1031: The Emirate of Al-Andalus

Far away in Damascus, the political struggles of the Caliphate were being resolved by a general massacre of the princes of the Umayyad dynasty, the successors of Muhammad, as the rival tribe of Abbasids replaced them on the throne. One Umayyad escaped—Abd ar-Rahman; he fled to Córdoba, well beyond the reach of the usurping Caliphs, and managed to establish himself there as the first leader of an independent Emirate of Al-Andalus. Under this new government, Muslim Spain grew strong and prosperous. Political unity was maintained only with great difficulty, but trade, urban life and culture flourished. Though their domains stretched as far as the Pyrenees, the Umayyad emirs referred to it all as *Al-Andalus*. Andalucía was its heartland and Córdoba, Sevilla and Málaga its greatest cities, unmatched by any others in western Europe. Toledo and Zaragoza in the north prospered greatly as well.

Much nonsense has been written about the history of 'Moorish' Spain. Whether glorifying or disparaging it, too often the age has been approached as if it were a foreign occupation. It cannot be emphasized too strongly that Al-Andalus was a *Spanish* culture. Somehow the arrival of Islam, Islamic art and Arab poetry energized the intact, though slumbering, culture of Roman Andalucía. Spaniards, Arabs, Berbers and Jews all made their contributions; here, however, they lived in relative harmony, and it would be impossible to disentangle them even if there were reason to try. For its wealth and sophistication, its poetry and scholarship, and its art and architecture, all far in advance of anything else Europe had to offer, we may take medieval Al-Andalus as the height of Spanish civilization.

The political foundation for this achievement was provided by Abd ar-Rahman III, who turned the emirate into the Caliphate of Córdoba in 929. When the boy Caliph Hisham II came to the throne in 976, effective power was seized by his chamberlain Muhammad ben Abd-Allah, better known as *Al-Mansur* ('the victorious'), who recaptured León, Pamplona and Barcelona from the Christians, and even raided Compostela, stealing its bells to hang up as trophies in the Great Mosque of Córdoba. Throughout this century, the military superiority of the Moors was great enough for them to have finally erased the tiny Christian kingdoms of the northwest had they cared to do so. If lack of determination was one flaw, another was an anarchic inability to create a modern state. Directly upon Al-Mansur's death in 1002, the Caliphate entered a fatal period of factional struggles and civil war. By 1031 the central authority had vanished for ever, and Al-Andalus broke up into a patchwork of petty kingdoms called the *taifas*.

The Christian states of the north were better organized, and despite their relative weakness, it was in this period that they laid the foundations of reconquest. Three small states in particular appeared, and each would one day be an important Christian kingdom. Under Alfonso I ('the Catholic', d. 757) and Alfonso II ('the Chaste', d. 842), little Asturias grew into the Kingdom of León. The Basques, independent for centuries already, developed the Kingdom of Navarre, reaching its height under Sancho the Great (d. 1035). The northeastern corner of the peninsula, the 'Spanish march' of Charlemagne's empire that today is Catalunya, attained its independence as the County of Barcelona, and began its career as a mercantile power in the Mediterranean under Ramón Berenguer II (d. 1131).

1031–1284: The Reconquista

With Al-Andalus hopelessly divided, these Christian kingdoms had their chance. A son of Sancho the Great gained possession of the border county of Castile in 1037 and made of it a kingdom, installing himself as Fernando I, later annexing León and making the Muslim states of Toledo and Zaragoza his vassals. Almost from the beginning, this new state of Castile and León was the scene of permanent civil war, but it was still strong enough to advance when it had a strong leader. Alfonso VI, with the help of the legendary warrior El Cid, captured Toledo in 1085. The loss of this key fortress-city, opening all central Spain to Christian raids, alarmed the kings of the *taifas* enough for them to invite in the Almoravids from North Africa, fanatical Muslim Berbers who had recently established an empire stretching from Morocco to Senegal. The Almoravid leader Yusuf crossed the straits and defeated Alfonso in 1086. Yusuf liked Al-Andalus so much he decided to keep it, and Almoravid domination lasted until 1147 when it was replaced by that of the Almohads, a nearly identical military state also from Africa, that grew up around the reforming fundamentalist zeal of a mystic named ibn-Tumart.

Like the Almoravids, the Almohads went quickly through the cycle of conquest, decadence and decay. The end for them, and for Al-Andalus, came with the Battle of Las Navas de Tolosa in 1212 when an army from all Christian Spain (and newly independent Portugal) under Alfonso VIII destroyed the Almohad power forever. Alfonso's son, Fernando III, reunited Castile and León for the last time, captured Córdoba (1236) and Sevilla (1248), and was made a saint for his trouble. Alfonso X 'the Wise', noted for his poetry and the brilliance of his court, completed the conquest of western Andalucía in the 1270s and 1280s, leaving the newly-formed Nasrid Kingdom of Qarnatah (Granada) as the only Muslim state in Spain. While all this was happening, the growing Kingdom of Aragón, incorporating the County of Barcelona, was completing the Reconquista in the east. Alfonso I 'the Battler' had taken Zaragoza as early as 1118 but it was left to the greatest Aragonese ruler, Jaume I ('the Conqueror', d. 1276) to expand Aragón's rule to Valencia, the Balearic Islands and Alicante.

It would be a mistake to see the early days of the Reconquista as a simple crusade: that was a myth invented in the reign of Isabel and Fernando. The age is as fascinating as it is complex. Before the coming of the fanatical Almoravids and Almohads, and the growth of the crusading idea in the Christian Church, Spanish Christians and Muslims usually had too much respect for each other to lapse into the kind of bigotry of an Isabel or Felipe II. Intermarriage was common; all the Castilian and Aragonese kings had some Moorish blood, and the mother of Abd ar-Rahman III was a Basque. Alfonso the Wise and many of the kings of Aragón were just as much at home in Arabic as in their own language, and a warrior like El Cid was just as happy serving the Muslim Emir of Zaragoza as Alfonso VI. Above all, it was a great age for culture. León and Toledo were beginning their cathedrals at about the same time as the Almohads were building La Giralda in Sevilla.

1284–1476: Aragón and Castile

These two states came to dominate the new Christian Spain. Aragón's career was perhaps the more spectacular. Out of Barcelona's navy and trade connections, it built an empire that included Sicily, Sardinia and even parts of Greece. As a formidable rival to Genoa, Pisa and Venice, Barcelona dominated the western Mediterranean until a long stretch of bad luck after 1330—plagues, bank collapses, and class strife directed against the big merchants—sent the city into a long economic decline that enabled Castile to gain the upper hand on the peninsula.

Castile itself, having swallowed up León, Galicia, and most of the reconquered lands, was an aggressive society of ever-greater importance in European affairs. The civil wars between Pedro I 'the Cruel' (d. 1369) and his brother Enrique de Trastámara brought in foreign intervention. Pedro had the support of the English, Enrique the French, and the Black Prince and Bertrand du Guesclin carried out a side-show to the Hundred Years' War on Spanish soil. Such dynastic feuds were still common, though none seriously damaged the kingdom. Castile based its prosperity on the *Honrado Concejo de la Mesta*, an enormous crown-chartered cooperative of sheep farmers that supplied Europe with much of its wool; the annual trade fairs at Medina del Campo were the busiest on the continent. Because of the experience of the Reconquista, when new hands were always needed to settle newly conquered lands, economic feudalism ended in Castile long before anywhere else in western Europe. Still, the nobility flourished, exempt from taxes and loaded with privilege. The Reconquista had seen the creation of three new knightly orders, those of Santiago, Calatrava, and Alcántara, created to replace the heretical Templars who were dissolved in 1312. The new orders, cooperating with an increasingly arrogant and worldly Church, gained great power and wealth in this period.

On the whole, the experience of the Reconquista seems to have had a negative effect on both kingdoms, particularly Castile. Religious bigotry became widespread in the 13th and 14th centuries: the first general pogroms against the Jews occurred in 1391. Above all, the years of constant warfare coarsened Castile, creating a pirate ethos where honest labour was scorned. In 1474, yet another civil war broke out upon the death of Enrique IV 'the Impotent', this time between the partisans of his (likely) daughter Juana 'la Beltraneja' and his sister Isabel.

1476–1516: The Catholic Kings

Isabel had already married Fernando, heir to the throne of Aragón, and when Fernando defeated Juana and her Portuguese allies in the 1476 Battle of Toro, the way was open for the unification of the two realms. They reigned together, collaborating in every decision; both were capable and intelligent, though Isabel, representing the stronger kingdom, had the final say. Fernando, a subtle statesman and excellent campaigner, did all the work. Under these two, the new Spain reached the height of its glory. In the unforgettable year of 1492, Columbus initiated the Age of

Discovery by reaching Hispañola and Fernando conquered Muslim Granada, finally completing the Reconquista. Later in their reign Fernando would annex Navarra, and the great general Gonzalo de Córdoba, 'El Gran Capitán', would conquer Naples and make Spain for the first time a leading player in European affairs. Also in 1492, the Catholic Kings expelled the Jews from Spain, some 150,000 of them. Soon afterwards, they created the Inquisition, in an age when most European countries were disbanding it. They also broke the agreements they had made with the Moors of Granada, instituting a policy that was little better than genocide. Fernando and Isabel's fierce bigotry was popular enough in the nation as a whole—there was plenty of confiscated property to be handed out to loyal supporters—and it set the tone for Spain's grisly history in the next two centuries.

1516–1700: The Age of Rapacity

Or, as historians once called it, Spain's 'Golden Age'. Modern historians entertain fewer illusions, and remind us that any golden age is in the eye of the beholder. In the 16th century Spain fought for hegemony over three continents, and succeeded only in destroying itself.

In an effort to build up their alliances against France, Fernando and Isabel had married their daughter Juana to the Habsburg Archduke Philip, son of the Holy Roman Emperor. The death of their other two children made Juana and Philip heirs to the throne, but Philip (called 'the Handsome') soon died, and Juana became deranged with grief. Whether she actually became permanently insane we do not know. Her son Charles arrived from Flanders in 1517, visited her just long enough to force her to sign papers of abdication, and then locked her up in a windowless cell for the next 40 years. Spain in its long history had suffered invasions and civil wars, plagues and famines, but never had it been forced to bear anything like the Habsburgs. This family had the good fortune to marry into half the thrones of Europe, and it was Charles' luck to inherit them all—Spain and its colonies, the Netherlands, Austria, half of Italy and a smattering of German principalities. To top it off, he bought himself election as Holy Roman Emperor, making him the most powerful ruler in Europe since Charlemagne. (In Spain he is Carlos I, though we know him better under his imperial title, Charles V.)

To the rest of Europe, Charles meant unending war, serving both his megalomaniac ambitions and his opposition to Protestantism. To Spain, a country he had never seen, Charles meant economic ruin. Almost immediately upon arriving, he and his Flemish minions emptied the royal treasury and shipped it overseas to bribe the German electors. This and other outrages occasioned the Comunero Revolt of 1520–21 in which the cities of Old Castile rose to defend their liberties—and their purses—but were eventually crushed by Charles' foreign troops. It was the beginning of Castile's decline, and 36 more years of expensive Habsburg imperialism ended all hope for recovery. Charles' wars came to nothing, and in 1556 he chucked it all for retirement at the monastery of Yuste in Extremadura.

The mess was inherited by his intelligent, pious and grandly neurotic son, Felipe II (one-time husband of Mary I of England), whose reign began with a national bankruptcy in 1556, the first of three. Silver from America kept Spain afloat, though little stayed in Spain long enough to do any good. Felipe had his successes, notably the great naval victory of Felipe's brother Don Juan over the Turks at Lepanto in 1571, but mostly the news was bad. The continuing revolt in the Netherlands eventually resulted in Dutch independence, and the failure of the Great Armada against England in 1588 finally put an end to Habsburg designs in the north.

At home, too, things were going very wrong. Felipe's religious mania turned Spain into the very picture of a modern totalitarian state. The Inquisition securely shut down the country's intellectual life. Book-burnings (as parodied in *Don Quixote*) became common, and Spaniards were forbidden to study overseas. The national movement towards *limpieza de sangre* ('purity of blood') resulted in a national manhunt for clerics and officials with a taint of Jewish ancestry, and oppression of the remaining Moors reached new heights of ferocity. Spanish behaviour in the New World was even more brutal; in the 16th century 80 per cent of the native population of Mexico and Peru died from disease and overwork in the fields and mines.

One family tradition of the Habsburgs was incest. Felipe's fourth wife, Anne of Austria, was at once his niece and the daughter of his first cousin. Not surprisingly, their son Felipe III was an imbecile, entirely under the influence of a favourite, the Duke of Lerma. His reign was distinguished by the final expulsion of the Moors in 1609. Most of them lived in Valencia, perhaps the most prosperous region in Spain at the time; the departure of its most skilled farmers ruined it. Felipe III married another cousin, and the result was Felipe IV. Not quite an idiot, this Felipe also had a better choice of favourite. The Conde Duque de Olivares was a flamboyant, tireless and confident reformer, but 20 years of hard work (1621–43) brought not a single noteworthy accomplishment. The opposition of the Catalans and the nobility, along with national exhaustion and lethargy, made reform impossible. In 1640 Catalunya and Portugal (annexed by Felipe II in 1580) revolted. The Portuguese eventually secured their independence, and crushing defeats at the hands of the Dutch, English and French (notably at Rocroy in 1643 during the Thirty Years' War) put an end to the age when Spain was taken seriously as a European power. Olivares went mad and died soon after.

Spain was dying with him. Under the Habsburgs, Spaniards had made contributions to European culture despite the terror of the times. The last great generation of Spanish artists, poets and dramatists, including Velázquez, Calderón, and Lope de Vega, were contemporaries of Felipe IV, but when they died there were no more to replace them. Economically, a wasteland had appeared. Spain's agriculture had been ruined, its mountains deforested, its manufacturers bankrupted. In the Middle Ages the plains of Castile had been the most densely populated part of Spain. By 1650 they had become as lonely and empty as you see them today, and their once thriving cities were reduced to relics of the past. We cannot credit the Habsburgs with all the blame. They could not have wrecked Spain so thoroughly without the help of a grasping, ignorant Church and nobility. Both found ample opportunity to enrich themselves in every Spanish reverse, while contributing less than nothing to the national life. These institutions had once combined to create the expansive, crusading ethos of medieval Castile; later, ironically, they conspired to assist in a national suicide. To close the book on the Habsburgs, there's drooling, staring Carlos II, who lasted 35 years. He spent the last few in trances and convulsions, while the police combed the back alleys of Madrid to find the 'sorceress' who a priest said had enchanted him. Surrounded by a cabal of exorcists, clairvoyants and witch-doctors, Carlos passed on in 1700, fortunately childless.

1700–1931: Bourbons, on the Rocks

A vacant throne attracted suitors, and prostrate Spain watched while they fought over it. The Austrian Archduke Charles had the support of England, while the French schemed for Philip of Anjou, a Bourbon, and the result was a general European commotion, the War of the Spanish Succession. The English agitated madly, and the Duke of Marlborough won great victories; in the end, though, they abandoned their Spanish and Austrian allies for possession of Gibraltar (seized in 1704), and the promise that the Spanish and French thrones would never be united. The new king, Felipe V, was put out at not being able to live in Paris, but he knew what Spain needed most—more palaces. He and his successors spent most of Spain's revenues in constructing a dozen mock-Versailles around Castile, and beyond that did their best never to offend the grandees or the Church. The one bright exception was Carlos III, who came to the throne in 1759. Carlos and his ministers, Floridablanca and Jovellanos, tried to reform everything but most of his efforts went down the drain with the succession of his son Carlos IV, as useless and stupid as any Habsburg.

The disruptions of the French Revolution interrupted the Bourbons' rococo daydream. Napoleon first threatened Spain, then enticed it into cooperating in his campaigns. The result was the 1805 Battle of Trafalgar, where nearly the entire Spanish fleet was destroyed under incompetent French leadership. Every Spaniard did his duty though, and today, with their invincible concept of personal honour, the Spaniards still take it as a kind of victory. Napoleon finessed Carlos IV into abdication in 1808, and when French troops attempted to kidnap the heirs to the throne in Madrid, the citizens responded with the famous revolt of the *Dos de Mayo*, brutally suppressed by General Murat.

In the Peninsular War that followed, French troops occupied all of Spain, and distinguished themselves by stealing as much gold and art as they could carry, and blowing up castles and historical buildings just for sport. British forces under Moore and later the Duke of Wellington arrived in 1809, won most of their battles, and generally conducted themselves disgracefully towards the population. The Spanish themselves recovered some self-respect by heroically resisting the French, notably at the siege of Zaragoza under Palafox in 1809. In 1812 a group of Spanish liberals met in Cádiz to declare a Constitution, and under this the Spanish fitfully conducted what they call their War of Independence. Victory came with the restoration of the Bourbons in 1814. The new king, Fernando VII, turned out to be a black-hearted reactionary who restored the Inquisition and invited back the Jesuits. A successful revolt against him in 1820 was suppressed by the French in 1823. In this decade most of Spain's American colonies achieved their independence—the mother country could do little to stop them. Fernando's death in 1833 occasioned the First Carlist War, in which liberals supporting the rights of the Infanta, Isabel II, fought the Church, reactionaries and the Basques under pretender Don Carlos. The liberals won, but their succeeding dictatorships accomplished little of value apart from the expropriation of the monasteries and the final extinction of the Inquisition.

Spain, by now, had become a sort of banana monarchy, where any ambitious general could issue a *pronunciamiento* and strive for power. Under a Catalan, General Prim, the First Republic was declared in 1868 but it soon succumbed to anarchy in Andalucía and a Second Carlist War as futile as the first. A *pronunciamiento* by General Martínez Campos restored the Bourbons in 1876 and liberal and conservative politicians cut a cynical deal under which they would alternate in power. Political frustrations with this arrangement helped the growth of new left-wing groups: Communists, Socialists, and the Anarchist CNT.

The outstanding feature of Spanish life in the late 19th century was the economic and spiritual blossoming of Catalunya. While the long-oppressed Catalans were rediscovering their language and culture, Barcelona attained the position of Spain's biggest and most modern city, its artistic leader and the great stronghold of Anarchism. The heavily industrialized Basque provinces began to assert themselves, too, and even Andalucía, where Anarchism was also strong, began to feel the winds of change. Once more regionalism became a political issue, as thriving peripheral areas began to challenge the moribund Castilian centre.

A crisis for Spanish life came with the embarrassing defeat in the 1898 Spanish-American War, and the loss of Spain's last important colonies. An informal group of truculent intellectuals, the 'Generation of '98', whose most famous members were Miguel de Unamuno and José Ortega y Gasset, began to examine closely their country's curious destiny. At the same time, Spain was once more becoming a force in European culture, producing Picasso, Gaudí, and a host of lesser figures. After a long hibernation, the creative juices were flowing once more. Spain stayed neutral in the First World War, and afterwards King Alfonso XIII entrusted the government to a genial, though rather repressive dictator, Miguel Primo de Rivera, who did much to bring the country's economy into the modern world in the optimistic decade of the 1920s. A newly-confident Spain demanded better; Primo de Rivera was dismissed with the onset of the Depression, and when municipal elections in 1931 showed an overwhelming victory for parties favouring a republic, Alfonso agreed to abdicate.

1931–9: The Second Republic and Civil War

In the beginning, the Second Republic was greeted with general euphoria, but the reforms of the leftist government under Manuel Azaña served only to bring the underlying conflicts of Spanish politics to the surface. To the reactionary upper classes, any reform was 'Bolshevik', while the Marxists and Anarchists saw the new government only as a prelude to revolution. Political violence ranged from an attempted coup by General Sanjurjo in Sevilla in 1932, to a series of peasant revolts and land seizures in the poorest areas of Andalucía. Basques and Catalans took advantage of the government's weakness to declare their autonomy. Reaction came when the abstention of many leftists in the 1933 elections brought the radical right into power. Moderate leaders like Azaña found themselves temporarily in jail, and an epic miners' revolt in Asturias was crushed with incredible brutality in 1934. The alarmed Left formed a Popular Front to regain power in 1936, but street fighting and assassinations were becoming daily occurrences, and the new government seemed powerless to halt the slide into anarchy. Most of the trouble was cause by rightist provocateurs, especially the violent new Fascist party, the Falange Española, led by José Antonio Primo de Rivera, son of the former dictator. The Left responded in kind, seizing the property of aristocrats, burning churches and forming armed militias. At this point the army decided to step in.

Spain's creaky military, with one officer for every six soldiers, had a long tradition of interfering in politics, dating from the scores of *pronunciamientos* (coups) of the 19th century. On 17 July 1936 simultaneous risings occurred across Spain, orchestrated by Generals Francisco Franco and Emiliano Mola. The government was panicked into inaction, but workers' militias took control of the situation in many areas. Also, a substantial part of the army remained loyal to the Republic, and instead of the quick coup they had expected the generals got a Spain divided into two armed camps. In the early stages of the war, the balance was swung by the Army of Africa, the only effective fighting force, made up of mercenary Moors who had campaigned in Spain's colonial wars in its North Moroccan protectorate. They quickly captured eastern Andalucía and Extremadura, and their presence made their commander, Franco, first among equals (Mola died in a car crash soon afterwards). The insurgents' hope for an early victory was thwarted by the militia's heroic defence of Madrid.

Almost from the beginning the Civil War became an international affair. Fascist Italy, Portugal, and Germany sent hundreds of aeroplanes and some 200,000 troops. Only Russia helped the Republic (all arms to be paid for in cash, of course; the Fascists were a little more liberal to Franco). The Communists also organized the famous International Brigade, though these were only a handful. The list of famous foreigners who participated in the war in one way or another is endless: Hemingway and George Orwell came as war-tourists; André Malraux organized an air squadron; Willy Brandt helped keep peace among the leftist factions while reporting for a Norwegian newspaper. Among the Communists, arrangements for volunteers were handled from Paris by Josep Broz (Marshal Tito), while future national Communist leaders like Walter Ulbricht of East Germany and Togliatti of Italy were agents in Spain.

The great imbalance in foreign help favouring Franco probably decided the war. British governments pursued a policy of appeasement and set up a 'Non-Intervention Committee', pressed the French into going along and ignored German and Italian intervention, while doing their best to keep any aid from reaching the Republic. Dissension among the Republicans themselves did not help. With Russia the sole arms supplier and Communist-run divisions the best disciplined troops, the Communists dominated the government in later stages. In late 1937 the Republic finally found a capable leader in Dr Juan Negrín, but it was already too late.

Franco's careful tactics probably dragged the war on longer than was necessary. The first serious Republican reverse was the fall of Málaga in February 1937, losing them Andalucía once and for all. Spaniards on both sides chuckled when the Italian attempt to mount a blitzkrieg on Guadalajara in the same month lost them most of a division as prisoners. The Germans introduced terror bombing at Gernika (Guernica), in April, in a campaign where Franco took the Basque provinces and Asturias. In December, the Republicans mounted an offensive in southern Aragón and another in July 1938 across the Ebro, where the Nationalists had reached the sea to cut the Republican zone in two. Both failed for lack of artillery and air support. After these last efforts, the Republic was finished; Franco conquered Catalunya in January 1939 and only token resistance continued in the centre. Madrid surrendered in March.

1939–75: Franco's Dictatorship

Some 500,000 Spaniards died in the war, more in mass killings behind the lines than in battle. When it was over, Franco proved more interested in revenge than reconciliation; even moderate Republican supporters found themselves in jail or forced labour camps. Franco by now was calling himself *Caudillo* (leader) and dressing in full Fascist regalia at public functions. By no means, though, did he convert Spain into a genuine Fascist state. Since the death of José Antonio Primo de Rivera in a Republican jail in 1936 the Falangists had been leaderless, though they greatly increased their numbers during and after the war. Franco manipulated them carefully, letting them organize Fascist-style vertical trade unions and 'syndicates', but they were gradually excluded from power when Franco guessed the Fascists would lose the Second World War. Franco's relations with the Axis were difficult from the start. Hitler came down from a 1941 meeting at Hendaye, intending to bully Spain into the war, but afterwards stated he would 'rather have his teeth pulled' than ever again talk to such a stubborn character.

Even had Franco been more willing, Spain was capable of little help. Industry and communications were in ruins, and parts of the country knew famine several times in the dark 1940s. Conditions did not improve until after 1953 when Franco signed a treaty with the United States, exchanging military base sites for a measure of international respectability and a huge transfusion of dollars. To please his new friends and at the same time avoid bankruptcy, Franco dismantled the cumbersome Fascist organization of the economy and encouraged a new generation of technocrats (many of them members of the secret Catholic society *Opus Dei*). Their reforms and the American loans began to pay off in the 1960s, when Spain experienced an industrial take-off that gave it the highest economic growth rate in the world—really just making up for lost time. The growth of tourism and remittances from half a million Spaniards working abroad helped as much as any new industry.

Economic advance, of course, meant social changes. Possibly the greatest was the mass migration of rural people from the south to the industrial cities. Between their experience in the cities and the influx of the tourists, millions of Spaniards were exposed to foreign ideas and influences for the first time. Such things usually mean trouble for dictators, but Franco proved stubborn enough to resist all pressure for change. As always, his regime depended entirely on Spain's three evil stepsisters: the Church, the Army and the landowners. All legal political factions, Falangists, Carlists and Monarchists were combined in the toothless Movimiento Nacional, but what Franco really wanted was to eliminate politics for ever. The Spaniards had other ideas. All the leftist groups had maintained clandestine organizations, even organizing a network of underground trade unions. Most groups were simply waiting for the old man finally to die; an exception was the Basques, who evolved the terrorist ETA. This first became prominent in 1973, when their master blasters assassinated Admiral Carrero Blanco, sending his limousine over the roof of a Madrid church where he was coming to attend Mass. Carrero Blanco had been the ageing dictator's strong man and best hope for the continuity of the regime. Franco found no one hard enough to replace him.

1975 to the Present: the Restoration of Democracy

Franco was a monarchist at heart, and back in 1969 he had declared Juan Carlos I, grandson of Alfonso XIII, to be his successor. In doing so he passed over Juan Carlos' democratically-minded father Don Juan; Juan Carlos seemed a pliable enough young man, and both Franco and the opposition expected him to carry on the old order. Franco died in 1975 and for a while the new King did nothing to excite anyone's suspicions.

Those who underestimated Juan Carlos, however, received a big surprise when he began confidently to move Spain back to democracy. His choice for Prime Minister, Adolfo Suárez, initiated a political reform bill that would establish a democratically elected *Cortes*. On the night of 18 November 1977, the nation watched spellbound on television while the disorganized Francoists in the old *Cortes* committed political suicide by approving it. In the months that followed, the trade unions and the Socialist and Communist parties were legalized, and the Francoist Movimiento disbanded. Press censorship was ended, and the first free elections in 32 years held, returning Suárez and his centralist party, the UCD, to power. The speed and orderliness of the transition astounded the world. Somehow, the long years of Franco's grey dictatorship had created a new maturity among the vast majority who desired democracy. They had been waiting for this opportunity for years, and no one did anything to ruin it. In the words of one perceptive foreign correspondent, Spain was 'a country whose society was open and democratic long before its institutions were'.

A new Constitution followed, one of the most liberal in Europe. Even more remarkably, the long heritage of Castilian centralism was undone once and for all by measures creating regional autonomy, making Spain a federal state like Germany or the USA. The new democracy easily survived the old guards' last hurrah, when Civil Guards under Colonel Antonio Tejero attempted a coup by occupying the *Cortes* in February 1981. Elements in the army were behind it, but they backed down when ordered to do so by the King. In 1982 the real transition came, when general elections were won overwhelmingly by the Socialists under Felipe González, a charmer from Sevilla with a chipmunk smile who has been called the 'best politician in Europe'.

Throughout the '80s, González maintained his popularity by staying as close as possible to the centre, while carefully nurturing the economy. In 1986, he overcame all the opposition by steering Spain into the European Community, winning a national referendum over NATO membership (something he had opposed four years earlier), and keeping his majority in two general elections. In the late '80s the rightist parties merged to form a common opposition, the Partido Popular (PP), led by a young, economically conservative former tax inspector named José María Aznar, while the Communists, finding their support dwindling with each election, reformed into the professedly democratic United Left (IU). Under González and the Socialists, Spanish prosperity increased steadily, growing closer to that of the other big nations of western Europe. The big problem was, and remains, an unemployment rate consistently over 20%, the highest in the EU.

The magic year 1992—the 500th anniversary of national unification and Columbus's voyage—was a chance for the Spaniards to show off the new Spain to the world, with Sevilla's World's Fair and the Barcelona Olympics.

In 1996, after 14 years in power, González's Socialists found themselves suffering the usual weariness and lethargy that come with a long term of office, besides suffering serious scandals over corruption and the GAL, so-called 'death squads' in the security forces which are accused of murdering Basque separatist (ETA) officials involved with terrorism. Spain takes its new democracy with admirable seriousness, and she can put on spectacles in politics as good as those in her fiestas. After the most recent attack, Madrid witnessed a silent, monster demonstration at night, led by González, Aznar and the other party chiefs marching together—in the middle of an electoral campaign. The next general elections resulted in a narrow victory for Aznar's Partido Popular, which has managed to steer a respectable course for the past three years, supported (for the most part) by the powerful national parties in the parliament. The success of the Good Friday agreements in Northern Ireland has inspired some serious soul-searching in the ETA, which declared a ceasefire in September 1998 while talks continue.

Art and Architecture

Pre-Roman

Early examples of Spanish art are among the oldest yet found—most notably the Upper Palaeolithic (12,000 BC) cave paintings at Altamira, near **Santander**. Prehistoric architectural remains are less remarkable. Neolithic cultures constructed dolmens along the coasts, especially in Galicia and Asturias; the best on the mainland are the three huge dolmen-chambers in **Antequera**, Andalucía, along with the site of Los Millares, near **Almería**. Galicia and Asturias are rich in foundations of Celtic *castros*, the best-preserved in **A Garda**. The Celts brought with them a talent for jewellery and metalwork, and under Roman rule made the stone bulls and boars called *verracos* found throughout Ávila province. The most interesting works can be found in the archaeological museums of **Córdoba**, **Sevilla** and above all, **Madrid**, where you can see the masterpiece of Iberian sculpture, the famous *Dama de Elche*.

Roman and Visigothic

Considering the literary and political figures Spain gave the Roman world, it's surprising that Roman Spain comes up so short in art. In the museums of **Madrid**, **Córdoba**, **Mérida** and **Barcelona** you'll see the usual copies of Greek sculpture, statues of emperors, and mosaics: some lovely mosaics have recently been uncovered at the Roman villa of Olmeda at **Pedrosa de la Viga** (Palencia province). Among Roman cities **Mérida** is by far the best preserved, although rivalled by **Tarragona** for interest. The aqueduct of **Segovia**, still intact, is one of the largest engineering works left from antiquity; the lofty **Alcántara** bridge in Cáceres province is also impressive. Other Roman ruins may be seen at **Italica** near Sevilla; there's also a reconstructed temple colonnade in **Córdoba** and an intact belt of Roman walls around **Lugo**.

Art under the Visigoths, what there is of it, was derivative of the Roman with a touch of barbaric dash. The Spanish rediscovered their talent for gaudy, intricate jewellery, best seen in the Archaeological Museum of **Madrid** ('the Treasure of Gurrazar') and the Museo de los Concilios y del Arte Visigotico in **Toledo**. A few churches survive, with the characteristic horseshoe-arch later adopted by the Moors: the most extraordinary of these is at **Quintanilla de las Viñas** south of Burgos, San Pedro de las Naves, near Zamora, the martyrium in **Palencia** cathedral, Recesvinth's church at **Baños de Cerrato** (south of Palencia), and the churches at **Terrassa** near Barcelona.

Moorish

The renaissance of culture in Spain began in the 9th century, with the reign of the great Abd ar-Rahman. Its inspirations were surprisingly varied: floral arabesques and detail from late Roman art, architectural forms from Syria, mosaics from Byzantium (often done by Greek artists), and the perfection of the already impressive Spanish heritage in metalwork and jewellery. The catalyst that made these disparate elements come together so brilliantly was Islam itself. Prohibiting figurative art, the religion led men to contemplate rhythms and patterns in nature. Islamic art carried on, without decadence or revolutions, until 1492 and beyond, shifting slowly like a kaleidoscope, constantly finding new forms to delight the eye and declare the unity of creation. In the time of the caliphate, before 1009, Moorish Spain excelled in architecture (the Great Mosque of **Córdoba**), and its artists became the consummate masters of the minor arts: elaborate woodcarving, metalwork and ceramics, including the *azulejo* tiles used in architectural decoration that have been a Spanish speciality ever since. The best collections are in the museums of **Granada** and **Córdoba**.

The age of the Almohads was a great time for architecture, exemplified by the Torre de Oro and La Giralda in the Almohad capital, **Sevilla**. Islamic art had its last efflorescence in Nasrid **Granada**, where the marriage of art and architecture was raised to a level of perfection in the Alhambra, built in stages throughout the 14th century. Granadan artists also worked for the Christian King Pedro in the Alcázar of **Sevilla**. Much Moorish work was wantonly destroyed after the Reconquista but, besides the sites mentioned above, many castles remain, notably the Alcazabas in **Málaga** and **Almería**. In the north, the Cristo de la Luz church (a former mosque) in **Toledo** and the Aljafería in **Zaragoza** are the outstanding buildings.

Asturian and Mozarabic Pre-Romanesque

In the 9th century, as the Moors in the south were beginning their golden age, the small Christian principalities of the north were developing an architecture as sophisticated and original as anything else in western Europe. Athough referred to as 'Pre-Romanesque', the monuments of the Kingdom of Asturias are in fact Romanesque, a century ahead of anything elsewhere. Having the cultured Moor for a neighbour and an enemy undoubtedly provided the Asturians with their impetus to build; lacking precedents, they created a new architecture from Roman survivals, along with Celtic decorative motifs and Islamic elements, such as the latticework screen windows. The greatest monuments are the Asturian churches in and around **Oviedo**. From the same period, there are interesting Mozarabic churches in the villages of **Soria** province (San Baudelio), **León** (San Miguel de Escalada), **Aragón**, and especially at **Melque**, near Toledo. This was also the period of the first great illuminated manuscripts: beautifully coloured copies of the *Commentaries on the Apocalypse,* written by Beato of the Mozarabic monastery of Santa María de Lebeña (Asturias), survive in **Girona**.

Romanesque

Romanesque, the first 'international style' of European art, anticipated in Asturias, took shape across the Pyrenees in the 11th century. A strong French influence came back to Spain along the pilgrimage road to Santiago de Compostela, where you can see scores of examples: **Jaca** cathedral in Aragón, **Santa María de Eunate**, **Sangüesa** and **Estella**, all in Navarra, the 'perfect Romanesque church' at **Frómista**, the Pantheon of St Isidore in **León**, and the great cathedral of **Santiago** itself. The Catalans were among the first to develop their own brand of Romanesque: straightforward and solid, distinguished by elegant square bell towers with ranks of paired windows. **Ripoll**, **San Cugat**, and most villages in the Pyrenees have impressive churches. Many churches were often part of a town's defences, such as the cathedrals at **Ávila**, **Tarragona** and **Sigüenza**. As elsewhere in Europe, this was an era of great creative freedom, and there are many regional styles besides Catalunya's: **Segovia**'s, for instance, with characteristic side porches, or the Byzantine cupolas of **Zamora** and **Toro**.

Sculpture, integrated in the architecture of a religious building, was an essential feature of the Romanesque. The Catalans excelled at it, especially at **Ripoll**, and there are many fine capitals, tympana and tombs along the pilgrimage road (Santo Domingo de Silos near **Burgos** has the best cloister), but the finest of all Spanish sculpture from the 12th-century is Master Mateo's tremendous Pórtico de la Gloria at **Santiago de Compostela**. The Catalans also had a head start in painting: in **Barcelona**, the Museu Nacional d'Art de Catalunya contains a magnificent collection of frescoes salvaged from tiny churches in the Pyrenees. The finest *in situ* Romanesque frescoes are in the Panteón de los Reyes in San Isidoro in **León**.

Mudéjar

In parts of the north, in the first lands of the Reconquista, Moorish influence and Moorish artisans survived, developing a new and unique art in the 12th century. One critic has called *mudéjar* the 'national style of Spain', combining the best of Moorish decorative arts—brickwork and *azulejo* tiles—and their love of elaborate geometric patterns with elements from the Romanesque and Gothic. The cloisters of San Juan de Duero at **Soria** and the brick churches at **Sahagún** near León are among the earliest examples, while **Toledo** has the best collection: several parish churches, town gates, and two lovely synagogues. Perhaps the grandest *mudéjar* works are the four great church towers of **Teruel**. Many other towns in southern Aragón—**Zaragoza**, **Calatayud**, and **Tarazona**—have good examples. In the south, the Alcázar in **Sevilla**, built for Peter the Cruel, is *mudéjar* at its most extravagant.

Gothic

The increasing bitterness of the Reconquista broke off many cultural relations between Christian and Moorish Spain; one result was that Moorish influences in architecture ended in Castile and León, allowing the growth of a Gothic aesthetic highly dependent on French originals. The three greatest Gothic cathedrals are in **León**, **Burgos** and **Toledo**. Catalan Gothic is another story altogether, emphasizing width and strength rather than height. The cathedrals of **Girona**, **Tarragona** and **Barcelona** are textbook examples. Barcelona also has Santa María del Mar, Catalan Gothic at its most sublime, and the Barri Gòtic, Europe's greatest concentration of secular Gothic architecture. Gothic penetrated Andalucía with the progress of the Reconquista, as the triumphant Spaniards refused to permit any continuity with the artistic legacy of the Moors. The results range from the simple parish churches of **Córdoba** to ponderous **Sevilla** Cathedral, the biggest Gothic church ever built. The style lingered in Spain longer than the rest of Europe—the last Gothic cathedrals are those of **Salamanca** and **Segovia** in the 16th century. Isabelline Gothic, late 15th-century Spain's ornate contribution to the style, corresponds roughly to the French Flamboyant or English Perpendicular, but is a distinctive product of a young, confident nation. You can see Isabelline Gothic at its best in **San Juan de los Reyes** in Toledo, San Gregorio in **Valladolid**, Santa María in **Aranda del Duero** (Burgos province) and Enrique Egas' Capilla Real in **Granada**. At the Cartuja of Miraflores in **Burgos**, Gil de Siloé's tombs mark the summit of Isabelline Gothic sculpture.

The 14th and 15th centuries were the first important age of Spanish painting, again mainly in Catalunya but also in Valencia. Works by a score of talented but little-known painters like Ferrer Bassá (d. 1348), Bernat Martorell (d. 1452), Jaume Huguet (d. 1492) and Bartolomé Bermejo (d.1498) can be seen in the Cathedral and museums of **Barcelona**, and also in the museums of **Vich** and **Valencia**.

Renaissance and the 'Golden Age'

Out of Isabelline Gothic came the early Renaissance style known as Plateresque ('silversmith-like') in the early 16th century, characterized by lavish sculptural decoration, especially elaborate façades, unrelated to the rest of the building. The best Plateresque is all over **Salamanca**, the University in **Alcalá de Henares**, the façades of the Hostel de los Reyes in **Santiago de Compostela** and the Hospital de San Marcos in **León**. Plateresque coincided with the height of Spanish sculpture. Many great works are anonymous, like the famous *Doncel* in **Sigüenza** cathedral; Gil de Siloé's son Diego (d. 1563) deftly combined sculpture and architecture in the cathedrals of **Granada** (where he was the master builder) and **Burgos** (tombs and the *Escalera Dorada*). High Renaissance grandiosity arrived with Italian-trained Pedro Machuca in 1527 (Palace of Charles V, **Granada**). The new trend eventually led to something well-suited to the grim age of conquest and Counter-Reformation, exemplified in Juan de Herrera's great **El Escorial** near Madrid and the Ayuntamientos of **Madrid** and **Toledo**. In Andalucía, Herrera and Diego de Siloé had a worthy follower in Andrés de Vandelvira, whose work can be seen in **Úbeda** and **Jaén**.

Spanish painting developed in the 16th century under the influence of the Italian Renaissance and the Flemish painters brought over by Charles V; both styles can be seen in the work of Pedro Berruguete (d. 1504) in the Prado, **Madrid**, and **Paredes de Navas**, near Palencia. His son, Alonso Berruguete (d. 1561) went a step further and introduced the emotional intensity of Italian Mannerism in painting and sculpture (works in **Valladolid** and **Toledo**). Alonso Berruguete was succeeded in Toledo by El Greco (d. 1614), a Cretan whose ecstatic Mannerist style may have been *sui generis*, but properly begins the history of a distinctively Spanish painting (works in the Prado, **Madrid** and **Toledo**). The 17th century was the Golden Age of Spanish painting. The clarity, virtuosity and naturalistic perfection of the Spanish school's greatest master, Diego Velázquez (d. 1660), stand out head and shoulders above the others. By the end of his career, in his masterpiece *Las Meninas*, he achieved a miraculous subtlety and shimmering vividness, more real than real: examined close up, however, the forms magically dissolve into blurs, as if Velázquez were making a statement on the nature of matter itself (Prado, **Madrid**). The restrained, direct, monumental spirituality of the saints of Francisco de Zurbarán (d. 1664) can be seen in the museums of **Cádiz**, **Sevilla**, the Prado and the cathedral of **Guadalupe**. Other painters limited themselves to orthodox religious commissions—either grim and disquieting (Ribalta, d. 1628; Ribera, d. 1652; and the outrageous Váldez Leal, d. 1690)—or saccharine mariolatry with floating angels (Murillo, d. 1682, many works in **Sevilla**; and architect-painter Alonso Cano, d. 1667, of **Granada**).

Baroque

Architecture in the 17th and 18th centuries followed two increasingly divergent strains—the plain and the fancy, as if Spain could not make up its mind to laugh or to cry over the troubles of the age. The Baroque, as Italy and other nations knew it, never really caught on, although Spaniards often borrowed ideas from it while inventing many original forms. The plainer faction, loath to give up the ideas or the Renaissance, is shown in such works as the Basilica del Pilar in **Zaragoza** and Alonso Cano's façade for **Granada** cathedral. The real interest is with the more decorative party; their amazing creations maintained the freshness and originality of Spanish architecture in the 1700s, while almost every other nation was losing its own. The ornate early works of this school were inspired by the earlier Plateresque (San Pablo at **Valladolid**, 1601). Later, influences would come from such disparate sources as the *mudéjar* and the wild Mexican Baroque (the towers of **Jerez de los Caballeros**). The 18th century spawned the extravagant forms of the 'Churrigueresque', named after the sculptor and architect José Churriguera (d. 1723). The finest Churrigueresque creations are the Plaza Mayor in **Salamanca**, Vicente Acero's **Guadix** cathedral, the Cartuja in **Granada**, churches in **Priego de Córdoba**, the Convento de Merced in **Córdoba**, the 'Transparente' in **Toledo** cathedral and the sublime, flaming Obradoiro façade of the cathedral at **Santiago de Compostela** by Fernando Casas y Novoa.

Good Spanish painting died suddenly and completely after the 1660s: real art would have to wait for the luminosity of Goya (d. 1828), ranking with Velázquez as one of Spain's greatest (in **Madrid**, the Prado and La Florida church). Goya had no worthy followers, but the works of 19th-century Romantic realists like Fortuny, Casas, de Madrazo, Zuloaga and Sorolla fill the museums of **Madrid** and **Barcelona**. Similarly, in architecture eclecticism took hold, resulting in neo-Moorish bullrings and Roman-style public buildings.

The 20th Century

The first sign of a rebirth in Spanish architecture occurred in Catalunya, with the advent of Barcelona's Universal Exhibition of 1888 and the first works of the specifically Catalan *modernista* style. The modernistas were part of the great Art Nouveau movement at the turn of the century, although in Catalunya the artists had another agenda: Catalan nationalism. All the members of the *modernista* triumvirate—Lluis Domènech i Montaner, Josep Puig i Cadafalch, and Antoni Gaudí—frequently made references back to the Middle Ages, when Catalunya possessed its own Mediterranean empire, but expressed their medievalism in the newest techniques in iron and brick and swirling asymmetrical decoration based on stylized natural forms. Gaudí (d. 1926), the most imaginative of the *modernistas*, has been recognized as a key architectural genius of the 20th century (most works, including the Parc Güell, the Pedrera, the Colonia Güell crypt and Sagrada Família are in or near **Barcelona**, others in **Comillas** (Cantabria), **Astorga** and **León**). Gaudí's co-worker Josep Maria Jujol was responsible for most of the magnificent tile mosaic-collages that decorate the buildings; his work, and that of scores of other architects and decorators, make wandering the streets of Barcelona a delight.

Barcelona's *modernista* movement proved to be a hothouse for some of the greatest artists of the 20th century. Pablo Picasso (d. 1973), was born in Málaga but spent his early manhood in Barcelona (many works in the Reina Sofía museum in **Madrid**, others in the Picasso Museum in **Barcelona**). In Paris, Picasso met his fellow Cubist Juan Gris (d. 1927) and Barcelona natives Julio González (d. 1942) and Joan Miró (d. 1983). Another surreal Catalan, the irascible painter Salvador Dalí (d. 1989), made his whole life a masterpiece of performance art and left his native **Figueres** a delightful museum. The Catalan, Antoni Tàpies (d. 1994), was an important innovator, especially in his use of everyday objects (**Fundació Tàpies**, Barcelona).

The coming of the Civil War and Franco put a quick end to Spain's prominence in the arts, and if recovery after Franco has come in fits and starts it hasn't been for lack of good will. The Museum of Contemporary Art in **Cuenca** was built to house works by Spanish abstract artists, beginning with Antonio Saura; another showcase is the new Centro de Arte Reina Sofía in **Madrid**. Elsewhere, look out for the works of the Basque Eduardo Chillida, the greatest living sculptor in Spain (**San Sebastián** and **Vitoria**). **Barcelona** especially has sought to recapture its old prominence, beginning in 1975 with the construction of Josep-Lluis Sert's beautiful Fundació Miró. Since then, no city anywhere has commissioned more works of public art (over 70 squares have been handed over to artists from around the world) and architecture (Norman Foster's Collserola tower for the Olympics, Isozaki's Palau Sant Jordi, or native Barcelonan Ricardo Bofill's airport terminal and Sport University) or has set up more galleries and museums to digest it all (most recently, Richard Meier's Museu d'Art Contemporani de Barcelona in the Barri Xinès). Barcelona's modern art status is now seriously challenged by Bllbao, seat of the fabulous new Guggenheim Museum, a sublime work of art in itself designed by Frank Gehry.

Sketches of Spain

Air and Light

We can tell you everything about cathedrals and palaces, cities and resorts, but setting the scene for them will prove somewhat harder. One of the delights of all the Mediterranean lands is the endless variety of qualities and colour in the sea and sky. Nowhere, perhaps, will they grab your attention as in Spain.

On the high central plains, where the air is thin, the sun becomes a manifest power. At noon, even on a cool day, it can seem like some diabolical ray, probing deep inside your brain. Always, it illuminates Spain with a merciless brilliance; Spanish writers recall it when trying to explain their country's literature and history. 'Spain', according to one, 'is a country where things can be seen all too clearly.' Spanish art could not be what it is without this light. In the Prado, you'll look at Goya paintings set under an impossibly lovely pale blue sky with clouds like the breath of angels. You'll probably blame the artist for picturesque excess—and then walk outside to find that same Castilian sky, and those same clouds, reproduced over your head. Madrid's air is equally renowned, though with somewhat less lyricism: 'it is like quick lime, drying and consuming a corpse in a trice', as one 18th-century traveller noted. Doctors believed the air was so potent that it would be toxic unless humans were there to dilute it with fetid exhalations. One worried doctor did a census and estimated that 10,000 turds a day (there was no sanitation) hit the streets of Madrid, much to everyone's relief. 'That which one shits in the winter, one drinks in the summer,' they used to say.

The winds, too, will make you take notice: each has its name and characteristics, and when the less gracious of them visit they seize the land like a conquering army. Andalucía and the south annually endure the African sirocco; walking into it is like opening the oven door. The *tramontana*, when it's angry, roars over the Pyrenees and knocks the Catalans' houses down. And springtime Cádiz is sometimes plagued with an utterly bizarre wind called the *solano* that gets under your skin like a scalpel. The effect it has on the female population is legendary: in the old days, they would converge on the beach en masse when the *solano* hit, taking off their clothes and jumping in the sea for relief while the local cavalry regiment stood guard. Today, ask the ladies of Cádiz about it and they'll just laugh.

Bats

A fine country for bats, is Spain. Almost everywhere in the country (but especially in Aragón and around Granada) you'll see clouds of them cavorting in the twilight, zooming noiselessly past your ears and doing their best to ensure you get a good night's sleep by gobbling up all the mosquitoes they can. Spaniards don't mind them a bit, and the medieval kings of Aragón even went so far as to make them a dynastic emblem, derived from a Muslim Sufi symbol.

Lots of bats, of course, presumes lots of caves, and Spain has more than its share. The famous grottoes of Nerja, Aracena, and Valporquero (near León) are only a few of the places where you can see colossal displays of tinted, aesthetically draped stalactites. Hundreds were decorated in one way or another by Palaeolithic man; even though the most famous, at Altamira, are closed to the public, you can still see some cave art by asking around for a guide in Albarracín in Aragón, in the villages west of Cuenca, at Puente Viesgo near Santander, or around Vélez Rubio west of Murcia. This last area, from Vélez as far west as Granada, actually has a huge population still living in caves—quite cosily fitted out these days—and in Granada itself you can visit the 'gypsy caves' for a little histrionic flamenco and diluted sherry.

In Spanish newspapers, you will not find accounts of the bullfights (*corridas*) on the sports pages; look in the 'arts and culture' section, for that is how Spain has always thought of this singular spectacle. Bullfighting combines elements of ballet with the primal finality of Greek tragedy. To Spaniards it is a ritual sacrifice without a religion, and it divides the nation irreconcilably between those who find it brutal and demeaning and those who couldn't live without it. Its origins are obscure. Some claim it derives from Roman circus games, others that it started with the Moors, or in the Middle Ages, when the bull faced a mounted knight with a lance.

There are bullrings all over Spain, and as far afield as Arles in France and Guadalajara, Mexico, but modern bullfighting is quintessentially Andalucían. The present form had its beginnings around the year 1800 in Ronda, when Francisco Romero developed the basic pattern of the modern *corrida*; some of his moves and passes, and those of his celebrated successor, Pedro Romero, are still in use today. The first royal *aficionado* was Fernando VII, the reactionary post-Napoleonic monarch who also brought back the Inquisition. He founded the Royal School of Bullfighting in Sevilla, and promoted the spectacle across the land.

In keeping with its ritualistic aura, the *corrida* is one of the few things in Spain that begins strictly on time. The show commences with the colourful entry of the *cuadrillas* (teams of bullfighters or *toreros*) and the *alguaciles*, officials dressed in 17th-century costume, who salute the 'president' of the fight. Usually three teams fight two bulls each, the whole taking only about two hours. Each of the six fights, however, is a self-contained drama performed in four acts. First, upon the entry of the bull, the members of the *cuadrilla* tease him a bit, and the *matador*, the team leader, plays him with the cape to test his qualities. Next comes the turn of the *picadores*, on padded horses, whose task is to slightly wound the bull in the neck with a short lance or *pica*, and the *banderilleros*, who agilely plant sharp darts in the bull's back while avoiding the sweep of its horns. The effect of these wounds is to weaken the bull physically without diminishing any of its fighting spirit, and to force it to keep its head lower for the third and most artistic stage of the fight, when the lone *matador* conducts his *pas de deux* with the deadly, if doomed, animal. Ideally, this is the transcendent moment, the *matador* leading the bull in deft passes and finally crushing its spirit with a tiny cape called a *muleta*. Now the defeated bull is ready for 'the moment of truth'. The kill must be clean and quick, a sword thrust to the heart. The corpse is dragged out to the waiting butchers.

More often than not the job is botched. Most bullfights, in fact, are a disappointment, especially if the *matadores* are beginners, or *novios*, but to the *aficionado* the chance to see one or all of the stages performed to perfection makes it all worthwhile. When a *matador* is good, the band plays and the hats and handkerchiefs fly; a truly excellent performance earns as a reward from the president one of the bull's ears, or both; or rarely, for an exceptionally brilliant performance, both ears and the tail. You'll be lucky to see a bullfight at all; there are only about 500 each year in Spain, mostly coinciding with holidays or a town's fiesta. During Sevilla's *feria* there is a bullfight every afternoon at the famous Maestranza ring, while the rings in Málaga and Puerto de Santa María near Cádiz are other major venues. Tickets can be astronomically expensive and hard to come by, especially for a well-known *matador*; sometimes touts buy out the lot. Get them in advance, if you can, and directly from the office in the *plaza de toros* to avoid the hefty commission charges. Prices vary according to the sun—the most expensive seats are entirely in the shade.

Castrum

In laying out their military camps, as in anything else, the Romans liked to go by the book. From Britain to Babylonia, they established hundreds of permanent forts (*castrum* in Latin) all seemingly stamped out of the same press, with a neatly rectangular circuit of walls and two straight streets, the *cardo* and *decumanus*, crossing in the middle. Many of these grew into towns—any place in Britain, for example, that ends in -chester or -caster.

In Spain, where the Roman wars of conquest went on for 200 years, there are perhaps more of these than anywhere else, and it's interesting to try and trace out the outlines of the Roman *castrum* while you're exploring a Spanish city. In Barcelona's Barri Gòtic, the plan is obvious, and in Ávila and Cáceres the streets and walls have hardly changed since Roman times. With a little practice and a good map, you can find the *castra* hiding inside Córdoba, Mérida, León, Zaragoza, Tarragona, Lugo and a score of other towns.

Churros

The Spanish breakfast is as deplorable as the French.

H.V. Morton

As James Michener wrote: 'Any nation that can eat *churros* and chocolate for breakfast is not required to demonstrate its courage in other ways.' These long, fluted wads of fried dough, looking like some exotic variety of garden slug, are an essential part of the Spanish experience—sooner or later every serious traveller will have to step into a *churrería* and face up to them. Properly made, they're as greasy as a crankcase and drowned in sugar. The hot chocolate that comes with them should be quite thick to offer some small degree of protection by coating the stomach lining. Spaniards down billions of them each year.

Pablo Picasso, who as a small boy in Málaga had trouble learning how to count because he could not believe a 7 was not an upside-down nose, recalled that *churros* always fascinated him, and were the first thing he ever tried to draw—which proves that *churros* are just as subversive aesthetically as they are in your stomach.

El Cid

In the Spanish pantheon El Cid Campeador comes in a close second to Santiago himself, but unlike Arthur, Siegfried, Roland and other heroes of national medieval epics, the Cid, Rodrigo Díaz de Vivar (1043–99), was entirely flesh and blood. Born in Vivar near Burgos, his unique title is derived from the Arabic *sayyidi* ('my lord'). Campeador means 'Battler', and his fame spread widely among both Moors and Christians (in his career he served both Alfonso VI of Castile and the Emir of Zaragoza); even before his death ballads celebrated his prowess. The greatest achievment of his life, the capture of Valencia from the Moors in 1095, took place when he was already 52 years old.

Through modern eyes, Rodrigo was little better than a gangster, but for the warrior class of the Reconquista, he served as a model of virtue—fearless, with an exaggerated sense of honour, devoutly Catholic and wholly pragmatic, a generous conqueror, devoted to his family, and a man who nearly always kept his word. The Cid was the perfect man for his time, living in the frontier society among Christians, Moors and Jews, where a king's powers were limited, and the main issues of the day were the simple pleasures of turf and booty.

For all that, 'O Born in a Happy Hour'—Rodrigo's other nickname—would not have had such a long shelf life, inspiring such diverse spirits as Corneille and Hollywood (where he was played, inevitably, by Charlton Heston) if there wasn't something more to his character. This comes through in the epic *Poem of the Cid,* composed around 1140, less than half a century after his death. For 500 years the actual poem was lost, until 1779, when the royal librarian, through some literary detective work, located a copy from 1307, appropriately enough in Vivar, the Cid's hometown. Not a single ounce of the magic or marvellous touches the text; the Rodrigo Díaz that emerges lies and cheats, but has a rustic sense of humour and a certain generous charm, always ready to praise another, happy to have his wife and daughters watch him 'earn his bread' fighting the Moors. You can't help liking the guy. His saga, though somewhat repetitive to read, is also the first known example of Spanish gift for realism that would reach its climax in *Don Quixote.*

Dr Fleming

Ask a Spaniard to name one famous Scot, and if you get anything more than a blank stare, it will likely be a mention of the inventor of penicillin. To the Spaniards he is one of the titans of science; there is a street named for him in almost every large town. Fleming has also become a sort of patron saint for two special groups in Spanish society. There are two monuments to the good doctor in Spain; one in front of the Ventas bullring in Madrid, and another in the Barri Xinés, the old red-light district of Barcelona.

Flamenco

For many people, flamenco is the soul of Spain—like bullfighting—an essential part of the culture that sets it apart from the rest of the world. Good flamenco, with that ineffable quality of *duende,* has a primitive, ecstatic allure that draws in its listeners until they feel as if their very hearts were pounding in time with its relentless rhythms, their guts seared by its ululating Moorish wails and the sheer drama of the dance. Few modern experiences are more cathartic.

As traditional music goes, however, flamenco is newborn. It began in the 18th century in Andalucía, where its originators, the gypsies, called one another 'flamencos'—a derogatory term dating back to the days when Charles V's Flemish (*flamenco*) courtiers bled Spain dry. These gypsies, especially in the Guadalquivir delta cities of Sevilla, Cádiz, and Jerez, sang songs of oppression, lament and bitter romance, a kind of blues that by the 19th century began to catch on among all the other downtrodden inhabitants of Andalucía.

Despite flamenco's relatively recent origins, Andalucían intellectuals such as Lorca and de Falla have always insisted that it was rooted deeply in the south's soil and soul, and many musicologists now believe they're right. According to a 7th-century archbishop, the first Sevillan guitar was shaped like the human breast, with chords 'that signified the pulsations of the heart'. The Moors of Andalucía based their instruments on these heartstrings and traditionally coloured the first string yellow, symbolic of bile. In 820, the famous Córdoba school of music and poetry was founded by Abu al-Hassan Ali Ibn Nafi, better known as Ziryab, the 'Blackbird'; Ziryab also added a fifth string to the guitar and coloured it red, for blood. The half-tonal notes and lyrics of futility of the *cante jondo,* or deep song, the purest flamenco, seem to go back to the Arab troubadours who followed Ziryab but it's impossible to prove— the Arabs knew of musical notation, but disdained it in their preference for improvisation.

In the Middle Ages, the gypsies, in their great migrations from India, arrived in Andalucía with the ecstatic rhythms and a few new tunes, met the *cante jondo* and the heart string guitar and flamenco was born. But just how faithfully the music of al-Andalus was preserved among the gypsies and others to be reincarnated as flamenco will never be known.

By the late 19th century, flamenco had gone semi-public, performed in the back rooms of cafés in Sevilla and Málaga. Its very popularity in Spain, and the enthusiasm set off by Bizet's *Carmen* abroad, began seriously to undermine its harsh, true quality. At the same time, flamenco's influence spread into the popular and folk repertories to create a happier, less intense genre called the *sevillana* (often songs in praise of you know where). When school-children at a bus stop in Cádiz burst into an impromptu dance and hand-clapping session, or when some old cronies in Málaga's train-station bar start singing and reeling, you can bet they're doing a *sevillana*. In the 1920s attempts were made to establish some kind of standards for the real thing, especially *cante jondo*, though without lasting results; the 'real, original flamenco' was never meant to be performed as such, and will only be as good as its 'audience'. This should ideally be made up of other musicians and flamenco *aficionados*, whose participation is essential in the spontaneous, invariably late-night combustion of raw emotion, alcohol, drugs and music, to create *duende*.

With so many intangible factors, your chance of getting in on some genuine soul-stirring flamenco are about as rare as getting in on a genuine soul-stirring bullfight. But perhaps it is this very fleeting, hard-to-pin-down quality that makes both arts so compelling in the midst of a programmed, homogenized world.

The Inquisition

> What a day, what a day
> for an *auto-da-fé*!
>
> Bernstein's *Candide*

Besides bullfighting and flamenco, it's one of the things Spain is most famous for, an essential part of the 'Black Legend' of the dark days of Felipe II. There's nothing to debunk and no need for a historical re-examination; the Inquisition was just as bloody and stupid and horrible as the Protestant propagandists of the day said it was. But what made them do it? Not surprisingly, the original motives were largely political. Fernando and Isabel re-introduced the Inquisition in 1480 as an institution entirely under the control of the crown, and they used it as a means to suppress dissent; with their powers strictly limited under the secular laws, they turned to the Church courts as a way to get at their enemies. Originally, under the direction of a passionate ascetic, the famous Torquemada, the Inquisition's victims were nearly all *conversos*, baptized Jews with wealth or important positions in government or church. Any of them found guilty of backsliding in the faith would have their property confiscated—if they weren't burned at the stake. Much of this booty went to finance the wars against the Moors of Granada.

In the decades that followed, though, the Inquisition took on a life of its own. From the 1530s on, with the Catholic powers in a panic over the onset of the Reformation, a succession of Inquisitors much worse than Torquemada expanded the Holy Office to every city, with a corps of secret agents and investigators estimated at 20,000. Though terror of it spread to every household, application was crazily inconsistent; the Inquisition saw nothing wrong with the opinions of Copernicus, but sent hundreds of poor souls to the stake for reading the Bible in

Spanish instead of Latin. Neither did the learned inquisitors care much for witch-hunting after the late 1500s. The following century saw an estimated 30,000 poor souls burned for witch-craft in Britain, against almost none in Spain. Whatever this says about human nature, it seems that by refusing to take witchcraft seriously, the Spaniards never allowed the hysteria a chance to take root. Still, there were victims enough to be found among the Christians. The first decade of the renewed Inquisition (after 1478) was thorough—5200 victims in Toledo alone in a single year, 1486. After the Jews and freethinkers were dealt with, the Inquisition began to look for new targets just to keep itself in business. Blasphemy went under their jurisdiction in the 1490s, and some secular crimes in 1517. At its height, the Holy Office became a state within the state, responsible to no one and dependent on continuous terror to keep its members in jobs.

Despite its cumbersome bureaucracy and a great pretence of legalism, the Inquisition was little better than a kangaroo court. Anyone denounced (even if it were by playful children) had a good chance of spending several years in solitary confinement while the Holy Office decided his or her case. Few were ever cleared, and even if they were they and their families were tainted forever. Torture was almost universal—as everywhere else in Europe in that grim age—and after it the accused would be lucky to get let off with a public recantation, a flogging and the loss of all his property. *Autos-da-fé* ('works of faith') were colourful public spectacles, preceded by much pageantry and preaching, where sentences were given out, before the unlucky ones, dressed in capes decorated with flames and devils and bearing signboards explaining their crimes, were led off to the stake. The last, and biggest, was a 14-hour affair with 120 victims, personally staged in Madrid's Plaza Mayor in 1680 by the insane Carlos II.

Santiago

No saint on the calendar has as many names as Spain's patron—Iago, Diego, Jaime, Jacques, Jacobus, Santiago, or in English, James the Greater. James the fisherman was one of the first disciples chosen by Jesus, who nicknamed him Boanerges, 'the son of thunder', for his booming voice. After the Crucifixion, he seems to have been a rather ineffectual proselytiser for the faith; in the year 44 Herod Agrippa beheaded him and threw his body to the dogs.

But Spain had another task in store for James: nothing less than posthumously leading a 700-year-old crusade against the peninsula's infidels. The first mention of the Apostle's relics in Spain appear in a 830 annex to the *Martirologio de Florus*, written in 806 in Lyon. From this a new history of James emerged: after his martyrdom, two of his disciples gathered his remains and sailed off with them in a stone boat (faith works wonders) to Iria Flavia in remote Galicia, where the disciples buried Boanerges in the nearby cemetery of Compostela. In 814, a shower of shooting stars guided a hermit shepherd named Pelayo to the site of James' tomb. Another legend identifies Charlemagne (who died in 814) with the discovery of James' relics: in the Emperor's tomb at Aachen you can see the 'Vision of Charlemagne', with a scene of the Milky Way, the *Via Lactea*, a common name for the pilgrims' road.

In 844, not long after the discovery of the relics, James was called into active duty in the battle of Clavijo, appearing on a white horse to help Ramiro I of Asturias defeat the Moors. This new role as Santiago Matamoros, the Moor-Slayer, was a great morale booster for the forces of the Reconquista, who made 'Santiago!' their battle cry. Ramiro was so pleased by his divine assistance that he made a pledge, the *voto de Santiago*, that ordained an annual property tax for St James' church at Compostela.

Never mind that the bones, the battle and the *voto* were all humbug; the story struck deep spiritual, poetic, and political chords that fit in perfectly with the great cultural awakening of the 10th and 11th centuries. The medieval belief that a few holy bones or teeth could serve as a hotline to heaven made the discovery essential. After all, the Moors had some powerful juju of their own: an arm of the Prophet Muhammad in the Great Mosque of Córdoba (possession of it was Abd ar-Rahman's justification for declaring himself Caliph in 929). Another factor in the early 9th century was the Church's need for a focal point to assert its control over the newborn kingdoms of Spain. A third factor was the desire to re-integrate Spain into Europe—and what better way to do it than to increase commercial and cultural traffic over the Pyrenees? Pilgrimages to Jerusalem and Rome were already in vogue; after the Dark Ages, the Church was keen to re-establish contacts across the old Roman empire it had inherited for Christianity.

The French were the great promoters of the *Camino de Santiago* (the Way to Santiago), so great in fact that the most commonly tramped route became known as the *camino francés*. The first official pilgrim was Gotescalco, bishop of Le Puy, in 950; others followed, including Mozarab Christians from Andalucia, who founded some of the first churches and monasteries along the road in the province of León. In the next century, especially once the Moors were pushed over the south bank of the Duero, the French monks of the reforming abbey of Cluny did more than anyone to popularize the pilgrimage, setting up sister houses and hospitals along the way. Nor were the early Spanish kings slow to pick up on the commercial potential of the road; Sancho the Great of Navarra and Alfonso VI of Castile founded a number of religious houses and hostels along the way and invited down French settlers to help run them.

The 12th century witnessed a veritable boom along the *camino francés*: the arrival of new monastic and military orders, including the Templars, the Hospitallers, and the Knights of Santiago; all vowed to defend the pilgrim from dangers en route. In 1130, Cluny commissioned Aymeric Picaud, a priest from Poitou, to write the *Codex Calixtinus*, the world's first travel guide, chock full of practical advice for pilgrims: tips on where not to drink the water, where to find the best lodging, where to be on guard against 'false pilgrims' who came not to atone for crimes but to commit them. The final bonus for Compostela came in 1189, when Pope Alexander III declared it a Holy City on equal footing with Jerusalem and Rome, offering a plenary indulgence—a full remission from Purgatory—to pilgrims on Holy Years (if you need one, the next holy years will be 1999 and 2004).

From the Tour de Saint-Jacques in Paris, the traditional gathering point for groups of pilgrims (there was more safety in numbers), the return journey was 800 miles and took a minimum of four months on foot. It was not something to go into lightly, but for many it was more than an act of faith, a chance to get out and see the world. Many pilgrims were ill (hence the large number of hospitals), hoping to make it before they died. Not a few were thieves, murderers and delinquents condemned by the judge to make the journey for penance. Dangerous cons had to do it in chains. To keep them from cheating or stealing someone else's indulgence (the *Compostelana* certificate), pilgrims had to have their documents stamped by the clergy at various points along the route, just as today (as a nice touch, the old stamps and seals have recently been revived).

An estimated half a million people a year made the trek in the Middle Ages (out of a European population of about 60 million), and even in the 18th century the pass at Roncesvalles still counted 30,000 pilgrims a year. But in the 19th century numbers fell dramatically; most of the monasteries and churches disappeared forever in the confiscation of church lands in 1837, either converted into stables or pillaged for their building stone. Yet in the 1970s, just when it seemed as defunct as a dodo, the pilgrimage made a remarkable revival, due to a number of factors—the modern world's disillusionment with conventional religion, the search for something beyond what over-organized day-to-day life and church attendance can offer, and more prosaically, the growth of ecological and alternative tourism. In 1985, UNESCO declared it the 'Foremost Cultural Route in Europe', helping to fund the restoration of the Romanesque churches that punctuate the trail. Although modern roads have changed the face of the pilgrimage forever, efforts have been made to create alternative paths for pedestrians, marked every 500m with a stylized scallop shell; new free or inexpensive *hostales* have sprouted along the way for walkers or cyclists. The pilgrims' quest is back in business.

Templars

One of the most provocative chapters of medieval history was written by the Order of the Knights Templar, founded during the First Crusade in 1118 by Hugues de Paynes. The 'Temple' of the knights, generally believed to be the Temple of Solomon, was actually the octagonal Temple of the Dome of the Rock, rebuilt by the Muslims in the 10th century—an octagonal design the Templars recalled in the construction of their own temples in London and in Spain, where the Order spread within a few years of its foundation.

The Order was both religious and military, and assisted the crusades, in Spain as well as in the Holy Land. They soon grew more powerful than the kings and popes they ostensibly served, and in 1307, France's King Philip the Fair and Pope Clement V conspired to dissolve the troublesome Order, Clement declaring it heretical and Philip coordinating the secret orders sent throughout Europe for all the Templars to be seized simultaneously at midnight on a certain date—a necessary ploy to ensure their defeat. The conspiracy succeeded and the Templars were captured unawares, imprisoned and made to face trumped-up charges of sorcery, black masses, orgies and sodomy. Some recanted to save their skins, but many, including the Grand Master, remained silent and were burned at the stake. Their immense worldly goods were, naturally, inherited by their enemies, as well as by the newer Order of the Knights of St John.

The dissolution of the Templars was a great loss for Spain, where they did their most important work, attempting a kind of syncretism between the peninsula's three great religions. In return for military services performed for the various kingdoms of Spain, the Templars would request castles and land, nearly always in the *juderías* (Jewish quarters) or among the Moriscos, to learn from their ancient traditions and to defend them from grabby Christians. Their other land requests frequently corresponded with holy sites connected to the peninsula's oldest religions, and their castles and churches that have survived are often fascinating for their mysterious symbolism and hints of the rites of initiation they once held.

Urbanización

Our dictionary translates this blandly as 'urbanization' but to the Spaniards, perhaps the most consciously urban nation in Europe, it encompasses a whole range of meanings. Especially in Castile, history, climate and economy have conspired to make Spain a land of city-dwellers, and they have contributed more to the art of city-building and city-living than is generally acknowledged. When the Moors reigned in Al-Andalus, and Córdoba was the largest and finest city in Europe after Constantinople, they set a pattern that would influence the cities of Spain for centuries. Enclosure was the key word: a great mosque and its walled courtyard at the centre, near a palace and its walled gardens. Along with the markets and baths, these were located in the *medina*, and locked up behind its walls each night. The residential quarters that surrounded the *medina* were islands in themselves, a maze of narrow streets where the houses, rich or poor, locked inwards into open patios while turning a blank wall to the street. Today the great mosques have been replaced by cathedrals, but their courtyards remain; in the cities of the south, famous for their decorated patios and winding lanes, much of this peculiar cellular quality of the Moorish towns survives.

Medieval Spain's most characteristic contribution to urban design is the *Plaza Mayor*. In its classical form, as seen in Madrid or Salamanca, this is an enclosed, rectangular space, surrounded by arcaded walks under buildings of an even height. Often the four sides are alike, as if they were walls of a single structure, giving the impression of a building turned inside-out. Such a square counts much more than just a knot in the web of streets; it is like a stage in the theatre, where public life can be acted out with the proper Spanish dignity. The analogy with the stage is no accident, for theatres in the great age of Calderón and Lope de Vega, such as the Corral de Comedias in Almagro, were perfect little Plaza Mayors in form, with balconies all around and the proscenium at the narrow end. Often in Spanish cities the Plaza Mayor will be replaced, or accompanied, by a *Calle Mayor* (though the name may be different). This is a long central street, arcaded on both sides; a good example survives in Alcalá de Henares. This form can trace its inspiration to the Moors, who learned it from the Romans.

Modern Spain, even in the worst of times, never lost its talent for city building. The world's planners honour the memory of Arturo Soria, who in the 19th century proposed the *Ciudad Lineal* as a new form for the industrial age, a dense ribbon of city, three blocks wide but stretching for miles, where everyone would be a block or two from open countryside, and transportation to any point made easy and quick by a parallel railway line. A Ciudad Lineal was actually begun northeast of Madrid, though it has long since been swallowed up by the expanding suburbs.

During the last 30 years, the time of Spain's 'take-off' into a fully fledged industrial economy, *urbanización* has continued at a furious pace—in all senses of the word. As migrants streamed into the cities during the 1960s, endless blocks of high-rise suburban developments grew up, ugly but unavoidable. To the people who moved into them from poor villages or ancient tenements, they must have represented an exciting new way of life. The name for these is *urbanizaciones,* and the Spanish also use the word for their big seaside vacation developments, where they package northerners into urbanized holidays on the beach.

Catalunya

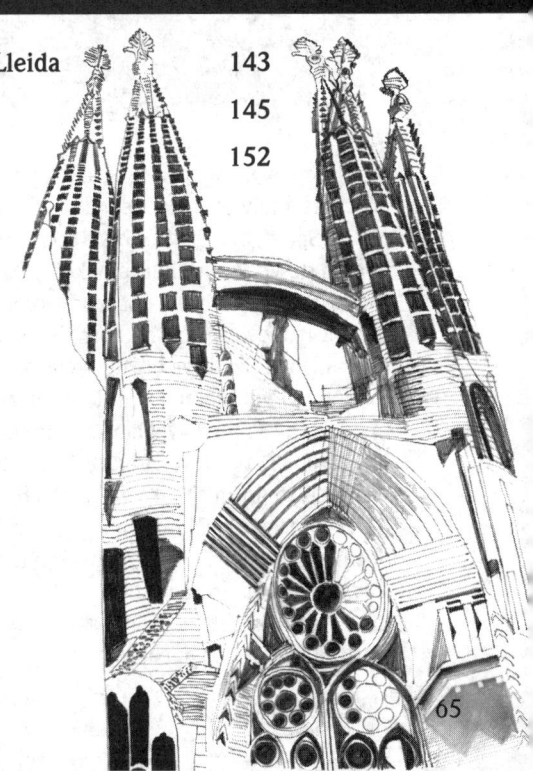

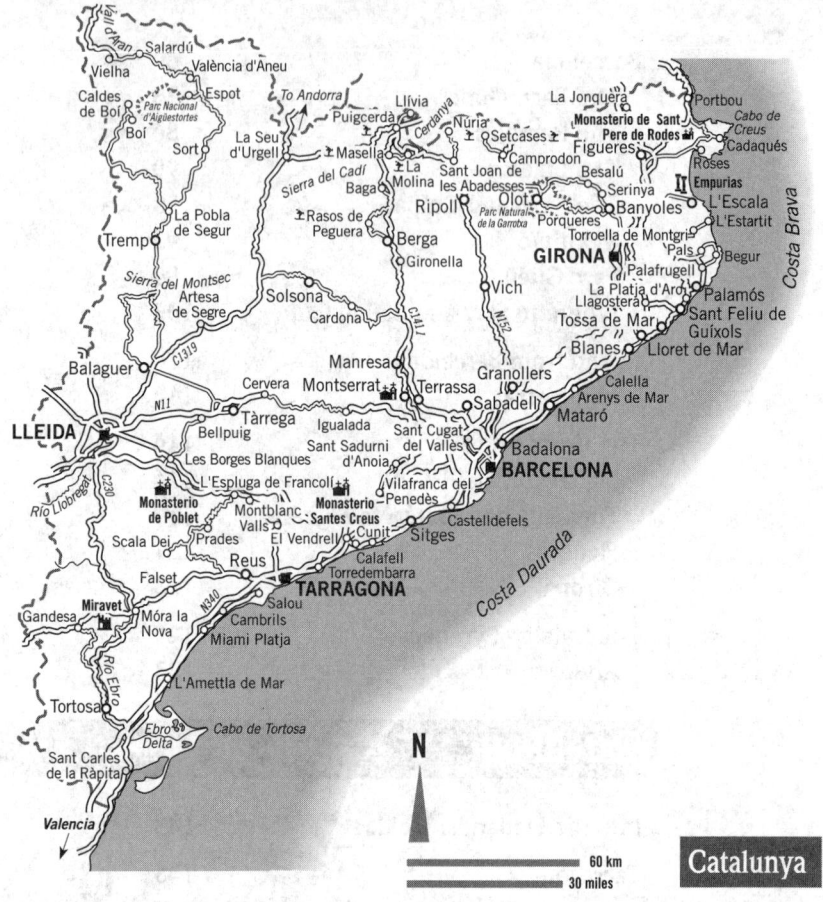

On the map, Catalunya (in Castilian Spanish, Cataluña; in English Catalonia) occupies a tidy triangle wedged between France, the Mediterranean and the rest of Spain, but that's where the tidiness ends. To the north the Pyrenees stretch down to dip their crooked toes in the sea, forming the fabled Costa Brava; to the south the flat sandy strands of the Costa Daurada peter out at the soggy morasses of the Ebro delta. In between, dead volcanoes and mountains shaped like pipe-organs squat inscrutably over a landscape littered with Iberian, Greek, Roman and Romanesque monuments. Enough monsters lurk in Catalunya's medieval cloisters to fill Carnegie Hall. Nowhere else in Spain has early 20th-century architecture (*modernista*, as the Catalans call it) bloomed so furiously, from Gaudí's Barcelona to wine cooperatives in the tiniest village. Spaniards and Hispanophiles tend to warn first-time visitors to Spain away from Catalunya; it's too heady, too 'fizzy', lacking the austere *sol y sombra* of the 'real Spain', whatever that may be. But to visit Spain and miss Barcelona, its best city, would be to miss the most exciting and dynamic spirit of present day Spain, the vanguard of modern Spanish culture.

In the old days the Spaniards kept Catalunya under an iron heel. Today, they worry that Barcelona's busy entrepreneurs are transforming the nation into a Greater Catalunya. Thirty years ago, flying the Catalan flag was a criminal offence; today it waves proudly over the Catalan Generalitat and also, thanks to an intrepid band of Barcelona alpinists, atop the highest peak of Mt Everest.

History

Catalunya has always been a round peg in a square empire; of all the medieval kingdoms that Fernando and Isabel wedded together, it had the most illustrious history. Tarragona was the capital of one of the three Roman provinces of Iberia, and Barcelona served as the first Visigothic capital in Spain in the 5th century. But the saga of its separate identity and language really began in 801 when Charlemagne's son Louis reconquered the northern part of 'Gothalanda' or Catalunya. In 874 (a year of notable coiffures) the Frankish king Charles the Bald granted independence to Count Wilfred 'the Hairy'. A marriage in 1137, between Count Ramón Berenguer IV and the heiress of Aragón, Queen Petronila, brought the Catalans the crown of Aragón, although each nation jealously retained its own parliaments and privileges, or *usatges*. These were the foundation of Catalunya's unique and extraordinary relationship between sovereign and citizen, manifest in the famous oath of allegiance to the king: 'We who are as good as you swear to you who are no better than we, to accept you as our king and sovereign lord, provided you observe all our liberties and laws; but if not, not.'

The Catalan Golden Age lasted from the 12th century, when the Reconquest of Catalunya was completed and the creative juices of the Catalans ignited in a remarkable burst of Romanesque and Gothic energy, to the 14th century, when Barcelona ruled an empire that included Sicily, Malta, Sardinia and most of modern Greece, not to mention Valencia, the Balearics and the modern French regions of the Cerdagne and Roussillon. Catalan merchants, who so often pop up in Boccaccio's *Decameron*, controlled Mediterranean trade and regulated it by the *Llibre del Consulat del Mar*, Europe's first maritime code, written under the great Jaume I in 1259.

Other nations soon adopted the Consulat, but by the 15th century Catalunya was running out of steam, devastated by plague, spectacular bank crashes, and the Genoese homing in on their Mediterranean markets. The Catalans hoped union with Castile would pump some much-needed vitality into the kingdom, although it soon turned out that subsequent heirs to the crowns of Castile and Aragón were more interested in squeezing all they could from Catalunya to finance their imperial ambitions. Especially grating was the codicil in Isabel's will prohibiting Catalan merchants from any dealings with the New World. For from the Castilians' point of view the Catalans were troublesome hotheads, always insisting on their *usatges* and shirking their share of the increasingly heavy national burden.

Catalan history is a chronicle of revolts and uprisings, both against Madrid and within Catalan society itself. In 1640 Catalunya cut itself loose from the Spanish fold and threw itself under the protection of France for 12 years. There it learned a lesson about the untrustworthy Bourbons that made it later support the claim of the Archduke Charles against Bourbon Felipe V in the War of the Spanish Succession. It was a mistake, and hopeless once the English abandoned their cause and made peace with France. Barcelona fell in September 1714, and with it all of Catalunya's privileges and autonomous government.

The Catalan Renaixença and Anarchism

Castilianization proceeded apace, especially among the upper classes who were busy making Catalunya Spain's leading industrial region. Then in the 1830s, just as literary Catalan was in danger of sinking into oblivion, the Romantic movements of the day played midwife to the Catalan *Renaixença*, or Renaissance, a literary crusade led by such poets as Jacint Verdaguer (1843–1902) and Joan Maragall (1860–1911) who helped to bridge the Catalan of the troubadour poets with the everyday language of the people. Concurrent with the *Renaixença*, a fervent nationalist movement rose that was embraced by all the parties of the political spectrum and influenced artists from Antoni Gaudí to Pau Casals. Just as Catalan culture began to revive, so did the workers. Catalan industrialists and the Church connived to squeeze factory workers to such a degree that anarchist doctrines took root in the cities as they did nowhere else in the world. Bombings, riots and church-burnings rocked Catalunya in 1835, 1909 and throughout the 1920s. Barcelona was the most radical city in Europe, 'Anarchism's rose of fire'.

In 1931, as soon as Alfonso XIII had left the country, Catalunya declared itself an independent republic in the Federation of Iberia. Since no such thing existed, the nationalists renamed their government the Generalitat after medieval Catalunya's parliament. Towards the end of the Civil War Catalunya became the Republicans' chief stronghold and, when Valencia fell, Barcelona served as the government's last capital, a time brilliantly evoked in Orwell's *Homage to Catalonia* (1938). And when the war was over, rather than submit to Franco, thousands of Catalans fled over the border to France and Andorra.

Franco dissolved the last remnants of Catalan autonomy, prohibited the public use of Catalan, books in Catalan, and the Catalans' most joyful expression of national unity, a circle dance called the *sardana*. The denizens of Barcelona society put their suits and ties back on—a risky manoeuvre in the heyday of the Republic—and went back to business. Migrants from the south had been flocking to Barcelona's industrial jobs since the turn of the century, and Franco did nothing to discourage them, hoping a tidal wave of poor Andalucíans would dilute Catalanism into a harmless eccentricity. Instead, the opposite has happened: second and third generation Andalucíans have turned into ardent Catalans. Franco was still warm in the grave when Catalunya burst out of the starting block to recreate itself as a nation. The Generalitat was restored, and Catalan was revived with a vengeance. Yet, common sense and clear headed pragmatism, what the Catalans call *seny*, is among their most exalted virtues when they're not tearing up the place. Instead of leaving Spain to form an independent Catalunya, modern Catalans are ready to co-exist—on their own terms.

Català: the Language

Català, or Catalan, is its own proper language, spoken by over six million people; the classic *faux pas* of the foreigner is to call it a dialect of Spanish. Catalan is a Romance language, closely related to Provençal or Occitan, the medieval languages of southern France. If you read French or Spanish, you'll be able to figure out many of the signs—but just try to understand *spoken* Català. Pronunciation is different from Spanish: the j's and g's are sounded as in French, x sounds like sh, ch is k and ll is a pure y (if not, the lls are separated, as in *Paral.lel*) and -ig at the end of a word is -tch, such as in *puig* (mountain), pronounced 'pootch'. You can usually warm the cockles of a Catalan's heart by asking '*Com es diu això en català?*' ('How do you say it in Catalan?').

Although Catalunya is officially bilingual, you'll find street signs and shops signs exclusively in Català: here the most important words to know are open/*obert* and closed/*tancat,* and the days of the week: Monday/*Dilluns*; Tuesday/*Dimarts*; Wednesday/*Dimecres*; Thursday/*Dijous*; Friday/*Divendres*; Saturday/*Dissabte*; Sunday/*Diumenge.*

Catalan Cuisine

Like the Basque kitchen, the Catalan has enjoyed considerable influence from beyond the Pyrenees and is rated one of the best in Spain. Not surprisingly, seafood is a main ingredient, in such well-known dishes as *zarzuela,* a seafood casserole; lobster with chicken; *suquet* (similar to bouillabaisse); any fish with *romesco* sauce (toasted hazelnuts, wine, nutmeg, paprika, garlic and olive oil) or *xapada,* with dried eels from the Ebro delta. *Botifarra*—pork sausage, black or white, with beans—is a staple, as is *escudella,* a hearty pork and chicken stew. In the autumn a Catalan's mouth waters for partridge with grapes, or goose with pears, or rabbit cooked with almonds or garlic sauce. Near Tarragona in the very early spring outdoor *calçotada* feasts are the rage, featuring lamb cutlets, sausage, wine and, the star ingredient, tender green onions grilled over the fire, which Catalans, discarding their usual dignity, slurp down, dressed in aprons and bibs. Excellent red wine and *cava* (champagne) are produced in Catalunya.

The Main Sights in Catalunya

Besides Barcelona, Catalunya has two fine provincial capitals: Tarragona with its interesting Roman ruins and Girona with its evocative medieval quarter. The playful Dalí museum, one of the most visited in Europe, is in Figueres, just off the Costa Brava. This is Spain's prettiest coast—if you have magic spectacles that can see through some of the worst speculative *urbanizaciones* anywhere. There's less drama along the Costa Daurada south of Barcelona, but as compensation there's Sitges, one of the hottest resorts on the Med. Inland, the Pyrenees are the highlight, especially majestic in Aigüestortes National Park, the secluded Vall d'Aran and even more secluded Vall de Boí, and most commercially in the Catalan principality of Andorra. Fantastically situated, Montserrat is perhaps Spain's best-known monastery; another, Ripoll, is a Romanesque gem. In the wine region, exotic *modernista bodegas* liven up sleepy medieval villages. Besides tripping the *sardana*, Catalans love to stack themselves up in towers, especially during fiestas. For the past two centuries otherwise normal men and boys called *castellers* have climbed on each others' shoulders to the eerie music of the '*grolla*', the best groups, from Valls and El Vendrell, attain eight or nine tiers of bodies.

Barcelona

> *Barcelona, the treasure house of courtesy, the refuge of*
> *strangers...unique in its position and its beauty. And although the*
> *adventures that befell me there occasioned me no great pleasure, but*
> *rather much grief, I bore them the better for having seen that city.*
>
> Don Quixote, Part II

And so are we all the better for having seen Barcelona, the capital of the Catalans, a city that goes about its business and pleasure with such ballistic intensity that you can't tell whether it's insanely serious or seriously insane or both. In 1975, three million Barcelonans danced in the streets like drunken banshees when they heard of Franco's death; the next day they rolled up

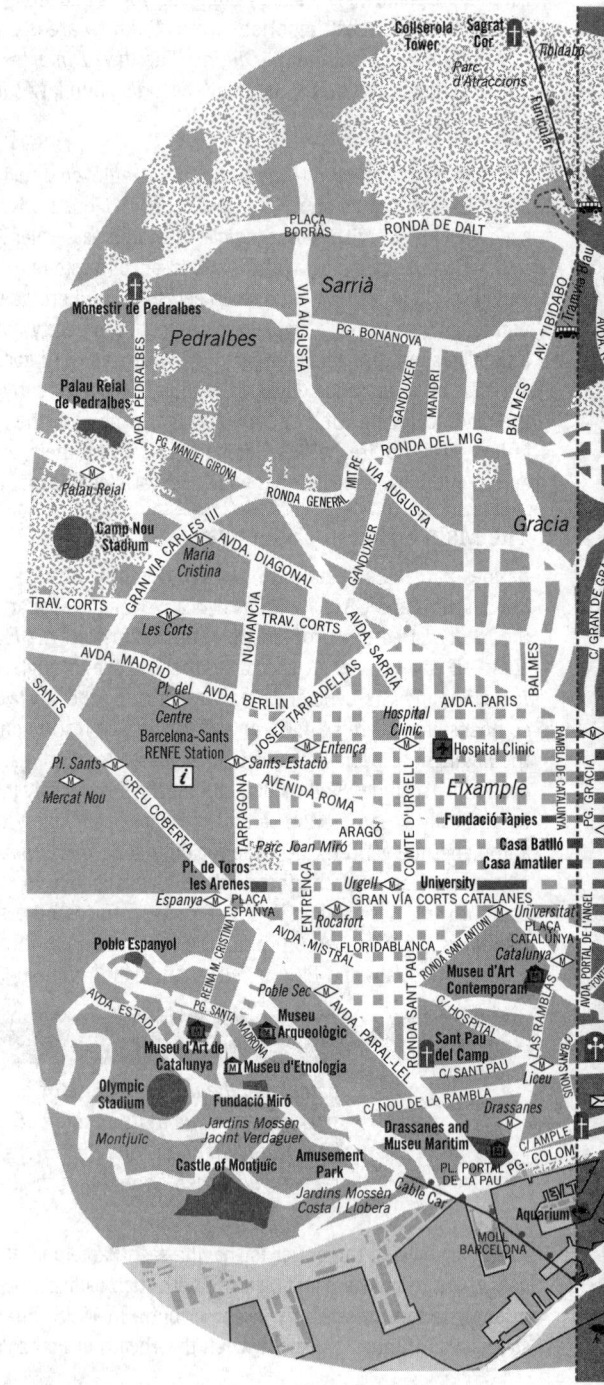

Coliserola Tower
Sagrat Cor
Tibidabo
Parc d'Atraccions

PLAÇA BORRÀS
RONDA DE DALT

Sarrià

VIA AUGUSTA
PG. BONANOVA

Monestir de Pedralbes

Pedralbes

AVDA. PEDRALBES
GANDUXER
MANDRI
BALMES
AV. TIBIDABO

Palau Reial de Pedralbes

PG. MANUEL GIRONA
RONDA DEL MIG

Palau Reial

RONDA GENERAL
MITRE
VIA AUGUSTA

Gràcia

Camp Nou Stadium

GRAN VIA CARLES III
AVDA. DIAGONAL
GANDUXER

Maria Cristina

TRAV. CORTS
Les Corts
NUMANCIA
TRAV. CORTS
AVDA. SARRIÀ

BALMES

C/ GRAN DE GRÀCIA

AVDA. MADRID
Pl. del Centre
AVDA. BERLIN
JOSEP TARRADELLAS
Hospital Clínic
AVDA. PARIS

SANTS
Barcelona-Sants RENFE Station
Entença
COMTE D'URGELL
Hospital Clínic

Pl. Sants
Sants-Estació
Mercat Nou
CREU COBERTA
AVENIDA ROMA

TARRAGONA
ARAGÓ

Eixample

Fundació Tàpies
Casa Batlló
Casa Amatler

RAMBLA DE CATALUNYA
PG. GRÀCIA

Parc Joan Miró
ENTENÇA
Urgell
University

Pl. de Toros les Arenes
PLAÇA ESPANYA
Espanya
Rocafort
GRAN VÍA CORTS CATALANES
Universitat
PLAÇA CATALUNYA

AVDA. MISTRAL
FLORIDABLANCA
RONDA SANT PAU
RONDA SANT ANTONI
Catalunya

Poble Espanyol

AVDA. M. CRISTINA
Poble Sec
AVDA. PARAL·LEL
Museu d'Art Contemporani

AVDA. ESTADI
REINA M. CRISTINA
PG. SANTA MADRONA
Museu Arqueològic
C/ HOSPITAL
LAS RAMBLAS
AVDA. PORTAL DE L'ÀNGEL

Museu d'Art de Catalunya
Museu d'Etnologia
Sant Pau del Camp
C/ SANT PAU
Liceu

Olympic Stadium
Fundació Miró
C/ NOU DE LA RAMBLA
Drassanes

Jardins Mossèn Jacint Verdaguer

Montjuïc
Castle of Montjuïc
Amusement Park
Drassanes and Museu Marítim
C/ AMPLE
PL. PORTAL DE LA PAU
PG. COLOM

Jardins Mossèn Costa i Llobera
Cable Car
Aquarium

MOLL BARCELONA

70

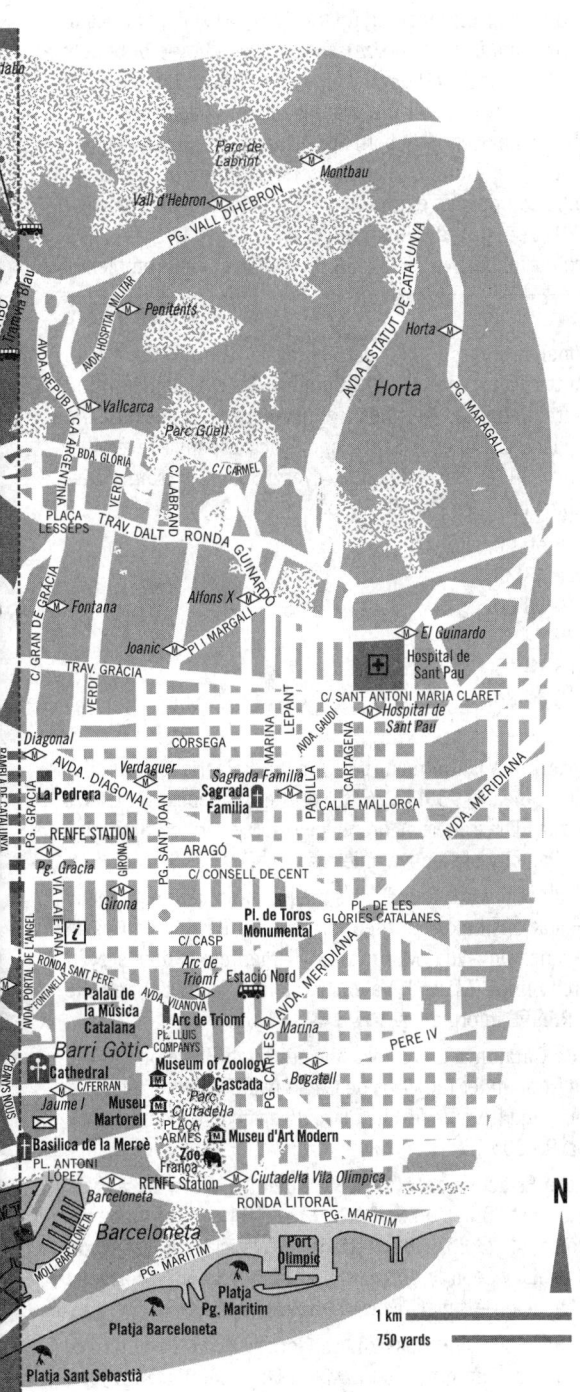

Barcelona

their sleeves and channelled their mad energy into making up for those 40 stale, flat years. They've just about done it: modern Barcelona fizzes and sizzles again like a bottle of bubbly Catalan *cava* spiked with a red pepper. With its superb legacy of *modernista* architecture, its business acumen and ambitious immigrants, its taste for the avant-garde and manic obsession with design, its position as the major publishing centre in both Spanish and Catalan, Barcelona is a little New York—and in many ways it is the only really successful modern city in old Europe. Nor is it shy about saying so. A compulsive exhibitionist, Barcelona held two great international fairs, in 1888 and 1929, and staged a humdinger of a show for the 1992 Olympics, bequeathing a permanent colourful, festive spirit to its incredible edifice complex.

Getting There

By air: Barcelona's international airport is El Prat de Llobregat, 12km to the south. Trains link it every 30 minutes from 6am to 10.30pm to Plaça Catalunya and Barcelona-Sants. The more frequent A1 Aerobus connects both domestic and International terminals with Plaça Catalunya, Sants, and Plaça Espanya (every 15 minutes from Mon–Fri 5.30am–11.15pm; weekends every 30 mins from 6am–11.20pm). For flight information, call © 93 298 38 38, or:

British Airways:	© 93 215 69 00.
Delta:	© 93 412 43 33.
Iberia:	© 90 240 05 00.
KLM:	© 93 379 54 58.
Spanair:	© 90 213 14 15.
TWA:	© 93 215 84 86.
Virgin Express:	© 90 046 76 12.

By sea: Barcelona's Estació Màritima is the main port for the Balearic islands. For information, contact Trasmediterránea © 93 443 25 32, or the Buquebus fast ferries © 93 481 73 60, both on Avda. Drassanes. A brand new ferry service now also connects Barcelona with the Italian city of Genova; information, © 93 295 70 65.

By train: Sants on the south side of town is Barcelona's main station, although many trains also stop at the RENFE stations linked to the more central Passeig de Gràcia Metro. The huge Estació de França on Avda. Marquès de l'Argentera is now served only by a few suburban, intercity lines (Madrid, Valencia, Lleida, Zaragoza) and the occasional international train. RENFE information, © 93 490 02 02.

Ferrocarrils de la Generalitat de Catalunya (FGC) has lines through Barcelona to the suburbs and beyond, departing from under the Plaça de Catalunya (for Sant Cugat and Terrassa, at least one every hour) and from under the Plaça d'Espanya (to Montserrat). For information on the FGC, © 93 205 15 15.

By bus: The main station is the Estació Nord, on Avda. Vilanova, near the Arc de Triomf, with departures for the Costa Brava on Sarfa, © 93 265 11 58; for Valencia, Murcia and Andalucía on Bacoma, © 93 231 38 01; Madrid, Valencia and Galicia on Enatcar, © 93 245 8856; for Castilla y León on Iñigo, © 93 231 0113; for Andorra, La Seu d'Urgell, Vall d'Aran and Lleida on Alsina Graells © 93 309 9518.

Other bus departures: for San Sebastián and Euskadi, on Gonce, Avda. Paral.lel 96, © 93 325 84 38; for Tarragona and southern Catalunya, on Hispania, Pg. Sant Joan

52, ℰ 93 231 27 56; for the Ebro delta, Hifesa, Numància 160, ℰ 93 322 7814. Juliá, Balmes-Pelai, ℰ 93 490 40 00, has a daily bus to Montserrat, departing at 9am and returning at 7pm. Eurolines buses to other European cities depart from next to Estació Sants, ℰ 93 490 40 00.

Getting Around

Barcelona's public transport authority, **TMB**, (ℰ 93 318 70 74) is efficient, cheap and user-friendly. Its **buses** run until 11pm—the 14 main lines also have special after-hours 'Nitbuses' (night, not lice)—and at each stop their routes and timetables are clearly posted. You can pay the 140 pts fare on board; the Nitbus is 190 pts. The city also has six underground (**Metro**) lines with muzak pumped into the stations and a sixth underground line operated by the FGC out of the Plaça Catalunya. As stylish as Barcelona is, its Metro is not, but it is certainly fast and cheap: trains run until 11pm, or 1am at weekends, and cost 140 pts a ride. For either the city buses or Metro you can save money by purchasing a 10-trip *tarjeta* in the Metro stations for 775 pts, or day-passes valid on the Metro, buses or FGC (450 pts for 1 day, 1510 pts for 3 days, 1700 pts for 5 days).

TMB also operates the **Tramvia Blau**, a refurbished old-fashioned streetcar, running from Plaça Kennedy to Plaça Dr Andreu (225 pts one way) and Barcelona's **funiculars**: to Tibidabo from Plaça Dr Andreu (350 pts one way) and to Montjuïc from Avda. Paral.lel (215 pts one way). From the latter funicular, you can continue to the Castell de Montjuïc on the **Teleférico de Monjuïc** (425 pts one way). Services grind to a halt on weekdays out of season; ring TMB for schedules.

From 28 March to 6 January, 9am–7.45pm, TMB operates the **Barcelona Bus Turístic** taking in the best known sights of the city: the whole journey takes 2 hours

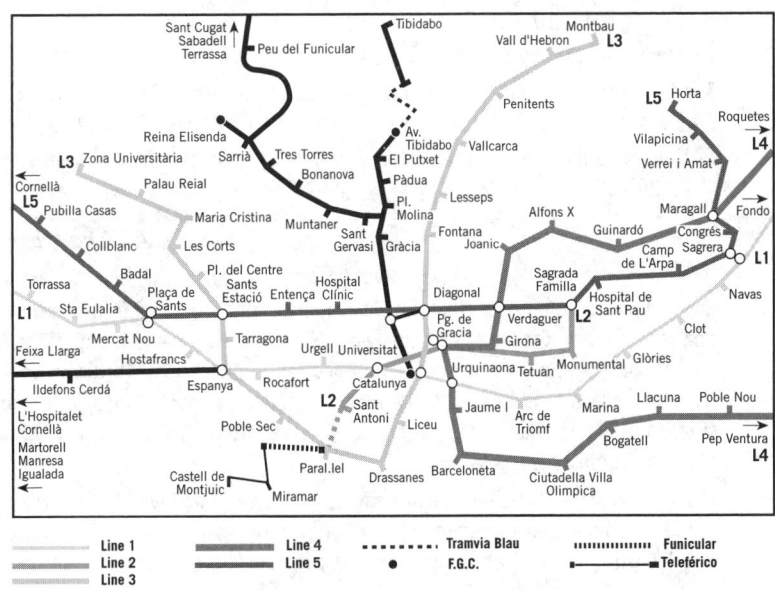

and runs every 20 to 30 mins, allowing you to get off and on at will. A one-day ticket (purchase it on the bus) is 1700 pts, two days (consecutive) 2300 pts and kids cost 1700 pts a day. You get a number of discounts with the ticket (the Poble Espanyol, for instance, is half price) that can make it excellent value.

Taxis are omnipresent and reasonable. If you can't find one, call ✆ 93 225 00 00 or ✆ 93 330 03 00; for cabs with disabled access, ring ✆ 93 358 1111.

Tourist Information

Barcelona's tourist offices distribute excellent detailed maps, transport maps, and a useful little booklet called *Top Tips*. If you need an answer to any question you may have on the city or its transport you can get it in English on ✆ 010.

Plaça Catalunya: (located underground on the Corte Inglés department store side of the Plaça), ✆ 93 304 31 35. *Open 9–9 daily.*

Palau Robert Passeig de Gràcia 107: ✆ 93 238 40 00, also has information on all of Catalunya. *Open Mon–Fri 10 am–7pm, Sat 10am–2.30pm.*

Sants Railway Station: ✆ *Open Oct–May Mon–Fri 8–8, Sat and Sun 8–2, June–Sept 8–8 daily.*

Ajuntament: Plaça Sant Jaume. *Open Mon–Sat 10–8, Sun 10–2.*

Airport: ✆ 93 478 47 04 or ✆ 93 478 05 65. *Open Mon–Sat 9.30–8, Sun 9.30–3.*

La Rambla 99: Palau de la Virreina, ✆ 93 301 77 75, specializing in city cultural information.

Other tourist kiosks are open in summer only in Plaça Catalunya, Passeig de Gràcia, by the Sagrada Família, Vila Olímpica and Port Vell.

other addresses

American Express: Carrer Rosselló 259 (Ⓜ Diagonal) ✆ 93 217 00 70 (open weekdays 9.30–6, Sat 10–12).

Central Post Office: Pl. d'Antoni López (at end of Via Laietana), ✆ 93 318 35 07.

Medical emergencies: ✆ 061. Two hospitals are Clínico, Casanova 143, ✆ 93 227 54 00; and S. Creu i Sant Pau, Avda. S. Antoni María Claret 167, ✆ 93 291 90 00.

Police: National, ✆ 091; municipal, ✆ 092. The main station is at Via Laietana 49, ✆ 93 290 30 00.

A Little Orientation

Barcelona is situated on a plain gently descending to the sea, wrapped in an amphitheatre of hills and mountains that keep its climate mild, protected from the north winds and tempered by the breeze off the Mediterranean. At the south end of the harbour rises its oldest landmark, a smooth-humped mountain called **Montjuïc**, once key to the city's defence and now its pleasure dome and Olympic 'ring'; on the landward side, the highest peak in the **Sierra de Collserola** is **Tibidabo**, with its priceless views and amusements.

Old Catalans may have bewailed their eclipse during the days of Imperial Spain, but moderns may be thankful that the lack of prosperity has left intact the historic centre or **Barri Gòtic**, the greatest concentration of medieval architecture in Europe. This is bounded on the southwest by **Las Ramblas**, Barcelona's showcase promenade; south of the Ramblas and north of Avda. Paral.lel, the **Barri del Raval** remains the most piquant, with the remnants of the once notorious red light district, the **Barri Xinès**. The large part of the map that looks as if it were stamped by a giant waffle iron is the **Eixample**, the 19th-century extension that quadrupled the size of Barcelona, and coincided with the careers of the *modernista* architects, whose colourful buildings brighten its monotonous chamfered blocks. Las Ramblas, Barri Gòtic and Eixample meet at an enormous node called **Plaça de Catalunya**, the geographical heart of Barcelona.

West of the Eixample the city has digested once independent towns like **Gràcia** and **Sarria** and spread as far up the hills as gravity permits. Meanwhile, Barcelona has turned its attention to its long neglected seafront: just south of **Barceloneta**, a planned popular neighbourhood from the 18th century, the **Port Vell** (old port), has been transformed into an urban playground, complete with the *de rigueur* aquarium at the Maremagnum, while to the north of Barceloneta the **Vila Olímpica**, founded to house Olympic athletes, is sweating urban hormones to become a swank address. The rest of the city is hardly being ignored: the Ajuntament (town hall) has filled some 80 public spaces, even in the city's dullest *urbanizaciones* from the Franco years, with art and fountains by artists from around the world, many of whom contributed designs for free. Keep your eyes open: you never know when you're going to run into a 15-foot bronze cat or inscrutable post-modernist froofroo.

The Barri Gòtic

Barcelona is designed for walking, both through space and time, and there's no better place for a pedestrian time traveller to begin than in the ancient heart of the city, the Barri Gòtic, enclosed between the 19th-century Vía Laietana and the curving Carrer Banys Nous. The Barri Gòtic's gentle hill, **Mons Tàber**, is Barcelona's 'acropolis', where the institutions of medieval Catalunya rose over the ruins of their ancient predecessors. The first of these predecessors was (some say) Hamilcar Barca, father of Hannibal, who founded a Carthaginian colony and named it *Barcino* after himself. The Romans, conquering in 133 BC, renamed it *Faventia Julia Augusta Paterna Barcino* by 15 BC—a mouthful that over the years became simply Barcelona. In the 4th century, the Romans enclosed their colony in lofty walls that may have failed to keep out the Visigoths in 415 but for the next 1000 years held tight to Barcelona's heart. When the city gravitated towards the port in the 16th century, it left a time-capsule behind on Mons Tàber.

The best introduction to the Barri Gòtic is to enter it by way of Plaça Angel (Carrer Jaume I and Via Laietana, Metro Jaume I). Here the **Roman walls and towers** (some 14m high) make cameo appearances in a mesh of medieval building, especially along the Carrer Sotstinent Navarro; one mighty tower was discovered hidden in a building only in 1968. More Roman walls are just up Via Laietana in the **Plaça de Ramón Berenguer el Gran**, overlooking an equestrian statue of the Templar count who married Barcelona to Aragón.

The Home of the Count-Kings: Plaça del Rei

Heading into the Barri Gòtic, the first right from Plaça Angel will take you into little Plaça del Rei, a handsome architectural ensemble that originally served as the enclosed courtyard of the Romanesque-Gothic **Palau Reial Major**, home of the Counts of Barcelona and later the kings of Aragón. The first residents were the twins, Ramón Berenguer II and Ramón Berenguer, who ruled alternately; the only way to tell them apart was that the first was surnamed the Towhead and the second the Fratricide (so you can guess what finally happened). The latter was twice captured by El Cid, and in a comic interlude in the epic was forced to eat himself sick to the Cid's amusement before he regained his freedom.

The first place to visit, however, is the **Museu d'Historia de la Ciutat** (*open Tues–Sat 10–2 and 4–8, July–Sept 10–8, Sun and hols 10–2, closed Mon; adm*). Housed in a 15th-century Gothic palace painstakingly moved here from Carrer de Mercaders to close off the square, the museum offers a fascinating subterranean stroll through Roman and Visigothic Barcino, discovered by accident in the 1930s; the houses are directly beneath the modern Carrer de los Comtes and the 4th-century Paleochristian baptistry and font is directly under the Cathedral. If there's not a special exhibition on, the ticket includes admission to the Palau Reial's magnificent **Saló de Tinell** ('Banquet Hall'), up the fan-shaped stair in the corner, where Fernando the Catholic (never a favourite in Barcelona, after he wed Isabel and subjected Aragón's interests to Castile) narrowly escaped an assassination attempt by a disgruntled peasant. In the Saló itself, according to tradition, he and Isabel received Columbus after his first voyage. If it's not true, it should be: the Saló deserves a good story. Built in 1362 by Guillem Carbonell, architect to Pedro 'the Ceremonious', its six huge rainbow arches cross a span of 17m, with wooden beams filling in the ceiling between; viewed from the corner of the hall, the arches appear to radiate from a single point. A fresco of a procession led by the king and bishop (*c.* 1300) from a former room is now in the antechamber. From the hall you can pass through to the apse of the lofty **Capilla Palatina de St Agata**. Built by Jaume II and his queen Blanche of Anjou, it houses the 1466 masterpiece of Jaume Huguet, the *Retablo del Condestable*, and what is claimed to be the stone where the breasts of Saint Agatha were laid when the Roman soldiers snipped them off in Catania.

Rising over the square is a curious skyscraper—five storeys of galleries built by Antoni Carbonell in 1557 and anachronistically named the **Mirador del Rei Martí** after the popular humanist king, to hide the unpleasant truth that it was really a spytower for the hated viceroy, or Lloctinent, a position set up by Fernando. Just left of the royal palace, the **Palau del Lloctinent**, also by Carbonell, is jam-packed with the Archives of the Crown of Aragón, one of the world's greatest collections of medieval documents, dating back to 844. Walk outside Plaça del Rei to Carrer de les Comtes, where its second façade is penetrated by a fine courtyard with a magnificent coffered ceiling over the stair. Nearby is the entrance to the **Museu Frederic Marés** (*open Tues–Sat 10–5, Sun and hols 10–2, closed Mon; adm*), occupying the part of the royal palace Fernando the Catholic gave to another of his popular gifts to Barcelona, the Inquisition. Incredibly, as big as it is, it contains only a fraction of the collections amassed by sculptor Frederic Marés, Spain's champion pack rat. His obsessive accumulations of the sublime and ridiculous are beautifully arranged: on the ground floor, 12th–14th-century polychrome wood sculptures of sweet-faced Virgins and stylized crucifixes; on the first floor, art from the Middle Ages to the 19th century (when the Baby Jesuses have real hair and dolly faces), intermingled with masterpieces, Montserrat memorabilia and colourful plaques of the Dance of Death, showing the Grim Reaper cavorting and reeling with ladies, monks and peasants. Your own brain will start reeling if you go upstairs, where the 16 rooms of the **Museu Sentimental** are swollen with scissors, fans, giant cigars, little lead Moorish and Christian soldiers and every kind of 19th-century junk in between.

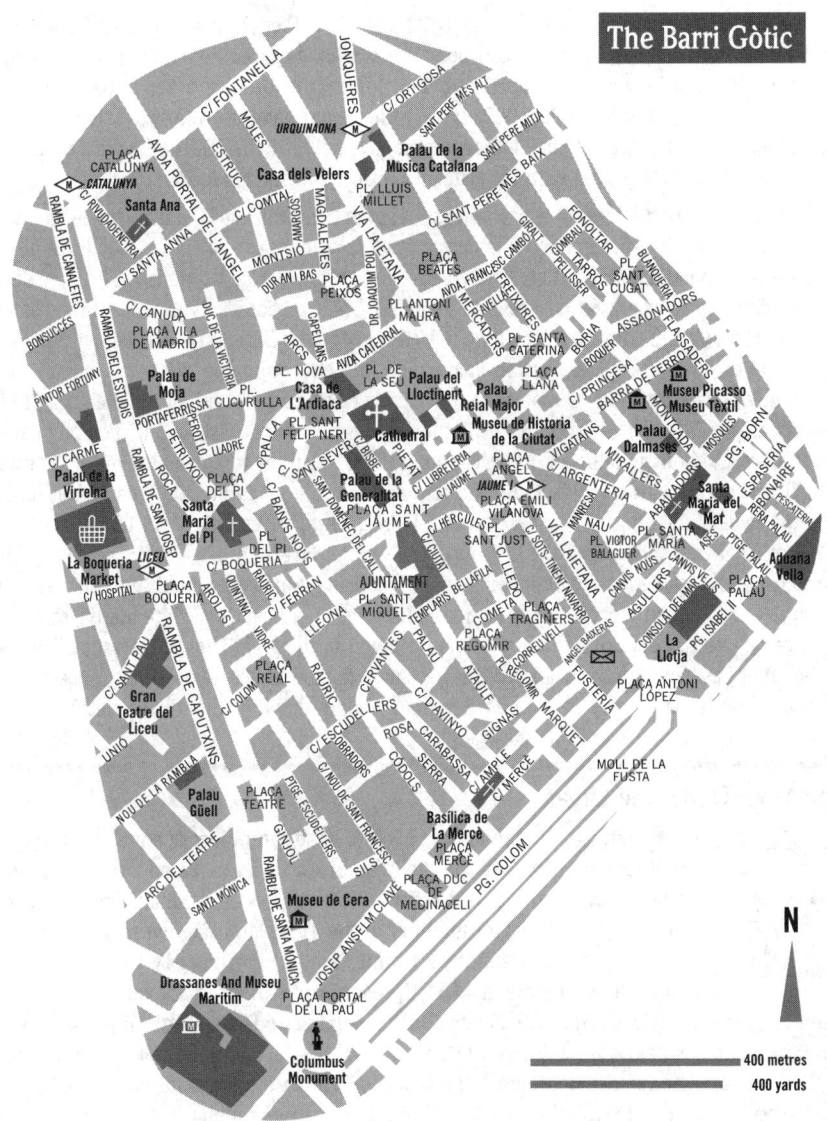

The Cathedral: La Seu

Carrer des Comtes continues around to the front of Barcelona's huge Gothic cathedral (*open 8–1.30 and 4–7.30*) which, with its fat apse, octagonal towers and spires, is hard to miss. It is, at least, the third church to stand on the site. The first was flattened in Al-Mansur's raid on the city in 985; of the second, a Romanesque church built by Count Ramón Berenguer I, only two doorways remain. The current model was begun in 1298 by Jaume II, and on Carrer des Comtes it's worth pausing by its portal of Sant Iu to see the carvings up on the left of St George and Barcelona's first count, Wilfred 'the Hairy', both killing dragons.

The façade of the cathedral, based on the 1408 plans by a French master named Carli, faces the **Plaça de la Seu**, a wonderful backdrop to the *sardanas* danced here on Sunday mornings and Wednesdays (*7–9pm*) but suspiciously not quite right for such a venerable church— perhaps because it was begun in 1882. It might not even have been finished then had the canons not feared the worst: during their moment of power in 1820, the Liberals proposed engraving the then blank wall with the Catalan Constitution and Civil Code.

Catalan Gothic is best known for its conquest of space—not through the dizzying height and light of French Gothic, but in its vast length and width. Although La Seu has only three aisles the architects made it look like five. One wonders what they would have made of the modern lighting that dispels its mysterious, cavernous gloom. The Cathedral's 29 chapels contain some beautiful High Gothic paintings, including the *Pietà* (1490) by Bartolomé Bermejo, his master-piece, one of the first oil paintings in Spain. The first chapel on the right, the magnificent star-vaulted **Sala Capitular**, contains the lucky crucifix borne by Don Juan on the mast of his flagship at the Battle of Lepanto in 1571; the curious S-shaped twist in Christ's body came about, they say, from dodging a Turkish cannon-ball. Stuck in the middle of the nave, the elab-orate 15th-century **Choir** (*adm: the ticket also includes the lift to the roof*) was emblazoned with the arms of the Kings of France, Portugal, Poland, Hungary and others in 1514, when the Emperor Charles V summoned the Knights of the Golden Fleece to Barcelona. The choir faces the elegant, low-vaulted **crypt** designed by the Mallorcan Jaume Fabre in 1339 for the relics of the 4th-century virgin martyr, Santa Eulàlia. Eulàlia lies in a beautiful white marble sarcoph-agus, carved with scenes of her martyrdom, attributed to the great Giovanni Pisano. The rest of the crypt has been curiously arranged to resemble theatre boxes—you almost expect poor Eulàlia to get up and perform. Ramón Berenguer I and his wife Almodis lie nearby in the humble painted caskets tacked on the wall.

The Moor Under the Organ

 Look under the organ for the Moor's head, an object of some mystery. Traditionally, it represents the head of Ali Baba, defeated at Lepanto, and on feast days in the past it vomited forth sweets for the children. In fact it may well be a distant memory of the Templars, who were a major force in medieval Catalunya. Count Ramón Berenguer IV the Great joined the Templars in 1131 in response to an emissary sent by the founder of the Templars himself, Hugues de Paynes (Hug de Pinós, himself probably a Catalan), whose shield bore a device of three Moors' heads, symbolic of knowledge and understanding—hence the Baphomet, the idol the Templars were accused of worship-ping. The Moor's head symbol (often blindfolded) pops up throughout the Mediterranean, especially the islands of Mallorca, Corsica and Sardinia. After Ramón Berenguer IV, the Templars continued to counsel and train the kings of Aragón (Jaume I the Conqueror was their star pupil), until Jaume II, builder of this cathedral, banned the Order at the end of the 13th century.

The Romanesque **Porta de Sant Severo** leads to a medieval oasis, the green garden of the **Cloister** begun in 1385. Its iron-grilled chapels were once dedicated to the patron saints of Barcelona's guilds ('Our Lady of Electricity' is still going strong) and many leading masters are buried in the floor. The lovely pavilion with a fountain is dedicated to St George, the blobby green figure on top. In the old days, for Corpus Christi (once a lavish holiday, when each guild competed to make the most elaborate or alarming floats) a hollow egg would be set to dance in the jet of water (*l'ou com balla*). Nor did anyone have to look far for an egg, because a flock of white geese natter away next to the fountain, with their little houses and pond. They have been there since anyone can remember, white symbols of Santa Eulàlia's virginity or a memory of the geese that saved Rome, or (most likely) just because. One chapel houses the **Cathedral Museum** (*open daily 10–1; adm*), with *retablos* and reliquaries retired from duty.

As you leave the cloister, don't miss its lovely Porta de Santa Eulàlia. This gives on to Carrer de Bisbe, which passes under a neo-Gothic bridge (1928) that links the 16th-century **Casa de los Canónigos** to the Generalitat. Before heading in that direction, opposite, to your right, is the medieval **Palau Episcopal**, with a fine courtyard, and Romanesque paintings along the upper patio. Beyond that, flanking Plaça de la Seu, the 11th-century **Casa de l'Ardiaca** (of the Archdeacon) has a pretty Gothic fountain splashing in its courtyard under lofty palm trees. More religious art, garments, silver and ceramics have been pensioned off in the **Museu Diocesà**, Plaça de la Seu 7 (*open Tues–Sat 10–1.30 and 5–8, Sun 11–2, closed Mon; adm*). Occasionally there's a flea market just below in **Plaça Nova**, where two Roman towers, renovated in the 12th century, once guarded a medieval gate to Barcelona. The square's **Col·legi d'Arquitectes** (1962), is decorated by a sketchy frieze of dancing Catalans by Picasso beneath the windows—his only public work of art in Barcelona, which claims him as her own.

Plaça de Sant Jaume

The third node in the Barri Gòtic, the **Plaça de Sant Jaume** is the heart of civic Barcelona. Originally Barcino's forum, where the main *cardo* and *decumanus* of the Roman town intersected, it was recarved out of a warren of streets in the 1840s along with Carrer de Ferrán. These days it's still something of a forum, an ongoing, face to face dialogue between the Catalan government, the Generalitat, and Barcelona city hall, the Ajuntament. Created by Jaume I in 1283, the Generalitat was made up of representatives of the three Estates of the Catalan *corts* (Church, military, and civilian) and in 1359 it assumed fiscal responsibility for the realm, making it Spain's first real parliament since Roman times. The **Palau de la Generalitat** was begun in the 15th century to give it a permanent seat. When Felipe V abolished the Generalitat, the palace became seat of the Real Audiencia, but its original role was never forgotten: from its balcony in 1931 Francesc Macià proclaimed the Catalan Republic (and the Spanish Republic, too). It was the home of the autonomous government until Franco, and since 1977 it has served its original function.

The Generalitat turns its oldest and fairest face towards Carrer del Bisbe, a façade built in 1416 by Marc Safont with human gargoyles and Catalunya's patron, St George, on the medallion over the door. On St George's Day (23 April—the one day when the general public is allowed in) a ceremony in the gallery kicks off the festival of the Book and the Rose founded in 1456 by the Generalitat: men give their true love a rose and women give their men a book.

Across Plaça de Sant Jaume, the Generalitat faces the **Ajuntament** from where the Council of a Hundred, also founded by Jaume I, ruled the city from 1272 to 1714 like an Italian Republic. The Ajuntament's classical façade, added in the 1840s, is as exciting as mashed potatoes, but the Gothic façade on the Carrer de la Ciutat still has some of its charm. The oldest part of the Ajuntament, the 14th-century **Saló de Cent**, is on top of a black marble stair, over-remodelled and off limits anyway. But if you can wheedle in, visit the **Alcadía**, where in 1929 the satirist

Xavier Nogués painted his vision of 19th-century Barcelona society, complete with *nouveau riche americano* and thrifty Catalan shopkeeper 'Senyor Esteve' (Carrer de Petritxol by Santa Maria del Pi has similar designs in tiles), and the **Saló de las Cròniques**, painted with golden murals by Josep Sert (1928) who decorated New York's Rockefeller Center.

From the Plaça de Sant Jaume, take the narrow lane to Carrer Paradí, the name of the summit of Mons Tàber, marked by an ancient millstone in the pavement. Here, past the Gothic court-yard of the Centre Excursionista de Catalunya, four impressive Corinthian columns and part of the podium from the 1st-century AD Roman **Temple of Augustus** have been trapped in a green walled hothouse.

El Call

In the Middle Ages, Barcelona's Jewish quarter (*El Call*) was to the west of Carrer Bisbe and Plaça de Sant Jaume. In the 11th and 12th centuries this little neighbourhood was the intel-lectual centre of Catalunya, home of its finest schools, doctors, translators, poets, astronomers and philosophers. The first sign of trouble occurred in 1243, when Jaume I ordered that El Call be set apart from the rest of the city, and that its residents wear special hats. At the same time, however, Jews expelled from other territories were made welcome here by the kings, to the extent that El Call incited a dangerous amount of working-class envy. In 1391, rumours that the Black Death had been brought by the Jews incited riots in the quarter that led to 300 deaths. King Joan I had the 22 instigators put to death, but could not halt the growing tide of anti-Semitism, and in 1424 the Jews were expelled from El Call, and the stones of their syna-gogues and cemeteries quarried for the construction of the Generalitat and other structures. On tiny Carrer de Marlet, off Carrer de Sant Domènec del Call, one stone remains, inscribed in Hebrew: 'Sacred foundation of Rabbi Samuel Hassareri, of everlasting life. Year 692.'

East of Plaça de Sant Jaume

From the north (or Gothic) side of the Ajuntament, Carrer de Hèrcules both recalls Barcelona's mythological founder and leads to the **Plazuela de Sant Just** and two palaces, **Moxió** and **Palamòs**. The latter, now housing the Gallery of Illustrious Catalans, was the grandest private address in medieval Barcelona, built in the 13th century atop the Roman wall, with a fine Romanesque patio. Here, too, is the parish church of the Kings of Aragón, **Les Sants Just i Pastor** (if the front door is locked, try the back), founded according to tradition by Charlemagne's son, Louis the Pious in 801. It is the last church in Spain to preserve its ancient privilege of 'Testimentos Sacramentales' bestowed by pious Lou himself, which gives an oath the power of notary or writ if said before the altar of San Félix. There is a fine 16th-century *retablo* by the Portuguese Pero Nunes, some lovely 14th-century stained glass and Visigothic capitals, pressed into service as Holy Water fonts.

In 1893 Joan Miró was born in, and later had his first studio in, a Parisian-style arcade called **Pasaje de Crédit**, built in 1879 between Carrer de Ferran and the 1514 Palau Centelles, on Baixade de Sant Miquel. Several old palaces on the Carrer de Avinyó, at the end of Baixade de Sant Miquel, were converted into brothels around the turn of the century; the ladies in one were the subject of young Pablo Picasso's 1907 *Les Demoiselles d'Avignon*, the unfinished manifesto of Cubism, a painting that was so incomprehensible even to other artists that it wasn't exposed publicly until 1937. If you walk along Avinyó, note the fine *esgrafiados* that embellish the houses at Nos.26 and 30.

North of Via Laietana, La Ribera was Barcelona's maritime quarter in the Middle Ages, when the sea came in as far as the Estació de França. It has a decidedly funkier atmosphere than the Barri Gòtic, never really recovering from Madrid's amputation of half of its streets in 1718 to construct the hated Ciutadella. Amid the genteel decrepitude, however, passes one of the highlights of Barcelona: **Carrer Montcada**, a street given in 1148 by Ramón Berenguer IV to a rich merchant named Montcada in return for services rendered. Montcada sold lots to his buddies and they created a medieval Millionaires' Row. The presence of big money led to the founding nearby of the *correus volants*—'flying runners', the origin of the Spanish postal service, first referred to in 1166. These earliest Catalan pony express riders, the *Troters*, were headquartered at the top of Carrer Montcada by the little Romanesque chapel of **Santa María d'en Marcús,** where they would ride in to be blessed before setting out.

In the 15th–17th centuries, the millionaires' descendants rebuilt their palaces, with walls right up to the street, making Carrer Montcada look like a gully. Today, most of the once secret palaces are museums or galleries, thanks to an initiative taken in 1963 to restore the loveliest mansion of them all, the 15th-century **Palau Aguilar** (with a patio by Marc Sanfont) and the adjacent Baró de Castellet and Meca palaces to house the **Museu Picasso** (*open Tues–Sat 10–8, Sun and hols 10–3, closed Mon; adm*), the best place in Spain to see the works of a Spaniard acclaimed as the greatest artist of the 20th century. The core of the collection, donated by Picasso's secretary, Jaume Sabartés, represents the master's early works, beginning with the drawings of an exceptionally gifted 8-year-old child in Málaga and his first major academic painting, *Science and Charity*, painted a few years later. This is followed by much of his Barcelona work, including a menu *à la* Toulouse-Lautrec for Els Quatre Gats (1900), where he had his first exhibition in 1901, the *Portrait of his sister Lola*, *Desemparats* and *The Madman*. Other works are from his Pink Period in Paris (1904–6), some Cubist paintings (1907–20) and 58 studies of Velázquez's *Las Meninas*, painted in 1957 and donated by Picasso himself.

Picasso and the Origins of Cubism

 Born in Málaga in 1881 and relocated with his family to Barcelona in 1895, Picasso was one of the first Andalucíans to thoroughly identify with his adopted city and become an honorary Catalan. From 1895–97 he studied at the School of Fine Arts in the Llontja where his father taught, then drifted into the city's Bohemian artistic milieu headquartered at Els Quatre Gats, where his precocious talent was recognized and encouraged by Barcelona's most famous painter of the day, Ramón Casas. Even so, Picasso never had much money in Barcelona and he knew at first hand about the impoverished, outcast subjects of his first, 'Blue' Period (1901–04), painted before he took off to Paris and invented Cubism. His interest in Cézanne's studies of structure and form have long been cited as the seeds for his monumental break with the past, but in 1990 (as critic Robert Hughes writes in his excellent book, *Barcelona* (1992) American artist Ellsworth Kelly hit on what may have well been another important inspiration behind Picasso's fragmentation and dissolution of form: the *trencadis*, or broken tiles, that Gaudí used to decorate so much of his architecture.

Just a few steps down at No.12 Carrer de Montcada, the **Museu Tèxtil i de la Indumentària** (*open Tues–Sat 10–8, Sun 10- 3, closed Mon*) is housed in the 16th-century Gothic Palau dels Marquesos de Lió, with a café in its attractive courtyard. Dedicated to textiles and fashion, its exhibits date back to the 3rd century and include rare embroideries from the kingdom of Granada, as intricate as the tile patterns in the Alhambra, a 16th-century Tournai tapestry of the Siege of Rhodes, Baroque shoes and socks, and classic frocks by Balenciaga. Another fine palace along Carrer de Montcada is at No.20, the 17th-century **Palau Dalmases**, the ground floor of which has been transformed into a café. The palace's flamboyantly carved stair, shows Neptune and his watery wife Amphitrite racing up the waves (and curiously, up the slope of the stair); opposite, the **Galerie Maeght**, in the 16th-century Palau dels Cervelló, has changing exhibitions and a large art shop.

Santa Maria del Mar

The east end of Carrer de Montcada runs into the Passeig Born and the apse of Santa Maria del Mar, the most perfect and pure expression of the Catalan Gothic anywhere. The place has long been holy: the first church here was built in the 4th century over an even older burial site, believed to hold the relics of Santa Eulàlia, martyred here in 303, which were later moved to the Cathedral. When Jaume I conquered Mallorca in 1235 he promised a temple to Mary, Star of the Sea, the patroness of his sailors, but his promise remained unfulfilled until Alfonso the Benign took Sardinia, the last Catalan territorial gain, and laid the first stone of the church in 1329.

By this time the portside neighbourhood of La Ribera was firmly established as one of the medieval suburbs or *vilanovas* that grew up outside the city walls along Carrer Argenteria, the main road from the Barri Gòtic to the port. As Catalan maritime interests grew more important, so did the population of sailors, porters, tradesmen and small merchants. Santa Maria was to be their parish church, and for 50 years all able-bodied men in the parish donated their labour to build it. In 1714 its interior was damaged during the French and Spanish bombardment; even graver, in 1936, Anarchists set it ablaze, its elaborate Baroque fittings feeding a fire that burned for ten days. Yet however wonderful the furnishings might have been, the current lack of any decoration at all enhances its sublime beauty.

Designed by Berenguer de Montagut, perhaps with the assistance of the Mallorcan master, Jaume Fabre, Santa Maria del Mar is a textbook lesson on Catalan Gothic. From the austere exterior it doesn't look like much at all, certainly not Gothic: a great dark mass, the façade around in Plaça Santa Maria is embellished only with a rose window, a simple relief of Christ with his hands up, like the victim of a hold-up, a pair of octagonal towers, wildflowers sprouting out of cracks in the stone; here, too, is a columned Gothic fountain with a garden on top. Enter (the door is in Passeig del Born) and what was closed in and austere on the outside opens up to a miraculous, immense spaciousness within, early evidence of the Catalan vocation for daring architecture. A minimum of interior supports hold up the vaults: the four simple octagonal piers of the nave standing some 13m apart—a distance unsurpassed in any other medieval building. Two aisles, equally lofty and half the width of the nave, have only simple niches for chapels between the buttresses. The whole converges on the semi-circular apse, the raised altar defined by a semi-circle of slender columns, like a glade in a forest, especially when the morning sun shines through them in radiant spokes. In the afternoon, the simple Romanesque statue of the Virgin is beautifully lit from beneath. At the foot of the altar, two stone reliefs depict the longshoremen who built the church. The stained glass windows date from every century; the best, from the 15th century, are of the Ascension and Last Judgement. Next to the church, a low wall and the fan-shaped **Fossar de les Moreres** marks the mass tomb of citizen resisters to the Bourbon troops of Felipe V in 1714.

Around Santa Maria del Mar: La Llotja

The neighbourhood around Santa Maria del Mar is undergoing a slow but steady process of gentrification. Most street names recall their medieval crafts or professions: C/Argenteria, for example, was the silversmiths' street, while C/Canvis Vells and C/Canvis Nous were the streets where money was changed on 'bancos' ('benches', hence the origin of the word 'bank'). The **Pla del Palau**, the neoclassical **Aduana Vella** (the old customs house, now occupied by the Guardia Civil) has a series of interesting murals in the Sala de Actos, portraying the reign of Carlos III, life in commercial Barcelona, and the sad adventures that befell Don Quixote in the city—where he was unhorsed and forced to give up knight errantry. Diagonally across Pla del Palau stands **La Llotja**, or the stock exchange (literally, 'lodge'). In the mercantile empire of the Catalans, a Llotja held the place of a secular cathedral, and vast sums were lavished on the building. Barcelona's was built by Pere Arbei for King Pedro 'the Ceremonious' in 1380. In 1802 it was slapped with a neoclassical facelift, although fortunately the great **Gothic hall** inside was left untouched. It was the oldest continuously operating stock exchange in Europe, until Barcelona's bourse moved most of its operations to Passeig de Gràcia in 1996. The gates to the old Llotja remain open on weekdays and no one minds if you discreetly step inside for a look around.

The grand old **Estació de França**, just south on Avda. Marquès de l'Argentera, has lost most of its train passsengers to the Estació de Sants, leaving it only a few trains a day; one of its new roles is hosting Barcelona's annual New Year's party. Between Santa Maria del Mar and the Parc de la Ciutadella, the trendy, bar-lined **Passeig del Born** was used for medieval tournaments (and probably witnessed Don Quixote's mishap). At its north end, another institution awaits a new role: the beautiful wholesale **Mercat del Born**, a striking iron structure with a roof of coloured tiles, designed by Josep Fontseré in 1876, which is destined by the year 2001 to begin life anew as the city's central library.

Parc de la Ciutadella

The year 1714 is a bitter date in the annals of Barcelona. In that year, after an extraordinary eleven-month resistance, the besieged city and independent Catalunya fell to the troops of Felipe V. To punish the city the Bourbon king moved its university to Cervera and demanded the evacuation (without any compensation) of much of La Ribera to construct, at Barcelona's expense, the Ciutadella, one of the most massive fortifications ever built in Europe. When the good Catalan General Prim took power in 1869, he gave the mastodon to the city, which immediately razed the hated symbol to the ground and made it into a park.

In 1888, Barcelona's progressive mayor Francesc de Paula Ruis i Taulet used the new park as the site of a Universal Exposition, which city historians believe was the key event that saved the city from sliding into provincial backwardness. It also served as a stage for architectural innovation, as do all good expositions—in this case, the colourful, eclectic *modernista* style. The main entrance of the park, on Passeig Lluís Companys, is dominated by a relic from the great fair: the **Arc de Triomf**, by Josep Vilaseca, a peculiar piece of *mudéjar*-style ceramic brickwork topped with four crowns that manifests, if nothing else, the eternal Catalan longing to be different—a longing shared by several other buildings around the Passeig, like the elephantine **Palau de Justicia**, with a façade made entirely of stone from Montjuïc, the **Grupo Escolar Pere Vila**, with its ceramic reliefs, and behind it the idiosyncratic **Compañia de Gas y Electricidad** of 1897.

The park itself is well used, especially at weekends when families come to paddle in the little boats under the **Cascada**, a monumental pile of rocks and mythological allusions by Josep Fonserè, who was assisted by Gaudí, a young student at the time. Gaudí is credited with the arrangement of the boulders and some of the decorative elements, as well as the graceful ironwork at the park's second gate, on Avinguda Marqués de l'Argentera. East of the lake was the fort's **Plaça d'Armes**, now a formal garden with the only surviving structures from the Ciutadella: a chapel, the Governor's Palace and the Arsenal. For the moment, it shares the space with the **Museu d'Art Modern** (*open Tues–Sun 9–7, closed Mon; adm*), featuring a fine introduction to 19th- and 20th-century Catalan *modernista* and *noucentisme* art, with paintings and sculptures by Casas, Fortuny, Nonell, Julio González, Nogués and Rusinyol, and furniture, including exquisite pieces designed for Domènech's Casa Lleó Morera. One striking new work is Josep Guinavart Bertram's 1979 *Contorn-Entorn*—a forest of sinister shapes and mobiles reminiscent of the great cactus garden on Montjuïc. Even if the museum moves, *El Desconsol (Despair)* 1907—Josep Llimona's famous Rodinesque nude (or rather, a copy)—will remain in her lily pond.

The Ciutadella also contains Barcelona's excellent, if a bit cramped, **Zoo** (*open daily Nov–Feb 10–5.30; Mar and Oct 10–6; April and Sept 10–7; May–Aug 9.30–7.30; adm exp*) with an aquarium. Near the zoo's aquarium stands the fountain of the pretty **Senyoreta del paraigua**, 'The lady with the umbrella', the symbol adopted by the city from the 1888 Exposition. Other survivors of the big fair line the park's under-the-lindens Passeig Tilers: the pretty **Umbráculo** (greenhouse for shade plants), and the iron and glass **Invernadero** (a winter greenhouse, which now has a very pleasant café installed in it), both by Josep Amargós, and, in between, the neo-Pompeian **Museu de Geologia**, Barcelona's first public museum, chock full of minerals, fossils and rocks from across Spain (*10–2, closed Mon; adm*). Best of all is the great brick **Castell dels Tres Dragons**, designed by Domènech i Montaner as the Universal Exposition's café-restaurant. This was the true herald of *modernista* architecture in 1888, with its innovative use of unorthodox materials and in its ceramic decoration—large blue and white shields decorated with stylized natural motifs that run under the battlements. These days a herd of stuffed beasts and bugs call it home; it's the **Museu de Zoologia** (*10–2, closed Mon; adm*).

Vila Olímpica and Barceloneta

Until the late 1980s, the seafront by Parc de la Ciutadella was occupied by Poblenou's dreary 19th-century industrial sprawl; like its great Mediterranean rival Genoa, Barcelona traditionally took no delight in its waterfront, and closed it off from public access between Barceloneta in the south and the Besos river in the north with train yards, warehouses, dumps, and little factories. Even if you could get to a beach, the water stank.

The need to house 15,000 athletes for the '92 Olympics combined with the city's need for space to play propelled the Ajuntament to undertake Barcelona's biggest urban renewal project this century. The coast was cleared to create the **Parc de Mar**, 5km of beaches for the public, and architects Oriol Bohigas, Josep Martorell and David Mackay were given the task of creating a **Vila Olímpica** that could be converted into housing (some 7000 apartments) after the games. The promise to make the new housing affordable was just a promise, and the few businesses that have moved into the American-style commercial area are not exactly your neighbourhood shop. What completes the jarring soulless suburban air of the Vila Olímpica are its wide, wide streets, its prominent car parks (even along the marina), its big desolate spaces between the traffic with outsize sculptures and fountains. This is one area of Barcelona that is clearly more friendly to cars than people.

There's no starker contrast to the Vila Olímpica than the city's 18th-century effort to build a planned neighbourhood by the sea. This is **Barceloneta**, 'Little Barcelona', a 15-minute walk south along the Passeig Marítim. After the destruction of some 2000 homes in La Ribera to build the Ciutadella, a French military engineer with the delicious name of Prosper Verboom designed a neighbourhood for the displaced on this 25-acre triangle of land, following the most progressive urban-planning ideas of the 18th century. The streets were laid out in a grid, with a market in the centre square and long, narrow blocks of houses, permitting every room to have a window and, as all houses were allowed only one floor, all had access to sunlight. Verboom's height prohibition was modified in 1837 and ignored ever since, so that most houses in Barceloneta have at least four floors. Traditionally inhabited by sailors' and fishermen's families, Barceloneta is still vibrant, densely populated, piquant and poor, and not very happy that most of its seafood restaurants have moved to the Vila Olímpica, which was supposed to have a certain amount of low-income housing, but doesn't. If by chance it's not undergoing one of its periodic mechanical overhauls, sail up to Montjuïc on the aerial cable.

Port Vell and Along the Seafront

What may bring the Barcelonans back to Barceloneta is the redevelopment of the old port, or Port Vell, just to the south. The **Palau de Mar**, overlooking the Port Vell Marina, has been rehabilitated into restaurant space and into the **Museu d'Història de Catalunya** (*open Tues–Thurs 10–7; Fri and Sat 10–8; Sun 10–2.30; closed Mon; adm*), designed to inform you all about Catalunya's history from the Palaeolithic era to the present. Up from here, the old Moll d'Espanya is occupied by a shopping centre, **Maremagnum**, an **IMAX cinema**, showing the usual IMAX mix of nature extravaganzas and rock concerts throughout the day, and an **Aquarium** (*open 10–9, 10–10 holidays; adm exp*). Don't expect a lot of bright colours, but the vast central tank, encircled by a 225ft viewing tunnel equipped with a slow human conveyor belt and serenaded by gentle New Age music and soothing patterns of silvery fish and sharks swimming all around and over your head, is a hell of a cure for stress. A wooden bridge, the **Rambla de Mar**, links the Moll d'Espanya to the foot of the Columbus monument (see below) and rotates to let sailing boats through; next to it, the **Moll de la Fusta** has become a favourite seaside promenade with restaurants and bars, the most famous, Gambrinus, topped by a 20ft fiberglass prawn designed by Xavier Mariscal, the cartoonist. The final stage of the Port Vell development is to be nothing less than a **World Trade Centre**.

At the foot of the Moll d'Espanya begins the seaside Passeig de Colom, where Cervantes lived at No.2 during his stay in Barcelona. Although the **Cervantes House** has been remodelled over the centuries, you can still see some 16th-century elements in the façade. Two blocks behind the Passeig de Colom runs the **Carrer Ample**, for several centuries the city's most aristocratic address, where Emperor Charles V, the kings of Hungary and Bohemia, and Barcelona's greatest merchants stayed and worshipped at the **Basilica de La Mercè**. Our

Lady of Mercy has been the patroness of Barcelona ever since she appeared in a vision to Jaume I, asking him to found a monastic order devoted to the deliverance of Christian captives held by Barbary pirates. The first church on the site dates from 1267, but has since been altered and rebuilt; its Gothic façade was actually transferred here from a church that had to be destroyed to make way for the Ajuntament's annex. The fittings are Baroque, but there's a fine statue of the Virgin, carved in 1361 by Pere Moragues. In September Barcelona holds a great fiesta de la Mercè, and when a football team from the city wins an important match, it sings a hymn of thanks to the Virgin.

Columbus and the Drassanes

Towering over the port in the Porta de la Pau is another souvenir of 1888, the **Monument a Colom** (Columbus Monument), which has the admiral high atop a 50m iron column, pointing out to sea. He's been married: in honour of 1992, Catalan conceptual artist and matchmaker Antoni Miralda fixed him up with the Statue of Liberty in New York, and talked Birmingham into supplying the wedding ring; Paris made Liberty's wedding gown and Valencia sewed the world's biggest pair of blue jeans for the groom. You can get into his brain for the overall view by taking the lift up (*open Tues–Sat 10–2 and 3.30–6.30, Sun 10–7; June–Sept daily 9–9; adm*). At the foot of the column you can catch a **bus nautic** (water bus) across Port Vell to Barceloneta or take one of the tour boats for a more extended visit of the port.

In a way it's ironic that Barcelona should honour the one man who led to the loss of its prestige and prosperity, as Spain turned from the Mediterranean to the riches from across the Atlantic. A far more fitting memorial to the city's own past is the **Drassanes**, or royal shipyards, Columbus' neighbour on the Porta de la Pau. Begun in 1255 by Pedro the Great, the yards took their present form in 1388, the construction costs shared by Pedro the Ceremonious, the city, and the Corts. Given to the city by the navy in the 20th century, the Drassanes is the largest and best-preserved medieval shipyard in the world and houses the **Museu Marítim** (*open Tues–Sun 10–7, closed Mon; adm*), devoted to Catalunya's proud seafaring history. Note especially the fascinating display of Mallorcan cartography from the Middle Ages (when that island had the most advanced map-making school in Europe), a 1971 full-scale replica of the Galera *La Real*, Don Juan's flagship at the 1571 Battle of Lepanto, ships' models, figureheads, painted seamen's chests, and a copy of the famous *Llibro del Consulat del Mar*, medieval Europe's first maritime code. A recent addition is the virtual reality 'Great Adventure of the Sea'.

Barcelona's Showcase Promenade: Las Ramblas

Columbus also marks the beginning of Barcelona's most famous street and one of the world's most urbane thoroughfares, the Ramblas. *Ramla* means 'sand' in Arabic, and long ago this is what it was, the sandy bottom of a torrent that passed just outside the walls of the medieval city. In the dry season it became Barcelona's major thoroughfare, where the butchers had their stalls, where employers came in search of day-labourers, and where the gallows bore their strange fruit. By 1366 the torrent was paved over, and at the end of the 18th century, after Barceloneta had been laid out, it was decided to make the Ramblas a park lane. Trees were planted and benches installed; cast-iron streetlights, kiosks and flower stalls were added in the 19th century. In 1859 the first of the plane trees was planted and thrived so well that the Barcelonans have a saying, 'to grow like a tree in the Ramblas'.

Day and night the Ramblas (there are actually five connected streets) are crowded with natives and visitors from every continent. Kiosks sell newspapers in every conceivable language, cafés, hotels, burger stands, and magically tacky souvenir stands have sprouted up; Catalan Elvis impersonators, unicyclists, flamenco buskers, and other street performers flock here in the evening. If not the 'real' Barcelona (as some point out, especially to visitors who neglect the rest of the city), the Ramblas have a big share of Barcelona's soul. And, like the rest of Barcelona since 1992, it has been tidied up, to the detriment of all the seedy sexy shops that once dominated the lowest *rambla*, **La Rambla de Santa Monica** (now they're squirreled away in the side streets). From the 15th to 18th century the area was a major producer of artillery, most notably of a colossal 35,420lb cannon named 'Santa Eulàlia' cast in 1463, which blew up into smithereens when fired for the first time. Charles V in his endless warfare showered so much business on the 12 foundries here that they were called his 'twelve apostles'. The foundries have since been supplanted by a wax museum, the **Museu de Cera**, where Nixon, Franco and Pinocchio keep company with newer dummies Charles and Di (*open Mon–Fri 10–1.30 and 4–7.30, summer 10–8; adm exp*).

The next *rambla*, **Rambla dels Caputxins**, defines the heart of Barcelona's old theatre district, of which the forlorn **Teatro Principal** is the sole survivor, heir of the first theatre on this site built by the Hospital de la Santa Creu, when Felipe II granted it a monopoly on dramatic spectacles to raise revenue. It was built in 1603, and has been rebuilt and burned and remodelled several times since (lastly in the 1980s). In the **Plaça del Teatre** stands a monument to Serafi Pitarra, the father of modern Catalan theatre, which you can learn all about in the **Theatrical Museum** in the nearby Carrer Nou de la Rambla 3 (*open daily 10–6 except Mon; adm*). The real reason to visit is the building itself, the only house by Gaudí that you can explore at leisure: the **Palau Güell**, his first major project for his patron, the financier Eusebi Güell, built in 1888 to coincide with the Universal Exposition. The exterior is restrained for Gaudí, with the exception of the swirling ironwork and the amazing roof, covered with a nubbly spire with a row of parabolic windows and topped by a lightning rod and a bat and forest of chimney and ventilator sculptures, each different and covered in what would become a signature medium for the architect, *trencadis* (broken tiles)—frustratingly, the only place to see it is from the top floor of the nearby Hotel Gaudí. Although badly damaged by Anarchists in the Civil War, much of the extraordinarily rare and precious materials Gaudí used in the rather morose Hispano-Moorish medievalish interior are still intact (with Güell, money was no object), and here and there you can see other signs of future Gaudí greatness—in the powerfully atmospheric crypt of a cellar, in the superb screen of parabolic arches by the *mirador*, in the three storey-high parabolic cupola over the main salon, forming a honeycombed beehive pierced with beams of light.

Another slight detour off the Ramblas, this time on the Passeig Colom to the right, leads into the arcaded oasis of the **Plaça Reial**, Barcelona's only square designed as a single set piece. When the Capuchin convent on the site was demolished in Mendizábal's suppression of the monasteries in 1837, architect Daniel Molina took advantage of the rare new space in the centre city to enclose it in harmonious neoclassical residences with shops and cafés on the ground floor. At the head of the Rambla dels Caputxins, on the edge of the theatre district, stood an institution that Barcelona was specially proud of: the 3500-seat **Gran Teatre del Liceu** (1860) one of Europe's largest and most sumptuous auditoria, with five huge, semi-circular balconies. For decades Spain's only opera house, presenting a regular season of grand opera, the Liceu often featured such home-grown virtuosi as Montserrat Caballé and Josep Carrers (José Carreras). In 1994, during last-minute work on a stage set, it caught fire and burned to the ground. Reconstruction of a clone is nearing completion, although it may well take until the middle of 1999 before the fat lady sings again. **Pla Boqueria**, with its colourful mosaic by Miró, marks the centre of the Ramblas. Here at No.82, the Caixa de Sabadells bank occupies the **Casa Quadros** (1896), an old umbrella maker's, studded with bright parasols and defended by a swirling dragon holding a bumbershoot designed by Josep Vilaseca. Opposite, another *modernista* shop, the **Antiga Casa Figueras**, still sells its fine cakes. There are two worthy detours south of Pla Boqueria, into the once piquant **Barri Xinès** or 'Chinatown'. The first detour, down Carrer de Sant Pau, leads in about five minutes to the 12th-century Romanesque **Sant Pau del Camp**, 'St Paul's in the Field'. The façade is decorated with reliefs of the hand of God, the Evangelists, and funny masks; if it's open, the tiny cloister with its paired columns and triple-lobed arches and garden is a charmer.

The second detour, just down Carrer de l'Hospital, leads to the **Antic Hospital de la Creu**, founded in 1024 and relocated in 1926 to Domènech's *modernista* complex near the Sagrada Família, leaving behind a mostly 15th-century complex. The two huge Gothic arches on either side of the courtyard are now the entrance to the Library of Catalunya, Barcelona's largest, with a million volumes. Just inside the former **Casa de Convalecencia**, the vestibule is richly adorned with magnificent 17th-century *azulejos* by Llorenç Pasoles; others can be seen on the stair leading to the chapel. Across the lane is the 18th-century Surgery College, now the **Real Academia de Cirugía y Medicina**, with an elliptical anatomical amphitheatre and the original marble dissection table in the centre that revolves so students could all have a good peek at the guts. The neglected cloister with its orange trees has some lively carvings if you don't mind the smell of urine. Across Pla Boqueria, Carrer Cardenal Casañas leads into the **Barri del Pi** (named after a pine tree), another of the medieval *vilanovas* that grew up outside the Roman walls. It separates the Ramblas from the Barri Gòtic and has its spiritual centre in the Plaça del Pi, where **Santa Maria del Pi** with its huge rose window broods like a cyclops.

Beyond Pla Boqueria the next *rambla*, **Rambla de Sant Josep**, is the most perfumed, lined with kiosks selling flowers and birds and miniature rabbits. On the left, a large *modernista* neo-Gothic arch beckons you into the lively century-old Mercat Sant Josep, better known as the **Boqueria**, founded in 1830 and still the place to find the freshest fish, fruit, meat, cheese and vegetables in Barcelona. Just up from the market, the ivory-coloured neoclassical **Palau de la Virreina** was built in 1778 for the Viceroy of Peru with the loot he skimmed off the fabulous silver mines of Potosí. He died not long after moving in and left the spread to his wife, the vicereine—hence its name. The city has converted it into an exhibition space and cultural information centre (*open Tues–Sat 10–8.30, Sun 10–2.30; call ahead ☎ 93 301 77 75 to see the palace's Catalan national coin collection*).

The next *rambla*, the **Rambla dels Estudis**, was named after L'Estudi General, or University, that once stood here, founded by Martin I and suppressed by Felipe V; nowadays the promenade is full of the whistles and chirps of its permanent bird market. Monuments on this segment include the 18th-century **Església de Belén**, its once Baroque interior blasted away in the Civil War; opposite, the arcaded **Palau de Moya**, from the same century, now houses the Generalitat's cultural bookshop. Further up, a right on to Carrer Canuda leads to the **Plaça Vila de Madrid**, with 2nd-century AD **Roman tombs** that once lined the road into the city; you can see how much the ground level has risen over the centuries. On the left, Carrer del

Bonsuccès will take you to Plaça del Angels and its glowing new **Museu d'Art Contemporani de Barcelona**, or 'MACBA' as it's popularly known, (*open Tues–Fri 12–8, Sat 10–8, Sun 10–3, Mon closed; adm*), designed by American architect Richard Meier, a pure white light-filled Mediterranean version of Paris' Pompidou Centre, its great glass front and ramps overlooking the roofs and laundry of the funky old Raval quarter. The core collection is formed by such lights as Antoni Tàpies, Caldar, Dubuffet, Barceló, Klee, Oldenburg, Raschenberg, and Christian Boltanski—don't miss his sinister bank vault-like *Réserve des suisses morts* (1991). Next to the museum, a former orphanage has been converted into the **Centre de Cultura Contemporani** (CCCB), Montealegre 5 (*open Tues, Thurs and Fri 11–2 and 4–8, Wed and Sat 11–8, Sun 10–3; adm*).

The last little segment of the Ramblas, the **Rambla de les Canaletes**, is named after a magical fountain dispensed beneath a pretty four-headed street light that forces all who drink of it to remain forever in Barcelona.

Around the Plaça de Catalunya and the Palau de la Música

This vast rather jumbly square is the nerve centre of Barcelona, dividing the medieval city and the 19th-century extension, or Eixample; nearly all the city buses and the Metro converge here under banks crowned with large neon signs and the Corte Inglés department store, a cross between a ferry boat and a radiator. In the centre are two illuminated fountains, a giant upsidedown stair on a pedestal dedicated to Francesc Macià, and among the tulips a wistful sculpture by Barcelona's own Josep Clará called *The Goddess*.

Behind the Banca d'España on Carrer de Rivudadeneyra, the plain Romanesque church, monastery and double-decker Gothic cloister of **Santa Ana** hosted the Cortes held under Fernando the Catholic—the last *cortes* before Aragón and Catalunya were tacked on to Castile. Near here at Carrer Montsió 3 (get there by way of Carrer S. Ana and Avinguda Portal de l'Angel), in a neo-Gothic house by Puig i Cadafalch, is the renowned **Els Quatre Gats** (The Four Cats), Barcelona's legendary *modernista* artsy intellectual café. Founded in 1897 by four artists, Rusinyol, Casas, Pere Romeu and Miquel Utrillo (father of Maurice), it published its own art review, held avant-garde puppet shows, recitals by young composers and exhibitions, including Picasso's first. When everybody who was anyone had passed through, the original Four Cats closed in 1903, and was replaced by the pious Catholic club, the Cercle Artistic de Sant Lluc, which counted Gaudí among its members. But now there's a new Quatre Gats, recreated with much of the original décor.

Continuing down Carrer Montsió, take a left onto Vía Laietana and then right onto Carrer Mes Alt Sant Pere for *modernista* architecture in its most delightful extreme: Lluís Domènech i Montaner's 1908 **Palau de la Música Catalana**, undulating, polychromatic, adorned with floral and musical motifs in tiles and mosaics, so ripe and rich they seemed cramped in the narrow streets. The interior (*if you can't get a concert ticket, you can book a tour, © 93 317 99 82*) is if anything more colourful, an exuberant epiphany of stained glass and ceramics, with a permanent hemicyclical stage set composed of half tile, half 3-D ceramic musical maidens in a background of *trencadis*. The proscenium is marked by flowing pumice sculptures of Beethoven and the Valkyries facing a forest and Josep Clavé. There's an old joke: one Catalan starts a business, two start a corporation, and three start a choral society. Josep Clavé was one of the founders of the *Orféo Català*, which paid for the Palau de la Música; these days it also serves as Barcelona's principal concert hall, in spite of its famously bad acoustics.

In the 18th and early 19th century, the Ciutadella and city walls built by the Bourbon king Felipe V after the city's defiant revolt in 1714 were a constant, humiliating reminder of Barcelona's subjection to Madrid. As the population grew and the industrial revolution took its first baby steps, the city became increasingly claustrophobic in its confines. Barcelona endlessly petitioned the government in reactionary Madrid to remove them, and finally succeeded in August 1854, during a brief interlude of liberalism. As soon as word reached Barcelona, a wild celebration filled the streets as every man, woman and child grabbed a tool and started hacking away at walls. The Bourbon wall was made of tougher stuff than the Berlin wall: it took ten years to dismantle, and was so despised that not a block of it was left in place to remind anyone that it had ever been there.

Now that it had room to grow, the city sponsored a competition for the plan of the new extension, or **Eixample**. The winning plan (imposed by Madrid—the city fathers had chosen another) was that of an engineer named Ildefons Cerdà, who designed a democratic grid with distinct chamfered corners at the intersections (to allow the new steam trams to turn more easily). But unlike most grid plans, especially American ones, Cerdà's idea wasn't to cut up property to buy and sell as easily as possible. He had Utopian visions: his abstract plan would eliminate social classes—there was no reason why one block should be better than another— and he planned markets, parks and social services for each modular set of blocks. Few city plans have been more hated, their intentions so thoroughly ignored by developers. With the 'Pla Cerdà' Barcelona quintupled in size over the next 50 years. Height and density restrictions soon went by the wayside; the trees and patio gardens destroyed. Only one of Cerdà's parks came into being (near the Sants station); his vision of the **Plaça de les Glòries Catalanes** (where the Eixample's three big boulevards, the Diagonal, the Meridiana and Gran Via des Corts Catalans meet like the Union Jack) as the throbbing centre of Barcelona life is only now taking shape with the completion of a new shopping centre, the Auditori Municipal by Rafael Moneo and the Teatre Nacional project by Ricardo Bofill. In spite of Cerdà's egalitarian intentions, social snobbery won out and, as Paris has its Right and Left Banks, Barcelona has its Right and Left Eixample, divided by the delightful linden-lined **Rambla de Catalunya** —an extension of Las Ramblas beginning in Plaça Catalunya. The Right Eixample is the more prestigious of the two sides: here, to make up for the enforced equality of the Pla Cerdà, *modernista* architects created visual fireworks to flaunt the status of their wealthy clients. Over the past decade the Ajuntament has gone out of its way to restore, clean off and preserve their fascinating legacy; if the Barri Gòtic is Europe's largest medieval neighbourhood, the Eixample holds its greatest trove of Art Nouveau buildings.

The Passeig de Gràcia and the Fairest of Discords

The greatest concentration of *modernista* masterpieces is along the Eixample's most elegant boulevard, the Passeig de Gràcia, the old road from the Barri Gòtic (and Plaça de Catalunya) to the once separate town of Gràcia. The beautiful street lamps arching half way over the street from white *trencadí* bases at once set the boulevard apart. If you love architecture, though, take the first right from the Passeig de Gràcia to Carrer de Casp, where at No.48 stands the **Casa Calvet** (1898), Gaudí's first apartment building—the ironwork detail, the two crosses, and the decorative elements presage his future masterpieces on the Passeig de Gràcia.

Beyond the Gran Via de les Corts Catalanes—one of the three wide avenues Cerdà designed through his grid—the stretch of the Passeig de Gràcia between Carrers Consell de Cent and Aragó is known as the **Manzana de la Discordia**—a pun on manzana, which means both 'apple' and 'block'; here every passer-by can play the role of the Trojan Paris and award his or her prize to the fairest of the three *modernista* beauties. The first, at No.35, is the **Casa Lleó Morera** (1905), Domènech i Montaner's most lavish residential building, beautifully decorated with sculpture by Eusebi Arnau. As the ground floor was destined to house a photographer's studio, Arnau covered it with nymphs and reliefs relating to electricity and cameras, all sacrificed in 1943 in the interest of larger shop windows; the original cupola and interior furnishings were removed as well (two nymphs, holding a camera and lightbulb, survive on the second floor). Next, three doors down at No.41, stands Puig i Cadafalch's Casa Amatller. In 1898 Amatller, Barcelona's Willy Wonka of a chocolate tycoon, hired Puig to give an existing apartment building the neo-Gothic treatment. Puig's neo-Gothic is like no one else's, with a façade wall decorated in discreet sgraffito, culminating in a remarkable stepped gable richly aglitter with blue, pink and cream tiles. Don't miss the sculptural details by Eusebi Arnau, including Catalunya's patron St George and the dragon, and if the library of Institute Amatller d'Art Hispanic is open (*Mon–Fri 10–1.30*) you can have a look inside at some of Puig's original furnishings.

Next door, the **Casa Batlló** was similarly a nondescript residential building of the Eixample when textile magnate Josep Batlló commissioned Gaudí to give it a facelift in 1904. Gaudí, a Catalan nationalist like every other *modernista* architect, transformed its flat façade into an allegory of St George and the dragon, covering the building with an unforgettable rippling, magical skin of different shades of blue ceramics and *trencadis* (by his great collaborator Josep Jujol i Gilbert), topped by an equally sublimely coloured roof—the dragon's scaly back. The characteristic Gaudí pinnacle with its bulb dome and cross is St George's lance, placed to the side to complement the symmetry of the adjacent Casa Amatller; the colourful *trencadi-* covered chimneys, invisible from ground level, look like the dragon's multi-spiked tail. If the door's open, take the lift (also designed by Gaudí) to the top and walk down the stair, hopefully obtaining a peek into the magnificent ceramic light-well.

Around the corner from the Manzana de la Discordia at Carrer Aragó 255, the Fundació Antoni Tàpies (*open Tues–Sun 11–8, closed Mon exc on holidays; adm*), is headquartered in Domènech's building for the publisher, Editorial Montaner i Simón (1880–85), an early example of his love for good bare Catalan brick and iron; the restorers updated it with a cloud of aluminium wire, in the spirit of Tàpies (1923–94), a great promoter of the use of everyday, common materials in art. Born in Barcelona and educated at law school, Tàpies turned to art during the Second World War, first producing paintings in a surrealist vein before turning to abstract works. Tàpies' imaginative use of mixed media—from scraps of paper and rags to furniture and musical instruments in his later works—made him the most influential artist to emerge in Spain after the 1940s. In 1984 he set up his foundation for the study of contemporary and non-Western art; the foundation displays a selection of Tàpies' art upstairs and changing exhibitions of other people's on the lower two floors.

Further up Passeig de Gràcia: La Pedrera

Casa Batlló created such a sensation that some even richer people immediately hired Gaudí to outdo himself a few blocks up the Passeig de Gràcia. Here he was given a large chamfered

Genius and Crank

Antoni Gaudí i Cornet (1852–1926) was one of the most innovative architects of any time, and his major works such as La Pedrera have been listed in Unesco's catalogue of World Heritage properties. Although Gaudí was regarded as an eccentric or even a hippies' architect in the 1960s, you don't have to be in Barcelona long to realize that his reputation has since been polished and used to fuel an industry of its own: you can take an all-Gaudí tour, purchase models of his benches in Parc Güell, or even build your own little Casa Batlló from a paper kit. Although classed as a *modernista*, Gaudí's creation of new forms and textures and his vision of decoration as being as integral to the structure as its walls or roof went far beyond anything built by his colleagues. No architect ever studied nature more intently; in his buildings, stone became organic, sensuous, dripping; iron was wrought into whiplash ribbons, trailing leaves and spider webs; the old Muslim art of covering surfaces with broken tiles (*trencadis* in Catalan) was given a new vibrant, abstract meaning, reaching a kind of epiphany in the Parc Güell. Gaudí ingenuously reinvented the almost impossible parabolic arch, last seen with the Hittites: he would create hanging models made of chains, suspend carefully measured weights from them, take photos from every angle and turn the photos upside down. Much of the mathematic work he and his colleagues had to do in those pre-computer days is mindboggling. He also had the luck to draw on a highly skilled, no longer existent craft base to give his imagination substance.

So it tends to come as a surprise to learn that Gaudí, whose very name in Catalan means 'delight', was the last man you'd want to invite over for dinner (to begin with, he was probably the only Catalan vegan who ever lived). Obsessive, morbidly pious, a nationalistic egomaniac, he regarded La Pedrera only as a pedestal for a 40ft-high statue of the Virgin Mary and a pair of angels, an idea his client prudently vetoed after the 1909 Tragic Week when Barcelona was still smoking from another of its periodic bouts of church burnings; the kind of wealthy industrialists who hired Gaudí made their bundles by keeping the working people of Barcelona so downtrodden that anarchism seemed to be their only hope. Gaudí didn't get it. La Pedrera was his last secular building (1910), before he devoted the rest of his life trying to expiate the church-torching sins of his fellow citizens by building the Sagrada Família.

virgin corner of the Eixample, and the result, the Casa Milà, was just what the Milàs ordered: the most extraordinary, singular apartment building ever, nicknamed *La Pedrera*, 'the stone quarry'. The five-storey stone façade undulates around the bevelled corner of the block without a hint of a right angle or straight line, a cliff sculpted by waves of wind, pierced by windows that look as if they had been eroded into the stone and balconies of forged iron spilling over the edges and twisted into naturalistic shapes based on kelp. This sea cliff of stone rises to a steep white foam of a roof, topped by chimneys and ventilators shaped like bouquets of visored knights in reddish stone and four fat globs of Cheeze Whiz (the stair exits) covered in white *trencadis*: the culmination of Gaudí's amazing roof installations, called the precursors of surrealism, expressionism, and cubism. The roof itself is supported by a great wavy tunnel of

Gaudí's catenary parabolic arches. The interior is nearly as striking as the façade, with its two irregular circular patios open to the sky linked by winding ramps, while below ground is Europe's first underground car park; originally Gaudí wanted residents to be able to drive to their doors. Long dark with grime, the façade has been cleaned up to reveal its original pale honey tones since 1986 by its owner, the Caixa de Catalunya, which holds exhibitions in the building and now offer tours of the interior and roof (*book for groups © 93 484 59 00*).

Around La Pedrera: Other Modernista Highlights

Just beyond La Pedrera, Avinguda Diagonal slices across the neat waffle of the Eixample. If in the Manzana de la Discordia you gave the prize to Puig i Cadafalch, two of his principal works may be seen just to the right, the neo-Gothic/Plateresque Palau Baró de-Quadras (1904) at Diagonal 373, now the **Museu de la Música** (*open Tues–Sun, 10–2, Wed 5–8, closed Mon; adm*) with a fascinating collection of antique and exotic instruments from the 16th century on, including one of Adophe Sax's original saxophones and a major collection of guitars. At Nos. 416–20, Puig's massive neo-Gothic apartment block, the **Casa de les Punxes** (1903–5), 'Spiky House', bristles with the pointiest witch's hat roofs ever, and needly spires rising out of its brick gables. Here, too, at No.442 is the **Casa Comalat** (1911) designed by one of Gaudí's followers, Salvador Valer, with an undulating rear façade and a magnificent entrance hall of tile and stained glass. If you awarded your apple to Domènech i Montaner, turn down Carrer Mallorca (between Passeig de Gràcia and Avda. Diagonal), where in 1893 he added the ceramic façade to the **Casa Montaner** (No.278), now the seat of the provincial government of Barcelona. At No.291, a *modernista* furniture showroom now occupies Domènech's **Casa Thomas** (1898), a neo-Gothic apartment house with the first examples of the architect's decorative ceramic appliqués.

The Sagrada Família

George Orwell, writing of the church burnings during the Civil War in his *Homage to Catalonia*, wondered why there was one that the mobs always spared, a peculiar one with spires shaped like bottles looming high over the Right Eixample. These 350ft bottles, of course, belonged to Gaudí's Sagrada Família. Slightly smaller than St Peter's in Rome, occupying an entire block of the Cerdà plan with its own Metro station (or you could simply continue up Carrer Mallorca from the Casa Thomas), the Templo Expiatorio de la Sagrada Família is surely the most compelling, controversial, ambitious—and most unfinished—piece of 20th-century architecture in the world.

The temple was begun in 1882, the brainchild of a bookdealer named Josep M. Bocabella Verdaguer, fervent follower of reactionary Pope Pius IX and founder of a society dedicated to St Joseph, devoted to expiating the sins of modernism. He originally hired another architect, Francesc del Villar, who planned a neo-Gothic church and got as far as the crypt when disagreements with Bocabella led to his replacement by Gaudí in 1883, when the architect was 31. Gaudí finished the crypt and then spent much of his remaining 43 years on the project, which grew grander and grander with each plan. For his last 15 years he accepted no other commissions, and actually lived in a hut on the construction site. When money ran low, he sold everything he owned for the project and spent his free time soliciting funds. He lived on bread and water and prayer.

Gaudí intended the Sagrada Família to be 'an immense palace of Christian memory' and spent much of his energy on making sure that every possible aspect of Catholic doctrine was expressed in some nook or cranny of the temple. There were to be three façades dedicated to the Birth (Naixement), Passion and the main one, to Glory; each façade would have four towers, symbolizing the twelve Apostles. Four higher towers would be dedicated to the Evangelists, and between them, a truly colossal tower symbolizing the Saviour, with a large tower to the Virgin on the side. Gaudí started on one façade, the Naixement, but absent-mindedly wandered in front of a streetcar in 1926 and died before he even saw that completed. He was buried in the crypt chapel. His followers attempted to have him canonized. By 1935, they had completed the façade according to his models. Orwell was wrong when he wrote that the Anarchists never damaged the Sagrada Família: in 1936 they made a point of breaking into the workshops and crypt and setting fire to every plan and model they found, and then broke open the tombs of Bocabella and Gaudí to add insult to injury.

And so the temple stood until 1954, when the Joseph society raised enough money to continue the project in the manner of Gaudí, instructing architects to guess the master's intent from a few surviving drawings. Architect Jordi Bonet and sculptor Josep Subirachs have completed the Façade of the Passion and have turned their attention to the enormous Gloria façade. Their work has offended purists, who believe the temple is best left as it was when Gaudí died, as a memorial to his unique genius; they also point out that Gaudí never even followed his own models, but was ever changing and revising his plans as he went along. One can only speculate whether Gaudí himself would have wished the construction stopped or continued over generations like the cathedrals of the Middle Ages. There is something depressing about the result: the recently completed Passion façade with its robotic sculptures by Subirachs is so dire a piece of kitsch it makes you feel queasy. Where the Naixement façade has Gaudí's unmistakable natural, textured organic style, as if it were some primordial growth, Subirachs's is mechanical, cheap and sinister. His magic square that adds up to 33 and the labyrinth are only bones tossed to medieval tradition.

Current plans are to complete the whole thing by the centenary of Gaudí's death—2026. Admission to the site includes the museum in the crypt, entered through the Passion façade on Carrer Sardenya (*open daily, 9–9 in summer, 9–6 in winter; adm*). The museum has photos, diagrams, plaster models, bits of sculpture (air pollution has already devoured many from Gaudí's day), and an astonishing reproduction of the scale model of chains used by Gaudí to build the Crypt Güell. For a small fee you can take the lift (*10–5.45*) up the Passion towers, for a vertiginous dreamlike ramble high over the city. The Avinguda Gaudí, decorated with neo-Gothic street lamps transferred from the Passeig de Gràcia, leads from the Sagrada Família through a neighbourhood called Camp de l'Arpa or 'Field of the Dolmen', recalling a long-lost megalith, to another (completed and useful) gargantuan *modernista* work, Domènech i Montaner's **Hospital de Sant Pau** (1902–30) covering over 100,000 sq.m or nine blocks of the Eixample and completed by his son after his death. If you fall ill in Barcelona, this is the place to go, but even if you're perfectly well it's a lovely place to visit.

South of the Sagrada Família, at Gran Via 749, the brick *modernista*-Moorish **Plaça de Toros Monumental** (1911) has three towers supporting huge yellow, white and blue ceramic dinosaur eggs. This is Barcelona's largest bullring and home of the **Museu Taurí**, with a collection of famous bulls' heads (*open daily April–Sept 10.30–2 and 4–7*).

Getting There

Every half hour **bus 61** from the Plaça d'Espanya Metro takes in most of the park, making a great loop from the Palau Nacional past the Poble Espanyol, the Olympic Stadium, the Fondació Miró to Plaça Dante, where the **telefèric de Montjuïc** continues up to the Castell and Parc d'Atraccions and where the **funicular** rises and descends from the Paral.lel Metro station. If the **aerial cable car** is working, you can travel to the Jardins de Miramar from the port of Barceloneta. Note that the *telefèric*, funicular, and cable car run only on weekends and holidays outside the summer. If you drive, watch out: every learner driver in Barcelona has their first lessons on Montjuïc.

Gently sloping up 215m between the city and the sea, Montjuïc is Barcelona's grandstand and playground, with more than enough attractions to fill a day and night. The origins of its peculiar name are much disputed: either it derives from 'Mons Jovis'—the mountain of Jupiter—or the large Jewish cemetery that used to be there, hence 'mountain of the Jews'. For most of Barcelona's history it was reserved for defence, but slowly but surely the city's green thumbs claimed it as their own, and in 1914 Barcelona made the entire north slope into Montjuïc Park, beautifully landscaped by Jean-Claude Forestier and N M Rubió i Tuduri. Its loveliness inspired the city fathers to hold an International Exposition to show it off, unfortunately just in time for the Depression. Style had evolved as well since the 1888 Universal Exposition initiated the *modernista* style; in 1929 Barcelona was in a period of neo-Mormonism. The mountain was the natural site for the 1992 Olympic stadium and sport palace.

Plaça d'Espanya and Around

The show begins in the round Plaça d'Espanya, marking the end of the Left Eixample and the wide boulevard of the **Parel.lel**, cutting down to the sea. This street has had a number of official names in its career, but has been known simply as the 'Paral.lel' ever since 1794, when it was discovered to lie exactly on the 41° 44' parallel—fascinating to the Barcelonians, whose city otherwise refuses to square with the compass. During the first half of this century, the Paral.lel was known as 'the Montmartre of Barcelona' for its music halls, several of which have survived to become local institutions. Where the Diagonal meets the Plaça d'Espanya is the city's smaller, older bullring, **Les Arenes**.

The main entrance to Montjuïc is guarded by a pair of tall **Tuscan Towers**, framing the grand view of the main exhibition palaces, lining the fairway up to the neo-Mormon Palau Nacional. Various trade fairs occupy the buildings throughout the year. In between, the **Font Màgica**, created by engineer Carlos Buigas for the 1929 exhibition, performs a dazzling aquatic ballet of colour and light while blue searchlights radiate a peacock's tail of beams from the Palau Nacional (*open May–Sept Thurs–Sun 9pm–midnight; Oct–May Fri and Sat 7–9; music and light show every 30mins*).

To the right of the fountains, the Ajuntament has reconstructed (1986) the cool, elegant **Pavelló Barcelona** (*open daily Nov–Mar 10–6.30; April–Oct 10–8; adm*), designed by Bauhaus architect Mies van der Rohe ('I would rather be good than original') for Germany's exhibit in the 1929 fair; inside the prize exhibit is Mies' Barcelona Chair.

The Museu Nacional d'Art de Catalunya

From the fountains, a never-ending stair (and outdoor escalators, put in for the Olympics, that crank up as you approach) leads up to the Palau Nacional, home of the remarkable **Museu Nacional d'Art de Catalunya** (*open Tues–Sat 10–7, until 9pm on Thurs, Sun and hol 10–2.30; adm*). It contains the world's foremost collection of medieval murals, rescued in the 1920s from decaying chapels in the remote Pyrenees—strikingly bold, expressive paintings, directly descended from the Byzantine murals and mosaics, with sharply delineated, brightly coloured forms and hieratic attitudes. The divine figures stare out hypnotically with riveting dark eyes, red circles on their cheeks, stylized stringy hair and weird elongated hands that look like flippers. In the most primitive, from the 11th-century San Miquel de Marmellar, the artist could hardly draw a face. The four finest are all from the 12th century: *Santa María de Taüll, Santa María d'Aneu, Sant Joan de Boí*, with jugglers and the Stoning of St Stephen and *Sant Climent de Taüll*, with its famous Pantocrator in his mandala, one of the most commanding, direct images in medieval art, accompanied by an unforgettable weird scene of David cutting off the head of a Goliath with a sausage body. The striking painted crucifix known as the *Majestat Batlló* portrays Christ, not in the exquisite agony favoured in the rest of Spain, but dressed like a king, open-eyed and serene, in a beautiful tunic, a conceit symbolizing the triumph over death. The Catalan gift for surrealism is expressed in the 12th-century Durro altar frontal—note especially St Quirze sawn in two.

There are secular murals of monsters from the palatine room of San Pedro de Arlanzer near Burgos and the ceiling of the chapter house of Sigena in Aragón (1200), damaged by fire in 1936 but still superb, its Old and New Testament figures inspired by English miniatures and Norman Sicilian mosaics.

Catalan Gothic art is equally well represented, with 13th-century murals of the Siege of Mallorca, beautiful works by master Jaume Huguet, and the refined *retablo* of the *Verge dels Consellers* by Lluís Dalmau. Standouts among the museum's later works are El Greco's *SS. Peter and Paul*, and paintings by Velázquez, Ribera and Zurbarán. When, at some point in the not so distant future, the Museu d'Art Modern is relocated here, the museum will offer a complete feast of old and new Catalan art.

Around the Palau Nacional

A short walk just west of the Palau Nacional, you'll find the **Botanical Gardens of Montjuïc** (*call in advance to request a visit, © 93 325 80 50*), the **Mirador del Llobregat** (one of several Montjuïc belvederes, this one with Josep Llimona's statue of a weary St George) and another relic of the 1929 fair, the **Poble Espanyol** (*open Tues–Thurs 9am–2am, until 4am Fri–Sat, 8pm Mon and until midnight on Sun; adm 950pts, under 14s 525 pts, free adm with a reservation at one of the nightclubs or big restaurants. In the summer there's a free bus from Plaça d'Espanya*). Conceived as an anthology of Spanish architecture with the slogan 'Get to Know Spain in an Hour', the replicas of famous buildings across the country were cunningly arranged with Disneyland deftness; souvenir and craft shops occupy every other building. Other attractions in the Poble Espanyol include showings of the *Barcelona Experience*, in smellavision (*hourly between 10.30–8*) or the museums (*both open 9–2*): the **Museu d'Arts, Indústris i Tradicions Populars**, with traditional rural and ethnographic exhibits, toys and religious items, and the **Museu de les Arts Gràfiques**.

Montjuïc's other attractions lie east of the Palau Nacional. Just behind it are the formal gardens of the Exposition's **Palacete Albéniz**, named after the Catalan composer and used to lodge visiting VIPs. Just downhill from here, the **Museu d'Etnologia** (*open 10–2, Tues and Thurs til 7, closed Mon*) has a fascinating collection from Morocco, Japan, Australia, Africa and especially Latin America—Amazonian shrunken heads with serious expressions, hot-pink skeleton dolls from Mexico, a Peruvian head deformer, and much more. Below this, the righthand stair leads down to the oldest gardens of Montjuïc, **La Roselada**, with its Font del Gat ('cat fountain') and the **Teatre Grec**, made from an old quarry in 1929 and used for summer theatre performances. A bit further down Passeig de Santa Madrona, in the 1929 Graphic Arts Palace, the **Museu Arqueològic** (*open Tues–Sat 9.30–7, Sun 10–2.30, closed Mon; free Sun*) concentrates on Palaeolithic to Visigothic Catalunya and contains an especially interesting collection from the Balearics—megalithic models and Carthaginian sculpture from Ibiza—and finds from the ancient Greek Empúries, Iberian vases and Roman mosaics of chariot races.

Further up, off the Avinguda de l'Estadi, begins the **Anella Olímpica**, with the Olympic swimming pool, the **Piscines Picornell** (bring your passport and some money if you want to swim) and the **Stadi Olímpic**, originally built for the 1929 fair. Barcelona made a bid to hold the 1936 games here, but lost out to Hitler's Berlin; in defiance it decided to hold a non-fascist 'People's Olympics', an event spoiled by another fascist named Franco, who revolted and began the Civil War the day before the games were to open. The whole interior was rebuilt to hold 70,000 for the 1992 games, preserving the façade of 1929 and its bronzes by Pau Gargallo. The gate is always open for a look around and a visit to the **Galeria Olímpica** (*open Apr–Sept 10–2 and 4–8, Sun 10–2; Oct–Mar 10–1 and 4–6, Sun 10–2, closed Mon; adm*), with videos of the extraordinary opening and closing ceremonies of the games. The adjacent covered sports arena, the **Palau Sant Jordi**, designed by Japanese architect Arata Isozaki, is one of the most beautiful in Europe and is used for sports and concerts alike. Tucked on the hill nearby is **Institut Nacional d'Educacio Fisica de Catalunya**, designed by Barcelona's own Ricardo Bofill. The tall white needly thing, death to any passing Zeppelin, is a telecommunications tower.

Fundació Joan Miró to the Castell Montjuïc

Avda. de l'Estadi continues to the **Fundació Joan Miró** (*open Tues–Sat 11–7, July–Sept; 11–8, Thurs until 9.30, Sun 10–2.30, closed Mon; adm*), in a beautiful white building bathed in natural light, designed in 1975 by Miró's friend Josep Lluís Sert, a student of Le Corbusier (and enlarged in 1986 by Sert's collaborator, Jaume Freixa). A native of Barcelona, Miró (1893–1983) moved to Paris in 1919 where he soon joined the surrealist movement, only to go a step beyond surrealism by evolving his own playful, personal language to express his mix of dream and reality (full of Catalanist imagery, according to Robert Hughes; apparently the Romanesque frescoes just over the way in the Palau Nacional were one of Miró's strongest influences). In 1940, Miró returned to Spain from France, settling for good in Mallorca in 1956, where over the years he planned the Fundació to create a forum for experimentation and study. It holds wide-ranging special exhibitions of contemporary art and a permanent collection of works made by artists in homage of Miró. The core, of course, is an excellent sampling of the artist's own paintings, sculptures, textile works and drawings made between 1917 and the 1970s. Not all are bright and colourful—most strikingly the lithographs of the *Barcelona Series*, inspired by the horrors of the Civil War.

To the east, beyond the Fundació Miró, are the **Jardins Mossèn Jacint Verdaguer** with a sculpture in honour of the Catalan national dance, the *sardana*. The neighbouring **Parc d'Atraccions** (*open June 24–mid-Sept Tues–Fri 6pm–11pm, Sat and Sun till midnight, weekends only in winter 6pm–9pm*) has not only a fun ferris-wheel, roller-coaster, and the 'Crazy Rat', but also the cable car that continues up to the **Castell Montjuïc**.

The first real castle on this site was thrown up in 30 days during the Catalan Rebellion in 1640, when the defenders won a stirring victory over the Castilian forces of Felipe IV. Since then the citadel has played a singularly unhappy role. In 1808, the French, disguised as allies, were admitted and took over without a shot; in 1909 the Anarchist founder of Barcelona's secular Modern Schools, Francesc Ferrer, was executed here following the 'Tragic Week' church burnings—even though Ferrer wasn't even in Barcelona at the time—causing a storm of protest throughout Europe.

A decade later in the infamous La Canadiense streetcar strike—Spain's worst and bloodiest, putting the lights out in Barcelona, causing severe food shortages, and shutting down 70 per cent of its industry—3000 workers were imprisoned in the castle. In October 1940, the President of the Generalitat, Lluís Companys, was captured by the Gestapo in France and handed over to Franco, who had him secretly taken to the castle and shot; a stone marks the spot. In 1960 the military ceded the castle to the city, which has used this haunted ground for its interesting **Museu Militar** (*open 9.30–7.30pm, closed Mon; adm*), based on the collection of models, maps, weapons and armour acquired by that emperor of packrats, Frederic Marés.

Below, near the aerial cable-car station at **Miramar**, you can enjoy an especially fine view of the city over a glass of beer. Next to the bar, incongruously overlooking the bustling docks, are the superb **Jardins de Mossèn Costa i Llobera**, with one of the world's outstanding collections of succulents, a towering cactus Manhattan interspersed with exotic specimens that look as if they have dropped in from another planet.

Into the Hills: Around the Edge of Barcelona

On the map, the ragged edges of the Eixample's grid mark its contact with older, once independent towns or hills that defy its modular grid. One of the ex-towns, Gràcia, is worth a visit for itself; other suburbs attracted moneyed Barcelona in the early 20th century, leaving some fine works by Gaudí to mark its passing, especially the sublime Parc Güell. Other sites are of more specialized interest: **Horta**, for instance, on the far northwest edge of Barcelona in the Collserola foothills, has its **Parc del Laberint** on Passeig del Vall de Hebrón. The park belongs to the lovely neoclassical country house of the Marques de Alfarràs, who in 1799 hired Italian architect Domenico Bagutti to lay out the formal gardens, lake, canals, an arbour and a cypress **maze**. These days access to the park is by way of the Olympic **Velódrom**, set in its own park with a sculpture-poem by Joan Brossa and a reconstruction of Josep Lluís Sert's **Pavilion of the Spanish Republic**, built as a cry of defiance in the midst of the civil war for the 1937 Paris Exposition Universal: the original housed Picasso's *Guernica*, Miró's lost mural of *El Segador*, Julio González's *Montserrat* and Calder's *Mercury Fountain*.

Bus no.27 from the Plaça d'Espanya will take you there, or the Horta Metro and bus no.85.

'Toto' (said Dorothy), 'I don't think we're in Kansas anymore.'

The Wizard of Oz

It is a characteristic paradox of Spain for it to contain within its borders both our century's greatest monument to Death—Franco's Valle de los Caídos—and its greatest evocation of the infinite variety and magic of life—Gaudí's Parc Güell, located south of Horta on one of Barcelona's great balconies, 'Bald Mountain', Mont Pelat (from the Lesseps Metro, walk 0.4km up the Travessera de Dalt, then turn left up the Carrer Labrand, or take bus no.24 from Plaça de Catalunya). The park owes its existence to tycoon Eusebi Güell, who bought two farms on Mont Pelat in 1902 to lay out an exclusive garden suburb. To give it tone and attract residents, he gave his pet architect free reign to create a grand entrance to the estate, a central plaza and market area for residents. For all that, Güell's experiment in property speculation was a flop; only two houses were ever built on his lots so he donated the Parc Güell to the city.

In the midst of the dull, not-so-hoity-toity *urbanización* that actually was built on Bald Mountain, the Parc Güell glows like an enchanted mirage. The entrance is flanked by two fairy-tale **pavilions** as bright as candy, crowned by sloping roofs of swirling coloured mosaics, cupolas, a magic mushroom and Gaudí's signature steeple with its double cross. The grand stair swoops past on either side of the most jovial **reptile** imaginable, clinging to the fountain and covered with brightly coloured *trencadis*. On top of the stair opens the remarkable cavernous Sala Hipóstila—Gaudí's covered market—better known as the **Hall of a Hundred Columns**, with its thick forest of Doric columns (actually there are only 86). The shallow vaults of the ceiling are covered with white *trencadis* and beautiful ceramic medallions by Jujol. The scalloped roof of the hall is rimmed with a brilliantly coloured ceramic collage—the first collage, ever—that also serves as the back of fantastic **serpentine benches** on the terrace above. Designed mostly by Jujol, great care went into the apparently random patterns of colour, words, and simple and abstract designs, creating new delights with each turn and change of perspective and light. Then there are Gaudí's extraordinary nubby rough stone **porticoes**, sloping in and out of the hillside, made of stone found on the site and fitted together to form sinuous passageways like no others on this planet with their curling walls and fanciful planters. No two columns are alike; one looks like Carmen Miranda holding a pile of rocks on her head instead of fruit salad.

Before settling into his hut by the Sagrada Famìlia, Gaudí lived for 20 years in a house by the park's Carrer del Carmel entrance.

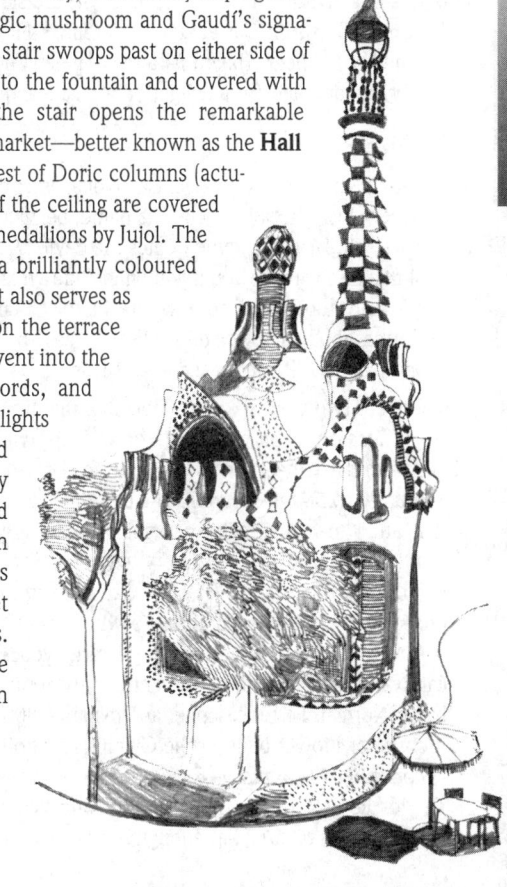

Designed by his associate Francesc Berenguer, it is now the **Casa-Museu Gaudí** (*open daily Mar–Oct 10–7, Nov–Feb 10–6; adm*) and contains plans and examples of the wonderful organic furniture that Gaudí designed for his houses. Just west of the Parc Güell, bus no.25 continues to one of the city's newer urban spaces, the **Parc de la Creueta del Coll**, with as its centrepiece a small artificial lake and beach, with sculptor Chillida's giant gentle claw, the *Elogi de l'aigua* ('praise water') suspended over the water.

Gràcia

Parc Güell lies within walking distance of the lively old town of **Gràcia**, which begins just north of the Diagonal: the FCG metro Gràcia will leave you near the centre, Plaça Gal.la Placidia, or take bus nos.22 or 24 from Plaça de Catalunya. Throughout the 19th century, Gràcia was a vortex for liberal and progressive ideas: workers, Anarchists, feminists, vegetarians, Protestants and ardent Republicans flourished here, formed societies and movements, and published an astounding number of periodicals (even one in Esperanto) and to this day Gràcia has a laid-back neighbourhood atmosphere, a nice contrast to the Barcelona of big art and monuments. **Plaça Rius i Taulet** is the spiritual heart of Gràcia, with its 100ft bell-tower adorned with symbols of the zodiac, invoked frequently as the town's symbol of liberty; nearby Plaça del Sol is the centre of Gràcia's nightlife. Farther up, by the Metro station Fontana, is Gaudí's first house, the **Casa Vicens** (1883), on Carrer de les Carolines Nos.18–24. Islamic in inspiration, its façade is adorned with chequerboard patterns of green and white tiles (the owner was a tile merchant) and brickwork, and has a delightful iron gate and fence of date-palm fronds.

Tibidabo

For an incomparable view over Barcelona, ascend the highest peak of the Collserola, the 550m Tibidabo, just west of the city. Its name, peculiar even by Catalan standards, comes from the Gospel of St Matthew, who quotes the devil, '*Haec omnia tibi dabo si cadens adoraberis me*' ('All this I will give to you if you will fall down and worship me'). Purists might claim the incident really took place somewhere in the Sinai, but a Catalan would counter 'What's so tempting about a rocky desert?' Whereas the view from here, encompassing Barcelona, Montserrat, the Pyrenees and even Mallorca is a tempting offer indeed.

There are two ways to get to Tibidabo: the direct Tibibus (*July and Aug only, every 30 mins from Plaça de Catalunya beginning at 11.30am*), or the FGC Metro to Avinguda del Tibidabo, and from there the Tramvia Blau to Plaça Dr. Andreu, where you can catch the **Funicular del Tibidabo** (*6.50am–8.40pm*). The best time to go is in the late afternoon on a clear day, as dusk falls and the lights begin to twinkle in the great city below. On the summit stands Enric Sagnier's neo-Mormon expiatory temple of **Sagrat Cor**, restaurants, a hotel and the **amusement park** (*open Tues–Fri 11–7, Sat and Sun 11–9; adm 1800 pts to ride everything*) offering one of the most panoramic ferris wheel rides imaginable. Admission includes the **Museu d'Autòmats del Tibidabo**, with grinning wooden fortune-tellers, mechanical bands and other carnival gizmos from the 19th century. Just south, another summit of the Collserola is occupied by Sir Norman Foster's slender and dynamic 800ft **Torre de Collserola**, a high-tech telecommunications tower built for the Olympics that offers vertiginous views down on Tibidabo itself (*open daily 11–2 and 4–7, winter weekends only; adm*). The new **Museu de la Ciència**, Teodor Roviralta 55, just off the Ronda de Dalt along the route of the Tramvia Blau (*open Tues–Sun 10–8; adm*) has enough hands-on science exhibits to keep children busy for a while.

South of Gràcia, things get more exclusive. The suburb of **Sarrià** has Barcelona's finest private schools; one of them, the **Convent of Santa Teresa**, Carrer de Ganduxer 41, was built by Gaudí in 1890. Although constrained by finances and the need to build quickly and functionally, he endowed the building with a distinctive rhythm of parabolic arches along the upper floor, and defined the corners with his favourite cross-crowned steeples. Sarrià is also the Barcelonans' favourite neighbourhood to play country squire, although no one's castle can better another Gaudí creation, **Torre Bellesguard**, at Carrer Bellesguard 46, built at the foot of the Collserola over a summer residence of King Martin I. Gaudí restored the medieval walls and built a tall, neo-Gothic villa on the site (1900).

To the south, another fashionable residential area, **Pedralbes**, the 'white stones', begins on the west side of Avinguda Diagonal; here at No.686, the **Palace of Pedralbes** (bus nos.7, 63, 67, 68, 74, 75 or ⓂPalau Reial), was another present to the city from the Güells. Alfonso XIII occupied it briefly, and Negrín made it his headquarters towards the end of the Civil War; from its window he must have watched all Barcelona turn out along the Diagonal in 1938 to bid farewell to the International Brigades as they marched away from a hopeless cause. These days the palace houses the beautiful if fragile **Museu de Cerámica** (*open Tues–Sun 10–3, closed Mon; adm*) with a collection garnered from the famous ceramic centres of the Crown of Aragón—Paterna, Teruel, Manises, Barcelona—as well as 13th-century Arab-Catalan works from Mallorca and ceramics by Picasso and Miró. The same ticket gets you into the **Museu de les Arts Decoratives**, containing tapestries, furniture, and handicrafts from the Middle Ages to the present, as well as a collection tracing the evolution of Spanish industrial design. The surrounding park is shaded by ancient trees; behind it, on Passeig Manuel Girona there is, lost all by itself, a fence and gate by Gaudí (1901), his first work without any historical reference. A more extensive work by Gaudí, the **Pabeliones Finca Güell** (1887), is at Avinguda de Pedralbes 7, near the intersection of Passeig Manuel Girona.

At the top of the Avinguda de Pedralbes, a cobbled lane leads up to the **Col.lecció Thyssen-Bornemisza**, housed in the renovated dormitory of the Gothic **Monestir de Pedralbes** (*open 10–2, closed Mon; adm; take bus no.22 from Plaça de Catalunya*). Although Madrid received the bulk of the Baron's collection, his Catalan beauty-queen wife made sure that 72 of his paintings settled in Barcelona. These include work by early Italian masters such as Lorenzo Daddi and Lorenzo Monaco, and Fra Angelico, whose sublime, ephemeral *Madonna of Humility* steals the show. There are smaller works by Lotto, Titian, Tintoretto, Veronese and a fairy-tale *Stoning of St Stephen* by Dosso Dossi, and later pictures by Giambattista and Giandomenico Tiepolo, Guardi and Canaletto; there's an excellent portrait by Velázquez of *Mariana de Austria* with her Habsburg face and a foxy *Santa Marina* by Zurbarán, and paintings by Rubens and Lucas Cranach (a *St George*, for Catalunya).

For a few more pesetas, your ticket can include an interesting tour of the convent itself, founded by Elisenda, the fourth wife of Jaume II, in 1326. A rare time capsule of 14th-century Catalan architecture, it was built quickly and has scarcely been altered since. The three-storey cloister with its slender columns, garden and fountains is serene and lovely, surrounded by the Poor Clares' tiny austere prayer cells and the small, irregular **Capilla de Sant Miquel**. This was beautifully frescoed in 1346 with the Seven Joys of the Virgin and the Passion by Ferrer Bassa, a follower of Giotto and founder of the Catalan School. Elsewhere you can visit the kitchen, refectory, stables and storeroom, where an intricate series of 3–D dioramas on the life of Christ by Joan Marí has been installed. The single-naved church contains the alabaster tomb of Elisenda and stained glass by Mestre Gil.

Barça and The Cause

Barça means FC Barcelona, the city's beloved football club, magnificently headquartered in their stadium of Camp Nou, on the other side of the Diagonal from Pedralbes' Palau Reial (Ⓜ Collblanc). You've probably seen their jerseys, caps, and banners for sale in every kiosk and souvenir stand and if you're a fan getting a ticket for one of its 120,000 seats for a match was probably one of your first concerns. If you don't succeed, you can always take some comfort in the excellent **Museu del Futbol Club Barcelona**, entrance gate 9 (*open Tues–Sat 10–6.30 and Sun 10–2)*. Barça are popular not only because they're consistently great (they performed the rare trick of winning the three European cups in 1992) but because back in the Franco years, they offered the best alternative to the invincible machine of Real Madrid, a club pumped full of money by the stodgy old dictator until it became the best in the world. Supporting Barça became an act of protest against the regime; for Catalans, forbidden even to speak their own language, it was one of the few outlets available to express any kind of national unity.

Like ice cream, nationalism comes in all kinds of flavours. Catalan nationalism is as strongly felt as any, but it's as practical and reasonable as vanilla—rather than become independent, Catalunya would prefer to take Madrid over through legal means. That's not all. Spend some time on the other side of the Pyrenees, and you'll find Catalans picnicking in the snow in January at Peyrepertuse, furiously taking notes at the castle of Salses, and measuring Perpignan's train station (the centre of the universe, according to Salvador Dalí). You just know they're agents from Barcelona, reconnoitring for the reconquest of greater Catalunya.

Shopping

There are roughly three main shopping areas in Barcelona: the **Barri Gòtic** for trendy streetwear, secondhand clothes, interesting junk, and antiques; the centre of the **Eixample** (around La Rambla de Catalunya and Passeig de Gràcia) for good quality clothes and jewellery, with the enormous **El Corte Inglés** department store in Plaça de Catalunya as a main focu, rivalled by a 6-storey Marks & Spencers; and **Sant Gervasi** (south of Gràcia and west of Avinguda Diagonal) for designer boutiques, many in the swanky avant-garde **L'Illa shopping complex** (on the Diagonal, between C/ Numància and C/ Entença). Serious shoppers hit Barcelona in January, when everything's on sale. If you're interested in the things Barcelona does best, check out **Vinçon**, one of Spain's top names in design and furniture, right next to **La Pedrera** (Passeig de Gràcia 96); Modernista BD Ediciones de Diseño, Mallorca 291, for the best in old and new furniture designs in Domènech's **Casa Thomas**; or **Insolit**, Diagonal 353 for a surreal touch. **Otranto**, at Pg. Sant Joan 142 and **Urbana**, Còrsega 258 have furnishings and architectural bits salvaged from *modernista* buildings; **Neocerámica**, C/Mandri 43, has the widest range of wall and floor tiles.

There are good places to stay all over Barcelona, with cheaper choices clustered in and around the Barri Gòtic. Sentimental travellers should stay on the Ramblas, 'the world's most beautiful street', Barcelona's favourite hotel address for the past century. If you arrive without a reservation, there are low cost booking services in the airport and Sants station and at the city's main tourist office on Plaça Catalunya. Prices are similar to those in Madrid.

The Ramblas and Around

At the top of the line there's the hyper-plush ★★★★**Le Meridien Barcelona**, Ramblas 111, ✆ 93 318 4432, ✉ 93 318 6200 (*luxury*), used to coddling finicky opera and rock stars. You can immerse yourself in stylish new Art Deco design at the ★★★★**Rivoli Rambla**, Rambla dels Estudis 128, ✆ 93 302 66 43, ✉ 93 317 50 53 (*expensive*), with a rooftop terrace and great views over the old centre. The classic ★★★**Oriente**, Ramblas 45, ✆ 93 302 25 58, ✉ 93 412 38 19 (*moderate*) occupies one of the street's oldest buildings, the former monastery of the Colegio de San Bonaventura, built in 1670. The cloister now gaily serves as the hotel ballroom. ★★★**Continental**, Rambla de la Canaletas 138, ✆ 93 301 25 70, ✉ 93 302 73 60 (*moderate*) has rooms with balconies over the Ramblas. ★★★**Gaudí**, C/ Nou de la Rambla 12, ✆ 93 317 90 32, ✉ 93 412 26 36 (*moderate*) has modern instead of *modernista* rooms, but offers views of the great roof of the Palau Güell. The ★★**Cuatro Naciones**, Ramblas 40, ✆ 93 317 36 24, ✉ 93 302 69 85 (*moderate*) opened its doors at the beginning of the 19th century and for the next 100 years was Barcelona's best hotel; it's not so bad nowadays, either, with individual air conditioning. On a leafy little square off the Pla. Boqueria is the★★★ **San Agustin**, Plaça Sant Agustí 3, ✆ 93 318 16 58, ✉ 93 317 29 28 (moderate); try for an attic room with beamed ceilings and views of the old city. Nearby, the ★★**Espanya**, C/ de Sant Pau 9-11, ✆ 93 318 17 58, ✉ 93 317 11 34 (*moderate*) has a beautiful ground floor decorated by Domènech i Montaner, with an alabaster chimney by Arnau and *sgraffito* by Casas and pleasant if not grand rooms. Further down the same street is the ★★ **Peninsular**, C/ de Sant Pau 34–36, ✆ 93 302 3138, ✉ 93 412 36 99 (*moderate*) with rooms set along curved balconies overlooking a spacious, light-filled inner patio. Around the corner, the ★★**Principal**, C/ Junta de Comerç 8 (near the Hospital de Santa Creu), ✆ 93 318 89 70, ✉ 93 412 08 19 (*moderate*) is simple but welcoming. **Las Flores**, Rambla de las Flores 79, ✆ 93 317 16 34 (*inexpensive*) is decent and has rooms with bath, or for a few pesetas more there's the bright, recently refurbished ★**Roma Reial**, in Plaça Reial, ✆ 93 302 03 66, ✉ 93 301 18 39 (*inexpensive*). Just off the Rambla, **Tamashiro**, C/ Hospital 93, ✆ 93 329 54 87 (*cheap*) is plain and basic.

The Barri Gòtic

The one upmarket hotel in the quarter, ★★★★**Colón**, Avda. Catedral 7, ✆ 93 301 14 04, ✉ 93 317 29 15 (*expensive*) is in a historic building and has fine views of the cathedral, a garage, air conditioning and other amenities. The relatively small ★★★**Suizo**, Plaça del Angel 12, ✆ 93 310 61 08, ✉ 93 310 40 81 (*moderate*) offers a carefully cultivated 19th-century ambiance and a beautiful bar. Near the Plaça Sant Jaume, *****Rialto**, C/ Ferrán 42, ✆ 93 318 52 12, ✉ 93 318 53 12, is exceptionally comfortable and near the Ramblas. In the same area, ***Rey Don Jaime I**, C/ Jaime I, 11, ✆ and ✉ 93 310 62 08 (*inexpensive*) offers good value and a touch of class. Not far from the city's old port is the *****Metropol**, C/ Ample 31, ✆ 93 310 51 00, ✉ 93 319 12 76, a 19th century hotel that was re-done for the Olympics. For a room with a view of the Roman walls try the ****Hs Layetana**, Plaça Ramón Berenguer el Gran 2, ✆ 93 319 20 12 (*inexpensive*) located in an attractive, 19th-century building but which can be a bit noisy with the nearby Via Laietana. Recommended cheaper choices include ****Hs Rembrandt**, near the Cathedral at Portaferrisa 23, ✆ 93 318 10 11; the friendly **Levante**, Baixada Sant Miquel 2, (near Plaça San Miquel) ✆ 93 317 95 65 (*inexpensive*), and **Lourdes**, C/ Princesa 14, ✆ 93 319 50 31 (*cheap*), a clean and pleasant bargain and nicer than the Pinar, in the same building. The small and cheerful **Maldà**, C/ del Pi 5, ✆ 93 317 30 02 (*cheap*) is located up two flights of stairs inside Barcelona's first shopping arcade, and though a bit hard to find, its sunny, quiet rooms are very good value.

Around the Gran Via de des Les Corts Catalanes and the Eixample

The *******Husa Palace**, Gran Via 668, ✆ 93 318 52 00, ✉ 93 318 01 48 (*luxury*) was known as the Ritz until 1995, but despite the change of owners and names, it remains Barcelona's classic grand hotel, as it has been since 1919, offering luxury in every sense of the word. The *******Claris**, C/ Pau Claris 150, ✆ 93 487 62 62, ✉ 93 215 79 70 (*luxury*) gives luxury a twist, blending refined modern design with a connoisseur's collection of ancient art treasures; discreetly located one street east of the Passeig de Gràcia. The *modernista* ******Condes de Barcelona**, Pg. de Gràcia 73, ✆ 93 484 22 00, ✉ 93 488 06 14 (*expensive*) is as stylish inside as out, and has great marble bathrooms; another summer *modernista* building now houses the ******Gran Hotel Havana**, Gran Via 647, ✆ 93 412 11 15, ✉ 93 412 26 11 (*expensive–moderate*), with an avant-garde décor inside. ******Regente**, Rambla de Catalunya 76, ✆ 93 487 59 89, ✉ 93 487 32 27 (*expensive*) is stylish, welcoming and quiet. ******Avenida Palace**, Gran Via 605, ✆ 93 301 96 00, ✉ 93 318 12 34 (*expensive–moderate*), is a favourite older hotel. *****Gran Via**, Gran Via 642, ✆ 93 318 19 00, ✉ 93 318 99 97 (*moderate*) is one of the few that has resisted the urge to remodel, preserving a touch of 19th-century grace from its courtyard to its lounge and the antique furnishings in the rooms. ****Hs Palacios**, Gran Via 629 bis, ✆ 93 301 30 79 (*inexpensive*) is centrally located and a good bargain. ****Hs Oliva**, Psg. de Gràcia 32, ✆ 93 488 01 62 (*at the top of the inexpensive category*) is the cheapest in the street that Gaudí made famous; the ****Hs Windsor**, Rambla de Catalunya 84, ✆ 93 215 11 98, is a bit dearer but also a bit nicer; book early in the summer.

By the Sea

Occupying one of the two Olympic towers of the Port Olímpic, the *******Arts Barcelona**, C/ Marina 19-21, ✆ 93 221 10 00, ✉ 93 221 10 70 (*luxury*) is in a class by itself, offering stunning views of the sea and city and a fantastic sea-side pool. Look for reduced weekend rates and other price packages.

Youth Hostels

Ring ahead for these to make sure there's room. None of the official IYHF hostels are very convenient, although **Hostel de Joves**, Pg. de Pujades 29 (next to the Parc de la Ciutadella) ✆ 93 300 31 04 (Ⓜ Arc de Triomf) is probably the nicest. If you arrive at Sants station, **Albergue Pere Tarrés**, C/ Numancia 149-151, ✆ 93 410 23 09 (Ⓜ Les Corts) is closest; **Albergue Mare de Déu de Montserrat**, Pg. de la Mare de Déu del Coll 41-51, ✆ 93 210 51 51 (ⓂVallcarca) is way out in the wilds. A more centrally located, privately run youth hostal, is the **Albergue Kabul**, Plaça Reial 17, ✆ 93 301 40 34, ✉ 93 301 40 34, with rooms that house from two to twelve people.

Eating Out

Barcelona doesn't dine quite as late as Madrid but almost; restaurants open at around 8 or 8.30pm and stay open until midnight—some much later. The range is vast: there are places that serve the very finest of Catalan cuisine and others that feed the masses with more hardy, standard fare. Alongside these native eating houses are also numerous restaurants from other regions of Spain and the world, with a reputed 600 Chinese restaurants sprinkled around town for good measure. As a general rule, book ahead for the expensive restaurants.

expensive

Gaig, Passeig Maragall 402, ✆ 93 429 10 17, (Ⓜ Vilapicina), is old and famous, having been under the culinary care of the Gaig family for four generations. Meals served are of a refined Catalan variety, with such delicacies as *arròs de colomí amb ceps* (pigeon in rice with wild mushrooms). **Vía Veneto**, C/ Ganduxer 10–12, ✆ 93 200 72 44 (FGC Ⓜ La Bonanova), has won several prizes for its exquisite and innovative Catalan dishes such as *pequeños calabacines en flor en salsa de hígado de oca* (tiny flowering zucchini in goose liver sauce) prepared by Josep Monje; *closed Sat lunch and Sun*. **Eldorado Petit**, Dolors Monserdà 51 in Sarrià, ✆ 93 204 55 06 (FGC Ⓜ Sarrià) is another award-winning restaurant in a lovely turn-of-the-century building, with an elegant bar and a menu that changes according to market availability and chef Luis Cruañas' refined muse; *closed Sun*. At **Neichel**, Avda. de Pedralbes 16, ✆ 93 243 84 08 (Ⓜ María Cristina), the elegant modern dining room is the perfect stage for some of the most creative and refined cuisine in Spain, prepared by French chef Jean-Louis Neichel; the magnificent cheese and pastry chariots that round off the meal are legendary; *set menus at 7700 and 9500 pts. Closed Sat lunch, Sun and Aug*. **Jaume de Provença**, C/ Provença 88, ✆ 93 430 00 29 (Ⓜ Hospital Clinic) offers Catalan cuisine at its most elaborate—a typical dish is fillet of turbot with saffron lobster; *closed Sun eve and Mon*. A pair of superb young Catalan chefs run **Ot**, C/Torres 25, ✆ 93 284 77 52, (Ⓜ Verdaguer), a small, comfortable restaurant in Gràcia with a five course menu that offers deliciously creative variations of traditional Catalan dishes; *closed Sun*. In the music-hall district, the warm, intimate **Ca l'Isidre**, Les Flors 12, ✆ 93 441 11 39 (Ⓜ Paral.lel) has long been a favourite of artists as well as King Juan Carlos of Spain, and serves lovely food based on the freshest ingredients. At the lower end of this price category you can dine well on *mariscos* or have a steak grilled at your table at **A La Menta,** Ps. Manuel Girona 50, (Ⓜ María Cristina) ✆ 93 204 15 49; or visit the atmospheric **Casa Leopoldo**, Sant Rafael 24, ✆ 93 241 30 14, in the Barri Xinès (Ⓜ Liceu), founded in 1933 and serving tasty grilled fish and oxtail stew; *closed Sun evening, Mon and Aug.* The famous **Set Portes,** Ps. Isabel II 14, ✆ 93 319 30 33, (Ⓜ Barceloneta) was founded in 1836 and is more popular than ever, serving delicious rice and seafood. **Le Bistrot,** Diagonal 640, ✆ 93 405 92 00 (Ⓜ Maria Cristina) is frequented by Barcelona's chic-set, serving very good French inspired Mediterranean food; downstairs there's a plush disco-bar to dance off the extra calories; *closed Sun.*

moderate

Reservations are a must at **Senyor Parellada**, Argenteria 37, ✆ 93 315 40 10 (Ⓜ Jaume I), where the night owls hang out to dine on *estofados, manitas de cerdo,* fish platters and old-fashioned recipes. *Closed Sun.* The popular **L'Olivé**, Muntaner 171, ✆ 93 430 90 27 (Ⓜ Hospital Clinic) serves traditional Catalan food emphasizing fish and fresh market ingredients; try the *fricandó*, a meat and veg stew. One of the best places for seafood in Barceloneta is **Can Ros**, Almiral Aixada 7, ✆ 93 221 45 79 (Ⓜ Barceloneta): while waiting for a main course of *paella* or arrós negre, sample some of the fresh seafood hors d'ourvres, or steamed mussels and clams in tomato sauce; *closed Wed eve.* **Compostela**, C/ Fernán 30 (Ⓜ Jaume I) draws crowds for its popular Galician specialities such as *pulpo* and *tetilla* cheese, for a meal or just *tapas; closed Tues.* The crowds that pack **La Targa Florio**, Villarroel 190, ✆ 93 430 72 79 (Ⓜ Hospital Clinic) lend proof to the claim that it's the finest Italian restaurant in Spain. Located in the vast, vaulted 13th century shipyards is **La Llotja**, Museu Marítim, Avda. Drassanes, ✆ 93 302 64 02 (Ⓜ Drassanes), a restaurant run by a local food critic and gourmet, serving very fine Catalan food, including a medieval dish of saffron and chicken intended to go with the setting. **Euskal Etxea**, Plaçeta Montcada, ✆ 93 310 21 85 (Ⓜ Jaume I) serves up the best Basque food in Barcelona. In the new Maremagnum complex on the Moll d'Espanya (Ⓜ Barceloneta), **Nautilus**, ✆ 93 225 80 51, has received excellent reviews for its inventive seafood dishes and views over the yachts.

cheap

Pinocho, in the Ramblas' Mercado de la Boqueria, ✆ 93 317 17 31 (Ⓜ Liceu), is run by a real character, who offers good home-cooked food and tapas in the fascinating hurly-burly of the market (*early morning to lunchtime only*). Up in Gràcia, **Flash-Flash**, Granada 25, ✆ 93 237 09 90 (Ⓜ Diagonal) serves a hundred different omelettes, although their potato *tortilla* remains Barcelona's special favourite. **Silenus**, C/Angels 8, ✆ 93 302 26 80 (Ⓜ Catalunya) is off the Ramblas en route to the MACBA, and serves market fresh international and Catalan food in a relaxed setting with contemporary art on the walls. **La Dentellière**, C/ Ample 26, ✆ 93 319 68 21 (Ⓜ Drassanes) has good simple food and fondues; *closed Sun and Aug.* **Rodrigo**, C/Argenteria 67, ✆ 93 310 30 20 (Ⓜ Jaume I) nearby the Santa Maria del Mar church offers excellent home-cooking at very reasonable prices, and though full meals are served only at lunch time, a wide selection of sandwiches are to be had at night. Barcelona's most famous pastry shop, **Mora**, Diagonal 409, ✆ 93 416 07 26 (Ⓜ Diagonal) serves delicious, economic meals; *closed Sun.* Vegetarians can find solace at the **Corts Catalans**, Gran Vía 603, ✆ 93 301 03 76 (Ⓜ Universitat) with a *1100-pts* daily *menú*, or at the **Biocenter**, C/ Pintor Fortuny 25, ✆ 93 301 45 83, (Ⓜ Liceu) which has a generous salad bar and various hot dishes to choose from. *Closed Sun.* Located off of the Plaça George Orwell is the Restaurante Pakistani, C/Carabassa 3, ✆ 93 302 60 25 (Ⓜ Drassanes) serving good, very cheap Pakistani food.

You can also easily make a good *inexpensive* meal trawling through tapas: some of the best are made at **Cal Pep**, Plaça Olles 8, by Plaça de Palau, ✆ 93 310 79 61 (Ⓜ Barceloneta) with a spectacular display of delicacies (sit-down meals are *expensive*); **Fats**, Rosselló 206, near the corner of the Rambla de Catalunya, ✆ 93 487 12 21 (Ⓜ Diagonal) features excellent high-calorie tapas and beer. In the Barri Gòtic, **Irati**, Cardenal Casanyes 17 (Ⓜ Liceu) offers exquisite reasonably priced Basque tapas and *pinchos* and *txacolis* wine. Tasty tapas or *inexpensive* meals can be had at the cosy and very pleasant **Pla de la Garsa**, Assaonadors 13, ✆ 93 315 24 13 (by C/ Princesa, Ⓜ Jaume I).

Entertainment and Nightlife

cinema, dance and theatre

There is always something to do in Barcelona, especially from June to August, when the Generalitat's Grec festival brings in concerts, theatre and dance at Montjuïc's Teatre Grec, the Plaça del Rei and other venues. The information centre for the Grec and other cultural events is the Palau de la Virreina on the Ramblas, ✆ 93 301 77 75. News stands sell the weekly *Guia del Ocio* (*125 pts*) with detailed listings of events; its Cine section has a list of films shown in their original languague (VO) and the excellent, unusual fare shown by the **Filmoteca de la Generalitat**, located in the Cine Aquitania, Avda. de Sarrià 33, ✆ 93 410 75 90 (Ⓜ Hospital Clinic). Dance fans can take in performances at the Generalitat's **L'Espai de Danza i Música**, Travessera de Gràcia 63, ✆ 93 441 31 33 (Ⓜ Diagonal). If you understand Spanish and/or Catalan, Barcelona offers some of the most innovative **theatre** in these languages anywhere with over 20 active theatres: you can buy tickets over the phone (✆ 93 310 12 12).

music

The free monthly music calendar, *Informatiu MUSICAL*, put out by the Amics de la Música de Barcelona (available at the tourist offices), lists daily performances of everything from the most classical to the most scurrilous country and western twangs. You can book tickets 24 hours a day for major classical music concerts before even leaving home (✆ 34 93 417 00 60) or within Spain (✆ 902 332 211). Until the Liceu is rebuilt, opera fans will have to hear their arias in other venues such as the beautiful 19th-century **Mercat des Flors**, the wholesale flower market converted into a theatre at 59 Lleida (Ⓜ Espanya), the magnificent **Palau de la Música Catalana**, Sant Francesc de Paula 2 (Ⓜ Urquinaona), and the brand new **Teatre de L'Eixample**, Aragó 140 (Ⓜ Urgell). There are so many different churches, cultural centres (often run by *caixas*, or savings banks) and other locales used for chamber music and recitals that it's impossible to list them all. For low-brow, sleazy kitsch, check out El Cangrejo, C/Monserrat 9, ✆ 93 301 85 75 (Ⓜ Drassanes) located in the Barrio Chino, with surreal, campy cabaret reviews.

Barcelona is a good town for jazz and salsa. Important jazz venues include **Luz de Gas**, Muntaner 246, ✆ 93 209 77 11, (FCG Ⓜ Muntaner), a large, happening club for jazz, rock, pop, salsa, and funk, with live music most nights; and **Blue Note**, in the Maremagnum complex on the Moll d'Espanya, ✆ 93 225 80 92 (ⓂBarceloneta). Plaça Reial (Ⓜ Liceu) has two small clubs with busy programmes of live jazz: **Jamboree** at No.17, ✆ 93 301 75 64 (which doubles later on in the evening as a disco for soul and hip-hop fans), and the little **Barcelona Pipa Club**, up on the first floor at No.3, ✆ 93 302 47 32, a private club for pipe smokers during the day and in the night open to all, hosting jam sessions and quality trios and quartets. Near the Plaça Reial is the **London Bar**, C/Nou de la Rambla 34, ✆ 93 318 52 61 (Ⓜ Liceu), in operation since 1910 and now a popular venue for blues, jazz and pop performances. In the Barri Gòtic, the small **Harlem Jazz Club**, Comtessa Sobradiel 8, ✆ 93 310 07 55 (Ⓜ Jaume I) has live swing, Celtic music, country and just about everything in between. **Costa Breve**, Aribau 230, ✆ 93 414 27 78 (FCG Ⓜ Gervasi) brings in an eclectic, wide variety of music from acid jazz, to African to rumba and '60s sounds. **La Boîte Mas i Mas**, Avda. Diagonal 477, ✆ 93 419 59 50 (Ⓜ Verdaguer) leans towards soul and blues.

Visiting rock and pop megastars perform in the Palau Sant-Jordi on Montjuïc while smaller fry play at **Zeleste, C/Almogavers 122**, ✆ 93 309 12 04 (Ⓜ Marina), **La Cova del Drac**, Vallmajor 33, ✆ 93 200 70 32 (FCG Ⓜ Muntaner), and **Club Apolo**, C/Nou de la Rambla 113, ✆ 93 309 12 04 (Ⓜ Paral.lel). Up on the north side of town **Savannah Músic Club**, Muntanya 16 (Ⓜ Sant Andreu) showcases local performers and informal jam sessions while hard rock rules at **Arzobispo**, Costa Brava 13.

Traditional Catalan music features at the **Centre Artesà Tradicionàrius**, Travessia de Sant Antoni 6–8 in Gràcia. Lastly, Raval's **Bodega Bohemia** at Lancaster 2 (Ⓜ Liceu) is Barcelona's answer to New Orleans' Preservation Hall, minus the jazz but with all your favourite cabaret tunes of yesteryear, sung by the stars of yesteryear.

after dark: bars and cafés

Barcelona's nightlife cranks up at around 10 or 11pm and at weekends lasts until a late breakfast, if you've got the energy (and money) to keep up. Note that bars offi-cially close at 2 or 3am, but if the ambiance is good the owner will close the door and let the party continue inside. Favourite spots for drinks and *montaditos* (tiny tapas on a slice of bread) are the Barri Gòtic, Gràcia, in the Eixample around the Passeig de Gràcia and the trendy Sant Gervasi (the district just south of Gràcia) where posing can get in the way of a good time. The Barri Gòtic is more relaxed. The Passeig del Born by Santa Maria del Mar is a favourite hangout: **El Born**, at No.29 (Ⓜ Barceloneta) is a friendly rendezvous, especially after midnight; nearby on the Moll de la Fusta is **Octopussy** (Ⓜ Barceloneta) a trendy dance bar with a large outdoor area that fills up with a bouncy young crowd after 1am. In the centre of things there's the popular **L'Antiquari de la Plaça del Rei**, Verguer 13 (Ⓜ Jaume I), a great place to sit out on a summer's night, or take in the café-concert, *Thurs–Sun*. Classical music comes with your drinks at **El Paraigua**, with a *modernista* décor from 1902 near the Ajuntament at Pas de l'Ensenyança 2 (Ⓜ Jaume I). For those looking for the latest sounds in elec-tronic dance, **Dot**, C/Nou de Sant Francesc 7, behind the Plaça Reial, is the place to be. On the other side of the Plaça at C/Ferran 23 is **Schilling**, a spacious, new café that is both popular and hip. North along the Rambla, **Café de l'Opera**, Rambla 74 (Ⓜ Liceu) has been fashionable for a century with theatregoers who now come to sit and watch the rebuilding of their beloved Liceu.

In the Eixample, El Otro, C/Valencia166 (Ⓜ Hospital Clinic) is a relaxed hangout for a young, likeable crowd. **La Fira** at C/Provença 171 (Ⓜ Hospital Clinic) is a bar of bizarre design, jammed full of fun house paraphernalia, including a row of warped mirrors in the entrance hall that could throw you off balance as you exit. For those looking for a modern, elegant place to sip a professionally made cocktail, there's **Zsa Zsa**, C/Rosselló 156 (FGC Ⓜ Provença).

Up in Sant Gervasi, **Flann O'Brien's**, Casanova 264 (Ⓜ Hospital Clinic) is a friendly place to hoist a pint and a great place to meet fellow English-speakers. The futuristic, video-flickering **Network**, Diagonal 616 (Ⓜ Hospital Clinic) is just about the opposite. For a place where you can rub elbows with uptown youth and get good tapas, try Mas i Mas, C/Marià Cubí 199 (FCG Ⓕ Muntaner), or the **Universal Bar**, Marià Cubí 182 (Ⓜ Fontana), offering 'drinks and design' (only in Barcelona!). In Gràcia, Plaça del Sol is the centre of action and the **Café del Sol** as the main grandstand for Gràcia's hipsters (Ⓜ Fontana). Nearby at Planeta 39–41, the New Age **La Ñola**, 'The Human Bar', offers 'visual, olfactory, auditive, gustative and tactile experiences'. The small **Zimbabwe bar**, C/Mozart 13 (Ⓜ Diagonal) plays non-stop reggae music, while down-to-earth beer lovers should make for the **Barcelona Brewing Co**. Sant Augustí 14 , where you can watch them make the contents of your beer glass.

Barcelona's popular *xampanyerias* serve Catalan champagne, *cava* as well as the French stuff, and elegant titbits from bitter chocolate to raw oysters. Try **El Xampanyet**, C/Moncada 22 (Ⓜ Jaume I), in the Ribera near the Picasso Museum; the **Casablanca**, Bonavista 6, in Gràcia; **Xampú Xampany**, Gran Via 702 (Ⓜ Girona), and **La Cava del Palau**, Verdaguer i Callís 10, near the Palau de la Música (Ⓜ Uriquinaona). **Languedoc Roussillon**, Pau Claris 77 (Ⓜ Urquinaona) is Barcelona's first oyster bar, featuring the fine bivalves from Bouzigue.

discos and clubs

Discos and clubs don't gear up for action until after midnight, and they stay open until 5am or later, especially on Friday and Saturday nights; drinks and/or the cover charge generally cost a bomb. The current favourites for serious dancing are the vast subterranean **Fellini**, Avda. Marquès de l'Argentera (Ⓜ Barceloneta), in the basement of the Estació de França, and the **Nitsaclub** in the Sala Apolo, C/Nou de la Rambla 113, ✆ 93 441 40 01 (Ⓜ Paral.lel). Dress-code police guard the door at chi-chi **Otto Zutz**, Lincoln 15, ✆ 93 238 07 22 (FCG Ⓕ Gervasi), which calls itself 'the New York-style disco where the beautiful people go'; a designer converted warehouse that opens at midnight, sometimes with good live music. **Velvet**, Balmes 161, ✆ 93 217 67 14 (Ⓜ Diagonal) has plush furnishings and '60s music for baby boomers.

Latin and salsa are favourite ways to work off a Catalan stew. **Antilla Cosmopolita**, Muntaner 244, ✆ 93 200 77 14 (FCG Ⓜ Muntaner) is the hottest place for salsa in all its forms, with superb live bands; on weekends, Caribbean immigrants flock to **Lagota2**, Via Laietana 5 (Ⓜ Jaume I) to dance their socks off. For the spiciest Cuban sounds, try **Gràcia Llatina**, Carrer de l'Or 19, ✆ 93 237 71 72 (Ⓜ Fontana). Down by the sea, at the perennial party held at the Maremagnum centre, there are a slew of latin bars on the first floor, including the **Mojito Bar**, ✆ 93 225 80 14, and the **Tropicana Bar**, ✆ 93 225 80 46, (both Ⓜ Drassanes). **Africa Monumental**, Gran de Gràcia (Ⓜ Fontana) plays what it says from 11pm onwards.

In a town obsessed with design, it's not surprising to find Barcelona well-endowed with completely over-the-top late-night high-tech multi-space music bars. The most famous must be Mariscal and Arribas' **Las Torres de Ávila**, in the Poblo Espanyol, ✆ 93 424 93 09, where amazement at the design and bill go hand in hand. **KGB**, Alegre de Dalt 55, ✆ 93 210 59 06 (Ⓜ Joanic), is a classic neo-Barcelona design creation, this one with a Cold War spy theme, and something of a traditional late late last stand. The more staid, fashionable **Mirablau**, Plaça Dr Andreu (by the funicular up to Tibidabo), ✆ 93 418 58 79, has tremendous views over the city to go with its cocktails. One of the most popular nightspots on the scene is the **Bikini**, C/Déu i Mata 105, ✆ 93 322 08 00 (Ⓜ María Cristina), under the convention centre of L'Illa on the Diagonal , the rebirth of the city's hottest spot in the '50s, where young fiancés Juan Carlos and Sofia danced the cha-cha-cha.

gay Barcelona

To find out the latest places to go after dark, try the general gay info hotline, ✆ 93 237 70 70, evenings only. Barcelona's gays and lesbians tend to share the same music bars: long-time favourites are the two floors of **Punto BCN**, Muntaner 63 (Ⓜ Universitat); **Este Bar**, C/Consell de Cent 257 (Ⓜ Universitat) a small, colorful place with a regular clientele; and **Bahia**, C/Seneca 12 (Ⓜ Diagonal), up in Gràcia. **Free Girls**, C/Marià Cubí 4 (FGC Ⓜ Muntaner) is a disco-bar that is popular with a young lesbian crowd. The liveliest gay disco at the moment is **Arena**, C/Balmes 32 (Ⓜ Passeig de Gràcia).

Inland from Barcelona: Sant Cugat del Vallés, Terrassa and Montserrat

Within easy striking distance of Barcelona are superb Romanesque and Visigothic churches, and the magnificent mountain monastery of Montserrat, 'the Catalan Miracle'.

Getting Around

Sant Cugat and Terrassa are easiest reached on FGC **trains** from the station under Barcelona's Plaça Catalunya; there are trains at least once an hour, and they take 30 minutes to Sant Cugat, and an hour to Terrassa. From Barcelona, there's a daily Juliá **bus** to Montserrat (departures at 9am, return 7pm, ✆ 93 490 40 00) leaving from Ronda Universitat 5 or FGC trains from the station under the Plaça d'Espanya, with weekday departures every hour starting at 9:07am with the last train at 17:07; Saturday, Sunday and holidays trains run every other hour beginnning 9:07am. Get off at the station Aeri de Montserrat, where you link up with the thrilling *teleferic* to the monastery (included in the 1500 pts return ticket). Trains return to Barcelona at 11.26am, 1.26, 3.26, 4.30, 5.26, 6.41 and 7.26pm.

Tourist Information

Sant Cugat del Vallés: Plaça de Barcelona 17, ✆ 93 589 22 88.
Terrassa: Plaça Eduardo Mariany, ✆ 93 788 44 00.
Montserrat: Plaça de la Creu, ✆ 93 835 02 01.

Sant Cugat and Terrassa

Northwest of Barcelona, over the Collserola mountains, **Sant Cugat del Vallés** (the Roman *Castrum Octavianum*), grew up around the Visigothic **Abbey de Sant Cugat** (*open 9–1 and 3–6, closed Mon; adm*). According to legend founded either by Charlemagne or his son Louis the Pious, the Gothic church that now stands is as austere as Barcelona's Sant Pi, with a great rose window and Lombard Romanesque tower. It's the late 12th-century cloister that makes the trip worthwhile, a Romanesque masterpiece, with 144 carved capitals depicting scenes from the New and Old Testaments by the monk Arnau Cadell; one capital with an inscription shows him at work. Another Catalan masterpiece, the *Retablo of all the Saints* by Pere Serra (1395), is in the small museum in the Chapter house, portraying the Virgin and Child in the centre with an angelic sextet, surrounded by most of the saints on the calendar.

Industrial **Terrassa**, 33km from Barcelona, is Catalunya's third-largest city and one of Spain's first textile manufacturers. Woollen cloth was the mainstay of the Catalans' medieval trading empire, and early examples from Terrassa and the rest of the world are displayed in the **Museu Textil**, Salmerón 25 (*open 9–6, Thurs 9–9, Sat and Sun 10–2, closed Mon; adm*), one of the most important collections of its kind in the world. Across the street is the **Museu Cartuja de Vallparadís** (*open 10–1.30 and 4–7, Sun 11–2, closed Mon and hols*), a 12th-century castle converted to a Carthusian monastery in 1344, housing a municipal museum with sculptures, ceramics and 19th-century paintings.

Best of all, however, is a rare and picturesque ensemble of three Visigothic-Romanesque churches in the **Parque de Vallparadís** near the Cartuja. Back when Terrassa was the bishopric of Egara in the 6th century, it was common for the functions of an episcopal church to be divided between separate buildings. **Sant Pere**, remodelled in the 12th century in the Lombard style, has a Visigothic triple-lobed apse and 10th-century stone *retablo* and murals. Square **Sant Miquel**, reconstructed in the 9th century, has a seven-sided apse and an elegant 6th-century baptistry in its centre, with a dome supported by Roman and Visigothic columns; the murals are from the 9th century.

The main church, **Santa Maria**, rebuilt in 1112 in the form of a Latin cross, is topped by an octagonal lantern and dome and incorporates the Visigothic apse with a horseshoe arch. It has excellent Gothic *retablos* by Huguet and 9th–12th-century frescoes; note especially the one in the apse of the murder of St Thomas of Canterbury (1170), painted only a few years after the fact.

Even then you haven't exhausted all of Terrassa's charms. An excellent alabaster *Burial of Christ* (1540) by Italian-trained Martí Diez de Liatzasolois is housed in a special chapel of the church of **L'Esperit Sant**. A magnificent 18th-century mansion, the **Casa Museu Alegre de Sagrera**, Font Vella 29 (*open Tues–Fri 11–2*), retains much of its original furnishings and a collection of Chinese art. A smattering of *modernista* industrial buildings add graceful notes to the newer parts of the city: on the Rambla d'Egara one of the best, the former Vapor Aymerich, Amat i Jover factory (1908) by municipal architect Lluís Muncunill, has recently been made into the **Museu de la Ciència i de la Tècnica de Catalunya** (*open Tues–Fri 10–7, Sat and Sun 10–2.30; July and August Tues–Sun 10–2.30*), dedicated to the history of Catalunya's industrial revolution; note the beautiful Catalan brick vaulted ceiling. Another fine building by Muncunill, the white **Masia Freixa** (1907) with an undulating roof and Gaudiesque parabolic arches, is in the Parc Municipal de Sant Jordi.

Strange, mystical Montserrat, the spiritual heart of Catalunya and symbol of Catalan nationalism looms 40km northwest of Barcelona up the River Llobregat. Its name means 'serrated mountain', an apt enough description of the isolated, fantastical 10km massif made of jagged pudding stone pinnacles rising precipitously over deep gorges, domes and shallow terraces, all so different from the surrounding countryside that it seemed as if heaven itself had dropped it there to prove all things are possible. It has often been compared to an immense shipwreck.

The mountain's history begins back in the Tertiary period, when powerful sea currents swept an immense pile of rubble here, which over the eons mixed with softer muck and hardened into a mass of stone. Miocene geological upheavals ten million years ago caused the sea around the mass to subside, leaving a mountain to be sculpted by the wind and rain into a hedgehog of phallic peaks with names like Cat Head, Nun, Salamander, Potato, Bishop's Belly, and a hundred others. Its human history is as fantastical: St Peter supposedly came here to hide an image of the Virgin carved by St Luke in a cave; in another grotto, the good knight Parsifal discovered the Holy Grail—a legend used by Wagner for his opera. In 880, not long after Christians regained the region, the statue of the Virgin (apparently hidden by someone, if not St Peter, before the advance of the Moors) was discovered on Montserrat and, as is so often the case, it stubbornly refused to budge beyond a certain spot. Count Wilfred the Hairy of Barcelona built a chapel to house it, and in 976 this was given to the Benedictines of Ripoll, who added the monastery. In the Middle Ages only Compostela attracted more pilgrims in Spain. A visit to Montserrat was essential before any major undertaking; Ignacio Loiola kept a vigil before the altar, consecrating his sword to the Virgin prior to founding the Jesuits in 1522. Independent and incredibly wealthy, Montserrat was favoured by Charles V, and his son Felipe II rebuilt the church. During the Peninsular War, Catalan guerrillas fortified it as a base, and in reprisal the French looted and sacked the monastery (1811).

As the Catalan Renaixença gathered steam, Montserrat became its symbol. In 1918, the first Bible in Catalan was printed here, and Verdaguer, Gaudí and Pau Casals were all fervent devotees of the Virgin. Under Franco, Montserrat was the only church permitted to celebrate Mass in Catalan, and thousands of couples ascended the mountain to be married in their own language. Even today Montserrat for Spaniards evokes the same image as Niagara Falls does for Americans as a traditional honeymoon destination, to receive the blessing of the *Moreneta* ('the little brown one'), as the Virgin is affectionately called, before undertaking the supreme adventure of marriage. It has also, like Niagara falls, become a favourite destination for daytripper crowds off the Costa Brava, not to mention mountain climbers and potholers. A disastrous fire in 1986 led in 1989 to the creation of the Montserrat Natural Park to restore and protect the mountain.

The monastery and the church can hardly compete with the fabulous surroundings. Only one side of the Gothic cloister remains intact, and Felipe's basilica lost most of its sumptuous furnishings to the French in 1811, although newer gifts fill nearly every corner of the church. The enthroned Virgin of Montserrat presides over the high altar; the statue dates from the 12th century and is believed to be a copy and coloured black to imitate the original idol. Pilgrims still come to worship her in droves on 27 April and 8 September. The famous boys' choir or **Escolanía**, founded in the 13th century—the oldest music school in Europe—still performs a *virrolei* and *salve* daily at 1 and 6.45pm, except during the month of July. The

Museu de Montserrat has two sections of gifts given to the monastery by the faithful. On the main square by the cloister there's a selection of Old Masters including an El Greco and a Caravaggio and archaeological finds (*open 10.30–1 winter and 10.30–2 and 3–6, summer; adm*); and a modern section on the basilica square (*open 3–6 winter and 10.30–2 and 3.30–6 summer*) with 19th-century paintings, especially by Catalans of the Renaixença movement.

Best of all, though, are the walks around the mountain, to its various caves and ruined hermitages. An easy walk called **Los Degotalls** takes in a wonderful view of the Pyrenees. A funicular ascends from the Plaça Santa Creu (*every 20 minutes, 10–7*) to the **Santa Cova**, where a 17th-century chapel marks the exact finding place of the *Moreneta;* another will lift you up to the **Hermitage of Sant Joan** from where you can take a spectacular walk in just over an hour up to the **Hermitage of Sant Jeroni**, the loftiest hermitage—traditionally the one given to the youngest and spryest hermit.

From the hermitage a short path rises to the highest peak in the range (1253m), offering a bird's eye view of the holy mountain itself, across to the Pyrenees, and over the sea to Mallorca if the weather's clear. Before leaving Montserrat, try a glass of the monks' *aromas de Montserrat*—a liqueur distilled from the mountain's herbs.

Montserrat ✉ 08691   **Where to Stay**

To get a real feel for Montserrat, stay overnight, but be sure to bring a sweater or coat, as it can get quite cold even in the summer. The monks operate two hotels: the ★★★**Abad Cisneros**, ✆ 93 835 02 01 (*moderate*), the honeymooners' special, and the cheaper ★★**Hs El Monestir** (same phone; *moderate*) open April to Oct with simpler rooms. There's also a **campsite** near the Sant Joan funicular, ✆ 93 835 02 51. Food is mediocre and overpriced at Montserrat, so you may want to bring a picnic.

South of Barcelona: Gaudí's Crypt, Castelldefels and Sitges

When Barcelonans want to sprawl on the beach they usually head south; Sitges is very much a petal of the Fiery Rose of Anarchism that fluttered down to the sea. On the way you can visit another unforgettable masterpiece by Gaudí, in the Colonia Güell.

Getting Around

For the Colonia Güell, Oliveras **buses** from Plaça Espanya will take you as far as the Ciutat Cooperativa; the nearest **train** station (FCG) is Molí Nou; if you're driving take the A2 to the Cinturó Litoral exit for Sant Boi de Llobregat and drive up the Llobregat river to Santa Coloma. Catalunya en Miniatura is easiest reached by car (just off Autopista A2, exit 3) or the FGC train from the Plaça Espanya to Sant Vicenç dels Horts, followed by a 1.6km walk. Trains from Barcelona's Estació de Sants depart every half hour for Castelldefels (the Castelldefels-Platja station is a minute from the beach) and Sitges (50mins from Barcelona).

Tourist Information

Castelldefels: Plaça de l'Esglesia, 1, ✆ 93 664 23 61.
Sitges: Sinia Morera, ✆ 93 894 42 51.

The Colonia Güell Crypt and Castelldefels

Labour and class disputes in Barcelona led industrial magnate Eusebi Güell to consider a little adventure in paternalism in 1890. Located in the country at **Santa Coloma de Cervelló**, the **Colonia Güell** was planned as a pseudo-worker's-cooperative (Güell was still boss) around a cotton goods mill, with houses, store, school and other buildings for the workers designed by Gaudí's assistants, Francesc Berenguer and Joan Rubió Bellver. The chapel on the estate, however, was too small, and in 1898 Güell asked Gaudí to design a larger church. The sketches for this look like a cross between Coney Island and the Emerald City of Oz, but once Eusebi Güell died in 1918, funds for the church dried up, and only the **crypt** was completed (*ring ahead to arrange a visit,* © *93 640 29 36*). Yet of all Gaudí's works, this magical primordial avant garde-grotto is the most innovative—a marvel of virtuosity and engineering. It has no right angles, no straight lines—the pillars bend at weird expressionist angles. If you've been to the museum of the Sagrada Família, you've seen the copy of Gaudí's complex dangling web of chains and weights that he photographed and reversed to help work out the incredibly difficult problems of stress and loads, inventing a form known as the hyperbolic paraboloid, something modern architects now do with the aid of sophisticated computers. Gaudí had only the thunder and lightning of his brainstorms, but he also had something else modern architects don't have: Catalan bricklayers. There is no steel reinforcing anything, anywhere: the whole thing is made of rough hewn stone and brick, primitive textures brightened here and there with stained glass and *trencadí* collages. Robert Hughes' description of Gaudí's architecture as 'a womb with a view' fits it to a T.

Nearby, in little Torrelles de Llobregat, **Catalunya en Miniatura** (*open 10–6, summer 10–7; adm exp*) offers the chance to see the 170 best monuments of Catalunya, all at once in the space of a few acres, from the perspective of a Gulliver. The highways and byways to the south meet the coast 20km south of Barcelona at **Castelldefels**, with a huge and popular stretch of sand. Pretty **Garraf**, further south, has a smaller beach and a fishing/pleasure port for lazing.

Sitges

Wedged between the Garraf massif and a lovely long crescent of sand, **Sitges** has been Barcelona's favourite resort ever since the *modernistas* flocked here at the turn of the century, led by painter Santiago Rusinyol (1861–1931). Rusinyol's love of jokes anticipated the archprankster Dalí and in his delightful summerhouse, **Cau Ferrat**, Carrer Fonollar 25 (in the old fishing village, on the seaside promontory) he sponsored his Festes Modernistes from 1892 to 1899, with theatre, exhibitions, concerts and events like a performance by an impostor of the famous Art Nouveau American dancer Loie Fuller—but no one was the wiser. Cau Ferrat is now a museum, with two paintings by El Greco (put into place during one of Rusinyol's parties), a superb collection of ironwork from the 10th to the 20th centuries, and drawings and paintings by Rusinyol, Casas, Miquel Utrillo and their contemporaries. Adjacent, the **Museu Maricel**, a hospital restored by Utrillo for American millionaire Charles Deering, is adorned with Gothic windows and door, and contains an eclectic collection of medieval to modern art, including a mural of the First World War by Josep María Sert. Another museum, the **Museu Romántico**, on C/ Sant Gaudenci 1 (in the centre of town), conjures up the elegance of the 19th century and its love of gadgets—not to be missed by music-box fans (*all three museums are open Tues–Sat 9.30–2 and 4–6, Sun 9.30–2*).

The extravagance of Rusinyol and his friends set the stage for Sitges' role as Barcelona's seaside cockpit of crazy good times, and as one of the biggest gay resorts on the Med. In the summer it seems that half of Europe's yuppies have washed up here, and new hotels built to accommodate them have changed the town forever. Yet Sitges retains two of its old traditions: an antique car rally to Barcelona on the first Sunday in March, and on Corpus Christi the streets of the old town are turned into stunning carpets of flowers. The new Sitges hosts the most outrageous carnival in Spain and an international festival of Theatre of the Vanguard in June. It also has nude beaches to the south, the first for straights and the second for gays called the Playas del Muerto—'the beaches of the dead'.

Sitges ✉ *08870*   *Where to Stay*

Sitges isn't for the staid nor the economy-minded, and don't expect to find a room without a reservation. Note that things quiet down considerably in the off season. The biggest and best positioned hotel on the beach, ★★★★**Terramar**, Psg. Marítim 80, ✆ 93 894 00 50, ✉ 93 894 56 04 (*expensive*) is comfortable and up-to-date (though it resembles a clumsily decorated birthday cake), offering its guests tennis, golf, a nice pool and garden. The new, huge ★★★★**Gran Sitges**, Avda. Port d'Aiguadolç, ✆ 93 811 08 11, ✉ 93 894 90 97 (*expensive*) has everything you could possibly want, including an indoor and outdoor pool. More atmospheric, ★★**Hotel Romàntic**, Sant Isidre 33, ✆ 93 894 83 75, ✉ 93 894 81 67 (*moderate*) is made up of three 19th-century villas linked together, close to the beach, with a romantic garden. Near the station, little ★★**El Xalet**, Isla de Cuba 33–35, ✆/✉ 93 894 55 79 (*moderate*) occupies one of the prettiest *modernista* houses in Sitges; book well in advance. The recently spruced up ★★**Madison Bahia**, near the beach and town centre at Parelladas 31-33, ✆ 93 894 00 12 (*moderate*), is also well-placed and comfortable. You can enjoy the delights and delirium of Sitges and still pay around *6000 pts* for a decent double at ★**Lido**, just back from the sea at Bonaire 26, ✆ 93 894 48 48; at ★★**Hs Termes**, Psg. Termes 9 (behind Plaça Espanya) ✆ 93 894 23 43; at **Parellades**, C/ de la Parellades 11, ✆ 93 894 08 01; or at **Internacional**, C/ Sant Francesc 52, ✆ 93 894 26 90, one of the few hostelries in Sitges that stays open all year.

Eating Out

You can get just about anything in cosmopolitan Sitges but, as it is a place where liquid diets dominate, you shouldn't expect anything especially refined. The long-established **Mare Nostrum**, at Psg. de la Ribera 60, ✆ 93 894 33 93 (*expensive–moderate*), serves a wide variety of imaginatively prepared fish and crustaceans (try the fresh cod steamed in *cava*) to go with its good wine list and a pretty seaside location. *Closed Wed.* Nearby **El Velero**, Psg. de la Ribera 38, ✆ 93 894 20 51 (*expensive*) sits on a rock overlooking the sea and also has a good name for good fresh seafood. *Closed Sun eve.* **Chez Jeanette**, C/Sant Pau 23, ✆ 93 894 00 48, serves good Catalano-French cuisine, while **La Masía**, Psg. Vilanova 164, ✆ 93 894 10 76 (*moderate*) serves the most authentic Catalan food in Sitges. Covering all options and price ranges is the ever popular **Los Vikingos**, offering fish, burgers, chicken and steaks—Marqués de Montroig 79, ✆ 93 894 96 87 (*inexpensive*).

The Costa Brava

The Costa Brava ('Rugged Coast') officially begins at Blanes and winds its serpentine way up to the French border. The 72km between Barcelona and Blanes has been dubbed the **Costa del Maresme**, which, although it lacks the scenic grandeur of its famous neighbour, has some fine beaches, especially at **Arenys de Mar** and **Calella de la Costa**—both well-equipped with hotels. But the real holiday madness lies farther north.

Those fortunate enough to have visited the Costa Brava in the 1950s invariably have fits when they contemplate what speculator-man has wrought on the 'Spanish Riviera'. For her part, Mother Nature was lavish, tipsy even, as she sculpted out one scenic cove after another beneath pine-crowned cliffs, tucking lovely sandy beaches among strange boulder formations and rocky wind-sculptures, where 40 years ago fishermen berthed their boats. The Costa Brava is within reasonable driving distance of most of western Europe, which has fallen for it in a big way. To keep up with burgeoning demand, accelerated by scores of package holiday companies, hotels have been tossed up on the shore in a tidal wave of concrete that shows few signs of abating—just try to get a room in season without a reservation. After the Costa del Sol, the Costa Brava is Spain's most visited shore, but virtually all of its trade is shoehorned into a much briefer season (mid-June to mid-September). If you're just passing through in the summer, consider staying in Girona or Figueres just off the coast, where accommodation is easier to find and bus connections to the beaches frequent.

Blanes to Pals

Getting Around

By train: Blanes is easiest reached by train from Barcelona's Estació de França.

By bus: From Blanes, buses make the 8km trip to Lloret; you can also take a SARFA bus, ☎ 93 265 11 58, direct to Lloret from Barcelona. Another SARFA bus from Barcelona passes through Tossa del Mar and the other coastal villages as far as Palafrugell and Begur. From Girona there are several buses a day from the bus station to Lloret and the coast; SARFA buses from Girona depart from the Plaça de Canalejas 4.

The best way to reach the more remote places is the 'Lancha Litoral', the **sea bus** that meanders up the coast from Lloret to Port Bou. It's slow, but it stops nearly every-where and takes in some lovely scenery without the hassle of traffic or bus schedules.

Tourist Information

Blanes: Plaça Catalunya 21, ☎ 972 33 03 48.
Lloret de Mar: Plaça de la Vila 1, ☎ 972 36 47 35.
Tossa de Mar: Avda. Pelegrí 25, ☎ 972 34 01 08.
Sant Feliu de Guíxols: Plaça del Monestir 54, ☎ 972 82 00 51.
Palamós: Psg. de Mar 22, ☎ 972 60 05 00.
Palafrugell: Carrilet 2, ☎ 972 30 02 28.

Beautiful but Overcrowded Beaches

Semi-industrial and an important fishing port, **Blanes** is where it all begins from Barcelona's point of view, with one of the coast's longest beaches and most popular camping areas. It sits at the foot of a hill, crowned by the ruins of the castle, and has a pretty botanical garden, **Mar i Murtra**, on the way to its most picturesque cove, **Sant Francesc**. Most visitors, however, descend on **Lloret de Mar**, the jam-packed, half looney fun-house of the Costa Brava, boasting an even longer beach and the coast's greatest concentration of hotels, all brimful of packaged people, most of whom come to drink something a mite stronger than 'Tea just like your Mum makes it' as one Lloret café proclaims. By now it must be Spain's most famous sign, and one that sums Lloret up precisely.

North of Lloret, **Tossa de Mar** is one of the prettiest towns on the Costa Brava. Its **Vila Vella**—a maze of alleys, stone and whitewashed houses, embraced by a 12th-century crenellated wall and towers—is a National Historical Monument. Besides the three village beaches, intimate pine and cork-shaded coves are within easy reach. The next town north, **Sant Feliu de Guíxols**, once a major cork exporter, now prides itself on its pretty Passeig Marítim and its 11th-century **Porta Ferrada**, a Mozarabic remnant of a long-vanished monastery. You can see a fine panorama of the nearby coast from the **Hermitage of Sant Elm**, and there's a good beach at Sant Pol, 2.4km away. Inland, at Romanyà de la Selva, stands one of Catalunya's most impressive megaliths, the **Cova d'en Daina**. Brash and modern, the **Platja d'Aro-S'Agaro** has little to recommend it beyond its fine beach. **Palamós** fares better in charm, with its fishing fleet and excellent sailing facilities; its Platja de la Fosca beach is safe for the smallest child. Farther north, **Palafrugell**, the most attractive of the villages, has managed to preserve some of its delight, despite the *urbanizaciones* which have sprung up on the surrounding hills. The village also provides a good base for a number of beaches and lovely coves, as well as the fishing villages of **Calella de Palafrugell, Llafranc and Tamaríu**, the latter enveloped in fragrant pine-woods. In Llafranc, walk up to the lighthouse for the scenic view over the bay; in the abandoned hermitage perched on the cliff, toss a coin in the bowl behind the door-grille and make a wish. Palafrugell is also convenient for visiting **La Bisbal**, a medieval town with a market on Friday and a ceramics centre. La Bisbal's Romanesque castle belonged to the Bishop of Girona, and it claims to have Catalunya's finest *sardana* dance band, the 'Cobla Principal'. A bevy of medieval hamlets surround La Bisbal. The oldest of these is **Ullastret**, former Iberian settlement and Greek colony, complete with a set of Cyclopean walls. A small museum in a 14th-century hermitage houses finds dug up by Ullastret's farmers. More recent walls, from the Middle Ages, completely surround nearby **Peratallada**.

Up on its hill, **Pals**, another attractive medieval ensemble (with a pine-shaded golf course) has its own beach, framed by a great tree-topped chunk of rock. Near here, Begur is known for the intense azure blueness of its coves, especially **Aiguafreda** and **Aiguablava**.

Where To Stay and Eating Out

Not only does the Costa Brava have hundreds of hotels, but it has more camping sites per square foot than anywhere in Spain. Most of the hotels in the big resort towns are block-booked by February, but if you come in May or September you should find a room. Otherwise, reserve as early as possible. Most places are open May–September.

Blanes ✉ 17300

Blanes has the big modern ★★★**Park Hotel Blanes**, on the Platja S'Abanell, ✆ 972 33 02 50, 🖷 972 33 71 03 (*expensive*), a good family hotel, with a pool and playground for the children, tennis, a pool and a garden. Cheaper, ★**Hostal Patacano**, on the sea at C/Xavier Brunet 3, ✆ 972 33 00 02 (*moderate*) has six pleasant doubles which are open all year, as well as the best restaurant in Blanes, with meals based on seafood and fresh vegetables (*4000 pts*). A good budget choice, ★**Hotel Rosa**, S. Pedro Martin 42, ✆ 972 33 04 80, is in modest surroundings. **Can Flores II**, Esplanada del Port, ✆ 972 33 16 33 serves decent cooked meals from morning till night.

Lloret de Mar ✉ 17310

In Lloret the star luxury hotel is the plush ★★★★**Santa Marta** on the Platja de Santa Cristina, ✆ 972 36 49 04, 🖷 972 36 92 80, adding a pool, pretty garden, tennis courts and a very good restaurant to its attractive seafront location. Near the main beach, the ★**Residencia Reina Isabel**, Venècia 12, ✆ 972 36 41 21 (*moderate*) is rare in that it stays open all year and offers rooms with more character than most. Another good bet (without a restaurant) is down the street: **Roca y Mar**, Venècia 51, ✆ 972 37 04 03 (*moderate*). *Open May–October.* For sea-views try the new and comfortable **Tropicana**, C/ Joan Llaverias 19, ✆ 972 36 41 30 (*moderate*). Lloret has a number of mediocre *hostales*, none of which stand out in any way. Typical are ★**El Ciervo**, Avda. Mistral 8, ✆ 972 36 52 33, and ★**Cotano**, Areny 18, ✆ 972 36 48 90. Both are in the centre, and have rooms with bath for around 4500 pts. One of the cheapest places to stay is **El Cuarto Escalón**, C/ Santa Catarina, ✆ 972 36 86 43, which offers basic rooms for around *2000 pts a double*.

Besides a wide selection of fish-and-chip shops in Lloret, there's good seafood at **El Trull**, Ronda Europa s/n at Cala Canyelles, 2km from Lloret, ✆ 972 36 49 28 (*expensive*), in a pretty garden setting (*6000 pts*). Those with large appetites can dress up and go to the Lloret **casino**, where on Friday and Saturday nights there's an all-you-can-eat buffet for *3000 pts*. Cheaper, and serving good seafood *al fresco*, is the rustic **Mas Vell**, San Roc 3, near the bullring, ✆ 972 36 82 20 (*moderate*).

Tossa de Mar ✉ 17320

In Tossa de Mar the most charming place to stay is the ★★**Diana**, Plaça d'Espanya 6, ✆ 972 34 11 16 (*expensive*), an old-fashioned villa with a pretty courtyard on the seaside promenade. In a more tranquil corner on the Passeig del Mar, the stone-built ★**Hotel Cap d'Or**, ✆ 972 34 00 81 (*moderate*) has a fine sea view. To get into either of these, do reserve very early. Less well known, but also offering more atmosphere than the typical Costa Brava hotel, is ★**Sant Pere** (*moderate*), located on the edge of Tossa on the Ctra. Sant Feliu, ✆ 972 34 03 71, with a garden. For a cheap *pensión*, try the pleasant **Moré**, C/ Sant Telmo 9, ✆ 972 34 03 39 (*around 3000 pts*).

For good seafood and *sopa de mero* (grouper), Tossa's **Bahía**, on the Psg. del Mar 19, ✆ 972 34 03 22 is the place to go (*moderate*). **Es Molí**, C/Tarull 5, ✆ 972 34 14 14, offers a well-rounded menu with outdoor dining during summer months and a fireplace in the winter. For live jazz in the summer, it's **La Tortuga**, a bar on San Raimundo de Penafort.

La Platja d'Aro-S'Agaro ✉ 17000

On the beach at La Platja d'Aro the **★★★★★Hotel de la Gavina**, Plaça de la Rosaleda, ✆ 972 32 11 00, 📠 972 32 15 73 (*luxury*) is in a sumptuous villa, with gardens, solarium, gym, tennis courts and an 18-hole golf course nearby. At the other end of the price range is **La Marina**, C/Ciutat de Palol 2, ✆ 972 81 71 82, a decent *pensión*.

Palafrugell and Llafranc ✉ 17200

Prices tend to be lower here. Palafrugell's coves, Calella and Llafranc and Tamariu, each have a handful of hotels. In Llafranc, the **★★★ Llevant**, Francesc de Blanes 5, ✆ 972 30 03 66, 📠 972 30 03 45 (*expensive*) is small, smart and has a good restaurant. More reasonable is the **★★Montecarlo**, Cesárea 14, ✆ 972 30 04 04, (*moderate*). *Open all year.* In Llafranc there are also a couple of good cheaper choices: the **★El Coral**, Coral 5, ✆ 972 30 03 95 (*moderate*) and the **★Hs Montaña**, Cesàrea 2, ✆ 972 30 04 04 (*moderate*). IIn Palafrugell a good budget choice, **Fonda L'Estrella**, C/ de les Quatre Cases 13, near Plaça Nova, ✆ 972 30 00 05, has modest rooms built around a quiet courtyard.The **Hs. Cypsele**, C/Ample 30, ✆ 972 30 01 92, in Palafrugell has a good Catalan restaurant (*moderate*). Also in Palafrugell, La Casona, Paratge la Sauleda 4, ✆ 972 30 36 61 serves good food at *moderate* prices, try the *arròs negre*.

Aiguablava ✉ 17000

Near Begur, in Aiguablava, there's the modern and magnificently sited **★★★★Parador Costa Brava**, ✆ 972 62 21 62. 📠972 62 21 66 (*luxury*) where guests—either of the hotel or just the bar—can enjoy one of the finest views on the entire coast. There's also a pool, and a charming beach just below. *Open all year.* In Begur itself, the **★★Bagur**, Comas y Ros 8, ✆ 972 62 34 00, 📠 972 62 29 38 (*moderate*) is located in the centre of town in a pretty building, with comfortable rooms. *Open all year.* A charming place to eat in Begur is Can Torrades, ✆ 972 62 28 82, situated in a 19th-century villa in town. The gourmet's choice in Aiguablava is **Les Acacies**, on the beach, ✆ 972 62 24 95, with an imaginative menu based on the specialities of the region (*expensive*)—excellent *paella* and *musclos a la marinera* (mussels).

Torroella de Montgrí to Figueres

Getting Around

All **trains** from Barcelona to France stop in Figueres, which is the centre of the **bus** network to the upper Costa Brava (though there are connections from Girona five times daily to L'Estartit and L'Escala). SARFA buses run five or six times a day from Figueres to Roses and Cadaqués. Port Bou and Llançà are easiest reached by trains to France. The **seabus** Lancha Litoral also serves the coast.

Tourist Information

L'Estartit: Psg. Marítim 47, ✆ 972 75 19 10.
L'Escala: Plaça de Les Escoles 1, ✆ 972 77 06 03.
Roses: Avda. Rhode 101, ✆ 972 25 73 31.
Cadaqués: Cotxe 2, ✆ 972 25 83 15.
Figueres: Plaça del Sol, ✆ 972 50 31 55.

Ancient Greeks and Spain's First Romanesque Church

The coastal road veers inland from Pals to the castle-crowned **Torroella de Montgrí**, with its rambling lanes lined with medieval and Renaissance buildings. A major port in the Middle Ages, it now lies some 5km inland. Its resort satellite, **L'Estartit**, is a haven for underwater enthusiasts, who can pester the sea creatures around the tiny offshore **Islas Medes**. From here the road turns inland again, by way of **Verges**, where on Holy Thursday night adults and children don skeleton costumes and cardboard skulls to perform the 'Dança de la Mort', their Hallowe'en caperings a memory of the Black Death of the 14th century.

L'Escala, on the south shore of the Gulf of Roses, lies 2km from ancient **Empúries**, founded by the Greeks from Marseilles some time around 600 BC. Later an important Roman port, it was captured by Scipio in the second Punic War, and inhabited until the 9th century when it was looted and burned by Norman pirates (*open in the summer 10–2 and 3–8, winter 10–1 and 3–5, closed Mon; adm*). The modern town dates from the 16th century when it was re-populated by fishermen and is famous nowadays for its anchovies. Empúries is as pleasant to visit for its site as for the visible remains. Closest to shore stood the Greek colony, with its market, streets, cisterns and temples. Further back, in the partially excavated Roman town, two grand villas have been discovered with fine mosaics, along with an amphitheatre. A small museum (*entry included in the ticket*) on the site explains how it may have looked.

Roses, another Greek foundation on the north end of the gulf, has nice long beaches and modern development spread along them. Far more intimate and scenic (and conscious of the fact) is **Cadaqués**, refuge of artists and writers—Salvador Dalí lived in nearby Port Lligat. More than the other resorts on the Costa Brava, Cadaqués has preserved the atmosphere that began to attract people in the first place, primarily because it's hard to reach by public transport, and if you're driving there's no place to park. The jewel-like beaches of Cadaqués are also too small to hold a coachload of tourists comfortably. Still, people come, especially in July and August for the International Painting and Music Festivals. Cadaqués lies at the tip of Cape Creus, where the Pyrenees meet the sea. At this geographical crossroads and ancient holy place, the 9th-century Catalans founded one of their most important monasteries, **Sant Pere de Rodes**, 'the cradle of the Romanesque' built over the ruins of a Roman temple of Venus Pirenaica. According to legend, when Rome was threatened by an invasion of infidels, Pope Boniface IV decided to send some of the Church's holiest relics, including the head of St Peter, out of the city for safe-keeping. The relics were brought to Cape Creus and hidden in a grotto in the Sierra de Rodes. However, when the emissaries who undertook the task returned to Rome, the threat had passed, and they were sent back to Spain to retrieve the precious relics—only to discover that the grotto had vanished. The monastery was then constructed on the site, dedicated to St Peter. What survives dates from 1022, a magically picturesque fortress-like ruin that is slowly undergoing restoration.

The views from the monastery over the coast are stunning. To get there, walk up from **Llançà**, which along with **El Port de la Selva** and **Port Bou** are clustered near the border of France, in a region called Alto (High) Ampurdán. One of the high things about it is the wind, the Tramontana, which rages through here, mainly in the winter—Port Bou has one of the more protected beaches if it kicks up while you're around.

Figueres: to Dilly-Dalí, Catalan Style

Figueres is the capital of Alto Ampurdán, transport hub for the northern Costa Brava, and a wind sock; in the spirit of the ancient Greeks who called their terrible Furies the Eumenides ('the kind ones'), the town has erected a statue of a woman about to be blown away and called it the **Monument to the Tramontana**. It's near Pujada Castell and Figueres' star attraction, nothing less than the 'the spiritual centre of Europe' as its creator proclaimed: everyone else calls it the **Museu Dalí** (*open daily July–Sept 9–7.15; Oct–June 10.30–5.15; adm exp*). Salvador Dalí, born in Figueres in 1904, created this dream museum in 1974 in a merrily crazy reconstruction of his hometown's old municipal theatre. The result is the most visited museum in Spain, after the Prado, with a catalogue intended to misinform, as the artist intended it. Inside, expect the outrageous: the former stage has a set by Dalí, accompanied by a full orchestra of mannequins; a coin-fed Cadillac waters its snail-covered occupants. Dalí himself, who died in Figueres in 1989, is entombed nearby, his mortal coils the final exhibit.

Life is Art is Life

 It's a shame that the old megalomaniac didn't live forever, because Dalí was one of the funniest characters Spain ever produced. Gifted with an impeccable academic technique, he became the most famous surrealist of all while still in his '20s when he painted his first, haunting 'hand-painted dream photographs' as he called them of melting watches and human bodies fitted with sets of spilling drawers, Dalí loved the camera, and was one of the first artists to get involved with the cinema, in his 1929–30 collaborations with Luis Buñuel (*Un Chien Andalou* and *L'Age d'Or*)—surrealist films that caused riots when they were premiered in Paris. During the Civil War he offered to go to Barcelona and run a Department for the Irrational Organization of Daily Life (only to be told: thanks anyway, it already exists).

If traditional Surrealists drew inspiration from the irrational well of the unconscious, Dalí claimed his came from 'critical paranoia'–a carefully cultivated delusion, a conscious suspension of rational thought, a way of art and a way of life. Dalí, with his alert moustache-antennae tuned into the outrageous, did it with the deadpan humour of a Buster Keaton. The serious art world considered him a publicity-mongering buffoon, who produced little of value after the 30s, and who broke nearly every taboo; he claimed to support Franco (although he lived in the USA between 1940–55), he painted religious kitsch (all the while arguing that Jesus Christ was made of cheese) and signed his name to anything, which in his reclusive, suffering old age in Figueras was exploited by art dealers. This museum is his vindication.

L'Estartit ✉ 17258

The ★★★**Panorama**, Avda. de Grecia 5, ✆ 972 75 80 92, ✉ 972 75 71 19, is a good place to bring the whole family without breaking the bank. It has a nice location on the beach, a pool and a garden (*10,000–12,000 pts*). *Open all year.*

L'Escala ✉ 17130

The ★★★**Nieves-Mar**, Psg. Marítim 8, ✆ 972 77 03 00, ✉ 972 10 36 05 (*expensive*) offers tennis, children's activities, and a pool in modern surroundings. Near the Greek ruins, the ★**Hotel Ampurías** on Afueras, ✆ 972 77 02 07 (*moderate*) is isolated and tranquil and on the beach. *Open April–Oct.*

Roses ✉ 17840

In Roses, there's the self-contained ★★★★**Almadraba Park**, on the Platja de Almadraba, ✆ 972 25 65 50, ✉ 972 25 67 50, the most chic and sleek on the upper coast. An air-conditioned room, heated pool, sauna, tennis courts and plush rooms can all be yours for *18,000 pts. Open all year.* Centrally located on the Platja Salata is the contemporary ★★**Marítim**, ✆ 972 25 63 90, with typical, pleasant rooms (open all year). It also has two swimming pools—one for the children as well. Roses has a few bargains for budget travellers—★**María de la Cinta**, Riera Ginjolers 22, ✆ 972 25 61 22, and **Puig Rom**, Plaça Levant 1, ✆ 972 25 41 33, both in the centre, with so-so rooms (with bath).

Roses can lay claim to one of Spain's finest restaurants: **Hacienda El Bulli**, located on a promontory over the lovely Cala Montjoi, ✆ 972 15 04 57 (*expensive*), where you can moor your yacht while dining. El Bulli has created many of its own recipes, prepared by a perfectionist chef whose menu varies according to season (*12,500 pts*). *Closed Mon and Tues, except in summer.*

Cadaqués ✉ 17488

In Cadaqués there's the smallish ★★★**Llane Petit**, Dr Bartoneus 37, ✆ 972 25 80 50, ✉ 972 25 87 78, a modern and very comfortable hotel with a garden on the beach of the same name (*16,000 pts*). The old ★★**Port Lligat** has fine views over Cadaqués and Port Lligat, ✆ 972 25 81 62, with a children's playground and pool. *Open all year.* In the heart of Cadaqués a less expensive alternative is the ★**Hostal Ubaldo**, Unión 13, ✆ 972 25 81 25 (*7000 pts*). *Open all year.* In Cadaqués the only *inexpensive* places are ★**Joker**, Avda. San Mauricio 8, ✆ 972 47 00 44, and ★**Ribot**, Rocas 6, ✆ 972 47 00 21. Of these, the Joker is the better deal—its rooms come with bath.

The most fashionable restaurant in Cadaqués is **La Galiota**, N. Monturiol 9, ✆ 972 25 81 87 (*expensive–moderate*), with good seafood and soufflés. If it's packed, as it often is in the summer, try **Sa Gambina,** Riba Nemesi Llorens s/n, ✆ 972 25 81 27, where good fish and rice dishes can be had, or **Don Quijote**, Avda. Caridad Seriñana 6, ✆ 972 25 81 41 (*moderate*), just outside Cadaqués, with a nice atmosphere and set menu with typical Spanish dishes for *around 4000 pts*.

Figueres ✉ 17600

The ★★★**Hotel Durán**, in town on Lasauca 5, ✆ 972 50 12 50, ▨ 972 50 26 09 (*moderate*) has cosy pleasant rooms, is open all year, and is the best place to stay if you'd like to be above one of the best and oldest restaurants in Catalunya. For something more modest, the **España**, La Junquera 26, ✆ 972 50 08 69 (*inexpensive*) has quite adequate doubles. The cheapest place to stay is the bare-bones **La Vinya**, Pl. Indústria 7, ✆ 972 50 00 49, with double rooms for *2500 pts*.

People drive in from miles around Figueres for one of the tables in the huge dining-room of the **Hotel Durán**, C/ Lasauca 5, ✆ 972 50 12 50, for meals like *zarzuela con langosta* (fish stew with lobster) at good prices (*4500–6500 pts*). Equally renowned is the **Ampurdán**, on Highway N11, at 1.5km north of Figueres, ✆ 972 50 05 62 (*expensive*) famed for its adaptations of regional specialities to the modern palate. Game dishes are a speciality, as are its mint salads and *taps de Cadaqués*—an incendiary rum cake (*5500–7000 pts*).

Girona/Gerona

Between the Costa Brava and the highest Pyrenees, the heart of the province of Girona is surprisingly untouristified, despite the hordes that descend on the Costa Brava and the ski resorts of the Pyrenees, bypassing its oasis of rolling green hills and occasional geological oddities. Yet it is tourism, more than anything, that has brought the province its new status as the wealthiest in all Spain.

Spread over a tumble of hills at the confluence of the Onyar and Ter rivers, the capital **Girona** (ancient *Gerunda*) is one of Catalunya's most atmospheric little cities. Its position has brought it a history tormented with sieges, most famously in 1809, when the city's inhabitants withstood 35,000 French troops for seven months, giving up only when their supplies were exhausted. Few of its embattled walls remain, however; like so many cities in Spain, Girona has burst its buttons in the last few decades.

Getting Around

Girona's **bus** (✆ 972 21 23 19) and **train** stations (✆ 972 20 70 93) are side-by-side on the Plaça d'Espanya in the Eixample; all trains between France and Barcelona stop here. Girona's airport receives international charters, but has no public transport linking it to the city itself. A taxi will cost about 1900 pts. Banyoles, Olot, Besalú and the Costa Brava can be reached by bus; services are run by a number of companies.

Tourist Information

Rambla de la Llibertat 1, ✆ 972 22 65 75.

The Old Town

Fortunately, Girona's **Old Town** has been lovingly neglected. Its dim, narrow streets and passages, its steep stairs, little plazas, archways, and solid stone buildings offer any number of elegant perspectives. In recent years, in an attempt to keep the Old Town from falling too deeply asleep, the town approved the placement of various departments of the University of Catalonia within its quarters, adding a bit of student verve to the area. Across the Onyar from the old town is Girona's Eixample—a miniature version of Barcelona's, complete with a handful of minor *modernista* buildings designed by poet Rafael Masó (see the **Casa Teixidor** and **Farinera Teixidor** in Carrer de Santa Eugénia). Cross between the two on the bridge called the **Pont de les Peixateries** for the much-photographed view of the houses built up directly over the river.

The main street of medieval Girona, the **Carrer de la Força** follows the Roman *Via Augusta*, the road of conquest. Narrow and winding, it seems to have changed little since the day when Girona's famous Jewish quarter, the **Call**, was defined by its southernmost reaches, around the steep alleys of Sant Llorenç and Cúndaro. Like the *calls* of Barcelona and Tarragona, the quarter came under the direct authority of the king, enjoying total autonomy from the municipal council, the *Jurats*—a situation designed to exacerbate tension, for the kings not only regarded the Jewish communities as a national resource and favoured them at the expense of others, but made use of these enclaves to meddle in city affairs. But before the decline into the 15th century, when the *Jurats*, egged on by a fanatical clergy and jealous debtors, managed to isolate the *Call* into a ghetto with only one entrance, Girona's Jews had founded an important school of Jewish mysticism, the *Cabalistas de Girona*. The most celebrated member, Moses Ben Nahman, or Nahmanides, was born in Girona in 1194 and helped diffuse Cabalistic studies throughout Europe. The old school of the Cabala has been opened as the **Centra Bonastruc Ça Porta**, 972 21 67 61 (*open daily in summer 10–9, until 6 in the winter, holidays 10–2; adm*) on Sant Llorenç, and just as the Muslims are building a new mosque in Granada, there are plans to refound the school. Carrer de la Força continues past the **City Museum** (with changing exhibits on the subject of cities) to the lovely **Plaça de la Catedral**, framed by the 18th-century **Casa Pastors** (law courts) and the stately Gothic **Pia Almoina**. From here a monumental Baroque stair leads up to the cathedral and its lofty **Torre de Carlomagno**.

The Cathedral

One of the masterpieces of Catalunya, Girona's cathedral surpasses the grandeur of the stair with the widest single nave in all Christendom—22m across. Originally planned as a typical three-aisled nave, work began early in the 14th century. A century later the master architect Guillem Bofill (ancestor of Ricardo Bofill, Catalunya's current architectural innovator) suggested an aesthetic and money-saving improvement: to add a single great nave to the already completed apse. His proposal was so radical that all the leading architects of Catalunya were summoned to a council to solicit their opinions as to whether or not such a cathedral would stand. The majority said no, but Girona let Bofill do it anyway.

Inside there are plenty of fine details, but it's the colossal Gothic vault, supported by its interior buttresses, that steals the show. The stained glass is recent, the heads of all the saints reduced to simple black ovals—a haunting effect. The *retablo* over the high altar is a 14th-century masterpiece of silverwork, surmounted by an equally remarkable silver-plated canopy, or baldachin. A ticket will get you into a small but exceptional **museum** (*open daily summer 10–2 and 4–7, in winter 10–2 and 4–6 weekdays; adm*), featuring the unique *Tapestry of Creation*, an 11th-century view of Genesis, with the Creator surrounded by sea monsters, the four wind-bags, the seasons, and Eve popping out of Adam's side. Then there's *Código del Beatus*, an illuminated commentary on the Apocalypse from the year 974, with richly coloured Mozarabic miniatures. The ticket also admits you into the trapezoidal Romanesque **Cloister**, with exquisitely carved capitals, including one of a giant rabbit menacing a man.

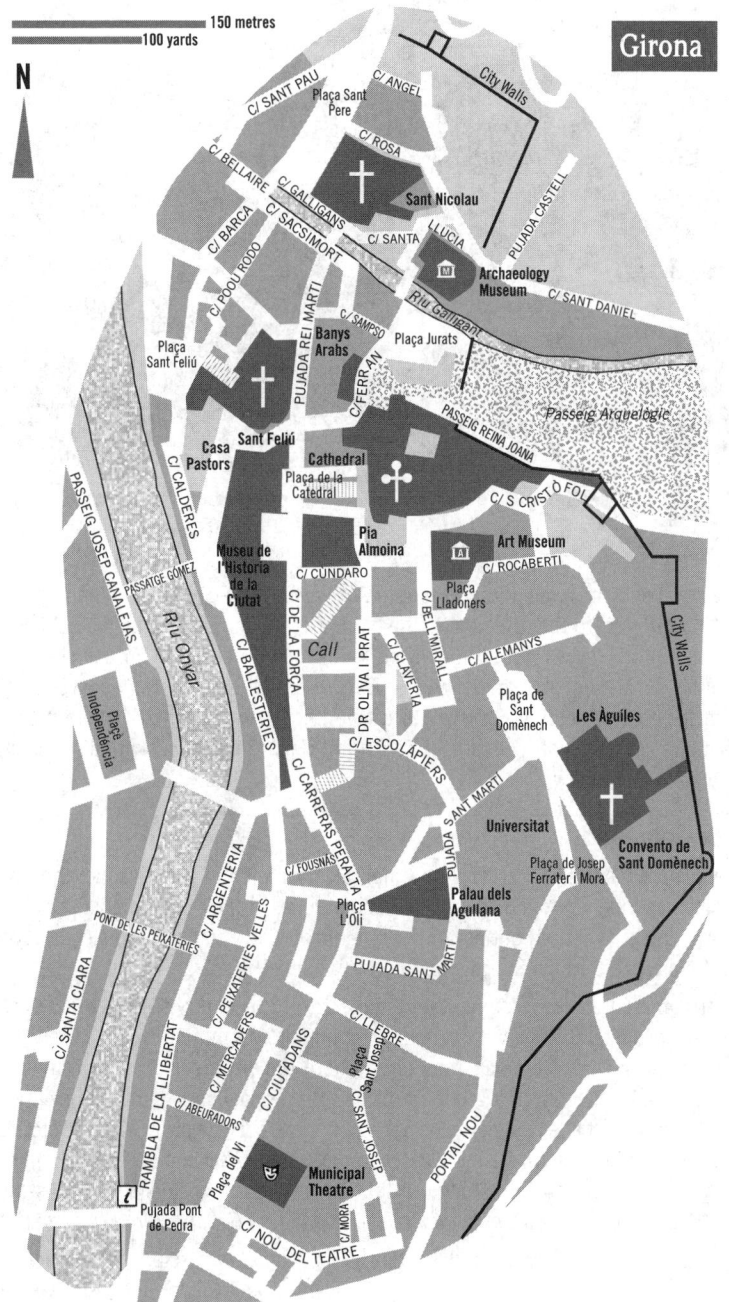

150 metres
100 yards

N

Girona

City Walls

C/ SANT PAU
C/ ANGEL
Plaça Sant Pere
C/ ROSA
C/ BELLAIRE
C/ GALLIGANS
Sant Nicolau
PUJADA CASTELL
C/ BARCA
C/ SACSIMORT
C/ SANTA LLUCIA
C/ POUU RODO
Archaeology Museum
Riu Galligant
C/ SANT DANIEL
PUJADA REI MARTI
C/ SAMPSO
Banys Arabs
Plaça Jurats
Plaça Sant Feliú
C/ FERRAN
Passeig Arqueològic
PASSEIG REINA JOANA
Casa Pastors
Sant Feliú
Cathedral
PASSEIG JOSEP CANALEJAS
PASSATGE GOMEZ
C/ CALDERES
Plaça de la Catedral
C/ S CRISTÒFOL
Museu de l'Historia de la Ciutat
Pia Almoina
Art Museum
C/ ROCABERTI
Riu Onyar
C/ BALLESTERIES
C/ DE LA FORÇA
C/ CUNDARO
Plaça Lladoners
City Walls
Plaça Independència
Call
C/ BELLMIRALL
C/ ALEMANYS
Plaça Independència
C/ DR OLIVA I PRAT
C/ CLAVERIA
Plaça de Sant Domènech
Les Àguiles
C/ ESCOLÀPIERS
PUJADA S SANT MARTI
C/ CARRERAS PERALTA
Universitat
Convento de Sant Domènech
C/ FOUSNAS
Plaça de Josep Ferrater i Mora
C/ ARGENTERIA
Plaça L'Oli
Palau dels Aguilana
PONT DE LES PEIXATERIES
C/ PEIXATERIES VELLES
PUJADA SANT MARTI
C/ SANTA CLARA
C/ MERCADERS
C/ CIUTADANS
C/ LLEBRE
RAMBLA DE LA LLIBERTAT
C/ ABEURADORS
Plaça Sant Josep
PORTAL NOU
Plaça del Vi
Municipal Theatre
Pujada Pont de Pedra
C/ NOU DEL TEATRE
C/ MORA

More medieval delights await in the **Museu d'Art** (*open Tues–Sat 10–7, in winter until 6pm, Sun 10–2; adm*) next to the cathedral in the old Episcopal Palace. Among the exhibits there's a beam from 1200, carved with funny-faced monks lined up like a chorus line, a beautiful 15th-century catalogue of martyrs and a *Calvary* by Mestre Bartomeu (13th century), portraying a serenely smiling Christ with a face like Shiva, ready to dance off the Cross. Upstairs, there are rooms of 19th- and 20th-century Catalan paintings, with a selection by the masters of Olot (*see* below).

Portal de Sobreportas

Back down the 90 steps to the Plaça de Catedral, turn left and pass through the **Portal de Sobreportas** and its two round towers. The huge stones of their bases predated the Romans, and there's a niche hollowed out on top for a statue of 'Our Lady of Good Death' invoked by the unfortunates led through the gate on their way to execution.

To the left stands Girona's most important temple, the 13th-century **Sant Feliú** at the head of its own flight of stairs. It has a curious spire, amputated by lightning, and is believed to have been built over an early Christian cemetery, where the city's patron saint Narcís suffered martyrdom. Inside the church are two Roman and six Palaeochristian sarcophagi with fine carvings. Turning right after the Portal de Sobreportas, a door in a plain wall leads to the 13th-century **Banys Arabs** (Arab baths), a 13th-century version of ancient Roman *hammams*, built by Morisco craftsmen and illuminated within by an elegant eight-sided oculus on white columns (*open daily except Mon, summer 10–7, holidays 10–2; winter 10–4; adm*).

Down the Pujada del Rei Marti and across the Galligans river stand two attractive 12th-century works—tiny **Sant Nicolau** with its three apses, and the former **Monestir de Sant Pere Galligants**, now the **Archaeology Museum**, with an extensive collection of medieval

Jewish headstones and a cloister that makes an interesting comparison with the cathedral's (*open daily except Mon, 10–1 and 4.30–7, Sun and holidays 10–2; adm*). From here the **Passeig Arqueològic** offers a garden-like stroll along the walls, with fine views over the pretty Vall de Sant Daniel from the ruins of the Roman **Torre Gironella**. Once through the Portal de Sant Cristòfol you can return to the cathedral or take Carrer dels Alemanys to the Plaça de Sant Domènec, with Girona's best-preserved ancient walls and all that remains of the city's old university, the Renaissance **Les Àguiles**, adorned with two eagles. Down the steps from this square is the beautiful **Palau dels Agullanas**, with its low arch spanning the junction of two stairs. From here, Carrer Ciutadans returns to the Plaça del Vi, with the 19th-century **Municipal Theatre**, where two Catalan *gegants* (giants) stand vigil in the courtyard, waiting for a holiday, when they're allowed to sally forth and menace the children.

Girona ✉ *17000*   ***Where to Stay***

The ★★★★**Melià Confort Girona**, Ctra. de Barcelona 112, ✆ 972 40 05 00, ✉ 972 24 32 33, is one of a chain, attracting Spanish businessmen and choosy tourists for the most luxury in town (*14,000 pts*). The best mid-range choice is the ★★**Pensión Bellmirall**, C/ Bellmirall 3, ✆ 972 20 40 09, a pleasant little charmer in the old town, near the cathedral, which has the best breakfast in Girona (*6000 pts*). *Open all year*. Also in the old town and open all year round, the ★★**Pensión Reyma**, Pujada del Rei Martí 15, ✆ 93 20 02 28, is pleasant and tranquil (*6000 pts*). The best moderate choice in the new part of town is the ★**Condal**, Joan Maragall 10, ✆ 972 20 44 62, near the train station, with comfortable modern rooms (*5700 pts*). ★**Margarit**, Ultònia 1, ✆ 972 20 10 66, is a decent *inexpensive* option for a short stay, and some of its simple rooms come with bath. There are some even cheaper *hostales* though some are rather gloomy. Try the popular **Pensión Viladomat**, C/ Ciutadans 5, ✆ 972 20 31 76. There's also a youth hostel at Ciutadans 9, ✆ 972 21 80 03.

Eating Out

Hearty Catalan specialities like *cannelonis* are one of the many treats at **L'Hostalet del Call**, near the cathedral at Batlle y Prats 4, ✆ 972 21 26 88, (*5000 pts*). *Closed Sun*. Locals will recommend **La Penyora**, C/ Nou del Teatre 3, ✆ 972 21 89 48 (*moderate*), where a first-class meal will cost around *4000 pts*. Another favourite in town is **Celler de Can Roca**, Ctra. Taialà 40, ✆ 972 22 21 57 (*moderate*), whose grim exterior hides a restaurant of very high quality (*5500 pts*). Probably the best restaurant in Girona is the well-designed **Albereda**, Albereda 9, ✆ 972 22 60 02 (*expensive*). They serve beautifully prepared food, especially *bacalao* dishes, at reasonable prices: rapefish and prawns with a parmesan gratin costs *2500 pts*. Across the Onyar from the cathedral is the Casa Marieta, Plaça Independència 5, ✆ 972 20 10 16, which serves up generous helpings of hearty fare, such as botifarra amb mengetes (porc sausage with white beans). Near the Museu d'Art is **Cipresaia**, General Fournas 2, ✆ 972 22 24 49 (*moderate*), with an elegant interior and muted atmosphere. **El Pou del Call**, C/ de la Força 14, ✆ 972 22 37 74 (*moderate*) is another good restaurant with reasonably priced dishes, well-beloved of locals.

Tourist Information

Banyoles: Passeig Industria 25, ✆ 972 57 55 73.
Olot: Mulleres 33, ✆ 972 26 01 41.
Besalú: Plaça de la Llibertat 1, ✆ 972 59 12 40.

Banyoles

No one thinks of lakes when they think of Spain, but there's a pretty one just north of Girona in the Garrotxa mountains called Banyoles. Banyoles town has a 13th-century porticoed square, and a copy of a Neanderthal jawbone found here in its **Regional Archaeological Museum** (*open July and Aug daily 10.30–1 and 4.30–8, Sept–June Tues–Sun 10.30–1.30 and 4–6.30; adm*), housed in the Gothic Pía Almoina. On the other side of the lake, the tiny village of **Porqueres** has a gem of a Romanesque church, **Santa María** (1182), and prehistoric cave paintings in nearby **Serinyà** (ask in Girona about opening hours). Buses take half an hour to make the trip from Girona.

Olot

Between Banyoles and Olot there's an odd landscape called the Garrotxa, pitted by 40 extinct volcanoes and endowed with a diaphanous light. The largest crater, **Santa Margarida**, is 350m across and lush with greenery, while another, **Sant Pau**, is barren and lunar. The beautiful beechgrove near Santa Margarida, **La Fageda dén Jordà**, is a great place for a picnic. The unique scenery inspired innumerable Catalan landscape painters, many centred in **Olot**, on the River Fluvià, which has been the centre of a small art colony since the founding of the School of Fine Arts in 1783. The **Museu Comarcal** (*open daily exc Tues 11–2 and 4–7, Sun 11–2*) in Olot's neoclassical Hospici features work by the 19th-century Olot school, whose painters took the rural scenes of Millet as their starting point. A stroll through town reveals sculpture by Josep Clarà and Miquel Blay and the ornate 1915 *modernista* **Casa de Solá Morales** by Domènech i Montaner. From Olot, take the C150 for the startling view of **Castellfollit de la Roca**, perched atop a basalt escarpment 59m over the Fluvià.

Besalú

On down the Fluvià (14km north of Banyoles) is one of Catalunya's purest, most uncommercialized medieval ensembles, Besalú. For one brief, shining hour, after its reconquest by Louis le Deboinair in 800, it ruled an independent county before being absorbed by the House of Barcelona in 1020. You can get there by way of a 12th-century **fortified bridge**, built at an unusual angle, with a tower at the bend, and eight arches of irregular shape and size.

On the far side of the bridge, where the Jewish **call** once stood, there's a Romanesque **Mikwah** (a ritual bathhouse connected to a synagogue), the only one ever found in Spain, and one of only three in Europe. Besalú has two 12th-century churches—**Sant Pere**, decorated by a pair of stone lions obviously carved from hearsay rather than an authentic model, and **Sant Vicenç**, its entrance prettily decorated with floral motifs. A domestic building of the period, **Casa Cornellà** (*open for hourly tours July–Sept Mon–Sat*) has been restored and furnished with antique tools and household items.

Where To Stay and Eating Out

Banyoles ✉ 17000

The best place to stay near the lake is the **★★Hostal L'Ast**, Psg. Dalmau 63, ✆ 972 57 04 14 (*moderate*) with a pool and adequate restaurant (*6200 pts*). Less expensive, but also near the lake, **★Can Xabanet**, Carmen 27, ✆ 972 57 02 52, is equally pleasant and has good meals for *2500 pts*. The cheapest place to stay is the **Ramiò**, Sant Esteve 34, ✆ 972 57 37 09, (*2300 pts*).

Olot and Besalú ✉ 17800

The moderately priced **★★★Borell**, Nònit Escubos 8, ✆ 972 26 92 75, is a good, small hotel in the center of Olot. For those on a tighter budget there's the **Stop**, Sant Pere Màrtir 29, ✆ 972 26 10 48 (*3200 pts*). Market fresh meals can be had at **Les Cols**, Ctra. de la Canya, Mas Les Cols, ✆ 972 26 92 09. *Closed Sundays.* In Besalú, you have the choice of three places, the **★Siqués**, Av. President Companys 6-8, ✆ 972 59 01 10, which harbors a very decent restaurant **Cal Parent**, the Venència, Major 8, ✆ 972 59 12 57, and the **Marià**, Pl. Llibertat 4, ✆ 972 59 01 06.

The Catalan Pyrenees

When the Bourbon Felipe V ascended to the Spanish throne, his grandfather Louis XIV haughtily declared (according to Voltaire): 'Il n'y a plus de Pyrenées!' History, of course, proved him sadly deluded, though these great mountains have suffered of late a good deal of mental erosion as Spain takes its place as an equal partner in Europe. For the Catalans and Basques, who live on both sides of the Pyrenees, the mountains have never been all that high, and when Madrid made things hot, it was customary to slip over the border to visit one's French cousin. Yet the difference between the French and Spanish Pyrenees is striking. The former are rugged and often forbidding and even at the beginning of May there can be a blinding whiteout of snow, while to the south green valleys bask in the sun. The mountains are gentler, more benign in Spain.

Spain divides its Pyrenees into three sectors: the Catalan, the Aragonese, and the Navarrese. Of the three, the Catalan Pyrenees have the easiest access and are the most visited, although innumerable tiny villages remain tucked away in the mountain folds on the banks of sparkling streams. Because of their remoteness, smugglers were spiriting away the masterpieces of their tiny Romanesque chapels as late as the 1920s—a practice halted by their removal to Barcelona's Museu Nacional d'Art de Catalunya. Some of Spain's best ski resorts are in Catalunya, as is the lovely national park, Aigüestortes.

Vic, Ripoll, Ribes de Freser and Puigcerdà are linked by RENFE **trains** to Barcelona eight times a day. Cardona is easiest reached by train from Barcelona to Manresa and then bus; Sant Joan is connected by **buses** running between Olot and Ripoll.

The hour-long rack railway ride from Ribes to Núria runs five times daily, connecting with the train from Barcelona.

Tourist Information

Vic: Plaça Mayor 1, ✆ 93 886 20 91.
Cardona: Avda. Rastrillo s/n, ✆ 93 869 27 98.
Ripoll: Plaça de l'Abat Oliba, ✆ 972 70 23 51.
Sant Joan de les Abadesses: Rambla Comte Guifré 5, ✆ 972 72 05 99.
Puigcerdà: Querol (baixos Ajuntament), ✆ 972 88 05 42.

Vic and Cardona

Vic, in the foothills of the Pyrenees, is an ancient town that served as the capital of the Ausetani Iberians and has been mildly important ever since; among its sights are the **cella** of a 2nd-century Roman temple, the picturesque **Plaça del Mercadal**, where markets have been held every Tuesday and Saturday since the 10th century, and a collection of Baroque houses and churches. In 1781 Vic saw fit to knock down its Romanesque cathedral and replace it with a neoclassical pile. To make up for the loss, the bishop hired Josep Maria Sert to cover the interior with remarkable and massive **golden murals**—a job the artist had to do again after the cathedral was set on fire in 1930. What you see here occupied him until his death in 1945, and in their evocation of the triumph of Injustice to Christ and Catalunya on the west wall (including the burning of the cathedral with his first paintings) resemble a modern man's Sistine Chapel. Here, too, are two 15th-century works which managed to escape restoration and the flames: an alabaster *retablo* and **tomb**, both by the same sculptor. Vic also preserves a major collection of medieval art in the **Museu Episcopal**, north of the cathedral on Plaça del Obispo Oliba (*open Mon–Sat 10–1 and 4–7, mid-Oct–mid-May 10–1 only, Sun 10–1*). It contains beautiful works by Jaume Huguet, Pedro Serra, Ferrer Bassa, Jaume Ferrer, Lluís Borrassà and Ramón de Mur and a famous stylized, wooden *Descent from the Cross* of Erill la Vall. If you're driving, head out along the Manresa road for an extraordinary view of Montserrat.

Cardona, to the west, is midway between Barcelona and Andorra. Spaniards know it as the Capital of Salt, for its nearby, unearthly **Salí**, a mountain of pure salt 80m high and 5km around the perimeter. On a hill high over the town itself is the attractive ensemble of a **medieval castle** of the powerful Dukes of Cardona (now a *parador*) and the Romanesque church of **Sant Vicenç**.

Ripoll and Sant Joan

One Romanesque masterpiece the smugglers couldn't cart off is in the Benedictine monastery in the otherwise dreary town of Ripoll, to the north of Vic. Founded by Count Wilfred the Hairy in 888, **Santa María de Ripoll** held a prominent position in early medieval Catalunya and was one of the great diffusers of Arab learning to the West, its vast library full of translations of classical texts. When the monastery at Montserrat was founded, it seemed natural to give it to the Benedictines of Ripoll. The church was begun in the 12th century, suffered a devastating fire in 1835 and was rebuilt. Surviving intact, however, is the great **west portal**, the most mature expression of Catalan Romanesque sculpture, a 'Stone Bible' that encompasses nearly the whole Book, with the zodiac and some monsters thrown in for good measure. The north wing of the two-storeyed **cloister** survived as well, with its elaborate capitals. Next to the monastery, in the 14th-century **Sant Pere**, the **Museu Pirineos** contains many of the firearms manufactured in Ripoll beginning in the 16th century, arms that were prized throughout Europe (*open Tues–Sun 9.30–1 and 3.30–6, till 7 April–Sept; adm*).

Just east of Ripoll, **Sant Joan de les Abadesses** on the River Ter is a medieval town named after the **Colegiata** also founded by Wilfred the Hairy, in 887, and likewise gloriously embellished in the 12th century. Architects from Aquitaine exerted a strong influence over Catalan builders, nowhere more so than on Sant Joan. In one of the chapels stands the church's most curious treasure, a wooden 15th-century *Deposition* nicknamed 'Las Brujas'—the witches—for the weirdness of its figures. More traditional is the lovely 14th-century alabaster **Retablo de Santa María la Blanca** and a fine Gothic cloister. Also in town, the dilapidated 12th-century **Sant Pol** is worth a look for its carved tympanum. The recently restored pretty **bridge** over the trout-filled Ter dates from 1140.

Núria, Llivia and Puigcerdà

Up the river Freser from Ripoll the small spa **Ribes de Freser** is the departure point for an extraordinary vertiginous journey by private rack railway (*cremallera*) to the attractive stone village of **Queralbs** and beyond to **Núria** (1270m), a lofty bowl-shaped valley and sanctuary. Like Montserrat, Núria is a favourite name given to Catalan girls. The 11th-century cult image in the grim sanctuary, **La Mare de Deu de Núria**, has recently been proclaimed the official Patroness of Winter Sport. Fittingly Núria has a ski station, while the valley provides lovely walks that skirt the edges of precipitous chasms. The high plain to the west, the **Cerdanya**, was divided between Spain and France by the Treaty of the Pyrenees in 1659, bestowing on France all the villages of Upper Cerdanya—but not the towns. Hence the anomaly of **Llivia**, an islet of Spanish territory 3km into France. Ancient *Julia Libyca*, a main town on the Roman highway *Strata Ceretana*, Llivia was the capital of the Cerdanya, but now is visited primarily for curiosity's sake (a neutral road links it to the Cerdanya's current capital, Puigcerdà) and to visit its **pharmacy**, said to be the oldest in Europe—dating from 1415—and now part of the municipal museum (*open Tues–Sat 10–1 and 3–6; until 7 April–Sept, Sun and holidays 10–2; adm*). Nearly every town in Spain has a palatial pharmacy with fancy woodwork, painted ceilings and antique jars—and this is the mother of them all. The medicines are stored not in cabinets, but ornate shrines, veritable *retablos* of drugs. Llivia also claims a heavily fortified church from the 1400s, now used for a summer music festival.

Puigcerdà, opposite Llivia, is a typical frontier town except in the winter when the skiers pile in; it's also the capital of Spanish ice hockey. There's a pretty lake with swans and paddle boats for hire, and the 13th-century parish church **Sant Domènec**, its walls decorated with medieval frescoes of unholy brutes dealing the saint a splitting headache.

Some 32km south of Puigcerdà, on the upper end of the new **Tunnel of Cadi** (Spain's longest) is the tiny town of **Baga**, one of the cradles of Catalan nationalism. Near the centre stands a statue of the knight Calcerán de Pinos, who was rescued from a Moorish prison in Almería by the miraculous intervention of the silver Byzantine cross reputedly brought over from the First Crusade and now kept in the 14th-century church of **Sant Esteban**.

Vic (Vich) ✉ 08500

About 14km outside Vic on the Carrer de Roda de Ter, there's the
★★★★**Parador Nacional de Vic**, ✆ 93 812 23 23, (*expensive*), a
charming idealization of a Catalan *masia*, or country house, located in a
pine-grove and overlooking a reservoir, with a pool, tennis and a good
restaurant. In Vic itself, there is the ★★Ausa, Plaça Major 4, ✆ 93 885
53 11, overlooking the town's central square, which on market days can be quite a
feast for the eyes and ears. Around the corner from the Roman temple is the Jordi
Parramón restaurant, Cardona 7, ✆ 93 886 38 15, in a large, old space and praised for
the fresh and creative quality of its cuisine.

Cardona ✉ 08261

The ★★★★**Parador Nacional Duques de Cardona**, ✆ 93 869 12 75, ✆ 93 869 16
36 (*expensive*) makes a stop in Cardona worthwhile. High over the town, it is part of
the castle founded in 789 by Louis the Pious. The Romanesque courtyard and chapel
are a museum, and the restaurant offers well-prepared Catalan specialities in a lovely
setting. The rooms are furnished with Catalan antiques.

Ripoll ✉ 17500

In Ripoll the most pleasant place to stay is 2km outside town, on the Barcelona road:
Solana del Ter, ✆ 972 70 10 62, ✆ 972 71 43 43 (*moderate*), a little resort unto
itself with rooms, a campground, tennis court, pool and children's playground in a
pleasant park-like setting. It also has Ripoll's best restaurant, featuring Catalan cuisine
(*4000 pts*). In town, there's the **Pension Monasterio**, Plaça Gran 4, ✆ 972 70 41
33, (*moderate*), not exactly for those in habit but close. Excellent meats from the grill
are on the menu at **Grill El Gall**, 3km off the N152, ✆ 972 70 24 51 (*moderate*). Up
at Núria there are campsites, a youth hostel and one *hotel*, the ★★★**Vall de Núria**,
✆ 972 73 20 00 (*expensive–moderate*) with nicely furnished rooms and a very good
restaurant serving mountain meals for *3000 pts*.

Sant Joan de les Abadesses ✉ 03000

There are three one-star *hostales* in Sant Joan, the nicest of which is **Ter**, C/ Vista
Alegre 1, ✆ 972 72 00 05, with the best location. It also has a good restaurant. **Llivia**
Llivia has one hotel, the ★★★**Llivia**, ✆/✆ 972 14 60 00 (*expensive*) with a pool and
tennis courts. There are also a couple of hostals, the better of the two being **Can
Marcellí**, Frederic Barnades 7, ✆ 972 14 60 96. The town's best restaurant, **Can
Ventura** on Plaça Major, ✆ 972 89 61 78 (*expensive*) is worth working up an
appetite for, especially if you walk over from Puigcerdà. The 18th-century building has
a charming rustic decor, and the menu features Cerdanya delights.

Puigcerdà ✉ 17520

In Puigcerdà there's a wide selection, including the ★★★**Chalet del Golf**, on the Seu
d'Urgell road just out of town, ✆ 972 88 09 62 (*expensive*), a cosy little spot by a
garden and the links. In Puigcerdà town, ★★**Hotel Del Lago**, Avda. Dr. Piguillem 7,

✆ 972 88 10 00 (*moderate*) has pretty views of lake and mountains. There is also the small and charming ★★★**Avet Blau**, Plaça Santa Maria 14, ✆ 972 88 25 52 (*expensive*). There are many inexpensive *hostales* by the train station and throughout town. The Internacional, La Baronia, ✆ 972 88 01 58, is mid-sized and well-priced. You can dine abundantly at the **Casa Clemente**, Avda. Dr. Piguillem 6, ✆ 972 88 11 66 (*moderate*), with filling meals for *2500–3200 pts.* A restaurant of international fame is located 4 km outside of town in Bolvir de Cerdanya at the five-star *luxury* hotel, **Torre del Remei**, Camí Reial s/n, ✆ 972 14 01 82.

Where To Ski

The six major ski installations east of Andorra are among Spain's most sophisticated and among the easiest to reach by public transport.

Vallter 2000, in Setcases near the French border, has 15 pistes, a slalom course, seven lifts and night illumination on some of the pistes, ✆ 972 74 05 77. There are five *hostales* in Setcases and four in nearby Camprodón. **Núria** has eight pistes—a couple over 4km long, and two teleskis. Besides the *hotel* at Núria (*see* above) there are many more down in Ribes, ✆ 972 73 03 26. **La Molina**, near the village of Plandas south of Puigcerdà, has 23 pistes (three very difficult), a 5km cross-country course, five jump ramps, and 20 lifts. There are 11 places to stay (four one-star) on the site, ✆ 972 89 20 31. **Masella**, also south and accessible from Puigcerdà, in Alp, is one of Spain's best, with a wide variety of pistes—88 altogether, and five hotels on the site, ✆ 972 89 01 06. **Rasos de Peguera**, Barcelona's favourite resort—125km from the big city—is further south, near Berga in Castellar del Riu-Montmajor. It has 14 pistes, two cross-country trails (5 and 10km) and five lifts. There are nine hotels in Berga; ✆ 972 821 13 08. **Port del Comte** is at La Coma, near Coll de Nargo to the west, with 31 pistes in excellent condition (four very difficult), a slalom, and four artificial slopes, two with grass for summer skiing. There are two hotels on the site; ✆ 972 811 09 50.

Andorra

The little **Principat de les Valles de Andorra** as it's officially known, is an independent historical oddity in the style of Grand Fenwick and the Marx Brothers' Fredonia, a little Catalan-speaking island of mountains measuring 468 square kilometres that has managed to steer clear of the French and Spanish since its foundation by Charlemagne. Its name is apparently a legacy of the Moors, derived from the Arabic Al-gandûra—'the wanton woman'—though unfortunately the story behind the name has been forgotten. Andorra has two 'co-princes', the President of France (as the heir of the Count of Foix) and the Bishop of La Seu d'Urgell in Catalunya. According to an agreement spelled out in 1278, in odd-numbered years the French co-prince is sent 1920 francs in tribute, while in even-numbered years, the Spanish co-prince receives 900 pesetas, twelve chickens, six hams and twelve cheeses. Napoleon thought it was quaint and left it alone, he said, as a living museum of feudalism.

Being Catalan, the Andorrans were always most adamant about preserving their local privileges, which they did through the **Consell de la Terra**, founded in 1419, one of Europe's oldest continuous parliaments. The citizens also claim to be the only people in the world who have avoided warfare for 800 years (surely a claim for 'small is beautiful'), though there was a close call in 1934, when a White Russian count proclaimed himself King Boris I of Andorra and declared war on the Bishop at Seu—a war the Bishop ended after two weeks by sending four Guardias Civils, who escorted King Boris to Barcelona and thence out of Spain.

Until the 1940s Andorra remained isolated from the world, relying on dairy-farming, tobacco-growing, printing stamps for collectors, and more than a little smuggling. This peaceful Ruritania began to change with the Spanish Civil War, with an influx of refugees and a new popular sport called downhill skiing. And then came the great revelation: why bother smuggling when you can get the consumer to come to you? For many Andorrans, it's simply been too much of a good thing; their traditional society, already swamped by emigrants (32,000 Spaniards and 4000 French and only 12,000 native Andorrans) has now all but disappeared under a wave of over 6 million visitors a year, most of whom are only passing through to purchase tax-free petrol, electronics gear, booze and American smokes, imported tax-free by Philip Morris and Reynolds, who ran the native tobacco growers out of business. In 1993, Andorra even gave up feudalism and voted for a constitution—although the co-princes still get their cash and cheese.

Outside the summer and peak ski seasons, however, Andorra slows down considerably; even in the summer a stout pair of walking shoes and a reasonable amount of energy can take you far away from the congestion, sophisticated sport complexes, highrise hotels and discos to some breathtaking scenery, a storybook land of green meadows and azure lakes, waterfalls and minute hamlets with stone houses drying tobacco on their south walls, clustered below Romanesque churches, with mountains towering overhead in all their grandeur, the silence broken only by the tinkling of cow bells.

Getting There

By air: There's a small airport near La Seu d'Urgell, 23km from Andorra la Vella, especially used by ski charters. The weather, however, is unpredictable, and there are plans for regular helicopter services between Barcelona, Andorra and Toulouse.

By train and bus: SNCF trains on the Toulouse–Perpignan–Barcelona line get as close as L'Hospitalet, with bus connections the rest of the way. Other buses to Andorra depart from Toulouse every morning and also from Ax-les-Thermes. From Perpignan you can catch the Villefranche train at 7.58am, which links up with the narrow-gauge *Petit Train Jaune* ('little yellow train') which passes through some awesome mountain scenery on its way to La-Tour-de-Carol, where a Pujol Huguet bus meets it at 1.35pm to go to Andorra, through the **Port d'Envalira**, at 2407m the highest pass in the Pyrenees.

Similarly, RENFE trains from Barcelona will get you to the French border at La-Tour-de-Carol where you can hook up with the Pujol Huguet bus, or you can take a bus direct from Barcelona to Andorra la Vella on the Alsina Graells bus line, © 93 265 68 66; there are two buses daily at 6.30am and 3pm. A mini-van taxi service also operates from Barcelona to Andorra, 4000 pts one way (call Andorra tourist office in Barcelona/Andorra for details).

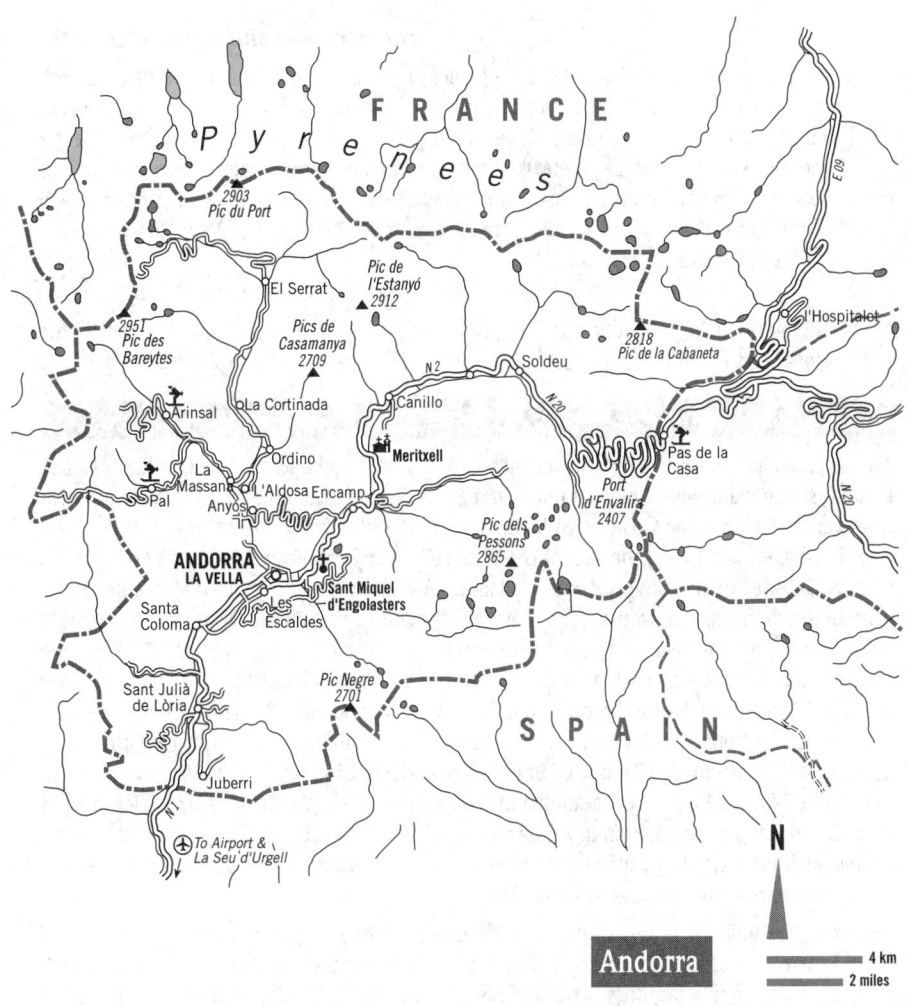

Andorra

▬▬▬	4 km
▬▬▬	2 miles

Tourist Information

Andorra la Vella: C/ Dr. Vilanova, ✆ (376) 82 02 14, ✉ (376) 82 58 23.

Andorra Tourist Office in Barcelona: C/Marià Cubí 159, ✆ 93 200 07 87, ✉ 93 414 18 63.

Andorra Delegation Tourist Office: 63 Westover Rd, London SW18, ✆ (0181) 874 4806.

The Syndicat d'Initiative sells a map of Andorra's campsites and mountain refuges (*refugios* and *cabanas*). Two trails (*sentiers de grande randonnée*) pass through Andorra: GR7 and GR75.

currency and shopping regulations

Although Catalan is the official language of Andorra, French and Spanish are well understood. French francs and Spanish pesetas are the currencies, and prices are always given in both (though if you plan to make some big purchases, you'll get a better exchange rate in pesetas). Entrance formalities are a breeze; the traffic tie-ups occur when you leave, and the Spanish and French police bring out their fine-toothed combs to make sure you're not carrying more than 300 cigarettes, five litres of wine, and a litre and a half of spirits.

telephone

If you're dialling an Andorran number from Spain, you must first dial 07, wait for the tone, and then dial the prefix ℡ 376– and the number.

Andorra la Vella

Andorra la Vella ('Europe's Highest Capital and duty-free shop') and the former villages of **Les Escaldes-Engordany** have melded into a vast arena of conspicuous consuming. Worth a visit, however, is the old stone **Casa de la Vall**, Calle de la Valle (*free guided tours Mon–Fri 10–1 and 3.30–6.30, Sat 10–1*), the seat of the Counsell de la Terra since 1580, and home of the famous **Cabinet of the Seven Keys**, containing Andorra's most precious documents, accessible only when representatives from each of the country's seven parishes are present. A folklore museum has been installed on the top floor. Andorra is famous for its Romanesque churches and bell-towers: a 40-minute walk south of Andorra la Vella will take you to the best one, the 11th-century **Santa Coloma**, with a unique, round bell-tower and Visigothic arches. A winding road from Escaldes (or ride on the *telecabina* from Encamp to the north) ascends to the isolated 11th-century **Chapel of Sant Miquel d'Engolasters**. Its fine frescoes, now in the Museu Nacional d'Art de Catalunya in Barcelona, have been replaced by copies, and its three-storey *campanile*, as often in Andorra, totally dwarfs the church. Beyond the chapel lies a forest and the pretty **Lago d'Engolasters** ('lake swallow-stars') where an old tradition states that all the stars in the universe will one day fall.

Exploring the hidden corners of old Andorra can be difficult if you're not walking or don't have a car to zigzag up the narrow mountain roads. Buses ply the two main roads through Andorra every couple of hours towards El Serrat, and more frequently towards Soldeu. **La Cortinada**, en route to Soldeu, is a good tranquil base, with only one very reasonably priced hotel, excellent scenery, and some of Andorra's oldest houses. In a 1967 restoration of its parish church, **Sant Martí**, some of the original Romanesque frescoes were uncovered. **El Serrat** is more touristy but worth a visit in the summer for the gorgeous panorama of snow-clad peaks from the **Abarstar de Arcalís** (via the ski resort). Another branch of the road from El Serrat leads to the three stunning mountain lakes of **Tristaina** in Andorra's loveliest and least developed northwestern corner, and site of its finest ski resort, Ordino-Arcalis.

Another destination reached by bus (on the Soldeu road) is **Meritxell**, the holy shrine of Andorra—an old Romanesque church standing in ruins since a devastating fire in 1972, and next to it, a new sanctuary housing a copy of the 11th-century Virgen de Meritxell, designed in 1976 by Barcelona's overrated superstar architect Ricardo Bofill. The Andorrans have their doubts about this gruesome hybrid of their traditional architecture with the modern, which may explain why the principality decided a few years ago against going ahead with a Bofill designed ski resort near Andorra la Vella. The lovely 12th-century church **Sant Joan de Caselles** is located on a hillside on the north edge of Canillo (the big village in these parts), its interior adorned with a Gothic *retablo*, painted wooden ceiling, and Romanesque paintings; the bell-tower has fine mullioned windows in the Lombard style.

Where to Ski

Andorra has abundant snow from December to April, combined with clear, sunny skies—a skier's heaven. It has six major installations: **Pas de la Casa-Grau Roig** (2050–2600m), just within the border with France, is the oldest (1952) and has 47 pistes, a slalom course, and several slopes for beginners as well as the advanced, night skiing, a medical centre; 29 lifts, four cafés and restaurants and 30 hotels; ✆ 80 10 60, ✉ 80 10 70. **Ordino Arcalís** (1940–2600m), near El Serrat, is perhaps the most dramatically beautiful and the best place to ski in Andorra. It has 24 pistes and 12 lifts, a medical centre, six cafés, restaurants and hotels in Ordino itself and more hotels in El Serrat; ✆ 85 01 21, ✉ 85 04 40. **Soldeu Tartar** (1710–2560m), near Canillo, is the biggest complex, with 28 slopes (some especially for children), 22 lifts, a 2km cross-country course, a surf park, a medical centre, two cafés and restaurants, 20 hotels and three self-catering apartment blocks; ✆ 85 11 51, ✉ 85 13 37, for piste condition ✆ 84 81 51. **Pal** (1780–2358m) near La Massana has 20 pistes and a slalom course in a splendid forest setting. Part-owned by the government, it is dedicated to preserving as much of the natural environment as possible. There are 14 lifts (two especially for the children's slopes); ✆ 83 62 36, ✉ 83 59 04. There are five cafés and restaurants, a medical centre, one hotel in Pal, and a number of others along the main road nearby. **Arinsal** (1550–2560m), next to the village of the same name, has 22 slopes, 14 lifts, a medical centre and six cafés and restaurants. There are four hotels in Arinsal and many others nearby; ✆ 83 62 36, ✉ 83 59 04. **La Rabassa**, near Sant Julià de Lòria, is a cross-country skiing station and features 15km of pistes through meadows and forests, separate pistes for snowmobiles, a children's snow park complete with snow slides, sleds and the like, a sports centre with pool, gym, sauna, etc. and horse-riding and guided ecology tours. There are rooms, a café and restaurant at the refuge which is approached by a good road. To book, call ✆ 84 41 50, ✉ 84 42 42, and for general information, call ✆ 84 34 52, ✉ 84 34 52. Note that Andorra's high altitude and even terrain make it especially good for ski trekking, or *ski randonnée*, with overnight accommodation in refuges around the rim of Andorra.

Sports and Activities

There are a number of sports complexes and facilities all over Andorra, providing an inescapable chance for holiday-fitness.

Andorra la Vella

Andorra's **sports complex**, ✆ 86 12 22, ✉ 86 45 64, is used for indoor sporting events and has a shiny multi-purpose court with stands for 5000 people. The **Mercure health centre**, Avda. Meritxel 58, ✆ 82 07 73, ✉ 82 85 52, is part of the Mercure hotel but is open to non-residents and offers saunas, swimming pool, tennis court, gym, solarium and, most usefully, pre-ski warm-up programmes and après-ski relaxation. **Serradells swimming pool**, Ctra. de la Comella, © 86 43 93, ● 86 77 99, is an Olympic size pool. *Open all year, from 7am–10pm in summer.* There is also a learning pool, gym, sauna, tennis courts and a snack bar.

Canillo

Palau de Gel, © 85 15 15, ● 85 15 65, is a giant skating-rink with the usual Andorran passion for lots of facilities: there is a swimmimg pool, gym, sauna, games room and much more, plus lessons for both ice-hockey and normal/'artistic' skating. There is even accommodation, but that's aimed at teams and pros.

Encamp

Encamp's **sports centre**, © 83 28 30, ● 83 20 04, has the usual facilities, plus some surprising ones, such as a library, exhibition hall, table-tennis, billiards, massage rooms, martial arts and a dance hall.

La Massana

In nearby Anyós the **sports centre**, © 83 64 63, ● 83 82 80, includes a shooting gallery, golf simulator, solarium, massage rooms, sunbeds, jacuzzis, Turkish baths and saunas as well as swimming pools, squash and tennis courts. *Open 8am–11pm.* A few kilometres north in L'Aldosa, the **sports complex**, © 83 72 75, ● 83 63 24, has both indoor and outdoor facilities along with its saunas, jacuzzis, vertical sunbed and an alarming sounding heart workout room. *Open from 10am–10pm.*

Sant Julià de Lòria

La Rabassa Shooting Range, © 84 37 47, ● 84 36 73, is a nice, new outfit with six semi-automatic posts, Olympic and universal pits, an armoured gun room and, comfortingly, a first-aid room. Archery is also available. Right in the centre of town is Sant Julià's **sports centre**, © 84 17 16, ● 84 47 16, which, along with the normal facilities, features an indoor climbing wall. Classes in everything from yoga to tae-kwondo and aerobics.

Escaldes-Engordany

A modern, mirrored, pyramidal structure houses **Caldea**, a hydrotherapy centre and spa near the centre of town at Parc de la Mola 10, © 80 09 99, ● 86 56 56. There are thermal water facilities, air baths, indoor and outdoor jacuzzies, hydromassage and many, many more watery things all within luxurious, aquatic surroundings.

Andorra ✉ *61699*   **Where to Stay**

Andorra now has some 300 hotels, the vast majority of them spanking new. In terms of glamour, the ★★★★**Roc Blanc**, Plaça de Co-Prínceps 5, Escaldes, © 87 14 00, ● 86 02 44 (*luxury*) takes the cake, with a five-storey atrium lobby and a glass elevator, sauna and a thermal spa with a number of treatment programmes offered, including two weeks of magne-totherapy to realign your electrons. The Roc Blanc's restaurant, **El Pi**, features a very good selection of French and Spanish dishes (*5000–6000* *pts/300 F)*. In Andorra la Vella, the ★★★★**Andorra Park**, 24 C/ de les Canals, ✆ 82 09 79, 🖂 82 09 83 is a charming little palace set in a park with a beautiful rockcut pool, croquet lawn, driving range and tennis court (*16,000 pts*). Its restaurant is one of the best in Andorra, with fresh pasta dishes and excellent Spanish and Chilean wines (*6000 pts*). The ultra-contemporary ★★★★★**Plaza**, María Pia 19, ✆ 86 44 44, 🖂 82 17 21 (*expensive*) is elegant and classy if right in the centre of the hubbub.

Moderate choices in Andorra la Vella are: ★★★**Pitiusa**, C/ d'Emprival 4, ✆ 86 18 16, 🖂 86 19 88, which is modern, central and quiet, on the edge of town; and ★★★**Xalet Sasplugas**, C/ La Creu Grossa 15, ✆ 82 03 11, 🖂 82 03 05, is even quieter and more traditional (around 10,000 pts). The newest of the new hotels in town is the well-equipped **Holiday Inn**, Prat de la Creu 88, ✆ 87 44 44, 🖂 87 44 45.

Cheaper choices include the ★★**Marfany**, Avda. Carlemany 99, ✆ 82 59 57, centrally located in **Escaldes**. It is long-established and comfortable, though only 24 of the 36 rooms have baths; the rest come with a shower (*5900 pts*). A good, clean hostal in Andorra la Vella is the Hostal del Sol, Plaça Guillemó, ✆ 82 37 01. Outside the capital hub there are numerous alternatives, which are especially convenient for skiers.

In La Cortinada, the simple La Cortinada, ✆ 85 01 51, is open all year and has a restaurant (*4500 pts*).

There are some eight year-round **campsites** dotted around Andorra and about half a dozen others that open only in the summer months. Most of the year round places have swimming pools and caravans or chalets to rent. In Andorra la Vella, the **Valira** campsite is at Avda. Salou, ✆ 82 23 84. There is another one near Santa Coloma: **Riberaygua**, Avda. d'Enclar 91, ✆ 83 66 99. Both have good facilities including electricity, restaurants, shops, plenty of shade and lots of hot water showers. The highest campsite is **Pla Naudi** at Canillo at 1600m, right beside the main road, ✆ 85 13 33, 🖂 85 12 80.

Eating Out

The better restaurants in Andorra tend to be French such as **La Bohême**, Av. Meritxell 1, 3rd floor, Andorra la Vella, ✆ 82 67 16, which serves fine fish and fowl dishes at 3000–4500 pts. Best known for its Gallic dishes is the **Molí dels Fanals**, C/ Dr Vilanova 9, ✆ 82 13 81 (*expensive*) in Andorra la Vella, located in an old mill with a garden terrace (*around 4000 pts*). *Closed Sun night and Mon.* Roast boar, apple pie and traditional French food are also served up at **Versailles**, on Cap. del Carrer 1, in Andorra la Vella, ✆ 82 13 31 (*4500 pts*). *Closed Sun and Mon lunch, 15 June–15 July.*

La Borda de l'Avi on the Arinsal road, ✆ 83 51 54, offers typical Andorran meals roasted in front of you on a wood fire (*4000 pts*). On the main road in Ordino is **Topic**, ✆ 83 76 50, which serves some 60 varieties of Belgian beer and a selection of fondues alongside a traditional menu for around 2500 pts. In Sant Julià de Lòria, the French restaurant **La Guingueta**, on the Rabassa road, ✆ 84 29 45, offers dishes like roast dove with foie gras and charcoal-grilled sea bass with cured ham in its rustic interior (*5000 pts*).

La Seu d'Urgell

Avda. Valira, ✆ 973 35 15 11.

La Seu d'Urgell, 9km south of Andorra and a good base for visiting the principality, is named after its cathedral (Seu), founded in the 8th century. Rebuilt in 1184 in the Lombard Romanesque style, it has a fine cloister, minus one gallery. The **Diocesan Museum**'s prize exhibit is an illuminated copy of Beatus de Liébana's 10th-century *Apocalypse* (*open Mon–Sat 10–1 and 4–6, Sun 10–1*; *Oct–May daily 11–1*). The rest of Seu isn't much, though there's some lovely scenery to the south through the **Garganta de Organyà**, a narrow, 600m walled gorge formed by the river Segre, now dammed up to form a long lake.

La Seu d'Urgell ✉ *25000*   ***Where to Stay and Eating Out***

In what's left of the town's old quarter in La Seu d'Urgell, there's the recently built ★★★**Parador Nacional de la Seu d'Urgell**, Sant Domènec 6, ✆ 973 35 20 00, ⏚973 35 23 09 (*expensive*) with a heated pool, and modern, air-conditioned, comfortable rooms and a worthy restaurant. All *paradores* are very good, but Seu's is topped by ★★★★**El Castell**, just outside town on the road to Lleida, located in an old castle, ✆ 973 35 07 04, ⏚ 973 35 15 74 (*expensive*). It has a pool and air conditioning as well as Seu's best restaurant, the very elegant *D'En Jaume*, with specialities like lobster tails in puff pastry as well as simple grilled meat dishes; delicious home-made ice cream tops the dessert list (*6500 pts*). *Closed 15 Jan–15 Feb.*

The small ★ **Andría**, Psg. Brudieu 24, ✆ 973 35 03 00/973 35 14 25 (*moderate*) is centrally located and offers comfortable rooms with bath. The **Habitaciones Europa**, Av. Valira 5, ✆ 973 35 18 56, lacklustre name aside, has clean, cheap rooms.

West of Andorra

The nearest RENFE station is in La Pobla de Segur, linked four times daily with the provincial capital of Lleida. From Pobla there are two buses to the Vall d'Aran; on the whole it's best to take one of the several direct buses from Lleida to Espot and the Vall d'Aran. There is also a direct bus to the Vall d'Aran from Barcelona at 8am from the main Estació de Nord terminal (10hrs). Transport into the Vall de Boí is plagued with uncertainties; it's best if you can drive.

Vielha: C/ Sarriulera 6, ✆ 973 64 01 10.

Parc Nacional de Aigüestortes and the Vall de Boí

For beautiful mountain scenery without the tax-free merchandise, head west to the heart of the Pyrenees and the **Parc Nacional de Aigüestortes i Estany de Sant Maurici**, created in 1955 and encompassing 230 sq km of forests, meadows, lakes and jagged snow-capped peaks,

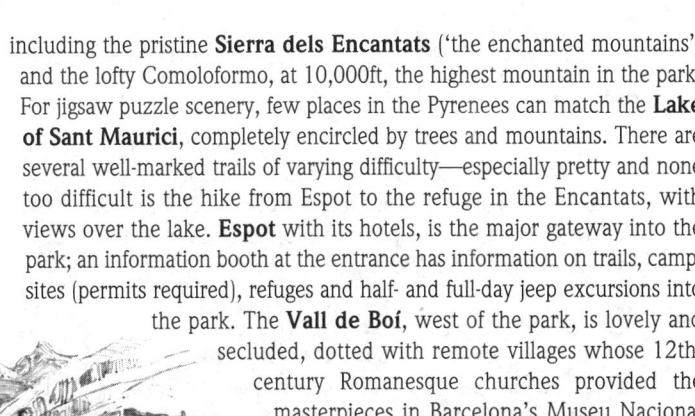

including the pristine **Sierra dels Encantats** ('the enchanted mountains') and the lofty Comoloformo, at 10,000ft, the highest mountain in the park. For jigsaw puzzle scenery, few places in the Pyrenees can match the **Lake of Sant Maurici**, completely encircled by trees and mountains. There are several well-marked trails of varying difficulty—especially pretty and none too difficult is the hike from Espot to the refuge in the Encantats, with views over the lake. **Espot** with its hotels, is the major gateway into the park; an information booth at the entrance has information on trails, campsites (permits required), refuges and half- and full-day jeep excursions into the park. The **Vall de Boí**, west of the park, is lovely and secluded, dotted with remote villages whose 12th-century Romanesque churches provided the masterpieces in Barcelona's Museu Nacional d'Art de Catalunya. Recently the exteriors of these slate-roofed churches and their stout square *campaniles* with storeys of mullioned windows (a style imported from Lombardy) have been restored, with replicas of their frescoes. Four of the best are within walking distance of Boí: **Sant Joan de Boí**, **Santa Eulàlia** with a six-storey tower in **Erill-la-Vall**, the curious **Santa María de Taüll** with its leaning tower, and best of all **Sant Climent de Taüll**, with its six-storey bell-tower and the most beautiful fresco copies. The western entrance to Aigüestortes park is through the spa **Caldes de Boí**, the most developed village in the quiet valley.

The Vall d'Aran

North of the park and the Vall de Boí, the western and eastern Pyrenean massifs join in a rugged embrace, enfolding the verdant 48km long **Vall d'Aran**. Almost inaccessible, it was first linked by road with the outside world in 1924, an aesthetic tragedy that has brought it thousands of massive electric pylons. For most of its history the valley was in practice independent, like Andorra, until Napoleon annexed it to France; it became officially part of Spain a few years later. Some of the older inhabitants still speak *Aranés*, a dialect not of Catalan, but of Gascon.

The valley's rubble houses are also unique, with their stepped gables, dormers, slate roofs, and carved wooden balconies. Many of them may be seen in **Vielha**, principal village of the upper valley (or Mijaran), all gathered in the shadow of its giant Romanesque-Gothic church and its octagonal tower. The inside is worth a look, especially for its dashing, 12th-century *Christ de Mijaran* that originally belonged to the once mighty monastery of Mitg-Arán. Of the monastery only a chapel remains, across the new-born river Garona, which swells into the great Garonne and flows into the Atlantic at Bordeaux. A mysterious monolith near the chapel suggests the site has long been sacred.

Besides trails and ski slopes, the Vall d'Aran has a number of other traditional villages and beautiful Romanesque churches, like the pretty hamlet of **Salardú** and the rustic village of **València d'Aneu**.

Espot ✉ 25597

In Espot there are four modest *hostales*: the ★**Roya**, Sant Maurici 1, ✆ 973 62 40 40, is a good bet, *open all year*, in a scenic location, and there's an adequate restaurant. Try also the **Sant Maurici**, Afores s/n ✆ 973 62 40 61, which, though both the smallest and cheapest place in town, has decent rooms, all very clean.

Boí ✉ 25528

In Boí, there's the moderately priced ★**Beneria**, on the Plaça Trayo, ✆ 973 69 60 30, a pleasant enough lodging open all year, and one of Boí's few restaurants (*2800 pts*) for simple but filling meals. Boí's best budget accommodation is probably at ★**Hostal Pascual,** by the bridge below the village, ✆ 973 69 60 14, which is *open all year* and always gives a warm welcome. The restaurant serves decent food.

A good place to eat is the cheap and delicious **Casa Higinio**, on the road to Taüll, ✆ 973 69 60 39. The grilled meats are worth trying; about *2500 pts* for a full meal. Nearby in Taüll, **Restaurante La Coma**, ✆ 973 69 60 25, has a very good reputation (*moderate*).

Vielha ✉ 25530

In Vielha there's a fortress of a *parador*, the ★★★**Parador de Valle de Arán** on N230 tunnel road, ✆ 973 64 01 00, ✆ 973 64 11 00, prettily located on a mountainside in a dense forest. It has a pool and a good restaurant serving Aranese specialities. Other moderately priced accommodation in Vielha includes the small ★★**Delavall,** Eth Pas d'Arro 40, ✆ 973 64 02 00, located near the centre of town. *Open all year.* The ★**Urogallo,** Av. Castiero 7, ✆ 973 64 00 00, is a bit bigger with rooms that cost a lot less, and a restaurant that serves standard, local fare. For cheaper quarters, you can try your luck at ★**De Miguel**, Plaça San Antoni, ✆ 973 64 00 63, where the rooms come without bath, or the tiny, four room, Busquets, Major 9, ✆ 973 54 02 38.

Vielha has a selection of restaurants, none of which are truly exceptional; Nicolàs, Castèth 10, ✆ 973 64 18 20, is noted for providing good value for money, while Era Mola, Marrec 8, ✆ 973 64 24 19, serves Aranese specialties, such as the olla Aranesa, a meat and vegetable stew. In the nearby village of **Escanyau**, you can indulge in hearty Aranese dishes at the **Casa Turnay**, ✆ 973 64 02 92, in the Plaça Major for 3000 pts; one of the Vall d'Aran's best restaurants. *Closed May–July.*

Salardú ✉ 25598

In **Arties** (near Salardú), there's the more intimate ★★★★**Parador Don Gaspar de Portolá**, Ctra. de Baqueira, ✆ 973 64 08 01, ✆ 973 64 10 01 (*expensive*) located in one of the more charming corners of the Vall d'Aran and close to the skiing at Baqueira-Beret. Also in Arties there's the very pleasant ★★★**Valartiés** II, Major 3, ✆ 973 64 43 64, ✆ 973 64 21 74 (*expensive*), especially cosy in the winter, with its fireplaces. *Closed May and Nov.* It also has a very fine restaurant, **Casa Irene**, ✆ 973 64 09 00, featuring dishes like duck with truffles for *4000–5000 pts.*

Baqueira-Beret, a clutch of ugly ski apartments just above Vielha, is one of Spain's most modern installations. It overlooks the Vall d'Aran and boasts 41 pistes (three very difficult), 19 lifts, two slalom courses, and a helicopter service to the peaks for new thrills. There are five hotels on the site; © 973 64 50 25, or in Barcelona, © 93 318 27 76. **Tuca-Betran** is also easily accessible from Vielha, offering a wide diversity of pistes (18 altogether, six very difficult), served by nine lifts. There is one four-star hotel at the station; © 973 64 08 55. **Super Espot**, near Aigüestortes National Park, offers 10 pistes (two very difficult), four lifts, and modest lodgings in the town of Espot; © 973 62 40 13. **Sant Joan de L'Erm** is 20km west of La Seu d'Urgell at Montferrer Castellbo, and concentrates on cross-country (Nordic) skiing with some very pretty courses; © 973 29 80 15.

Into the Flatlands: West of Barcelona to Lleida

Getting Around

By train: Lleida, Bellpuig, and Cervera are linked by most trains between Barcelona and Madrid. The RENFE station in Lleida is on Avda. Francesca Macià and Rambla Ferran.

By bus: Buses from the Pyrenees usually terminate in Lleida; the bus station is on the Avda. de Blondel.

Tourist Information

Lleida: Av. Madrid 36, © 973 27 09 97, 973 27 09 49.

Cervera and Bellpuig

In the Middle Ages Lleida was famous for its university but, like Barcelona's, it was closed by a vengeful Felipe V, who combined the two institutions to create a third, Bourbon university in between the two at **Cervera**. This lasted until 1841, when the university returned to Barcelona, leaving behind a monumental university ghost town, now partly used as a cultural centre. Besides the strange forlorn buildings, there are three churches worth a visit: **Sant Domènch** for its cloister, the Romanesque **Santa María** with fine Catalan artwork, and the mysterious round **Sant Pere le Gros** (1079), thought to have served as a funerary chapel/pilgrim initiatory temple. The environs of Cervera are dotted with seldom-visited medieval hamlets, like **Biosca**, **Olujas** and, an hour's walk from Olujas, **Montfalcó Murrallat**, with a baker's dozen houses encompassed by a vast wall and a ruined Moorish castle.

Bellpuig contains in its parish church the marvellous Italian Renaissance marble tomb of Ramón Folch de Cardona, Viceroy of Sicily, by Giovanni di Nola. Ramón's armoured effigy rests its head on a helmet, while the sarcophagus is decorated with a robust pagan scene.

Lleida/Lérida

Lleida, or Lérida on Castilian maps, lies along the river Segre in the midst of Catalunya's most extensive plain, or *huerta*. Its Celtic founders called it *Illizurda*, and against the Carthaginians they fought perhaps the first of many battles that scar the city's history. During one war—the

Spanish Succession—the defenders saw fit to convert the magnificent cathedral, **La Seu Vella**, into a barracks, leaving the town to build a new, far less imposing edifice in the town below.

La Seu Vella (*open Tues–Sat 9.30–1.30 and 3–6.30, till 5.30 in winter, Sun 9.30–1.30; adm*) is mightily positioned, within the walls of the Moorish-built fortress, **La Zuda**. Begun with Templar assistance in 1203, it is a prime example of the Transitional style from Romanesque to Gothic, with a colossal octagonal tower and a 14th-century Mozarabic portal to the south called *dels Fillols*, 'of the Children'. Major restoration work, begun in the 1940s, revealed a lovely Romanesque-Gothic **cloister** of exceptional grace, its twelve arches woven with stone tracery like snowflakes; no two are alike. Its unusual position, in front of the church, recalls the patio of the mosque that once stood here. The nave looks almost brand new after its restoration; note the lingering Moorish influence in the carved capitals.

The rest of Lleida isn't much. On Carrer Major you'll find the dull new Cathedral, across from the **Hospital de Santa María** (1512) built around an elegant 15th-century patio, and, just off Carrer Major, the 13th-century **Paheria**, or town hall, with a museum of local history; it conserves a rare 11th-century Catalan codex of laws, *Les Constitucions* (*open 10–2 and 6–8, closed Sat and Sun*). Just to the southwest is the **Castel de Gardeny**, seat of the first territory granted the Knights Templar in Spain (1149), with a Romanesque chapel of Santa María.

Where to Stay and Eating Out

expensive

You can have four-star splendour at three-star prices at Lleida's **Comtes de Urgel**, Avda. de Barcelona 17, © 973 21 23 00, @ 973 20 24 04. It has an equally splendid restaurant, **El Sauce** (*moderate*). **Hotel Pirineos**, Gran Passeig de Ronda 63, © 973 27 31 99, @ 973 26 20 43 (*12,000 pts*), has rooms at around the same prices and is also comfortable.

moderate

Near the centre of Lleida there's the fairly large and pleasant ★**Hotel Ramón Berenguer IV**, Plaça Ramón Berenguer IV 3, © 973 23 73 45. There's a good collection of *pensiones*, too—**Mundial**, Plaça Sant Joan 4, © 973 24 27 00, is fairly typical at *4000 pts* for a decent double. Near the bus station there's the adequate ★**Rexi**, Avda. de Blondel 56, © 973 27 07 00. The rooms are nothing special, but the showers are good and hot. Another good bet is the smallish Santiago, Alcalde Costa 15, © 973 26 97 95.

cheap

Caribe, Anselm Clavé 20, © 973 24 35 84, has rooms with or without showers.

Eating Out

Lleida is fortunate to be blessed with one of Catalunya's best restaurants, the **Forn del Nastasi** on Salmerón 10, © 973 23 45 10 which offers an extensive four-part menu including very good seafood, charcoal grills, and house specialities (*5000–6000 pts*). *Closed Sun nights and Mon as well as the first two weeks of August.* Also good is **La Huerta**, next to the market just below La Seu Vella, © 973 24 24 13 (*moderate*), specializing in provincial dishes and using local ingredients (*3000 pts*).

La Mercè, Avda. Navarra 1, ☎ 973 24 84 41 (*moderate*) has a very good reputation. You can find a cheaper meal at the friendly **Casa Lluís**, Plaça de Ramón Berenguer IV 8, ☎ 973 24 00 26. *Closed Sunday nights and Mondays.*

Tarragona

Tarragona, 'the Balcony of the Mediterranean', is one of Spain's oldest cities and one of the best situated, a mighty rampart of a town 60m above the sea. The Iberians fortified it so well that many of the later Roman and medieval buildings, as if shedding old skins, rise from bases of their huge, rough-hewn blocks. The Romans were quite fond of Tarraco, as they called it, and lavished on it the entire province of Tarraconensis, or Hispania Citerior. Over the years, they made it the most elegant city on the Iberian peninsula; the poets Martial and Pliny praised its superb climate, fertile fields and delicious wines. Augustus relaxed here after his 26 BC campaign in the north of Spain. By the 2nd century AD it had 30,000 inhabitants.

A well known legend has St Paul preaching in Tarragona. The Visigoths made it one of Spain's leading bishoprics in the 5th century; St Hermenegild, a prince of the Visigoths who converted to Catholicism, led the city in a revolt against the Arian heresies of his father King Leovigild, who had him martyred. During Moorish rule, Tarragona is said to have been almost entirely Jewish, to the extent that when it was retaken by Ramón Berenguer IV, the new cathedral was built by Jewish architects. After peaking in the 14th century, the city declined into a backwater. Modern Tarragona has spread far beyond the walled enclosure on the hill; it owes its revival to wine and the growing popularity of the Costa Daurada.

Getting Around

By train: Tarragona is frequently linked with Barcelona and Valencia by rail, as well as with Madrid, Zaragoza and Lleida, several times a day. The RENFE station is just below the Balcó del Mediterrani.

By bus: Rambla Nova 40. Buses depart from the vicinity of the Plaça Ponent, near the Municipal Forum. For the Aqueduct, take the El Salvador bus (every 20 minutes from Prat de La Riba). Nearly any bus going up the coast will let you off at Tamarit Castle and beach.

Tourist Information

Provincial office: Carrer de Fortuny 4, ☎ 977 23 34 15.

Municipal: C/ Mayor 39, ☎ 977 24 50 64.

In the summer, there are information booths in the Plaça Imperial Tarraco, Portal del Roser, and Paseig de Sant Antoni.

Upper Tarragona

Like Barcelona, Tarragona's main promenades are called the Ramblas—the Old (*vella*) and the New (*nova*). The **Rambla Nova**, decorated with *modernista* buildings, divides old Tarragona from the new and begins at the **Balcó del Mediterrani**, its famous 320ft-high balcony overlooking the sea and Tarragona's beautiful beach. Looking the other way is a statue of King Pedro III's great admiral-privateer Roger of Llauria, who conquered Sicily for the crown of Aragón. Below the Balcó, in a garden setting, are the ruins of the **Roman Amphitheatre** and, in the ruined 12th-century **Santa María del Miracle**, traces of a 6th-century Visigothic church built to commemorate Fructuosus, Augurius and Eulogius, who were martyred here on a pyre. Continuing up and around the Balcó, the Plaça del Rei and the lst-century BC **Praetorium** are up to the left (*open June–Sept Tues–Sat 10–8; Oct–May Tues–Sat 10–5.30; Sun all year 10–3; adm 400 pts, including the two museums*). Popularly called the Castle of Pilate—like Sevilla, Tarragona likes to claim Pontius Pilate—the Praetorium was really the one-time residence of Augustus and Hadrian, and later the Kings of Aragón. The French destroyed a good part of it, but left the tower that has been opened as the **Museu d'Historia de Tarragona**, devoted to the urban evolution of the city. Next to the Praetorium, the **Museu Arqueològic** (*same opening hours*) has an especially fine array of Roman mosaics, including a famous one of Medusa, a terracotta mask that looks like the Roman Kilroy, an erotic oil lamp and more.

What remains of Tarragona's **Jewish quarter** is near the museum, in the picturesque narrow arched lanes around the Plaçet Angels, where the synagogue once stood. Beyond this is the Plaça del Forum and the remains of the northeast corner of the tremendous (200 by 300m) Roman **Provincial Forum**. This square gives on to the lovely 14th-century arcaded **Carrer Merceria**; where it intersects with the Carrer Major, the city has restored the fine, 17th-century **Casa Consistorial** as a museum and information office.

The Cathedral

Open July–Oct Mon–Sat 10–7; March–June and Oct–Nov Mon–Sat 10–12.30 and 4–7; Nov–March Mon–Sat 10–2.

A stairway from the Carrer Major ascends to Tarragona's cathedral, a masterpiece of the Transitional style, begun in the 12th century and completed in the 15th. The principal façade, shut in by the surrounding streets and lacking the pinnacles planned for it, presents a mastodontic aspect, compensated for by a magnificent rose window and fine 13th-century statues of saints, bishops and martyrs. More than the other great Catalan cathedrals, Tarragona has preserved its mystical gloom—which makes it difficult to see the magnificent marble *Retablo de Santa Tecla* in the Capilla Mayor, a 1430 work by Pere Johan honouring Tarragona's patron saint, a convert of St Paul. Near the predella the details become increasingly minute and include tiny spiders and butterflies, as fine as filigree. There's a 16th-century organ, and the 14th-century **Chapel of Santa María de los Sastres** (of the tailors), a humble profession in the Middle Ages, but wealthy enough here to have endowed the Cathedral's finest chapel. Next to it, a door leads into the enormous **Cloister**, decorated with 12th-century sculpture that alone is worth the trip to Tarragona. Moorish influences are evident in the geometric panels that fill the spaces below the arches; on the west side there's even a niche resembling a *mihrab* dated 960. The scenes over the door are especially robust and, among the fanciful capitals, don't miss the one just to the right as you enter, depicting two scenes from the medieval fable of the clever cat who feigns death to outsmart the cautious mice hiding in the rafters. The jubilant mice descend to put puss on a bier for the funeral, only to face an unexpected feline resurrection. The highlight of the **Museu Diocesano** off the cloister (*open Mon–Sat 1–7*) is a 15th-century tapestry of medieval life, *La Bona Vida*.

To the Passeig Arqueològic

From Carrer Major, take a left turn on to the aristocratic Carrer Cavallers. At No.14, the Gothic **Casa Castellarnau** (*open June–Sept Tues–Sat 10–8; Oct–May Tues–Sat 10–5.30;*

Sun all year 10–3; adm) has been restored and opened as a museum; as in the seignorial palaces in Barcelona, the courtyard and stair are especially fine. Near the end of Carrer Cavallers is the picturesque **Plaça del Pallol**, where Gothic buildings were built over ruins of the huge Provincial Forum. In the walls, the **Portal del Roser** is one of six megalithic gates; note the double axes and Iberian letters (ancient masons' marks?) carved into the Cyclopean blocks. Beyond the Portal del Roser begins the **Passeig Arqueològic** (*open 10–1.30 and 4.30–6.30, summer 10–8)*, the other star attraction of Tarragona, where through a manicured garden you can get the best view of the walls—rugged Iberian blocks at their base, tidy Roman stone added by the Scipios on top, surrounded by walls put up by the English during the War of the Spanish Succession. The best part of the Passeig is near the **Minerva Tower**, where a bronze statue of Augustus, donated by the Italians in 1936, looks on authoritatively.

Lower Tarragona

Near the Rambla Vella (at the end of Vía de L'Imperi Romà) the **Plaça de la Font** occupies much of the ancient circus; in the houses on surrounding streets big pieces of it are embedded in the walls. On the other side of the Rambla Nova (take Carrer Canyelles down to Lleida) are the columns and foundations of Roman Tarraco's smaller, porticoed **Municipal Forum**, where city business was transacted (*open April–Sept Tues–Sat 10–8, Sun 10–3; Oct–March Tues–Sat 10–5.30, Sun 10–3; adm)*. Further down, on the banks of the river Francolí (from the Rambla Nova take the Avinguda Ramón i Cajal) a huge **Roman-Palaeo-Christian Necropolis** was unearthed during the construction of a tobacco factory. Used between the 3rd to 5th centuries, the necropolis is the richest yet discovered in Spain, producing a large number of funerary monuments and mosaics, from the pagan Romans to the Visigoths. A couple of interesting crypts remain *in situ*, while the best artefacts are in the adjacent **Palaeo-Christian Museum** (*open June–Sept Tues–Sat 10.30–2 and 4.–7, Sun 10–2; rest of the year Tues–Sat 10–1.30 and 4–7, Sun 10–2; adm)*. Note the strange Lions' Sarcophagus, an ivory doll from the 4th century, and the mosaic of Optimus. Tarragona has one of the finest beaches of the Costa Daurada, the **Platja del Miracle**, and another good one that's usually less crowded at **La Rabassada**, 1.6km to the north. Tarragona's lively fishermen's quarter, **El Serrallo**, a 20-minute walk from the Rambla Nova is the place to go for good seafood and tapas.

The Roman Environs of Tarragona

Spain's finest Palaeo-Christian monument, however, is 5km from Tarragona, just beyond Constanti in a vineyard in Centcelles: the **Mausoleo Romano de Centcelles** (*open Tues–Sat 10–2 and 4–6, Sun 10–2)*. In the 4th century, a substantial Roman villa was converted into a basilica dedicated to St Bartholomew. Also north of Tarragona, just off the main road to Valls in the village of El Salvador, are the remains of a two-tiered 123m-high Roman aqueduct called **Les Ferreres**, a graceful golden beauty that supplied the ancient city with water from the Gayà River.

Up the coast along the ancient **Vía Augusta** are three other Roman monuments. At 6km stands the impressive 9.2m **Torre de los Escipiones**, thought to be a funerary monument to the two famous Scipio brothers, Publius and Gnaeus, who died fighting the Carthaginians in 212 BC; the figures in relief represent military deities. At 8km a monolith marks the centre of the Roman stone quarry, the **Cántara del Médol**. At 20km the **Arco de Barà**, a triumphal arch, spans the ancient road, erected for some forgotten victory in the 2nd century.

Tarragona's hotels fill up quickly in the summer, so book or start searching early in the day—or make a day-trip from Barcelona.

expensive

★★★★**Imperial Tarraco**, Rambla Vella 2, ✆ 977 23 30 40, 📠 977 21 65 66, is Tarragona's finest hotel, pleasantly located in the old town, but offering such amenities as a pool and air conditioning throughout. *Open all year with a considerable off-season discount.*

moderate

★★★Astari, Vía Augusta 95, ✆ 977 23 69 00, 📠 977 23 69 11, is near the sea and in the style of a typical resort—with a pool, tennis, garden and terraces, and rooms with balconies. ★Residencia España, Rambla Nova 49, ✆ 977 23 27 12, has very nice modern rooms on Tarragona's favourite promenade.

inexpensive–cheap

A good place to look for the cheapest *fondas* and *hostales* is Plaça de la Font or Rambla Vella. Try the Forum, Plaça de la Font 37, ✆ 977 23 17 18. If you want to be near the beach there are a few *inexpensive* choices like ★**El Callejón**, Vía Augusta 213, ✆ 977 23 63 80, *open June–Oct*, or **El Torreón**, on the same street, ✆ 977 20 77 65. Even cheaper is **Pensión Mar i Flor**, C/ Gral. Contreras 29, ✆ 977 23 82 31, near the train station, which has large modern rooms and friendly service.

Eating Out

The area's most famous restaurant, **Sol Ric** (*expensive*) is a 20-minute walk from the Rambla Nova, on Vía Augusta 227, ✆ 977 23 20 32. Seafood is the speciality, from the simple to the elaborate—for something different, try a dish with spicy *Romesco* sauce (a mixture of peppers, almonds or hazelnuts, garlic and Priorato). Sol Ric has a comprehensive wine list and outdoor dining in a lovely garden in the summer (*4000 pts*). *Closed Sun eve and Mon.* The **Merlot**, Cavallers 6, ✆ 977 22 06 52, blends French and Mediterranean cuisines. For more variety—and lower prices—spend an evening in the bars in El Serallo: **La Suda** and **La Áncora** both make excellent seafood *tapas*. One of the better known and more inspired restaurants of the district is the **Club Nàutic**, Serallo s/n, ✆ 977 24 00 68, again featuring excellent seafood for *3500 pts*.

For typical southern Catalan dishes, head 1km out of town to Larga beach and **El Trull**, Ctra. Barcelona Km 255, ✆ 977 23 55 38, in a converted old Catalan house, where, surprisingly enough, fish doesn't make an appearance on the menu (*3000 pts*). If it's seafood you're after, try **Cal Marti**, ✆ 977 21 23 84 (*moderate*), or **Cal Brut**, ✆ 977 21 04 05 (*moderate*), both on Sant Pere down in the harbour. Two good land-food haunts are just off the Rambla Nova: **Les Coques** (*closed Sun*), on C/ Baixada del Patriarca 2, ✆ 977 22 83 00, with Catalan specialities like rabbit *à la Catalã* for *3000 pts*; and the less expensive **Pizzeria Cal Faune** (*cheap*), C/ Girona 11, with a good curry (and other) pizzas as well as omelettes, pasta, and a long dessert menu. You also have several Chinese restaurants to choose from.

Getting Around

By train: The six trains a day between Lleida and Tarragona/Barcelona stop at L'Espluga de Francolí, Montblanc and Valls; another train, three times a day, goes to Falset and Móra la Nova (for Miravet, Gandesa and El Pinell), on the route between Tarragona and Zaragoza.

By bus: The bus from Tarragona (departs at 12 noon from the Plaça Fomet) stops at Poblet and returns at 5. Other destinations are served by provincial buses out of Tarragona; the tourist office has schedules.

Tourist Information

L'Espluga de Francolí: Torres Jordi 16, ✆ 977 74 04 56.
Montblanc: Hortalans 4, ✆ 977 86 22 91.
Vilafranca del Penedés: Cort 14, ✆ 93 892 03 58.
Valls: Plaça del Blat 1, ✆ 977 60 10 50.

Reus

One of the liveliest towns in the province, Reus is especially rich in beautiful *modernista* buildings, thanks to the mayor who invited Domènech i Montaner to build several structures in town, like the 1901 **Casa Navàs** in the central Plaça del Mercadal, with a façade decorated by Gaudí's cousin and a beautifully preserved interior lavish with floral motifs. In the outskirts he also built, as a prelude to his great Hospital de Sant Pau in Barcelona, Reus' **Institut Pere Mata** (1897–1912), a psychiatric hospital, richly decorated with blue and white ceramics.

The Cava of Penedés

Tarragona province encompasses three of Spain's finest wine-growing areas: Tarragones, El Priorat, and Penedés. Penedés is famed for its white wines and *cavas* (Spanish champagnes); one town, **Sant Sandurí de Noia**, is the Jerez of *cava*, packed with *bodegas* full of the bubbly and sprinkled with *modernista* buildings. Two of these, **Caves Freixenet** (1920s) C/ Joan Sala 2, ✆ 93 891 70 00 and **Caves Codorniu**, Avda. Codorniu, ✆ 93 818 32 32, welcome visitors who just drop in. The Codorniu cellars, said to be the world's largest producer of sparkling wines, are in a superb *modernista* cathedral of parabolic arches by Puig i Cadafalch (1896–1906) built over a labyrinth of 16km of cellars. Another important town in the region, **Vilafranca de Penedés**, also has numerous *modernista* works. It is the home base of Spain's greatest winemaking family, the Torres, and has a wine museum, the **Museu del Vi**—just one of six specialized museums in Plaça Jaume I, housed in a 12th-century palace (*all six open 10–2 and 4–7, Sun 10–2; June–Sept, Tues–Sat 9–9, closed Mon*); others include art, geology, ornithology and archaeology. Items in the last come from the Ibero-Roman-medieval ruins of **Olèrdola**, surrounded by 2nd-century BC walls and only a short walk from Vilafranca.

El Priorat

El Priorat is red-wine country, producing some of the world's most potent vintages—up to 24 per cent proof. These formidable vineyards were first cultivated by the monks at the Carthusian priory **Scala Dei**, in the heart of the region. It never recovered after the dissolution of the monasteries in 1831 and has been gracefully falling apart ever since. **Falset**, the modern capital of El Priorat, has, like so many of the region's villages, a lovely *bodega* done in the *modernista* style by a disciple of Gaudí, César Martinell (1888–1973); Falset's **Bodega Cooperativa** dates from 1919. Other *bodegas* by Martinell, all worth seeing not only for their architecture but for the chance of buying some wine, include those at **Rocafort de Queralt** (with an interior reminiscent of the Sagrada Família), **Sarral**, **Barbara de la Conca** (which also has a good Templar castle), and **Montblanc** (*see* below). Two of the finest are across the Ebro in the Terra Alta wine district: the **Cooperative Agricola**, a fascinating play of parabolic brick arches and vaults, in **Gandesa**, and in cliff-top **El Pinell de Brai**, Martinell's masterpiece **Celler del Sindicat Agricola** (1922) adorned with an *azulejo* frieze of the grape harvest and drunken hunters by jovial Xavier Nogués. Another *modernista*, Pere Domènech, built the *bodega* in **L'Espluga de Francolí**.

Poblet

From medieval L'Espluga de Francolí, it's a lovely 40-minute walk to the famous Cistercian **Monastery of Santa María de Poblet**, founded by Ramón Berenguer IV in 1151 to commemorate the end of the Reconquista in Catalunya. Poblet was for centuries the principality's most powerful and privileged monastery. Openly dissipated and corrupt in later years, Poblet was so despised that when the monks were suspected of harbouring Carlist sympathies in 1835, the locals had the excuse they needed to avenge centuries of maltreatment. In their fury they wrenched apart the buildings and fed its famous library to the flames. The ruins of Poblet stood overgrown with wild flowers until the 1940s, when a band of Italian Cistercians reclaimed the monastery and beautifully restored it. They offer guided tours (*daily 10–12.30 and 3–6*). Within the castle-like walls you can see the huge **wine cellar**, befitting a worldly monastery; a lovely, evocative **cloister** in the late Romanesque style; the fine Gothic **Chapter House**; the **Dormitory**; the Refectory and **Kitchen**. Poblet was 'Catalunya's Escorial' for its many **tombs of the kings of Aragón**, wonderfully restored by sculptor-collector Frederic Marés (*see* 'Barcelona', p.76). Among those interred in the great cathedral-like church are Alfonso I el Batallador (d. 1134) and Jaume I 'the Conqueror' (d. 1276).

Montblanc

Near Poblet and L'Espluga de Francolí, Montblanc is an enchanting medieval village with well-preserved 14th-century walls and a river spanned by a Gothic bridge. At the main gate a map points out the sites; the best are the Catalan Gothic parish church **Santa María**, with a Plateresque façade, and the Romanesque **Sant Miquel**; between the two stood Montblanc's Jewish quarter. Like Tarragona itself, its province had a majority Jewish and Morisco population in the early Middle Ages.

South on Montblanc's Carrer Major, just outside the town walls, stands the ruined **Convent of Sant Francesc**, with a large 14th-century church until recently used as a winemaker's warehouse. Yet this monastery produced one of Catalunya's medieval geniuses, Ansèlm Turmeda (1352–1425), who as a young friar left his Order, moved to Tunis, and converted to Islam with a new name: 'Abdallah at-Tarjuman al-Mayurqí—'the Mallorcan interpreter'. Like Catalunya's greatest mystic, Ramon Llull, Turmeda was a native of Mallorca, and like Llull was greatly attracted by the Islamic and Sufic thought that lingered in Spain with the Moriscos. Turmeda took Llull's 'heresies' a step further by actually converting, but his books commanded such respect (among them, *La Tuhfa* in Arabic, *The Dispute with an Ass* in Catalan, and a book of moral parables called *El Fransèlm*, long-used as a text in Catalan schools) that the Church refrained from condemning him, and instead tried very hard to earn propaganda points by luring him back to the fold. It failed, and Abdallah died a good Muslim and was buried in a holy tomb in Tunis, where he is worshipped as a Sufi saint.

Prades

Between Poblet and Scala Dei is Prades, another fine, walled medieval town in the mountains. In the centre, in the pretty, arcaded **Plaça Major**, stands the unusual spherical **Fountain of Prades** (if it gives a *frisson* of *déjà vu*, you've seen a copy in Barcelona's Poble Espanyol). The source of the fountain is unknown, but it has never in known memory run dry. **Siurana de Prades**, on the road to Cornudell, is even more romantic, with its Arab castle perched atop a cliff known as 'the Balcony of El Priorat', ancient stone-built houses, and a primitive Romanesque chapel down by the river gorge. The castle was the Moors' last stronghold in Catalunya, where they held out until 1153. A third important monastery in the province is nearby: **Santes Creus**, anciently walled and of elegant proportions. Like Poblet it was founded by Ramón Berenguer IV, in 1158, devastated in 1835, and since carefully restored. Particularly lovely is the **church**, completed in 1221 and containing the tombs of all the notables not buried in Poblet, including Pedro III (d. 1285).

Valls

Valls is famous through Catalunya for the daring and skill of its *castellers* (human towers), and its club, the Xiquets de Valls, is so good that the town erected a monument, depicting the *castellers* all piled up on top of each other. A good time to see the real thing is at the city's midsummer festival in June or during the *Firagost* (the first part of August, when local farmers offer their best produce and flowers to Mother Earth). The most interesting streets in Valls belong to its **Call**, the Jewish quarter, still reached via its medieval arch and still well preserved; also worth a look are the Gothic **Sant Joan Baptista** and the **Chapel des Roser**, with a 17th-century portrayal in *azulejos* of the Battle of Lepanto. In the village of **Vistabella**, in the agricultural region of La Secuita between Valls and Tarragona, Gaudí's colleague Josep M. Jujol designed an eccentric little *modernista* church, **El Sagrat Cor** (1918–23), its roof spiked with a needle-sharp bell-tower.

The Templar Castle of Miravet

Across the Ebro from Móra la Nova stands Miravet, site of one of Spain's most remarkable Templar castles, one of the many gifts to the Order from Ramón Berenguer IV. One of their tasks was to safeguard the region's Moriscos, who enjoyed nearly total religious and economic freedom in return for their rents and taxes. The castle is located on a 308m precipice over the river, and may be reached by a narrow path beginning at Carrer Blanc. In the deathly silence that hangs over the place you can explore the Templars' Romanesque chapel, with a spiral stair to the tower, the dormitory and refectory, and large vaulted rooms believed to have served as *bodegas* and granaries—although, curiously, no one has ever found a trace of a chimney or kitchen. The upper patio is called the Patio de la Sang ('of the blood'—here the last Templars of Miravet were beheaded after resisting the order to disband in 1308). There are wonderful views over the Ebro and the village below.

Most visitors to this area base themselves in Tarragona, but for a tranquil night or two away from the coast one of the more pleasant places to stay is Montblanc.

expensive

If you're driving, there's the scenic **★★Hotel Coll de Lilla**, Ctra. Nacional 240, ✆ 977 86 09 07, 🖩 977 86 04 23, on the road to Lilla. Its 12 pretty rooms are air-conditioned, with TV and bath. It also has a good restaurant, specializing in game dishes and, from Dec–March, *calçatada* (grilled green onions and lamb, *4000 pts*).

moderate

The **★Ducal**, Francesc Macià 11, ✆ 977 86 00 25, has cosy doubles with bath for *5700 pts*. There's also a handful of *hostales* in Espluga. **★★Del Senglar**, Plaça Montserrat Canals, ✆ 977 87 01 21, is the pick of these, in the centre of the village, open all year, with a garden and decent restaurant. Another pretty place to stay, near the monastery of Santes Creus, is **★Hs. Grau**, Sant Pere III 3, ✆ 977 63 83 11.

inexpensive

In Montblanc centre, there's the amiable **★Hs. dels Àngels** on the Plaça Angels, ✆ 977 86 01 73. In Falset, you can sleep cheap at the **Fonda Nacional**, Av. Catalunya 8, ✆ 977 83 01 57, which also has a decent restaurant.

Eating Out

A good place to eat in Montblanc is the **Fonda Colom**, Ctra. de Civadeira 5, ✆ 977 86 01 53, with Catalan cuisine for *3500 pts*. Heading 6km out of town on the road to Valls, **Les Fonts de Lilla**, ✆ 977 86 03 03 (*expensive*) serves local cuisine in an attractive rustic setting. *Closed Mon eve, Tues and mid-June–mid-July*. Near Valls on the road to Montblanc, is the Masia Bou, ✆ 977 60 04 27, a highly praised eating house, especially popular for its *calçotadas*—roasted spring onion parties.

The Costa Daurada

Spain's 'Golden Coast' stretches from Barcelona to the southern tip of Tarragona province and, while its beaches are often long and even gold-coloured, they lack that most elusive quality in people and resorts—charm. The surrounding scenery tends to be featureless, the *urbanizaciones* are ugly or sleepy, or both, and unless you have young children who require nothing more than good castle-building sand, shallow sea, and their peers for a perfect holiday (most of the visitors are Spanish and French families) you may want to limit yourself to a nod from the train window.

Getting Around

Cunit, Calafell, Torredembarra, Tamarit, Salou, Cambrils, L'Ametlla de Mar and Tortosa are all served by three **trains** a day between Valencia and Barcelona; the larger stations see considerably more action. Sant Carles de la Ràpita is linked by **bus** with Tortosa almost every hour.

Calafell: Sant Pere 29–31, ✆ 977 69 29 81, ✉ 977 69 29 81.
Cambrils: Plaça Creu de la Missió, ✆ 977 36 11 59.
Salou: Plaça Jaume I, ✆ 977 35 01 02, ✉ 977 38 07 47.
Torredembarra: Avda. Pompeu Fabra 3, ✆ 977 64 45 80.
El Vendrell: Dr. Robert 33, ✆ 977 66 02 92, ✉ 977 66 59 24.
Tortosa: Plaça del Bimil-lenari, ✆ 977 51 08 22.
Sant Carles de la Rápita: Plaça Carles III 13, ✆ 977 74 01 00, ✉ 977 74 43 87.

Cunit to the Ebro Delta

For the record, from north to south, **Sitges** (*see* 'Around Barcelona', p.114) is by far the most interesting and exciting resort of the Costa Daurada. Nearby **Cunit** is staider and boasts an exceptionally long, seldom crowded beach. A few miles inland, **El Vendrell**, like Valls famed for its *castellers*, was the birthplace of the great cellist and composer Pau Casals, a Catalan nationalist (he refused to speak anything but Catalan in public), whose opposition to Franco forbade him from ever seeing his beloved home after the Civil War. In 1979 his remains were brought from Puerto Rico and interred in El Vendrell's cemetery. A bequest from the maestro turned his family home in **Sant Salvador** on the sea into the **Casals Museum,** devoted to his life, works, and memorabilia, and constructed an auditorium next door.

Near Sant Salvador there's the vast beach, **Coma-ruga**, lined with holiday villas, and **Calafell**, a modest resort with a blank-walled castle as landmark. A ruined castle gave **Torredembarra** its name, and it has one of the coast's best—if busiest—beaches. Another lovingly restored 11th-century castle containing a fine museum of antiques stands right next to the beach at **Tamarit**. South of Tarragona sprawls the Costa Daurada's Miami Beach-style resorts, **Salou**, and nearby **Cambrils**. The next resortlet south took a shortcut by simply dubbing itself **Miami Beach**. Beyond Platja Miami it's desolate, literally, until the little fishing village-cum-resort of **L'Ametlla de Mar**. If developers have their way, the desolation won't last too much longer. Catalunya's challenge to Paris' Euro Disney, **Port Aventura**, is a 115-hectare theme park near Salou (*open Mar–Oct;* ✆ *977 77 90 90*). Beyond stretches the **Ebro delta** (Ebre in Catalan), as one writer described it, 'a strange amphibious landscape in the sea itself'. Malarial and abandoned until the beginning of this century, the delta is divided into rice paddies and dotted with *barracas*, farmhouses with thatched roofs, recalling the Valencian homeland of many of the rice farmers. A major southern European wetland and natural park (information office at **Deltebre**), it is fun for bird watchers, but otherwise a fitting anticlimax to the 746km of the Ebro, which, as great rivers go, is a bit of a bore (though it has given its name to the entire peninsula), from the days when the Greeks knew it as the Iberus and the people on its banks as Iberes.

Tortosa

Tortosa is the most important city here, and with much of the surrounding farmland in its municipal boundaries, it claims to be Spain's second-largest city. No one seems to like it much. The Catalans regard it as somehow peculiar, and the natives prefer to call themselves Tortosans and not Catalans. The Battle of the Ebro, the last Republican offensive in the Civil War, took place here, and Tortosa, on the front line for a year, suffered considerable damage. A monument commemorating the battle, which cost 35,000 lives, was erected by the river.

If fate brings you to Tortosa, there are two sights worth your time. The **Cathedral** has a charming Gothic interior and several fine chapels, especially that of the city's patroness, Nostra Senyora de la Santa Cinta (Our Lady of the Holy Ribbon). The citadel, **La Zuda**, was a Templar stronghold in the 12th century, when Tortosa's Moors, Jews and Christians lived in exemplary harmony. Walk through the **Eixample**, the new part of Tortosa, an area thick with *modernista* buildings.

On the southern tip of the delta, **Sant Carles de la Rápita** is the last resort on the Costa Daurada, splendidly located on Europe's largest natural harbour, **Los Alfaques**. The good Bourbon Carlos III (after whom the town is named) wanted to take advantage of nature's gift and make this a great seaport but, like so many of his fine plans, it was buried with him.

Where to Stay

Nearly all the hotels on the Costa Daurada close from October to May.

Calafell ✉ 43820

In Calafell, a pleasant family-resort hotel, the ****Canadá**, C/ Mossèn Jaume Soler 44, ☏ 977 69 15 00, ✆ 977 69 12 55 (*expensive–moderate*) has a pool, playground, and a reasonable restaurant. For less, but minus the restaurant and pools, try ***Salomé**, C/ Narcís Monturiol 19, ☏ 977 69 01 00. Excellent Italian food and pizzas may be had at **Da Giorgio**, Ángel Guiméra 4, ☏ 977 69 11 39 (*around 4500 pts*).

Torredembarra ✉ 43830

In Torredembarra the place to stay is ****Morros**, C/ Pérez Galdós 15, ☏ 977 64 02 25, ✆ 977 64 18 64, a beach hotel in the traditional style. *Open March–Sept.* Beautifully located on the sea, the **Morros** restaurant on Narcís Monturiol, ☏ 977 64 00 61, serves delicious seafood specialities (*4500 pts*). *Closed Sun eve.*

Salou and Cambrils ✉ 43840

In Salou it's hard to tell one hotel from the next; in Cambrils you'd do well to stay at *****Hs. Rovira**, Avda. Diputació 6, ☏ 977 36 09 00, ✆ 977 36 09 44. *Open all year.* It's as comfortable as the others by the beach, but has no restaurant, leaving you free to dine out. In Cambrils there are three great seafood restaurants run by the Gatell dynasty of chefs: **Casa Gatell**, Psg. Miramar 26, ☏ 977 36 00 57 (*expensive*), *closed Sun eve*; **Ca'n Gatell**, Psg. Miramar 27, ☏ 977 36 03 31 (*expensive*), *closed Mon eve and Tues*, and **Eugenia**, Consolat de Mar 80, ☏ 977 36 01 68, *closed Wed and Thurs lunch*—all in the *4000–5000 pts range* for a full-course meal, and worth it.

Tortosa ✉ 43500

Perhaps the only reason to stay in Tortosa is to sample its fine *parador* ******Castillo de la Zuda**, ☏ 977 44 44 50, ✆ 977 44 44 58 (*expensive*), set in the great Templar citadel, with sterling views and a restaurant specializing in Catalan dishes.

Sant Carles de la Rápita ✉ 43540

In Sant Carles de la Rápita the ***Juanito Platja**, Paseig Marítím, Platja Miami, ☏ 977 74 04 62, is on the front line of Miami Beach, rooms for *6900 pts*. The big prawn meals are famous at **Augusti**, Pilar 2, ☏ 977 74 04 27 (*moderate*).

Valencia and the Levante

The Fallas, Valencia

The modern autonomous region called *Comunitat Valenciano* covers what was once the third kingdom of the Crown of Aragón, reconquered for the Christians by Jaime I in the 13th century. It was a valuable asset, for the seemingly interminable Huerta de Valencia is Spain's single most fertile garden plot, irrigated since Roman times by the waters of the Turia. The Levante, or 'East', as this region is commonly known, has the highest rural density in Europe, with over 800 inhabitants per square kilometre, and their capital, Valencia, is Spain's third city and one of its most prosperous. This is the land of oranges and rice, and the home of the national dish, *paella*, which tastes better here than anywhere else. It is also the home of Costa del Azahar, with its string of modern resorts, and the Costa Blanca, which has entered the big league with the Costas Brava and Sol.

Most of the Christians who settled the new kingdom of Valencia were Catalan and, like the Catalans, the Valencians have their Generalitat and a long Republican tradition. Over the centuries, their language has evolved into a new creature, *valenciano*, which in the fierce parochialism of post-Franco Spain is flaunted as an entirely different tongue. There's hardly a signpost that hasn't had the Castilian names wiped out and replaced by the Valencian equivalent, or merely splattered by paint bombs to express discord.

But for many it is Valencia's light that best defines the region, a clear, diaphanous light called *La Clara* that artists love, that illuminates the characteristic blue-tiled steeples and cupolas, and casts a spell over the Albufera, the great lagoon and rice paddy south of the city, where changing patterns of light and colour are worthy of a Monet.

Valencia

The city of Valencia is an acquired taste. Those who arrive with visions of orange blossoms dancing in their heads will be disappointed once they leave the RENFE station (one of Spain's loveliest, a confection of ceramic oranges, tiles, and glittering mosaics of orange goddesses), for the first impression is of a bustling metropolis, where grand bridges span a non-existent river and two magnificent gates stand shorn of the stupendous walls destroyed to let the city expand drably in all directions. A trip through the old quarter is usually enough to dispel any initial misgivings, and if you linger a little longer, you'll begin to feel the charged atmosphere. There is an intensity in Valencia, a feeling that suggests if a revolution in Spain were to erupt, it would begin here. This smouldering feeling actually ignites every March in what must be the world's greatest pyromaniac's ball, *Las Fallas*, where hundreds of satirical floats, painstakingly built in the streets and quarters of the city, are burnt in a saturnalia of gunpowder and fireworks.

History

As Mediterranean cities go, Valencia is a newcomer, founded in 138 BC specifically to settle a band of defeated legionaries from Lusitania, who called it Valentia Edetanorum. It prospered under the Moors, who irrigated the fertile Huerta with an elaborate system of canals and made the local ceramics industry famous. When the Almoravids took the city from the Moorish king of Valencia in 1092 the latter allied himself with El Cid, who captured 'Bright Valencia' in 1094 and ruled the city as a personal fief until his death five years later. Its permanent Reconquest had to wait until 1238, a joint Aragonese-Catalan venture under Jaime I. Most of the Moors stayed on to work in agriculture and, by the 17th century, they constituted a third of the kingdom's population. Their happy idyll ended when Ottoman ships threatened the coast and the archbishop of Valencia, Juan de Ribera, conjured up fears of a Morisco-Turkish conspiracy. Madrid in its paranoia believed everything it heard, and in 1609 the Moors had to go. Valencia, which until then had been one of Spain's most prosperous cities, thriving on the silks and crops produced by the Moors, suffered a near-total economic collapse. Worse came when Valencia, like Catalunya, picked the wrong side in the War of the Spanish Succession.

In the 1860s and 1870s, Valencia took a leading role in the Republican movement; at the same time, in a progressive mood, it tore down its great 14th-century walls as a public works project to give jobs to the needy. During the Civil War it served as the Republicans' capital after the government had fled from Madrid, a period remembered by plaques throughout the city. Valencia was also the birthplace of novelist Vicente Blasco Ibáñez (1867–1928), author of *Four Horsemen of the Apocalypse* and fine descriptive tales from the Huerta like *La Barraca* and *Entre Naranjos*.

Getting There

By air: There are regular flights between Valencia and Madrid, Ibiza, Mallorca and the Canary Islands. The airport is 8km west of town in Manises, ✆ 96 370 95 00. Iberia's office is at C/ de la Paz 14, ✆ 96 352 05 00. British Airways can be found at Plaza Rodrigo Botet 6, ✆ 96 351 22 84. Bus no.15 leaves Valencia's bus station hourly for the airport, though on Sundays this service doesn't exist: get a bus to Manises and take a taxi from there (*500 pts*).

By sea: Valencia's port is 5km from town and has frequent connections with Mallorca, Minorca and Ibiza, and the Canaries. For ferry information call the *estación marítima* on ✆ 96 367 65 12. Trasmediterránea's office is at Avda. Manuel Soto Ingeniero 15, ✆ 96 367 39 72. Bus nos.19 or 4 goes directly to the port from Pza. del Ayuntamiento.

By train: The RENFE station is only a couple of blocks from the Pza. del Ayuntamiento, ✆ 96 352 02 02. There are eight trains a day from Madrid, via Cuenca or Albacete; three connections with Zaragoza, five to Alicante, and eight to Barcelona and Castellón. There are also trains nearly every hour to Játiva.

A fast, efficient local train service (FGV) links Valencia to the villages of the Huerta. There are connections to Lliria, Buñol, Paterna and Villanueva de Castellón, from the underground station in Plaza de España.

By bus: Valencia's bus station is across the Turia at Avda. de Menéndez Pidal 3, ✆ 96 349 72 22 or ✆ 96 349 12 50; catch bus no.8 from across the street for the Pza. del Ayuntamiento. There are connections from here to most of the major cities of Spain, to the resorts along the coasts to the north and south, and a Eurolines bus direct to London. Autocares V. Edo go from Valencia to Castellón, Tarragona and Andorra once a day. In the summer there are buses to El Salér from the Plaza Porta del Mar every half hour.

Estacion del Norte, Jativa 24, ✆ 96 352 85 73.
Provincial office, Calle de la Paz, ✆ 96 394 22 22.
Municipal office, Pza. del Ayuntamiento, ✆ 96 394 04 17.

The **British Institute:** C/ General Sanmartín 7, ✆ 96 351 88 18.

The **hospital** is on Avda. Cid, ✆ 96 379 16 00.

The main **post office** is at Pza. del Ayuntamiento 24, ✆ 96 351 67 50. *Open Mon–Sat 9am–9pm and Sun am.*

The Cathedral

Looking at a map, it's easy to trace the line of the walls that once embraced old Valencia and find the heart of town, the **Plaza de la Reina** (Plaza Zaragoza). Here the **Cathedral** was built over the Great Mosque in 1262, and given for a partner the sturdy, octagonal, minaret-like tower called the Miguelete, or **El Micalet** in *valenciano*, completed by Pere Balanguer in 1429. If the thought of climbing 200 steps up a narrow spiral staircase doesn't dismay you, the top of the Micalet offers lovely views over Valencia's gleaming ceramic domes and the Huerta (*open daily 10–1 and 4.30–7; adm*). There are 13 bells in the Micalet, the largest weighing over five tons and dedicated on Michaelmas—hence the tower's name. The Cathedral has suffered a number of changes over the years: the main Baroque portal on the Plaza de la Reina is stale toast compared to the Romanesque **Portal de Palau** and the Gothic **Puerta de los Apóstoles** (1354), facing the Plaza de la Virgen and adorned with sculpture and a star of David (locally called the Salomó) in the rose window.

If you happen to pass by the Puerta de los Apóstoles on a Thursday at noon, you'll see a crowd gathered around eight seated men in black shirts. They are Valencia's famous **Tribunal de las Aguas** (Water Jury), where all disputes related to the Huerta's irrigation water are settled. The eight-member Tribunal has been elected every two years, ever since it was founded in 960, in the reign of Caliph Abderrahman III of Córdoba. Conducted in *Valenciano*, none of the proceedings is ever written down, nor is there any appeal if a user is fined—not in pesetas, but in the medieval currency, *lliures valencianes*. The water laws of Valencia are so fair they were copied by the rest of Spain and Spanish America in the 19th century.

The **interior** of the cathedral has been restored (since 1939) to reveal as much of its Gothic structure as possible. Best of all is the elegant, 14th-century lantern, where two stories of alabaster windows radiate a soft light over the crossing. The Sala Capitular is now a **museum** (*open Mon–Sat 10–1 and 4.30–7; adm*), where you can see a Virgin by Correggio and a macabre painting by Goya that foreshadows his 'Black Paintings' in the Prado—three grinning demons whisper into the ear of a graphically depicted corpse, while St Francis Borgia wards them off with a crucifix. The museum also contains a lovely gold and coloured enamel Pax Tablet by Benvenuto Cellini and, for a climax, nothing less than the alleged chalice used in the Last Supper, one of several possible Holy Grails floating around Europe.

According to legend, St Peter took the chalice to Rome, where it became a keepsake of the popes. In the 3rd century, when Pope Sixtus II was about to be martyred during Valerian's persecutions, he entrusted it to his disciple Lawrence, who sent it for safe keeping to Huesca in Aragón. When the Moors invaded, the chalice was hidden in the mountains, where the monastery of San Juan de la Peña (*see* p.205) was built to house the now bejewelled relic. In 1399 King Martín persuaded the monks to hand it over, and it ended up here for safe-keeping.

Great as this relic is, the faithful of Valencia put greater trust in the heavenly power of intervention of 'Our Lady of the Forsaken' who resides next door in the round **Basilica de Nuestra Señora de los Desamparados**. In the 14th century, a band of pilgrims appeared at the door of a charitable brotherhood and requested four days' food and lodging in a locked room without windows. Four days later, when the door was unlocked, the pilgrims had vanished, leaving behind the statue. Adorned with a radiant diamond crown and surrounded by a thousand flickering candles, this Virgin made by angels is Valencia's patron saint.

The Generalitat and the Gates

Across lovely Plaza de la Virgen stands the **Generalitat of the Kingdom of Valencia** (1510) (*open Mon–Fri 9am–8pm*), now again serving its original function as the seat of the comunitat's council. The exterior is plain, but within are two chambers with wonderful *artesonado* ceilings, the **Salón Dorado** and the especially lovely **Salón de Cortes** with its *azulejos* and frescoes of 1592 representing a meeting of the assembly. To see them you need to make an appointment, © 96 386 34 61 (*Mon–Fri 9–2*); an English-speaking guide can be arranged.

From here Calle Serranos leads to the **Torres de Serranos** (*open Tues–Fri 9–1.30 and 4–6, Sat 9–13.30*), the massive survival of the 14th-century walls. From the river the gate looks solid and imposing; from the rear it looks like a stage prop, hollowed out with platforms and stairs. The gate that formerly stood to the east along the river next to a Templar church (now a Guardia Civil barracks) was the famous Gate of El Cid, through which the Cid's corpse, decked out in warlike array and propped up on his faithful horse Babieca, led the attack on the Moorish besiegers who had taken courage from rumours of his death—in the film *El Cid*, this was Charlton Heston's best scene. A second muscular souvenir of Valencia's walls, the **Torres de Cuart** (1460), is just west of the Generalitat.

Plaza del Mercado

This square, where old Valencia held its *corridas* and *autos-da-fé*, is an exceptionally fine ensemble, although during market hours, when it's jammed with triple-parked lorries, it goes unnoticed. Befitting an agricultural queen, Valencia's **Municipal Market** is the city's true royal palace, Spain's largest and most beautiful market, a confection of iron and glass, topped with a parrot-and-swordfish weathervane. Inside, the astounding cornucopia of the *huerta* is on display; sometimes you find oranges weighing up to 3kg apiece.

Opposite the market stands another cathedral of commerce, the 15th-century Flamboyant Gothic **Lonja de la Seda** (silk exchange) (*open Tues–Fri 9–2 and 4–6, Sun 9–1.30*). Twisted, rope-like columns support the ogival arches in the main hall, where a Latin inscription along the walls reads 'I am a famous building that took fifteen years to build' and exhorts the merits of honest trade. A spiral staircase ascends to the **Salón del Consulado del Mar** or maritime law courts, topped by a magnificent *artesonado* ceiling. Across from the Lonja stands the plaza's third monument, **Los Santos Juanes**, a medieval church with a Plateresque façade.

Behind the Lonja peers the second of Valencia's monumental towers, the 17th-century hexagonal **Tower of Santa Catalina**. Next to it, in the Plaza de Santa Catalina two famous **Horchaterías** will sell you a glass of Valencian tiger milk, *Horchata de chufa*, made from

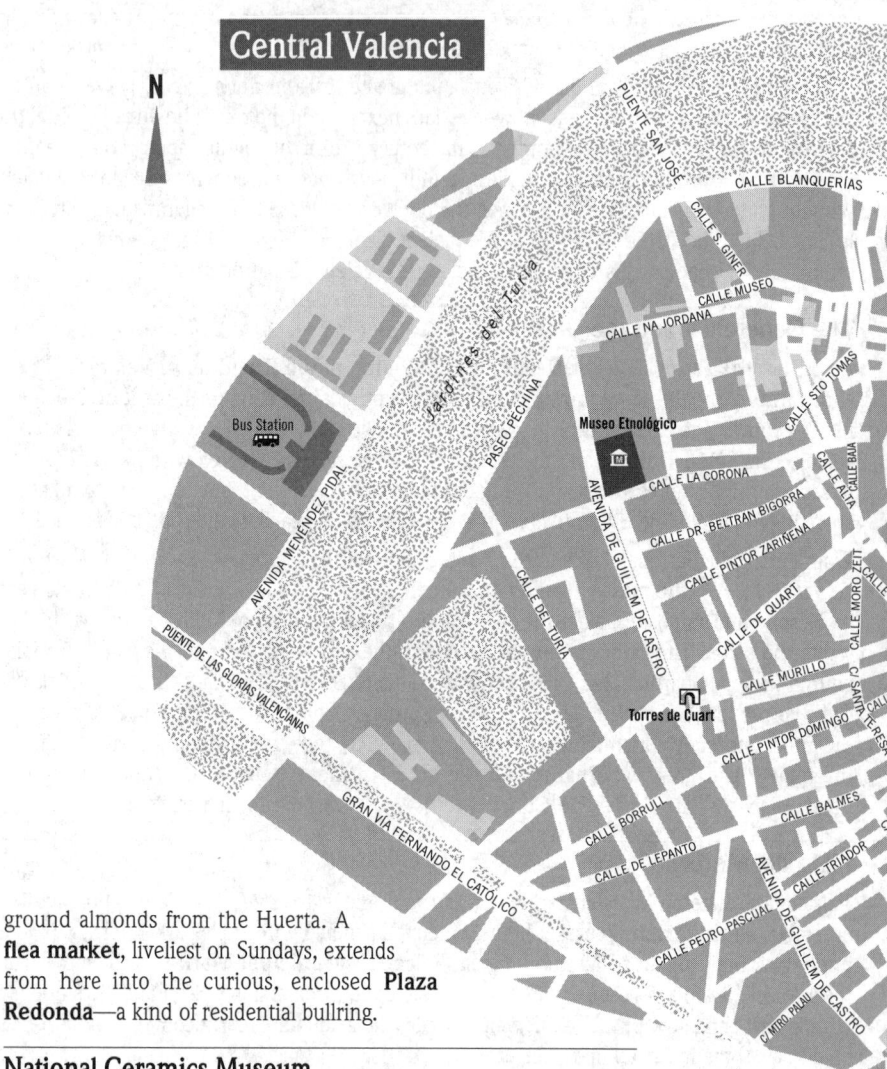

N

ground almonds from the Huerta. A
flea market, liveliest on Sundays, extends
from here into the curious, enclosed **Plaza
Redonda**—a kind of residential bullring.

National Ceramics Museum

From here, Calle de La Paz passes the Baroque **S. Martín**, its gutted interior another
victim of the Civil War. An alley in front of it leads to the 18th-century **Palacio del
Marqués de Dos Aguas**, an outlandish Baroque wedding-cake with an amazing alabaster
portal designed by Hipólito Ravira, who died a lunatic shortly after its completion. It now
houses the **National Ceramics Museum**, which has an exceptionally rich collection of
azulejos, many with humorous or whimsical scenes (one portrays a giant mosquito chasing a
dog). The 'popular' 18th- and 19th-century ceramics from Manises on the third floor are
strangely reminiscent of Picasso, whose works are concentrated in their own room. The oldest
plates and bowls come from Paterna, decorated with green motifs from the 13th and 14th
centuries, and blue up to the 15th. There's a beautiful all-tiled Valencian kitchen and three

lovely 18th-century carriages, a collection of ex-libris designs from the 1920s, and on the top floor the zany Gallery of Humorists, which fascinates even if you don't get the jokes.

Plaza del Patriarca

Two blocks east, the Plaza del Patriarca was named after the **Colegio del Patriarca**, founded by Bishop Juan de Ribera, the arch enemy of the Moriscos. There is a small but choice collection of paintings, including three El Grecos and Ribaltas, a Hugo Van der Goes and a book of miniatures once belonging to Philip the Handsome, with a scene of 15th-century golfers (*open daily 11–1.30, adm*). Next to it is the 1830 building of the 15th-century **University**, whose library contains a copy of probably the first book printed in Spain, the 1474 *Les Trobes en Lahors de la Verge Marie*.

Adjacent to the Patriarca, the 16th-century church of **Corpus Christi** is decorated with *azulejos* and offers some genuine Spanish Catholic hocus-pocus during its Friday morning service. As the priests chant the *Miserere*, the painting over the altar—*The Last Supper*, by Ribalta—sinks away, to be replaced by a series of four curtains that are parted at the climactic moment to reveal a starkly illuminated crucifix of the 1400s.

From here walk down the Calle de La Paz to the Glorieta and turn left for the grand church of **Santo Domingo** *(open Tues–Thurs 10–12)*. Some tough customers have called its cloister home, beginning with St Vicente Ferrer, perhaps Spain's most ferocious religious bigot, and recently, General Milans del Bosch, mastermind of the abortive coup in February 1981, who called out the tanks in Valencia in support of his stooge Tejero, as the latter shot up the Cortes in Madrid. Although the cloister remains a barracks, you can see the porch designed by Felipe II (who was no great shakes as an architect) and the Gothic **Capilla de los Reyes**, with the elegant 16th-century tombs of Rodrigo Mendoza and his wife.

Across the Turia

From Santo Domingo stretches Valencia's most attractive bridge, the **Puente del Real** which once spanned the unpredictable Turia. This river either trickled or flooded once it reached Valencia (after being 'bled' by the canals of the *huerta*) and so often inundated the city that in 1957 Valencia lost its patience and dug it a new channel.

Across the Puente del Real it's a short stroll to the **Museo de Bellas Artes** *(open daily exc Mon 9–2.30 and 4–6; Sat, Sun and holidays 9–2)*, with a smattering of good works among the forgettable—there's a self-portrait by Velázquez, paintings by Ribalta, Pinturicchio *(Our Lady of Feveís)*, El Greco *(St John the Baptist)*, a triptych by Hieronymus Bosch *(The Mocking of Christ*—the original centrepiece is in the Escorial), medieval Valencian art, and the only painting attributed with certitude to Valencia's 15th-century Rodrigo de Osona. The upper floors are haunted by some astoundingly lurid Spanish Impressionism. Next to the museum you can recover from it all among the roses in the **Jardines del Real** *(open daily 6–10)*, and perhaps visit its cramped **zoo** *(open daily 10–6; adm)*. The heart of modern Valencia is the large, triangular **Plaza del Ayuntamiento**, its bustling life tempered by the sweet scent of flowers from numerous stalls. From here you can catch bus no.13 to the **Fallas Museum** on Plaza Monteolivete 4, *(open Tues–Sat 10–2)* which can give you a hint of what you're missing if you aren't in Valencia between 13 and 19 March.

Nights of Fire

Throughout the world, the spring equinox is a popular time to light bonfires to welcome the new season, but no one does it with more enthusiasm than the *valencianos*. The holiday began to take its present form in the 18th century, when as a rite of spring local carpenters and artisans would ceremoniously burn the wooden poles that had supported the lamps they needed in the winter. Because 18 March is also the feast of St Joseph, the patron of carpenters, the rite took on a festive air, and the *valencianos* began to dress up the old poles as satirical effigies called *ninots*. Neighbourhood competions for the best effigy soon developed, and residents joined in, contributing money towards the *ninots*, hoping theirs would be bigger and more humorous than the *ninot* from the next plaza.

In the festival's present form, the *ninots* are merely small scale models for the *fallas* or 'torches' themselves—huge papier-mâché tableaux, some several stories high and redolent with satires that spare no one and need no translation. Fat women, politicians, naked girls and bug-eyed tourists are peppered throughout; slick TV announcers tempt with trays of sausages and coffins. You can spend the week as the *valencianos* do, strolling though the city to see the *fallas*, or their *ninots* all on display in La Lonja, where the best are given prizes. *Barracas* (typical Valencian houses with thatched roofs) are set up throughout the city, dispensing doughnuts and chocolate to the passing throng. Every day at 2pm in Plaza del Ayuntamiento an ear-splitting string of fireworks, *Las Mascaletas*, is set off. In the afternoon the first bullfights of the Spanish calendar take place, and every night there are more fireworks. On the 18th, a huge offering of flowers takes place in the Plaza de la Virgen, the blooms forming a massive skirt for the statue of the Virgin made by angels.

The 19th is the long-awaited *Nit de Foc,* the Night of Fire. The prize-winning *falla* is brought to the Plaza del Ayuntamiento, and all are strung with firecrackers. Around midnight, in a prearranged order, the *fallas* and *ninots* are ignited one after another in a tremendous city-wide holocaust, or *cremá*. The prizewinners are burned last, ending up with a huge pyre in Plaza del Ayuntamiento that goes up while hundreds of tons of fireworks blast and scream and thunder overhead. Of all the months of work and millions of pesetas that went into Las Fallas, only the first prize *ninot*, the *Ninot Indulat*, is spared the flames of the *cremá* and installed in the 'Pantheon-hospice' of the museum.

Valencia's Beaches and the Albufera

Valencia has two municipal beaches, **Levante** and **Malvarrosa** (bus nos.19 or 4 from the Plaza del Ayuntamiento) but they are as polluted as they are convenient. Levante, however, is the place to go for fresh seafood; the Avenida de Neptuno alone has some 27 restaurants.

Further south and far more pleasant and cleaner are the beaches at **Pinedo** and **El Saler**. El Saler is the best base for visiting the **Albufera**, Spain's largest fresh-water lagoon, separated from the sea by **La Dehesa**, a narrow sandbar shaded with pine groves. September is a good time to come, when the Albufera's emerald green rice paddies turn to gold. Wildfowl (and duck hunters) flock here from September to March, and the waters are plied by scores of eel fishermen, some in their stately old-fashioned sailing boats. The Albufera is most dramatic at dusk, when the soft colours change by the second. To get here, take a white or blue bus from Pza. Porta del Mar. You can hire boats from the little dock behind El Saler beach. Prices vary, so shop around.

Valencia ✉ *46000*   ***Where to Stay***

In Town

It usually isn't too hard to find a room in Valencia, except during Las Fallas. Most of the better hotels are clustered around the Plaza del Ayuntamiento; otherwise good budget rooms can be found in narrow, dimly lit streets in the older part of town and around the train station.

★★★★**Astoria Palace**, Pza. Rodrigo Botet 5, ✆ 96 352 67 37, ✉ 96 352 80 78, resides in a quiet square off the Ayuntamiento and has luxurious interiors and smooth service. The restaurant is good too. ★★★★**Reina Victoria**, C/ Barcas 6, ✆ 96 352 04 87, ✉ 96 352 04 87, lies just off the Plaza del Ayuntamiento, and is the elegant *grande dame* of the city's hostelries, in an attractive Victorian monument; its air-conditioned rooms are a godsend in the summer.

moderate

★★★**Excelsior**, Barcelonina 5, ✆ 96 351 46 12, ✉ 96 352 34 78, is also just off the big square, its clean modern rooms also blessed with air-conditioning, and it's a lot cheaper. ★★★**Hotel Inglés**, Marqués de Dos Aguas 6, ✆ 96 351 64 26, ✉ 96 394 02 51, is in the same price range, and while lacking the air-conditioning offers much more in the way of style and old-fashioned atmosphere; at night the street is very quiet. ★★★**Hs Mediterráneo**, Avda. Barón de Cárcer 45, ✆/✉ 96 351 01 42, also conveniently located, is small, friendly and cool in the summer.

inexpensive–cheap

★★**Hostal Bisbal**, C/ Pié de la Cruz 9, ✆ 96 391 70 84, is right at the market's front door; noisy during the day but quiet at night. The owners speak English. ★★★**Hs Florida**, C/ Padilla 4, ✆ 96 351 12 84, one block west of the Ayuntamiento, is a middle-range *hostal* with comfortable rooms, decent services and air conditioning.

★**Universal**, C/ Barcas 5, ✆ 96 351 5384, is a basic, faded but well scrubbed *hostal*, just off the Plaza del Ayuntamiento. ★**Hospederia del Pilar**, Mercado 19, ✆ 96 391 66 00, is clean, friendly and pleasant in the middle of the old town, with a lobby resembling an elementary-school classroom. A ginger cat stalks the ★**Hostal El Rincón**, C/ Cardá 11, ✆ 96 391 60 83, which is almost opposite the Pilar and marginally cheaper. The large rooms have well-scrubbed stone floors and comfortable beds. If they're both full, try the pleasant **Pension París** at C/ Salva 12, ✆ 96 352 67 66.

Out of Town

★★★★**Parador El Saler**, Playa del Saler, ✆ 96 161 1186, ✉ 96 162 7016 (*expensive*) is located among the sand dunes and pine forests of the Dehesa near Saler. Contemporary, air-conditioned and next to a fine 18-hole golf course and pool, with plush rooms. ★★**Patilla II**, C/ Pinares 10, ✆ 96 183 03 82 (*moderate*) is also prettily located on Saler beach, small, with TVs in each room, and open all year. A cheaper option on Playa de Neptuno at no. 22 is ★**Tres Cepas**, ✆ 96 371 51 11 (*cheap*) which provides decent and clean budget rooms at *4300 pts* for a double.

Eating Out

Any city that boasts such an array of international restaurants, from Persian to Mongolian, deserves to be taken seriously. Valencians are rightly proud of their rice dishes, from the famous *paella* to other lesser-known dishes like *arros a la banda* and *arros en fesols i naps*. Another Valencian favourite, baby eels (*angulas*) from the Albufera, figures on many menus. Remember that many of Valencia's restaurants close for the month of August, as in most Spanish cities.

Two good places in the new part of town specialize in Valencian cuisine. One of the city's oldest restaurants, **El Romeral**, Gran Vía Marqués del Turia 62, is on the big boulevard south of the Plaza Puerta de la Mar, ✆ 96 395 15 17 (*4500 pts*). *Closed Mon and Aug.* For class and innovative cuisine, the place to go in Valencia is **Ma Cuina**, just south of the train station and bullring on Gran Vía Germanías 49, ✆ 96 341 77 99; the menu always changes but Valencian rice and Basque dishes are permanent features (*4500 pts*). **La Hacienda**, C/ Navarro Reverter 12, ✆ 96 373 18 59 is considered one of the best restaurants in Valencia, with specialities like truffle soup and Grand Marnier soufflé (*7500 pts*).

moderate

One of the best places for *paella* in town is **Navarro**, C/ Arzobispo Mayoral 7, near the Plaza del Ayuntamiento, served in a small and traditional interior with beaming service. The wine list is also quite good (*3000 pts*). On Levante beach try **Chicote**, Avda. de Neptuno 34, ✆ 96 371 61 51, where good seafood reigns and the rice dishes will inspire you. Try *arros a banda*, rice cooked in fish stock. A meal with wine will set you back around *2500 pts*. *Closed Mon and 15 Nov–15 Dec.*

cheap

That typical little Spanish restaurant you've been looking for might just be **Setabis**, Pza. Dr Collado 9 near the Zona de la Lonja, ✆ 96 391 62 92, popular for its 950 pta *menú del día*, with excellent *paella*. The seriously impoverished go to **Comidas Eliseo**, C/ Conde Montores, off Plaza Tetuán. Two courses with bread and a drink will barely singe your pocket at 575 pts. If you prefer your rice with soy sauce, there's a handful of Chinese restaurants in the city. Try the popular **Mey Mey**, Historiador Diago 19, ✆ 96 384 07 47, which has a good reputation. *Closed Aug.* A lovely little vegetarian restaurant nestles in the heart of the Barrio del Carmen: **La Lluna**, C/ San Ramón, with imaginative veggie dishes. *Closed Aug.*

tapas bars

A great, cheap and authentic place to eat is **Serranos**, C/ Blanquerías 5, ✆ 96 391 70 61, by the Torres de Serrano. The plain and bustling interior is full of young Valencians enjoying the efficient service and tucking into a wide range of perfect tapas. If you go for a variety of *porciones*, you'll be hard pushed to spend more than 1000 pts, including a bottle of wine. Also worth a visit in the Barrio del Carmen is **Café-Bar Pilar**, C/ Moro Zeit 13, off Plaza del Esparto, ✆ 96 391 04 97, which has been serving up steaming mussels and snails with the beer since 1918. Chuck the shells into buckets lurking under the bar.

Some other inexpensive dining spots where you'll find good-value tapas and *bocadillos* are **Damy**, Mistral 7 (*closed Mon*) and **Bar Manoli**, Luis Oliag 6, which also offers a popular, cheap *paella*. A bar which serves *agua de Valencia* (the region's traditional cocktail made from champagne, vodka and orange juice) is the juice bar **Naturalia**, C/ del Mar 12, where the lampshades are upside-down straw hats. There is a menu of fresh fruit-juice cocktails, with or without alcohol; crêpes provide stomach lining. Apart from pitchers of *agua de Valencia*, you can get jugs of *agua naturalia*, which is the same alcoholic mixture but with pineapple juice instead of orange. Open till around 2am.

Culture (two little theatres) and bars are slowly reclaiming the alleys of the old town; the city could help them along a bit by adding a few watts to the street lights. That doesn't deter the Valencians from their fun, however: they have been in the grip of *bacalao* fever for a few years now. That's not an unhealthy obsession with a dried fish: *bacalao* is also the Spanish name for the techno music which has ruled the east coast and the island of Ibiza since the late 1980s. Valencia has a serious clubbing reputation throughout Spain, no mean feat in a land so good at staying up all night. The Barrio del Carmen is very lively at night with the smarter and more expensive bars edging up to Pza. del Esparto and noisier local haunts starting on C/ Alta, around Pza. San Jaume. Here the street life itself can keep you entertained all night as various local characters shimmer through the Barrio. Watch out for Blancita, a tiny and ancient lady who's always dressed in white with a variety of objects pinned to her chest, including her false teeth. She roams the streets, attracting small change while her reputation grows out beyond the Barrio. The younger, wilder crowd head for the disco bars and restaurants of the Pza. Xuquer and Pza. Honduras, whilst the more sedate swingers congregate around the Gran Vía Marqués del Turia and the Avda. Jacinto Benavente. In the summer months, the bars of Malvarrosa beach groove all night: the best is the barn-like **Vivir sin Dormir** on Avda. de Neptuno. There are also some huge outdoor nightclubs sheltering the young and beautiful of Valencia; don't even bother to arrive before 3am. If you can get to the suburb of Alboraya, the favourite disco of the moment is **Arena**, C/ Emilio Baró, also used as a band venue.

Original-language films can be seen at Filmoteca cinema, Pza. del Ayuntamiento.

Around Valencia: Sagunto (north)

In 219 BC Hannibal initiated the Second Punic War by taking the Greek city and Roman ally of Sagunto (24km north of Valencia), which proved no easy task—after an eight-month siege, the defenders, unable to hold out any longer, made a huge bonfire where they burnt their belongings, their wives and children and themselves. Historical hindsight suggests Hannibal ought to have taken the hint and driven his elephants back home. Although Rome easily took Sagunto back from Carthage five years later, the town never recovered its former importance, although the Moors added the great walls of the citadel over the Roman foundations, and the Spaniards added a giant steel mill. In 1902 the composer Joaquín Rodrigo was born in Sagunto.

The modern town is sprinked with traces of ancient Sagunto—some of the arcades in the **Plaza Mayor** are supported by its columns. Some medieval houses remain in the **Judería** where, according to Sephardic tradition, the first Jews settled in Spain in 100 BC. Calle del Castillo leads up to the **Roman Theatre**, a 2nd-century creation where spectators had fine views over the sea. Recent US$6m improvements by the Generalitat—the addition of a 82ft stage and new limestone seats—have caused a vast international controversy. The idea was to make it a venue for opera and other performances, but all the locals hate it and have sued to have the improvements undone. Next to it is a modest **Archaeology Museum** and the road up to the drawbridge of the huge, rambling **citadel** (*open Tues–Sat 10–2 and 4–7; Sun 10–2*), its half-mile of walls draped over the ancient acropolis. You can pick out the foundations of Roman temples and French buildings from the Peninsular War and ruins left by every king of the mountain in between. The views over the deep green *huerta* are excellent. A bus from Sagunto heads down to its beach, which isn't bad if you don't mind looking at the steel mill.

Some 30km north of Sagunto, at Vall D'Uixo you can take a journey to the centre of the earth at the **Cuevas de San José**, where boats sails through crystal clear subterranean waters under an impressive display of stalactites.

Játiva (south)

Játiva (or Xátiva) is an hour's trip from Valencia (frequent trains make the trip), across the *huerta* and past many a dilapidated but stylish orange warehouse. Located on a pair of vine and cypress-clad hills in the midst of these fertile flatlands, Játiva is one of the most scenic villages in the *país valenciano*, best known for the three natives it exported to Italy: Ribera, known as Lo Spagnoletto in Naples for his short stature, and the two Borgia Popes, Calixtus III and the much-maligned Alexander VI, both born here when the family relocated from Borja in Aragón. Játiva (its Moorish name) was such a headache to Felipe V that when he finally captured it in 1707 he burnt much of it and renamed it San Felipe for himself, just so the inhabitants would never forget who was boss. He is remembered to this day in the **Museum of the Almundi**, where his portrait has been hung upside down. He is suspended alongside a few paintings by Ribera (1591–1652) and a diverse selection of works received from the Prado. The Museum also exhibits an equally wide-ranging collection of archaeological finds, with many fine Islamic remains. All are housed within the 16th-century **Almundìn** (granary) on Carrer de la Corretgeria (*open Tues–Sat 10–2*).

In the historic centre, **Plaza del Seo** is dominated by a Renaissance **Colegiata** even bigger than Valencia's cathedral, with several fine marbles and donations from the Borgias. Across the square from the church is Játiva's prettiest building, the **Municipal Hospital**, its Plateresque façade serenaded by a charming angelic chamber orchestra over the door. The road up to the castles passes **San Félix**, the town's Visigothic cathedral, remodelled in the 13th century; it has a fine set of 15th-century paintings from Valencia, recycled Roman columns and a stoup made from a marble capital. The **castle** that crowned Játiva dates from the 15th century but was mostly demolished by Felipe V. From the ramparts you can see across the *huerta* to Valencia and the sea (*open Tues–Sun 10–2 and 4.30–8*).

Costa del Azahar

The 'Orange Blossom Coast', as the shore of Castellón and Valencia provinces has been dubbed, is true to its name, lined through most of its length with orange groves; Castellón itself has a *huerta* as rich as Valencia's, and so flat the *valencianos* call it La Plana, the plain. While there are long stretches of sand, few of the beaches here are anything to write home about. Pockets of villas and flats occupy the better stretches, but there are fewer hotels than you'd imagine.

Getting Around

By train: RENFE has frequent services up the coast from Valencia and down from Tarragona; there are stations at Burriana, Villareal, Castellón, Benicasim, Oropesa, Alcalá de Chivert, Benicarló and Vinaroz.

By bus: There are two buses a day from Valencia's bus station and from Castellón to Montanejos. Peñíscola, Benicarló, and Vinaroz are linked by a municipal bus every hour; there are also three direct buses between Castellón, Benicarló and Vinaroz on weekdays (six in the summer), departing from C/ Trinidad 166. On Sundays the only direct bus linking Castellón to Peñíscola leaves from the same place. Three other buses link Castellón and Valencia in a 1½hr express service. Municipal buses leave Castellón's Plaza Hernán Cortés for the beaches from Grao de Castellón to Benicasim every 15mins in the summer.

Two buses a day from Castellón and Vinaroz go to Morella, which is itself a terminus for buses that go once or twice a day to the villages of the Maestrazgo. Buses from Castellón pass through them all as well; get timetables from the tourist office.

Tourist Information

Castellón: the very helpful office is at Pza. María Agustina 5, ✆ 964 22 10 00, ✉ 964 22 77 03.

Peñíscola: Pso. Marítimo, ✆ 964 48 02 08.

Benicassim: C/ Medico Segarra 4, ✆ 964 30 09 62, ✉ 964 30 01 39, *benicassim@gva.es*, www.gva.es/benicassim.

Castellón de la Plana

Between Sagunto and Castellón there's little to see. **Burriana** is one of Spain's major orange ports; if you're driving through, stop to see the portal of the 16th-century parish church, flanked by two curious bears. Inland, **Villareal de los Infantes** is a busy citrus centre, founded in 1272 by Jaime I, who laid out its streets in a neat grid. Best among the beaches here are **Playa de Nules** and **Playa de Chilches** near Almenara, but it's far more delightful to head inland up the River Mijares that irrigates the Huerta of Castellón. Before it reaches the plain, the Mijares passes through a deep, forested ravine, especially lovely around **Montanejos**, where you can paddle about in the clear, shallow water under the cliffs. So reputed are the waters here (for treating digestive disorders and poor circulation) that a spa and treatment centre have been set up.

Castellón is not one of Spain's prettier provincial capitals, but it has a fine series of sandy beaches stretching from **Playa del Serrallo** (with a golf course) north to **Benicasim**. In town itself, the **Provincial Museum of Fine Arts** in C/ Caballeros (*open Mon–Fri 9–2; Sat 10–12*) has good paintings by Ribalta, Ribera and Sorolla, and good modern ceramics from the region. In the **Convento de las Capuchinas**, C/ Nuñez de Arce 11 (*open daily 4–8*) there are 10 saints attributed to Zurbarán (or copies of lost works by the master). The Gothic cathedral, flattened in the Civil War, has been rebuilt stone by stone. Castellón also has something other Spanish towns don't: a collection of tiny volcanic islets, the **Islas Columbretes**, 43km out to sea but still in its municipal boundaries. Although not much more than rocks themselves, they are very popular with underwater fishermen, who can hire out excursion boats from **Oropesa**, the next town and beach north of Benicasim.

North of Oropesa the road is forced away from the coast by the rugged Sierra de Irta, dotted with castles and towers. The finest of these, **Alcalá de Chivert**, is an enormous ruin that once belonged to the Templars.

Burriana ✉ 12530

For a good seafood meal in Burriana, the **El Morro**, C/ Dona Puerto s/n, ✆ 964 58 60 33 (*expensive*), right on the port, is the local favourite for rice and seafood, but it's a little pricey—*6000 pts. Closed Sun.*

Montanejos ✉ 12448

Montanejos has four modest *hostales*; the pick of the lot, prettily located near the small spa, is **★Rosaleda de Mijares**, Ctra. Tales 28, ✆ 964 13 10 79. But the lure of a cure can make this a popular spot; if the Rosaleda is booked, try **★★Hotel Xauen**, Avda. Fuente Banos 26, ✆ 964 13 11 51, ✆ 964 13 13 75, *xauen@hotelxauen.com.*

Castellón ✉ 12000

Castellón's accommodation is of a generally good standard with some good bargains in all price categories. The poshest hotel is the modern **★★★★Intur**, C/ Herrero 20, ✆ 964 22 50 00, ✆ 964 23 26 06, with a gym for the health-conscious (*15,000 pts*). The place to stay if you've brought along the clubs is the **★★★Hotel del Golf**, located on the Grao's Playa del Pinar, ✆ 964 28 01 80. Besides golf, it offers tennis, a pool, and air-conditioned rooms in contemporary surroundings. *Closed 15 Oct–15 March.* The **★★Hotel Doña Lola**, C/ Lucena 3, ✆ 964 21 40 11, is small and very comfort-able. Great service and a good restaurant compound its charms. Less expensive, the **Hs Los Herreros**, Av. Del Puerto 28, ✆ 964 28 42 64, is well-located on the beachfront.

The classic place to dine in Castellón is the **Casino Antiguo**, Puerta del Sol 1, ✆ 964 22 28 64 (*moderate*), a private club with a public dining room, classic Valencian rice dishes and good seafood (*4000 pts*). **Peñalen**, C/ Fola 11, ✆ 964 23 41 31 (*moderate*) is another restaurant serving superbly prepared food to enthusiastic Spanish (*3500 pts*). *Closed Sun and 15 Aug–15 Sept.* More excellent seafood can be consumed at the charming **Rafael**, C/ Churruca 28, ✆ 964 28 21 85 (*expensive*), right off the fisherman's docks in El Grao, where you can watch the fleet come in (*5500 pts*). *Closed Sun.* For some unfussy and deeply authentic food, visit **Casa Teresa**, C/ Lope de Vega 4, ✆ 964 20 15 20 (*cheap*), which serves up steaming plates of specialities which includes game in season (*2000 pts*). *Closed Sun.* For deli-cious rice, including a tasty *arroz negro*, head straight for **Tasca del Puerto**, Avda. del Puerto 13, ✆ 964 23 60 18 (*cheap*).

Benicasim ✉ 12560

Here you get less value for your money. A good bet is the **★★★Intur Azor**, right on the beach, Avda. Gimeno Tomás, ✆ 964 39 20 00, ✆ 964 39 23 79, *open from Mar–Nov*, and offering its guests tennis, golf, and pool facilities for *10,000 pts*. Just a little further from the beach, **★★Hotel Eco Avenida**, Avenida Castellon 2, ✆ 964 30 00 47, ✆ 964 30 00 79, provides a pleasant haven with swimming pool for a better price, (*4–5000 pts*). Benicasim has a fair choice of restaurants; the best option for seafood on the beachfront is **Villa del Mar**, Ps Maritimo Pilar Coloma 2/4, ✆ 964 30 28 52. It is

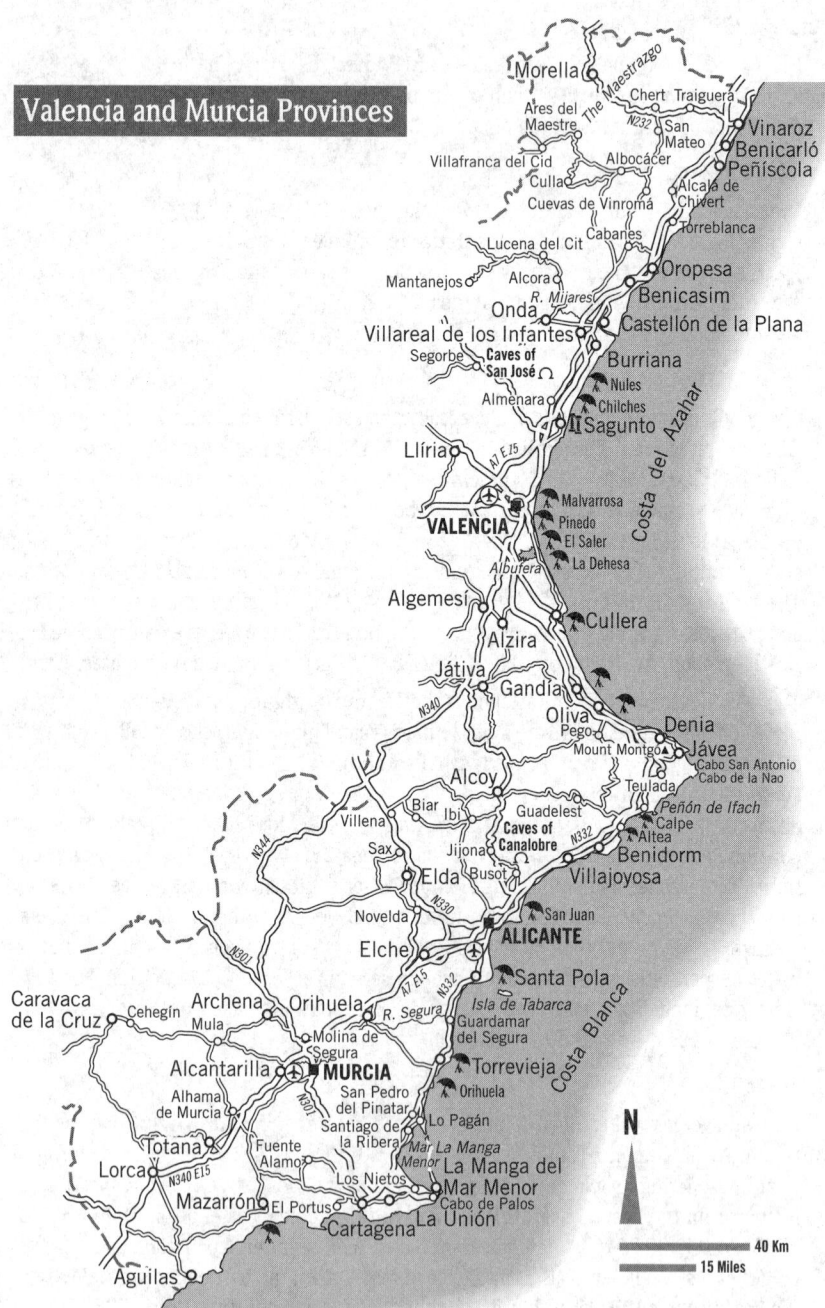

Valencia and Murcia Provinces

Morella
Ares del Maestre
Villafranca del Cid
Culla
Cuevas de Vinromá
Lucena del Cit
Mantanejos
Alcora
Onda
Villareal de los Infantes
Segorbe
Caves of San José
Almenara
Llíria
VALENCIA
Algemesí
Alzira
Játiva
Gandia
Oliva
Pego
Alcoy
Biar
Villena
Ibi
Sax
Jijona
Elda
Busot
Novelda
Elche
ALICANTE
Caravaca de la Cruz
Cehegín
Archena
Mula
Orihuela
Molina de Segura
Alcantarilla
MURCIA
Alhama de Murcia
San Pedro del Pinatar
Totana
Fuente Alamo
Santiago de la Ribera
Lorca
Mazarrón
El Portus
Los Nietos
Cartagena
La Unión
Aguilas

The Maestrazgo
Chert
Traiguera
N232
San Mateo
Vinaroz
Benicarló
Peñíscola
Albocácer
Alcalá de Chivert
Torreblanca
Cabanes
Oropesa
R. Mijares
Benicasim
Castellón de la Plana
Burriana
Nules
Chilches
Sagunto
A7 E15
Malvarrosa
Pinedo
El Saler
La Dehesa
Albufera
Cullera
N340
Denia
Jávea
Mount Montgo
Cabo San Antonio
Cabo de la Nao
Teulada
Peñón de Ifach
Guadelest
Calpe
Caves of Canalobre
Altea
Benidorm
Villajoyosa
N332
N330
San Juan
N344
N340
N301
R. Segura
Isla de Tabarca
Guardamar del Segura
Santa Pola
Costa Blanca
A7 E15
N332
Torrevieja
Orihuela
Lo Pagán
Mar Menor
La Manga del Mar Menor
Cabo de Palos
La Manga
Costa del Azahar

N

40 Km
15 Miles

170

worth an excursion into the hills behind the town to find **Desierto de las Palmas**, Pola Desierto Palmas s/n, ✆ 964 30 09 47 (*cheap*), near a 17th-century Carmelite monastery of the same name. The restaurant has panoramic views to the coast, overlooking palm groves and aromatic shrubs and trees tended by the monks.

Oropesa ✉ 12594

For more reasonable prices, stay instead at Oropesa, where a small but good beach hotel like ★★★**El Cid**, Las Playetas, ✆ 964 30 07 00, offers rooms in a pretty location, pool, tennis and a garden. *Open April–end Sept.* Another option on Oropesa's beach is ★★**Hs Oropesa Sol**, Avda. Madrid 11, ✆ 964 31 01 50. It's unremarkable but clean and comfortable (*under 5000 pts*). *Open April–end Sept.* A pricier alternative is the **Parador de Oropesa**, Pza. del Palacio 1, ✆ 964 43 00 00, ✆ 964 43 07 77, set in a feudal palace.

Peñíscola

The belle of the Costa del Azahar, Peñíscola has been called Spain's Mont St Michel for its location on a rugged promontory anchored to the mainland by a sandy isthmus. Intensive tourist development along the isthmus keeps Peñíscola from looking as strikingly isolated as it once did; still, the heavily fortified medieval town, with its cobbled streets and castle, forms one of the prettiest scenes to grace a Spanish postcard. The Phoenicians, its first settlers, called it Tyriche, because it reminded them of Tyre; the Romans regarded it in the 3rd century BC as the boundary between their colonies and Carthage's. Hamilcar Barca used the town as his headquarters, and here his son Hannibal, chafing under Roman constraints, resolved to make war on the upstart young empire. Jaime I won Peñíscola from the Moors and handed it over to the Templars, who built the castle. When the Order was dissolved, the town passed to the Knights of Montesa, who inherited all the Templars' possessions in the Kingdom of Valencia. They never spread outside Valencia, and according to most historians, quietly went about practising the same heresies and rituals that had condemned their predecessors.

The Knights of Montesa sheltered and protected Peñíscola's best-loved historical personage, Papa Luna, the last of the anti-Popes of Avignon, who reigned under the name Benedict XIII. Born in Aragón, Pedro de Luna (1338–1423) seems to have been a formidable character. After having been chased from Avignon by French troops and condemned for heresy, he spent the rest of his life issuing anathemata and ex-communicated everyone who wronged him, refusing even in his 90s to renounce his title of Benedict XIII. His obstinacy gave rise to the modern Spanish idiom, *mantenerse uno en sus trece*, 'to maintain one's thirteen', or as we would say, 'he stuck to his guns'. One of the gates into Peñíscola still bears his coat of arms.

The **Templar's Castle** (*open daily 10–2.30 and 4–8.30 in summer*), where Papa Luna resided, has been vigorously restored and contains the few relics left by his stay in its fine Gothic halls. One of his papal bulls issued here confirmed the 1411 foundation of St Andrew's University in Scotland. The façade of the 18th-century church near the castle is adorned with curious military symbols. Beware that in July and August, elbow room in Peñíscola's narrow streets is at a premium, the streets made even narrower by wall-to-wall souvenir stands that never seem to close. In the midst of this, restaurants claim their own bit of pavement to set tables and placards on. Yet from a distance it is always enchanting, especially at night when the walls and castle are bathed in golden light.

Benicarló, Peñíscola's mainland connection, has a Baroque church, with a Valencian dome frosted with blue *azulejos* and a tower. **Vinaroz** nearby is a small but important fishing-port, famed for its sturgeon and lobsters; its Baroque church has an equally colourful portal.

Where to Stay and Eating Out

Peñíscola ✉ 12598

Peñíscola's ★★★★**Hostería del Mar**, on Avda. Papa Luna 18, ✆ 964 48 06 00, 📧 964 48 13 63, is widely acclaimed as the best on the promenade (*around 14,000 pts*). *Open all year.* Splash out on a medieval banquet with music and dancing. Typical beach fare in Peñíscola, with fine views of the promontory, is ★★**La Cabaña**, Avda. Primo de Rivera 29, ✆ 964 48 00 17. It has many neighbours, all more or less the same. Of the cheap hotels on Peñíscola's promontory, the finest is ★**Hs del Duc**, located in an old mansion in the centre of town on C/ Fulladosa 10, ✆ 964 48 07 68. *Open April–Sept.*

There are many restaurants all over Peñíscola, covering all price ranges. On the promontory try **Casa Severino** at Urb. Las Atalayas, ✆ 964 48 07 03 (*moderate*), which offers the provincial speciality, *paella marinara*, with dining on the terrace overlooking the sea (*4000 pts*). *Closed Wed in winter.*

Benicarló ✉ 12580

In Benicarló the best place to stay and eat is the ★★★**Parador de Benicarló**, Avda. Papa Luna 3, ✆ 964 47 01 00, 📧 964 47 09 34, a modern establishment with pool, garden and air-conditioned rooms; the restaurant features the freshest of seafood and Valencian specialities. Much cheaper is ★★**Hotel Rosi**, Dr Fleming 50, ✆ 964 46 00 08, with the advantage of being close to the centre of town and the beach. Benicarló's best budget accommodation is just beside the Plaza del Mercado, at ★**Hs Belmonte**, Pio XII 3, ✆ 964 47 12 39 (*around 3500 pts*). Benicarló has some decent restaurants: try the air-conditioned **El Cortijo**, Avda. Méndez Núñez 85, ✆ 964 47 00 75 (*expensive–moderate*), which has a wide range of fresh seafood. *Closed Mon and the first two weeks of July.*

Vinaroz/Vinaròs ✉ 12500

Vinaroz has the small and perfectly formed **El Pino**, C/ San Pascual 47, ✆ 964 45 05 53. Eat the locally caught catch of the day when you can: the fish and seafood here is fresh and excellent. Try **Casa Pocho**, C/ S.Gregorio 49, ✆ 964 45 10 95 (*moderate*), a friendly place (*closed Tues*), or the smarter **El Langostir ○ de Oro**, C/ San Francisco 3, ✆ 964 45 12 04 (*expensive*).

The Maestrazgo

Inland from Peñíscola is a region called the Maestrazgo, which translates as 'the jurisdiction of a grand master of a military order'; and of Grand Masters you can take your pick between the Templars, the Knights of Montesa, and the Knights of St John, all of whom resided here. It is a rugged, picturesque place, especially the Upper Maestrazgo (*see* **Aragón**, p.198). The Lower Maestrazgo, while not as wild or remote, has a number of fascinating medieval villages.

Easiest to reach, on the Vinaroz–Zaragoza road, picturesque **Morella** is surrounded by medieval walls that look as if they were raised yesterday and surmounted by a steep, isolated rock and a mighty castle. Of the four gates leading into the city, the 14th-century **Puerta de San Miguel** is the most impressive. Of the churches, the **Basílica de Santa María la Mayor** (1330) with its finely carved portals and stained glass is not only the finest in town, but perhaps of the whole *país valenciano*. Inside (*open daily 12–2 and 4–6*) a magnificently carved marble spiral staircase ascends to the raised *coro*, where the balustrade has a frieze of the Last Judgement. The small museum stars a *Madonna* by the serene Italian painter Sassoferrato and a 15th-century Valencian *Descent from the Cross*. The steep streets of Morella are lined with tall whitewashed houses with wooden balconies. Just below the castle is an old **Franciscan monastery** with a museum in its fine 13th-century **cloister**. From here you can take a path up to the castle itself, with magnificent views; to the north look for the **Gothic aqueduct**, built in the 14th century when Roman techniques were a dim memory.

From the extremely pretty San Mateo a minor road heads 22km south to **Albocácer**, a Templar town with a ruined castle; near this, just off the road from San Mateo is a **Calvario**, an outdoor version of the Stations of the Cross or symbolic journey along the Via Dolorosa. A typical one has a chapel atop a hill, reached by a winding path marked by intermittent shrines. The Maestrazgo is famous for its Calvarios, but Albocácer's is exceptional—a virtual maze of low, whitewashed, stone walls. Another one in maze form may be seen in the **Cuevas de Vinromá** just to the southeast. While the rest of Europe underwent the pangs of the Second World War, Spaniards were reading about the chapel atop the Cuevas de Vinromá's Calvario, where the Nationalists manufactured a miracle—several appearances of the Virgin, no less, who mouthed the philosophy of José Antonio Primo de Rivera and declared that Heaven, in league with Hitler, would soon clear the earth of the Marxist-Jewish menace that threatened it with extinction. In the euphoria of post-Civil War victory, there were plans to make the village the Lourdes of Spain, but when the Vatican remained silent on the matter and the war took its course, the miracles quickly dried up. Nowadays the only 'sight' in the old village is its prehistoric cave paintings.

Two other scenic medieval towns, formerly Templar possessions, are **Culla** and **Ares del Maestre**. The latter is built around a cheese soufflé of a rock, 1,318 m high, near some excellent palaeolithic art in the **Cova Remigia**. The cave lies just along the road to another pretty village, **Villafranca del Cid**, which like several other places in the Maestrazgo recalls in its name the Cid's frequent raids in the region. The villages of the Maestrazgo celebrate various saints throughout August, their *fiestas* usually being spread over a long weekend and involving minor bull-running during the day and much jollity in the evenings.

Where to Stay and Eating Out

Morella ✉ 12300

Morella is the only town in the Maestrazgo well-prepared for visitors, though the majority of the villages mentioned above have rooms above bars, or modest *hostales*. Castellón's tourist office can provide you with a list. Best in Morella is the ****Cardenal Ram**, Cuesta Suñer 1, ℮ 964 17 30 85, located in a restored palace, like a budget *parador*, with fine rooms near the centre for *7500 pts*. It also has a good restaurant. For the same price, you could choose to stay in cosy comfort at the new and beautifully furnished ★★★**Hotel Rey Don Jaime**, C/Juan Giner 6, ✆/☎ 964 16 09 11, with superb mountain views. Also in Morella is the welcoming **Hs La Muralla**, C/ Muralla 12, ✆ 964 16 02 43, which is clean and cheerful.

10km outside Morella, the delightful 16th-century **Palau dels Osset**, Pza Major 16, ✆ 964 17 75 24, ☎ 964 17 75 56 (*expensive*) offers all the luxuries in a restored palace in the tiny medieval village of Forcall.

An even better restaurant than the Cardenal Ram's is **Mesón del Pastor**, Cuesta Jovani 5, ✆ 964 16 02 49 (*cheap*), which features the local cuisine of the mountains—lots of pork and lamb with curds and honey (*cuajada y miel*) for dessert (*1500–2000 pts*). *Closed Wed.* For tapas try the bar **Vinatea** on the main road Els Porxos, which harbours a variety of **bakeries** and **cafés**.

The Costa Blanca

The 'White Coast' of Spain started out as a refuge from the intensity of the Costa Brava, where pioneering Germans, followed by the British and French, could have an inexpensive if unexciting holiday. Not as beautiful as the Costa Brava, nor as physically monotonous as the Costa del Sol, the Costa Blanca is no longer inexpensive, and every year more sports activities and nightclubs accompany a growing number of hotels and apartment blocks—especially in the Babylon of Benidorm.

Getting Around

There are at least 15 local trains daily between Valencia and Gandía, the terminus of the coast line. The Valencia–Alicante train, however, goes inland, through Játiva; another branch from Valencia terminates in Alcoy via Játiva (three a day). There are frequent RENFE buses between Valencia and Alicante as well, some direct on the *autopista*, others stopping at the resorts along the Costa Blanca.

The Costa Blanca is also well served by its own narrow-gauge line (FGV) out of Alicante (15 a day, once an hour), with stations at Denia, Teulada, Calpe, Altea, Benidorm and the beaches north of Alicante. Several buses a day link Denia with Jávea, connecting with the train. FGV information: Denia, ✆ 96 578 04 45; Benidorm, ✆ 96 585 18 95; Alicante, ✆ 96 526 27 31.

Denia is also a port with ferry links on the Flebasa line to Ibiza; for information, ✆ 96 578 40 11 in Denia or freephone ✆ 900 177 177. PITRA also operate ferries, for information, call ✆ 96 642 31 20. Both offices are on the harbour front.

Tourist Information

Gandía: Avda. Marqués de Campo, ✆ 96 287 77 88.
Denia: Pza. Oculista Büigues 9, ✆ 96 642 23 67.
Jávea: Pza. Almirante Basterreche 24, ✆ 96 579 07 36.
Calpe: Avda. Ejércitos Españoles 66, ✆ 96 583 69 20.
Altea: C/ Sant Pere 9, ✆ 96 584 41 14.
Benidorm: Avda. Martínez Alejos 16, ✆ 96 5853224.

The Costa Blanca officially begins at Denia; en route there are great rice plantations and minor beaches with the notable exception of the busy resort of **Cullera**, which is populated by energetic Spanish families and has a nice beach. Next is **Gandía**, set back a couple of miles from the sea. The town once belonged to the Borgia dukes, a more polite branch of the family than the band who caused so much trouble in Italy; in the 15th century they settled down in the fine Renaissance **Palace of the Dukes**. The fourth duke of Gandía, Francisco Borgia, renounced the worldly vanities his family was famous for and became a Jesuit and saint. The palace now belongs to the Jesuits; the tourist office can tell you how to get in for a tour. There are frequent connections to the over-developed beach. **Oliva**, 4km away, is a little quieter.

Just within Alicante province, Denia is squeezed between Mount Montgó and the sea. The Greeks built a temple of Artemis here, and the town is named for her Roman alias Diana. Only the ruined **castle** over the town evokes Denia's pre-tourist history, but the town with all its villas is one of the quieter on the Costa Blanca, and there are fine views from atop Mount Montgó. **Jávea**, nestled beneath the villa-covered capes of San Antonio and San Martín, has preserved more of its old character, and although it has only two small beaches, it is well endowed with scenic marine grottos and dramatic coves. Next are the fairly quiet beaches of **Teulada**, and then the not-so-quiet but excellent sands of **Calpe**. The Greeks called Gibraltar 'Calpe' and this Calpe, too has it own mighty Rock, the **Peñon de Ifach**, swept by body-scarred beaches on either side and bored with a tunnel to let you mount to the summit— 327m over the sea below. **Altea** is quieter, located on a natural balcony over the sea; its stony beach isn't as good but does form a series of coves, including a nudist beach. The others are popular with families. Its church has a fine blue-tiled Valencian dome.

Where to Stay and Eating Out

Gandía ✉ 46700

In Gandía, the swanky hotels are on the beach, and the modest, inexpensive ones in the town. In the first category the ★★★★**Bayren I**, Pso. de Neptuno 62, ✆ 96 284 03 00, ✆ 96 284 06 53, stands out, with a pleasant pool and dancing in the evening (*15,000 pts*). It has an annex, the ★★★**Bayren II**, on C/ Mallorca 19, ✆ 96 284 07 00, with cheaper rates. In Gandía town, the ★★**Hotel Mengual**, Pza. del Mediterráneo 4, ✆ 96 284 21 02, is a pleasant choice (*7000 pts*). Most of the restaurants in Gandía are on the beach: **La Gamba**, on the Ctra. Nazaret-Oliva, ✆ 96 284 13 10 (*moderate*), has a garden-terrace as a pretty setting for its delicious seafood (*4000 pts*). At the **El As de Oros**, Pso. de Neptuno (*expensive*), shellfish are the speciality (*5500 pts*). *Closed Mon.*

Jávea/Xàbia ✉ 03730

Jávea boasts the finely situated ★★★**Parador de Jávea**, Playa del Arenal, ✆ 96 579 02 00, ✆ 96 579 03 08, air-conditioned, with a pool and palm-filled garden and good restaurant focusing on the dishes of the Levante (*14,000–16,000 pts*). If you can't swing the *parador*, the ★★**Hs Jávea**, in the middle of town on Pío X 5, ✆ 96 579 54 61, is small and friendly. The best budget accommodation is the popular ★**Hs La Favorita**, C/ Magallanes 4, ✆ 96 579 04 77.

The resoundingly popular **Azorin**, Toni Llido, ℗ 96 579 44 95, at the centre of the action near the port, dishes out huge plates of shellfish for a nice price. About 1km from the town, on the road to the wicker and wood-working town of Gata, **La Casita de Paco**, Carretera de Gata, ℗ 96 579 59 09, serves wholesome portions of fine local-style cooking; their *fideos* is especially good. Alternatively, an *expensive* treat halfway between Javea and Calpe, **The Girasol**, ℗ 96 574 43 73, provides fine international cuisine in elegant surroundings.

Calpe/Calp ✉ 03710

There are numerous multi-complex, variously starred hotels in Calpe, but for a better bargain try the **★Hs El Parque**, in the centre at C/ Portalet, ℗ 96 583 07 70. Its simple but clean rooms go for *2500–3500 pts*. The food in Calpe's restaurants, like nearby Benidorm's, tends to be international: good French dishes are featured at **Los Zapatos**, C/ Santa María 7, ℗ 96 583 15 07 (*3500 pts*). *Closed Tues.* For an extraordinary range of pancakes, try **Bora Bora**, Av. Del Puerto, ℗ 96 583 31 77.

Altea ✉ 03590

In Altea, there is luxury on the beach in the form of **★★★Cap Negret**, Ctra. Valencia, ℗ 96 584 12 00, with a range of facilities including a pool. A good bet on the beach is the **★★Hotel Altaya**, Generalísimo 113, ℗ 96 584 08 00; the pleasant and very comfortable rooms have sea views. The service is helpful and friendly. There are a few budget *hostales* grouped behind the main square.

For gourmets only, **Monte Molar** just outside Altea on Ctra. Valencia, ℗ 96 584 15 81 (*expensive*) serves some delicate and imaginative dishes—snails with wild rice, duck with mushrooms and bilberry sauce; the terrace looks onto the sea (*6000 pts*). In Altea itself, you could try **Sant Pere 24** on Carrer Sant Pere 24, ℗ 96 584 49 72 (*moderate*). A cool and pleasant place, it specializes in rice dishes, mostly for two people: the *arroz de langosta* is splendid. **Raco de Toni**, La Mar 127, ℗ 96 584 17 63, also excels in rice and fish dishes. Good tapas can be found in the old town around the Plaza de la Iglesia, the best area for atmospheric open-air dining, especially at **La Capella**, C/ San Pablo 1, ℗ 96 668 04 84.

Denia ✉ 03700

In Denia, the **★★Hotel Rosa**, C/ Marinas 197, ℗ 96 578 15 73, is a pleasant, seaside, family-orientated resort, with pools for the adults and children, a playground, tennis and restaurant (*8500 pts*). The **★Hs Noguera**, Marinas Pda Estaño, ℗ 96 647 41 07, offers nice enough rooms on Marinas beach; anyway the price is right at *4000 pts* for a double room. The place to eat in Denia is **El Trampoli** (*moderate*), Playa Les Rotes (where most of Denia's restaurants may be found), with a delicious menu of Valencian rice and seafood for *4500 pts*, ℗ 96 578 12 96. **Gavila**, C/ Marqués de Campo 55, ℗ 96 578 10 66 (*expensive*) serves more of the same in a cool setting. The food is perfectly cooked. A cheaper option is the buttercup-yellow **Bitibau**, C/ San Vicente del Mar 5, ℗ 96 642 25 74 (*moderate*) which inhabits a typical narrow street and has a more international menu.

Benidorm

The undisputed giant on the Costa Blanca, Benidorm has become synonymous with high rises and package tourism. The 6.4km-long and generously wide sandy beach has something to do with it, and the ensemble of skyscrapers huddled together in a dense forest is awesome in a Manhattanish way; certainly it has a verve most other costa resorts lack—as well as more discotheques and Las Vegas-type shows.

Behind Benidorm (you can perhaps see it best from the *autopista*) there is a peculiar mountain with a neat, square notch taken out of it—a notch shaped exactly like the islet off the coast. An old Spanish legend recounts that a giant once lived near Benidorm. After many years of loneliness, he found a lady love. She fell ill and told the giant that she would die when the sun went down that day. In despair the giant watched the sun sink behind the mountain, then at the last minute wrenched out a piece of the summit and hurled it into the sea to give his beloved another minute of life. True or not, geologists have confirmed that the islet and mountain are at least made out of the same kind of rock. Inland from Benidorm, it's 27km to the very pretty medieval village of **Guadalest** with its much-ruined castle perched high atop a pinnacle. To capture it, Jaime I wrote that he had to attach wings to his soldiers' armour; the modern visitor can climb up through a tunnel. **Alcoy**, further west, celebrates St George's Day with a Battle of Christians and Moors commemorating a personal appearance of the saint in a 1276 battle. It's been going on so long there's a museum of the holiday, as well as local costumes, armour, etc. at the **Casal de Sant Jordi**.

Villajoyosa is the last big resort before Alicante, but despite the pretty white nucleus of its old town it manages to have the least character.

Sports and Activities

When you've had enough of the beach, the Costa Blanca will entertain you in other ways. Nearly every town has its **tennis** courts; Altea, Benisa (near Calpe), Jávea and Torrevieja (south of Alicante) have **golf** courses as well. There are **watersports** of all kinds, especially at Benidorm which has waterskiing facilities, boat rentals, sailing and diving on offer. Windsurfing is popular all along the coast. Near Pego (by Denia), the **Safari Park Vergel** is for those with cars only—the lions and tigers run about freely; there's also a dolphin show and many children's activities; open all year, © 96 575 02 85. Benidorm has a permanent **fun fair** just off the access route to the *autopista*, and a **marine park**, Aqualandia, © 96 586 40 06, with lots more fun for the kids (*under 3s get in free, adm 1575 pts for adults, 1200 for kids; a bus leaves every half hour from Plaza Triangular*). The **Go-Kart** craze has really caught on in Spain, and there are circuits everywhere. The modern **Casino Costa Blanca** is between Benidorm and Villajoyosa; all along the old coastal road from Alicante are **shopping centres** with big parking lots (open and abandoned), scruffy putting courses and bowling alleys. Yachtsmen should obtain from the tourist offices the detailed folder on *Instalaciones Náuticas* on the Costa; another big folder, *Deporte y Cultura*, details every possible activity on the coast, from deep-sea diving to choral societies. There are **cruises** to look at the offshore islands in boats or half-submerged submarines with glass bottoms (©. 96 585 00 52) and to Calpe, leaving from the port at 9.30am.

There are so many hotels in **Benidorm**, and so many of them so similar and so booked up with packagers in the summer, that it's hard to tell them apart. Off-season you can get excellent rates—as little as half those in the high season. Don't bother to turn up in August without a booking.

Good value for money ★★★**Los Alamos** (*moderate*), located near the beach and the heart of Benidorm on Avda. Gerona, ✆ 96 585 02 12, has a pool and garden. In the same category, but a bit further back from the sea, is the attractive ★★**Hotel Don José**, Ctra. Del Alt, ✆ 96 585 50 50. *Open Mar–Oct*. A third choice isn't stylish, but it's centrally located and has a pool: ★**Hs Nacional**, C/ Verano 9, ✆ 96 585 04 32 (*inexpensive*). *Open April–Oct*. Budget accommodation tends to be clustered near the centre of town, away from the sea.

There is no accommodation in **Guadalest**.

Eating Out

The posh place to dine in Benidorm is **Tiffany's** (*expensive*), Avda. del Mediterráneo 51, ✆ 96 585 44 68, with high-class international cuisine (*4000 pts*). *Closed 7 January–7 February*. Similarly expensive and delicious is **I Fratelli**, Avda. Dr Orts Llorca 21, ✆ 96 585 39 79, with a few regional dishes too (*4500pts*). Also international, with a good atmosphere and terrace dining in the summer is **La Caserola** (*moderate*), Avda. Bruselas 7, ✆ 96 585 17 19 (*3500 pts*).

For good-value seafood at a similar price, try **La Palmera**, Casa Paca Nadal, Avda. De Severo Ochoa s/n, ✆ 96 585 32 82. *Closed July and August*. In Benidorm's old town—the tiny, pre-holiday fishing village—**El Calpi** (*cheap*), Pza. de la Constitución, is a good bet for tapas.

Entertainment and Nightlife

Benidorm counts its pubs, night clubs, and discotheques by the score; there are close to a hundred discos alone. Most are international in flavour and stay packed all night, only disgorging their crowds when the need for a fried egg breakfast grows too strong. Otherwise you can generally choose any form of entertainment that catches your fancy: from English to German and Scandinavian pubs, American-style bars, nightclubs in which you are serenaded by Spanish guitar and establishments in which you can let loose with your own version of bath-time favourites with a karaoke machine. Perhaps to compensate for all this, Benidorm sponsors a Festival of Spanish Song.

Alicante/Alacant

Alicante is the air gateway to the Costa Blanca, and many of the two million people who fly in here decide to go no further. Unlike the other resorts on the coast, Alicante is a real Spanish city, with an air all of its own along its seaside promenades and narrow back streets. It never tires of letting you know that, year after year, it has the warmest and sunniest winters in all Europe. And charter flights in January or February can be cheaper than the heating bills you would pay staying at home.

By air: Alicante's *El Altet* airport is 10km from the city, ✆ 96 528 50 11. Besides charters from northern Europe, it handles a large number of regular domestic flights from Madrid, Barcelona, Palma, Ibiza, Sevilla, Las Palmas, Tenerife, Bilbao and Vitoria. Iberia's office is at Avda. Federico Soto 9, ✆ 96 520 60 00. Airport buses, no.C6, leave from C/ Portugal, by the bus station, every hour on the hour from 7am–10pm (100 pts).

By train: RENFE's station in Alicante is on Avda. Salamanca, ✆ 96 592 0202; the ticket office is at Explanada de España 1, ✆ 96 521 98 67. There are frequent connections with Murcia (*see* below).

By bus: Alicante's bus station is at the corner of C/ Portugal and C/ Italia, ✆ 96 513 07 00. There are frequent connections all along the Costa Blanca; also to Granada, Almería, Barcelona, Jaén, Málaga, Sevilla, Madrid and Valencia. There are also international buses to assorted European destinations.

Bus no.C1's route continues past the FEVE station to the Playa de San Juan and Playa de Muchavista, and takes in most of Alicante's discotheques as well. It runs approximately every 15mins and on summer weekends, all night.

There are buses down the coast from Alicante; connections between Torrevieja and points south are also very frequent from Murcia (*see* below).

<hr>

Tourist Information

Municipal office: Pza Ayuntamiento 1, ✆ 96 514 92 80.
Provincial office: Explanada de España 2, ✆ 96 520 00 00.
In the bus station: C/ Portugal 17, ✆ 96 592 98 02.

The **hospital** is on C/ San Juan, ✆ 96 590 8300. The **post office** can be found at Plaza Gabriel Miró; a **telephone office** is on Avda. Constitución 10.

Trasmediterránea operate **ferries** to Ibiza, Explanada de España 2, ✆ 96 514 25 51, ✉ 96 520 45 26.

<hr>

The Castle, Cathedral and Around

Alicante was the mightiest citadel of the Kingdom of Valencia, and judging by the powerful **Castillo de Santa Bárbara** that crowns the city, it still is. An English garrison spent most of Spain's wars here; Felipe V blew both castle and troops up in 1707, but it was later restored, and is fun to explore for itself and the stunning views it commands (*open daily exc Mon, 10–sundown in the summer; access by lift from the Paseo de Gomis, just above the Playa del Postiguet*).

Below the castle is Alicante's lively and jovial old quarter, **Santa Cruz**, encompassing the **Catedral San Nicolás de Bari** (1662), a strong, well-proportioned church covered with red graffiti (*open daily 7.30–12.30 and 5.30–8*). The interior has been restored since its destruction in the Civil War. Republican passions burned white hot in Alicante—the founder and patron saint of the Falange, José Antonio Primo de Rivera, was imprisoned in a local convent and hurriedly executed when the locals feared the Republican government might order him freed. At the end of the war, some 15,000 Republicans waited on the docks in vain for the

Republican Navy to rescue them from Nationalist reprisals. Several hundred, it is said, committed suicide. Behind the cathedral is a **Nativity Museum**, with 380 Christmas cribs (*open daily except Mon 10.30–2 and 4.30–8.30; Sun, am only*).

The **Ayuntamiento** in Calle R. Altamira has an elegant Baroque façade and is near the **Museum of 20th-Century Art**, just off pedestrian Calle Mayor, with works by Picasso, Braque, Gris, Miró and others (*open summer 10.30–1.30 and 6–9; winter 10–1 and 5–8 ; closed Mon and Sun pm*). Near the train station, the Palacio de la Diputación on Avda. de la Estación, houses the town's **archaeology museum**, with prehistoric finds and remains from the Carthaginian wars (*open weekdays 9–2, closed Sat and Sun*).

Alicante's Beaches

Most visitors, when they're not lounging on Alicante's fine beaches, are strolling down the shady **Explanada de España** with its flamboyant mosaics. The **Playa de El Postiguet**, at the end of the Explanada, can get very, very crowded in the summer, and sometimes it seems just as many people take the bus or train 6.5km north to bigger and cleaner **Playa de San Juan**. The FGV train up the coast passes some **quiet coves** such as the small beach near Amerador station. It's possible to explore on the ride: just keep your eyes peeled and be prepared to jump off quickly when a nice beach catches your fancy.

Between Alicante and San Juan beach, you can visit the **Monasterio de La Santa Faz**, built to enshrine the supposed handkerchief that Santa Veronica loaned to Christ as he carried the Cross—although for authenticity it has to compete with a similar handkerchief in the Vatican (*open 9–12 and 4.30–sunset; take the bus no.C-3 from Plaza del Mar*). A secondary road off the coast leads to Busot and the **Caves of Canalobre** (24km from Alicante), with stalactites and strange formations, where concerts are held occasionally in the summer (*open daily 10.30–8.30, winter 11–6.30, for information ring ☏ 96 569 92 50*).

Valencia ✉ *03000*   ***Where to Stay***

In Alicante, hotels of all categories are spread throughout town, but the most popular are near the Explanada. The cheapest are around Santa María church.

expensive

On the beach, in a huge, self-contained complex, is the ★★★★**Meliá Alicante**, Playa de El Postiguet, ☏ 96 520 50 00, ✆ 96 520 47 56, with restaurants, pools, and shops.

moderate

A few blocks from the Explanada, the ★★★**Hotel Cristal**, C/ López Torregrosa 9, ☏ 96 514 36 59, was named after its crystal façade. All rooms are attractive, and come with bath and air conditioning. It's popular with businessmen. ★**El Alamo**, C/ San Fernando 56, ☏ 96 521 83 55, doesn't look like much from the outside, but has pleasant rooms within, although the street it's on is infamous in Alicante for drugs and prostitution. More reasonable is the **Hs Galicia**, C/ Arquitecto Morell 1, ☏ 96 522 50 93, two blocks from the bus station in a modern building.

inexpensive–cheap

A nice budget *hostal*, the ★★**Montecarlo**, C/ San Francisco 20, ☏ 96 520 67 22, is near the heart of town and near the beach. A very special place to stay, **Pensión Les**

Monges, First Floor, C/ Monjas 2, ✆ 96 521 50 46, behind the Ayuntamiento, has fine rooms with satellite TV, music, air conditioning and parking.. The owner, Pedro, is as charming as his establishment. Very good value at *3000–4200 pts.* Those on a tight budget will not find anywhere else like **★Pension Versalles**, C/ Villavieja 3, ✆ 96 521 45 93. Its handful of large rooms are arranged around a jasmine-scented, vine-canopied courtyard, set with tables and a TV in the evenings. There are shared bathrooms, a kitchen and a very mellow atmosphere.

Eating Out

expensive

The best restaurant in Alicante, **Delfín**, Explanada de España 12, ✆ 96 521 49 11, serves delicious Alicantino versions of Valencian rice dishes, innovative international dishes and excellent seafood, with fine views of the sea (*6000 pts*). **Dársena** boasts an even more scenic location on Pso. del Puerto just off the Explanada, ✆ 96 520 75 89; it has a bright shiny interior and delicious rice dishes (*4500 pts*). **Nou Manoulin**, C/ Villegas 3, ✆ 96 520 03 68, is housed in old brick wine cellars close to the ancient centre of town, and offers delicious local delicacies. Elegant **Piripiri**, Oscar Espla 30, ✆ 96 522 79 41, also makes the most of regional dishes. Try the *fideos*, a northern Alicante speciality which uses vermicelli noodles instead of rice (*5500 pts*).

moderate

Another restaurant with a sea view from its terrace is **La Goleta**, Explanada de España 8, ✆ 96 521 43 92, specializing in seafood rice dishes and mixed grills, with a good set menu for *2500 pts.* Galician specialities are a must at **O'Pote Galego**, Pza. Santísima Faz 6, ✆ 96 520 80 84, with excellent grills and *merluza a la gallega* (*3500 pts*). **Bar Luis**, C/ Pedro Sebastián 7, ✆ 96 521 14 46, is cool and elegant with a notable wine cellar: bottles line the walls. The international menu has firmly Spanish roots and unusual dishes are created with real flair. Try the lasagne with spinach, prawns and salmon. Their tapas are excellent. Reasonable for this standard at around *5000 pts. Closed Sun.*

cheap

One of Alicante's great bargain eateries in San Juan is **Regina**, Avda. Niza 19, ✆ 96 526 41 39, with good tapas, *paella* and seafood. The set menu is only *850 pts*, but even if you go all out you'll spend less than *2000 pts.* **Mesón Labradores** on C/ Labradores is very popular for its great tapas; it's typically Alicantian inside with *azulejo* walls busy with pictures and ceramics. Calm staff conjure tables out of nowhere in the midst of the bustle. *Closed Mon.* Another favourite, this time with the colourful locals of the old Santa Cruz quarter, is **Rincón de António**, Patronato de Santa Cruz just above the Pza. del Carmen. You won't meet any other tourists at this tapas bar; there is no menu here and the friendly owner is happy to give you a good selection for *around 800 pts.* The best streets for shopping stem from the main drag, especially Avenida Maisonnave and Calle Gerona; the latter is also home to **Croissanterie Chantal**, which serves delicious homemade cakes and fresh fruit juices.

The tiny and unusual **Bodega Las Garrafas**, squeezed between the modern convenience cafés, at C/ Major 33, is filled with all things ancient—a cash till on the counter and an eccentric collection of oil lamps, cow bells and even a British police helmet hanging from the ceiling. The walls are covered with pictures of the owner with famous visitors over the last 40 years: Hemingway and Dalí are there. The area around Pza. del Carmen and below San Cristóbal, known as **El Barrio**, comes alive with bars after 1am. In the summer the place to be is San Juan beach, which is overrun with all-night bars and discos. The FGV train runs all night as far as Altea.

Around Alicante

Getting Around

By bus: There are buses from Alicante to Elche, from Mon–Fri, 7am–9pm every half hour, on Sat and Sun from 8am–9pm every hour. The company is MOLLA.

The bus company BAILE connects Alicante with Santa Pola hourly, on weekdays from 7.30am–9pm, on weekends from 9am–9pm.

COSTA AZUL buses go south from Santa Pola from 7am–8pm every 2hrs.

Tourist Information

Elche: Pza. del Parc, ✆ 545 2747.
Orihuela: Francisco Díez 25, ✆ 530 2747.
Santa Pola: Pza. Diputación 6, ✆ 669 2276.
Torrevieja: Pza. Ruiz Capdepont, ✆ 571 5936.
Los Alcázares (Mar Menor): C/ Fuster 63, ✆ 817 13 61.
La Manga del Mar Menor: Urb. Castillo del Mar, San Javier, ✆ 814 18 12.
San Pedro del Pinatar: Parque de los Reyes de España, ✆ 818 23 01.

Jijona and Villena

In Alicante you may have noticed shops stacked to the ceiling with *turrón*, a nougat sweet made of local almonds and honey. Nearly all of it comes from **Jijona**, on the main road to Alcoy (try the 1880 *Crema de Fijona*), where a **Turrón Museum** will show you how it's made. This is a busy region: nearby **Ibi** makes most of Spain's toys. One company claims to be the world's largest producer of dolls' eyeballs. West of Ibi there are picturesque **castles** crowning the villages of **Biar**, **Sax** and, strikingly, **Villena**, where the huge, square-towered citadel dates from the 15th century, as do many of the old noble houses. Villena's Gothic church of **Santiago** is decorated with fluted columns and strange motifs, while the Ayuntamiento (1707) has a gracious courtyard and an **Archaeology Museum**. Unlike many dusty provincial collections, this one is worth a detour for the **Treasure of Villena**—a hoard of solid gold bracelets, tiaras, bowls and rings discovered near the town in 1963. The pieces have been dated back to the Bronze Age (1000 BC) and were made by the ancestors of the Iberians.

Elche/Elx

Elche, 20km west of Alicante, makes two claims on the world's attention. First, Spain's most famous piece of ancient art was unearthed here, *La Dama de Elche*, now in Madrid's

Archaeology Museum. Secondly, it has the only date-palm grove in Europe. The Moors planted the first palms, and now the approximately 200,000 trees nearly surround Elche. Although they produce a crop of dates (no other palms in Europe do), they are economically more valuable for their fronds, which are tied up to bleach a pale yellow and shipped throughout Spain for Palm Sunday. Often you'll see one tied to a balcony, not because the owner has forgotten to take it down after Easter, but because the fronds are widely believed to ward off lightning. The palms are best seen in the **Huerto del Cura** just east of town on Calle Federico García Sanchis, where you can pay your respects to the unusual, seven-branched Imperial Palm, thought to be around 150 years old (*open daily 9–9*).

The Lady of Elche bust was discovered in 1897 in **La Alcudia** south of town. Since then further excavations have revealed nine successive civilizations, documented by a small **museum** on the site (*Ctra. Dolores, 2km from town; open 10–2, closed Mon*). The blue-domed **Basílica de Santa María** has an elaborate 17th-century Baroque façade; ask to climb the tower for the view across the palm plantations. Just north of the cathedral, in a restored 15th-century palace on the edge of the municipal park, another **Archaeology Museum** has a copy of La Dama de Elche, along with finds from prehistoric, Phoenician and Roman times. There's also a Greek headless torso of Venus (*open daily except Mon 10–1 and 4–8*). On Plaza de Arrabal a small **Museum of Contemporary Art** contains paintings, sculptures and ceramics by modern Valencian artists (*open daily except Mon 10–1 and 5–8*).

Orihuela, also on the road to Murcia, is an oasis—a prosperous town in its own very fertile *huerta*. It's worth a stop for its idiosyncratic **Cathedral** (*open mornings till 1 and from 4–6*). Finished in 1355, its interior is a fantasy of spiralling pillars and corkscrew-rib vaulting; the **cathedral museum** has a Velázquez and other masters in its fine collection (*open daily 10–1.30 and 5.30–7.30*). The town also has an **ethnographic museum** on Plaza Mayor, with a display of local crafts (*open daily 11.30–1 and 5–7*). Of the many 19th-century **palacios** the one housing the tourist office can be viewed (*open Mon–Fri 10.30–1.30*). The tourist office staff will show you round.

South of Alicante

The landscapes south of Alicante are mostly flat and not especially attractive, though in February the blossoming almonds provide a pretty lace edging. The resorts to the south are also less exciting. **Santa Pola**, the largest, has good beaches and a landmark, fortified **Isla de Tabarca**, which you can visit on an excursion boat. **Guardamar del Segura** is more scenic with its palms and pines; **Torrevieja** has modern hotels going up everywhere. To the south there are some tranquil beaches, as yet not too developed, belonging to **Orihuela**.

Further south, into the Murcia region, the unusual **Mar Menor** is a warm, shallow and salty lagoon, covering 170 sq km, and dotted with islets. It's separated from the sea by a narrow, beach-lined strip of land called **La Manga** ('the sleeve') where most of Murcia's holiday development has taken place. Along La Manga you can choose between the calm and warm beaches on the Mar Menor, or the cooler beaches along the Mediterranean. Moorish kings would come to the Mar Menor for their ritual 'nine baths'; today some of the ancient pools are still used in **San Pedro del Pinatar** for rheumatism therapy. Because of its warmth the Mar Menor is also used as a great prawn nursery, where Spain's favourite snacks may be harvested right up to the beginning of winter. These resorts are all very popular with the Spanish.

Elche ✉ 03200

In Elche, there's an associate *parador*, the ★★★★**Huerto del Cura**, Porta de la Morera 14, ✆ 96 545 80 40, 🖅96 542 19 10, with cabins in the palm grove. There's a pool and tennis courts; all rooms are air-conditioned and have private bars. Within easy walking distance of the Parque Municipal and palm groves, the simple but clean ★★**Candilejas**, c/ Dr Ferran 19, ✆ 96 546 02 83, is fine for an overnight stay. Elche claims three clean and relatively unspoilt beaches on the outskirts of town, where it is possible to find good cheap accommodation; **Hs. Maruja** at La Marina, ✆ 96 541 91 26, is basic but clean and well-situated at the water's edge.

The restaurant of the *parador*, **Els Capellans** (*expensive*) is considered the town's finest, and has views over the palms; some desserts are made with local dates. The restaurant in the **Parque Municipal** (*moderate*) specializes in rice dishes under the palms, for around *3500 pts*. **Mesón El Granaino** is done out in traditional style, across the river at Josep María Buch 40, ✆ 96 546 01 47 (*moderate*), serving varied *paellas, cocidos* and the local speciality *tarta de almendra* (*4000 pts*). *Closed Sun.*

Orihuela ✉ 03100

In Orihuela itself try the large and pleasant ★★**Hostal Rey Teodomiro**, Avda. Teodomiro 10, ✆ 96 674 33 48. Right on Orihuela's beach, Dehesa de Campoamor, the ★★★**Montepiedra**, ✆ 96 532 03 00, has a pretty pool and garden.

Santa Pola ✉ 03130

A good restaurant in Santa Pola is **Batiste** on Playa de Poniente, ✆ 96 541 14 85 (*moderate*), the best place to eat seafood (*3500 pts*).

Torrevieja ✉ 03180

On the coast, ★★**La Cibeles**, Avda. Dr. Marañón 26, ✆ 96 571 00 12, is a pleasant, *moderate,* central beach *hostal.*

Mar Menor ✉ 30380

Around the Mar Menor, the most luxurious and pricey accommodation is on La Manga, like the huge ★★★★**Cavanna**, Gran Vía de la Manga, ✆ 968 56 36 00, 🖅 968 56 44 31, with a pool, tennis and children's activities between the two seas. Rooms are air-conditioned. *Open May–Sept.*

In Los Alcazares, **Hotel Corzo**, Avda Aviacion 8, ✆ 96 57 51 31, is a smart option close to the beach, with bed and breakfast between *6000–10,000 pts*. A charming budget choice in the same area, ★**Pension San Diego**, has cheap rooms without bath amid a profusion of flowers and antiques.

There are many restaurants around here. Between Lo Pagàn and Santiago de la Ribera beaches, a popular choice is **Pezuela** (*cheap*), Entidad de Población, which has a sea-facing terrace—watch novice windsurfers fall into the water as you tuck into tapas or good *paella* for around *1000 pts*.

The Comunidad de Murcia

In the division into autonomous regions of post-Franco Spain, no one wanted Murcia, so it became its own little region. In opinion polls, with questions like 'who would you like your daughter to marry?' the Murcians always come out at the very bottom. They don't really deserve it; they just happen to have been the first emigrants looking for work in Barcelona at the turn of the century. On the other hand the Moors, who gave it its name, *Musiyah*, loved it well and farmed its *huerta*; most Muslim scholars would say that Ibn Al-Arabi of Murcia (1165–1240), mystic and poet of love, was the greatest Spaniard that ever lived.

Getting Around

By air: Murcia's airport is located near the Mar Menor in San Javier, © 968 57 05 05, and has daily connections with Madrid and Barcelona. Iberia's office is at Avda. Alfonso el Sabio, © 968 24 00 50. The RENFE station (Estación de Carmen) is south of town, on C/ Industria (bus nos.9 and 11 will take you to the centre); © 968 25 21 54. There are connections with Águilas, Cartagena, Lorca, Alicante, Valencia, Albacete, Madrid and Barcelona.

By train: A narrow-gauge train links Cartagena with Los Nietos (near Cabo de Palos and its beaches) once every 1½hrs, a service complemented by hourly buses between Cartagena and Cabo de Palos run by FEVE.

By bus: Murcia's central bus station is on the west edge of town on Plaza de Casanova, © 968 29 22 11 (good tapas in the station bar). There are buses throughout the day to Orihuela, Caravaca, Lorca, Cartagena, Águilas and Mazarrón; less frequently towards the Mar Menor: San Pedro, Los Alcázares, Cabo de Palos and La Manga del Mar Menor. Also connections with Granada, Sevilla, Almería, Mojácar, Barcelona, Málaga and Torrevieja.

Tourist Information

Murcia: C/ Alejandro Seiquer 4, © 968 21 37 16, *only open from 9–2 in August*.
Cartagena: in the Ayuntamiento, © 968 50 64 83.
Águilas: Pza. Antonio Cortijo s/n, © 968 41 33 03.
Mazarrón: Avda. Dr. Meca 20 (Edif. Bahía Mar), © 968 59 44 26.

Murcia Town

Whatever other Spaniards may think, Murcia is a congenial little city. The **Cathedral**, not far from the river, is easy to find by its lofty, unusual **tower**, built by four different architects between 1521 and 1792; ask the museum custodian to open the door if you'd like to climb up. The cathedral itself has a fine Baroque façade and Gothic portals on either side. The interior is a mixture of styles and is especially notable for its 15th-century **Vélez Chapel**, an exuberant Plateresque national monument. An urn on the main altar contains an odd relic—the innards of Alfonso the Wise. In the Cathedral **museum** (*open daily 9–1 and 4–8*) a Roman sarcophagus relief of the muses shares space with a collection of religious artefacts.

From the cathedral head up the pedestrian Calle de Trapería, where, at the first block, stands the **Casino** (club), a charming 20th-century glass-topped arcade in the Alhambra style. On the far side of the Gran Vía Escultor Salzillo, Murcia's main street, you'll find the **Salzillo Museum**

(*San Agustín 1, closed Mon; open Tues–Sun 9.30–1 and 4–7*), dedicated to the works of Murcian sculptor Francisco Salzillo (1707–83) who made many of the *pasos*, or floats, used in Murcia's *Semana Santa* processions, which make it one of Spain's best. The **archaeology museum**, Pso. Alfonso X 5, houses a good collection of Iberian artefacts and Roman sculptures and coins (*open 9–2 and 5–8; Sat 11–2; closed Sun*). The **Museo de Bellas Artes**, Obispo Frutos 12, (*open summer 9–2, Sat 11–2, closed Sun; winter 9–2 and 5–7.30, Sat 11–2, closed Sun*) has a collection of paintings dating from the 15th century, including a *St Jerome* by Ribera.

Lorca, Caravaca and Moratella

Lorca, the prettiest town in Murcia, is on the main road between Granada and Almería. It was an outpost against the Moors of Granada and a small artistic centre. An **archaeological museum** resides in the Palacio del Marqués de Esquilache, with local finds from the Bronze Age and Iberian settlements. Lorca is famed for its *Semana Santa* celebrations which are particularly lively on Good Friday, with a sumptuous show of the triumph of Christianity.

Caravaca, further north and more out of the way, sits under a hill crowned with the large **Real Alcázar–Santuario de la Vera Cruz**. In 1231 (13 years before Caravaca was reconquered by the Christians), the Moorish lord asked a priest he had imprisoned to perform a mass so that he could see what it was like. The priest reluctantly agreed, and gathered together all the necessary items when he realized he had no cross. He was about to call it all off when two angels brought one in through the window. The Sanctuary, with its pink Baroque façade, was built in the 17th century to house this relic, but it was stolen during the Civil War and never found (though the Vatican sent a copy containing a sliver of the True Cross). After the Reconquista, Caravaca was donated to the Templars who are vividly remembered in the village's unique fiestas.

If you have come this far, it is worth making the journey 14km further to the ancient village of **Moratella**. Set on a high plateau, and seemingly indifferent to tourism, this old town is nonetheless well-preserved and welcoming. The steep streets wind towards a crumbling Arabic fortress and the impressive edifice of the 16th-century Church of the Asuncion, where most of the locals gather to gossip on moonlit nights.

Cartagena

Cartagena was the major city of the Carthaginians in Spain, who honoured it by naming it after their own capital. It prospered by dint of its gold and silver mines, and it was a major blow to Hannibal when Scipio Africanus besieged and captured it. It next made history when Francis Drake raided the port and snatched its guns in 1585. When the message of the First Internationale reached Spain, it was eagerly received here; revolts by radicals in Cartagena and Alcoy in 1873 led to the downfall of Spain's first Republican Government. The Civil War inflicted more damage; nor does the presence of a major naval base improve its appearance.

Cartagena's port is dominated by its **Arsenal** (1782) and decorated with an early (1888) submarine, Isaac Peral's big white torpedo called the *Cartagena*. The old town, with Roman ruins and dilapidated houses, is clustered around the woebegone, ruined 13th-century cathedral. The best thing to do is head further up to the **Castillo de la Concepción** for the fabulous view, or west to the beaches—there's a nudist one at **El Portus** and a fine one east at **Cabo de Palos**.

Mazarrón, further west, is near more beaches and full of Spanish holiday homes and the **Enchanted City of Bolnuevo**, an area of strange, wind-eroded rocks and pinnacles. Ruined watchtowers from the 16th century guard the coast to **Águilas**, the last resort before Andalucía. The Tartessians were the first to found a city here, on a promontory overlooking two bays, but Barbary pirates caused its abandonment until 1765 when Carlos III and the Count of Aranda laid out a new, modern town. English mining interests in Águilas shipped away iron ore but left behind the game of football, which the locals claim (as do the Bilbaínos) they played before anyone else in Spain.

Where to Stay and Eating Out

Murcia ✉ 30000

In Murcia, there are two elegant choices in the heart of the city. ★★★★**Hotel Conde de Floridablanca**, Corbalán 7, ✆ 968 21 46 26, 🖷 968 21 32 15, is in an air-conditioned Baroque palace in the old town (*12,000 pts*). More modern, and also air-conditioned (a definite plus when the torrid *leveche* wind blows in the summer) is the ★★★★**Rincón de Pepe**, Pza. Apóstoles 34, ✆ 968 21 22 39, 🖷 968 22 17 44, with the most comfortable rooms in town (*16,000 pts*). ★★★★**Arco de San Juan**, Pza. de Ceballos 10, ✆ 968 21 04 55, 🖷 968 22 08 09, is modern and comfortable (*14,500 pts*). ★★**Hispano I** on the pedestrian Trapería 8, ✆ 968 21 61 52, also offers comfortable air-conditioned rooms for a nicer price (*7500 pts*). ★★★**Pacoche Murcia**, Cartagena 30, ✆ 968 21 33 85, is centrally located with the bonus of its own garage (*8000 pts*). Cheaper and cool too, ★**Hs Pacoche**, C/ González Cebrián 9, ✆ 968 21 76 05, is a bit ageing, but the price is right: *4500 pts*. Over Murcia's old bridge is ★★**Pensión Segura**, Pza. Camachos 19, ✆ 968 21 12 81, which offers comfortable rooms from *3000 pts*.

An added attraction of the **Rincón de Pepe** (*see* above) is that the same management runs the restaurant downstairs (*expensive*), by all accounts the finest in Murcia; try the seafood or Murcian roast lamb (*5000 pts*). Traditional local cuisine, with a menu changed daily and pretty brick decor, can be found at the slightly cheaper **Los Apóstoles**, Pza. Apóstoles 1, ✆ 968 21 77 79, (*4000 pts*). *Closed August*. **Paco's**, on C/ Alfaro 7, ✆ 968 21 42 96 (*moderate*) serves solid Spanish fare (*around 3000 pts*). **Bocatta's Todo 100** at Platería 44, a small square with a kiosk, offers very cheap fuel food, run by nice people and with a friendly atmosphere. For gorgeous wholemeal seed bread go to the health-food shop **Alegría**, Pza. San Antolín 4, ✆ 968 29 09 10, near the bus station.

If you are entering the **Natural Park of the Sierra de Espuña**, between Murcia and Lorca, stay at the ★**Hs Tánger** in Alhama de Murcia at Avda. Ginés Campos 2, ✆ 968 63 06 99. Near the small walled town of Aledo, the **Hotel el Pinito Oro**, ✆/🖷 968 48 44 36 is reasonable,with fantastic views across the mountains and a swimming pool. The restaurant serves decent mountain-style fare.

Lorca ✉ 30800

★★★Hotel Alameda, C/ Musso Valiente 8, ✆ 968 40 66 00, has much nicer rooms than looks likely from the outside, and is so well-located that it might make the price worthwhile (8000pts). Of the innumerable cheap hostels in Lorca, the ★**Ciudad del**

Sol, in the centre at C/ Galicia 9, ✆ 968 46 78 72, beats the competition in August with its air-conditioned, modest rooms. You can get good regional cuisine in pleasant surroundings at **Casa Roberto,** also in C/ Musso Valient. Cheaper is **Barcas Casa Cándido**, C/ Santo Domingo 13: it has a very good daily menu for *around 1000 pts*.

Cartagena ✉ 30200

In Cartagena one of the best places to stay and eat is **★★Los Habaneros**, San Diego 60, ✆ 968 50 52 50, centrally located, air-conditioned, and there's a decent restaurant specializing in fish (*3500 pts for a meal*). A slightly cheaper and central option is the atmospheric **★★Hotel Cartagenera**, C/ Jara 3, beside the Plaza Tres Reyes, ✆ 968 50 25 00. The best tapas in Cartagena is at **La Tartana**, opposite the cinema on Moreria Baja, ✆ 968 50 00 11, 🖷 968 52 21 31, or at the **Barlovente** in C/ Cuatro Santos 33, ✆ 968 50 66 41 (*moderate*)—fresh local fish for around *3500 pts* a full meal.

Mazarrón ✉ 30800

In the Puerto de Mazarrón, **Hotel Guillermo II**, C/ Carmen 7, ✆ 968 59 04 36, has pleasant rooms and good service, with a decent restaurant as well. The **Urena Hotel**, ✆ 968 49 00 61, is a fine, moderately priced holiday choice by the beach (*around 6000 pts*). *Open April–Sept.* It is near the port, opposite the well-situated **Miramar** restaurant, Playa de la Isla, ✆ 968 59 40 08, serving good-value shellfish platters. Mazarrón has a selection of generally unremarkable restaurants; try popular **Virgen del Mar**, Pso. De la Sal, ✆ 968 59 50 57 (*moderate*), with good rice and seafood dishes. **El Puerto**, ✆ 968 59 48 05, is another favourite for fish dishes on Plaza del Mar.

Águilas ✉ 30880

In Águilas you can't do better than the **★★★Carlos III**, C/ Rey Carlos III 22, ✆ 968 41 16 50; small, prettily located near the sea with modern clean rooms bursting with facilities and popular with Spanish families. Open all year. There are cheaper places on the beach, one being **★★★Hotel Bahia**, Playa de la Reya, ✆ 968 54 40 00, 🖷 968 59 06 09, which has nice rooms with views of the sea, set near an impressive flight of ceramic steps. The new **★★Pension Cruz del Sur**, Constitiucion 38, ✆ 968 41 01 71 is close to the beach and extremely good value.

Good seafood can be had at **Ruano**, Urb. La Kabyla 9, ✆ 968 41 96 09 (*moderate*). Try the delicious *tortilla de marisco Ruano*, which is huge and bursting with seafood. The *menú del día* is good value at *1000 pts*.

Moratella

If you want to stay, the options are limited in this little town. **Pension Reyes**, C/ Tomas el Cura, ✆ 968 73 03 77, above a popular local bar of the same name, has pleasant rooms, including a family room with five beds, at an exceptionally cheap price. In Caravaca de la Cruz, the **Hotel Central**, Gran Via 18, ✆ 968 70 70 55; the atmosphere is a little impersonal but the rooms are good for under *8000 pts*.

Aragón

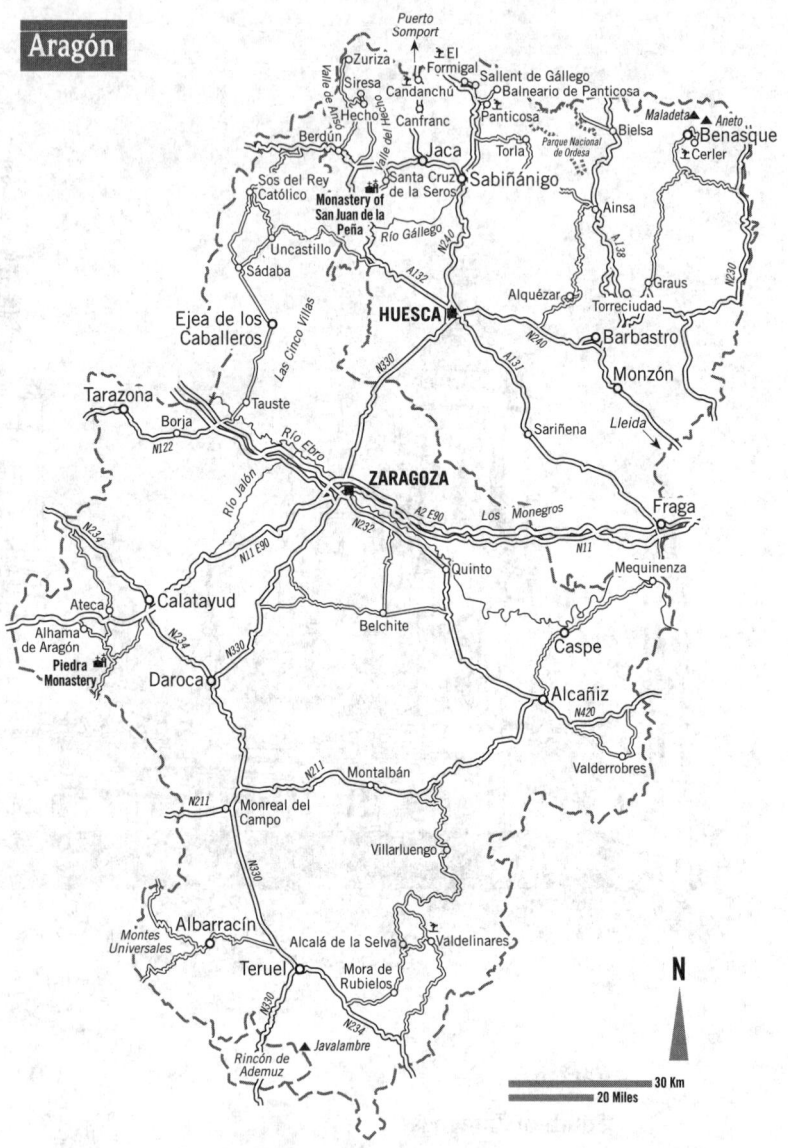

Aragón

Puerto Somport
Zuriza
El Formigal
Sallent de Gállego
Siresa
Candanchú
Balneario de Panticosa
Valle de Hecho
Hecho
Canfranc
Panticosa
Maladeta ▲ ▲ Aneto
Benasque
Berdún
Valle del Roncal
Jaca
Torla
Parque Nacional de Ordesa
Bielsa
Cerler
Sos del Rey Católico
Santa Cruz de la Seros
Sabiñánigo
Ainsa
Monastery of San Juan de la Peña
Río Gállego
Uncastillo
A138
Sádaba
Graus
N330
Ejea de los Caballeros
Las Cinco Villas
Alquézar
Torreciudad
Tarazona
Tauste
HUESCA
N240
Barbastro
Borja
Río Ebro
N122
Río Jalón
N330
A131
Monzón
ZARAGOZA
Sariñena
Lleida
N234
A2 E90
Los Monegros
Fraga
N232
N11 E90
N11
Quinto
Mequinenza
Ateca
Calatayud
Belchite
Alhama de Aragón
N234
Caspe
Piedra Monastery
N330
Daroca
Alcañiz
N420
N211
Montalbán
Valderrobres
N211
Monreal del Campo
Villarluengo
N330
Montes Universales
Albarracín
Alcalá de la Selva
Valdelinares
Teruel
Mora de Rubielos
N330
N234
Javalambre
Rincón de Ademuz

N

30 Km
20 Miles

Most people going between Madrid and Barcelona see only the bleak plain of the Ebro out of the window and have little desire to see any more. Yet, the best of Aragón lies off the beaten highway, in the seldom explored mountains in the south and in the Pyrenees, here at their highest and most majestic, offering almost endless hiking and skiing possibilities. Another attraction is the villages, some of Spain's most medieval and remote, often set against unforgettable scenery. Although an Aragonese nationalist was elected to the Cortes for the first time in 1986, the region has historically been a kind of buffer-state between the Catalans and Basques and their aspirations for independence. In the old days, the Aragonese, the most stubborn of Spaniards and boasting the oldest and some of the most liberal *fueros* or privileges, were not so tractable—Felipe II had to put down a major revolt. Union with the Catalans in 1137 brought the Crown of Aragón a Mediterranean empire and international renown.

At Aragonese fiestas, you're likely to see some brisk hoofing in the national dance, the *jota*, not one of Spain's more elegant ballets, but certainly one of the most energetic. In the Pyrenean valleys, sword dances are still performed. The region produces considerable quantities of wine—Cariñena is perhaps the best, and served in many restaurants, along with hearty mountain cuisine and game dishes in season.

Zaragoza

Zaragoza, the capital of Aragón, is centrally located and, if not the most charming of cities, it has seduced the Aragonese, who have emptied the countryside to move here. It can get bitter in the winter and too warm in the middle of summer; still, it's the best base for visiting Aragón.

Getting Around

By air: Zaragoza's airport receives a number of ski-orientated charters from London in the winter, and domestic flights from most points in Spain all year round. The airport is some 20km west of town, © 976 34 90 50. Iberia's office is at C/ Bilbao 11, © 976 21 34 18. The airport bus leaves from Pza. de Aragón, © 976 34 38 21.

By train: The train station is the modern Estación Portillo on Avda. Clavé, © 976 28 02 02. There's a ticket office at San Clemente 23, © 976 23 38 02. Trains go frequently to Madrid and Barcelona. Also, four times a day to Huesca, Jaca and France (Canfranc); Teruel and Valencia; Pamplona and San Sebastián; and Logroño and Bilbao.

By bus: Buses can leave from anywhere. Points east and Catalunya are the domain of Agreda Automóvil, Pso. M. Agustín 7, © 976 22 93 43 (not far from the train station); for Huesca and Jaca: La Oscense, Pso. M. Agustín 84, © 976 22 93 43, or Irigoyen, Allué Salvador 4, © 976 22 37 21; for Soria, Borja and Tarazona: Therpasa, Gral. Sueiro 22, © 976 34 31 58; for the Basque country: Conda, Avda. de Navarra 81, © 976 33 33 72. Buses to Alicante, Valencia and Murcia: Arión Express, Asalto 53, © 976 20 05 23. Continental routes are operated by, among others, Julia, Hernán Cortés 6, © 976 23 87 73. For others, check at the tourist office.

Local buses, TUZSA, have a booth on Pza. de España, © 976 22 64 71.

Tourist Information

Torréon de la Zuda, Glorieta de Pio XII, © 976 39 35 37 (provincial office);
Plaza de Sas, © 976 29 84 38;
Plaza del Pilar, opposite the Lonja, © 976 20 12 00/91 (municipal office).

A Real Pillar of the Church

Don Quixote made it within sight of Zaragoza but refused to enter (because another author's false Don Quixote had been there already!). Even so, he enjoyed one of the best sights the city can offer: the view of its great towers and domes from the distance. Close up, Zaragoza reveals itself to be a busy city of over half a million people; over 70 per cent of all Aragonese call it home. Located on the Ebro, in the midst of a fertile *huerta*, it has been prominent ever since the Romans, who gave it its name—Caesar Augusta.

One peculiarity of Zaragoza is that it has two cathedrals, forcing the bishop to shuttle back and forth every six months. Newer and decidedly larger, the 17th-century **Basílica de Nuestra Señora del Pilar** (*open daily, summer 6am–9.30pm; winter 6am–8.30pm*) rises from the banks of the Ebro on the spot where, according to legend, the Virgin appeared on a pillar to St James (Santiago) and required a church to be built. From a distance it looks as if she got an Imperial Ottoman mosque instead, complete with four 'minarets' and a hierarchy of 11 domes. There's nothing like it elsewhere in Spain. The interior manages to be both vast and overdone. Goya had a hand in painting the domes, most notably the one called *Saint Mary, Queen of Martyrs*. A 14th-century, darkened image, adorned with countless diamonds and other gems, stands on the jasper pillar, on which the Virgin was transported to Spain by angels; she is the patroness of the Guardia Civil (during the Civil War she was also Captain General of Zaragoza, and defused two Republican bombs dropped on the basilica which hang like trophies in her chapel). Best of all is the 16th-century *reredos* of alabaster by Damián Forment, who adorned many of Aragón's churches; Goya's sketches for the domes are in the **Museo Pilarista** next to the basilica (*open 9–2 and 4–6*).

At the far end of the Plaza del Pilar stands the old cathedral, **La Seo**, a crazy quilt of styles—a *mudéjar* wall of brick and tile on the outside, but within, a lovely alabaster *retablo* from the 15th-century and charming capitals carved with children. Unfortunately it seems to be inteminably closed for restoration. The nearby **Tapestry Museum** displays 15–18th-century French and Flemish works. A third monument, the Renaissance Exchange or **Lonja** (*open if an exhibition is on, Tues–Sat 10–2 and 5–9, Sun 10–12, closed Mon*) stands on the Plaza del Pilar in between the cathedrals; if it's open, step in to see its hall of tall Ionic columns, under which Aragón's grain dealers once met. Modern grain dealers sell seeds outside in the plaza to pilgrims, who over the centuries have helped create Spain's plumpest pigeons.

Downtown Zaragoza

On the far side of the plaza, across from La Seo, the provincial tourist office is shoe-horned into **Zuda tower**, a vestige of the medieval walls, adjacent to fragments of the wall of Caesar Augusta that once bristled with 200 towers. From here, walk up Avenida C. Augusto to Calle San Pablo and **San Pablo** church, topped by the most beautiful of Zaragoza's many towers, a 13th-century *mudéjar* work; inside there's a wooden *retablo* by Damián Forment. Avenida C. Augusto continues up to the main thoroughfare, El Coso; near the corner the **Audiencia** is guarded by two fierce giants with clubs and topped with a tympanum portraying the Triumph of Caesar. This was the ancestral home of the Luna family, which produced not only Viceroys, but an anti-Pope (*see* 'Peñíscola') and an operatic villain (*see below*).

Continue down El Coso, past the **Plaza España** and **Paseo Independencia**, the heart of city life, to Calle Rufas. This will take you to the **Plaza de Los Sitios** (of the Sieges) commemorating Zaragoza's heroic resistance to Napoleon's troops in 1808. In 1908 the city held a Hispano-French centenary fair, for which the monument and an exhibition palace, now the **Museum of Zaragoza**, were erected (*open Tues–Sat 9–2, Sun 10–2*). The ground floor is devoted to archaeological exhibits, including bronze tablets in Iberian and Latin, while upstairs the best of the paintings are by Goya, a native of Fuendetodos, 50km south of Zaragoza.

Back towards the Paseo Independencia via Calle Costa, the church of **Santa Engracia** was founded by Fernando and Isabel, whose images kneel over the door; in the crypt, two 4th-century Palaeo-Christian sarcophagi are said to contain the remains of scores of local martyrs who must be wedged in like sardines in a can. From Santa Engracia, cross the large Plaza Aragón and Plaza Paraíso for Zaragoza's version of Barcelona's Passeig de Gràcia, the **Paseo Sagasta** where you'll find out what local *Modernistas* were up to—No.11, the **Casa Juncosa** by Ricardo Magdalena (1906) is the best Art Nouveau work in the city. Near the Plaza Paraíso, the bank Caja de Ahorros de Zaragoza houses the reconstructed 14th-century **Patio de la Infanta**, an elegant Renaissance work with medallions portraying the kings of Spain, that originally formed part of the palace of Gabriel Zaporta, one of Charles V's biggest financiers.

The Alijafería

Open summer Tues–Sat 10–2 and 4–8, Sun 10–2, closed Mon; winter Tues–Sat 10–2 and 4.30–6.30, Sun 10–2, closed Mon.

Zaragoza's prime attraction, the **Alijafería** is a short walk from the train station (alternatively, take bus no.23 from the Basílica del Pilar or Plaza Aragón). This palace, begun as a defensive work in the 9th century, later served as a residence of the local Berber-Moorish dynasty (its name is derived from the emir Abu Ja'far Ahmad) and after the Reconquista, of the Aragonese kings. Until 1706, it was the seat of the Aragonese Inquisition, an institution set up by the Catholic kings and regarded by the Aragonese as an underhand attempt by the Castilians to sidestep the special privileges, or *fueros* of Aragón—and to prove their point, the Zaragozans murdered the first Inquisitor in the cathedral. Destroyed and misused for centuries since, restoration work on the Alijafería has been going on since the 1940s.

Walk around the huge walls to the entrance by the tiny jewel-like **Mosque**, in itself the best piece of Moorish architecture outside Andalucía. The oldest part of the Alijafería, the Moorish **Torre del Trovador**, provided the set for Antonio García Gutiérrez's play, *El Trovador* (1830), and Verdi's opera, *Il Trovatore* (1853), where Manrico was imprisoned by the nasty Conde de Luna. The Gothic additions—notably the stair and throne room with their fine *artesonado* ceilings—were added by Fernando and Isabel.

Zaragoza ✉ *50000*   **Where to Stay**

One of the prime places to look for a room in Zaragoza is in the back alleys between Alfonso I and Don Jaime, particularly on C/ Méndez Núñez and the streets around it, the area known as El Tubo.

expensive

For years Zaragoza's ★★★★**Gran Hotel**, C/ Joaquín Costa 5, © 976 22 19 01, ✆ 976 23 67 13, was the city's finest and, after extensive renovations, this elegant *grande dame* can reclaim her laurels; its air-conditioned, beautifully furnished doubles go for *14,000 pts.*

If it's hot and you're not a Rockefeller, try the **★★Conde Blanco**, C/ Predicadores 84, ✆ 976 44 14 11, 🖷 976 28 03 39, with air-conditioned rooms a block from the Ebro (*7000 pts*). The **★★Hotel Las Torres**, Plaza del Pilar 11, ✆ 976 39 42 50, 🖷 976 39 42 54, has rooms with views of the basilica (*around 7000 pts*). **★★★El Príncipe**, C/ Santiago 12, centrally located off the Plaza del Pilar, ✆ 976 29 41 01 (*9000 pts*). **★★Hotel Sauce**, C/ Espoz y Mina 33, ✆ 976 39 01 00, at the heart of El Tubo, has modern rooms with air conditioning, heating and video for around *9000 pts*.

inexpensive

Even cheaper *pensiones* and *fondas* may be found in El Tubo. **★Pensión Rex**, C/ Méndez Núñez 31, ✆ 976 39 26 33, has simple, large rooms for *under 2500 pts*. **★★Pensión Fernando el Católico**, C/ Fernando el Católico 17, ✆ 976 35 62 88, is one of the best cheapies and very popular (*2500 pts*) .

Eating Out

Aragonese cuisine is substantial and simple, with lots of beans, potatoes, eggs, lamb, and codfish. One favourite, *cabrito asado* (roast kid), is one of many Aragonese dishes served at the **Bodega de Chema**, Latassa 34, ✆ 976 55 50 14 (*expensive*), where Spaniards go on their nostalgia trips; it's also a good place to try Aragón's wine—order a Cariñena; *meals 5000 pts*, best book ahead. Many Aragonese will only recommend one restaurant when it comes to eating cheaply and well: the **Bodegón Tío Faustino**, Don Teobaldo 14, ✆ 976 39 09 60 (*moderate*), where you can get a good meal for *under 3000 pts*. A similarly moderately priced place is **Casa Emilio**, Avda. Madrid 5, ✆ 976 43 58 39; be sure to try their delicious fresh fish. The **Asador León Rojo**, Lon Laga 2, ✆ 976 31 49 00 (*moderate*) is popular for its excellent grills (*4000 pts*). **La Matilde**, Casta Alvarez 10, ✆ 976 44 10 08 (*expensive*) serves a range of classic French dishes for *around 5000 pts*. *Closed Sun*. One of the province's best restaurants is **La Casa del Ventero**, Pso. 18 de Julio 24, ✆ 976 18 51 87 (*expensive*), in the village of Villanueva de Gállego, 14km north of the city. Although known as a French restaurant, there are still many tasty Aragonese dishes on the menu (*4500 pts*). *Closed Sun, Mon*. **La Zanahoria**, C/ Tarragona 8, near the train station (*cheap*) translates as carrot and the decoration follows this theme with green and orange bannisters. The small, mellow and friendly vegetarian restaurant serves very good value, delicious dishes: try the blue cheese soufflé at *850 pts* or vegetable curry at *600 pts*.

tapas bars

The inhabitants of Zaragoza claim their tapas bars can give Madrid and Sevilla a run for their money. Many of the bars are scattered around El Coso, in the heart of the city. The following stand out: **Casa Juanico**, C/ Sta Cruz 21; **Belanche**, C/ Romea s/n; and **Casa Colas**, Mártires 10. **Los Victorinos**, C/ Lahera 4, is small and overflowing with character: don't let the bulls' heads on the walls put you off their great tapas. In the Barrio de Portillo area the **Café Madrid** may not appeal to all in its plain vastness, but the choice of watering holes around here is ample.

For fresh bread, try **Chipen** on the corner of C/ Alfonso I with C/ Prudencio.

West of Zaragoza: Tarazona

Not a few towns in Spain (we could mention Barcelona) give the impression of having just been dropped down from outer space. Tarazona, with its startling *mudéjar* towers hanging over the cliffs, is certainly one of them. Most of these are in the older quarter of town, across the Rio Queiles—the churches of **La Magdalena, La Concepción** and **San Miguel**. Tarazona is famous for its 16th-century **Ayuntamiento**, with reliefs of the capture of Granada across the façade; another landmark is the old, arcaded bullring, with its arches bricked up and turned into apartments (like the one in Tangier). Tarazona's **Cathedral** is odd too, with a dome like La Seo's in Zaragoza, a tower like La Giralda's in Seville, and several other styles mixed in. On the way to Zaragoza, the road and railway line pass **Borja**, in the middle of a big wine-growing region. The peculiar crag with chimneys sticking out of it is explained as the ruins of Borja castle, the ancestral home of that celebrated family of schemers and connoisseurs of poison, the Borgias, petty-noble hoodlums in Aragón before they hit the big time in Renaissance Italy.

South of Zaragoza

Southern Aragón is a case of the blind man and the elephant—your opinion of it will depend entirely on which corners of it you come to first. The landscape is a jumble of awful, barren plateaux, scrublands and green, fertile valleys. Unfortunately there are more of the former, and this region, now as always, is one of the poorest in Spain. More serious battles of the Civil War were fought here than anywhere else in the country, and that certainly did not help. **Belchite**, once an important town and now a ghostly ruin, was a victim of bitter house-to-house fighting in the 1938 Ebro offensive. The ruins include a Romanesque church and some fine old buildings, and the government has left them standing as a reminder.

Getting Around

If you're relying on public transport, expect frustrations. This is a sparsely populated region, and both buses and trains are infrequent and slow.

By train: There are about four daily; you can get to either Zaragoza or Valencia from Teruel, with no really interesting stops in between; in Teruel, ✆ 978 60 26 49.

By bus: The bus station is on Ronda 18 Julio in Teruel; the most frequent destination is Zaragoza, ✆ 978 60 10 14, but there will be a daily bus to Cuenca and Madrid, to Valencia, ✆ 978 60 34 50 and to most of the provincial towns. In the Maestrazgo, the bus service is informal; it's no place to be in a hurry.

Down the Ebro

The Zaragoza–Valencia road, following the turgid Ebro, passes through mostly non-descript towns. **Caspe** can show a **Roman mausoleum** in its town square, relocated from lands flooded by the big Mequinenza reservoir, which turns the Ebro into an impressive lake for some 48km. Most of **Mequinenza** was drowned, too, but the remainder has a finer lakeside location than ever before. The well-preserved medieval **castle** above the town now belongs to the local electric company. **Alcañiz**, to the south, is a big town, with little to show the folks who stay in the *parador*, installed in the 12th-century **castle** that once belonged to the Order of Calatrava. The 16th-century Ayuntamiento and Lonja buildings on the Plaza Mayor are the only sights. If you're heading towards the coast, tiny **Valderrobres** is worth a detour for its improbably grand **Santa María la Mayor** (12th-century) with a beautiful rose window, along with a castle of the kings of Aragón, a Renaissance Ayuntamiento, and a pretty main street along the Río Matarraña.

From Calatayud to Teruel

Sooner or later you'll pass through **Calatayud**, an important road and railway junction, but it's a dour and shabby place and there's little reason to stay. Calatayud (from the Arabic 'castle of Job') specializes in octagonal *mudéjar* church steeples; **Santa María La Mayor** has the best of them, along with an ornate Plateresque-*mudéjar* façade. Nearby, on the Sigüenza road, **Ateca** has a converted mosque for its main church, **Santa María**, with a later *mudéjar* tower much like those you'll see in Teruel. This one leans a little. There's a detour to the south to the **Piedra Monastery**, a 13th-century Cistercian house. Most of it is a hotel now, but the surroundings, with plenty of trees and a 150ft **waterfall** along the Río Piedra, has to be the garden spot of all southern Aragón.

South from Calatayud, **Daroca's** pride is its **walls**, with 114 towers in varying states of decay. The gates are well-preserved and impressive. Charles V built them; Daroca was a thriving town in his time, as evidenced by several fine *mudéjar* churches, a lovely fountain called the **Fuente de Veinte Caños** ('20 spouts') outside the walls, and a 1km **tunnel** dug under a mountain to carry off flood waters—a very unusual fit of public works for 16th-century Spain. The tunnel was not an entirely original idea, as a curious history details tunnels being dug around Daroca throughout the 8th, 9th and 10th centuries. They were designed to carry water from the mountainside to the early Yemeni settlers, who were the original tribal founders of the town. A later quirk of Darocan history evolved from a miracle that took place during the ousting of the Arabs on the 23rd of February 1239. Legend tells how a local priest was in the midst of celebrating a mass for the soldiers who were to fight for Christian virtue, when the Arabic foe made a surprise attack. The Priest hastily hid six consecrated hosts, that were intended for the army captains, in a shroud. But the battle was bitter and bloodthirsty, and when the shroud was opened, all the hosts had turned to blood. The Santismo Misterio de Daroca became widely known, and almost two centuries later King Ferdinand and Elisabeth I decorated the shroud with a golden frame, said to have been made from the first gold brought from the Americas.

About 20km before Teruel, a side road follows the valley of the Río Turia up into the Montes Universales. The town of **Albarracín** is the centre of this bare and rocky district. There are no churches to attract visitors here, but the town itself is a national monument, one of the least-changed old towns of Spain. Its oldest streets are fairy-tale medieval, with narrow, cobbled lanes and half-timbered houses with projecting balconies leaning at precarious angles over them. Albarracín has an unusually long circuit of walls—not because the town was ever bigger than now, but to protect it from attacks from the dominating hillsides. As befits a fairytale town, Albarracín has a number of legends attached to it, one concerning the **Torre de Doña Blanca** which perches above the town. The ghost of a beautiful enchanted princess appears every full moon at midnight, dressed in white, to bathe in the river Guadalaviar. She fell in love with a young Jewish man, but it was a forbidden love and she dutifully expired from longing in her tower.

Tourist Information

C/ Tomás Nogués, just off C/ Ramón y Cajal (the main street), ☎ 978 60 22 79.

As a provincial capital, Teruel looms large on the Spanish map. From up close, however, it is small and a little woebegone. Already a poor backwater, Teruel suffered as much as any Spanish city in the Civil War. In the freezing winter of 1937 (Teruel is famous for these), the Republicans fought their way up the steep slopes and took the town. Just two weeks later the Nationalists did the same and got it back. Since then the town has been repaired and a little prosperity has seeped in. The reason for visiting is to see the best *mudéjar* churches in Spain— four of them, with tall glorious towers of delicately patterned brick and tiles. Teruel kept a large Moorish population after the 12th-century Reconquest, and it was Moorish craftsmen who gave the city its pride and its symbol.

If you come by train, you'll get an immediate introduction to Teruel *mudéjar* in the **terrace steps**, built in the 1920s, a long, elegant (though poorly maintained) stairway leading up from the station to the town. At the top, the most elaborate of the *mudéjar* towers is just a block to the left: that of **El Salvador** (*open daily 11–2 and 5–7*), built right over the street with a narrow arch to let pedestrians pass. Like minarets, the towers of Teruel are always separate from their churches. **San Martín**, the next tower, also has an arch underneath; it's a few blocks north down Calle Santiago. The tower of the **Cathedral** (*open daily 11.30–2 and 5.30–9*) pales by comparison, but it compensates with a unique, *mudéjar*-style brick dome.

Heartbreak in Old Teruel

San Pedro is the fourth *mudéjar* tower, and below it a little chapel has been built to house the remains of **Los Amantes de Teruel** (*open Mon– Sat 10–2 and 4–7, Sun 10–2*). Diego de Marcilla and Isabel de Segura were the star-crossed lovers of the old story. He had six years to go out and win his fortune; on the appointed day Isabel's impatient father married her off when Diego failed to appear. He did make his fortune, but was then captured by the Moors and held in Valencia by Queen Zulima, who told Isabel he was dead. On his release, he was recaptured by bandits in the pay of Zulima. He escaped, but arrived in Teruel one day late, and there was nothing left for the lovers to do but expire in each other's arms. The same tale is told in Boccaccio's *Decameron*, only the lovers are named Girolamo and Salvastra; scholars never get tired of speculating whether Teruel's lovers were the source for Boccaccio, or if some local light simply invented the story. There can't be fewer than a hundred other versions of this folk-tale motif floating around Europe: you can take your pick. You may also join young honeymooners in visiting this shrine of sorrow. Their effigies are beautifully sculpted, holding hands between the sarcophagi, and you can peek at the mummified remains if you care to. Meanwhile Spanish children have their nursery rhyme:

> *Los Amantes de Teruel,*
> *Tonta ella y tonto él.*
> (The lovers of Teruel—she was crazy and him too.)

Teruel really is an unlikely honeymoon destination, but besides its *mudéjar* towers it has a few other things to see. The **Provincial Museum** is an interesting diversion: it is housed on four floors of the recently restored 16th-century palace of the provincial Casa de Comunidad, Plaza Fray Anselmo Polanco s/n, ℗ 978 60 01 50 (*open Tues–Sat 10–2 and Tues–Fri 4–7*) The **Fountain of the Torico**, a bull with a star between its horns, is the symbol of the city, in the quiet Plaza Mayor; from there it's a short walk to the northern end of town and **Los Arcos**, a 16th-century aqueduct you can walk across, the work of the same French engineer who dug the tunnel at Daroca. There are no stories about the peculiar, eight-sided tower called the **Castillo de Amberes** nearby; nobody seems to know who built it, or why. Behind it, near the bus station, the streets around Plaza Judería provide the most incongruous sight in Teruel on Saturday nights, when all southern Aragón's fast crowd congregates at the scores of hole-in-the-wall bars. How does one little old-fashioned province get so many bikers?

Ademuz and the Maestrazgo

Quite a few of them speed in from these two pockets of quiet villages, where by day you're more likely to see shepherds with their flocks. If you're headed for Madrid or Cuenca, you'll pass through the **Rincón de Ademuz**, a spot of land that was independent through much of the Middle Ages, and now survives as an island of Valencia province within Aragón. The villages, such as Ademuz and Castielfabib, are among the least modern in Spain, and the countryside in the valley of the Río Turia is lovely.

In the **Maestrazgo**, between Teruel and Valencia, the scenery is wilder and the villages a little more colourful, with pointed arches overhanging the streets and Moorish *ajimez* windows. **La Iglesuela del Cid** is perhaps most characteristic, but tiny **Mirambel** is prettier; the town has recently won a national prize for the restoration of its modest monuments, including the old half-timbered gatehouses. Mirambel is reached through vertigo-inducing **Cantavieja**, a Templar foundation that was a stronghold of the Carlists in both their rebellions. Cantavieja preserves an imposing 16th-century church and Ayuntamiento, and if you have a car you may enjoy the view from a famous **mirador** outside the town called 'Muela Monchen'.

Where To Stay and Eating Out

Southern Aragón sees few tourists, but you can find modest accommodation in all the towns and villages mentioned in this section.

Alcañiz ✉ 44600

Alcañiz has its ★★★**Parador La Concordia** in the castle, one of the most beautiful *paradores* in the country, Castillo de los Calatravos, ℗ 978 83 04 00, 🖷 978 83 03 66, with air-conditioned doubles (*expensive*). Also in Alcañiz the **Meseguer** on the edge of town, Avda. Maestrazgo 9, ℗ 978 83 10 02, 🖷 978 83 01 41, is very ordinary from the outside but has comfortable air-conditioned rooms and the best restaurant in town. Packed every night, it specializes in fish dishes and local game (*menú del día 1000 pts*).

Valderrobres ✉ 44580

Tiny Valderrobres, surprisingly, has a hotel, the ★**Querol**, Avda. Hispanidad 14, ℗ 978 85 01 92 (*moderate*).

Ateca

It's worth going out of your way to spend a night at the★★★**Monasterio de Piedra**, mentioned above, near the hamlet of Nuévalos, near Ateca, ✆ 976 84 90 11, ✆ 976 84 90 54 (*expensive*); the old monastery among the gardens has been converted into a first-rate hotel, with a pool, tennis courts, and a good restaurant.

Daroca ✉ 50360

The **Posada del Almuni**, Grajera 7, ✆ 978 80 06 06, ✆ 978 80 11 41, is an exquisitely restored 16th–17th-century palace, offering very reasonable rates (around *8000 pts*). The excellent restaurant features wonderful desserts. Less extravagant accommodation can be found at **El Ruejo**, Calle Mayor 88, ✆ 978 80 09 62; a little old and creaky, but the spacious rooms are arranged around a pretty courtyard (*4500 pts*).

Albarracín ✉ 44100

Albarracín is becoming a small resort, as its charming streets and mountain views begin to attract visitors; its quality hotel is the ★★★**Albarracín**, also in a restored building, in C/ Azagra, ✆ 978 71 00 11, ✆ 978 60 53 63 (*moderate*). Near the old town centre, the ★★**Dona Blanca**, has comfortable rooms with balconies (*moderate*). The best place to eat is the small **El Rincón del Chorro**, C/ del Chorro 15, ✆ 978 71 01 12 (*moderate*), all rough walls and hanging hams. The portions are huge. There is a good vegetable and soup section: try the *pisto*, vegetables baked with eggs.

Teruel ✉ 44000

The ★★★**Parador de Teruel** is nothing special, and inconveniently located outside the city at Aptdo. 67, ✆ 978 60 18 00, ✆ 978 60 86 12 (*expensive*). In town, the most comfortable spot is the ★★★**Reina Cristina**, Pso. Generalísimo 1, near San Salvador tower, ✆ 978 60 68 60, ✆ 978 60 53 63 (*expensive*) though it's a bit pricier. Otherwise, the swish new **Hotel Plaza**, Plaza Tremedal 3, ✆ 978 60 86 55, (*expensive*) in the city centre provides a good line in comfort and is a bargain by comparison, with significantly lower rates at the weekend (*expensive*). Teruel has more modest lodgings in a quiet, central location; try the **Hs Aragon**, Calle Santa Maria 4, ✆ 978 60 13 87, or the **Hs Continental**, C/ Juan Perez 9, ✆ 978 60 23 17.

To help ward off the effects of its cold winters, typical Teruel cuisine relies heavily on soups and stews, all washed down with strong, wholesome wines. The area is also known for its cured hams, which you'll see dangling from most food-shop and *bodega* ceilings. Teruel itself is not really noted for outstanding restaurants; you can, however, get better than average fare at **Torre del Salvador**, C/ Salvador 20, ✆ 978 60 52 63 (*moderate*), near the San Salvador tower (*3500 pts*). **La Parilla**, San Esteban 2, ✆ 978 60 59 23 (*moderate*) is popular and full of character. In Rubielos de Mora, an hour's drive southeast of Teruel on the C232, the **Portal del Carmen** (*expensive*) is set in a 17th-century Carmelite convent.

Cantavieja ✉ 44140

Cantavieja has the hotel **Balfagón Alto Maestrazgo**, Avda. del Maestrazgo 20, ✆/✆ 978 18 50 76 (*around 6000 pts*), and the simpler, cheaper **Fonda Julián**, García Valiño 2, ✆ 18 50 05 (*cheap*).

Anywhere else, especially in the Maestrazgo, you'll likely find only the sparest of *fondas* or rooms over a bar. In any season but summer remember to ask if there's heat, for this province has the worst climate in Spain.

Northern Aragón

Besides ski slopes, Northern Aragón's prime attractions are its unspoilt medieval villages and mountain scenery. Public transport to nearly all points is possible but often time-consuming; the service is good but infrequent. Don't come with a tight schedule or a plane to catch in a couple of days—unless you have a car.

Getting Around

Monzón is on the railway line between Lleida and Zaragoza (three a day). Barbastro and Monzón are also on the bus route between Huesca and Lleida (three times a day). Las Cinco Villas are served from Zaragoza by bus (Autobuses Cinco Villas, Avda. de Navarra 80, ✆ 976 33 33 71 in Zaragoza). Sos del Rey Católico is easiest to reach, via any Pamplona–Zaragoza bus; RENFE buses from Zaragoza station will take you right there four times a day. Huesca and Jaca are easiest reached by train from Zaragoza (for bus connections, *see* 'Zaragoza').

In Huesca the train station is on C/ Zaragoza (information, ✆ 974 24 21 59); the bus station on the Avda. del Parque 3 (information, ✆ 974 21 07 00). To get to the Castillo de Loarre, catch the bus to Ayerbe and get off at Loarre—then walk 6.5km. There are only two connections a day so plan in advance.

In Jaca the train station (information, ✆ 974 36 13 32) is at the northern end of C/ Juan XXIII. A local bus makes connections to the centre of town. The bus station is more convenient, on Avda. Jacetania behind the cathedral (for information ✆ 974 35 50 60). From Jaca there's a daily bus to Ansó and Hecho, and two buses daily to Pamplona, Zaragoza via Huesca and Biesca—30km to Torla and Ordesa Park—but ask at Jaca's tourist office before you take it and hitch the rest of the way; plans are afoot for some kind of shuttle. You may just want to rent a car and save yourself the hassle.

Benasque may be reached from Monzón (with its train station, ✆ 974 40 12 44); buses are more frequent during the ski season: the bus station is on Avda. Lérida, ✆ 974 40 06 32. Jaca runs a fairly good shuttle service to the resorts in the winter.

East: Barbastro, Monzón and Torreciudad

Tourist Information

Barbastro: Pza. de Aragon s/n, ✆ 974 30 83 50, 🖷 974 30 83 51, *turismo@barbastro-ayto.es*
Monzón: Pza. Aragón, ✆ 974 40 48 54.
Torreciudad: Santuario Torreciudad, ✆ 974 30 40 25.

One of Aragón's more remote corners, this is a good place to see the difference irrigation has made to the land. **Los Monegros** (just to the south of Monzón) provides the 'before' picture—a wasteland as dry and barren as anyone could wish. **Barbastro** is the largest town in the desolation; its 16th-century **Cathedral** has a polychrome alabaster *retablo* by Damián

Forment (*open all day in summer; in winter 9–1 and 6–8.30*). Buses from here go 13km to **Alquézar**, one of Aragón's most picturesque villages, crowned by a well-preserved 12th-century **castle** and large **Colegiata** (16th-century).

Monzón, the other large town of the region, was a very important Templar enclave. It came their way as part of a deal: when the King of Aragón, Alfonso el Batallador, died without an heir in 1131, the Aragonese nobles were shocked upon reading his will to discover that he had bequeathed the kingdom to the Sepulchre of the Lord in Jerusalem and its guardians, the Knights Templar. The nobles quickly talked Alfonso's brother, Ramiro the Monk (Ramiro II) into taking the Crown. He dutifully married, sired a daughter, married her off at age two to Count Ramón Berenguer IV of Barcelona and went back to his monastery. Ramón Berenguer could now add 'King of Aragón' to his titles, and he generously compensated the slighted Templars with Monzón and many other properties. Ramón Berenguer's descendant, Jaime I, the Conqueror, received his education here, in the ruined **castle** that still dominates the town.

Near Graus, on the banks of a lake, **Torreciudad** has had a shrine of the Virgin since the 12th century. One of its most fervent devotees was Escrivá de Balaguer (d. 1975), an Aragonese priest who in 1928 founded the Opus Dei—a shadowy organization of ultra-conservative Catholic technocrats that ran most of Spain in the later Franco years. It has since spread to some 80 countries around the world, with the blessing of John Paul II, who beatifed Escrivá in 1992. Some of Opus Dei's rites, like flagellation, are downright medieval; and yet their main concerns are education (they run a university in Pamplona) and getting their members or sympathizers into the upper echelons of business and government—the organization came close to taking over Spain in the 1970s and Mexico in the 1950s.

Las Cinco Villas

Tourist Information

Ejea de los Caballeros: Pza. de la Magdalena, ✆ 974 66 11 00.

West of Zaragoza the region of Las Cinco Villas was named after five villages promoted to the status of towns by Felipe V in gratitude for their help during the War of the Spanish Succession. The five (Tauste, Ejea de los Caballeros, Sádaba, Uncastillo and Sos del Rey Católico) all offer picturesque ensembles of old buildings and quiet atmosphere.

Tauste, closest to Zaragoza, boasts a fine *mudéjar* church of the 13th century, the convent of **Las Clarisas** and, a few kilometres away over the mountains, the sanctuary of **Sancho Abarca**. Among its fine 16th-century houses, **Ejea de los Caballeros** has a fortified Romanesque church, **San Salvador** (1222) with a stork-topped tower, more befitting a castle than a church, and beautiful Romanesque sculpture in one of the two fonts. The first Aragonese Parliament is said to have been formed in the church of **Santa María**. In **Sádaba**, there's a 16th-century church in Aragonese-Gothic style and a large, square 13th-century castle just outside town, outwardly in good condition, but a wreck inside.

The last two of the Cinco Villas, nearer the Pyrenees, are the most rewarding. **Uncastillo** seems entirely medieval, its houses adorned with proud escutcheons on steep streets crowded beneath the great ruined castle. Arcaded **Plaza del Campo** is the centre, near the most interesting of Uncastillo's numerous churches, Romanesque **Santa María la Mayor** with a fine carved façade and a battlemented Gothic tower. There are remains of a Roman spa by the hot springs at **Los Bañoles**.

Sos added 'del Rey Católico' to its name in 1924, honouring Fernando, who was a baby here. It is the most visited town of the five and the most beautiful; a wander through its old streets reveals a snapshot of its history, from the Romanesque and Gothic windows of its houses, to the sweeping view from the esplanade near the castle church. Like Uncastillo it has a number of noble mansions, most importantly, the **Palacio de Sada**, birthplace of Fernando and now a museum, housing artworks and historical odds and ends related to the king. Go inside Romanesque **San Esteban** to see the 14th-century frescoes in its crypt.

Where to Stay and Eating Out

Barbastro ✉ 22300

The best place to stay is the **Pirineos**, C/General Ricardos 13, ✆/✉ 974 31 00 00 (*moderate*), where the atmosphere is relaxed and peaceful and the service is good. There is a collection of cheap hostales—the ★**Roxi**, Corona de Aragón 21, ✆ 974 31 10 64, is well run and in the middle of town. The **Palafox**, ✆ 974 31 24 61, next door, is a little more expensive but worth it for the extra comfort. **L'Arrabal**, Avda. Pirineos 7, ✆ 974 31 16 73 is the favourite for eating out. It is small and simple, but the food is good for the price. 3km out of town, on the road to Huesca, the food is almost as good as the views at **El Pueyo**, in the restored ancient monastery of Santuario de El Pueyo, ✆ 974 31 50 79. Situated near a pretty 14th century church, the restaurant looks out over the Pyrenees and Natural Park of the Sierras de Guara.

Monzón ✉ 22400

In Monzón, the ★★**Vianetto**, Avda. de Lérida 25, ✆ 974 40 19 00, ✉ 974 40 45 40 (*moderate*) has both air conditioning and one of the town's best restaurants (*meals around 3500 pts*). The small **Bellomonte**, Avda. de Lérida 87, ✆ 974 40 20 44 (*inexpensive*) is very comfortable and has a decent, cheap restaurant.

Ejea de los Caballeros ✉ 22100

The pleasant **Cuatro Esquinas**, Salvador 4, ✆ 974 66 10 03, is tucked away behind the church and has a bustling little restaurant.

Sos del Rey Católico ✉ 50680

The modern **Parador Fernando de Aragón** (*moderate*) is in a traditional, stone and wood-beamed building, ✆ 974 88 80 11, ✉ 974 88 81 00, signposted from the village square. It's not huge and so has a friendly and cosy atmosphere. With double rooms costing *under 10,000 pts*, it's very reasonable too, and has quite a good restaurant (*3500 pts for a meal*).

Also in Sos, **Fonda Fernandino** (*cheap*) is the budget traveller's dream. Housed in an old mansion with a huge foyer, a grand ceiling and a sweeping staircase, the large rooms are comfortable and very clean. The simple restaurant serves tasty food under the beady eye of a boar's head (*meal at around 2000 pts, double room 3000 pts*). For meals, a less expensive choice than the *parador* is the **Vinacua**, ✆ 974 88 80 71, on Plaza del Mesón, serving Aragonese dishes (*3000 pts*).

Huesca: C/ General Lasheras 5, ✆ 974 22 57 78.

Huesca, the provincial capital of northern Aragón, is unlovely but prosperous—it sits in the middle of its own fertile *hoya* (irrigated farmland), and is within easy striking distance of some of the loveliest scenery in Spain, from the central Pyrenees to many green, forested valleys dotted with blue glacial lakes. Spaniards associate Huesca with the *Legend de la Campana* ('of the bell'), illustrated by a painting in the **Ayuntamiento**: faced with rebellious nobles Ramiro II ('the Monk'—*see* above) summoned them to his palace to ask their advice on a bell he meant to cast, so big that it would be heard throughout all Aragón. As the nobles filed in, one by one, the monkish king had their heads cut off. Ramiro II's admirers claim it's a load of hooey, but you can visit the actual **Sala de la Campana** underneath the **museum** in the Plaza de la Universidad (*opening after extensive restoration in 2000, daily except Mon 9–2, holidays 10–2*), in a building that began its life as a Moorish alcazar, and served for many years as the palace of the kings of Aragón, then in 1354 as a university. Exhibits range from the prehistoric to medieval Aragonese painting.

Ramiro II and his brother Alfonso el Batallador are buried in Huesca's oldest church, the 12th-century **San Pedro el Viejo** on Calle Cuatro Reyes; the cloister's capitals have some fine carvings of monsters (*open daily 10–2*). The lovely late Gothic **Cathedral** has a landmark octagonal tower, and a west portal topped by an unusual *mudéjar* gallery; within is another of Damián Forment's great alabaster *retablos*. The **cathedral museum** holds mainly primitive art from the region (*the museum is open daily 11–1 and 4–6, closed Sun; the cathedral is open daily 9–1 and 4–6.30*).

Huesca is the base for visiting Aragón's showpiece **Castillo de Loarre** (*open daily except Mon, 10–3.30 and 4–7, in the summer opening is extended to 8pm*), an 11th-century military masterpiece on a rocky eminence overlooking the great plain of Aragón. The castle, built by Sancho Ramírez, the great king of Navarre, so perfectly fits into its surroundings that it approaches environmental art. It has been lovingly restored and is exciting to explore; outstanding are its three great towers—La Vigía, el Homenaje, and la Reina—and a gem of a Romanesque **chapel**. If you pass through nearby **Ayerbe**, stop to see the **Gothic palace** of the local Marqués.

Huesca ✉ *22000*   ***Where to Stay***

The best hotel in Huesca, ★★★**Pedro I de Aragón**, Avda. del Parque 34, ✆ 974 22 03 00, 🖷 974 22 00 94 (*expensive*) has air-conditioned rooms with TV and a swimming pool, an option to consider in the summer months. One of the prettier places to stay is the ★★★**Hotel Sancho Abarca,** Pza. de Lizana 15, ✆ 974 22 06 50 (*moderate*), small and near the old centre.

Another very comfortable establishment is the **Lizana**, Pza. de Lizana 6, ✆ 974 22 07 76 (*inexpensive*), which is perfect in its simplicity. Of the cheap places in Huesca, ★**Augusto**, Ainsa 16, ✆ 974 22 00 79, a short distance from the Lizana, is small and very friendly.

Huescan specialities include *pollo a la chilindrón* (chicken in a sauce of onion, garlic, pepper and tomato), *ternasco* (lamb roasted with garlic and potatoes), *salmorrejo* (eggs with pork cutlets). The local wine comes from the area east of Huesca, Somontano, and is noted mostly for Alcañón, a light, fruity white.

The best food in Huesca town is at **Las Torres**, C/ Maria Auxiliadora 3, ✆ 974 22 82 13 (*expensive*), which serves imaginatively prepared Aragonese and some international dishes. Old ladies quiver in the corner of **La Campana**, Coso Alto 78, ✆ 974 22 95 00 (*moderate*), a sombre looking place that serves a superlative *cabritillo asado en horno de leña*—baby kid baked in a traditional wood oven. The *menú del día* is good value at *1500 pts*. Other good choices serving local specialities are **Casa Vicente** (*moderate*), Plaza de Lérida 2, ✆ 974 22 98 11, and **Ordesa** (*moderate*), Padre Huesca 14, ✆ 974 22 77 65 (*meals for around 3500–4000 pts*). If your funds won't stretch that far, try **Hervi**, Santa Paciencia 2, ✆ 974 24 03 33 (*cheap*), a busy, friendly bar/restaurant in the centre, with excellent tapas and a decent *menú del dìa* for *1000 pts*. Nearby, the best tapas in town are served by two bars within a few metres from each other: **Ricocu**, between Argensales and San Orencio, and **Pozal**, just around the corner. Veggies should check out **Ceres**, C/ Padre Huesca 37 (*cheap*), an 'alternative' stronghold. *Closed Sun*.

At **Esquedas**, 28km north of Huesca on the A132 in a converted country house, **Venta del Sotón** (*expensive*), Ctra. Tarragona-San Sebastian, Km 226, ✆ 974 27 02 41, serves excellent *chorizos y las longanizas a la brasa*, Aragonese baby kid with artichokes, *pollo al chilindrón* and salted beef dishes for *around 6000 pts*.

Jaca

Tourist Information

Avda. Regimiento de Galicia 2, ✆ (974) 36 00 98.

The attractive, bustling little town of Jaca, only 30km from France, is the only real town in Aragón's Pyrenees and is nearly everyone's point of departure for the mountains to the north and east (far more rugged and less exploited than Catalunya's Pyrenees) and to the secluded valleys and villages to the west. If you're heading north to France at the end of your Spanish holiday, it's your last chance to pick up some Spanish wine and that *paella* pan you've been meaning to buy all along.

In the Middle Ages, Jaca was also a point of departure—for Santiago de Compostela. Pilgrims taking the Aragonese road would cross the mountains near Canfranc, then the next day make for Jaca before turning west. Even earlier, Jaca served as the first capital of Aragón when in 760 it was regained from the Moors. In 795, when the Moors tried to take it back, the women defended it so fiercely they never tried again, an event commemorated each May by a mock battle between groups of local ladies. French influence crossed the border with the pilgrims, and, in Jaca, Spain's very first Romanesque church, the **Cathedral**, was constructed at the beginning of the 11th century. Although meddled with over the years it's still impressive; note the finely carved capitals, and the silver shrine of Santa Orosia, Jaca's patron saint, who was martyred by the Moors for refusing to renounce her faith (*open daily 9–2 and 4–9*). The **Diocesan Museum** (*open daily except Mon, 11–1.30 and 4–7*), in the cloister—when it reopens after restoration—is especially worthwhile, featuring many Romanesque frescoes garnered from abandoned chapels in the Pyrenees. Jaca's other principal monument, the pentagonal **Ciudadela**, was begun by Felipe II after the Aragón revolt—one of the numerable headaches faced by His Majesty the Bureaucrat (*open daily 11–12 and 4–5*). Take a stroll along the ramparts of the Camino Monte Pago for fine views of the River Aragón, or walk down to the handsome medieval **Puente de San Miguel** on the pilgrims' road, 1km from town. Before setting out on excursions, check at Jaca's tourist office, a goldmine of information on the Pyrenees: it can also sell you a good hiking map.

East of Jaca: Ordesa National Park

Tourist Information

There's a summer information office at the entrance of Ordesa Park, in Bielsa and at Torla in the Ayuntamiento, © 974 48 61 52.

In the misty dawn of Aragón this was the county of Sobrarbe. Much of its heart is now part of the **Parque Nacional de Ordesa**, created in 1918. One of Spain's most beautiful, the park is crowned by the **Tres Sorores**, 'the three sisters'—three mountains over 3080m high. In the late spring, hundreds of waterfalls cascade towards the Río Arazus in the valley, and in summer edelweiss adorns the slopes. There are trails through the poplar groves for strollers and 300m cliffs for alpinists; the most beautiful is the 6–7hr **Soasso Circle** route along the Río Arazus then up the valley for some spectacular scenery over the gorge, climaxing in the **Mirador Calcitarruego**. Anyone in reasonable shape can make it, but you should wear hiking boots and take a lunch. Provisions are obtainable in **Torla**, a small stone village at the entrance of the park, with plenty of accommodation as well. Just north of Torla, on the other side of the pretty, narrow gorge **Garganta de Escalar**, lies the now rather decrepit spa resort of **Balneario de Panticosa**, with mineral springs providing cures for dodgy tummies, bad backs and respiratory problems.

South of the park, **Ainsa** was the capital of the ancient kingdom of Sobrarbe and is the loveliest town in the region. Its walled old centre is criss-crossed with medieval streets and an elegant **Plaza Mayor** overlooks the new quarters below, now interspersed with an ample supply of restaurants, hotels, discothèques and boutiques. **Bielsa**, near the French border, is the departure point for the 15km hike along the **Valle de Pineta**, Ordesa's 'twin' valley, on the banks of the Río Cinca. A pre-Romanesque hermitage, a lake and glacier and magnificent views (and fewer fellow-hikers) are some of the highlights. Farther east, the mountains become so formidable that the Spaniards call them **Los Montes Malditos** (the 'cursed mountains'). The tallest of the Pyrenees are here: **Aneto** (3404m) and its sister peak, Maladeta (3308m). **Benasque** is the base for visiting them, for summer climbs and hikes, or winter skiing. The village itself, of stone houses with slate roofs, is hemmed in by the mountains and wonderfully picturesque and tranquil.

West of Jaca

In 724, the nobles of Sobrarbe gathered at the remote **chapel of San Juan de la Peña** and solemnly vowed to rid Aragón of the Moorish invader, and ever since then the old monastery has been the chief shrine of the Aragonese Reconquista. According to legend, the chalice of the Last Supper (now in Valencia) was hidden here for centuries; the old monastery (*open Tues–Sun 10–1.30 and 4–7,* © *974 34 80 99*), under an overhanging cliff, has two levels. The crypt, with traces of fresco, is actually the original 9th-century Mozarabic chapel, while upstairs the 12th-century Romanesque church is full of kings; in the 18th century Carlos III had many of the earlier rules of Aragón and Navarra re-interred here with regal fittings. The 12th-century cloister—or the half of the cloister that has survived—is the main reason for coming, magnificently and fancifully carved by the Maestro de San Juan de la Peña. The hamlet of **Santa Cruz de la Serós**, (*open 11–1 and 4–6; adm*) a short walk away, had an auxiliary convent, its surviving 11th-century church modelled on Jaca's cathedral.

Berdún was a day's journey for the pilgrim from Jaca. The beauty of the area, and its abundant and unusual plant and bird life, inspired an English artist, John Boucher, to found a field studies centre for painters, bird watchers, botanists and architects, amateurs and professionals alike.

This is the region of **Old Aragón**, and there are two secluded valleys here which have changed little since the Middle Ages. The eastern one, the **Valle del Hecho**, was the birth-place of Alfonso el Batallador and still preserves its ancient Aragonese dialect; the principal village, **Hecho**, couldn't be more charming or better sited. In July and August, Hecho and the surrounding hills turn into a contemporary sculpture garden as part of the 'Simposio de Escultura y Pintura Moderna'. It has spawned an open-air gallery of sculpture, set west of the village and affording great views over the valley. There is an **ethnographic museum** near the village church (*open 11–2 and 6–9*). The nearby hamlet of **Siresa** is an easy walk away; Alfonso el Batallador was educated here in the monastery of the ancient church of **San Pedro de Siresa**, currently under restoration. A number of lovely hikes begin here.

In the **Valle de Ansó** the old villagers speak yet another near-vanished dialect, and it's one of the few places in Spain where you may catch sight of a woman in her traditional costume any day of the week. Some of Ansó's houses are adorned with inexplicable symbols—thought to be a memory of the valley's once sizeable population of *agotes*, the mysterious pariahs of the Pyrenees, believed to be the descendants of Visigoths, Moors, Cathar heretics or, most commonly and erroneously, lepers. They lived on both sides of the Pyrenees under apartheid laws of segregation until the late 18th century and have since vanished without a trace. Ansó is a bit more conscious of its own whitewashed charms than Hecho; a **museo etnológico** (*open 10.30–1.30 and 4–8; adm*) of odds and ends may be visited in the old church on the Plaza de San Pedro. Ansó is a good base for hikes in the beautiful **Valle de Zuriza**, 13km north.

Where to Stay and Eating Out

Jaca ✉ 22700

In Jaca, the **★★Conde Aznar**, Pso. de la Constitución 3, © 974 36 10 50, ✆ 974 36 07 97, is traditionally comfortable and sports a garden. Its restaurant is also good (*see* below). The modern **★★Hs La Paz**, © 974 36 07 00, is set on lovely C/ Mayor 39 (*7000 pts*). Just off the Calle Mayor, **Hs Somport**, Echegaray 11, © 974 36 34 10, is cheaper.

Another cheap option is **Hs París**, Pza. de San Pedro 5, © 974 36 10 20, near the cathedral. The tourist office has a list of *casas particulares* (rooms in private houses).

For your last meal on Spanish soil before hitting the French border, there are a few places in Jaca worth a visit: **La Cocina Aragonesa**, C/ Cervantes 5, ✆ 974 36 10 50 (*expensive*) is the Conde Aznar's well-regarded restaurant. It's posh: the sort of place people speak in hushed voices, and the food is wonderful. *Closed Thurs.* **Meson Serrabio**, ✆ 974 36 24 18, also serves excellent regional cuisine, with a *menù del dìa* for *around 3000pts.* Another good choice for Aragonese cuisine is **Mèson El Rancho Grande**, C/ del Arco 2 (*moderate*). Cheaper, and worth a visit even if you are a dedicated carnivore, **El Arco**, C/ San Nicholas 4, is a family-run vegetarian restaurant, serving an inventive and delicious menu. Jaca is good for tapas; for a superb range, from prawns to country-style pies, try **La Nicolasa**, on Escuelas Pias 3, ✆ 974 35 54 12.

Torla ✉ 22376

In Torla, by Ordesa Park, you are guaranteed a mountain view. ★**Viñamala**, Falás 5, ✆ 974 48 61 56, is open all year and has a pool. Torla has the *fonda* **Ballarín**, Capuvita 11, ✆ 974 48 61 55, with fairly decent rooms for *under 3500 pts.*

Balneario de Panticosa ✉ 22661

If you're thinking of taking the waters at Balneario de Panticosa, the ★★★**Gran Hotel**, ✆ 974 48 71 37, offers good facilities for *8000 pts*—swimming pool, tennis and sauna, and very comfortable rooms.

Ainsa ✉ 22330

In Ainsa, there's little in the way of cheap accommodation. The best bet is ★**Apolo XI**, Ctra. Campos s/n, ✆ 974 50 02 81.

Bielsa ✉ 22350

If you want comfort in Bielsa after your mountain hikes, there's the modern ★★★**Parador de Monte Perdido**, Valle de Pinetar, ✆ 974 50 10 11, 🖷 974 50 11 88, with 24 rooms and a restaurant serving mountain specialities.

Benasque ✉ 22440

Benasque has several relatively posh places along Ctra. Anciles; in town, try ★**Hotel El Puente II**, San Pedro, ✆ 974 55 12 79, with mountain views. There are decent restaurants attached to Benasque's hotels. A nice café is **Filly** (*cheap*), opposite the Red Cross station on the road leading up to the peak. It has good tapas, light meals and a delicious selection of filled croissants.

Valle del Hecho ✉ 22720

In Hecho, a decent mid-range choice is ★**De la Val**, Cruz Alta 1, ✆ 974 37 50 28 (*6000 pts*). **Casa Blasquico**, ✆ 974 37 50 07 (*moderate*) identifies itself only as *pensión* at Pza. de la Fuente 1. Its small restaurant has a big, nationwide reputation: the imaginative menu is a real treat (*closed Sept*).

Valle de Ansó ✉ 22700

In Ansó the choice is limited; you can get a bed for 6000 pts at the charming old **Fonda Estanés**, Pso. Chapitel 9, ✆ 974 37 01 46. Guests enjoy use of the garden and good prices in the popular little restaurant, which specializes in fish dishes.There is also the **Aisa**, Plaza Domingo Miral 2, ✆ 974 37 00 09, which will give you a pleasant room without bath for *4000 pts*. **Posada Magoria**, next to the Estanés, © 974 37 00 49, is all low ceilings and wooden beams, very much a traditional house, and comfortable to boot, with good home-made, home-grown vegetarian meals.

Where to Ski

Northern Aragón offers Spain's most varied and challenging skiing, and facilities are mostly up-to-date and quite reasonable compared to other installations in Europe; a bit out-of-the-way, they are also likely to be less crowded.

Package deals are available in Madrid, Barcelona, Zaragoza and from travel agents anywhere in Aragón. All rent equipment.

Cerler, near Benasque, has very modern facilities including five restaurants, two discos and five bars, and 25 pistes on the highest slopes the Pyrenees can offer. There are two hotels at the resort (and 14 other places to stay in Benasque), an ice palace and a wide range of other activities; © 974 55 10 12. Benasque also has **La Maladeta**, a series of downhill runs and cross-country trails, but you have to make your own way up there. **Astún**, near Jaca and the Canfranc rail station, has 22 pistes (15 difficult, three very difficult), two slalom courses (one giant), and easy transport from Jaca; © 974 37 30 34. **Candanchú**, Astún's older sister on the other side of Canfranc, offers 22 pistes, cross-country skiing, 24 lifts and four hotels at the station and bars, cafés and discos; easy transport from Jaca; © 974 37 31 92. **El Formigal**, near Sallent de Gállego, has 27 very open pistes without obstacles (one is 7km long), served by one *telecabina* and 17 other lifts. Most of the courses are rated difficult; © 974 48 81 25. There's a slalom course, lots of recreational facilities and eight hotels at the station. **Panticosa**, also near Sallent de Gállego (Sabiñánigo, between Jaca and Huesca, is the closest train station—40km distant), has 14 pistes, a slalom course and eight hotels and the most bars and restaurants at the station; © 974 48 81 25. **Valdelinares** is the only ski resort in southern Aragón, on the Sierra de Gúdar, near Teruel. There are four pistes and a slalom course and four hotels at Virgen de la Vega, 8km away, © 978 80 10 14.

The Basque, Navarra and La Rioja

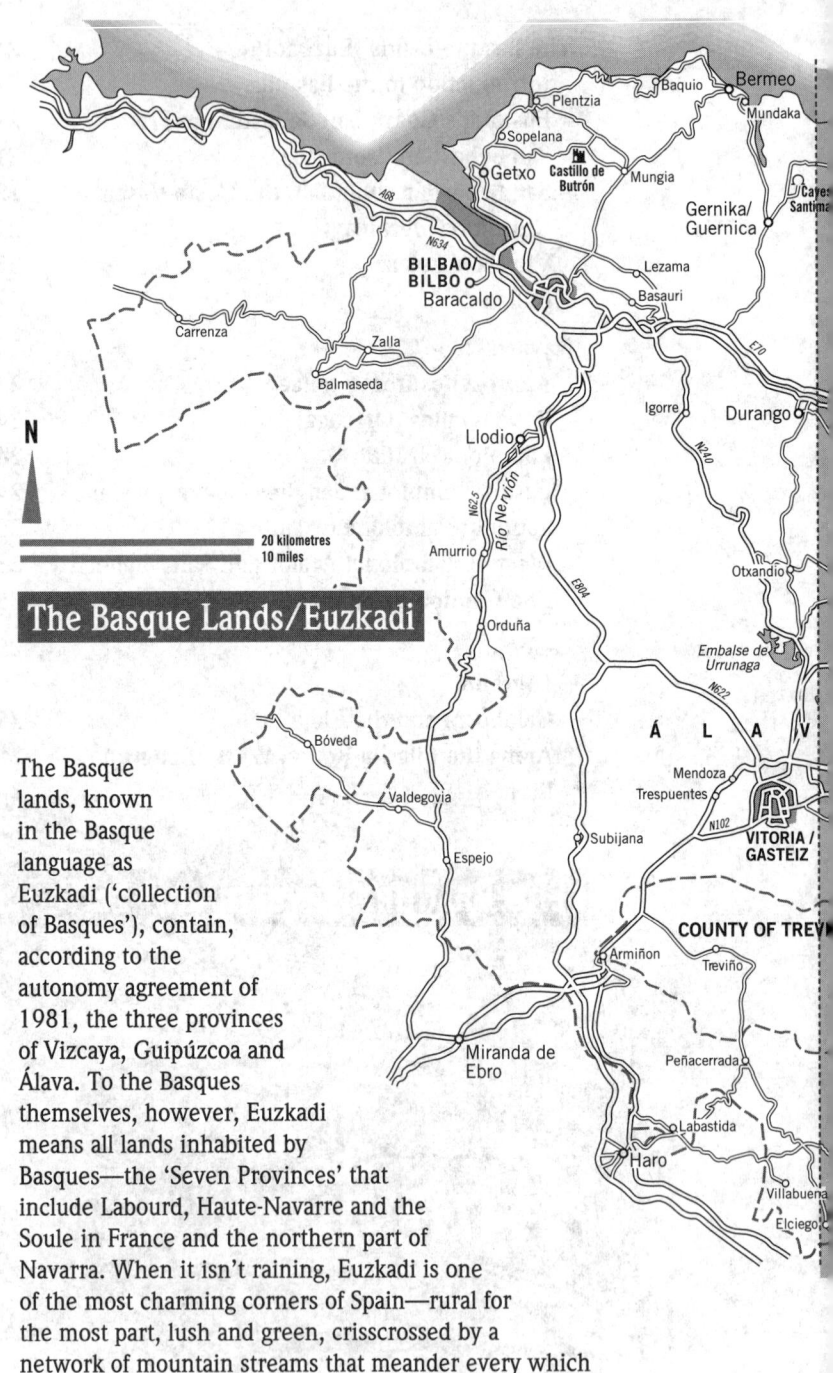

The Basque Lands/Euzkadi

N

20 kilometres
10 miles

The Basque
lands, known
in the Basque
language as
Euzkadi ('collection
of Basques'), contain,
according to the
autonomy agreement of
1981, the three provinces
of Vizcaya, Guipúzcoa and
Álava. To the Basques
themselves, however, Euzkadi
means all lands inhabited by
Basques—the 'Seven Provinces' that
include Labourd, Haute-Navarre and the
Soule in France and the northern part of
Navarra. When it isn't raining, Euzkadi is one
of the most charming corners of Spain—rural for
the most part, lush and green, crisscrossed by a
network of mountain streams that meander every which

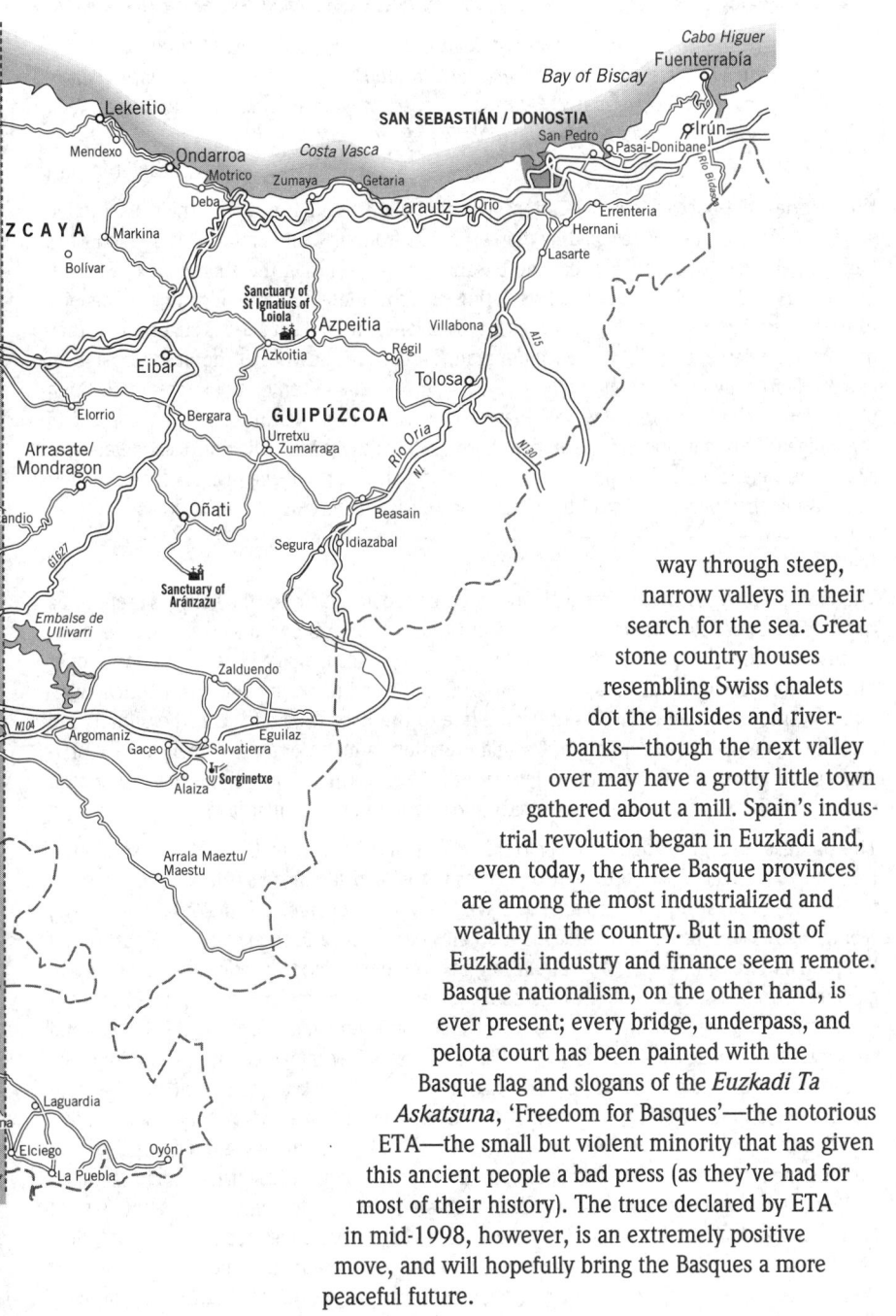

way through steep, narrow valleys in their search for the sea. Great stone country houses resembling Swiss chalets dot the hillsides and riverbanks—though the next valley over may have a grotty little town gathered about a mill. Spain's industrial revolution began in Euzkadi and, even today, the three Basque provinces are among the most industrialized and wealthy in the country. But in most of Euzkadi, industry and finance seem remote. Basque nationalism, on the other hand, is ever present; every bridge, underpass, and pelota court has been painted with the Basque flag and slogans of the *Euzkadi Ta Askatsuna*, 'Freedom for Basques'—the notorious ETA—the small but violent minority that has given this ancient people a bad press (as they've had for most of their history). The truce declared by ETA in mid-1998, however, is an extremely positive move, and will hopefully bring the Basques a more peaceful future.

Nomansland, the territory of the Basques, in a region called Cornucopia, where the vines are tied up with sausages. And in those parts there was a mountain made entirely of grated Parmesan cheese on whose slopes there were people who spent their whole time making macaroni and ravioli.

The Decameron, VIII

Wild stories like Boccaccio's have often been told about the Basques and their inscrutable ways, but the conclusions reached by many scholars from many different fields are almost as hard to believe. It seems likely that the Basques are no less than the aborigines of Europe, having survived in their secluded valleys during the great Indo-European migrations of peoples from the east thousands of years ago; recent discoveries in Euzkadi's caves suggest that they may even be descendants of Cro-Magnon man. Tests have shown that the Basques have an extraordinarily high proportion of type A 'European' blood; an even more extraordinarily high proportion—the highest in the world—have blood with a negative Rh factor, characteristic of the indigenous prehistoric European race. Basques have slight but telling physical differences from their neighbours. Not only are they bigger and stronger, but the distinct shape of their skulls is matched only by those of their ancestors, buried under dolmens in 2000 BC.

History

The Basques have no written records, and in other people's histories they always seem to be causing trouble. The Romans conquered but did not tame them, and respected them as soothsayers. Visigoths, Moors and early Christian kingdoms managed even less control over them. Medieval clerics railed against them for fleecing and harassing pilgrims. Political organization into towns and Christianity came late to the Basques, and when they finally did agree to recognize the suzerainty of Castilla it was on terms that retained their *fueros* (privileges) and ancient laws, one of which was that every king upon being crowned should come to Gernika and swear under the sacred oak tree to uphold their laws.

The Basques (except for those in Navarra) lost their *fueros* in retaliation for their support of Fernando VII's reactionary brother Don Carlos in the Carlist wars (1876). Around the same time Euzkadi began to industrialize, and while many prospered, the majority of workers, seeing their traditional society threatened on all sides, flocked to the newly raised banner of Basque Nationalism. When the Republican government offered the Basques autonomy in exchange for their support in the 1930s, they jumped at the chance, despite reservations about the government's secularism (the Basques have always been among Spain's most fervent and conservative Catholics). When the Civil War broke out, they remained loyal to the Republic and even the priests fought side by side with the 'reds'. To break their spirit, the German Condor Legion practised the world's first saturation bombing of a civilian target, at Gernika. Franco later singled out the Basques for reprisals of all kinds, outlawing their language and running the region as a police state, so that even the thousands of Castilians who immigrated to Euzkadi to work in the factories felt oppressed enough to sympathize with Basque Nationalist goals. Since Franco, the democratic government has done much to right past grievances in Euzkadi—the Basques were the first to gain their autonomy, their own police and their own independent TV station. The region is bilingual: Basque is taught in the primary schools, and amnesty was granted to any member of the ETA who renounced violence. But terrorism continues unabated, and it will take many years before the ETA lose their support, or as Mao put it, 'pond for the fish to swim in'. Still, the large majority of Basques vote their aspirations through the PNV (*Partido Nacional Vasco*) rather than the political wing of the ETA, *Herri Batasuna*, and on the whole they are progressive—left on most issues (strongly anti-nuclear and anti-NATO). After all that, it must be said that the Basques are an extremely friendly people, and they will make sure you enjoy your stay in their beloved Euzkadi.

Basque Culture

Basques have always played an important role in Spanish affairs, far out of proportion to their numbers. They were great sailors and explorers, shipbuilders and whalers, *conquistadors* and pirates, and nowadays they run most of Spain's banks. Basque whalers are said to have landed in the Americas before Columbus (whose pilot was a Basque); Basque sailors helped the English conquer Wales, built the Spanish Armada, fought in the American revolution and founded a number of Spanish colonies including the Philippines and the city of Buenos Aires. The conquistador Lope de Aguirre (so well portrayed by Klaus Kinski in Herzog's film *Aguirre, the Wrath of God*) and Pedro de Ursua were Basques; the Basque captain Sebastián Elcano became the first man to sail around the world. Two of Spain's most influential saints, St Ignatius de Loyola and St Francis Xavier, were also Basque.

Traditional Basque culture is full of stories about the countless dolmens in the region, erected as houses by the 'gentiles', or *jentillak*, friendly giants who lived side-by-side with the Basques. If the rest of Spain used to tell tales about the magical Moors and their hidden treasures, the Basques, who had little contact with the Moors, did the same with their gentiles. The *jentillak* are said to have taught the Basques some special skills, like cultivation, but one day, when strange omens appeared in the sky, they all disappeared under a dolmen, saying 'Kixmi (Jesus Christ) is born, our time is over.' They've never been seen again, although in some villages especially strong, tall people are said to be descendants of the *jentillak*. Strength, endurance, agility and competitiveness are traditional Basques virtues in work, dancing and especially sports. The Basques invented *pelota* (*jaï alaï*), that combines two Basque loves, agility and gambling—although originally *pelota* seems to have been a sacred sport, played against the church wall. Less sacred but widespread are log-splitting, wrestling and heaving mega-kilo concrete weights over one's shoulders. Traditional Basque instruments include the *txistu*, a three-holed flute played with one hand while the other hand beats out the rhythm on a tambour. To accompany their music the Basques dance some of the most furiously athletic dances in the world, especially the *Bolant Dantza* (the Flying Dance) or the *Espata Dantza* (sword dance). Traditional dances in costume can be seen on most Sundays in village squares.

Basque Cuisine

Basques love to eat, and when they're not running banks or lifting weights, they're opening restaurants, not only in Euzkadi but throughout Spain. Basque cuisine relishes imaginative sauces; perhaps the most famous Basque dishes are *ttoro*, a fish soup, and squid in its own ink (*chiperones*)—reputedly the only one in the world that's all black, and better than it sounds. Basque chefs work wonders with elvers and cod, salmon and the famous *txangurro*—spider crab; Basques like to wash it down with *txakoli*, a tangy wine. Southern Álava produces an excellent Rioja, and you can top off your meal with a tipple of deadly Basque hooch, *pacharán*.

It's only 20 minutes by bus from San Sebastián to Irún or Fuenterrabía on the frontier; connections are frequent by bus and train and not a few people watching their pesetas stay in Irún (or in France) rather than in the more pricey capital. If you're not in a hurry, take the narrow-gauge 'El Topo' for a leisurely ride through some fine scenery.

Irún: Puente de Santiago (Barrio de Behobia s/n), ✆ 943 62 26 27, and in the train station, ✆ 943 61 67 08.

Fuenterrabía (Hondarribia): Javier Ugarte 6, ✆ 943 64 54 58.

Fuenterrabía

If you're driving to San Sebastián you can take the coastal road along **Monte Jáizkibel**, offering superb views over the Bay of Biscay, the French coast and the Pyrenees. It begins at the charming border village of **Fuenterrabía** (Hondarribia), endowed with a fine, wide, and protected sandy beach. Fuenterrabía glows with colour—in its brightly painted houses, especially along Calle San Nicolás, in its balconies loaded with flowers, and in its fishing-fleet that has not been afraid to take on France in the EU's battle of fishing rights. The town has had its share of sieges—you can still see the ancient walls and a **castle of Charles V**, now a *parador*. In the evening, head out towards the lighthouse on Cabo Higuer—the northeasternmost corner of Spain—for views of the sunset over the bay. **Irún**, up the Bidasoa, is the uncharming frontier town, with only plenty of cheap accommodation to recommend it. Inland you can flee the bustling coast for the serene **Valley of Oyarzun**, one of Euzkadi's rural beauty spots, with the pretty villages of **Oyarzun**, **Lesaka** and **Vera (Bera) de Bidasoa**.

Just east of San Sebastián, the long ribbon town of **Pasajes de San Juan** lines the east bank of a fjord, with picturesque old houses. Victor Hugo lived in one for a while, and the Marquis de Lafayette lodged in another before sailing off to aid Britain's American colonists in their revolution. Philip built part of the Invincible Armada here, although now business affairs are handled by San Juan's ugly step-sister across the fjord, **Pasajes de San Pedro**.

Fuenterrabía ✉ 20280

The castle that housed so many kings and dukes on French business over the centuries has been converted into the ★★★**Parador de Hondarribia**, Pza. de Armas 14, ✆ 943 64 55 00, 🖷 943 64 21 53, and is prettily situated. Smaller, but just as noble, the ★★★**Pampinot**, Kale Nagusia 5, ✆ 943 64 06 00 (*expensive*) has eight rooms in a restored 15th-century mansion in the heart of the old quarter. In the *moderate* and *inexpensive* ranges there are few choices (actually, rooms are a better bargain across the border in Hendaye, though Fuenterrabía would make a more pleasant stay). The ★★**San Nicolás** has attractive, functional rooms right on Pza. de Armas 6, ✆ 943 64 42 78.

Of the small number of *hostales*, a dependable and relatively cheap one is the **HSR Alvarez Quintero**, C/ Alvarez Quintero 7, © 943 64 22 99. **Ramon Roteta**, Villa Ainara, Irún 1, © 943 64 16 93 (*expensive*) offers gracious dining in a lovely villa with a garden, grand cuisine and superb deserts. *Closed Sun eve and Thurs.* Next to the sea, the **Arraunlauri**, Pso. Butrón 3, © 943 64 15 81 (*moderate*) is the best bet, offering simple fish dishes and other scrumptious seafood.

Irún ✉ 20300

At the top of the range, try the **★★★Alcazar**, Avd Iparralde 11, © 943 62 09 00, ◉ 943 62 27 97 (*expensive*). The **Hs Irún**, at Zubiaurre 5, 943 61 16 37, has decent rooms with or without bath at the cheapest rates in town. Near the train station, the **★★Lizaso**, Aduana 5-7, © 943 61 16 00, is a good bargain. The **Romantxo** on Pza. de Urdanibia, © 943 62 09 71(*moderate*) has good home cooking. **Larretxipi**, Larretxipi 5, © 943 63 26 59, has excellent fish. A number of places nearby are cheaper.

San Sebastián/Donostia

Long before there were any 'costas', wealthy Spaniards spent their summers bathing at San Sebastián (*Donostia* in Basque) following in the footsteps of the Queen Regent María Cristina, who made it all the rage in 1886. It's been a classy place to go ever since, a lovely, relaxed, Belle Epoque resort in a spectacular setting, built around one of the peninsula's most enchanting bays, the oyster-shaped Bahía de La Concha, protected by a wooded islet, the Isla de Santa Clara, and Monte Urgull, the hump-backed sentinel on the easternmost tip of the bay.

Sheltered within the bay is the magnificent golden crescent of the **Playa de la Concha**, San Sebastián's largest beach; on its western end stands a promontory topped by the mock-Tudor **Palace of Miramar** of María Cristina. A tunnel under Miramar leads to the **Playa de Ondarreta**, a traditional Society retreat. Ondarreta itself meets a dead-end at seaside **Monte Igueldo**, crowned by a **Parque de Atracciones** (attainable by road or funicular), with spectacular views over San Sebastián. On the shore near the base of the funicular stands one of the most successful monuments of modern Spanish sculpture, Eduardo Chillida's **Comb of the Winds**; the sculptor's house is on the cliffs above. Nearly all the city built around these beaches dates from the 19th century; San Sebastián is an ancient place, but has been burnt to the ground 12 times in its history, lastly by Wellington's drunken soldiery, who celebrated the conquest of the town with murder and mayhem.

Getting Around

By air: San Sebastián's airport to the east, near Fuenterrabía, © 943 65 88 00, has connections to Madrid and Barcelona. The bus to the airport, Fuenterrabía and Irún departs from Plza. Guipuzkoa, © 943 64 13 02, every 12 minutes—note that this is really the bus for Fuenterrabía, and lets you off across the road from the airport.

By train: RENFE trains depart from the Paseo de Francia, in Gros, from Estación del Norte, © 943 28 30 89. There are frequent connections with Irún and Hendaye, Paris, Burgos and Madrid; less frequent trains to Barcelona, Pamplona, Salamanca, Vitoria, Zaragoza and León. *Talgos* whizz all the way to Madrid, Málaga, Córdoba, Algeciras, Valencia, Alicante, Oviedo and Gijón. The two narrow-gauge lines have neighbouring stations on the C/ de Easo: Topo trains, © 943 47 08 15, depart from

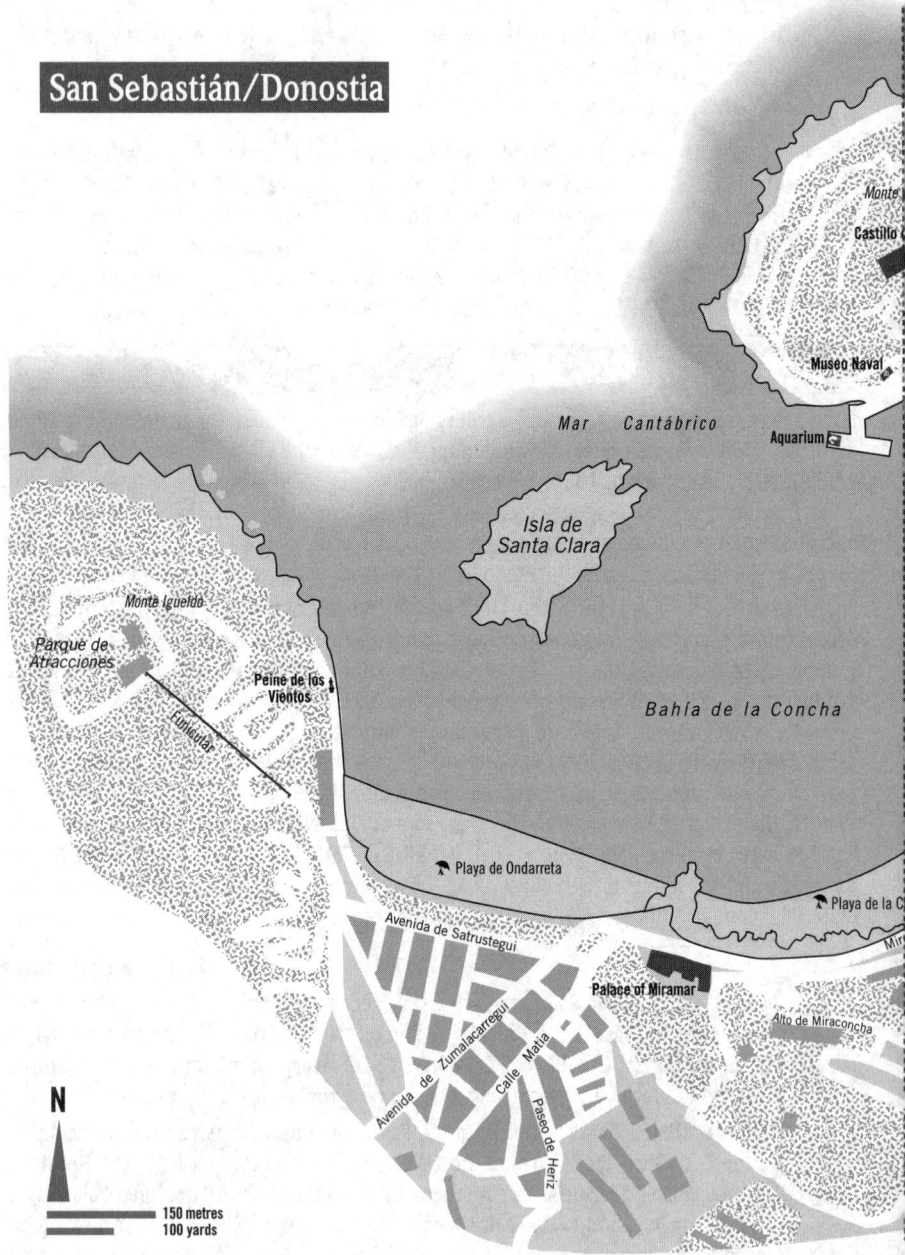

San Sebastián/Donostia

Monte

Castillo

Museo Naval

Mar Cantábrico

Aquarium

Isla de
Santa Clara

Monte Igueldo

Parque de
Atracciones

Peine de los
Vientos

Bahía de la Concha

Funicular

Playa de Ondarreta

Playa de la C

Avenida de Satrustegui

Palace of Miramar

Alto de Miraconcha

Avenida de Zumalacarregui

Calle Matia

Paseo de Heriz

N

150 metres
100 yards

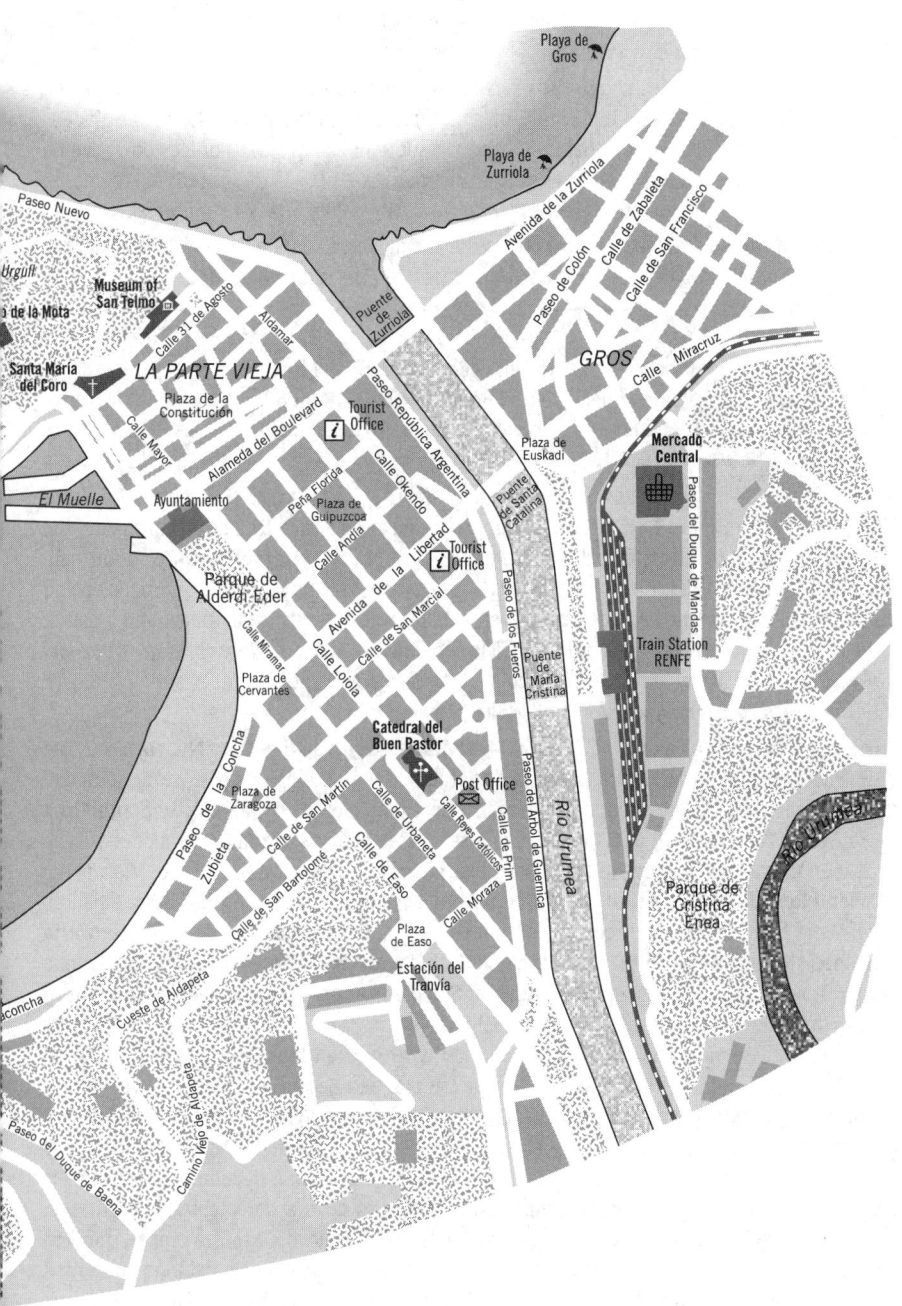

the Estación del Tranvía for Hendaye, going by way of Oyarzun. Eusko Trenbideak-Ferrocariles Vascos, (Feve-Eusko Tren), ✆ 943 45 01 31, depart from Estación de Amara less frequently for Bilbao, stopping everywhere on the way.

By bus: A bewildering number of small bus companies leave from the station on Pza. de Pío XII on the southern end of town, a block from the river. The ticket office is nearby on C/ Sancho el Sabio 33, though some lines have their offices on Paseo de Vizcaya. There are 19 bus lines in San Sebastián itself (✆ 943 28 71 00); no. 16 goes to Igueldo and the funicular (*daily in summer 10am–10pm, every 15 minutes*).

Motor **boats** make excursions out to the Isla de Santa Clara every half-hour from the port, where you can also rent a rowing boat to do the same yourself.

Tourist Information

Municipal: on the river, C/ Reina Regente, ✆ 943 48 11 66.
Basque Government: Pso. de los Fueros 1, ✆ 943 42 62 82.

La Parte Vieja and Monte Urgull

Most of the action in town takes place beneath Monte Urgull in the narrow streets of **La Parte Vieja**, or old town. From **La Concha** beach, its entrance is guarded by a beautiful square, the **Parque de Alderdi Eder**, and the enormous 19th-century **Ayuntamiento**, or town hall, formerly the casino. What remains of the city's fishing-fleet may be seen in the harbour behind the Ayuntamiento, an area rimmed by souvenir shops, pricey tourist restaurants, and a pair of salty museums: the recently-refurbished **Museo Naval** (*open daily exc Mon, Tues–Sat 10–1.30 and 5–8.30, winter 10–1.30 and 4–7.30, Sun 10–2*) and, at the far end of the port, the **Aquarium** (*open daily exc Mon 10–8.30*).

From here you can stroll along the outer edge of **Monte Urgull** on the Paseo Nuevo, a splendid little walk between turf and surf. In the late afternoon, when the light is best, stroll up one of the numerous paths to the summit of the rock where the half-ruined **Castillo de Santa Cruz de la Mota** (16th century) and an ungainly kitsch statue of Christ (from the Franco era) keep an eye on the holiday-makers on La Concha beach below. The centre of La Parte Vieja is the arcaded **Plaza de la Constitución**; within a few blocks of this local centre of Basque nationalism stand San Sebastián's three best monuments—the hyper-ornate façade of **Santa María del Coro** (18th century) on Vía Coro, the fine Gothic **church of San Vicente** on San Vicente and, nearby, the old Dominican **monastery of San Telmo**, now the fascinating **Museum of San Telmo** (*open daily exc Mon 10.30–1.30 and 4–8, summer 10.30–1.30 and 5–8.30, Sun 10–2; adm*). The monastery's church is adorned with golden murals by the Catalan artist Josep Sert (1930) on the history of the Basque people. Old Basque tombstones, with round heads adorned with geometric patterns, are lined up in the cloister. Upstairs the museum contains three El Grecos, two bear skeletons, Basque lucky charms and amulets, Basque sports paraphernalia, the interior of a Basque cottage and more. The main attraction of La Parte Vieja is its countless bars, where the evening crowds hasten to devour delectable seafood tapas. Eating is the city's greatest obsession, and there are societies devoted to the preparation and devouring of enormous Basque meals. A fun excursion is to gather some good food and row it out to **Isla de Santa Clara** for a picnic (*in summer there is a regular ferry to the island from El Muelle, the dock behind the Ayuntamiento; boats run from 10am to 8pm*).

San Sebastián is not the place to look for bargains, and many of the cheapeɪ *hostales* and *fondas* are packed full of university students most of the year. In general, the farther back you are from the sea, the less expensive the accommodation will be.

expensive

For a touch of Belle Epoque elegance, one of Spain's best hotels is the old *grande dame*, ★★★★★**María Cristina**, Pso. República Argentina 4, ✆ 943 42 49 00, ✆ 943 42 39 14, looking onto the Río Urumea's promenade, a short walk from La Concha. The city's other most luxurious address, the ★★★★**Hotel Londres y Inglaterra**, on La Concha beach at Zubieta 2, ✆ 943 42 69 89, ✆ 943 42 00 31, has splendid views, first-class service, and plenty of charm, as well as one of the city's best restaurants (*meals around 3500 pts*). Quiet, small, comfortable, and located halfway up Monte Igueldo, the attractive ★★★**Gudamendi**, Barrio de Igueldo, ✆ 943 21 40 00, ✆ 943 21 51 08, has quite spectacular views.

moderate

San Sebastián being the posh resort it is, most *hostales* here fall into the moderate price category, and there are plenty of chances for a simple double room for *5000 pts*. One well-run place right in the centre is the ★**Hs Eder II**, on the Alameda del Boulevard at the edge of the Parte Vieja, ✆ 943 42 64 49. Nearby, the ★★**Ozcariz**, Fuenterrabía 8, ✆ 943 42 53 06, is in a noisy location but very welcoming.

inexpensive

The best you'll find will be at the higher end of the inexpensive range, and there are a fair number of them both in the Parte Vieja and in the centre. In the old town, the **Hs Kaia**, at C/ Puerto 12, ✆ 943 43 14 42, has little going for it but the price; rooms with bath or without. Places in the centre seem much the same, without the atmosphere. Good bargain choices include the **Hs Easo**, C/ San Bartolomé 24, ✆ 943 45 39 12, and the old-fashioned **Hs La Perla**, C/ Loiola 10, ✆ 943 42 81 23. The best camping option is up on Monte Igueldo, the **Camping de Igueldo**, Paseo Orkelaga, ✆ 943 21 45 02, though it's quite expensive. At the end of Ondarrena beach, at the foot of the road up Monte Igueldo, there is a youth hostel, **La Sirena**, ✆ 943 31 02 68; it's the cheapest place in town.

Eating Out

As eating is the municipal obsession, it's not surprising that the city can claim three of Spain's most renowned, award-winning restaurants, the cathedrals of Basque cuisine: **Arzak**, Alto de Miracruz 21, ✆ 943 27 84 65, offers a constantly changing menu of delights (its *8500 pts menú de degustación* may be the best choice in this book for a big splurge). **Akelare**, in the Barrio de Igueldo, ✆ 943 21 20 52, combines exquisite meals with a beautiful setting and views over the sea (*8000 pts*). The third culinary shrine, **Nicolasa** on Aldamar 4, ✆ 943 42 17 62, founded in 1912, specializes in classic Basque cookery and offers a large choice of dishes (*7500 pts*). *All three close Sun eve and Mon, as do most restaurants in the city.*

ood, and slightly less expensive, restaurants are **Urepel**, Pso. de Salamanca 3, 42 40 40, serving fine Basque food at *moderate* prices. Another superb choice, lizing in grilled fish and meat and with a huge wine cellar, the **Rekondo**, Pso. ueldo 57, ℰ 943 21 29 07, offers elegant dining for around *6000 pts*.

hon, San Marcial 40, ℰ 943 42 75 07, fills up fast with diners in search of a wide variety of reasonably priced seafood and other dishes on the *900 pts menu*. The **Bar Tamboril**, C/ Pescaderia 2, 943 42 35 07 offers tasty *pintxos*, while the **Bodegón Alejandro**, C/ Fermin Calbetón 4, ℰ 943 47 77 37 has a decently priced menu; for something cheaper, follow the crowds through the tapas bars of the Parte Vieja.

Entertainment and Nightlife

The centre of the serious party action is C/ Reyes Católicos (nicknamed Reyes Alcohólicos), and the surrounding streets south of the cathedral, where the cars are shut out on weekends and everyone does it in the road. Bars with live music are mostly in the Parte Vieja, such as the **Be Bop**, on Paseo de Salamanca (jazz), **Kelly's**, Plaza Nafarroa Bera 3, an Irish pub enjoying its moment in the sun, and the **Café Remember Rock**, C/ Republica Argentina s/n, with live rock shows.

Etxekalte, C/ Mari 1, has two floors of club/dance music and is almost always chock full. Late night bars and clubs are found around the end of Onderreta beach.

San Sebastián to Bilbao: the Costa Vasca

Getting Around

The coast is served by frequent buses from San Sebastián and Bilbao; the narrow-gauge Eusko Trenbideak line stops four or five times a day at Zarautz, Getaria, Zumaya, Deva and Durango; another branch runs out of Bilbao to Bermeo via Gernika.

Tourist Information

Zarautz: Nafarroa Kalea, ℰ 943 83 09 90.
Getaria: ℰ 94 314 01 03. *Open in summer only.*
Zumaya: ℰ 94 314 33 96. *Open in summer only.*
Lekeitio: ℰ 94 624 33 65. *Open in summer only.*
Gernika: C/ Artekale 8, ℰ 94 625 58 92.

Zarautz and Getaria

Most of the **Costa Vasca** is simply beautiful and it's worth your while taking the old coastal highway for the views. The first major town to the west of San Sebastián, **Zarautz**, is a big resort, first popularized by more summering royalty—King Baudouin and Queen Fabiola of Belgium. The first ship to make it all the way around the world, the *Vitoria*, was built here— and the man who sailed it, Sebastián de Elcano, came from the nearby fishing port of **Getaria**; a huge monument in his honour is as much of a landmark here as the rat-shaped islet **El Ratón** that shelters the harbour. Getaria has been compared to a Cornish fishing village, and besides its old charm it has two little beaches and a fine early 15th-century church of **San Salvador** containing a ship model and unusual altar. It also produces Euzkadi's finest *txakoli* wine.

The First Man to Sail around the World

In the great age of discovery, no Spanish or Portuguese captain worth his salt would set out without a Basque pilot, the heirs of centuries of experience in whaling boats off Europe's westernmost shores—they may have actually found the American coast in medieval times, and kept the knowledge a closely guarded secret. Columbus took a Basque pilot, and Elcano had the post of second-in-command to Magellan. In 1519, Charles V backed the Portuguese navigator Ferdinand Magellan's attempt to find a quick western route to the Indies by sailing southwest around the newly discovered continent of America to the Molucca islands, then cutting back to Spain around the Cape of Good Hope. Charles gave Magellan five ships, and in August they set forth from Seville. One ship turned back before attempting the Straits that took Magellan's name (October 1520). If already dismayed by the distances involved just crossing the Atlantic, Magellan must have been appalled at the extent of the Pacific. Even worse, by the time his little fleet made it to the Moluccas in 1521 a civil war had just broken out, which through tragic accident numbered Magellan among its victims. Elcano took over the helm of the expedition and sailed halfway around the world to Seville in the only surviving ship. He arrived in October 1522, the holds stuffed to the brim with spices.

In spite of his singular feat, Elcano was destined to remain forever in Magellan's shadow—except of course in the eyes of his fellow Getarianos. Besides the aforementioned monument, they erected a statue of Elcano just outside the gate of the old town, and stage a historical re-enactment of his homecoming every four years. Below the monument lies Getaria's port, sheltered by a peninsula and an islet known for its shape as El Ratón, the mouse.

From the coastal road, you wouldn't think there was much to Getaria at all. Yet pass through the old gate next to the monument, and you will find one of the loveliest villages of Euzkadi, hugging the steep slope down to the harbour. Whenever the Getarianos go to Mass in the **church of San Salvador**, in the centre of the old town, they step on his grave, located just inside the door. Elcano was lost in the Pacific in 1526, so there probably isn't much of him in there anyway. The next town east, **Zumaya** is reached by a scenic stretch of road nicknamed the **Balcony of Cantabria**, from which it descends to Zumaya's long, serene **Zuloaga Beach** with its pine trees; it was named for the Basque painter Ignacio de Zuloaga, whose stone house, just behind the beach, is now the **Zuloaga Museum** (*open Jan–Sept, Sun only 10–2; adm*) with a fine collection of El Grecos and Goyas and two saints by Zurbarán, displayed in a charming setting. Next to the house, the 12th-century chapel and cloister of **Santiago Echea** was a shrine for pilgrims taking the coastal route to Compostela. Zumaya itself is a pleasant town with relatively few tourists, and has another beach to the west—**San Telmo**, a dramatic swathe of sand under steep red cliffs, known for the strength of its pounding surf.

After Zumaya the main road dives inland, but you can continue along the old winding coastal road to **Deva** and **Motrico**. Motrico is set back from the quiet beach of **Saturrarán**. Crossing from here into Vizcaya province at **Ondárroa** used to mean paying duty at the provincial customs house. The village is another pretty fishing-port, but most people press on west to **Lekeitio** (Lequeitio), with its better beaches, **Isuntza** and **Carraspio** further out. Lekeitio still catches more fish than tourists, despite its gorgeous situation under the Cantabrian hills.

The ancient, sacred city of the Basques is mostly rebuilt now, and most of the inhabitants are too young to remember the horror that occurred one market day in 1937. But beyond the beautiful setting in the Mundaka valley and the oak tree by the old Basque parliament building (**Las Casas Juntas**), there's not much to see. The **tree**, the seedling of the ancient oak under which Spanish kings would swear to uphold Basque liberties (remnants of its 600-year-old trunk can be seen under a nearby pavilion), miraculously survived the saturation bombing as a potent symbol of freedom and hope, not only for the Basques, but for everyone—Gernika shocked the world because it was the first time modern technology was used as a tool of terror. About 5km east of Gernika, the **Cueva de Santimamiñe** has Euzkadi's best paleolithic art (*open for free guided tours Mon–Fri, 10, 11.15, 12.30, 4.30, 5.30, only 15 people allowed on each so come early*). Guernica lies at the head of a pretty, pine-forested estuary, the Ría de Gernika, with a number of small, sandy beaches—at **Laida** and **Laga** near the mouth of the Ría, and **Pedernales** and **Mundaka** on the western shore. **Bermeo**, near Mundaka, is Euzkadi's largest fishing-port, a colourful, working town that makes few concessions to tourism, although it has a fine collection of seafood restaurants. Just to the west, off the shore of **Baquio**, the hermitage-topped islet of **San Juan de Gaztelugatxa** is linked to the mainland by an artificial bridge. In the old days it supported a castle; the best one remaining in the vicinity is the 11th-century **Castillo de Butrón**, rebuilt in fairy-tale style in the 19th century and located in the wooded hills (*open daily exc Mon 10–8, Sun 11–6.30; adm*).

Inland

From San Sebastián the main road leads to **Tolosa**, a riverside town tainted with the aroma of paper mills. Tolosa is famous for its sweets and offers a **Museo de Confitería**, but you may prefer to carry on up to **Régil**, a pretty mountain town with beautiful views from the Col de Régil (C6324). This picturesque road winds up to the ancient village of **Azpeitia** and the nearby **Sanctuary of St Ignatius of Loiola** (Iñigo López de Loyola), where in 1491 Ignatius was born, the last of 13 children of a noble family and the future founder of those intellectual stormtroopers of Christ, the Jesuits. The actual house, built by the saint's grandfather after a four-year exile among the Moors, is a fortress-like *mudéjar* structure. Next to it stands a large ornate basilica, the work of the Italian Baroque architect Carlo Fontana, with relics, Ignatius's death mask, and scenes from the life of the general of the Church Militant.

Southwest of Tolosa, there's the pretty mountain village of **Segura**, and further on, **Oñati**, capital of the Pretender Don Carlos in the nasty Carlist wars. This was one of the few towns in Euzkadi to be ruled by a noble, and it retained its independence until 1845. For many years Oñati had the only Basque university, founded in 1540; its building has a beautiful Plateresque façade and a plain and distinguished Renaissance courtyard. Oñati is also known for its number of well-preserved medieval palaces, one of which saw the birth of conquistador Lope de Aguirre. The parish church of **San Miguel** (15th century) contains a number of treasures, including the alabaster tomb of the university's founder, Bishop Zuázola de Avila, attributed to Diego de Siloé, and an attractive Plateresque cloister. Other noteworthy buildings include the **Ayuntamiento** and the Franciscan **Convento de Bidaurreta**, but perhaps the greatest charm is the town's setting in a rich, rolling valley, dominated in the distance by the bluish pointed peaks of Mount Amboto and Udalaitz.

A scenic road up from Oñati climbs in 9km to the **Sanctuary of Aránzazu**. Here, a shepherd found an icon of the Virgin by a thorn bush and a cow bell. The church that h it has been rebuilt innumerable times since, lastly in 1950—a curious temple of Basq modernism in a lonely and rugged setting, its towers covered with a distinctive skin of pyramidical concrete nubs that look like meat mallets on end.

Where to Stay and Eating Out

Zarautz ✉ 20800

Zarautz can be as pricey as San Sebastián. ★★★★**Karlos Arguiñano**, Mendilauta 13, 943 13 00 00, is a formidably *expensive* modern hotel, but its restaurant is one of the best dining places along this stretch of coast, with sophisticated seafood dishes and a warm, welcoming atmosphere. As for accommodation, the more reasonable ★**Sol y Mar**, Avda. de Navarra 50, ✆ 943 83 23 19 (*moderate*) is a trim modern building with in-room TV. The **Camping Talai-Mendi**, an *inexpensive* and quiet campsite, is near the beach at Monte Talai-Mendi, ✆ 943 83 00 42.

Getaria ✉ 20808

In Getaria you can lodge near the beach at the ★★**Hs San Prudencio**, ✆ 943 14 04 11, a good bargain for the area; *inexpensive* rooms without bath. Getaria is a good town not only for seafood, but for drinking *txakolí* wine, grown in the nearby hills. You can taste it at any of the restaurants that crowd the harbour, including the **Kaia Kaipe**, upstairs at Gral. Arnao 10, ✆ 943 14 05 00, along with good Basque seafood and good views (*4000 pts*). **Elkano**, Herrerieta 2, ✆ 943 14 06 14, boasts the best grilled fish.

Zumaya ✉ 20808

No hotels here, but some of the bars in the main square have *inexpensive* rooms. **Jesuskoa** in Zumaya's Barrio de Oikina, ✆ 943 86 17 39, has good grilled fish meals.

Lekeitio ✉ 48280

The recently opened **Emperatriz Zita**, C/ Santa Elena Etorbidea s/n, ✆ 946 84 26 55, ✆ 946 24 35 00 (*expensive*) is a modern palace of a place built over the ruins of the home of the last Austro-Hungarian empress.

There's also the fine little **Piñupe**, Avda. Abaroa 10, ✆ 946 84 29 84 (*moderate*), or the more *expensive* ★★**Beitia**, Avda. Abroa 25, ✆ 946 84 01 11 (*moderate*). Good, abundant fish dinners are served at **Zapirain**, Igualdegui 3, ✆ 946 84 02 55 (*moderate*).

Gernika ✉ 48300

Near Gernika's Santimamiñe caves there's the **Lezika**, a fine restaurant located in an 18th-century Basque chalet in a charming woody grove (*moderate*); and in town itself **Zimelea Etxea**, Carlos Cangoiti 57, ✆ 946 25 10 12 (*moderate*). Accommodation is limited to the simple ★★**Gernika**, Carlos Gangoiti 17, ✆ 946 25 03 50, and the very similar **Boliña**, C/ Barrenkalle 3, ✆ 946 25 03 00 (*both moderate*).

resort at the edge of the Ría near Bermeo has one of the loveliest hotels in
n: the **Atalaya**, Itxaropen Kalea 1, © 946 17 70 00, ℻ 946 87 68 99
/e). Located right on the river, this is one of those glorious Basque buildings of
' ago with glass galleries all around. It has small but lavishly appointed rooms,
w.... ....llite TV and minibars.

Vitoria/Gasteiz

Vitoria has style. It also has the air of a little Ruritanian capital—because it is one. The seat of
the inland province of Álava, and since 1980 the capital of autonomous Euzkadi, Vitoria has
grown to be one of Spain's modern industrial centres, a phenomenon that has so far done little
harm to one of the most surprisingly urbane cities in the nation. Although Wellington soundly
defeated the forces of Joseph Bonaparte here in 1813, Vitoria's name has nothing to do with
victory, but recalls the height (*Beturia* in Basque) on which the city was built. In the Middle
Ages this was a hot border region between the kingdoms of Navarra and Castile. Navarrese
King Alfonso VI founded a fortress and town here in 1181, but the Castilians managed to
snatch it away from them soon after. Like everything else in medieval Castile, Vitoria boomed,
and extended itself logically in concentric rings of streets—oddly enough, a plan exactly like
Amsterdam's, without the canals. Hard hit by the wars and plagues of the 1300s, Vitoria stag-
nated for centuries, and began its recovery only with the industrial boom of the 1890s. It has
preserved itself beautifully throughout, probably an important factor in getting Vitoria named
the Basque capital in the autonomy agreement of 1981. The important thing to know about
Vitoria is the *Fiesta de la Virgen Blanca*, on the 4th of August. It's a typically berserk six-day
Spanish blowout, with champagne everywhere, lots of high-powered fireworks, and parties
until dawn, but the image of it that sticks in the mind is *Celedón*, a dummy in a beret and
workman's clothes. Celedón holds an umbrella aloft, which is attached to a wire from the top
of the cathedral tower; from this he descends as gracefully as Mary Poppins, gliding across
the Plaza to start the festival. On the morning of the 10th he glides up the wire and pops
magically back into the bell tower, and it's all over for another year.

Getting Around

Foronda **airport**, 7km west of Vitoria, has connections with Madrid and Barcelona
(© 945 16 35 00). Trains between San Sebastián and Madrid pass through Vitoria,
and Salvatierra is a stop along RENFE's Vitoria–Pamplona run. Otherwise you'll have
to take the bus, or hitchhike. Generally the more remote the area, the more likely you
are to get a ride—friendly locals will often stop and ask you if you want a lift.

Vitoria's stylish **train** station is at the head of C/ Eduardo Dato, six blocks from the
old town. The **bus** station is at C/ Los Herran 50, © 945 25 84 00, a short walk east
of the old town. There are regular services to San Sebastián, Bilbao and Logroño, as
well as to the provincial villages, and because of the city's position on the main route
north from Madrid, you can get a bus to nearly anywhere from here—Bordeaux,
Paris, Germany and even London.

Though small, Vitoria can be a puzzle if you are driving. Most of the centre is a closed-
off pedestrian zone, and parking is hard to find.

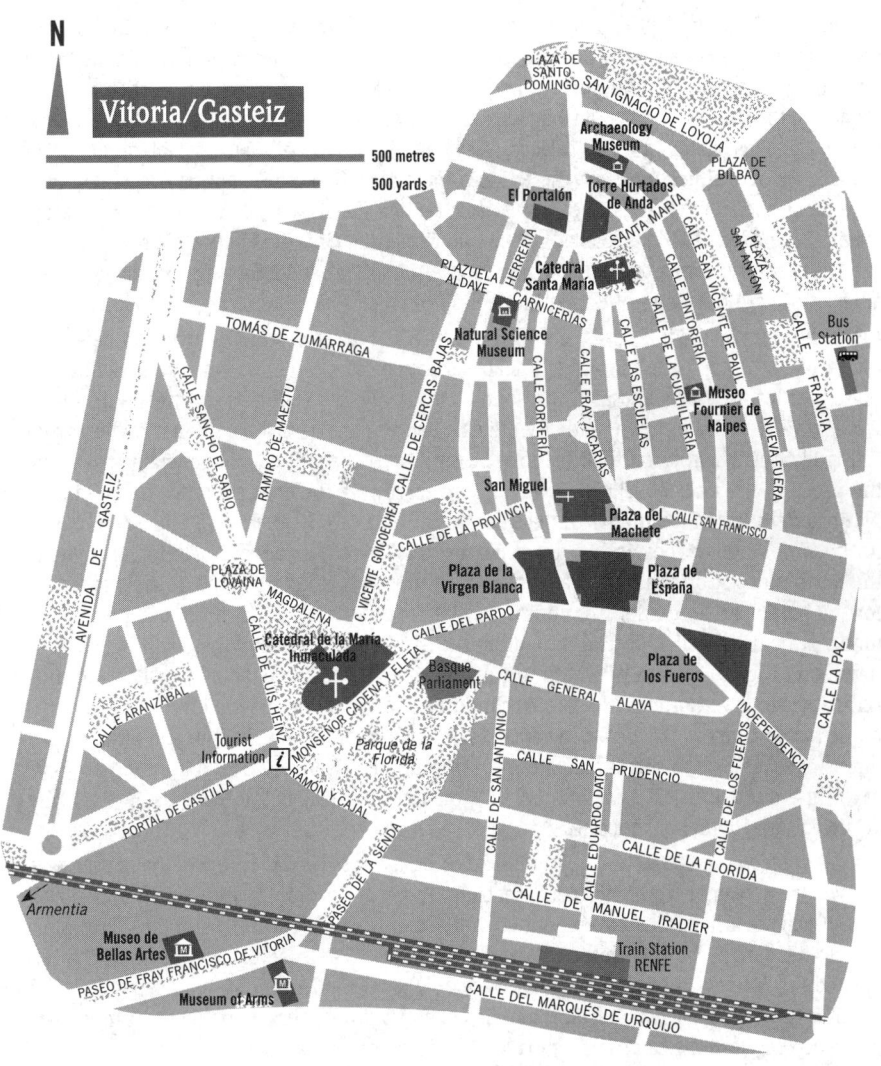

N

Vitoria/Gasteiz

500 metres
500 yards

PLAZA DE SANTO DOMINGO
SAN IGNACIO DE LOYOLA
Archaeology Museum
PLAZA DE BILBAO
El Portalón
Torre Hurtados de Anda
SANTA MARÍA
PLAZUELA ALDAVE
HERRERÍA
Catedral Santa María
CARNICERÍAS
CALLE SAN VICENTE DE PAÚL
CALLE PINTORERÍA
TOMÁS DE ZUMÁRRAGA
Natural Science Museum
CALLE DE LAS ESCUELAS
CALLE DE LA CUCHILLERÍA
Bus Station
CALLE SANCHO EL SABIO
RAMIRO DE MAEZTU
CALLE DE CERCAS BAJAS
CALLE CORRERÍA
CALLE FRAY ZACARÍAS
Museo Fournier de Naipes
NUEVA FUERA
CALLE FRANCIA
AVENIDA DE GASTEIZ
C VICENTE GOICOECHEA
CALLE DE LA PROVINCIA
San Miguel
Plaza del Machete
CALLE SAN FRANCISCO
PLAZA DE LOVAINA
MAGDALENA
Plaza de la Virgen Blanca
Plaza de España
Plaza de los Fueros
CALLE ARANZABAL
CALLE DE LUIS HEINTZ
MONSEÑOR CADENA Y ELETA
Catedral de la María Inmaculada
CALLE DEL PARDO
Basque Parliament
CALLE DE LOS FUEROS
CALLE LA PAZ
RAMÓN Y CAJAL
Tourist Information
Parque de la Florida
CALLE GENERAL ALAVA
INDEPENDENCIA
PORTAL DE CASTILLA
CALLE DE SAN ANTONIO
CALLE SAN PRUDENCIO
PASEO DE LA SENDA
CALLE EDUARDO DATO
CALLE DE LA FLORIDA
Armentia
CALLE DE MANUEL IRADIER
Museo de Bellas Artes
PASEO DE FRAY FRANCISCO DE VITORIA
Train Station RENFE
Museum of Arms
CALLE DEL MARQUÉS DE URQUIJO

Tourist Information

Parque de la Florida, ✆ 945 13 13 21.

There is a **market** on Thursdays, in Plaza de Abastos; also a flea market on Sundays in Plaza Nueva, and a clothes market on Wednesdays and Thursdays in C/ Arana.

La Parte Vieja

The old city, with its old core of neat, concentric streets, begins with **Plaza de la Virgen Blanca**, a delightful example of asymmetrical medieval town design. Adjacent to it, the enclosed and studiously symmetrical **Plaza de España**, or Plaza Nueva, provides a perfect contrast; this grand neoclassical confection was built at the height of Spain's flirtation with the

Enlightenment, in the 1780s, and now houses mostly city offices. Plaza de la Virgen Blanca is the centre of Vitoria's big party on 4 August, and it takes its name from the statue in the niche over the door of **San Miguel**, the 14th-century church that turns a graceful portico towards the top of the square. Behind San Miguel, Calle Fray Zacarías leads into the medieval streets; this was the high-status street for palaces, as evidenced by two 16th-century Plateresque beauties, the **Palacio Episcopal**, and the **Palacio Escoriaza-Esquivel**, built by a local boy who became physician to Charles V; this one has a refined Renaissance courtyard with a marble loggia. Take a left at C/ La Soledad for the old cathedral, **Catedral Santa María**, also from the 14th century, with a beautifully carved western doorway and impressive central nave, the aisles lined with the tombs of Vitoria's notables from medieval times.

Just behind the cathedral on C/ del Herrería, the **Torre de Doña Otxanta** is a defensive tower of the 15th–16th centuries. Italian early Renaissance cities, with their skylines of skyscraper-fortresses, set a fashion that found its way to other countries—fortresses like these were private castles in town, and city officials had to fight hard to keep their owners from acting like rustic barons on their manors, bossing everyone around and generally disturbing the peace of the neighbourhood. Now fully restored, the tower is home to the province's **Natural Science Museum** (*open weekdays 10–2 and 4–6.30, Sat 10–2, Sun 11–2, closed Mon; adm*). Another conspicuous tower nearby, the **Torre Hurtados de Anda**, lurks just to the north on C/ Correría: this is a blank-walled fort with a half-timbered house planted on top—a proper urban castle. Continuing northwards to C/ Correría, a rambling brick and timber structure called **El Portalón**, built in the early 1500s, is one of the oldest buildings in town, and it gives an idea of what most of Vitoria must have looked like at the time. Just across the street at Correría 116, the **Archaeology Museum** occupies a lovely half-timbered house (*same hours as the Natural Science Museum*) containing Roman finds and Basque 'star' tombstones, as well as some fascinating medieval finds. There are over a hundred artificial caves in the province of Álava, and exhibits recount the story of the religious hermits who occupied some of them a thousand years ago.

Palaces are fewer in the eastern quarter of old Vitoria, across C/ Las Escuelas; the houses here are generally plainer, though older, especially those in the former **Judería**, the medieval Jewish neighbourhood that covered much of this area. On C/ Cuchillería, in the Plateresque Palacio Bendaña, Spain's biggest manufacturer of playing cards (an old Vitoria speciality) has opened the **Museo Fournier del Naipe** (*open Tues–Fri 10–2 and 4–6.30, Sat 10–2, Sun 11–2, closed Mon*). The collection includes plenty of Tarot decks; originally there was no difference between the cards for fortune telling and those for playing games.

The New Cathedral and the Museum

The tourist information office shares the pretty **Parque de la Florida**, Vitoria's monumental centre, with the stern, no-nonsense **Basque Parliament** building (*© 945 24 78 00*, if you want to sit in the gallery and watch them deliberate) and the remarkable 'new cathedral', the **Catedral de la María Inmaculada**. Here, the Basques showed their devotion to the Middle Ages by building a completely 'medieval' building, by medieval methods, beginning in 1907. Most of it is already finished, though there is enough decorative work undone inside to last them another century or two. Vitoria is a city of unexpected delights; one example, is one of the most resplendent Art Deco petrol stations in all Spain, just behind the cathedral. Another, a few blocks east on Calle Eduardo Dato, is the fantastical **RENFE station**, done in a kind of

Hollywood Moorish style with brightly coloured tiles. The city is also currently finishing a new embellishment: **Plaza de los Fueros**, a new square just east of Plaza de la Virgen Blanca designed and decorated by Eduardo Chillida. Parque de la Florida, laid out in 1855, retains much of the Romantic spirit of its times, with grand promenades, hidden bowers and overlooks. It was the centre of the city's fashionable district, and a shady walkway from the southern end of the park, the Paseo de la Senda, takes you to the elegant **Paseo de Fray Francisco de Vitoria**, lined with the Hispano-Victorian mansions of the old industrialists. One of these houses, the **Museo de Bellas Artes** (*open weekdays 10–2 and 4–6.30, Sat 10–2, Sun 11–2, closed Mon; adm*), features a well displayed collection ranging from early paintings to Picasso and Miró, with a handful of great Spanish masters in between, all in a beautifully restored space with original features such as a Tiffany-style stained-glass skylight.

Some of the finest works are of the type museums here call '*Escuela Hispanoflamenca*', paintings from the early 16th century, at a time when the influence from the Low Countries was strong here; most are anonymous, and it is impossible to tell which country the artist was from. One of the finest works, a triptych of the Passion by the 'Master of the Legend of Santa Godelina', shows the same sort of conscious stylization as an Uccello; the longer you look at it, the stranger it seems. Medieval painted carved wood figures are well represented, and there are three paintings by Ribera, including a Crucifixion. As in all Basque museums, Basque painters are well represented. Up the Paseo at No.3, the Museum of Arms (*open weekdays 10–2 and 4–6.30, Sat 10–2, Sun 11–2, closed Mon; adm*) houses suits of armour, medieval weapons, and dioramas and displays on Wellington's victory at the Battle of Vitoria. Seeing the last of Vitoria's little secrets means a pleasant 20-minute walk to the southwest (from the Paseo de Fray Francisco, take Paseo de Cervantes and Avenida de San Prudencio; this is part of the *camino francés*, one of the Santiago pilgrimage routes), to the **Basílica of San Prudencio**, in Armentia, a village swallowed up by the city's suburbs. The church was built at the end of the 12th century, with a fine doorway and curious reliefs and capitals carved inside.

West of Vitoria, you can visit Roman ruins including a long, 13-arched bridge at **Trespuentes**, near the remains of a town, the **oppidum of Iruna** (*open daily exc Mon 11–2 and 4–8, Sat 11–3, Sun 11–2; winter 11–3, Sun 10–3; adm*). Two km away at Mendoza, near the airport on the A3302, a 13th-century defensive tower with great views over the countryside has been restored to house the **Museo de Heráldica** (*open daily exc Mon 11–3, May–Oct 11–2 and 4–8, Sun 11–2; adm*), Spain's only museum dedicated to the origins of heraldic escutcheons; the exhibits give special attention to the histories of the great families of the Basque country.

Vitoria ✉ *01000*   **Where to Stay**

expensive

In Vitoria, the best value among the several large hotels in the new part of town is the ★★★**General Álava**, Avda. Gastéiz 79, ✆ 945 22 22 00, 🖂 945 24 83 95, with modern, comfortable rooms with TV.

moderate

Vitoria offers a wide range of choices for about *6000 pts*, mostly catering to businessmen. The ★**Achuri**, C/ Rioja 11, ✆ 945 25 58 00, 🖂 945 26 40 74, is well equipped. Near the rail station, ★★**Dato** 28, C/ Dato 28, ✆ 945 14 72 30, 🖂 945 23 23 20, is convenient and imaginatively furnished; it's a good bargain too.

There are quite a few of these, mostly in the Casco Viejo: the **★La Riojana**, C/Cuchillería 66, ✆ 945 26 87 95, is one of the cheapest. A few others are the **Savoy** C/ Prudencio María Verástegui 4, ✆ 945 25 00 56; the **La Paz**, La Paz 3, ✆ 945 13 96 66; the **Portal de Vergara**, Portal de Vergara 20, ✆ 945 26 04 70.

Eating Out

Most of the good bars and restaurants in Vitoria are in the old town—especially good is **El Portalón**, Correría 151, ✆ 945 14 27 55 (*expensive*), with tables on three floors of a 16th-century building and traditional Basque food. Other less expensive places to look out for, all serving excellent Basque cuisine for around *4000 pts*, are **Mesa**, Chile 1, ✆ 945 22 84 94 (*closed Wed*); **Zabala**, Mateo de Moraza 9, ✆ 945 23 00 09; and **Olarizu**, Beato Tomas de Zumarraga, 54, ✆ 945 24 77 52. The best and most popular pizzeria in town is run by a former cycling champ named Galdós: **Dolomiti**, C/Ramón y Cajal, ✆ 945 23 34 26, also does Italian dinners (*1500 pts*). **Kintana**, C/Mateo de Moraza 15, ✆ 945 23 00 10, specializes in fresh game dishes.

Nightlife

Vitoria has its share of nightlife, mostly in the Parte Vieja, though C/ Dato near the station can also be noisy after hours. Some of the clubs, a few on C/ San Prudencio, for example, stay open until 6 or 7 in the morning. For grown-ups, there is the **Café Caruso**, a coffee house on C/ Enrique de Eguren 9, which has occasional concerts and exhibitions. Currently the most popular disco is **El Elefante Blanco**, Plaza San Antón; for salsa, the place is **Salsumba**, C/ Tomás de Zumárraga. Alternative music of all sorts (though mostly rock) can be found at **Gaztetxe**, C/ Fray Zacarías.

Between Vitoria and Bilbao

There are several tempting old towns between the two provincial capitals. **Ochandio** was the original Basque iron town, a fact commemorated by a statue of the god Vulcan in the main square. **Elorrio** is an attractive village of grand palaces and impressive little squares, adorned with a set of unique **crucifixes** from the 15–16th centuries. The one on the west is especially good, carved with a frieze of people. From the centre it's a lovely walk out to the hermitage of **San Adrián de Argiñeta**, where you can see the 9th- and 10th-century **tombs of Argiñeta**, carved out of rock, some adorned with pinwheel-like stars. It's another 6km to **Durango**, a name that conjures up cowboys and Westerns in the New World. It has an attractive Baroque centre behind its **Portal de Santa Ana**, an ornate survival from the old walls, and two good churches: **San Pedro de Tavira** and the porticoed **Santa María de Uribarri**.

North of Durango, in the heartland of old Basque traditions, is the minute village and valley of **Bolívar**, from whence came the family of the great Liberator of South America, Simón de Bolívar, honoured by a monument that dwarfs the village square. Near the old parish church of **Santo Tomás** you can see the 'Cattle Trial Yards' and the huge stone weights hauled by oxen at festivals. **Markina**, further north, is nicknamed the 'University of *Pelota*'; its historic *frontón* has produced champions who have made their mark around the world. Near Markina, on the right bank of the Río Artibay, stands the fascinating hermitage of **San Miguel** de **Arretxinaga**, housing an altar built by the giant *jentillak* (or, according to some, fallen from heaven as a meteorite) that consists of three huge boulders sheltering a statue of St Michael. It is an uncanny place, and has another 'Cattle Trial Yard' next to the church.

Where to Stay and Eating Out

Unlike the coast, this is definitely not tourist country, and you'll find only simple accommodation anywhere near the A8.

Durango ✉ 48200

Though it's the biggest town in the area, don't count on workaday Durango either for a place to stay or a meal. It has one mid-range *hostal*, the **★★Hs Juego de Bolos**, San Agustinalde 2, ✆ 946 81 10 99.

On C/ San Antonio in Berriz, just outside Durango, **Josu Mendizabal**, ✆ 946 22 50 70, runs a very popular restaurant with plenty of fresh seafood.

Markina ✉ 48200

Here you can get a good night's sleep at the central **★★Vega**, Abesúa 2, ✆ 946 16 60 15 (*moderate*). For dinner, there is **Niko**, San Agustín 4, ✆ 946 16 89 59, good cooking on a bargain 900 pts menu.

Bilbao/Bilbo

Tucked into the deep lush folds and clefts of Euzkadi's coastal range, where the river Nervión, once a notorious industrial by-product and now almost clean enough to support fish, discharges its last effluents in the flushing tides of the coast's deepest estuary, you'll find **Bilbao**. The name is Bilbo in Basque, but its inhabitants prefer to call it lovingly the *botxo*, Basque for hole, or orifice. The orifice was originally a scattering of fishing hamlets, huddled on the left bank of the *ría* where the hills offered some protection from the Normans and other pirates. In 1300, when the coast was clear of such dangers, the lord of Vizcaya, Diego López de Haro, founded a new town on the right bank of the Ría de Bilbao. It quickly developed into the Basques' leading port, trading Vizcaya's iron to France and Castile's wool to Flanders. In 1511 the merchants formed a council to govern their affairs, the Consulado de Bilbao, an institution that survived and thrived until 1829. The 19th century had other treats in store: the indignity of a French sacking in 1808 and the brunt of two Carlist revolts, during one of which the city was besieged by the Carlists. But this century also made Bilbao into a city. Blessed with its iron mines, forests, cheap hydraulic power and excellent port, Bilbao got a double dose of the Industrial Revolution. Steel mills, shipbuilding and other associated industries sprang up, quickly followed by banks and insurance companies. Workers from across the country poured into the tenements, and smoke clogged the air. The resemblance to Pittsburgh was striking; it still is. After being crushingly punished by Franco for its support of the Republicans, Bilbao gradually grew back to its former prominence as the industrial centre of Spain.

Of late, the rusting machinery has been removed and the once-seedy dock area, gentrified. Meanwhile Greater Bilbao/Bilbo/*botxo*, with its population of over a million, the sixth city of Spain and its greatest port, not to mention the sister city of Boise, Idaho, is not twiddling its thumbs awaiting obsolescence. Thanks to banking, insurance and such less obviously dirty business, the economy is doing pretty well, and the city has embarked on an ambitious redevelopment programme, reclaiming vast areas of the centre formerly devoted to heavy industry. The visually striking, hugely popular Guggenheim museum, opened in October of 1997, has by itself significantly boosted the city's economy, attracting almost a million and half visitors in its first year. Other new projects include a concert hall, a convention centre (completed in 1998), a library, a park, an hotel, offices and residential buildings all to be built on the site of the old shipyards; a metro, with sleek modern stations designed by Norman Foster, was completed in 1995. Bilbao may well be one of the cities of Europe's future; come back in a few years and see.

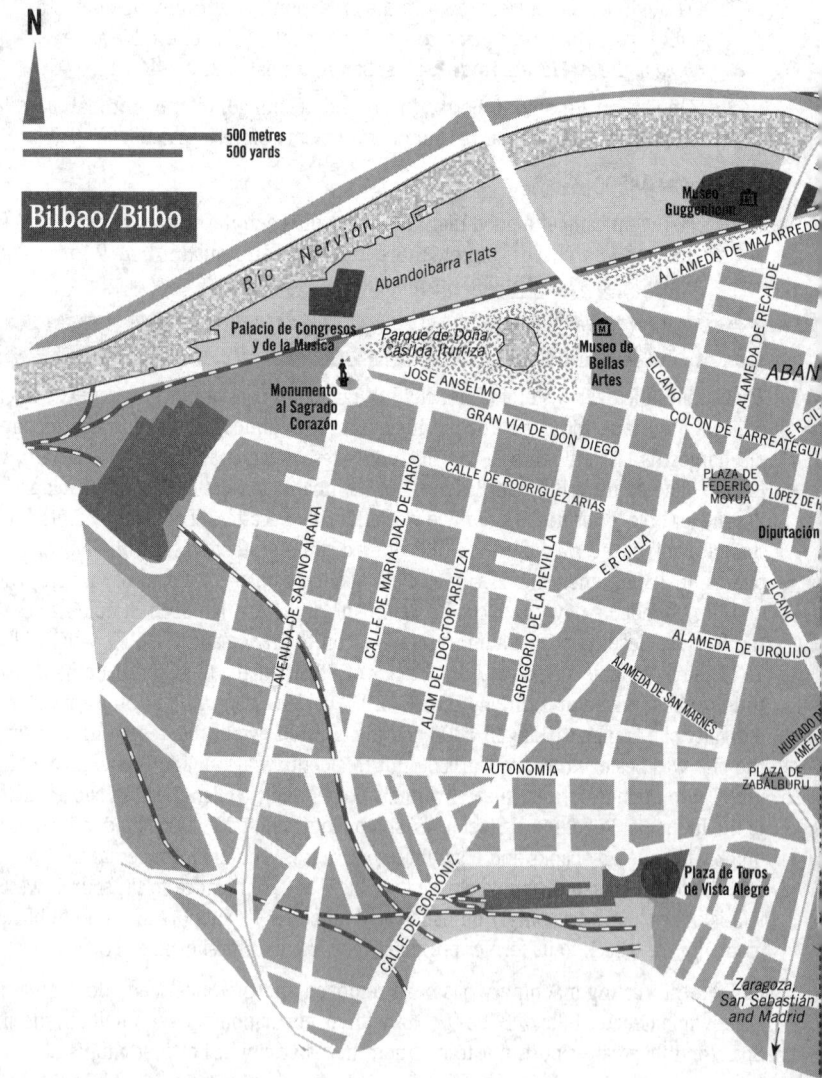

By air: Bilbao's Sondika airport is the busiest in northwest Spain, with daily flights from London, Brussels, Frankfurt, and Milan, and to most airports in Spain, including Santiago and Vigo (for information, ℂ 944 86 93 00/01). The airport is 10km north and approximately a 2000 pts taxi ride away from the centre; a bus service to the airport (from C/ Sendeja, ℂ 944 75 82 00) runs roughly every 45 minutes.

By train: Bilbao has several train lines and about a dozen stations, although as a non-suburban commuter you have to be aware of only four of them. The main RENFE station, with connections to France, Madrid and Galicia is known either as Estación de Abando, Plza. Circular (ℂ 944 23 86 23) or de la Naja, Bailen 1 (ℂ 944 15 74 01). Next to Abando at Bailén 2, but facing the river with a colourful tile front, is the Estación de la Concordia, where scenic, narrow-gauge FEVE trains come and go to Santander, Oviedo, and El Ferrol (ℂ 944 23 22 66). The pretty little Estación Atxuri, at Atxuri 8 in the Casco Viejo, is used by the Basque regional line, Eusko Trenbideak (ℂ 94 433 95 00) for connections to Donostia/San Sebastián, by way of Durango, Gernika, Bermeo, Zarautz and Zumaya. Eusko Trenbideak also offers the easiest way to Bilbao's beaches at Getxo and Plentzia, although from their other station at Plaza San Nicolás, in the Casco Viejo near the Plaza Nueva.

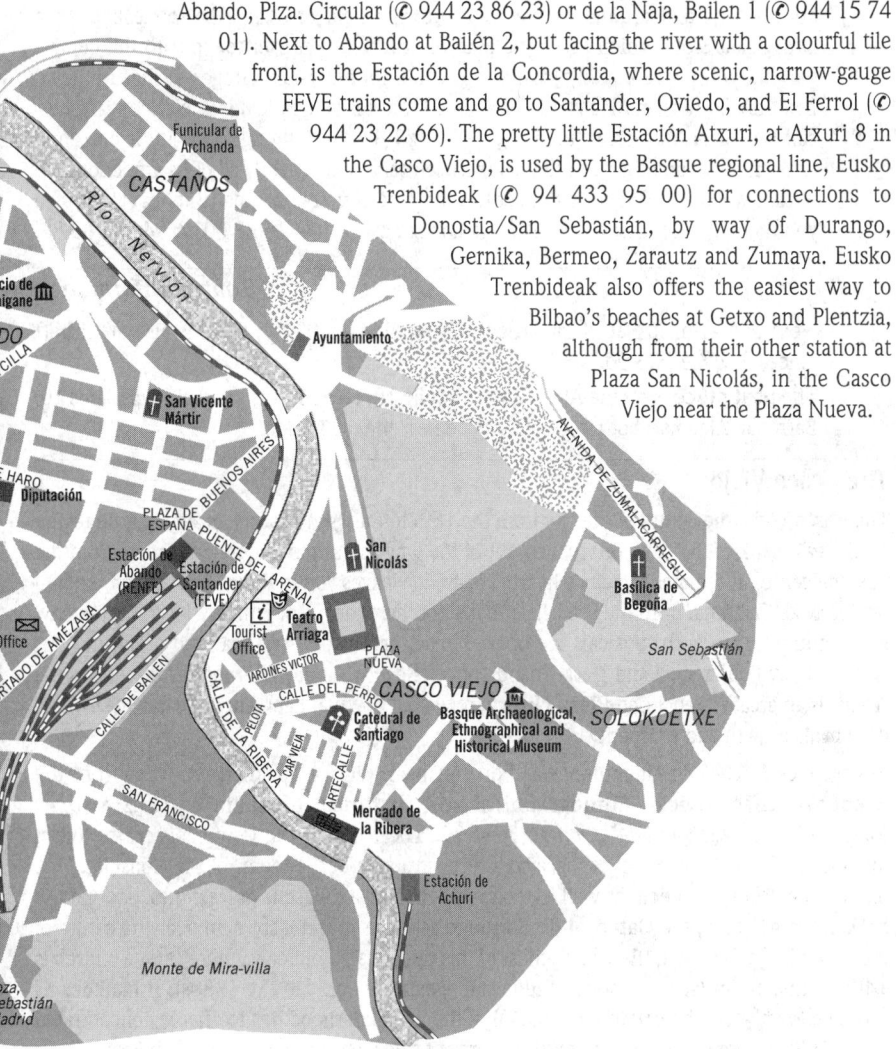

By bus: Bilbao has recently opened a central bus terminal, the Termibus C/ Guturby 1, © 944 39 50 77. Almost all bus lines arrive and depart from the Termibus. The exceptions are:

Grupo Ansa bus lines, C/Autonoma 17, © 944 44 31 00, which runs services to Balmaseda, Barcelona, Burgos, León, and Madrid.

La Union bus lines, C/Henao 29, © 944 24 08 36, which has buses to Vitoria.

Getting Around

Bilbao's excruciatingly complex topography of hills and valleys makes it a beast to negotiate by car; miss one turn, and you may have to circle around 40km (no exaggeration!) back and around, only to end up in a field of orange barrels called Asua Crossroads from which few have ever returned. If you ever make it to the centre, parking will prove equally frustrating; you'll find city-run garages at Plaza Nueva, Instituto Correos and Plaza del Ensanche. If the car you parked in the street vanishes, call the Grúa Municipal (towing), © 944 23 46 41. Although the city is currently excavating an underground to unclog its central arteries, nearly all of its attractions are within walking distance in the centre; the efficient city bus line (Bilbobus) will take you there if you're elsewhere. For a radio taxi, call © 944 16 23 00, © 944 44 88 88.

Tourist Information

Next to the theatre at Plaza Arriaga s/n, © 944 16 02 88; there is also an airport office, © 944 53 23 06.

The **post office** is on the Alameda de Urquijo 19; **telephones** are at Buenos Aires 10, Barroeta, Aldamar; both in the Ensanche near the rail station.

The Casco Viejo

The Casco Viejo, the centre of the city from the 15th to the 19th century, is a snug little region on the east bank of the Nervión; tucked out of the way across the Puente del Arenal from the bustling centre, it remains the city's heart. The bridge leaves you in **Plaza de Arriaga**, known familiarly as *El Arenal* from the sand flats that stood here long ago. Fittingly for a Basque city, its monuments are both musical, the opera house, or **Teatro Arriaga**, and a glorious Art Nouveau pavilion in steel and glass—band concerts every Sunday afternoon. Adjacent to the Arenal is an arcaded, enclosed **Plaza Nueva**, now a bit down-at-heel, but in its day the symbol of Bilbao's growth and prosperity.

Philosopher Miguel de Unamuno was born on nearby Calle La Ronda, not far from the **Basque Archaeological, Ethnographical and Historical Museum** on Cruz 4 (*open Tues–Sat 10.30–1.30 and 4–7, Sun 10.30–1.30*). Located in an old Jesuit cloister, this offers for your perusal a scale-model of Vizcaya, a reconstruction of the rooms of the Consulate, the old merchants' organization, as well as tools, ship-models and Basque gravestones. Around the back of the museum, the **Catedral de Santiago** sends its graceful spire up over the centre of the Casco Viejo. Begun in the 1200s, most of this understated but elegant grey stone church is 14th–15th-century Gothic (though the façade was added only in the 1880s). It matches its setting perfectly. All the colour and animation the neighbourhood has to offer is concentrated in the 1929 Mercado de la Ribera on the riverfront, the largest covered market in Spain.

The 'Seven Streets' being closely hemmed in by cliffs, Bilbao's centre migrated over the bridge as the city grew up, while garden suburbs grew up on the cliffs. Behind the large **church of San Nicolás**, off El Arenal, an elevator ascends to the upper town, from where it's a short walk to the Viscayans' holy shrine, the **Basílica de Begoña** with its unusual spire stuck on an early 16th-century church. Inside, a venerated statue of the Virgin holds court with some huge paintings by the slapdash Neapolitan Luca Giordano, probably the most popular painter of his day. There are fine views of the old town below.

The Ensanche

Nobody in the 19th century had a sharper sense of urban design than the Spaniards, and wherever a town had money to do something big, the results were impressive. Like Barcelona, Bilbao in its industrial boom years had to face exponential population growth, and its mayors chose to plan for it instead of just letting things happen. The area across the river from Bilbao, the '**Anteiglesia de Abando**', was mostly farmland in the 1870s when the city annexed it. A trio of planners, Severino de Achúcarro, Pablo de Alzola and Ernest Hoffmeyer, got the job of laying out the streets for what came to be known as the **Ensanche**, or 'extension', and they came up with a simple-looking but really rather ingenious plan, with diagonal boulevards dividing up the broad loop of the river like orange sections.

The Ensanche begins across from El Arenal; just over the bridge from the old town, a statue of Bilbao's founder, Diego López de Haro, looks benignly over the massive banks and circling traffic in the **Plaza de España**. This has become the business centre of the city, with the big grey skyscraper of the Banco Bilbao Vizcaya, built in the '60s, to remind us who is the leading force in the city's destiny today. The RENFE station occupies one corner of the square; you'll have to walk around behind it on the riverfront to see one of the city's industrial age landmarks: the tiny Bilbao-Santander rail station, a charming Art Nouveau work with a wrought iron and tile façade, designed by Severino de Achúcarro. The vast desolation of tracks and sidings behind these two stations, wasted space at the heart of the city, is about to be reclaimed as the centrepiece of Bilbao's ambitious facelift—the Intermodal, a huge commercial project to be built on air right over the tracks. A new station under an elliptical glass dome is also envisaged.

From Plaza de España, the main boulevard of the Ensanche extends westwards: the **Gran Vía de Don Diego López de Haro**. A block to the north, the façade of the **Corte Inglés** department store is one vast high relief mural evoking the industry and history of Bilbao. The centre of the Ensanche scheme is Plaza de Federico Moyúa, better known as **La Elíptica**. The Hotel Carlton here, still one of the city's posh establishments, served as the seat of the Basque government under the Republic and during the Civil War. From La Elíptica, C/ Elcano takes you to the **Museo de Bellas Artes**, on the edge of the large and beautiful Parque de Doña Casilda Iturriza, between the Gran Vía and the tourist office (*open 10.30–1.30 and 4–7.30*). It contains a worthy collection ranging from Flemish paintings (Metsys' *The Money Changers* is one of the best) to Spanish masters like Velázquez, El Greco, Zurbarán and Goya, to modern art by Picasso, Gauguin, Léger and the American Impressionist Mary Cassatt, and efforts by 19th- and 20th-century Basques. Overflow from the Guggenheim has brought more visitors, and the museum is currently being enlarged to accommodate them. The park itself is an agreeable place to spend an hour or two, with exotic trees carefully labelled, a lagoon, and a new light-and-colour bauble called the 'Cybernetic Fountain'.

The 'Guggenheim Effect'

Just behind the above-mentioned park is the **Abandoibarra flats**, site of the old Euskalduna Shipyards, once the city's biggest employer. For years abandoned and barren indeed, it has now become Bilbao's biggest riverfront redevelopment, bookended by the **Museo Guggenheim**, Avenida Abandoibarra 2, ℗ 944 35 90 80 (*open daily exc Mon 11–8; July and Aug 11–9; adm*) and the **Palacio de la Música y de Congresos Euskalduna**. Stocked with the finest 20th-century art, the Guggenheim (or 'gugen' as it's known locally) is a coup for Bilbao. Attendance rates have vastly exceeded those projected, and long queues to get in—up to an hour—have become frequent, especially at the weekend. Designed by the noted American architect Frank O. Gehry, the museum has been described variously as a titanium clipper ship with all sails up, a cauliflower, a grounded spaceship from Alpha Centauri, and an immense soufflé. Whatever the description, its highly visible titanium shell has won almost universal approval. The museum's collection, shared with the Guggenheim collections in New York and Venice, is of course another reason to visit the site. On permanent display are works by De Kooning, Pollock, Klee, Kandinsky and many others; special exhibitions of world-class 20th century and contemporary artists are also regularly shown.

Bilbao ✉ *48000*   ***Where to Stay***

The 'Guggenheim Effect' has filled Bilbao's hotels to the brim with the kind of educated culture-seeking tourist other cities dream of, so book in advance.

expensive

Bilbao has quite a few luxury hotels, catering for the businessmen who pass through. Many stay at the ★★★★ **NHVilla de Bilbao**, Gran Vía 87, ℗ 944 41 60 00 or the ★★★★★**Lopez de Haro**, Obispo Orueta 2, ℗ 944 23 55 00. There is also the famous ★★★★**Carlton**, Pza Federico Moyúa 2, ℗ 944 16 22 00, as well as the ★★★★**Ercilla**, C/Ercilla 37–39, ℗ 944 10 20 00, both centrally located in the Eixample. Across the river from the Guggenheim is the ★★★**Conde Duque**, C/ Campo Volantin 22, ℗ 944 45 60 00, at the low end of this price category.

moderate

The average visitor would probably prefer to stay in the Casco Viejo—there are several choices on C/ Bidebarrieta, including the ★★**Hs Hostal Arana** Bidebarrieta 2, ℗ 944 15 64 11, with comfortable modern rooms. The ★**Arriaga**, off Plaza Arriaga at C/ Ribera 3, ℗ 944 79 00 01, is similar in qualtity though a bit more expensive. Both of these hotels have parking, an important consideration in this crowded town. There is also the ★★**Cantabrico**, C/ Miravilla 8, ℗ 94 415 28 11, just below Monte Miravilla, and on the other side of town, the ★★**Estadio**, C/ J. Antonio Zunzunegui 10, ℗ 944 42 42 41.

inexpensive

Most of the inexpensive rooms will be found in the Casco Viejo. ★★**Hs Hostal Gurea** C/ Bidebarrieta 14, ℗ 944 16 32 99, has nice simple rooms (with bath), and just around the corner by the cathedral at Lotería 2, ℗ 944 15 07 55, there's the friendly ★★**Roquefer**, in an old building with high ceilings and nice showers down the hall. Another good bet is the ★★**Don Claudio**, C/ Hermógenes Rojo 10, ℗ 944 90 50 17.

This city may not get as wild about cuisine as San Sebastián, but eating is still a pleasure in Bilbao—you can splurge at the city's finest, the traditional and sumptuous **Bermeo**, C/ Ercilla 37, ✆ 944 10 20 00; if it's on the menu, this is the place to try one of the ultimate Basque treats, *cocochas*—the 'cheek and throat' of a hake in a garlic and parsley sauce (*7000 pts*).

For the purest Basque cuisine, look for the strangest names: **Zortziko**, Alameda de Mazzarredo 17, near Plaza de España, ✆ 944 23 97 43, serves innovative dishes with a wide variety of Rioja wines (*menu 3500 pts/ 6000 pts*).

Guría, Gran Vía 66, ✆ 944 41 05 43, is another old favourite, though quite expensive (*8500 pts*). **Goizeko-Kabi**, C/ Particular de Estraunza 4–6, ✆ 944 41 50 04, has the right-sounding name and sure enough offers excellent cooking to match.

You can eat very well for less at **Aitxar**, C/ María Muñoz in the Casco Viejo, with good seafood and typical dishes for about *1000 pts*, or **La Granja**, an attractive old place on Plaza de España (*moderate*).

Amboto, C/ Jardines, is a seafood place off Plaza Arriaga that specializes in *merluza* (hake) in a delicious sauce made from crabs (*1500–2000 pts*). A good *1500 pts* menu offering *nouveau Basque cuisine* can be found at **Metro Moyúa**, Gran Vía 40, ✆ 94 424 92 73.

For snacks, sandwiches and *platos combinados* until late, there is **Café Gargantua**, on C/ Barrenkale (*inexpensive*).

Nightlife

Fans of Bertolt Brecht and Kurt Weill will be disappointed to learn that 'Bill's Ballhaus in Bilbao' was only a figment of their imagination. Nightlife is generally limited to weekends, in the streets of the Casco Viejo. C/ Barrenkale is a busy place with a number of clubs; in the Ensanche, there are more on C/ Pérez Galdós.

The big techno-disco in town is called **Distrito 9,** on C/ Ajuriagerra.

Navarra

Navarra is a good introduction to the Spanish plurals, the 'Spains' combining a sizeable, often nationalistic Basque minority up in the misty western Pyrenees and a conservative, non-Basque Navarrese majority tending the sunny gardens of the Ebro valley flatlands to the south. The combination (in Spain both sides are known as tough cookies lacking polish) hasn't always been comfortable, and only now that much of the population has abandoned the countryside have tensions between the two groups loosened up. As everyone must know by now, much of this 'loosening up' is concentrated in Pamplona, the capital both groups share, into an ecstatic week-long bacchanalia of inebriated recklessness, bull-running and partying known as 'Los Sanfermines'.

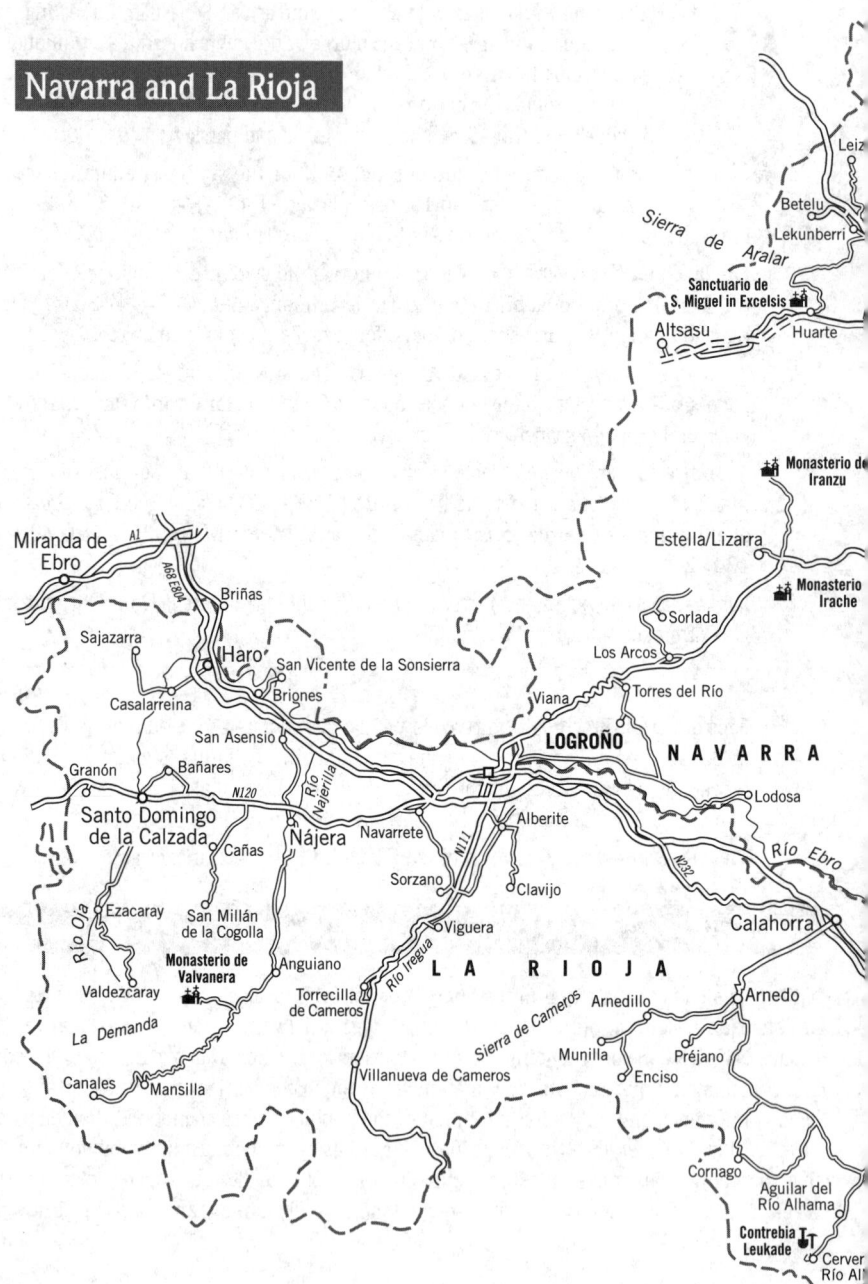

Navarra and La Rioja

Leiz
Betelu
Sierra de Aralar
Lekunberri
Sanctuario de
S. Miguel in Excelsis
Altsasu
Huarte

Monasterio de
Iranzu

Miranda de
Ebro
A1
A68 E804
Briñas
Estella/Lizarra

Monasterio
Irache

Sajazarra
Sorlada
Haro
San Vicente de la Sonsierra
Los Arcos
Casalarreina
Brignes
Viana
Torres del Río
San Asensio
LOGROÑO
NAVARRA
Granón
Bañares
Río Najerilla
Lodosa
N120
Santo Domingo
de la Calzada
Cañas
Nájera
Navarrete
Alberite
Río Ebro
Ezacaray
Sorzano
Clavijo
N232
San Millán
de la Cogolla
Viguera
Calahorra
Monasterio de
Valvanera
Anguiano
Río Iregua
LA RIOJA
Valdezcaray
Torrecilla
de Cameros
Arnedillo
Arnedo
La Demanda
Sierra de Cameros
Munilla
Préjano
Canales
Mansilla
Villanueva de Cameros
Enciso

Cornago
Aguilar del
Río Alhama
Contrebia
Leukade
Cerver
Río Al

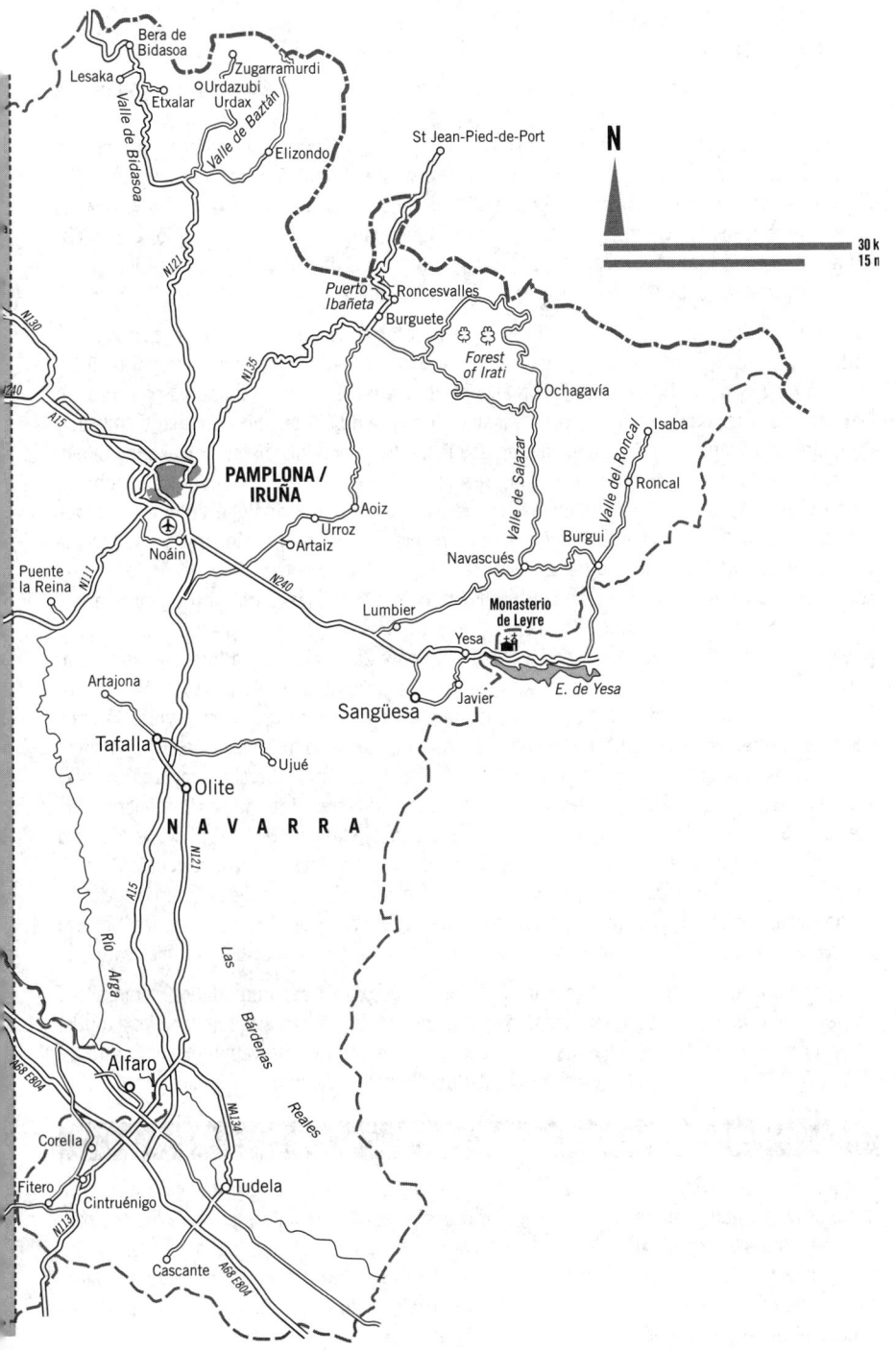

N

30 k
15 n

A Potted History

To understand the standoffish, weird, James Dean rôle Navarra traditionally plays, you need a bit of Spanish history, which is full of the phrase 'except Navarra'. Even in 'the nation of nations' the region has stood apart ever since 605, when the Franks tried to harness it as part of the Duchy of Vasconia, a huge untenable territory that extended from the Garonne to the Ebro. Charlemagne himself came down in 778, either to discipline the unruly duchy or to force it to join his fight against the Moors, and after razing the walls of Pamplona he went stumping back to France—except for his rear guard, which the furious Basques of Pamplona ambushed in 778 at the pass of Roncesvalles ('Valley of the Thorntrees').

Charlemagne taught the Navarrese that owing nothing to nobody was the way to go, and within a few years of his passing they created the independent kingdom of Navarra. Its most talented king, Sancho III 'the Great' (1004–34), firmly established the *camino francés* through Navarra and controlled much of French Basque country and Galicia, and pocketed Castile and León after the death of its last count, setting up his son Fernando I as the first to take the title of 'King of the Spains'. The centre was too precocious to hold, and by the time of Sancho IV (1054–76) Navarra was once again a fierce rival of Castile, but avoided entanglements—marital or martial—by playing the French card. 'The Flea between Two Monkeys', as it became known, was ruled by three different French dynasties between 1234 and 1512, when Fernando the Catholic slyly demanded that Navarra let his armies march through to France. His demand, as he anticipated, was refused and he used the refusal as an excuse to grab Navarra south of the Pyrenees. France was left with only Basse Navarre, a thimble-sized realm but one that gave her a long line of kings, with the accession of Henri IV (1589–1610). Fernando kept the Navarrese happy by maintaining their *fueros* (or privileges), which in practice gave the region an independence enjoyed by no other in Spain; it was ruled by a viceroy, minted its own coins and had its own government. Napoleonic and Liberal attempts to do away with the *fueros* in the cause of central unity turned the Navarrese into fierce reactionaries and the most ardent of Carlists (supporters of the pretender, Carlos III). In the 1930s Navarra rejected the Republic's offer of autonomy; instead, the Navarrese Carlist *requetés* in their distinctive red berets became among Franco's best troops, fighting for their old privileges and Catholicism—just as the Basques were, only on the Republican side. Franco rewarded Navarra by leaving the *fueros* intact, making it the only autonomous region in Spain until his death.

Note: Navarra has made efforts to improve reasonably priced accommodation. Traditional houses have been restored as *casas rurales*, or bed and breakfasts: write to the Pamplona tourist office for their *Guía de Alojamientos de Turismo Rural*. A central reservation office, © 948 22 93 28, ● 948 21 20 59, will book beds for pilgrims along the Camino de Santiago.

Approaches from France: Down the Valleys of the Pyrenees

The Navarrese Pyrenees don't win many altitude records, but they're green, wooded and shot through with legends, many lingering in the mists around Roncesvalles, for centuries the pass most favoured by French pilgrims. Much of Navarra's Basque population is concentrated in the three valleys of Roncal, Salazar and Baztán where seemingly every house in every hamlet is emblazoned with a coat of arms—for the Basques have traditionally considered themselves all equal and therefore all noble.

By bus: There are no trains here; and usually the buses from Pamplona go only once a day. La Tafallesa, ✆ 948 22 28 86, and La Roncalesa, ✆ 948 30 02 57, both serve the Valle del Roncal; they stop at Yesa, near the lake, and 4km from the monastery of Leyre (*see* below). For the Valle de Salazar, Río Irati has one bus daily to Ochagavía, ✆ 948 22 14 70. For Roncesvalles, you can go to Burguete and walk 3km (La Montañesa, ✆ 948 21 15 84). La Baztanesa, ✆ 948 22 67 12, serves the Valle de Baztán.

Tourist Information

Ochagavía: ✆ 948 89 00 04.
Roncal: Ayuntamiento, ✆ 948 47 51 36.

The Eastern Valleys: Valle del Roncal and Valle de Salazar

Like many Pyrenean valleys, the Roncal was so remote for centuries that the central authorities were content to let it run its own show. Time has changed a few things: timber logged on its thickly forested slopes now travels by truck instead of careering down the Esca River, and the valley's renowned sheep's cheese, *queso de Roncal*, is now made in a factory (but according to farm traditions). Mist often envelops **Isaba**, the Valle del Roncal's biggest town, gathered under its fortress church of **San Cipriano** (1540). Every 13 July since 1375, at stone frontier marker no.262, the mayor of Isaba and his colleagues don traditional costume to meet their counterparts from France and ask them for the 'Tribute of the Three Cows', in exchange for the right to graze their herds in the Valle del Roncal in August—something both sides used to kill for before the annual tribute was agreed on. Isaba provides an excellent base for exploring the magnificent mountain scenery: hike up Navarra's highest peaks, **Pic d'Anie** (8200ft) and **Mesa de los Tres Reyes** (7900ft), or make the most beautiful walk of all, into the Parque Natural Pirenáico to the **refugio de Belagua**, set in a stunning glacial amphitheatre. **Roncal**, once the capital of the valley, is a pretty village surrounded by pine forests. The great, amiable Basque tenor Julián Gayarre (1844–90) lies buried in a suitably high operatic tomb just outside town; the **Casa-Museo Julián Gayarre** (*open Tues–Sun 10–1.30 and 5–7, 4–6 in winter; adm*) contains costumes and photos from his glory days. The sparsely populated **Valle de Salazar** is much less visited but just as lovely, abubble with trout streams, beech forests and old white stone Basque chalet-like *caserónes*. **Ochagavía** is a good base for walks: the GR11 leads into the vast beech and ancient yew **Forest of Irati**, the largest primeval forest in the Pyrenees, with majestic Mt Orhi (6618ft) as a backdrop. Irati forest is haunted by the ghost of Jeanne d'Albret, queen of Navarra and mother of Henri IV, a nasty, diehard Protestant fanatic. Poisoned in 1572, Jeanne tours her old domain on windy nights with an escort of Basque *lamías* or nymphs, with whom she never would have been caught dead while still alive.

Where to Stay and Eating Out

Valle del Roncal ✉ 31680

In Isaba, the new, luxurious ★★★**Isaba** Ctra. Roncal s/n, ✆ 948 89 30 00, 🖷 948 89 30 31 (*moderate*) has the most modern rooms in the valley, as well as a sauna and gym. ★**Hs Lola**, at Mendigatxa 17, ✆ 948 89 30 12 (*moderate*) has good rooms and a good restaurant; **Pensíon Txiki**, Mendigatxa, 17, ✆ 948 89 31 18 (*moderate*) offers reasonable half-board rates, as does the even *cheaper* **Pensión Txabalkua**, Izargentea 16, ℰ 948 89 30 83. At the mountain refuge **Venta de Juan Pito**, Puerta de Belagua, ℰ 948 89 30 80, you can try inexpensive local dishes such as *migas pastor* (fried bread) and Roncal cheese. In Roncal try the ***Hs Zaltua**, Castillo 23, ℰ 948 47 50 08 (*moderate–inexpensive*), or **Pensión Begoña**, Castillo 118, ℰ 948 47 50 56 (*inexpensive*).

Ochagavía ✉ 31680

Most accommodation in the Salazar valley is in *casas rurales;* or there's the ***Hs Ori-Alde**, ℰ 948 89 00 27, featuring Basque cooking in the kitchen (*open July–Oct*); the ***Hs Laspalas**, ℰ 948 89 00 15, is open all year (*both moderate*). The restaurant **Auñamendi**, Plza. Guarpide 1, ℰ 948 89 01 89 (*moderate*) has some inexpensive rooms and serves a good asparagus and prawn pudding and trout with ham. In Oronz, just south of Ochagavía, the new ****Hs Salazar**,C/ Mayor s/n, ℰ 948 89 00 53 (*moderate*) has a pool and pretty views.

Roncesvalles (Orreaga)

Of all the passes over the Pyrenees, introverted Roncesvalles was the most renowned in the Middle Ages. French pilgrims would mumble verses from the *Chanson de Roland* as they paid their respects to the sites associated with Charlemagne and his nephew Roland, then say their first prayer to another gallant knight, Santiago. From Roncesvalles' Colegiata it's 781km to Compostela, a distance the fittest pilgrims could cover in 20 days. The Colegiata had a sad, has-been look back in the 1970s, when the medieval floods of pilgrims had dried to a trickle of eccentrics. No one predicted that in the 1990s the number of pilgrims who stopped to have their documents stamped would grow by the thousands each year, especially in the last Holy Year, 1993. The years 2000 and 2004 have also been pronounced Holy Years.

Tourist Information

Roncesvalles: Antiguo Molino, ℰ 948 76 01 93.

Up the Colegiata

The pilgrims' routes from France converged at the busy frontier town of **Valcarlos**, where Charlemagne was camping when he heard Roland's horn Oliphant warning of danger. Charlemagne was too far away to rescue his rear guard, but they were all dead anyway; Roland puffed so hard on his horn that he blew his brains out. From Valcarlos the road winds up through lush greenery to **Roncesvalles** and its zinc-roofed **Colegiata**, a French-style Gothic church consecrated in 1219. The front of the church caved in under the snow in 1600 and was replaced by a cloister, with a 14th-century chapterhouse housing the **tomb of Sancho the Strong**. The stained glass shows a scene from his 1212 victory over the Moors at Las Navas de Tolosa, and the chains are among those that bound 10,000 slaves around the emir's tent.

The **museum** (*open summer and weekends 11–1.30 and 4–6, or by appointment,* ℰ 948 76 00 00; *adm*) contains such rare medieval treasures as the emerald which fell from the emir's turban when giant King Sancho burst into his tent at Las Navas de Tolosa (surely it was a sight enough to scare the emerald off anybody), an 11th-century *pyx*, or golden box used to hold the host, a reliquary called 'Charlemagne's chessboard' (*c.* 1350) for its 32 little cases, each designed to hold a saintly titbit, and a *Holy Family* by Morales.

An easy path from the monastery leads up to the **Puerto Ibañeta** (1057m) where the Basques (converted into Moors in the *Chanson*) dropped boulders on the Franks. **Burguete** (Auritz) and **Espinal** (Auritzberri) were the pilgrims' next stops and are still good places to stay.

Roncesvalles ✉ 31650

If you want to stay in comfort **★★Hs La Posada**, ✆ 948 76 02 25 (*moderate*), has 11 spacious rooms in the Colegiata, with a fine restaurant located in the medieval inn that formerly served the pilgrims. **★Hs Casa Sabina**, ✆ 948 76 00 12 (*moderate*), next to the monastery gate, has six pleasant rooms, and good Navarrese cooking. In Burguete, 3km away, **★★Hs Loizu**, ✆ 948 76 00 08, offers plenty of atmosphere for its moderate rates; or try one of several *casas rurales* or restaurants with rooms.

Western Valleys: Valle de Baztán and Valle de Bidasoa

Frequent rains off the Atlantic make the valleys west of Roncesvalles so lush that they're called the 'Switzerland of Navarra'. Both are dotted with unspoiled Basque villages and quietly beautiful scenery that wasn't always so quiet: in the early 17th century, the **Valle de Baztán** had a legendary colony of witches who held their black Sabbaths in the vast **Cuevas de Zugarramurdi**, carved by the Infernuko Erreka (Hell's Stream). In 1609 the Logroño Inquisition tortured 13 'witches' to death and ignited six others at an *auto da fé*. There are other caves: the lovely stalactite **Cuevas de Urdax** just south at Urdazubi/Urdax has guided tours in the summer. **Elizondo**, the chief village in the Baztán valley, has an informal tourist office in C/ Jaime Urrutia where you can pick up a map that pinpoints the historic houses; one of the best, in **Arizcun**, 7km west, belonged to Pedro de Ursúa, leader of the search for El Dorado up the Amazon in 1560. Further south a road turns east to France through the spectacular **Izpegui pass** (summer only).

Navarra's westernmost Pyrenean valley, the **Valle de Bidasoa**, embraces streams filled with salmon and trout and the main San Sebastián–Pamplona road. Buses between the two offer a chance to visit charming old Basque villages such **Vera (Bera) de Bidasoa**, where the home of the anarchistic Basque novelist Pío Baroja (1872–1956) is now an ethnographic museum (✆ 948 63 00 20). **Lesaka**, equally pretty, claims one of the best preserved fortified feudal houses in Navarra. Further south, **Zubieta** and **Ituren** are famous for a carnival rite that could have been invented by Dr Seuss: men called the *Ioaldun* dress up in dunce's caps and lacey smocks, and tie a pair of noise-making *polunpak* (giant bells) to their backs, nestled in furry sashes. Thus arrayed, the *Ioaldun* make a *zanpantzar*, or march from village to village, their *polunpak* jangling as they walk.

Urdazubi/Urdax ✉ 31711

Sitting out on the terrace at **Menta**, on the Dantxarina road, ✆ 948 59 90 20 (*moderate*), you can feast on a superb mix of French and Navarrese dishes; good wine list too. *Closed Mon eve and Tues.* **Hostal Irigoienea**, C/ Salvador, ✆ 948 59 92 67 (*moderate*) is a charming place to stay.

The modern ★★★**Baztán**, on the main road, ✆ 948 58 00 50, 🖷 948 45 23 23, has panoramic views, a pool and a garden. *Closed Dec–Mar.* ★★**Hs Saskaitz**, M. Azphilikueta 10, ✆ 948 58 04 88, 🖷 948 58 09 92 (*expensive*) is cosy enough in the centre of town. For something cheaper, try **Pensión Eskisaroi**, ✆ 948 58 00 13 (*moderate*), which also does *inexpensive* dinners.

Elizondo is famous for its *txuri-tabeltz*, a stew of lamb's tripe, served most days at **Galarza**, C/ Santiago 1, ✆ 948 58 01 01 (*inexpensive*), a haven of traditional Baztanian cuisine and cheese, a rival to Roncal. *Closed Tues.* Livestock still baa and moo on the ground floor of the **Casa Rural Urruska**, 10km away in Barrio de Bearzún, ✆ 948 45 21 06; the simple but solid home-cooking attracts hungry clients from all down the valley.

Pamplona/Iruña

Whether you call it Pamplona, the town founded by Pompey in 75 BC, or by its older name Iruña, which means simply 'the city' in Basque, the capital of autonomous Navarra sits on a strategic 1400ft pimple on the beautiful fertile plain, its existence as inevitable as its nickname, the 'Gateway of Spain'. For a few years in the 730s, Abd al Rahman used it in reverse, as the gateway to France, until Arab dreams of Europe were hammered at Poitiers. Over the next decades the Vascones regained control of Pamplona, clobbered Charlemagne after he burnt their walls, and set up their own king. In 918 the Moors came back and razed Pamplona to the ground again. To encourage rebuilding, Sancho III the Great invited his subjects in French Navarre to come and start trades in what became the two new districts of Pamplona, San Cernín and San Nicolás. The fact that the three districts of the city were practically independent and had their own privileges led to violent rivalry, so much so that in 1521 the French Navarrese unsuccessfully besieged Pamplona in an effort to regain San Cernín and San Nicolás. Wounded while fighting for Castile was a certain Captain Íñigo López de Recalde, who convalesced in Pamplona, got religion in a militant way and founded the Jesuits.

Pamplona seems to have been naturally conducive to that sort of thing, with a reputation for being crazily austere, brooding and puritanical. For anyone who knows the city only for throwing the wildest party in Europe, this comes as a shock of *desfase* or maladjustment, a word that means (and gleefully celebrates) the unresolved contradictions that coexist in post-Franco Spain. Stern Catholicism is part of the city's fabric. 'From the top to the bottom of Pamplonese society, I have found the whole place poisoned by clerical alkaloid,' grumped Basque philosopher Unamuno. 'It oozed out of every corner…one drop in the eye is enough to infect you forever.' In the 1950s, the secretive Opus Dei, Christianity's ultra-conservative fifth column, chose Pamplona to build their Universidad de Navarra. In the 1960s the city's new tennis club still built separate swimming pools for men and women. Thirty years later, a new Pamplona prides itself on setting up Spain's first shelter for battered women, the first city workshops for training disadvantaged youth and the first urban rubbish recycling programme. 'Pamplona is a city that gives much more than it promises', said Victor Hugo. It certainly will if you come the second week of July for the Sanfermines, but expect it to take as well: your money, your watch, your sleep and a lifetime supply of adrenalin.

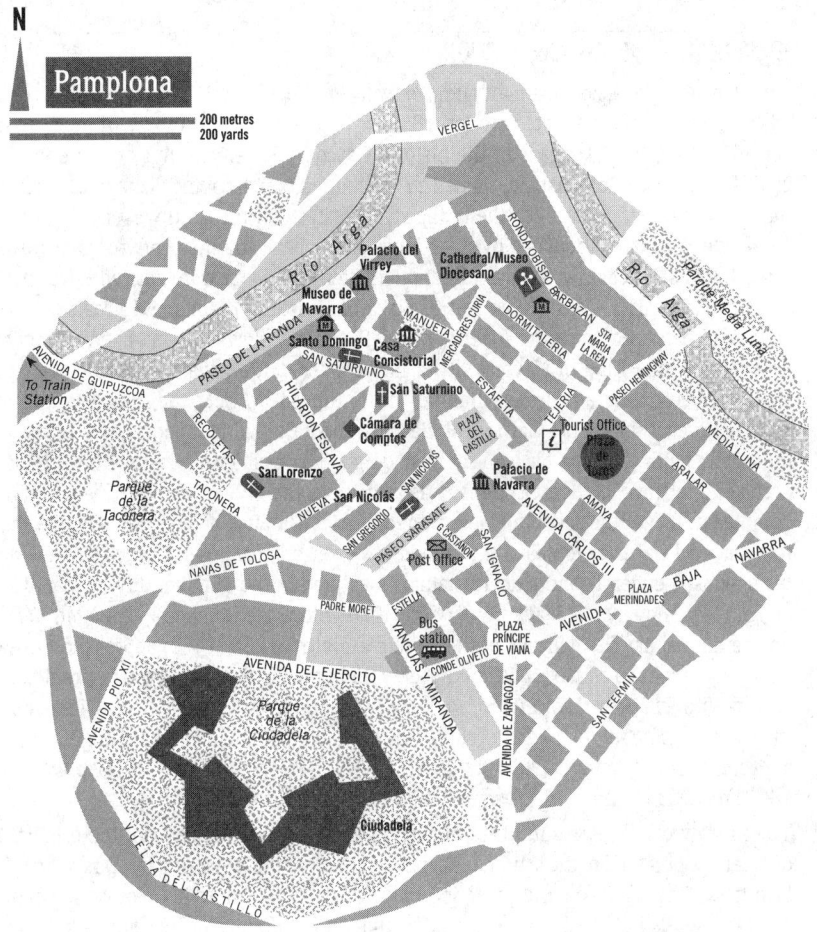

Getting Around

By air: Pamplona's airport is 9km south of the city, ✆ 948 16 87 00, with connections to Madrid, Barcelona and Santander. The cheapest way to get to the airport is to take a Beriainesa bus from the bus station (every half-hour) to Noaín, which drops you a few hundred metres from the airport.

By train: Pamplona's train station is 2km out of town on Avda. San Jorge. Bus no.9 makes connections from the centre every 10 mins, ✆ 948 13 02 02; tickets and information can also be had at the railway office in town at C/ Estella 8, ✆ 948 22 72 82.

By bus: The bus station is in town, near the citadel, at C/ Conde Oliveto 8; information ✆ 948 22 38 54. Besides provincial connections, there are three buses to Vitoria, four to Bilbao, three to San Sebastián, four to Zaragoza, and two to Huesca and Jaca.

Tourist Information

C/ Duque de Ahumada 3, off Plaza del Castillo, ✆ 948 22 07 41, ✉ 948 21 20 59. There is a **market** every morning except Sundays at the Plaza de los Burgos.

A Walk through the Casco Viejo

Pamplona was squeezed in a tight girdle of walls until the early 1900s, when the city spread in all directions and accumulated around 185,000 inhabitants in the process. But for all its 20th-century flab, the vital organs in the historic Casco Viejo remain intact, beginning with the city's heart, **Plaza del Castillo**, shaded by the knitted boughs of the plane trees, circled by too many cars, framed by arcades sheltering stylish cafés. Off the southwest corner extends the **Paseo de Sarasate**, populated by stone kings and queens and the overwrought **Monumento a los Fueros**, erected by popular subscription after Madrid tried to mess with Navarra's privileges back in 1893. Off the east end of Plaza del Castillo, the narrow streets jammed with shops and bars were once the *Judería*, where Pamplona's Jews, 'a gentle and reasonable race' according to the King of Navarra, lived unmolested until Navarra was gobbled up by the Castile of Fernando and Isabel. Behind these, tucked up near the ramparts, the gracious 14th–15th-century Gothic **Cathedral** hides behind a dull-witted, neoclassical façade, slapped on in the 18th century by a misguided do-gooder; a shame because the original front, according to travellers' descriptions, was as lusty as the one at Cervatos (*see* p.276). When completed, it was the second-largest cathedral in Spain after León's, and suitable shelter for the beautiful alabaster tombs of the cathedral's sponsors, big-nosed Carlos III 'the Noble' and his big-nosed queen Leonora de Trastámara, sculpted in the 15th century by Jean de Lomme of Tournai. The kings of Navarra were crowned before the Romanesque *Virgen del Sagrario* on the high altar. The delicacy of the Gothic **cloister** (1280–1472) approaches gossamer in stone and reaches a climax of decorative bravura in the justly named **Puerta Preciosa** (1325), carved with a superb *Dormition of the Virgin*. Off the cloister, the **Museo Diocesano** (*open mid-May to mid-Oct 9–2; adm*) occupies the refectory and kitchen where pilgrims once dined and contains two remarkable reliquaries—the 1258 *Relicario del Santo Sepulcro* and the 1401 *Relicario del Lignum Crucis*, adorned with precious stones.

The narrow old lanes around the cathedral belong to the **Navarrería**, the original Basque quarter, populated in the Middle Ages by cathedral builders and farmers who tilled the bishop's lands. Here on the promontory you'll find the most impressive segment of the surviving **walls** built by Felipe II, with a reputation for impregnability so powerful that no one tried to challenge their reputation until the French tried to hole up here against Wellington; the views stretch for miles over the plain. Just west, the 13th-century **Palacio del Virrey** started out as the royal palace and now houses the local military government. Through the attractive **Portal de Zumalacárregui**, the **Museo de Navarra** (*open 10–2 and 5–7, Sun 11–2, closed Mon; adm*) occupies a huge 16th-century hospital and contains everything from Roman mosaics to an ivory coffret from Leyre made in Córdoba in the 11th century and a fine portrait of the Marqués de San Adrián by Goya. Just below the museum, wooden barricades remind you that this is the beginning of the *encierro*; the bulls leave their corral near Plaza Santo Domingo and head up C/ Mercaderes and Estafeta. Follow their route and you'll come to Plaza Consistorial and the colourful baroque **Casa Consistorial**, topped with jaunty allegorical figures. Pamplona's nobles built their finest escutcheoned palaces just off this square, along C/ Zapatería and C/ Mayor. Plazas de Consejo and San Francisco, set diagonally opposite each other, are also worth a look, the latter with a *modernista* hotel converted into a bank. Nearby in C/ Ansoleaza, the well-preserved Gothic **Cámara de los Comptos Reales**, the kings' mint in the 12th century, has a magnificent porch opening onto a vault and patio with some original decorations intact.

The *francos*, invited to Pamplona by Sancho the Great, lived just to the south in their two rival quarters named after, and defended by, 13th-century churches that doubled as fortresses. These are **San Saturnino** (or San Cernín) in C/ San Saturnino and **San Nicolás** in lively, bar-lined C/ San Nicolás; a plaque by the former marks the site where the first Pamplonans were converted by San Saturnino. Further west, **San Lorenzo** is best known for its chapel dedicated to San Fermín, built by the city in 1717, where his bust reliquary quietly resides 51 weeks of the year, presiding over weddings; so many Pamplonese want to be married under his protective eye that there's a two-year waiting list.

Pamplona is well endowed with parks: good for naps during the fiesta. The oldest, the French-style **Parque de la Taconera**, closes out the west end of the Casco Viejo and has one of the city's nicest cafés, the **Vienés**, in a charming old kiosk. Just south, the star-shaped **Ciudadela**, built on the orders of Felipe II, is now a green park inside and outside the steep walls. The prettiest garden, **Parque Media Luna**, lines the river east of the city and has a path ending at the medieval bridge used by the pilgrims. The park in front of the **Plaza de Toros**—the third largest in the world—was renamed Paseo Hemingway and has a grizzled bust of the writer whose *The Sun Also Rises* (1926) made Pamplona a household word.

Pamplona's Annual Meltdown: Los Sanfermines

 Before Hemingway there was Fermín, son of a Roman senator and first bishop of Pamplona. His family had been converted by San Saturnino (or Sernin, or Cernín) of Toulouse, who was martyred by being dragged about by a bull. Fermín, for his part, travelled as a missionary to the Gauls and was beheaded in Amiens for his trouble. Some time between then and 1324, when Pamplona held its first fiesta, Fermín decided to take bull-fighters under his saintly cape; by 1591 his festival had found its current dates and form. Although it's the insanely dangerous running of the bulls that has made Los Sanfermines world-famous, it's only a tiny portion of the nine days of nonstop revelling when 'Pamplona becomes the world capital of happiness', a state of hyper-bliss fuelled by three million litres of alcohol. A year.

There is some order to the madness. The Sanfermines officially open at noon on 6 July, when thousands of Navarrese in their festival attire (white shirts and white trousers or skirts, red sashes and red bandanas) gather in front of the town hall to hold their bandanas aloft as a rocket called *El Chupinazo* is fired off the balcony and a city councillor cries in Spanish and Basque: 'People of Pamplona! Long live San Fermín!' The city explodes with a mighty roar, while popping tens of thousands of champagne corks. In the afternoon the giants and big heads (*gigantes y cabezudos*) leave their 'home' in the bus station. The eight 13ft plaster giants supported by dancers date from 1860 and represent kings and queens, whirling and swirling the minuet. They are accompanied by the *cabezudos* and *kilikis*, big-headed figures in tricorn hats, with names like Napoleon and Patata, who wallop children on the head with foam rubber balls tied to bats. This is also the prerogative of the *zaldikos*, the colourfully dressed men wearing cardboard horses around their waists; all are accompanied by dancers, *txistularis* (Basque flutes) and *gaiteros*. At four o'clock a massive scrum, the *Riau Riau,* begins when members of the Corporación de San Fermín dressed in all their finery try to proceed 400m down the Calle Mayor to the chapel of San Fermín at San Lorenzo's for vespers, but everyone else tries to prevent them in a gung-ho defiance of authority, to the extent that it's often late at night before the Corporación achieves its goal. After a first night of carousing and dancing in the streets, the dawn of 7 July and every following day is welcomed with the *dianas*, a citywide wake-up call performed on screeching pipes. The *encierro*, or running of the bulls, begins daily at 8am, but if you want a good place to watch, wedge yourself into a spot along the route—Cuesta de San Domingo, Mercaderes and Estafeta—at least an hour earlier. Before running, the locals sing a hymn to Fermín and arm themselves with a rolled-up newspaper to distract the bull's attention, since the animals—1200lbs of muscle and fury—charge at the nearest moving object, ideally at a flung newspaper instead of a falling runner. A rocket goes up as the first bull leaves the corral; a second rocket means that all are released; and a third signals that all have made it to the bullring—on a good run the whole *encierro* only lasts three minutes. The most dangerous moments are when the runners and bulls have to squeeze into the runway of the bullring, or when a bull gets loose from his fellows and panics. People get trampled and gored every year; if you run you can hedge your bets by running on weekdays, when it's less crowded, and by avoiding the *toros* of the Salvador Guardiola ranch, which have the most bloodstained record. The spirit of abandon is so infectious that, even if you come determined not to run, you may find yourself joining in on a self-destructive spur of the moment. Women do defy the authorities and run, although the police try to pull them out. During the *encierro* the lower seats of the bullring are free (again, arrive early), except on Sunday; from here you can watch the bulls and runners pile in and, afterwards, more fun and games as heifers with padded horns are released on the crowd in the ring. The bullfights themselves take place daily at 6.30 in the afternoon—tickets sell out with the speed of lightning and are usually only available from scalpers. The *sombra* seats are for serious aficionados, while members of the 16 *peñas* (clubs devoted to making noise and in general being as obnoxious as possible) fill up the *sol* seats and create a parallel fiesta if the action in the ring isn't up to snuff or create pandemonium if it is. Afternoons also see other bull sports that are bloodless (for the bull, at any rate): the dodging, swerving *concurso de recortadores* or leaping *corrida vasca-landesa*.

At night fireworks burst over the citadel and the *toro de fuego* or 'fire bull' carried by a runner and spitting fireworks chases children down the route of the *encierro*. Then there's the midnight *El Estruendo de Irún*, led by an enormous drum called the *bomba*, in which hundreds of people gather and let loose in an ear-bashing sonic disorder. At midnight on 14 July Pamplona winds down to an exhausted, nostalgic finale, a ceremony known as the *Pobre de mí*; everyone gathers in front of the town hall (or in the Plaza del Castillo for the livelier, unofficial ceremony), with a candle and sings 'Poor me, poor me, another San Fermín has come to an end'. As the clock strikes twelve everyone removes their red scarves and agrees, like Hemingway, that it was 'a damned fine show' and promises to do better and worse next year. Die-hards party on until 8am the next day, and perform one last feat, the *encierro de la villavesa*: the bulls are all dead so they run in front of a bus.

During San Fermín, hotel prices double and often triple, supplemented by scores of overpriced rooms in *casas particulares*, advertised weeks ahead in the local newspapers, *Navarra Hoy* or *Diario de Navarra*. The tourist office has a list of these as well; prices range around *5000 pts* a night. If you end up sleeping outside, any of the gardens along the walls or river are preferable to the noisy, filthy, vomit-filled citadel. Keep a close eye on your belongings (petty criminals, unfortunately, go into overdrive along with everyone else during the fiesta) and check in what you don't need at the bus station's *consigna*; everyone else does too, so get there early. Two free campsites are set up along the road to France, but again, don't leave anything there you might really miss. If you stay outside Pamplona and drive into town, beware that breaking into cars is epidemic but discerning: thieves took our toothbrushes, Tampax and travel iron but left everything else.

luxury

Conveniently located a short walk from the old town, ★★★★**Iruña Palace Los Tres Reyes**, Jardines de la Taconera, ✆ 948 22 66 00, @ 948 22 29 30, pampers its well-heeled guests with every possible convenience and an indoor heated pool and tennis.

expensive

Maisonnave, C/ Nueva 20 (next to Pza. San Francisco) ✆ 948 22 26 00, @ 948 22 01 66, offers comfort and prestige and a peaceful garden in the back. Another good choice in the centre, ★★★ **Europa**, just off Pza. Castillo on C/ Espoz y Mina 11, ✆ 948 22 18 00, @ 948 92 35, is one of Pamplona's prettiest choices with its flower bedecked balconies, some overlooking the *encierro* action in Estafeta; the restaurant, one of the city's finest, is run by the same management as the Alhambra's (*see* below). **Yoldi**, Avda. san Ignacio 11, ✆ 948 22 48 00, @ 948 21 20 45, has long been the favorite of *toreros* and aficionados in general. The small, quiet, cozy Eslava, Pza, Virgen de la O, ✆ 948 22 22 70, @ 948 22 51 57, is run by a friendly family and has views over the walls of Pamplona. At Berrioplano, 5km from Pamplona on the Guipúzcoa road, ★★★**NH El Toro**, ✆ 948 30 22 11, @ 948 30 20 85, has quiet rooms in a traditional-style mansion, overlooking a statue group of the *encierro*.

moderate

There's not a lot in this range: Hemingway always stayed at Pamplona's oldest hotel, ★**La Perla**, Pza. Castillo, ✆ 948 22 77 06, @ 948 21 15 66, at least as long as room 217 was available; the others, recently renovated, still have their high ceilings and plaster mouldings from 1880. ★**Hs Bearán**, San Nicolás 25, ✆ 948 22 34 28, @ 948 22 34 28, is one of the few decent *hostales*, where doubles come with baths. A pair of sisters run ★★**Hs Príncipe de Viana I and II**, in the same building on Avda. Zaragoza 4, ✆ 948 24 91 47, @ 948 24 91 46, some rooms with, some without baths.

inexpensive

Cheaper *hostales* and *fondas* are mostly on C/ San Gregorio and C/ San Nicolás. The least inexpensive hostal, **Hs Casa García**, C/ San Gregorio 12, ✆ 948 22 38 93, offers 10 double rooms without bath, and an adequate *menú del día* in its restaurant.

Located in an 18th-century palace, **Casa Santa Cecilia**, C/ Navarrería 17, © 948 22 22 30, provides one of the nicest cheap sleeps under lofty ceilings in huge rooms. **Otano**, San Nicolás 5, © 948 22 50 95, has been popular for years for its nice rooms with baths, and a good inexpensive restaurant-bar. The nearest camp site, **Excaba,** is 7km north, © 948 33 03 15.

Eating Out

Pamplona's classic, **Josetxo**, C/ Príncipe de Viana 1, © 948 22 20 97 (*expensive*), has been a local gourmet institution for 40 years. Try to book one of the small Belle Epoque dining-rooms upstairs, and try the chef's prize *solomillo a la broche con salsa de trufa* (steak fillet on a spit with truffle sauce). *Closed Sun and Aug*. The excellent **Hartza**, C/ Juan de Labrit 19, © 948 22 45 68 (*expensive*), is famous for its *bonito encebollado* (tuna with onions), hake dishes and homemade desserts. *Closed Sun eve, Mon, and mid-July–early Aug*. At the fashionable **Alhambra**, C/ Bergamín 7, © 948 24 28 66 (*expensive*) look for imaginative dishes: potatoes stuffed with truffles and scampi and homemade desserts; good *menú degustación* at *4400 pts. Closed Sun*. At the family-run **Rodero**, C/ E.Arrieta 3, © 948 21 12 17 (*expensive*), delicious dishes are based on Navarrese, Basque and French recipes. *Closed Sun and Aug*.

On weekends half of Pamplona drives 11km out towards Irún to dine at **Sarasate**, © 948 33 08 20 (*moderate*) in a traditional *caserío* with a fireplace for winter dining and a terrace in the summer. Near Parque Media Luna, the **Chalet de Izu**, Avda. Baja Navarra 47, © 948 22 60 93 (*moderate*) has plenty of swish atmosphere and good *menús*. For a big grilled meat and wine feast, try **Asador Olaverri**, C/ Santa Marta 4, © 948 23 50 63 (*moderate*); for Navarrese-style seafood, try **Erburu**, C/ San Lorenzo 19, © 948 22 51 69 (*moderate—inexpensive lunch menú*). **Casa Sixto**, C/ Estafeta 81, © 948 22 51 27, is well known for its succulent home-cooked game dishes. *Closed Oct*. The chef at **La Campana**, C/ Campana 12, © 948 22 00 08 (*inexpensive*) takes special pride in preparing unusual recipes such as chicken in champagne.

Other *inexpensive* choices include **Casa Paco**, C/ Lindatxikía (behind San Nicolás church), © 948 22 51 05, a favourite for lunch since the 1920s; **Urricelqui**, C/ Jarauta 30, © 948 22 21 46, even older, a good bet for liver or mushroom dishes, and another **Sarasate**, C/San Nicolás 19, © 948 22 57 27, for the best vegetarian meals in Pamplona. *Closed Sun and evenings, except Fri and Sat*.

cafés and bars

At the last count Pamplona had some 700 bars, or one for every 280 inhabitants, many of whom seem to be always in them, day and night. There are elegant cafés, most famously the 1888 *modernista* **Café Iruña**, a fixture on the Plaza del Castillo, where you can also tuck into inexpensive light meals until 2.30am.

The **Mesón del Caballo Blanco**, near the cathedral in Redín, is an atmospheric old stone house with a terrace, a delightful place to linger; in winter sandwiches are served around the fireplace. **Roch**, C/ Comedias, is small, lively and usually packed at the start of *la marcha*, thanks in part to their superb *fritos de pimiento* tapas. Favourite late-night bar-crawling zones in the Casco Viejo are C/ San Nicolás and San Gregorio, San Lorenzo and Jarauta, and Navarrería, the latter still popular with the Basques and alternative Pamplonese. **El Cordovilla**, one of the bars here, claims to make the biggest *pinchos* (kebabs) in the world.

East of Pamplona: Sangüesa, Javier and Leyre

Pilgrims from Mediterranean lands would cross the Pyrenees at Somport in Aragón and enter Navarra at Sangüesa, home of one of the very best Romanesque churches and one of the craziest palaces in all Spain, but these days, if the wind's wrong, the pong of the nearby paper-mill hurries visitors along; note that if you go by bus from Pamplona (La Veloz Sangüesina, © 948 22 69 95) there are only three a day and you'll be stuck with the stink longer than you might like.

Tourist Information

Javier: © 948 88 03 42.
Sangüesa: © 948 87 03 29.

Sangüesa

Sangüesa was a direct product of the pilgrimage, purposely moved from its original hilltop location in the 11th century to the spot where the road crosses the River Aragón. In 1122 Alfonso el Batallador, king of neighbouring Aragón, sent down a colony of *francos* to augment Sangüesa's population, and ten years after that ordered the Knights of St John to build a church well worth stopping for: **Santa María la Real**. This possesses one of the most intriguing and extraordinary portals on the whole Camino (unfortunately the street in front is quite busy, so you have to look at it between the cars), so strange that some writers believe that its symbols (knotted labyrinths, mermaids, two-headed beasts symbolizing duality, etc.) were sculpted by *agotes* or by a brotherhood of artists on to something deeper than orthodox Catholicism; even the damned are laughing in the *Last Judgement* on the tympanum. Below, the elongated figures on the jambs show stylistic similarities to Chartres cathedral, although again the subjects are unusual: on the left the three Marys (the Virgin, Mary Magdalene and Mary Solomé, mother of St James), on the right Peter, Paul and Judas, hanged, with the inscription *Judas Mercator*. The upper half of the portal is by another hand altogether, crossed by two tiers of Apostles of near-Egyptian rigidity and another Christ in Majesty surrounded by symbols of the four Evangelists. If the church is open, ask the sacristan to show you the capitals in the apse, hidden behind the Flemish Renaissance *retablo*. Note the well in the corner: not something you find every day inside a church. Walk around to see the beautiful carved corbels on the apse and the octagonal tower.

Sangüesa's arcaded Rua Mayor is lined with palaces, including the **Casa Consistorial** behind this is the austere 12th-century, twin-towered Palacio del Príncipe de Viana. The 12th-century church of **Santiago** has a huge battlemented tower and carved capitals and conserves a large stone statue of St James. The slightly later, Gothic **San Salvador** has a pentagonal tower and a huge porch, sheltering a carved portal; its Plateresque choir stalls come from Leyre. Around the corner in C/ Alfonso el Batallador, the brick **Palacio Vallesantoro** catches the eye with its corkscrew baroque portal and the most extraordinary wooden eaves in Spain, carved with a phantasmagorical menagerie that makes the creatures on Santa María look tame.

Javier and Leyre

Sangüesa is the base for visiting two holy sites. **Javier**, 13km away, is topped by a picturesque, over-restored castle, the birthplace in 1506 of St Francisco de Xavier, apostle of the Indies and Japan. Though the castle is now a Jesuit college, you can take the tour (*open 10–1 and 4–7; adm*) and learn a lot about St Francis Xavier and castles—this one dates back to the 11th century, was wrecked in 1516, and restored after 1952. Perhaps most fascinating is the fresco of the *Dance of Death*, a grim reminder of the Black Death.

Just north of Javier at **Yesa**, the Río Aragón has been dammed to form the vast **Yesa Reservoir**. A road from here leads up to the **Monasterio de San Salvador de Leyre** (*open 8am–9pm*), founded in the 8th century and reoccupied in 1950 by the Benedictines, who began a restoration programme that obscures much of the older building. Visits begin in the pre-Romanesque **crypt**, where it looks as if the church is sinking into the ground; the columns are runty stubs weighed down by heavy block capitals that stand at about chest level. Above, the church, harmonious, light and austere, is the perfect setting for the Benedictines' beautiful Gregorian chant. The bones of the first ten kings of Navarra lie in a simple wooden casket. The west portal, the **Porta Speciosa**, is finely carved with a mix of saints and monsters. A 10-minute walk up, the **Fountain of San Virila** affords a magnificent view of the artificial lake and sierra. Leyre's 8th-century abbot Virila came up here to pray for a peek into infinity so often that he was granted his wish, by the lovely warbling of a bird. To the abbot, the vision was a sublime moment, but when he went down to tell his monks he found that all had changed—his eternal second had lasted 300 years.

The Sierra de Leyre divides the Roncal and Salazar valleys, and there are two splendid gorges quite close at hand: the **Foz de Lumbier**, formed by the Irati river, and the even more spectacular 1000ft, sheer-sided **Foz de Arbayún**, home to Spain's largest colonies of rare griffon vultures, birds with 8ft wingspans; you can nearly always spot them floating around the roadside belvedere between Navascués and Lumbier.

Where to Stay and Eating Out

Sangüesa ✉ 31430

The cosiest places to stay are ★★**Yamaguchi** on the road to Javier, ✆ 948 87 01 27 (*moderate*), with a pool and nice restaurant, and the cheaper ★★**Hs Las Navas**, C/Alfonso El Batallador 7, ✆ 948 87 00 77 (*inexpensive*). The Basque **Asador Mediavilla** on the same street, ✆ 948 87 02 12 (*moderate*) serves delicious charcoal-grilled fish and meat with excellent local wine. *Closed Sun eve and Tues.*

Javier/Leyre ✉ 31411

You can stay and eat next to the castle in the antique ★★★**Xavier**, ✆ 948 88 40 06, ✆ 948 88 40 78, or do the same rather more basically at ★**El Mesón**, ✆ 948 88 40 35, ✆ 948 88 42 26 (*both moderate*).

At Leyre, the former pilgrims' hostel is now the charming ★★**Hospedería de Leyre**, ✆ 948 88 41 00, ✆ 948 88 41 37 (*inexpensive*), the perfect antidote to stress; its restaurant specializes in traditional Navarrese cuisine. *Open Mar–Nov.*

The green valleys of the Pyrenees are a distant memory south of Pamplona; here the skies are bright and clear, the land arid and toasted golden brown after the last winter rains, except for the green swathes of vineyards of La Ribera, cradle of Navarra's finest freshest rosés.

Getting Around

By train: Most trains between Pamplona and the main junction of Alsasua stop at Huarte-Araquil; trains linking Pamplona and Zaragoza call at Tafalla, Olite and Tudela. Conda (✆ 948 21 10 08) stops at Tafalla, Olite and Tudela on the way to Zaragoza.

Tourist Information

Olite: ✆ 948 71 24 34.
Tudela: Gaztambide, Esq. Carrera 11, ✆ 948 82 15 39.

There are **markets** in Tafalla on Plaza Navarra on Fridays; in Olite in Paseo del Portal on Wednesdays; in Fitero in Plaza San Raimundo on Tuesdays and Fridays.

Tafalla, Artajona and Olite

In the 17th century, a Dutchman named E. Cock described Tafalla and Olite as the 'flowers of Navarra' and both have determinedly crowed Cock's sweet nicknames ever since. Old **Tafalla** has wilted a bit over the centuries, but it still has an impressive Plaza Mayor and claims one of the finest and biggest *retablos* in the north: a masterpiece by Basque artist Juan de Ancheta tucked away in the austere church of **Santa María**. West of Tafalla, **Artajona** has the air of an abandoned stage set: majestic medieval walls with startlingly intact crenellated towers defend little more than the 13th-century fortress church of **San Saturnino**. This has a tympanum showing the saint exorcising a woman, watched by Juana de Navarra and Philip the Fair of France, while the lintel shows Saturnino's martyrdom with the bull. The walls, rebuilt in the 1300s, were first constructed between 1085 and 1103 by the Templars and canons of Saint-Sernin (San Saturnino) of Toulouse, at a time when the Counts of Toulouse were among the chief players in Europe, leading the First Crusade and fighting side by side with the Cid.

Olite, south of Tafalla, is dwarfed by its huge, battlemented, lofty-towered **Castle of Carlos III**, built for the king of Navarra in 1407 (*open Mon–Sat 10–2 and 6–8, winter 4–5, Sun 10–2; adm*). Hanging gardens were suspended from the great arches of the terraces, and there was a '*leonera*' or lion pit, and a busy set of dungeons; the Navarrese royal families led messy, frustrated lives. At night the whole complex is illuminated with a golden light, creating a striking backdrop to performances in the summer Festival of Navarra. The castle's Gothic chapel, **Santa María la Real** (*open 9.30–12 and 5–8*), has a gorgeous 13th-century façade and the Romanesque church of **San Pedro** (*same hours*) has a portal adorned with two large stone eagles, one devouring the hare it has captured (symbolizing force) and the other representing gentleness. East of Tafalla and Olite, the striking medieval village of **Ujué** is set on a hill, where a shepherd, directed by a dove (*ujué*), found the statue of the black Virgin now housed in the 13th-century Romanesque-Gothic church of **Santa María**. The doorway has finely carved scenes of the Last Supper and the Magi and the altar preserves the heart of King Carlos II of Navarra. Every year since 1043, on the first Sunday after St Mark's day (25 April), the Virgin has been the object of a solemn pilgrimage that departs from Tafalla at 2am.

Tudela

Founded by the Moors, Tudela, the second city of Navarra and capital of La Ribera region, was the last town in Navarra to submit to Fernando the Catholic, and it did so most unwillingly. Before the big bigot, Tudela had always made a point of welcoming Jews, Moors and heretics expelled from Castile or persecuted by the Inquisition, and it was no accident that its tolerant environment nurtured three of Spain's top medieval writers: Benjamin of Tudela, the great traveller and chronicler (1127–73); the poet Judah Ha-Levi of the same period; and doctor Miguel Servet (1511–53), one of the first to write on the circulation of the blood.

Don't be disheartened by Tudela's protective coating of dusty, gritty sprawl, but head straight for its picturesque, labyrinthine Moorish-Jewish kernel, around the elegant 17th-century **Plaza de los Fueros**; the decorations on the façades recall its use as a bull ring in the 18th and 19th centuries. The Gothic **Cathedral** (*open 8.30–1 and 4.30–8*) was built over the Great Mosque in the 12th century and topped with a pretty 17th-century tower. The north and south portals have capitals with New Testament scenes, while the west portal, the **Portada del Juicio Final**, is devoted to the Last Judgement, depicted in 114 different scenes in eight soaring bands. The Flamboyant Gothic choir is delightfully carved with geometric flora, fauna and fantasy motifs; note, under the main chair, the figures of two crows picking out the eyes of a man—the dean who commissioned the work refused to pay the sculptors the agreed price. The main altar has a beautiful Hispano-Flemish *retablo* painted by Pedro Díaz de Oviedo; the chapel of Santa Ana, patroness of Tudela, with a cupola that approaches baroque orgasm. The 13th-century cloister, with twin and triple columns, has capitals on the life of Jesus and other New Testament stories, while the *Escuela de Cristo*, off the east end of the cloister, has *mudéjar* decorations. Among the best palaces are the **Casa del Almirante** near the cathedral and, in the C/ de Magallón, the lovely Renaissance **Palace of the Marqués de San Adrián**. An irregular, 17-arched, 13th-century bridge spanning the Ebro still takes much of Tudela's traffic.

Just east of Tudela is a striking desert region straight out of the American Far West known as the **Bárdenas Reales**, where erosion has sculpted steep tabletops, weird wrinkled hills and rocks balanced on pyramids. The best way to see it (and not get lost) is by the GR13 walking path, crossing its northern extent from the Hermitage of the Virgen del Yugo.

Where to Stay and Eating Out

Tafalla ✉ 31300

★★**Hs Tafalla**, on the Zaragoza road, ✆ 948 70 03 00, 🖅 948 70 30 52 (*moderate*), has nice rooms and food, especially when the dishes involve asparagus, lamb and hake. *Closed Fri.* Atxen Jiménez, the chef at **Tubal**, Plaza de Navarra 2, ✆ 948 70 08 52 (*expensive–moderate*) draws in diners from Pamplona and beyond with her delicious variations on classic Navarrese themes—*menestra de verduras* and innovations such as crèpes filled with celery in almond sauce. *Closed Sun eve, Mon and late Aug.*

Olite ✉ 31390

Next to the Castle of Carlos III is the 13th-century Castillo de los Teobaldos, now converted into the ★★★**Parador Príncipe de Viana**, ✆ 948 74 00 00, 🖅 948 74 02 01 (*expensive*). A garden, air-conditioning and beautiful furnishings make castle-dwelling a delight, as do delicious Navarrese gourmet treats in the dining-room. Little **Casa Zanito**, Rúa Revillas, ✆ 948 74 00 02 (*moderate*), offers simple, cheerful rooms and excellent meals, based on market availability, topped off with good home-made desserts. **Gambarte**, Rúa del Seco 13, ✆ 948 74 01 39 (*inexpensive*) is pleasant and also serves the most reasonably priced food in town.

Ujué ✉ 31390

The place to dine has long been the terrace of **Mesón las Torres**, ✆ 948 73 81 05 (*moderate*), serving Navarrese taste treats and Ujué's special candied almonds.

Tudela ✉ 31500

Unfortunately there aren't any places to stay in the old town, and elsewhere prices are high: **Hs Remigio**, C/ Gaztambide 4, ✆ 948 82 08 50, and *Hs Nueva Parrilla**, Carlos III el Noble 6, ✆ 948 82 24 00, 🖷 948 82 25 45 (*both moderate*) are the only two that don't ask an arm and a leg. Tudela is the chief producer of the ingredients of Navarra's famous *menestra de verduras*: delicious asparagus, artichokes, peas, celery and lettuces. Book a table at **Casa Ignacio**, Cortaderos 9, ✆ 948 82 10 21 (*moderate*), to taste them at their freshest. *Closed Tues and 15 Aug–15 Sept.*

Alternatively, try **Choko**, Pza. de los Fueros, ✆ 948 82 10 19 (*moderate*), with pretty views. *Closed Mon*. **La Estrella**, C/ Carnicerías 14, ✆ 948 82 10 39 (*inexpensive*) has good home-cooking based on garden vegetables.

Cintruénigo ✉ 31592

The most seductive reason to stop in the village is to dine *chez* **Maher**, C/ La Ribera 19, ✆ 948 81 11 50, for delicious Navarrese dishes with an imaginative nouvelle cuisine touch: traditional *menú 3000 pts*, or for a splurge opt for a *menú degustación*.

West of Pamplona: Aralar and San Miguel in Excelsis

Navarra's magic mountain, **Aralar**, is a favourite spot for a picnic or Sunday hike, gracefully wooded with beech, rowan, and hawthorn groves. It has been sacred to the Basques since neolithic times, when they erected 30 dolmens and menhirs in the yew groves around Putxerri, the biggest concentration of neolithic monuments in all Spain. On top is Navarra's holy of holies, the **Sanctuary of San Miguel in Excelsis** (*open 9–2 and 4 to sunset*), on a panoramic north–south road that climbs over Aralar between Huarte-Arakil and Lekunberri.

The story goes that in the 9th century, Count Teodosio de Goñi was returning home from the war when he met the devil in disguise who warned him that his wife was unfaithful. The knight stormed into his castle, saw two forms lying in bed and slew them both. When he ran out he met his wife returning from Mass, who told him that she had given his own aged parents the bed. Horrified, Teodosio went to Rome to ask the Pope what penance he could possibly do, and the Pope had a dream that he should wear chains in solitude until God showed his forgiveness. Thus bound, Teodosio lived on Mt Aralar as a hermit when, one day, a dragon emerged from a cave. Teodosio implored the aid of St Michael, who appeared with his sword in hand, and spoke to the dragon in perfect Basque: '*Nor Jaunggoitkoa bezaka?*' ('Who is stronger than God?'). The dragon slunk away, and the archangel struck off the knight's chains and left a statue of himself—an angelic figure with a cross on its head and an empty glass case where the face ought to be.

In art Michael is often shown with a spear, not slaying as much as fixing dragons to the earth: these are sources of underground water. And sure enough, the Sierra de Aralar is karstic and hollow; under the sanctuary there's a subterranean river that makes moaning dragonish sounds, feeding an icy lake under a domed cavern. The gloomy stone chapel on top, built by the Count of Goñi, was consecrated in 1098 but has had an empty air ever since French Basques plundered it in 1797, when they knocked off St Michael's head (or so say apologists who find the crystal head too weird). You can see the chains worn by Teodosio de Goñi and the enamelled Byzantine *retablo*; the only comparable work in Europe is the great altarpiece in St Mark's in Venice. Tentatively dated 1028, it was probably originally stolen in Constantinople by a Crusader and sold to Sancho the Great, who donated it to the chapel.

Where to Stay and Eating Out

The pilgrims' hostel next to the church of **San Miguel de Aralar**, © 948 56 10 66, is rugged and comfortable enough but isn't famous for its food. In Lekunberri, **★★Hs Ayestarán II**, C/ San Juan 64, © 948 50 41 27 (*moderate*) has a pleasant old-fashioned atmosphere, tennis, children's recreational facilities, a pool and garden; *menús* feature home-cooked stews, stuffed peppers and codfish with almonds.

Just west, between Betelu and Azpirotz, the **Asador Betelu** attracts hordes of diners. Right in the centre of Leiza, you can sleep and eat reasonably at **★Hs Basa Kabl**, © 948 51 0 1 25 (*moderate*). The lively **Taverna Oilade** functions as the town beanery, bar, mess hall and gambling den; good fish soup and other filling dishes (*inexpensive*).

The *Camino de Santiago*

Few places in Europe can boast such a concentration of medieval curiosities as this stretch of the road, where the mystic syncretism of the Jews, Templars, pagans and pilgrims was expressed in monuments with secret messages that tease and mystify today.

Getting Around

By bus: La Estellesa buses, © 948 21 32 25, from Pamplona stop at Puente le Reina and Estella (with a fancy neo-Moorish station) en route to Logroño five times a day.

Tourist Information

Estella: © 948 55 40 11.
Puente de la Reina: © 948 34 08 45.
Los Arcos: © 948 44 10 04.
Viana: © 948 44 63 02.

From Pamplona to Estella

A short turn off the N111 (about 15km from Pamplona) leads to the old village of **Obanos**, and 1.6km beyond that village to a lonely field and **Santa María de Eunate** (*open 10–1 and 4.30–7, closed Mon*), a striking 12th-century church built by the Templars. The Templars often built their chapels as octagons, but this one was purposely made irregular, and is surrounded by a unique 33-arched octagonal cloister—hence its name 'Eunate' (the Hundred Doors). Many knights were buried here, and it's likely that its peculiar structure had deep significance in the Templars' initiatory rites. There are only a few carved capitals—some little monsters, and pomegranates on the portal, which oddly faces north. During its restoration, scallop shells were discovered along with the tombs—the church served as a mortuary chapel for pilgrims. The lack of a central keystone supporting the eight ribs inside hints that Arab architects were involved in the building; the Romanesque Virgin by the alabaster window is a copy of the one stolen in 1974. The *camino francés* from Roncesvalles and the *camino aragonés* converged at the 11th-century bridge in **Puente la Reina**. The village hasn't changed much since the day when pilgrims marched down the sombre Rúa Mayor, passing through the arch of another Templar foundation, **El Crucifijo**, a church with Celtic interlaced designs on the portal and two naves. The smaller nave was added to house a 14th-century German crucifix left by a pilgrim, where the Christ is nailed not to a cross but to a Y-shaped tree.

Estella/Lizarra, known as Estella la Bella for its beauty, was a favourite pilgrimage stopover. It owes its foundation in 1090 to a convenient miracle: nightly showers of shooting stars in the same place on a hill intrigued some shepherds, who investigated and found a cave, sheltering a statue of the Virgin—a spot now marked by the **Basílica de Nuestra Señora de Puy**. The Virgin is still there, but the old basilica was replaced in 1951 with a concrete and glass star-shaped church. Below, the arcaded main **Plaza de Santiago** is the town centre, while just to the south, the 12th-century **San Miguel** sits on a rock atop its original set of steps. March right up them for the magnificent portal, where Christ in majesty holds court among angels, Evangelists and the Elders. On the left St Michael pins the dragon; on the right an angel shows the empty tomb to the three Marys. Near San Miguel, Estella's medieval bridge crosses over to the 12th-century **San Sepolcro,** with a fascinating façade added in 1328. The tympanum has an animated Last Supper, Crucifixion, Resurrection and what looks to be the harrowing of hell; statues of the apostles flank the door; one holds a stack of pancakes. The main street here, Calle de la Rúa, is lined with palaces, most notably the Plateresque brick **Casa Fray Diego**. Off to the left, the 12th-century synagogue was converted into **Santa María de Jus del Castillo**, where the apse is decorated with a rich assortment of Romanesque modillions. The church is dwarfed by the adjacent 13th-century monastery of **Santo Domingo**, now a retirement home. Further up, a 16th-century fountain under a canopy of linden trees in **Plaza de San Martín** makes a delightful place; beyond, the 12th-century **Palacio de los Reyes de Navarra** is one of the best preserved civic buildings from the period. One capital bears the oldest known depiction of Roland, fighting the giant Ferragut.

Stairs leads up to the 12th-century **San Pedro de la Rúa** , defended by a skyscraper bell-tower. The Moorish-inspired foiled arch of the portal is crowned by a relief of St James in a boat with stars, blessed by a giant hand emerging from the water. Inside, the church has a unique column made of three interlaced 'serpents' and, in the Baroque chapel to the left, St Andrew's shoulder-blade; the story goes that the Bishop of Patras took it with him for good luck while making the pilgrimage in 1270. Luck failed him in Estella, where he died and was buried in San Pedro's cloister, along with his relic. The apostle's shoulder-blade wasn't going to have any of this, and made itself known by a light that appeared over the tomb. Of the cloister, only two galleries survive, but the capitals are especially good.

Estella is an important producer of D.O. Navarra wine, and the most interesting *bodega* is the Benedictine **Monasterio de Irache,** 2km west at Ayegui *(open 10–2 and 5–7, Sat and Sun*

9–2 and 4–7, closed Mon). First recorded in 958, it received a generous endowment from Sancho the Great, who helped finance one of the very first pilgrims' hospitals here. It has an austerely beautiful Romanesque church under a Renaissance dome: the original Romanesque north door is decorated with hunting scenes. The sumptuous Plateresque cloister has grotesque and religious capitals. The small **wine museum** preserves Irache's 1000-year-old custom of offering free drinks to pilgrims.

From Estella to Logroño

After Estella, the pilgrims walked to **Los Arcos**, with an arcaded plaza and a 16th-century church, Santa María, with a cathedral-size Gothic cloister, carved choir stalls and frantic Baroque *retablos*. **Torres del Río**, the next stop, has a tall and striking octagonal church, **Santo Sepolcro**, built by the Knights of the Holy Sepulchre; like Santa María Eunate, it may have been a mortuary chapel for pilgrims. Just before La Rioja, **Viana** fits a lot of monumentality into a small space, including splendid mansions and an elegant 17th-century **Casa Consistorial**, crowned with a huge escutcheon, and the 13th–14th-century church of **Santa María**, hidden by a magnificent concave Renaissance façade designed by Juan de Goyaz (1549). The Gothic interior is airy and lovely, culminating in an intricate Baroque retable. A marker in front of the church marks the last resting place of Cesare Borgia (1475–1507). When Julius II, arch-enemy of the Borgias, was elected pope in 1503, Cesare's conquests in Italy were lost and he fled to Aragón, the cradle of the Borgias, only to be imprisoned by Fernando the Catholic. Navarra (he was married to the king's sister) proved to be his only refuge, and he died in Viana, fighting Castilian rebels.

Where to Stay and Eating Out

Puente la Reina ✉ 31100

The stone and timber ★★**Mesón del Peregrino**, on the Pamplona road, ✆ 948 34 00 75, ✉ 948 34 11 90 (*moderate*) has cosy, air-conditioned rooms and a pool, and serves up excellent meals. *Closed Mon.* ★**Hs Puente**, in the centre, ✆ 948 34 08 468 (*moderate*) has some cheaper rooms without bath. **Fonda Lorca** in the main plaza is the cheapest of all.

Estella ✉ 31200

The largest and most comfortable, the ★★★**Irache**, is 3km away on the Logroño road in Ayegui, ✆ 948 55 11 50, ✉ 948 55 47 54 (*expensive*), and offers air-conditioning and a pool. ★**Hs Cristina**, C/ Baja Navarra 1, ✆ 948 55 07 72 (*moderate*) is run by a kindly woman. For less try ★**Pensión San Andrés**, C/ Mayor 1, ✆ 948 55 04 48 (*inexpensive*). Cheapest is the **Fonda Izarra**, C/ Calderín, ✆ 948 55 06 78. **La Cepa**, Pza. Fueros 8, ✆ 948 55 00 32 (*moderate*) specializes in regional cuisine, with *menús degustación* at *3–4000 pts. Closed Mon and eves exc Fri and Sat.* The medieval **La Navarra**, Gustavo de Maeztú 16, ✆ 948 55 10 69 (*expensive–moderate*) is another good bet, perhaps more for its atmosphere than food, which is good if a bit pricey.

Los Arcos ✉ 31210

A pair of choices here: ★★**Hotel Monaco**, Pza. del Coso 22, ✆ 948 64 00 00 (*moderate*), and the slightly dearer ★★**Hs Ezequiel**, La Serna 14, ✆ 948 64 02 96 (*moderate*), where pilgrims get a 10% discount.

Viana ✉ 31230

The avant-garde décor of **Borgia**, Serapio Urra, ✆ 948 64 57 81 (*expensive–moderate*) is Aurora Cariñanos' temple of personal, imaginative cuisine, with dishes such as *pochas con caracoles al tomillo* (fresh haricot beans with snails and thyme), and an excellent cellar. *Closed Sun and Aug.* **La Granja**, Navarro Villoslada 19, ✆ 948 64 50 78 (*moderate– inexpensive*) is central and average.

La Rioja

La Rioja, the smallest autonomous region in Spain (5000 sq km), may be named after the river Oja, one of the seven tributaries of the Ebro, but to most people it means wine, wine and more wine. The banks of the Ebro are frilly with vineyards and pinstriped with rows of garden vegetables on the plains of Rioja Baja around Calahorra. In the Sierra de la Demanda in the southwest, mountains are high enough to ski down; in the gullies of Rioja Baja, dinosaurs once made the earth tremble, or at least left their curious tracks in a prehistoric bog, which petrified for posterity. Later Riojans began the history of Castilian Spanish as a written language and contributed to the invention of Santiago, with a first sighting of the battling Son of Thunder at Calvijo, and miracles and saints along its stretch of the pilgrimage road.

Logroño

Half of all the 250,000 Riojans live in Logroño, their shiny, up-to-date capital. It began under the Visigoths as *Gronio*, the 'ford', but really bloomed only with the advent of the pilgrimage, when a stone bridge was built over the Ebro by San Juan de Ortega.

Getting Around

By train: Several trains a day link Haro, Logroño, and Calahorra on the Bilbao-Zaragoza route. The RENFE station is at C/ Calvo Sotelo 9, ✆ 941 21 38 56

By bus: Several buses a day run to Burgos (via the towns on the pilgrims' route), Zaragoza, Vitoria, Pamplona and Rioja's villages. In Logroño the bus station is at Avda. de España 1, ✆ 941 24 35 72, and the train station (with a left luggage office) is nearby in Pza. de Europa, ✆ 941 23 17 37.

Tourist Information

Kiosco del Espolón, ✆ 941 26 06 65.
There is a **market** for country produce and products at Mercado del Campo, Marqués de la Enseñada 52. *Open Tues and Fri 8–2.*

A Walk Around Logroño

Logroño is a big long sausage of a town, but the interesting bits are concentrated in a small area near the Ebro. Barely an arch survives of San Juan's first bridge, which was replaced in the 1800s by the **Puente de Hierro**, or iron bridge. Just off this the pilgrims would pass in front of the 16th-century fountain and lofty Gothic **Santiago**, the oldest church in town. This was rebuilt in 1500, with a single nave a startling 53ft wide and still standing, in spite of the fact that its architect had no confidence in his handiwork and left town as soon as it was completed. It has a Renaissance *retablo*, and at the front a mighty 18th-century statue of Santiago Matamoros ('St James Moor-killer') rides a steed with *cojones* as big as beach balls.

The skyline of Logroño is stabbed by church towers, including two slender 18th-century Churrigueresque towers by Martín de Beratúa that frame the magnificent baroque façade of the cathedral, **Santa María de la Redonda** in Plaza del Mercado, a front that belies the Gothic-inspired gloom inside (*open 8–11 and 6–8*); the rotundity of its name (the first Romanesque church was octagonal) is recalled in an exuberant round rococo altar. Near here, in a high-security strong box, is the *Tabla de Calvario*, supposedly painted by Michelangelo for his friend and muse Vittoria Colonna. Logroño's most distinctive landmark is its nubby pyramidal 'Needle' , the 149ft 13th-century spire atop the lantern of **Santa María de Palacio**, a church said to have been founded by no less than Emperor Constantine. If it's open, pop in to see the Renaissance choir stalls, the 13th-century *Nuestra Señora de la Antigua*, and what remains of the Gothic cloister. Another tower, brick 11th-century *mudéjar* this time, looks over **San Bartolomé** with a ruggedly carved, time-blackened 14th-century Gothic façade; the smooth white interior, recently restored, has lovely shallow choir vaults.

The 17th-century Palacio del General Espartero in Plaza San Agustín now holds the **Museo Provincial de La Rioja** (*open 10–2 and 3–9, Sun and hols 11.30–2, closed Mon*), full of art from disappeared churches (14th-century painting from San Millán and *San Francisco with Brother Lion* by El Greco), Flemish coffers and orphaned academic 19th-century paintings from the Prado's storerooms. There are a number of wine cellars in the area, including **Bodegas Marqués de Murrieta**, at Ygay, Ctra. de Zaragoza, Km 403, ✆ 941 25 81 00, founded in 1872 and famous for its 35–40-year-old *Gran Reservas* .

Logroño ✉ 26000 **Where to Stay**

Logroño has a surprising number of spanking new hotels. There is also the antique ★★★★**Carlton Rioja**, Gran Vía del Rey Juan Carlos I 5, which offers a taste of old world charm, ✆ 941 24 21 00, 📠 941 24 35 02 (*expensive*). The ★★★**Ciudad de Logroño**, Menéndez Pelayo 7, ✆ 941 25 02 44, 📠 941 25 43 90 (*moderate*) is central, modern and comfortable, with views over  a park. ★★★**Hotel Murrieta** Marqués de Murrieta 1, ✆ 941 22 41 50 (*moderate*) is small, central and welcoming. Near the cathedral, the handsome ★★★**Hs Marqués de Vallejo**, Marqués de Vallejo 8, ✆ 941 24 83 33 (*moderate*) has recently been restored and offers reasonable half-board rates. Cheaper choices include ★★**Hs la Numantina** , C/ Sagasta 4, ✆ 941 25 14 11 (*moderate*) and ★**Hotel Isasa**, C/ Doctores Castro Viejo 13, ✆ 941 25 65 99 (*inexpensive*).

Eating Out

Logroño's (and La Rioja's) best restaurant is **La Merced**, Marqués de San Nicolás 109, ✆ 941 22 11 66 (*expensive*), exquisitely set in an elegant 18th-century palace, with superb food and a vast *bodega* containing 40,000 bottles of the finest Rioja. The *rabo estofado al vino Rioja* is excellent and the 6500 pts *menú degustación* is a delight. *Closed Sun eve and 1–20 Aug.*

The original, lovingly restored Merced *bodega* just opposite is now the **Mesón Lorenzo**, ✆ 941 20 91 30 (*moderate*), with good food and wine. For a delicious *menestra*, go where the locals go: **El Cachetero** on C/ Laurel 3, ✆ 941 22 84 63 (*moderate*): arrive early because it fills up fast. *Closed 15 July–15 Aug.* **Las Cubanas**, C/ San Agustín 17, ✆ 941 22 00 50 (*inexpensive*) owes its popularity to excellent regional cuisine, its friendly atmosphere and good value. *Closed Sat eve and Sun.* **Zubillaga**, C/ San Agustín 3, ✆ 941 22 00 76, offers succulent roast meats and fish, and treats like leek and gambas *pastel*. *Closed Wed and 1–25 July.* For tapas, try C/ Laurel and C/ San Juan.

Calahorra and the Rioja Baja

Down the Ebro, east of Logroño, La Rioja Baja is flat, fertile, and endowed with a sunny Mediterranean climate. Olive oil and wine are the two mainstays of the economy, with the kind of peppers the Spanish devour by the kilo coming in a close third. Few tourists pass through here, and those who do are mostly dinosaur fanciers.

Tourist Information

Calahorra: Ayuntamiento, ✆ 941 13 09 32.
Arnedo: Ayuntamiento, ✆ 941 38 10 80.

There are **markets** in Calahorra on Pza. del Raso on Thursdays; in Alfaro on Fridays; in Cervera de Río Alhama on Fridays; and in Arnedo on Mondays and Tuesdays.

Calahorra

Calahorra, capital of Rioja Baja, owes its contented look to its rich *vega* of orchards and vegetables, and has been inhabited for so long (since palaeolithic times) that St Jerome speculated that it was founded by Tubal, grandson of Noah. In 187 BC the town was grabbed by Rome, then in a dispute between Pompey and Sertorius in AD 72 it held out against Pompey until all the defenders died of starvation, a fanaticism that gave rise to the expression 'Calagurritan hungers'. The Romans rebuilt it, and Calahorra returned the favour by giving Rome Marcus Fabius Quintilian (42–118), its first professor of rhetoric. Although an episcopal see since the 5th century, Calahorra's **Cathedral** has been fussed with frequently. Behind a fruity, floral neoclassical façade pasted on in 1700, the nave with graceful star vaulting is a product of 1485. The Plateresque cloister houses the **Museo Diocesano** (*open 12–2 Sun and hols only*) with a 12th-century Bible and 15th-century Custodia called *El Ciprés*, made of gold and silver, donated by Henri IV. The church of **San Andrés** has a Gothic portal illustrating the triumph over paganism and the arch **Arco del Planillo** is the only gateway surviving from the Roman walls; other bits of Calagurra are further up, along panoramic Camino Bellavista.

Down the Ebro from Calahorra, **Alfaro**'s chief monument is its twin-towered **Colegiata de San Miguel**, built in the 16th and 17th centuries and reminiscent of colonial churches in South America. But the Colegiata's chief claim to fame are its lodgers: it has more stork nests on its roof than any other in Spain, a colony of some 250 birds. Rioja Baja also has Europe's largest concentration of dinosaur tracks, or ichnites—5000 footprints dating back 120 million years when the denizens of the Cretaceous (post-Jurassic) period stomped through the marshes. Conditions for preserving their prints in these broken hills were excellent: a different sort of mud filled in the tracks, preserving the impression after the mud below was turned to stone. In the Middle Ages, the ichnites were said to be the hoofmarks of Santiago's horse. The best places to find them are in **Préjano** just east of Arnedillo and the Los Cayos gully at **Cornago**. **Enciso** has the largest number, especially at the Valdecevillo bed; others are just north in **Munilla** in a gully called Peñaportillo.

Where to Stay and Eating Out

Calahorra ✉ 26500

The modern ★★★**Parador Marco Fabio Quintiliano**, Parque Era Alta s/n, ✆ 941 13 03 58, ▦ 941 13 51 39 (*expensive*) is near the scanty Roman ruins of Calagurris, with good views, comfortable rooms and air-conditioning; like all *paradores*, it has a good restaurant serving regional and international cuisine. ★★**Chef Nino**, C/ Padre Lucas 2, ✆ 941 13 31 04 (*moderate*) is new, central and air-conditioned; the restaurant serves an excellent Basque-Riojan *2000 pts menú*. For something a little cheaper, try ★**Teresa**, C/ Santo Domingo 2, ✆ 941 13 03 32 (*inexpensive*). Calahorra's best-known restaurant, **La Taberna de la Cuarta Esquina**, Cuatro Esquinas 16, ✆ 941 13 43 55 (*moderate*) is justly renowned for its well-prepared fish, game and vegetable dishes and reasonably priced wines. *Closed 6–31 July.* **Casa Mateo**, Pza. del Raso 15, ✆ 941 13 00 09, serves a tasty *menestra* and other dishes at the lowest prices in town.

Enciso ✉ 26580

In a little red 19th-century house, the **Posada de Santa Rita**, Ctra. de Soria 7, ✆ 941 39 60 66 (*inexpensive*) is a cosy place to stay, with a small library devoted to dinosaurs. If it's a weekend or holiday, **La Fábrica**, Ctra. de Soria 10, ✆ 941 39 60 51 (*inexpensive*) offers delicious meals based on game dishes, served in an atmospheric old flour mill.

Along the Pilgrim Route: West of Logroño

Beyond Logroño, the segment of the Camino de Santiago that crosses La Rioja is short but choice and full of interest, even though only a fraction of the monuments a 12th-century pilgrim would have known remain intact. A nearly obligatory detour remains: the famous pair of monasteries at San Millán de la Cogolla.

Tourist Information

Nájera: C/ Carmen, ✆ 941 36 16 25. *Open in summer only.*
San Millán: ✆ 941 37 30 35.
Santo Domingo: C/ Zumalacárregui, ✆ 941 34 22 34.

Navarrete and Nájera

Eleven km west of Logroño, **Navarrete** makes ceramics and rosé wine, and merits a stop for its medieval gate to the hospital of San Juan de Arce, doing duty as the entrance to the cemetery and decorated with lively capitals—of St Michael and the dragon, a pair of picnicking pilgrims, and Roland grappling with the giant Ferragut. The 16th-century church of the **Asunción**, attributed to Juan de Herrera, contains an elaborate Churrigueresque *retablo* and a triptych by Rembrandt's student Adrian Ysenbrandt.

Nájera has an illustrious pedigree. After the Moors flattened Pamplona in 918, the kings of Navarra moved here to keep an eye on the upstart kingdom of Castile. In 1052 one of them, García III (son of Sancho the Great), was hunting when he saw a dove fly past. He sent his falcon after it and followed the birds through the trees into a cave, from which a bright light emanated; inside he found the dove and falcon cooing side by side and a statue of Virgin and Child, a jar of fresh lilies, a lamp and a bell. To celebrate the miracle, García founded a church by the cave, which was rebuilt in the 15th century as the monastery of **Santa María la Real** (*tours 9.30–11.30 and 4–7.30; adm*). A beautiful Flamboyant Gothic door leads into the lovely Gothic-Plateresque Claustro de los Caballeros, its 24 arches half veiled by intricate sculpted screens, carved to imitate lace; no two are alike. The solemn 15th-century church has an enormous 17th-century *retablo* holding the miraculous statue of the Virgin. Originally she wore a large ruby. This was pinched by Pedro the Cruel in 1367 to pay the Black Prince for whipping the French army of his brother Enrique de Trastámara. The ruby now glows on the State Crown of England, but it cost the Black Prince his life—from a Spanish fever.

At the entrance of the holy cave are 16th-century tombs of the 10th–12th-century dynasties of Pamplona and Nájera, among them the original **sarcophagus** of Sancho III's 21-year-old wife Blanca, a magnificent Romanesque tomb, carved with a Christ in Majesty, the Massacre of the Innocents, and the death of the queen. Up the spiral stair is the remarkable Isabelline Gothic **choir** (1493–95); painted kings and queens create a charming *trompe l'oeil* effect.

San Millán de la Cogolla: Yuso and Suso

From Nájera it's a 17km detour south to **San Millán de la Cogolla**, a village that grew up around two monasteries, Yuso ('the lower') and Suso ('the upper'). St Millán (473–574) spent much of his 101 years living in the caves on the hill, and in the 7th century his followers built a monastery at **Suso**, signposted up a 2km narrow road (*open 10.30–1.15 and 4–7.15*). Carved out of a hill, the shadowy, atmospheric little church has a cloister, where Gonzalo de Berceo (b. 1198) the first poet to write in Spanish, loved to sit. The church was damaged by al-Mansur in the 11th century and rebuilt with Romanesque and Visigothic arches. Its tomb, with its recumbent alabaster effigy of San Millán, has been empty since 1053, when García III decided to take Millán's relics to Nájera; but the oxen pulling the cart refused to budge another inch once they reached the bottom of the hill. Here García built a new monastery called **Yuso** (*long guided tours by the monks from 10.30–1.30 and 4–6.30, closed Mon*) rebuilt in the 16th century and nicknamed the 'Escorial of La Rioja'. The monastery is proudest of its anonymous 10th-century monk who, while writing a commentary in his Latin text, the *Emilian 60 Codex*, and lapsed for 43 words into the vernacular—the first known use of Castilian: it's engraved on stone in the **Salón de Reyes**. The small **museum** contains Yuso's prizes: the ivory reliquary chests of San Millán and San Felices de Bilibio (1063).

Santo Domingo de la Calzada and its Chickens

Pilgrims especially looked forward to Santo Domingo de la Calzada, a delightful walled village that owes its name and existence to the first road saint, a shepherd named Domingo (1019–1109) who devoted his life to building bridges and *hostales*, making him the patron saint of engineers and public works, hence *de la Calzada* ('of the causeway'). His **church**, now the Cathedral of **La Rioja** (*open 10–2 and 3.30–7*)was founded on land donated in 1098 by King Alfonso VI, a pilgrimage booster who came in person to lay the first stone.

Reconstruction began in 1158 and took centuries to finish: the neoclassical façade is matched by a 243ft-(69m-)tower built by Martín de Beratúa in 1762. The Gothic interior is lavishly decorated, but what everyone remembers best are the rooster and hen, cackling in their own late Gothic **henhouse**. Their presence recalls the miracle that took place in Santo Domingo's *hostal*: a handsome 18-year-old German pilgrim named Hugonell, travelling with his parents, refused the advances of the maid, who avenged herself by planting a silver goblet in his pack and accusing him of theft. Hugonell was summarily hanged while his parents sadly continued to Compostela. On the way back, they passed the gallows and were amazed to find their son still alive. They hurried to the judge and told him; the judge, about to dig into a pair of roast fowl, scoffed their son was as alive as the birds on his table, upon which both cackled and flew away. The church is filled with beautiful art, especially the magnificent tomb of Santo Domingo by Felipe de Vigarni (1529) and the huge *retablo mayor* (1540), the last and best work of Damián Forment.

Where to Stay and Eating Out

Nájera ✉ 26300

****Hostería Monasterio de San Millán**, ✆ 941 37 32 77, 🖃 941 37 32 66, is situated in the monastery itself, with a good restaurant. On the Najerilla river, ****San Fernando**, Pso. San Julián 1, ✆ 941 36 37 00, 🖃 941 36 33 99 (*moderate*) is centrally located, or try the serene *Hs Hispano**, La Cepa 2, ✆ 941 36 36 15.

In the old town, **Pensión El Moro**, C/ Mártires 21, ✆ 941 36 00 52, is the cheapest. **El Mono**, C/Mayor 43, ✆ 941 36 30 28 (*moderate*) is Nájera's favourite for monkfish stuffed with lobster. A few doors down, lovely family-run **Los Parrales**, ✆ 941 36 37 35 (*moderate*) has a summer terrace. To the south the **Abadía de Valvanera** (*see* above) has simple rooms, ✆ 941 37 70 44; peace and quiet guaranteed.

Santo Domingo ✉ 26250

Grim on the outside but lovely within, the ****Parador de Santo Domingo de la Calzada**, Pza. del Santo 3, ✆ 941 34 03 00, 🖃 941 34 03 25 (*expensive*) occupies the pilgrim's *hostal* built by Santo Domingo; the restaurant serves a delicious *3700 pts* menú. ***Hs Santa Teresita**, C/ Pinar 2, ✆ 941 34 07 00 (*moderate–inexpensive*), is a pleasant guesthouse run by Cistercian nuns or, for something cheaper, try *Hs Río**, Echegoyen 2, ✆ 941 34 00 85 (*inexpensive*).

There is a pair of good restaurants specializing in regional cuisine: the well-known **El Rincón de Emilio**, Pza. de Bonifacio Gil 7, ✆ 941 34 09 90, with a *1500 pts* menú and **El Peregrino**, with a garden at Avda. Calahorra 19, ✆ 941 34 02 02, which has similar prices. *Closed Mon.*

Rioja Alta

To the north along the Ebro lies the Rioja Alta, a lush region of abrupt natural features rising above rolling hills, carpeted with vineyards and roads lined with brash spanking new wine *bodegas* that speak of La Rioja's rising reputation, and just might lose their sharp kitsch edge over the next 200 years.

Haro: Plaza Hermanos F. Rodríguez, ✆ 941 31 27 26 (summer only), ✆ 941 31 22 70. There is a **market** on Tuesdays and Saturdays on Arco de Santa Bárbara.

Haro

Haro is a bustling working wine town built around a large arcaded square. Its chief monuments are a handful of noble houses, the attractive **Casa Consistorial** (1775) and the 16th-century church of **Santo Tomás** up in Plaza Iglesia, bearing a handsome, recently restored Plateresque façade with sculpture and reliefs in several registers, paid for by the Condestables de Castilla. Since 1892, Haro's **Estación Enológica**, C/ Bretón de los Herreros 4 (just behind the bus station), has tested new winemaking techniques; its **Wine Museum** (*open Tues–Sun 10–2 and Sat 4–7*) offers detailed explanations of the latest high-tech processes used in La Rioja. For a far less serious initiation in Rioja, come on 29 July when San Felices is celebrated with a *Batalla del Vino*, that takes place 3km from Haro at the **Peña de Bilibio**, below the rock formation of the Conchas de Haro. Archaeologists have recently discovered a 10th-century church and the ruins of a Roman town, Castrum Bilibium, or Haro la Vieja, just under the rocks.

Rioja in the Bottle

Spain's only DOC (AOC) classified wine, La Rioja tastes like no other: soft, warm, mellow, full-bodied, with a distinct vanilla bouquet. The Phoenicians introduced the first vines, which after the various invasions were replanted under the auspices of the Church. The arrival of masses of thirsty pilgrims proved a big boost to business, much as mass tourism would do in the 1960s and '70s. Despite a long pedigree, the Rioja we drink today dates from the 1860s, when growers from Bordeaux, their own vineyards wiped out by phylloxera, brought their techniques south of the border and wrought immense improvements on the native varieties. By the time the plague reached La Rioja in 1899, the owners were prepared for it with disease-resistant stock. During the First World War, when the vineyards of the Champagne were badly damaged, the French returned to buy up *bodegas*, sticking French labels on the bottles and trucking them over the Pyrenees. Rioja finally received the respect it deserved after Franco passed on to the great fascist parade ground in the sky. In the last 20 years, *bodegas* have attracted buyers from around the world and prices have skyrocketed. La Rioja's growing area covers 48,000 hectares and is divided into three sub-zones: Rioja Alta, home of the best red and white wines, followed by Rioja Alavesa (on the left bank of the Ebro in Alava province) known for its lighter, perfumed wines, and the decidedly more arid Rioja Baja, where the wines are coarse and mostly used for blending—a common practice in La Rioja. The varieties used for the reds are mostly spicy, fruity Tempranillo (covering some 24,000 hectares alone), followed by Garnacha Tinta (a third of the red production, a good alcohol booster) with smaller portions of Graciano (for the bouquet) and high-tannin Mazuela (for acidity and tone). Traditional Rioja whites are relatively unknown but are excellent, golden and vanilla-scented like the reds: Viura grapes are the dominant grape, with smaller doses of Malvasía and Garnacha Blanca. Unlike French wines, Riojas are never sold until they're ready to drink. DOC rules specify that La Rioja's Gran Reserva, which accounts for only 3% of the production, spends a minimum of two years maturing in American oak barrels (six months for whites and rosés) then four more in the *bodega* before it's sold. *Reservas* (6% of the production) spend at least one year in oak and three in the *bodega*. *Crianzas* (30% of the production) spend at least a year in the barrel and another in the bottle. The other 61% of La Rioja is *sin crianza* and labelled CVC (*conjunto de varias cosechas*, combination of various vintages): this includes the new young white wines and light reds (*claretes*) fermented at cool temperatures in stainless steel vats, skipping the oak barrels and losing some vanilla tones.

Haro is the growing and marketing centre for the wines of Rioja Alta, with a clutch of *bodegas* near the train station. While most *bodegas* welcome visitors, they usually require advance notice. An exception is **Bodegas Bilbaínas**, C/ Estación 3, © 941 31 01 47, usually open mornings and late afternoons. In the same area along Costa del Vino, you'll find the celebrated cellars of the **CUNE** (or CVNE, © 941 31 06 50), home of a fine bubbly; **López de Heredia**, © 941 31 01 27, makers of one of the best Riojas, *Viña Tondonia* ; the vast, French-founded **Rioja Alta**, Avda. Vizcaya, © 941 31 03 46, with 25,000 barrels; the even larger **Federico Paternina**, © 941 31 05 50, founded in 1896 by the Plaza de Toros; and **Martínez Lacuesta Hnos**, C/ Ventilla 71, © 941 31 00 50, is in the old gas company. Among the shops, **Selección Vinos de Rioja**, Pza. Paz 5, © 941 30 30 17, offers tastings and a wide variety of different Riojas; likewise the aptly named **La Catédral de los Vinos**, Casa Quintin, C/ Sto Tomás 4 just off the Plaza de la Paz.

Where to Stay and Eating Out

Haro ✉ 26200

Superbly restored and centrally located, ★★★★**Los Agustinos**, C/ San Agustín 2, © 941 31 13 08, ◉ 941 30 31 48 (*expensive*) occupies a former Augustinian monastery that later served as a prison. Along the highway, overlooking Haro, modern ★★★**Iturrimurri**, Ctra. N. 124 Km 41, © 941 31 12 13, ◉ 941 31 17 21 (*expensive–moderate*) is plain, comfortable and has a pool. The very basic ★**Hs Aragón**, La Vega 9, © 941 31 00 04, is probably your only bet for a *cheap* sleep. At **La Kika**, C/Santo Tomás 9, © 941 31 11 81 (*moderate*) the kitchen changes its repertoire daily, so there's no set *menú*—rely on the waiters' suggestions; reservations are a must. Since 1867, **Terete**, C/ Lucrecia Arana 17, © 941 31 00 23 (*moderate*), has filled Haro with the divine aroma of its famous roast lamb and huge choice of other dishes; good *1500 pts menú. Closed Sun eve, Mon and Oct.* Traditional mushroom, fish and vegetable dishes are the prizes at the two dining rooms of **Beethoven I and II**, C/ Santo Tomás 3-5 and Pza. de la Iglesia 8, © 941 31 11 81 (*all moderate*).

Briñas ✉ 26200

★**El Portal de La Rioja**, Ctra. De la Victoria 42, © 941 31 14 80, has, in addition to just barely moderate rooms with bath, an excellent restaurant (*moderate*) serving chops grilled on vine cuttings (*chuletas al sarmiento*), a craft shop and a wine museum with century-old bottles.

Cantabria, Asturias and Galicia

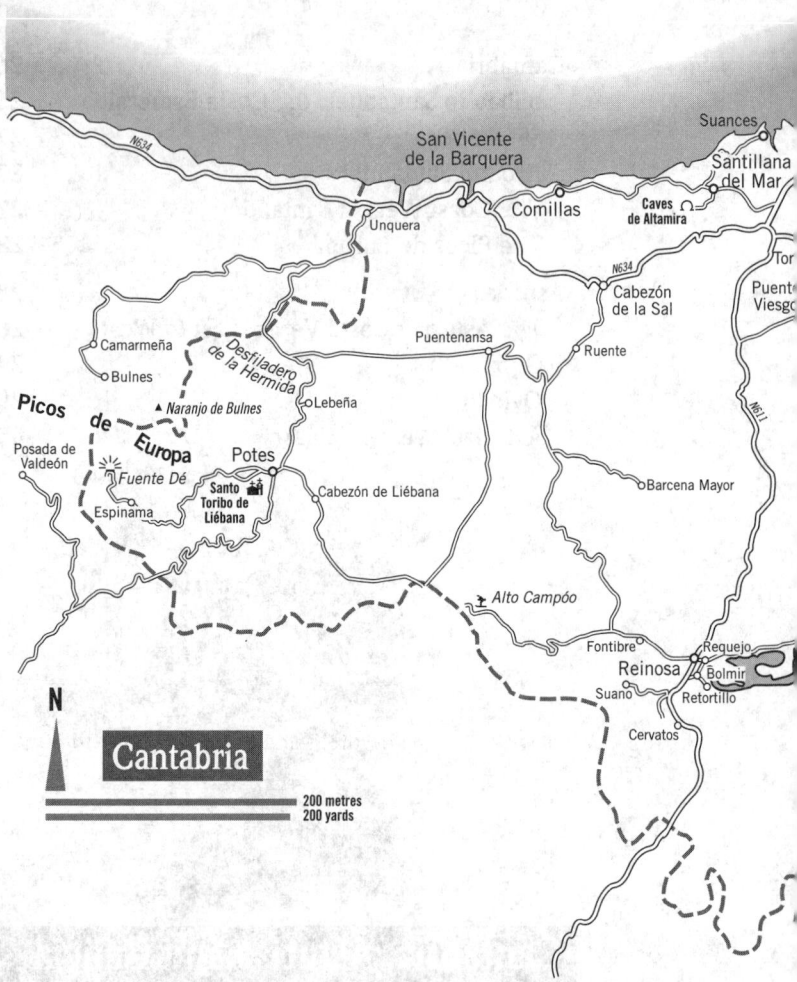

Cantabria

Spain's steep emerald-green dairy-land, Cantabria is wedged between the extraordinary Picos de Europa, the Cordillera Cantábrica and a coastline of scenic beaches. Santander, the capital and only large city, is a major summer resort and, while there are a handful of other tourist spots (Laredo, Comillas, and the medieval Santillana del Mar), much of Cantabria is serenely rural, claiming to have the highest density of cows in Europe. The majority of the bovine population lives indoors, and in the evening the most common Cantabrian sight is the farmer or his wife, often wearing wooden clogs, driving home an ox-cart laden with grass which they have cut from their several Lilliputian plots of land scattered over the hills. On rainy winter

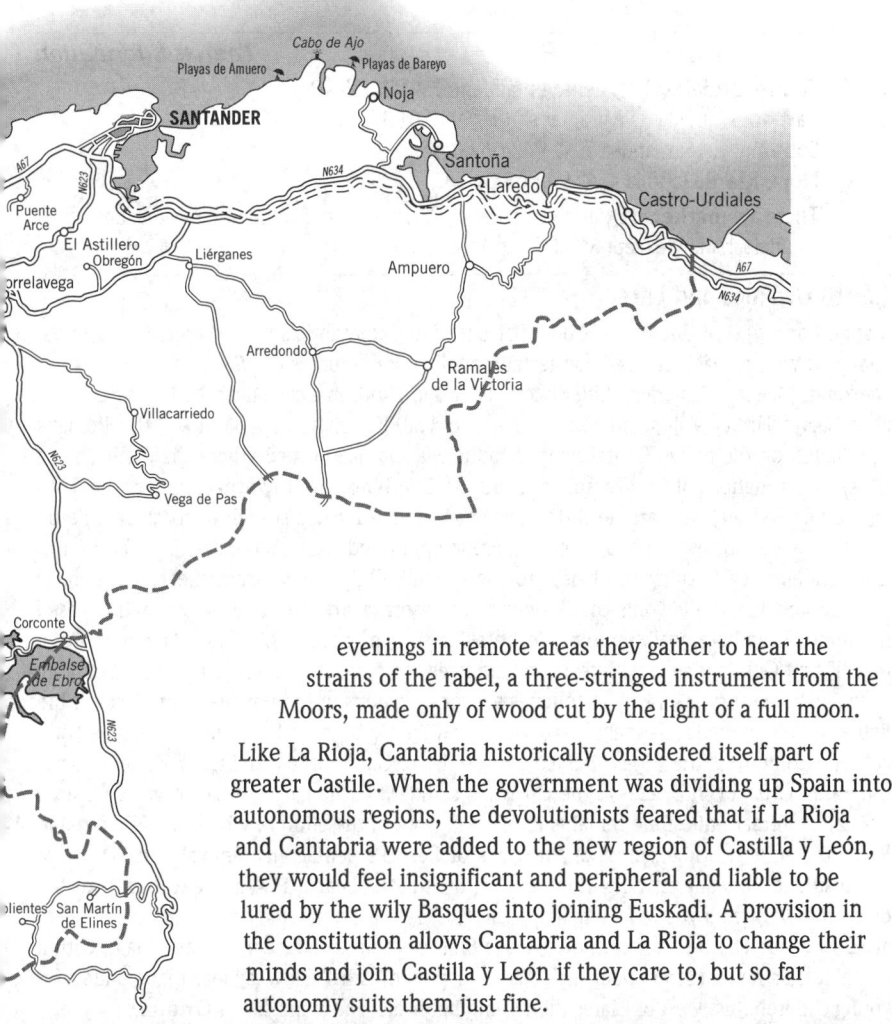

evenings in remote areas they gather to hear the strains of the rabel, a three-stringed instrument from the Moors, made only of wood cut by the light of a full moon.

Like La Rioja, Cantabria historically considered itself part of greater Castile. When the government was dividing up Spain into autonomous regions, the devolutionists feared that if La Rioja and Cantabria were added to the new region of Castilla y León, they would feel insignificant and peripheral and liable to be lured by the wily Basques into joining Euskadi. A provision in the constitution allows Cantabria and La Rioja to change their minds and join Castilla y León if they care to, but so far autonomy suits them just fine.

Bilbao to Santander: the Costa Esmeralda

If this eastern stretch of coast is all you see of Cantabria, you may think what you have just read about rural serenity is pure fiction. This seems to be the busiest coast in all northern Spain in the summer and especially at the weekend, when half of Bilbao is out here looking for a bit of beach and seems to end up on the endless sweep of sand at Laredo.

Getting Around

By train: The two daily FEVE trains between Santander and Bilbao stop near Laredo; Pza. de las Estaciones s/n, © 942 21 16 87.

By bus: Several Turytrans buses a day run along the coast between Santander and Bilbao; from Santander they depart from Pza. de las Estaciones s/n, © 942 21 19 95.

Castro Urdiales: Pza. del Ayuntamiento, ✆ 942 85 90 07.
Laredo: Alameda de Miramar s/n , ✆ 942 61 10 96.
Santoña: C/ Santander 5, ✆ 942 66 00 66.
Noja: Pza. de la Villa 1, ✆ 942 63 00 38.
There are **markets** in Castro Urdiales on Thursdays; in Laredo at the Mercado Municipal, daily except Sundays.

Castro Urdiales and Laredo

Just an hour west of Bilbao, Castro Urdiales is one of Cantabria's most scenic fishing-ports, endowed with a beach and seafood restaurants that draw hordes of *bilbaínos* every summer weekend. Magdalenian-era graffiti, discovered in the 1960s in a cave near the Plaza de Toros, date Castro Urdiales' first inhabitants back to 12,000 BC. In ancient times, the Romans muscled in on the native Cantabrians to found *Flavióbriga*, located where the castle stands today. A stronghold of the Templars in the Middle Ages, the town declined in the 14th century as Pedro I and Enrique II de Trastámara fought for this stretch of coast. It suffered even more grievously in 1813 when the French punished Castro's resistance in the War of Independence by burning most of it to the ground. Only a few streets near the harbour escaped the flames, beyond the 18th-century **Ayuntamiento**, at the top of the Paseo Marítimo. From here, walk up to the fortress-like church of **Santa María de la Asunción**, a magnificent Gothic temple with massive buttresses and pinnacles. Constructed almost entirely in the 13th century, its Templar touches are most obvious in the unusual symbolism of the figures carved in the lovely frieze wrapped around the top of the church. Inside there's a 13th-century sculpture of the *Virgen Blanca* and a series of Gothic woodcarvings. You can also see the *Santa Cruz*, or 'holy cross', the Christian standard at the battle of Las Navas de Tolosa (1212). A Roman milestone remains in place in front of the church, while over the striking Roman/medieval bridge, most of the walls of Castro's pentagonal **Templar castle** have survived and now shelter a lighthouse. Castro Urdiales' beach, **Playa Brazomar**, is at the other end of town; if you're feeling like peeling, there's also a naturist beach just outside town at **El Pocillo.** The best beach, however, is 8km west up to **Islares**, a small village with a magnificent strand of sand under the cliffs, interspersed with shallow lagoons that are ideal for young children. Just west of Islares there's another beach and camp site at **Oriñón**.

Cantabria's biggest resort, **Laredo**, has little in common with its namesake on the Río Grande. The scenery in fact isn't too different, but on its streets there is hardly a cowboy alive or dead to be seen. This Laredo does have an old town, hidden somewhere among the *urbanizaciones*, but you'll remember it mostly as a somewhat brash and totally modern holiday playground. People from Bilbao and Madrid and France love it, and it does have its charms. Laredo was the Roman *Portus Luliobrigensium*, the place where the Romans finally subdued the last die-hard Celtiberians in a great sea battle. The medieval Puebla Vieja over the harbour was walled in by Alfonso VIII of Castile to safeguard the region from pirates; its 13th-century church **Santa María de la Asunción** has five naves (rare for the period) and curiously carved capitals. The late-Renaissance **Ayuntamiento** in Plaza Cachupín is said to mark the location of the harbour quay the megalomaniac Emperor actually stepped on; behind it is the attractive tiled market building erected in 1902. *Urbanizaciones* have marched nearly to the tip of Laredo's wide, sheltered pride and joy: **Playa de Salvé**, a gentle 3-mile-long crescent of sand.

West of Laredo, heading towards Santander, the parade of beaches continues: **Santoña** is another fishing-port resort and hometown of Juan de la Cosa (b.1460), the cartographer who accompanied Columbus on his second voyage to America (1493) and is remembered with a suitably large monument. Santoña also claims that its shipbuilders made the *Santa María* for Columbus. Another lovely area, **Noja**, has another stretch of fine, sandy beaches and a considerable villa and apartment *urbanización* along the shore. According to local legend the village takes its name from Noah; the Ark washed up on one of the mountains nearby. The rest of the way to Santander there are plenty of unexploited beaches: the **Playas de Arnuero**, near the lighthouse at Cape Ajo, and the **Playas de Barayo**, west of Ajo.

Where to Stay and Eating Out

Castro Urdiales ✉ 39700

If you're just looking for a place to stay over or hang out for a day or two, Castro will prove much more interesting than Laredo, though inexpensive places are hard to find. There are two plum choices by the town beach (*both expensive*): the luxurious and tranquil ★★★**Las Rocas**, Avda. de la Playa s/n, ✆ 942 86 00 04, ✇ 942 86 13 82, near the beaches, and the stylish ★★★**Miramar**, Avda. de la Playa 1, ✆ 942 86 02 00, ✇ 942 87 09 42, which offers comfortable rooms, attentive service and excellent views of the cathedral from its second-floor restaurant. The antique ★★**El Cordobés**, C/ Ardigales 15, ✆ 942 86 00 89, is prettily located in the Mediavilla. ★**Hs Alberto**, near the town park on Avda. de la República Argentina 2, ✆ 942 86 27 57, is cheap and cheerful.

The well-known **Mesón El Marinero**, in the historic Casa de los Chelines next to the fishing port at La Correría 23, ✆ 942 86 00 05, is the place to go for heaping plates of delicious, fresh seafood at reasonable prices—for less than the typical *4000 pts* meal, feast on a wide selection of tapas at the bar. For roast sucking pig or a seafood grill (*15,000 pts for two*), make your way to Castro's second culinary shrine, **El Segoviano**, La Correría 19, ✆ 942 86 18 59 (*6000 pts average*). Bar and nightlife in Castro Urdiales is concentrated along C/ de la Rúa and the Paseo Marítimo.

Islares ✉ 39798

There's a large comfortable campsite by the beach, the **Camping Playa Arenillas**, and one pleasant little *hostal*, the ★★**Hs Arenillas**, ✆ 942 86 07 66 (*moderate*), quiet and near the beach.

Laredo ✉ 39770

Hotels in Laredo are small and fairly dear, and reservations are essential in the summer. Newest is the modern, mid-size ★★★**Miramar**, Alto de Laredo s/n, ✆ 942 61 03 67, ✇ 942 61 16 92 (*moderate; expensive in high season*), with huge windows to take in the huge sea views. ★★★**Risco**, C/ La Arenosa 2, ✆ 942 60 50 30, ✇ 942 60 50 55, has commodious rooms enjoying superb views of the protected bay and beach and a restaurant generally rated as Laredo's top seafood palace, featuring elaborate creations such as a *capricho* of lobster, chicken breasts and figs (*moderate*). ★★**Montecristo**, C/ Calvo Sotelo 2, 942 60 57 00 (*moderate*), is one of the better beach hotels in town. *Open mid-April to mid-Sept.*

Near Playa de Salvé, **Squash**, Avda. Reina Victoria s/n, © 942 60 40 69, has nothing to do with the game, but instead offers both modern hotel rooms near the beach and furnished apartments for five persons (*20,000 pts in high season*). ****Hs Ramona**, C/ General Mola 4, © 942 60 53 36, is another reasonable *moderate* choice. In the centre, you won't find a better deal than the ***Hs Salomón**, C/ Menéndez Pelayo 11, © 942 60 50 81, with immaculate rooms and wooden floors. For anything under *4000 pts*, ask at a bar.

Some of the best seafood you'll find in the coastal towns are informal outdoor places on the docks, often run by fishermen's families. At the far end of Laredo's fishing port, there's the popular **El Rincón del Puerto**, a few long tables next to a grill, where you can feast on fresh sardines, prawns, striped tuna, *paella*, fish soup and other delicacies, and happily spend anything from *1500 to 5000 pts*. Another good place for simple seafood gratification is **Playa**, Avda. de la Victoria, © 942 61 22 03. For cheaper eats try **Asador Orio**, Avd. José Antonio 10, © 942 60 70 93 (*1000 pts menu*).

Santander

The capital of Cantabria, Santander has a lot in common with San Sebastián—a large city beautifully situated on a protected bay, popularized by royalty as a summer resort. The story has it that Queen Isabel II first came down in the 1860s in the hope that the sea air would help with a bad dose of the clap. Again, after the First World War, it was *the* fashionable place to go for Madrileños, especially with the founding of an international summer university (named after Menéndez Pelayo, Santander's favourite son and Spain's greatest antiquarian), offering holiday-makers highbrow culture to complement its wide beaches. Still, despite this and its widely acclaimed International Music Festival in August, Santander lacks the excitement and *joie de vivre* of San Sebastián. The Santander of the festivals shows a bright and modern face to the world, but the real atmosphere of the place is still best represented by the pigeon-spattered statue of Franco in the centre and the grey streets still named after Nationalist hoodlums of the Civil War.

Getting There

By air: Santander's airport is 7km away at Maliaño (no buses), with daily connections to Barcelona and Madrid. Iberia's office is at Pso. de Pereda 18, © 942 22 97 00; Aviaco's is at the airport, © 942 25 10 07.

By ferry: From Santander, Brittany Ferries sail to Plymouth twice-weekly from mid-March to mid-December, once weekly in January and February. For information in Santander, call © 942 36 06 11, or visit the ticket office at the Estación Marítima.

By train: The train stations are both on Pza. de las estaciones s/n. RENFE, © 942 21 23 87, has connections with Madrid, Palencia, Reinosa, Segovia and Valladolid. The narrow-gauge FEVE, © 942 21 16 87, has trains to Bilbao, Oviedo, Torrelavega and Unquera; unfortunately they miss the coast east of Santander, which is served by buses.

By bus: The central bus station is conveniently opposite the train stations on Navas de Tolosa, © 942 21 19 95. Connections include: Continental Auto to Burgos, Madrid and Ontaneda-Vejores; Turytrans to nearly all the coastal towns and resorts, and to Bilbao, Zarauz, San Sebastián, Llanes, Oviedo, Gijón, Vitoria and Pamplona ; Intercar to Galicia, Asturias and Euskadi; Fernández to León and Autocares de

Cantabria to Logroño. The main line up to the Picos de Europa is Palomera, with runs to Potes and Fuente Dé. Within Santander itself there are frequent buses and trolleys (nos.1, 2 and 7) that run from the centre to El Sardinero 20 minutes away.

Lanchas Reginas runs the **boat service** to the beaches across the bay, with departures every 15 minutes from 10.30am to 8.30pm from the Muelle de Ferrys, two blocks from the cathedral. They also offer excursions around the Río Cubas.

Radio **taxi**, ✆ 942 33 33 33, or ✆ 942 23 23 23.

Tourist Information

Pza. de Velarde 5, ✆ 942 31 07 08, ✉ 942 31 32 48, at the centre of the beach strip, and at the Jardines de Pereda, in the city centre facing the port, ✆ 942 21 61 20.

Markets: in Plaza de la Esperanza behind the Ayuntamiento: Tuesdays, Wednesdays, Fridays and Saturdays for food; Mondays and Thursdays for clothes. Plaza de México: Mondays, Wednesdays, Fridays and Saturdays for food; Tuesdays and Fridays for clothes (by the bull ring at the end of Calle de San Fernando).

The Cathedral and Museums

In the centre, Santander's much-altered and rebuilt **Cathedral** is interesting mostly for its early Gothic crypt; this now forms the separate church of **Santísimo Cristo**, where a glass floor has been installed over the remains of a Roman building. The **Museo de Prehistoria y Arqueología**, next to the Provincial Council on C/ Juan de la Cosa (*open Mon–Sat 9–1 and 4–7, Sun 11–2; adm*), has exhibits devoted to Cantabria's prehistoric cave-dwellers, including tools, reproductions of their art, and two disc-shaped star tombstones the size of tractor tyres made just before the Roman conquest, discovered in the valley of the Buelna. Near the Ayuntamiento, the **Museo de Bellas Artes** (*open daily 10.30–1 and 5.30–9, Sun 11–1; adm*) has, besides a contemporary art collection of dubious merit, a Zurbarán and several Goyas, including a portrait of Ferdinand VII, which the city commissioned to flatter the king. Nearby, the **Casa Museo de Menéndez Pelayo** (*open weekdays only 9.30–1; guided tours every half-hour*) has an extensive collection of books donated to the city by the scholar himself. Behind the Ayuntamiento, the iron and glass **market** is definitely the most colourful sight Santander has to offer, especially the pride of the town: the glorious fish market.

On the way out to the beaches, Avenida Reina Victoria passes Santander's new **Museo Marítimo del Cantábrico** (*open daily exc Mon 11–1 and 4–7, Sun 11–2; in winter 10–1 and 4–6, Sun 11–2; adm*), with an array of model ships, exhibits in the local maritime tradition, and an **aquarium**.

El Sardinero

The 1941 fire destroyed most of Santander's character but it spared the suburb of **El Sardinero**, with its fine twin beaches, imaginatively named **Primera** (First) and **Segunda** (Second), backed by the enormous Belle Epoque **casino**, recently refurbished in an effort to revive some of the city's lost panache. El Sardinero is separated from the working end of the city by the beautiful **Peninsula de la Magdalena**, a city park fringed by two more splendid beaches, the **Playa de la Magdalena** and the **Playa del Promontorio**. The Tudor-style **Palacio de la Magdalena** at the end of the peninsula was a gift from the city to Alfonso XIII; when the king accepted it, Santander's return to fashion as a summer resort was guaranteed.

Santander

N

1 kilometre
1/2 mile

Today it is part of the International University. Besides the beaches in the city, there are several miles of golden dunes across the bay at **Somo**, **El Puntal** and **Pedrena**, linked every 15 minutes by boat from the centre of town; **Playa las Atenas** nearby is a naturist beach. Just west of Santander at Liencres, there is another fine and very popular beach, **Valdearenas**. The **Parque de la Naturaleza de Cabárceno** (*opening hours change regularly; call © 942 56 37 36 for information; adm exp*), is 10km south of the city at Obregón, a bit of land wasted by strip mining has been recycled into an attractive and enormous zoo.

Santander ✉ 39000

Where to Stay

July, August and September are the busy months here, especially the first two, when the music festival and International University are in full swing. Prices are as high as in San Sebastián, though there are plenty of *casas particulares* to preserve your budget. Hang around the bus and train stations and someone will probably lead you to one.

expensive

Santander's most elegant establishments are all on the back side of town by the beaches, starting with the lovely *modernista* ★★★★★**Hotel Real**, Pso. de Pérez Galdós 28, ℡ 942 27 25 50, ✉ 942 27 45 73, located near the Playa de la Magdalena and offering marvellous views over the bay, fine rooms and a fine garden. The popular ★★★**Hotel Sardinero**, Pza. de Italia 1, ℡ 942 27 11 00, ✉ 942 27 16 98, is conveniently located near the beaches of Sardinero and the casino. On Avda. Reina Victoria, the main street facing the beaches, ★★★★**Rhin**, ℡ 942 27 43 00, ✉ 942 27 86 53, enjoys a smart location. A recent addition to the ranks of luxury in town is the ★★★★ **Castelar**, C/Castelar 25, ℡ 942 22 52 00, in the city centre with sea views.

moderate

The recently remodelled ★★**Méjico**, Calderón de la Barca 3, ℡ 942 21 24 50, is central and pleasant. Also centrally located is the ★★**San Glorio**, C/ Ruiz Zorilla 18, 942 31 29 62. ★**Hotel Residencia Carlos III**, Adv. Reina Victoria 135, ℡ 942 27 16 16, is comfortable and a good bargain, while the **Piñamar**, C/ Ruiz de Alda 15, ℡ 942 36 18 66, is modern and functional and located near the train station.

The cheaper hotels have gained a certain notoriety for being either dreary or rip-offs. A safe one is ***Hs Gran Antilla**, C/ Isabel II 8, 942 21 31 00. At El Sardinero *inexpensive* places are difficult but not impossible to find: try ***Hs Castilla**, Avda. Joaquin Costa, *Ⓒ* 942 27 22 00, or ****Hs Rocamar**, Avda. de los Castros 41 (a street where there are several other choices). **Camping Bellavista** is located by the Cabo Mayor lighthouse, *Ⓒ* 942 27 48 43.

Eating Out

Unlike San Sebastián, Santander is hardly known for its cuisine. The seafood, however, is always good, and the traditional place to get it is at the rather piquant **Barrio Pesquero**, an area rebuilt after the fire, just behind the train stations. One of the best places here is the **Casa José**, C/ Mocejón 2, with a good *menú del día* for *1200 pts*. Another favourite in the barrio is **La Gaviota**, where you can try the seafood *menú del día* for *800 pts*; at either you can also just order a plate of whatever delicacy has come home with the fishermen for *600–1600 pts*. To get a feel for traditional fare, there's the **Bodega Cigaleña**, C/ Daoiz y Velarde 19, *Ⓒ* 942 21 30 62, a typical, dark *bodega* which harbours a wine museum.

Around the beaches, restaurants tend to be more elaborate in every way. The fashionable **La Sardina**, C/ Dr Fleming 3 in El Sardinero, *Ⓒ* 942 27 10 35 (*expensive*) offers imaginative renderings of traditional dishes such as *bacalao* with red peppers, in a very pretty setting. Less formal dining can be found at **Bodega del Riojano**, Río de la Pila 5 (north of the Jardines de Pereda), *Ⓒ* 942 21 67 50 (*moderate*), one of Santander's typical *bodegas* in the old quarter, also serving tapas. Specialities are *rabo de buey* (ox tail), *morcillo estofado* (a blood sausage stew), and stuffed peppers. *Closed Sun eve.* Near the Ayuntamiento, **La Casona**, C/Cuesta 6, *Ⓒ* 942 21 26 88 (*moderate*) is an old favourite that has accumulated a huge collection of paintings on its walls; excellent grilled meats and seafood. More seafood in sumptuous displays is on offer in numerous eateries in the Puerto Chico, between the centre and the beaches. Especially good are the **Bar del Puerto** on Hernán Cortés 63 (*3000 pts*) and **Iris**, at Castelar 5 (*3500 pts*). Nearby is **Zacarías**, C/ Hernán Cortés 38, *Ⓒ* 942 21 06 88, offering a total '*mar y montaña*' Cantabrian culinary experience, including the region's excellent cheeses.

Entertainment and Nightlife

Since 1951 the August **Festival Internacional de Santander** has showcased an extraordinary variety of music and dance from around the world. Along with all the big-league culture, popular Spanish and Latin American song, dance, magic shows and fireworks take place every night in August at the Auditorium and the Finca Altamira. For information contact the Oficina del Festival, Palacio de Festivales de Cantabria, C/ Gamazo s/n, 39004, Santander, *Ⓒ* 942 21 05 08/*Ⓒ* 942 21 03 45/*Ⓒ* 942 31 48 19/*Ⓒ* 942 31 48 53, *✉* 942 31 47 67. Tickets are on sale in advance from the ticket booth at the Palacio de Festivales, from any branch of the Caja Cantabria bank, or from the special Festival booth in the Jardines de Pereda, *Ⓒ* 942 31 33 42 (*open 11–2 and 5–8*).

Nightlife is concentrated in two places: first the proper *marcha* grounds in the old town, with a vast number of bars and clubs around C/ de la Pila and Plaza de Cañadío. This is the place where you're most likely to find live music and a raucous good time. One old and pleasant bar with good snacks and sometimes live music is **La Conveniente**, C/ Gómez Oreña. Nearby are some of the flashier discos, including **Malaespina**, C/ Santa Lucía 40, and **El Cairo** at C/ Moctezuma 4, which run until dawn. The **Rockambole** on C/ Hernán Cortés 10, has plenty of space to party until rosy fingered aurora appears. For those wanting to avoid the strictly young scene, there's the classic La Luna, C/ General Mola 35. For a typical wine *bodega* full of big old barrels, try the **Casa La Montaña** on C/ Vargas, the park boulevard northwest of the Renfe and Feve train stations. More staid entertainment can be had around El Sardinero; the Plaza de Italia attracts the older set, while the overdressed young in search of fun head for the bars and discothèques in Calle Panamá. At the lavish **Gran Casino** you can risk your pesetas from 7pm to 4am (dress up and bring your passport).

Shopping

Santander is a good shopping city, where it's easy to while away an afternoon strolling along such streets as C/ San Francisco in the city centre and others in the vicinity. A good place for quality shoes and other leather goods is **Lucio Herrezuelo**, C/ Calvo Sotelo 23. On the pedestrian-only streets, C/ Arrabal and C/ del Medio, are some good clothing boutiques, as well as local arts and crafts galleries.

Around Santander

South of the capital the land gradually rises to the Montañas de Santander, a pretty, hilly region with only a handful of villages. There are plenty of wide open spaces along these high roads of the old County of Castile, but there are a few attractions besides the solitude: caves of prehistoric art, untouched forests, the source of the Ebro and one of the sexiest churches in Europe.

Getting Around

By bus: Reinosa's bus station, at the south end of town, is served from Santander by García, ✆ 942 75 40 67, and Alsa, ✆ 942 75 40 67; Ansa goes to Bilbao (summer only, ✆ 942 75 28 13). Donato, ✆ 942 12 20 47, links Reinosa to Espinilla and La Lomba in the Alto Campóo.

Tourist Information

Torrelavega: Ruíz Tagle 6, ✆ 942 89 29 82.
Reinosa: Avenida Puente Carlos III, ✆ 942 75 52 15.

There is a **market** in Reinosa on Mondays.

The Caves of Puente Viesgo

If you haven't made an appointment in advance to see the caves of Altamira, you can at least get into Cantabria's second most spectacular set of prehistoric grottoes at **Puente Viesgo**. There are five caves altogether, but the only one open to the public is the Cueva de Castillo (*Tues–Sat 10–2.15 and 3.30–6.30, closed Sun; adm, EU passport holders get in free; children under 13 strictly not admitted*). Decorated with graceful line drawings of stags, horses and other animals, this ensemble is believed to predate the even more eloquent art at Altamira.

Reinosa, on the rail line, is the main hub in this part of the Cantabrian mountains, with most of the area's hotels and restaurants. The source of northern Spain's longest river, the **Nacimiento del Ebro**, is signposted just to the northwest in **Fontibre** (on the road to Espinilla); you can clamber down in the trees to stick your toes in the stream gurgling out of the ground. The river has barely begun when, just on the other side of Reinosa it is dammed to form a massive reservoir, **Embalse del Ebro**, the grass on its jagged shore cropped by herds of horses and dairy cows, following the outline of a prehistoric lake. **Corconte**, on the eastern end of the lake, bottles mineral water next to an old spa.

The most beautiful part of the region lies west of Fontibre, in the virgin valleys of the **Saja National Reserve**, where beech, oak and birch forests follow the courses of clear streams. Real explorers can make for **Suano** and the **Población de Suso**, villages that figure on few maps, but can claim a large number of dolmens, a huge cromlech and the ruins of a Templar castle. The region's most important ski installation, **Alto Campóo**, lies to the west in the village of Hermandad Campóo de Suso.

South of Reinosa you'll find good Romanesque churches—in **Bolmir** and more significantly in **Retortillo**. Retortillo is near the scanty remains of the Roman city of **Julióbriga**, once the most important city of Cantabria. Set amidst the low walls is the church, with a unique sloping stair leading up to its campanile. Over the door note the carving of two animals shaking hands. But the most extraordinary Romanesque church of all is further south in **Cervatos**: the singular 12th-century **Colegiata**, at the top of a newly cobbled lane. It has a tympanum with an oriental design, a frieze of lions and, carved on to the corbels and capitals in the apse, unabashedly erotic figures that a respectable guidebook hesitates to describe.

South of Cervatos the road to Burgos (S614) soon meets up again with the Ebro. It's a lovely road, with lots of trees and local swimming holes by tiny villages. One of the largest is **Polientes**, with a roadside statue of a spotted dog and one of Cantabria's 'rupestrian churches' in a cave, although here little old ladies have set up a table by the altar to play cards. Follow the road and Ebro southeast to an even more remote region and the 12th-century church at **San Martín de Elines**, with a lofty cylindrical tower, keyhole windows and more fascinating modillions and carvings by the same school as Cervatose. If you've made it this far, it would be a shame not to continue towards Orbaneja del Castillo and the splendid, spectacular **canyons of the Ebro** (*see* p.344).

Where to Stay and Eating Out

Puente Arce ✉ 39478

One of the best restaurants in Cantabria can be found at this village, 12km inland from Santander on the road to Torrelavega. **El Molino**, Ctra. General s/n, © 942 57 50 55, ✆ 942 57 52 54 (*expensive*) is in an old mill on the river, with valuable oil paintings on the walls, excellent fish (an *ensalada cantabrica* with seafood and lots of ginger), a large selection of wines and a monumental *5000 pts* gastronomic menu. *Closed Sun eve and Mon, except in summer.*

Puente Viesgo ✉ 39478

If you have come to see the caves, you can stop at the ★★★**Gran Hotel Puente Viesgo**, Blvd. de la Iglesia, © 942 59 80 61, ✆ 942 59 82 61 (*luxury*), a sumptuous modern establishment connected to a spa that's good for your rheumatism and neurological troubles; swimming pool, sauna and all the amenities. More realistically, try **★★HR Carrion** at neighbouring Alceda, © 942 59 40 16. There is a good country restaurant in San Vicente de Toranzo, south of Puente Viesgo: the **Méson El Cazador** (*moderate*) offers boar, pheasant and other game dishes.

Reinosa ✉ 39200

★★★Vejo, in the newer part on Avda. Cantabria 83, © 942 75 17 00, ✆ 942 75 47 63 (*moderate*) is the most comfortable place in town, with a garden, bar and good restaurant. The more economical **★★San Cristóbal**, 16 de Agosto 1, © 942 75 17 68 (*inexpensive*) has simple, bathless rooms. If you're driving, a scenic place to stay is **★La Casona**, in Nestares, © 942 75 17 88 (*inexpensive*), an old inn on the Reinosa–Cabezón de la Sal highway.

The Coast West of Santander

This lush seaside stretch has been spared any Laredo toadstools, and what tourist development there is remains fairly discreet. When the summer hordes have vanished and the little windy roads belong to you alone, it is haunting in a fairylike way. Even in the rain.

Getting Around

By train: FEVE trains out of Santander go as far as Torrelavega, with frequent bus connections to Santillana. Another FEVE station is 3km from San Vicente—a lovely walk if you're not carrying too much luggage.

By bus: Suances, Santillana, Comillas and San Vicente are linked around 6 times daily to Santander by La Cantábrica de Comillas or SA Continental buses from Santander's main bus station.

Tourist Information

Suances: Plza. Del Generalisimo 1, © 942 81 09 24.
Santillana del Mar: Pza. de Ramon Pelayo s/n, © 942 81 82 51.
Comillas: Aldea 6, © 942 72 07 68.
San Vicente de la Barquera: Avda. Generalísimo 20, © 942 71 07 97.
Cabezón de la Sal: Pza. de Ricardo Botín s/n, © 942 70 03 32.

There are **markets** in Suances on Tuesdays; Torrelavega on Wednesdays; Comillas on Thursdays; San Vicente and Cabezón on Saturdays.

Santillana del Mar

The tour buses disgorge their hundreds daily upon this tiny village (which despite the 'del Mar' is not on the sea), and in summer it can be a ghastly tourist inferno, with no place to put your car for a mile around. If you come at all, do it out of season, or spend the night after the day-trippers have all gone. Santillana is at once an evocative medieval town of grand palaces and a country village of dairy farmers, whose pastures lie on the hills just beyond the mellowed stone and half-timbered houses that line Santillana's one street.

The village is famous as the birthplace of Spain's favourite fictional rogue, Gil Blas, and home of the real Marqués de Santillana, Íñigo López de Mendoza, the Spanish Sir Philip Sidney, a warrior and poet and courtly lover whose house still stands on the Calle del Cantón. Other houses have equally noble pedigrees; an archduchess of Austria owned the one across from the **Colegiata**. The latter is a 12th-century masterpiece, dedicated to St Juliana (or Iliana), an Anatolian martyr under Diocletian whose remains have lain here since the 6th century, and who gave her name to the town; the monks who built the cloister for themselves owned most of the town and ran its affairs until the 1400s. The church has a fine weather-beaten façade, rebuilt in the 1700s with bits and pieces of the Romanesque original tacked on; inside, the impressive altar is made of silver from Mexico—plenty of the *hidalgos*' younger sons went off to America to make their fortune, and many of the family mansions in the village are *casas de indianos*. There is a beautiful cloister, with capitals carved with biblical and hunting scenes (*open 9–1 and 4–7.30; adm*).

The ticket to the cloister will also get you into the **Museo Diocesano** (*across town near the parking lot; open 10–1 and 4–7*) installed in the 17th-century **Convento de Regina Coeli**, Gothic in style, displaying an exceptional collection of ecclesiastical artefacts from all over Cantabria, some of Templar origin, and all perfectly restored by the nuns. In the eloquent **Plaza Ramón Pelayo**, the tower house of Don Borja holds one more museum, **Cantabria y la Mar en la Historia**, devoted to the region's seafaring past, and making up in a way for the town's anomalous name 'del Mar' when it's actually 3km from the sea. On the same plaza stands the **Ayuntamiento**, rebuilt in 1770, and from the same century, the Palacio de Barreda-Bracho, now the Parador Gil Blas. Fifteen or so years ago, residents of Santillana still kept cattle on the ground floors of their homes and sold delicious rich milk by the glass and tasty *bizcocho* (cake) by the piece to tourists. You'll see less of that today, but there are still plenty of souvenirs to buy. Fox tails seem to be in fashion. If you're in a hurry to get to the promised Mar, the closest beaches are at **Suances**, just 5km away; it's a fishing village and a small resort, though the sea here isn't the cleanest.

The Caves of Altamira

From Santillana you can walk up to Altamira in 20 minutes, though don't expect to get in unless you've written years in advance (Centro de Investigación de Altamira, Santillana del Mar, Santander ✉ 39330) and are one of the 20 chosen ones permitted the 15-minute glimpse at one of the sublime masterpieces of Upper Palaeolithic art. Still, an extraordinary number of people show up at the caves almost with the fervour of pilgrims to pay homage to the genius of the artists of *c.* 12,000 BC, who covered the undulating ceiling with stunningly exuberant, vividly coloured paintings of bison, horses, boars and stags. Only at Lascaux, up at the northern end of the Franco-Cantabrian arc of Magdalenian cave painting, will you find such powerful, masterful technique; the movement and strength in the coiled, startled and galloping bisons, the attentive deer, the frisking horses are simply awesome. As they say, 'This is the infancy of art, not an art of infancy.'

The story of the discovery of Altamira, however, is a parable of perceptions. As at Lascaux, an ancient landslide sealed the entrance of the caves and tunnels (and more or less vacuum-packed the paintings) until it was rediscovered by a hunter and his dog in 1868. In 1875, Don Marcelino de Sautuola, an amateur prehistorian, was intrigued by the black drawings on the walls in the outer rooms, and over the years explored them, in 1879 taking his nine-year-old daughter María along. The child wandered a little deeper into the caves, and lifted her eyes to the superb polychrome paintings. Although no one had ever seen the like, the Marquis at once recognized the ceiling for what it was: a ravishing work of genius from the Stone Age. Excited, he published a description of Altamira but, rather than receiving the expected response of awe and wonder from the 'experts' in the field, de Sautuola was mocked, ridiculed, viciously attacked, and even accused of forging the paintings; the scholars simply refused to believe that people who used stone axes were capable of painting, one of the 'civilized arts'. Undaunted, the Marquis held his ground, insisting Altamira was for real and died heartbroken in 1888, vilified and as forgotten as the caves themselves. Fifteen years later, the discovery of a dozen painted caves in the Vézère valley in the Dordogne led to a change of mind, beginning in 1902 with one expert, E.Cartailhac, making a public apology to de Sautuola's memory in his *Mea Culpa d'un Sceptique*. Although the 'white disease' caused by the moisture in the breath of visitors has restricted admission to the caves, you can do the next best thing at Altamira—see the video and photos in the fascinating **museum** (*open 10–1 and 4–6, closed Sun; adm*) installed on the site. You can also explore a small stalactite cave which is prettily lit to emphasize nature's wonders as compensation for the inaccessibility of the more fragile works of man.

Comillas, with a Little Modernista Madness

Definitely *the* place to be on this stretch of the coast, the seaside resort of Comillas offers a bit of Catalan quirkiness in a gorgeous setting, framed by two endearing beaches—the **Playa Comillas** just below town and the longer **Playa de Oyambre**, a 20-minute walk away. Comillas' old town, with its rough cobbled streets and arcaded mansions, has been a quiet watering-hole for the Madrid and Barcelona aristocracy for a long time; the latter brought along their favourite architects in the 19th century to add a *modernista* flair.

The Instant Marquis

 The Spain of the Industrial Revolution is a land not very well known, but if the nation's capitalists never could match the mills of the Midlands or Massachusetts in the 19th century they certainly produced some marvels, and some incredible robber-baron careers. Antonio López was a local boy who went off to Cuba and made a fortune in shipping and slaves (slavery wasn't abolished in Spanish-run Cuba until 1886), and then moved out and made another pile running a monopoly: the Philippine National Tobacco Company. He came back home and purchased the title of Marquis of Comillas. The new Marquis' son married the daughter of Joan Güell, the richest man in Barcelona, who had also started in Cuba and ended up as Spain's biggest textile magnate. If the name is familiar, you're thinking of Antoni Gaudí's famous surreal Güell Park in Barcelona. Like Cosimo de' Medici in old Florence, this robber baron had a talented aesthete to succeed him, whose sponsorship of Gaudí sparked the golden age of *modernista* architecture in Catalunya. It was the Güell connection that brought Gaudí to Cantabria, where he helped with the López family palace in 1878 and came back to build El Capricho in 1883. The centre of the López interests was Barcelona, where they ran factories, banks and the Trasatlántica shipping line (which later fell into the grasp of the greatest of all Spanish robber barons, Juan March, and still runs most of the Spanish island ferries). The Lópezes lived on the Ramblas in Barcelona, but they spent their summers here,

bringing along their Catalan friends and making Comillas a genteel upper-class resort; locals called them the 'Trasatlánticos'. López's castle-like summer mansion, on the hill overlooking the town, was one of the most spectacular private homes in its day, and the centre of the glittering social season Comillas knew at the turn of the century. But modern capitalist glories never seem to last more than a generation or two, and today López's palace stands as empty, weird and forlorn as *Citizen Kane*'s Xanadu.

The peculiar legacies of the robber barons are up on the hills to the west of the village centre. A walk up a garden path takes you to Gaudí's **El Capricho**, built for a relation of the Marquis', and recently restored and pressed into service as a restaurant (*see* below). If not one of the architect's more ambitious works, it is an utterly delightful house, exciting the envy of the crowd of Spanish tourists usually milling about it. The main feature is an eccentric, perfectly non-functional tower, half-lighthouse and half-minaret.

Next to El Capricho you can have a peek through an iron gate at the **summer palace of the Marqués de Comillas** though a better view can be had from the main coastal road leaving the village. A work of another Catalan, Gaudí's friend Joan Martorell, this ponderous palace in a quirky *modernista* neo-Gothic is protected by an imitation castle wall with oubliettes. Next to it, the Marquis' **chapel** adds the perfect touch of discreet surrealism to the ensemble. The third member of this singular trio stands on the opposite hill, across the main road through Comillas, but it commands the views for miles around. The **Universidad Pontificia** (*open daily 9–3; adm*) begun in 1883, with a plan by Martorell and some financial help from Antonio López. The sumptuous main building was decorated by a third major figure of Catalan modernism, Lluis Domènech i Montaner, who also created the wonderfully florid **Monument to Antonio López**.

San Vicente de la Barquera, the next resort to the west, is still as much a fishing port as a holiday retreat, though it's hugely popular with Madrileños in summer—you won't find a place to park your car. Marvellously sited on a hill in the last elbow-bend of the wide and marshy Río Escudo (arriving on the coastal road from the west provides the best view), it is linked by a long causeway to the eastern coast, near the town beach. The older, upper town is dominated by the rose-coloured parish church **Nuestra Señora de los Ángeles**, a 13th-century transitional work containing the finely sculpted Renaissance tomb of the Inquisitor Antonio Corro. Below, interwoven branches of plane trees add a French touch to the main plaza. Every quarter of an hour the bell tower of the church San Vicente booms out a recording of the first phrase of Schubert's *Ave María*, guaranteed to drive you nuts. The locals claim an enemy of their town had it installed—with any luck it will be a bad memory by the time you get there.

Where to Stay and Eating Out

Santillana ✉ 39330

At the top of the list there's the wonderfully atmospheric ★★★**Parador Gil Blas** on Pza. Pelayo 11, ✆ 942 81 80 00, 🖷 942 81 83 95 (*expensive*), with medieval rooms; reserve well in advance in season, and request a room on the first or second floor. A good second choice, ★★★**Hotel Altamira**, on C/ Cantón 1, ✆ 942 81 80 25 (*expensive–moderate*) is installed in another palace nearby, with a patio and garden. Both have elegant dining-rooms, especially the *parador*. For something *moderate*, try **Conde Duque**, ✆ 942 81 83 36, ✉ 942 84 01 70, in a restored medieval building with its own parking. Ask at the tourist office for a list of *casas particulares*, though many of them are in the newer suburbs en route to Altamira; or else, head for C/ Los Hornos or Avda. Le Dorat, which have plenty of rooms. **Camping Santillana**, ✆ 942 81 82 50, just north of the village, is one of the pricier camp sites in this area, but it has all the amenities including a pool and tennis courts.

The restaurant of the **Altamira** may be the best in town, with big plates of roast meats (and some seafood). If you happen to be in Santillana at the weekend you can feast on local and mountain specialities—everything from *fabada* to grilled *langostinos* (craw-fish) at **Los Blasones**, Pza. de la Gándara 8, ✆ 942 81 80 70, for *1500 or 2500 pts*, or at **La Robleda**, C/ Revolgo, ✆ 942 81 83 36, for a little less; otherwise there are good tapas and reasonably priced meals in the bar nearest the Colegiata.

Comillas ✉ 39520

The ★★★**Casal del Castro**, San Jerónimo, ✆ 942 72 00 36, ✉ 942 72 00 61 (*expensive–moderate*) is in the centre of town in a fine old building with a pretty garden and rooms. *Open April–mid-Sept.* The ★★**Hs Esmeralda**, C/ Antonio López 7, ✆ 942 72 00 97 (*moderate*) is a good second choice close to the beach. Alternatively, try ★**Fuente Real**, C/ Sobrellano 19, ✆ 942 72 01 55 (*inexpensive*). The tourist office has a list of *casas particulares* for something cheaper.

Comillas is the only place where you can dine in a building by Gaudí, in **El Capricho de Gaudí**, Barrio de Sobrellano, ✆ 942 72 03 65 (*expensive*). The interior, if not entirely as the master planned it, has been beautifully restored. The food is a work of art as well, mostly seafood with a *nouvelle cuisine* touch; the *4000 pts menu* is a bargain. Ring ahead as it's usually booked solid in season. Just outside the grounds, the **Fuente Real**, with its ancient sign and décor of *azulejo* tiles, has been a favourite for well over a century, a cheerful seafood place with outside tables (*1200 pts menu*). **Adolfo**, Pso. Garelli s/n, ✆ 942 72 20 14, is another good choice with traditional cooking for a few more *pesetas*.

San Vicente de la Baquera ✉ 39540

The modern ★★★ **Miramar**, Paseo de la Barquera 20, ✆ 942 71 00 75, has great views of the bay and the Picos de Europa; the restaurant sits you in the spot to enjoy the vista. ★★**Luzón**, Ctra. Santander-Oviedo, ✆ 942 71 00 50 (*moderate*) is a solid, square stone inn smack in the centre of town facing the tidal basin. ★**La Paz** nearby on C/ del Mercado 28, ✆ 942 71 01 80 (*inexpensive*) has recently been remodelled and offers stylish, if bathless, rooms. **Camping El Rosal**, ✆ 942 71 01 65, is conveniently located near the beaches, on the main road just outside San Vicente. As for dinner, expect more seafood, notably at a place called **Boga-Boga**, Pza. José Antonio, ✆ 942 71 01 35 (*expensive*), where the award-winning chef turns out the sort of Cantabrian recipes you've never imagined: red peppers stuffed with *langostinos*, for instance. For a less serious seafood attack, you can do well for *3500 pts* at **Maruja** on Avd. Generalísimo s/n, ✆ 942 71 00 77.

They are not the highest mountains in Spain, or even in the Cantabrian-Pyrenean *cordillera*, but the Picos de Europa have a certain cachet. So many peaks, packed closely together in a small area, make a memorable landmark for Spain's northern coast. No one knows where the name came from, though it may have been that these mountains, visible far out to sea, were the first sight of the continent for Atlantic sailors. To the Asturians they are known as the Urrieles. Thank Asturian ecologists for their efforts in keeping Spain's most beautiful mountains enchanting and unspoiled: what development there is (ski resorts, hotels) is in western Cantabria and northern León. The Picos are divided by rivers into three tremendous massifs— **Andara**, mostly in Cantabria, **Urrieles**, in the middle, and **Cornión**, to the west. The highest peak, Torre de Cerredo, stands 8606ft—not all that much as mountains go. But for sheer beauty and rugged grandeur, for the contrast of tiny rural villages in fertile green valleys against a backdrop of sheer, twisted stone peaks crested with snow the year round, the Picos de Europa are hard to beat.

The range seems to have been dropped from heaven, especially for hikers; there are trails for Sunday walkers and sheer cliffs for serious alpinists. Hiking boots, however, are universally recommended because of frequent patches of loose shale on the trails and slopes. If you're going for an extended holiday in the Picos, get the detailed maps published by the Federación Española de Montañismo, generally available at Potes, the main base for visiting the mountains. The guide *Picos de Europa* by Robin Collomb (West Col, Reading) is a great help, and up-to-date detailed information on guides, itineraries and mountain *refugios* (free overnight shelters) is available from the **Federación Asturiana de Montañismo**, C/ Melquiades Álvarez 16, Oviedo, ✆ 942 21 10 99.

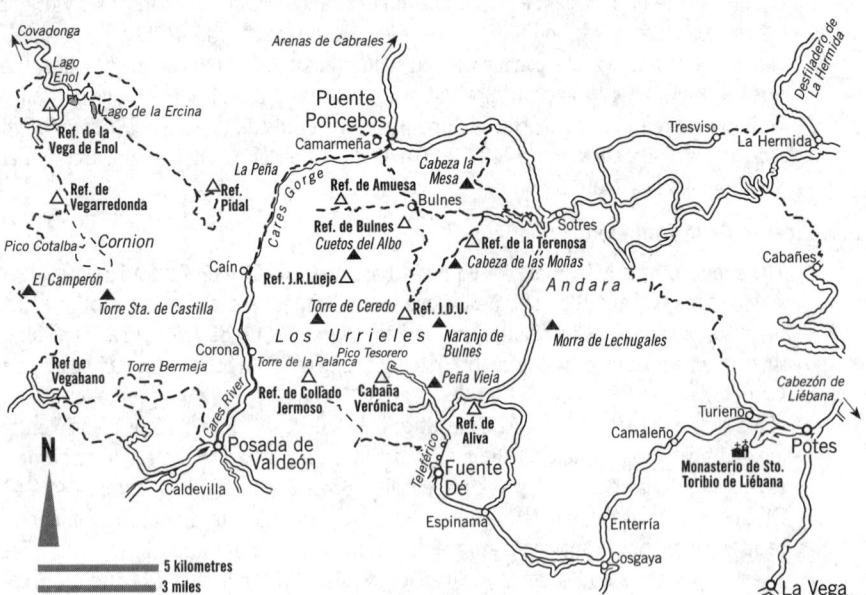

Hiking in the Picos is practical only from the end of May to October, but even then you may get a soaking—the Picos are only 32km from the rainy Atlantic seaboard. Bring warm clothes and a lightweight plastic poncho, a sleeping bag and food for nights in the refuges, and a pair of binoculars to take in the wonderful array of wildlife and birds.

Getting Around

By bus: There are two buses (one in the winter) daily between Santander and León that stop at Potes and Lebeña; departures are more frequent from Unquera (five buses daily to Potes). From Potes there are three buses from the central square to Fuente Dé and the *teleférico*; jeeps make the link between the upper station of the *teleférico* to the refugio de Aliva if you're not up to the walk. Also, a stable in Turieno next to Potes offers several guided riding excursions in the Picos. If you want to do it yourself, *Viajes Wences* and other firms in Potes rent mountain bikes. There are daily buses between Arenas and Cangas along the northern rim of the Picos, and a Land Rover connection between Arenas and Poncebos. Cangas itself may be reached once daily by bus from Riaño; there are also a couple of buses daily from Oviedo to Cangas and Covadonga.

Posada de Valdeón is most easily reached from León, via Riaño or Portilla de La Reina (once a day).

Tourist Information

Unquera: (Val de San Vicente) Residencial Tina Mayor, ✆ 942 71 72 82.

Potes: C/ Independencia s/n, ✆ 942 73 07 87 (for more detailed information and maps try Bustamente's on central Pza. Capitán Palacios, an excellent source for all books on the area—everything from hiking trails to works by Beato de Liébana).

Arenas de Cabrales: Ctra. General, ✆ 985 84 52 84.

There are **markets** in Unquera on Tuesdays and in Potes on Mondays.

Potes and the Valley of Liébana

The eastern mountains of the Picos are the most visited and the most accessible. The main entrance from the coast begins at **Unquera** (a FEVE stop on the coast to the west of San Vicente de la Barquera); the N621 from here climbs up through the **Desfiladero de La Hermida**, a dramatic, high, narrow gorge walling in the River Deva, and the tiny hamlet of **La Hermida**. The road climbs up from here into the idyllic little valley around the town of **Lebeña**, with its parish church—the 10th-century Mozarabic **Santa María**—signposted south of the village on the N62. This is one of the finest pre-Romanesque churches, a little jewel in the middle of nowhere that is the perfect expression of the strange little mountainous state of Asturias and, perhaps, its dreams of future greatness.

Two venerable companions, an olive and yew tree, stand next to the church; they were both planted at the time the church was built—over a thousand years ago. **Potes**, the capital of the Valley of Liébana, is the metropolis of the Picos, where you can garner information, catch buses, change travellers' cheques and stock up on supplies. For all the tourist traffic Potes is still a gracious town, with stone arcades to shelter the cafés on the main street and a warren of medieval lanes behind. There are also a number of jeep excursions on offer. The main monument in Potes itself is the 15th-century **Torre del Infantado**, a massive, square defensive-residential work in the centre of town.

The most popular excursions from Potes include the 4km trip up to the **Monasterio de Santo Toribio de Liébana**. Don't miss it, because this is the only place in Cantabria where a visit will earn you an indulgence—time off from purgatory. It is a long-established pilgrimage site, allegedly the home of the world's largest chunk of the True Cross. In its earliest days the monastery was ruled by the Abbot Beato de Liébana, whose *Commentaries on the Apocalypse* were popular in Spain throughout the Middle Ages: in the cloister here you can see a full set of copies of one of them—mad and brilliant pictorial prophecies from an age when people were convinced the world would soon be meeting its end. The nearby **mirador de Santo Toribio** takes in splendid views over the Andara massif. Another, longer, walk south will take you through **Cabezón de Liébana**, where some of the houses have coats of arms, and two medieval bridges cross over to the lovely church of **Santa María de Piasca**, built in 1172 with fine Romanesque carvings on the capitals within. The monastery was shared by monks and nuns, which was typical for the mountains but unusual elsewhere.

From Fuente Dé to Arenas de Cabrales

The classic excursion from Potes is to take the bus west up to the stunning old village of **Espinama** and, 1.6km beyond, to **Fuente Dé**. Here you can catch the *teleférico* for an awesome, vertigo-inducing ride 2568ft up the sheer cliff to the **mirador del Cable** (*the teleférico runs daily, July–Sept 9–8 ; adm; in peak season, arrive very early or you'll get stuck waiting, maybe for hours*). Once at the top, walk 4km up to the **Refugio de Aliva**, a popular modern version of the old mountain refuge; a path from here leads down to Espinama—a pleasant day's circuit. From Espinama, you can make a longer, more serious hike through the eastern and central massifs north to **Sotres**, a good day's work (jeep excursions also available from Espinama). The landmark near here, in the Central Massif of the Urrieles, is **Naranjo de Bulnes** (Pico Urriello on some maps), a distinct sheer-sided, tower-like pinnacle, loved and hated by daredevil alpinists. From Sotres, a long day's hiking will bring you to **Arenas de Cabrales**, renowned for its stinking mountain cheese, and the most important village in the region, with buses to Cangas and Land Rovers to **Poncebos** (*see* below).

The Divine Gorge

Between Poncebos and Caín, the **Cares Gorge** (better known as simply the 'Garganta Divina') extends north to south across the Picos. It is a spectacular 26km walk over sheer drops down to the Río Cares, made relatively easy by a footpath sculpted into the mountainside. The classic approach is from **Caín** in the south, itself linked to civilization (i.e. the fine mountain village of **Posada de Valdeón**) by a regular four-wheel-drive service. Walking south from Poncebos isn't much more strenuous—but you risk either spending the night in Caín, which has no lodgings, or walking the 9km further south to sleep in Posada. Other possible walks from Poncebos are to **Camarmeña** and **Bulnes**, two of the most remote villages in the Picos. Bulnes has a *refugio*; both villages have knockout views of the Naranjo de Bulnes. The aforementioned Posada de Valdeón is the chief village of the **Valley of Valdeón**, highest in the Picos and a serenely magnificent place to rest up in before or after the Cares Gorge; here tiny farming villages and their rustic granaries, or *hórreos,* built on stilts to protect their contents from moisture and mice, look like mere toys under the loftiest mountains in the Picos. One of the most stupendous views of these is from the **Mirador del Tombo**, 1.6km from Posada. The **Chorco de los Lobos** nearby was used to trap the mountains' most fearsome predator, the now rare wolf.

It may be paradise for hikers, but there's no need to rough it. Nearly every village in the Picos has at least one *casa particular* or *fonda* or a place to camp, and you can purchase supplies or dine out in a traditional restaurant. Every village has its specialities, and the shops under the arches on the main street of Potes are treasurehouses of the mountains' finest; you can purchase local cheeses (especially *cabrales*) and charcuterie, honey in various original flavours and especially *orujo*, the clear Cantabrian firewater sold in dangerous-looking little bottles all over town. It's made from grape stems after the wine harvest, like French *marc* or Italian *grappa*.

Potes ✉ 39570

Potes has by far the most in the way of accommodation. The top of the line is the ****Picos de Valdecoro**, at C/ Roscabao, ✆ 942 73 00 25, ✎ 942 73 03 15, and the modern, stone-built ****Infantado**, on the Fuente Dé road, ✆ 942 73 09 39, ✎ 942 73 05 78 (*both moderate*). The small ****Pico de Europa**, C/ San Roque 6, ✆ 942 73 00 05, ✎ 942 73 20 60, is run by a friendly, knowledgeable fellow whose son studied culinary arts with the famous master Juan Mari Arzak and prepares excellent meals in the hotel restaurant. The budget choice, ****Hs La Serna**, C/ La Serna 9, ✆ 942 73 09 24, has the only rooms with bath for *under 3500 pts* in town; ****Hs Rubio**, C/ San Roque 31, ✆ 942 73 00 15, is slightly more expensive, but has rooms in an attractively restored village house. **Camping El Molino**, 9km south of Potes at La Vega, ✆ 942 73 04 89, offers *inexpensive* sites in a pleasant setting. For dinner, **Camacho** has an honest *1000 pts* menu including *fabada*, trout and other local treats.

Fuente Dé ✉ 39588

Since 1965, the magnificently sited *****Parador Río Deva**, ✆ 942 73 66 51, ✎ 942 73 66 54 (*expensive–moderate*), has been a part of the Picos experience. A modern building at the end of the *teleférico*, many of its rooms have grand views; the hotel organizes jeep excursions up into the peaks, and its restaurant specializes in mountain dishes. (*2500 pts menu*). You could do just as well, immersed in equally stunning mountain scenery, at the modern *****Hotel del Oso**, ✆ 942 73 30 18 or the beautiful stone original ****Del Oso Pardo**, 10km east at Cosgaya: both owned by the Rivas family, ✆ 942 73 04 18, ✎ 942 73 01 36 (*both moderate*). A bonus is the superb mountain cuisine: try the trout and cheese cake (*tarta de queso*) or the *3000 pts menu*.

Espinama ✉ 39500

About 7.5km up from Espinama, the **Refugio de Aliva** has a restaurant and 24 rooms available on a first-come, first-served basis (*inexpensive*). Ring in advance, ✆ 942 73 09 99. A Land Rover from Espinama will take you up (for other *refugios* in the Picos, ask at the Potes tourist office). *Open 15 June–30 Sept.*

Posada de Valdeón ✉ 24915

Posada has several *casas particulares*, some fine *fondas* and the ****Hs Abascal**, El Salvador, ✆ 987 74 05 07. (*2000 pts.*)

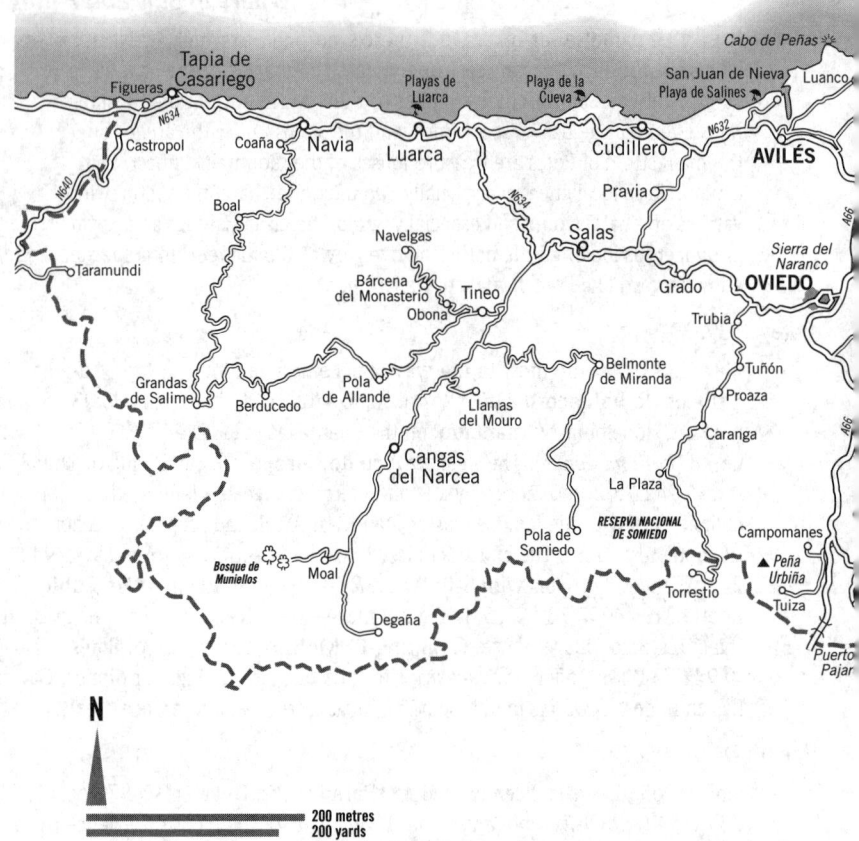

N

200 metres
200 yards

Asturias

The Principality of Asturias is the Spanish Wales, a rugged country of mines, stupendous mountains and a romantically beautiful coastline. The inhabitants have traditionally been a hardy lot, beginning with the Iberian tribe of Astures who gave their name to the province and defied both the Romans and Visigoths. Yet the proudest date in Asturian history is 718, when a band of Visigoths, led by the legendary Pelayo, defeated the Moors in the misty mountain glen of Covadonga, officially beginning the Reconquista and founding the first tiny Christian kingdom in Muslim Iberia. Their beautiful churches are Asturias's chief artistic patrimony; the language they spoke, *el Bable*, or 'Babel', survives only as a dialect against the modern dominance of Castilian, its direct descendant. Since the 14th century, the Spanish heir-apparent has borne the title of 'Prince of Asturias', a practice initiated by John of Gaunt when his daughter married the son of Juan I. Not long after John of Gaunt's day, Asturias fell into an obscurity that lasted centuries. The discovery of iron ore and coal in the 19th century rapidly

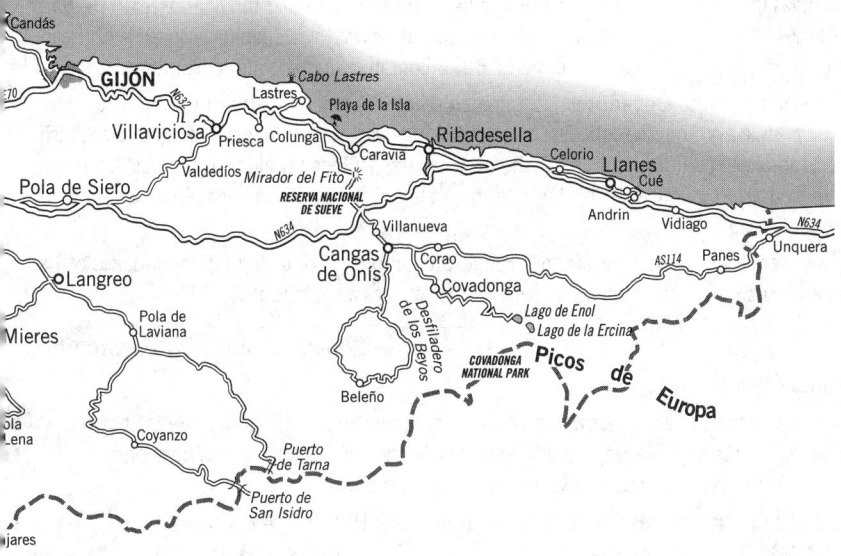

transformed its traditional agricultural economy into a mining one with radical tendencies. These brought about the second great date in Asturian history: an epic miners' revolt in October 1934.

The modern autonomous region of Asturias is in its quiet way one of the most progressive in Spain. One of the last areas to be touched by tourism, it is fighting to maintain its integrity and environment against big developers who would exploit the magnificent Picos de Europa and the coast; instead, Asturias would have you stay in a rural village, to learn something of its culture and architecture. In 1985, the Asturian wildlife protection fund received the European Preservation of Nature (FAPAS) prize for its efforts to preserve the rare Cantabrian bear and the capercaillie from extinction. At least once, visit an old Asturian *chigre* or *sidrería* to taste the local poison 'sidra' (cider)—natural but dangerous stuff always poured at arm's length to give it the proper bounce. If you drink enough of it, it even begins to taste good.

The Asturian Side of the Picos de Europa: Cangas and Covadonga

The salmon-filled Río Sella defines the west edge of the western Massif de Cornión, which in its northernmost reaches forms part of **Covadonga National Park**. Most easily reached from Ribadesella on the Asturian coast, or through the stunning narrow gorge **Desfiladero de los Beyos** (N625) from León and Riaño, the region lacks the high drama of the mountains further east, but is nonetheless green and tranquil, and for Spaniards constitutes a pilgrimage.

Cangas de Onís claims to be the first capital of Christian Spain, where the Asturian kings set up shop right after their victory at nearby Covadonga. The most beautiful things in Cangas de

Onís are the high **medieval bridge** (erroneously called 'Roman') with its great arch spanning the Río Sella, and the **Capilla de Santa Cruz**, where the kings worshipped. It was built over a dolmen, and according to legend its founder was Favila, the successor of Pelayo. The original building may really be as early as the 5th century, though it was completely rebuilt in the 15th.

From Cangas it's 3km north to **Villanueva**, where Alfonso I founded the **Monasterio de San Pedro** in 746. Now deserted, it has a 12th-century doorway, with capitals carved with bear-hunting scenes. East of Cangas, the **cave of Buxu** contains rare paleolithic paintings.

From here it's 10km to **Covadonga**, dominated by an enormous 19th-century basilica. Here Pelayo, son-in-law of Roderick, the last Visigothic king, and 300 followers managed to ambush a small Moorish expedition and defeat them, according to legend. Next to the basilica is the **cave** where Pelayo fought with his back to the wall and now rests in peace in a sarcophagus next to his wife.

From Covadonga it's a beautiful 20km through the national park to the mountain lakes of **La Ercina** and **Enol**, with the huge Peña Santa mountains as a backdrop.

Where to Stay and Eating Out

Cangas de Onís ✉ 33550

Cangas has pricey hotels and a score of *hostales* where the going rate is about *6000 pts* in high season, considerably less the rest of the year; one central one is the ★**Piloña**, De San Pelayo 19, ✆ 985 84 80 88.

Lucky souls can get one of the four rooms at ★**El Sella**, Avda. Castilla, ✆ 985 84 80 11 (*inexpensive*), which also offers a decent restaurant with a *1500 pts menu*. For something more substantial, *fabada* and other Asturian dishes are to be had at **Casa Juan**, Avda. de Covadonga (*moderate*).

Covadonga ✉ 33589

Accommodation is scarce; there's the ★★★**Hotel Pelayo**, ✆ 985 84 60 61, ✆ 985 84 60 54, basic and perhaps a bit overpriced (*expensive in season, otherwise moderate*), and a number of bars and restaurants that hang out camas signs along the main road.

The restaurant **La Cabaña**, out on the road to Covadonga, ✆ 985 84 82 84 (*moderate*) is in an old stone house decorated in traditional Asturian style, serving winter warmers such as *cabritu asado*, or roast kid, together with some seafood dishes. *Closed Thurs.*

Hospedería del Peregrino, 200m below the sanctuary in Covadonga, ✆ 985 84 60 47 (*moderate*), has a well-deserved name for its *fabada*, seafood and mountain dishes which include freshly caught salmon.

The Asturian 'Costa Verde': East to West

Although the Picos attract mountaineers and hikers from all over the world, the very attractive coast of Asturias sees relatively few foreigners. There are over 50 sandy beaches, most of them on unmarked roads just off the main coastal N632; some have spectacular locations, and a few can offer relative peace and quiet even in the middle of August. It's a mountainous and rugged coast for the most part, and the lack of a good road along it (until recently) has kept development to a minimum.

By train and bus: FEVE trains along the coast take in much of the marvellous scenery. Five trains a day run between Santander and Oviedo, with stops at Unquera, Colombres, the beaches at Nueva and Villaharmes and Ribadesella. To continue up the coast from here you'll have to take a Gijón-bound bus. FEVE has frequent connections between Gijón and Avilés, and west to Cudillero, Luarca, Soto de Luiña and Ortigueira. ALSA buses link all these towns with Oviedo as well, while RENFE links Gijón with Oviedo, Madrid, Barcelona and the rest of the peninsula.

By car: Turning the old N632 along the coast into a reasonable route has been the biggest road project in this part of the country for some years. Most of it is already finished, and getting around is not a problem—except perhaps for some tight and twisty stretches between Cudillero and Luarca.

Tourist Information

Llanes: Alfonso IX, La Torre ✆ 985 40 01 64.
Ribadesella: Ctra. Piconera, ✆ 985 86 00 38.
Villaviciosa: Parque Vallina, ✆ 985 89 17 59.
Gijón: C/ Marqués de San Esteban 1, ✆ 985 34 60 46.
Avilés: Ruiz Gómez 21, ✆ 985 54 43 25.

There are markets in Llanes on Tues; in Ribadesella and Villaviciosa on Wed; and in Avilés on Mon.

Llanes to Villavciosa

This eastern section of the coast is well endowed with beaches and quiet coves, especially around Llanes, a lively resort with good beaches nearby. East of Llanes, near Vidiago and the **Playa de France**, there's a peculiar Bronze Age monument called **Peña-Tú** or the 'Cabeza del Gentil' (the gentile's head). Even older are the cave drawings in the **Cueva del Pindal** near Colombres (*open Wed–Sun 9.30–1 and 3–5.30; adm; guided tours in Spanish although guide speaks good English*). **Ribadesella**, at the mouth of the meandering Río Sella, makes an excellent base for forays along the coast or into the western Picos. Split in two by the river and bridge, with a picture-postcard backdrop of mountains, Ribadesella has a handful of old streets, a long protected beach, and plenty of chances for hiking, pony trekking, canoeing and fishing. The beaches lie just across the Sella to the west of town. Just outside town are the stalactitic **Tito Bustillo Caves** (*open 10–1 and 3.30–5.15, sometimes closed weekends*), where some 15–20,000 years ago the residents painted the walls with stylish animals and humans in the Altamira fashion, worth a visit although their sienna, purple and black tones have faded.

Further west, into what is officially known as the Costa Verde, you'll find quiet beaches in the tiny hamlets of **Caravia** (Baja and Alta), and near **Colunga**: **La Isla**, **La Griega** and **Lastres**. Equally renowned for its clams and *sidra*, Lastres's stack of red-tile-roofed houses and noble mansions overlooks one of Asturias' most picturesque fishing harbours. Some rare Asturian horses, descendants of the hardy creatures used by the Romans for mountain duty, survive in the **Reserva Nacional de Sueve**, 3km south of Colunga, where you'll also find the **Mirador del Fito** with splendid views of the Picos de Europa and the coast.

Apple orchards line the coast around **Villaviciosa**, the cider capital of Asturias, set at the mouth of a deep *ría*. Villaviciosa was the first town in Spain to see the face of their new king, Charles V, who was sailing to Santander from his home in Flanders and was blown off course. Some of Asturias' best churches lie in the vicinity: the Romanesque **San Juan de Amandi** is noted for its beautiful sculpture with graceful geometric patterns on the portal and capitals.

Valdedios, nine km southwest, was the religious centre of the region, and has two ecclesiastical gems: the oratory of **San Salvador**, built in 893 by Alfonso III and the 11th-century basilica of **Santa María** (better known as El Conventín). When it's time for a swim, there are two beaches near Villaviciosa to choose from: long **Rodiles**, and **Tazones**, a picturesque fishing village across the *ría*.

Where to Stay and Eating Out

Llanes ✉ 33500

Most hotels and restaurants are spread along the beaches, such as ★★★**Montemar**, C/ Jenaro Riestra, ✆ 985 40 01 00 (*moderate*), with modern, comfortable rooms with all amenities. At the same rate, though, you can stay in a 17th-century palace in Llanes itself: ★★★**Don Paco**, Parque Posada Herrera, ✆ 985 40 01 50 (*high moderate*). It's quiet, with a small garden, and the main hall of the mansion is now an elegant restaurant, serving mostly seafood (*3500 pts*).

Less expensively, there is another hotel with four rooms in a pleasant old house: ★★**Hs Los Barquitos**, C/ La Concepción on the eastern edge of town, ✆ 985 40 26 12 (*moderate*). Both Llanes and the villages near the beaches have plenty of inexpensive *hostales*, such as the good-value ★**Hs Migal**, ✆ 985 40 12 01, in the pretty village of Cué. In Ribadedeva, some 18km east of Llanes, there is the ★★★ **Mirador de la Franca**, Playa de la Franca, on the 634 (E70), ✆ 985 41 21 45, ✉ 985 41 21 53 (*expensive–moderate*), a comfortable place with restaurant and tennis court, beside a fine beach.

The best places for dinner, as always on the coast, are on the harbour; **Mirentxu**, a bit classier than the others, does the seafood Basque-style for about *2500 pts*; in season there are also some wonderful instant restaurants, nothing more than a shelter and a few tables, where you can get anything finned at bargain rates. A few kilometres outside Llanes is the popular **Casa Moran**, at Puente Nuevo, on the road from Posada to Robadella, ✆ 985 40 74 85 (*moderate*), with a traditional menu featuring items like *fabada asturiana* and roast lamb. *Closed Tues.*

Ribadesella ✉ 33560

Ribadesella has more accommodation than most villages around the coast, and you can choose the posh, air-conditioned, beach-side splendour of the ★★★★**Gran Hotel del Sella**, La Playa, ✆ 985 86 01 50 (*expensive–moderate*), with a pool, tennis courts and garden—a bit of Costa del Sol luxury on the Atlantic. *Open April–Sept.* Two moderate-priced *hostales* offer rooms and delicious food: the ★★**Hs Apolo**, by the beach on C/ Gral. Franco, ✆ 985 86 04 42, with bathless doubles for 3200 pts and good *inexpensive* seafood; and the ★**Hs El Pilar**, near the bridge, ✆ 985 86 04 46, with tennis, garden and spiffier rooms; the restaurant features Asturian home-cooking (*both moderate*). The ★★**Boston**, C/ El Pico 7, ✆ 985 86 09 66, has off-season doubles with bath for *4000 pts.*

Possibly Ribadesella's best restaurant, **Bohemia**, Gran Via, ✆ 985 86 11 50 (*moderate*) offers plenty of seafood but also a chance at something else for a change, in dishes such as the *entrecôte* with *cabrales* cheese. For tapas and cider, the place to go is the noisy and convivial **Sidrería Corasceo** facing the harbour.

Lastres ✉ 33330

This growing resort can still be your best bet for a peaceful place to while away a few days. There are *casas particulares* and rooms over bars, along with the ★★★**Halcón Palace**, C/ Cofiño Arriondas, ✆ 985 84 13 12 (*moderate*), a new hotel in a restored 18th-century mansion located in the hamlet of Cofiño up in the hills with sea views.

Villaviciosa ✉ 33300

It may be away from the beaches, but Villaviciosa can provide an agreeable night's stay, especially at **La Casona de Amandi**, out in the country at Amandi, ✆ 985 98 01 30 (*expensive*), a *casa de indiano* (a house built by a returned emigrant to the Americas); today it is a thoroughly charming eight-room hotel in a lovely formal garden. The owners were antique dealers, and the rooms are decorated with their finds. Good if modest choices in town include the ★**Carlos I**, Pza. Carlos I, ✆ 985 89 01 21, and the ★**Manquín**, Pza. Santa Carla, ✆ 985 89 05 06 (*both moderate*). The latter has quiet rooms and a restaurant that occupies a pretty square with a fountain; seafood and properly poured cider for *2500 pts.* The **Sol**, C/ Sol, ✆ 985 89 11 30, has plenty of soul indeed, provided by an ancient proprietor, a former guitarist, who stands at his bar and plays 1930s jazz records all day (he can talk about them all day too); very nice rooms at bargain rates.

Gijón

With some 250,000 people, Gijón—*Xixón* in Asturian dialect—is the largest city in the Principado, a gritty hardworking port that also offers long beaches. A major industrial centre, it had to be almost totally rebuilt after the Nationalists devastated it in the Civil War. The centre of town occupies the isthmus leading to the newer quarters; there you will find the enclosed and arcaded **Plaza Mayor**, surrounded with cafés and restaurants. Behind it are the recently discovered **termas romanas**, some ruins including part of a 2nd-century baths complex, notable for its under-floor hypocaustal central heating. This is the start of the main beach, the **Playa de San Lorenzo**. In the new town, the **Museo del Pueblo de Asturias** displays a host of bagpipes from Celtic northwestern Spain and around the world, as well as a workshop (*Mon–Sat 10–1 and 5–8, Sun and hols 11–2; adm*). Adjacent is a **Museo Etnográfico** (*same hours*) where you can learn how to make cider in the traditional way, and what *horreos* (raised granaries) are used for.

Up the headland is the pretty fishing port of **Candás**, an old tuna-fishing village famous for its *corridas marineras*— bullfights in a flooded ring that are unique in Spain. **Luanco**, just up the coast, had similar beginnings, but has now become much more of a resort.

Avilés, to the west, is another large and friendly industrial town but, unlike Gijón, it has a well-preserved historic centre worth exploring: look especially for the arcaded **Plaza de España,** and the expressively sculpted 16th-century fountain, **Caños de San Francisco,** in little Plaza San Nicolás, next to the 13th-century church of **San Nicolás de Bari.** Just north of Avilés, an old lighthouse guards the entrance to the *ría,* at **San Juan de Nieva,** and a long, gorgeous beach at **Salinas.**

Where to Stay and Eating Out

Gijón ✉ 33200

Most people don't stay in Gijón, though for an overnight stop there's no shortage of choice. The ★★★★**Parador Molino Viejo,** in the pretty Parque Isabel La Católica, ✆ 985 37 05 11, 🖅 985 37 02 23 (*expensive*) has the best rooms in town with all the usual facilities (except a pool, but the beach is a 10-minute walk) and serves Asturian suppers in its restaurant. A good place in the centre is the ★★**Asturias,** located on the quiet, enclosed Plaza Mayor, ✆ 985 35 06 00 (*moderate*). The cheapest *hostal* in Gijón is the ★**Hs Narcea,** ✆ 985 39 32 87,with basic, bathless rooms for 2200 pts.

Touristically Gijón may have little going for it, but at least it has some of the best restaurants in Asturias. **La Pondala** on Avda. Dionisio Cifuentes 27, in the suburb of Somió, ✆ 985 36 11 60 (*expensive*) has been going for nearly a hundred years. Specialities are the rice and seafood dishes—try the *arroz con almejas* and the delicious *merluza rellena de mariscos* (hake filled with shellfish), or, for more conservative palates, straightforward dishes like roast beef with potatoes, washed down with some vintage wines. You have a choice of three smart dining rooms and, in summer, dining on the garden terrace. *Closed Thurs.* Also in Somió you'll find **Las Delicias,** Barrio Fuejo by the Evaristo Valle museum, ✆ 985 36 02 27 (*expensive*), another long-established upmarket eatery which mixes surf and turf—*lubina al horno* (sea-bass from the oven), *medallones de solomillo, escalopines de ternera a la sidra*—and very good service. *Closed Tues.*

For something kinder on the pocket but just as interesting to the taste buds, go to **Torremar,** C/Ezcurdia 120 (one block back from the beach), ✆ 985 33 01 73 (*moderate*), serving seafood and Asturian dishes including *fabes con almejas*—broad beans with clams. For a less ambitious dinner the area around the Plaza Mayor is definitely the place to go: try the convivial **Sidrería Plaza Mayor** on C/ Recoletas (*1500 pts for fish and cider*), or the very similar **Casa Fernando** next door: the *cazuela*'s nice here, and they do *bacalao* most days too.

Avilés ✉ 33400

This unlikely destination has a few good restaurants. **San Félix,** Avda. de los Telares 48, ✆ 985 56 51 46, is an old *sidrería* that is now a restaurant in classic Spanish style, serving classic seafood (sea-bass in champagne, no less) for around 5000 pts.

At least stop for a drink at the **Café Colón,** C/ de la Muralla, the town's gathering spot where Avilés's history is spelled out in modern murals.

The ancient and modern capital of Asturias, Oviedo is a working town with a fine cathedral, a university almost 400 years old, and two of Europe's most exquisite pre-Romanesque churches. Founded by Fruela I in 757 as a fortress guarding the key road over the mountains to the coast, Oviedo served as the capital of Christian Spain until the Asturian kings conquered León in 1002. The city suffered terribly in the insurrection of 1934 and during the Civil War. It used to earn a living from the surrounding coal and iron mines, but today Oviedo definitely has the look of a place where people stamp papers for a living.

Getting Around

By train: Oviedo has three train stations, all near the centre of town. The RENFE station, with frequent connections to Gijón and less frequent links to León, Barcelona, Burgos, Zaragoza, Pamplona, and to Madrid, Valladolid and Palencia, is at the head of the main street C/ Uría, ✆ 985 25 02 02. FEVE trains to Santander depart from the neighbouring station on Avda. Santander, ✆ 985 334 224 15; trains for Pravia and the western coast to El Ferrol leave from the other FEVE station, on C/ Víctor Chavarri near the cathedral, ✆ 985 29 76 56.

By bus: Most buses, including those of ALSA, the biggest company, with services throughout Asturias and to Madrid, Sevilla, Barcelona, Valladolid and Valencia as well as Paris, Geneva, Zürich and Brussels, set off from Pza. Primo de Rivera, at the end of C/ de Fray Ceferino near the train station; ✆ 902 42 22 42. Buses to nearby villages in Asturias depart from the FEVE station for Santander.

By car: Parking can be a pain in Oviedo, as can getting around in general. Almost all of the old centre is closed to traffic; as a last resort there is a parking garage underneath the Campo de San Francisco.

Tourist Information

Pza. de Alfonso II El Casto 6, just by the cathedral, ✆ 985 21 33 85.

The **post office** is on C/ Alonso Quintanilla; **telephones** are at C/ Foncalada.

There is a **market** on Thursdays, and a flea market on Sundays, both in Plaza del Fontan.

The Cathedral

The middle of Oviedo (take C/ Uría from the station) is occupied by the tranquil, shady **Campo de San Francisco** where you can feed the ducks. From here C/ San Francisco leads to the oldest part of the city, and the asymmetrical **Cathedral**, an attractive Gothic temple from the 14th century, its lovely tower with its delicate stone latticework is Oviedo's landmark. In the Capilla Mayor look for an enormous florid 16th-century *retablo* of the Life of Christ sculpted by Giralte of Brussels. Best of all, a door in the right transept leads to the original church of Alfonso el Casto, now known as the **Cámara Santa** (*open daily except Sun, 10–1 and 4–7; adm, free Mon*), strange and semi-barbaric, with fine carvings of the Apostles on the capitals of the outer chamber and disembodied heads on the walls. The inner chamber, is thought to be unaltered since Alfonso el Casto built it in 802 to house the relics of Visigothic Toledo rescued after its capture by the Moors. Today it contains the cathedral's precious treasures: the *Cruz de la Victoria*, supposedly borne by Pelayo at Covadonga, and pictured today on Asturias's coat of arms; the *Cruz de los Angeles* (808), a golden cross embedded with huge rubies and carved gems, reputedly made by the angels themselves and donated by Alfonso II; and a beautiful, silver-plated reliquary chest of 1073. Oviedo cathedral was always famous for its collection of relics—a phial of the Virgin Mary's milk and one of Judas' thirty pieces of silver; most of these are kept here too.

The Asturian Pre-Romanesque Churches

Oviedo has the finest of Asturias's post-Visigothic pre-Romanesque churches. Enjoying the patronage of its kings, this little capital can claim the beginnings of medieval architecture, a sophisticated art that seems to have come out of nowhere in a time when most of Christian Europe was still scratching its carrot rows with a short stick. The major influence clearly comes from North Africa or the Middle East, via Christian refugees from those newly Islamized countries. Hints of later Byzantine elements can be seen in many of the details, but this is all—Byzantium was 3000 miles away. Even with these influences, much in these provocative prototypes that never made it to the assembly line is original and beautiful. In 1985 UNESCO declared them the best architecture produced in 9th-century Christian Europe, to be protected as part of the 'Patrimony of Humanity'.

Alfonso el Casto built the oldest of these, **San Julián de Los Prados** (also called *Santullano*), northeast of the centre; C/ de Martínez Vigil will take you there from the back of the cathedral (*open daily exc Mon, 11–1 and 4.30–6; Nov–April, 12–1 only*). This is a simple, solid building with three square apses, a secret compartment in the wall, and interesting murals by an artist who learned his craft from studying monuments left by the Romans.

However, if you're pressed for time, head in the opposite direction up the Cuesta de Naranco, a hill overlooking the town (facing the RENFE station, turn left to the sign at the bridge over the tracks and continue 3km; city bus no.6 makes cameo appearances as well, starting from C/ Gil de Jaz, between the station and the Campo San Francisco). The two churches here, **Santa María de Naranco** and **San Miguel de Lillo**, can be found halfway up the mountain with a view over Oviedo (*open Mon-Sat 10–1 and 3-5, Sun-Mon 10-1; adm*). Both of these churches were built by Alfonso el Casto's successor, Ramiro I; incredibly, the perfectly proportioned Santa María is believed to have been part of the king's summer palace. Built of a fair golden stone and set in a small clearing, it is an enchanting building, supported by unusual flat buttresses and flanked by two porches. The lower level is believed to have served as a waiting chamber and bath; the upper, with a rough-hewn altar on the porch, was the main hall. Inside are blind arches of subtly decreasing height, topped by round medallions. Just up the road, San Miguel is a more traditional cruciform church, although of stunted proportions after an ancient amputation removed two-thirds of the original length.

Oviedo ✉ 33000

Where to Stay

expensive

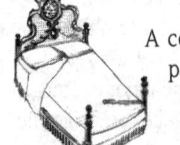

A couple of blocks from the Parque de San Francisco, a lovely 17th-century palace has been converted into the ★★★★★**Hotel de la Reconquista**, C/ Gil de Jaz 16, ℂ 985 24 11 00, ℮ 985 24 11 66, a plush luxury hotel of the highest order, and highest prices; all rooms with satellite TV and air conditioning. **Gran Hotel España**, C/ Jovellanos 2, ✆ 985 22 05 96, is elegant and conveniently situated downtown. For half as much ★★★**La Gruta**, on the west end of town at Alto de Buenavista, ✆ 985 23 24 50, ✆ 985 25 31 41, is snazzy, immaculate and offers the best views in town.

moderate

Best options in this category include ★**Favila**, near the cathedral at C/ Uría 37, ✆ 985 525 38 77, and **La Ovetense**, C/ San Juan 6, ✆ 985 522 08 40.

inexpensive

These cluster on and around C/ Uría, near the RENFE station. One of the best is the family-run ★**Hs Belmonte**, C/ Uría 3, ✆ 985 24 10 20. If they're full, try ★★**Hs Alteza**, ✆ 985 24 04 04, down the street at No.25.

It would be more fun to stay in the old centre, notably at the ★★**Hs Arcos**, ✆ 985 521 47 73 (*cheap*), just off the Plaza Mayor on C/ Magdalena 32; some rooms with bath.

Eating Out

There are plenty of restaurants and tapas bars in Oviedo, but the oldest and best is **Casa Fermín** near the park at San Francisco 8, ✆ 985 21 64 97 (*expensive*), offering classic Asturian cuisine and seasonal Spanish regional dishes, in a refined atmosphere (*2900 pts menú*).

Other good choices are **Los Arcos** at C/ Fray Ceferino, ✆ 985 29 52 02, or **El Raitán**, ✆ 985 21 42 18, which specializes in grilled meats—a dozen different kinds, on the special *3400 pts menú de carnes* in the evening.

Hearty Asturian stews and good *fabadas* bubble away at all the *sidrerias* (*inexpensive*) around C/ Gascona. Good recommendations are **Villaviciosa**, ✆ 985 20 44 12 and **La Pumarada**, ✆ 985 20 02 79.

Entertainment and Nightlife

Oviedo is one of the few places in which you will find anything beyond the usual all-night drinking and chattering. It's the centre of Asturian rock, and you can see what the local groups are getting up to in the desperate-looking clubs all along C/ Rosal, one street south of the Campo de San Francisco and the university.

Otherwise, the action is on the nearby streets in the old town, with more clubs and bars for the younger set: Pza. Riego, Pza. del Fontan, C/Canóniga and C/ Ildefonso Martínez. Asturian separatists hang out at **Xalabam**, C/ Postigo Alto 8; there are many discos in this area and elsewhere in town, including Lo Real, C/Cervantes 19, which has some of the best DJ programming to be found anywhere in Spain. Other discos that also function as venues for live acts are Sala Estilo, C/ Joaquin Bubela 8, and Stravaganza on C/ Santa Clara. One fun place is the **Cervecería Asturianu** on C/ Carta Puebla, with every different kind of beer and whisky imaginable, with décor that includes pieces of the Berlin Wall.

For simply drinking and chattering, the best bet is the informal places around Fontan where tables magically appear on the street every sundown, or else **Salsipuedes**, with an outdoor terrace on Ildefonso Martínez.

The principality, beyond the coast and the Picos, is *terra incognita* for most foreigners—a hilly, wooded land of small mining towns and agricultural villages, crisscrossed with walking paths. Much of it is protected, especially in the national hunting preserves that cover the northern slopes of the Cordillera Cantábrica. The coast is excellent—rugged cliffs, few tourists, plenty of shellfish and beaches everywhere. Public transport is limited throughout the area, and you'd do well to rent a car—and pack a big lunch—before setting out. Be sure to pick up one of the large detailed maps at the tourist office in Oviedo.

Getting Around

By bus: All the main towns can be reached by bus. ALSA buses from Oviedo, Pza. Primo de Rivera, © 985 28 12 20, go to Salas, Puerto de Somiedo, Cangas del Narcea, Tineo and Pola de Allande. Empresa Fernández, Aniceto Sala, Oviedo, © 985 23 83 90, has buses to Mieres, Pola de Lena and Turón; there are also a half-dozen or so a day down the western coast to Cudillero and Luarca, and as many from Gijón. Alcotán, C/ Padre Suárez 27, Oviedo, © 985 21 76 17, has buses to Pola de Laviana. The RENFE train between Oviedo and León stops at Pajares and Pola de Lena.

By car: If you're driving when the snow is flying, it's essential to call ahead for road conditions, © 985 25 46 11. If you want to rent a car, the main companies in Oviedo are along C/ Ventura Rodríguez, where you can shop around for the best deal.

Tourist Information

Salas: Pza. de la Campa, © 985 83 09 88.
Tuñón: © 985 76 10 61.
Tineo: Calle Mayor, © 985 80 01 87.
Cangas del Narcea: Pza. Asturias 33, © 985 81 17 21.

There are markets in Mieres on Sundays; Pola de Siera on Tuesdays; Tineo on Thursdays and Cangas del Narcea on Saturdays.

Southeast of Oviedo

Southeast of Oviedo, the AS244 passes **Pola de Laviana**, a typical Asturian copper-mining town, on its way to Reres National Reserve and the beautiful mountain pass, **Puerto de Tarna**. From a point just south, a lonely mountain path leads up to **Beleño**, on the edge of the Picos de Europa, where the reward is a fine panorama over the mountains. The next pass to the west, **Puerto San Isidro**, has a major ski installation (both passes can be reached by bus from Pueblo de Lillo in León province). **Coyanzo**, some 12km below the pass, is set near an idyllic little gorge, the **Hoces de Río Aller**.

Directly south of Oviedo, along the train route and recently built highway to León (an engineering marvel Spain is not a little proud of), the views become increasingly magnificent as you ascend to the dramatic **Puerto de Pajares**, another ski spot on the border with Léon. But before you get there, look for the signs 6km south of **Pola de Lena** for another of Ramiro I's lovely churches, the hilltop **Santa Cristina de Lena**, a cruciform temple built around 845, with blind arches similar to Santa María de Naranco, Visigothic decorations and an intricate iconostasis of Mozarabic inspiration (the key is available in the house below by the bridge).

The landmark in this part of the Cantabrian mountains is the jagged-peaked 7855ft **Peña Ubiña**, which sturdy walkers can tackle in around 4 or 5 hours from **Tuiza de Arriba** for incomparable views over the Picos de Europa and Somiedo (to reach Tuiza, take the side road from the highway at Campomanes). From Pajares, you can make the much shorter climb up the 5580ft **Pico de los Celleros**.

Up to the *Cordillera,* and Somiedo National Park

Southwest of Oviedo, in the highest part of the Cantabrian mountains, is the wild **Reserva Nacional de Somiedo**, where boar roam and deer and bears play on the banks of eighteen glacial lakes. One approach to it is by way of **Trubia**, a village known mostly for its enormous armament works. Ten km south of Trubia on the road to the park you can stop at **Tuñón** for one of the last of the 'Asturian' churches, **San Adrián**, built by Alfonso III (866–910). Inside are some of the oldest frescoes anywhere in Spain, traces of sun symbols over the altar and zigzag motifs taken straight from the Grand Mosque of Córdoba. The lady in the tobacco shop opposite has the key, but the only guide is the unusually friendly bat that lives in the choir. Further south, **Proaza** has a number of medieval buildings; it is separated from the next village, **Caranga**, by a pretty gorge you can walk through, the **Desfiladero del Teverga**. The road continues south through **La Plaza**, site of the interesting 12th-century **Colegiata de San Pedro**, where elements of Asturian pre-Romanesque combine with early French Romanesque; on the capitals are sculpted local animals, and there are two 18th-century mummies.

From La Plaza, the road south cuts through a magnificent forest to the Puerto Ventana, perhaps the least-used Asturian mountain pass. Just on the other side of the pass, from the Leonese village of **Torrestio**, you can hike in 3 hours into the lovely heart of Somiedo and its mysterious lakes, where *xanas*, or mermaids, guard the sunken treasures they use to please their lovers on the night of St John. Somiedo isn't really a park, but a hunting preserve. Despite all the mining this part of the Cordillera Cantábrica is one of the most unspoiled and natural in Spain. For one thing, it has a healthy population of bears (there are almost none in the Pyrenees) and even a few wolves; both are protected by law though they have few friends among the farmers and shepherds. Somiedo also has plenty of deer and boar, chamois and many species of eagle, kite, harrier and buzzard, including the rare lammergeier or bearded vulture, the largest bird of prey in Europe.

A second approach to Somiedo is via the N634, the main road west from Oviedo. This will take you through the fat village of **Grado**, where everybody comes on Wednesday and Sunday for the markets, and **Salas**, with its medieval monuments and palaces. The surrounding countryside is rich in picturesque *hórreos* (granaries), and to the west are the lovely pasturelands and hills around **Navelgas** and **Bárcena del Monasterio**. From Salas you can head south and follow the valley of the Pigüeña to the Somiedo Park. The big village in this iron-mining area is **Belmonte de Miranda** (C633); a curiosity in the region is the **Machuco de Alvariza** (near Belmonte village), an oak-built hydraulic hammer used in the 18th-century iron works. Many *vaqueros* still live in the vicinity—some of their conical-roofed *pallozas* (huts), along with several Celtic *castros* (hill forts) lie further up towards **Pola de Somiedo**, the chief town in the district. Pola de Somiedo stands at the head of the four-hour path to Somiedo's fourth lake, the **Lago del Valle**, passing several *pallozas* on the way. South of Pola are the ancient thatch-roofed hamlets of **Santa María de Puerto** and the remote **La Pornacal** (trail from Villar de Vildas).

The Dress Rehearsal

The event of the century in Asturias was the epic miners' revolt of 1934, a full-scale battle that eerily prefigured the Spanish Civil War. Because of the large numbers of workers in mining and industry, Asturias was politically the odd man out, an island of belligerent Marxists in the middle of the arch-conservative northwest. Mining and metalworking go way back in Asturias, but really took off at the beginning of the 20th century, when *indianos* forced home by Spain's loss of Cuba and the Philippines began to invest their money here. In the First World War, Spanish neutrality made for a boom in the mining areas, one which collapsed in the 1920s, leaving Asturias with the angriest proletariat in Spain. Along with the Basques and Catalans, Asturians were strong supporters of the Republic when it appeared in 1931 but, for many of their leaders, the new regime was only a stepping-stone to Socialism. The depression increased popular discontent, but what really set the workers boiling was the radical right-wing national government elected in 1934. Under Prime Minister Gil Robles, it began dismantling all the reforms of its leftist predecessors and openly postured for the restoration of the monarchy. On 4 October 1934 the trade unions declared a general strike in Asturias in protest. Barcelona and Madrid also rose up but failed to follow through, leaving the Asturians on their own and in a fighting mood. The main centres of the revolt were Mieres, Sama and Oviedo, but it was the munitions works at Trubia, near Somiedo, that turned the strike into a war. The workers occupied it and seized some 30,000 rifles inside. Soon there was a 30,000-man 'Red Army', and a revolutionary committee was formed to govern the province. The government sent in a dependable general named Mola, leading a force made up mainly of Moroccan troops—northern Morocco was still a Spanish protectorate. The Moors were mercenaries who had fought against their own people, but they were fiercely loyal to their commander, a certain Francisco Franco. Franco, a Galician married to an Asturian woman, felt right at home. He had already led troops, using the Spanish Foreign Legion, to crush a general strike in Asturias in 1917. The Legion was also present in 1934. An outfit not much like the romantic French version, this one was now led by a fascist psychopath named Millan Astray, famous for his missing arm and eye-patch. As for the Moors, some of them must have enjoyed the irony of a Spanish commander, an heir to Pelayo, bringing them to a place where they hadn't set foot for a thousand years. The government had to make its point, and the revolt was crushed quickly and with the utmost ferocity. Many of the mining towns were thoroughly wrecked, and the troops slaughtered nearly 1300 Asturians in reprisals after the surrender on 19 October. A year and a half later, after new elections brought the leftist Popular Front to power, the coup that began the Civil War started with the same cast of characters: General Mola, who was to be the new dictator, but who died in an air crash at the start; the Foreign Legion; and the inevitable Francisco Franco, whose Moroccans won him the title of *caudillo* (leader). The best-equipped and trained forces in Spain, they used their practice in Asturias to get the jump on the disorganized government and citizens' militias, and gained control of much of Spain within a month, an advantage that helped assure the Nationalists' final victory.

West of Oviedo: Ancient Pottery and Primeval Forests

Back on the main route west from Oviedo, after Salas the next village is **Tineo**, a great trout-fishing area crossed by a branch of the Santiago pilgrimage route. A number of medieval churches survive from that era—Tineo's 13th-century parish church and the ruined monastery and church of San Miguel in nearby **Obona**. Further south, a dirt road leads up to the tiny borough of **Llamas del Mouro**, where potters, isolated from the rest of the world, still create the shiny black ceramic jugs and bowls made by their Celto-Iberian ancestors. The pieces are fired in the ancient style, in circular ovens buried in the earth. Three of these are still in use.

Cangas del Narcea, the largest town in southwest Asturias, is modern and has little to waylay you; head instead further south to **Pico de la Masa** (near Puerto del Connio) for the view over the magnificent 5000-hectare **Bosque de Muniellos**, one of Europe's last and most extensive forests of primeval oak and beech. A strictly protected wildlife preserve, the forest is the last refuge in the world of the rare *urogallo*, a funny-looking kind of capercaillie with red eyebrows. The trail through the forest begins at **Tablizas**, a short hike from Moal; the hike takes about five-and-a-half hours and will leave you mourning for the ancient times, when (they say) a squirrel could cross the whole of Iberia without ever touching the ground. Like Altamira, Muniellos is accounted such a threatened treasure that only 20 people a day are allowed in it; write in advance to the Agencia de Medio Ambiente del Principado de Asturias, 1 Plaza General Ordóñez, Oviedo 33007. East of Muniellos lies the **Reserva Nacional de Degaña**, another lovely, wooded area, with pretty meadows and small lakes formed by glaciers. In the Roman era Degaña was heavily mined for its gold.

Gold was also mined in the most westerly zone of the province, around **Pola de Allande** and **Grandas de Salime**, both enchanting villages. Grandas has a partially Romanesque church, San Salvador, and a **Museo Etnográfico y Escuela de Artesanía**, with exhibits on country life in old Asturias and craftworkers present weaving and carving wood. In **Celón**, 5km from Pola, there's a fine 12th-century church, **Santa María**, with good frescoes and carvings. One of Asturias' best-preserved Celtic *castros* is up on **Pico San Chuis** to the west near Berducedo, whose ancient inhabitants, like the modern, exploited the region's minerals.

Where to Stay and Eating Out

There are hotels and *hostales* in the villages along the N634, but up towards the Somiedo Park expect only *casas particulares* and not a lot of those.

Mieres ✉ 33600

Mieres, on the Oviedo–León road, offers a good stopover at **★★Hs Villa de Mieres**, C/ Teodoro Cuesta 33, ✆ 985 46 70 04 (*inexpensive*); and good home cooking in modern, smart surroundings at **Casa Villa**, C/ Aller, ✆ 985 46 00 33, serving Asturian favourites for *around 3000 pts.*

Salas ✉ 33600

Salas is a convenient stopover on the N634, with a few inexpensive *hostales* over bars. The **★★Castillo de Valdés**, Pza. Campa, ✆ 985 83 10 37, is a restored 16th-century palace (*rooms moderate*); its restaurant is the local dining hot spot, serving imaginative Asturian dishes, including locally fished salmon, for *around 2500 pts.* There are basic **camp sites** within the Somiedo Park at Valle de Lago and Saliencia.

Cangas del Narcea ✉ 33800

Cangas has the widest range of choices in this region. The best places to stay are the ★**Peña Grande**, out on the main road, ✆ 985 81 23 92 (*moderate*), with a restaurant; the ★**Hs Acebo**, C/ Hermanos Flórez 1, ✆ 985 81 05 46; and the small ★★**Hs Virgen del Carmen**, C/ Mayor 46, ✆ 985 81 15 02, with eight *inexpensive* rooms.

Tineo ✉ 33870

Here you'll find three *hostales*, each with only a handful of rooms. ★★**Don Miguel**, El Viso, ✆ 985 80 03 25, and ★**Casa Lula**, El Crucero, ✆ 985 80 16 00, both have rooms for around *7000 pts*. The least expensive *hostal* in Tineo, ★★**Hs Casa Sole**, on the main road, ✆ 985 80 60 44, offers nice rooms with or without baths.

Where to Ski

Valgrande Pajares, 3km from the Busdongo train station, offers 15 slopes from the very difficult to the very easy, 10 lifts and two chairlifts, ✆ 985 49 61 23. The closest hotels are in León province, at La Pola de Gordón and Villamanín. **San Isidro** (León province) is near Puebla de Lillo, and offers three very difficult runs in the Cebolledo circuit, as well as five of average difficulty and four easy ones; there's a chair lift and seven ski lifts, ✆ 985 73 50 66. There are a couple of hotels at Puebla de Lillo, but no public transport. Other ski installations in the area are at San Emiliano, on the slopes of Peña Ubiña, at **Lietariegos Pass**, and **Maraña**, near Riaño in León.

Asturias' Western Coast

The Asturian coast west of Avilés could well be the best chance in this book for a peaceful and agreeable seaside holiday. The shoreline itself does not seem dramatic until you see it close up—wild cliffs of jumbled, glittering metamorphic rock, mixed in with long stretches of beach where you can easily find uncrowded spots even on August weekends. Cudillero and Luarca happen to be two of the most delightful seaside villages on earth, and there are plenty of isolated beaches all along the rugged coast between them.

Tourist Information

Cudillero: Pza. de San Pedro, ✆ 985 59 01 18.
Luarca: Olavarrieta 27, ✆ 985 64 00 83.
Navia: El Muelle, ✆ 985 47 37 95.
Tapia de Casariego: Pza. de la Iglesia, ✆ 985 47 29 68.
Castropol: Los Callejones, ✆ 985 63 51 13.
Taramundi: Avda. de Galicia, ✆ 985 64 67 01.

There are **markets** in Cudillero and Navia on Fridays; Tapia de Casariego on Mondays and Fridays.

Cudillero and Luarca

The first resort west of Avilés, **Cudillero** is well protected from the tourist hordes by its geography; the only way into this fishing village is its narrow, cobbled main street, which snakes down almost vertically for 3km before reaching the impossibly picturesque little harbour at the bottom of the cliffs. There are few hotels but, except for the summer days when it fills up with Madrileño day trippers, Cudillero would be a perfect place to hide out for a few days. If you have a car you can find plenty of good beaches nearby, especially the broad **Playa de la Cueva** (visible from a high viaduct on the coast highway, though in fact miles away from it).

Luarca, with its sheltered harbour at the mouth of the Río Negro, is a little more tourist-orientated, but it is still in every respect the most satisfactory place for a holiday on Spain's northern coast. The village was an important place in medieval times, first as a whaling port and then from trade with the Americas. The best way to see it is to follow the first signposted road in from the east—a back road that will take you to the cemetery, high on a cliff with a stunning view over the village below. Luarca is still an important fishing port, mostly for tuna, and the harbourfront ensemble makes a pretty photograph. Old Luarca stretches inland from there, with some stately palaces from the 17th and 18th centuries, and old quarters with narrow alleys climbing up the steep hills. There is an acceptable beach right in the centre of Luarca, but for something special head for **Playa del Barayo**, a beautiful natural area to the west.

Continuing westwards, **Navia** is the next fishing village. Southwest of here at **Coaña** you can visit the extensive remains of another Celtic *castro*—foundations of stone walls, paved streets and the circular foundations of houses. The similarity between these and the *vaquero* huts led some to believe that the *vaqueros* were a lost Celtic tribe. Near the main road, there's a monolith carved with the star symbol so widespread in northern Spain. The Asturian coast ends with **Castropol**, another attractive fishing port sheltered on the broad Ría de Ribadeo. Inland, south beyond Vegadeo, tiny **Taramundi** up in the mountains has long been famous for the manufacture of knives; pocket knives with carved and painted wooden handles made here are another popular Asturian souvenir.

Where to Stay and Eating Out

Cudillero ✉ 33150

The best place to sleep is an old inn, **★La Lupa**, in San Juan de la Piñera (2km east of the village), ✆ 985 59 00 63 (*moderate*). **★★Azpiazu** is the best known hotel at Playa de Aguilar, ✆ 985 58 32 10. It specializes in seafood, and has a breezy summer terrace. In the village itself, there's **★San Pablo**, C/ Suárez Inclán, ✆ 985 59 11 55 (*moderate*), and not much else; ask around the bars for *casas particulares*, though if you have a car you'll see plenty of modest *hostales* hanging their signs out on the roads. Restaurants line the tiny harbour: the **Taberna del Puerto**, ✆ 985 59 04 77 (*moderate*), with excellent seafood, and the less expensive **El Remo**, which does a good *paella*.

In a lovely setting with a view of the sea and mountains, Concha de Artedo has one of the many pretty beaches in the area (off the coastal road west of Cudillero): **Casa Marino**, ✆ 98 559 01 86, serves top-class seafood, and a memorable *zarzuela de mariscos y pescados* (shellfish and fish casserole) for around *3500 pts*.

Luarca ✉ 33700

The one swanky hotel is the bright, central and airy **★★★Gayoso**, Paseo Gómez, ✆ 985 64 00 54 (*moderate*). The few others are nearby, including the **★Hs Oria**, ✆ 985 64 03 85, around the corner on C/ Crucero; clean rooms with bath. A bit dearer but still good, the **★Hs Rico** is nearby on Pza. Alfonso X, ✆ 985 70 05 59 (*inexpensive*). The closest camp ground is the *inexpensive* **Los Cantiles** at Villar, on the cliffs above Luarca, ✆ 985 64 09 38. As at Cudillero, for dinner you need look no further than the row of seafood restaurants that line the harbour; nearly all of them have outside tables to enjoy the view.

La Mesón del Mar, on the far end, offers a wonderful seafood *menú gastronómico* with a bit of everything in the day's catch, well worth the *3800 pts*. The least expensive on the harbour (no tables outside) is a good one: **La Dársena**, where a full dinner costs about *2100 pts*.

One of the best hotel-restaurants in the area is 6km west of town on the N634, the **★★Casa Consuelo** at Otur, ✆ 985 64 08 44 (*moderate*), where the food served in the large dining rooms attracts people from miles around with classic Asturian *fabada* and cider (*1500 pts menú*).

Figueras del Mar ✉ 33793

At the farthest western limit of Asturias, near Castropol, you'll find the region's loveliest hotel, the **★★Palacete Peñalba**, El Cotarelo, ✆ 985 63 61 25 (*expensive*). Set in a glorious Art Nouveau mansion designed by a follower of Gaudí, it is a listed monument, and retains its gardens and much of its original furnishings; all rooms have TV and minibar.

Galicia

If Asturias is Spain's Wales, then Galicia is in many ways its Ireland, for many years so far removed from the mainstream of Spanish life and history it might just as well have been an island. Here the Celtic invaders of 1000 BC found their cosiest niche, in the same kind of rain-swept, green land facing the setting sun that their brethren had settled farther north in Brittany and Cornwall. The Moors left no mark in Galicia, having been expelled in the 8th century by the kings of Asturias—who promptly turned their attention to the richer spoils of the south.

While the rest of the north expanded into the newly won lands of the Reconquista, the Galicians, or *Gallegos*, were hemmed in by Portugal and forced to turn inwards, dividing their land into ever smaller and smaller holdings with every generation. Famines were common, and as soon as the New World was discovered, they emigrated in droves—even today Galicia is one of the poorest regions in Spain. Yet few places in Spain have such a lasting charm. The coastline is pierced by a dozen estuaries, or *rías*, wild and scenic in the north, and in the south, sheltering serene beaches (Galicia has some 772 of these) and tiny coves, perfect for the smuggling that has long been a mainstay of the economy. Rivers in deep, narrow valleys with fantasy names—the Éo, the Ulla, the Lor, the Sil and Jallas—spill down wild mountains on their way to the sea. Bright green gardens cover every inch of cultivable land, although a third of the acreage is wasted by the granite walls each *Gallego* has erected around his own little plot. Many cottages have granaries (*hórreos*), monumental pieces of granite set up on pillars to protect the grain from rodents and wet, with vents to permit air to circulate, topped by a gabled roof with crosses. Early travellers mistook them for hermitages.

Because of the endless division of land, much of Galicia is covered higgledy-piggledy with farms and houses in some 31,000 'villages' (most with populations of 100–200), sprinkled here and there with the showy bungalows of the *americanos* who made their fortunes in Argentina. Many older houses, especially in A Coruña, have balconies closed in by glass 'crystal galleries', adorned with elaborate white mullions. Another distinctive feature of Galicia is the sculpted granite crosses at the crossroads. Some apparently guided pilgrims, or marked out the high roads, or fulfilled vows, or perhaps even served the same geomantic organization as Neolithic menhirs and dolmens, only carved into acceptable Christian forms. In the Rías Baixas, and especially along the rivers leading into them, you'll see the stately manor country villas the *Gallegos* call *pazos*, from the Roman *palatio*.

Galicia's language, Gallego, is chock-full of x's (pronounced 'sh') and closely related to Portuguese, and spoken by a greater percentage of the population than Basque or Catalan are in their respective regions. Even García Lorca penned verses in Gallego, inspired by the language of Alfonso the Wise's masterpiece, the *Cantigas de Santa María* and the evocative poetry, reminiscent of Emily Dickinson's, by Rosalía de Castro (1837–85). Rosalía was a key figure in the *Rexurdimento* (literary renaissance), inspired by the Catalans, and like theirs, a forerunner of Spain's nationalist movements.

Culturally, Galicia has always looked to its ancient roots. The national instrument, the *gaita*, is very similar to Breton or Irish bagpipes, and *Gallegos* like nothing better than to blow it at festivals. Celtic influences are also strong in Galicia's festivals (many associated with death and evil spirits). Irish immigrants in the 16th century introduced lace-making (*camarinhas*), still done by older women all along the coast.

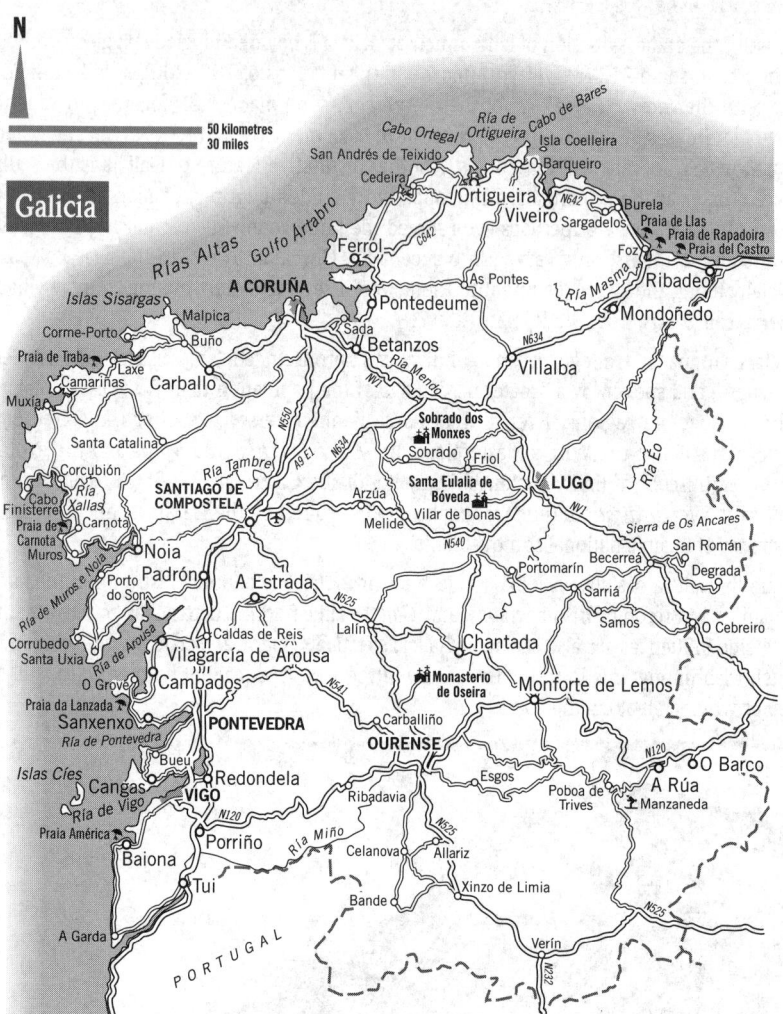

Galician Cuisine

Eating is one of the great pleasures of Galicia; in Spain, *Gallego* restaurants command as much respect as Basque. The estuaries are rich in an extraordinary array of seafood, from the famous scallops of Santiago and lobster to creatures unique to Galicia such as *zamburiñas* scallops. Another favourite served in every town are *empanadas*, large flat flaky pies filled with eels or lamprey (the most sought after; try it before you knock it), sardines, pork, or veal. Turnip greens (*grelos*) are a staple, especially in *Caldo Gallego*, a broth that also features turnips and white beans; in winter, the heartier *lacón con grelos* holds pride of place. Galicia produces Spain's best veal and good cheeses, such as Roquefort-like *cabrales* and *gamonedo*. A tapas meal to make a *Gallego* weep includes grilled sardines, *pulpo a la gallega* (tender octopus with peppers and paprika), roasted small green peppers (*pimientas de Padrón*), with chewy hunks of bread and lightly salted breast-shaped *tetilla* cheese, washed down with white Ribeira wine.

For dessert try *tarta de Santiago* (almond tart), and to top it all off, a glass of Galician fire water, *aguardiente*—served at night after a meal to ward off evil spirits—properly burned (*queimada*), with lemon peel and sugar.

The Coast West of Asturias: As Mariñas de Lugo

In the Spanish drive to leave no coast unchristened, this wild Atlantic-thundered northernmost stretch of Galicia is known as As Mariñas de Lugo after the provincial capital Lugo. It surrenders every so often to admit sandy beaches decorated with storm-chiselled cliffs and rocks; until very recently, deplorable slow roads conspired to keep it a secret.

Getting Around

Besides buses originating from Lugo, Gijón and A Coruña, the slow FEVE choochoo from Gijón or Oviedo makes several leisurely trips a day along the coast to Ferrol, stopping at Ribadeo, Foz, Burela, Viveiro, Covas, O Barqueiro and Ortigueira.

Tourist Information

Ribadeo: Praza de España, ✆ 982 10 06 89.
Viveiro: Puerta de Carlos V, ✆ 982 56 04 86.

There are **markets** in Mondoñedo on Thursdays and Sundays; in Foz on Tuesdays; in Viveiro on Mondays, Thursdays and Saturdays; and in Cedeira there is a fish market daily, and a market for other food on Wednesdays and Saturdays.

Ribadeo, Foz and Mondoñedo

Galician *rías*, or estuaries, are usually named after their largest towns. The first *ría* west of Asturias, **Ribadeo**, is named after a piquant old fishing town, where palm trees and the delightfully eclectic **Casa Morena** of 1905 lend it a lost Californian air. The hermitage atop **Monte de Santa Cruz**, 2km south of Ribadeo, offers splendid views of the Galician-Asturian coastline, guarded by a folksy monument to the Galician bagpiper; in early August Santa Cruz pipers from across Galicia gather here in an ear-splitting eisteddfod. West, the tiny lobster fishing village of **Rinlo** is the gateway to the long sandy beach known either as the **Praia del Castro** or **As Catedrais** after its rock formations in the sea. Other pretty beaches dwarfed by towering cliffs, **Praia de Rapadoira** and **Praia de Llas** lie further west by **Foz**, a workaday industrial fishing port at the mouth of the Rio Masma.

If Foz is no prize, **Mondoñedo**, 18km to the south up the Masma valley offers some consolation. Mondoñedo was founded in 1117, in the diocese of San Martín de Mondoñedo. It became the capital of its own little province in the 15th century. The granite **Cathedral** was begun in 1219 and when the time came to slap on a baroque façade, it was done with surgical discretion, preserving the Romanesque portal and Gothic rose window in harmonious blind arches. The interior is still late Romanesque and decorated with remarkable 14th-century frescoes of the *Massacre of the Innocents*; there's a wonderful organ with trumpets (1710), and a painted Gothic statue known as the *Virgen Inglesa*, brought over from St Paul's in London for safekeeping during the Reformation. On the pretty *Alameda*, the baroque church **Os Remedios** is decorated with grand Churrigueresque *retablos* and lots of candles, too, for the remedies in its name are said to be usually granted.

Between Mondoñedo and Foz, the Benedictine **Monasterio de Vilanova de Lourenzá** dates from the 10th century, but became wealthy enough in the 17th and 18th centuries to finance a church façade by granite wizard Fernando de las Casas y Novoa that was never quite finished. The graceful interior gives the lie to the idea that Spanish baroque means dark, gloomy and heavy. In the chapel of Santa María de Valdeflores you can make a wish while stroking the bones of the monastery's founder, Conde Gutierre Osorio.

Las Rías Altas: West of Foz to Viveiro, O Barqueiro and Ortigueira

From Foz, a brief inland detour will take you to the impressive, mightily buttressed 11th-century **San Martín de Mondoñedo**, a rare Romanesque church left untampered with over the centuries. Heading west on the coast, you can pay your respects to the **Citanía de Fazouro**, a well-preserved Celtic *castro*; the similar Castro do Chan, near the pretty fishing-port of **Burela**, yielded the unique golden torques in the Lugo museum. Just inland from Cervo, **Sargadelos** had one of Spain's earliest ironworks and a famous Royal Ceramics Factory. It reopened in 1970 as the **Cerámica de Sargadelos** (*open Mon–Fri 8.30–1 and 4.30–6*) manufacturing traditional blue and white jugs and avant-garde works; if you're sticking around the area you can take a ceramics course in August by writing ahead.

Beyond Cervo and Sargadelos, the Rías Altas, or Upper Estuaries, begin in earnest, offering some of the best wild and windy coastal scenery in Iberia. Fragrant eucalyptus groves dot the coast around **Viveiro**, at the head of its lovely *ría*. Viveiro is the choice place to stay in the Rías Altas, sheltered by its partly ruined medieval walls from the ravages of the Atlantic, automobiles, and time itself. In the 18th century it imported linen from the Baltic in exchange for Galician agricultural goods but these days its outer fishing port **Celeiro**, on the opposite side of the estuary, deals mostly in sardines. Three medieval gates survive, along with the fancy **Puerta de Carlos V** (1548) on Avda. Galicia, erected to curry favour with Charles V. Inside, the narrow lanes and pretty **Praza de Pastor Díaz** are paved in granite and lined with medieval houses sucking in light through their *solanas*, while the austere but pure 12th-century Romanesque **Santa María del Campo** provides a town centrepiece. Viveiro has some ravishing beaches: the sand plain of **Covas** sweeping out to a treetopped rock 'castle', **O Faro** facing the ocean, and **Xilloi** and **Ares** near Celeiro, where legend has it an ancient city sank into the sea for refusing to hear the preaching of St James. You can get a good overview from the mirador atop **San Roque**, the mountain just behind Viveiro. To the west, the rugged **Isla Coelleira**—'rabbit island'—has been forlorn and desolate ever since the Templars, who took refuge there from the pope's pogrom, were massacred one night in 1307 by the lord of Viveiro.

The next estuary west, the Ría do Barqueiro, provides a magnficent setting for the little hamlet of **Vicendo** and its pretty azalea gardens, the wide beach at **Arealonga** and, over the *ría*, for **O Barqueiro**, a bijou lobster port, in a landscape of piney fjords. A road leads down the *ría* to more beaches and to the tiny fishing hamlet and fabulous curling sandy beach of **Bares**, the northernmost settlement in Spain, marked by a lighthouse and blocks of walls from the days when it served as a port for Phoenician ships en route to the tin mines of Cornwall.

Ortigueira, on the pine-wooded east bank of the Ría de Santa María de Ortigueira is a peaceful, unremarkable town (except during its annual Festival del Mundo Celta) with white sandy beaches that never get too crowded. On the west bank of the *ría* (cross the river at Mera) the long toes of the Sierra de Capelada extend down to Cape Ortegal, where the fishing village of **Cariño** is the last to look over the Cantabrian sea.

Cliffs, Lizards and Cedeira

West of Cariño the road takes in spectacular views of the 612m cliffs of the **Garita de Herbeira** en route to the village and tiny sanctuary of **San Andrés de Teixido,** perched on savage, wave-battered cliffs. Wild horses roam the meadows and woodlands here, and pilgrims flow in year round, for as the saying goes, '*A San Andrés de Teixido, que no vai vivo vai morto*' 'if you don't go while alive, you'll go dead'—reincarnated as a lizard or toad, creatures which are never harmed in the village. On 8 September, the dead are given a formal invitation to the festival, when colourful dough figures are baked to be consumed before Mass, and pilgrims who over the past year had a close brush with the Grim Reaper are carried to the church in coffins. Buy an amulet or *santera* of the saint, or enquire about San Andrés' famous love herb, which in the good old days was consumed in large quantities after mass as a prelude to a general orgy. A corniche road continues to the lovely town and port of **Cedeira,** which marks a series of stunning beaches and lagoons that stretch to Ferrol. The Ría de Cedeira is lined with beauty spots: the lofty **Mirador de Peña Edrosa,** the lighthouse at **Punta Candelaria,** and to the west, the gorgeous setting of the hermitage of **San Antonio de Corveiro.**

Where to Stay and Eating Out

Ribadeo ✉ 27700

In a scenic, quiet spot overlooking the *ría*, the ★★★**Parador de Ribadeo,** C/ Amador Fernández, ✆ 982 12 88 25, ✇ 982 12 83 46 (*expensive*) is comfortable and has fine views; the restaurant features the day's catch. The cheapest decent place in Ribadeo is the ★**Hs Galicia,** C/ Virgen del Camino 1, ✆ 982 12 87 77 (*cheap*). The beaches west towards Foz are well supplied with camp sites. If you prefer a 'casa de campo', **Huerta de Obe** at Ctra. Santa Cruz, ✆ 982 12 87 15 (*expensive*) has lots of services including swimming pool. At **Oxardín,** C/ Reinante 20, ✆ 982 11 02 22 (*moderate*), sit amid greenery and feast on baked oysters or turbot with clams (*longuerirós*). *Closed Mon in winter.*

Mondoñedo ✉ 27740

★**Montero,** Avda. San Lázaro 7, ✆ 982 52 17 51(*moderate*) has pleasant doubles, although for character, opt for the recently restored ★**Montero II,** across from the cathedral at C/ Candido Martínez 8, ✆ 982 52 10 41 (*moderate*). The small, simple ★**Hs Padornelo,** C/ Buenos Aires 1, ✆ 982 52 18 92, has *cheap* rooms with or without bath. For a simple, filling, *inexpensive* dinner try **Avoltiña,** Ctra. Lorenzana.

Viveiro ✉ 27850

Note that most places offer big discounts off season. There's a clutch of hotels along Covas beach, among them the smart ★★**Las Sirenas,** ✆ 982 56 02 00, ✇ 982 55 12 67 (*expensive*), with rooms, and flats and studios sleeping up to four. In the countryside, in Galdo, there is el **Pazo da Trave,** ✆ 982 59 81 63 (*expensive*), a luxurious old stately home. Little ★**Hs As Areas II,** Avda. de Santiago 22, ✆ and ✇ 982 55 05 23 (*moderate*), is another comfortable choice. In the centre, try ★★**Hs Vila,** C/ N. Montenegros 57, ✆ 982 56 13 31 (*moderate*). **Vivero,** C/ Melitón Cortiñas 16, ✆ 982 56 00 18, serves up plates of *marisco*. For tapas in a friendly atmosphere, try **Pepe** in the same street.

Pilgrims who made it as far as Villafranca del Bierzo (*see* p.376) had to gird their loins for one last trial: the Puerto Pedrafita in the Sierra de Ancares. This is Galicia at its wildest, driest and bleakest, deceptively covered with blooms in the spring, but the haunt of werewolves and witches in the evening—a zone apart, bound in dreams and legends. The regional government, the Xunta de Galicia, has recently restored the atmospheric old *camino francés* and placed yellow scallop-shell markers every 500m. The *camino* itself rarely coincides with the highways, making this last leg of the journey especially pleasant for walkers; to really maintain the medieval mood, Galicia's fierce sheepdogs are still in place with medieval sheepdog attitudes, just asking for a buffet from a stout pilgrim's staff.

Getting Around

The towns in this section are served by bus from Lugo (the station is just outside the Roman walls in Praza de Constitución, ✆ 982 22 39 85, buses from Lugo to León pass through Becerreá and Pedrafita. Lugo and the junction at Monforte de Lemos are linked by rail to León, A Coruña, Ourense and Vigo, with speedy Talgos to Zaragoza, Barcelona, Bilbao and Irún. Lugo's station is in the new part of town on Pza. Conde de Fontao, ✆ 982 22 21 41; take the steps down and walk along Rúa de Castelao to the walls. There's a RENFE office at Pza. Maior 27, ✆ 982 22 55 03.

Tourist Information

Lugo: Praza Maior 27, ✆ 982 23 13 61.

O Cebreiro, Os Ancares, and the Pilgrim's Road

After Villafranca, the road ascends relentlessly to the 1100m pass at **Pedrafita**. Here, in 1809, Sir John Moore's troops fleeing to A Coruña, with Marshal Soult's terrible army in hot pursuit, nearly rebelled. Discipline had already vanished in Villafranca, where the soldiers had sacked, raped and looted the homes of their Spanish allies; at Pedrafita and at **O Cebreiro**, another 200m up and a famous brunt of blizzards, hundreds of men froze to death. Such was their haste that the soldiers threw thousands of pounds in gold—the army's pay—over the cliff, along with hundreds of horses, while all the women and children camp followers were abandoned in the icy wilderness. It was one of the blackest pages in the history of the British army, and it was almost miraculous that Moore was able to restore order and continue to the coast.

Today O Cebreiro has a huge parking lot to allow everyone to enjoy the tremendous views (in good weather) and have a look at the village's Celtic *pallozas*, oval stone huts topped with conical straw roofs. A cluster of four *pallozas* now houses the **Museo de Artes y Costumbres Populares** (*usually open 12–2 and 5–7*). A Benedictine monastery, **Santa María del Cebreiro,** was built over an old Celtic temple. Pilgrims never failed to pay their respects in its squat slate church, where one of the greatest miracles of the road took place: in the late 13th century, an old priest, tired of celebrating Mass for just one shepherd in the winter, was grumbling away during the Transfiguration when he and his parishioner were astonished to see the host transformed into flesh and the wine into blood. The miraculous chalice is displayed in the right aisle with the miraculous paten and a silver reliquary for the blood and flesh donated by celebrity pilgrims Fernando V and Isabel I in 1489.

O Cebreiro and the mighty mountains to the north form part of the **Reserva Nacional de Os Ancares**, part refuge of the rare capercaillie (especially around Degrada) and part hunting reserve of roebuck and boar. Several of the tiny villages lost in the bosom of the range also have *pallozas,* a few still inhabited by diehards—**Villarello, Cervantes, Doiras** and, best of all, **Piornedo,** which can only be reached by foot from Donís. **Becerreá,** on the Lugo road, is the main base for excursions into Os Ancares. From O Cebreiro, the *camino* ascends vertiginously to **O Poio** pass (1337m), but from here it's all downhill through mountain meadows, chestnut groves and tiny hamlets, where most of the pilgrims' chapels and *hostales* have survived only in name. During the construction of the cathedral of Santiago at Compostela, every medieval pilgrim would pick up a chunk of limestone in the quarries outside Triacastela, and carry it 100km to the Castañeda kilns to be melted into mortar.

One branch of the *camino* passes down the Ouribio valley to the huge Benedictine **Abadía de San Xulián** at **Samos** (*open 10.30–1 and 4.30–7*), where the hospitable old monks always seem glad to see visitors. Founded in 655, abandoned with the arrival of the Moors but rebuilt a few years later, the abbey had a famous library in the Middle Ages. The tiny slate chapel of San Salvador is from the 9th century, but the medieval monastery burned down in the 16th century, and its replacement in 1951, leading to the reconstruction of the two cloisters, one late Gothic and the other, larger, very strict and buttoned-down Spanish baroque. In the centre flows the lovely Fountain of the Nereids, said to be the work of Velázquez. There's a recent statue of Padre Feijóo, who founded the monastic **church** with profits from his essays.

The two branches of the *camino* meet in **Sarriá**. In its a quietly aloof medieval core, there's a ruined castle, the little Romanesque church of San Salvador and a pilgrims' hostel in the **Convento de los Mercedarios**, where the church has Isabelline Gothic frills. **Portomarín** was a pilgrims' halt protected by the Templars, but even they couldn't have fended off the waters of the Minho, when the river was dammed in the 1960s submerging the village. However, old Portomarín's porticoed main street plan was salvaged in a new Portomarín, along with the pretty façade of **San Pedro** and the Romanesque tower church of **San Nicolás**. The villagers continue to do what they've always done best: supply Galicia with excellent *aguardiente*—firewater which they not only distil but drain during the nightly *marcha.*

And the Last Leg of the Camino

At **Vilar de Donas**, 'Ladyville' (just off the pilgrim's road 15km west of Portomarín), the 13th-century granite church of **San Salvador** has a ruined Gothic cloister and a pretty Romanesque-Gothic portal; inside the granite walls are green from the damp, while the rounded apse is embellished with 15th-century paintings. The altar stone is carved with the miracle at O Cebreiro, with Jesus emerging out of the chalice; the 15th-century baldachin in the transept is one of the few to survive intact in Galicia. San Salvador was once the seat of the Knights of Santiago in Galicia (note the crossed swords, the symbol of the order, on the tombs).

If it weren't for the proximity of Santiago itself, the last two days' march along the *camino* would be disappointing, especially for the modern pilgrim. The old road passes over a medieval bridge at **Furelos**, before arriving in **Melide**, with its endearing Praza do Convento and ancient roadside cross, marking the geographic centre of Galicia. Just outside Melide, you'll find a dolmen, the **Pedra de Raposo** and the crumbling church Santa María with 15th-century murals in the apse, perhaps by the same artist as Vilar de Donas. **Arzúa** was the traditional last overnight stop, 30km from Compostela.

These days Santiago's airport is the dominant feature of **Labacolla** ('Wash Arse'), 8km from Compostela where 'for the love of the Apostle' the pilgrims would bathe in the stream. Another 5km would take them up to the now desolate hill (Km 717 along the *autopista*), **Monte del Gozo** or Mountjoy, and the long-awaited sight of the towers of Santiago. The first member of each pilgrimage band to sight the cathedral towers was called the 'King', a proud title that was passed down as a surname; if yours is King, Leroy or Rey, the chances are you had a sharp-eyed ancestor. These days Santiago's sprawl and traffic conspire to make the last few kilometres a hellish welcome to a heavenly goal.

Where to Stay and Eating Out

O Cebreiro and Os Ancares ✉ 27600

Near the *pallozas*, **★★Hs San Giraldo de Aurillac**, ✆ 982 36 71 25 (*inexpensive*), now a *mesón*, offers authentically medieval rooms in a Benedictine convent. Sturdy stone **★★Hs Piornedo**, in Cervantes, ✆ 982 36 83 19 (*moderate*) has lovely views over the mountain. Other lodgings in Os Ancares are in Becerreá: **★Hs Herbón**, G. Jiménez 8, ✆ 982 36 01 34 (*inexpensive*), and the **★★Hs Rivera**, Avda. Madrid 86, ✆ 982 36 01 85 (*moderate*), outside town. Both are basic *hostales* open all year; a couple of bars in town serve meals as well. **Casa de Aldea Valiña**, ✆ 982 36 71 25 (*moderate*), in a farmhouse whose living room ocupies the former '*palloza*', is an excellent choice.

Sarriá ✉ 27600

Sarriá has plenty of choices, starting with **★★★Alfonso IX**, Peregrino 29, ✆ 982 53 00 05, ✉ 982 53 12 61 (*expensive*), with a good restaurant. For less, **★★Hs Londres**, Calvo Sotelo 153, ✆ 982 53 24 56, ✉ 982 53 30 06 (*moderate*) has doubles with baths. **Casa Nova de Rente**, Barbadelo, ✆ 982 18 78 54, offers nice rooms in a countryside environment for a good price.

Detours off the Camino: Lugo

Lugo, may be the capital of Spain's poorest province, but it happily dozes away in cosy retirement on the banks of the Minho after a career of some consequence. Its Celtic name *lug* means either the sun god or sacred forest, and when the Romans took it over in the 2nd century AD, they renamed it Lucus Augusti, made it the capital of their province of Gallaecia and endowed it with a remarkable dark slate corset of **walls**, the best preserved ancient fortifications in Spain, just over 2km long and 28ft (8.5m) high and interspersed with 85 rounded towers. For all that, Lugo was grabbed by the Suevi in the 5th century, the Visigoths in 585, and the Moors in the 8th century. Four ancient gates (and six modern ones) pierce the dark fastness. Pilgrims would enter the southern Santiago gate to visit Lugo's **Cathedral**, built in 1177 and encased in a baroque skin that offers a modest prelude to the great façade and three towers at Santiago de Compostela. Inside there are fittings from every century: a Romanesque chapel and another from 1735, lavish and baroque in the shape of a rounded Greek cross, dedicated to the Virgen de los Ojos Grandes, 'Our Lady of the Big Eyes', designed by Fernando de las Casas, master of the Obradoiro façade at Compostela. Glass protects a beautiful walnut *coro* carved with a proto Art Nouveau flair by Francisco Moure (1590–1621), whose detailed scenes include an anatomy lesson.

Next to the cathedral, elegant Praza Santa María holds the handsome 17th-century **Bishop's Palace**, built in the style of a typical *Gallego pazo*. Just west, **Praza do Campo** with its fountain was the Roman forum; Lugo's medieval neighbourhood, **La Tinería**, extends here around Rúa Cruz and Rúanova. Just north of Prazo do Campo, the formal Alameda gardens give onto the Praza Maior, site of Lugo's rococo Ayuntamiento. Rúa da Raiña heads north to big and busy **Praza de Santo Domingo**, with two Gothic churches: 14th-century **Santo Domingo** and 16th-century, *mudéjar*-influenced **San Francisco**. The delicate cloister and refectory now house the interesting **Provincial Museum** (*open Sept–June 10.30–2 and 4.30–8, Sat 11–2, closed Sun; July and Aug 11–2 and 5–8, Sat 10–2, closed Sun*) containing Celtic and Roman finds. Lugo's beauty-spots are along the Río Minho, the most beautiful of Galicia's rivers; in the **Parque Rosalía de Castro**, just outside the Santiago gate and a favourite rendezvous during the evening *paseo*, the *mirador* has magnificent views of the valley. Near here are the brick vaults of the **Termas Romanas**, or Roman hot baths, now part of a modern complex.

Santa Eulalia de Bóveda, and a Mystery

Some 16km southwest of Lugo (take the Ourense road for 4km, then bear right towards Friol and follow the signs) is the extraordinary 4th-century subterranean chapel of Santa Eulalia de Bóveda, built over a Celtic temple as a Roman nymphaeum, and later as a mausoleum (*open for guided tours in Spanish, Oct–May 11–5, June–Sept 11–7; Sun and hols 11–2, closed Mon*). Discovered in 1962, steps lead down to what must have been an antechamber of some kind. A horseshoe arch with mysterious reliefs of female dancers on one side and the healing of a man on the other leads into a vaulted room with a shallow pool in the centre (perhaps used for immersion baptisms by the early Christians), decorated with colourful winsome murals of birds and trees, variously dated 4th or 8th century—just predating the pre-Romanesque churches of Asturias. The columns by the pool were found nearby and re-erected around the rim; under the pavement, an efficient drainage system kept the water clear. According to the guide, stones carved with the sun, moon and stars were found here and taken to Rome, and the only known building similar to Santa Eulalia is in the Ukraine, and just as mysterious. According to popular belief, the right wall of Santa Eulalia once contained the tomb of Galicia's first 'saint', Prisciliano, whose doctrines, `a syncretism of old Celtic and Christian beliefs, attracted many followers in Galicia and León but upset the Church. For one thing, Prisciliano believed works of the spirit obliterated sexual differences, and that monks and nuns should live together. His followers walked barefoot to stay in contact with the earth's forces, were vegetarians, did a bit of sun-worshipping on the side and retreated to hermitages.

Another rewarding excursion from Lugo is northwest to the evocative ruins of **Sobrado dos Monxes** (*open 10.15–1.15 and 4.15–6.15*), Galicia's greatest monastery, founded by the Cistercians in 1142. Although the original building hasn't survived, a fresh handful of monks have been doing what they can with government funds to preserve the massive towered baroque church, the lovely if rotting choir stalls, originally in the cathedral of Santiago, and the monumental, ogival **kitchen**; also intact are the 13th-century chapel dedicated to the Magdalen, a sacristy (1571) by Juan de Herrera, a 12th-century chapter-house or Sala Capitular, and three 17th- and 18th-century cloisters, wreathed in lichens and wild flowers. Villalba, farther north, was the capital of the Terra Cha, ruled by the Andrade family, who left behind their powerful 15th-century octagonal castle, now an exceptionally nice *parador*.

Lugo ✉ 27000

At the top of the scale, the ★★★★**Gran Hotel Lugo**, Avda. Ramón Ferreiro 21, ✆ 982 22 41 52, ✆ 982 24 16 60 (*expensive*) offers a pool, piano bar, air conditioning, a good seafood restaurant (Os Marisqueiros) and a pizzeria. Within the walls, the ★★★**Méndez Núñez**, Reina 1, ✆ 982 23 07 11, ✆ 982 22 97 38 (*moderate*) has modern rooms, or you can have a view of the walls at the ★★**Hs Mar de Plata**, Ronda Muralla 5, ✆ 982 22 89 10. ★**Hs Parames**, Rúa do Progreso 28, ✆ 982 22 62 51 (*inexpensive*) is decent and central, and has a popular restaurant with a *900 pts* menu. Although Lugo boasts of quirky delicacies such as pancakes with pig's blood, it has good seafood restaurants; two of the best are nearby in Rúa da Cruz, **Alberto** ✆ 982 22 83 10, offers classic and modern Galician dishes (*closed Sun*), and the older **Verruga**, ✆ 982 22 98 55 (*closed Mon*); both have good *2300 pts menus*. **Campos**, Rúa Nova 4, ✆ 982 22 97 43, has traditional *Gallego* sucking-pig, octopus and delicacies such as *pimientos del Piquillo* filled with seafood (*menus from 1300 pts*).

Vilalba ✉ 27400

The crenellated ★★★**Parador Condes de Vilalba**, Valeriano Valdesuso, ✆ 982 51 00 11, ✆ 982 51 00 90 (*expensive*) bestows on its visitors feudal fancies—the windows in the 3m-thick walls were made to shoot arrows at attackers far below. Book early to nab one of its 6 rooms, all centrally heated, with modern necessities like TVs and minibars. The restaurant in the cellar offers baronial dining on free-range capons, fresh Galician produce and wine. *Closed Dec.* For half as much, check into modern, functional ★★★**Villamartín**, Avda. Tierra Chá, ✆ 982 51 12 15, ✆ 982 51 11 35 (*moderate*).

Monforte de Lemos ✉ 27400

The most pretensions are on offer at the ★★**Hs Puente Romano II**, Paseo del Malecón, ✆ 982 41 11 68 (*moderate*), but there are also nicely priced rooms at the ★★**Hs Río** near the centre at R. Baamonde 30, ✆ 982 40 18 50 (*cheap*). For reliably delicious *Gallego* cuisine, try **O Grelo**, Chantada 16, ✆ 982 40 47 01 (*moderate*).

Castroverde ✉ 49110

Pazo de Vilabade, ✆ 982 31 30 00 (*expensive*) is one of the nicest '*pazos*' in Galicia.

Santiago de Compostela

The original European tourist destination, Santiago de Compostela still comes up with the goods. Not only does it boast a great cathedral where pilgrims are promised 50 per cent off their time in Purgatory, but the moss-stained baroque city is pure granite magic, a rich grey palette of a hundred moods crowned with curlicues. The university keeps the ancient streets and especially the bars full of life year round and fuels the raw *urbanización* that engulfs the perimeters. Expect rain—the city never fails gently to remind you that the showers are good for granite, fostering the elegant patina on its monuments and the micro-gardens that sprout out of the stone.

History

The story goes that in the year 813, a bright star led Pelayo, a hermit shepherd, to the forgotten tomb of St James the Greater, the legendary apostle of Spain. The place was named Compostela, a corruption of the Latin *Campus stellae* 'Field of the star'. Of course apostles don't compost like everyone else, and the remains of James were just what Christian Spain required at the dawn of the Reconquista. Local bishop Theodomir confirmed the relics' authenticity and built a chapel. So many pilgrims began to arrive that an even larger church was needed and supplied by Alfonso III the Great in 896. This in turn fell to Al-Mansur and his Moorish armies when they swept through in 997; Al-Mansur took the bells to the Great Mosque at Córdoba, but left the Apostle's tomb alone, awed by the piety of a single monk, who fearlessly knelt there and prayed during the battle. Sometime in these early days James the humble fisherman was given a new posthumous role as Santiago Matamoros, hero of the entirely apocryphal Battle of Clavijo of 844. This legend was 'confirmed' in a 12th-century document known as the *Privilegio de los Votos de Santiago*, purporting to be by Ramiro I of Asturias, the grateful victor of Clavijo, vowing a tax in perpetuity to the saint's church in Compostela (a tax annulled only in 1834). The new tax paid for the present cathedral. By 1104, Compostela was made an archbishopric; in 1189, Alexander III decreed it a Holy City, on a par with Jerusalem and Rome. In 1236, Fernando III the Saint brought back Santiago's bells from the Great Mosque. In 1589, with Drake ravaging the coast, Santiago was tucked away for safekeeping, but in a fit of amnesia, no one could remember where. Still, the pilgrims came, and only in the 19th century did a cathedral workman stumble across the most important relics in Spain (1879). How to make sure they were genuine? An authenticated apostolic bone chip from Pistoia was sent over and fitted the notch in the skull like a hand in a glove.

On years when the 25th of July, Santiago's feast day, happens to land on a Sunday, a Holy Year is proclaimed and the city launches into a year's worth of festivities. 1999 is such a year and visitors should keep an eye out for music, dance and street activities that celebrate all things *Gallego*—both traditional and contemporary. A special Santiago hotline has been set up to provide information on events: ✆ 981 54 19 99. If you miss the action in 1999, you'll have to wait for the next Holy Year in 2004. *For listings of events, call ✆ 981 58 25 25.*

Getting Around

Santiago's airport, ✆ 981 59 75 00, is at Labacolla, 11km to the east. It has regular flights to Barcelona, Madrid, Sevilla, Santa Cruz de Tenerife, Bilbao, Santander and San Sebastián, as well as direct flights to London, Paris, Amsterdam, Geneva and Frankfurt. Iberia's office is at Gral. Pardiñas 36, ✆ 981 57 20 24; there are buses to the airport from the station run by the Empresa Freire, ✆ 981 58 81 11.

Santiago's train station is a 10-minute walk from the centre at the end of Rúa do Hórreo, ✆ 52 02 02, with daily connections to Madrid, Ourense, A Coruña, Vigo, Zamora and other points. The bus station is way out on San Cayetano, ✆ 981 58 77 00, at the opposite end of town from the train station; city bus 10 links it to Praza de Galicia. Buses go to nearly all points in Galicia, especially the Rías Altas.

Tourist Information

Rúa de Vilar 43, ✆ 981 58 40 81.

There is a daily **market** (*exc Sunday*) in the covered market in Praza de San Félix.

Santiago de Compostela

N

100 metres
100 yards

CAMPO DAS HORTAS

RÚA DAS HORTAS

RÚA DAS CARRETAS

CRUZEIRO DO GAIO

Hospi
Hosta
Reyes

AVENIDA DE COMPOSTELA

San Fructuoso

Pazo
de Rajo

PRAZA DO OBRADOIRO

RÚA DO POMBAL

Colegio de
San Jerónimo

PASEO DE FERRADURA

TRAVESA DE FONSECA

Colegio
Mayor de
Fonseca

Post Office

Santa Susana

CAMPO DE SAN CLEMENZO

RÚA DA RAIÑA

RÚA DO VILAR

Colegio de
S. Clemenzo

AVENIDA DE FIGUEROA

RÚA DO FRANCO

Tourist
Information

Iglesia del Pilar

Santa María
Salomé

CARREIRA DO CONDE

RÚA DA SENRA

PRAZA
DO TORAL

RÚA DAS ORFAS

RÚA DE MONTERO RÍOS

FONTE DE SANTO ANTONIO

PRAZA DE
GALICIA

Train
Station

Santa María
del Sar

Irresistibly all roads in Compostela lead up to the towering granite magnet of the Cathedral of Santiago, the town's *raison d'être* and culmination of the pilgrim's journey. Approach it from the enormous Praza do Obradoiro, the 'Square of Works', also known as Praza de España, where for centuries the cathedral's stone masons liberated the soul of Galicia's stone and made it sing and blaze like a baroque bonfire. In the rain and mists, at morning or sunset or the heat of the day, the cathedral façade changes its tune; it cries out for a new Monet to paint its moods during the course of the day or, perhaps even better, a composer.

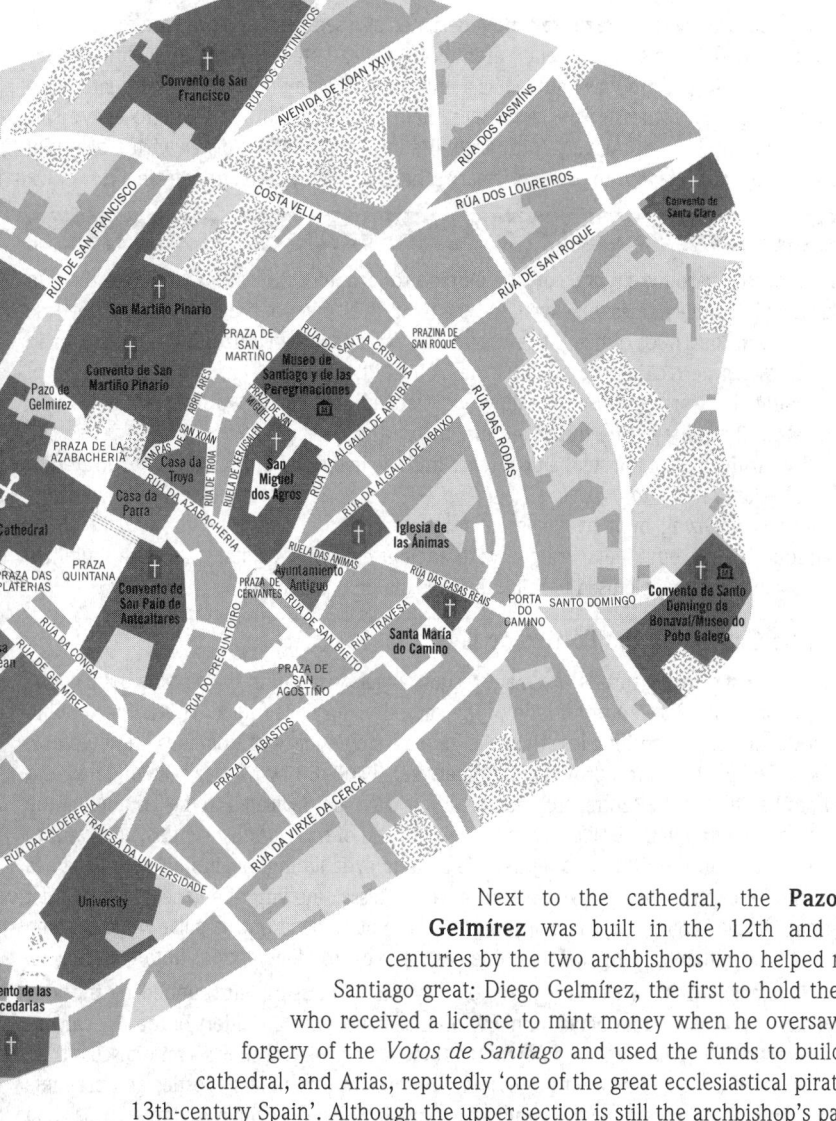

Next to the cathedral, the **Pazo de Gelmírez** was built in the 12th and 13th centuries by the two archbishops who helped make Santiago great: Diego Gelmírez, the first to hold the job, who received a licence to mint money when he oversaw the forgery of the *Votos de Santiago* and used the funds to build the cathedral, and Arias, reputedly 'one of the great ecclesiastical pirates of 13th-century Spain'. Although the upper section is still the archbishop's palace, you can visit the lower medieval rooms, especially the huge Romanesque dining-hall, where the corbels are carved with delicious scenes of a medieval feast.

Continuing around the square, the Plateresque **Hospital Real** (1501–9) was constructed for poor pilgrims by Fernando and Isabel with the booty from taking Granada in 1492. Built by Enrique de Egas, its façade concentrates its embellishments in a few key spots, in its long baroque balconies added in 1678, and especially in the crowded Gothic Renaissance altarpiece of a doorway. A Christian's Who's Who from Adam and Eve on up fill the chiselled niches. A hospital until 1953, it was converted into a five-star *parador*: at least have a drink down in the bar—the former hospital morgue.

The enormous 18th-century **Pazo de Rajoy**, designed as a seminary and now the town hall, is pure Parisian neoclassicism, by French architect Charles Lemaur. Next, the 16th-century **Colegio de San Jerónimo** was founded as a university, where priests could learn languages to hear the pilgrims' confessions. Classes were held just behind in the **Colegio Mayor de Fonseca**, built by Juan de Álava (1546) around a lovely, peaceful cloister with a beautiful *mudéjar* ceiling, still a favourite place for weary scholars to enjoy a breath of fresh air.

The Cathedral of Santiago

And back to that baroque firecracker, the Obradoiro façade of the cathedral where the two towers shoot like huge flames to heaven. On the right, the Tower of the Bells was built by José Peña de Toro in the 1600s, while the left-hand one was added by Fernando Casas y Novoa in the 1750s, when he tackled the main façade. A lively triple-ramp stair leads up to a pair of doors, arranged to form a cross in stonework; stacked above are two calm windows in a shallow arch like the eye of a hurricane just before the front peaks in a flickering crest of granite fire. At the foot of the steps a door leads into the delightful **crypt of Master Mateo** or 'Catedral Vieja' (*11–1 and 4–6, Sun 10–1 and 4–7, adm; keep your ticket for the treasury, cloister and museum*), built by the great master builder to distribute the weight of his Romanesque façade, but so elaborately, with ancient columns, capitals, and fine sculpture under the vaults that people used to think this was the first cathedral.

Inside the Cathedral: the Pórtico de la Gloria

Perhaps the most startling surprise for many visitors awaits just within the busy baroque doors, where the original 12th-century façade of the cathedral survives intact. This is the sublime **Pórtico de la Gloria**, nothing less than the greatest single piece of Romanesque sculpture, anywhere. Sculpted in warm brown granite between 1168–88 by Master Mateo (dated and signed on the lintel of the central arch) its three doorways are dedicated to the Triumph of the Apocalypse, full of movement, life and rhythm; if the end of the world is like this, you want to be there. Nearly all the 200 or so figures are smiling or laughing, beginning with St James himself on the central pillar, carved with the tree of Jesse, showing the genealogy of Christ from Adam to the Virgin Mary; so many pilgrims have put a hand on the pillar while bending to kiss the base in thanksgiving that the stone has the five worn indentations from their fingers.

Above St James, Christ in Majesty raises both hands in blessing, surrounded by the four Evangelists, Apostles and an ogival rainbow of musicians—the 24 Elders of the Apocalypse (plus a few stand-ins), each with a different instrument on his lap as they seem to discuss their hopes for another gig during an intermission. On the two side pillars apostles and prophets chat pleasantly together, among them the famous laughing Daniel, who is said to owe his good humour to the loveliness of Queen Esther, whom he eyes across the way; Chinese monsters grimace on the lowest frieze. The door on the right is dedicated to heaven and hell, mostly, and depicts children suffering the torments of the damned with their parents—on the surface a powerful psychological trick to make parents toe the line—while the scenes above the left door are even more elusive. After drinking in this most eloquent draught of medieval happiness, pilgrims would line up behind the central pillar before the curly-haired figure of Master Mateo, who is humbly kneeling to offer the cathedral to God; his nickname, '*O Santo dos Croques*', 'Saint Bump-on-the-Head', comes from the millions who have bowed their heads to touch Mateo's in the hope that some of his genius would rub off.

The **Romanesque interior** of the cathedral is essentially as Master Mateo left it, a long, majestic, barrel-vaulted nave lined with galleries. The silver high altar glimmers in the penumbra, visible since the 1940s when the enclosed baroque choir was removed. Of the chapels along the nave the most important is the first on the right, the 16th-century **reliquary chapel** and Royal Pantheon, with medieval tombs of Galicia's royal family, and reliquaries containing bits of the True Cross and the head of St James the Lesser, who was occasionally purposefully confused with James the Greater for propaganda ends. Next on the right is the cathedral **Treasury**, aglitter with the silver hammer used to pound open the Holy Door in Holy Years, silver scallop shells, a score of other showy religious trappings and a celebrated 16th-century monstrance. When you get right up to it, the glow-in-the-dark 17th-century high altar, lavishly coated with Mexican silver, turns out to be a pointless piece of tomfoolery, its cast of knick-knack characters borrowed from a giant's Christmas tree. Just over the altar itself sits a stiff idol, a 12th-century statue of Santiago, the patron saint of Spain. The thing to do is climb the narrow stairway behind the altar, kiss the statue's robe and receive a holy card (for the certificate of indulgence, the *compostellana*, pilgrims should apply with their documents to the *Oficina arzobispal*, in the back of the cathedral). Below the altar you can pay your respects to the saint's bones in the 19th-century silver crypt; the outer, rounded wall here survives from Alfonso III's 9th-century church, while the inner wall is believed to be Roman.

To the side of the high altar, notice the ropes and pulleys suspended from the octagonal dome from which, on high feast days, the **Botafumeiro**, the world's largest censer, is suspended and swung with terrifying force across the entire length of the transept in a comet-like arc of perfumed smoke and sparks. Weighing in at 54kg, the Botafumeiro is a smaller brass version of the original silver model made in 1602 and pilfered by Napoleon's troops: it takes eight men, the *tiraboleiros*, to swing it on a system invented in the Middle Ages. Don't miss it if you're in town on a holy day, and try not to think about the time when Catherine of Aragón attended Mass and the Botafumeiro broke loose and flew out of the window. The ten chapels radiating like petals from the ambulatory are all worth a look, especially the Romanesque **Capilla de San Salvador**, where pilgrims received Communion. Off the north transept, a doorway topped with a 13th-century relief of the Magi leads into the Romanesque **Capilla de la Corticela**. Off the south transept, a 16th-century Gothic-vaulted **cloister** big enough for a football match holds the **Cathedral Museum** and **Library**; the former has an illuminated 12th-century *Codex Calixtus* and the latter contains the Botafumeiro when it's not in use. The **Sala Capitular** contains the cathedral's impressive collection of tapestries. There are, however, pretty views to be had from the upper rooms across the Praza do Obradoiro.

Around the Cathedral

Although low key after the Obradoiro façade, the cathedral's other entrances each deserve a look. Circumnavigating the Pazo de Gelmírez, you'll come first to the split-level **Praza das Platerías**, named after the silversmiths whose shops once filled the arcades. The double **Puerta de las Platerías** is the only one to remain essentially unchanged from the Romanesque cathedral. Locals use the doors as a short cut across town, as their ancestors did in the Middle Ages, when cathedrals were covered public squares as much as religious shrines. From here you can gaze up at the ornament-laden 80m **Berenguel** designed by Galician humanist Domingo de Andrade in the 1710s to hold the town clock. The *praza*'s geometric baroque **Chapter House** and the **fountain of the horse** were both designed by Fernández Sarela.

Past the bulk of the Berenguel is the enclosed **Praza da Quintana**; the upper level is named 'of the living' and the lower 'of the dead', recalling the Roman cemetery that once occupied the spot. Alongside the square runs the stern, unforgiving façade of the **Convento de San Paio de Antelares,** 'Pelayo before the Altars', containing a **Museo de Arte Sacro** (entrance around back, *open summer only 10–1 and 4–7*), where a celebrity Virgin holds the Child in one hand and thumps a devil with the other.

In the lower square is the **Puerta Santa**, opened only during a Holy Year, or Año Xacobeo, when St James' Day—25 July—falls on a Sunday; 1999 and 2004 have aslo been declared Holy Years. The doorway of 1611 consists of 24 compartments, each pigeonholing a carved figure from the Romanesque choir. The handsome 17th-century **Casa de la Parra** is one of the prettiest in Santiago, decorated with grapes.

The north façade faces **Praza de la Azabachería** ('of the jet-makers'),where pilgrims bought souvenirs; you couldn't have your photo taken next to St James back then, but you could get little black figures of the Apostle with yourself praying at his feet. In the Middle Ages, the square was the favourite rendezvous for French pilgrims, who would bathe in the long-gone Fountain of Paradise, before entering the Cathedral for the first time through the French Door, unfortunately obliterated by the dullest of the 18th-century facelifts the cathedral underwent.

The Gallop to the Scallop

The very first thing a medieval pilgrim did upon arriving in the city was stop in the Barrio de los Conchieros, buy a scallop, eat it (this is where French pilgrims learned to make *coquilles St Jacques*, after all) and stick the shell on the turned-up brim of his or her hat—visible proof that they had made it at last; strict laws forbade the selling of scallops anywhere else along the *camino*. By the 16th century, the real shell was replaced by a fancy souvenir replica, either in silver or in jet.

The scallop, that tasty bivalve that thrives in the *rías* of Galicia, has been associated with the Santiago pilgrimage since the early Middle Ages. In Compostela, as usual, they can explain it with a miracle: a young *Gallego* , on the eve of his wedding, was spirited into the sea by his wayward horse and believed drowned, although in truth the horse was running along the waves to meet the stone boat bringing the body of St James to Galicia. When the bridegroom returned, escorting the boat, his body was covered with an armour of milk-white shells, so amazing the locals that they converted at once to the new faith. Its Spanish name, *venera*, calls up associations with the vagina and Venus, the goddess of love, who was born of the seafoam and surfed ashore on a giant scallop shell. For pilgrims, the shell also symbolized the end of the journey, the resurrection and unity in the world—the sea from which it came, the earth in its stony hardness, and the sun in its radiant lines.

It's hard to think of another symbol so polyvalent, embracing sex, death, dinner and spiritual wholeness—not to mention a multinational company peddling the Super or Unleaded souls of the dead dinosaurs that fuel the way.

San Martín Pinario

Another attraction in Praza de la Azabachería was the chance for destitute pilgrims to hang their rags on an iron cross and pick up new clothes from the Benedictines at San Martín Pinario, founded in 912 as the special protector of the Apostle's tomb. Inside, the vast Claustro de la Portería with its elegant fountain was completed by Casas y Novoa, while just beyond is an extraordinary, floating 17th-century staircase with Aztec decorations under a baroque dome. Beyond, the huge barrel-vaulted church is the stage for Casas y Novoa's *retablo mayor*, a feverish blast of intricate gilded detail, a nightmarish vision of total paradise marked by the merciless destiny of the unbelieving Moors stage left and right. Casas y Novoa was also responsible for the almost as frantic Capilla del Socorro on the right side of the nave. The stately, colonnaded 18th-century church façade facing Praza San Martín grows like an altarpiece above a sunken baroque staircase designed by a Dominican named Manuel de los Mártires, all granite ribbons squirming below the level of the pavement, like nothing else in Spain.

In Praza San Miguel, the 14th-century Gothic Pazo de Don Pedro contains the **Museo de Santiago y de las Peregrinaciones**, (*open daily exc Mon, Tues–Fri 10–8, Sat 10.30–1.30, and 5–8, Sun and hols 10.30–1.30*). For a real eyeful of local baroque, walk north to Rúa de San Roque, where the startling façade of **Santa Clara** by Simón Rodríguez almost jumps out.

Elsewhere in Santiago

The founders of the two great mendicant orders of the 13th century both made pilgrimages and personally founded monasteries. In 1214, St Francis founded the **Convento de San Francisco**, and St Dominic founded the rather larger **Convento de Santo Domingo de Bonaval** during his pilgrimage in 1220. Behind the baroque façade hides a handsome Gothic church from the 1300s and the chapel of the Pantheon of Illustrious Gallegos, last resting-place of poet Rosalía de Castro and the caricaturist Castelao (died 1950), the Goya of the Civil War. The convent and cloister house the **Museo do Pobo Galego** (*open 10–1 and 4–7, closed Sun; adm*) with a good ethnographic collection and a memorable **triple spiral staircase**, a stunning architectural *tour de force* by Domingo de Andrade. Off the Azabachería, Rúa de Troya is named after the venerable **Casa de la Troya**, base for the local *tunas*, bands of student minstrels, who play Galician-Celtic music around the Praza da Immaculada. In arcaded Rúa Nova is the little church of **Santa María Salomé** with a Romanesque door under a Gothic arcade. In parallel **Rúa do Vilar**, Santiago's arcaded main shopping street, the **Casa do Dean** has a fine baroque portal; at the Confitería Mora (No.60), pick up a delicious *tarta de Compostela,* made with chocolate bumps in honour of the Santo dos Croques. For the classic view of Santiago's towers and roofs, walk along the **Paseo da Ferradura**, a leafy 19th-century park where old men will take your photo with cameras nearly as old as themselves.

Santa María del Sar

After being thoroughly baroqued by the centre of Santiago, take a Romanesque break at the 12th-century Santa María del Sar, a mile south of the **Convento de las Mercedarias**. Alone in its meadow, Santa María is a jewel of Spanish architecture, with a different slant—literally. The piers and arches along the high barrel-vaulted nave have leant back at a startlingly precarious angle as long as anyone can remember. It may well have been done intentionally like the *campanile* of Pisa. Don't miss the remarkable carvings by Master Mateo along one gallery in the **cloister** (*open Mon–Sat 10–1 and 4–6, summer till 10pm*).

Finding a place to stay at any price is easy in the city that has received visitors for 1100 years; even during the high holy day of 25 July you'll probably be met at the bus or train station by landladies luring you to their *hostales* or *casas particulares* for around *2000 pts* a head.

luxury–expensive

Poor pilgrims used to stay in the magnificent 15th-century ★★★★★**Hs Los Reyes Católicos**, Praza del Obradoiro, ✆ 981 58 22 00, 📠 981 56 30 94, but since 1954 it has been reserved for visitors with well-padded wallets, the luxurious *ne plus ultra* of Spanish *hostales* and one of Europe's best hotels. The trendiest place to stay, modern, central ★★★★★**Araguaney**, Alfredo Brañas 5, ✆ 981 59 59 00, 📠 981 59 02 87, offers every conceivable service, except perhaps easy parking—a headache in the *casco viejo*. ★★★★**Hotel Compostela**, Hórreo 1, ✆ 981 58 57 00, 📠 981 56 32 69, is a grand old granite hotel still offering a touch of class for *14,000 pts*.

moderate

For a cheerful Catholic atmosphere near the centre, get a room at the former Franciscan Missionary College, ★★★**Hogar San Francisco**, Campillo de San Francisco 3, ✆ 981 58 16 00, 📠 981 57 19 16. ★★**Hs Universal**, Pza. de Galicia 2, ✆ 981 58 58 00, is a solid no-surprises provincial hotel only 100m from the *casco viejo*. Try **Pazo de Xan Xordo**, ✆ 981 88 82 59, in Lavacolla, if you prefer to stay out of town. Or likewise, there's the Casa Grande de Cornide, ✆ 981 80 55 99, in Calo-Teo off the Padron road, run by a friendly duo in a lovely setting with a swimming pool.

inexpensive

On Santiago's prettiest street, ★★**Hs Suso**, Rúa del Vilar 65, ✆ 981 58 66 11, a pilgrims' favourite, is run by a jovial fellow who may have something to do with the tasty tapas in the bar downstairs. A lovely patina of age adorns the charming ★**Hs La Estela**, by the cathedral on Raxoi 1, ✆ 981 58 27 96. The **Hospedaje Rodrigues,** Pinos 4, ✆ 981 58 84 08, offers kitchen privileges to guests.

Eating Out

Eating in Santiago is a pleasure—competition is keen and the food has to be good to succeed. Rúa del Hórreo has the biggest concentration of restaurants. Classic eateries include **Anexo Vilas** on the Avda. de Villagarcía 21, ✆ 981 59 83 87, where an informal tapas bar serves delicious seafood and *empanadas*, while a dining room upstairs shows Gallegan cuisine at its very best. For pudding, try the *Postre Xacobeo*, followed by a local digestif made from apples or peaches (*menu 4000 pts*). *Closed Mon.* Another brother runs the equally worthy bastion of *Gallego* cuisines, **Vilas**, in a turn-of-the-century house at Rosalía de Castro 88, ✆ 981 59 10 00; similar prices. *Closed Sun.* For tradition mixed with international, seasonal dishes, try **Don Gaiferos**, Rua Nova 23, ✆ 981 58 38 94 (*expensive*), with a beautiful vaulted dining room. *Closed Sun.* **Tacita de Juan**, Hórreo 31, ✆ 981 56 32 55 (*expensive*) offers *nouvelle cuisine* made from the freshest Galician ingredients (*menu 4500 pts*). *Closed Sun.*

For a special treat, drive out 8km to Vedra in the Valle de Ulla, where **Roberto**, San Xulián de Sales, © 981 51 17 69 (*expensive*, but not outrageous) prepares some of the most delicious dishes in all Galicia in a lovely country villa. *Closed Sat and Sun eve.*

Alameda, Porta Faixera 15 1Ě, © 981 58 47 96 (*moderate*) serves up hearty Galician fare—all types of *empanadas*, and local wines. For good value, **A Roda**, Rodríguez de Viguiri 7, © 981 58 70 50 (*moderate–inexpensive*) is one of the best. For a feast of fresh seafood that won't break the bank, drive out to **Pampín**, Puente Espino at Calo-Teo on the Padrón road, © 981 80 31 70 (*inexpensive*). Also out of town is the **Cierto Blanco**, © 981 54 83 83, serving superb seafood.

bars and nightlife

Santiago's lively bars offer a wonderful way to eat and drink a rainy night away. The area around Rúa Franco is the centre of the evening *marcha*, where **El Franco** at No.28 is a typical place to start with your first *aperitivo*. *Raciones* or tapas of octopus with peppers and paprika are the speciality at the **Mesón do Pulpo**, Vista Alegre 30; **O Gato Negro**, Raiña, has delicious eel pies. **Bodeguilla de San Roque**, San Roque 13 (near Santa Clara) serves wine with plates of delicious breast-shaped *tetilla* cheese and ham. For jazz with your drinks, try **La Borriquita de Belém**, San Paio, near the cathedral, while chocolate-lovers should try the hot chocolate or chocolate cocktails served nearby at **Metate**, Colexón de San Paio, a former chocolate factory. The prettiest café in town, **Derby**, Huérfanos 29, hasn't changed its décor since the 1920s.

Live music and other happenings can be taken in at the **Casa de las Crechas**, located behind the cathedral. The beautiful people of Santiago meet at **Casting**, the disco in the aforementioned hotel **Araguaney**; **Ruta 66** on C/ Perez Constanti is a popular place with plenty of action, while ultra-modern **Ultramarinos** at the entrance of the Puerta del Camino is where the young and trendy hang out.

Back to the Rías: the Golfo Ártabro

Two of Galicia's most important ports, Ferrol and A Coruña, occupy either end of the 20km Golfo Ártabro, savagely bitten out of the northwest coast. You can get there by dawdling west along the Rías Altas (*see* p.305–6) or by racing up the A9 motorway from Santiago.

Getting Around

By air: A Coruña's airport is 9km away at Alvedro, © 981 18 72 00, with connections to Madrid, Barcelona and Sevilla. There's an airport bus into town.

By train: Ferrol and A Coruña are linked by RENFE with Pontedeume and the main junction at Betanzos, Santiago, Ferrol, Lugo, Vigo, Padrón and Villagarcía de Arosa. In A Coruña the station San Cristóbal is a bit out of the way on Avda. Joaquín Planelles, © 981 15 02 02—best to take bus no.1 from the nearby bus station to the historic centre. There's also a RENFE travel office on Fontán 3, © 981 22 19 48. In Ferrol, RENFE and FEVE share the same station, © 981 37 13 04 and © 981 37 04 01.

By bus: A Coruña's bus station is on Caballeros near the RENFE station, © 981 23 96 44; El Rápido buses serve Betanzos and Monfero. Ferrol's buses leave from the train station, © 981 32 47 51 and go to Betanzos, Viveiro, Foz, Ribadeo and Lugo.

Ferrol: Magdalena 12, ✆ 981 31 11 79.

Pontedeume: Avda. Saavedra Meneses 2, ✆ 981 43 02 70.

A Coruña: Dársena de la Marina, ✆ 981 22 18 22.

There are **markets** in Pontedeume on Saturdays; in Betanzos on Tuesdays, Thursdays and Saturdays; in A Coruña Monday–Fridays (Mercado San Agustín).

Ferrol and Pontedeume

Plump on the big fat Ría de Betanzos, swollen by four rivers, the salty city of Ferrol was named after its lighthouse (*faro*). Gently, slowly, the port city has dropped the article 'El' from the front of its name and the 'del Caudillo' stuck on the back in honour of Francisco Franco, born here in 1892, son of a naval supply officer who grew up to be the youngest general in Spanish history before his career as dictator. Ferrol has a pretty enough medieval core, a large planned 18th-century geometric, neoclassical quarter, the legacy of Felipe V who greatly boosted Ferrol's fortunes, and a modern quarter that looks like a Simcity computer game. The best thing to do is just wander among the pretty houses with 'crystal galleries' and the casino and gardens. A pair of castles on the slender waist of the *ría* defend the naval base.

South of Ferrol, the charming medieval town of **Pontedeume** was once the preserve of the Counts of Andrade, who built and collected the tolls from their great bridge over the Ría Eume. There are a couple of beaches along the *ría* (the Praia Perbes is a good one) and off the NVI to Betanzos, **San Miguel de Breamo** (1137), with its façade pierced by a window in the shape of an 11-point star and capitals to warm the cockles of any Romanesque diehard's heart.

Betanzos

Rising steeply over the head of yet another small estuary, lovely Betanzos is a far more ancient place, a Celtic village that grew into the Roman port of Brigantium Flavium. It thrived into the 18th century, when the Mandeo and Mendo rivers washed in so much silt that they stole Betanzos' seacoast. Progress stopped, leaving a time capsule: houses and mansions of all sizes with wrought-iron balconies or *solanas* line the narrow lanes that wind up the hill from the habour's medieval gates. Life revolves around the charming, monumental **Praza de García Hermanos,** its central ornament a statue of two Indianos and a replica of Versailles' Fountain of Diana. Most of the surrounding buildings are from the 18th century, including a neoclassical palace now used as the National Archives of Galicia; this runs a small but interesting historical **Museo de las Mariñas** (*open 5–8, Sat 11–1*). The three attractive churches are just off the square: the 14th-century **Santa María del Azogue**; 15th-century **Santiago,** with a figure of Santiago Matamoros on the tympanum; and Gothic **San Francisco**, inspired by the basilica at Assisi. Rather than take the NVI directly to A Coruña, follow the pretty scenery along the Ría de Betanzos up to the local resort of **Sada**, to see its boardwalk and **La Terraza**, the finest *modernista* building in Galicia, designed by López Hernández, a curious pavilion made of glass and giant music stands. The road to A Coruña passes the **Pazo de Meirás**, residence of Galicia's greatest novelist, Countess Emilia Pardo Bazán, and later Franco, whose descendants still own it; further along, just offshore on a wooded islet, the 17th-century **Castillo de Santa Cruz** once defended A Coruña and now awaits a new rôle.

Occupying the length of the Ría da Coruña and the southwest fringe of the Golfo Ártabro, A Coruña is the liveliest city in Galicia, its big (pop. 230,000), exuberant, commercial capital with character to spare. Sprawling over a peninsula and attached to the mainland by a thin neck of land, it has beautiful windswept beaches facing the Atlantic and a magnificent sheltered harbour in the estuary that has made its fortune and paid for all its hypnotic wall of windowed balconies or *solanas* that gave A Coruña its nickname 'Crystal City'. A Coruña's relationship with Britain goes back to its first settlers, Phoenician merchants who imported tin from Cornwall. The Romans called it Ardobicum Corunium, and tenuously associated it with Hercules, who performed one of his Twelve Labours (stealing the cattle of Geryon) down in Cádiz on the other side of Spain and reputedly had a hand in building the lighthouse. The Suevians and the Moors took turns running the show until 1002; in the Middle Ages, English pilgrims to Santiago often landed here, among them Chaucer's Wife of Bath and his patron John of Gaunt, who arrived in 1386, though unsuccessfully, to claim the Spanish throne for his wife, daughter of Pedro the Cruel. On 22 July 1588, an Armada of 130 enormous galleons, manned by 10,000 sailors and 19,000 soldiers set sail from A Coruña to meet defeat at Gravelines and storms around Scotland; by the time the Armada limped home, only 76 half-wrecked galleons pulled into port, minus 15,000 soldiers.

In the 'Groyne'

The classic view of A Coruña is of its harbour along **Avenida de la Marina**, lined with a solid wall of crystal galleries set in white balconies, a window cleaner's vision of hell. It is magical to sail into, just as Drake fearlessly did in 1589, swooping down in the night with 30 ships to rub salt in Felipe's wounds. Only a young girl named María Pita stood in the way, not only raising the alarm to save the city but somehow swiping Drake's flag in the process. In gratitude A Coruña gave her name to its biggest, busiest square, **Praza María Pita** where the older part of A Coruña—what old British seadogs called 'the Groyne'—begins.

Near the harbour at Rúa Tabernas 13, Countess Emilia Pardo Bazán was born in 1851; the mansion now houses the **Royal Gallego Academy** and a small **museum** dedicated to the novelist (*open Mon–Sat 10–12*). For pilgrims who sailed into A Coruña, the 12th-century over-restored Romanesque church of **Santiago** was their first stop. The **Colegiata de Santa María del Campo**, begun in the 1210s and finished in the 1400s, stands at the top of the square. Its sculptors were star-struck: star decorations run along the roof and on the west façade; the triple portal has a carving of the Three Magi. Over the north door two angels stand by as someone seems to fall out of the sky with either star symbols or perhaps Ezekiel's wheel of fire, whirling up in the cosmos. Inside are some fine Romanesque tombs, polychrome statues and just to the left of the altar, another star, carved on a capital. Just down from here, the little Plazuela de Santa Bárbara is A Coruña's most charming, site of the **Convento de Santa Barbara** (1613), where cloistered Poor Clares live behind the portal. Behind this, the **Convento de Santo Domingo** has two excellent baroque chapels from the 17th century, especially the Capilla de la Virgen del Rosario, sheltering the Crystal City's patroness.

Santo Domingo stands on the edge of the evocative **Jardín de San Carlos**, set in the walls of the old fortress of San Carlos. It contains the granite tomb of Sir John Moore, who in 1809 led the routed, dispirited British army across Galicia with the French on his tail. At Elviña, just before A Coruña, he sent most of his troops ahead to board ships for home, just as Marshal Soult launched into a vicious attack; Moore managed to stall the French long enough for 15,000 of his men to embark under Soult's nose, an operation that has been called a precursor to Dunkirk. Just opposite, A Coruña's busy military history is remembered in the **Museo Militar** (*open 10–2*) in the old church of San Francisco. From here, bus no.3 will take you out 2km to the northernmost tip of the peninsula and the 104m **Torre de Hércules**, A Coruña's proudest symbol (*open 10–2 and 4–6, closed Sat afternoon and Sun*). Built in the 2nd century AD in the time of Trajan, it's the oldest continuous working Roman lighthouse, but with an external skin from 1791. Bring a pep pill: it's 242 steps to the top for the splendid view of the city and ocean from 300ft up. Within walking distance from the Jardin de San Carlos, the Paseo do Parrote leads out to **Castillo de San Antón**, last rebuilt in 1779. It now defends artefacts from the Iron Age, the Celtic *castros*, Romans, and Middle Ages in the **Museo Arqueológico** (*open 10–3 and 4–9, closed Mon; adm*).

In the newer part of A Coruña (beyond Praza de María Pita) the ex-Maritime Consulate in Praza do Pintor Sotomayor (off the Rúa Panaderas) houses the **Museo de Bellas Artes** (*open 10–2, in summer also 4–7; adm*), with a collection of European paintings, sculptures, ceramics and coins dating from the 17th century. The **Casa de las Ciencias** in Parque de Santa Margarita has a planetarium and museum dedicated to the world of science, technology and nature (*open 10–7, Sun 11–3.30, closed Mon*). On Paseo de Ronda near the stadium is the ultra-modern **Domus**, or Museum of Man, designed by Arata Isozaki and dedicated entirely to the human body. On the other side of the isthmus lie A Coruña's beaches: the **Praias de Ríazor** and **Orzán** fill up in summer. Quieter (except in August), cleaner and prettier strands are outside the city at **Santa Cristina**, **Bastiagueiro**, **Santa Cruz**, **Mera** and **Lorbe** (this last is the farthest from town, 16km away).

Where to Stay and Eating Out

Ferrol ✉ 15400

Franco saw to it that his home town got a **★★★Parador do Ferrol**, Almirante Fernández Martín, ✆ 981 35 67 20, 🖨 981 35 67 20 (*expensive*); its ageing nautically decorated rooms have handsome views over the *ría*. **★★★ Hotel Suizo**, Dolores 17, ✆ 981 30 04 00, 🖨 981 03 06 (*expensive*) is located in a modernist building and has a pleasant café. If you're driving, little **★★★Pazo da Merce**, Ctra. Fene at Neda, ✆ 981 38 22 00, 🖨 981 38 01 04 (*expensive*), is a prettier place, a 17th- and 18th-century manor with *ría* views and a pool.

★★Hs Almendra, Almendra 4, ✆ 981 35 81 90, is a good *moderate* choice; cheaper rooms are concentrated on Pardo Bajo near the station. Along the waterfront at Neda, a 10-minute drive out towards Ortigueira, **Casa Tomás**, ✆ 981 38 02 40, is a favourite with specialities straight from the *ría*: *jurelos en escabeche* (fresh sardines in oil, garlic, basil and wine vinegar) and crayfish from the grill (*menu 3800 pts*). Closed Sun eve and Mon. In town, **Borona**, Dolores 52, ✆ 981 35 50 99 (*moderate*) isn't much to look at but serves delicious *nouvelle cuisine*. Closed Sun. **Pataquiña**, Dolores 35, ✆ 981 35 23 11, offers heaps of *Gallego* specialities; try their *salsa Pataquiña*, a delectable mixture of shrimp and crab cooked in brandy and garlic (*menu 2000 pts*).

Betanzos ✉ 15300

⋆Los Ángeles, Los Ángeles 11, ℰ 981 77 15 11, ● 981 77 12 13 (*moderate*) is modern, but not exactly full of character, while the best bargain, **⋆Hs Barreiros**, Argentina 6, ℰ 981 77 22 59 (*cheap*) has simple rooms and a good cheap restaurant, Mesón dos Arcos. **Casanova**, Pza. García Hermanos 15, ℰ 981 77 06 03 (*moderate*), in a rustically romantic setting, serves up tasty salmon and lamprey dishes for the bold.

A Coruña ✉ 15000

A Coruña fills up in the summer, so arrive early or book ahead. The best-located and most luxurious hotel in the city, **⋆⋆⋆⋆Finisterre**, Pso. del Parrote 20, ℰ 981 20 54 00, ● 981 20 84 62 (*expensive*) overlooks the sea and has pools, tennis courts, a nursery, playground and a casino. **⋆⋆⋆Riazor**, Avda. Pedro Barrié de la Maza 29, ℰ 981 25 34 00, ● 981 25 34 04 (*expensive*) is a pleasant, less costly alternative with a fine beachside location and modern rooms. Near the Torre de Hércules, with frequent buses into the centre, **⋆⋆⋆Ciudad de La Coruña**, Polígono Adormideras, ℰ 981 21 11 00, ● 981 22 46 10 (*expensive*) has modern rooms, all with sea views. **⋆⋆Hs Mar del Plata**, Pso. de Ronda 58, ℰ 981 25 79 62 (*moderate*), has pleasant rooms with bath; **⋆⋆España**, Juan de Vega 7, ℰ 981 22 45 06, ● 981 20 02 79 (*moderate*) is central if a bit noisy. Cheaper central places include the well-kept **⋆Hs El Parador**, Olmos 15, ℰ 981 22 21 21 (*moderate*); **⋆Hs Palacio**, Pza. de Galicia 2, ℰ 981 12 23 38 (*inexpensive*); **⋆Hs Centro Gallego**, La Estrella 2, ℰ 981 22 22 36 (*inexpensive*), and two no-name *hostales* on Zapatería by Santa María do Campo.

Seafood rules menus here and two of the best places to eat it are **Coral**, near the port at La Estrella 2, ℰ 981 22 10 82, for exceptional, delicately prepared shellfish and a classy setting (*menu 4000 pts*), *closed Sun except in summer*, or the long-established **Casa Pardo**, Novoa Santos 15, ℰ 981 28 00 21 (*menu 4000 pts*), famous for melt-in-your-mouth monkfish dishes. *Closed Sun.* **A La Brasa**, Juan Flórez 38, ℰ 981 27 07 27 (*moderate*), as its name implies, specializes in meat and fish sizzling from the grill; if there are two of you, work up an appetite and order the *punta trasera de ternera a la parrilla*, a whopper of a succulent steak with baked potatoes. **La Marina**, Avda. de la Marina 14, ℰ 981 22 39 14, is a popular place offering solid fish and regional dishes for *around 2800 pts*. *Closed Sun eve, Mon and June.*

For less, try **A Penela**, María Pita 9–12, ℰ 981 20 19 69, a typical 'taberna' and restaurant. The bar zone around Rúa Franja and Praza María Pita keeps going well into dawn when the fishing fleet pulls in and everyone goes down to watch the auctioning of the catch, the Muro, a strange ritual featuring fast-talking *Gallegos* and fish you've never seen before.

West of A Coruña: A Costa da Morte

Before tourism invented the Costa del Sol and the Costa Blanca, the Galicians dubbed this region down to Finisterra the 'Coast of Death' after its number of drownings, shipwrecks and ancient Celtic memories; from the end of the west, from the end of the Milky Way, Celtic warriors would sail out to their reward in the seven-towered castle of Arianrhod. The scenery along this wild land of the setting sun is romantic, the waves are dramatic, and the beaches pale and inviting; only the water is icy cold.

A Coruña and Santiago are the main bases for transport to the Costa da Morte, but buses are not all that frequent, and if you intend to visit more than one destination in a day, study bus schedules before setting out. Carballo, 35km southwest of A Coruña, is the main bus junction for the coastal villages.

Ría de Corme e Laxe

Heading west of A Coruña and Carballo, **Buño** is Galicia's traditional pottery town *par excellence*. The road north of Buño ends up at **Malpica**, where the granite cliffs west of A Coruña first relax their vigilance. A former whaling-port, Malpica is partly sheltered by the windswept Sisargas islets, populated only by a large seabird nursery. Appropriately enough, the Costa da Morte has some fine dolmens, or Neolithic tombs, beginning with Malpica's **Pedra de Arca**. The nearest swimming is to the southwest, at the sheltered **Praia de Niñons**, passing by way of the romantic little ivy-shrouded castle known as the **Torres de Mens**, next to a tiny Romanesque chapel decorated with erotic figures.

Corme Porto, a picturesque fishing village to the west, has a reputation for being a law unto itself, a nest of resistance to Franco's Guardia Civil goons even into the 1950s. Ask directions to the **Pedra da Serpe** at Gondomil, a snake carved in the stone believed to date from the Phoenicians and connected to the legend of St Adrian, the local St Patrick, who is said to have gathered all the snakes in Galicia here and given them a mighty kick into the ground, where they disappeared. It has a fine white beach and dunes and a more sheltered strand, the **Praia de Balarés**. **Laxe**, a pleasant fishing village across the estuary from Corme, has a white beach, safe even for children; for something more remote, continue south along the coast to the enormous **Praia de Traba**. There are two intriguing dolmens on the road to Bayo, 5km inland: signs point the way to the **Dolmen of Dombate**, with engravings of a ship inside on the right and the **Pedra Cuberta**, another kilometre south, with a 6.2m chamber.

Ría de Camariñas

After some very rugged coast, the rocks relent to admit another *ría* shared by the remote fishing hamlets of Camariñas and Muxía, both renowned for intricate bobbin lace. From little, white, and increasingly trendy **Camariñas** you can walk 5km to Cabo Villán and its lighthouse, a wild piece of savage, torn coast, which makes you feel small and that civilization is far away, although perhaps less so now that a set of experimental windmills have been erected to harness the wild winds that whip the cape. **Muxía** has always been a bit more important, as the proud escutcheons on the houses testify. It is also the holy city of the Costa da Morte, with its seaside sanctuary of **Nostra Señora de la Barca**, where the Virgin Mary herself is said to have sailed in a ship of stone when Santiago was preaching in these parts (it wasn't her only Spanish holiday: she made a similar appearance riding a stone pillar in Zaragoza). Ship-shaped votive offerings dangle throughout the church. Parts of the Virgin's own magic boat may be seen around the church, including the hull, the Pedra de Abalar, which moves whenever a person completely free of sin stands on it.

Ría de Corcubión and the End of the World

Further south, a byroad off the C552 leads up to the lighthouse at **Cabo Touriñán**, where, as the plaque states, and notwithstanding Finisterre, you are standing on the westernmost point of continental Europe. Another branch of the road leads to the huge (and hugely exposed) beach, the **Praia do Rostro**, before continuing south to the little ports of **Cée** and **Corcubión**. White beaches are sprinkled under the pines, among them **Praia Sardiñeiro** with a few bars and restaurants. Beyond lies the traditional westernmost point of Europe, the granite houses of **Finisterre** (or Fisterra) huddled like barnacles on the rocks around the church of the miracle-working Christ of the Golden Beard, who came out of the sea. According to tradition, these same waters contain the city of Duyo (or Dugium), which sank beneath the waves at the same time as Pompeii went under the lava. Two km beyond is **Cape Finisterre** with its lighthouse, the world's end, where the Roman legions and pilgrims from Santiago came to gaze at the sun sinking into the limitless horizon. At the foot of the cape, pilgrims would visit the Romanesque church and the '**Ara Solís**', evoking the mysteries of life, death and resurrection. For the best overviews, take the road up to **Vista Monte do Facho** where sterile women used to rub up against a menhir until an 18th-century bishop ordered it destroyed.

From Cée, the C550 follows the coast around to **Ezaro**, a wild, picturesque place where massive granite boulders of 600m Mount Pindo, 'the Celtic Olympus', have mysterious engravings and ruins of ancient shrines. South, beyond the cute granite port of **Pindo**, the dune-backed beach of **Carnota** is the longest in Galicia (it also holds a more gloomy record for drownings: even if you think you're a strong swimmer, beware).

Where to Stay and Eating Out

The gastronomic prize of the the Death Coast is barnacles, or *percebes*, which cost a fortune; people who gather them from the shore are washed away so often that they can't buy insurance.

Malpica ✉ 15113

By the beach, ****Hs J.B.**, ✆ 981 72 02 66 (*moderate*), is comfortable enough and open all year; in the centre, ***Hs Panchito**, Pza. Villar Amigo 6, ✆ 981 72 03 07 (*moderate*) is adequate. For reasonable fresh seafood, **San Francisco** is *inexpensive* and good. In Barizo, ***Refuxio das Garzas**, ✆ 981 72 17 60, has a restaurant and a fine location.

Camariñas ✉ 15123

Of the *hostales*, ***Hs La Marina**, M. Freijó 4, ✆ 981 73 60 30 (*inexpensive*), is nearest the sea and has the best views and restaurant; both ***Hs Plaza**, Real 12, ✆ 981 73 61 03 (*moderate*), and ***Hs Triñares II**, Area da Vila, ✆ 981 73 61 08 (*moderate*) have a handful of rooms with bath.

Corcubión ✉ 15100

Beautifully located near the sea, *****El Hórreo**, Sta Isabel, ✆ 981 74 55 00, 🖷 981 74 55 63 (*expensive*) is the largest and most pretentious hotel on the Costa da Morte; it has a pool and garden. Also **** Las Hortensias,** Playa de Quenxe, ✆ 981 74 50 25.

For fresh fish and simple good food **Casa Leston**, Ctra. Finisterre, at Sardiñeiro, ✆ 981 74 73 54 (*moderate*) can't be beaten.

Finisterre ✉ 15155

At the end of the world **★Finisterre**, Federico Ávila 8, ✆ 981 74 00 00 (*moderate*) is the largest and nicest place to check into; the same owner runs the cheaper **★Hs Cabo Finisterre**. Cheapest of all is **★Hs Rivas**, Ctra.Faro, ✆ 981 74 00 27 (*inexpensive*). In the same road try **Don Percebe**, ✆ 981 74 05 12, for bountiful seafood. **Los Tres Golpes**, C/ Huertas 9, ✆ 981 74 00 47, serves excellent shellfish, featuring lobster.

Into the Rías Baixas

The Lower Estuaries, or Rías Baixas/Bajas, almost at once have tamer, greener scenery; here the ocean is predictably warm enough to maintain a regular holiday trade. These less exposed, less continuously 'flushed' *rías* can, however, get a bit dirty in the innermost coves.

Getting Around

RENFE trains between A Coruña and Vigo pass through Padrón and Vilagarcía. There are hourly buses (7am–9pm) from Santiago to Noia and O Grove. From Vilagarcía buses leave for Isla de Arousa.

Tourist Information

Vilagarcía de Arousa: Avda. Juan Carlos I, 37 baixo, ✆ 986 50 15 68.
Cambados: Rúa Novedades.
O Grove: In the port, ✆ 986 73 14 15.

There are **markets** in Noia on Thursdays and Sundays in Rúa do Mercado; in Vilagarcía on Tuesdays and Saturdays; in Cambados on Thursdays.

The Ría de Muros e Noia

Under Monte Costiños on the north edge of the *ría,* **Muros** is a fine, old-fashioned, granite *Gallego* town, with narrow, arcaded lanes, a palatial market, and a fountain with a stone turtle, all stacked under its Gothic parish church. There's a good beach at **Louro**, 'the golden', 1.6km from Muros on the tip of the cape. Inland, **Entines** has the shrine of miracle-working **San Campio**. After making the ritual walk around the crucifix (six times clockwise, three counterclockwise) you can pay a visit to Campio in person, or so it seems; an early Christian martyr brought from Rome in the 18th century by a bishop of Santiago, his skeleton has been lovingly covered with wax and dressed in a centurion's costume so that he looks as if he were sleeping. **Noia** (or Noya) is full of legends, beginning with its name, after Noah, whose dove is said to have found the olive branch here while his ark anchored on the holy Celtic mountain of Barbanza. This local Mt Ararat is adorned with numerous dolmens and in Noia itself you can visit the mysterious cemetery next to the Gothic **Santa María a Nova** (1327) where guildsmen between the 10th and 16th centuries left headstones carved with symbols far more pagan than Christian. Another church, early 15th-century **San Martín**, has a good rose window carved into its fortress-like façade; opposite, the **Pazo de Tapal** dates from the same period. Often windy beaches and lagoons dot the coast of the *ría* south from Noia. From **Oleiros** you can drive up to a pair of miradors (498m) for great views, or visit the exceptional dolmen, **Axeitos**—an enormous rock measuring nearly 16 m sq, supported by eight smaller ones. At the tip of the headland, **Corrubedo** has a proud set of dunes, the highest in all Galicia, constantly sculpted by the wind.

Ría de Arousa to Pádron

The Ría de Arousa is touristically the most developed of all Galicia's estuaries. The first town you come to, **Santa Uxia** (or Eugenia) **de Ribeira**, combines tourism with its status as Spain's top coastal and underwater fishing port. Remains of a Phoenician port are nearby at Aguiño, while further south, the **Isla de Sálvora** is a haunt of mermaids. The rest of this shore has quiet beaches; **A Póboa do Camaniñal** has some stately homes. At the head of the estuary, at the mouth of the blood-sucking lamprey-rich River Ulla, **Padrón** is the raggle-taggle capital of Galicia's favourite vegetable tapa, midget green *pimientas de Padrón*. Padrón has plenty of legendary baggage to accompany its peppers: it is ancient *Iria Flavia*, the port where Santiago's disciples sailed with their precious cargo, anchoring their stone boat to a stone 'memorial pillar' (*pedrón*), now displayed under the altar in the 17th-century church of **Santiago**. The stone boat was met by a pagan queen, Lupa, who mockingly gave the Christians two wild bulls to transport the coffin. When yoked the bulls turned into peaceful oxen; the astonished Lupa converted at once and was baptized by Saint James himself, who popped out of his coffin in the oxcart to do the job. On the Carretera de Herbón on the fringes of town, the **Casa-Museo de Rosalía** (*open 9–2 and 4–8, adm; closed Mon*) was the home of Galicia's favourite poet Rosalía de Castro (1837–85), the illegitimate daughter of a priest, who unhappily married historian Manuel Murguía, had six children, wrote beautiful poetry in *Gallego* and died young of cancer. The big town on the south bank is **Vilagarcía de Arousa**, the glossy base for Galicia's drug-smuggling barons; the woodsy, sand-fringed **Isla de Arousa** is reputedly the chief drop-off point for Colombian cocaine in Europe. All this nefarious underworld activity seems far away in **Cambados**, an atmospheric noble town with plenty of old family crests and a lovely granite paved square. It is the capital of Albariño, the ideal fruity dry lightly sparkling wine that goes perfectly with Galicia's seafood; on the first Sunday of every month the lovely gardens of its *parador* host a wine festival. From Cambados, the C550 circles down to the family resort of **O Grove**, linked by a bridge to **Isla A Toxa** (de la Toja), a pine-clad islet that first became famous when a donkey left for dead was miraculously restored after a few days. Now adorned with a casino and 9-hole golf course, A Toxa is designed for people with bags of money, leaving O Grove for those who don't, but know how to have a good time.

An Excursion Inland from Vilagarcía to the Manor of the Goose

From Vilagarcía, the N640 leads in 12km to the old spa town of **Caldas de Reis**, founded by the Romans. If you forgo drinking the waters, which promise marriage within a year, at least take a walk through the charming *alameda* and botanical gardens. Farther along, 8km east of the centre of **A Estrada** (the largest rural municipality in Spain, no less), you can visit the exterior of the most lavish country villa in all Galicia, the sumptuous 18th-century **Pazo da Oca**, a thoroughly enchanting mix of granite, lichens and greenery.

Where to Stay and Eating Out

Muros/Noia ✉ 15250

> ★★**Hs La Muradana**, Avda. de la Marina, ✆ 981 82 68 85 (*moderate*) is a good place to eat and sleep, although the best value for money must be ★**Hs Ría de Muros**, Avda. Castela, ✆ 981 82 60 56 (*moderate*). In Noia, the friendly ★★**Hs Ceboleiro**, Avda. Galicia 15, ✆ 981 82 05 31, has the best restaurant, with meals at around *2500 pts*.

Padrón ✉ 15900

Fanciest here is ★★★**Scala**, Pazos, ✆ 981 81 13 12, ✉ 981 81 15 50 (*moderate*), but of all the places to stay, ★★**Hs Casa Cuco**, Avda. de Compostela, ✆ 981 81 05 11 (*moderate–inexpensive*) has the best name going, and rooms with or without bath. In Cornide, you'll find **La Casa Grande de Cornide**, ✆ 981 80 57 51, a *pazo-hostería* from the XVIII century with suites, library and a museum. The culinary star of Padrón, the superlative **Chef Rivera**, Enlace Parque 7, ✆ 981 81 04 13, is your chance to dine on José Rivera Casal's superb, seasonal dishes (if you're not squeamish, the lamprey *empanada* is exquisite) and a delightful mix of traditional *Gallego* and international cuisine (*menu 2700 pts*). In Rois, don't miss **Casa Romalla**, ✆ 981 81 12 10, a favourite of Spanish novelist and Nobel prize-winner, Camilo José Cela.

Vilagarcía de Arousa ✉ 15900

Prices here are over the odds. Set in a pine wood, the 17th-century ★★★★**Pazo O Rial**, O Rial, Ctra. Vilagarcía-Cambados, ✆ 986 50 70 11, ✉ 986 50 16 76 (*expensive*), is sweet and quiet and near the sea, with a pool and satellite TV. ★**Hs 82**, Pza. de la Constitución 13, ✆ and ✉ 986 50 62 22 (*moderate*) is small but more than pleasant, and there are several others along the waterfront. For dinner, splurge on a memorable experience at **Chocolate**, located 2km away in Villajuán (Vilaxoán), ✆ 986 50 11 99 (*expensive*), Galicia's most famous restaurant, where divine grilled fish or tender Texas-sized steaks are prepared by the flamboyant owner, accompanied by famously bad service; tributes to the restaurant from celebrities and VIPs line the walls. There are also 18 attractive rooms that will set you back *7000 pts* a double. The day's catch gets the home-cooked treatment at **Loliña**, Alameda 1 in Carril, ✆ 986 50 12 81 (*moderate*), served in a sun-baked courtyard. *Closed Sun eve, Mon and Nov.*

Cambados ✉ 36630

The ★★★**Parador de Cambados Albariño**, Paseo de Cervantes, ✆ 986 54 22 50, ✉ 986 54 20 68 (*expensive*) occupies an old country *pazo* with a beautiful garden and a restaurant featuring seafood. ★**El Duende**, Ourense 10, ✆ 986 54 30 75, ✉ 986 54 29 00 (*moderate*) offers a nice, cheaper alternative by the sea, or for a bit more, there's ★**Hs Europa**, Ourense 12, ✆ 986 54 37 25, ✉ 986 54 37 61 (*moderate*). **O Arco**, Real 14, ✆ 986 54 23 12, remains the classic place to dine, with a good *1700-pts menú*, or surrender to the tender loving culinary care of **Maria José**, Pza. das Rodas 6, ✆ 986 54 22 81, who makes a mean *sopa de mariscos*.

O Grove/A Toxa ✉ 36980

You can rub shoulders with the likes of Julio Iglesias at the ★★★★★**Gran Hotel La Toja**, Isla A Toxa, ✆ 986 73 00 25, ✉ 986 73 00 20 (*luxury*), and enjoy golf, tennis, a spa, heated pool and everything else in a park setting, for *27,000 pts* a night in the summer; for less than half as much, you can bask in almost as much luxury at ★★★★**Louxo**, ✆ and ✉ 986 73 02 00 (*expensive*). In O Grove proper, ★★★**Bosque Mar**, Reboredo 93, ✆ 986 73 10 55, ✉ 986 73 05 12 (*expensive*) is a pleasant family place with a garden and pool; ★★★**Mar Atlántico**, Pedras Negras San Vicente do Mar, ✆ 986 73 80 61, ✉ 986 73 82 99 (*moderate*) is similar, with tennis courts. ★**El Besugo**, González Besada 102, ✆ 986 73 02 11, ✉ 986 73 07 87 (*moderate*), on the road to Toxa, has simple, clean rooms with bath. Nearby, **Posada del Mar**, Rúa Castelao 202, ✆ 986 73 01 06 (*moderate*) has fine views and good seafood croquettes, now served by its third generation; a similar pedigree accompanies the slightly cheaper **Casa Pepe**, Rúa Castelao 149, ✆ 986 73 02 35, again specializing in seafood.

Rías Baixas: Pontevedra to Tui

Nothing to the south is as tourist-orientated as the Ría Arousa, though the hotels of the Ría de Pontevedra fill up fast enough in the summer with vacationing Spaniards and Portuguese. The scenery is domesticated, green and pretty. Most of the beaches are safe even for the kids. Pontevedra, the provincial capital, is a handsome confection of granite, the best urban architecture in Galicia after Santiago itself.

Getting Around

In Pontevedra the RENFE station, ✆ 986 85 13 13, and bus station, ✆ 986 85 24 08, are next to each other, but a long walk along Alféreces Provisionales; a municipal bus can take you into town. Frequent buses serve the main *ría* villages.

Tourist Information

Sanxenxo: Avda. Generalísimo, ✆ 986 72 02 85.
Pontevedra: General Mola, ✆ 986 25 08 14.

There is a **market** in Pontevedra in the Mercado by the river, daily except Sunday.

The Ría de Pontevedra

The end of the Salnés peninsula dividing the Arousa and Pontevedra estuaries is occupied by the tremendous sweep of the **Praia da Lanzada**, one of Galicia's finest beaches. Nearby **Portonovo** and its neighbour **Sanxenxo** are jumping little resorts, with beaches like sugar and a chamber-of-commerce claim that they get more sun than the rest of Galicia. **Combarro** has a famous view of its *hórreos* lined up along the shores of the *ría*. Roads from Sanxenxo or Combaro go up to the abandoned medieval **Monasterio de Armenteira**, where the Virgin favoured a monk named Ero: one morning, while listening to the song of a bird, he was granted a look into eternity. To him the ecstasy lasted but a few minutes, but upon returning to the monastery he found that centuries had passed. The rose window on the main façade of the church is believed to have been a mandala for meditation and the carved archivaults around the door are *mudéjar*. Look for the peculiar masons' marks on the walls. Just before Pontevedra, the **Monasterio de Poio** was founded in the 7th century by San Fructuoso, a member of the Visigothic royal family, who caused a sensation by walking across the water to the islet of Tambo to rescue a sinking boat. In the oldest part of the church is the tomb of yet another unorthodox Galician saint, Santa Trahamunda, whose body floated to Galicia in a stone boat from Córdoba; note her statue, clutching an Andalucían palm tree.

Pontevedra

Pontevedra is the perfect genteel granite *Gallego* town. Its streets are shaded with arcades, its squares are marked with stone crosses. Ancient tradition states that it was first called *Helenes*, founded by Teucer (Teucro), who fought at Troy. *Teucro* means 'Trojan' in Castilian, and there is, in fact, a Teucro who fits the bill, a son of Scamander, who is recorded as leading a band of Cretans to western Spain to found a colony. It is significant that he named the city after Helen, the sister of the twins Castor and Pollux, the favourite gods of Roman warriors. The cult of the warrior twins inspired the soldiers of the Reconquista in the apocryphal tradition that St James was the twin brother of Jesus. As if this weren't enough, Pontevedra also (along with Mallorca, Barcelona and Corsica) claims to be the birthplace of Columbus; there's a statue to him at the west end of the Alameda looking towards the ocean and the Americas.

Pontevedra's promising mythological progress was stymied back in the Middle Ages, when the Río Lérez silted up the port. By the time of Columbus, all the marine business had moved south to Vigo, leaving a compact, endearing and exceptionally vibrant **Zona Monumental**, its showcases all within a stone's throw of the Praza da Peregrina. Here is the tall, twin-towered18th-century **Virgen La Peregrina** church, built in the shape of a scallop, to house a statue of the city's patroness. Behind the Virgen La Peregrina, there's a lovely 16th-century fountain in a small garden and the 13th- and 14th-century church of **San Francisco** with some good tombs, while across the street arcaded Praza da Ferrería is a favourite hangout for Pontevedrans. From here, Calle Pasantería descends to Pontevedra's most perfect little granite square, the **Praza da Leña**; on one side two old houses have been joined to form the **Museo Provincial** (*open 10–1.30 and 4.30–8, Sun 11–1, closed Mon*). There are other pretty little squares tucked in the streets to the northwest, among them **Praza de Teucro** with its crystal galleries, named after the city's putative father. On the corner with Praza de España and the Alameda are the romantic, ivy-draped late 13th-century ruins of the **Convento de Santo Domingo** (*open Tues–Fri 10–2*); the leafy Alameda and adjacent **Jardines de Vincenti** are favourite spots for the evening's *paseo*.

If Pontevedra has a drawback it tends to be olfactory, a strong pong which wafts in when the wind's up from the massive paper mill to the south which usually puts people off from exploring further. Persevere. Near **Mogor** are some of the most important petroglyphs in Spain, a labyrinth and spirals carved by the Celts. Another 15km further down the C550s, **Bueu** is a sleepy fishing village with two *hostales*, a great base from which to explore the surrounding beaches. The sands continue down towards the tip of the cape, **Hio**, site of Galicia's most elaborate stone crucifix, sculpted out of a single block of granite in the 19th century by José Cerviño of Pontevedra, with a Descent from the Cross and souls in Purgatory.

Where to Stay and Eating Out

Sanxenxo/Sangenjo ✉ 36000

There are scores of places, but just try to get one in the summer without a reservation. Some of the best are along Praia de Silgar, such as the modern fashionable ★★★**Rotilio**, Avda. do Porto 7, ✆ 986 72 02 00, ✉ 986 72 41 88 (with a superb seafood restaurant), and the welcoming ★★**Hs Minso**, Avda. do Porto 1, ✆ 986 72 01 50, ✉ 986 69 09 32 (*both moderate*).
★**Montalvo**, Praia Montalvo, ✆ 986 72 30 28 (*moderate*) is a reasonable if unremarkable place, although the restaurant is more than adequate. ★**Panadeira**, Praia da Panadeira, ✆ 986 72 37 28 (*moderate*) is a friendly little place in a pretty spot.

Pontevedra ✉ 36000

In the centre, ★★★★**Galicia Palace**, Avda. de Vigo 3, ✆ 986 86 44 11, ✉ 986 86 10 26 (*expensive*) is comfortable but not that luxurious, although it does have a garage;

prices are only a smidgeon higher than the ★★★**Parador de Pontevedra**, Barón 19, ✆ 986 85 58 00, 🖂 986 85 21 95 (*expensive*). This offers a chance to sleep in a *Gallego pazo* from the 11th century, with a magnificent stone staircase and a garden. For something less, try ★★★**Virgen del Camino**, Virgen del Camino, ✆ 986 85 59 04, 🖂 986 85 09 00 (*expensive*), comfortable and with a garden. ★**Madrid**, Andrés Mellado 10, ✆ 981 86 51 80 (*moderate*) is near the centre, but rooms are on the dingy side. The Mercedarian monks up at the **Monasterio de Poio**, 2km from Pontevedra, run an *inexpensive* guesthouse, ✆ 986 77 00 00.

Pontevedra has one of the leading restaurants in Galicia, **Casa Solla**, 2km out of town on the road at San Salvador de Poio, ✆ 986 85 26 78 (*expensive*), famous for its great devotion to traditional recipes, the freshest seafood and meat dishes, matched by excellent service. *Closed Thurs and Sun eve.* In town, **Doña Antonia**, Soportales de la Ferrería 4 (on the first floor), ✆ 986 84 72 74 (*expensive*) has a well-deserved reputation for imaginative dishes. *Closed Sun.* **Casa Román**, Avda. Augusto García Sánchez (south of the centre), ✆ 986 84 35 60, prides itself on select ingredients, especially shellfish (*menu 3500 pts*). *Closed Sun eve.* **Castaño**, Rúa Sapos 8 (by the Alameda), ✆ 986 85 09 52, is famous for its *empanada* (*2000 pts*). For less, choose one of the four daily dishes prepared at **Chipen**, Rúa de la Peregrina (*1400 pts*). Pontevedra has plenty of opportunities to eat cheaply in the bars in the Zona Monumental: **La Navarra**, Princesa 13, serves a range of wines and snacks; **A. Picota**, Rúa de la Peregrina 4, serves tasty charcuterie and cheese; **O Merlo**, Santa María 2, and **Rianxo**, on Panantería, have great tapas to go with your carafe of chilled Albariño.

The Ría de Vigo

The Ría de Vigo is the economic star of Galicia's estuaries: it narrows at Rande then widens again to form the sheltered inlet of San Simón, site of one of Europe's largest oyster beds. At the mouth of the estuary, the enchanting Cíes islets (a national park) protect the port and enable mussel farmers to moor their wooden platforms safely in the estuary, where the molluscs incubate on suspended in the water. Vigo itself has become the largest city in Galicia.

Getting Around

By air: Vigo's airport is 8km from town, with connections to major Spanish cities and Lisbon, ✆ 986 27 05 50.

By bus and train: This sector of the coast is well served by buses, and there are several trains daily between Pontevedra and Vigo and beyond. The train station is at the top of Rúa Alfonso XIII, a 15-minute walk uphill from the port, ✆ 986 43 11 14. Frequent buses depart from the bus station near Praza de España, a couple of blocks down from the train station; for information, ✆ 986 37 34 11.

By boat: Weekdays from 6am–10pm and Sundays from 9am–10.30pm, ferries (taking foot passengers only) sail every half-hour to Cangas, every hour to Moaña and 6 times daily from mid-June to mid-Sept to the Islas Cíes from Vigo's Estación Marítima near El Berbés (Vapores de Pasaje, ✆ 986 43 77 77). For the Cíes, buy your ticket to the islands as soon as you arrive; by law only 2200 people a day can make the crossing and boats fill up fast. In the summer, there's also a morning boat from Cangas to the Cíes.

Cangas: Rúa Real, ✆ 986 30 50 00.
Vigo: Las Avenidas, by the port, ✆ 986 43 05 77.
Tui: Ponte Trines, ✆ 986 60 17 89.

There are **markets** in Cangas on Fridays; in Baiona on Mondays; and in Tui there is a *Gallego* /Portuguese market on Thursdays.

Vigo

Nothing less than Spain's premier fishing port, Vigo occupies a privileged hillside spot that attracted both ancient Phoenician and Greek seamen. Its name comes from the Roman *Vicus Spacorum*, but the city claims that its true founder was an early 12th-century troubador, Martín Codax. In 1702, the English surprised a joint Spanish and French treasure fleet just returned from the New World and captured some of the ships. But 11 were sunk or run aground near the tiny islets by the suspension bridge; some sources say the silver had already been unloaded, but they haven't stopped treasure-seekers from looking. For all that, there's not much to 'see' in Vigo beyond the fine views towards the sea, although the old part of town hugging the fishing port, the **Barrio del Berbés**, is thick with atmosphere and rough, cobbled streets. As in A Coruña, there's a lively fish auction by the waterside at the crack of dawn. Look at the noblemen's palaces in López Puigcerver (**Calle Real**); from **Parque del Castro**, on top of the city, enjoy a great view of the *ría* from the modern monument to the Galeones de Rande. The municipal museum Quiñones de León is in the 17th-century **Pazo de Castralos** (*open Tues–Sat 10–8, Sun 10–1, closed Mon*) in the southwest of town, in the geometric gardens of the **Parque Quiñones de León**. Vigo also claims Galicia's sole **zoo** (*open 11–2 and 3.15–7, Sun 10–9*), along the road to the airport.

South of Vigo to the Ría de Baiona

Vigo's main beaches, white **Praia de Canido** and **Praia Samil**, are just west and often crowded, but the main lure is **Baiona** (Bayona), down the coast, one of Galicia's choice resorts, topped by the walls of the medieval **Castillo de Monterreal**. The coast is embellished with little beaches of soft sand, namely Ladeira, Santa María and the magnificent crescent of **Praia América**; the latter is named after the fact that Baiona was the first place in Europe to learn that Columbus had discovered a New World when the little *Pinta* sailed into its port. To the south, **A Garda**, at the mouth of the Río Minho, has a clutch of nouveau-riches *americanos'* bungalows. People have lived there for much longer, however, up in the excavated Celtic *castro* on **Monte Santa Tecla**, a 40-minute walk up from the village. This was one of the most important fortified hill settlements in Spain, inhabited from the 7th century BC up to the Roman period. Farther up there's a Neolithic stone circle, and at the very top a church with a small **archaeological museum** (*open 11–2 and 4–7.30, closed Mon*). The nearest beach is at **Camposancos**, 3km from A Garda, overlooking the mouth of the wide, wooded Río Minho, Galicia's prettiest river and the frontier between Spain and Portugal.

Tui

One of the seven ancient capitals of Galicia, Tui is picturesquely piled upon its acropolis; like Pontevedra, it claims to have been founded by wandering Greeks after the Trojan War. It was the capital of the Visigoth King Witiza in 700, and has seen many battles and border skirmishes with Portugal. Tui's granite lanes and houses are crowned by the military profile of the **Catedral de San Telmo** with its powerful walls and keep, which did double duty as Tui's castle. It has a fine Romanesque porch and a portal of 1225, carved with the Adoration of the Magi, one of the finest Gothic works in Galicia, by French-trained sculptors. The interior contains the relics of San Telmo, otherwise known as Pedro González of Astorga (confessor of King Saint Fernando of Castile) who died while working among the seafolk of Galicia in 1246. He is the patron saint of Spanish sailors, who confused his name with their first patron St Elmo (or Erasmus), who sends sailors his lucky fire to light upon their masts, igniting even their finger-tips without burning them. His tomb, accredited with 203 miracles, oozes a vinegary gunk much prized as a cure-all. Among Tui's smaller churches are **Santo Domingo** (1415), its interior a mix of pre-Romanesque and Gothic and **San Francisco**, with a Portuguese baroque chapel. In half an hour you can walk from the centre of Tui to the lovely Portuguese walled town of **Valença do Minho**, crossing an iron bridge built by Gustave Eiffel.

Where to Stay and Eating Out

Vigo ✉ 36200

Luxuriate on the beach in the ★★★★**Gran Hotel Samil**, Apartado 472, 5km south on the Praia de Samil, ✆ 986 24 00 00, ✆ 986 23 14 19 (*expensive*), with a pool and tennis courts. ★★★★ **Bahía de Vigo**, ✆ 986 22 67 00, ✆ 986 43 74 87, has great views of of the port and the *ría*. Modern ★★★**Ensenada**, Alfonso XIII 7, ✆ 986 22 61 00, ✆ 986 43 89 72 (*expensive*) is in the centre and has fine views. ★★**Nilo**, Marqués de Valladares 8, ✆ 986 43 28 99, ✆ 986 43 44 74, is a good *moderate* choice, just up Rúa Carral, a good place to look for cheap sleeps: try ★★**Hs Savoy**, Carral 20, ✆ 986 43 25 41 and ★**Hs Carral**, Carral 18, ✆ 986 33 49 27 (*both inexpensive*).

Eating out is an excellent reason for sticking around Vigo. To every kind of seafood and shellfish add the delicacies from the River Minho. **Síbaris**, Avda. García Barbón 122, ✆ 986 22 15 26 (*expensive*) has first quality cuisine in an upmarket, intimate setting. *Closed Sun.* Up at **El Castillo**, Monte del Castro, ✆ 986 42 12 99, exquisitely grilled fish and meat are the specialities (*menu 4200pts*). *Closed Sun eve and Mon.* Out near Praia Samil, **Timón Playa**, Canido 2, at Corujo, ✆ 986 49 08 15, looks across to the Islas Cíes,(*menu 3800 pts*). *Closed Sun.* For piles of good seafood (and some beef dishes), go to **Puesto Piloto Alcabre**, Avda. Atlántida 98, ✆ 986 29 79 75 (*moderate*), overlooking the sea. *Closed Sun eve.* For seafood or roast leg of lamb, the long-established people's choice in Vigo is **El Mosquito**, Pza. da Pedra 4 (near the port) ✆ 986 22 44 11 (*moderate*). For something different, **José Luis**, Avda. Florida (out by the stadium; take a taxi), ✆ 986 29 95 22 (*moderate*) serves excellent game and Basque dishes and has a good list of Riojas. *Closed Sun.* Good cheap food is plentiful in the bars of El Berbés and along the Gran Vía in the centre.

Baiona ✉ 36300

The ★★★★**Parador Conde de Gondomar**, Monte Real, ✆ 986 35 50 00, ✆ 986 35 50 76 (*expensive*) is Galicia's finest, housed in a modern reconstruction of a typical Galician *pazo* within the medieval walls of Monterreal, in a lovely park. ★★**Hs Tres**

Carabelas, Ventura Misa 72, ✆ 986 35 54 41, 📠 986 35 59 21, is a fine old inn on a narrow cobbled lane in the middle of town, with prices at the top of this category. Baiona has wide choice of cheaper options, among them **★Hs Mesón del Burgo**, Barrio del Burgo, ✆ 986 35 53 09, and **★Hs La Anunciada**, Elduayen 16, ✆ 986 35 55 90, 📠 986 35 55 34 (*both moderate*). **O Moscón**, Alférez Barreiro 2, ✆ 986 35 50 08, is known for its lobster (*bogavante*); otherwise prices are *moderate*.

A Garda ✉ 01300

★★Convento de San Benito, Pza. de San Benito, ✆ 986 61 11 66, 📠 986 61 15 17 (*moderate*) is set in a renovated 16th-century monastery with a lovely restaurant, **Os Remos**, serving a delicious lobster and rice dish. Stay near the top of Monte Tecla in the delightful **★Pazo Santa Tecla**, ✆ 986 61 00 02 (*moderate*). *Open June–Sept*. Or try portside **★Hs Martirrey**, José Antonio 8, ✆ 986 61 03 49 (*inexpensive*). Good fish soups wait at family-run **El Gran Sol**, Malteses 32 (*inexpensive*). *Closed Sun*.

Tui ✉ 36700

Overlooking the Minho, the refined **★★★Parador San Telmo**, Avda. Portugal, ✆ 986 60 03 09, 📠 986 60 21 63 (*expensive*) is located in a large reproduction of a typical *Gallego pazo* 1km below town, with a garden, tennis and pool; **★★★Colón Tuy**, Colón 11, ✆ 986 60 02 23, 📠 986 60 03 27 (*moderate*) offer similar facilities for less. **★Hs Generosa**, Calvo Sotelo 37, ✆ 986 60 00 55 (*cheap*) has fine rooms without bath, or try **★Hs San Telmo 91**, Avda. de la Concordia 88, ✆ 986 60 30 11 (*moderate*) all rooms with bath. **O Cabalo Furado**, Pza. Generalísimo, ✆ 986 60 12 15 (*moderate*) offers good home-cooking. *Closed Sun*. If you're looking for something special, look into **Abadía do Pelouro Aixeto**, ✆ 986 62 90 24 (*expensive*), in Caldelas de Tui (12 km from Tui), with two delightful apartments available.

Up the Minho to Ourense

Galicia's least known and only land-locked province is an introspective place, with more valleys, they say, than towns, descending to form the *rías* from the great tableland of Castile. The province is famous for wine, hot springs, and Spain's walking sarcophagus, Julio Iglesias.

Getting Around

Ourense is the main hub here, with **trains** to Santiago, Lugo, A Coruña, Vigo, Ribadavia, León and the rest of Spain. RENFE's Estación Empalme is across the river, ✆ 988 21 02 02; tickets also on sale at Rúa do Paseo 15, ✆ 988 21 46 04 .

The **bus** station is 1km from the centre on the Vigo road, ✆ 988 21 60 27.

Tourist Information

Ribadavia: Praza Mayor, ✆ 988 47 12 75.
Ourense: Curros Enríquez 1, ✆ 988 37 20 20.

There are **markets** in Ourense on the 7th and 17th of each month; in Allariz on the 1st and 15th of each month; in Ribadavia on the 10th and 25th of each month; and in Verín on Wednesdays and Fridays.

From Tui to Ribadavia

Both the train and road follow the wooded banks of the Minho, offering one more chance to cross into Portugal, on the ferry from Salvaterra do Minho to Monção. To the east, the river takes on a wide and elegiac quality, around the beginning of the wine-growing region of Ribeiro. Ribeiro's charming 15th-century capital, **Ribadavia**, has the best-preserved Jewish *barrio* in Galicia, a web of lanes around the church of Santiago. Ribadavia has a beautiful **Praza Mayor** and interesting Romanesque churches: a tree grows out of the belltower of the **Oliveira** church, **San Juan** has a 13th-century *cruceiro*, while the **Convento de Santo Domingo**, occasional residence of the kings of Galicia, has a fine Gothic church and simple cloister. Learn about the local wines at the **Museo del Ribeiro** (*open 10–1 and 5–8*) or visit the ruined **Castillo de los Condes de Ribadavia**, still an impressive pile of walls, towers, and tombs carved into the rock. From Ribadavia, it's 5km to the curious hilltop **Monumento de Beade** (or **Calvario**), with three granite crosses, overlooking a cluster of *hórreos*, and a bit further, the 8th-century, Asturian-style church of **San Ginés (Xens) de Francelos** with a unique decorative programme by the entrance arch, a mix of Mozarabic and Visigothic elements. South of Ribadavia, the village of **Celanova** is built around a vast **Praza Mayor**. The venerable **Benedictine monastery of San Salvador** holds a gargantuan *retablo* of 1697 and the choir is a masterpiece of Gothic carving. An even older church is 26km to the south on the N540 in **Bande**: the rural Visigothic chapel of **Santa Comba**, overlooking the reservoir of Limia. East of Celanova (and south of Ourense on the N525) the medieval town of **Allariz** is a monument in itself and site of two more Romanesque churches: **Santiago** with an unusual round apse and **San Esteban**, on the way to the ruins of the castle. Between Allariz and Ourense, the ruined 12th-century **Santa Mariña das Aguas Santas** (a 15-minute walk from the village; bring a flashlight) has steps down to its crypt—actually a corridor dolmen, constructed of boulders.

Ourense (Orense)

Continuing up the Río Minho, Ourense puts its best face forward, greeting visitors with a graceful **Ponte Romano**, the biggest stone bridge in Spain. It was built by the Romans and rebuilt on the ancient piers in the 13th century by Ourense's bishop. It is still used, to put it mildly: traffic is Ourense's day-in, day-out nightmare. If you can find a place to park, or don't mind walking a mile in from the bus or train stations, you can see what first attracted the Romans: the steaming hot springs, *Aquae Urentes*, known by the Visigoths and Suevi as Worm Sea (hence *Ourense*). The main source, **Las Burgas**, still steams out of the neoclassical fountain at a constant, nearly boiling temperature midway down Rúa do Progreso. Up from here, the arcaded **Praza Maior** is Ourense's historic core and hub of its social life, and the old episcopal palace in Praza Maior houses the **Museo Arqueológico Provincial** (*open 9.30–2.30, closed Mon*). In the corner of Praza Maior, the **Cathedral** was begun in the 12th century and is entered by way of the **Pórtico del Paraíso**, a 13th-century reproduction of Santiago's great Pórtico de la Gloria. The high altar contains the reliquary of St Martin of Tours, while the florid baroque chapel houses Ourense's oddest attraction, the Santísimo Cristo who has real hair and a fabric body; according to legend it was made by Nicodemus and floated ashore near Finisterre. The **Museo Catedralicio** (*open 11.30–1 and 4.30–7*) has one of the first books printed in Galicia and the 'Treasure of San Rosendo'—rare 10th-century chess pieces carved out of rock crystal.

Around Ourense

The monumental Cistercian monastery of **Oseira** (*open daily 9.30–12.30 and 3.30–5*), off the N525, was founded in 1137 by four hermits. The monastery façade has a gigantic Churrigueresque doorway and the odd crest of two bones with the tree of knowledge. The most majestic scenery in these parts begins just east of Ourense, heading up the Minho along the N120, where the cliffs over the river rise ever steeper. At **San Esteban**, dominated by the Romanesque **Monasterio de Ribas de Sil** and its three atmospheric cloisters, the Sil flows into the Minho, and along the latter are wild gorges to walk along. The nearly as dramatic C536 east of Ourense goes up to **Esgos**, where a small byroad leads to the ruined, abandoned monastery and church of **San Pedro de Rocas**, founded by followers of Prisciliano in 573. The road rises up higher and higher to **Puebla de Trives**, where there's even a ski resort, **Manzaneda**, with 10 different pistes of all degrees of difficulty, served by a chair lift and three other ski lifts (call ✆ 988 31 08 75 to see if there's any snow). If you're heading southwest from Ourense towards Bragança or Zamora, you may want to stop in the old walled town of **Verín**, capital of the wine-growing Monterrey valley; don't pass up the chance to try a bottle of Verín red—as long as you aren't driving anywhere. This highest-octane Galician wine can pack 14 per cent alcohol.

Where to Stay and Eating Out

Ribadavia ✉ 32000

★Hs Evencio, Avda. R. Valcárcel 30, ✆ 988 47 10 45, has a pool and garden to delight its guests. **★★Hs Oasis**, Ctra. N 120, ✆ 988 47 16 13, has pleasant rooms with views and a no-frills but fine, *inexpensive* restaurant (*both moderate*).

Ourense ✉ 32000

★★★★Gran Hotel San Martín, Curros Enríquez 1, ✆ 988 23 56 90 (*expensive*), has large, air-conditioned rooms. A few paces away, **★★★Sila**, Avda. de la Habana 61, ✆ 988 23 63 11, ✇ 988 23 60 25 (*moderate*) has cheerful rooms. If you've got a car, the new **★★★Auriense**, at O Cumial Xeixalbo, ✆ 988 23 49 00, ✇ 988 24 50 01, offers a pool and tennis in a quiet setting. Cheaper choices in the centre are **★Río Minho**, Juan XXIII 4, ✆ 988 21 75 94 (*moderate*), and **★Hs San Miguel II**, San Miguel 14, ✆ 988 23 92 03 (*cheap*), next door to one of Ourense's best restaurants, **San Miguel**, San Miguel 12, ✆ 988 22 07 95 (*expensive–moderate*), specializing in seafood fresh from the coast served in the traditional *taza*. *Closed Tues.* **Carroleiro**, San Miguel 10, ✆ 988 22 05 66, offers a simple, good *1500 pts menu. Closed Mon.*

Pobra de Trives ✉ 32600

The 18th-century **★★★Pazo Casa Grande**, Marqués de Trives, ✆/✇ 988 33 20 66 (*moderate*) has seven atmospheric rooms that share a private chapel. The **★★Queixa**, ✆ 988 30 97 47, ✇ 988 31 08 75, is up at the ski resort of Manzaneda.

Verín ✉ 32600

Four km outside Verín, the **★★★Parador de Verín**, ✆ 988 41 00 75, ✇ 988 41 20 17 (*expensive*) is located next to the 13th-century castle; its restaurant has seafood and other *Gallego* treats. You can look up at the castle and *parador* from the *inexpensive* **★Dos Hermanas**, Avda. de Sousas 106, ✆ 988 41 02 80.

Castilla y León

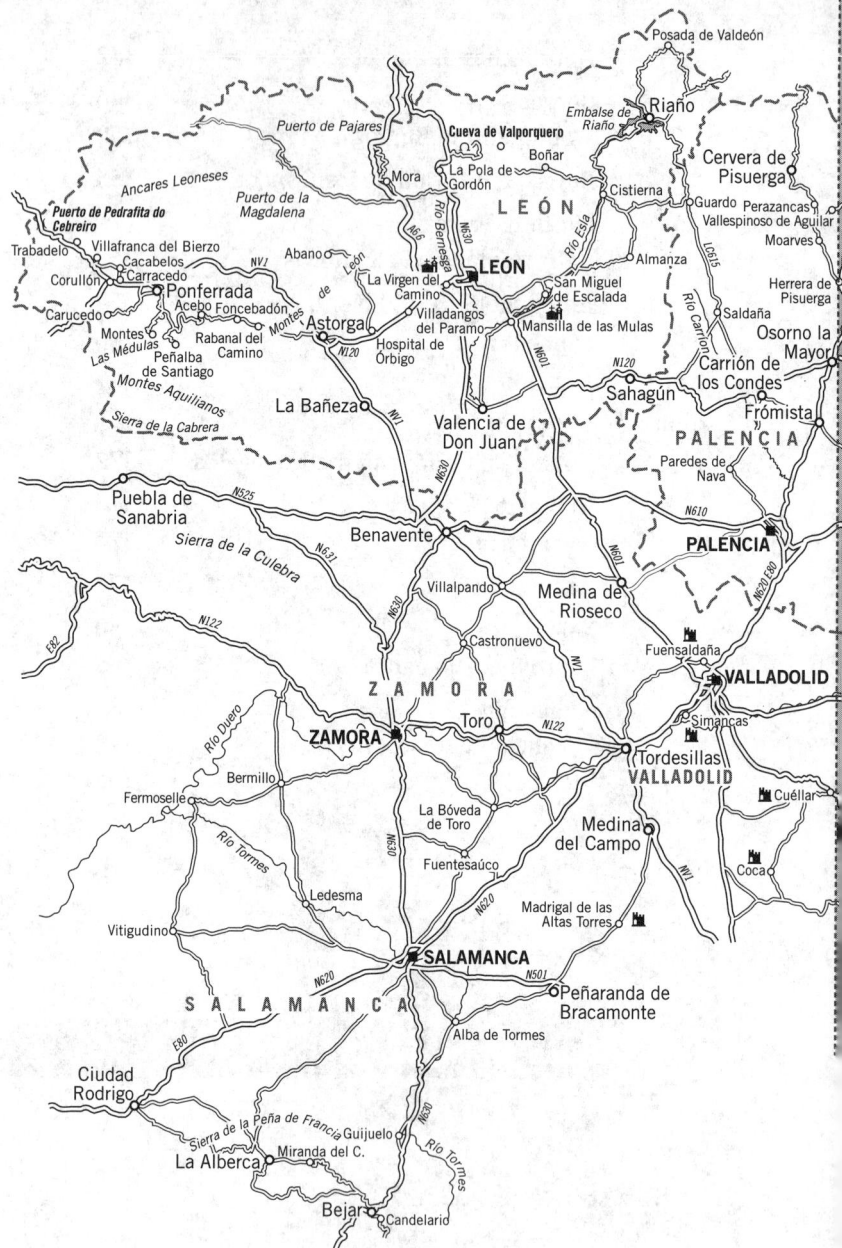

Old Castile and León encompasses two ancient kingdoms of the *meseta*—a flat, semi-arid table-top 700—1000m above sea level—where the climate, summed up in an old Castilian proverb, is nine months of winter and three months of hell. It looks like no other place in Europe: endless rolling dun-

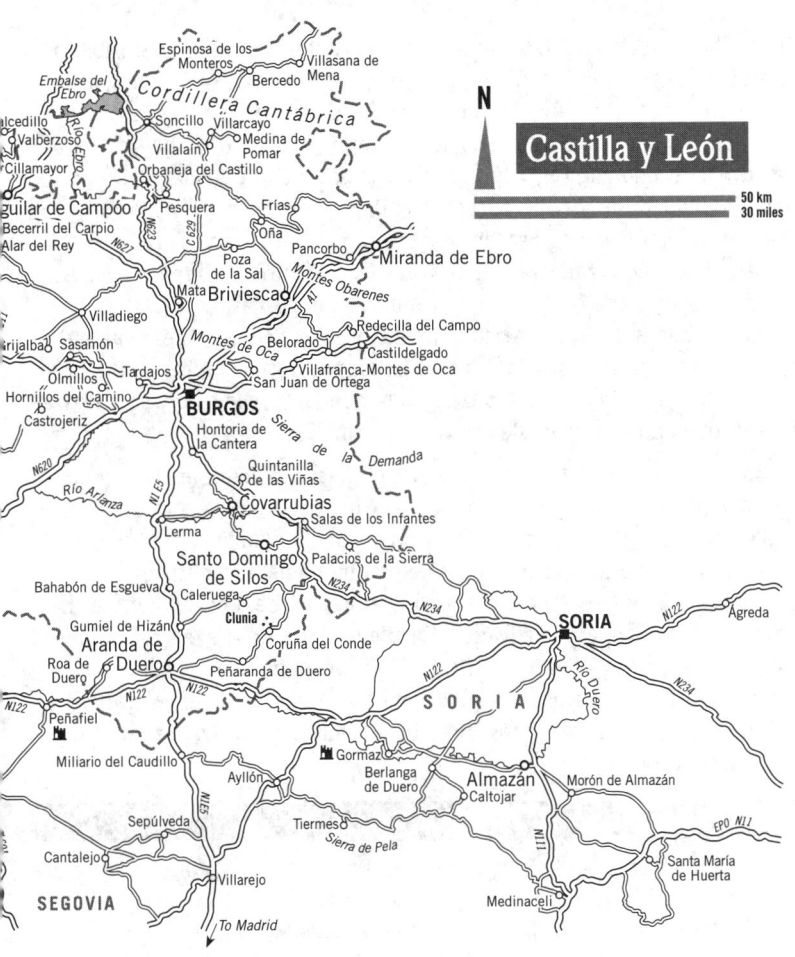

Castilla y León

N

50 km
30 miles

coloured plains, spotted with scrub and patches of mountains, but few trees;
during the mindless free-for-all of the Reconquista nearly all of the forests
were axed. Depending on your mood you will find the *meseta* romantic and
picturesque, or brooding and eerie, but you'll never forget it. From this
unlikely land, however, came the culture, language, and people who would
dominate in their day not only the nations of Iberia, but a good part of two
continents. Even today Burgos, seat of the first counts of Castile, is the
headquarters of all that is pure Castilian and *castizo*, down to proper lisping
pronunciation of the name of its hero, the Cid, or 'El Theed'.

In early times Castile not only resembled America's Far West, but played the
same kind of frontier rôle twice in European history. After the Romans
whipped the native Iberians, retired legionaries were given land to raise

wheat. The Visigoths followed in their tracks, but the Moors found little to like and conquered Old Castile without settling it. The Christian kingdoms to the north erected a string of border fortifications that gave the region its name Castile ('land of castles') sometime around 800. In 882 the first part of Castile was reconquered by Alfonso III of Asturias; two years later, Diego Porcelos founded Burgos and became the first count of Castile. According to the medieval *Romance de Fernán González*, the Good Count Fernán González obtained Castile's independence from Asturias-León in the 10th century by selling the king of Asturias a horse and goshawk. The king, lacking any handy cash, promised Fernán González he'd pay him double the price for every day that he didn't pay. The king forgot his promise, and by the time the cunning Fernán González reminded him, the sum was so extraordinary that all the king could do was give him Castile.

Fernán González formed his fledging state into seven counties, the *Antiguas Merindades de Castilla*. Unlike the feudal Christian kingdoms to the north, Castile was settled by free men or *hidalgos*, each of whom owned their farms and bore the responsibility for defending them. The difficulties in repopulating the empty land were greatly eased by the development of the *camino de Santiago*, especially after Castile was 'tamed' by the reconquest of Toledo by Alfonso VI and the Cid in 1085. It set off a medieval boom: settlers moved in, churches, hospitals and towns sprouted all along the road. Most have been collecting dust since Charles V sucked them dry in the 16th century.

Approaches to Burgos

This section covers the approaches to Burgos from the east and north, whether you approach along the pilgrims' road from La Rioja, quickly on the *autopista* from Bilbao, or through the magnificent mountains scenery of the Cantabrian range from Santander.

Getting Around

There are frequent buses from Burgos to Belorado and less frequently to Miranda de Ebro, a major railway junction. At least one bus a day goes up to Briviesca, Oña, Frías, Espinosa de los Monteros, and Poza de la Sal.

Tourist Information

Miranda de Ebro: on the Madrid–Irún road, ✆ 947 31 18 86.

Along the *Camino*, from Redecilla to Burgos

After Santo Domingo de la Calzada in La Rioja, the pilgrimage road enters Castile at medieval **Redecilla del Campo**, an old strip frontier town whose church, **Virgen de la Calle**, contains a sublime 12th-century baptismal font, intricately carved with the towers and windows of a city presumed to be Jerusalem. West, the leather-making town of **Belorado** attracts a different kind of pilgrim these days with its factory outlets, although its former vocation is recalled in two churches, built in the 1500s in the wide, airy Catalan Gothic style. The deeply forested Montes de Oca mark the traditional border of Castile. At their foot, **Villafranca Montes de Oca** once succoured pilgrims in its 14th-century Hospital de San Antón. If Villafranca seems forgotten, head up the pine-forested slopes to even more lonely **San Juan de Ortega**, a hamlet named after the builder-saints. The surviving, original apse of the church (1142) proves his skill as an architect: an elegant design of gracefully slender round columns and three receding arches around alabaster windows. Inside, San Juan is buried in a magnificent tomb, with an effigy and delightful cartoon-like scenes from his life, crowned by an Isabelline Gothic baldachin, paid for by Isabel the Catholic herself, who got pregnant for the first time in 1477 after praying by the saint's Romanesque tomb (now down in the crypt). At 5pm, on the day of the spring and autumn equinoxes (21 March and 22 September), pilgrims come to see the *Milagro de la Luz*, when a sunbeam illuminates the womb of the lovely Virgin of the Annunciation, carved on a triple capital in the crossing.

To Burgos from Bilbao: the Gate of Pancorbo

The Bilbao—Madrid motorway A1 runs into Castile by **Miranda de Ebro**, a major town, where glass balconies hang over the river. The 16th-century church of Santa María is Miranda's most beautiful monument, while the Ebro itself sculpted the stunning gorge, the **Hoces del Sobrón** through the Montes Obarenes. From here the road and train funnel dramatically through the pass at **Pancorbo**, for V. S. Pritchett 'a place of horror, for the rock crowds in…and at the top has been tortured into frightening animal shapes by the climate'. A ruined Moorish castle and an 18th-century fort that played a role when Wellington chased the French through the gorge in 1813 survive above the homely old town. At Pancorbo truck drivers tuck into *sopa castellano* to steel themselves for their all-night ride to beat the heat of the *meseta* beyond. Or as Pritchett put it: 'Pancorbo is the moment of conversion. Now one meets Spain, the indifferent enemy.' It's not so bad, really.

Between Pancorbo amd Burgos, **Briviesca** is peaceful enough, with a rectangular plan that served as the model for several towns in South America; its octagonal church, **Santa Clara** (1565), has star vaulting and a florid carved *retablo mayor* (a rare, unpolychromed one, with a central figure dreaming of the tree of Jesse).

Northeast Approaches: Oña

The bulge on the map in northeast Burgos province is the cradle of Old Castile, a place of curiosities and remarkable scenery. North of Briviesca, **Oña**, '*La Villa Condal*', had one of the first castles of Castile and was granted its *fueros* or privileges in 950 by Fernán González. In 1033, Sancho the Great of Navarra, heir of Castile, ordered the royal stronghold replaced by the Benedictine **Monasterio de San Salvador** to serve as his royal pantheon, a status he encouraged by spending his dying days in Oña. Rebuilt in 1640 and decorated with four squat kings who would look perfectly at home on a deck of cards, the monastery is now used as a psychiatric hospital. The town, however, offers guided tours of its **church** (*open 9–12 and 4–7; adm*). The entrance is through the 15th-century Pórtico de los Reyes, carved with figures of kings; beyond stands the oldest Romanesque façade in Castile (1072), with Flemish-Gothic paintings just inside, and a *mudéjar* door. Although the walls of the narrow church date from the 11th century, the interior was redone in the 15th by Fernando Díaz. His starry dome, measuring 400 sq m, is the largest in Spain after Tarragona's; below, flanking a florid 18th-century *retablo* is the magnificent **Panteón Real**. Sancho the Great (d. 1035) is here, among others, their tombs arranged by Fernando Díaz into charming little temples, decorated with paintings by Fray Alonso de Zamora. The **museum** in the sacristy contains the excellent alabaster tomb of Bishop Lope de Mendoza, by Italian Mannerist master Leone Leoni, and a fragment of 10th-century cloth once belonging to Sancho the Great, embroidered with Arabic writing, the figures of an alchemist and the horse and goshawk of Castile's independence. The **cloister,** built by Simón de Colonia in 1508, is a rich piece of Isabelline Gothic, and presiding over the door is the Gothic statue of Santa María de Oña, sovereign against worms in Infantes.

Up the Ebro: Frías, Medina de Pomar and the Ebro Canyons

East of Oña, built high over the banks of the Ebro, medieval **Frías** is one of the most striking villages in Castile: a ruined 12th-century castle spirals up a rocky outcrop known as 'the Molar' high above the hanging whitewashed houses, arcaded lanes and intimate vegetable gardens, reached by a magnificent **medieval bridge**, complete with its mighty gate and central guard tower. Between Oña and Frías, turn north 16km at Trespaderne for 12th-century **San Pantaleón de Losa**, a curious hermitage set over the village on a huge boulder resembling a capsized boat. Ships and dragons' heads decorate the capitals. North of Trespaderne, **Medina de Pomar** has a powerful, two-towered castle built in the 14th century by the Velascos, the hereditary Constables of Castile; a *mudéjar* stucco frieze in the main hall is decorated with inscriptions in Gothic and Arabic letters. The Constables founded the **Convent of Santa Clara** in 1313, and lie buried under alabaster effigies in its early Gothic church. Santa Clara's lovely 16th-century Capilla de la Concepción has a *retablo* by Diego de Siloé and Felipe de Vigarni.

Up the Ebro from Oña, near Puente-Arenas, **San Pedro de Tejada** (*open April–Oct 9–1 and 4–7, other times 10–2 and 4–6*) is an excellent Romanesque church, decorated with flagrantly erotic sculptures and a good portal. Further up, **Villarcayo** was the capital of one of Fernán González's original counties, but it was burned in the First Carlist War. Only bits of its medieval past survive, especially in the **Museo-Monasterio de Santa María la Real de Vileña** (*open Sun 10.30–11.30 and 4.30–6.30*), founded to hold the fragments of the 13th-century Cistercian monastery that burned down in 1970. Villarcayo is in striking distance of a pair of sites associated with the judges of Castile, who in the 8th and 9th centuries played a role somewhere between chieftain, lawmaker and general sage. One, *juez* Laín Calvo, was buried in the hermitage of the Virgen de la Torrentera in **Villalaín**; when disinterred all were amazed at the giant stature of his body, which turned to dust on contact with the air. The church, with a square apse and inscription dated 1130, has a lovely portal and interesting murals. Sculptures of the five judges of Castile decorate the doorway of the Renaissance church in nearby **Bisjueces**. North of Villarcayo in **Torme**, the 12th-century Romanesque church of Butrera has fascinating capitals and an excellent relief of the Three Magi.

To the northwest, you can pick up the 6318 into the mountains (*see* below). For the Ebro Canyons, however, cut over to **Soncillo**, then drive southwest through the Puerta de Carrales towards Ruerrero. The cliffs grow increasingly majestic and fantastical as you drive towards **Orbaneja del Castillo**: vultures and eagles circle high over the ruddy canyon walls, sculpted by eons of wind and rain to form soaring bridges, castle walls, haunted towers or hollow snaggle-toothed caves. In Orbaneja an enchanting waterfall cascades, even in August; from here the road curls up to the N623, the main Santander–Burgos highway.

The N623 is not an unattractive route, but for something even better, pass it by and cross the Ebro at **Pesquera de Ebro**, make your way east to Pesadas de Burgos and turn right onto the C629. For the next 14 km the road is surreal—perfectly straight, in the middle of absolutely no where, yet each kilometre is systematically marked off with an impressive 10ft monument in stone—all identical, all bearing no identification whatsoever. The sensation of wandering across the middle of a games table for giants is confirmed when, after the last monument, you turn east and it's as if the world has suddenly dropped out beneath your feet, leaving you to wind down, down, down, the edge of the table, with tremendous views across to the ruined **Castillo de las Rojas**, piled high on a rocky outcrop. The castle, where Charles V shamelessly imprisoned the ambassadors of Pope Clement in 1528, defends **Poza de la Sal**, a town founded by the Romans, who first extracted salt from its marshes along the Río Torca Salada. In its web of tiny lanes there's a Gothic church with a Baroque façade, the 18th-century salt administration offices, a pair of old gateways and a panoramic view from Plaza Nueva; along the river, the old salt works are near a Roman aqueduct that supplied the village wash basin.

The Far Northeast Corner: in the Cordillera Cantábrica

Near Soncillo the 6318 leads into the secret corner of Burgos province; if you're coming from the north, the N629 from Laredo will take you straight there. Some day, the most extraordinary attraction, the massive cave complex of Ojo Guareña by Quintanilla-Sotoscueva, with its prehistoric paintings, will be open to visitors, but at the time of writing you can only get as far as the Hermitages of SS. Bernabé and Tirso, set on a panoramic esplanade with their façades built into the cliffs; inside are 17th- and 18th-century paintings and ex-votos. The 6318 continues east to medieval Espinosa de los Monteros, with its 14th-century Castillo de los Condestables on the far bank of the river Trueba, and the Constable's elegant Baroque palace.

On the other hand, if you venture east, Romanesque churches are your reward: San Miguel at **Bercedo**, with a good portal and carved; a 12th-century Templar church of Santa María, at **Siones**, with an elegant double archway in the apse, strange and beautiful capitals, and a Visigothic baptismal font; and San Lorenzo at **Vallejo de Mena**, founded by the Knights of St John, with a gallery of arcades along the top of the south façade and a handsome apse.

Where to Stay and Eating Out

Villafranca Montes de Oca ✉ 02600

El Pájaro, Ctra. Logroño–Burgos, ✆ 947 58 20 01 (*inexpensive*) is your best bet for a simple room and a meal along this stretch of the pilgrims' route; there's also the restored Hospital de la Reina for pilgrims.

Pancorbo/Briviesca ✉ 09240

Hotel-restaurants line the highway at Pancorbo, but the best bet is just in on the edge of the old town: **Casa Rural El Ferial**, San Nicolás 59, ✆ 947 35 42 76 (after 9pm), an *inexpensive* bed and breakfast overlooking a little garden; the owners, Vicente Cardiñanos and his wife, must be the most hospitable people in Castile. In Briviesca, **★★El Valles**, Ctra. Madrid–Irún km 280, ✆ 947 59 00 25, ✆ 947 59 24 84 (*moderate*) has long been a favourite stopover; in town **El Concejo**, Pza. Mayor 14, ✆ 947 59 16 86 (*expensive–moderate*) is set in a 15th-century mansion and serves a tasty leek and prawn *pastel* and imaginative desserts; good wine list. *Closed Mon.*

Medina de Pomar ✉ 09500

***Las Merindades**, Pza. Somovilla, ✆ 947 11 08 22 (*moderate*) is located in a pretty, historical building with the village's best, moderately priced restaurant downstairs; try the *solomillo a los ajos tostados* (sirloin with toasted garlic).

Burgos

First it must be said that Burgos is a genteel and quite pleasant town, its river, the Arlanzón, so filled with frogs in the spring and early summer that they drown out the traffic with their croaking; and that the favourite promenade, the Paseo del Espolón, is one of Spain's prettiest, adorned with amazing topiary hedges. Burgos contains one of the greatest collections of Gothic art and monuments in southern Europe, and it is the city in all Spain where you are most likely to see a nun riding a bicycle. Yet throughout much of its history, Burgos' role has been that of a stern military camp, from the day of El Cid Campeador to Franco el Caudillo who, during the Civil War, made Burgos his temporary capital, the city where, it was said, 'the very stones are Nationalist'. Here, in 1970, Franco held the infamous Burgos trials in which sixteen Basque separatists (two of them priests) were tried in a kangaroo court. Six were sentenced to death, though outraged world opinion convinced Franco to commute the sentences.

The Kingdom of Castile was born in Burgos, and it is fitting that the city itself began as a castle erected on the Moorish frontier in 884. By 926 it was ready to take its first step away from Leonese rule, electing its own judges; in 950, one of the judges' successors, Fernán González, declared his independence as Count of Castile. His descendant, Fernando I, elevated the title to king and married the heiress of León. Burgos remained sole capital of Castile until 1087, when Alfonso VI moved to Toledo (one reason must have been to put some distance between himself and the overbearing Cid). The frontier was moving southwards, and though most Spanish kings managed to spend some time here, this city that had done so much to create the ethos of Spain now found itself something of a backwater. But Burgos has always remained true to the cause and is still the most aristocratic, the most pious, most polite, most reactionary city in Spain.

Getting There

By train: RENFE is on Avda. Conde Guadalhorce, across the river from the cathedral, ✆ 947 20 35 60; tickets are also dispensed from the office at Moneda 21, ✆ 947 20 91 31. Burgos is on the main rail line from Irún to Madrid (connections to Pamplona, Vitoria, Bilbao, Valladolid, etc.), with less frequent links with Zaragoza, Palencia, León, and A Coruña; also to Salamanca, Barcelona, Málaga, Madrid, Córdoba and Vigo on various Talgos.

By bus: The bus terminal is on C/ Miranda, across the river from the Arco de Sta María, ✆ 947 26 55 65; there are daily buses to León (one), Santander (three), Madrid (seven), Soria, San Sebastián and Vitoria (four or more), and the provincial villages. Even if there may be only one bus a day to villages not on a main route, such as Frías, they're often conveniently timed for a day trip.

Tourist Information

Plaza de Alonso Martínez 7, ✆ 947 20 31 25.

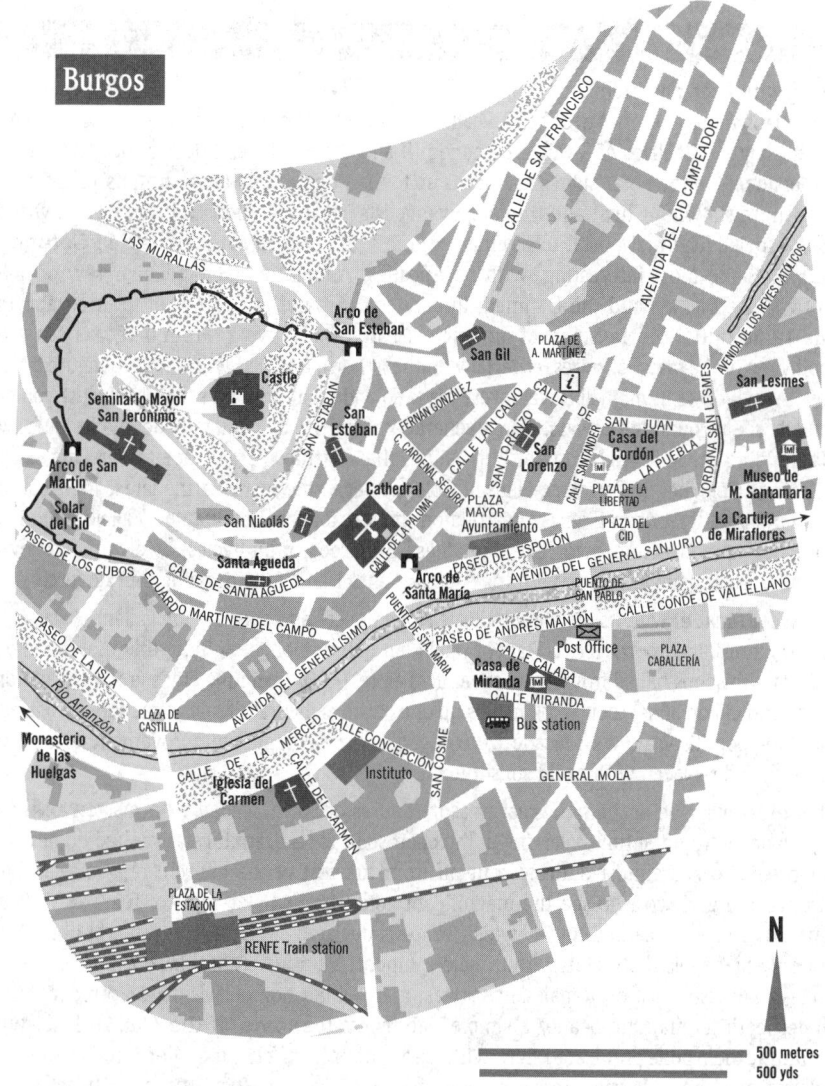

Arco de Santa María

Burgos' glistening white, fairy-tale front door, the **Arco de Santa María**, was originally part of the medieval walls, but after the Comunero revolt it was embellished to appease Charles V; triumphal arches like this were a Renaissance conceit, and they were especially favoured by the vainglorious and ambitious Charles. The Emperor himself is portrayed in a Burgos pantheon that includes its first judges, King Fernán González, and El Cid. The arch was designed by Francisco de Colonia and Juan de Vallejo, two artists you are going to know well before you leave Burgos—along with Francisco's father Juan, responsible for the great open-work spires of the Cathedral, looming just behind the arch.

Along with León and Toledo, Burgos has one of Spain's greatest Gothic cathedrals, one of the most diaphanous churches ever built—half of stone, half of light and air. In 1221, in honour of his marriage to Beatrice of Swabia, Fernando III and the English bishop Maurice laid the first cornerstone. On the north side, a stair leads up to the **Puerta del Sarmental**, its 13th-century tympanum showing Christ and the four Evangelists (sitting studiously at their desk, writing the Gospels). The first portal to be finished, the south-side **Puerta Alta de la Coronería** (1257), is the most interesting, with its Apostles, Almighty, and a peculiar row of mere mortals, the Blessed and the Damned, in between. Around the corner of the transept, the **Puerta de la Pellejería** is part of the original 13th-century work. From here you can get a good view of the forest of spires, especially on the lantern, adorned with scores of figures. Note how the windows in the bell towers were made so wide that from most points of view you can actually see through the towers. Three generations of the Colonia family devoted themselves to moulding the soft grey stone of Burgos into these virtuoso stone lace towers and spires. Colonia is Cologne, in Germany; Hans of Cologne began the works in the late 1400s, and his son Simón and grandson Francisco carried on the job, followed by Juan de Vallejo, who built the Platersque crossing tower. At night these hundreds of pinnacles, as electric as any of Gaudí's, are illuminated along with the Arco de Santo María for a dazzling tour de force.

The **west façade**, with its huge but delicate stone tracery and over-the-top gallery of statues of Spanish kings, incorporates two Stars of David, an unintentional reminder that more than one of Burgos' bishops hailed from a Jewish family before 1492, as did the city's greatest sculptors, Diego and Gil de Siloé; their work makes up one of the cathedral's main attractions. Tragically, the three portals of the west façade were destroyed in the name of improvement in the 18th century, and replaced with pallid substitutes.

The **interior** is one of the two great treasure-houses of Spain, loaded with masterworks and superb detail from the tiniest carving in the choir stalls to its beautiful star-vaulted domes. The enclosed **choir** is almost entirely shut off from the rest of the church, but you can peer through the grill work to see the magnificent gold-trimmed star vault of Juan de Vallejo's **lantern**, under the central tower, which Felipe II declared couldn't have been built by men, but only by angels. Four stately round piers support a profusion of intricate carved decoration—a Spanish twist on Renaissance styles, married harmoniously into a Gothic building. Underneath its majestic beauty a simple slab marks the **tomb of the Cid and his wife Ximena**, their bones relocated here with great pomp in 1921. The other tomb in the *coro* belongs to Bishop Maurice, topped by his enamelled copper effigy; try to get in to see the magnificent carving on the wood and inlaid stalls—unabashed pagan figures on the seats, New Testament scenes above. They were done by Felipe de Vigarni, who also sculpted the dramatic scene on the ambulatory behind the main altar.

De Vigarni also carved the Tomb of *Don Gonzalo de Lerma* in the 16th-century **Capilla de la Presentación**, to the right of the choir. To the left, the **Chapel of Santa Ana** has a wonderfully ornate *retablo* of the Tree of Jesse by Gil de Siloé and a fine Bishop's tomb by his son Diego. One of Diego de Siloé's masterpieces, the diamond-shaped, drippingly Plateresque **Golden Stair** (1523), is the most strikingly original feature of the interior, the perfectly proportioned solution to the Puerta Alta, 7.7m above the floor of the cathedral.

Buffalo Jesus and the Fly-catcher

The two features of the interior that everyone remembers, though, are just inside the west door. First, to the right as you enter, is the plainest but most venerated, the glass-doored **Capilla del Santo Cristo**, where ladies in mantillas gather to worship one of the strangest cult idols any religion has conjured up—the 13th-century **Cristo de Burgos**, a figure made of old buffalo hide (long reputed to be human skin), real hair and fingernails (according to an old tale, both had to trimmed every few days) dressed in a green frock and warm to the touch. Both the head and arms can move, like a doll; these were probably somehow manipulated to impress the faithful, back in the age of miracles. Nearly as famous is the 15th-century mechanical clock across the nave near the roof, the **Papamoscas** ('fly-catcher'), a grinning devil who pops out of a hole in the wall to strike the hour. The most spectacular chapel, the octagonal **Capilla del Condestable**, was attached to the apse by Simón de Colonia for the tombs of the Constable of Castile, Pedro Hernández de Velasco, and his wife in 1482–94. The tombs face the elaborate altar by Vigarni and Diego de Siloé. Velasco clutches his sword even after death; his lady's little dog sleeps at her feet. Velasco was Constable during the conquest of Granada, whose Moorish craftsmen inspired the great, geometric star-vaulting. The chapel has its own sacristy full of trinkets and a wonderfully voluptuous auburn-haired *Magdalen* by Giampetrino, a pupil of Leonardo da Vinci. This being Burgos, she's usually locked up; you'll have to ask the man in the souvenir shop to open the door. The nearby **Sacristía Mayor** is adorned with one of the cathedral's lighter scenes, a Baroque bubble bath of a heaven. Off the cloister, the **Museo Diocesano** (*daily 9.30–1 and 4–6.30; adm*) contains the Cid's marriage agreement and the famous leather-bound coffer the Cid filled with sand, then passed off as gold as security to two Jewish money-lenders, who made him a sizeable loan.

Around the Cathedral

Just northwest of the cathedral on Calle Fernán González, **San Nicolás de Bari** contains an incredible wall-sized alabaster *retablo* by Francisco de Colonia (1505), depicting 36 scenes from the Bible and more angels than could dance on a head of a pin. Plain 15th-century **Santa Águeda**, on Calle Santa Águeda, is the successor of the church where the Cid forced Alfonso VI to swear on a silver lock that he had nothing to do with the assassination of his brother Sancho—an iron copy of the lock is hung over the door inside. Burgos' **castle** was blown up by the French in 1813 and little remains to be seen up here besides the fine view of the city. It is reached through the horseshoe **Arco de San Esteban**. Also near the arch are two 14th-century Gothic churches: **San Esteban** and **San Gil**, both with fine interiors. Near San Gil, in Plaza Alonso Martínez, a grim little building called the **Capitanería** is guarded by military police and covered with commemorative plaques. This was the Nationalist capital during the Civil War; here Franco assumed total power and directed his campaigns in the north. Calle Santander is Burgos' main shopping street; at its head is the **Casa del Cordón**, named after the rope (really a Franciscan monk's belt) carved over the door in honour of St Francis. This palace was built by the Condestable de Velasco in 1485. Fernando and Isabel received Columbus here after his second voyage, and 18 years later, an ageing Fernando sent Ponce de León off to discover the Fountain of Youth.

Nearby, the attractive, arcaded **Plaza Mayor** has recently been refurbished and pedestrianized, although the shady **Paseo del Espolón** along the riverfront is the city's real centre; at the far end, a mighty equestrian **statue of the Cid** with the flowing beard no one dared to pull seems ready to fly off its base and attack any enemy crossing **San Pablo Bridge** towards the Plaza Primo de Rivera. The bridge itself is embellished with stone figures of the Cid's wife, his companions and a Moorish king. Across the bridge the lovely **Casa Miranda** (1545) houses the **Museo de Burgos** (*open daily exc Mon 9.45–1.50 and 4.15–7, Sat and Sun 10–2; adm*) with an archaeological collection.

Monasterio de Las Huelgas

On the outskirts of Burgos lie two of Spain's richest monasteries, both well worth a visit. A 20-minute walk to the west will take you to the Cistercian convent of Las Huelgas (*open daily exc Mon, 10.30–1.15 and 4–3.45, Sun am only; adm*), founded by Alfonso VIII in 1187 at the behest of his wife Eleanor: back then, *Las Huelgas Reales*, the monastery's true name, meant 'the royal repose'). The abbess of Las Huelgas enjoyed more power and influence than any other woman in Spain except the Queen herself, until her powers were revoked in the 19th century. In 1219 San Fernando III started the custom of Castilian kings of going to Las Huelgas to be knighted into the Order of Santiago—not by any inferior, mind you, but by Santiago himself; in the cloister you can see the statue of the saint with a moveable arm holding out a sword made especially for the purpose. Guided tours (in Spanish) will take you through the English-Gothic church: statues of Alfonso VIII and Eleanor kneel before the altar, and there's a curious painted iron pulpit of 1560 that gyrated to allow the priest to address the nuns in the choir or congregation. The church also serves as a Pantheon of Castilian kings and royal ladies.

The French, as usual, desecrated the tombs, though the one they missed, that of Alfonso X's son Fernando de la Cerda, produced such a fine collection of goods as to form the nucleus of Las Huelgas' **Museo de Ricas Telas**, a fascinating collection of fabrics and medieval dress, showing considerable Eastern influences. These are not the only Moorish touches in Las Huelgas: note the geometric tomb of the Infanta Doña Blanca, the peacock and stars in the *mudéjar* **cloister**, and the **Capilla de Santiago**. The grand **Sala Capitular** contains a trophy from Alfonso VIII's Battle of Las Navas de Tolosa—the lovely silk flap of the Moorish commander's tent—and Don Juan's banner from Lepanto, which he gave to his daughter Ana, abbess of Las Huelgas. If the guide's in a good mood, he'll play a scale on the well-tuned columns in the halls. Noble and wealthy pilgrims would receive a fair welcome at Las Huelgas, but for the needs of poor pilgrims Alfonso VIII also built the **Hospital del Rey**, a short walk from Las Huelgas, with a 16th-century Plateresque gateway and a court.

La Cartuja de Miraflores

Burgos' second great monastery is a half hour's walk to the east, through a lovely park of shady trees. **Miraflores** (*open daily 10.15–3 and 4–6, Sun 11.20–12.30, 1–3 and 4–6*) was founded by Juan II in 1441 and is still used as a monastery, so you can see only the church, built by the Colonia family; yet this alone contains more great art than many a cathedral. Here Isabel la Católica commissioned the great Gil de Siloé to sculpt the **tomb of Juan II and Isabel of Portugal** as a memorial to her parents, and after four years of steady work he created the most elaborately detailed tomb of all time, 'imprisoning Death inside an alabaster star' as a local guidebook poetically put it. Instead of a chisel, it looks as if Siloé used a needle to sew the gorgeous alabaster robes of the effigies—Juan pensive, his wife reading a book. Isabela owed her succession to the death of her brother, and as a posthumous thank-you had

Siloé carve his memorial as well. The **tomb of the Infante Don Alfonso** portrays the young prince (1453–68) kneeling at prayer surrounded by a wonderfully playful menagerie of animals, putti and birds entwined in the vines. Master Siloé also did most of the gilt *retablo* of the high altar, said to be made with the gold that Columbus had presented to the Catholic kings at the Casa de Cordón. There are other works of art: a lovely *Annunciation* by Pedro Berruguete, the carvings on the stalls of the lay brothers' choir (the middle section of the Carthusian church's traditional three divisions—the monks' choir is in the front, the general public in the back, by the painting of the Virgin sending the infernal spirits packing). In the side chapel there's a wooden **statue of St Bruno** carved by the Portuguese Manuel Pereira, so lifelike 'it would speak if it weren't a Carthusian monk' as the *burgaleses* like to say.

Below Miraflores and 10km further down the road is the **Abbey of San Pedro de Cardeña**, founded in 899 and now a Trappist monastery (*open 10–1 and 4–6, Sun 12–1.30 and 4–6; adm*). Here the Cid left his family when banished by Alfonso VI, and here he requested to be buried by his wife Ximena. The French stole the bones and when the Spanish government finally got them back it was to inter them in the more secure precincts of the cathedral. You can visit the original tombs with their effigies in a chapel off the **Cloister of Martyrs**, where 200 Benedictines were beheaded during a 10th-century Moorish raid. The Cid's faithful charger Babieca is buried just outside the gate.

Burgos ✉ *09000*

Where to Stay

expensive

Just outside Burgos on the Madrid road, the ★★★★★**Landa Palace**, ✆ 947 20 63 43, ▨ 947 26 46 76, is a member of the prestigious Relais et Châteaux and provides a memorable stay in an over-the-top pseudo-medieval tower furnished with antiques, an indoor atrium and swimming-pool, and beautiful rooms. A meal in the Landa's equally palatial restaurant, the region's finest, will set you back some *6000 pts*. There is also a bar/cafetería with excellent tapas. In the centre of Burgos, the ★★★★**Hotel Condestable**, Vitoria 8, ✆ 947 26 71 25, ▨ 947 20 46 65, is the city's traditional old favourite in an elegant setting. ★★★★**Hotel Almirante Bonifaz**, Vitoria 22 and 24, ✆ 947 20 69 43, ▨ 947 20 29 19, has similar rooms in the centre of town. ★★★**Del Cid**, Pza. Santa María 8, ✆ 947 20 87 15, ▨ 947 26 94 60, magnificently located opposite the cathedral, has well equipped rooms, garage space and a secret tunnel to their excellent restaurant.

moderate–inexpensive

The charmingly old-fashioned ★★**Norte y Londres** on Pza. Alonso Martínez 10, ✆ 947 26 41 25, ▨ 947 27 73 75, is another lovely old building with glass balconies, ★★★**Cordón**, La Puebla 6, ✆ 947 26 50 00, has rooms bordering on *expensive*. Stay near the river in the ★★**Hilton** (not related to the chain), Vitoria 165, ✆ 947 22 51 16, situated near the park (*inexpensive*). Right off the Plaza Mayor, the ★**Hs Hidalgo**, ✆ 947 20 34 81, a well-kept and old fashioned *hostal*, is on a street that is (at least at night) relatively quiet. The ★**Hs Victoria**, San Juan 3, ✆ 947 20 15 42, is nothing special but priced right; the same could be said for the faded but tolerable ★**Castellano** on Laín Calvo, just north of the Plaza Mayor. There is also a youth hostel, the **Residencia Juvenil Gil de Siloé**, Avda. General Vigón, ✆ 947 22 03 62.

Eating Out

For a medieval atmosphere in a 15th-century building facing the cathedral and delicious, roast sucking-lamb, the **Mesón del Cid**, Pza. Santa María 8, ℭ 947 20 87 15, is the place to go. The dining-rooms are on various levels throughout the building, which held one of Spain's first printing presses (*menu 3500 pts*). Just inside the Arco de Santa María, the **Corral de los Infantes** offers Castilian specialities like *olla podrida* and 'medieval lentils' for *1600 pts*; outdoor dining in the summer. The Chinese restaurant next door has inexpensive *platos combinados*. **Gaona**, Virgen de la Paloma 41, near the cathedral, ℭ 947 20 61 91 (*moderate*) has Basque cooking; the peppers stuffed with cod is a treat. Just north of the cathedral on Huerta del Rey, the **Mesón el Cardinal** has a wide array of fancy *bocadillos* and seafood tapas. Near the statue of the Cid, the **Casa Alonso** on Calatrava offers a nice *1000-pts menu*: paella, merluza, stuffed pork chops or Castilian snails. The most popular place in town, **Casa Ojeda**, Vitoria 5, ℭ 947 20 90 52, has the best tapas in its bar and good local cuisine *(around 2500 pts)*. Not to be missed are the *morcillas*, black pudding with either onion or rice. They are one of Burgos's main contributions to Spanish cooking.

Southeast of Burgos

In the mountainous region southeast of Burgos on or off the N234 towards Soria, Covarrubias and Santo Domingo de Silos are firmly marked on the tourist map, but you'll need a car to take in the prizes just off the beaten track such as San Quirce or the Visigothic church of Quintanilla de las Viñas.

Getting Around

Transport here is mostly non-existent. There are several buses daily from Burgos to Aranda de Duero, and in general one a day to Santo Domingo de Silos, Caleruega, Lerma, and Covarrubias, but that's about it.

Tourist Information

Lerma: in the centre, ℭ 947 17 01 43.

A Scatological Abbey and a Visigothic Beauty

The **Abadía de San Quirce** is not easy to find; signposts guide you from **Hontoria de la Cantera**. Founded by Count Fernán González after his defeat of the Saracens on this spot, in 929, the church conserves its original structure, with a fortified tower in the centre; the west door has 11 modillons showing the Creator, Adam and Eve, Cain and Abel and in between, earthy reliefs of men defecating, with inscriptions reading *io cago* and *mal cago* (I shit, and I shit badly), reminiscent of the anarchical shitting figure, the *cagoter*, that accompanies every Catalan Christmas crib. Other reliefs decorate the north door and modillons supporting the charming bubble of an apse, illuminated by two round bull's eye windows and a regular Romanesque window, which was probably originally a bull's eye as well; inside (*open only the first Tues of each month, 9.30–6*) the capitals are carved with the legend of San Quirce and a naked woman who suckles serpents, with lions on either side.

From **Quintanilla de las Viñas**, 4km up under the steel toned Montes de Lara and the ruins of the Castilla de Lara, the gold-stoned Visigothic **Nuestra Señora de las Viñas** drinks up the sun (*open 9.30–2 and 4–8, winter 9–4; closed Mon, Tues and the last weekend of each month; if no one's there, try the guardian's house, marked Turismo 1km south*). This is nothing less than the last Visigothic basilica in Spain, dated 7th century or just before the invasion of the Moors. Made of large blocks incised with Christian graffiti, only the square apse and part of the transept have survived the past 1300 years: the exterior of the former is beautifully girdled with friezes of animals and birds, and what are believed to be the monograms of the founders. Inside, on the triumphal arch, there's another bird frieze and a rare example of Visigothic syncretism: angels with rocket wings, Byzantine in style or perhaps even more like the winged figures on Roman tombs, holding up portraits identifying Christ with the moon (a bearded figure, with a crescent moon LVNA on his head like horns) and the Virgin (or Church) with the sun SOL. Blocks in the apse show heavily coiffed, symmetrical but inexplicable 'astral' figures, sculpted by another artist who had trouble getting the arms and hands on right.

San Pedro de Arlanza, Covarrubias and Santo Domingo de Silos

South of Quintanilla de las Viñas, the Arlanza river runs through a valley known in the 10th century as the Valley of Towers, the frontier of Old Castile, pushed this far south by 'the Good Count' Fernán González. His exploits are described in an epic poem, written in the 13th century by a monk in the romantically ruined abbey of **San Pedro de Arlanza**, founded by the count's father, Gonzalo Fernández, in 912.

Medieval **Covarrubias** is Old Castile's half-timbered showcase of porticoed squares and lanes, guarded by the only surviving 10th-century Mozarabic tower in the Valley of Towers, the sturdy **Torreón de Doña Urraca**. The ex-Colegiata, **San Cosme y San Damián** (*open 10.30–1.30 and 4.30–6.30, weekends 10–2 and 4–7, closed Tues; adm*) was rebuilt in 1474 as the pantheon for the Infantes de Covarrubias; in 1848, the remains of Fernán González and his wife Sancha were transferred from San Pedro de Arlanza and placed next to the altar in a 4th-century Roman sarcophagus. The 17th-century organ, one of the most beautiful in Spain, still works, although you'll have to attend mass to hear its sweet sound.

South of Covarrubias, the star attraction in these parts is **Santo Domingo de Silos** (*open 10.30–1.15 and 4.30–7, Sun and hols 4.30–7; adm*), a Benedictine monastery founded in 954 by Fernán González and ruled in the next century by the abbot who gave it its name. Rebuilt after al-Mansur burned it to the ground, the monastery was refounded in the 19th century by French Benedictines, who have made it famous for Gregorian chant (*sung at 9am Mon–Sat and noon on Sun, and at 7pm*). A double compact disc of Gregorian Chant from the monastery was a Christmas number one in 1992, and still sells well. The monks have inherited the most beautiful Romanesque **cloister** in Spain, built around an ancient cypress tree. The lower section dates from the late 11th to early 12th centuries and has fascinating capitals carved by a sculptor versed in motifs of the Córdoba caliphate. On the corners of the cloister, eight large reliefs on the life of Jesus are in a similar style; one shows the only known representation of Christ dressed in pilgrim's garb. The cloister's *mudéjar* ceiling, painted with scenes of everyday life in the Middle Ages, has been restored. Off the cloister, the **museum** houses Mozarabic illuminations, the Romanesque tympanum from the first church, a 12th-century paten with Roman cameos, and the 18th-century **pharmacy**. After all this, the neoclassical **church**, rebuilt in the 18th century, seems dull.

A mere 2.5km south of Santo Domingo towards Caleruega, the **Desfiladero de la Yecla**, a spectacular narrow gorge full of vultures, hawks and buzzards, has been fitted with wooden walkways. **Caleruega** was the birthplace in 1170 of another canonized Domingo, the one who made the heavenly big time, Santo Domingo de Guzmán, founder in 1216 of the Dominicans or Black Friars, who took on the job of the Inquisition. The exact spot of the saint's birth is marked in the crypt of the church of Dominican Madres.

Way Down South in Burgos Province

The N1 south of Burgos to Madrid passes through **Lerma**, another town on the Arlanza river, founded by the son of Fernán González in 978. It owes its impressive appearance to the Duke of Lerma (Francisco Gómez de Sandoval y Rojas), who ruled Spain between 1598 and 1618 for Felipe III. It was the Duke's idea to expel the Moriscos, and devote a part of the proceeds from their expropriated property into making Lerma a unique monumental complex, with at least six monasteries and the **Palacio Ducal**. This is linked by a flying walkway to the **Colegiata de San Pedro**. Inside, the church contains its original organ of 1616 and a statue in bronze of the archbishop of Sevilla, the uncle of the Duke. The tourist office (*see* above) offers guided tours of the town (*11–2 and 5–7*). Much further south, **Gumiel de Hizán** has a fine 15th-century parish church with monumental stairs and a beautiful Renaissance *retablo*. Gumiel marks the northern limits of D.O. Ribera del Duero, the largest and finest wine region in Castile, producing a variety of reds, especially from a local grape known as *tinto del país* ; mixed with garnacha, malbec, merlot and cabernet sauvignon, it becomes a fresh rosé, a purplish young wine or a mellow aged wine. **Aranda de Duero**, the third town of the province, has a number of old *bodegas* and a pair of good churches: **Santa María** has a beautiful portal attributed to Simón de Colonia and an excellent Renaissance *retablo*.

Downriver, the Augustinian **Monasterio de la Vid** ('of the vine', *open 10–1 and 4–7.30*) boasts an 18th-century Baroque façade with spiralling leaves and roses on the sides of the elegant belfry and octagonal dome. East of Aranda, picturesque **Peñaranda de Duero** is built around the sprawling castle of its medieval lords, who in the safer 16th century decided to move down into the Plaza Mayor. A Plateresque portal marks their **Palacio de los Zúñiga y Avellaneda** (*open 10–1.30 and 4–7, closed Mon*), built around an elegant two-storey patio; rooms are adorned with superb *artesonado* ceilings and plasterwork. Around the corner, a 17th-century **Botica de Jimeno** is the second oldest pharmacy in Spain, in the same family for seven generations. North of Peñaranda, the isolated 11th-century **Ermita del Santo Cristo** is made out of stones cannibalized from Roman **Clunia** (just north, near Peñalba de Castro, where the guardian lives; *open 10–2 and 4–8. winter 5–7, closed Sun pm and Mon*). Founded in the reign of Augustus, it counted 30,000 inhabitants at its peak. In AD 69 Galba, Governor of Nearer Spain, rose up here against Nero and was proclaimed Emperor by his legionaries; the Senate concurred, leaving Nero to run himself through. Clunia was abandoned with the fall of Rome, leaving the forum, theatre, baths, temples, and houses with mosaics.

Where to Stay and Eating Out

Covarrubias ✉ 09346

★★★**Arlanza**, Plaza Mayor 11, ✆ 947 40 30 25, ✉ 947 40 63 59 (*moderate*) occupies a handsome old mansion in the centre of town; its restaurant serves medieval banquets of trout and roast lamb every

Saturday night with music and ancient Castilian dances; book ahead. Another fine old house contains **Galin**, Pza. Doña Urraca, ✆ 947 40 30 15 (*inexpensive*), serving an authentic *olla podrida* for ridiculously low prices (*1300-pts menú*). *Closed Tues in winter.* **Torreón de Doña Urraca**, Pza. Doña Sancha, ✆ 947 40 31 08 (*moderate*) has a delightful terrace. *Open only in summer.*

Santo Domingo de Silos ✉ 09610

The charming **★★★Tres Coronas**, Pza. Mayor 6, ✆ 947 38 07 27, ✆ 947 38 80 25 (*moderate*) is located in a 17th-century house, with 16 intimate rooms; its restaurant, **Casa Emeterio**, features Castilian cuisine (*menú 2200 pts*). Near the famous cloister, **★★Arco de San Juan**, Pradera de San Juan, ✆ 947 38 07 94 (*moderate*) is quiet and offers a delightful garden; family-run **Méson Asador**, C/ Principal, ✆ 947 39 00 53, has *inexpensive* rooms and food. Men can eat and sleep for a song (well, almost) in the monastery by ringing the Padre Hospedería, ✆ 947 38 07 68.

Aranda de Duero ✉ 09400

Business travellers en route to Madrid stop in Aranda's functional hotels near the highway; most have cheap weekend rates. **★★★Los Bronces**, Ctra Madrid–Irún km 160, ✆ 947 50 08 50, near the Burgos exit, and **★★★Tres Condes**, at Avda. Castilla 66, ✆ 947 50 24 00, ✆ 947 50 24 04, are typical (*both moderate*).

There are two special places to eat, however: **Mesón de la Villa**, Pza. Mayor 3, ✆ 947 50 10 25, serves some of the best food around, including poultry and garden vegetables raised on the owner's farm, accompanied by the finest Riojas (*around 4000 pts*). *Closed Mon.* The second is **Rafael Corrales**, Carrequemada 2, ✆ 947 50 02 77, an *asador* that opened in 1902 serving baby lamb baked in a wood oven, washed down with Ribera del Duero. *Closed Thurs.*

Along the Pilgrimage Route: Burgos to Carrión de los Condes

If the medieval pilgrim survived the storms, cut-throats and wolves at Roncesvalles, the Navarrese who exposed themselves when excited, and the dupers and fleshpots of Burgos, then they faced the flattest, hottest and most monotonous landscape in Europe. With nothing to look at, one becomes introspective and meditative, receptable to enlightenment. Off the highways, 20th-century intrusions are rare; hamlets of adobe houses, church towers crowned with storks and huge dovecotes powerfully evoke the Middle Ages.

Getting Around

Buses run from Burgos to Aguilar de Campóo and Cervera de Pisuerga, to Palencia, Frómista, Sahagún, Saldaña and Carríon (on the Burgos–León route), to Sasamón and Grijalba. Frómista can also be reached by train from Palencia or Santander.

Tourist Information

Frómista: Pso. Central (summer only).
Carrión de los Condes: Pza. Santa María (summer only).

From Burgos to the Puente de Fitero

Like many towns along the road, **Sasamón**, 33km west of Burgos, takes pride in its churches, especially **Santa María la Real**, with an exact 12th-century copy of the Sarmental door on the cathedral of Burgos; it has a good if damaged cloister and a statue of St Michael attributed to Diego de Siloé. Of the 15th-century **San Miguel**, only the portal survives with its seven archivaults isolated in a field like a lost triumphal arch. East, at **Grijalba**, the 13th-century Gothic church of Santa María de los Reyes has plenty of gargoyles and carved capitals with New Testament themes; inside, the ribs of the vaults are painted with alligators. The 12th-century font is supported by a lion and serpent.

The main road, however, heads south of Tardajos to pass right through the haunting, ravaged remains of the 14th-century **Monasterio de San Antón**, its once magnificent vaults hanging miraculously in the void. Its monks were famous for treating pilgrims afflicted with 'St Anthony's fire' or erysipelas, inflammations on the body, at the time associated with leprosy. Westward is the medieval castle and village of Castrojeriz, that once had seven hospitals and a residence of Pedro the Cruel along Calle de los Peregrinos. The finest church, Gothic **Santa María del Manzano**, is named after the apple tree trunk where a statue of the Virgin was found when Santiago, on his white horse, leapt from the castle to the tree; note the horseshoes on the door. San Juan, built next to a 12th-century tower, conserves a half-ruined 14th-century cloister with an *artesonado* ceiling. West of Castrojeriz the ruthless horizons of the *meseta* come into their own. The last hill for miles, the windswept Alto de Mostelares (900m) looks over the Pisuerga river, spanned by the **Puente de Fitero** with 11 arches, built in the 11th century by pilgrimage-promoter Alfonso IV. Little **Boadilla del Camino**, the first village (9km) on the west bank, has a beautiful 15th-century Gothic column in its plaza decorated with scallops. The parish church has a curious Romanesque baptismal font on twelve baby columns and decorated with swastikas and solar symbols.

Frómista

Six km west, **Frómista** has been a key pilgrims' stop since the days of the *Codex Calixtinus* for its 'perfect Romanesque church', golden **San Martín** (*open 10–2 and 4.30–8, winter 3–6.30*), founded in 1035 by the widow of Sancho the Great. Restored in 1893 by the arch-restorer of France, Viollet-le-Duc, San Martín is now a national monument stripped of all its trappings. Two slender round turrets buttress the west door; inside the proportions of the three-aisled, three-apsed, barrel-vaulted interior crowned by an octagonal tower satisfy the soul. But just as noteworthy is the extraordinary amount of sculpted detail inside and out, on the modillons and capitals; the original 11th-century carvings are superb and easy to distinguish from the fond fancies of the restorers, who based their work on medieval sarcophagi and marked their work with an R. The whole is a tantalising book of hundreds of medieval symbols and occult messages; a pair of binoculars comes in handy and a crick in the neck is probably unavoidable. Of Frómista's other churches, note especially the 16th-century **Santa María del Castillo** with its elaborate painted Hispano-Flemish *retablo* with 29 panels.

Beyond Frómista, the tawny little villages of Palencia merge into the tawny earth. One, **Villalcázar de Sirga**, was once a thriving town and key Templar possession. At the start of the 13th century the Templars built the enormous church of **Santa María la Blanca**, with what must be the tallest porch in Spain to shelter a richly decorated double portal with a double frieze (if closed, find the sacristan who lives around the corner on the street left of the church). Pilgrims would make a beeline to the Capilla de Santiago and its miraculous Virgin, who looks a little worse for wear, with her peasant features and headless child, but modern visitors tend to head straight to the beautifully carved tombs sculpted by Antón Pérez de Carrión of the Infante Don Felipe (son of Fernando III the Saint) and his second wife, Leonor Ruiz de Castro, curiously gagged. Here too is the tomb of a Knight Templar, with his hawk and sleeping lion: a rare burial, as most Templars were buried face down in the earth without a casket. The magnificent *retablo mayor* was painted by the school of Berruguete.

Where to Stay and Eating Out

Castrojeriz ✉ 09110

**El Méson, Cordón 1, ✆ 947 37 74 00 (*moderate–inexpensive*) offers a handful of rooms in an old mill (and a new annex), a peaceful setting and simple favourites like trout stuffed with ham in the dining room.

Frómista ✉ 34440

Hostería de Los Palmeros, Pza. San Telmo, ✆ 979 81 00 67 (*expensive*) began its career as a *hostal* for pilgrims, although the medieval has been seasoned with several styles since; furnished with antiques, its rooms are complemented by a fine restaurant with an *artesonado* ceiling; dinners around *3500 pts. Closed Tues except in summer.* ***Hs San Telmo**, Martín Veña 8, ✆ 979 81 01 02 (*moderate*) is a good second choice; **Fonda Marisa**, ✆ 979 81 00 23, costs even less and cooks up good cheap *menús.*

Villalcázar de Sirga ✉ 34400

There's nowhere to stay except at the pilgrims' shelter behind the town hall, but a charming old *posada* awaits for lunch or dinner, the very popular **Mesón Villasirga**, Pza. Mayor ✆ 979 88 80 22, featuring baked sucking-pig with almonds and other Castilian favourites (no cat, we promise) for *2800 pts. Open daily May–Oct, other times Fri, Sat, and Sun only; book at weekends.*

North of Frómista: the Románico Palentino

If you've the time or inclination, you could do worse than take a wander off the beaten track into the northern part of Palencia province, into the foothills of the Cantabrian mountains, known as the Románico Palentino for its rare collection of some 200 mostly untouched Romanesque churches (nothing less than the greatest concentration in Europe). It seems that masons brought in to build churches along the *camino* came up here to build churches in the new villages, founded to repopulate the region. Aguilar de Campóo, linked by bus from Burgos or Palencia, or train from Santander, makes the best base for exploring, although you really need a car and that most elusive object of desire: a good map of Spain. The Ministerio de Fomento's road atlas is the best.

Tourist Information

Aguilar de Campóo: Pza. Mayor 33, ✆ 979 12 20 24 (July and Aug only).

North to Aguilar

Northwest of Alar del Rey (on the Santander–Palencia N611) you can easily see two of the finest Romanesque works in the region. **San Andrés de Arroyo** (*open summer 9.30–1.15 and 4.15–7.15, winter 9.30–12 and 3.15–6.15*), a Bernardine convent founded in 1190, has an interesting little museum; the entrance to the chapterhouse is beautiful and the cloister has extraordinary twin columns and capitals, decorated with interlacings and exotic flora. The second church, golden-stone **Moarves de Ojeda**, has a superb portal, with a Christ in a mandorla, four Evangelists and twelve Apostles; the capitals are crowded with people and inside there's a 13th-century baptismal font. Other prime stops on the Romanesque trail are north of Moarves: **Vallespinoso de Aguilar**, where a fortified 12th-century hermitage on a rock has a cylindrical tower and pretty door, and **Barrio de Santa María**, a handsome village where the Ermita de Santa Eulalia is a pristine 13th-century church with a lovely apse and the narrowest windows in Spain, complete with 13th-century murals inside.

Alternatively, if you stick to the N611, north of Alar del Rey, you'll find in **Santa María de Mave** a church founded in 1208 with a fine portal, an octagonal lantern and Renaissance murals in one of its three apses; its monastery has been converted into a charming hotel (*see* below). The church in **Olleros de Pisuerga** to the west is some 300 years older, a rare example of a Spanish church carved into the living rock. Further north, a kilometre from Aguilar, **Lomilla** has a Romanesque church with a 14th-century calvary.

Aguilar de Campóo

Set in the green mountain valley of the Río Pisuerga and next to a large man-made lake, Aguilar de Campóo is a picturesque town of cookie-bakers and decidedly leaning, medieval houses with big bold coats-of-arms. The Aguilar, or eagle, of its name refers to its rocky limestone outcrop, its eagle's nest, crowned by a ruined five-towered castle built in the 11th century. At the foot of the castle, the **Hermitage of Santa Cecilia** (get the key in the *casa rectoral*) was founded in 1041, and has exceptional capitals: one shows the Massacre of the Innocents by 11th-century knights in fishscale armour. In the arcaded Plaza de España, the Gothic **Colegiata de San Miguel** has the Renaissance mausoleum of the Marquesses of Aguilar and a **museum** (*open 10–1 and 5–8*) full of tombs and sculptures. Two km west of Aguilar, the Cistercian monastery of **Santa María la Real** (1213) has more excellent capitals and a good cloister; in 1988 it won a Europa Nostra award for its restoration and now shelters a **Centre of Romanesque Studies**, with a unique collection of models of the region's churches (*open 10–3 and 4–8, Sat and Sun 11–2 and 5–7*).

Romanesque Routes North of Aguilar

The road directly north of Aguilar takes in more Romanesque charmers: the 12th-century church at **Matalbaniega**, with two decorated portals, carved modillons and unusual caryatids holding up a window. **Cillamayor**'s Romanesque church has a funerary hypogeum; at **Revilla de Santullán**, the church has a handsome portal with its fifteen figures, sitting at desks like members of the board, and other sculptures that verge on the pornographic. Further along, the village of **Brañosera** claims to be one of the oldest municipalities in Spain, with its charter dating back to 824; its Romanesque church has a good 12th-century portal. **San Cebrián de Muda**'s 12th-century church has Renaissance murals.

West of Aguilar, **Cervera de Pisuerga** was once an important frontier settlement, but has retired to its meadows and old family manors. Its recently restored 16th-century Gothic church, **Santa María del Castillo**, built on the medieval citadel, has a fine Hispano-Flemish *retablo* by Felipe de Vigarni and a beautiful painting of the *Adoration of the Magi* by Juan de Flandres. Three km away, at **Ruesga**, there are huge views across the mountains, and a *parador* to enjoy them.

Where to Stay and Eating Out

Aguilar de Campóo ✉ 34800

★★★**Valentin**, Avda. Generalísimo 21, ✆ 979 12 21 25 (*moderate*), is a scenic mountain hotel in an elegant old building (in need of a lick of paint) with a garden and good restaurant; or there's the less expensive ★★**Villa de Aguilar**, Alférez Provisional, ✆ 979 12 22 25 (*moderate*). In Santa María de Mave, 12km from Aguilar, the serene ★★**Hostería El Convento**, ✆ 979 12 36 11 (*moderate*) occupies a lovingly restored Benedictine monastery, the perfect place to sleep in, if you're doing the Romanesque route. Delicious, simple and satisfying food awaits at **Cortés**, El Puente 39, ✆ 979 12 30 55: menus for under *2000 pts*, or you can splurge on the *caldereta de pescados y mariscos* (seafood stew for two) for *8000 pts*.

Cervera de Pisuerga ✉ 34840

Up on the edge of the Picos near man-made lakes and newborn rivers, the modern ★★★**Parador Fuentes Carrionas**, Ctra. de Ruesga, ✆ 979 87 00 75, 🖷 979 87 01 05 (*expensive*) makes a plush headquarters for nature-lovers, with a good restaurant. Plaza España has a couple of *inexpensive* choices, among them, ★**Siglo XX**, ✆ 979 12 29 00, with average food. For a meat orgy, **Gasolina**, by Plaza Mayor, ✆ 979 87 07 13, will fill you up with offerings from its oven and grill for *under 3000 pts*. For something sweet, **Uko**, Ukaldo Merino 15, is famous across Spain for its puff pastries.

Along the Carrión River

West of Frómista, into the *campos góticos*, the Visigothic plains, the *camino* continues to Carrión de los Condes, which also occupies one of Old Castile's chief north–south arteries. Palencia and environs were more important in Roman and Visigothic times than now; among the things to see are two Roman villas and the oldest dated church in Spain.

Getting Around

Carrión de los Condes is connected by bus with Frómista and Palencia at least twice a day. Palencia is easy to leave: there are frequent trains to Burgos, Valladolid, Ávila, Madrid and Santander (via Frómista and Aguilar de Campóo); trains to León call at Paredes de Nava. The RENFE station is at Jardinillos, ✆ 979 74 30 19. The bus station is nearby, on Avda. Dr. Simón Nieto.

Tourist Information

Palencia: Mayor 105, ✆ 979 74 00 68.

Back on the Pilgrim Track: Carrión de los Condes

West of Villalcázar de Sirga, Carrión de los Condes is named after the river Carrión and not for putrefying nobility, although it can't be denied that the Infantes or Counts of Carrión, who married the Cid's two daughters, were genuinely rotten villains; after picking up their big, glittering dowries, they beat their wives and tied them to oaks and left them for dead. The outraged Cid gathered up a posse, killed the Counts, and found his daughters new, even more princely husbands. The wicked Infantes are buried in the lovely Renaissance cloister of **San Zoilo**, a Benedictine monastery by the river, founded in 1047, when the Emir of Córdoba sent the 4th-century relics of Zoilo to the Count of Carrión. It looks its best on Friday nights, when the monastery hosts medieval dinners complete with troubadours; to book, © 979 88 00 50.

Over the 16th-century bridge from San Zoilo, the heart of Carrión has two worn 12th-century Romanesque churches that preserve interesting portals: **Santiago**, in the Plaza Mayor, with its Christ in Majesty and apostles and representatives of 22 medieval guilds, including soldiers bashing each other and contortionists. **Santa María del Camino** has a capital on the portal depicting the Tribute of 100 Maidens that the Castilians sent yearly to the Moors; other figures are of Samson fighting the lion and women riding beasts. The interior is out of kilter, although whether it was done so intentionally (like Getaria, for instance) is hard to fathom; it could just be falling over. During the great days of the pilgrimage, the town produced two men of genius: Rabbi Shem Tov Ardutiel (Sem Tob), author of the *Danza General de la Muerte*, who died in 1370, and Íñigo López de Mendoza, the Marqués de Santillana, the Renaissance poet. Lastly, just off the road before the province of León, you can visit the 3rd-century AD **Roman villa** at **Quintanilla de la Cueza** for its colourful mosaic floors and the heating system or hypocausts, protected by a shelter; there's a small museum on the site with finds.

South along the Carrión to Palencia

Paredes de Nava was the birthplace of painter Pedro Berruguete (d.1504), who worked in Urbino and introduced the Renaissance style to Spain as court painter to Fernando and Isabel, and of his son Alonso (d.1561), a pupil of Michelangelo, who brought mannerism back with him and served as court painter to Charles V. A few of the Berruguetes' paintings, including a *retablo mayor* by Pedro, remain in **Santa Eulalia**, with its delicious bell tower. The adjacent **museum** (*open 11–2 and 4–7*) has an impressive collection of works by other Renaissance masters (Gil de Siloé, Juan de Flandres, Juan de Juni, etc.).

Palencia

Palencia is one of the bigger wallflowers in the garden of Spain's provincial capitals, although in 1185 Alfonso VIII made it the site of Spain's first university (in 1239 it was removed to Salamanca). Part of the blame for Palencia's failure to thrive rests squarely on the shoulders of Charles V who, after sucking the city dry to pay for the bribes he needed to be elected Holy Roman Emperor, rubbed out the city's prospects and privileges in revenge for its leading role in the Comunero revolt. The one thing they couldn't take away from Palencia is its Gothic **cathedral**, nicknamed *La Bella Desconocida* ('the Unknown Beauty'), in Plaza San Antolín (*open 10.30–1 and 4–6.30, Sun and hols 9–2; adm to crypt and museum*). The exterior is austerely plain except for two portals; Juan de Flandres' Renaissance *retablo mayor* is the prize in an interior that has remained more or less unchanged–a lack of Baroque curlicues and rolling eyeballs is a tell-tale sign of decline in a Spanish town. The oldest part of the crypt (673) is the only known surviving example of a Visigothic martyrium, built by King Wamba before he was shuttled off to a monastery. Among the highlights in the museum is an early *San Sebastián* by El Greco and a fine *Virgin and Child* by Pedro Berruguete. Don't miss the clock in the transept, where a Lion and Knight strike the hours with gusto. To the south, 11th-century **San Miguel** is a fine little ogival Romanesque church, where the Cid married his Ximena. East of Calle Mayor, the 16th-century **Santa Clara** has a famous *Cristo Yacente* that elicited the comment from the ultra-pious Felipe II: 'If I had faith, I would believe that this was the real body of Christ.' Until the archaeology museum reopens (ask at the tourist office) you can take some comfort in the privately-run **Museo de la Calzada**, just off C/ Mayor on C/ Barrio y Mier 10 (*open 12–2 and 7–9, closed Thurs and Sun*) where Juan Carlos's personal cobbler displays pairs of his Majesty's shoes, along with other celebrities' footwear.

Ten km south of Palencia in the village of **Baños de Cerrato** (2km from Venta de Baños), the Visigothic King Reccesvinth (he of the famous golden crown with dangling letters spelling his name) founded the sturdy church of **San Juan de Baños** back in 661 (*open 10–1 and 4–7, closed Mon; Patricio, the guardian, lives just opposite*), the purest example of Visigothic architecture to come down to us. Fretwork windows and a carved doorway (and a belfry, added by the restorers) relieve the simple stone exterior. Inside, the nave is divided by rows of horseshoe arches, and the capitals, doorways, and the apse are discreetly decorated with finely carved 8-pointed crosses (*croix pattées*), scallop shells, and palms. Reccesvinth's rather complex dedicatory inscription survives intact on the triumphal arch, framed by modillons decorated with diving eagles. In its use of pleasing, robust architectural volumes and the concentration of intricate detail in a few places, San Juan has been called the first Spanish church. Recent excavations uncovered 58 7th-century tombs and the original plan of the church, with its three apses standing out separately like fork prongs. The Baños of its name refers to a nearby curative spring, closed in by two Visigothic arches and restored in 1941.

North of Carrión de los Condes: Saldaña and a Roman Villa

From Carrión de los Condes, the C615 follows the river Carrión up to **Renedo de la Vega** and the ruins of the monastery of Santa María de la Vega, a *mudéjar* work of 1215. Further north, towards Lobera, a sign points the way to **Pedrosa de la Vega** (1.5km), where the 3rd–4th-century Roman **Villa of Olmeda** was discovered in 1968 (*open winter 11–1.30 and 4–6, summer 10–1.30 and 5–7, closed Mon*) with its perfectly preserved polychrome mosaic floors, with geometric designs and mythological scenes. Nearby, in the pretty medieval village of **Saldaña**, the church of San Pedro houses finds from the ongoing excavations. Saldaña's ruined 11th-century castle was the residence of Doña Urraca, sister and advisor of Alfonso VI; the 15th-century Gothic **San Miguel** has a *retablo* attributed to Gil de Siloé.

Where to Stay and Eating Out

Carrión de los Condes ✉ 34120

There are pleasant rooms and a restaurant at the monastery **San Zoilo**, ✆ 979 88 11 45, ✉ 979 88 10 90, or try ***Hs La Corte**, Santa María 34, ✆ 979 88 01 38 (*moderate*), with a good restaurant. Rooms are cheap at **El Resbalón**, C/ Marqués de Santillana, ✆ 979 88 00 11, which also serves filling *menús* for around *1000 pts* including wine and dessert. South of Carrión in Villoldo,**Estrella del Bajo Carrión**, Ctra. Palencia-Riaño, ✆ 979 82 70 05, @ 979 82 72 69 (*moderate*) is a comfortable family hotel with a large garden; good meals at around *3000 pts.*

Palencia ✉ 34000

***Rey Sancho de Castilla**, Avda. Ponce de León, ✆ 979 72 53 00, @ 979 71 03 34 (*expensive*) has recently been restored and offers a number of diversions—swimming, tennis, TV, bingo—and activities for children. For the same price and facilities (though no pool) ***Castilla La Vieja** is another sound choice on Avda. Casado del Alisal 26, ✆ 979 74 90 44, @ 979 74 75 77. **Monclús,** Menéndez Pelayo 3, ✆ 979 74 43 00 (*moderate*) is comfortable and good value.

Lorenzo, Casado del Alisal 6, ✆ 979 74 35 45 (*moderate*) cooks up the most traditional food in town, cooked by mama 'La Gorda'; among its specialities is *pisto*—creamed tomatoes, peppers, onions; *menús 3700 pts. Closed Sun.* **Casa Damian**, Ignacio Martínez de Azcoitia 9, ✆ 979 74 46 28 (*moderate*) serves up steaming bowls of Castilian *menestra de verduras*, its speciality, and other regional dishes. Closed Mon. For something cheaper, there's **Ecuador-Casa Matías**, Martín Calleja 19, with hams, sausages and wines, and **Taberna Plaza Mayor**, for *raciones* of gambas.

Along the Pilgrims' Road to León

The *camino de Santiago* continues its flat way towards León. Framed by the Cordillera Cantábrica to the north and the lower, softer Montes de León to the west, the province was a refuge for Mozarabs from Andalucía in the first days of the Reconquista, and what remains of their monasteries are among the finest monuments along the whole road.

Getting Around

Sahagún is linked by trains between Palencia and León and less frequently by buses between León and Carrión de los Condes.

Tourist Information

Valencia de Don Juan: Pza. del Generalísimo 1, ✆ 987 75 04 64

Sahagún and its *Mudéjar* Bricks

During the 12th century, when Sahagún was the seventh official stop of the *Codex Calixtinus*, it had a population of 12,000 and artificially concentrated so much wealth in the middle of nowhere that it earned the nickname the 'Las Vegas of the Middle Ages'. Today a mere 3000 souls try to fill up the dusty plaza mayor, the darkened old porticoes and forlorn chewed-up houses. Sahagún's rise and fall went hand in hand with that of Spain's most powerful Benedictine abbey, **San Benito**. The seeds of its future glory were sown in the 11th century when Sancho III of Castile snatched León, the inheritance of his brother Alfonso, and locked Alfonso up in the abbey. But Alfonso made a secret pact with the abbot of San Benito, who helped him escape and take refuge in Moorish Toledo. In 1072, Sancho was assassinated and Alfonso was crowned king of Castile and León.

Like Henry VIII, Alfonso VI married his way through six wives; those from Aquitaine and Burgundy put him into contact with Cluny—the great promoter of the Santiago pilgrimage. Never forgetting the help he received at Sahagún, the king refounded San Benito in 1080 under the new Cluniac reforms and poured money into the abbey, and a new pilgrims' hospital. In its heyday San Benito even minted its own coins; in 1534 its theological school had the status of a university. Felipe II brought it low by moving the school to Navarra's Monasterio de Irache in 1596 and constraining the abbey to pay nearly all of its rents to the crown. In the 18th century two fires finished off what remained, leaving only a 17th-century portal, now a decorative city gate at the west end of town, and the adjacent ruins of the 12th-century Gothic **Capilla de San Mancio**. Smaller bits of San Benito are in the **museum** in the **Monasterio Santa Cruz** *(open 10–2.30 and 4.30–6.30, closed winter)*: the tombs of Alfonso VI and a few of his wives and the great silver *custodia* by master Enrique de Arfe, which makes official appearances only for Corpus Christi but the nuns will show it if you ask.

What Sahagún never had was a ready supply of building stone, which led the craftsmen who immigrated here from the Moorish lands to develop an architecture in brick, a medium that permitted new decorative patterns and delicacy. The first example, **San Tirso** *(open 10.30–1.30 and 5–8, Sun 10–1.20, closed Mon)*, was built near the monastery in the first decade of the 12th century, with its squat, tapering skyscraper-tower rising out three round apses. **San Lorenzo** is just a little later and more obviously Moorish in design, but its interior was redone in the 18th century (the chapel has Renaissance reliefs by Juan de Juni); both churches have porticoes for the famous markets Sahagún once held. In 1259 the Franciscans built the much damaged **Santuario de La Peregrina**, just outside the town on the N620, the third and latest *mudéjar* church, applying the new brick techniques to Gothic; inside some lovely bits of the original stucco work survive. Five km south of Sahagún, on the Río Cea's bank, two sisters founded **San Pedro de las Dueñas** in the 10th century, with a beautiful Renaissance crucifix by Gregorio Fernández and 18 top-notch Romanesque capitals from the church's 1109 rebuilding, begun in stone and continued in brick by *mudéjar* craftsmen. Another road from Sahagún, the C611, leads in 6km to the mighty, well-preserved 16th-century castle at **Grajal de Campos**.

San Miguel de Escalada

This whole region was the new frontier back in the early days of the Reconquista, when the kings of Oviedo had just added León to their title. Among the first pioneers on the scene were Abad Adefonso and his companions, refugees from Córdoba, who in 913 founded the beautiful church of **San Miguel de Escalada** (just before Mansilla de las Mulas, take the road northeast 8km). A lovely portico of horseshoe arches, an *ajímez* window and a heavy 11th-century tower mark the exterior, while the interior (hopefully reopened after a major restoration) is proof in golden limestone that the Cordovans never forgot the classic symmetrical Roman basilica form and its proportions. Delicate horseshoe arches divide the three aisles, and separate the transept and triple apse from the main body of the basilica (like the Byzantines, the Mozarab liturgy called for a screen between the holy precinct and the parishioners). The capitals have simple palmette designs; luxuriant floral and geometric reliefs with lions and peacocks eating grapes decorate the chancels and friezes; over the door you can make out the highly elaborate if faint dedicatory inscription. The ceiling, a later *mudéjar* addition, bears the arms of León and Castile.

Southwest of Mansilla, **Valencia de Don Juan** was named after its first duke, the son of Alfonso the Wise, and is worth a detour for a theatrical 15th-century **castle**, which rises from the banks of the Río Esla and is featured on all León's tourist brochures, with its massive walls (on one side only, like a stage set) broken by a series of slender turrets and crenellations. The surrounding Esla *vega* is one of the most fertile swathes of the province, producer of Valdevimbre-Los Oteros, a light, fruity rosé wine, fermented in curious bunker-like *bodegas*.

Where to Stay and Eating Out

Sahagún ✉ 24320

★Hs Alfonso VI, C/ Antonio Nicolás 6, ✆ 987 78 11 44 (*moderate*), is one of the smarter choices in town, or there's the colourful **Fonda Asturiana**, ✆ 987 78 00 73 (*cheap*), with good food. Santa Cruz's **★Hs Hospedería Benedictina**, ✆ 987 78 00 78 (*moderate*) has sparkling rooms with bath.

Valencia de Don Juan ✉ 24200

In the centre of town**★★Villegos II**, C/ Palacio 10, ✆ 987 75 01 61 (*moderate*) is an intimate family hotel with a garden pool. Nearby, in the oldest house in town, **★★Hs El Palacio**, C/ Palacio 3, ✆ 987 75 04 74 (*moderate*) is a charming little inn, decorated with antiques and a document saying that King Felipe III once slept here. Run by Asturians, it also has an excellent *sidrería* and good home-cooking. *Closed Oct–May.*

León

*León tuvo veinticuatro reyes
antes que Castilla leyes*

(León had 24 kings before Castile even had laws)

Radiant under the famous spires of its cathedral, León is a singularly happy city of clean boulevards shaded by horse-chestnut trees: one of the few places in Spain to achieve modern *urbanización* with grace and elegance. Part of the credit for this must go to its hyperactive City Hall, which blankets the city with posters depicting itself as a friendly lion, advising the Leonese to ride the bus, recycle their glass and not to blaspheme. The founding of a university has given the old city a transfusion of young blood.

History

Although the lion has long been the city's symbol, its name actually comes from *Legio Septima Gemina*, the Roman Seventh Legion, established here in AD 68 when Galba built a fort to guard the plain and the Roman road from Zaragoza. Reconquered from the Moors in the 850s by Ordoño I of Asturias (850–66), León changed hands several times again before Ordoño II (914–24) moved his capital here. Even then, factionalism in the royal family left the city prey to Moorish re-reconquests until 1002. After this last Moorish hurrah, León, rebuilt and refortified, reconquered Castile. But just as León eclipsed Asturias, Castile—first a county, then a separate kingdom—eclipsed León. In 1252, under Fernando III el Santo, the union of the two kingdoms was finalized. Castile never looked back, but for León, the marriage spelt nothing but decline: the nobles went off to the court in Burgos and the people left to settle the new frontiers gained by the Reconquista.

Into this vacuum of power and influence stepped the Church: the pilgrims' road became the chief source of income. Medieval pilgrims eagerly looked forward to León, with its Hilton of a *hostal*, where they could catch their breath for the last leg of their journey. Broken and crushed during the Comunero revolt against Charles V, León sank into oblivion until the invention of the railway made its mines viable once again. These in turn declined, leaving León its share of autonomy atavists who, remembering the good old days of the 10th and 11th centuries, preach '*León sin Castilla*' (León without Castile). As yet their movement has little support—it's too much like a mother rejecting her own child.

Getting Around

By train: León's main Avda. de Ordoño II crosses the Bernesga river to meet the RENFE station, © 987 22 37 04. There are frequent connections with Burgos, Palencia, Medina del Campo, Madrid, Astorga, Ponferrada, Ourense and Lugo. The Transcantábrico journey to Bilbao begins at 8.50am at the FEVE station, Avda. Padre Isla 48, © 987 22 59 19, stops for a half-hour lunch at Mataporquera near the Picos de Europa and arrives at Bilbao at 7.12pm, stopping everywhere in between; regular trains depart for Oviedo and Gijón nine times a day through some magnificent mountain scenery and at least 500 tunnels.

By bus: Buses, © 987 22 62 00, depart from the terminal south of the RENFE station, on Pso. Ingeniero Sáenz de Miera, for the villages in the province and Oviedo, Burgos, Santander, Salamanca and Madrid.

Tourist Information

Plaza de Regla 4, across from the cathedral, © 987 23 70 82.

The Cathedral

The Spaniards call this, the most splendid articulation of French Gothic in Spain, *La Pulchra Leonina* ('Belle of León'), a cathedral so remarkable that it would stand out even in France for its daring and superb walls of stained glass. A like amount of glass caused Beauvais, its closest rival in window-acreage, to collapse, a disaster León has managed to avert so far by increasing support to the walls: expect some scaffolding. Although Calahorra in La Rioja claims the most storks' nests, León comes in a close second with some 100 families.

In 1204, Alfonso IX began a new church in warm golden stone in unheard-of dimensions, modelled on the soaring Gothic cathedrals of Chartres and Rheims. His successor, Fernando III, worried by the expense, tried to limit its size, but the Leonese responded by putting up their own money for the construction, and by the 15th century it was more or less finished. Outstanding 13th-century sculpture decorates the north, south, and especially the **west portal** with its three finely carved tympana—the one in the centre illustrates a lively scene of the Last Judgement, the devils boiling the sinners beneath a triumphant Christ. The exterior, however, pales before the soaring spectacle of the **interior**, stripped in the 19th century of all its Baroque frosting, leaving it bare and breathtaking, especially when the late-afternoon sun streams in to ignite the richest and most vivid stained glass imaginable, 1800 square metres of it, all glowing reds and golds, greens and violets, all by Spanish artists. The oldest glass, in the chapels around the apse and the great rose window in the front of the twelve Apostles, dates from the 13th century.

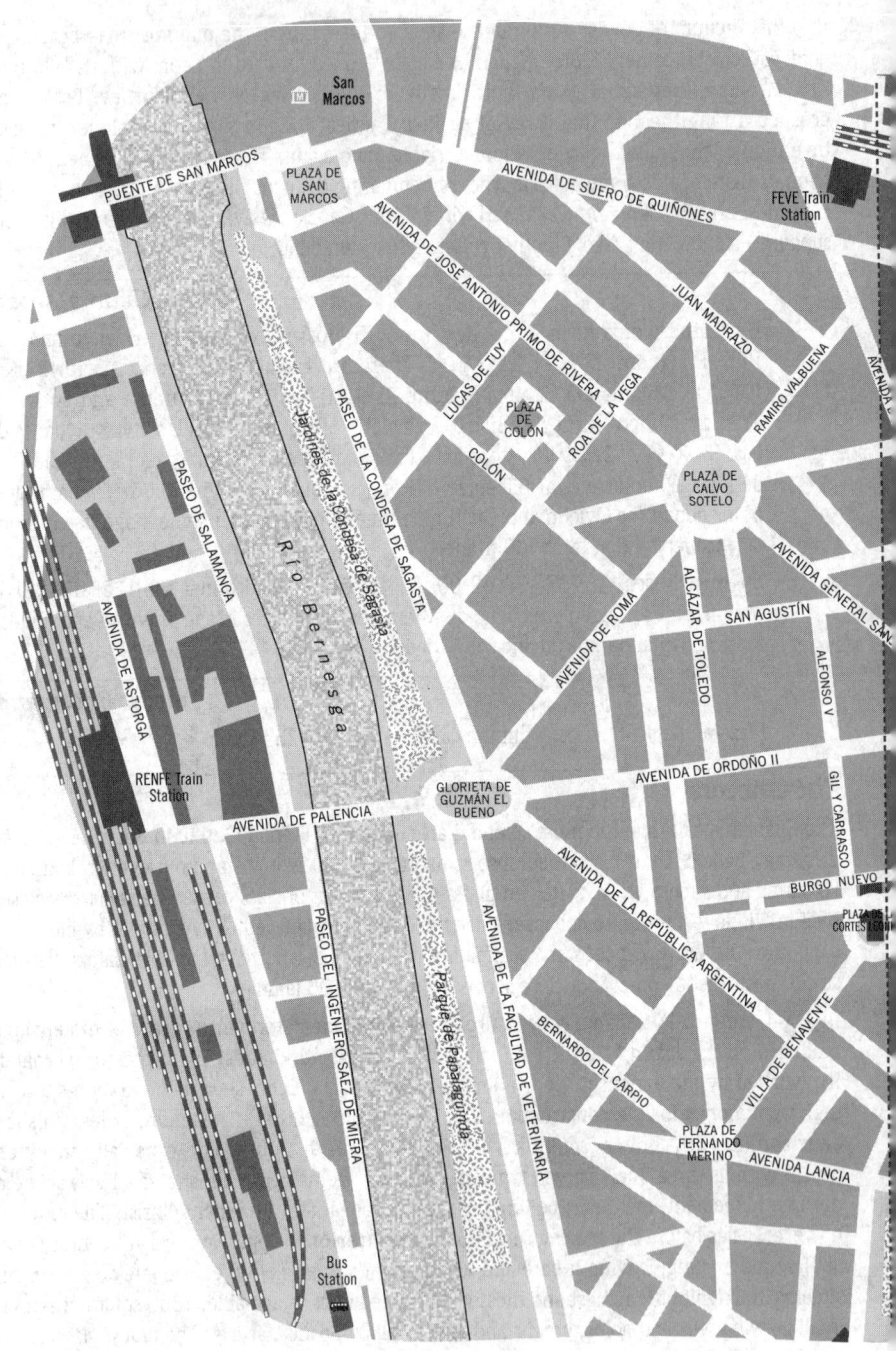

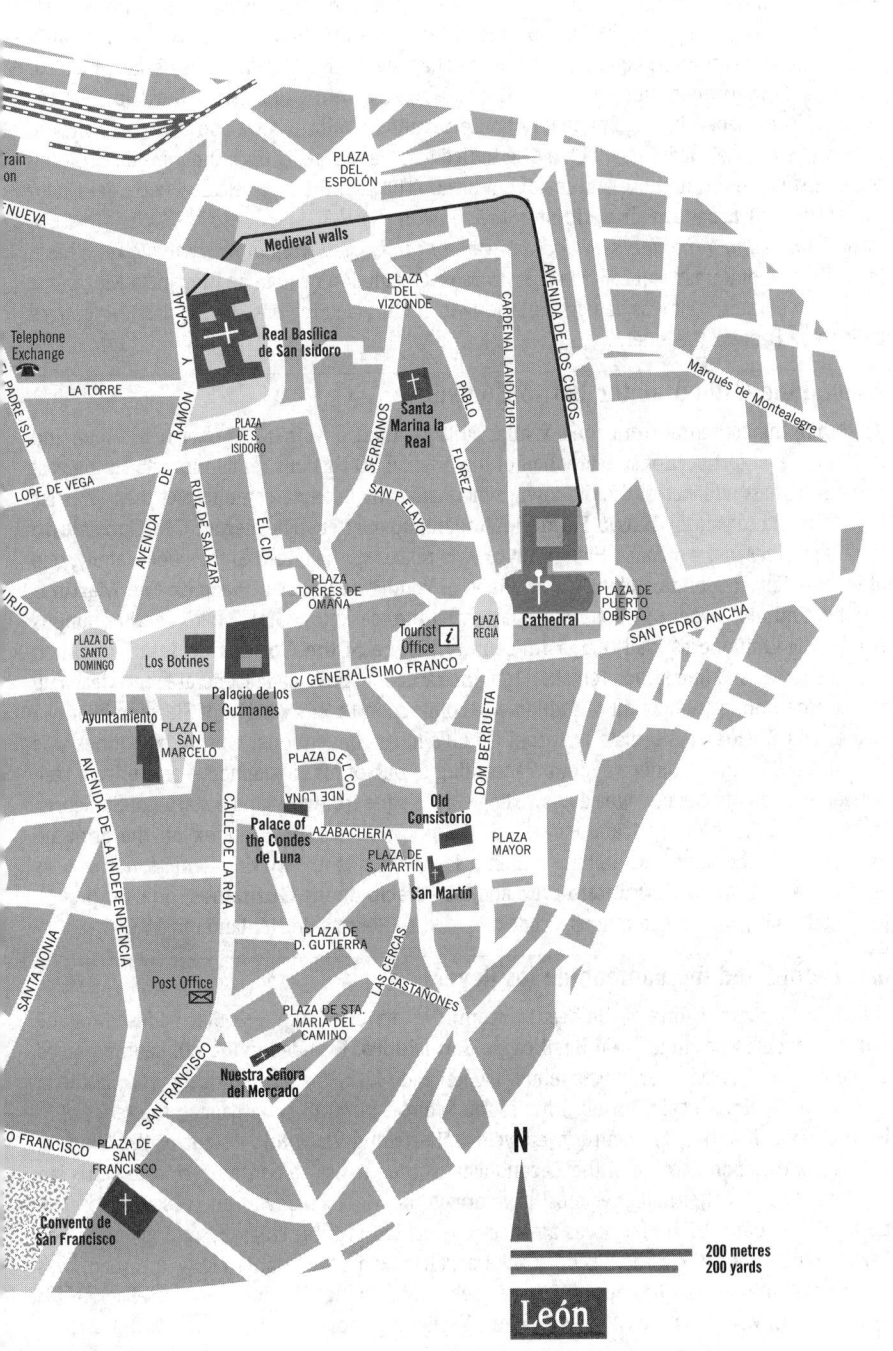

rain
on

NUEVA

Telephone
Exchange

LA TORRE

PADRE ISLA

LOPE DE VEGA

RJO

PLAZA DE
SANTO
DOMINGO

Ayuntamiento

AVENIDA DE LA INDEPENDENCIA

SANTA NONIA

Post Office

SAN FRANCISCO

O FRANCISCO

PLAZA DE
SAN
FRANCISCO

Convento de
San Francisco

PLAZA
DEL
ESPOLÓN

Medieval walls

CAJAL

RAMÓN Y

AVENIDA DE RAMÓN

RUIZ DE SALAZAR

EL CID

Real Basílica
de San Isidoro

PLAZA
DE S.
ISIDORO

PLAZA
DEL
VIZCONDE

SERRANOS

Santa
Marina la
Real

SAN PELAYO

PABLO

FLÓREZ

CARDENAL LANDÁZURI

AVENIDA DE LOS CUBOS

Marqués de Montealegre

PLAZA
TORRES DE
OMAÑA

Los Botines

Palacio de los
Guzmanes

PLAZA DE
SAN
MARCELO

CALLE DE LA RÚA

PLAZA DE EL
CONDE LUNA

Palace of
the Condes
de Luna

AZABACHERÍA

PLAZA DE
S. MARTÍN

San Martín

PLAZA DE
D. GUTIERRA

LAS CERCAS

LAS CASTAÑONES

PLAZA DE STA.
MARIA DEL
CAMINO

Nuestra Señora
del Mercado

Tourist
Office

PLAZA
REGIA

Cathedral

C/ GENERALÍSIMO FRANCO

DOM BERRUETA

Old
Consistorio

PLAZA
MAYOR

PLAZA DE
PUERTO
OBISPO

SAN PEDRO ANCHA

N

200 metres
200 yards

León

If you can draw your eyes from the soaring walls of glass, note the choir in the centre of the nave, set behind an ornate triumphal arch of a façade and embellished with 15th-century alabaster carvings by Juan de Badajoz the elder; its midsection of glass was added fairly recently so you can see straight through to the altar, swimming in reflections of the windows. The *retablo mayor* contains an excellent Renaissance painting of Christ's Burial by Nicolás Francés. The chapels in the ambulatory house beautiful Gothic tombs, and there's an altar to Nuestra Señora del Dado, at which a disgruntled gambler allegedly once flung his dice, hitting the Christ Child on the nose and making it bleed. Through the Plateresque Puerta del Dado, the **cathedral museum and cloister** (*open Mon–Fri 9.30–1.30 and 4–7, Sat 10–1.30, closed Sun; adm; if the doors are locked, wait for the harried woman with the big keys*) has a big collection of Romanesque Virgin Marys; also a Crucifixion by Juan de Juni and a Mozarabic Bible. The cloister itself was damaged in the 14th century and reworked with classical motives by Juan de Badajoz the elder.

Around the Cathedral: the Barrio Húmedo

Alongside the cathedral run León's **walls**, built by Alfonso XI in 1324 over the Roman and early medieval fortifications; nearly half of the original 80 bastions remain intact. To the east extend the narrow lanes of the old town, where so many Leonese come to wet their whistles that everyone calls it the **Barrio Húmedo**, 'the humid quarter'. The elegant **Old Consistorio** (1677) presides in the arcaded **Plaza Mayor**, where a tower belonged to the Ponce family, one of whom went to Florida seeking the Fountain of Youth; the adjacent **Plaza de San Martín** is the most humid corner of the humid quarter. By the market in Gral. Mola, another famous family, the Quiñoneses, had their 14th-century **Palace of the Condes de Luna**, of which only the tower and fine façade remain. From the cathedral, busy Calle General Franco leads up to Plaza de Botines, where all of sudden you come upon León's version of Sleeping Beauty's castle, **Los Botines** ('the spats'). Antoni Gaudí's most conventional work, Los Botines was built in 1891—'in a moment of doubt' according to one of his biographers—as a private residence, with pointy turrets, typically swirling Gaudiesque ironwork and a statue of St George (patron of Gaudí's native Catalunya) over the door, where, by the look on the grinning dragon's face, the saint is scratching him in just the right spot. Two fine Renaissance palaces are here too: the arcaded **Ayuntamiento** and the **Palacio de los Guzmanes** (now the provincial Diputación), with a sumptuous façade designed by Rodrigo de Hontañón in 1559.

San Isidoro and the Panteón de los Reyes

If León's cathedral is one of the best in Spain, the city can claim a similar pedestal for the Romanesque frescoes in its **Real Basílica de San Isidoro**. Founded in the 9th century, razed to the ground by al-Mansur, it was rebuilt by Fernando I, the first to unify León and Castile in 1037 and the first to call himself 'King of the Spains'. In 1063 León bagged the relics of St Isidoro of Sevilla, that 6th-century, encyclopedia-writing Visigothic doctor of the Church, whose bones, upon hearing of the Reconquista, started to ask to be transferred to Christian territory. These chattering bones must have driven the Moors in Sevilla crazy, so they packed them off to León; the basilica was at once rededicated to him, enlarged and given its bell tower. Once here, the gentle Isidoro, like a half dozen other saints along the road, was conscripted into Reconquista duty; you can see him over the side door, on horseback in his bishop's gear, whacking the Moor with John Wayneish gusto.

The façade has two entrances; the church is entered through the righthand, 11th-century Puerta del Perdón topped by a tympanum sculpted with the Descent from the Cross, the Three Marys and the Ascension. This is the first Door of Pardon along the *camino de Santiago*; pilgrims too ill or weak to carry on, could touch the door and receive the same indulgence granted to those who made it to Compostela. The barrel-vaulted interior with its foiled arches, desecrated by the French in the Peninsular War, is a heavily restored disappointment; of the 12th-century original only the transept capitals and chapel remain.

The more ornate Puerta del Cordero, its tympanum carved with the Sacrifice of Isaac, leads into the narthex of the church, the **Panteón de los Reyes** (*open 9–2 and 3–8, winter 10–1.30 and 4–6.30, Sun 9–2, closed Mon; adm*), founded by Fernando I. Its two small groin-vaulted chambers are supported by elaborately carved capitals (Daniel in the Lions' Den, the Resurrection of Lazarus), and the ceiling and walls are covered with extraordinary vivid frescoes from the 12th century, among the best preserved Romanesque paintings anywhere still in their original setting. Stylistically similar to the 5th-century frescoes and mosaics in Santa Costanza (which all the pilgrims to Rome would have visited), Christ Pantocrator and the Evangelists, with human bodies and animal heads reign over scenes of the shepherds, the Flight to Egypt, the Last Supper, the Tears of St Peter, the Seven Cities and Seven Lamps of the Apocalypse. Best of all, there's an allegory of the months, beginning with the two-headed Janus, Roman god of the door, who looks both backward and ahead at the 'hinge' of the old and new years.

Although the French desecrated the tombs and burned the library, they missed the treasures in the Pantheon's **museum** (*same hours*): St Isidoro's original silver reliquary, the gem-studded chalice of Doña Urraca (made from two Roman cups), and lovely Mozarab caskets covered with ivories and enamels. The library, rebuilt in the 16th century by Juan de Badajoz, has an illuminated Bible of 960 that somehow escaped the French firebugs.

The Hospital de San Marcos and the Archaeology Museum

León's third great monument lies at the end of the garden along the riverside Paseo Condesa de Sagasta. The **Hospital de San Marcos** was built in 1173 as headquarters for the Order of the Knights of Santiago, charged with the pilgrims' protection; at their hospital the weary, blistered pilgrim could rest up for the rigours ahead. In 1514, when the powerful Knights were more devoted to their own status, they set about rebuilding their headquarters thanks to an enormous donation by Fernando the Catholic—a payoff for electing him to the post of Grand Master and surrendering their semi-autonomy to the Crown. Over the 16th to 18th centuries the hospital was given its superb 330ft Plateresque façade, its frieze of busts, niches (the statues were never completed), swags, scallop shells, pinnacles, and reliefs culminating in the portal topped by Santiago Matamoros and the arms of Charles V, who inherited the title of Grand Master from Fernando. Used after 1837 as a barracks, the building was several times condemned by the city until 1961, when the government purchased it, and invested a fortune to create Spain's most beautiful luxury hotel. Non guests can partake at the bar, and visit the upper choir of the adjacent church of **San Marcos** with its cockleshell façade.

The chapterhouse and sacristy by Juan de Badajoz the younger contain the **Provincial Archaeology Museum** (*open 10–2 and 5–7.30, Sun 10–2, closed Mon*), with a small but prize collection: the 11th-century ivory Carrizo crucifix, enamels from Limoges, a Mozarab cross given by King Ramiro II in 940 to Santiago de Peñalba, the Corullón calvary, three pairs of beautiful capitals from the first Mozarab church at Sahagún, medieval weapons and mementoes of the Roman Seventh Legion, and artefacts discovered in a Punic necropolis near the Maragato village of Santa Colomba de Somoza—a key discovery in unravelling the origins of the Maragatos (*see* below).

León ✉ 24000

Where to Stay

The luxurious *parador*, the ★★★★★**Parador San Marcos**, Pza. San Marcos 7, ℭ 987 23 73 00, ✆ 987 23 34 58 (*luxury*) is not only Spain's best hotel, it is a veritable antiques museum in its public rooms—even the bedrooms are furnished with unique pieces. There are less expensive rooms in the modern building behind, with views over the river and gardens. The attractively designed ★★★★**Alfonso V**, C/ Padre Isla 1, ℭ 987 22 09 00, ✆ 987 22 12 44 (*expensive*) is the newest hotel in town (and nearly as pricey as the San Marcos). In the new part of town, the very modern ★★**Quindós**, Avda. José Antonio 24, ℭ 987 23 62 00, ✆ 987 24 22 01 (*moderate*) is arty and comes with excellent service. By the river, ★★**Riosol**, Avda. de Palencia 3, ℭ 987 21 66 50, ✆ 987 21 69 97 (*expensive*) is large and pleasant. León has a good choice of cheaper places, although most are on busy streets: ★**Paris**, Generalísimo 20, ℭ 987 23 86 00, near the cathedral, is an old palace, though the rooms are modern; ★**Hs Guzmán el Bueno**, López Castrillón 6, ℭ 987 23 64 12, in the old town is one of the quieter choices (*both moderate*). Within walking distance of the RENFE station, ★**Hs Londres**, Avda. de Roma 1, ℭ 987 22 22 74 (*moderate*) is comfortable and convenient; ★**Hs Oviedo**, Avda. Roma 26, ℭ 987 22 22 36, is similar (*cheap*). León's youth hostel, **Residencia Juvenil Infanta Doña Sancha**, Corredera 4, ℭ 987 20 22 01, is at the south end of town, and has a pool.

Eating Out

León is famous for sweetbreads and black puddings (*morcilla*), game dishes and garlic soup with trout. **Casa Pozo**, Pza. San Marcelo 15 (near the Ayuntamiento), ℭ 987 22 30 39, specializes in both trout and salmon and prime fresh ingredients (*menu 3000 pts*). *Closed Sun eve and 1–15 July*. **El Faisán Dorado**, Cantareros 2, ℭ 987 25 66 09 (*expensive–moderate*) has a good name for excellent game and lobster dishes, and friendly service; good wine list too (*menu 1800 pts*). *Closed Sun eve and Mon*. **Bodega Regia**, Gral. Mola 5, ℭ 987 21 31 73 specializes in simple, traditional dishes at reasonable prices (*2000-pts menú*). *Closed Sun*. In the Barrio Húmedo, Plaza San Martín is the bopping headquarters not only of bars and tapas but also *inexpensive* restaurants; try the 12th-century **El Nuevo Racimo de Oro** at No.8, ℭ 987 25 41 00, which has a good bar and plenty of atmosphere; good Leonese cuisine as well (*around 2500 pts*). *Closed Sun in summer and Wed rest of the year*. The same management also runs the less expensive **Mesón Leonés del Racimo de Oro**, Caño Badillo 2, ℭ 987 25 75 75, specializing in regional dishes like roasts and Serrano ham; the tables overlook a patio and the *bodega* dates back to the 12th century. *Closed Sun eve and Tues*. **Fornos**, C/ Cid 8 (*moderate–inexpensive*) has long been a favourite for its lively atmosphere. Closed Sun eve and Mon.

Two distinct regions fill the area between León and Galicia: between Astorga and Ponferrada **La Maragatería**, the homeland of the Maragatos, and west of Ponferrada **El Bierzo**, a unique mountainous region, with some of the province's prettiest wooded valleys, distorted and eroded by mining and a favourite abode for 10th-century hermits.

Getting Around

RENFE links Astorga and Ponferrada with León, Lugo and beyond, four times a day, although note that for Astorga the station is a long hike, while buses go to the centre. Astorga is the point of departure of buses for La Maragatería; Ponferrada for El Bierzo; and León for the villages in the south. The Cueva de Valporquero is accessible only by car, although there are often excursions organized from León.

Tourist Information

Astorga: Ayuntamiento, Plaza de España, © 987 61 59 47.
Ponferrada: Gil y Carrasco 4, © 987 42 42 36.

North of León

Northern León province encompasses the southern slopes of the Cordillera Cantábrica and the Picos de Europa and one of Spain's best caves, the **Cueva de Valporquero**, 46km from León through the spectacular gorges of the Torio river (*open 10–2 and 4–7; adm; bring non-skid shoes and a jacket*). The caves have no prehistoric art, but 4km of colourful galleries with little lakes, esplanades, a stalactite 'cemetery', chamber of wonders, and striking sheer cliffs. Another beauty spot is the **Puerto de Pajares** (1379m), the lofty pass in the Cordillera Cantábrica used since antiquity as the main gate between León and Oviedo. The Leonese gateway to the Picos de Europa is **Riaño**, from where you can visit the **Valle de Valdeón** and **Valle de Sajambre**.

Along the Pilgrimage Road to Hospital de Órbigo

On the N120, not far from the industrial sprawl west of León, is, for better or worse, the only modern chapel along the *camino de Santiago*: La Virgen del Camino, a concrete box built in 1961 by Brother Coello de Portugal. It has all the air of a middle American college library, but houses a much venerated 16th-century statue of the Virgin in a Baroque *retablo*; the stained-glass workshop at Chartres produced the ugly windows, and Catalan sculptor Subirachs contributed the weird emaciated bronze figures of the Virgin and the Apostles that cover the front. One of the bridges the pilgrims crossed, the 13th-century **Puente del Paso Honroso**, still stands parallel to the N120, 23km west of León in a tranquil green setting. Things weren't so tranquil back in July 1434, when Don Suero de Quiñones and his nine companions vowed to hold the bridge for the 13 days preceeding 25 July, the feast day of Santiago, and challenged every passer-by to declare his lady, Leonor de Tovar, the fairest in the land. If they refused to admit it, they had to joust. As it was a Holy Year, the road was crowded with pilgrims, and 727 men took up the challenge (no one recorded how many refused). The incident, the last hurrah of Spanish romantic chivalry, has gone down in history as the Paso Honroso; many scholars believe the story of Don Suero de Quiñones was an inspiration for Cervantes' Don Quixote.

Astúrica Augusta was an important administrative centre for the Romans, close to the mines and a main station along their celebrated Vía de la Plata, the 'silver road' that ran from Sevilla to Galicia, to transport the gold of the Bierzo, the silver of Galicia and the copper of Asturias. Like León, Astorga had its own bishopric by the 3rd century; like León it remained important in the Middle Ages because of the pilgrimage. It has genteelly declined since the 18th century, helped along by a bit of pillaging in the Peninsular War.

The best way to approach Astorga is to circle the centre, still belted by half of its robust Roman-medieval **walls**, and enter on the northwest side of town, where the **Catedral de Santa María** and Bishop's palace looming over the walls make a startling impression. Begun in 1451, the cathedral took until the 18th century to complete, with too many cooks along the way; even the colour of the stone in the towers doesn't match. The façade was inspired by the cathedral in León, only here the ornamentation is floridly Baroque: intricate garlands, reliefs of the Descent from the Cross, the Adulterous Woman, and the Expulsion of the Merchants from the Temple. All the interest in the interior is concentrated in the *retablo mayor*, in marble high relief, by Gaspar Becerra (1520—70), an Andalucian who studied with Michelangelo. Off the neglected cloister, the **Museo Diocesano** (*open daily 10–2 and 4–8; adm*) houses some fine medieval pieces—including a 10th-century casket of gold and silver that belonged to Alfonso III, a figure of Santo Toribio by Gaspar Becerra and a 12th-century painted tomb. Astorga seemed like a dusty, declining nowhere to Juan Bautista Grau y Vallespinós when he arrived as its new bishop. In 1887, hoping to give his see a dynamic jump start into the 20th century, he commissioned the most imaginative architect he knew, his friend and fellow Catalan, Antoni Gaudí, to build him a new **Palacio Episcopal.** The rest of Astorga had deep reservations about the *modernista* fairy tale castle; once the bishop died in 1893, the public's hostility was so violent that Gaudí quit and refused to return to Astorga. Without his input, this pale asymmetrical castle (completed only in 1963), built more or less in the shape of a Latin cross, with sharp pointed towers and turrets, a moat and a huge sloping front, lacks the detail and colour that characterize Gaudí's work in Barcelona. Instead of a bishop, the palace now houses the **Museo de los Caminos** (*open daily 11–2 and 3.30–6.30; adm*), a collection of pilgrimage paraphernalia and art (note the mean-looking she-devil and Santiago in the Renaissance altarpiece from Bécares) along with some equally mean-looking examples of contemporary provincial art. For a hint of Gaudí's intentions, don't miss the magnificent atmospheric throne room with its discreet stained glass.

Maragato Mysteries

 Before leaving, look at the top of the cathedral apse, decorated with the figure of a Maragato named Pero Mato, who fought with Santiago at the battle of Clavijo. Astorga is the 'capital' of the Maragatos, who have lived here and in the villages to the west for as long as anyone can remember. Until the 19th century, they were muleteers and carriers, transporting nearly all the goods between Castile and Galicia, a line of work forced on them by their stubborn, almost uncultivatable land; their name has been traced back to the Latin *mercator*, or merchant. Their honesty and industry were proverbial and no one hesitated to trust them with huge sums. Until recently they wore their ancient

costumes: broad-bottomed breeches called *zaraguelles* and red garters for the men; for the women, a crescent-shaped cap covered with a mantle and heavy earrings. They kept to themselves, marrying only other Maragatos, and at Corpus Christi and the Ascension, all would gather in Astorga and at 2pm would begin a dance called El Canizo and finish at exactly 3; if any non-Maragatos attempted to join in, the dance would stop at once. Who were the Maragatos? Common beliefs that they were Celts, Visigoths or Berbers who came over in the 8th century and held on to this enclave after converting to Christianity have been called into question by Dr Julio Carro, who in the late 1950s discovered a Punic necropolis near the village of Santa Colomba de Somoza west of Astorga—hardly where you'd expect to find one, because the Phoenicians were sailors and León isn't exactly on the coast. Among the finds were figurines nearly identical to those found at Punic sites in Ibiza and dressed in a style similar to the Maragatos. Carro's conclusion, based on his discoveries and on Maragato cultural traditions, was that the Maragatos descended from Phoenicians and Iberians enslaved by the Romans to work the gold mines of El Bierzo. The Maragatos themselves agree, and to thank Carro for discovering their true origins, they put up a stone plaque to him in Quintanilla de Somoza.

In reality, the only other Maragatos you're likely to notice as such are the two *jacquemart* figures, Zancudo and Colasa, who bang the hour atop the attractive 17th-century **Ayuntamiento** at the east end of Astorga; in front of it you can descend into the Roman slaves' prison, the **Ergástula**, where the Maragatos' ancestors languished. In **Plaza Roma** you'll find ruins of Roman houses, some with pretty mosaics.

West of Astorga

The mostly ruined villages of the Maragatería have been in decline ever since the railway took over the Maragatos' ancestral occupation, but **Castrillo de los Polvazares** (6km from Astorga) has been restored to the verge of being twee, with old stone houses now mostly holiday homes, a score of roadside crosses and a main cobbled street built wide for mule trains. West of Astorga, pilgrims tackled the wild Montes de León, climbing up to **Foncebadón**. At the top of the 1504m pass stands the spindly **Iron Cross**, planted by a pilgrim untold years ago. Later pilgrims have added, one by one, the mound of slate stones at its foot, just as the Celts would 'give' stones to roadside shrines to placate the dangers ahead.

Where to Stay and Eating Out

Astorga ✉ 24700

★★★**Hotel Gaudí**, Pza. Eduardo de Castro 6, ✆ 987 61 56 54, ✉ 987 61 50 40 (*expensive*), is by far the finest place to stay, near the cathedral; its good, moderately priced restaurant with a fancy marble floor features several Maragato dishes and fish. ★★**Hs La Peseta**, Pza. San Bartolomé 3, ✆ 987 61 72 75 (*moderate*) is central and boasts the best restaurant in Astorga, where you can sample the wines of El Bierzo with the Maragatos version of cocido, which, unlike others, serves the meat before the soup and vegetables. The reason: the muleteers never knew how long they would be able to stop to eat, and so got the meat down first. *Closed Sun eve.*

El Bierzo

In the old days the Romans dug for gold in these hills; the modern Leonese extract the iron and cobalt. El Bierzo has bleak mining towns, lovely mountain scenery and tobacco fields, charming villages that time forgot, and ancient hermitages—its isolation and warm climate (the mountains shield it from the worst of the *meseta* and Atlantic)—attracted so many anchorites that it was known as the Thebaid of Spain. After the Iron Cross the pilgrims' road descends into El Bierzo by way of **Acebo**, with its still flowing pilgrims' Fountain of the Trout along its one street. From Acebo it's 5km south to **Compludo**, a tiny isolated hamlet, where San Fructuoso, the first holy man in El Bierzo, founded his first monastery in 614. Although this is now long gone, San Fructuoso's forge, the remarkable **Herrería de Compludo** still works as well as it did in the 7th century using the stream to turn its great wheel.

Ponferrada

Both the easy NVI or the dramatic, lonely pilgrims' track over the Montes de León lead to **Ponferrada**, originally a Roman mouthful known as Interamnium Flavium. It is the largest town of El Bierzo, and sums up the region's split personality, part of it mine-blackened, and slag-heaped, the other half medievally pretty. The town's name comes from a long-gone bridge with iron balustrades, erected over the Sil for the pilgrims by the local 11th-century Bishop Osmundo. On the east bank of the Sil stands Ponferrada's proudest monument, the 12th-century **Castillo de los Templarios** (*open 10.30–1.30 and 4–7, Sun am only, closed Mon*), its triple ramparts built to defend the pilgrims from the Moors; its fairy-tale gate and towers were added later, in 1340. In 1811 the French went out of their way to vandalize it, resulting in heavy restoration. Here and there you can see Templar crosses and *taus* carved on the walls. While building the castle, the Templars discovered a statue of the Virgin in the heart of a holm oak tree, now enshrined in the **Basilica de Nuestra Señora de la Encina** (1577), with a good *retablo mayor*. Sitting on a hill, 2km south on the Madrid road, the minute church of **Santo Tomás de las Ollas** is a curious Mozarabic church, with horseshoe arches and best of all, an elliptical ten-sided apse encircled with blind arcading.

Into the Valley of Silence

South of Ponferrada, the Oza river winds through the beautiful **Valle del Silencio** where, from the 7th century to the 10th, hermits took up their abode under the dramatic white flanks of Monte Aquiana, a mountain sacred to the Celts. Most of the hermits were Visigoths from Andalucía, come to spread the writings of San Isidoro of Sevilla. One of these was San Fructuoso, founder of the monastery of **San Pedro de Monte** in the village of **Montes** (to get there, take the road to San Esteban de Valdueza for 8km, then turn left 14km on a narrow, hairpinning road that follows the river Oza; at the end of the road, it's a steep 500m walk up). Reinhabited in 890 by St Genadio of Andalucía and his monks, the ruins are mostly 12th century, although Genadio's 919 dedication is still embedded in the wall and some of the original Asturian style capitals are intact.

The real jewel of El Bierzo, the little Mozarabic church of **Peñalba de Santiago** (*open 10.30–1.30 and 4–7, closed Sun afternoon and Mon*), is a bit farther on in a spectacular setting at the head of the valley (take the left turning over the river, and leave your car at the entrance of the little medieval hamlet). Founded by Saint Genadio and dedicated in 913, its perfect proportions are reminiscent of Palaeochristian basilicas in Africa, as is its shape: rectangular with three cupolas and two apses rather oddly facing one another. The rough stone and slate exterior doesn't prepare you for the refinement and fine craftsmanship inside, beginning with a pretty double-arched portal crowned by two horseshoe arches. A track leads up to the hermit's cave of San Genadio for the magnificent view down onto the church and its tower, surrounded by a huddle of slate roofs.

Las Médulas

Carucedo, 20km southwest of Ponferrada, is the point of departure for an unusual journey through an ancient ecological disaster, **Las Médulas**. In the first century AD, the Romans noted the soft red soil was sprinkled with gold and minium (or red lead, used for painting), but to extract it meant sifting through thousands of tons of earth. Labour back then was no problem: some 60,000 slaves were brought in to dig a complex network of galleries, wells, dams and canals—one over 40km long—to erode away the soil. The work was gruelling and dangerous, and thousands died over the next two centuries in moving an estimated 300 million tons of earth to extract 90 tonnes of gold. Whole hills collapsed in the process, and new ones of left-over tailings were piled up by the slaves, leaving behind a landscape like a row of jagged red spinal cords—or medullas. There's a natural balcony over Las Médulas from Orellán; from the village of Las Médulas, 4km from Carucedo, you can take a stroll (bring sturdy shoes) past the ancient canals, galleries, rock needles and surreal caves—a natural disaster perhaps, but a strangely beautiful one.

North of Ponferrada: the Ancares Leoneses

North of Ponferrada, a lonely road heads north to Vega de Espinareda and the beautiful, densely forested, mountainous Ancares Leoneses, now under the jurisdiction of the National Park. The park not only protects a number of endangered species—a few brown bears, Iberian wolves, roe deer, and capercaillie—but also a dying way of life in its 27 remote mountain hamlets, with their traditional architecture and *pallozas*, straw-topped round stone huts first built by the Celts. The best examples may be seen along the tiny roads up the Ancares river valley. Nearly all the hamlets are cloaked in chestnut groves, which until a couple of decades ago provided much of their food.

West of Ponferrada: the Valle del Bierzo

After Ponferrada the pilgrimage road enters the Valle del Bierzo, the bed of a dried-up lake, surrounded by a ring of mountains. Its microclimate is warm, damp yet shot with sunlight, ideal for cultivating the vines of D.O. El Bierzo. Don't miss a brief detour 3km south of Cacabelos to the **Monastery of Santa María de Carracedo**, founded in 990 in a pastoral setting, this time by Bermudo II the Gouty of León. At the end of the 18th century the monks decided to begin a large neoclassical church. It was only partially finished in 1811 when the French marched through and effectively put an end to the project, leaving half of a new church and much of the old intact, pieced together, restored and roofed over for the monastery's 1000th birthday. By the church are the remains of a little **palace** built by Alfonso IX in the early 1200s, to house his wife Teresa of Portugal and his two daughters after the Pope annulled his marriage. The claims of the princesses to the throne were a powerful reason behind the union of León and Castile declared by Fernando III el Santo—Alfonso IX's son from his second marriage.

Villafranca del Bierzo

The *Codex Calixtinus*' tenth stop on the *camino de Santiago*, **Villafranca del Bierzo** is one of the most attractive small towns along the whole road, embraced on all sides by mountains, built at the confluence of the Burbia and Valcarce rivers. As its name suggests, the town was founded by the French in the 11th century and in its heyday it had eight monasteries and six pilgrims' hospitals; today it makes wine and lodges visitors to the region. On the hill where pilgrims entered Villafranca is the well-preserved 16th-century **Castillo de los Marqueses de Villafranca** and the 12th-century **Santiago**, a simple Romanesque church but an important one, with the second Puerta del Perdón along the road. Pilgrims too weary or ill to continue had only to touch the door to achieve the same indulgences as they would at Compostela. Some then keeled over dead and were buried in the adjacent cemetery. All of the church's eroded decoration is concentrated around the Puerta del Perdón; you can make out three kings on horseback, a Crucifixion and Christ in Majesty. The pilgrims would descend from the church and castle to walk along wide, atmospheric **Calle del Agua** ('Water Street', from when the street was often flooded by the Burbia). The Plaza Mayor was set higher up away from danger, and near this you'll find the church of **San Francisco**, all that remains of a monastery founded by St Francis during his pilgrimage. It has a magnificent 15th-century *mudéjar artesonado* ceiling, much of which has been recently restored. Down on the banks of the Burbia, **La Colegiata de Santa María** (*open 10–2 and 4–8*) was built in 1544 to designs by Rodrigo Gil de Hontañón. Construction continued into the 18th century, when the money ran out, leaving the nave cut short. Nevertheless the part-Gothic and part-Renaissance interior is uncommonly grand; note especially the chapel of the Trinity and a reliquary by Juan de Juni.

Where to Stay and Eating Out

Ponferrada ✉ 24400

The largest and best-endowed hotel is ★★★★**Del Temple**, Avda. de Portugal, *۞* 987 41 00 58, *✆* 987 42 35 25 (*expensive*), located in a pseudo-Templar castle, with a swimming pool; beware that it can be noisy. ★★★**Bérgidum**, Avda. de la Plata 2, *۞* 987 40 15 12 (*expensive/moderate*), offers contemporary comforts.

Most of the cheaper choices are in the new town: ★**Madrid**, on main Avda. de la Puebla 44, *۞* 987 41 15 50 (*moderate*); ★★**Hs Marán**, Avda. A. López Peláez 29, *۞* 987 41 63 51 (*inexpensive*); and ★**Hs La Madrileña**, on the same street at No.4, *۞* 987 41 28 14 (*cheap*). **La Fonda**, *۞* 987 42 57 94, in Pza. Ayuntamiento, uses local ingredients to create interesting dishes (try the *gambas* with bacon); *menus 1600 pts. Closed Sun eve.*

Villafranca del Bierzo ✉ 24500

The ★★★**Parador de Villafranca del Bierzo**, Avda. de Calvo Sotelo, *۞*987 54 01 75, *✆* 987 54 00 10 (*expensive*) is not one of the chain's showcases, but more like a comfortable motel in a scenic locale. Family-run ★**Hs Casa Méndez**, Pza. de la Concepción, *۞* 987 54 24 08 (*moderate*) has good home cooking to go with its *inexpensive* rooms. The excellent **Eurbia**, La Granja, *۞* 987 54 05 85 (*moderate–inexpensive*) serves delicious *cocidos*, roasts and fish.

Zamora is a fine old city on the banks of the Río Duero, boasting a golden necklace of small Romanesque churches and a jewel of a cathedral. Despite these treasures, it's off the main tourist route—even in June it's very likely that you'll have it to yourself.

Needless to say, this wasn't always the case. Zamora 'the well-walled', under the great shepherd-chieftain and escaped Roman slave Viriato, was a nightmare for the Romans. In 1072, the siege of Zamora was a nightmare for the Cid, who at the time served as a standard-bearer to Sancho II of Castile. Sancho was besieging his sister Urraca, whom the Cid refused to fight as she was his foster sister; in the end Sancho was treacherously murdered and succeeded by his brother Alfonso VI. The city joined the Comunero revolt under Antonio de Acuña, the last great battling bishop, who had seized his bishopric in Zamora by force against the mayor. When the Comuneros collapsed, he was thrown out of town—only to acquire a private army, capture Toledo and proclaim himself archbishop.

When Franco, like Charles V, faced dissenting priests, he built a notorious prison in Zamora to contain them all—more were imprisoned here, it is said, than in the whole of the Warsaw Pact countries.

Getting Around

By train: Zamora's Plateresque train station lies at the bottom of the hill on C/ Tres Cruces; several regular trains and Talgos daily link Zamora to Madrid, Ávila, Galicia, Puebla de Sanabria and Toro.

By bus: From the bus terminal (a couple of blocks north near the bullring) buses depart hourly for Salamanca and less frequently to Toro, Valladolid, Madrid and Barcelona; there are four a day to Benavente, and two to Fermosella.

Tourist Information

Santa Clara 20, © 980 53 18 45, ✆ 980 53 38 13.

The Churches

The dusty Plaza Viriato, with a dramatic statue of Viriato and a battering ram called '*The Roman Terror*', is the core of old Zamora; on the map, the town's many churches circle the plaza like the numbers on a clock. All are lovely, if not spectacular, and specific ones to aim for are Santa María la Nueva behind the old hospital (now the Diputación Provincial), with its unusual 8th-century capitals in the Byzantine style and Museo de la Semana Santa (*open Mon–Sat 10–2 and 4–8, Sun 10–2; adm*) where the Virgins and Jesuses of the *pasos* hang out 51 weeks of the year. If the hospital is at 'noon' on the Plaza, at one o'clock you have Santiago de Burgos; at three o'clock San Andrés with a fine interior and *artesonado* ceiling; at six o'clock Santa María de la Orta, built by the Templars, with a *mudéjar* arcaded cornice.

Calle Ramos Carrion (at nine o'clock) leads towards the cathedral, passing by way of the 1160 La Magdalena with its pretty rose window and sculpted portal, to San Ildefonso, with photogenic arches, buttresses and a Flemish triptych, brought over by Charles V.

The Cathedral

At the far west end of Zamora stands the Cathedral, crowned by its striking fish-scale Byzantine dome, and corner turrets. Inside are some fine ironwork grills and wonderful carved choir stalls—pious images on the backs, and indecorous scenes hidden away below, vignettes of amorous nuns and monks that were censored for years. The **museum** off the cloister (*11–2 and 4–7, closed Sun; adm*) contains a treasure that even the most respectable cathedral would envy—the magnificent **Black Tapestries,** masterpieces of the weaver's art, made in Flanders in the 15th century. The 'black' refers to the sheer density of stitches and detail put into the scenes of the Trojan War, the battles of Hannibal, and the Parable of the Vine, where everyone swans about in elegant Renaissance finery.

Zamora ✉ *49000*   ***Where to Stay***

The ★★★★**Parador Condes de Alba de Aliste,** Pza. de Viriato 1, ✆ 980 51 44 97, ✆ 980 53 00 63 (*expensive*) is one of the most atmospheric and elegant in all Spain, located in the 15th-century ducal palace, with a lovely courtyard; public rooms are furnished with antiques and coats of armour and even the bedrooms have a pleasant old feel; there's a swimming-pool the *parador* shares with the public and a restaurant serving the finest of local cuisine. The new ★★★**Dos Infantas**, Cortinas de San Miguel 3, ✆ 980 53 28 75, ✆ 980 53 35 48 (*moderate*) is conveniently located and offers comfortable rooms.

For more atmosphere, but the odd chance of a ghost or two, you can stay in a 16th-century palace of the Inquisition where Pizarro once slept: the comfortable ★★★**Hostería Real de Zamora**, Cuesta de Pizarro 7, ✆/✆ 980 53 45 45 (*moderate*), near the Puente de Piedra; all rooms have satellite TV and minibars. ★**Hs La Reina**, C/ La Reina 1, ✆ 980 53 39 39 (*inexpensive*) is good, honest and cheap. In a modern building at Benavente 2, ★**Hs Luz**, ✆ 980 53 31 52 and ★**Hs Chiqui**, ✆ 980 53 14 80, both have inexpensive doubles with bath.

Eating Out

Pizarro, in the aforementioned Hosteria Real (*low expensive*) is a lovely, atmospheric place to dine, especially in the courtyard on a summer's night, with a fountain built into the rockface splashing away; on Saturday nights there's usually live classical music. The menu features Basque and Zamoran specialities; try the rabbit. **Paris,** on the east side of town at Avda. Portugal 14, ✆ 980 51 43 25 (*expensive*) has a delightful inner garden and some of the best food in Zamora with a wine list to match. **Las Aceñas**, in a lovely old mill, has reasonably priced local specialities: Aceñas s/n, ✆ 980 53 38 78 (*moderate*). You can eat well for less, just off Plaza Mayor at the elegant **España**, Ramón Alvarez 3, ✆ 980 53 17 31; *menus for 1000 pts.*

Around Zamora

Zamora divides itself as a province between the **Tierra del Pan** (bread land) north of the Duero and **Tierra del Vino** (wine land) south of the river, which sums it up quite well. The wheat-growing Tierra del Pan has the most to see: northwest near Galicia, there's the pretty glacial lake, **Lago de Sanabria**, 1000m above sea level and the centrepiece of Spain's newest national park. **Puebla de Sanabria** is the main town, located on a cliff over the river Tera, dominated by a well-preserved 15th-century castle; in the parish church, note the four curious slate figures in 11th-century dress. **Benavente**, an ancient city on a promontory between the Esla and Orbigo, had one of Spain's most elaborate alcázars, built in the 15th century; unfortunately only the **Torre de Caracol** ('snail tower') survived the fire set by Napoleon's troops and now houses a *parador*. There are a couple of interesting 12th-century churches: **San Juan del Mercado** contains an unusual image of the Virgin holding a Templar cross in a wheel, while **Santa María de Azoque** has a more orthodox Annunciation tableau.

Near the Portuguese frontier (from Zamora, take the N122 towards Alcañices, and turn off towards the village of El Campillo) the 8th-century **San Pedro de la Nave** stands isolated in a field, a late Visigothic masterpiece transported stone by stone from the banks of the Elsa when the river was dammed in 1931. Built of rosy limestone in the form of a Greek cross, with a tower-lantern rising out of the crossing, its exterior is decorated with a frieze of vines and birds. The imposing interior is richly embellished with some of the finest and last Visigothic sculpture: more friezes with faces, solar symbols and birds, and superb carved trapezoidal capitals carved with powerfully modelled figures of the apostles, of the sacrifice of Isaac, interrupted by a big hand from stage left, and Daniel in the lions' den, or rather in the lions' lake, according to the Latin inscription above (LAQUM LEONVM); the prophet stands ankle deep in water, which the two big cats happily lap.

South of the Duero in the Tierra del Vino the most important town is **Fermosella** on the Portuguese border, the last refuge of Bishop Acuña's Comuneros. The imposing Gothic parish church contains a collection of Romanesque and Gothic statues.

Where to Stay and Eating Out

Puebla de Sanabria ✉ 49300

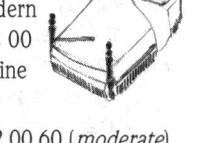

There are quite a few places to stay in, where holiday-makers come to swim in the lake and fish in the streams of the park. The modern **★★★Parador Puebla de Sanabria**, Ctra. del Lago 18, ✆ 980 62 00 01, ✆ 980 62 03 51 (*expensive*) is actually near to the town, with fine views and as usual a good restaurant.

For less, try **★★Hs La Trucha**, Padre Vicente Salgado 10, ✆ 980 62 00 60 (*moderate*), all rooms with bath, or **★Galicia**, Animas 22, ✆ 980 62 01 06 (*cheap*), for beds without frills and a restaurant.

Benavente ✉ 49600

The **★★★★Parador Rey Fernando II de León**, Paseo Ramón y Cajal, ✆ 980 63 03 04, ✆ 980 63 03 03 (*expensive*), has been elegantly furnished in the Torre del Caracol, complete with an *artesonado* ceiling brought in from another demolished monument.

★★Avenida, Avda. Gral. Primo de Rivera 17, ✆ 980 63 10 31 (*moderate*), is comfortable enough and open all year. **Paraíso**, Obispo Regueras 70, ✆ 980 63 26 85, (*inexpensive*), is adequate with showers down the hall.

Spain's great medieval university town, Salamanca, is also one of the country's charmers, a dream city of golden stone, embroidered into a thousand tiny Plateresque details and later put into Baroque curling irons by the prolific Churriguera family. Although the university was ranked in the Middle Ages as one of Europe's finest, it began to decline in the strict clericalism and intolerance initiated by Felipe II; Francoism, virulently anti-intellectual, was almost a death blow, although the glamour of Salamanca's name continues to lend it status. But there's nothing like thousands of students to keep a town awake, and their lively presence complements the serene magnificence of Salamanca's monuments.

Getting Around

By train: Salamanca's train station is a 20-minute walk north of the centre via Plaza de España, in the Plaza de la Libertad, ℰ 923 22 57 42; there are trains to Ávila and Madrid, Ciudad Rodrigo and into Portugal; others go up through Valladolid and Burgos to Irún, or to Zaragoza and Barcelona.

By bus: The bus station is a 15-minute walk from the Plaza Mayor in the Avda. de Filiberto Villalobos 73–85, ℰ 923 23 67 17; there are 13 buses daily to Zamora (fewer at the weekends), two to León, four to Valladolid, one to Cáceres and twelve *rapidos* to Madrid. Two or three buses a day go to Galicia, the Basque Country, Barcelona, Sevilla and Cádiz. Frequent buses go to Ciudad Rodrigo and surrounding villages.

Tourist Information

Casa de las Conchas, Rúa Mayor s/n, ℰ 923 26 85 71, ✉ 923 26 24 92.

Municipal information booth: Plaza Mayor 10, ℰ 923 21 83 42.

Plaza Mayor

Despite its prominent place in Spanish history, Salamanca is not a big town, and you can walk nearly everywhere from the central **Plaza Mayor**. This endearing urban heart of gold was built at the beginning of the 18th century, a happy collaboration by Alberto Churriguera and Andrés García de Quiñones, members of Salamanca's two great Baroque dynasties. Like most of Salamanca's monuments, the plaza is made of *piedra de Villamayor*—a fine grained sandstone that is pale, moist, and easy to handle when freshly quarried, but when left in the sun slowly hardens and darkens to a deep, golden-brown patina. The Plaza Mayor is Salamanca's public stage and general meeting-place, and in the evening the whole city relaxes in the cafés spilling out of its shady arcades, on occasion entertained by the *Tunas*, the bands of student minstrels in Renaissance costume. The plaza doubles as a Spanish hall of fame, with busts of the national greats—and schmucks like Franco—carved on medallions around the arcades.

South of the plaza, the Rúa Mayor passes another Salamantine landmark, the 16th-century **Casa de las Conchas** ('House of the Shells'), which now houses the Tourist Information office. Built by Dr Talavera Maldonada, a member of Fernando and Isabel's royal council and a Knight of Santiago, he covered the whole surface with the scallop-shell symbol of St James, giving the house a wonderful nubby texture; shells are even incorporated in the iron grills over the windows. The great, domed **La Clerecía** (1750) nearby belonged to a Jesuit seminary, and nowadays to the Universidad Pontificia; only the patio is accessible.

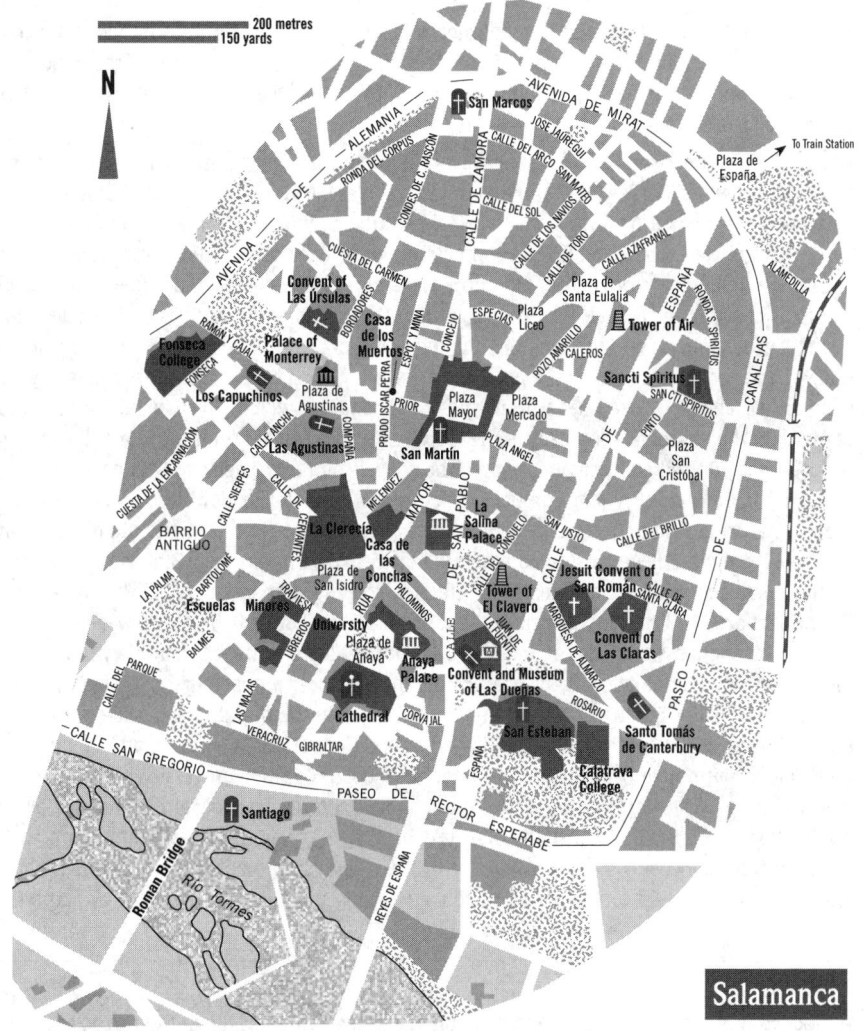

Salamanca

The Cathedrals

Both Old and New Cathedrals are open daily 10–2 and 4–8; ticket required for the Old Cathedral.

Rúa Mayor continues down to the Plaza de Anaya and Salamanca's two cathedrals. These are built side-by-side; from the outside at least the much larger New Cathedral dominates. One of Gothic's last hurrahs, it is adorned with pinnacles, cosmic Plateresque details (even an elephant makes an appearance) and a bell tower modelled after the one in Toledo. It was completed in 1560 as a symbol of Salamanca's aspirations and prestige—just as the terror and intolerance of the times were undermining both. Inside, the New Cathedral is lofty and elegant. Among its chapels near the main altar is the talisman *Christ of the Battles*—a simple Romanesque image carried by the Cid and invoked before his battles, surrounded by some of the frothiest Baroque imaginable. Underneath lies the tomb of Bishop Jerónimo, the Cid's chaplain and founder of the old cathedral. Another chapel, next to the door of the old cathedral, is crowded with wooden sculptures of every conceivable saint; in its window is the inevitable Spanish *memento mori*—Death.

Dwarfed in comparison, the Romanesque **Old Cathedral** makes itself known from the outside through its **Torre del Gallo**—an unusual silvery 'fish-scale' byzantine dome, flanked by turrets and topped by a rooster. Built in 1160, its magnificent Romanesque interior is a work that the New Cathedral failed to surpass. Brightly lit by the windows at the base of the dome, the rich colours of Nicolás Florentino's *retablo mayor* are wonderfully vivid, its 53 paintings crowned by an awesome vision of the Last Judgement. Paintings on the side walls depict various miracles—including one that occurred during the building of this very cathedral, when a stone block fell on the head of a mason, inflicting only a headache (judging by his expression). The block itself hangs from one of the columns, which have beautiful capitals. In the back of the church a door leads to the **Capilla de San Martín** with the late 13th-century frescoes of saints and another Apocalypse. The chapels off the former cloister (modernized to death in the 18th century) are especially interesting. The first, the **Capilla de Talavera**, has unique star-vaulting, the tattered standard of the Comuneros—a rare memento of the great revolt—and the privilege, bestowed when the chapel was built in the 12th century, of celebrating Mass according to the Mozarabic rite (*see* Toledo Cathedral, p.493). The **Capilla de Santa Barbara** (1340) has in its centre the tomb of Bishop Lucero—he of the well-worn feet, polished by countless anxious candidates for Doctorate degrees. It was customary to pass the night before the examination in the chair before the altar, feet propped up on the bishop's in a vigil of study. The examiners would come to the chapel in the morning and grill the student, who, if successful, would leave in a triumphal procession, attend a bullfight and, mixing the bull's blood with olive oil, inscribe his name on the cathedral or university building for all posterity to see. The **Capilla de Los Anayas** contains another bishop's tomb, enclosed by an ornate *verja* (iron grill); against the wall is a beautifully crafted 14th-century organ with *mudéjar* designs, believed to be the oldest in Europe. The **chapter house**, where the Knights Templars were tried for heresy in 1316, contains a museum featuring paintings by Fernando Gallego (a 15th-century native of Salamanca).

The University

A block from the cathedral is the **Patio de las Escuelas**, with a statue of the mystic and poet Fray Luis de León, Salamanca's most famous professor. This is the main entrance to the university, founded as the Escuelas Salamantinas in 1218 by Alfonso IX of León. From that moment its growth was prodigious; with the union of León and Castile it incorporated the fledging university of Palencia; in 1254 Alfonso the Wise endowed it with a law school and professorships; the following year Pope Alexander ranked it in the same category as Oxford, Paris and Bologna. At its peak it enrolled 10,000 students in 25 colleges, boasted one of Europe's best faculties of astronomy—consulted by Columbus before his famous voyage—and the first woman professor, Beatriz de Galindo (1457–1535), who taught Queen Isabel her Latin. One of Spain's most prominent thinkers of the 20th century, the Basque Miguel Unamuno, taught classics here and served as rector into the Civil War.

During the Peninsular War the French demolished 20 of the colleges, but fortunately spared the **University** and its unsurpassed Plateresque façade; in a low medallion over the door are smug portraits of Fernando and 'Elisabetha' and the elegant Greek inscription: 'From the Kings to the University; from the University to the Kings'. Inside (*open Mon–Sat 10–1.30 and 4–6.30, Sun 10–1; adm*) the old lecture-rooms are placed around a two-storey cloister, linked by a gorgeously carved **Renaissance stair**, where giant insects frolic with bishops popping out of pots. On the ground floor the **Lecture Hall of Fray Luis de León** has been perfectly preserved since the day in 1573 when the professor, in the middle of a lecture, was carted off by the Inquisition. For five years he languished in a dire prison cell; upon his release, he returned here and without further ado, calmly resumed his lecture with 'As we were saying yesterday. . .' In the same room, Unamuno, who at first had given Franco some much-needed intellectual backing, claiming the Nationalist rising was 'necessary to save Western Civilization', had his famous confrontation with the lunatic Falangist Millán Astray. Chairing a Columbus Day commemoration in 1936, Unamuno listened to a string of speeches in praise of Franco, then stood up and denounced both sides for their atrocities. Astray went berserk, bellowing 'Death to the intellectuals' while his bodyguards drew their arms. Franco's wife, present at the ceremony, saved Unamuno from the Falangist fury, though he was dismissed from his post as rector and died in disgust two months later. He is remembered in the **Casa-Museo Unamuno** by the door (*open Tues–Fri 11–1.30 and 4.30–6.30, Sat and Sun 10–2*).

Your ticket will also get you into the **Escuelas Menores** ('the Lesser Schools'–i.e. for non-aristocrats), equally endowed with a fine cloister; one room contains Ferdinand Gallego's, *Sky of Salamanca*, a beautiful scene of the zodiac salvaged after the Lisbon earthquake in 1755. Next to it, the **Museo de Bellas Artes** (*open Tues–Sun 9–2*) contains an eclectic collection and *artesonado* ceilings. The most interesting piece, an anthropomorphic menhir from the 10th century BC, is in the foyer, while in the courtyard are *verracos* and *cerdos* (swine), Celtiberian gravestones similar to the ones found around Ávila. From here you can walk down to the Río Tormes, spanned by a beautiful 400m **Roman bridge**, and guarded by a headless *cerdo*. The brick Romanesque-*mudéjar* church of **Santiago**, with its three elegant apses, sits on the city side of the bridge; cross over for the classic view of Salamanca's cathedral and towers.

Convento de Las Dueñas and Convento de Santa Clara

Behind the cathedral, at the head of Salamanca's main shopping street, the Gran Vía, the Convent of Las Dueñas was founded in 1419 for the Dominican Mothers. In the 16th century, an unusual five-sided **cloister** (*open daily 10–2 and 4–7*) was added, its upper gallery adorned with capitals carved by some Plateresque Edvard Munch—disturbing, nightmarish, twisted torsos, skulls, and hundreds of shrieking faces of the damned. Across from Las Dueñas stands another Plateresque masterpiece, **San Esteban** (*open daily 9–1 and 4–7.30*) with a façade as filigreed and delicate as that of the University; inside it has a tranquil cloister, and a huge wedding-cake of a *retablo* by José Churriguera. The frescoes near the upper choir are unintentionally funny, depicting rows of martyred saints, all holding their heads like a queue of bewildered waiters. Behind this is another Romanesque church, **Santo Tomás de Canterbury**, the first in the world dedicated to St Thomas, erected just three years after his martyrdom by English residents of Salamanca. On the other side of this is the newest star in Salamanca's art constellation, the 13th-century **Convento de Santa Clara** (*open Mon–Fri 9–2 and 4–7, Sat and Sun 9.30–2; adm*)—a beautiful set of 13th–18th-century frescoes were found under coats of white wash, and a superb polychrome 14th-century ceiling found behind a false one in the church, and another one, from the Renaissance, in the cloister.

Elsewhere in Salamanca

West of the Plaza Mayor, the triangular **Plaza de Agustinas** is one of the city's scenic corners, framed by the **Convent of Las Agustinas** (containing the well-known *Immaculada* by Ribera) and the ornate 16th-century **Palace of Monterrey**. A block down is the **Casa de las Muertes** ('House of the Dead'), named after the skulls incorporated in the Plateresque façade. Unamuno died in the house next door, at No.4, and his neo-Rodinesque statue, broods across the square. The church of the **Convento de Santa Ursula** just to the north of the square houses a magnificent tomb of Archbishop Alonso Fonesca by Diego de Siloé. Further north at the end of C/ Zamora **San Marcos** is an unusual round Romanesque church (1202). Two towers from great aristocratic solars survive as landmarks east of the Plaza Mayor: the **Tower of Air** with its elaborate windows, and the **Tower of El Clavero** with a picturesque crown of turrets. As you stroll through the city, look for the brass door-knockers shaped like a hand—the *Mano de Salamanca*, a memory of the Islamic charm, the 'Hand of Fatima'.

Salamanca ✉ *37000*

Where to Stay

expensive

The ★★★★**Parador de Salamanca**, Teso de la Feria 2, ✆ 923 26 87 00, 🖷 923 21 54 38, is located just across the Roman bridge with a fine view of the city's enchanting skyline. One of Spain's newest *paradores*, it offers a pool, garden and air conditioning. In the centre, in a late 15th-century palace, the ★★★★**Palacio de Castellanos**, C/ San Pablo 58, ✆ 923 26 18 18, 🖷 923 26 18 19, has a lovely patio and plush rooms. Historic ★★★**Las Torres**, C/ Concejo 4, ✆/🖷 923 21 21 00, has some rooms with balconies over the Plaza Mayor and a good restaurant.

moderate

Best here is ★★**Amefa**, Pozo Amarillo 18-20, ✆ 923 21 81 89, 🖷 923 26 02 00, a luxurious charmer in the centre of town. ★★**Emperatriz**, C/ Compañia 44, ✆ 923 21 92 00, is located in a pretty monumental building, with TV in every room. If they're full-up try the up-to-date ★★**Don Juan**, Quintana 6, ✆ 923 26 14 73, 🖷 923 26 24 75.

inexpensive

★**Hs Tormes**, Rúa Mayor 20, ✆ 923 21 96 83, stands out by dint of its great location, between the Plaza Mayor and University; the rooms are clean and pleasant, and you can eat cheaply in its small restaurant. Failing that you could try ★**Hs Alianza III**, Avda. Villamayor 2, ✆ 923 26 83 60, or ★**Hs Valencia**, Pso. San Antonio 5, ✆ 923 26 98 64. There are scores of inexpensive *fondas* and *pensiones*: **Lisboa**, Meléndez 1, ✆ 923 21 43 33, and **Marina**, Doctrinos 4, ✆ 923 21 65 69, are excellent.

Eating Out

Just of Plaza Mayor you'll find one of Spain's best French restaurants, **Chez Victor**, Espoz y Mina 26, ✆ 923 21 31 23 (*expensive*) with imaginative, creative cuisine, especially the duck and game dishes. Top the evening off with the 20-year-old port. *Closed Mon, Sun eve, and Aug*. On the same street at No.20, **Le Sablon**, ✆ 923 26 29 52 (*moderate*) has an excellent reputation for its equally French-influenced cuisine and elegant desserts.

Closed July. A traditional Salamanca favourite, **La Montaraza**, José Jáuregui 9, © 923 26 00 21 (*moderate*) serves up a heaving board of tapas, or meals with oven-baked soup (*tostón de horno*), cod, and cheese cake. *Closed Mon and Aug.* Arrive early if you want a table at little **Rio de la Plata**, Pza. Peso, © 923 21 90 05, with excellent turbot *a la plancha* and a *2400-pts menu. Closed Mon and July.* You can easily eat for less, thanks to the student population, in spots like the **Roma**, C/ Ventura Ruiz Aguilera 10, near the Plaza Mayor, © 923 21 72 67, with meals *under 1000 pts*; there are many other places like it.

Around Salamanca

The province of Salamanca for the most part resembles a northern extension of Extremadura. A good part of the land is devoted to raising fighting bulls, who roam vast fields dotted with holm oaks. Spain's most remote villages are located in Salamanca's sierra—reputedly some of them hadn't even heard of God until the 20th century.

Getting Around

There is only one train a day from Salamanca to Ciudad Rodrigo, and it leaves town at an ungodly 5am; otherwise you'll have to rely on buses from Salamanca to Ciudad Rodrigo, Alba de Tormes, Ledesma, Béjar and the villages of the Sierra. Connections exist, if not particularly often. Remember, life is a journey, not a destination.

Tourist Information

Ciudad Rodrigo: Pza. de las Amayuelas 6, © 923 46 05 61.

Béjar: Pso. Cervantes 6, © 923 40 30 05.

Northwest of Salamanca, there's some very green, un-Castilian scenery and even a couple of beaches along the fetching Río Tormes all the way to **Ledesma** at the tip of the **Embalse de Almendra**, a vast reservoir formed by a dam on the Tormes, close to its confluence with the Duero. Ledesma is a pretty, walled town with a pretty Plaza Mayor, a couple of medieval churches and a Roman bridge. Upriver, the **Arribes del Duero** is a region of steep, 300m-walled canyons, lakes and rugged hills. **Saucelle** is a pretty village to aim for, in the centre of a large almond-growing area.

Ciudad Rodrigo

On the Portuguese frontier, Ciudad Rodrigo was captured from the Moors in the early 12th century and named after Count Rodrigo González Girón, who led its resettlement. A magnificent set of walls added in 1190 is still almost intact; Spaniards are fond of aerial views of the city, enclosed in its perfect multi-pointed star. During the Peninsular War, Wellington took it from its French occupiers after a bitter, 11-day siege, earning himself the Spanish title of Duque de Ciudad Rodrigo from the grateful King Fernando VII. Since then much of the damage inflicted by British guns has been restored, although the breach in the walls near the Cathedral has been preserved as a memory. This side of the elegant Gothic **Cathedral**, built soon after the conquest by Count Rodrigo, took a licking. Its other portals are still in good nick; note especially the twelve figures from the Old Testament over the south door, and the beautiful Portico del Perdón on the main façade. Inside, under the complex vaults of the nave, the **choir stalls** are the work of the fertile imagination and delicate chisel of Rodrigo Alemán (who is also credited with the naughty choir in Zamora), and there are more imaginative carvings in the **cloister**, added in 1325, from the 14th and 16th centuries (*open 11.30–1.30 and 4–7; adm*). Ciudad Rodrigo has a charming, 17th-century **Plaza Mayor** with an unusual **Ayuntamiento** that seems more Latin American than Spanish, perhaps not too surprisingly as many of the city's Renaissance palaces were built by men who had made their fortunes with the *conquistadores*. One of the highlights of the city is the 2.4km walk around the **medieval walls** and the wonderful views from the **castle of Enrique II**.

South of Salamanca

Between Salamanca and Ávila, set in a pretty *vega*, pottery-making **Alba de Tormes** has a history bound up with the proud Dukes of Alba and Santa Teresa, who in 1571 founded the **Convento de las Carmelitas** with the Duke's support. She returned to the convent to die, and her remains (or at least her heart and arm) are venerated in the church; a beautiful relief over its door depicts the Annunciation, with the Angel Gabriel carrying a caduceus like the god Mercury. Of the Dukes' castle, only the **Homage Tower** remains. When the Grand Duke was in residence, Lope de Vega's plays were often premiered before being performed in Madrid; some of its 16th-century frescoes have been restored.

In the rugged **Sierra de Béjar** and the **Sierra de la Peña de Francia** in the southern extreme of the province, tiny villages were secluded for centuries. They are wonderfully atmospheric places, their narrow medieval streets lined with leaning, half-timbered houses, refreshingly cool in the summer when par-boiled Spaniards ascend, seeking relief from the plains of Extremadura and Castile. Most beautiful and most visited is **La Alberca**, a gem of a village (and now a national monument) in a magnificent setting. The parish church has a unique pulpit of coloured granite, and if you're lucky, you'll run into one of the village's celebrations, when the women don the most ornate costumes in Spain; when they're not dressing up, they're stitching gorgeous, primitively exuberant embroideries. Some 2km south of La Alberca, the road rises to **El Portillo** pass, marking the beginning of the magnificent **Valle de Las Batuecas**, a Natural Park with needle-like peaks and its own lush microclimate; bring a picnic. The road winds dramatically down to the bottom of the valley, where the river banks around the **Monasterio de los Carmelitos** (early 1600s) have prehistoric rock paintings amid the outlandish formations. North of La Alberca, an equally winding road ascends the conical **Peña de Francia** (1730m), a favourite goal of walkers, where a Gothic church houses an image of a Virgin discovered by a French pilgrim; the views again are stupendous and in the summer there's a restaurant/bar. Other beautiful old villages of the Sierra are **El Cabaco**, 10km from La Alberca, **Mirador de Extremadura** and **Candelario**, 4km from the major town of **Béjar**, which itself boasts some fine streets and the Palacio de los Duques, with a lovely Renaissance patio. If the above are too cosmopolitan, try **Miranda del Castañar**, 37km from Béjar or the even smaller **San Martín del Castañar**, or head south into **Las Hurdes** (*see* p.502).

Where to Stay and Eating Out

Ledesma ✉ 37000

Ledesma's only hotel belongs to a large, fairly modern spa, the ★★★Balneario de Ledesma, © 923 57 02 50 (*moderate*). *Open mid-March to Nov.*

Ciudad Rodrigo ✉ 37500

The ivy coated ★★★**Parador Enrique II**, Pza. Castillo, ✆ 923 46 01 50, ✉ 923 46 04 04 (*expensive*), has its entrance just under the Homage Tower; intimate and charmingly furnished, it enjoys lovely views (try to get room 10 with a round dome) and runs the best restaurant in town; try the city's speciality, stuffed lamb shoulder (*paletilla de cordero rellena*). ★★★**Conde Rodrigo**, Pza. de Salvador 9, ✆ 923 46 14 08, ✉ 923 46 14 08 (*moderate*), by the cathedral in a lovely old palace, is a close second to the *parador* (in summer, ask for a room in the back). The **Madrid**, C/ Madrid 20, ✆ 923 46 24 67, has good cheap rooms. A clutch of eateries lines the Salamanca–Portugal road and there's great tapas in **El Sanatorio** in the Plaza Mayor.

Alba de Tormes ✉ 37800

You can get a fine, air-conditioned double in a quiet corner of town at the ★★**Alameda**, Avda. Juan Pablo II, ✆ 923 30 00 31 (*moderate*); it also has a very reasonable restaurant, with full meals for *1500 pts.*

Villages of the Sierra

The villages of the Sierra are mostly unspoiled, but hardly undiscovered, and if you'd like to stay over in summer, you'll need a reservation. Béjar has the Sierra's best hotel, ★★★**Colón**, Colón 42, ✆ 923 40 06 50 (*moderate*), with a bar, garden and restaurant, and the cheaper, welcoming ★**Comercio**, Puerta de Avila 5, ✆ 923 40 02 19 (*low moderate*). In Alberca the best hotel is ★★**Las Batuecas** on the road to Las Batuecas, ✆ 923 41 51 88, ✉ 923 41 50 55 (*moderate*), a fine place amid the chestnuts and cherry trees with a decent restaurant; ★★**Paris**, La Chanca, ✆ 923 41 51 31 (*low moderate*) is also good. In Candelario the ★★**Hs Cristi**, Pza. Béjar 1, ✆ 923 41 32 12 (*moderate*) is the village 'Ritz' (Nov–May open weekends only). If you come out of season, the best bet is the ★**Hs El Pasaje**, Las Eras s/n, ✆ 923 40 32 10, with eight comfortable rooms for *4200 pts*, with bath. In Miranda de Castañar, ★**Hs Condado de Miranda**, Parajela Perdiza, ✆ 923 43 20 26 (*inexpensive*, all rooms with bath), has one of the town's two restaurants (*1200 pts*). **La Posada de San Martín**, in San Martín del Casañar, ✆ 923 43 70 36, is a new restaurant with rooms in the centre, with good meat dishes and desserts (*moderate*). *Open Holy Week–Oct.*

Valladolid

Valladolid, sovereign of infirmity
The priest's early death, the maggot's Compostela.

Such was the opinion of Guillem de la Gonagal, the 16th-century 'François Villon of Extremadura', said to have died in a brothel here in 1546. The judgement seems harsh for a city that has experienced so much of Spain's history and culture. Felipe II was born in Valladolid, and Columbus died here in 1506, impoverished and almost forgotten. Valladolid was twice capital of Spain, and Cervantes wrote the first part of *Don Quixote* in a little house on Calle del Rastro. Valladolid has attractions that almost make it worth a short stay, but to see them you'll have to pay a price. For all its history, Valladolid is a stupefyingly ugly city, and probably always has been. Lately it has enjoyed considerable industrial growth, becoming the largest city of Old Castile. Many writers have blamed it for destroying much of its older quarters in the process, but this is one city where you may want to cheer on the wrecking crews. The new developments are neither better nor worse than elsewhere in Spain, but the old, an amorphous blot of shabby alleys and ghastly misbegotten churches, will not be the memory of Spain you would wish to take home with you. Nobody in Valladolid seems unhappy to see it go. But if you want to see San Pablo church and the Colegio San Gregorio, two of the most unusual architectural fantasies in all Spain, steel yourself and plunge in. Valladolid hosts a film festival every November, the country's second biggest after San Sebastian.

Getting Around

By train: Lots of trains pass through Valladolid, with regular connections daily to all the cities of Old Castile and León (except Soria and Segovia) as well as Galicia and the northern coast. There are always at least eight daily trains to Madrid, some passing through Ávila. In this region, there may be quicker connections than you see up on the boards at the station. Always ask at the information desk or the ticket counter; all trains pass through the big junction at Medina del Campo, and by changing there you may reach your destination faster. In Valladolid the station is on the southern edge of town, on the Paseo de Campo Grande (for information © 983 22 33 57 or, in the centre at the RENFE office at Atreo de Santiago 3, © 983 22 28 73).

By bus: The bus station is a 10-minute walk west of the train station, at Puente Colgante 2, under a highway overpass, © 983 23 63 08, with connections to the same places, also Soria, Barcelona and provincial towns like Toro, Tordesillas and Arevalo.

Tourist Information

On the other side of the Campo Grande from the train station, Pza. de Zorrilla 3, © 983 35 18 01.

The City

Most people's introduction to Valladolid will seem innocuous enough; both the bus and train stations are near the **Campo Grande**, a large park on the eastern edge of town. From here, follow the pedestrian Calle de Santiago to the city centre and the **Plaza Mayor**, grimy but not unpleasant, with most of the restaurants and cheap hotels on or around it. In the 16th century the plaza earned renown for spectacular *autos-da-fé*, a practice inaugurated by Felipe II in 1559 after a secret community of religious freethinkers was discovered in the town. Heading west down San Francisco Ferrari, you'll come to the **Cathedral**. It was begun in 1580 as one of the first works of Juan de Herrera, and in the 1720s Alberto Churriguera was given a chance to try and complete it. This combination of Spain's apostle of austerity and its most exuberant Baroque master explains the mess you see; plenty of hacks have monkeyed with it since, but quite understandably the city has given up; the cathedral will never be finished and fair-sized shrubs are already growing out of the cornice. Just behind it is a small 14th-century Gothic jewel, **Santa María la Antigua**; its Italian Romanesque tower survives from an earlier church.

San Pablo and San Gregorio

It is hard to explain the presence of these two buildings in Valladolid (they are next to each other on the Plaza de San Pablo, just down Calle de las Angustias from the cathedral)—their façades are as eccentric as Toledo Cathedral's Transparente, and completely unlike anything else in Spain. Both façades are huge curtains of sculpture, woven with fantastical forms and ornate decoration, completely disregarding the norms of religious architecture. **San Pablo**, where Felipe II was baptized, had its façade added in 1601. The big coat-of-arms also displayed on it is that of the Duke of Lerma, who picked up the bill. Its great lions and dozens of saints and angels seem like figures of some mechanical clock, ready to come alive at the stroke of the hour. The Castilian Cortes often met here, and the interior is full of tombs of Spanish notables, but there hasn't been much to see inside since the thorough looting done by the French in 1809. Napoleon could have overseen the job himself; he made the **Capitanía General** across the square, a former royal palace, his headquarters on his visit to Spain.

San Pablo's anonymous sculptors were undoubtedly inspired by the earlier (1496) Isabelline Gothic **Colegio de San Gregorio**, very similar in conception. Its architect, Mattias Carpontera, is said to have committed suicide just before the façade was completed. At its centre a pomegranate tree, commemorating the conquest of Granada, springs from a fountain full of cherubs. Ragged wild men with clubs called *maceros* guard the doors, a curious fashion copied in other Spanish churches, such as Ávila cathedral.

Museo Nacional de Escultura

Inside, the Colegio San Gregorio has been restored to house this large collection (*open 10–2 and 4–6, Sun 10–2, closed Mon*). The name is a little misleading; it's all religious sculptures, taken from churches in Valladolid and elsewhere in Castile. Very little is of any merit—Alonso Berruguete's statues from an enormous *retablo* in the first three rooms, the anonymous 1463 **Retablo de San Jerónimo** and some 15th-century choir stalls up on the second floor by Diego de Siloé. The rest, room after room of gaping Virgins and blood-splattered Christs, will either make you queasy or make you laugh. A French immigrant, Juan de Juni (*c. 1540*) is the master of this, and his *El Entierro de Cristo* is rivalled only by Gregorio Fernández's *Cristo Yacente* in the expression of anguish and depiction of wounds. The school's restored chapel has a lovely statue of *Death* himself; in the cloister, restorers of the 1880s tried to clear the air with some silly fanciful **gargoyles**, which are more fun than anything in the museum.

Other Museums

Both Cervantes' and Columbus' houses have been turned into museums, the **Casa de Cervantes** (Rastro 7, *open daily except Mon, 10–3.30, Sun 10–2*) and **Casa de Colón** (C/ Colón, *open daily except Mon, 10–2 and 4–6, Sun 10–2*). Better than these, the old **Philippines Convent** behind the Campo Grande has a **Museo Oriental** (*open Tues–Sat 4–7, Sun 10–12; adm*), with works acquired during centuries of missionary work in the Far East—nine rooms filled with fine paintings and porcelain from China, and three more with folk art of the Philippines and elsewhere.

Valladolid ✉ *47000*   ***Where to Stay and Eating Out***

Rooms in Valladolid are pricey. If you must stay, you can indulge at the recently reno-vated ★★★★**Olid Melia**, Pza. San Miguel 10, two blocks from San Pablo, ✆ 983 35 72 00, 📠 983 33 68 28 (*expensive*), the best in town. Good moderate-priced choices include the well appointed ★**Feria**, Avda. Ramón Pradera, ✆ 983 33 32 44, 📠 983 33 33 00, ★★**El Nogal**, Conde Ansúrez 10, ✆ 983 34 02 33, 📠 983 35 49 65, which also has a reputed restaurant, and ★**Enara**, Pza. de

España 5, ℗ 983 30 03 11. You'll find a wide choice of cheap dives in the back streets around the Pza. Mayor, or the very respectable **Dani**, ℗ 983 30 02 49, and **Dos Rosas**, ℗ 983 20 74 39, run by sisters on different floors at C/Perú 11, near Campo Grande and the train station. The Pza. Mayor and cathedral area is the best place to look for restaurants. Near Cervantes' house, the excellent **Mesón Panero**, Marina Escobar 1, ℗ 983 30 70 19 (*moderate*) prides itself on game dishes in season, Vallodolid codfish stew and tasty *patatas a la importancia* (fried in batter with garlic). *Closed Sun.* In the same area **El Figón de Recoletos**, Recoletos 3, ℗ 983 39 60 43, is another reliable restaurant, typically Castilian, serving the city's finest roast lamb (*lechazo asado*) from the woodburning oven: *4000 pts* for two. *Closed Sun and mid July–mid Aug.* **Santi**, Correos 1, ℗ 983 33 93 55 (*moderate*) is in a 16th-century inn and serves up tasty homemade stews and good wines.

Around Valladolid

In the heartland of Castile you would expect castles, and these are the major attraction of the flat, monotonous country around Valladolid. Few ever served any military purpose, apart from intimidating the populace and defending the nobility during the civil wars. That they survived while so much else has been lost is a key to Castile's history. In the 15th century this was indeed the heartland, a region of new towns whose prosperity was based on the *Mesta*, that peculiar half-corporation, half-cooperative that kept all Europe supplied with prized merino wool. The Habsburgs destroyed the region's economy for ever, and towns like Toro and Tordesillas, that figured so prominently in the chronicles of Fernando and Isabel, never fulfilled their early promise.

The Comunero Revolt

At the end of the Middle Ages, in the 1400s, Europe was opening up and looking for new horizons. No economy in this period was better prepared to discover a New World than Castile's. A new urban society had appeared, based around the great trade fairs of Medina del Campo, Badajoz, Sevilla and Cádiz, and on some of Europe's biggest, most advanced manufactures: cloth from Segovia, Toledo, Palencia and Cuenca, metalwork from Valladolid, leather from Córdoba and Toledo, not to mention Castile soap. Art and culture were thriving, and in this period Spain was on the verge of attaining a prominence in Europe that it had never before known.

A real change in Spanish society came with the conquest of Granada in 1492. Suddenly there was plenty of other people's land to be grabbed, and the grandees of the north used gangster methods against the Muslims and each other to get it. They soon found that such methods worked equally well against their old enemies, the mercantile towns, back home and launched into an orgy of assaults against city rights and riches. Nobles used legal trickery to snatch vast areas of land from the towns, then proclaimed new tolls everywhere, nothing more than protection rackets in the countryside they controlled. To gain a slice from the profits of trade, they resorted to daylight robbery and kidnapping of merchants and town officials, with a veneer of legality provided by the nobles' ancient rights to hold courts of law.

Fernando and Isabel did little to stop any of this, and things got worse under the ineffectual regencies that followed Fernando's death in 1516. Spain had lost control of its destiny; the strings were pulled from Flanders by the ministers of the heir, Charles V. Charles himself, only 16, cared for nothing but hunting, but the men who manipulated him saw Spain as a cash cow, and they milked it as much as possible to finance Habsburg ambitions of universal monarchy. Now the towns had two gangs after what was left of their wealth. The situation was becoming serious; the depredations of the Habsburgs caused a national financial collapse in 1519. In Castile, the area that suffered the most, rebellion was in the air.

What came to be called the Comunero Revolt (for the *comunes*, or free towns) started on 30 May 1520, with a revolt of the wool workers in Segovia. They lynched Rodrigo de Tordesillas, delegate to the Cortes, and chased all royal officials out of town. The Spanish army was off in the Pyrenees annoying the French, so the way was clear for the revolt to spread; by July Salamanca, Toro and Toledo had joined, and a *junta* was formed at Ávila. On Aug 20, the government tried to seize a store of rebel weapons at Medina del Campo (shades of Lexington and Concord!) but the local minutemen beat them back, a victory that inspired most of the other Castilian towns to join. Tordesillas was taken, and became the rebel capital.

The *junta* had great hopes for mad Juana, the rightful queen and mother of Charles; a 'recovery' two years earlier saw her completely in control of her faculties (if indeed she had ever lost them). Though sympathetic to the rebels, in the end she refused to sign a declaration deposing Charles. This was the turning point. Now the private armies of the nobles felt free to go on the warpath once more against the towns. They recaptured Tordesillas for Charles in December, and the end came when the returned royal army met the rebel army at Villalar on 23 April 1521. Though numerically superior, the rebels lost for lack of cavalry; their leader, Juan de Padilla, was captured and killed in the aftermath. The king, whose position was still uncertain, turned his most conciliatory face to the rebels. The survivors were pardoned in 1522, and Charles even decreed some of the reforms the Comuneros had demanded. But with the end of the revolt, the rape of Castile's towns and business became a *fait accompli*. Had the Comuneros won, Spain might well have developed the same kind of progressive economy and society as England and France, and avoided the terrible decline of the coming centuries; its history, and the world's, would have been very different.

Medina del Campo stands as a symbol of so much that went wrong. Once one of the greatest trade fair towns of the continent, merchants from as far as Germany and England made the annual trip here over the Pyrenees to expedite the trade in wool, Vizcaya iron and Toledo silk. Medina's fairs inaugurated the use of letters of exchange among merchants—the beginning of modern banking—and the city's financiers arranged the exchequers of all Castile's kings up to Charles V. The Habsburg bankruptcies put an end to all this, and Medina dwindled to an insignificant village in just over a century. Spain's biggest sheep-market is still held here, but there's little to see of the old Medina—Charles V's army razed it to the ground. **La Mota Castle** survives, east of town; Queen Isabel often stayed here, and in the town itself is a small palace where she died in 1504.

Madrigal and Toro

Some 30km south, **Madrigal de las Altas Torres** makes a fine sight, with its crumbling 14th-century walls rising above the plain. There's little left inside them, but you can visit Isabel's birthplace here at the Convento de las Angustias (she wasn't born in a nunnery; the building incorporates an old palace of Isabel's family). **Toro,** north of Medina on the Zamora—Valladolid road, has a site almost as picturesque, on red cliffs above the Duero; it has grown old more gracefully than Madrigal. Toro's landmark is a remarkable 12th-century Romanesque Colegiata, with a broad 16-sided Byzantine *cimborio* over the crossing, similar to those in Zamora and Salamanca—and nowhere else. The Colegiata's west front, the Pórtico de la Gloria, is one of the best works of Spanish Romanesque sculpture. The Battle of Toro, fought during the civil war that followed the death of Enrique IV, inaugurated Spain's 'golden age' by making Fernando and Isabel undisputed masters of the country. Fernando's army did not really defeat the partisans of Juana la Beltraneja; the battle was a draw, but Juana's Portuguese supporters gave up and went home, ensuring Isabel's hold on the throne of Castile.

Tordesillas

Like Toro, Tordesillas was once a thriving town, its name synonymous with the Pope Alexander Borgia's 1494 Treaty of Tordesillas that divided the discoveries in the New World between Spain and Portugal. Its better days are recalled in its lovely arcaded **Plaza Mayor**, in **San Antolín**, with a Plateresque tomb and a magnificent *retablo* by Juan de Juni, and a fine little museum of sculpture, and most of all in the **Convent of Santa Clara**, (*open daily except Mon, 10.30–1.30 and 3.30–7, Sun, am only; adm*), the last abode of Isabel's daughter, Queen Juana the Mad. Her son, Charles V, kept her locked up here for 46 years under guard: intent on keeping Castile for himself, he allowed Juana no visitors to confirm or deny the rumours that she was sane. Parts of Santa Clara were begun as a palace by Alfonso XI in 1340; his son, Pedro the Cruel, converted it into a convent. The **Patio de San Pedro** and the **Capilla Mayor** offer some of the most lavish *mudéjar* work in Castile, with colourful *azulejos*, lattice-work façades and a remarkable *artesonado* ceiling. North of Tordesillas and Mota del Marquéz, **San Cebrián de Mazote** has a lovely early 10th-century Mozarabic church, with three aisles divided by horseshoe arches with superb carved capitals and a painted ceiling. Nearby **Torrelobatón** has a fine medieval castle, and near Zaratán (20km west of Valladolid) the church of **Santa María de Wamba** preserves its original Mozarabic arches.

As for castles, there are fine ones at **Fuensaldaña**, **Simancas** (this one has housed the state archives of Spain since the time of Charles V) and **Cuéllar**, a village famous for its annual *encierro*, or 'running of the bulls'. **Coca Castle** may be the strangest in Spain, a 14th-century stronghold of notorious local tyrants, the Fonseca family. This flight of *mudéjar* fancy with unique fluted turrets looks as if it was built much more for decoration than defence.

Where to Stay and Eating Out

Tordesillas has a ★★★**Parador Nacional** in a modern building in the pines on highway 620, ✆ 983 77 00 51, ✉ 983 77 10 13 (*expensive*), but it gets stiff competition from ★★★**El Montico**, on the same highway, towards Salamanca, ✆ 983 77 07 51, ✉ 983 77 07 51 (*expensive*), in a restored farmhouse, with a pool and tennis, and a charming restaurant. The best place to dine in Tordesillas, **El Torreón**, Dimas Rodríguez 11, ✆ 983 77 01 23 (*moderate*) does all the Castile basics under a repro 15th-century ceiling from Santa Clara. Madrigal has a decent inexpensive *hostal*, the ★**Madrigal**, on the road to Peñaranda, ✆ 983 32 08 78, and there are a few modest hotels each in Medina del Campo, Toro and Simancas. Medina del Campo has a pair of good restaurants: **Monaco**, superbly set in Pza. España, ✆ 983 81 02 95 (*inexpensive*), with simple dishes and an excellent *1200-pts menu*; **Continental**, Pza. Mayor, ✆ 983 80 10 14 (*inexpensive*), has been in business for over 50 years, thanks to its good home-cooking.

From Valladolid to Soria

Coca Castle has a worthy competitor at **Peñafiel**, on a narrow ridge overlooking the Duero. This ship-shape (literally) white castle, built in 1466 to follow the crest of its difficult site, is 214m long and only 24m wide, giving it the appearance of a stage set (*open Tues–Sun 11–2.30 and 4–6, summer til 8; adm*). Wander through the old village streets by the Plaza del Coso, which serves as a bullring during Peñafiel's fiesta on 15 August.

The road to Soria generally follows the Duero, and the countryside becomes considerably greener and prettier in the neighbourhood of **El Burgo de Osma**. This town, important until the 1700s, has shrunk into one of the truly beautiful villages of Castile, with bits of its old walls crumbling beneath the trees, and fields and gardens encroaching on its very centre. It also has an exceptional little **Cathedral** (*open 10–1.30 and 4–7*) with a beautiful 13th-century Gothic façade; the tower, Burgo de Osma's landmark, is a Baroque addition, and there are some arches of the original Romanesque church and a harrowing Cruxifixion within, among a hotch-potch of different styles. Its founder, San Pedro de Osma, is entombed inside in a 13th-century sarcophagus covered with lively and colourful medieval scenes. The **musuem** contains a major collection of illuminated manuscripts, especially the *Beato*, a 1065 codex of commentaries on the Apocalypse. Burgo de Osma is not the original town here; its predecessor, Osma, was a Roman city called *Uxama*, but has now declined to a tiny hamlet just a short distance away. Both are overlooked by a ruined **castle** on Roman foundations. Just over 14km north of town, there is some wild and rugged scenery around the **Canyon of the Río Lobos**; here, just outside Varo, the church of **San Juan de Otero** (now called San Bartolemé) was built in the 12th century by the Templars. In this isolated spot the Templars could afford to express some of their heretical doctrines in the design. One of the windows is in the form of an inverted pentangle, and there are other unusual geometric forms and patterns inside.

From Burgo de Osma, it's a short jump to Soria (on the way, stop at **Calatañazor**, a perfect medieval Castilian time capsule). But better still, consider a detour through the fascinating and little visited country to the southeast, in the valley of the Duero.

The Upper Duero

The landscape, if you're not alert for it, may pass without notice, but you'll find it sticks in your memory after you go. Most of Soria province is like this—unusual, intense shades of green and gold, wrinkled hills ploughed into subtle patterns of furrows, bare mountains topped with crumbling castles. The towns and villages, little changed since the Middle Ages, come in the same gold and brown as the hills. Most are genteel and decaying, seemingly ready at any moment to seep back into the land that gave them birth.

Heading south from Burgo de Osma, you meet the Duero under the walls of **Gormaz Castle**, a huge, half-ruined, barbaric-looking pile built by the Moors in the 10th century. The walls are half a mile around, and worth the climb for the fine Moorish gateway and the view. From Gormaz, a long detour to the south will take you to **Termancia** in a small patch of mountains called the Sierra de Pela, near the village of Tiermes. This was an important Celtiberian town, and though unexcavated it's an exceedingly strange site, with tunnels and stairs and caves dug out of the bare rock; scanty ruins of the Roman Termancia that succeeded it can be seen below.

The next town up the river from Gormaz, **Berlanga de Duero**, has a squat, round-towered castle, arcaded streets and medieval gates, and the fine, plain early Gothic **Colegiata**. Friar Romas de Berlanga, the town's favourite son, is buried here. He was a 16th-century Bishop of Panama, who changed the course of history by introducing bananas into the New World from Africa. Best of all, 8km south in **Casillas de Berlanga**, you can visit a Mozarabic jewel, the 10th-century **Ermita de San Baudelio de Berlanga**, a grey stone cube in an austere land-scape, built as an outpost on the frontiers of New Castile (*open 10.30–2 and 4–6, summer 5–9, Sun 10.30–2, closed Mon and Tues*). Since antiquity, the cube has represented the element earth; inside, the central palm pillar, radiating horseshoe arches, supports the celestial sphere. A mini-mosque of horseshoe arches, symbolizing the dark forest of the soul, leads to Baudelio's holy cave; the chapel on top, suspended between heaven and earth, was the ideal place for a holy man to live and pray. Most extraordinary of all, hidden away just under the roof and above the top of the central palm pillar, is an enchanting kiosk, just big enough for one person, symbolic of paradise and accessible only by ladder—Jacob's ladder. Frescoes of animals and hunting scenes decorate the walls, but the best ones have been spirited away to the Prado.

Almazán, a growing town of some 6000 people, second-largest in the province, has managed to keep nearly all its medieval walls and gates, as well as the 12th-century church of **San Miguel**, with a Moorish dome of interlaced arches. A nearby village, **Morón de Almazán**, has a lovely plaza surrounded by a Renaissance church and palaces. South from Almazán, you meet the main Madrid–Barcelona road and rail line at **Medinaceli**; 3km from the new town, its dusty half-deserted core survives defiantly on a hill, with eschutcheoned palaces and a Roman **triumphal arch**, the only triple one in Spain. Some 30km east, **Santa María de Huerta**'s Cistercian monastery was founded in 1162 by Alfonso VII, shut down in 1853 and repopulated by the order in 1927. It is like a small museum of Gothic architecture and sculpture, with a fine chapel and beautifully vaulted century refectory (*open 9–1 and 3–7 except Mon*).

Where to Stay and Eating Out

El Burgo de Osma ✉ 42300

★★★**II Virrey**, Calle Mayor 4, ✆ 975 34 13 11, ✆ 975 34 08 55 (*expensive*) offers the luxury of a four-star hotel. Family-run ★**Virrey Palafox**, Universidad 7, ✆ 975 34 02 22, ✆ 975 34 08 55 (*moderate–inexpensive, without bath*), has a restaurant, renowned for Castile's classics (*menu 1800 pts*). ★★**Hs Casa Agapito** C/ Universidad 1, ✆ 975 34 02 12, is a real bargain at *2500 pts for a double with bath. Open Mar–Nov*).

Berlanga de Duero ✉ 42360

Try the ★★**Fray Tomás**, Real 16, ✆ 975 34 31 36, or ★★**Hs La Hoz**, Postigo 42, ✆ 975 34 31 36, both *moderate*; the latter has a good restaurant.

Medinaceli/Santa María de Huerta ✉ 42240

Medinaceli has the best restaurant in these parts: the family-run **Los Llaves**, in the Plaza Mayor, ✆ 975 32 63 51, in a prettily restored building; for a change from pork, try the *bonito en rollo; menu 3800 pts. Closed Sun eve and Mon.* In Santa María, the privatized *parador* ★★★**Santa María de Huerta**, ✆ 975 32 70 11, ✆ 975 32 70 11 (*expensive*) has been completely renovated and endowed with a health and natural beauty centre; on a far more modest scale, in the tiny village, **Pensión Santa María**, Mayor 50, ✆ 975 30 70 31, has *inexpensive* rooms with bath.

Soria

It may be one of Spain's smallest provincial capitals, but Soria will seem like a metropolis after the bitsy villages of the rest of the province. It is a town of distinction, full of early medieval monuments in a beautiful setting among forested hills overlooking the Duero.

Getting Around

By train: Soria's only train service runs five times a day to Madrid, and twice daily to Pamplona; it's easy to reach Zaragoza or Bilbao, though, with a change at Castejon del Ebro. You'll have to take a cab to the station, outside Soria; there's no bus. RENFE information: ✆ 975 21 10 95.

By bus: The city has a new bus station, on the western edge of town, with a few daily runs to Logroño, Pamplona, Zaragoza, Barcelona, Burgos, Valladolid and Madrid–and also to Burgo de Osma, Almazán and, less regularly, to the smaller villages of the province. There are also two daily direct buses from Burgo de Osma to Madrid.

Tourist Information

Pza. Ramón y Cajal, ✆ 975 21 20 52.

Around the Centre of Soria

Soria's centre, connecting the old town with the new, is the **Plaza Ramón y Cajal**. The plaza faces a big park, the **Alameda de Cervantes**, with perhaps Spain's only public tree-house, and the **Museo Numantino** (*open May–Oct Tues–Sat 10–2 and 5–9, Sun and hols 10–2, closed Mon; Nov–April Tues–Sat 10–2 and 4.30–7, Sun and hols 10–2, closed Mon; adm*) with finds from the ancient city of Numantia (*see* below). Soria's two finest medieval churches stand at the northern and southern edges of the old town: **San Juan de Rabarera** on Calle Caballeros (*c.* 1200), with an unusual apse, in transition from Romanesque to Gothic, and **Santo Domingo** on Calle La Aduana Vieja (*c.* 1160), with a spectacular carved tympanum over the west portal, displaying hundreds of figures of saints and angels. Behind the Plaza Mayor, Calle Real traverses the old town, passing two 13th-century churches on its way to the Duero—the ruined **San Nicolás** and **San Pedro**, the latter with a beautiful Romanesque cloister.

San Juan de Duero

Soria's riverfront, strung between two hills (one has a monastery, the other a *parador* and a ruined castle), is an attraction in itself, a lovely, peaceful spot with groves of poplars, an island, and a weir on the lazy Duero. You can rent canoes from the bar next to the old stone bridge, or cross to the other side and see **San Juan de Duero**, founded by the Knights of St John around 1200. The arcade of its ruined **cloister**, standing strangely alone in a field, is unlike any other in Spain—half of it Gothic, the remainder intertwined pointed arches that look from a distance like spiral loops. The church next to the cloister is still in good shape, with vivid scenes of the Massacre of the Innocents on its capitals. A small **museum** has been installed (*open Nov–March 10–2 and 3.30–6; April, May, Sept and Oct 10–2 and 4–7; June–Aug 10–2 and 5–9*). Medieval Soria was an important Jewish city, and many of the artefacts—headstones and sarcophagi, mostly—are reminders. Take a walk down the avenue of poplars on the eastern bank of the river, and you'll pass two other old monuments: the 13th-century **San Polo** church, a Templar foundation built right over the road (now a private home) and, further on, the octagonal **Hermitage of San Saturio**, romantically set into a cliff over the river. It isn't surprising that these sites should be out of the ordinary. As the Templars would have known, this corner of the Duero must have been a holy site since remotest antiquity. Forget the made-up story of a San Saturio, hermit and patron of Soria—and don't even bother guessing who San Polo might have been. It was the common early Christian practice to appropriate ancient deities and turn them into saints. For Saturio and Polo, read Saturn and Apollo.

Numancia

> *Open Nov–March Tues–Sat 10–2 and 3.30–6; April, May, Sept and Oct Tues–Sat 10–2 and 4–7; June–Aug Tues–Sat 10–2 and 5–9; Sun and hols open 10–2; closed Mon.*

In this ancient city, 19 years of the Iberian Arevaco tribe's struggle against the Romans culminated in one of the famous events of antiquity. A year-long Roman siege in 132 BC seemed on the verge of success when the people of Numancia chose not to accept the inevitable. Instead they set fire to their town with themselves in it, a grand gesture of heroic defiance that Spanish poets and politicians haven't yet tired of talking about. There's little to see on the site (6km north of Soria); a few straight streets and foundations from the later, Roman town on a hillside overlooking the modern village of **Garray**, and traces of the four miles of walls. In northern Soria province, you can trace the source of the Duero into a landscape of grey mountains and pine forests. Vinuesa, off the Burgos road, is a beautiful, untouched village on route to the sequestered Laguna Negra ('black lagoon') and the Sierra de la Hormaza.

Where to Stay and Eating Out

Named after the poet who lived in Soria, the little ★★★**Parador Antonio Machado**, ✆ 975 21 34 45, ✆ 975 21 28 49 (*expensive*) heads the list of the city's hotels, a modern but comfortable place among the ruins of the old castle. Central ★★★**Husa Alfonso VIII**, Alfonso VIII 10, ✆ 975 22 62 11, ✆ 975 21 36 65 (*moderate*), is a fine historical building; quiet ★★★**Leonor**, Pza. Mirón, ✆ 975 22 02 50, ✆ 975 22 99 53 (*moderate*) has fine views. ★★**Viena**, García Solier 5, ✆ 975 22 21 09, is a good place to spend the night (*moderate with bath, less without*). Most of the *cheap fondas* off Pza. Ramón y Cajal will not disappoint: try **Fonda Ferial**, Pza. del Salvador 6, ✆ 975 22 12 44.

Among Soria's restaurants, **Maroto**, Paseo del Espolon, ✆ 975 22 40 86, stands out, with unusual dishes like mushroom and truffle soup (*menu 3000 pts*). **Mesón Castellano**, Pza. Mayor 2, ✆ 975 21 30 45, has a good name for its excellent local cuisine (*2000 pts*). **Capri**, C/ San Benito 8, ✆ 975 22 12 84, has better than average meals for *around 1500 pts.*

Madrid

Sifting through all the books that have ever been written about Spain, opinion on this unlikely capital seems about evenly divided. Some writers are sure it's the heart and soul of the nation, but the dissent has been coming in ever since the city has been on the map; many follow Richard Ford in counselling that the less time you spend in Madrid, the better you'll like it. Like Bonn or Washington, it is an entirely artificial capital, created on the whim of the early Habsburg kings. The city has great museums, wide boulevards and a cosmopolitan air. It doesn't have a beautiful setting, or a tolerable climate, or many noteworthy churches or monuments—it's difficult to imagine a capital more impoverished architecturally.

So why stay long, when fascinating places like Toledo and Segovia are just a short train-ride away? Art is one reason; not surprisingly, the city of Velázquez and Goya and connoisseur Habsburg and Bourbon kings has one of this planet's greatest hoards of fine paintings stored in its museums. Old Madrid, the area around the Plaza Mayor that has changed little since the 17th century, would be another. The biggest reason for many, though, will be that Madrid is better equipped than any city in Spain to give you a good time. The madrileños proudly claim their city stays up later than any in Europe; there's good cause to stay up, with an infinite variety of tapas bars, nightlife and attractions that may make you forget all about Velázquez and Goya.

History

Settlements have come and gone here since the Palaeolithic era, but the first permanent town seems to have been built by the Arabs, who constructed a fortress Alcázar on the site of today's Palacio Real, and a small circuit of walls that extended only as far as the Plaza Mayor and the Plaza Isabel II. Their name for it, *Mayrit*, came from the Matriz, a little stream that ran in the valley where the Calle de Segovia is now. Mayrit met the Reconquista in 1083, two years before Toledo; El Cid may have been around to assist Alfonso VI in its capture. The walls were extended in the 11th and 12th centuries. The new southern gate, the Puerta del Sol, gave its name to the square that later replaced it, standing at the centre of Madrid today.

One strange interlude in the city's history came in the 1380s, when King Juan I gave the city in fief to the exiled last king of Little Armenia, Leon VI. In the centuries that followed, the town's growth was steady and slow. Royal patronage came first with Enrique IV, who tacked a Renaissance façade onto the old Moorish Alcázar to make it one of his palaces, but it was Charles V who first began to spend much time here; both he and his son Felipe II found the climate eased their bad cases of gout. Up to that time Spain had had no real capital. The Cortes traditionally alternated its meetings in all the Castilian cities, so that none would be offended, and the necessity of an occasional royal presence in all of Spain's diverse regions made vagabonds of all the earlier kings. Felipe declared Madrid the permanent capital in 1561, giving the Habsburg monarchy a strong, central, specifically Castilian capital from which to combat the separatist tendencies of the outlying regions, and at the same time creating a counterweight to the contentious older cities of Castile, most of which had supported the Comunero revolt just 40 years earlier.

Unfortunately, neither the Habsburgs nor the Bourbons went out of their way to replan or embellish their capital. Besides palaces, their only important contributions are the two great parks, the Retiro and the Casa de Campo, that define the eastern and western boundaries of the old town and help so much to make Madrid habitable. Most travellers of that era, from the 16th to 18th centuries, write of Madrid as crowded, unpleasant, even unhealthy; sanitation and other urban amenities did lag far behind other European capitals of the day. The city must have seemed a curious juxtaposition of a sophisticated royal court, with its palaces and gardens, on top of an overgrown Castilian provincial town. Nevertheless, in this era Madrid was home to Velázquez and Goya, to Calderón and Lope de Vega, as well as many other important figures of the 'Golden Age of Spain'.

Politically the city learned to speak for itself in 1808, in the famous revolt of the 'Dos de Mayo'. When Napoleon's men attempted to kidnap the Spanish royal family, a spontaneous patriotic uprising occurred; though soon suppressed by the French, it has been a golden memory for the Spanish ever since. Madrid's next chance for heroism came with the Civil War. In the early days of that conflict, four Nationalist columns, including most of Franco's Army of Africa, advanced to positions within sight of the Royal palace (General Mola mentioned a 'fifth column' of sympathizers supposedly hidden within the city: it was just propaganda, but a new phrase was born). Bitter street fighting in the western suburbs continued until March 1937. At first, the defence of the city was almost entirely in the hands of the newly formed Socialist, Communist and Anarchist militias. Their untrained fighters, many women among them, wore street clothes, held meetings to discuss tactics with the officers, and some actually commuted daily to the front on the Metro, or in cars commandeered from the wealthy. The Republican government soon fled to Valencia, but as the world watched in suspense, Madrid held. '*No pasarán*'—'they shall not pass'—was the famous slogan, coined by La Pasionara, and the city became a symbol that caught the imagination of Europe, the first community in that dark time to make a successful stand against fascism. In November 1936 the International Brigades and the first squadrons of Soviet aeroplanes began to arrive, and they helped defeat the last Nationalist attempts to encircle the city.

Before the Civil War, Madrid had grown into a bright and cosmopolitan cultural capital; its cafés and clubs frequented by the artists and writers of the 'Generation of 1898' as well as politicians and the Spanish élite. Though most of the glitter, as well as the substance, disappeared under 40 years of Franco, the city grew tremendously. The Franco government, determined to see their capital outstrip Barcelona, encouraged new industry and migration from other corners of Spain. Though the city flourished, the environmental cost was high; once lovely boulevards were flattened into urban motorways, and the outskirts of the city were disfigured by the wasteland of factories, junkyards and shantytowns you see today.

After Franco's death in 1975, however, Madrid's civic pride was allowed to resurface. As the Seventies gave way to the Eighties, and the traditionally puritanical and austere Spaniards woke up to the attractions and pleasures of economic success, the city found itself at the cutting edge of a social revolution. Earning (or otherwise acquiring) vast sums became a fashionable compulsion, and the popular press coined the term '*los beautiful people*' for the new, money-flaunting jetset that filled Madrid's restaurants and *terrazas*. The early 1980s became known as the *movida*, when bars sprang up throughout the city, legalized drug consumption flourished, and under a socialist government's patronage the arts underwent not so much a renaissance, as a resurrection.

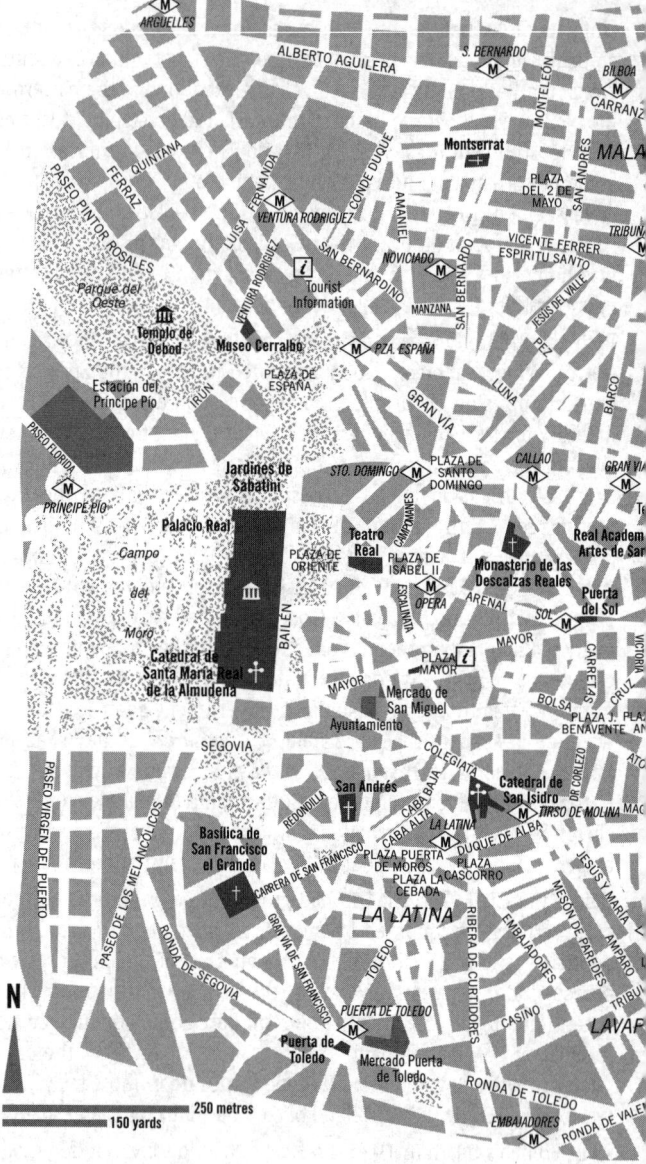

Madrid

Enrique Tierno Galván, who was elected Mayor of Madrid in 1979, was seen by many as the sponsor and orchestrator of the city's great cultural revival. A remarkable mayor, he dedicated himself to improving the city's quality of life; he planted thousands of trees, created new parks in the outlying districts, repaired some of the damage done by the traffic planners, and even found some water to direct through the dusty stream bed of the Manzanares. *Madrileños* called Tierno 'The Old Professor' for his habit of lecturing them on the importance of trees and greenery, and all of them, regardless of politics, mourned his death in 1986.

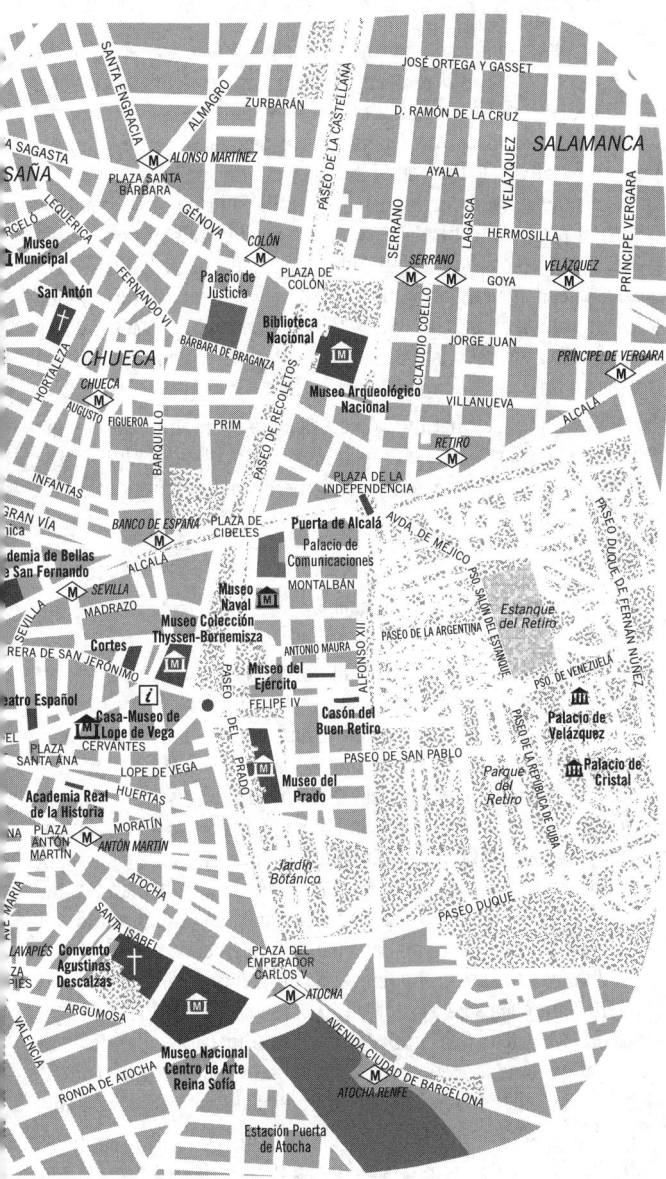

The Spanish economy grew faster than that of any other member country in the first five years after Spain joined the European Community, and, as property prices soared, Madrid benefitted from much needed investment. Art-fever gripped the city with the growth of ARCO, Madrid's annual contemporary art fair, the opening of the Reina Sofía modern art museum and the acquisition of the famous Thyssen-Bornemisza collection. In 1991, the right-wing Partido Popular gained control of Madrid's regional parliament, and, under Mayor José María Alvarez del Manzano, one of their first priorities was to set about making final preparations for Spain's golden year of celebrations, 1992. Barcelona had won the Olympics, Seville was hosting the World Fair, and Madrid came a poor third as European Cultural Capital. As it turned out, Madrid's contribution to the 1992 celebrations was not particularly remarkable; many of the projects planned to mark the event, such as the Opera House, were unfinished (it has, however, since been completed). But it was at the end of the year that the real blow came. For three years Spain's socialist government had been artificially warding off economic slump by pouring money into construction projects to furnish the nation for the celebrations. Even before the year-long fiesta was over, recession hit hard, with all the usual trappings—high unemployment, high interest rates, and currency devaluation. Nobody appreciated this sudden downturn, and, in the 1993 general election, the PSOE, their name already blackened by corruption scandals, lost control of the greater Madrid area. In 1996, the PP won the general elections. For the future, the right's hold on the capital looks assured.

Madrid has now come to terms with the fact that the boom years are over; although city life has lost the hedonistic, opportunistic sparkle and easy glamour that distinguished it in the eighties, the Madrileñan spirit is not dampened easily, and there's as much optimism as caution built into their image of the future.

Getting There

Madrid is smaller than most great European capitals, and getting into and out of the centre is surprisingly easy and convenient.

By air: The Aeropuerto de Barajas, Madrid, is 13km northeast of the city centre, off the N11 highway. Fast, air-conditioned buses (white with yellow and green stripes) run between Barajas (national and international terminals) and the underground bus terminal at Madrid's Plaza de Colón, 500m north of Retiro Park, every 12 minutes except between 1.50 and 4.45 in the morning, taking around 15mins when the traffic is reasonably clear. The fare is 380 pts one way—infinitely preferable to a very expensive taxi ride (expect to pay about 2,500 pts for the same journey by taxi, *see* 'Getting Around'). Airport bus information: © 91 431 61 92. A metro line is planned for Barajas by the end of 1999, part of an ongoing plan to extend the underground rail system. The airport has two banks where you can change foreign currency (BEX and Caja de Madrid), and a Visa/Mastercard cashpoint. Avis, Hertz, Europcar and Atesa all have car hire offices here. There's also a post office (*open Mon–Fri 8–8, Sat 8–1*), a RENFE office (*open 8am–9pm, © 91 305 85 44*), a small tourist office which has maps and some information, and a Brújula accommodation office (*see* 'Tourist Information'). The left luggage office is opposite the international terminal (*open daily, 7am–midnight, © 91 305 61 12*).

Airport information:© 91 305 83 43/4/5/6; local police:© 91 305 43 81; lost and found:© 91 393 60 00.

By train: All long distance trains now leave from just two stations: Estación de Atocha and Estación de Chamartín. **Atocha,** newly refurbished and quite close to the city centre at the southern end of the Paseo del Prado, handles AVE trains to and from Córdoba and Sevilla, Largo Recorrido (long distance) trains to and from Lisbon, Valencia, Andalucía and all points south, plus trains on the Regionales (short distance), and Cercanías (local) rail networks. **Chamartín,** just past Plaza Castilla at the northern end of the Paseo de la Castellana, is also fairly new and has the air of a shopping mall. It takes most of the trains to and from France, and those serving northern and central Spain, plus some local trains. There's a metro stop at both Atocha and Chamartín, but the quickest way to travel between the two stations is via the underground section of the main rail line, with stops at Recoletos (just northwest of the Retiro park) and Nuevos Ministerios (on the Paseo de la Castellana, 2.5km north of the Plaza de Cibeles). Many trains to and from distant places use it to hit both Atocha and Chamartín, and you may jump on any train that does to get from one to the other.

Tickets can be bought at the main RENFE office at C/ Alcalá 44, (*open Mon–Fri, 9.30–8*). For all RENFE enquiries, call ✆ 91 328 90 20. RENFE offers telephone reservations: for an extra *500 pts*, they will messenger the ticket to you, as long as it's within the capital. AVE information: ✆ 91 534 05 05.

By bus: Most, but not all, inter-urban and international buses use the big new **Estación Sur de Autobuses**, at C/Méndez Alvaro, close to the metro station of the same name. A big exception is the Auto-Res company, which has its own terminal at Pza. de Conde de Casal 6 (Ⓜ Conde de Casal, southeast of Retiro Park, ✆ 91 551 72 00) with services to Cuenca, Valencia, Extremadura, and parts of Castile. Continental Auto, C/ Alenza 20 (head north from Ⓜ Ríos Rosas) takes you up to Burgos and the Basque country; they also have a terminal at Avda. de América 34 for buses to Alcalá de Henares, Guadalajara and Sigüenza. For other towns close to Madrid, check the 'Getting There' sections for those towns.

Information: Estación Sur, ✆ 91 468 42 00; Auto-Res, ✆ 91 551 72 00; Continental Auto, ✆ 91 533 04 00 (C/ Alenza 20) or ✆ 91 356 23 07 (Avda. de América 34). Of course the Tourist Office can always tell you how to get where you want to go.

left luggage

As well as at Barajas airport (*see* 'By air', above), there are public *consignas* at Estación Sur (*open Mon–Fri, 6.35am–11.45pm*), Atocha (*open daily, 7am–11pm*) and Chamartín (*open daily, 6.30am–12.30am*).

Getting Around

Madrid's buses and metro operate on the same ticket, with a single price for all journeys, costing 130 pts. A '*bono*', for ten trips, costs *670 pts*.

By metro: The metro has been undergoing a massive expansion plan in recent years. New stations are constantly springing up. By the end of 1999, not only will Barajas Airport have a metro station, but a cross-town line will extend from Fuencarral in the north to Aluche in the far south. The metro's main faults are that it's a little colourless and connections are often inconvenient. Get an up to date map of the system at any station; study it carefully before setting out. There are so many stops and lines in the centre of the city, it's easy to be tricked into taking a half-hour ride (with a change or two) for a distance that could be covered in 10 minutes on foot. For navigation, you have to know your line number, and the name of the terminus in the direction you want to travel. As convenient as it is, try not to use the metro too much. There often isn't much need. However, unlike many other cities, it is safe and well used, even late at night. Trains run from 6am to 1.30am. Stations are distinguished by a red diamond over the entrance, as in Barcelona. For metro information, call ✆ 91 552 59 09.

By taxi: Madrid's local government-regulated taxis are white with a red diagonal stripe on each front door, and a sign saying 'Libre' if they're free. Any city taxi that has a meter (some don't—they're best avoided) is expected to use it, but don't be surprised if the fare comes out a little higher: there are surcharges for luggage, for the airports and bus and railway stations, for journeys at night (11pm–6am), and for leaving the city limits. As elsewhere in Spain, taxis are cheap enough; the average ride in the city centre costs well under *1000 pts.*

By bus: Only a few EMT bus lines will be of use to the visitor—but buses can be preferable to the metro if you want to see Madrid. Many buses go through the Plaza de Cibeles, Puerta del Sol and Plaza de Callao, where there are information kiosks which sell *bonobus* tickets. *Estancos* and news-stands also sell them. You enter the bus at the front, pay the driver or validate your ticket, and leave by the doors in the middle. Some drivers may object if you try to bring large suitcases on board. The sequence of places served from each stop is usually clearly marked. Buses run from 6am to midnight, after which there is a skeleton night service through the city, leaving from Plaza de Cibeles and Puerta del Sol every half hour until 3am, and every hour from 3–6am.

Useful lines:

Line 1: Moncloa–Pza. de España–Gran Vía–Pza. de Cibeles–Puerta de Alcalá–C/ Velázquez or C/ Serrano–C/ Ortega y Gasset (Salamanca district).

Line 3: Pza. de Alonso Martínez–C/ Fuencarral or C/ Hortaleza–Puerta del Sol–C/ Arenal or C/ Mayor–Pza. de San Francisco–Puerta de Toledo.

Line 14: Pza. de Conde de Casal–Atocha–Pso. del Prado–Pso. de Recoletos–Pso. de la Castellana—Chamartín.

Line 19: C/ Velázquez or C/ Serrano–C/ Alfonso XII (Retiro Park)–Atocha–Palos de la Frontera (Estación Sur bus terminus).

Line 33: Pza. de Isabel II–Casa de Campo: Parque de Atracciones, Parque Zoológico (funfair and zoo).

Tourist Information

The main office is close to the Prado at C/ Duque de Medinaceli 2, ✆ 91 429 49 51 (*open Mon–Fri 9–7, Sat 9–3*). At the bottom of the Torre de Madrid, the big skyscraper on the Plaza de España, there is a smaller office, ✆ 91 541 23 25 (*open Mon–Fri 9–7, Sat 9.30–1.30*). There are branch offices (don't count on their being open) at Barajas airport (✆ 91 305 86 56) and Chamartín station (✆ 91 315 99 76) (both supposedly *open Mon–Fri 8–8, Sat 8–1*). The city of Madrid has an office right on the Plaza Mayor, opposite the Casa de la Panadería, ✆ 91 366 54 77 (*open Mon–Fri, 10–8, Sat, 10–2*). Brújula, the agency that specializes in helping find lodgings for visitors, has an office on the 6th floor above the tourist office in Plaza de España, ✆ 91 559 97 05, and booths at Barajas and Chamartín. The tourist offices usually have up-to-date lists of hotels and *hostales* in Madrid.

While in Madrid, keep an eye out for the Columnas Informativas scattered about town, with maps and all sorts of information posted. They have a way of turning up miraculously when you're lost. Madrid also has a city information phoneline: dial ✆ 91 010, or ✆ 91 366 66 06 from outside the city (*Mon–Fri 8.30–9.30*).

Great Britain: C/ Fernando el Santo 16, ✆ 91 319 02 00, Ⓜ Alonso Martínez.

USA: C/ Serrano 75, ✆ 91 577 40 00, Ⓜ Rubén Darío or Serrano.

Canada: C/ Núñez de Balboa 35, ✆ 91 431 43 00, Ⓜ Núñez de Balboa.

Australia: Pso. de la Castellana 143, ✆ 91 579 04 28, Ⓜ Pza. de Castilla or Cuzco.

New Zealand: Pza. de la Lealtad 2, ✆ 91 523 02 26, Ⓜ Banco de España.

Ireland: C/ Claudio Coello 73, ✆ 91 576 35 00, Ⓜ Serrano.

post and telecommunications

The main post office is the Palacio de Comunicaciones on the Plaza de la Cibeles (*open Mon–Fri 8–10, Sat 8.30–10*). In central Madrid there are also post offices at: El Corte Inglés, C/ Preciados, Ⓜ Sol; C/ Hermosilla 103, Ⓜ Goya; C/ Mejí Lequerica 7, Ⓜ Alonso Martínez, *all open weekday mornings*. Postboxes, marked *Correos y Telégrafos*, are yellow; collections are generally Monday to Friday only. You can make local, national or international calls from any of the modern-style phone boxes that accept coins, credit cards or phone cards (sold in *estancos* and post offices), or from the Telefónica offices at Gran Vía 28, Pso. de Recoletos 41, or at the Palacio de Comunicaciones. Stationery shops are the best places from which to send faxes; Telefónica offices also offer a fax service.

banks

Most international banks have major branches around the Calle de Alcalá or in the Salamanca district. Banks are typically open *Mon–Fri 8.30am–2.30pm, and Sat 9–1*. Most will change foreign currency, even if they don't have a sign saying *Cambio*.

American Express

Pza. de las Cortes 2, ✆ 91 322 55 00, Ⓜ Banco de España, *open Mon–Fri 8.30–4.30pm*; also at C/ Francisco Gervás 10, ✆ 91 572 03 03.

lost and found

Objetos Perdidos, Pza. de Legazpi 7, ✆ 91 588 44 00.

emergency services

Madrid has a single number for all emergency services (fire, police, ambulance): ✆ 112

Orientation

Madrid goes on and on—today it is home for 4 or 5 million people, but almost everything of major interest to any traveller will be found within one mile of the **Puerta del Sol**. The areas of Madrid which will be of most interest to the visitor run westward from the Retiro park, just north of the Plaza de Cibeles, along either the C/Alcalá or Gran Vía to the Plaza de Oriente, home of the newly opened opera house and the Royal Palace. Nearby is the **Plaza de España**, a modern square laid out during the Franco regime. Back over on the east, near the Retiro and the broad boulevard called the **Paseo del Prado**, can be found the '*triángulo del arte*', the three art museums of the Prado, Thyssen, and Reina Sofia. The Puerta del Sol sits squarely in the centre, and the oldest quarter of the city, around the **Plaza Mayor**, is just to the east of it. Keep these landmarks in mind, and learn a few of the main streets, and you'll not get too lost—Madrid isn't nearly as complicated as it looks on the map.

Ten streets meet here, as well as three metro lines and dozens of buses; however you're travelling in Madrid, you're soon likely to cross the 'Gate of the Sun', the centre of Spain. All distances in the nation are measured from the marker in front of the old **Casa de Correos**, now the home of the Comunidad de Madrid, Madrid's regional government. The gate (*puerta*) from Alfonso's walls is long gone, and the plaza is chaotic, dirty and crowded as it always has been, but it endears itself to the *madrileños* in a way no formal plaza with a postcard view ever could. Here, at the mouth of a shopping street (the Calle de Carmen), stands a sculpture of their own emblem, the **Oso y Madroño** (bear and strawberry tree). It's a small, unshowy bronze, a low-key symbol of community identity, now rather upstaged by an equestrian **statue of Carlos III**, set up on a plinth between two fountains in the middle of the square. Nothing that is *auténtico* in Madrid ever strays far from the Puerta del Sol, and the spider's web of narrow streets around it; jammed into this tight-knit district are scores of curious shops and family businesses that have been running for generations, while the *tascas* south of the plaza, their windows piled high with shellfish and other delicacies, are some of the oldest and best-known bars in town. From here, you'll have the choice of heading either west to the old town and the Palacio Real, or east to the Retiro and the museums. It's almost a tradition for visitors to Madrid to begin with a morning in the Prado, one of the half-dozen great museums of the world, and the major attraction Madrid has to offer. If that's your destination, the Carrera de San Jerónimo on the eastern end of the square will take you right to it.

The Cortes

Along the way, if you blink you may miss the **Cortes** (1850), also known as the Palacio del Congreso or the Congreso de los Diputados, the home of the Spanish parliament. Many cities one-tenth Madrid's size have larger and more elegant post offices. Certainly, few nations would be content to house their lawmakers in such a dowdy structure; from it we can see how little Spaniards thought of their corrupt governments of the 19th century. Today, important sessions of the Cortes are broadcast on the radio, and it was on one such occasion in February 1981 when the right-wing zealot, Civil Guard Colonel Tejero, and his men stormed in, shooting off their pistols while the nation listened. Tejero held the Cortes hostage for 24 hours, finally surrendering when it became clear that the majority of the army was supporting the King and democracy. The following day saw the biggest demonstration in the city's history, led by the leaders of all the political parties, marching arm-in-arm down the Calle de Alcalá.

The Paseo del Arte: Madrid's 'Golden Triangle'

If the Prado wasn't already enough to make Madrid a major art destination, the re-opening of the Reina Sofía Art Centre in 1990 and the nation's permanent acquisition of the Thyssen-Bornemisza collection in 1992 removed all doubt. Madrid is rightly proud of its 'golden triangle' of art treasures—three superb museums all within strolling distance of each other, linked by the leafy Paseo del Prado.

The three collections complement each other neatly. The **Museo del Prado** is best known for its hoard of masterpieces of Spanish painting from the 12th to the early 19th centuries, and it also holds rich collections of 15th–17th century Flemish painting, and Italian art from Fra Angelico, Raphael and Botticelli to Tintoretto, Titian and Caravaggio. Its annexe, the **Casón**

del Buen Retiro, covers the 19th century. The **Museo Nacional Centro de Arte Reina Sofía** picks up the thread with its permanent collection of 20th century art (the centrepiece of which is Picasso's masterwork *Guernica*), and its ground-breaking exhibitions of modern works. The newcomer on the scene, the **Museo Collección Thyssen-Bornemisza**, is a remarkable collection of work spanning eight centuries. Its highlights include early Italian paintings, 17th-century Dutch works, and paintings by 20th-century masters including Braque, Mondrian, Picasso and Warhol. Fortuitously, it manages to fill in a few of the gaps left by the Prado and the Reina Sofía, with collections of impressionism and post-impressionism, German expressionists such as Munch, Schiele and Kandinsky, and a restrained but well-informed selection of pop art and geometrical abstracts.

As the Prado, the Reina Sofía and the Thyssen are such near neighbours, many visitors are tempted to hop between them, relishing the change in atmosphere, but it would be impossible to do justice to all three museums in a short visit. Don't even think about trying to 'do' the Paseo del Arte in a single day unless you are likely to be satisfied with a mere snippet of each.

Museo del Prado

Paseo del Prado, © 91 420 28 36, ® 91 420 07 94, ⓜBanco de España. Open: Tues–Sat 9–7, Sun and hols, 9–2, closed Mon; adm 400 pts, concessions 200 pts, free Sat after 2.30 and Sun; adm includes entry to the Casón del Buen Retiro; 'Paseo del Arte' voucher allowing one visit to each of the Paseo del Arte museums, 1050 pts.

When, in the early 19th century, the Spanish royal house realized that the paintings adorning its various palaces added up to perhaps Europe's greatest artistic treasure, it was resolved to bring all of them together under one roof. Credit for the creation of the Museo del Prado goes to Fernando VII, that most hated of kings, who took over this rambling neoclassical structure which had been intended as a natural history museum when it was begun in 1785, and opened the collections to the public in 1819. Since then the building has been restored several times, but the collections have changed little. The Spanish noble families who collected paintings in centuries past are likely still to have them; the habit of donating to museums never took root as much here as in the rest of Europe. For the best of the Prado we can thank the practised eyes of Charles V, Felipe II and Felipe IV. Whatever else history can blame them for, they knew good painting when they saw it.

Today, the Prado has a space problem. The exhibition areas are only large enough to display a fraction of the museum's vast collection, and among its 'unseen' canvases are significant works by a good number of the Spanish Old Masters. There was considerable disgruntlement when in 1993 the government invested an unprecedented (though bargain) sum in acquiring the Thyssen collection while apparently neglecting the Prado's arguably more pressing needs. Expect crowds, especially at weekends, but don't be dismayed by huge mobs at the entrances; they're likely to be disorganized tour groups counting heads, and you should be able to pass right through. The earlier you go, the less you'll have to contend with. The best place to begin a comprehensive visit to the collections is to enter at ground level by the Puerta de Goya (Goya gate) at the north end of the main building, the Edificio Villanueva, but if you want to head straight for the most spectacular of the Spanish Old Masters you can take a short cut up the steps and enter at first floor level, or, if you want to avoid the queues, there's a secondary entrance (the Puerta de Murillo) at the southern end.

The Collections

12th–16th-century Spanish Art

The first ground floor rooms are devoted to medieval religious works. Don't be in too much of a hurry to see Velázquez; some of the best art in the Prado is here, including some 12th-century murals from Segovia and three stunning 14th- and 15th-century *retablos*: the *Archbishop Don Sancho de Rojas* by Rodríguez de Toledo, the *Legend of St Michael* by the Maestro de Arguis, and *The Life of the Virgin and St Francis* by Nicolás Francés. This rich collection of early Spanish painting continues with Renaissance-influenced works such as Fernando Gallego's eerie *Cristo Bendiciendo*. Pedro Berruguete contributes a scene of an *Auto-da-Fé presided over by Saint Dominic* that is almost satirical, with bored church apparatchiks dozing under a baldachin while the woebegone heretics are led off to the slaughter. Bartolomé Bermejo's portrait of *St Dominic enthroned as Abbot of Silos* stands out for sheer dramatic realism: the saint is shown seated on a monumental throne surrounded by figures representing the three theological and four cardinal virtues.

Flemish, Dutch and German Schools

Even before Felipe II, who valued Flemish art above all others, the Low Countries' close commercial and dynastic ties ensured that some would turn up here. Today the Prado's collection of Flemish art is almost as unmissable as its Spanish collection. The works are arranged roughly chronologically, beginning with the 15th-century Primitives, including paintings by Robert Campin and breathtakingly detailed work by Rogier van der Weyden. Weyden's *Descent from the Cross* (c. 1435) is astonishing, framed like a scene from a mystery play, in which Gothic stylization is all but forgotten in favour of the realistic visual representation of a whole spectrum of human emotions. Within the tight confines of the composition the figures just float off the surface of the panel. There is a copy of this painting at El Escorial.

The biggest crowds, though, will be around the works of Hieronymous Bosch (1450–1516, known in Spain as 'El Bosco'). His psychological fantasies, including *The Garden of Earthly Delights*, *The Hay Wain*, *The Adoration of the Magi* and the table in the centre of the room decorated with *The Seven Deadly Sins* are too familiar to need any comment. Felipe II bought every one he could get his hands on, and it should not be surprising to find the most complex of all Spanish kings attracted to this dark surrealism as we moderns are. More works by Bosch can be seen in Felipe's apartments at El Escorial. If you like Bosch, you should also get to know his countryman Joachim Patinir, some of whose best work can also be found in this section. Probably no other museum has such a large complement of terror to balance its own beauty; between Goya (*see* below), Bosch and the other northern painters and the religious hacks, a trip to the Prado can seem like a long ride in a carnival funhouse. If you approach it in this way, the climax will undoubtedly be *The Triumph of Death* by Pieter Brueghel the Elder (1525–1569), with its phalanxes of leering skeletons turned loose upon a doomed, terrified world. To Felipe II, who is said to have kept a crowned skull on his night table, it must have seemed a deeply religious work. The Dutch, though, in the middle of their war of independence, would probably have been reminded of the horrors of intolerance and militant religion that were searing contemporary Europe—much of it emanating from this very city.

Rubens (1577–1640), another favourite of the Spanish monarchs, is well represented here, with his epic *Adoration of the Magi* dominating a whole roomful of florid biblical paintings, and his chubby *Three Graces* among other mythological subjects in an adjacent gallery. A room nearby contains the famous collaboration of Brueghel the Younger and Rubens, the *Allegory of the Five Senses*, a complete universe of philosophy in its five enormous canvases. Rubens' works are followed by those of later Flemish masters: delicate portraits by Anton van Dyck (1599–1641), complex studies by David Teniers such as his paintings-within-a-painting work *Archduke Leopold William in his picture gallery*, and, tucked away in a room full of small canvases, one of the greatest works of Brueghel the Younger, the untitled 'snowy landscape'.

The Prado's small Dutch collection consists mostly of 17th-century hunting scenes, still lifes, and the like, but there is one good Rembrandt (1606–69), a dignified portrait of a regal woman thought to be *Artemisia*, wife of King Mausolus. German paintings, too, are few, but they are choice. Albrecht Dürer's rather presumptious *Self Portrait* (1498), for example, is an interesting work, painted at a time when self-portraits were uncommon (artists were considered unworthy subjects), and composed in a style that is often compared to Leonardo da Vinci's *Mona Lisa* (a copy of which hangs in the Italian section), although it was actually painted five years earlier. Interesting too are Dürer's companion paintings of *Adam* and *Eve*, Hans Baldung Grien's angular Teutonic *Three Graces* and sinister *Three Ages of Man and Death*, and works by Cranach and Mengs.

Italian and French Schools

In the Prado's Italian collection, there are several paintings by Raphael (1483–1520), all religious subjects; from Fra Angelico (1397–1455) an intensely spiritual *Annunciation*; and an unusual Botticelli (1444–1510) trio of scenes from Bocaccio's Decameron, *The Story of Nastagio degli Onesti*. Andrea del Sarto, Mantegna, Antonello da Messina, Veronese, Caravaggio, Tintoretto and Correggio, among the other Italian masters, are all represented, and there are rooms full of Titians, including two portraits of the artist's patron, Charles V. Titian (*c.* 1490–1576) never painted anything small, and perhaps his biggest canvas of all is *La Gloria*, a colourful, preposterous cloud-bedecked imagining of the Holy Trinity that gently nudges the boundaries of kitsch. Charles (who is also in the picture, sometimes called his 'Apotheosis'), is said to have gazed upon this picture constantly while on his deathbed. Among the 17th- and 18th-century French works on display are paintings by Poussin and Watteau.

16th–17th-century Spanish Art

To appreciate the genius of Domenikos Theotocopoulos, better known as El Greco (1540–1614), there is no substitute for a visit to the museums of Toledo, but there are some fine examples of what are sometimes called his 'vertical pictures' in the Prado, including *The Annunciation* and *The Adoration of the Shepherds*, mannerist depictions of biblical figures with elongated limbs and faces. El Greco was also a skilled portraitist and his *Nobleman with his Hand on his Chest* is particularly haunting. By the 17th century, the religious pathology of the age becomes manifest, notably in a disturbing painting by Francisco Ribalta of the crucified Christ leaning down off the Cross to embrace St Bernard. Elsewhere, St Bernard comes in for more abuse, this time at the hand of Alonso Cano, who illustrates the old tale of the praying saint receiving a squirt of milk in his mouth from the breast of an image of the Virgin.

Other, uneven, works by Spanish Baroque masters fill a dozen galleries: José de Ribera (1591–1652), Francisco de Zurbarán (1598–1664) and Bartolomé Esteban Murillo (1618–1682) among others. Ribera was a follower of Caravaggio's style and he used dark colours, starkly lit, to suggest pious asceticism, pain, suffering, and earthy sensual pleasure. His paintings of mythological and religious subjects (such as *St Andrew* and *The Martyrdom of St Philip*) are shot through with sinister undercurrents; he was particularly keen on using scruffy urchins and decaying beggars as models in order to inject warts-and-all realism into his work. Zurbarán was a Sevillian contemporary of Velázquez, but was totally unlike him in style. The Prado has some examples of his finely worked still lifes; these have a sacramental quality, with everyday objects laid out like devotional offerings. Murillo churned out plenty of sentimental tosh, some of which has found its way here, but his *Holy Family* (1650) is sweet and unaffected; it is a lovingly painted moment, showing the toddler Jesus playing with a small dog, gently encouraged by his doting parents.

Velázquez

On a day when there are as many Spaniards as foreigners in the Prado, the crowds around the works of Diego de Silva y Velázquez (1599–1660) can be daunting. Many Spanish consider their countryman to be the greatest artist of all, and you may find his several rooms here, the largest Velázquez collection by far, to be a convincing argument. Many of the works have recently been cleaned or restored, making the audacity of his use of light and colour stand out even more clearly. Almost all of his best-known paintings are here: *Los Borrachos* (The Drunkards), *Las Hilanderas* (The Spinning-Women), and *The Surrender of Breda*, which the Spaniards call *Las Lanzas* (the Lances). There are portraits of court dwarves, such as *Francisco Lezcano*, in which he gave his small sitters an air of humanity and dignity generally denied them in daily life (dwarves were employed as court jesters and were treated much like children, or worse). Also present are the royal portraits: lumpy, bewildered Felipe IV, a king aware enough of his own inadequacies to let Velázquez express them on canvas, appears in various poses—as a hunter, a warrior, or simply standing around wondering what's for dinner. Of his children, we see the six-year-old *Infante Balthasar Carlos* in a charming, mock-heroic pose on horseback, and again at the age of 16. It was this prince's untimely death soon after the latter portrait that gave the throne to the idiot Carlos II. His sister, the doll-like Infanta Margarita, appears by herself and in the most celebrated of all Velázquez's works, *Las Meninas* (the Maids-of-Honour, 1656), a composition of such inexhaustible complexity and beauty that the Prado gives it pride of place. In it, not only does Velázquez capture eloquently the everyday atmosphere of the Spanish court (the little princess, her bizarre entourage, and, unseen except for in a mirror in the background, her royal parents), he also turns the then-accepted artistic limits of perspective and dimensional space inside out. Velázquez painted himself in the picture, but the red cross on his tunic, the badge of the Order of Santiago, was added by King Felipe's own hand, as a graceful way of informing the artist of the honour he was conferring on him.

Goya

Like Velázquez, Francisco de Goya y Lucientes (1746–1828) held the office of court painter, in this case at the service of an even more useless monarch, Carlos IV. Also like Velázquez, he was hardly inclined to flattery. Critics ever since have wondered how he got away with making his royal patron look so foolish, and the job he did on Carlos' wife, the hook-nosed, ignorant and ill-tempered Queen Maria Luisa, is legendary. In every portrait and family scene, she comes out looking half fairy-tale witch, half washerwoman. Her son, later to be the reactionary King Fernando VII, is pictured as a teenager, and Goya makes him merely disagreeable and menacing.

Among the other famous Goyas you may compare the *Maja Desnuda* and the *Maja Vestida* (the Naked and Clothed Majas), and the *Dos de Mayo* and *Los Fusilamentos de Moncloa*, the pair commemorating the uprising of 1808 and its aftermath. The latter, much the better known, shows the impassioned patriots' faces caught in the glare of a lantern, facing the firing squad of grim, almost mechanical French soldiers. Nothing like it had ever been painted before, an unforgettable image and a prophetic prelude to the era of revolutions, mass politics and total war that was just beginning, inaugurated by the French Revolution and Napoleon. The setting is Madrid's Casa de Campo, and the spires of the old town can be made out clearly in the background. Representing his early work, Goya's remarkable *cartoons*—designs for tapestries to be made by the Royal Factories for the king's palaces—provide a massive dose of joy and sweetness, with their vivid colours bathed in clear Castilian sunshine. Most, such as *El Quitasol* (the Parasol) and *La Fiesta de San Isidro* are idealized scenes of festivals or country life, and the creatures inhabiting them seem less Spaniards than angels.

In stark contrast are some of the Prado's greatest treasures, its collection of Goya's *Pinturas Negras* ('Black Paintings'), late works which are separated from the others by a staircase as if it were feared they would contaminate the sunnier paintings upstairs. All the well-known images of dark fantasy and terror are here: *Saturn Devouring One of his Sons*, *Duel with Cudgels*, *The Colussus (Panic)*. One, a nightmarish vision of the procession at Madrid's festival of San Isidro, can be compared with another, naturalistic painting he did of the festival that can be seen upstairs.

Casón del Buen Retiro

> *C/ Alfonso XII 28, ⓒ 91 420 26 28, ⓮ 91 429 29 30, ⓜRetiro. Opening times as Museo del Prado, above.*

The Prado's collection of 19th-century Spanish art is housed in an ungainly 17th-century building intended as a ballroom for Felipe IV (part of the Palacio del Buen Retiro), near the entrance to the Retiro Park. Its ground floor Grand Salon, where the largest and most impressive canvases are hung, retains its original over-the-top Baroque ceiling, painted by Luca Giordano. The Casón del Buen Retiro is far more famous for the paintings it has lost (notably Picasso's *Guernica*) than for the paintings it still holds. Many of these differ little from the bland naturalistic art of the rest of 19th-century Europe, but there are enough little-known gems in the collection to make it worth a visit if you have some time to spare.

Painters like Mariano Fortuny (1838–1874), Joaquín Sorolla (1863–1923) and the Madrazo family were popular in their day, and are well represented here: the collection opens with a blockbusting neoclassical work by José de Madrazo, his *Death of Viriazo*. Outstanding in a clutch of portraits by Vicente López is a fascinating study of *Goya*, holding his palette and brushes and looking grumpy, and a frank portrait of the blind and decrepit but sweet-faced *Infante Don Antonio*. In each, López expertly captures the essence of the sitter in the set of their facial features, rather than by merely recreating their environment or their pose. On the way upstairs to the Romantic section of the collection is a huge canvas by José Casado del Alisal, *The Surrender of Bailén*, painted in homage to Velázquez' *The Lances*. The Romantic works include paintings by Eugenio Lucas, Leonardo Alenza and Francisco Lameyer, all powerfully influenced by Goya; and Federico de Madrazo's wonderfully wry, flirtatious *Countess of Vilches*, in a room full of stuffy portraits. Among the works by Fortuny is his *Old Man Naked in the Sun*, a study of old age in all its gnarled glory; and Sorolla's sandy-bottomed *Children at the Beach* is a wonderful, luminously lit evocation of boyhood. A few rooms on both the first and the ground floors contain landscapes; of these Santiago Rusiñol's modernist *Garden in Aranjuez* will strike chords in anyone who has visited the gardens of Aranjuez' royal palaces.

The climax of a visit to the Casón del Buen Retiro is without a doubt the Grand Salon, where *Guernica* once hung, now replaced by monumental works by José Moreno Carbonero, Francisco Pradilla, Antonio Gisbert, Eduardo Rosales and others. Carbonero's *Prince Charles of Viana* depicts a cowed prince in a shambolic library, dusty and neglected, resigned to a hermit-like life having been passed over for the Aragonese throne; and his *Conversion of the Duke of Gandía* shows remarkable emotional control, especially for an artist of only 24 years. Here the putrefying corpse on display is Isabella, wife of Charles V. To say that Pradilla's *Doña Juana the Madwoman* and Gisbert's *Execution of Torrijos and his Comrades* are chilling in their realism does them both scant justice; these are among these artists' finest works. Last in the collection is Juan Gris' *Portrait of Josette*, looking forlorn and left-behind; it should have followed the other 20th-century works to the Reina Sofía but the insistence of its donor, the collector Douglas Cooper, keeps it in the Prado.

Museo Nacional Centro de Arte Reina Sofía

C/ Santa Isabel 52, ☎ 91 467 50 62, ▣ 91 539 68 24, Ⓜ Atocha. Open Mon–Sat, 10–9, Sun, 10–2.30, closed Tues; guided tours Mon, Wed, 5pm, Sat, 11am; adm 400 pts, concessions 200 pts, free Sat after 2 and Sun; 'Paseo del Arte' voucher allowing one visit to each of the Paseo del Arte museums, 1050 pts.

With the continuing success of ARCO, Madrid's annual contemporary art fair, founded in the early 1980s, and with promising work emerging from local artists, the *madrileños*' active interest in modern art has never been at such a high. It was partly in order to satisfy this popular passion that the Spanish government set about providing their capital with a world-class 20th-century art museum, to replace the old Museo Español de Arte Contemporáneo.

Conversion of Madrid's defunct General Hospital, near Atocha station, began in 1980 and the Centro de Arte Reina Sofía opened to the public in 1986. Cynics muttered that the timing of the opening was no more than a vote-catching ploy in this, an election year, since the building wasn't actually ready—the air conditioning, for example, was woefully inadequate. After this abortive inauguration, it was back to the drawing board, and, four years and several more millions later, a second opening ceremony was held. The building, graced by its three new landmark glass lifts (or 'crystal towers'), was by now fully equipped to house both temporary exhibitions and a permanent collection of art; all it lacked was a quorum of internationally famous paintings. It was two more years, however, before the Reina Sofía really made its debut as an art centre to be reckoned with: in 1992, Spain's golden year, Picasso's *Guernica* was moved here from the Prado's annexe, the Casón del Buen Retiro. The move was a controversial one. It had been Picasso's wish that New York's Museum of Modern Art should return the painting to Spain when liberty was restored there, and that it should hang in the Prado, as a gesture towards the modernization of that collection. His wish was granted in 1981, and millions of Spaniards made the pilgrimage to the Prado to see a part of their history denied them under 40 years of dictatorship. When the Spanish government proposed the removal of the painting to the Reina Sofía, there were bitter objections from Picasso's surviving relatives, but these were over-ruled in the interests of the fulfilment of a master plan: the Prado was to hold the Old Masters, the Casón del Buen Retiro the 19th-century art, and the Reina Sofía the 20th-century works, with *Guernica*, arguably this century's most famous painting, taking pride of place. It is hung, behind ominously thick bullet-proof glass, in a large room that has more of the air of a shrine than of a gallery.

One of the Reina Sofía's greatest assets is the huge amount of space it has at its disposal. As well as having plenty of room for its permanent collection, it has large gallery spaces for temporary exhibitions. There is also an excellent bookshop, a decent café/restaurant, an oasis of a sculpture garden, a library, a music archive and education unit, and enough supplementary resource areas to fully justify its status as an energetic multimedia community arts centre.

The Main Collection

The Reina Sofía's permanent collection contains works by every one of Spain's most celebrated 20th-century artists, which together amount to solid evidence, if any were needed, to back up the nation's claim to the title of contemporary creative super-power. Pablo Picasso, Salvador Dalí, Joan Miró, Juan Gris, Julio González, Antoni Tàpies, José Gutiérrez Solana and Antonio Saura are all represented. The paintings, sketches and sculptures occupy the second floor of the building and are grouped, room by room, chronologically and according to stylistic or conceptual affinity; you'll find you have to weave about a little to follow the intended order of the rooms.

Picasso's stern-faced *Woman in Blue* (1901) presides over the opening rooms, which aim to set the scene for the avant-garde works to come. This painting had a lucky escape from oblivion when Picasso disowned it after it failed to receive much recognition at a show; years later it was discovered by a private collector. In Solana's *Tertulia del Café de Pombo* (1920) we are given a sombre glimpse of that typically Madrileñan institution of the late 19th and early 20th century—the *tertulia*, a gathering of intellectuals in a city café. Solana includes himself in the coterie. The next, small, room is devoted to Julio González (1876–1942); sketches line the walls but it's the sculpture—thirteen pieces in rows like cups in a trophy cupboard—that is remarkable, given that González was the first to render iron an artistic medium and to speak as much with void space as with solid material. There is more superb avant-garde sculpture in the Cubist section, the work of González' colleague Pablo Gargallo (1881–1934): fluid traceries, deconstructed busts and skin-skeletons in bronze and iron. In a room containing a whole wall full of works by Juan Gris, it is one small Picasso that dominates, his *Still Life (Dead Birds)* (1912). Nearby are three early works by Dalí, showing him dabbling in the Cubist style—fascinating precursors to the better known works exhibited later in the collection. Significant numbers of Spanish artists took up residence in Paris between the wars and a room groups together a selection of their output, including sweetly nostalgic works such as the evocative *Joy of the Basque Country* (1920) by Daniel Vázquez Díaz and *Cadaqués Landscape* (1923) by Dalí. These two paintings show fascinating similarities in structure and style.

The Reina Sofía's collection of mature surrealist art kicks off with a room full of minor names, including Ramón Marinello's wonderful *Figures in Front of the Sea* (1936)—organic plaster and wood reliefs in simple white—plus some supernatural looking Miró portraits, but it is easy to be distracted from these with *Guernica* just a room away. Picasso (1881–1973) began work on *Guernica* in May 1937, in immediate response to the events of the previous month. When the German Condor Legion practised its new theory of saturation bombing on the Basque town of Guernica in April 1937, Franco most likely had not been informed. Nevertheless, the

Nationalists were forced to create an elaborate lie—they said the Communists had planted bombs in the sewers—and it became the official version up until Franco's death. As for the painting itself, there are as many interpretations as critics; *Guernica* is much more than a moment of terror caught in the glare of an electric bulb. As can be seen from Picasso's preliminary sketches displayed on either side of the painting, the fallen horse and rider in the centre were in the artist's mind from the beginning. In them perhaps we can see the origins of Guernica's destroyers: the man on horseback, the bully, the crusader, the *caudillo*, meeting a bad end from his own designs, while Picasso's primaeval bull looks dispassionately on.

In a room that groups together realist works is an interesting juxtaposition of three works by José de Togores (*Nudes on a Beach*, 1922), Velasco (*Adam and Eve*, 1932) and Balbuena (*Nude*, 1932), each exhibiting an obsessive, almost architectural interest in the smooth rendering of the human form. Salvador Dalí's famous *Girl's Back* (1925) completes the sequence. Dalí's best-known works are given a whole room to themselves; particularly outstanding are *Girl at the Window*, *The Enigma of Hitler* and *The Great Masturbator*.

The Spanish art scene in the 1940s was characterized by a desire to rebuild and regroup in the wake of the Civil War. Post-war trauma is evident in some of the '40s works exhibited here; more optimistic and flippant is Eugenio Granell's *The Pleasure of the Bath* (1943). As the Forties gave way to the Fifties a more liberal mood of catharsis took hold and among the works from this period are spikey scuptures by Eduardo Chillida and Pablo Serrano; ripped, rucked and daubed fabric works by Millares; and stark textured monochromes by Tàpies, Cuixart and others. These are followed by a room of 1970s Mirós—if you're a fan of his earlier work these may disappoint, but there are some interesting, primevally figurative sculptures made of *objets trouvés*—and a room of constructive art, including boxy sculptures by Jorge de Oteiza from the 1950s. The remaining rooms, titled Proposals, are a wonderful mixed bag of relatively recent works including Picasso's spontaneously charming *Painter and Model* series; Tàpies' texture studies; Soto's rather staggering *Yellow and White Extension*; and Schnabel's vast, lucid *Buen Retiro Ducks* series, painted as a gift to the Spanish people.

Museo Colección Thyssen-Bornemisza

Palacio de Villahermosa, Paseo del Prado 8, ☏ 91 420 39 44, ✉ 91 420 27 80, Ⓜ Atocha or Banco de España. Open Tues–Sun 10–7, closed Mon; adm 600 pts, concessions 350 pts; 'Paseo del Arte' voucher allowing one visit to each of the Paseo del Arte museums, 1050 pts.

The directors of the Reina Sofía, reeling from the media response to the controversies surrounding their early policies, were glad to have the spotlight eased off them for a while in 1993, when everyone's attention switched up the road to the Villahermosa Palace. Thanks to the persuasiveness of his wife, Carmen 'La Tita' Cervera, a former Miss Spain, Baron Hans-Heinrich Thyssen-Bornemisza had already decided on Madrid as the temporary home for the cream of his unique collection of art (Madrid having outbid other cities including London, represented by none other than Prince Charles). In 1993, the arrangement was made permanent: the Spanish government purchased the collection for the extremely reasonable sum of 44,000 million pesetas. Despite the recession, and the further millions required to convert the palace building to receive the collection, the acquisition seemed to represent an unmissable opportunity to boost Madrid's, and Spain's, already high profile on the international art scene.

The collection, started in the 1920s by the present baron's father, Baron Heinrich Thyssen-Bornemisza, is idiosyncratic, eclectic and fun, and offers a fascinating insight into the personal taste of two men with a magpie-like compulsion. Like a prized and precious stamp collection, the museum contains a little of everything—there's an entry on practically every page of art history, from the religious works of 13th-century Italy to the brash output of Europe and the US in the 1960s and '70s—with the Barons' particular favourites represented in larger quantities (they liked 19th-century American painting; you might not). The present Baron Thyssen is a standard bearer of art for the modern world and his is widely regarded as the world's finest private art collection after that of the British Royal Family. He has claimed that he learned all he knows about art appreciation simply by hanging his pictures up and looking at them; with an approach as honest and pragmatic as this it is wholly consistent that he decided to make it possible for the general public to share his enjoyment of his collection.

The architect Rafael Moneo had a shell of a building out of which to create the gallery spaces, and his finished work, the walls washed in a warm cross between salmon and terracotta and bathed in a very pleasing balance of natural and artificial light, is extremely successful. The chronological sequence of works begins on the top floor (reached by the lift or stairs towards the centre of the building) and works its way, anticlockwise, downwards. The sequence was arranged like this so that the modern works could benefit from being hung in the high-ceilinged ground floor rooms. In the basement is a café and a space for temporary exhibitions.

Second Floor

The collection opens with one of its highlights, a treasure trove of gems of primitive and medieval Italian religious art, including a hauntingly simple and lovely 13th-century statue of the Madonna and Child, and some 14th-century gilded panels of exquisite beauty. These are followed by 15th-century works from the Low Countries, among them Jan van Eyck's stirring and brilliantly executed monochrome *Annunciation Diptych* (*c.* 1435–1441), depicting stone sculptures of the Angel Gabriel and the Virgin Mary with the Holy Spirit fluttering above her head in the shape of a dove. *Clothing the Naked* (*c.* 1470) by the Master of Saint Gudule offers an interesting illustration of the development of perspective techniques: a courtyard recedes, like a stage set, behind the figures in the foreground. Rogier van der Weyden's tiny, immaculate *Madonna Enthroned* (*c.* 1433), showing the Virgin in a stone alcove carved with New Testament scenes, is a fascinating point of reference for his large, slightly later work, *The Descent from the Cross*, which hangs in the Prado. Beside this is Petrus Christus' symbolic masterpiece, *Our Lady of the Dry Tree* (*c.* 1450). The next room contains 15th-century Italian works such as Bramantino's spooky, cadaverous *Resurrected Christ*.

Early Renaissance portraits form another high point of the collection. There are plenty of familiar faces here, including Holbein's *Henry VIII* (*c.* 1534–36), Memling's *Young Man at Prayer* (*c.* 1485), Campin's uncompromisingly crisp *Stout Man* (*c.* 1485) and Messina's *Portrait of a Man* (*c.* 1475–76), whose eyes fix you with a direct, intelligent gaze. There is also a *Portrait of Giovanna Tornabuoni* (1488) by Domenico Ghirlandaio, one-time tutor to Michaelangelo, who includes a Latin inscription behind the sitter's elegant neck alluding to the duality of the outer and inner aspects of beauty; it translates as: 'if art could portray character and virtue, no painting in the world would be more beautiful'.

Alongside the Villahermosa Gallery, devoted to the decorative arts, are a row of galleries containing 16th-century paintings. Vittore Carpaccio's *Young Knight in a Landscape* (1510) is one of the Thyssen's most famous works, remarkable for its richly detailed allegorical back-drop. Among the German works is Dürer's *Jesus among the Doctors* (1506), a brilliant, oppressively compact composition built around a central motif of two pairs of hands: the youthful ones of Jesus and the sinewy ones of one of the six suspicious-looking priests that seem to be closing in on him. In the same room is another of the Thyssen's signature works, Hans Baldung Grien's *Portrait of a Woman* (1530). Among the 16th- and 17th-century paintings in the following rooms are classic works by El Greco and Titian, Caravaggio and Ribera, followed by Baroque canvases, and, as the collection takes a diversion into 18th-century Italy, a couple of Venetian views by Canaletto. The 17th-century Dutch paintings on display include one of the museum's many interesting juxtapositions: Matthias Stom's *The Supper at Emmaus* (*c.* 1633–39) and Hendrick ter Brugghen's *Esau Selling his Birthright* (*c.* 1627) both lend intense drama to climactic biblical moments by casting them in candlelight.

First Floor

A series of rooms are devoted to 17th-century Dutch painting, the best and most endearing of which show jolly, ribald scenes from peasant life, such as Frans Hals' skittish *Fisherman Playing the Violin* (*c.* 1630). These are followed by rococo and neoclassical works including some of the few English paintings to be found in Madrid: a portrait by Sir Joshua Reynolds, and one by Gainsborough. Next comes an even more unusual collection, possibly the only one of its kind in a European museum: paintings by 19th-century American artists. It's a mixed selection, from chocolate-boxy autumnal sunsets by Frederic Edwin Church, John Frederick Kensett and Jasper Francis Cropsey to an innovative still life by John Frederick Peto, *Tom's River* (1905), displaying a bold sense of composition that was way ahead of its time. Among other 19th-century European works are three Goyas including the delightful *El Tio Paquete*; there is also a fine work by John Constable, *The Lock*, 1824, full of silvery highlights and rich colours, a fitting prelude to the selection of impressionist paintings, which is sadly rather slim (although it does contains a lovely Renoir, his *Woman with a Parasol in a Garden*). The post-impressionists and Fauve painters are rather better represented: a gloriously lurid Van Gogh, a Cézanne *Portrait of a Farmer* (1901–6), relaxing cross-legged in dappled blue shade, some Degas ballerinas, an example of Gauguin's ethnic preoccupations (*Mata Mua*, 1892), and some riotously coloured works by Dufy, Derain and Vlaminck.

The Thyssen's collection of expressionist painting is particularly strong. Some of its leading exponents are here: Ernst Ludwig Kirchner (1880–1938), Max Beckmann (1884–1950) and Egon Schiele (1890–1918). Otto Dix's quasi-photographic *Hugo Erfurth with a Dog* stands out in a room full of confident works. From Christian Schad there is his discomforting *Portrait of Doctor Haustein* (1928), a tense, psychologically charged work in which the doctor of the title stares out at the viewer, his very smooth hands clasped off-centre, while behind him looms the menacing, distorted shadow of his mistress with a hint of smoke at her lips. Doctor Haustein's infidelity was one of the factors that pushed his wife to suicide; he himself took poison in 1933 rather than be captured by the Gestapo.

Ground Floor

A radical change in atmosphere marks the beginning of the Thyssen's collection from the experimental avant-gardes. There is plenty of space to appreciate the scale of the Mondrians (two of them, *Composition I* (1931), and *New York City, New York* (1942)) and Filonov's astoundingly complex untitled canvas. Cubism is represented by its three brightest stars,

Georges Braque, Pablo Picasso and Juan Gris. A section entitled 'The Synthesis of Modernism' contains Chagall's delightful, dreamlike *The Rooster* (1929), and more paintings by Picasso and Braque, plus glittering works by Ernst, Klee, Kandinsky, Léger and Miró, followed by American modernists: Mark Rothko, Georgia O'Keeffe, Jackson Pollock.

Along with a Magritte and other surrealist works, Baron Thyssen got his hands on an excellent Dalí, his *Dream caused by the Flight of a Bee Around a Pomegranate a Second before Awakening* (1944), but it is the very last section that contains arguably the best work in the whole museum: Richard Estes' multi-layered slices of New York (*Telephone Booths*, 1967); a characteristically disturbing Francis Bacon (*Portrait of George Dyer in a Mirror*, 1968); an unforgettable Lichtenstein (*Woman in the Bath*, 1963), in which every dot really is painted by hand to look like a screened print; a Hockney (*In Memoriam of Cecchio Bracci*, 1962), and a startling Tom Wesselmann (*Nude No.1*, 1970).

Parque del Buen Retiro

In the days of Felipe IV, this entire area was a royal preserve, including a fortress, a palace (of which only the Casón del Buen Retiro survives) and this park, begun by the Conde-Duque Olivares in 1636 for Felipe. Apart from growing smaller—it once extended westwards to the Paseo del Prado—the Retiro has changed essentially little since, an elegant, formal garden, perfect for the decorous pageants and dalliances of the Baroque era. Visit the Retiro in spring, when the tulips and horse-chestnut trees are in bloom; failing that, come on any Sunday, when all Madrid comes to see the flowers, concerts and other impromptu entertainments. If you would like a carriage ride, wait at the little cabin marked '*servicio de simones*' near the entrance opposite Calle Antonio Maura. The centre of the Retiro is a broad lagoon called **El Estanque**, where you may rent canoes or paddleboats. No king ever did less to earn such a grandiose memorial than Alfonso XII (1874–86), but that's him up on horseback decorating the eastern end of the Estanque. In the 17th century, this was a favourite spot for royal diversions: water pageants and plays. One of the best remembered was a royal performance of Calderón's *Polifemo y Circe* and *Los Incantos de Circe* in 1663; artificial islands were built for the action, while the audience sat around the edge of the Estanque. The whole of it took nine hours, including battles, sea voyages in miniature galleys and Odysseus' trip to the Underworld.

Other attractions of the Retiro include the **Palacio de Velázquez** and the great, glass **Palacio de Cristal** (Crystal Palace), built in the 1890s; both have a regular schedule of cultural exhibits and shows. Among the 160-odd hectares (400 acres) of the Park are cool fountains, a Japanese garden, and towards the south, a seemingly endless expanse of quiet paths among old shady trees and gardens where you can easily forget you're in the centre of a major metropolis. Sandwiched between the Retiro's southwestern corner and the Paseo del Prado is the **Real Jardín Botánico** (Botanical Garden), Plaza de Murillo 2, (*open daily, 10–7, winter, 10–dusk*), a particularly special urban oasis which was commissioned by Carlos III in the 18th century. An estimated 30,000 plants, many of them from far-flung corners of the globe, are grown here.

Museums near the Prado and Retiro Park

This neighbourhood was Madrid's fashionable centre for three centuries, and consequently attracted quite a few museums, devoted to all manner of things. Museums are about all there is here to interest the visitor these days, for this is one of the duller corners of Madrid.

Closest to the Prado, the **Museo del Ejército** (Army Museum), C/ Méndez Núñez 1, © 91 522 89 77, ⓜ Retiro (*open Tues–Sun 10–2, closed Mon; adm 100 pts, concessions 50 pts, free Sat*) pokes its scores of old cannons menacingly out at the surrounding apartment blocks. Most of the exhibits are from better days: armour and arms from the conquistadors, and from the nearly invincible infantry that made Spain a European power in the days of the Catholic Kings. El Cid's sword is here, and Boabdil el Chico's tunic, among rooms full of shiny military bric-a-brac. The Carlist and Napoleonic wars are covered, and the Civil War, too—you can get the Army's side of the story. At the moment, a question mark hangs over this museum's future, as it might be evicted and the building used as extra space for the Prado's massive collection. More interesting is the **Museo Naval** (Naval Museum), Pso. del Prado 5, © 91 379 50 55, ⓜ Banco de España (*open Tues–Sun 10.30–1.30, closed Mon; free*), in a corner of the Ministry of Defence offices. Whatever relics of the age of explorations were not locked away in Seville's Archive of the Indies ended up here. Some of the most fascinating are the maps and charts, not simple sailors' tools, but lovely works in which art and scholarship are joined. The 1375 *Atlas Catalan* is one of these, and Juan de la Cosa's *Mapa Mundi* of 1500 is the earliest Spanish map to show parts of the American coast. Another, made by Diego Rivera just 29 years later, has almost all of the Americas' Atlantic coasts, and some of the Pacific, a tribute to the work Spanish explorers had done in such a short time. Much of the Naval Museum is given over to ships' models. Some are wonderfully detailed and precise, giving real insight into the complexity and artfulness of the age of sail. Columbus' *Santa Maria* is one of these, and it is a reminder of the Admiral of Ocean Sea's achievement to see how small and frail his craft really were.

Just around the corner, the **Museo de Artes Decorativas** (Museum of Decorative Arts), C/ Montalbán 12, © 91 522 17 40, ⓜ Banco de España (*open Tues–Fri 9–3, Sat, Sun, hols, 10–2, closed Mon; adm 400 pts, concessions 200 pts, free Sat after 2, Sun*), has a comprehensive collection of furniture, costume, ceramics, and work in wood, textiles, gold and silver from the 15th to the 20th century—six floors of it, in fact, covering every aspect of Spanish design. One favourite exhibit is the lovely, tiled 18th-century Valencian kitchen on the top floor. Five minutes' walk west of the Prado on a corner of Calle de las Huertas, the **Academia Real de la Historía** (Royal Academy of History), C/ León 21, © 91 239 82 69 (*open irregularly, call for information*), maintains a small museum with some paintings by Goya, Iberian and Roman antiquities and religious art of the Middle Ages. Two streets north, the **Casa-Museo de Lope de Vega** (House of Lope de Vega), C/ Cervantes 11, © 91 429 92 16, ⓜ Antón Martín or Sevilla (*open Mon–Fri 9.30–3, Sat 10–2, closed Sun, hols, all Aug; adm 200 pts, free Sat*) has been restored by educated guesswork to how it might have looked when that great and very prolific dramatist lived there, from 1610 to his death in 1635. This is also the old neighbourhood of Cervantes (1547–1616). Though he and Lope de Vega were said to have been bitter enemies since the days they served together in the wars against the Turks, Cervantes lived on the same street, on the corner of Calle de León. *Don Quixote* was first printed nearby on Calle Atocha, and its author is buried in an unmarked grave in the Convento de las Trinitarias Descalzas, on Calle de Lope de Vega.

North of the Prado: Plaza de Cibeles to Plaza de Colón

Since the Bourbons, this area has been the most self-consciously monumental corner of Madrid, spread with impossibly wide boulevards and traffic-filled plazas, and not much fun for walking. The Paseo del Prado meets the Calle de Alcalá at Madrid's grandest roundabout, the **Plaza de la Cibeles**, where streams of traffic swirl around Ventura Rodríguez' fanciful fountain (completed in 1780) of the goddess Cybele in a carriage drawn by lions. The elaborate marble pile on the southeastern side of the plaza is nothing more than the city's main post office, named, appropriately enough, the **Palacio de Comunicaciones**. In a city as unimaginative in its architecture as Madrid, such a flagrant example of the movie-palace style popular under Dictator Primo de Rivera in the 1920s truly stands out. *Madrileños* have been making fun of it since it was built; one of the nicknames it has acquired is 'Nuestra Santa de Comunicaciones'. Buying a stamp has never felt so glamorous. East of here, the Plaza de la Independencia has for a centrepiece the stately Baroque **Puerta de Alcalá**, a sort of triumphal arch with no triumph to commemorate, built during the reign of Carlos III. Before Madrid's last set of walls was demolished in the last century, this was the actual gate on the road to Alcalá de Henares.

Joining the Paseo del Prado to the main stretch of Madrid's great north–south artery, the Paseo de la Castellana, is the Paseo de Recoletos, built in the 1830s and 1840s. Along its shady flanks are some of Madrid's most celebrated traditional cafés, among them the **Café Gijón** and **El Espejo**. In the Madrid of the 19th century, architectural tastes favoured the grandiose, and there is no better example, perhaps, than the florid pile on the Paseo de Recoletos that houses the **Biblioteca Nacional** (National Library), Pso. de Recoletos 20, *©* 91 580 7800, **Ⓜ** Colón (*open Mon–Fri 9–9, Sat 9–2*) and the **Museo Arqueológico Nacional** (National Archaeology Museum), Serrano 13, *©* 91 577 7915, **Ⓜ** Serrano or Colón (*open Tues–Sat 9.30–8.30, Sun 9.30–2.30, closed Mon; adm 400 pts, concs 200 pts, free Sat after 2.30, Sun*). By any measure, the Museo Arqueológico is the only comprehensive archaeology museum in Spain. If you can read a little Spanish, the explanations posted around the exhibits will provide a thorough education in the obscure comings and goings of Spain's shadowy prehistory. Not that the museum is limited to Spain—there is a surprisingly good collection of Greek vases, and an Egyptian room full of mummies and gaping school-children, along with some very fine jewellery and engraved seals. Many of the Greek and Egyptian relics were actually found in Spain, testimony to the close trade relations ancient Iberia enjoyed with the rest of the Mediterranean world.

A visit to this museum, however, is really a pilgrimage to the first and greatest of the great ladies of Spain, *La Dama de Elche*. Nothing we know of the history and culture of the Iberians can properly explain the presence of this beautiful 5th-century BC cult image. As a work of art she ranks among the finest sculptures of antiquity. Pre-Roman Spain was one of the backwaters of the Mediterranean, and while it would be sacrilege in Spain to suggest this lady was the work of a foreign hand, the conclusion seems inescapable. The dress and figure have much in them that is reminiscent of some eastern Mediterranean image of Cybele, and the Greeks could often capture the same expression of cold majesty on the face of an Artemis or Ariadne or Persephone. Elche, where the bust was discovered, was then in the Carthaginian zone, and that meant easy access to all the Mediterranean world; an artist from anywhere could conceivably have turned up to execute the high priests' commission. Nevertheless, many experts disagree, and find in *La Dama*'s unapproachable hauteur something distinctly Spanish. She holds court these days from a large glass case on a pedestal in the museum's main hall; when the hordes of school-children run up, pressing their noses on the glass and shouting, as thousands of them do every day, you will see the lady's expression intensify into a look of chilly disdain that is a wonder to behold. She shares the room with her less formidable cousins, the very few other Iberian goddesses that have ever been found, including the 4th-century *Dama de Baza* and the *Dama de Cerra de Los Santos*.

The Iberians of the Bronze Age were at least up-to-date in metalworking, and the collection of small expressionistic bronze figurines shows a fine talent; these are similar in many ways to the famous bronzes from the same period found in Sardinia. Spain's entry into the literate world is chronicled in a host of inscriptions from all over the country. Scholars think the language was related to modern Basque, and not surprisingly they haven't completely deciphered any of them. From the Romans, there are indifferent mosaics and copies of Greek sculpture, along with larger-than-life statues of emperors. The bronze tablets from AD 176, inscribed with the laws and orations of Septimus Severus, would have been set up in public places—a landmark in the development of political propaganda. The practice was begun by Augustus and used by several of the more energetic emperors that followed. There are also working models of the Roman catapult and ballista (a kind of gigantic crossbow) if you've ever wondered how they worked.

Spanish early Christian art is one of the Archaeology Museum's surprises. The architectural sculpture and mosaics show a strong and original sense of design, and a tendency to contemplative geometry that seems almost Islamic. The Visigoths haven't much to offer outside the Treasure of Gurrazar, a collection of vigorously barbaric bejewelled crowns and crosses, all in solid glittering gold, that were found in the Visigothic capital, Toledo. King Reccesvinth's crown (*c.* 650), the richest of all, has his name dangling from it in enamelled golden letters; to the mainly illiterate Visigoths, these must have seemed like magic symbols. A small number of Moorish and medieval Christian works complete the collection.

Outside, near the gate, a small cave has been dug to house replicas of the famous rock paintings of Altamira, very artistic representations of bisons, bulls, and other animals in red and black. The museum has gone to great lengths to copy the atmosphere of the real cave (which is now, except by special arrangement, closed to the general public)—the lighting is so realistically dim, you can barely make out the pictures.

Across the Calle de Jorge Juan from the Archaeology Museum, the **Jardines del Descubrimiento** is one of Madrid's new parks, and the great blocks of sandstone decorating it are all part of an interesting modern **Monument to Columbus**, carved with reliefs and quotes from the explorer's journals. Below the gardens, underneath the waterfall-at-the-end-of-the-world, is the **Centro Cultural de la Villa**, an arts centre with a theatre and large discussion area. Behind is a more old-fashioned Columbus monument, in the broad crossroads called the **Plaza del Colón**.

South of the Prado

In this direction, the Paseo del Prado passes the Jardín Botánico towards the shadowy districts around **Atocha**. It's not immediately obvious, but the broad square in front of the station, the Glorieta de Carlos V, represents one of the most significant environmental victories of civic-minded Madrid of the 1980s. Relatively recently, the entire plaza was buried under a ghastly, multi-level highway interchange *madrileños* called the 'scalextric' after the model racing car circuit. Mayor Tierno saw it dismantled just before he died. The original wrought iron and glass structure of Atocha station dates from the 1880s, and the station put in 100 years of faithful service until at last it was earmarked for a facelift, including major re-modelling to provide a terminal for the new Madrid to Sevilla AVE link. In 1992 Atocha re-opened as a shining new temple to rail travel, complete with an indoor shopping and eating centre which has as its centrepiece an acclimatized tropical garden, with nervous looking goldfish swimming in pools beneath soaring palm trees. Steam filters down onto this mini urban jungle through ducts in the roof. The effect is spectacular; it's a pity, then, that the glass panels in the ceiling don't let in enough light (this is boosted by banks of artificial lights), and, when planting the garden, the designers chose exotic palms rather than local ones, so many of the trees are struggling to survive.

Southeast of Atocha, you may visit a handicrafts workshop fit for kings. In the Palacio Real, El Escorial, and in all the other royal residences around Madrid hang works of the **Real Fábrica de Tapices** (Royal Tapestry Factory), C/ Fuenterrabía 2, ✆ 91 551 34 00, Ⓜ Menéndez Pelayo (*open Mon–Fri 9–12.30, closed Sat, Sun, all Aug; adm 200 pts*). Ever since Felipe IV founded it in the 1640s, the weavers of the Real Fábrica have served the Spanish elite's love of fine, pictorial tapestries—not only decorative, but a positive asset to any draughty palace during the chill Castilian winters. Its best-known productions, of course, are those woven to the designs Goya created when he was court painter, the cartoons for which are now hanging in the Prado. They are still the favoured subjects today. You may watch the master weavers at work on any weekday morning, and those with gargantuan bank accounts may even order a genuine tapestry as a souvenir.

Old Madrid

Shoehorned into a tight half kilometre between the Puerta del Sol and the Palacio Real is a solid, enduring Castilian town, often known as 'El Madrid de las Austrias' because most of it was built under the reign of the Habsburgs, and as evocative in its own way as Segovia or Toledo. Old Madrid has changed little since Goya painted its delicate skyline of cupolas and spires. Neither menaced by modern office blocks nor done up picture-pretty for the tourists, the quarter has enjoyed the best of possible fates—to remain as it was. Its residents are perhaps poorer than the city average but their presence keeps the place a living neighbourhood, loud, busy and unkempt, but still Madrid's best and cosiest refuge from the cosmopolitan noise of the rest of the city.

Plaza Mayor

Few squares in Spain are lovelier, and none is better used. Between concerts, festivals, political rallies and the popular Sunday market for stamps, coins, and trinkets, something is likely to be on when you visit. If there isn't, at least someone will be strumming a guitar on the pedestal of Felipe III's equestrian statue while all Madrid passes through and the tourists observe from the cafés. In the old days it was much the same. Kings of Spain were crowned here, and they would often return to preside over fiestas, bullfights, *autos-da-fé*, even archaic knightly tournaments. Although the Plaza is as old as Madrid, the present buildings were completed in 1619 for Felipe III. During events, the city council would rent the balconies from their owners to seat the distinguished visitors. Kings traditionally took their places in the elegant building with twin spires on the north side, the **Casa Panadería**, so called after the bakery that preceded it on the site. Its façade was decorated with colourful murals in the late 17th century and these were restored in 1992. Take time to look in the shop windows. Besides some of Madrid's best restaurants and ancient but still popular *tascas*, the streets around the Plaza Mayor are home to the queerest shops in all Spain. Just outside the Plaza there's a place that sells comic books from around the world; another, on the Calle Mayor, features Guardia Civil regalia and little ceramic statues of Franco. Off the Calle de Toledo is a shop claiming to sell the biggest sizes of ladies' lingerie in the world. Its lovingly designed window displays may well be the most unforgettable sight Madrid can offer.

Plaza de la Villa, La Latina and Lavapiés

Just a couple of hundred metres west of the Plaza Mayor, on Calle Mayor, some of Madrid's oldest buildings can be seen around the **Plaza de la Villa**. The **Ayuntamiento**, built in 1640 by Gomez de Mora, the same architect who created the Plaza Mayor, is one of Madrid's finest buildings. Across the square, the 15th-century **Torre de los Lujanes** once served as a prison for no less a personage than King François I of France. This monarch, bitterest enemy of Charles V and Habsburg ambition, was captured by the Spanish at the Battle of Pavia in Italy in 1525. He spent a few months as Charles' unwilling guest here, and won his release by signing a treaty and agreeing to marry Charles' sister; once safely over the border, he said it was all a joke, and he and Charles were at war for most of the next 20 years. Near the square, at Calle Mayor 59, is a rare example of blooming Art Nouveau, a style that was never as popular in this serious city as elsewhere in Spain. The old house next door was once home to Calderón de la Barca. Just a few yards west, the streets around the charmingly rickety glass-and-steel **Mercado de San Miguel** (San Miguel Market) make up the busiest and most colourful corner of old Madrid.To the south, the Plaza del Humilladero, the Plaza de Cascorro, and the Plaza Tirso de Molina are centres of the **La Latina** neighbourhood, the heart of old Madrid and a run-down but pleasant place for a stroll. Every morning, but especially on Sundays, the stretch of Calle de Ribera de Curtadores south of Cascorro is home to Spain's best known and longest running flea market, **El Rastro** (*see* 'Shopping', p.430).

Bordering the Rastro to the east is **Lavapiés**, perhaps Madrid's most distinctively *castizo* district (*castizos* being the *madrileño* equivalent of London's cockneys). Lavapiés is also the base for many of the city's fringe theatre companies. As such, it is a colourful and characterful, if not wholly salubrious, area. At C/ Tribulete 12 is **La Corrala**, a part-preserved example of a late 19th-century tenement block built around an open courtyard.

A Few Old Churches and a Nunnery

Despite its four centuries as capital of Catholic Spain, Madrid amazingly does not have a single church worth going out of your way to visit. It didn't even have a proper cathedral until the official opening in 1992 of the **Catedral de Santa María Real de la Almudena**, C/ Bailén, © 91 542 22 00, **Ⓜ** Opera (*open Mon–Sat 10–1.30 and 6–8.45, Sun 10–2 and 6–8.45; mass daily at noon and 8pm, Sun, at 11, 12, 1.30 and 8*). It was over 100 years in the building; the delays were political and bureaucratic and the cathedral has never been much loved. Nevertheless, its dedication was marked with some ceremony, with, in June 1993, the Pope making a visit to honour the new cathedral with his blessing (feted by enthusiastic Madrileño Catholics who showered him with yellow and white confetti, made, true to Madrid's public commitment to recycling, from chopped-up phone directories). Founded on the site of the old Almudena Mosque, the most beautiful part of this bulky, ungainly building is its high ceiling of triangular panels painted with Moorish-inspired patterns in muted earthy reds, browns and greens. Overall, the cathedral feels light and airy, but empty; the abstract stained glass adds much needed splashes of colour. Before 1992, Madrid had a stand-in cathedral in the shape of the huge, twin-towered **Catedral de San Isidro**, C/ Toledo 7, near Puerta Cerrada, ✆ 91 369 23 10, Ⓜ La Latina (*open Mon–Sat 8.30–12.30 and 6.30–8.30, Sun and hols, 9–2 and 5.30–8.30*), really a monastery church, built for Madrid's Jesuit community in the 1620s, with an elaborate Churrigueresque façade added later. This church was dedicated to Madrid's patron saint by Carlos III, and Isidro's remains are still here. A few streets away, on the Plaza de la Paja, the **Iglesia de San Andrés** is more typical of the blank, severe style of Madrid's older parishes. San Andrés was burnt during the Civil War, and both it and the Plaza have recently been restored. The city has a plan of rehabilitation here that it hopes will lead to a rebirth of interest in this quiet, pretty corner of town. Madrid's largest church, the **Basílica de San Francisco el Grande** (1785, restored 1890) is at the foot of the Carretera de San Francisco (Pza. de San Francisco, ✆ 91 365 38 00, Ⓜ Puerto de Toledo; *open summer, Tues–Sat 11–1 and 5–8; winter, 11–1 and 4–7.*) With a dome almost 30m in diameter, it does live up to its name, but there's little more to say for it, only that it too is under restoration.

North of the Calle Mayor, off Calle Arenal, is the **Monasterio de las Descalzas Reales** (Pza. de las Descalzas, ✆ 91 542 00 59, Ⓜ Sol or Callao, *open Tues–Thurs, Sat, 10.30–12.30 and 4–5.30, Fri 10.30–12.30, Sun, hols, 11–1.30, closed Mon; adm 650 pts, concessions 250 pts, free Wed*). To visit it, you'll have to submit to a guided tour, but there are paintings by Brueghel and Zurbarán inside, and several centuries' accumulation of rich tapestries, furniture, art and holy relics. The convent, from the 17th century, is the branch office of the order founded by Santa Teresa, the shoeless (*descalza*) Carmelites, sworn to poverty and pious observance. When Charles V's daughter, Juana of Austria, entered, though, fashion was not far behind, and the Royal Barefoots soon became the richest prestige nunnery in Christendom, attracting even a German empress for a short stay. You may notice one of the dusty portraits is of Charles' sister, the one François I agreed to marry. You'll see what changed his mind.

Palacio Real (Royal Palace)

> C/ Bailén, ✆ 91 542 00 59, Ⓜ Opera. Open, summer, Mon–Sat 9–6, Sun and hols, 9–3; winter, Mon–Sat 9.30–5, Sun and hols 9–12; adm 850 pts, concessions 350 pts, free to EU passport holders on Wed. Tours are given in English and other languages.

Any self-respecting Bourbon had to have one. Felipe V, who commissioned it in 1738, had to be talked out of an even grander version by his wife, who thought 2800 rooms would probably meet her needs. The palace entrance is off the now pedestrianised Plaza de Oriente, lined with statues of the earliest Spanish kings; originally intended to go on the building (they were too heavy). The guided tour doesn't take you through all 2800 rooms, but it takes you through plenty all the same; a mild delirium soon sets in, and one loses count. Each has a tapestry from the Real Fábrica, portraits of bewigged sycophants, a nice inlaid table, a half-ton chandelier, and indolent mythological deities painted on the ceiling. If you're serious about such things, persevere, and you will be rewarded with works by El Greco and Goya, as well as Rubens, Van der Weyden and Watteau, and many other favourites of the age. One room is full of gold clocks, and if your tour is lucky enough to hit it at noon, you can hear them all go off, a delicate symphony of bells and chimes.

Originally this was the site of the Moorish Alcázar, converted by Enrique IV into Madrid's first Royal Palace. It was here that Velázquez lived and painted for Felipe IV, and many of his works are infused with the atmosphere of its old, dark chambers. A great fire occasioned the 18th-century replacement, very much in the style of Versailles and other contemporary palaces. The exterior is grand and elegant enough, the effect heightened by its setting on a bluff above the Manzanares. Alfonso XIII was the last king to use the Palace as a residence. Juan Carlos' tastes are much more modest; he lives quite comfortably at the suburban Zarzuela Palace, without any semblance of an old-style court. The Palace is used today only for important state occasions; during these it will be closed.

Tickets are sold separately for the **Armería Real** (Royal Armoury), and the **Museo de Carruajes** (Museum of Carriages), both situated in the palace grounds. The Armoury is interesting. Charles V, living in an age when the medieval manner of warfare was rapidly becoming obsolete, had a truly Quixotic fascination for armour. His collection makes up most of what you see today. Some of the suits and weapons are functional, but most were never meant to be anything but decorative, something a king could cut a fine figure in on campaigns or in the old-fashioned jousts that were still popular with the nobility. Two formal parks make up the grounds of the Palacio Real, the **Campo del Moro** towards the Manzanares, and the smaller **Jardines Sabatini**. The southern wings of the palace enclose a courtyard big enough to hold the entire Plaza Mayor, buildings and all.

The Royal Opera House

Plaza de Isabel II, **Ⓜ** *Opera.*

In 1997, Madrid's Teatro Real opera house reopened after a 72-year break. Built in 1850 under the reign of Isabel II, the theatre closed in 1925, supposedly for refurbishment. Civil war followed by 40 years of Franco (who couldn't even be bothered to finish off construction of the nearby cathedral) puts the delay into context. Political infighting delayed reconstruction for more than a decade. From the outside, the building is little changed, although the area around it has undergone a revival, with a pedestrian area extending over to the Royal Palace. The opera house offers a varied programme, and seat prices are, by British and American standards, reasonable, with top seats weighing in at 20,000 pts, and a seat in the gods for 800 pts.

Ermita de San Antonio de la Florida

Pso. de la Florida 5, **Ⓒ** *91 542 07 22,* **Ⓜ** *Príncipe Pío. Open Tues–Fri, 10–2 and 4-8, Sat–Sun, 10–2, closed Mon and hols; adm 300 pts, concessions 200 pts, free Wed.*

From the Campo del Moro, you can walk a few blocks up the bank of the Manzanares, flowing gamely with its borrowed water, to a plain, tiny chapel tucked between the river and the railyards of the Estación de Príncipe Pío. Few tourists ever find their way up here, but inside is one of the milestones of Spanish art. In 1798, Goya was commissioned to do a series of frescoes on the walls, ceiling and dome, and he did them in a way no church had ever been decorated before. St Anthony, in the dome, is clearly recognizable, but that is Goya's only concession to the usual conventions of religious art. The scores of figures with which he covered the ceilings seem almost to be the same faces from his celebrated cartoons, only instead of angelic *madrileños* they have become angels in fact. Every one has the quality of a portrait; the peaceful rapture expressed in their faces has at its source nothing the Church could give, but a particular secret perhaps known only to Goya. The artist is buried here, and the church has become his monument. Week-long festivities around the 13th of June, San Antonio's day, close off the paseo at night, with traditional stalls, food and drink, and processions.

Around the Plaza de España and the Gran Vía

This is Madrid's shopping and business district replete with awkward skyscrapers, grand imperial cinemas with hand-painted billboards, American hamburger joints, and unyielding traffic swarms. You're likely to pass through the broad **Plaza de España**, with its famous Cervantes monument and bronze figures of Don Quixote and Sancho Panza, at least once; a tourist office is located here at the bottom of the Torre de Madrid. Pretty as it is, the Plaza is not a place to linger too long; a lot of Madrid's low-life congregate here. Just off the Plaza the **Museo Cerralbo**, C/ Ventura Rodríguez 17, ✆ 91 547 36 46, Ⓜ Ventuara Rodríguez or Plaza de España (*open Tues–Sat 9.30–2.30, Sun 10–2, closed Mon and hols; adm 400 pts, concessions 200 pts, free Wed and Sun*), is one of Madrid's several private collections that have become museums in their original settings—in this case, the home of a Marqués who died in the 1920s. There are paintings by Ribera and El Greco, and the lots of ambient bric-a-brac.

Running north west down from Pza España is the beautifully landscaped **Parque del Oeste**, complete with **La Rosaleda**, gardens where international rose exhibitions are held in spring each year. For a centrepiece, this park has just what you least expected, an Egyptian temple of the 4th century BC. The **Templo de Debod**, ✆ 91 409 61 65, Ⓜ Ventura Rodríguez or Plaza de España (*open Tues–Fri 10–1 and 4–9, Sat–Sun 10–1, closed Mon and hols; adm 300 pts, concessions 200 pts, free Wed*) is nothing very elaborate, but it is genuine. The Egyptian government sent it, block by block, as a gift of appreciation for Spanish help in the relocation of monuments during the building of the Aswan dam. However far it has strayed from the Nile, the little temple seems cheerfully at home, orientated to the same sunrise, looking over the peculiar city below. In July 1936, this spot was occupied by the Montaña Barracks, scene of one of the earliest and bloodiest events of the Civil War. When the government decided to arm the popular militias, they found that the bolts for most of the rifles available were locked away in the barracks, held at the time by a group of rebellious officers and Falangists. After a brief siege, some miners from Asturias managed to blow a hole in the walls, and the barracks was stormed by a mob, who killed most of those inside, throwing many alive from second story windows.

Casa de Campo

When the Habsburgs decided to make Madrid their capital, they didn't give much thought to amenities. One of their tricks was to chop down every tree of the forests that once surrounded Madrid; they sold them as firewood all over Castile, and used the money to embellish their palaces. Felipe II, an avid hunter like most of the Habsburgs, soon regretted this, and he had this tract of several square miles reforested. There was no altruism in Felipe's motives. He simply wanted a royal hunting preserve, but the Casa de Campo was the happy result, a stretch of quiet countryside, just a short walk (or bus or metro ride) from the centre of the city. The most interesting views of this park—and of the Manzanares and the Palacio Real with the city beyond—are from the cable car (**teleférico**, *open daily, in summer, 11am–dusk; winter, weekends and hols, noon–dusk*) that runs there from the Parque del Oeste. Within the Casa de Campo's boundaries are the **Parque de Atracciones** funfair and amusement park, ✆ 91

463 29 00 (*open daily, in winter Sun–Fri noon–11pm, Sat noon–1am; in summer, Sun–Thurs noon–11pm, Fri–Sat noon–3am*) where the admission fee includes most of the rides, including the 'Flume Ride', 'Top Spin' and 'Looping Star' rollercoasters, and the **Parque Zoológico**, ✆ 91 711 99 50 (*open daily, in summer 10–9.30; in winter 10–7.30; adm*), the star of which is Chulín, the first panda to be born in captivity in the West. Although rarely visible, the panda's surroundings are at least roomy, which is more than can be said for most of the zoo's inhabitants. The zoo also has a new 1.8 million-litre tropical aquarium, complete with hammerhead and other sharks.

North of the Puerta del Sol

The area immediately north of the Puerta del Sol is central Madrid's main middle-of-the-road shopping district, with pedestrian precincts crammed with chain stores. The broad, dignified Calle de Alcalá sweeps out of the Puerta del Sol to the northeast, and here, housed in the former Palacio Goyeneche, is the **Real Acadamia de Bellas Artes de San Fernando**, C/ Alcalá 13, ✆ 91 522 14 91, Ⓜ Sol or Sevilla, (*open Tues–Fri 9–7, Sat–Mon and hols, 9–2.30; adm 200 pts, concessions free*). The façade was stripped of all ornament in 1773. The rooms display a fascinating selection from the last five centuries of Spanish painting including important works by Murillo and Sorolla, a set of 20 Picasso etchings and eight remarkable life-size portraits of monks by Zurbarán. Among the Goya canvases on display is his famous *El Entierro de la Sardina* (The Burial of the Sardine), which depicts the riotous fiestas marking the end of carnival. The Burial of the Sardine continues to this day in the capital and elsewhere in Castile, with a mock funeral party of weeping women carry a coffin bearing a large papier-mâché sardine through the streets, down to the Casa de Campo, then set fire to it, to commemorate the occasion when the starving townspeople of Madrid received a long-awaited consignment of fish; on discovering, to their dismay, that it was completely rotten, they burnt it on the spot.

The Spanish Match

 Spain in the 17th century made itself the true homeland of the picaresque, the inspiration for the first novels, and Spaniards set the fashions and the manners for all Europe in the age of Baroque. Life was a stage, and a man wasn't a man until he'd gone out and had an adventure—even if he was the son of a king. In Calle de las Infantas, just north of the Gran Vía, there stands an old residence called the 'Casa de las Siete Chimeneas', the house of seven chimneys. In 1623, this house belonged to John Digby, Earl of Bristol, in Spain on government business, and in March of that year it received a very unusual lodger—none other than the 21-year-old Prince of Wales, the future Charles II. With his friend the Duke of Buckingham, Charles had travelled to Spain incognito, under the names of 'John Brown and Tom Smith'. The Earl, who was keeping an eye on Charles for his father, James I, wrote home that the pair were 'sweet boys and dear virtuous knights, worthy to be put in a new romanso'. The visit had a purpose; Spain and England were enjoying a rare period of peace, and there was talk of marrying Charles to the Infanta Doña Maria. Naturally, he wanted to have a look at her first. Riding to Spain was the easy part; getting into the court of Philip IV, who didn't much care for Protestant heretics, proved much harder. Charles first saw his Infanta

when their coaches passed in a Madrid street; later, go-betweens managed to contrive a meeting during the *paseo* on the Prado—Charles would know her by the blue ribbon in her hair. When word of this got out, Charles' presence could no longer be kept a secret; more and more English were arriving all the time to see the show, including King James's celebrated fool, Archie Armstrong. Finally the king consented to a state entrance for Charles in the biggest spectacle Madrid had to offer, a gala bullfight in the Plaza Mayor with all the court in attendance, watching from the balconies.

Charles apparently liked what he saw, for he tried without success to surprise the Infanta in the Casa del Campo, where she and her friends were out at dawn gathering May dew. But this is history, not a romanso, and politics made it a match never to be. Charles stayed in Madrid for six months; he met Velázquez and Van Dyck, and went back home with presents from the royal family that included paintings by Titian and Correggio, an elephant, an ostrich and five camels.

Off the northen side of Gran Vía lie the neighbourhoods of Malasaña and Chueca. A jumble of crowded streets, which by day are home to locals, and by night thronged with revellers. Malasaña still lives off its reputation as the epicentre of the *movida* years, and every other doorway seems to be a club. The town hall has cleaned the place up recently, and cleared out many of the badly parked cars, turning the area into a more or less pedestrian area. Chueca has prospered in its role as the capital's gay district, with trendy bars, restaurants and shops (not all of which are exclusively gay by any means). It's the real Madrid, and a perfect setting for the city's very good **Museo Municipal** (Municipal Museum), C/ Fuencarral 78, ✆ 91 588 86 72, Ⓜ Tribunal (*open Tues–Fri 9.30–8, Sat–Sun, 10–2, closed Mon and hols; adm 300 pts, concessions 200 pts, free Wed*). Housed in the 18th-century Hospicio de San Fernando, with an exuberant Churrigueresque portal by Pedro de Ribera, the museum has been renovated and greatly expanded in recent years. More *madrileños* come here than tourists, and you can sense their growing civic pride as you watch them scrutinizing the old maps and prints, pointing out landmarks and discussing how their city has changed. The collection is large, and you can learn as much as you care to about Madrid and its history. Spaniards love to make room-sized models of their cities, and there is one here that accurately reproduces the Madrid of the 1830s.

The heart of the Malasaña district is the **Plaza de Dos de Mayo**, the scene of the bloody insurrection of 2 May 1808, which Goya later immortalized on canvas. As the *madrileños* held out against the Napoleonic troops, one of the casualties was a young local seamstress, Manuela Malasaña, and the district now bears her name.

Moncloa and the Ciudad Universitaria (University City)

Miguel Primo de Rivera always liked to think of himself as a great benefactor of education, and it exasperated him that Spain's university students spent most of the 1920s out in the streets calling him names. He began this sprawling, suburban campus in 1927, partly to appease them but mostly to get them out of town. This institution, the nation's largest, began as the Complutensian University, founded by Cardinal Cisneros in Alcalá de Henares. After it moved to Madrid, its buildings stood in the quarter north of the Gran Vía, where many may still be seen. Primo de Rivera's new campus was unfinished when the Civil War broke out; in the battles for Madrid the University found itself in the front line, providing a potent symbol of the nature of the war as Franco's artillery pounded the halls of knowledge to rubble. Franco rebuilt them after the war in a stolid, authoritarian style. Today the campus is green and well-kept but as dull to visit as it must be for the students who attend it.

There are two museums near the southern end of the Ciudad Universitaria. The **Museo de América**, Avda. Reyes Católicos 6, © 91 549 26 41, Ⓜ Moncloa (*open Tues–Sat 10–3, Sun and hols, 10–2.30, closed Mon; adm 400 pts, concessions 200 pts, free Sat after 2 and Sun*), emerged like a butterfly in 1994 after a renovation programme lasting 12 years. In its new incarnation the museum is cool, elegant, and beautifully designed. On display is one of Europe's largest collections of artefacts from the Aztecs, Incas, Maya, and other indigenous New World cultures, many of them plundered in the time of the conquistadors, but many more acquired much later by more honourable means. Among the most beautiful are gold ornaments from Colombia and Costa Rica, some over 1000 years old, and ancient Peruvian and Chilean textiles. The museum holds an extremely rare post-Classic Mayan codex, the Códice Tro-Cortesiano, a document relating in symbols (*glyphs*) news of the Spanish arrival, and a replica of this is on display. Spanish engravings depicting indigenous South Americans as fantastical giants, headless monsters or cheerful cannibals give a fascinating insight into the popular state of mind at the dawn of the Age of Exploration, and a series of 16th- to 18th-century maps illustrate graphically the rapid growth of Western knowledge of this alien territory. The museum also covers aspects of contemporary Latin American culture, and there are film showings highlighting current social and cultural issues in the context of the past.

Nearby, just off the Avenida de la Victoria, is the **Museo Nacional de Antropología**, Avda. Juan de Herrera 2, © 91 549 71 50, Ⓜ Moncloa (*open Tues–Sat, 10–6, Sun and hols, 10–2, closed Mon*), formerly the Museo de Etnología and moved from near Atocha to the building that used to house the Museo Español de Arte Contemporáneo (MEAC). As well as a permanent exhibition on physical and cultural anthropology that includes a few bizarre curiosities, this museum frequently hosts special exhibitions on individual regions or cultures. Just outside the Museo de América is the **Faro de Madrid** (*open, summer, daily, 10.30–1.45 and 5–7.45; winter, daily, 10.30–1.45 and 4.30–7.15; adm 200 pts, concessions 100 pts*), an inland lighthouse designed by Salvator Pérez Arroyo to be exactly 92 metres high, opened as part of the 1992 celebrations. A lift will whizz you up to the observation platform for fine 360° views.

Salamanca Quarter and Museo Lázaro Galdiano

Ever since Madrid's last city walls were knocked down in the 1860s, opening this district to development, Salamanca has been Madrid's fashionable address. Today much of its cheerless grid of swanky avenues bears an eerie resemblance to the neighbourhoods around New York's Park Avenue, with a scattering of old mansions, trendy show-offs peering in the windows of the Calle de Serrano boutiques, illegally parked cars with diplomatic licence plates, and concierges walking other people's Pekineses. Many of the surviving mansions have a certain Victorian panache, but the only building in Salamanca that really stands out is the US Embassy on Calle de Serrano, done in that style only possible to American embassies, half fortress and half kitchen appliance.

You'll pass by it on the way to one of Madrid's best museums, the **Museo Lázaro Galdiano**, C/ Serrano 122, ✆ 91 561 60 84, Ⓜ República Argentina or Avda. de América (*open Tues–Sun 10–2, closed Mon and all Aug; adm 300 pts*). The founder, who died in 1948, had a better eye and deeper pockets than the other Madrid collectors whose homes have been turned into museums. Among the 37 rooms of art, he assembled one work by nearly every important Spanish painter, two visionary paintings by Hieronymous Bosch, a Rembrandt portrait and, something you won't see much of in any other Spanish museum, English paintings, including works by Gainsborough, Turner and Reynolds.

Galdiano's tastes were remarkably eclectic, and on the ground floor articles from the Moors, Byzantines, Persians and Celts share space with medieval enamels, swords and armour, and early clocks and watches. In summer, night-time tours are available.

Peripheral Attractions

There's not much reason to leave the central area of Madrid, but a few museums in the outlying districts may catch your fancy. The **Palacio Real de El Pardo**, Ctra. de El Pardo, ✆ 91 549 00 59 or 376 15 00 (*open Mon–Sat 10.30–6, Sun and hols 10–1.40; adm 650 pts, concs 250 pts, free Wed*) another overdone Bourbón palace, built by Carlos III, stands in a planted forest some 13km north of the centre. Franco used it as his residence throughout the dictatorship, and now it is open to guided tours. Indeed, the palace offers the only glimpse of how the dictator worked, with his office left as it was when he died.

Madrid's main bullring, the **Plaza de Toros Monumental de Las Ventas**, along the Calle de Alcalá 0.8km east of the Retiro, is the busiest and most prestigious in Spain. Around the back is the **Museo Taurino**, Pza. de Las Ventas, Patio de Caballos, ✆ 91 725 18 57, Ⓜ Ventas (*open Tues–Fri 9.30–2.30, Sun 10–1, closed Sat and Mon*; *adm*), the largest and most complete museum of bullfighting, with special exhibitions on famous *toreros* like Manolete, who met the horn in this ring in 1947.

South of Atocha, the century-old Delicias station has been converted into the **Museo Nacional Ferroviario** (National Railway Museum), Pso. de las Delicias 61, ✆ 91 527 31 21, Ⓜ Palos de la Frontera (*open Tues–Fri 10–5.30, Sat–Sun 10–3, closed Mon and hols*, adm 450 pts), with RENFE's oldest and proudest warhorses (some from the 1840s) shined up to look as good as new.

If you were interested in the works of the 19th-century painter Sorolla shown in the Casón del Buen Retiro, then visit the Valencian painter's house at the **Museo Sorolla**, C/ Gen. Martínez Campos 37, ✆ 91 310 15 84, Ⓜ Iglesia (*open Tues–Sat 10–3, Sun 10–2, closed Mon; adm 400 pts, concs 200 pts; free Sat after 2 and Sun*).

Finally, the Museo Municipal has a new rival in the **Museo de la Ciudad** (City Museum), C/ Príncipe de Vergara 140, ✆ 91 588 65 99, Ⓜ Cruz del Rayo (*open Tues–Fri 10–2 and 4–6, Sat–Sun 10–2, closed Mon; adm free*), a permanent exhibition tracing Madrid's evolution as a city, past, present and future, including videos, 3D reconstructions and interactive displays. Despite the modern gadgetry the museum's content is all rather dry but it hosts regular, more interesting, temporary exhibitions on topical issues.

The best public open-air swimming pools in Madrid are the **Piscinas de la Casa de Campo** (*open daily in summer, 10.30–8; adm 450 pts, 250 pts concessions*), on the southern edge of the Casa de Campo, a stone's throw from Lago metro. There are three outdoor pools here, including an Olympic-sized pool and a shallow pool for kids, set among landscaped gardens. Topless sunbathing is permitted. The smaller pool at the Casa de Campo complex is also a gay hangout. For an energetic afternoon out not too far from the city, kids can go wild at **Aquópolis**, Ctra. de la Coruña Km 25, ✆ 91 815 69 11 (*open daily in summer 12–7, free shuttle buses from Cine Coliseum, Pza. de España, 11–12am*), supposedly the biggest water park in Europe, with huge slides and wave machines.

Madrid's bullring, the **Plaza de Toros Monumental de Las Ventas**, sometimes referred to simply as Las Ventas, at C/ Alcalá 237, ✆ 91 356 22 00, Ⓜ Ventas, has the biggest schedule of any in Spain, and is the place you're most likely to catch up with a *corrida* on your trip. The season officially opens in May with daily bullfights during the Feria de San Isidro; from then on there are fights at 7pm every summer Sunday, and towards the end of the season, in September, there are daily bouts once again during the Feria de Otoño. The best way to get tickets is to go to the ring early on the day of the event—there are places in central Madrid that sell them in advance, but at a higher price. Tickets from Las Ventas go for *1000–12,000 pts*, depending on *sol* or *sombra*, proximity to ring, etc.

Madrid has a racetrack, the **Hipódromo de la Zarzuela**, Ctra. de La Coruña Km 7.8, ✆ 91 307 01 40, out in the northern suburbs near El Pardo, with night racing from 10pm on summer Saturdays, a major social outing for the *madrileños*. Basque *jai-alai* is played at the **Frontón,** C/ Doctor Cortezo 10, Ⓜ Tirso de Molina, and there are a number of golf courses in the metropolitan area, none of them cheap, the best equipped being the Club de Campo Villa de Madrid, Ctra. de Castilla km 3, ✆ 91 357 21 32. Real Madrid, the 'government's' football club in the Franco years, now struggles manfully to keep up with Barcelona, its traditional rival; they play at the **Estadio Santiago Bernabéu**, Pso. de la Castellana 104, off C/ Concha Espina, ✆ 91 344 00 52, Ⓜ Lima Add. The capital's other major team is Atlético de Madrid, who play at the **Estadio Vicente Calderón**, C/ Virgen de la Puerta 67, ✆ 91 366 47 07, Ⓜ Pirámides.

Finally, if you feel like throwing your money away, there is the **Casino de Madrid**, Ctra. de La Coruña km 28.3, ✆ 91 856 11 00 (*open Mon–Thurs, 2pm–4am, Fri–Sat, 2pm–5am. There is a free bus service from Plaza de España 6 or Plaza de Colón*).

Shopping

fashion

Madrid has not one fashion centre, but several, each with its own distinctive character. For designer labels, the streets to head for are those criss-crossing the self-confidently prosperous Salamanca district, north of the Retiro: Serrano, Goya, Claudio Cuello, Velázquez and Ortega y Gasset (Ⓜ Serrano, Velázquez, Núñez de Balboa). Spain's best-known names are here, including **Adolfo Domínguez**, Serrano

18, ✆ 91 577 82 80, Ⓜ Serrano, with sober, beautifully cut clothes for men and women; **Agatha Ruiz de la Prada**, Goya 4, ✆ 91 577 27 11, Ⓜ Serrano, offering more expressive, outgoing designs; and **Sybilla**, C/ Jorge Juan 12, Madrid's legendary fashion trail-blazer, who keeps on creating exciting collections. Here too are the international fashion celebrities, such as **Chanel, Kenzo, Giorgio Armani** and **Gianni Versace** (all on C/ Ortega y Gasset).

No trip to Madrid is complete without taking in **Loewe**, Serrano 26, ✆ 91 435 30 56, Ⓜ Serrano. Among the best designed, and most expensive, leather goods in Spain, along with dinky, more affordable accesories for men and women. For delicate underwear, **Meye Maier**, Jorge Juan 12, ✆ 91 575 36 54, Ⓜ Retiro.

For affordable mainstream fashion for men and women, the Calle de la Princesa between Argüelles and Moncloa metro stations is the best hunting ground, with particularly rich pickings at sale time. Shoe shops abound: **Bravo**, C/ Princesa 58, for quality designs; **Camper**, C/ Princesa 75, for more rugged styles; and **Iris**, C/ Princesa 70, for rock-bottom prices. There is a branch of the department store **El Corte Inglés** here, near Argüelles metro, and branches of Madrid's favourite fashion chains, such as **Mango**, C/ Princesa 68, selling relaxed fashions with individual touches, and **Zara**, C/ Princesa 45. Most Madrileñan women have at least one or two Zara outfits in their wardrobe though not all would admit it—the shop specializes in young fashions and designer copies at affordable prices.

Madrid's more *outré* street fashion shops are more scattered. At **Buggin**, Pza. de Cascorro 7 (Ⓜ La Latina, *open on Sundays to catch the nearby Rastro trade*), the assistants bop about to pounding techno among the display of club clothes—currently tiny T-shirts and dayglo mini backpacks. **Marihuana**, C/ Duque de Alba, Ⓜ Tirso de Molina, sells biker fashion—heavy metal band shirts, skull hip flasks and goblets, chunky watches, and Harley Davidson branded gear. Finally, if you're planning a night on the town and nothing less than a skin-tight zebra print skirt will do, make a bee-line for **Glam**, C/ Hortaleza 62, Ⓜ Gran Vía. **Marks & Spencers** is big in Spain. The four-floor emporium on Serrano 52, ✆ 91 520 00 00, Ⓜ Serrano, has everything from undies to chicken tikka sandwiches.

books, records and news

La Casa del Libro, Gran Vía 29, Ⓜ Gran Vía, claims to be Spain's largest bookshop—there's several floors of it, including an English language section. For scholarly and obscure matters about Spain in any language, try **Meissner**, C/ Ortega y Gasset, Ⓜ Núñez de Balboa. Most Madrid bookshops have a small selection in English. For English titles, the capital's best shop is **Booksellers**, José Abascal 48, ✆ 91 442 7959, Ⓜ Rios Rosas. There is an excellent travel bookshop, **Añosluz**, C/ Francisco de Ricci 8, Ⓜ Argüelles, which will have any specialized books on Spain as well as guides and maps to all cities.

The French chain **FNAC** has a characteristically massive branch off the Puerta del Sol at C/ Preciados 28, Ⓜ Callao, Sol, with row upon row of CDs, videos, video games, books, magazines and newspapers, and a concert ticket agency. **Madrid Rock**, Gran Vía 25, Ⓜ Gran Vía, is also large but somehow less overwhelming.

Foreign newspapers are sold at the larger stands around the Puerta del Sol, Gran Vía, Calle de Alcalá, Plaza de Cibeles, and in the Salamanca district.

specialities

If you don't make the trip to Toledo, which has almost as many tacky gift shops as tapas bars, you can simulate the experience in Madrid at two neighbouring shops, **El Escudo de Toledo**, Pza. Canovas del Castillo 4, and the self-deludingly named **Objetos de Arte Toledano**, Pso. del Prado 10, Ⓜ Banco de España, by splurging on decorated swords, penknives, and souvenir ashtrays. All branches of **El Corte Inglés** have a souvenir department.

For something genuinely Spanish, original and tasteful, the porcelain produced by Galican cooperative **Sargadelos**, C/Zurbano 46, ℗ 91 310 48 30 is among the most distinctive anywhere, and notable for its lovely deep blues and translucent whites. Modern designs based on traditional themes.

For the widest selection of flamenco recordings, as well as books on the subject, and even those dancing shoes you now need, **El Flamenco Vive**, C/Unión 4, ℗ 91 547 39 17, Ⓜ Opera, is essential.

Those who have acquired a taste for salt cod can stock up at **La Casa del Bacalao**, C/ Marqués de Urquijo 1, Ⓜ Argüelles, a tiny, traditional, marble-floored emporium of the stuff. The best place for olive oil is the exhaustively stocked **Patrimonio Comunal Olivarero**, C/ Mejía Lequerica 1, Ⓜ Tribunal, and for *turrón*, the almond nougat that was once made by Toledo's religious communities, you can do no better than **Casa Mira**, Carrera de San Jerónimo 30, Ⓜ Sol, an ancient shop which also sells all sorts of other luscious goodies.

Casa Seseña, C/ Cruz 23, Ⓜ Sol, an unassuming, reserved sort of shop, is the place to go for traditional *madrileño* velvet-lined capes, mantillas and beautifully embroidered Manila shawls, and Spanish guitars are made at the **Guitarrería Manzano**, C/ Santa Ana 12, Ⓜ La Latina, and sold at **Garrido-Bailén**, C/ Bailén 19, Ⓜ Opera, which has a stock of musical instruments from all over the world. For both traditional and modern ceramics and tiles from some of Spain's best craftsmen, head for **Cerámica El Alfar**, C/ Claudo Coello 112, Ⓜ Núñez de Balboa, or **Antigua Casa Talavera**, C/ Isabel la Católica 2, Ⓜ Santo Domingo.

Madrid has surprisingly few shops devoted to ethnic *artesanía* from Latin America, but it's worth paying a visit to **Ayllu**, C/ Sombreretel, Ⓜ Lavapiés, for textiles and jewellery, or to **El Quetzal de las Indias**, C/ Mayor 13, Ⓜ Sol; for something rather special, the shop at the **Museo de America**, Avda. Reyes Católicos 6, Ⓜ Moncloa, has a small, but beautifully chosen, selection of gifts.

markets

Madrid's most celebrated flea market is **El Rastro**, which takes over the La Latina district every Sunday morning, starting at Plaza de Cascorro and flooding down the Calle de Ribera de Curtidores and into the neighbouring streets and squares. The best time to visit is early in the morning, from autumn to spring: in summer the crowds are thicker and the spread of stalls thinner, and by mid-morning it's already hot. Once devoted solely to antiques and curios (this is the speciality of many of the permanent shops in this district), there are now stalls selling all sorts of junk—cheap shoes, jewellery, belts and bags; second-hand, ethnic, and new-age fashions; plants; household goods; pirate tapes; and rack after rack of sunglasses. If it's antiques and curios you're after, head for the Calle Mira el Río Baja and its neighbours. There are good bric-a-brac stalls in the Pza. del General Vara de Rey, and a few more upmarket shops in the sadly characterless **Mercado Puerta de Toledo**, Ronda de Toledo 1. The Pza. del Campillo del Mundo Nuevo is the place for plants and old books. Now that the Rastro has become as popular with tourists as with *madrileños*, the bargains are harder to come by, but if you've the time, and room in your suitcase, the shops and stalls are worth a look. The Rastro has long suffered a bad reputation for street crime, hence the heavy police presence, but if you are careful with your belongings you should have nothing to fear.

The **Mercado de Antón Martín**, C/ Santa Isabel 5, Ⓜ Antón Martín, is one of the most central of Madrid's bustling *castizo* food markets, with two floors of permanent stalls selling all manner of fresh produce (*open 9–2 and 5.30–8.30*). The **Mercado de San Miguel**, Pza. de San Miguel, Ⓜ Sol, also very central, is smaller but worth visiting for a glimpse of its bizarrely ornate ironwork exterior. Market shoppers should be aware that the melée round a busy stall is actually the Madrileñan version of an organized queue. The convention is that each new arrival calls out *¿Quién es el último?* ('Who's last?') in order to find out their place in the serving order—often the cue for a great deal of good-natured argy-bargy and verbal jostling for position. Nobody would dream of standing in line.

Madrid ✉ *28000*   ***Where To Stay***

With some 50,000 hotel rooms in Madrid, there are always enough to go around. Regrettably, few are at all interesting. If it's reliability or familiarity you're looking for, there are all the world's big chains to choose from, even a Holiday Inn, off an avenue named after General Perón (★★★★**Holiday Inn Madrid**, Pza. Carlos Trías Bertrán, ✆ 91 597 01 02, ✉ 91 597 02 92, Ⓜ Lima), or you could stay at any of a hundred other three, four- or five-star hotels—all pleasant and well-staffed, and all pretty much the same. Many are along the Gran Vía and other major streets; convenient but often intolerably noisy.

At the top end of the scale, Madrid has well over a third of all the luxury hotels in Spain. You could always pamper yourself at the Ritz, but only, needless to say, if money is no object—if you'd be inclined to wonder whether any hotel suite can possibly be worth 176,000 pts a night (the 'royal suite' is even more expensive) then this is definitely not your kind of place. At the other extreme, finding a good, cheap room for the night is not a problem if you're prepared to share a bathroom; otherwise you'll be hard pressed to find a double for under 4000 pts.

luxury

The ★★★★★**HGL Ritz**, Pza. de la Lealtad 5, ✆ 91 521 28 57, ✉ 91 523 09 44, Ⓜ Banco de España, has been open for less than a century but is arguably Spain's most celebrated hotel. Elaborately Belle Epoque in style, the bedrooms and suites are elegant and the public rooms unashamedly grand. The restaurant buffet table groans splendidly, and anyone can enjoy the famous *terraza*, particularly for afternoon tea or Sunday brunch.

The French Baroque style ★★★★**Palace Hotel**, Pza. de las Cortes 7, ✆ 91 429 75 51, 🖷 91 429 82 66, Ⓜ Banco de España or Sevilla, traditionally the Ritz's arch-rival, opened just a few years later than the Ritz but has a much more modern ambience and attitude.

Much more intimate is the ★★★★★**HGL Santo Mauro**, C/ Zurbano 36, ✆ 91 319 69 00, 🖷 91 308 54 77, Ⓜ Alonso Martínez, in the leafy Chamberi district, a century-old French-style mansion that has recently been painstakingly restored and fabulously well decorated, adding individual touches such as in the conversion of the lovely old library into a restaurant.

The ★★★★★**HGL Villa Magna**, Pso. de la Castellana 22, ✆ 91 576 75 00, 🖷 91 575 31 58, Ⓜ Rubén Darío, is the favourite of visiting celebrities and political luminaries. One of the two presidential suites comes complete with its own sauna and white grand piano. The hotel, which is close to the swanky designer shops of C/ José Ortega y Gasset and C/ Serrano, is in a modern building on the site of an old palace, with centuries-old cedars in the garden.

expensive

Madrid has plenty of pricey hotels—there's a large international expense-account crowd to keep them filled. They provide comfort but not necessarily character, and for a special treat you'd be better off looking elsewhere. A glowing exception is the well-established ★★★★**Gran Hotel Reina Victoria**, Pza. Santa Ana 14, ✆ 91 531 45 00, 🖷 91 522 03 07, Ⓜ Sol, whose greatest claim to fame is that it's a bullfighters' favourite. Minibuses carrying clutches of them, resplendent in their fighting regalia, regularly pull up outside the wedding-cake façade on summer weekends. The hotel is also conveniently placed close to Sol, and the Huertas, Santa Ana neighbourhood, one of the capital's main nightlife areas.

Another good choice is the ★★★★**Gran Hotel Conde-Duque**, Pza. Conde Valle de Suchil 5, ✆ 91 447 70 00, 🖷 91 448 35 69, Ⓜ San Bernardo, which has large rooms and suites, including one with a hydromassage bath, and a breakfast room overlooking gardens. For a bit of peace a stone's throw from the Gran Vía there's the ★★★★**Santo Domingo**, Pza. de Santo Domingo 13, ✆ 91 547 98 00, 🖷 91 547 59 95, Ⓜ Santo Domingo, which offers modern comforts in a pleasant old building.

★★★★**Hotel Eurobuilding**, C/ Padre Damián 23, ✆ 91 345 45 00, 🖷 91 345 45 76, Ⓜ Cuzco, is, despite the ponderous name, a good choice for a business visit—it's uncompromisingly modern, convenient for Chamartín, and it has a large outdoor pool.

As hotel pools go, however, the Eurobuilding's can't match the legendary rooftop pool of the sober and dignified ★★★★**Hotel Emperador**, Gran Vía 53, ✆ 91 541 28 00, 🖷 91 547 28 17, Ⓜ Callao—it's just about big enough to swim and sunbathe in comfort and is surrounded by stunning city views. Non-residents can swim for an entry fee of 800 pts.

Old Madrid ✉ 28000

moderate

Not far from the Emperador but a step down in price is the ★★★★**HR Mayorazgo**, Flor Baja 3, ✆ 91 547 26 00, ✇ 91 541 24 85, Ⓜ Pza. de España, offering stylish, international, anonymous comfort. The ★★★**HR Reyes Católicos**, C/ Angel 18, ✆ 91 265 86 00, ✇ 91 265 98 67, Ⓜ Puerta de Toledo, in a very nice old neighbourhood near the basilica of San Francisco El Grande, is small, personal, and a good bargain for the services offered, as is the ★★★**Carlos V**, C/ Maestro Vitoria 5, ✆ 91 531 41 00, ✇ 91 531 37 51, Ⓜ Sol, an otherwise unexceptional place which is nonetheless popular, probably thanks to its location, a mere hop from El Corte Inglés.

inexpensive–cheap

One of the most atmospheric places to experience Madrid is ★★**HS La Macarena**, Cava de San Miguel 8, ✆ 91 365 92 21, ✇ 364 27 57, Ⓜ Opera, just off the Plaza Mayor, tucked in a street full of ancient bars and restaurants (including fake Mexican eatery El Cuchi, whose awning proclaims, memorably, 'Hemingway Never Ate Here'), and tall buildings pitched at such a slope they look as though they'll topple over at any minute. On Calle Arenal, there are two acceptable and inexpensive *hostales* across the street from one another: ★**HSR Capricornio**, C/ Arenal 23, ✆ 91 542 16 45, Ⓜ Sol, and ★**HSR Caritel**, Arenal 26-3°izqda, ✆ 91 547 31 29, Ⓜ Sol, both with rooms for *4000–5300 pts.*

★★**HSR La Torre**, C/ Espoz y Mina 8-3°, ✆ 91 532 43 03, Ⓜ Sol, is probably the best value option in this area (*5000 pts*), a bright, squeaky-clean *hostal* which includes large twin rooms with fabulous balconies, giving views, opposite, of rooftop gardens, and, down the street to the left, the Puerta del Sol's landmark Tío Pepe advert.

Near the Prado ✉ 33344

moderate

For a chance to stay close to the Retiro Park, a good choice would be the ★★★★**HR Alcalá**, C/ Alcalá 66, ✆ 91 435 10 60, ✇ 91 435 11 05, Ⓜ Príncipe de Vergara,which is well-established, friendly, and reasonably priced.

inexpensive

★**HSR Coruña**, Pso. del Prado 12-3°dcha, ✆ 91 429 25 43, Ⓜ Banco de España and ★**HSR Sudamericana**, Pso. del Prado 12-6°izqda, ✆ 91 429 25 64, Ⓜ Banco de España, are two of the friendliest and quietest lodgings in Madrid, occupying the same fine old building with leafy views towards the Prado. ★★**HS Cervantes**, C/ Cervantes 34-2°, ✆ 91 429 83 65, Ⓜ Banco de España, is also clean, bright and friendly.

★★**HSR Corberó**, C/ Cervantes 34-1°izqda, ✆ 91 429 41 71, Ⓜ Banco de España, has small doubles with bathroom and TV for around *5000 pts*, and, in the next door block, mini-apartments with living room and kitchenette, which sleep up to four and are excellent value at *7000 pts*. Although the building it's in is tatty, the ★★**HS Armesto**, C/ San Agustín 6-1°dcha, ✆ 91 429 90 31, Ⓜ Sevilla, is a tidy *hostal* with small but sweet, feminine rooms.

Around Calle Huertas and Plaza Santa Ana ✉ 28000

The boisterous area of tapas bars and restaurants east of the Puerta del Sol offers dozens of good value hotels and pensions, many on the Plaza Santa Ana itself.

moderate

The ★★★**Hotel Inglés**, C/ Echegaray 8, ✆ 91 429 65 51, 🖷 91 420 24 23, Ⓜ Sevilla, would be a good choice for anyone attracted to the lively Santa Ana area and looking for more comfort than the local *hostales* can provide.

inexpensive–cheap

The friendly **Hostal Cervantes**, C/Cervantes, 34, ✆ 91 429 27 45, Ⓜ Antón Martín, is not at the cheap end of the scale, with a double costing *6,500 pesetas*, but is better than many hotels.

★**HSR Santa Ana**, Pza. Santa Ana 1-2°dcha, ✆ 91 521 30 58, Ⓜ Sol, is a small and clean if slightly tatty *hostal* right on the square. The owner, Marta, and her huge Siamese cat are both very friendly, and some rooms have lovely sunny balconies.

The landlady at **Pensión Romero**, C/ León 13-3°, ✆ 91 429 51 39, Ⓜ Antón Martín, is also very amiable; this too is a family flat, complete with small excitable dog.

★**HSR Vetusta**, C/ Huertas 3-1°, ✆ 91 429 64 04, Ⓜ Sol, has a balcony dripping with geraniums, and good value rooms (some for *4000 pts*).

Around Calle Fuencarral and Calle Hortaleza ✉ 28000

This district, close to the nightspots of Malasaña and the Gran Vía, has much to offer: hectic streets, quiet squares, mainstream cinemas, typically Madrilenian *castizo* bars, ancient shops and markets, international restaurants, cheap *comedores*, colourful nightspots and gay hangouts. On the flipside, there are certain streets, especially near Gran Vía metro, where not everyone will feel comfortable after dark: the area has more than its fair share of drug dealers and prostitutes.

moderate

In a city which abounds with very plain hotels, the ★**Hotel Mónaco**, C/ Barbieri 5, ✆ 91 522 46 30, 🖷 91 521 16 01, Ⓜ Chueca, in the heart of the living, breathing Chueca district, is a real find. Anyone investigating room 123, with its huge, splendidly ornate ceiling mirror and its bathroom decorated with cavorting nudes, will not be surprised to learn that in its heyday in the 1920s this hotel was in fact a fashionable and upmarket brothel. Despite some rather shoddy restoration, many of the rooms retain their lavish mock-Baroque decor, and it's worth asking to see a few—some are shabby but wonderful, some are just plain shabby, but they're all different. Room 127 has starred in a number of films, videos and magazine articles. The standard rate of *8500 pts* a double is well worth it if you manage to land a room you really like.

★★**HSR Santa Bárbara**, Pza. Santa Bárbara 4, ✆ 91 446 93 08, 🖷 91 446 23 45, Ⓜ Alonso Martínez, is on one of central Madrid's most pleasant squares.

inexpensive–cheap

Walk up C/ Fuencarral or C/ Hortaleza and you'll find an enormous choice of low-cost *hostales*. One of the classier cheap places at the noisy, grubby Gran Vía end of the district is the very pleasant **★★HSR América**, C/ Hortaleza 19-5°, ✆ 91 522 64 48, 📧 91 522 64 47, Ⓜ Gran Vía, high enough up for you not to be aware of the buses thundering by below. It has a clean, lived-in atmosphere and a jolly, efficient landlady; there's a TV lounge and a sunny balcony off the entrance hall.

Other choices include **★HS Zamoran**, C/ Fuencarral 18-2°izqda, ✆ 91 532 20 60, Ⓜ Gran Vía, which has a TV in the communal hall area and a good atmosphere, and **Hostal Sil**, further up Fuencarral at No.95, Ⓜ Bilbao, ✆ 91 448 8972, which is quieter, and well run. All rooms have television, and air conditioning for the very reasonable sum of *5,000 pts.*

★HS Palacios and **★HS Ribadavia**, C/ Fuencarral 25-2°/3°dcha, ✆ 91 531 48 47, two spotless *hostales* both run by the same people, are also very good value at *3000–3500 pts.*

Eating Out

No place in Spain except perhaps the Costa del Sol can offer such a wide choice. Besides the country's best gourmet restaurants, you can sample the cuisine of every region of Spain and a score of other lands without straying half a mile from the Puerta del Sol. Most of the old well-known establishments are in Old Madrid.

expensive restaurants

Madrid has a plethora of expensive restaurants offering every type of international cuisine. The established names include **Zalacain**, C/ Alvarez de Baena 4, ✆ 91 561 59 35, Ⓜ Rubén Darío, often described as Spain's best restaurant, and among the best in Europe (it has three Michelin stars to prove it). It matches superb food with impeccable service, to give you the experience of a lifetime (*set menu 9500 pts. Men are required to wear a jacket and tie*).

Jockey, C/ Amador de los Ríos 6, ✆ 91 319 24 35, Ⓜ Colón; **El Amparo**, Callejón de Puigcerdá 8, ✆ 91 431 6456, Ⓜ Serrano; **Lhardy**, Carrera de San Jerónimo 8, ✆ 91 521 33 85, Ⓜ Sevilla; and **Horcher**, C/ Alfonso XII 6, ✆ 91 522 07 31, Ⓜ Retiro, have reputations to match their prices; if you eat at any of these places the bill won't fall on the kind side of *10,000 pts.*

However some top-quality restaurants have emerged over the last few years with cooking that is just as inventive if not better. For '*nueva cocina*' there is **El Cenador del Prado**, C/ Prado 4 (just off Pza. Santa Ana), ✆ 91 429 15 61, Ⓜ Sevilla. It has a dining room which feels like a conservatory, and imaginative dishes that attract Madrid's knowing, smart set.

Another place with a highly inventive cook, this time Japanese (he prepares Japanese-influenced Spanish dishes cooked in classic French style) is **El Mentidero de la Villa**, C/ Santo Tomé 6 (Plaza Alesas), ✆ 91 308 12 85, Ⓜ Colón. The romantic atmosphere is matched by exceptional service, ambience and food. Try the marinated salmon, stuffed *chipirones* and entrecôte, and the trifle which remains unsurpassable (from *5000 pts*). The lunchtime set menu, at *2500 pts*, is one of the capital's best-kept secrets. For a special type of neo-colonial atmosphere try **La Parra**, C/ Monte

Esquinza 34 (near the British Embassy), ℗ 91 319 54 98, Ⓜ Rubén Darío. The tiled dining room is magnificent and the food spicy and Andalucían (*4500 pts upwards*). If the stiff formality of Madrid's top restaurants is not really your style, you're likely to appreciate **Viridiana**, C/ Juan de Mena 14, ℗ 91 531 52 22, Ⓜ Retiro, a short saunter from Madrid's Paseo del Arte, which serves excellent wine and creative cooking in a more relaxed atmosphere.

For exceptional hotel cooking, head for the **Grill Neptuno**, Palace Hotel, Pza. de los Cortes 7, ℗ 91 429 75 51, Ⓜ Banco de España. The fresh terrine of *foie gras* and the sea bass wrapped in thin layers of smoked ham are highly recommended (*6500 pts*).

For Spanish atmosphere, there is **La Fuencisla**, C/ San Mateo 4 ℗ 91 521 61 86, Ⓜ Tribunal (tucked away behind an inconspicuous bar just up from the Museo Romántico), whose humble dining room is considered to be the best *taberna* in Madrid, serving classic Spanish food and classic wine (*5000 pts*).

An excellent Galician restaurant with a top-class reputation for fresh seafood, simply and deliciously presented, is **O'Pazo**, C/ Reina Mercedes 20, ℗ 91 553 23 33, Ⓜ Lima. Especially good are the oysters and *merluza*. **Moaña**, C/ Hileras 4 (off C/ Arenal), ℗ 91 548 29 14, Ⓜ Sol, also Galician, is another good choice.

Book days in advance for what many describe as one of the finest restaurants in Madrid, **Or-Dago**, C/ Sancho Dávila 15, ℗ 91 356 71 85, Ⓜ Ventas, serving Basque dishes to as near perfection as you'll get outside that region. An alternative for French-Basque influenced cooking is **Hontoria**, Pza. del General Maroto 2, ℗ 91 473 04 25, Ⓜ Legazpi, a small homely restaurant with great atmosphere and decor.

Excellent Basque meals for around *5000 pts* are served at the **Asador Frontón**, Pza. Tirso de Molina 7, ℗ 91 369 16 17, Ⓜ Tirso de Molina, run by a former *frontón* star. Top quality ingredients go into the house specialities which include roasted fish and huge grilled chops; there's a reasonably priced lunchtime *menú* and the place is full every day.

A constant crowd also attests to the popularity of **Casa Lucio**, C/ Cava Baja 35, ℗ 91 365 32 52, Ⓜ Latina, something of a Madrid institution, with an extensive menu that will give you the opportunity of splashing out on more expensive items like seafood, but to show their generosity of spirit also includes some cheap fillers at the lower end of the menu.

El Amparo, Puigcerdá 8, ℗ 91 431 64 56, Ⓜ Serrano/Goya, has already earned a Michelin star in its short life. At the cutting edge of modern Basque cuisine, this really is a foodies' paradise: starting with the décor in this charmingly restored house with different salons, quite simply everything is done to perfection. Try the fresh tuna and lobster mousse, followed perhaps by grilled Dover sole with spinach and seafood sauce with a touch of saffron.

C/Reina Mercedes, up in the business district the Castellana, offers two of the capital's best Galician restaurants, **Combarro**, Reina Mercedes 12, ℗ 91 554 77 84, sits alongside **O Pazo**, at No.20, which both fly their own seafood down from Galicia (*both around 8000 pts*).

Santa Ana/Huertas ✉ 28000

Domine Cabra, Huertas 54, ✆ 91 429 43 65, Ⓜ Banco de España, offers creative cooking in a sophisticated but relaxed atmosphere. **Hyloghi**, Ventura de la Vega 3, ✆ 91 429 73 57, Ⓜ Sevilla/Sol, has been going strong for more than 60 years. The secret of its success is simple: attentive service, good ingredients, unpretentious home cooking, and large portions.

Despite being tucked away in a side-street opposite the Palace Hotel, **Paradis**, Marqués de Cubas 14, ✆ 91 429 73 03, Ⓜ Banco de España, is one of the capital's most popular restaurants. It's also one of Madrid's few Catalan eateries, and probably the best. As you'd expect, the décor is classy, the service faultless, and the food, with superb cod, as well as rice dishes, and an unsurpassable *fideos* with goose liver is quite simply top notch.

Malasaña/Chueca ✉ 28000

C/Reina (Ⓜ Gran Vía) between Chueca and Gran Vía, is a world unto itself, with two of the capital's best cocktail bars (*see* below), and a host of good restaurants, from Valencian to Japanese. **El 37 de la Reina**, at No.37, ✆ 91 532 94 71, Ⓜ Chueca, is intimate and exquisitely decorated. The food is simple, mainly Spanish, with the emphasis on lighter dishes. A few doors down is **Robata**, C/Reina 31, ✆ 91 521 85 28, one of the capital's best Japanese restaurants. Choose between eating at the sushi bar, at a table, or in one of the four private salons, on tatami.

La Barraca, at Reina 29, ✆ 91 532 71 54, offers good value, authentic paella, along with other rice dishes and a magnificent *fideos*—a macaroni version of paella. **Divina**, Colmenares 13, ✆ 91 531 37 65, is, like so many places in Chueca, nominally gay. Very much a place for the bright young things, the restaurant offers a limited set menu at a very reasonable *3500 pts*, which guarantees high standards.

Tienda de Vinos, also known as 'El comunista', C/Augusto Figueroa 35, ✆ 91 521 70 12, Ⓜ Chueca, has been around as long as anyone can remember. Under Franco, it was a haunt of lefties and intellectuals, and now attracts an old crowd of regulars, mixed in with many younger foreigners and Spaniards, charmed by its time warp feel and good food (*under 2,000 pts*).

For a complete change of atmosphere, further down the same street is **Momo**, at Augusto Figueroa 41, ✆ 91 532 71 62, caters mainly to Chueca's enormous gay contingent, but is just as likely to be filled with middle-aged ladies in town for a bit of theatre. The food is good value, and unpretentious. Round the corner, on C/Barbieri 15, is **La Chocolatería**, ✆ 91 521 00 23, which offers simple, home cooking in a relaxed atmosphere. What's more, you can get served until 1.45 am. And they've got a piano.

Salamanca ✉ 37000

With no other dish on the menu at midday, and with the sole option of bream in the evenings, few would disagree that **La Taberna de Daniela**, General Pardiñas 21

℗ 91 575 23 29, Ⓜ Goya, serves the capital's best *cocido*. Don't even think about just turning up: booking is essential, but well worth it.

Alkalde, Jorge Juan 10, ℗ 91 576 33 59, Ⓜ Goya, doesn't open Saturday evenings for some perverse reason. The rest of the time this old-style Basque restaurant is always full. Excellent fish dishes, stews and tapas. *Best to book.* **Casa Portal**, a couple of streets away on Doctor Castelo 26, ℗ 91 574 20 26, offers fine Asturian cooking in a relaxed atmosphere. The *fabada* is rated among the capital's best, and don't forget to order still cider. The waiter will pour it from shoulder height into a special glass, giving it fizz.

Nicolás, next door to the French embassy at Villalar 4, ℗ 91 431 77 37, Ⓜ Retiro, is something of a secret. Very much a labour of love on the part of owner Juan Antonio Méndez, who discovered the culinary arts late in life. **Club 31** on Alcalá 58, ℗ 91 531 00 92, Ⓜ Retiro, is in many ways a less formal, less expensive version of its wealthier elder brother, **Jockey**, and the food is just as good.

Old Madrid ✉ 28000

No visit to Madrid is complete without savouring the capital's traditional dishes, based on Castilian cooking, among them *cocido*, roast suckling pig, tripe, salt cod, and bean stews. A slew of restaurants on Cava Baja, south of the Plaza Mayor, offer old-fashioned hearty fare (Ⓜ Latina for all). Try **La Posada de la Villa**, Cava Baja 9, ℗ 91 366 18 80, a restored 19th-century former *posada*, or lodging house. **El Schotis**, Cava Baja, 11, ℗ 91 365 32 30, doesn't look too promising from the outside, but it has a loyal clientele. **Casa Lucio**, at Cava Baja 35, ℗ 91 365 32 52, is popular with politicians and television personalities, and serves traditional Madrid food. At the centre of the neighbourhood's gastronomic revival, the street now boasts more than a dozen restaurants, with one or two infiltrators such as **Julián de Tolosa**, Cava Baja 18. One of the best *asadores*, or grilled meat restaurants, in the capital, the décor makes the most of the open beams and raw brickwork.

Botín, C/ Cuchilleros 17 (just south of the Plaza Mayor), ℗ 91 366 42 17, Ⓜ Sol, claims to one of the oldest restaurants in the world. Dating back to 1725, it is very popular with American and Japanese tour parties in search of the taste of Hemingway. **Casa Ciriaco**, C/ Mayor 84, ℗ 91 548 06 20, Ⓜ Sol, another Castilian taberna, offers simple but first rate home cooking Try their speciality, *Gallina en pepitoria* (chicken casserole with wine and almonds).

A taste of real Madrileño cooking means a visit to the **Taberna de Antonio Sánchez**, C/ Mesoón de Paredes 13, ℗ 91 539 78 26, Ⓜ Tirso de Molina, where the extensive tapas display starts the ball rolling. Especially good are the stews, at very affordable prices. **La Abacería de la Villa**, Villa 3, ℗ 91 541 78 76, Ⓜ La Latina is on a little street winding up from the C/Segovia (not short of restaurants itself) to the C/Mayor. Just nine tables, and an adventurous menu, with delights such as cheese pancakes and fresh pasta with wild mushrooms, or ray in red wine.

Can Punyetes, in a small side street running from C/Mayor towards the Plaza de Oriente is half bar, half restaurant, with a range of simple Catalan specialities in a convivial, noisy, and youngish atmosphere. **Tía Dolly**, in Amparo 54, ✆ 91 527 33 26, is one of the capital's better-established Argentine restaurants, offering fresh pasta daily, and Argentine specialities such as *matahambre*, cold meat rolled over vegetables, and *pionono*, a kind of savoury roly-poly.

Popular with the younger set who have opted to live in the old quarter, and who appreciate the charming surroundings as much as the home-made grub, is *La Cacharrería*, C/ Moreria 9, ✆ 91 365 39 90, Ⓜ Latina, serving lovely salads, a selection of meats, including duck with raspberry sauce and succulent roast beef, and for dessert a tangy *tarta de limón*.

cheap

The best way to lunch economically in Madrid is to forget proper restaurants and take advantage of one of the hundreds of cafes and bars which offer a *menú del día*, between 1.30 and 3.30pm. A board outside will indicate what's on offer. Anywhere in the centre of town will do; after all, they are catering to office workers and labourers who can't make it home for lunch, but who still want home cooking.

vegetarian

Madrid used to be a veggie's nightmare. Things have changed, and the capital boasts a wide selection, many of them excellent value. **El Granero de Lavapiés**, C/ Argumosa 10, ✆ 91 467 76 11, Ⓜ Lavapiés, has a *1000 pts* menu, but only opens for lunch. **Artemisa**, C/ Ventura de la Vega 4, ✆ 91 429 50 92, Ⓜ Sevilla, is one of the capital's oldest, with a branch at Tres Cruces 4, ✆ 91 521 87 21, Ⓜ Gran Vía, although the menu is not overly imaginative. El Estragón, Plaza de la Paja 10, ✆ 91 365 89 82, Ⓜ La Latina, is a new addition, with a relaxed, American feel, and a distinctive, creative menu.

Gula Gula has two branches, neither exclusively vegetarian, but with a fine selection of salad buffets. Following the success of the first on GranVía 1, ✆ 91 522 87 64, Ⓜ Sevilla, another opened round the corner on Infante 5, ✆ 91 420 29 19, Ⓜ Sevilla. Both attract a large and camp gay crowd, with singing, dancing waiters and drag shows. **La Mazorca**, Paseo de Infanta Isabel, ✆ 91 501 70 13, Ⓜ Atocha, is a homely place with a chimney which offers a good respite from the hustle and bustle of the nearby Reina Sofia musuem.

open air eating

Eating out in the open is an option in the Spanish capital right through the year. Try any of the restaurants around the lake in the Casa de Campo, Ⓜ Lago, for lunch.

A short walk up from the lake, still in the Casa de Campo, is **El Urogallo**, a recently opened Asturian restaurant with a beautiful terrace opening out onto views of the Madrid skyline. They offer a terrific menu at midday for *1300 pts*.

La Plaza de Chamberí, Plaza de Chamberí 10, ✆ 91 446 06 97, Ⓜ Bilbao, is a delight on a summer's evening. **El Viajero**, Plaza de la Cebada 11, ✆ 91 366 90 64, Ⓜ La Latina, serves the finest Uruguayan beef, as well as good salads and crepes and puts tables outside in the summer.

An essential part of Madrid nightlife is the *tapeo*, which means going from bar to bar in a particular neighbourhood, nibbling on tapas, while sipping on a cold beer or a glass of wine. Beware, tapas can be expensive; the days when bars dished up anything more substantial than a few peanuts or a slice of tortilla with your drink are long gone.

The best areas for tapas bars are Chueca and Malasaña, the old centre, from Sol over to Plaza Mayor and on to Opera, Huertas and Plaza Santa Ana, Lavapies and La Latina.

As good a starting point as any in Chueca is **La Bardemcilla**, Augusto Figueroa 47, ✆ 91 521 42 56, Ⓜ Chueca is run by Monica Bardem, the youngest of the acting family clan. The tapas bear the names of assorted films that Javier (*Jamón Jamón*) and co have appeared in. Crowded, but unpretentious. **Santander**, down the road, at C/ Augusto Figueroa 26, ✆ 91 522 49 10, Ⓜ Chueca, is worth visiting for its abundant selection and low prices.

Over in Malasaña, on the other side of C/Fuencarral, start your tapas tour in **Albur**, Manuela Malasaña 15, ✆ 91 594 27 33, Ⓜ Bilbao: good wine, imaginative tapas and a relaxed atmosphere. Then, wind your way through Malasana to end up in **El Maño**, La Palma 64, ✆ 91 521 50 57, a beautifully restored 1920s *bodega* for fine tapas, a good selection of wines and prices to match.

At Sol, nip round the corner from the Corte Inglés to **Casa Labra**, C/Tetuán 12, ✆ 91 531 00 81, Ⓜ Sol. Dating back to the end of the last century, this spit and sawdust place is packed out with hungry shoppers guzzling down the tasty house speciality, deep fried cod chunks and *croquetas*.

At **La Taberna** de Antonio Sánchez, C/ Mesón de Paredes 13, ✆ 91 539 78 26, Ⓜ Tirso de Molina, you'll find a very traditional bar where the customers enjoy fine tapas under the beady eyes of stuffed bulls' heads. En route, stop off at **Casa del Abuelo**, C/ Victoria, off C/ Cruz, Ⓜ Sol, which has been specializing in prawns and powerful red wine since 1906.

The area known as the Madrid of the Austrias, which runs from the back of the Plaza Mayor over to the church of San Francisco Grande on Bailén, has gone upmarket in recent years. The thing to do is the '*ruta del vino*'. Start off at Cava Baja, and meander up to the Plaza Cebada, taking in, among others, **La Taberna de los Cien Vinos**, Nuncio, 17, ✆ 91 365 47 04, Ⓜ La Latina, and **Tapasentao**, Almendro 27, ✆ 91 364 07 21, Ⓜ La Latina, which has no bar. You sit down and write out what you've had on a slate. No cheating though. **Delic**, Plaza de la Paja, ✆ 91 364 54 50, Ⓜ La Latina, is the new face of tapas, with cold soups, canapés, juices, homemade pasta and ham.

Huertas and Santa Ana is a mecca for tapas lovers, among the highlights are **La Moderna**, Plaza Santa Ana 12, ✆ 91 420 15 82, Ⓜ Sol, and **El Lacón**, C/ Manuel Fernández y González 8, ✆ 91 429 60 42, Ⓜ Sevilla, a down-to-earth Galician place with a rustic-feeling, bright white interior, which serves great *calamares tinta* (squid in ink) and *sepia plancha* (griddled cuttlefish).

On the same street, **La Trucha**, C/ Manuel Fernández y González 3, ✆ 91 429 58 33, Ⓜ Sevilla, specializes in smoked fish, Andalusian style: try a *verbena de ahumados*, a plateful of luscious smoked delicacies.

Casa Alberto, C/ Huertas 18, Ⓜ Antón Martín, is a traditional bar with an air of antiquity that is popular with locals and tourists; the bar itself is cooled the old-fashioned way with cold running water flowing along a stainless steel channel.

The **Taberna de Dolores**, Pza. de Jesús, Ⓜ Antón Martín, is a very popular old bar with a beautiful mosaic-tiled facade. Here you can choose from a short menu of pricey (*about 300 pts each*) but delicious canapés to accompany your beer: best are the tiny offerings of smoked ham and cheese, anchovy and tomato, and *pez espada* (smoked swordfish) on slices of bread.

It's easy to tapa hop in Lavapies and La Latina. Try **Casa Montes** at Lavapiés 40, ℗ 91 527 00 64, for good wines and tasty bites such as cured duck or chorizo. Up the road, the **Taberna del Avapiés**, Lavapiés 5, ℗ 91 539 26 50, has lots of seats, wine and different tapas, such as *cecina* (cured beef) and garlicky cod. One of the capital's best-kept tapa secrets is to be found at **Tomás**, Tabernillas 23, ℗ 91 365 10 25, Ⓜ La Latina. The strict opening hours for this illustrious bar (*1.15 –3pm and 8pm–10pm, closed Saturday and Wednesday nights*) are because Tomás is a football fan. Try the vermouth, with anchovy on cheese.

cafés, bars, and interesting places to drink

Café society in Madrid includes everyone who cares to participate. With one bar for every 96 inhabitants, according to the last census, there's always somewhere to go, from beloved ancient holes in the wall which haven't been decorated since the time of Alfonso XII, to chic boulevard cafés where the Madrileñan *jeunesse dorée* discuss movies and modern art. You'll find one close to your hotel in which you'll happily send an entire afternoon down the drain, but here are some of the most interesting and famous.

The **Café Gijon**, Pso. de Recoletos 21, ℗ 91 521 54 25, Ⓜ Banco de España, dates from 1888 and is seeped in history: it is here that Madrid's writers, artists, philosophers and political theorists have always gathered to engage in the discussion meetings that became known as *tertulias*.

Other legendary haunts of Madrid's intellectual class include the **Café Comercial**, Glorieta de Bilbao 7, ℗ 91 521 56 55, Ⓜ Bilbao, a veritable institution which, like the Gijón, is over a century old, with devoted regulars; and **Chicote**, Gran Vía 12, ℗ 91 532 67 37, Ⓜ Gran Vía, an Art Deco haven which never closed during the Civil War, and, in recent years, has had its original 1940s furnishings immaculately restored. Chicote was famous for his cocktails and this was his bar.

The **Café-Restaurante El Espejo**, Pso. de Recoletos 31, ℗ 91 308 23 47, Ⓜ Colón, is not authentically old (it opened in the 1970s), but it too tries to recreate the atmosphere of the old *tertulias*. It's a pretty place, with a glass pavilion and a café terrace where, in summer, a pianist churns out honeyed improvisations on 'My Way', 'Misty' and the like.

Madrid's celebrated fine arts centre has a large café, the **Café de Círculo de Bellas Artes**, C/ Marqués de Casa Riera 2, Ⓜ Banco de España, which looks rather like a cross between a ballroom and an old-fashioned dentist's waiting room, but is one of the most relaxed places to linger in the city centre. It has an ostentatious *terraza* on the Calle de Alcalá which is open all year. The centre itself houses exhibition spaces and a library, and the annual masked ball held in the upstairs banqueting rooms is one of the highlights of the Madrileñan social calendar (for information on shows, workshops and events, call ✆ 91 531 77 00).

It's all too easy to let the hours slip by at the **Nuevo Café Barbieri**, C/ Ave María 45, ✆ 91 527 36 58, Ⓜ Lavapiés, a beautiful old café, yellowed with age, with huge, Baroque wall mirrors, and a civilized atmosphere. Soothing by day (symphonies play in the background and there are speciality coffees and infusions to enjoy over a newspaper) and quietly sophisticated and sociable by night, this café also offers occasional film screenings. It's in the Lavapiés district, itself apparently barely touched by the ravages of the 20th century, and full of traditional local bars and cafés.

A good tea-time hideout in the very centre of Madrid is **La Mallorquina**, Puerta del Sol 8, Ⓜ Sol—while the busy shop downstairs sells pastries and gaudily wrapped sweets, upstairs there's a salon which is just the place to sip a cup of something in comfort and quietude while gazing out over the hubbub of the Puerta del Sol below.

La Luiza, Pza. Santa Ana 2, Ⓜ Sol, is cool for cakes, with broad glass-fronted displays of *pastelerías* and *bollerías*, and a bar where you can sit and dunk the leg of a croissant in your coffee. Chueca's gay crowd favour the **Café Figueroa**, C/ Augusto Figueroa 17, ✆ 91 521 16 73, Ⓜ Chueca, a chatty, relaxed turn-of-the-century café.

One of the most pleasant places to watch the sun go down is the **Café Moderno**, Pza. de Comendadores, Ⓜ Noviciado, on a traffic-free square with a playground in the middle; as the light fades and the children are bundled away to supper, locals mellow out over their *copas*.

Meanwhile perhaps the most glorious views in all Madrid, particularly at sunset, are to be had from the shady terrace of **El Ventorillo**, C/ Bailén, Ⓜ La Latina, which overlooks the Jardines de Las Vistillas, Nuestra Señora de la Almudena and the Campo del Moro, with the sierra in the distance, and which serves good, simple meals. There are also lovely views of green parkland and the distant Guadarramas from the *terrazas* along the Paseo del Pintor Rosales, on the east side of the Parque del Oeste.

Not far away from El Ventorillo is **El Anciano**, C/ Bailén 19 (across from the Palacio Real), ✆ 91 559 53 32, Ⓜ Opera, a very old and picturesque wine shop, and another very *típico* old bar near the centre is **Casa Manolo**, C/ Jovellanos, Ⓜ Sevilla (near the Teatro de Zarzuela). The **Bodega Ángel Sierra**, C/ Gravina, Pza. de Chueca, Ⓜ Chueca, is also a classic place to drink—it's a traditional *vermut* bar, with house vermouth on tap.

The Plaza Santa Ana area is always full of high-spirited drinkers and a favourite place to meet people is **Viva Madrid**, C/ Manuel Fernández y González, Ⓜ Sevilla, one of Lorca's old haunts, which retains its gorgeous tiled façade; inside there are more coloured tiles, carved wood, and caryatids, plus the obligatory free-flowing beer taps.

Equally popular is **Los Gabrieles**, C/ Echegaray 17, ✆ 91 429 62 61, Ⓜ Sevilla, a handsome, cool, ancient (19th-century) bar, lined with decorative tiles, and full of loud music and lively company. The prices here double after 5pm.

Or there's **La Venencia**, C/ Echegaray 7, ✆ 91 429 73 13, Ⓜ Sevilla, an ancient sherry bar with a macho atmosphere, serving countless varieties of sherry from rows of bottles and vats. Near here is **No se lo digas a nadie**, C/ Ventura de la Vega 11, ✆ 91 429 75 25, Ⓜ Sevilla, a multi-purpose venue with a café/disco/bar which was once almost exclusively women-only but now welcomes lesbians and gays; it hosts private parties, drag shows, and other entertainments, and it doubles as an occasional meeting place for militant action groups.

Back on the Santa Ana trail is the **Cervecería Alemana**, Pza. Santa Ana 6, ✆ 91 429 70 33, Ⓜ Sol, a perfect German-Spanish beerhall and one of Hemingway's many old watering holes.

Further north, the **Cervecería Santa Bárbara**, Pza. Santa Bárbara 8, ✆ 91 319 04 49, Ⓜ Alonso Martínez, is packed with twenty-somethings at weekends.

C/Reina is host to two of the capital's best cocktail bars: **Cock**, at C/Reina 17, ✆ 91 532 28 26, is hideously expensive, but unique in its 1920s fake country house décor, while **del Diego** has attentive service and imaginative food and drink. The **Palacio de Gaviria**, Arenal 9, ✆ 91 526 60 69, is a 19th-century palace turned into macro venue, its many salons are home to a range of moods and musics. It attracts an international crowd.

The **Centro Cubano**, Claudio Coello 41, ✆ 91 575 82 79, Ⓜ Serrano, boasts an excellent restaurant behind its anonymous doors. Its bar also serves the best *mojitos* and *daiquiris* in town. Not for lovers of Fidel, though.

Malasaña has undergone gentrification in recent times, and is no longer the rough and ready area it once was. It still largely attracts an under 30s crowd though, drawn to such famous bars as **Louie Louie**, C/de la Palma 43, Ⓜ Noviciado, where you'll have to knock to get in, or **La Vía Lactea**, C/Velarde 18, Ⓜ Tribunal, still stuck in an early eighties timewarp, but none the worse for it.

Malasaña also has some lovely cafes to while away the hours: **Cafe Ruiz**, C/Ruíz 11, ✆ 91 446 12 32, Ⓜ Bilbao, or **Café Isadora**, C/Divino Pastor 14, ✆ 91 445 71 54, Ⓜ Bilbao. The Art Deco **Café Manuela**, San Vicente Ferrer, Ⓜ Tribunal, holds storytelling nights.

Entertainment and Nightlife

theatre

Madrid's theatre tradition has never matched Barcelona's, and over the last decade, the capital has fallen further behind. Classical theatre is kept alive at the **Teatro de la Comedia**, C/Principe, ✆ 91 521 49 31. The main event on the dramatic arts calendar is the Festival de Otoño, the autumn arts festival, which runs for a month in November and December, and still manages to attract a diverse international offering.

The state-funded **Centro Dramático Nacional** at the Teatro María Guerrero, C/Tamayo y Baus 4, ✆ 91 310 29 49, Ⓜ Colón, mixes modern pieces with works by standard 20th-century playwrights. Madrid's alternative scene has taken a bashing since the glory days of the eighties when the socialists heavily funded the arts, however the **Alfil**, C/del Pez 10, ✆ 91 521 58 27, Ⓜ Noviciado, offers a wide range of comedy and satire, while the **Sala Olimpia**, Pza de Lavapiés, ✆ 91 527 46 22, Ⓜ Lavapies, puts on dance and theatre to packed houses.

opera

Opera buffs can now enjoy a visit to the **Teatro Real**, Pza Isabel II, ✆ 91 516 06 06, Ⓜ Opera, the capital's opera house, finally restored after many years' delay. Across the other side of the city, the **Auditorio Nacional de Musica**, C/Principe de Vergara 146, ✆ 91 337 01 00, Ⓜ Cruz del Rayo, attracts international orchestras, and is home to the Orquesta Nacional de España. The **Teatro de la Zarzuela**, tucked away in Jovellanos 4, ✆ 91 429 82 25, Ⓜ Banco de España, is a Belle Epoque gem. Beautifully restored, it stages opera and a variety of concerts.

Zarzuela, Spain's unique light opera, fills the summer gap, with programming from June to September. Open air performances (albeit by amateurs) are held at **La Corrala**, C/Tribulete 12, Ⓜ Lavapies, in July and August. There is no phone booking, just turn up at 10pm. More information will be available from the tourist office.

Other performances are staged at the **Centro Cultural de la Villa**, Jardines del Descubrimiento, Pza Colón, ✆ 91 575 60 80.

flamenco

Madrid is also arguably the best place in Spain to see flamenco. The capital holds at least two festivals a year, and venues such as **Casa Patas**, C/Cañizares 10, 369 04 96, Ⓜ Tirso de Molina, and Suristán, C/de la Cruz, 532 39 09, Ⓜ Sevilla, regularly feature well-known acts.

Good flamenco, particularly dance, can be found at some of the *tablaos*—flamenco shows, usually with dinner and drinks, despite their touristy feel. Among the better *tablaos* are **Corral de la Morería**, C/ de la Morería 17, ✆ 91 365 84 46, Ⓜ La Latina, and **Café de Chinitas**, C/Torija 7, 547 15 01. They can be pricey though, at around *5,000 pts* a head.

Soleá, C/Cava Baja 34, 365 33 08, Ⓜ La Latina, was once a scruffy little bar attracting local would-be flamenco singers who would put on impromptu performances. The new joint, across the road, still attracts amateurs—some of whom are very good—but lacks the atmosphere of its former locale. Still worth a visit though.

cinema

Madrileños are avid film-goers, perhaps because the cinema is still so much cheaper (*500–800 pts*) here than in other European capitals. Spanish cinema has had its ups and downs over the last 20 years, and now seems to have established itself, with respectable domestic audiences, even in the face of Hollywood blockbusters. The capital has more than half a dozen original version cinemas, four of them— *multicines*—clustered around the Pza de los Cubos at Pza España: **Princesa**, **Renoir**, **Alphaville**, and **Lumiere**. See the daily papers for details. If you want that neighbourhood film feel, try the *cine de verano* open air screen at the Parque de la Bombilla, C/Quintana 22, ✆ 91 541 58 00.

Nightclubs and Bars

The first time visitor to Madrid, probably drawn here by the three major art museums, is often surprised by the intensity of the capital's nightlife, which at weekends takes over the city centre and lasts through into the dawn of Sunday morning. If you're serious about staying the course, the key to it all is not to start too early, i.e. before midnight. So get that siesta in. Actually, Madrid's nightlife nicely illustrates Khruschev's addage that quantity is its own quality. Madrileños favour their own established locals, where they are known, or they search for places where the famous hang out. Areas like Huertas and Santa Ana, or Malasaña and Chueca, or Argüelles, Bilbao are popular because people like to visit at least half a dozen places, before ending up in somewhere around three or four to see the night out. Now that the right wing Partido Popular is firmly ensconced in the town hall and the regional government, as well as at national level, licensing hours are more strictly observed, with many places closing at their required time of 2.30 or 3am.

Although new places open and close all the time, Madrid's club scene is fairly traditional, with most punters interested in just having a good time, and most places resistant to new trends in music; instead playing their own eclectic blend.

Joy Eslava, C/Arenal 11, ✆ 91 366 37 33, Ⓜ Sol, maybe the capital's best-known *discoteca*, but it's far from the trendiest. More fashionable is **Club 69**, Marqués de Riscal, 11, ✆ 91 308 27 36, Ⓜ Rubén Darío, with its drag queens and deep house. The smart young things go to the very upmarket **Empire**, Paseo de Recoletos 16, ✆ 91 431 54 27, Ⓜ Colón.

Down by the river is **La Riviera**, C/Virgen del Puertro, ✆ 91 544 89 23, Ⓜ Puerta del Angel, which hosts some of Madrid's best concerts and attracts an over 25s crowd to its almost open air complex. Salsa is still popular, and Madrid's Caribbean population grows every year.

If you want to dance, try the **Café del Mercado**, Ronda de Toledo 1, ✆ 91 365 87 39, Ⓜ Puerta de Toledo, it attracts a mixture of Spaniards and Latins. **Calentito**, Jacometrezzo 15, ✆ 91 547 00 81, Ⓜ Callao, is small, frenetic, always crowded (if not it's still too early), and has go-go dancers on the bar.

live music

Best for live jazz is the Café Central, Pza del Angel 10, ✆ 91 369 41 43, Ⓜ Sol. It attracts some of the best names to its genuine café atmosphere. **Clamores**, over at C/Albuquerque 14, ✆ 91 445 79 38 has jazz and flamenco, as well as local singer/songwriters. Down the road from the Cafe Central is **Populart**, Huertas 24, ✆ 91 429 84 07, which has jazz and blues, and rock. It can get very crowded, especially at weekends. Close by, **Suristán**, Cruz 7, ✆ 91 532 39 09, Ⓜ Sevilla, has emerged over the last couple of years as a venue with one of the most imaginative booking policies, attracting the best names in flamenco, blues, and salsa.

For more down to earth pub rock try the gigantic **Irish Rover**, Avenida de Brasil 7, ✆ 91 556 09 83, Ⓜ Cuzco. Flamenco fans will warm to **Candela**, C/Olmo 1,

℃ 91 467 33 82, Ⓜ Antón Martín, a sleazy late night bar which attracts a heady mix of gypsies, flamenco artists, locals, and foreigners looking to lose themselves in Spain: very much a wee hours joint.

More genteel, attracting local folk talent, is **Libertad** 8, C/Libertad 8, ℃ 91 532 11 50, Ⓜ Chueca, but arrive early, it's tiny and fills up quickly.

gay

Chueca, predominantly gay, is overflowing with bars. The **Café Figueroa**, C/Augusto Figueroa 17, ℃ 91 521 16 73, Ⓜ Chueca, is open throughout the day, until late, and is a good starting off point. Rick's, Pza Vazquéz de Mella, Ⓜ Chueca, and has an easy-going atmosphere. Those looking for something a little more hardcore might try **Refugio**, Doctor Cortezo 1, Ⓜ Tirso de Molina, famous for its foam parties and other thematic nights. Madrid's lesbian scene has picked up recently, with half a dozen clubs, mostly tolerant of accompanied men. **Truco**, Pza de Chueca, ℃ 91 532 89 21, Ⓜ Chueca, is great fun in the summer, with tables on the square.

chocolate and churros

Tradition demands that a night on the tiles ends up with chocolate and churros. Try the oldest and best known, **Chocolatería San Ginés**, Pasadizo de San Ginés 5, Ⓜ Sol. Fit to bursting around dawn, as revellers take much needed carbohydrates on board. The posh crowd over in Salamanca frequent the **Churrería San Ildefonso**, Lope de Rueda 41, ℃ 91 574 50 19, Ⓜ Ibiza, from 4.30am on.

Around Madrid

Beyond the caprice of Charles V and Felipe II, Madrid's location made it the logical site for Spain's capital. Not only is Madrid roughly central to the country as a whole, but its growth filled a vacuum at the centre of a region containing many of the most important cities of 16th-century Spain. Felipe's new capital thus had a sort of ready-made Île-de-France around it, a garland of historic and lovely towns, each with something different to offer the visitor.

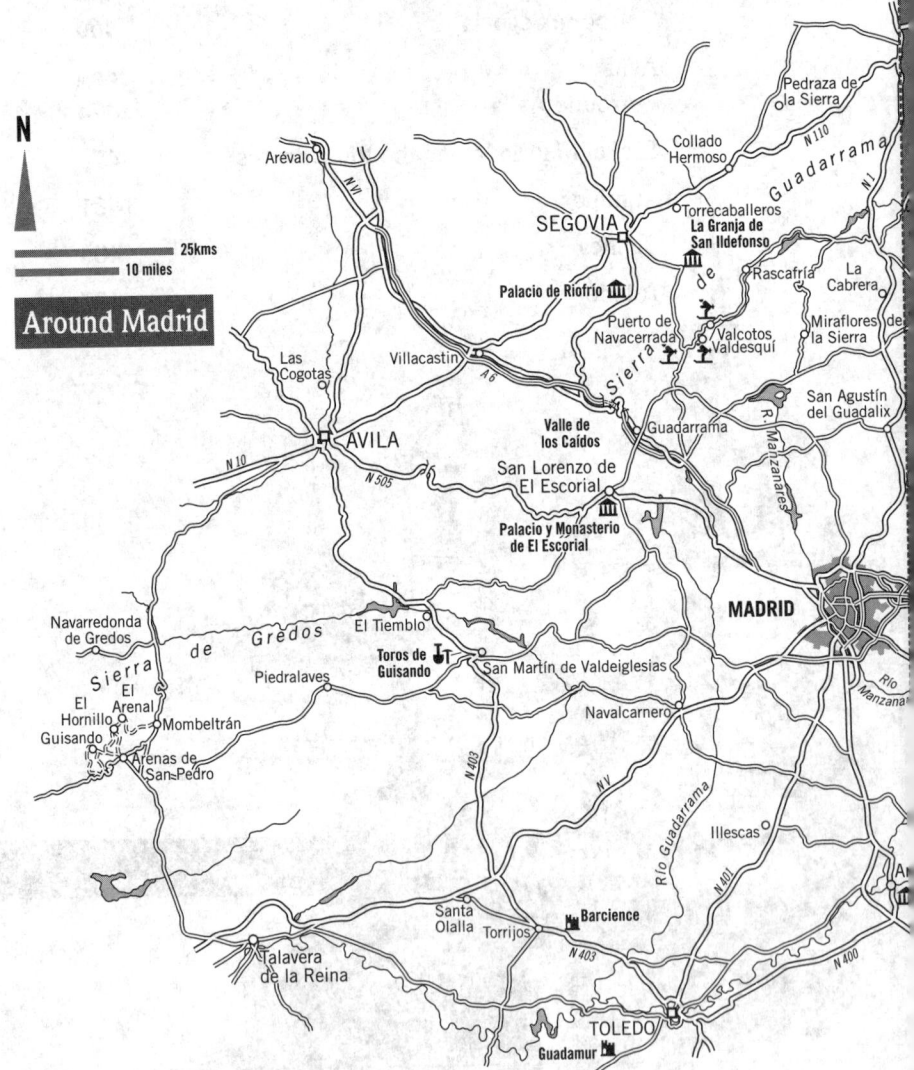

N

25kms
10 miles

Around Madrid

Arévalo

Pedraza de la Sierra

Collado Hermoso

SEGOVIA
Torrecaballeros
La Granja de San Ildefonso

Guadarrama

Palacio de Riofrío

Rascafría
La Cabrera

Puerto de Navacerrada
Valcotos
Valdesquí
Miraflores de la Sierra

Las Cogotas

Villacastín

Sierra de

San Agustín del Guadalix

ÁVILA

Valle de los Caídos

Guadarrama

San Lorenzo de El Escorial

R. Manzanares

Palacio y Monasterio de El Escorial

MADRID

Navarredonda de Gredos

Sierra de Gredos

El Tiemblo

Toros de Guisando

San Martín de Valdeiglesias

Río Manzana

El Hornillo
El Arenal
Guisando
Mombeltrán
Piedralaves

Navalcarnero

Arenas de San Pedro

Río Guadarrama

Illescas

Santa Olalla
Torrijos
Barcience

Talavera de la Reina

TOLEDO
Guadamur

Everyone goes to **Toledo**, of course, and romantically beautiful **Segovia** also comes in for its share of travellers. But beyond these, you may also conveniently use Madrid as a base for visiting **Ávila**, resolutely medieval behind its famous walls, the distinguished old university town of **Alcalá de Henares**, quiet, seldom-visited **Sigüenza**, the steep citadel of **Cuenca** with its cliffside houses, the royal palaces at **Aranjuez**, or **El Escorial**. Whenever Madrid's traffic, cacophonous nightclubs, and endless museum corridors become too much, any of these towns can provide a day's diversion and a little peace and quiet. And if Madrid is just the kind of metropolis you're trying to get away from, you can always set yourself up in one of them— and make a day-trip to Madrid.

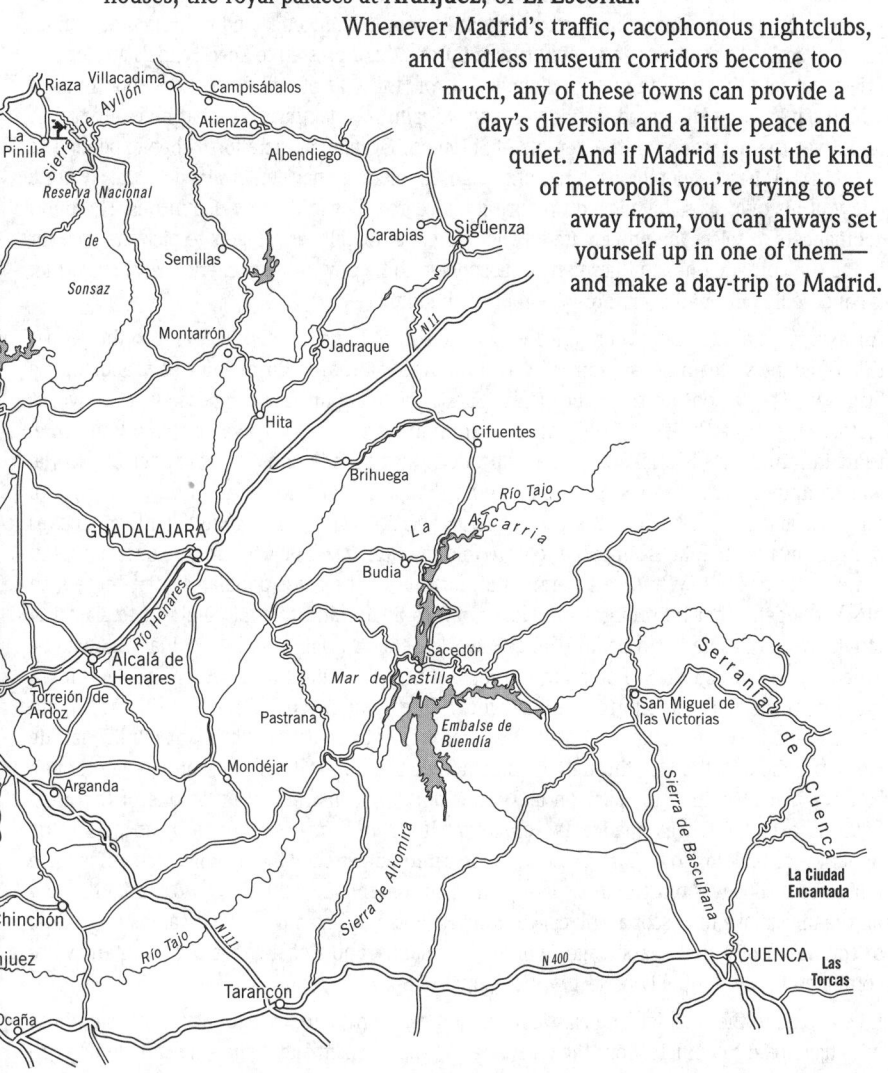

451

El Escorial

The Spaniards aren't shy; they matter-of-factly refer to Felipe II's combination palace-secretariat-monastery-mausoleum as 'the eighth wonder of the world'. Any building with a façade 200m wide and 2673 windows is entitled to some consideration, but it's not so much the glass and stone of the Escorial that make it remarkable, but the neurotic will of the king who conjured it up. This is the vortex of Spain, full of magnificence and poison, a folly on an imperial scale. To the Protestants of northern Europe, hard pressed to keep Felipe's armies and priests at bay, this building was a diabolic horror, the seat of evil on earth. Felipe himself would have calmly disagreed (for he was always calm), explaining that what he really had in mind was the re-creation of the Temple of Solomon. Despite all the effort Felipe expended in stamping out heretical opinions in his long reign, he seems to have entertained on the sly quite a few of his own, possibly picked up during his years spent in the Low Countries. He found geomancers to select the proper site for the millennial temple, astrologers to pick the date for laying the corner stone, and hermetic philosophers to help with the numerical mysticism that is supposedly built into every proportion of the building.

An *escorial* is a slag-heap. There once was some sort of mine on this site—and so the proper title of Felipe's dream-house translates as the Royal Seat of the Royal Saint Lawrence of the Slagheap. The reasons for the dedication to San Lorenzo are unclear. Supposedly Felipe won a victory on the saint's day in 1557, at St Quentin in Flanders, and vowed to build him something in return; this is unlikely, as the dedication wasn't made until 10 years after El Escorial was completed. An even less probable tale has Felipe's architects planning this rectangle of buildings and enclosed courtyards as an echo of the saint's gridiron attribute (San Lorenzo was roasted alive on one; he is supposed to have told the Romans: 'You can turn me over now; I'm done on this side'). While San Lorenzo is not one of the most popular saints, there's an obscure legend that he brought the Holy Grail to Spain, and this may help to explain the tangled web of esotericism behind Felipe's work. Felipe's original architect, Juan Bautista de Toledo, had worked on St Peter's in Rome; you may find that these two chilly, overblown symbols of the Counter-Reformation have much in common. Work commenced in 1563, but Bautista died four years later, and the Escorial was entrusted to his brilliant pupil, Juan de Herrera, who saw the task through to its completion in 1584. It kept him busy; even though Herrera had little time to spare on any other buildings, his reputation as one of the great Spanish architects was made. By creating the *estilo desornamentado*, stripping the Renaissance building to its barest essentials, he captured perfectly the nation's mood of austere militancy. Felipe was more than pleased, and as he contemplated the rising work from the spot on the hills above the Escorial still called 'King Philip's Seat' he must have dreamed just a little of the dawn of a new classic age, where Christianity and Renaissance achievement were combined in the spiritually perfect world empire of Spain.

If you come to the Escorial for a classic revelation, you'll have to settle for dry classicism; those who have read too much about the dark side of Felipe's Spain and come expecting a monkish haunted house will be equally disappointed. As huge as it is, there's nothing gloomy or menacing about the Escorial. Its crisp lines and soft grey-granite combine for an effect that is tranquil and airy both inside and out. Everything is remarkably clean, as if dust and age had been banished by royal decree; somehow the Escorial looks as bright and new as the day it was completed.

By train: Trains to El Escorial (Cercanías line C 8a or Regionales line R 1, direction Ávila) start from Madrid-Atocha, and also stop at Madrid-Chamartín. The journey takes about an hour, and there are usually hourly departures in the daytime, and more at peak times, so it would be possible to combine Ávila with El Escorial for a slightly hectic day-trip. The trains arrive at the neighbouring village of El Escorial and are met by local buses for San Lorenzo and the monastery. The alternative to this short bus ride is a gentle 2km walk uphill from the station, along a fragrant avenue shaded by chestnuts and pines, past the Casita del Príncipe (*see* below). RENFE information, Madrid: ✆ 91 328 9020; El Escorial: ✆ 91 850 53 90.

By bus: Keep in mind that the proper name of the town beside the monastery is San Lorenzo de El Escorial, and it appears that way in bus schedules. The bus, nos.661 and 664, is faster than the train, and is run by Herranz, ✆ 91 543 36 45 or ✆ 91 850 53 90, from bay 3 of the Intercambiador de Transportes (bus interchange) next to the Moncloa metro stop in Madrid, to the stop in Pza. Virgen de Gracia in San Lorenzo, very near the monastery (*buses every half hour in the morning, every hour thereafter, daily, journey time 1hr*). Herranz also has a once-daily service from San Lorenzo to the Valle de los Caídos, allowing enough time to see the place (the journey takes 20mins). Tickets are sold from a little office in a bar on C/ Reina Victoria; the bar also has bowling lanes, so you can get in a few frames while reflecting on Habsburg eccentricity.

By car: From Madrid take the NVI (Ctra. de La Coruña) northwest, then the M505.

C/ Floridablanca 10, ✆ 91 890 15 54, near the bus station.

Palacio y Monasterio de San Lorenzo el Real de El Escorial

Open Tues–Sun 10–7; closed Mon; adm exp; free for EU passport holders on Wed.

El Escorial is managed by the Patrimonio Nacional. They sell tickets, guidebooks and souvenirs inside the north entrance. They also run guided tours, in various languages, for which there is no extra charge; if you want to join one, you may be asked to wait for a large enough group to gather. If you prefer, you can explore the complex independently, in any order you like (the official tour route is clearly signposted). However, without any guidance, you may miss out on a lot of intriguing details, such as the many manifestations of Felipe's obsession with mystical patterns in designing and building the place. You may also find, as you make your way from chamber to chamber and up and down dim stone staircases, that you quickly lose all sense of direction, and fail to appreciate, for example, the strategic location of the royal mausolea and Felipe's apartments in relation to the Basilica. (James Michener was not ashamed to admit he came here twice without realizing it had a church, though a 13,000 sq m basilica with a 90m high dome would elsewhere be hard to miss.) Admission to the Basilica only is free—you can walk right in, through the monumental western entrance, under the statue of San Lorenzo with his gridiron, and from here, along the central axis of the complex, the symmetrical grandeur of Bautista and Herrera's plan will begin to unfold.

Palacio de los Borbones (Bourbon Palace) and Nuevos Museos (New Museums)

The official tours begin in the northeastern quarter of the Escorial, a quarter never used by Felipe II, but converted by the Bourbons Carlos III and Carlos IV into a royal residence. These two do not seem to have had any interest in Felipe's conception of the Escorial, but used it only as a sort of glorified hunting-lodge. Not surprisingly, they refurbished these rooms as a similar, though smaller version of the Bourbon Royal Palace in Madrid. The **Bourbon Apartments,** with their tapestries after works by Goya and others, have now been restored to their former splendour, and they form a pleasant contrast to the austerity of their surroundings. Sadly, one of the most interesting rooms, the **Hall of the Battles**, with its fresco nearly 62m long representing every detail of the 1431 Battle of Higuerela, a victory of King Juan II over the Moors of Granada, is under restoration and closed to the public.

Downstairs is an exhibition of some of the machinery and tools used to build the complex, plus architectural drawings and scale models tracing the progress of the construction work through its various stages of completion. Upstairs again, the **New Museums** occupy a long corridor along the eastern walls, with windows looking out over intricate knot gardens. Much of Felipe's collections of paintings is displayed here, including works by Bosch, Patinir and Dürer; later additions include a Velázquez.

Palacio de Felipe II

Such is the reputation Felipe earned for himself—the evil genius of the Inquisition and all—that it comes as a genuine surprise to visit the little palace he tacked onto the back of the Escorial for himself. Few kings anywhere have ever chosen a more delightful abode: a few simple rooms reminiscent of the interiors from paintings of Vermeer, with white walls, Delft-blue tiles, and big windows opening to gardens and forests on all sides. These rooms suggest that Felipe's famous self-isolation had less of monkishness about it than the desire of a cultured, bookish monarch to ensure the necessary serenity for the execution of the royal duty he took so seriously. Felipe did not like courtiers, and he didn't care to go out. Alone with his trusted secretaries, he governed the affairs of his empire meticulously, reading, re-reading and annotating vast heaps of documents and reports. Aesthete and mystic, he approached politics with the soul of a clerk, and each of all the long list of mistakes he made was decided upon with the greatest of care.

It was here that Felipe received nervous, respectful ambassadors on a throne 'hardly grander than a kitchen chair'. Here, in his perfect temple, where the wisdom of Solomon was to be reborn, they brought him the news of the Armada's disaster, the national bankruptcies, the independence of the Netherlands, and all the little pinpricks in between. Here he endured the wasting disease that killed him, stinking so badly that neither servants nor visitors could bear his presence. He made sure his bed was situated right above the High Altar of his Basilica, and had a spy-hole cut in the bedchamber wall so that he could observe the endless Masses and bad art down below. With only that crowned skull on his night table to keep him company, here he awaited the reward of the virtuous.

The art and furnishings of the apartments may not necessarily be an accurate representation of Felipe's tastes, but there is a copy Felipe had made of Bosch's *Hay Wain*, one of his favourites, the original of which hangs in the Prado. In the throne room, be sure to see the marvellous inlaid wood **doors**, decorated with *trompe-l'oeil* scenes and architectural fantasies, done by an anonymous German artist of the 16th century; they are among the most beautiful things in the entire Escorial.

Mausoleums, Sacristy, Chapter House and Library

An opulent but narrow staircase leads down to the **Panteón Real**, situated beneath the Basilica's High Altar. All manner of stories have grown up around this pantheon of bad kings. Carlos II, it is said, spent whole days down here, ordering the gilded marble tombs to be opened so that he might gaze on his mummified ancestors. As in the Basilica, the most expensive stone from around the Mediterranean was used in its construction; the red jasper of the pavement and pilasters is so hard it had to be cut with diamond-tipped saws. The adjacent room is called, charmingly, the **Pudrería**, where Habsburg and Bourbon potentates spent 20-odd years mouldering until they became sufficiently dried out for their interments. Royal relations fill a maze of corridors beyond the Pantheon of the Kings, guarded by enormous white heralds with golden maces. Don Juan, victor of Lepanto, is the best known of them, though the tomb everyone notices is the tall, marble wedding-cake that was built to hold 60 baby princes and princesses; it is now more than half full. Don Juan, the father of the current king, Juan Carlos I, is the most recent addition. Don Juan got in, despite never having ruled, largely on the say so of his son. Beyond are the **Sacristía** (sacristy) and **Salas Capitulares** (chapter houses), which house some of the Escorial's collections of religious art.

One other section that may be seen is the **Biblioteca** (library) entered by a stair near the Escorial's main gate. Felipe's books meant as much to him as his paintings. His librarian, Benito Arias Montano, contributed much to the esoteric conception of the Escorial, and he built Felipe one of the largest collections of Greek, Hebrew and Arabic philosophical and mystical works in Europe. His agents watched over all the book-burnings of the Inquisition, and saved from the flames anything that was especially interesting. That his hoard of 40,000 volumes survives almost unchanged since Felipe's day is due only to the benign neglect of the generations that followed; 18th-century travellers reported that the monks watching over the collection were all illiterate. The frescoes of 1590–2 that cover the vaulted ceiling, by the Italian Pellegrino Tibaldi, are an allegory of the seven liberal arts, portraying seven of the famous philosophers and scientists of antiquity. The large globe of nested spheres in the centre of the library is Felipe's orrery, used in making astronomical calculations.

Basilica and Patio de los Reyes (Patio of the Kings)

Once inside the huge, square church, you will quickly become aware of the heightened atmosphere of a holy-of-holies. With very few windows, the Basilica was purposely kept dark as a contrast to the airiness of the rest of the Escorial. No church in Spain is colder inside; even in the hottest days of July the thin air seems pure distilled essence of Castile. Just inside the entrance, in the narrow **lower choir**, note the unusual ceiling and its 'flat vaulting', an architectural trick of very shallow vaulting that creates the illusion of flatness.

From here, the eye is drawn to the bright *retablo*, framed in darkness. Its paintings are by several then-fashionable Italian artists, including Pellegrino Tibaldi, who like Juan Bautista was a pupil of Michelangelo. Above them all is a golden figure of Christ on the Cross, and at its foot a tiny golden skull that stands out even across the great distance; its hollow eyes seem to follow you as you pass through the Basilica. These are really only of gilded bronze; if they weren't, they wouldn't be here. Originally the Basilica was full of real gold ornaments, and the precious stones of the Tabernacle were some of the most valuable that the Spanish royal house possessed. Napoleon's troops did a thorough job of looting El Escorial in 1808, making off with them all. Connoisseurs that they were, they left the artwork in peace. Notable are the gilded bronze ensembles to the sides of the altar, the families of Charles V and Felipe II (with all three of his wives) at prayer. Beneath the high altar is the *primera piedra*, the cornerstone of the Escorial. The west doors of the Basilica open onto the **Patio de los Reyes**, which is the Escorial's main courtyard, named after sculptures by Monegro representing six mighty Kings of Judah which adorn the church's western façade. On the far side of the courtyard is the west gate, the main ceremonial entrance to the Escorial, and to the right and left are the *colegio* and the monastery, which are both still in use, and are not open to the public. The two statues in the centre represent David and Solomon.

Beyond the Monastery

Two little country houses within walking distance of the Escorial are included in the admission ticket. The **Casita del Príncipe** and the **Casita de Arriba** (also known as the Casita del Infante), both built in the 1770s for Carlos IV, are tasteful, cosy and full of pretty pictures, and worth a visit if you just can't get enough of those Bourbons or you have time to kill before the bus comes. The Casita del Príncipe has neat, well-tended gardens in typically Spanish style, with box hedges laid out in knot patterns, and roses and shrubs flourishing among the fruit trees in the ancient orchards. It's worth taking a field guide to European trees on the walk down to the Casita del Príncipe: the **bosquecillo** has some magnificent examples, many well over 100 years old. Fans of Romantic architecture will enjoy a walk round the **Terreros** neighbourhood which runs down behind the Victoria Palace Hotel: there are several good value restaurants around here which cater to locals with summer houses in the area.

San Lorenzo de El Escorial

Since the building of the Escorial, a pleasant little town has grown up here. San Lorenzo has held on to its village atmosphere despite having an air of sophistication thrust upon it thanks to the presence of a private university and an influx of well-to-do settlers. *Madrileños*, keen to escape their city of baking concrete, are drawn here not only by the palace but also by the beauty of the setting in the cool, forested foothills of the Guadarramas. San Lorenzo is a much more attractive commuter base than any of Madrid's fringe of new-town suburbs, and, for urbanites, it's a popular summertime resort. The town boasts a tiny, exquisite theatre, the **Real Coliseo**, which was founded by Carlos III. It's a short walk from the Escorial at C/ Floridablanca 20, © 91 890 44 11.

Valle de los Caídos

> *Death is the patron saint of Spain.*
>
> Váldez Léal

If you're one of those who came to the Escorial expecting freakishness and gloom, don't be disappointed yet. From the town, there's a regular bus service to Francisco Franco's own idea of building for the ages. The **Valley of the Fallen** is supposedly meant as a memorial to soldiers from both sides of the Civil War, but it was old Republicans and other political unfortunates languishing in Franco's jails who did the work in the 1950s, blasting a 245m tunnel-like church out of the mountainside, and erecting a 150m stone cross above. The crowds of Spaniards who come here in a holiday mood on any weekend seem to care little for history or politics; they linger at one of Spain's most outrageous souvenir stands, then take the children up the funicular railway to the base of the cross. For local colour, there'll be a few ancient widows in black who come every week, and perhaps a pair of maladjusted teenagers in Falangist blue shirts. If you find yourself in the area around November 20th, make the trek: it's the anniversary of the **generalísimo's** death, attracting a strange mixture of followers.

The **cross**, held up by faith and structural steel, is claimed to be the largest in the world. Around its base are a series of titanic sculptured figures in some lost, murky symbolism: lions, eagles and pensive giants lurch out above you. The view takes in the hills and valleys for miles as well as the monastery Franco built for the monks who look after the **basilica** below.

This cave church is impressive, in the way the palace of a troll-king might be. The nave goes on and on, past giant, disconcerting Fascist angels with big swords, past dim chapels and holy images, finally ending in a plain, circular altar. José Antonio Primo de Rivera, founder of the Falangists, is buried here. His original interment in the royal crypt of the Escorial was too much even for many of Franco's supporters, and he eventually had to be moved here. Franco is here too; the company he chose for his last resting-place is perhaps the last word on what kind of man he really was. **Franco's tomb** is a plain stone slab on the floor near the altar, opposite José Antonio's. The gentlemen behind you in sunglasses and Hawaiian sports shirts are, if you haven't guessed, plain-clothes policemen, waiting for someone to try and spit on the old Caudillo.

El Escorial ✉ *28280*   **Where to Stay**

expensive

Visiting nabobs check in at the once-grand ★★★★**Victoria Palace**, C/ Juan de Toledo 4, ✆ 91 890 15 11, 🖷 91 890 12 48. Now restored to its former glory, the best rooms face south, away from the monastery and over the woodlands.

moderate

The ★★**Hotel Miranda Suizo**, C/ Floridablanca 20, ✆ 91 890 47 11, has been restored, losing something of its former Swiss charm, but comfy nonetheless, and with lovely views of the monastery. The café downstairs retains the original alpine feel and attracts a genteel clientele who tuck into an afternoon tea of hot chocolate with *picatostes* (basically soldiers of fried bread dipped in sugar).

A reasonably priced option is the ★★**Hs Cristina**, C/ Juan de Toledo 6, ✆ 91 890 19 61, a friendly place with a small garden and a restaurant.

inexpensive

An alternative budget choice is the ★★**Hs Vasco**, Pza. de Santiago 11, ✆ 91 890 16 19; it also has a good, *inexpensive* restaurant—a consideration in this town where dining isn't cheap.

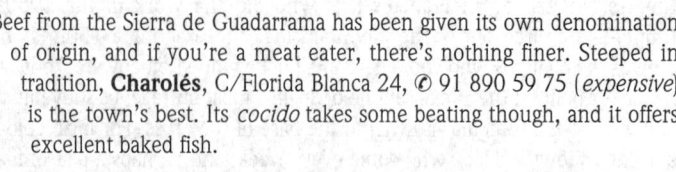

Beef from the Sierra de Guadarrama has been given its own denomination of origin, and if you're a meat eater, there's nothing finer. Steeped in tradition, **Charolés**, C/Florida Blanca 24, © 91 890 59 75 (*expensive*) is the town's best. Its *cocido* takes some beating though, and it offers excellent baked fish.

On the pretty Plaza de la Constitución, the **Fonda Génara**, Plaza San Lorenzo 2, (*moderate*) offers a terrific midday menu at around *1000 pts*. The **Erriuga**, Ventura Rodriguéz 7, © 91 890 61 36 (*moderate*) is a pleasant wine bar/restaurant which attracts a mainly local crowd. The cooking here is lighter, with the emphasis on game and fish.

As with much of the Sierra de Guadarrama, El Escorial holds its town fiestas during the first two weeks of September. The town's patron saint is the pretext for much fun on August 10th with processions and a fair at the entrance to the Casita de Arriba.

Segovia and Ávila

For whatever cool breezes refresh Madrid in its torrid summers, thank the **Guadarramas**, the chain of low mountains north of the city that stretches from Ávila in the west almost as far as Soria. Its highest peaks are near Madrid, and the snow on them lasts often until May or June. The Guadarramas have a near monopoly of pretty scenery in this part of Spain; though the heights are drab and grey, the lower regions contain green patches of forest and pastureland with a bit of the same alpine ambiance found in the Pyrenees and Cantabrian chains.

Once over the crests of the Guadarramas, the traditional boundary between the two Castiles, you're back in the medieval atmosphere of Old Castile, with its Romanesque churches, flocks of sheep and lonely castles. Two of its cities, Ávila and Segovia, are within easy reach of Madrid and could make convenient day-trips. Segovia, though, one of the most beautiful cities of Spain, is a place where you may wish to spend more time.

Segovia

Three distinct cultures have endowed this once-prominent town with three famous monuments. The Romans left Segovia a great aqueduct, and the age of Emperor Charles V (Carlos I of Spain) contributed an equally famous cathedral. The third, Segovia's Alcázar, should be as well known. Though begun by the Moors and rebuilt in the Middle Ages, its present incarnation is pure 19th-century fantasy, a lost stage set from a Wagnerian opera. Segovia has its other monuments—a unique style of Romanesque church, and the *esgrafiado* façades of its old mansions, but the memory the visitor takes away is likely to be mostly a fond impression. The delicate skyline silhouetted on a high narrow promontory between two green river valleys gives the city the appearance of a great ship among the rolling hills of Castile. To enter it is to climb into a lost medieval dream-Spain of unusually quiet streets, where the buildings are all of a single, lovely shade of warm, tan stone, making all old Segovia seem a single work of art.

When the Emperor Trajan built the aqueduct in the early 2nd century, Segovia was already a venerable city. Under Rome, and later the Visigoths and Moors, it attained little distinction, but it survived. After it fell to the Christians in the 11th century, Segovia blossomed in the great cultural and economic expansion of medieval Castile. Its Romanesque churches and palaces were built on the profits of an important textile industry, and by the time of the Catholic kings it was one of the leading cities of Spain.

Like most of Europe's medieval cities that have survived intact, Segovia's present-day serenity hides a dark secret. The economic policies and foreign wars of Charles V and Felipe II ruined Segovia as thoroughly as the rest of Old Castile, and it is only the four centuries of stagnation that followed that allow us to see old Segovia as it was.

Getting There

By train: Unless you've a hankering for slow, uncomfortable train journeys, Segovia is better reached by bus. There are nine trains every weekday and seven daily at weekends from Madrid-Atocha (Regionales line R 2, via Villalba de Guadarrama), leaving at two minutes past the even hours, plus 3.02pm. The journey takes just over 2hrs. All trains pass through Madrid-Chamartín about 15mins after leaving Madrid-Atocha. The journey takes you through some rugged, craggy scenery, and there are good views of the huge cross of the Valle de los Caídos as the train approaches Los Molinos. Trains back to Madrid leave Segovia at 55 past the even hours. Segovia station is in the modern part of town, about 20 minutes' walk from the old city, or a short ride by local bus. RENFE information, Madrid: *©* 91 328 90 20, Segovia: *©* 921 42 07 74.

By bus: La Sepulvedana, a comfortable, modern fleet, runs 15 buses every weekday (fewer at weekends) from Paseo de la Florida 11, Madrid, to Segovia's bus station on the central Paseo Ezequiel González. The buses are much quicker than the train, taking around an hour, but cost a little more. La Sepulvedana information, Madrid: *©* 91 530 48 00, Segovia: *©* 921 42 77 07.

Segovia also has bus connections to Ávila (twice on weekdays, once on Sat and Sun), Valladolid, La Granja, and all the villages in Segovia province.

Tourist Information

The main tourist office is at Plaza Mayor 10, *©* 921 46 03 34, *✉* 921 44 27 34; even if it's closed, there's plenty of information posted up on the doors and windows outside. There's another office by the viaduct at Plaza del Azojuego 1, *©* 921 44 02 05, *✉* 921 42 09 08.

Plaza Mayor and the Cathedral

Although new districts have grown out past the Roman aqueduct to the south and east, the **Plaza Mayor** (the former Plaza Franco) remains the centre of the old town, with its arcades and cafés. From here, the **Cathedral** (*open daily in summer 9–7; in winter Sun–Fri 9.30–1 and 3–6, Sat, hols, 9.30–6*) is just a stone's throw away. This has been called the 'last Gothic cathedral' of Spain; most of the work was done between 1525 and 1590, though parts were not completed until the 18th century. Segovia's old cathedral had been burned during the Comunero revolt, and Charles V contributed much to its replacement as an act of reconciliation. Juan Gil de Hontañón, who designed the Catedral Nueva at Salamanca, carried further here the tendencies of his earlier work. Segovia is finer in form and proportion than Salamanca,

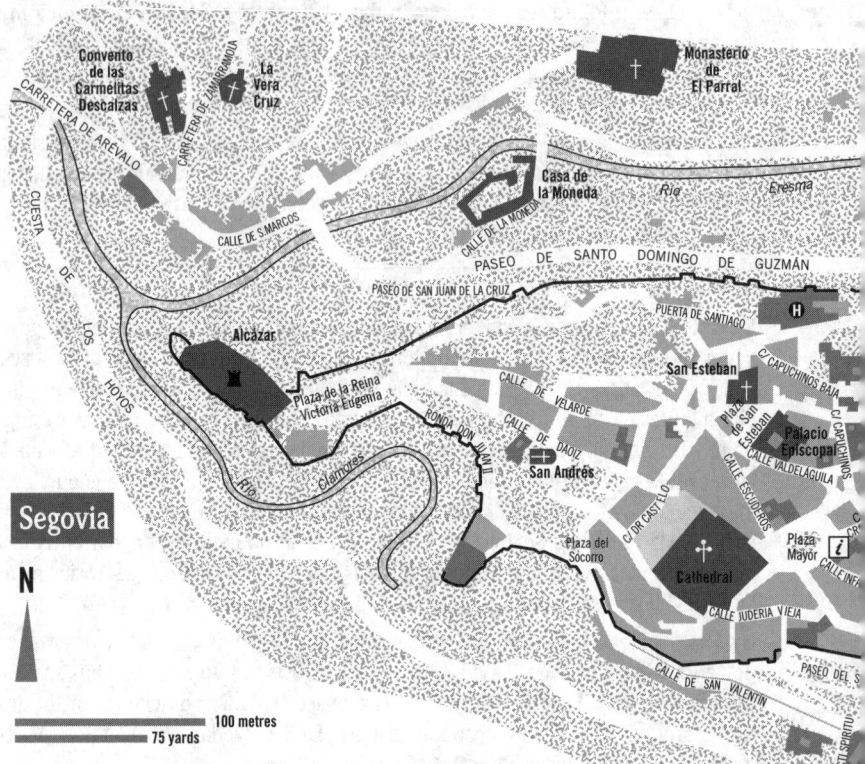

Segovia

N

100 metres
75 yards

and less encumbered with ornament, expressing the
national mood of austerity in grandeur in much the same way as El
Escorial. The best parts of this cathedral are the semicircular eastern end,
where an exuberant ascent of pinnacles and buttresses covers the chapels behind
the main altar, the unique squarish bell-tower and an elegant dome over the choir.
The latter two are Renaissance elements that fit in perfectly; in an age of architectural
transition it was the greatest part of Juan Gil's accomplishment to make a harmonious
combination of such diverse elements. The architect chose to be buried in the spare, well-lit
interior. There's little to see on the inside–a comment on the hard times 16th-century Segovia
had come into—and the small **museum** (*adm 200 pts*) inside is almost painful to visit. See the
cloister, though, if it's open; this is part of the original cathedral, built in the Isabelline Gothic
style by Juan Guas and moved here and reassembled after it survived the fire.

Alcázar

Open summer, 10–7, winter, 10–6; adm.

The **Alcázar**, jutting out on its cliffs over the confluence of the Río Eresma and the smaller
Clamores, was one of the great royal residences of Castile when Segovia was at the height of
its prominence. Alfonso the Wise spent much of his reign here, as did other kings of the 12th
and 13th centuries. By the 19th, though, the old, forgotten castle had declined into a military

school; in 1862, some young cadets set fire to it, in the hope they might be transferred to Madrid. No one, it seems, bothered to record the name of the architects who oversaw the Alcázar's restoration in the 1880s. Even worse, some writers have sniffed that the job they did is 'not authentic'. Just because these forgotten heroes of the picturesque saw fit to turn the Alcázar into a flight of fancy worthy of the Mad King Ludwig, with pointed turrets and curving crenellated walks, some people find fault. The German tourists look puzzled, and a little

disappointed to find a castle on the Rhine in Castile; still they admit it's a very good Rhine castle. The Alcázar is *better* than authentic.

As if the architects had ordered them for effect, sombre ravens perch on the turrets and walls. The people of Segovia who look after the castle have joined in the fun, fitting out the interior in a fashion that would make the characters of any Sir Walter Scott novel feel quite at home. There are plenty of 14th-century cannons and armour, an harquebus or two, stained glass and dusty paintings of Visigothic kings. Some of the interiors survived the fire; there are fine *artesonado* ceilings in the Sala de Las Piñas and in the throne room, built by Enrique IV but furnished as it might have been in the days of Fernando and Isabel. The **Plaza** at the Alcázar's entrance, with old mortars left over from the days of the military school, was the site of Segovia's original cathedral.

Old Quarters and Romanesque Churches

Between the Cathedral and Alcázar lies the oldest district of Segovia. The *esgrafiado* work on some of the houses is a local speciality; a coat of stucco is applied, then scraped away around stencils to make decorative patterns. In a small plaza just west of the Cathedral stands the finest and most representative of Segovia's Romanesque churches, the 13th-century church of **San Esteban**, with a lively bell-tower in the Italian style. The arcaded porch around two sides of the church is the trademark of Segovia's Romanesque architecture. Porches like this adorned all the old churches, and most likely the old cathedral as well; in the Middle Ages they were busy places, serving as the centres of business and social life the way arcaded streets and squares do in other Spanish towns. Across the plaza is the **Palacio Episcopal** (Archbishop's Palace), its plain façade enlivened only by the reliefs of a serpent-woman and other curious medieval fancies over the entrance.

Within Segovia's walls, the streets meander languidly; to meander along with them is a treat, and fortunately the old town is small enough so that you will never get entirely lost. The medieval parish churches are everywhere: **San Andrés**, a solid, simple work from the 12th century on the Plaza Merced; the church of **La Trinidad** on the Plaza de Doctor Laguna, off

Calle de la Trinidad, with an interior restored to something like its original appearance; **San Martín** on Calle Juan Bravo and **San Juan de los Caballeros** on the Plaza de Colmenares, both smaller versions of San Esteban (though both are older) with the characteristic arcades and towers. Calle Juan Bravo is named after the Segovian military leader of the Comunero revolt, who was executed after the defeat at Villalar in 1521. Segovia remembers enough of its ancient pride and liberty to keep him as a hero to this day, and his statue can be seen in the plaza. Nearby, the **Casa de los Picos** is another Segovia landmark, a 14th-century mansion with a façade like a waffle-iron, with protruding stone diamonds, a style copied in many later buildings in Spain and even one famous church in Naples.

One of Segovia's finest churches is outside the walls, near the centre of the new town on Avenida de Fernández Ladreda. **San Millán** is also the oldest, but the capitals of its arcade, charmingly sculpted with scenes from the Bible and from everyday life, have survived much more clearly than at the other churches.

The Aqueduct

Nothing else remains from Roman Segóbriga, but for the city to have merited such an elaborate water-supply it must have had nearly as many inhabitants as modern Segovia's 50,000. Trajan, one of the Spanish emperors of the Roman Empire, most likely ordered its construction. Its two-storey arcade rises 39m over the busy Plaza Azoguejo below, making it the tallest surviving Roman aqueduct.

The Romans, antiquity's master plumbers, did not build it there just to show off. An aqueduct's purpose is to bring water from a distant source, in this case the Río Frío, several kms to the east. Over the length of it a constant downward slope must be maintained to sustain the flow, and wherever it crosses a valley like this an arcade must be built to keep the flow level. The actual water-course, a channel cut into the stone and lined with lead, is at the very top. What you see here is only a small part of the system; the Romans built an underground water course from here to the Alcázar, and from the other end you can follow the arcade, ever shallower as the ground rises, up Calle Fernán García from the Plaza Azoguejo and right out of the city.

Note the notches cut into the rough stone on the arcade; these allowed for attaching scaffolding for the higher levels, and for block and tackles to hoist up the heavier stones. The Romans never cut corners; this was built for the centuries to come, and most likely would have survived unchanged had not several of the arches been destroyed in a siege by the Moors in the 11th century. Some 400 years later, Queen Isabel hired the monks of El Parral monastery to oversee the reconstruction, and when they had finished, they replaced the little statue of Hercules that had stood in a niche over the centre with an image of the Virgin Mary.

A Templar Church and a Rogue's Retreat

Do not by any means leave Segovia without a walk through the valley of the Eresma. Through either of the old *mudéjar* gates in the city's northern walls, the road leads down to the river through willow and poplar woods dotted with wild flowers. Following the road under the walls of the Alcázar, you cross the river and arrive at the church of **La Vera Cruz** (*open summer, Tues–Sun 10.30–1.30 and 3.30–7; winter, Tues–Sun 10.30–1.30 and 3.30-6, closed Mon and all Nov; adm*), one of the most interesting surviving Templar foundations, standing on a low hill in open countryside.

The church was built in 1208, and with the dissolution of the Templars in 1312 it became a regular parish church. The last few centuries have seen it abandoned, and its relic of the True Cross (*la vera cruz*), a sliver of wood, moved to the little village of Zamarramala, 1.6km away. Today the church is used by a Catholic brotherhood that grandiosely styles itself the 'Knights of St John'. Like many Templar churches, this one is round, with 12 sides; at its centre is the two-storeyed chamber, the 'inner temple' where the Templar secret rites took place, as opposed to the 'outer temple' which belonged to the common Church rituals.

None of the paintings or furnishings are as old as the Templars, but one 15th-century picture of the Last Supper, with the apostles seated at a round table, is worth a look. You may climb the bell-tower for one of the best views of Segovia and the Alcázar, taking in a number of churches and monasteries nearby in this holy valley, now largely unused.

The closest, the 17th-century **Convento de las Carmelitas Descalzas** (*open daily 10–1 and 4–7*) has the tomb of the gentle St John of the Cross—or what's left of him since, like that of any Spanish saint, his corpse was chopped up finely for holy relics.

To reach the most interesting of the monasteries, **El Parral** (*open daily 10–12 and 4–6.30*), retrace your steps from the Vera Cruz to the river and continue up the opposite bank. On the way you'll pass the remains of the **Moneda**, or mint, where American gold and silver were turned into coins before 1730.

El Parral's founder, Juan Pacheco, Marqués de Villena, ranks among the slipperiest of all Castilian court intriguers. A protégé of the famous favourite Álvaro de Luna during the reign of Juan II, he played a rôle in the wars between the partisans of Isabel and Juana la Beltraneja by taking first one side, then the other, and occasionally both. He apparently chose this site because it had brought him luck—he had killed three men here in duels. In its day, El Parral was famous throughout Spain for its woods and gardens. The place is still lovely, and the long-neglected church has been restored, with a number of interesting tombs of famous Segovians (and some of the Marqués' illegitimate children).

Segovia ✉ *40000*

Where to Stay

expensive

Segovia's ★★★★**Parador Nacional**, Ctra. de Valladolid, ✆ 921 44 37 37, ✉ 921 47 37 62, is not convenient unless you have a car (it's 2km out of town), and it's in a plain modern building. On the other hand, it has fine views of the town, a pool and one of the best restaurants of any *parador*. Still, to experience Segovia the better choice would be ★★★**Los Linajes**, C/ Doctor Velasco 9, ✆ 921 46 04 75, ✉ 921 46 04 79, in what certainly must be one of the most serenely pretty locations of any hotel in Castile, on the northern walls overlooking the valley of the Eresma. It has a terrace, and is only a short walk from the cathedral.

For a room overlooking the Plaza Mayor, try the small, elegant ★★★**Infanta Isabel**, C/ Isabel la Católica 1, ✆ 921 44 31 05, ✉43 32 40. One of Segovia's new hotels, the ★★★★**Los Arcos**, Pso. de Ezequiel González 26, ✆ 921 43 74 62, ✉ 921 42 81 61, though lacking the character of the hotels in the old city, is good value if you're looking for every possible modern convenience.

Best in this bracket is **Las Sirenas**, C/ Juan Bravo 30, ✆ 921 43 40 11, 🖂 921 43 06 33, a stately establishment with air-conditioning and TV in all rooms. The **Hs Plaza**, C/ Cronista Lecea 11, ✆ 921 46 03 03, 🖂 921 46 03 05, is a reasonable alternative, small, clean and close to the Plaza Mayor. Another good option is the **Hs El Hidalgo**, C/ José Canalejas 3-5, ✆ 921 42 81 90, a *hostal* with a restaurant in an old building just by San Martín.

inexpensive–cheap

Less expensively, there are the **Pensión Aragón**, ✆ 921 46 09 14, and the **Hospedaje Cubo**, ✆ 921 46 09 17, both at Plaza Mayor 4, reached through a door to the right of the Herranz bookshop. The Aragón is a little dingy but the Cubo is spotless; both charge around *2400 pts* for a double room with shared bathroom.

Eating Out

More than anywhere else in Castile, Segovia takes dining seriously, and the streets around the Plaza Mayor and the Aqueduct are packed with dimly lit *típico* restaurants, each with a window heaped with a luxuriant display of fresh fish, furred and feathered game, bunches of thyme, rosemary and lavender, glistening heaps of offal, and, taking pride of place, a freshly butchered piglet. Here master *asadores* of reputation, bedecked in ribbons and medals, serve up Spain's best *cochinillo* (roast sucking-pig, traditionally only 21 days old and so tender that you can cut it with the blunt edge of a plate), along with roast milk-fed lamb and other formidably heavy Castilian specialities.

Heading the list for 50 years or so now has been the **Mesón de Cándido** Pza. Azoguejo 5, ✆ 921 45 59 11 (*expensive*), with its picturesque exterior (shown on most of Segovia's tourist brochures) beside the aqueduct. The late Señor Cándido was the expert—he used to write cookbooks on Castilian cuisine—and he played host to all the famous folk who have ever passed through Segovia (autographed photos on the walls, of course, to prove it). Dinners here will set you back *4000 pts.*

The young contender in Segovia is the **Restaurante José María**, off the Plaza Mayor at C/ Cronista Lecea 11, ✆ 921 46 11 11, 🖂 921 46 02 73 (*moderate*), where everything is first-rate (try the breaded frogs' legs, another local treat) and the prices kept relatively low. José María, who started his career as an apprentice under Cándido, is passionate about Castilian wines; he is the man responsible for bringing Segovia's excellent Ribera del Duero reds into the spotlight by serving them as his house wine, and he now owns his own vineyard, not far from the legendary vineyards of Pesquera and Vega Sicilia.

Other renowned *asadores* hold court at the **Casa Duque**, C/ Cervantes 12, ✆ 921 43 05 37 (*expensive*), **La Oficina**, C/ Cronista Lecea 10, ✆ 921 43 16 43 (*moderate*) and **El Bernardino**, C/ Cervantes 2, ✆ 921 43 32 25 (*moderate*). If you fancy something a little more creative, try **La Cocina de Segovia**, Paseo Ezequiel González 26, ✆ 921 43 74 62 (*moderate*).

Less expensive restaurants abound, in the same central areas, like the **Restaurante Lazaró** on C/ Infanta Isabel (cheap *menú del día*, but you can get *cochinillo* here, too), and similar places on Calle Juan Bravo and the Plaza de San Martín. Sensitive souls should lay off the *sopa castellana* (spicy garlic soup served with a poached egg), especially in the cheaper places, where it's made with enough grease to lubricate a locomotive. It's not bad, though.

After all that food, a short walk up to the Plaza Mayor wouldn't do any harm. Among the rows of cafes under its portals, **La Concha** is the best, with tables and chairs outside.

Around Segovia

Another Bourbon Palace: La Granja de San Ildefonso

Open, summer Tues–Sun 10–6; winter Tues–Sat 10–1.30 and 3–5, Sun 10–2; closed Mon; adm, no charge for EU passport holders on Wed; gardens open summer 10–8; winter daily 10–6.

La Granja ('the farm') is one of the works of Felipe V, he of the insatiable appetite for palaces. The building has a certain rococo elegance of the sort American millionaires love to copy, but its fame has always been its **gardens**. Felipe originally conceived La Granja as a scaled-down version of Versailles (his father, Louis XIV's, palace) and the gardens, laid out in the 1740s, completed the picture. There are some 28 hectares (70 acres) of them, with remarkable fountains everywhere, decorated with pretty pagan deities. However, there is only one day of the year when they all work, and it's worth watching them come alive: August 25th.

The palace itself is furnished in 18th-century French style, and contains an impressive collection of Spanish and French tapestries and some spectacular cut-glass chandeliers. You can visit the Crystal Factory where these were made, in the village of **San Ildefonso** (La Real Fábrica de Cristales, *open Wed–Sun 11–8, closed Mon and Tues; adm*).

La Granja is an easy excursion from Segovia, only 11km southeast of town. To get there, take a bus or follow the N601 (Carretera de la Granja) to San Ildefonso.

Ten km south of Segovia, El Palacio de Riofrío (*same hours as La Granja*) is on a side road, off the N603. Here Isabella Farnese, Felipe V's second wife, let her taste for all things Italian run riot after Felipe's death. She intended to use this palace and hunting lodge as a bolt-hole in the event of her being turfed out of La Granja. Work began in 1752. Rebaglio, her architect, brought echoes of Madrid's Palacio Real to a building which would otherwise have had an overwhelmingly feminine feel, with its pink walls and pretty wooded parkland. Part of the palace is now a hunting museum.

Turning northwards off the N110 a few kilometres on, you come to **Pedraza de la Sierra**, an exceptionally beautiful walled village with a lovely medieval castle (*open Wed–Sun 11–2 and 4–6, closed Mon–Tues*) and a jumble of antique shops. The arcaded main square serves as a bull ring for the villagers' September *corridas*, and plays host to an international music festival every year between July 5–11, while some 25,000 candles light the village up at night.

If you carry on the N110 to Riaza, just past the town you'll see a south turning indicating the *Hermita Hontanares*. Along this road lie a series of villages which tell the story of the depopulation of rural Spain throughout the 1950s and 1960s all too graphically. The so-called *pueblos negros Segovianos* of El Muyo, Serracín and Becerril have begun to attract weekenders, but many of the houses, constructed of slate, are tumbling down.

Further on lie the *pueblos rojos* of El Negredo, Madriguera and Villacorta; so called because of the clay soil which blows everywhere, leaving the houses with a fine red dust coating. These villages, barely inhabited, lie among some of Spain's finest holm oak forests, with the sturdy Sierra de Ayllón as a backdrop.

Where to Stay and Eating Out

If all that roast flesh from Segovia is palling, then it's worth thinking about lunch in La Granja. **Zaca,** ✆ 921 47 00 87 (*moderate*) is a small eatery only open at midday. Stews are the speciality. *Booking is essential at weekends.* The village also boasts the charming ★★**Hotel Roma**, Roma 2, ✆ 921 47 07 52. Set right at the entrance to the palace, this could be a quieter and cheaper bet than Segovia if you have a car .

Segovians are such enthusiastic gastronomes that they're more than happy to travel a kilometre or 20 in order to indulge themselves in a gargantuan roast lunch at a celebrated farmhouse restaurant in one of the Guadarrama mountain villages. One such eating place is **La Posada de Javier**, Ctra. Segovia-Soria, ✆ 921 40 11 36 (*moderate*), in the typical Castilian village of **Torrecaballeros**, 10km north east of Segovia on the N110. This is a perfect place to sample local specialities such as *judiones de La Granja*, butter beans stewed with *chorizo* and various extremities of pork, or *cordero asado*, lamb roasted in a wood-fired oven. It's not cheap (a quarter roast lamb, to serve two, is *3900 pts*) but it's extremely popular and it's best to book. The village also has a handful of hotels.

Further up the Soria road is the village of **Collado Hermoso**, a good base from which to plan a hike in the Guadarramas. This village boasts a small, friendly hotel, in what was once a watermill, the ★★**Molino de Río Viejo** (*moderate*), Ctra. Segovia-Soria Km 172, ✆ 921 40 30 63, ✆ 921 40 30 63. The owners run excursions on horseback in the sierra and the surrounding countryside.

Pedraza de la Sierra acts as another magnet for *segoviano* and *madrileño* foodies, with roast lamb fans flocking to **El Yantar de Pedraza**, Pza. Mayor, ✆ 921 50 98 42 (*expensive*), which overlooks the square, and, even better, **La Olma**, Pza. del Granado 1, ✆ 921 50 99 81 (*expensive*) to sample all the usual delicacies, brilliantly prepared. There are two superb hotels in the village, ★★★**El Hotel de la Villa**, C/ Calzada 5, ✆ 921 50 86 51 (*expensive*), and ★★**La Posada de Don Mariano**, Pza. Mayor 14, ✆ 921 50 98 86, ✆ 921 50 98 86 (*expensive*), both in old buildings full of character, and both well worth the money.

Ski Resorts

For winter visitors to Madrid suffering from a build-up of oppressive car fumes, a lungful of crisp mountain air could be the perfect antidote. There are four skiing centres near Segovia which are within easy reach of the capital. These resorts are all quite low-key, and experienced skiers looking for a challenge would find the pistes disappointing, but they have plenty to offer beginners or near-beginners. All four resorts have ski schools and equipment hire facilites. For recorded information on snow conditions, call © 91 350 20 20.

Sierra de Guadarrama

The three ski resorts in the Guadarramas between Segovia and Madrid are particularly popular with *madrileños*, as they're easy day-trips; if you'd like to join them, take the N601, the scenic road that runs from Segovia to Collada-Villalba via San Ildefonso-La Granja; or take any train on the Madrid–Segovia line (R 2 or C 8b), disembark at the small resort of Cercedilla, and take the funicular up to Puerto de Navacerrada or Puerto de los Cotos.

Puerto de Navacerrada (information: © 91 262 10 10) offers the most challenging skiing in the Guadarramas, with 16 pistes for skiers at various levels of skill, plus a slalom and a cross-country course. The resort has 12 lifts, and is at an altitude of 1760m, with the highest pistes starting at 2222m. The neighbouring resorts of **Valcotos** (information: © 91 435 15 48) and **Valdesquí** (information: © 91 515 59 39) are slightly higher than Puerto de Navacerrada, a few kilometres up the C604 towards Rascafría. They're small resorts with simple facilities. Valcotos, in the Cotos mountain pass, has the prettiest location; it has seven pistes and eight lifts. Valdesquí generally has the best snow of the Guadarrama resorts, and is good for beginners; it has 23 pistes and 10 lifts.

Sierra de Ayllón

For intermediate skiers, **La Pinilla** (information: © 921 55 03 04) is a popular choice. This resort is in the middle of the Sierra de Ayllón, 10km south of the pleasant town of Riaza, which is 72km north east of Segovia on the N110. La Pinilla has 16 pistes, running from 2273m down to 1500m, and 12 lifts.

Where to Stay and Eating Out in the Ski Resorts

The only resort which has hotels close to the slopes is **Puerto de Navacerrada**; here the choice is between the rather modest ***Pasadoiro**, Ctra. de la Granja, Puerto de Navacerrada, © 91 852 14 27 (*moderate*), and the simple but comfortable *****Hs Nueva Venta Arias**, Ctra. de la Granja, Puerto de Navacerrada, © 91 852 11 00 (*moderate*).

The fashionable place to stay is the town of **Navacerrada**, downhill from Puerto de Navacerrada, where there is more of a choice of lodgings, such as the ******Arcipreste de Hita**, Ctra. Madrid-León, Km 52, © 91 856 01 25 (*expensive*), which has excellent facilities including a sports and fitness centre, the *****La Barranca**, Valle de la Barranca, © 91 856 00 00, ✆ 91 856 03 52 (*moderate*), a favourite venue for business conventions, and the ***Hs Mayte**, Avda. de Madrid 5, © 91 856 02 97 (*inexpensive*), which has 12 rooms with shared bathroom facilities.

When it comes to eating in Navacerrada, Felipe has the monopoly. **Asador Felipe** has a summer terrace and the best beef, lamb and suckling pig. Across the road, **Restaurante Felipe** offers wild mushrooms in autumn and winter, as well as excellent fish. **La Fonda Real**, up the hill towards the Puerto de Navacerrada offers fabulous views and traditional Castillian cooking.

A good alternative if you're skiing at Valcotos or Valdesquí and have transport would be to stay in the village of **Rascafría**. Probably the best value here is the rather charming, doll's-house-like ****Los Calizos**, Ctra. Miraflores-Rascafría, Km 22.8, ✆ 91 869 11 12, ◉ 91 869 11 12 (*moderate*); for those seeking a little more luxury there is the ******Santa María del Paular**, C/ El Paular, ✆ 91 869 10 11, ◉ 91 869 10 06 (*expensive*) in the converted wing of an ancient Benedictine monastery; and for those on a tight budget a good choice would be the ***Hs Porfirio**, Avda. del Paular 9, ✆ 91 869 10 92 (*inexpensive*).

The nearest hotels to La Pinilla are in **Riaza**: the ****Casaquemada**, C/ Isidro Rodríguez 18, ✆ 921 55 00 51 (*moderate*), the ****La Trucha**, Avda. Doctor Tapia 17, ✆ 921 55 00 61, ◉ 921 55 00 86 (*moderate*), which has a pool, and the simple but very reasonably priced ***Hs Los Robles**, C/ Médico Valentín Gil 6, ✆ 921 55 00 54 (*cheap*), which has some double rooms with basin for *1900 pts.*

Ávila

For two cities so close together and with so much history in common, Segovia and Ávila could hardly appear more unlike. Chance, with a little help from the geography, has made them into stone images of complementary sides of the Spanish character. Secure on its natural hilltop fortress, Segovia had the leisure to become a city of kings and merchants, aesthetic and relaxed and full of trees. Ávila stands more exposed, and it has always had the air of a frontier camp, coarse and ugly, a city first of soldiers, and later of mystics.

Ávila's **walls** are its main attraction, the only complete circuit of fortifications around any Spanish city. Though medieval, they rest on Roman foundations, and their rectangular layout is the classic form of the Roman *castrum*. For Rome, this was a frontier post against the Celtic tribes they had displaced from the area, and after the 8th century Ávila found itself performing the same role in the constant wars between Moor and Christian. Through most of the 11th century it was the front line, often changing hands, until Alfonso VI decided in 1088 to construct these walls, built between 1090 and 1099, and make the town a secure base for further Christian advance.

Except for Saint Teresa, who was a native and spent much of her career as a writer and monastic reformer behind Ávila's walls, the town has been heard from but little since. For a proper view of the walls, though, you'll have to cross the River Adaja, leaving town on the Avenida de Madrid, and onto the N501, turning right over the bridge.

Getting There

Ávila is a little under 2hrs from Madrid by train or bus.

By train: Unlike Segovia, a train journey to Ávila is worth the effort, with spectacular scenery and a quicker ride. Trains on the Regionales line R 1 from Madrid, running roughly once an hour from Atocha and more frequently from Chamartín (via Villalba de Guadarrama and El Escorial) arrive at the station in the new town on Avda. José Antonio, a 10-minute walk from the city's old walls. Most of the trains to and from Galicia, Asturias, Salamanca and even the Basque provinces and Burgos pass through here. RENFE information, Madrid: ✆ 91 328 9020; Ávila ✆ 920 25 02 02.

By bus: The city bus station is nearby on the Avenida de Madrid. Buses from Madrid are run by Automóviles de Ávila, ✆ 91 530 3092, twice a day from Estación Sur, C/ Méndez Álvarez (Ⓜ Méndez Álvarez) (✆ 91 468 4200); and by Empresa Larrea, ✆ 91 530 4800, three times a day from Pso. de la Florida 11. There are regular bus connections from Ávila to Segovia and Salamanca, and to all the provincial towns mentioned below, plus less regular services to points outside the province.

Tourist Information

Pza. de la Catedral 4, across the square from the cathedral, ✆ 920 21 13 87, ✉ 920 25 37 17.

San Vicente

Modern Ávila has almost completely forsaken the old walled town. The bus and train stations are out in the eastern extension, and however you arrive you are likely to approach the historic centre from this direction. Here, just where the Avenida de Portugal reaches the walls, is the Romanesque **Basílica de San Vicente** (*open summer, Tues–Sun 10–1 and 4–7; winter, Tues–Sun 4–6, closed Mon*), the most interesting of Ávila's churches. Parts of it are as old as the late 12th century, including the fine sculptural work on the west portal. San Vicente was another native of Ávila, who was martyred along with his sisters, SS. Sabina and Cristeta, during the persecutions of Emperor Diocletian in 306. There's more graphic, vigorous sculpture inside, where scenes of San Vicente on the rack and suffering other tortures decorate his sarcophagus. The church, probably succeeding an earlier Visigothic structure, was built over the site of the martyrdom, and if the attendant will agree to take you down to the crypt you can see the rock where the Romans did them in. Watch out for snakes; there's a legend of a serpent who guarded the saints' graves while Ávila was occupied by the Moors. A custom grew up whereby the people of Ávila would come down here to make bargains and swear oaths; if they lied, the serpent would come out and sting them (the only recorded victim was a bishop). Also down in the crypt is a much-venerated icon called **Nuestra Señora de la Soterana** (Our Lady of the Underground).

Los Verracos

This part of town, just east of the walls, is really as old as anything inside. A block from the walls, at Pza. de los Navillos 3, just off the Plaza de Italia, an old ecclesiastical residence called the Palacio de los Deanes has been converted into Ávila's very good **Museo Provincial** (*open Tues–Sat 10–2 and 5–8, Sun 10–2, closed Mon*), with a folk-costume and crafts collection, Roman artefacts and some fine local medieval pictures—displayed where you can see them much more clearly than in Ávila's dim churches.

The museum provides a good introduction to an interesting aspect of Ávila's ancient history. Ávila was a busy place when the Celts lived here, something as close to a capital or religious centre as this determinedly non-urban people cared to have. Remains of their castles and monuments can be seen all over the countryside, as well as hundreds of unique stone grave-markers called *verracos* (boars), carved in the shape of boars or bulls. These continued to be erected under Roman rule, as late as AD 300, and some carry Latin inscriptions, such as 'to the gods Manes and Titillo'.

Two blocks south, outside the **Puerta de Alcázar**, main gate of the old town, is the **Plaza de Santa Teresa**, the only really lovely corner of Ávila, with most of the modest restaurants and hotels nearby. The church here with the lovely rose window is **San Pedro**, from the 13th century.

The Walls

Calle San Segundo runs along the eastern side of the fortification, towards the Puerta de Alcázar. In this section of the walls, you will see some stones with Roman inscriptions, and a good many others with a rectangular niche and a groove cut into them. These were the bases of the *verracos*, and the niches held the ashes of the departed chiefs and warriors. The Castilians dragged in dozens of them to help build their walls, with 88 towers and nine gates. (A few *verracos* can be seen in the Plaza Calvo Sotelo, just inside the Puerta de Alcázar.) Though simple, the walls were up-to-date for the military needs of the 11th century; an engineer from Rome was called in to help with the design. The distinctive rounded towers, typical of ancient Roman fortifications, are called *cubos*, but the biggest bulge, facing Calle San Segundo, comes as a surprise. It is the apse of Ávila's cathedral, built right into the walls as if to symbolize the Church Militant of old Castile, helping man the battlements of the Reconquista.

It's a pleasant 2.4km walk around the walls; on the southern and western sides they face open country, and the setting is sufficiently medieval to have been used for the shooting of several movies. On the narrow west end, they overlook old bridges spanning the River Adaja and the 12th-century church of **San Segundo**, yet another local saint, who supposedly converted Ávila in the 1st century. If you wish to have a look at Ávila from the top of the walls, the only entrance is in the garden of the *parador*, inside the northern face of the walls.

The Cathedral

Open summer, daily 10–1 and 3–6; winter daily, 3–5.

It isn't much, though one of the earliest Gothic churches in Spain, and though a king of León (Alfonso IX, 1188–1230) once lived here in sanctuary during a civil war. From the front it has no character at all, apart from the two bizarre stone wild men with clubs, added in the 18th century, who guard the portal. Ávila's cathedral, half-church and half-fortress, does however have a little stage presence. The critics like to speak of Gothic architecture at its best as an eloquent argument for the Christian faith; this church was for a people who needed no convincing. Strong and plain, it has the air of an outsized chapel for warrior knights. The men of the Reconquista adorned it richly inside as if it were their treasure-house, and they lined its walls with niches for tombs where they expected to be buried.

Some of the sculpted tombs are among the best works in the cathedral, and there are some good reliefs in the north portal, and paintings and sculpture inside from quieter times when the wars of the Reconquista had passed on. One work very famous in Spain is the tomb of a learned 15th-century bishop named Alfonso de Madrigal (better known as *El Tostado* for his swarthy complexion), with a statue of the bishop deep in his books, wearing robes carved with finely detailed scenes from the scriptures.

Although Ávila has been a backwater for many centuries, a wander round the walled city is revealing. Like many a city in Castile, Ávila is quietly prosperous, and a host of ironmongers, gentlemen's outfitters and corner shops testifies to an economy which has little need of tourists - although they are more than welcome. And, little by little, its weedy lots and ruins are being restored. Ávila's summer fiestas, which take place between 17 and 25 July, do liven the place up though, and its high altitude make it a pleasurably cool place in July and August. October 15th sees processions and festivities in honour of Saint Teresa.

Ávila's Doctors of the Soul

The people of Ávila celebrate Santa Teresa de Ávila's memory as ostentatiously as the Corsicans do Napoleon's. Even if it were possible to escape hearing about her for a while, there would still be the ubiquitous, nasty, candied egg-yolks called 'Yemas de Santa Teresa' to remind you. A traditional speciality of the local nuns, they are sold in every shop in town.

Teresa Sánchez de Cepeda y Ahumada was born into a wealthy family of Jewish converts in 1515. She got religion young; at seven, after reading the *Lives of the Saints* she talked her brother into running away with her to be maryred by the Moors. An old stone cross called *Las Cuatro Postes*, just across the Adaja from the town, is the spot where their uncle caught the children and brought them back. Teresa had to wait until she was 18 before she took her vows as a Carmelite, and she lived 22 uneventful years in her convent until she had the famous vision that set her off on her career as a mystic—an angel pierced her heart with a burning arrow during prayer—unforgettably depicted in Bernini's statue in Rome, portraying Teresa in a state of eternal orgasm.

Usually Teresa's union with God was more down to earth. Shortly after her first mystical experience, she had a second while praying at the chapel of Nuestra Señora de la Soterana in San Vicente, which bade her to reform the lax Carmelite order and return it to its original regime of poverty and simplicity. The subterranean Virgin also had her take off her shoes, and wearing sandals became the symbol of the new *descalzada* (shoeless) Carmelites. Teresa then spent much of her life on the road, founding and reforming 32 convents in Castile and Andalucía. Her first male convert was a 21-year-old theology student from Fontiveròs, near Ávila, named Juan de Yepes, who became Teresa's confessor and the spiritual director of the *descalzadas.* One of the best things he did was order Teresa to write her autobiography, the frankest, most spontaneous, humorous and likeable account composed by any saint on the calendar.

In 1578 still-shod (Calced) Carmelite timeservers, who spitefully labelled Teresa 'the roving nun', denounced both her and her confessor Juan to the Inquisition. Both were confined to Toledo, separately, and wrote to each other daily—the disappearance of their correspondence is considered one of the greatest losses in Spanish letters. For it was in Toledo that the two wrote their classical works of mysticism: Teresa's *Inner Castle* was based on her vision of a glittering castle of seven abodes, each a stage that the bride/soul must pass on the road to heaven to the ultimate union with God. The Church disapproved of her books when she died in 1582, but it saw fit to canonize her in 1622, repackaging the honest mystic into a miracle worker and an object of popular devotion whose chopped-off fingers soon became prized holy relics.

Juan—the future St John of the Cross—suffered far worse indignities. The Calced members of his Order imprisoned him in a dungeon for nine months, a period of forced reflection that resulted in his first poem, *En una Noche Oscura (The Dark Night of the Soul)*—one of the masterpieces of Spanish literature. Like all his poetry, *The Dark Night* was ripe for misinterpretation because of its several levels of meaning, including the carnal; Juan assigned religious concepts genders and used often ambiguous erotic imagery to make potent poetic points with an extraordinary economy. He wrote fewer than 1000 lines in his whole life but into those fit a complete exposition of Catholic mysticism, expressed allegorically in unrivalled songs of love and nature, poems that create moods rather than merely describe them.

Although Juan managed to escape from prison when the Calced and Discalced Orders were officially separated, he made an obscure end in 1591, dying from abuse and starvation after years of suffering in the monastery at Úbeda, persecuted even on his deathbed by the prior, who had nuns sign affidavits against him. He and his poetry were vindicated when he was canonized in 1726 and made a Doctor of the Church in 1926, an honour St Teresa herself became the first woman to enjoy in 1970, putting Ávila in the record books as the only town to produce two Doctors of the Church.

In her writings, Santa Teresa had little kind to say about Ávila; apparently it was not a place where reforming ideas were very welcome. Nevertheless, Ávila is happy to show off memories of her life in a number of convents about town. On the spot where she was born they built the **Convento de Santa Teresa** (*open daily 9–1 and 3.30–8.30*), just inside the southern gate. There is a squat church in the Herreran style, with a collection of relics and paintings of imagined scenes from the saint's life. More of these can be seen at the **Convento de la Encarnación** (*open summer, Wed–Mon 9.30–1 and 4–7; winter, Wed–Mon 3.30–6; closed Tues*) where she lived for 27 years, just north of the walled town on Calle de la Encarnación, and at the **Convento de Las Madres** on Calle del Duque three blocks east of the Plaza de Santa Teresa.

Avila ✉ *05000*

Where to Stay

expensive

At the luxury end of the scale, Ávila's ★★★**Parador Raimundo de Borgoña**, C/ Marqués Canales de Chozas 2, ✆ 920 21 13 40, ✉ 920 22 61 66, has a worthy competitor in the ★★★★**Gran Hotel Palacio de Valderrábanos**, Pza. de la Catedral 9, ✆ 920 21 10 23, ✉ 920 25 16 91. Both are in converted Renaissance palaces. The *parador*, named after the man responsible for the building of Ávila's celebrated walls, has an excellent restaurant; the Valderrábanos, beautifully decorated with antique furnishings, has a warmer atmosphere.

moderate

In the middle range, the preferred choice is the ★★★**Hs El Rastro**, Pza. del Rastro 1, ✆ 920 21 12 18, ✉ 920 25 16 26, a place with character in the shadow of Ávila's walls; the rooms are plain but there's a garden and a very popular restaurant, the Mesón del Rastro (*see* below). If El Rastro is booked up—as many of Ávila's hotels are likely to be in July and August—try the **Hotel Jardín**, C/ San Segundo 38, ☏ 920 21 10 74, also in an old building near the walls. If you're prepared to spend a little more in order to sleep in an ancient palace, but can't quite stretch to the prices of the *parador* or the Valderrábanos, you are likely to appreciate the ****Hostería de Bracamonte**, C/ Bracamonte 6, ☏ 920 25 12 80, in a building steeped in history and an interior full of 18th-century tapestries.

inexpensive

Most of Ávila's inexpensive *hostales* can be found near the railway station on Avda. José Antonio, but you'd do better to take the time to find one closer in. In the old city, the **Hs Elena**, C/ Marqués Canales de Chozas 1, ☏ 920 21 31 61, a slightly hectic place across from the *parador*, has double rooms with bath for *4500 pts*, and the ****Hs Las Bellas**, C/ Caballeros 19, ☏ 920 21 29 10, equally central, charges *4000 pts*.

Eating Out

Ávila is full of good, solid, inexpensive restaurants: more than you would expect in a small town with lots of tourists. Most are near the eastern end of the walls, inside or out. At **El Rincón**, Pza. de Zurraquín 15, ☏ 920 21 31 52 (*moderate*), you can get *cochinillo* and other Castilian specialities for a reasonable price. Others worthy of mention are **Doña Guiomar**, C/ Tomás de Victoria 3, ☏ 920 21 37 89 (*moderate*), for inventive cooking and friendly service; **Casa Patas**, C/ San Millán 4 (*cheap*), just off the Plaza de Santa Teresa, for tapas and simple meals, and **Los Leales** (*moderate*), Plazuela de Italia, ☏ 920 21 13 29 (*moderate*), near the museum. For some classy, classic Castilian food, try the **Mesón del Rastro** (*moderate*), Pza. del Rastro 1, ☏ 920 21 12 18 (*moderate*)—here they serve authentic local dishes such as veal, pickled trout, roast lamb, and *judías de Barco* (bean casserole with *chorizo*). Outside the city walls, on the banks of the Río Adaja, **El Almacén**, Ctra. de Salamanca 6, ☏ 920 21 10 26 (*expensive*), also serves regional favourites, as well as imaginative variations on traditional themes.

Around Ávila

Verraco-spotting

One of the best places to see a large number of the Iberian Celts' mysterious boar- and bull-shaped gravestones is about 50km south of Ávila, beyond the village of El Tiemblo on the N 403. The site is called **Los Toros de Guisando**. At an assembly here in 1468, King Enrique IV was forced to accept Isabel's right to the throne of Castile. Only 6km north of Ávila, there are more *verracos* around the scanty remains of **Las Cogotas**, an ancient Celtic fortress whose inhabitants gave the advancing Romans problems for centuries.

North of Ávila

Heading towards Valladolid, the terrain stretches out into a high plain, with wide sweeps of green and yellow cereal fields. One of the more interesting villages in this part of the province is **Arévalo**, about 50km north of Ávila. Arévalo appears little changed since the 1600s, with its walls, old churches, and bridges across the Río Adaja. There's been a cattle market here longer than anyone can remember.

Sierra de Gredos

Around Ávila, the countryside is pretty and often quite unusual—green, rolling hills broken by rocky outcrops that often have the appearance of ancient ruins. Further south, Ávila province is bounded by the **Sierra de Gredos**, a craggy adventure playground of a region, heaven for hikers, climbers, mountain bikers, watersports enthusiasts and the like. A good number base themselves in **Arenas de San Pedro**, which has become the '*capital de Gredos*', a 70km drive southwest from Ávila. Set among the dark, spare mountains, this is a pretty village full of trees, with a little square castle right next to the Plaza Mayor. It's well known for finely crafted leatherwork and ceramics. The fiestas here during the last week of August attract locals and visitors alike. Near Arenas, on twisting mountain roads with staggering views, are the medieval villages of **Guisando**, (not to be confused with the Toros de Guisando), **El Hornillo**, **El Arenal** and **Mombeltrán**, which has a very well-preserved 14th-century castle.

For information on the multitude of activities in the Sierra de Gredos, contact: Oficina de Turismo, C/Triste Condesa, ✆ 920 37 23 68.

Sierra de Gredos ✉ *28000*   **Where to Stay and Eating Out**

expensive

★★★**El Parador de Gredos**, Ctra. Barraco-Béjar, 3.2km from **Navarredonda de Gredos**, ✆ 920 34 80 48, 📠 920 34 82 05, was Spain's first ever *parador*. It's an old stone hunting lodge set in a beautiful pine forest on the north edge of the mountains, not far from El Pico Almanzor, which is the range's highest peak at 2592m. The room rates here are lower than those of many *paradores*, and there is a good restaurant.

moderate

All the mountain villages have at least one or two modest *hostales* and restaurants to choose from. One of the more comfortable is ★★**Hs Pepe**, in **Guisando**, C/ Linarejos 4, ✆ 920 37 09 18.

inexpensive

Two pleasant places to stay in **Arenas de San Pedro** are the ★**Hs El Castillo**, Ctra. de Candeleda 2, ✆ 920 37 00 91, and the tiny ★**Hostería Los Galagos**, Pza. del Condestable Dávalos 2, ✆ 920 37 13 79.

In **Mombeltrán** you could try ★**Hs Albuquerque**, Pza. de la Soledad 2, ✆ 920 38 60 32 for rooms and good, simple meals, or ★**Hs Prados Abiertos**, Ctra. Ávila-Talavera, Km 72, ✆ 920 37 09 18.

There is another simple retreat in **Navarredonda**, ★**El Refugio de Gredos**, C/ Pajizo, ✆ 920 34 80 47. All these *hostales* offer a double room with bath for *around 4000 pts*.

Arévalo has a few *hostales* and *pensiones*, and an excellent Castilian restaurant, the **Asador Las Cubas**, C/ Figones 9, ✆ 920 30 01 25 (*moderate*).

The best place for food in Arenas de San Pedro is **El Bodegón**, Plaza Conde Dávalos 4, ✆ 920 37 18 20 (*inexpensive*), where the emphasis is on home cooking.

The railway line that trundles out of Madrid in the direction of Zaragoza and Barcelona follows the course of the Río Henares all the way to its source, near the provincial border of Guadalajara and Soria. Trains passing this way stop at towns which have stood on the river for centuries, such as **Alcalá de Henares**, famous for its ancient university, and **Guadalajara**, in the heart of the Alcarria. Northeast of Guadalajara the line cuts through dazzling fields of sunflowers on the way to the graceful town of **Sigüenza**. It's a pleasant journey, through plenty of open countryside which, thanks to the river, is splashed with green even in the driest of summer months.

Getting There

By train: There are six or seven trains a day to Sigüenza on the Regionales line R 9b from Madrid-Chamartín; some of these stop at Madrid-Atocha, and all pass through Alcalá de Henares and Guadalajara. The journey to Sigüenza takes around 2hrs. Alcalá and Guadalajara are also served by Cercanías trains from Madrid-Chamartín and Madrid-Atocha, four times an hour for Alcalá and every half hour for Guadalajara. RENFE information, Madrid: ✆ 91 328 90 20; Alcalá de Henares: ✆ 91 888 01 96; Guadalajara: ✆ 949 21 28 50; Sigüenza: ✆ 949 39 14 94.

By bus: This is one case where the train is so convenient that you needn't worry about buses, unless you're based near the terminus at Avenida de América 34, from which Continental Auto, ✆ 91 533 0400, runs a frequent service to all three towns.

Tourist Information

Alcalá de Henares: at Callejón Santa María 1, ✆ 91 889 26 94.
Guadalajara: at Pza. Mayor 7, ✆ 949 22 06 98.
Sigüenza: at C/ Cardenal Mendoza 2, ✆ 949 39 12 62.

Alcalá de Henares

Anyone from the Arab world would recognize the name's origin straightaway—*al-qalat*, a fortress—and it was the Moors who began this town, on the site of the abandoned Roman city of Complutum. In the 12th century, warrior bishops from Toledo captured it for Christianity and built it up; the long tradition of Church control may be one of the reasons Cardinal Jiménez de Cisneros founded his great Complutensian University here in 1508, an institution that almost immediately rivalled Salamanca as the foremost centre of learning in Spain.

In 16th-century Castile, it was possible for a man like Cisneros to be on one hand an imperialist and a disturbingly fierce religious bigot, and on the other a champion of the new humanist scholarship that was sweeping Europe. For a brief, brilliant period the University became one of the intellectual lights of the continent; its great achievement, indeed its main reason for being, was the creation of the Complutensian Polyglot Bible, the first authoritative scholarly edition in modern Europe, with Latin, Greek, Hebrew and Aramaic originals in parallel columns. Even today it remains the standard work for biblical scholars; in its day it created an academic revolution. Among the University's graduates in Spain's golden age can be counted Calderón, Lope de Vega and Ignatius Loyola.

Through the 17th and 18th centuries the University's degeneration was gradual but complete, and half its buildings lay in ruins by 1837, when the sad remnants were moved to Madrid. Some of the old colleges were used as the Communist headquarters during the Civil War.

Economic recovery in the 1970s and 1980s brought a change of fortune to Alcalá, which became one of the fastest growing cities of Spain, through industrial growth and the presence of a huge US air base nearby at Torrejón (a popular rendezvous for anti-NATO protesters from Madrid). Many of the old academic buildings were restored, and the university re-opened its doors to students in 1977. Cisneros would have been delighted—the re-establishment of his university brought Alcalá's dormant intellectual and cultural interests back to the surface and made it a lively city once more.

Alcalá's centre is the leafy, pleasant **Plaza de Cervantes**, with a bandstand at one end and gossipy cafés at the other. Touching its edge is the arcaded **Calle Mayor**, Alcalá's busy, pretty old main street, which comes alive with yet more café tables after the shops shut on summer evenings. The University buildings are spread all over town, but the best of them, the **Colegio Mayor de San Ildefonso**, is just off the Plaza de Cervantes; it has a wonderful Plateresque façade by Rodrigo Gil de Hontañón (the architect who also worked on the cathedrals of Segovia and Salamanca), with the arms of Cisneros (note the swans—*cisnes*).

Inside are the **Capilla Universitaria**, a Plateresque chapel, and a famous hall called the **Paraninfo** with an *artesonado* ceiling, used for graduation ceremonies and other congregational occasions. Other noteworthy buildings are the **Colegio de la Palma** on Calle de los Colegios and the **Casa de los Lizana**, with its brave stone lions, on Calle Postigo. Most of the University colleges are built in a very austere, Herreran style, as are Alcalá's churches.

On the Calle Mayor is a small museum devoted to Alcalá's most famous son, Miguel de Cervantes. The **Museo Casa Natal de Cervantes** (Cervantes' Birthplace) (*open Tues–Fri 10.15–1.45 and 4.15–6.45; Sat–Sun, 10.15–1.45, closed Mon*) is a lovingly kept reconstruction of the house in which the author was born. It's furnished to look like a mid-16th century family dwelling, and in an upstairs room there is a display of rare editions of Cervantes' works and other ephemera.

Modern Alcalá's only monument is on the street leading from the railway station. The **Hotel Laredo** or *Quinta de la Gloria* is an incredible confection of brick Moorish arches and turrets piled up by some forgotten madman of the 19th century. Its style is not really 'neo-*mudéjar*' as the sign says, but more honestly 'hyper-*mudéjar*'.

Guadalajara

The next stop up the rail line from Madrid, this once great town of New Castile was almost completely wrecked during the long battles for Madrid during the Civil War, but rebuilt as a modern, industrial city. The only reason to stop is the **Palacio de los Duques del Infantado**, Pza. de los Caídos 1 (*open Tues–Sat 10.15–2 and 4–7, Sun 10.15–2, closed Mon*) built by Juan Guas in 1461 for the founder of what was to become one of Spain's most powerful noble houses, the Mendozas. Among its members it counted statesmen, authors, even a Viceroy of New Spain. The palace, in the Plateresque style, has a façade and courtyard florid enough to please any duke. Most of the palace has been restored or rebuilt, and it now houses a provincial art museum.

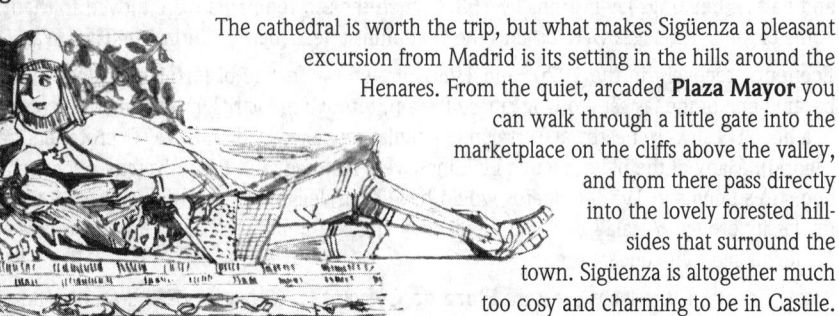

The cathedral is worth the trip, but what makes Sigüenza a pleasant excursion from Madrid is its setting in the hills around the Henares. From the quiet, arcaded **Plaza Mayor** you can walk through a little gate into the marketplace on the cliffs above the valley, and from there pass directly into the lovely forested hillsides that surround the town. Sigüenza is altogether much too cosy and charming to be in Castile.

The **Cathedral** has a good deal in common with the one in Ávila; both were built at about the same time and both show the influence of the French Gothic with a distinctive Castilian twist. Like Ávila's it stands honest and foursquare—a castle with rose windows. They are very good rose windows, especially over the north portal, but the best things are inside. In the chapel of the Arce family is the tomb of Martín Vázquez de Arce, a young man who died in the wars with Moorish Granada in 1486. An unknown artist carved his figure in alabaster on the top of the sarcophagus, gently smiling and musing over a book. The image, as evocative of the medieval world as any passage from Tennyson, has become so well known it is referred to simply as *El Doncel de Sigüenza*. *Doncel*, in this case, means a king's page; Arce was an attendant of Fernando and Isabel. His crossed legs are not just an expression of nonchalance. It was a convention of Spanish medieval art, used to show that the deceased had died while fighting for the faith.

To stroll through the rest of Sigüenza will require a little climbing up narrow streets to the **castle** that dominates the town. Like Guadalajara, Sigüenza suffered greatly in the Civil War. The castle, now a *parador*, and the Plaza Mayor have been almost completely restored, but plenty of bullet scars can still be seen on the cathedral tower. Several other Romanesque and Gothic churches, all quite plain, have also been restored, including the 12th-century San Vicente on Calle del Jesús. Across the Plaza Obispo Don Bernardo from the cathedral there is a museum, the Museo Diocesano del Arte Sacro, with works by El Greco and Zurbarán and some early religious art. The second sunday in May sees a spectacular romería, or religious procession, from Sigüenza seven kilometres to the sanctuary of Barbatona.

Around Guadalajara and Sigüenza

The region east of Guadalajara known as the **Alcarria** was made famous by Spain's Nobel prize-winning writer Camilo José Cela in his rather pompous 1940s travel classic, *Viaje a la Alcarria* (1948). Set among the rugged hills is the village of **Pastrana**, capital of the region, a jumble of mossy-roofed houses watched over by its **Colegiata**, which houses a museum containing some remarkable 14th-century tapestries. Further north, both the NII highway and the Madrid—Zaragoza railway line pass the impressive, round-towered 15th-century **Castillo de Jadraque**, built by the Dukes of Osuna. Other ancient villages in this region, around the Río Henares and its tributaries, include **Hita**, which holds an annual medieval festival at the end of June, and **Brihuega**, a fortified village with much of its old walls still intact.

For those with transport, Sigüenza is the perfect starting point from which to explore the **Ruta Románico Rural**, northwest of the city, a picturesque route linking pretty medieval villages that seem barely touched by the passing centuries. Fine examples of Romanesque architecture abound, such as the church of **San Salvador** in the village of **Carabias**, and the very beautiful **Ermita de Santa Coloma** in **Albendiego**, at the foot of the Sierra del Alto Rey. Particularly interesting are the churches that blend Romanesque styles with *mudéjar* influences, such as **San Bartolomé** in **Campisábalos**, and the parish church of **Villacadima**, whose door is decorated in very Moorish botanical and geometrical patterns. The highlight of this route is the town and castle of **Atienza**, once an important fortified stronghold, strategically located with commanding views of the valley it dominates. At the height of its influence in the 12th–13th centuries, the town had 15 churches; five of these survive, Romanesque again. West of Cogolludo, the little parish church of **Beleña de Sorbe** has a fine portal carved with the twelve months and a relief of Joseph fleeing Potiphar's wife.

Where to Stay and Eating Out

Alcalá de Henares ✉ 28800

Alcalá's best known hotel is the ★★★**El Bedel**, C/ San Diego 6, ✆ 91 889 37 00, 📧 91 889 37 16 (*expensive*) which has an excellent location close to Cardinal Cisneros' famous Colegio Mayor de San Ildefonso—central, but quiet. Most hotels in Alcalá are quite a walk from the action around the Plaza de Cervantes; an exception is the ★★**Hs Miguel de Cervantes**, C/ Imagen 12, ✆ 91 883 12 77, 📧 91 883 05 02 (*moderate*), opposite the Convento de la Imagen on a street which runs between the C/ Mayor and C/ Santiago. Similar in price is the ★★**Hs El Torero**, Puerta de Madrid 8, ✆ 91 889 03 73 (*moderate*), in a historic building just outside the old city's western gate. There are several one-star establishments and *fondas* around the railway station, such as ★**Hs Jacinto**, Pso. de la Estación 2, ✆ 91 889 14 32 (*inexpensive*).

The town has one restaurant so well-known that it attracts a regular clientele from Madrid. The **Hostería del Estudiante**, C/ Colegios 3, ✆ 91 888 03 30 (*expensive*) is a *parador* restaurant in an annexe of the Colegio Mayor, faithfully restored to recreate a 16th-century atmosphere, right down to the oil lamps and uncomfortable chairs. Traditional Castilian cuisine is studiously maintained, and if you're up to spending a small fortune on dinner in this corner of Castile, this is the place. Lower-priced alternatives, both of which serve good quality, inspired meals, are **La Cúpola**, C/ Santiago 18 (*moderate*), in a converted 17th-century convent, and **La Parilla**, Pza. de los Santos Niños (*inexpensive*). Visitors to the Colegio Mayor, Pza. de San Diego, are at certain times able to eat at its superior **Cafetería Rectorado**, ✆ 91 855 41 40 (*cheap*), perhaps Alcalá's best-value eatery; in this glassed-off corner of the historic Patio de los Filósofos, generous platefuls of standards such as *gazpacho*, salads, grilled *merluza* and chicken roasted in wine cost next to nothing. For those with a sweet tooth, a visit to the **Convento de San Diego** on Calle Beatas 7 is a must. The nuns of the Santa Clara order make the most exquisite *almendras garapiñadas*: almonds, toasted in thick chewy toffee, made fresh every week.

Guadalajara ✉ 19000

There are far more pleasant places to stay than Guadalajara within easy reach. The best facilities the town has to offer are at the ★★★**Hotel Alcarría**, C/ Toledo 39, ✆ 949 25 33 00, ✉ 949 25 34 07 (*expensive*), and the ★★★**Husa Pax Hotel**, Ctra. Madrid-Barcelona km 57, ✆ 949 22 18 00, ✉ 949 22 69 55 (*expensive*), both on the outskirts of the centre. The ★**España** (*moderate*), C/ Teniente Figueroa 3, ✆ 949 21 13 03, is better value, in a 19th-century palace in the centre. For basic, cheap lodgings, also quite central, there is the ★**Hs Arroyo**, C/ Gonzalo Herranz 2, ✆ 949 21 11 23 (*inexpensive*).

The finest ingredients go into creative variations on classical cuisine at **Amparito Roca** (*expensive*), C/ Toledo 19, ✆ 949 21 46 39, and Castilian favourites are normally on the menu at **Casa Victor**, C/ Bardeles 6, ✆ 949 21 22 47 (*moderate*). Other places to seek out local specialities such as *cabrito a la barreña* (spit-roast kid), garlic soup, and *bizcochos borrachos* (rum babas) are plentiful around the Plaza Mayor and Plaza Bejanque areas.

Sigüenza ✉ 19250

The ★★★★**Parador Castillo de Sigüenza**, Plaza del Castillo, ✆ 949 39 01 00, ✉ 949 39 13 64 (*expensive*), has been, in its time, a Visigothic fortress and a Moorish alcázar; the Christians stormed it in the 12th century and turned it into a bishop's palace; now, a recent restoration from the ground up, it's a rather stark and forbidding hotel. The décor follows spartan themes (bare stone, weaponry), and the rooms are arranged around the *patio de armas*. Down near the station, the ★★**Hs El Doncel**, Pso. de la Alameda 3, ✆ 949 39 00 01, ✉ 949 39 00 80 (*moderate*) appears cramped and shabby and is far from cheap, but the rooms themselves are decent, with bath and television; while the ★**Hs Venancio**, C/ San Roque 1, ✆ 949 39 03 47 (*inexpensive*) has adequate, old-fashioned rooms which share a large tiled bathroom, for *3000 pts*.

Visitors to the town are often directed to the **Restaurante Calle Mayor**, C/ Mayor 21, ✆ 949 39 17 48 (*moderate*), where the house specialities include *chipirones rellenos* (stuffed squid), *cabrito al ajo* (kid with garlic), and *cordero asado* (roast lamb). Other good places to try the local lamb are the **Restaurante Medieval Segontia Asador**, C/ Portal May or 2, ✆ 949 39 32 33 (*moderate*), and the **Mesón La Cabaña**, Ctra. de Soria Km 5, ✆ 949 39 16 15 (*moderate*). **El Laberinto**, Pso. de la Alameda, is always full of locals and has an unusually wide choice of dishes on its set menu; there are plenty of cafés and bars on this street, and in the ancient and rather lovely Alameda Park itself.

Around Guadalajara and Sigüenza

If you get to **Brihuega**, there's a good inexpensive *pensión* there, ★★**P El Torreón**, (*cheap*) Pso. María Cristina 6, ✆ 949 28 03 00, and a welcoming restaurant, **El Tolmo**, Avda. de la Constitución 26, ✆ 949 28 04 76 (*expensive–moderate*), where they will be delighted to let you sample the local variation of *bacalao*—*bacalao a la alcarreña*. There are also simple *pensiones* in **Pastrana** and **Jadraque**. The **Hostería Princesa de Éboli** in Pastrana, in the converted Convento de los Monjas de Abajo, © 91 555 7272 (*moderate*) serves excellent meals, and is packed at weekends. The **Hospederia Real**, in the Franciscan Convento del Carmen © 949 37 10 60 (*expensive*), at the entrance to the town, is just as good, and in as lovely a setting.

Aranjuez: Yet Another Bourbon Palace

Palaces open summer, Tues–Sun, 10–6.15, winter, Tues–Sun 10–5.15; closed Mon; adm exp, free for EU passport holders on Wed; gardens open summer, Tues–Sun 8–8.30; winter Tues–Sun 8–6.30, closed Mon.

There has been a royal residence in Aranjuez since the days of Felipe II. His palace, built by Bautista and Herrera, the architects of El Escorial, burned down in the 17th century, and we can only wonder what sort of pleasure-dome those two grinds could have created. Felipe V began the replacement at the same time as he was building his palace at La Granja. It is hard to tell the two apart. Like La Granja, Aranjuez is an attempt to emulate some of the grandeur of Versailles; it isn't surprising, with Louis XIV meddling in Spain's affairs at every step, that the junior Bourbon wanted to show that he, too, was somebody. Aranjuez is a natural location for a palace. The water of the Río Tajo makes it an oasis among the brown hills, on the threshold of La Mancha. Centuries of royal attention have given the area more trees than any other corner of Castile, and even today it is famous in Spain for its strawberries and asparagus. A small town has grown up around the palace since the 16th century.

The first week of September sees spectacular fiestas based around the *motín de Aranjuez*. This celebrates the uprising of 1808, when, in the face of the French invasion, the locals rose up to overthrow the then prime minister, Godoy, who had advised Carlos IV to flee to America as part of his own evil schemes to gain power. The mob attacked Godoy's palace in Aranjuez, and the king was forced to sack him and then abdicate in favour of his son. This is considered the inspiration for the uprising in Madrid which followed on 2nd May of that year. The fiestas attract big crowds, many dressed in period costume.

Getting There

By train: Cercanías line C 3 trains from Madrid (Atocha) run to Aranjuez twice hourly, so there's no problem in getting there or back. To make a special outing of it, you could pay the extra to take the **Tren de la Fresa** (strawberry train), a real steam train that chuffs from Atocha to Aranjuez and back once a day during the summer months. A local bus will take you right from Aranjuez station to the palace; if you'd rather walk, turn right out of the station, then left down the avenue. RENFE information, Madrid: © 91 563 02 02, Aranjuez: © 91 891 02 02.

By bus: Buses from Madrid, run by AISA, © 91 527 12 94, leave hourly from Estación Sur, C/Méndez Álvaro, Ⓜ Méndez Álvaro. © 91 468 42 00. Buses from Madrid to Chinchón are run by La Veloz, © 91 409 76 02, from a stop near their office at 49 Avenida Mediterráneo (Ⓜ Conde de Casal). Departures in both directions leave hourly on the hour on weekdays and Saturdays, and roughly every 90mins on Sundays. The journey takes 50mins.

Plaza de San Antonio 9, ℰ 91 891 04 27.

As at La Granja, the prime attractions here are the **gardens**, full of sculptural allegory, and fountains in the most surprising places, shady avenues and walks along the Tajo, even an informal garden of the sort that were called 'English gardens' in the 18th century. They'll drag you through a guided tour of the **Palacio Real**, packed full of chandeliers and mirrors, with collections of porcelain, fancy clocks and court costume of the period. Among the gardens is another small palace, the **Casa del Labrador**, modelled after the Petit Trianon, and along the river a **museum of boats**; the conscientious Carlos III built the structure as part of a forgotten project to make the Tajo navigable, but his successors turned it into a boathouse, and their pleasure craft are on display.

Chinchón

Aranjuez fills up with day-trippers at weekends, and more than a few also make their way to Chinchón, a pretty village of faded terracotta-coloured roofs and steep streets. After the noise and bustle of Madrid, Chinchón feels rustic in the extreme. The village huddles on a hillside, exposed, and winter mornings are frequently crisp with frost, while in summer nothing moves under the glare of the midday sun. *Anís*, the aniseed flavoured liqueur, is not quite as popular in Spain as it is in the south of France, but the Spaniards down their share of it; much of it is made here in Chinchón. If you approach the village by the main route from Madrid, you will pass one of the larger distilleries a few kilometres before you arrive.

Chinchón is also famous for its picturesque, largely restored **Plaza Mayor**, which has served as a location for quite a few movies. Hemmed in by the higgledy-piggledy tiered wooden balconies of its surrounding buildings, it feels rather like a medieval theatre. The square is converted into a bullring during the fiestas of San Roque in mid August. Presiding over the Plaza Mayor, the village church of **La Asunción** treasures a painting of the Assumption of the Virgin by Goya.

Where to Stay and Eating Out

Aranjuez ⊠ 28300

Not many tourists stay in Aranjuez, as it is so close to Madrid. There are two decent, reasonably priced places near the centre, the well equipped ★★★**Isabel II**, Avda. Infantas 15, ℰ 91 891 09 45 (*moderate*) and the ★★★**Mercedes**, C/ Ducachia 15 (Ctra. de Andalucía), ℰ 91 891 04 40 (*moderate*) which is very close to the palaces, is surrounded by gardens, and has a pool.

Cheaper options include the ★★**Hs Las Infantas**, C/ Infantas 4, ℰ 91 891 13 41 (*moderate*), and the ★**Hs El Rusiñol**, C/ San Antonio 76, ℰ 91 891 01 55 (*inexpensive*), in an old house with some rooms without private bathroom for under *3000 pts*.

Such has been the boom in tourism over the last decade, that most restaurants can't get local strawberries and asparagus, nevertheless, that's what people come here to eat. And they figure prominently on most of the town's restaurant menus. Most of them are expensive, though, and you may settle for *fresas con nata* (strawberries and cream) from one of the little stands around town, although the cream won't be real either. Many restaurants have elegant settings along the riverfront, like **La Rana Verde**, C/ Reina 1, ✆ 91 891 32 38 (*moderate*), where paying the extra for one of the fish or game specialities is preferable to the simple set menu.

Casa Pablo C/ Almíbar 42, ✆ 91 891 14 51 (*moderate*) takes the cuisine and the wine a little more seriously, and is a little more expensive. Casa Pablo makes a welcome change from the usual fare, with inventive, international, nouveau-inspired cuisine making it very popular. The recommended place for very fresh fish and seafood as well as wood-fired roasts is **El Molino de Aranjuez**, C/ Príncipe 21, ✆ 91 892 42 15 (*expensive*), a restaurant in the wing of an ancient palace.

Chinchón ✉ 28370

The ★★★★**Parador de Chinchón**, Avda. Generalísimo 1, ✆ 91 894 08 36, ✆ 91 894 09 08 (*expensive*) is quite exceptional. An atmosphere of cool serenity pervades the cloisters and stairways of this beautiful 17th-century monastery, with its lovely box-scented garden planted with roses and fruit trees. The rooms are pretty, with simple tiled floors and painted bedsteads.

You can't stay closer to the Plaza Mayor than at the welcoming, spotless ★★**Hs Chinchón**, C/ José Antonio 12, ✆ 91 893 53 98 (*moderate*), where the all rooms have TV and air-conditioning, and room 1 has a dramatic view over the square and the hillsides beyond. There's a bar and restaurant downstairs. Uphill from the Plaza Mayor, on the way to the municipal swimming pool, is the **Hs La Cerca**, C/ Cerca 9, ✆ 91 893 50 82, which has plain but neat and clean double rooms for *6000 pts.*

Many of the historic buildings on the Plaza Mayor are restaurants; one of the best is the **Mesón de la Virreina**, Pza. Mayor 28, ✆ 91 894 00 15 (*moderate*), good for local specialities like roast lamb and pork, *sopa castellana* or *pisto manchego* (the local answer to ratatouille). The **Restaurante La Columna**, ✆ 91 894 05 02 (*moderate*) is also on the Plaza Mayor, but it doesn't have views over the square; however it does have an extremely pretty galleried patio inside, and it is well worth visiting for its excellent, very reasonably priced *menú del día.*

Chinchón has no shortage of *mesones* specializing in spit-roasted or wood-fired brick oven-roasted joints; two of the most well known are the **Mesón de la Cerca**, C/ Cerca 9, ✆ 91 894 13 00 (*moderate*), next door to the *hostal* of the same name, and the **Mesón Cuevas del Vino**, C/ Benito Hortelano 13, ✆ 91 894 02 85 (*moderate*), built in centuries-old caves. A good place to sip a glass of *anís* is the **Bar Los Huertos**, C/ Generalísimo 3, a bar with a large, pleasant courtyard graced with a fountain and a spreading fig tree.

Cuenca

East of Aranjuez, the empty northern corner of La Mancha gradually rises into an attractive, rolling countryside, the foothills of the **Serranía de Cuenca**, a low, dishevelled chain that marks the traditional boundary between New Castile and Aragón. Cuenca, one of the most unusual and dramatic fortress-cities of Spain, stands at the base of this chain. On the way, anyone interested in Roman Spain who can't make it to Tarragona or Mérida may want to take the detour southeast of Tarancón to **Segóbriga**, an important city for the Iberians and Visigoths as well as the Romans. The 3rd-century theatre, amphitheatre and some other buildings have been excavated, and there is a small museum on the site.

Getting There

By train: Cuenca isn't really a comfortable day-trip from Madrid, unless the slow trains (2–3hr trip) and quirky RENFE schedules hold no terrors for you. There are six trains every weekday and four trains on Saturdays and Sundays from Madrid-Atocha on the Regionales line R 10, direction Valencia. RENFE information, Madrid: ✆ 91 328 9020, Cuenca: ✆ 969 22 07 20.

By bus: The bus service, Auto-Res, ✆ 91 551 72 00, departs eight times a day (at roughly 2hr intervals, journey time 2 hrs) from Pza. Conde de Casal 6 in Madrid (Ⓜ Conde de Casal) to the bus station on C/ Fermín Caballero in Cuenca.

Tourist Information

Glorieta González Palencia 2, ✆ 969 17 88 00.

Depending on how you enter Cuenca, you may not see the old town at all when you arrive. A fair-sized modern city fills up all the space in the valley of the Río Júcar that once held medieval Cuenca's market gardens. Nearly all the hotels and restaurants are down here, but to see the real Cuenca, you'll have either to do a very stiff climb or to take the city bus up from Plaza de la Trinidad, near the confluence of the Júcar and the little Huécar. Old Cuenca waits upon a high rock between the two valleys, a position that helps to explain the city's history. Save only a few odd sackings, at the hands of Alfonso VIII and during the Napoleonic Wars, Cuenca has been quiet for a long time, guarded by its nearly impregnable setting. The cliffs are steep, particularly on the Huécar side, and the **casas colgadas**, 'hanging houses', draped over them are the town's most prominent and picturesque feature.

Once you're up, you can rest while regarding the **Torre de Mangana**, the last remnant of the town's Moorish alcazaba; no one is quite sure whether it was a minaret or part of the fortifications. It's hard to find, on a rise tucked behind the main street, Calle Alfonso XIII. That street leads to the **Plaza Mayor**, passing underneath the arches of the lovely 18th-century **Ayuntamiento**. The Plaza Mayor, with its cafés and plane trees, would be perfect but for the screamingly atrocious façade of the **Cathedral** (*open daily, 9–2 and 4.30–7.30*). Inside, the church reveals itself as an austerely graceful Gothic work of the 12th century, but the front was rebuilt in the 1660s as someone's bright idea of what Gothic really ought to have looked like. The original features of the interior are worth a look inside, with some noble tombs, stained glass and sculpture; note the very unusual subjects portrayed on the inside of the north transept. The **treasury** contains two paintings by El Greco. Just behind the cathedral, on Calle Canónigos, there is a small **Museo Arqueológico** (*open Tues–Sat 10–2 and 4–7; Sun, 10–2; closed Mon*) with finds from Segóbriga, Valeria and other Roman sites around Cuenca.

Cuenca has two bizarre fiestas: on 21 September, wild cows are let loose in the main square and on the night of Good Friday, the Turbas, or *borrachos*—drunks—take to the streets to represent the Jews who condemned Christ and, in a sort of legitimised Saturnalia, get blind drunk, strip off, and blaspheme in public without punishment.

Museo de Arte Abstracto Español

C/ Canónigos, open Tues–Fri 11–2 and 4–6, Sat 11–2 and 4–8, Sun 11–2.30; closed Mon.

Some of the most decorative of the hanging houses perched on the cliff's edge have been converted into one of Spain's most unusual museums, the Spanish Museum of Abstract Art. Many visitors come to Cuenca expressly to see this audacious undertaking, showing off the avant-garde in a medieval setting, and the museum has acquired an international reputation. Only Spanish contemporary artists are represented, and while only fervent devotees of the abstract may spend much time on the paintings, anyone will enjoy the views from the old wooden balconies high above the Huécar. The houses—several of them have been connected for the museum—are interesting in themselves, though restored in a trendy manner with white walls and exposed beam ceilings.

The museum, now 25 years old, is one of the many projects of the Juan March Foundation, one of the most important forces in the Spanish art world. Its founder, the late Juan March, is worth a mention. Spain's greatest robber baron, a poor boy from Mallorca, made his fortune in contraband tobacco, eventually almost running the state tobacco monopoly out of business. After that he cornered the Spanish shipping business (with his Transmediterranea Line), put the entire Spanish coast guard on his payroll, stole the Barcelona street-car service from the foreign syndicate that built it, and still found time to assist British intelligence in two world wars. The Republic finally managed to land him in jail, but friends who visited him there reported finding March's private chef in attendance, tapestries on the cell walls, and three newly installed telephone lines. In return for the annoyance, March arranged all the financing for the Nationalist war effort in 1936. He died in 1962, from injuries received in the crash of his Cadillac, and his billions are now building hospitals around Spain and buying up abstract art.

The Devil's Handprint

On the opposite side of Cuenca, facing the Júcar, a road called the Ronda de Júcar leads down into the valley past a number of old churches, monasteries and shrines, a corner of Cuenca that has been a holy place probably for millennia. Past the chapel of Nuestra Señora de las Angustias, patroness of the city, there is a small sunken garden with an unusual stone cross, decorated at the base with radiant suns. There's a legend in Cuenca of a young wastrel, long ago, who was seduced by a mysterious lady into arranging a midnight tryst outside the walls (at Halloween!). Lost in her charms, he did not realize that he was about to become the subject of old legend until he slid his hand up her dress and saw the cloven hoof—for she was the Devil himself, concealed in femininity. The wastrel escaped with his life only by reaching the refuge of this cross just as the fiend was about to snatch him, and you may see the mark of the Devil's hand on it today. More prosaically, you may consider the hand to be a symbol from some discreet and long forgotten heresy, perhaps a version of the Islamic 'Hand of Fatima', a common symbol in the Middle East that survives in Salamanca and other cities of Spain in the form of door-knockers.

The Hoz del Huécar

Returning to the Huécar side of the town, just behind the apse of the Cathedral near the Abstract Art Museum, there is a long, narrow footbridge called the **Puente de San Pablo** that begins one of the most beautiful walks you can take in this part of Spain, over the gorge (*hoz*) of the Huécar and then down into it, passing through pine-woods and fields along the river-bank with a view of the *casas colgadas* high above. Only from here does it become apparent just how unusual some of these are. What seemed like simple houses from on top turn out to be the lobbies of upside-down medieval skyscrapers (*rascacielos* as the Cuencans call them), hanging down as many as 12 storeys on the side of the cliff. The road along the Huécar re-enters the city at the picturesque **Calle de los Tintes**, a boundary between the old Cuenca and the new.

Excursions From Cuenca

The rough mountains of the Serranía de Cuenca are full of natural curiosities, which can be seen best with a car and a little determination. By taking a loop of backroads north and east of the city you can visit the **Ciudad Encantada** (*open daily, sunrise to sunset*), near Villalba de la Sierra, a region of curious wind-blown rock formations among pine woods. Some, like the 15m 'big lump' are balanced precariously on narrow stems, like mushrooms; others have acquired names like the 'elephant' and the 'sea of stone'. To the southwest, **Las Torcas** are a group of strange, conical sinkholes, formed by the action of underground streams; some have filled up from below to become small lakes. The truly determined may find their way to the palaeolithic **cave paintings** near the village of Villar del Humo, interesting though not as well preserved as the caves of Altamira. They are quite a way off even the back roads; ask at the tourist office in Cuenca if they may still be visited, and for explicit directions.

The road east from Cuenca, heading for Teruel, is wonderfully scenic, especially after it passes through the Valley of Ademuz into Aragón. The Castilian section is called the **Vía Pecunaria**, the old 'cattle road'; there are more sheep than cattle grazing on its hillsides these days, but this is still one of the more traditional and out-of-the-way corners of Spain.

Cuenca ✉ *16000*

Where to Stay

expensive

The ★★★★**Parador de Cuenca**, Pso. Hoz del Huécar, ✆ 969 23 23 20, 🖷 969 23 25 34, is set in the former Convento de San Pablo which has been painstakingly restored. The building perches on the cliff across the Huécar gorge from the *casas colgadas*.

Most hotels are in the new, lower town, like the ★★★★**Alfonso VIII**, Parque San Julián 3, ✆ 969 21 25 12, across from the Parque de San Julián.

moderate

Surprisingly, perhaps, it's possible to stay in a *casa colgada* overlooking the Huécar gorge without paying the earth for the privilege. You could head for the ★★★**Leonor de Aquitania**, C/ San Pedro 60, ✆ 969 23 10 00, which has marvellous views from its *cafetería* and from its more expensive rooms.

The ★★**Posada de San José**, C/ Julián Romero 4, ✆ 969 21 13 00, in some converted 17th-century houses is stuffed with interesting old furniture and curios.

Most of the cheaper hotels and *hostales* are on Calle Ramón y Cajal, on the way from the railway station to the old town, including the ★**Hs San Isidro**, C/ Ramón y Cajal 32, ✆ 969 21 11 63, a modern place which has decent rooms with shared bathroom facilities, as does the ★**Hs Del Pilar**, C/ Ramón y Cajal 35, ✆ 969 21 16 84 (with heat—essential in the winter).

Eating Out

Cuenca's best restaurant for classic Castilian cuisine is, by consensus, the **Figón de Pedro** (*expensive*), C/ Cervantes 15, ✆ 969 22 45 11, with such specialities as *morteruelo*, made with grated pig's liver, traditionally finished off with a glass of *resolí*, a local potion of brandy, oranges, cinnamon and coffee. The Figón de Pedro can't, however, beat the **Mesón Casas Colgadas**, C/ Canónigos, ✆ 969 22 35 09 (*expensive*) for its stunning location in the old city, actually in one of the hanging houses and with inspiring views over the Huécar gorge.

Casa Marlo, C/ Colón 59, ✆ 969 21 38 60 (*expensive*) is another good choice, for its welcoming atmosphere and inventive menu (partridge stew with figs and aubergine and mushroom pie are featured). The **Taverna de Pepe**, C/ Tintes, ✆ 969 22 49 19 (*moderate*), in a lovely setting by the river, specializes in seafood. Some of the less expensive restaurants are good; the **Baviera** on C/ Hurtado de Mendoza (*cheap*) has a set menu that often includes river trout, and you can get by for even less at the **Fonda Tintes**, C/ Tintes (*cheap*).

Toledo

No city in Spain has seen more, or learned more, or stayed true to itself for so long through the shifting fortunes of a discouraging history. Under the rule of Madrid the usurper, though, the last 400 years have been murder for Toledo; its pride humbled, its talents and achievements dried up, this city with little political or economic function is entirely at the mercy of the tourists. It would be a ghost town without them. It isn't Toledo's fault that it has become a museum city, but it carries out the rôle with considerable grace. Its monuments are well-scrubbed, its streets lively and pleasant, and the city summons a smile and a welcome for even the most befuddled package tourist. No matter how you come to Toledo, you'll be glad when you finally arrive. The surrounding countryside, once all irrigated farmland or forest, is a desolation, a desert with a tinge of green. Toledo has a beautiful setting on a plateau above the Río Tajo, and its little plazas and narrow streets are like an oasis in brick and stone.

History

Toledo was a capital of sorts when the Romans found it, a centre for the local Celtiberian tribes called the Carpetani. As a Roman town, Toletum did not gain much distinction, but scanty remains of temples and a circus, still visible just north of town off the Avenida de la Reconquista, indicate it must have been fairly large. The Visigoths made it their capital in the 6th century; their palace may have been on the site of the Alcázar, but they were not great builders, and relatively little is left from their two centuries of rule.

Toledo

Circo Romano

AVENIDA DE CARLOS III
CALLE OCAÑA
AVENIDA DE LA RECONQUISTA
CALLE ESCALONA
CALLE LA DIPUTACIÓN
AVENIDA DEL DUQUE DE LE.
LA DIPUTACIÓN
PASEO DEL CIRCO ROMANO
PASEO DE CANÓNIGOS
Paseo de Merchán
PASEO DEL CRISTO DE LA VEGA
PZA. ALFONSO VI
Puerta de Bisagra
C/ LA CAV
AVENIDA PUENTE DE LA CAVA
C/ ALFONSO VI
PUENTE DE LA CAVA
Puerta del Cambrón
Santiago del Arrabal
REAL DE ARRABAL
LAS CARMELITAS
CUESTA DE LA GRANJA
CALLE REAL
Puerta del Sol
SANTA LEOCADIA
LA MERCED
CAL
C/ CARRET
Monasterio de S. Juan de los Reyes
PINTOR M. ALIAS MORENO
COLLEGIO DE DONCELLAS
PZA. PADILLA
PZA. STA. CLARA
PZA. CARMELITAS
Mezquita del Cristo de la Luz
LOS REYES CATÓLICOS
ESTEBAN ILLÁN
PZA. S. VICENTE
LOS ALFILERITOS
C/ E RIOS MENOR DE
NÚÑEZ DE
Museum of Contemporary Art
CALLE ANGEL
S. CLEMENTE
Post Office
TOLEDO DE
Sinagoga de Sta. Maria la Blanca
LAS BULAS
Museo de la Cultura Visigótica
PZA. AMADOR DE LOS RIOS
NUNCIO VIEJO
C/ COMERCIO
Sinagoga del Tránsito and Museo Sefardi
PZA. BARRIO NUEVO
Santo Tomé
PZA. DE VALDECABALLEROS
ALFONSO X
JESÚS Y MARIA
Palacio Arzobispal
Cathedral
PLAZA MAYOR
MAG
Casa Museo de El Greco
JUAN DE DIOS
STO. TOMÉ
Taller del Moro
LA TRINIDAD
PLAZA AYUNTAMIENTO
SIXTO
JUAN LABRADO
Palacio de Fuensalida
TRÁNSITO
DEL MORO
TALLER
Posada de la Hermandad
PASEO DEL TRÁNSITO
Ayuntamiento
POZO AMARGO
PZA. CABE
CALVARIO LOS DESCALZOS
PZA. DE SAN CRISTÓBAL
PZA. DEL REY D. PEDRO
PZA. FUENTES
PZA. SAN JUSTO
CUESTA DE S.
SAN LORENZO
PZA. DE STA. CATALINA
AVE. MARIA PLEGADERO
C/ SACRAMENTO
LAS RECOGIDAS
PASEO DE LA C
CARRERAS DE SAN SEBASTIÁN
PZA. DON FERNANDO
PZA. DE SAN LUCAS
San Lucas
Río Tajo
PUENTE DE SAN MARTÍN
PZA. ANDAQUE

N

300 metres
300 yards

King Roderick and the Tower of Hercules

Toledo is full of stories. One of the oldest speaks of a tower, built by Hercules, that stood on the edge of the city. No one knew what was in it, and it became a tradition for every Spanish king to add a new padlock to the scores of them that already secured the tower's thick brass door.

Roderick, that scoundrel who was to be the last of the Visigoths, neglected this, and was confronted one day by two magicians in mysterious dress to remind him of his duty. Roderick's curiosity was piqued, and instead of carrying on the old custom he resolved to find out what was inside the ancient tower. The bishops and counsellors did their best to dissuade him, but in the end Roderick had the centuries' accumulation of locks pried off, one by one, and threw open the brass door. An air as chill as death issued from inside, but the king entered, alone, and climbed a narrow stair to the top of the tower. There he met the figure of a bronze warrior, larger than life, swinging a great mace back and forth and barring his entrance to the tower's inner chamber. Still undaunted, the king commanded it to stop and it obeyed. Behind it lay a chamber with walls covered in gold and precious stones, empty save for a small table bearing a small chest. This the king opened greedily, finding nothing inside but a large folded linen scroll. He saw that it was covered with scenes of battle; as he unrolled it the figures on it came to life, and Roderick saw his own army go down to defeat at the hands of unknown invaders in outlandish costume. While he blinked in astonishment at the moving pictures, a loud crash like thunder sounded from the depths of the tower; he dropped the linen scroll and hurriedly fled, escaping just in time to see an eagle with a burning brand in its claws soaring over Hercules' tower. With a scream it dropped the flame directly over it, and in scarcely more time than it took Roderick and his knights to heave a sigh, the tower burnt to the ground. Then, a great flock of birds flew up from the ashes and sped off to the four winds.

Of course the invaders were the Moors; both Toledo and Roderick fell to them in the year 716. The beauty and strangeness of the old legend betray its Moorish origins, and Toledo, under its new masters, was about to embark on a career that itself would become the stuff of legends. Here, long before the Crusades, the Christian and Islamic worlds first met, in a city renowned throughout the Mediterranean world for learning. A school of translators grew up over the centuries in which Arab, Jewish and Christian scholars transmitted Greek and Arabic science, as well as Islamic and Jewish theology and mysticism, to the lands of the north. The first medieval troubadours most likely gained some inspiration from the Arab originals here. Toledo, conveniently close to the mercury mine at Almadén, became a centre for the study of alchemy. Schools of occult philosophy and mathematics proliferated, attracting students from all over Christian Europe. One was Sylvester II, the late 10th-century Pope, who was said to have stolen a famous book of magic while he was a student in Toledo, and was accused during his papacy of consulting with a prophetic magic 'head' of gold called a 'Baphomet' (the same charge that was later raised against the Templars).The chroniclers claimed a population for Moorish Toledo of some 200,000 people, over three times as large as it is today. Even so, it was never a centre of political power, and to the sultans and emirs of Al-Andalus it meant little more than the central bastion of their defence line against the rapacious Christians of the north. In a moment of inattention they lost it to Alfonso VI and El Cid.

The conquest of the city in 1085 was never reversed, and tipped the balance of power irreparably against the Moors. For a long time, Toledo under Castilian rule continued its role as a city of tolerance and scholarship, and its Moorish and Jewish populations easily accommodated the Christian settlers introduced by the Castilian kings. Alfonso the Wise was born here, and he did much to make Toledo's learning and experience become Spain's in common. After the accession of Fernando and Isabel, however, disasters followed thick and fast. The church and the Inquisition were given a free hand, and soon succeeded in snuffing out Toledo's intellectual lights. The expulsion of the Jews, and later the Moors, put an end to the city's long-established culture, and the permanent establishment of the capital at Madrid ended for ever the political importance Toledo had enjoyed in medieval Castile. To make matters worse, Toledo had been a focal point of the Comunero revolt, and suffered greatly after its suppression. By the 18th century the city had become an impoverished backwater, and except for the famous siege of the Alcázar during the Civil War, little has happened there since. Long ago, Toledo made its living from silk and steel; the silk industry died off with the expulsion of the Moors, and the famous Toledo blades, tempered in cold water from the Tajo, are only a memory except for the cheap versions the tourists buy. The visitors keep this town going, though the Toledans despair when the convoys of tour buses from Madrid stuff themselves through the tiny streets throughout July and August. Do not be discouraged; relatively few people spend the night, and after museum hours the old town becomes surprisingly tranquil.

Getting There

By train: Toledo is off the main road and rail lines, and it's hard to get there from anywhere but Madrid. That, however, is easy enough; there are nine trains a day at one to two hourly intervals from Madrid-Atocha to Toledo's charming *mudéjar*-style station east of town (Regionales line 9 f, journey time 60–85mins). Any city bus will take you from the station into the centre. RENFE information, Madrid: © 91 563 02 02, Toledo © 925 22 30 99.

By bus: There is also a convenient bus service run by Empresa Galiano Continental, *©* 91 527 2961, with departures every half hour from Estación Sur, C/Méndez Álvaro, Metro Méndez Álvaro *©* 91 468 42 00.

Tourist Information

Just outside the Puerta de Bisagra (Bisagra Gate), *©* 925 22 08 43, *✉* 925 25 26 48, on the road from Madrid (stop on your way if you can, so you won't have to make the steep trip down again).

Around the Plaza de Zocodover

The name, like the *souk* of a Moroccan city, is from the Arabic for market, and this square—triangle, really—has always been the centre of Toledo. Despite bearing the brunt of Toledo's success as a tourist destination (a McDonald's now dominates one side), the square endures as a favourite place for residents to meet up and exchange gossip, and a traditional market is still held here on Tuesdays. On the long, eastern edge of the triangle, the stately building with the clock is the seat of the provincial government, rebuilt after it burned down during the Civil War. From the archway under the clock, stairs lead down to the Calle Cervantes and the enormous, fascinating museum contained within the 1544 **Hospital de Santa Cruz**, C/ Cervantes 3, (*open Tues–Sat 10–6.30, Sun 10–2, closed Mon*), a building by Enrique de Egas with a wildly decorated façade. A little bit of everything has been assembled here: archaeological finds from Toletum, paintings and tapestries, Toledo swords and daggers. The building itself is worth a visit, its long airy halls typical of hospitals of the period, with beautiful ceilings and staircases. Spanish medicine was quite advanced in the 16th century (most of the physicians were Jewish and exempt from the persecutions) and the surroundings were held to be an important part of the cure. Notable among the displays are Don Juan's huge standard from his flagship at the Battle of Lepanto, paintings by El Greco (*Santiago, Saint John*, an *Assumption*, and a *Crucifixion* with a view of Toledo in the background), some eccentric holy scenes by the 16th-century Maestro de Sigena, and a sculptural frieze from a pre-Roman Toledo house. A lovely 15th-century Flemish tapestry, the *Tapiz de los Astrolabios*, shows the northern constellations in a kind of celestial garden; other tapestries detail scenes from the life of Alexander the Great.

Just around the corner of Calle de la Concepción, the chapel of **San Jerónimo** is one of the best examples of Toledo's 16th-century *mudéjar* churches.

Gates of the Town

North from the Plaza de Zocodover, the Cuesta de las Armas is the old main road to Madrid. The street descends gradually, past the **Mirador**, to the **Puerta del Sol**, a pretty gate-house from the 12th century. In the 14th century, the Knights of St John rebuilt it and added the curious relief medallion, much commented on as a late example of Toledan mysticism; it shows the sun, moon, and a large triangle around a scene of San Ildefonso, patron and 4th-century bishop of Toledo, receiving a chasuble woven by angels from the hands of the Virgin. According to local legend, it was presented in return for a treatise the saint wrote on the meaning of the Immaculate Conception. Further down, in the old quarter called the **Arrabal** outside the Moorish walls, is another fine *mudéjar* church, a joyous excess of pointed arches and towers done in brick, the 11th-century **Santiago del Arrabal**. In the 1480s, this was the church of San Vicente Ferrer, the anti-Semitic fire-eater whose sermons started regular riots and helped force the expulsion of the Jews. Here the modern road curves around the **Nueva Puerta de Bisagra**, more like a palace than a gate with its pointed spires and courtyard. Charles V built it, strictly for decoration, and added his enormous coat of arms in stone after the Comunero wars, to remind the Toledans who was boss.

Just outside the gate, the city's tourist office is on the edge of a large park called the **Paseo de Merchán**, on the other side of which stands another 16th-century charitable institution converted into a museum, the **Museo Hospital de Tavera**, Avda. de los Duques de Lerma (*open daily, 10.30–1.30 and 3.30–6*), lovingly guarded by three old ladies. Cardinal Tavera was a member of the house of Mendoza, a grandee of Spain, and an adviser to Charles V. His collection, including his portrait among several works by El Greco, and the memorable *Bearded Woman* by Ribera, share space with objects and furnishings from the Cardinal's time.

The Alcázar

> *C/ General Moscardó, open Tues–Sat 9.30–1.30 and 4–5.30, till 6.30 Fri, Sun, 10–1.30 and 4–5.30, closed Mon.*

Romans, Visigoths and Moors all had some sort of fortress on this spot, at the highest point of the city. The present plan of the big, square palace-fortress, the same that stands out so clearly in El Greco's famous *View of Toledo*, was constructed by Charles V, though rebuilt after destructions in the Napoleonic Wars and again in the Civil War. The second siege was a bitter one, and gave Toledo's Alcázar the curious fate of becoming the holy-of-holies for Spain's fascists and Francoists. Toledo declared for the Republic in July 1936, but a number of soldiers, civilians and Guardia Civil barred themselves inside with the idea that the coup would soon be over. Instead, what they got was a two-month ordeal, with Republican irregulars keeping them under constant fire. When the Nationalists began to exploit the brave defence for propaganda, the Republicans got serious, and finally Asturian miners succeeded in collapsing most of the fortress with dynamite charges. Still the defenders held out, under the leadership of Colonel José Moscardó, in the ruins and underground tunnels, until a relief column finally arrived in September. The courage shown by the men of the Alcázar was quite real, but Francoist Spain was never content to leave it at that. The climax of the visit here is Colonel Moscardó's office, where plaques in 19 languages record a telephone conversation in which the Republican commander threatened to kill Moscardó's son, whom he had captured, if the Alcázar did not surrender. With his son on the line, Moscardó intoned 'Shout *Viva España* and die like a hero!' The story is a blatant copy of that of Guzmán el Bueno in Tarifa. In this case, it's all a fake, and Moscardó's son was later found alive and well in Madrid.

The trip through the dungeons is interesting, with relics such as the old motorcycle that was hooked up to a mill to grind flour for the defenders, and the spot where two babies were born during the siege. The corridors are covered with plaques sent from overseas to honour the memory of the besieged soldiers, contributed by such groups as the Chilean army and an association of Croatian Nazis in exile.

Mezquita del Cristo de la Luz

From the Plaza de Zocodover, Calle Comercio leads off towards Toledo's great cathedral; on the way, you'll notice a big street sign proclaiming Calle de Toledo de Ohio, decorated with the Ohio state seal in *azulejos* (Toledans are proud of their little sister on Erie's shore, with its newspaper called the *Blade*; few of them have probably ever seen it). You may consider a detour here, up typically Toledan steep, narrow streets, to the church of **Cristo de la Luz**, in reality a mosque built around 980 and incorporating elements of an earlier Visigothic church. When Alfonso VI captured the city (the story goes), he and El Cid were making their triumphal entrance when the king's horse knelt down in front of the mosque and refused to move. Taking this as a portent, the king ordered the mosque searched, and a hidden niche was discovered, bricked up in the walls, with a crucifix and a lamp that had been miraculously burning since the days of the Visigoths. The tiny mosque, one of the oldest surviving Moorish buildings in Spain, is an exceptional example of their work.

The Cathedral

Open daily, 10.30–2 and 4–6.30; museum open Tues–Sat 10.30–1 and 3.30–6, Sun, 10.30–1, closed Mon.

This isn't a building that may be approached directly; most of its bulk is hidden behind walls and rows of old buildings, with corners peeking out where you least expect them. The best of its portals, the **Puerta del Reloj**, is tucked away in a small courtyard where few ever see it, at the end of Calle Chapinería. Circumnavigating the great building will take you all through the neighbourhood. On Calle Sixto Romano, behind the apse, you'll pass an old inn called the **Posada de la Hermandad**, seat of a permanent militia-police force called the 'Holy Brotherhood' that kept the peace in medieval Castile. Coming around Calle Hombre de Palo, past the cathedral cloister, you pass the entrance used today, the **Puerta del Mollete** (muffin) where bread was once distributed to the needy.

Finally, arriving at the Plaza Ayuntamiento (still often referred to as the Plaza del Generalísimo) you may enjoy the final revelation of the west front. It's a little disappointing. Too many cooks have been at work, and the great rose windows are hidden behind superfluous arches, over three big portals where the sculpture is indifferent but grandiose. Before too long, the interest fades; look across the square and you'll see one of Spain's most beautiful city halls, the 1618 **Ayuntamiento**, by El Greco's son, Jorge Theotocópoulos.

Don't give up on the cathedral yet; few Gothic churches in Spain can match its interior, unusually light and airy and with memorable works of art in every corner. Some 800 fine stained-glass windows from the 15th and 16th centuries dispel the gloom. Sculpture takes the place of honour before painting, unlike in most other cathedrals of Spain. Some of the best work is in the Old Testament scenes around the wall of the *coro*, at the centre of the Cathedral (note the interesting versions of the Creation and story of Adam and Eve). The *coro*'s stalls are famous, decorated with highly detailed scenes from the conquest of Granada, done just three years after the event by Rodrigo Alemán. Behind the *coro* is the freestanding **Chapel of the Descent**, dedicated to San Ildefonso; with its golden pinnacle it seems to be some giant monstrance left in the aisle. Another oddity is the 30ft-tall painting of St Christopher on the south wall. The **Capilla Mayor**, around the main altar, contains some fine sculpture. A famous statue on the left-hand wall is that of Martín Alhaga, a mysterious shepherd who guided Alfonso VIII's army through the mountains before its victory at Las Navas de Tolosa, then disappeared; only the king saw his face, and he directed the sculptor at his work. On the right, another statue honours the memory of Alfaqui Abu Walid. When Alfonso VI conquered Toledo, he promised this Moorish *alcalde* that the great mosque, on the site of the cathedral, would be left in peace. While he was on a campaign, however, the bishop and the king's French wife Constance conspired to tear it down; upon his return the enraged Alfonso was only dissuaded from punishing them by the entreaties of the generous Moor. Behind the altar, the beautiful *retablo* reaches almost to the vaulting.

The Transparente

Even in a cathedral where so much is unusual, this takes the cake. Early in the 18th century, someone decided that Mass here would seem even more transcendent if somehow a shaft of light could be directed over the altar. To do this a hole was chopped in the wall of the Capilla Mayor, and another in the vaulting of the ambulatory. The difficult question of how to reconcile this intrusion was given to the sculptor Narciso Tomé and his four sons, and in several years' work, they transformed the ungainly openings into a Baroque spectacular, combining painting, sculpture and architecture into a cloud of saints, angels and men that grow magically out of the cathedral's stones—many of the figures are partly painted, partly sculpture fixed to the walls. The upper window becomes a kind of vortex, through which the Virgin at the top and all the rest appear in the process of being vacuumed up to heaven. Even those who usually find Baroque extravagance a bore will at least raise a smile for the Transparente, completed in 1732. Antoni Gaudí would have approved, and it's hard to believe he did not gain just a little of his inspiration from this eccentric masterpiece. Near the Transparente, the ratty old bit of cloth hanging from the vaulting is a Cardinal's hat—cardinals in Spain have the privilege of hanging them wherever they like before they die. It is one of several in the cathedral. Toledo's archbishop is still the Primate of Spain, and of cardinals it has known quite a few.

The Mozarabic Chapel

After the Christian conquest of Toledo, a dispute arose immediately between the city's old Christians and the officious Castilian prelates over which form of the liturgy would be used in Masses: the ancient Mozarabic form descended from the time of the Visigoths, or the modern, Church-sanctioned style of the rest of Europe. Alfonso, as any good Crusader might have done, decided on a trial by combat to decide the issue. The Mozarabic champion won, but the Churchmen weren't satisfied, and demanded a trial by fire. So they ignited some prayer-books. The Roman version was blown from the flames by a sudden wind, the Mozarabic wouldn't burn, and Alfonso decreed that the two versions of the faith would co-exist on equal footing. Though the numbers of those faithful to the Mozarabic liturgy have dwindled, their Mass is still regularly celebrated in the large chapel in the southwest corner of the cathedral, built by Cardinal Cisneros, a friend and protector of the Mozarabs. You'll be lucky to see it; this chapel, the only home of the oldest surviving Christian ritual in Western Europe, is usually locked up tight. Other sections of the cathedral are open by separate admission, from the enormous souvenir stand inside the Puerta del Mollete. The **Treasury** has little of interest, though the 3m-high silver reliquary does not fail to impress. In the **Sala Capitular**, a richly decorated room with a gilt *artesanado* ceiling, you can see some unusual frescoes and portraits of all Toledo's archbishops. El Greco painted the frescoes and altarpiece of the **Sacristy**, and there are other works of his, as well as a Holy Family by Van Dyck, and a gloomy representation of the arrest of Christ by Goya that makes an interesting contrast to his famous *Los Fusilamientos de Moncloa* in the Prado.

Here the streets become even narrower and more winding; it's surprising just how long you can stay lost in a town only 1 sq km in area. Just three intractable blocks northwest of the cathedral, the 13th-century church of San Román has been converted into the **Museo de los Concilios y de la Cultura Visigótica** (Museum of the Councils and Visigothic Culture), C/ San Clemente (*open Tues–Sat 10–2 and 4–6.30; Sun, 10–2; closed Mon*), the only one of its kind in Spain. 'Councils' refers to the several General Councils of the Western Church that were held in Toledo in the days of Visigothic rule, but the majority of the museum's exhibits are simple Visigothic relics, jewellery and religious-artworks. Some of the buckles, brooches and carved stones show an idiosyncratic talent, but the lesson here is that the artistic inspiration of Spain did not really change in the transition from Roman to Visigothic rule—only there was much less of it. The building itself is much more interesting, half-Christian and half-Moorish, with naive, original frescoes of the Last Judgement and the 12 Apostles in a garden. Painted angels and saints peer out from the ceilings and horseshoe arches.

There is a small **Museo de Arte Contemporánea** (*open Tues–Sat, 10–2 and 4–6.30; Sun, 10–2; closed Mon*) just two blocks west of here, at C/ Bulas Viejas 13.

The Judería

As long as the streets continue to slope downwards, you'll know you're going in the right direction. The **Judería**, Toledo's Jewish quarter before 1492, occupies a narrow strip of land overlooking the Tajo in the southwestern corner of the city. El Greco too lived here, and the back streets of the Judería are a concentration of some of old Toledo's most intruiging and interesting monuments.

The church of **Santo Tomé**, on the street of the same name, is unremarkable in itself, but in a little chamber to the side, surrounded by souvenir stands, they'll show you El Greco's *El Entierro del Conde de Orgaz* (The Burial of the Count of Orgaz). The tourists come here in greater numbers than to any sight in Toledo, and more nonsense has been written about this work, perhaps, than any other Spanish painting. A miracle was recorded at this obscure count's burial in 1323. SS. Stephen and Augustine themselves came down from heaven to assist with the obsequies, and this is the scene El Greco portrays. A group of the Count's friends and descendants had petitioned Rome for his beatification, and it is perhaps in support of this that El Greco received the commission, over 200 years later. The portrayal of the burial has for a background a row of gravely serious men, each one a notable portrait in itself (the artist is said to have included himself, sixth from the right, and his son, the small boy in the foreground, and some commentators have claimed to find even Lope de Vega and Cervantes among the group of mourners). Above, the earthly scene is paralleled by the Count's reception into heaven.

This painting is perhaps the ultimate expression of the intense, and a little twisted, spirituality of 16th-century Castile. Its heaven, packed with grim, staring faces, seems more of an inferno. Nowhere in the work is there any sense of joy or release, or even wonder at the miraculous apparition of the saints. It is an exaltation of the mysteries of power and death, and the longer you look at it, the more disturbing it becomes.

The **Casa-Museo de El Greco**, not far away at C/ Samuel Leví 3 (*open Tues–Sat 10–2 and 4–6; Sun 10–2; closed Mon*), is where the painter lodged for most of the years he lived in Toledo. Domenico Theotocópoulos, a Cretan who had studied art in Venice, came to Spain hoping to find work at the building of El Escorial. Felipe II didn't care much for him, but 'the Greek' found Spanish life and Spanish religion amenable, and spent the remainder of his life in Toledo. The city itself, as seen from across the Tajo, was one of his favourite subjects (though his most famous *View of Toledo* is now in the Metropolitan Museum of Art, New York). The best parts of the restored house are the courtyard and tiled kitchen; only a few of El Greco's paintings here are of special merit—notably a portrait of *St Peter*, another favourite subject.

The **Taller del Moro** (Moor's Workshop), just around the corner from Santo Tomé church on C/ Taller del Moro (*open Tues–Sat 10–2 and 4–6.30; Sun 10–2; closed Mon*), gets its name from the days it spent as a shop for the cathedral workmen. The building itself is an interesting work of *mudéjar* architecture; inside is a collection of the sort of things the craftsmen made. Next door is the 15th-century **Palacio de Fuensalida**, which has been restored and is now the private residence of the President of Toledo. (Visits are possible in small private groups; contact the custodian at the palace.)

The Synagogues

Not surprisingly, in a city where Jews played such a prominent and constructive role for so long, two of Toledo's best buildings are synagogues, saved only by good luck after centuries of neglect. **La Sinagoga de Santa María la Blanca** (*c.* 1180), Pza. de Barrionuevo (*open Sat–Thurs 10–2 and 3.30–6; Fri 10–2 and 3.30–7*), so called from its days as a church, is stunning and small, a glistening white confection of horseshoe arches, elaborately carved capitals and geometric medallions that is rightly considered one of the masterpieces of *mudéjar* architecture. Just as good, though in an entirely different style, is the **Sinagoga del Tránsito**, Pso. del Tránsito (*open Tues–Sat 10–1.45 and 4–5.45; Sun, 10–1.45; closed Mon*), built by Samuel Leví, treasurer to King Pedro I (the Cruel) before that whimsical monarch had him executed. The synagogue is much later than Santa María la Blanca, and shows the influence of the Granada Moors—the interior could be a room in the Alhambra, with its ornate ceiling and carved arabesques, except that the calligraphic inscriptions are in Hebrew instead of Arabic, and the Star of David is interspersed with the arms of Castile and León. The building now houses the **Museo Sefardí** (Sephardic Museum), assembled out of a few surviving relics around the city. Elements of Jewish life and culture such as wedding costumes, a *torah*, and a *shofar* are displayed with explanatory notes, to reacquaint Spaniards with a part of their heritage they have quite forgotten.

Monasterio de San Juan de los Reyes

> *Pza. de San Juan de los Reyes; open daily, in summer 10–1.45 and 3.30–7; in winter, 10–1.45 and 3.30–6.*

Before the conquest of Granada, Fernando and Isabel built a church here with the intention of making it their last resting-place. The architect was Juan Guas, working the perpendicular elegance of Isabelline Gothic to perfection in every detail. Los Reyes Católicos wanted no doubt as to whose monument this was; their F and Y monogram, coats-of-arms, and yoke-and-arrows symbols are everywhere, even on the stained glass. There's little of the elaborate furnishings of

Toledo's cathedral here, but one of the side chapels contains one of the most grotesque, emaciated carved Jesuses in Spain. The exterior of the church is famous, with its western wall covered with the chains of prisoners released from the Moors during the Granada campaigns. The **Cloister**, surrounding a peaceful courtyard where a lone orange tree keeps meditative company with a lone pine, is another of Toledo's architectural treasures, with elegant windows and vaultings on the lower level. The same merry band of 1880s restorers who did Valladolid's San Gregorio were let loose here, and if you go up to the second floor and gaze up from the arches you will see the hilarious collection of **gargoyles** they added—all manner of monsters, a farting monk and a frog riding a fish; see if you can find the cat.

South of the City

The **Plaza de San Juan de los Reyes Católicos**, in the front of the church, has a wide prospect over the valley of the Tajo; from here you can see another of Toledo's fancy 16th-century gateways, the **Puerta del Cambrón**, and the fortified, medieval **Puente de San Martín**. If you would like to take the measure of this famous town from a little distance, on the other side of the Tajo there's a peripheral road called the **Carretera Circunvalación** that will give you more views of Toledo than El Greco ever did. On its way it passes a goodly number of country houses called *cigarrales*, the *parador*, and finally, the 14th-century **Castillo de San Servando**, rebuilt from an older Templar foundation. Beneath the castle, the old **Puente de Alcántara**, even better than the Puente de San Martín, will take you back across the Tajo in the neighbourhood of the Plaza de Zocodover.

Toledo's Countryside

It isn't pretty, and most of the attractions are castles—over 20 of them within a 48km radius of the city. **Guadamur** and **Barcience**, both west of Toledo, are two of the most interesting. Among the towns and villages, **Talavera de la Reina** is a famous pottery centre, and **Illescas** has five El Grecos on display in its **Hospital de la Caridad**. **Orgaz** and **Tembleque**, on the threshold of La Mancha, are suitably ancient and evocative; each has an interesting Plaza Mayor. At Melque, on a back road southwest of Toledo, is one of the oldest churches in Spain, the 9th-century **Santa María de Melque**.

Toledo ✉ *45000* **Where to Stay**

Even though most visitors don't stay overnight (it's their loss!), you may need a reservation in July and August.

expensive

At the top of the list, there's the showcase ★★★★**Parador Conde de Orgaz**, Cerro del Emperador, © 925 22 18 50, @ 925 22 51 66, south of the city. It's inconvenient for visiting the sights, but the El Greco-esque view of the city from the terrace is superb, and there is a very good restaurant. Nearby and also overlooking the city is the ★★★★**Hotel Doménico**, Cerro del Emperador, ©925 25 00 40, @ 925 25 28 77, artistically decorated and surrounded by olive groves. A less expensive option is the ★★★**Hostal del Cardenal**, Pso. Recaredo 24, © 925 22 49 00, @ 925 22 29 91, just outside the city walls, with a terraced garden and a good atmosphere, but it's a bit of a hike up to the sights.

You can enjoy another good view from the town (though not in every room) at the elegant and correct ★★★**Carlos V**, C/ Trastamara 1, Pza. Horna Magdalena, ✆ 925 22 21 00, 📠 925 22 21 05, tucked away on a quiet street near the Alcázar and Plaza de Zocodover.

Otherwise, in the middle range, you have a choice between the modern and pleasant ★**Imperio**, C/ Cadenas 7, ✆ 925 22 76 50, and the agreeable if a little cramped ★**Hs Las Armas**, C/ Armas 7, ✆ 925 22 16 68, both central. A better value option at the bottom of this category is the new and friendly ★★**Pensión Santa Úrsula**, C/ Santa Úrsula, just downhill from the Plaza de El Salvador.

inexpensive

Among Toledo's cheapest are the ★★**Hs Labrador**, C/ Labrador 16, ✆ 925 22 26 20 (not the brightest of places but with 40 rooms there's usually a vacancy) and a few other *hostales* scattered about town, like the ★**Hs Santa Bárbara**, Avda. Santa Bárbara 8, ✆ 925 22 02 98, and the **Pensión Lumbreras**, C/ Juan Labrador 9, ✆ 925 22 15 71, which has good views over the city from the top floor rooms.

Eating Out

Dining in Toledo is largely a matter of avoiding overpriced tourist troughs. You'll get your money's worth (*over 3000 pts*, though) at the fine restaurant of the **Hostal del Cardenal** (*moderate—see above*). As elsewhere in Toledo, stuffed partridge is a speciality, well-hung and gamey the way the Spaniards like it. **Venta de Aires**, C/ Circo Romano 25, ✆ 925 22 05 45 (*moderate*) also serves traditional Toledano fare. You can eat kosher at the **Sinai**, on C/ Reyes Católicos in the Judería (*moderate*), with a menu of Jewish and Moroccan specialities.

La Lumbre, C/ Real del Arrabal 3, ✆ 925 22 03 73 (*expensive*) mixes local cooking with French-inspired dishes; this is one place where vegetarians generally have plenty to choose from, such as onion tart, leek pie, and mushroom-stuffed artichokes. The **Asador Adolfo**, C/ Granada 6, ✆ 925 22 73 21 (*expensive*) is considered to be Toledo's best restaurant and is the place to go for truly flamboyant dining; equally good is **El Ábside**, C/ Marqués de Mendigorrín 1, ✆ 925 21 32 02 (*expensive*), located in a 15th-century mansion, where the house specialities include fresh leeks with prawns.

Inexpensive restaurants are not as hard to find as you might think; there's a small colony of them along the C/ Barrio Rey, just off the Plaza de Zocodover, including **Maravilla**, Pza. de Barrio Rey 5, ✆ 925 222 33 00 (*cheap*), a reliable choice for good, basic cooking. **Hierbabuena**, Cristo Luz 9, ✆ 925 222 39 24 (*moderate*) offers light, imaginative cooking with a hint of vegetarian. **La Abadía**, on the corner of Nuñez de Arce and San Nicolás (*cheap*) can get a bit hectic, but that's part of the appeal.

One of the prettiest places in which to enjoy a drink is the tiny square off C/ Santo Tomé; here the **Cafetería Nano** sets tables out under the trees. Lastly, you should try Toledo's old speciality *mazapán*, made from almond paste and sugar.

Castilla la Nueva: Extremadura and La Mancha

First-year students of Spanish often think Extremadura means 'extremely hard', a translation that seems all the more true once they find out that this was the native land of those hard men—Pizarro, Cortés, Balboa and hundreds of others like them—who sailed to 'conquer' the New World for Spain at the expense of the Aztecs and Incas. Actually Extremadura means 'beyond the Douro River'—the territory conquered by the kings of León and held for centuries as a buffer zone between Christians and Moors.

And hard as it may seem to its natives, who have left vast tracts of countryside empty for the bright lights of the city and jobs in Germany, Extremadura is not without a sweeping kind of beauty, one of endless rolling fields of wheat, dappled by the shadows of the evergreen holm oak, cork trees and olives. Blue mountains sunder the horizon; sleek black bulls share their pastures with storks, whose shaggy nests give a hairy toupé to church towers and castle turrets in the region. Villages consist of low, whitewashed rows of houses, snaking over the contours of the hills, or towns filled with palaces embellished with the huge coats of arms of the *nouveau-riches conquistadores*.

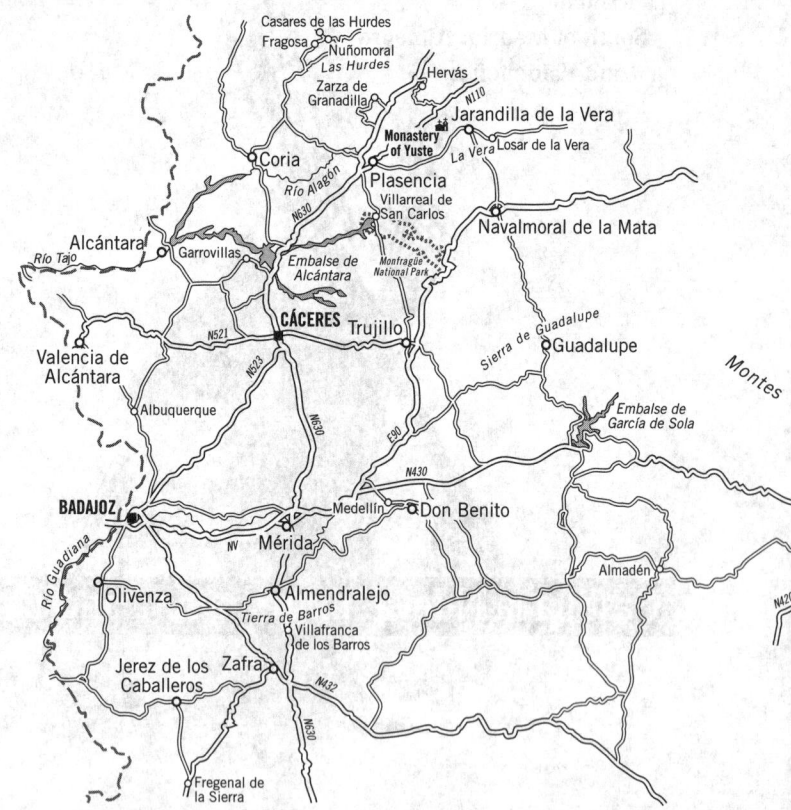

The jewels of Extremadura are its cities Cáceres, Trujillo and Zafra, the extensive Roman ruins at Mérida, the famous shrine of Guadalupe and the Monastery of Yuste, where the jaded Charles V retired from the Empire he bullied so hard to create. And lovers of scenic, out-of-the-way places can hardly do better than Las Hurdes, and the mountains and valleys to the north.

Upper Extremadura

Getting Around

By train: Cáceres is the transport hub here, with rail links to Mérida, Badajoz, Lisbon, Madrid, Sevilla, Zafra—but not to Salamanca, though many maps still show the connection. Plasencia has three daily connections to Madrid and Badajoz, one daily with Mérida and Cáceres. Palazuelo is the nearest station to Monfragüe National Park—20km from its entrance at Puerta Serrana. The RENFE station in Cáceres, © 927 23 37 61, at Ctra. Nacional 630, is 3km from the Plaza Gral. Mola; a city bus connects the two every 20 minutes or so.

By bus: There are several connections daily between Salamanca, Plasencia and Cáceres by bus, and three daily to Trujillo (the bus station is just off the main Madrid–Cáceres road on C/ Badajoz); one daily from Cáceres and two from Trujillo to Guadalupe. There are also several express connections between Cáceres and Madrid (4hrs), and two RENFE buses that pass through the city daily on the way between Badajoz and Irún. Cáceres' bus station is opposite the train station on the road to Sevilla, N630, about 1.5km from Pza. Gral. Mola. A free bus connects you with the city every half hour or so (© 927 24 59 50).

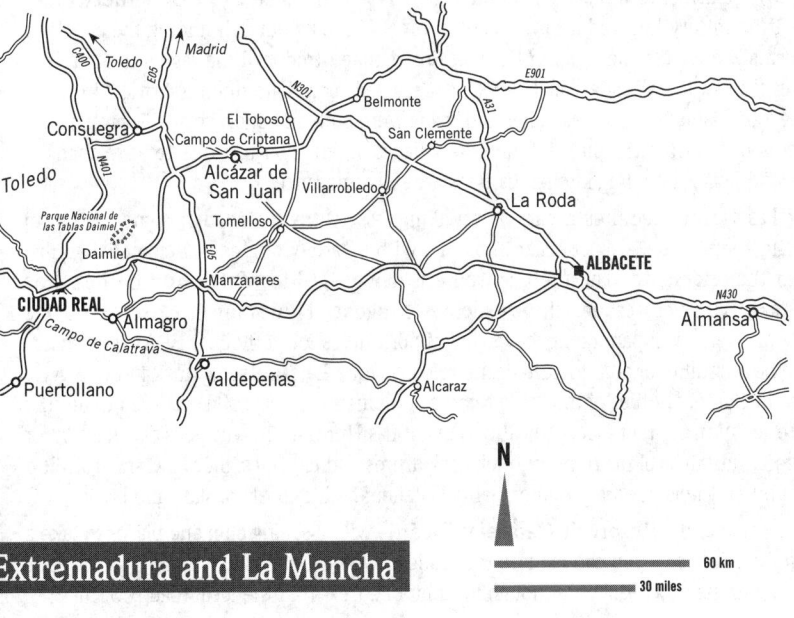

Extremadura and La Mancha

Las Hurdes: If you're driving, C512 and C515 are the main roads through the region; if you're taking the bus from Plasencia (the bus station is near the river, not far from the Puente Nuevo), be prepared for some hiking; the few buses up that way tend to go no further than Pinofranquedo or Caminomorisco, the two largest villages in the Lower Hurdes. Three buses a day go from Plasencia to Hervas, Yuste and La Vera, as well as services to the village of Coria. Alcántara and Garrovillas are most easily reached from Cáceres.

Tourist Information

Cáceres: Pza. Mayor 37, ✆ 927 24 63 47.
Plasencia: Plaza de la Catedral s/n 17, ✆ 927 42 27 66.
Trujillo: Pza. Mayor, near the steps, ✆ 927 32 26 77.
Guadalupe: Pza. Mayor, ✆ 927 15 41 28.
Mérida: Paseo José Alvarez de Buruaga s/n, ✆ 927 31 53 33.

In the summer there is also an information booth in **Pinofranqueado**.

Las Hurdes

The northernmost zone of Extremadura is scenically the best and one of the least-known corners of rural Spain. The sierra of the southern Salamanca province (*see* p.386) extends south into a wild untamed region split by three valleys called **Las Hurdes**. For the Spanish the name is a dark shadow, a legendary place ruled by demons, where the inhabitants of the 40 tiny hamlets were brute savages, running about naked, devoid of religion, eating raw chestnuts, and practising everything from polygamy to cannibalism. A popular tale has a pair of noble lovers, somehow encountering the disapproval of the Duke of Alba, fleeing to Las Hurdes, only to be discovered a short time later in a state of dire bestiality. The demons were exorcized by a Carmelite monastery founded in 1599 in the valley of **Las Batuecas** (*see* p.386), but the misery lingered into this century; in 1932 Luis Buñuel, finding the appalling poverty surreal, shot a film here, *Land Without Bread*, that introduced the region to the rest of Spain. Over the last few decades Las Hurdes has received special attention to bring it into line with the rest of Spain: new schools, dams and roads were built and efforts made to prop up the local economy. Yet, from the outside, the little villages of whitewash and slate have changed little, and wild boars trampling kitchen gardens are still a nuisance.

Exploring Las Hurdes requires a car, or a willingness to tramp through some delightful scenery. The countryside is spectacular in places, with a variety of greens welcome if you've come from the arid south. The prettiest route is along the **Río Malvellido** in the **Altas Hurdes**, taking in picturesque villages such as **Fragosa, Nuñomoral, Casares de las Hurdes**, with wonderful panoramic views and opportunities for potholing. **El Asegur** stands out for the best traditional architecture of the region, while **La Huetre** is stuck in the biggest time warp. El Gasco, another of the more remote settlements, has a 160ft waterfall under the **Chorro de la Miancera**, one of the beauty spots of Las Hurdes. The village is also known for its handicrafts and musical instruments, including drums and bagpipes. Stop in **Cambroncino** to see the church the locals are proud of, Santa Catalina, built entirely of slate and brick.

On the other side of the **Reservoir Gabriel y Galán**—with a sailing club and places to take a cool dip in the summer—you can explore the castle-crowned **Granadilla**, Spain's most genial ghost town, with nearby beaches, although it's a bit of a trek from the local road (C513).

Going north, this road joins the N630 near **Hervás** in a pretty region of cherry orchards; the village has one of the best preserved *aljamas* (Jewish quarters) in Spain, complete with a ruined synagogue and crooked half-timbered houses. Not surprisingly, the community owed much of its prosperity to the protection of the Templars, who aided in the conquest of Extremadura and were rewarded with large tracts of land. Worth a quick visit are the churches of Santa María de Aguas Vivas and San Juan Bautista. In the immediate countryside rambling paths lead up the mountain slopes, swathed with oaks and dotted with streams. The countryside around Hervás is a hunting area, principally for deer, wild boar and rabbit.

Plasencia and Yuste

When Alfonso VIII of León founded this settlement, he declared '*placeat Deo et hominibus*' ('may it be pleasing to God and men'), from whence came its name Plasencia, which Alfonso hoped would attract much-needed settlers to the frontier. It does have a fine location, in a bend of the Río Jerte, and its walls, no longer needed, have been entirely integrated into the houses. The odd silhouettes of two **Cathedrals** dominate Plasencia, twice begun and twice unfinished. The pointy Gothic bulk of the 'new' one is more interesting inside, boasting a fine *reja* (1604) and more choir stalls by the ever-inventive and ever-profane Rodrigo Alemán. The older of the two cathedrals, begun in the 13th century, has a peculiar Salamanca-Zamora-style dome over its Sala Capitular. The nearby **Museo Etnográfico** on C/ Trujillo (*open Wed–Sat 11–2 and 5–8, Sun 11–2*) has a collection of local costumes, crafts and farming tools . In the **Plaza Mayor**, a couple of blocks away, a funny man in green strikes the hours atop the **Ayuntamiento**; if you can get in, take a look at the *artesonado* ceiling in the main hall. Spanish tourists, on the other hand, come from far and wide to visit the **Museo de Caza** (Hunting Museum) in the 16th-century Palacio del Marqués de Mirabel on Plaza San Nicolás, with a large collection of weaponry and associated paraphernalia (*open all day in summer*).

Yuste

Plasencia is the easiest base for visiting the **Monastery of Yuste** (*open Mon–Sat 9.30–12.30 and 3.30–6.30, Sun 9.30–11.30 and 3.30–6.30 in summer; 9.30–12.30 and 3–6 in winter; adm, free Thurs am*). The bus goes as far as the picturesque old village of **Cuacos**; from there it's a 2km walk uphill to the monastery. After ruling a hefty percentage of the Western world for 40 years, Charles V chose this isolated corner of Extremadura for his final retirement, accompanied by his cat and parrot, his friend the engineer and clockmaker Torriano de Cremona and 100 servants. Whatever excesses and seeds of disaster were sown by the old egomaniac during his reign, his retirement captured the popular imagination; here the world-weary emperor, discomfited by gout (you can still see his gout chair, and the ramp especially constructed to give him easy access to his apartments), could fish, feed the ducks and look out over the Gredos mountains. Although Yuste was ruined after the depredations of the Peninsular War and suppression of the monasteries, Charles' apartments have been maintained as they were when he died in 1558, still draped in black (but minus his cartloads of Titians and Flemish tapestries); from his deathbed he could hear Mass in the church below.

Cuacos and the pretty villages to the east in the **Valle de la Vera** are tobacco towns, and you can often see the local product hanging from the medieval arcades and carved wooden balconies. In **Jarandilla de la Vera**, the castle where Charles lived while waiting for his quarters at Yuste to be completed, is now a *parador*. Other pretty villages in the valley are **Villanueva de la Vera**, with a fine plaza, and **Losar de la Vera**, with many dilapidated 16th-century houses. The best time to visit the Valle de la Vera is in April, when the whole area is alive with cherry blossom. Failing that, try and catch the Pero-Palo fiesta in Villanueva de la Vera on Shrove Tuesday. It may not match Rio for size, but the essence of carnival is definitely here. Nearby is **Valverde de la Vera**, with architecture even more splendid than Villanueva. The night before Good Friday sees a silent, sinister procession of *empalaos*—literally 'beaten' penitents, each tied to a plough.

We'll Be Glad When You're Dead, You Rascal You

 One of the unpleasant side-effects of the new humanistic learning of the Renaissance was the flood of self-indulgence and vanity it loosed on an unsuspecting Europe. If Man was the measure of all things, then plenty of spoiled princes were willing to follow their egos and make royal jackasses of themselves—think of Henry VIII. It's a shame that no director has ever explored the cinematic potential of Henry's contemporary, Charles V. He would have a plot loaded with violence and intrigue, the Renaissance for a backdrop, and a villain nobody in the theatre would ever forget. To his apologists and propagandists, Charles of Habsburg represented the dream of a universal Catholic monarchy, the heir of the Romans and Charlemagne; many of his subjects preferred to see him more as the Antichrist. Charles always tried to act more like the latter, in his decades of endless marching about Europe, disturbing the peace and bullying everybody about. Charles' latter-day appetite for food, it seems, was as great as it had once been for provinces and money, and there are hints that the real reason for his surprise abdication in 1556 was to spend more time caring for his digestion, in order to stuff himself as much as possible without aggravating his gout too much. The only thing that kept him going so long at Yuste, according to one observer, was a faithful steward who would 'interpose himself between his master and an eel pie, as in other days he would have thrown himself between the Imperial Person and the point of a Moorish lance'. Besides eating, Charles' other retirement hobbies were piety and death. The monks were paid to keep up a perpetual nattering in the church adjacent to his bedroom, so that the Emperor could stare at Titian's *La Gloria* (now in the Prado) and doze off in daydreams of sanctity; the poor brothers also had to assist in the constant rehearsals of his funeral that Charles loved to stage. At one of these, in 1558, he caught a chill and died.

Coria and the Bridge of Alcántara

Located just north of the Río Alagón, a tributary of the Tajo, **Coria** can claim a **Roman bridge** (although water no longer flows beneath it), a lovely **castle** with a pentagonal tower, and a **Gothic cathedral** with a refined interior; the treasure here is allegedly nothing less than the tablecloth used at the Last Supper. At **Alcántara**, where the Alagón joins the Tajo, a dam was built creating the vast **Embalse de Alcántara**, one of several irrigation schemes of the Badajoz Plan, designed to bring the dry but fertile lands of Extremadura under cultivation. Alcántara in Arabic means 'the **bridge**', a name given by the Moors for the remarkable example that now spans the dry gorge below the dam. Built under Trajan in the year 105, the bridge has six lofty arches, the highest ever built by the Romans, and still makes a brave sight complete with a triumphal arch in the middle. Alcántara was the headquarters of the Order of Alcántara, founded to defend the frontier in the 12th century; Grand Masters' tombs may be seen in the 13th-century church, and ruins of the knights' castle remain above the town. But the prettiest church in town belongs to the 16th-century **Convento de San Benito**, with a fine, recently restored Plateresque façade.

East along the reservoir lies **Garrovillas**, site of a Templar convent. Its **Plaza Mayor** is an undulating, whitewashed work of art; its 15th-century church of **San Pedro** has a curious façade. Near Cañaveral, turn off for Torrejoncillo; 4km further on are signs to the **Convento del Palancar**, the smallest monastery in the world. Still used by Franciscan monks, and open for visits, the cloister is so small you can touch the facing walls with outstretched arms.

Further east, **Monfragüe National Park** was created in 1979 to protect the unusual flora and fauna of this remote region—Iberian lynxes, boars, foxes, badgers, black storks, imperial eagles and several kinds of vulture. Although most of the park is inaccessible, many of the animals can be seen around **Villareal de San Carlos**, a village in the centre of Monfragüe, founded by Carlos III to police the notorious bandits who haunted the region. A booth in Villareal has information on trails, the best bird-watching spots and camping. The name of the park is derived from the crusading knights of the Order of Montfrag, who had their headquarters in the once mighty and now mighty ruined **Castello de Monfragüe**, located at the south end of the park by the scenic **Sierra de Peñafalcón**; a statue of the Virgin brought from Palestine by the Knights is still the subject of local devotion.

Cáceres

The provincial capital, Cáceres, is the most atmospheric of Extremaduran cities. Three sides of its large, central **Plaza Mayor** face the attractive, lively, whitewashed new town, home of the region's university; the fourth side adjoins the nearly perfectly preserved **Roman-Moorish walls and towers** that enclose a beautiful 16th-century city inhabited mainly by storks, swallows and bats. Much of it was built with gold from the Americas, and seemingly little has happened to it since the *conquistadores* returned to flaunt their wealth before their fellow citizens. If you come out of season, or in the dead of night, its cobbled streets seem as enchanted and timeless as Sleeping Beauty's castle. The **Torre Bujaco**, dominating the Plaza Mayor, is almost entirely Roman, and it's a startling experience to be in Cáceres during a fiesta, when the fireworks (and frightened storks) come careening off its roof just over the heads of the crowd below. The gate next to it, the **Arco de Estrella**, is an 18th-century addition by one of the prolific Churrigueras. Immediately to the right looms the huge, decrepit **Casa de Toledo-Montezuma**, home of the descendants of Cortés' follower Juan Cano and his wife, the daughter of Montezuma. All of the narrow streets near here converge in the elegant **Plaza de Santa María**, with a fine Gothic church of the same name containing a beautiful 16th-century *reredos*. Among the many lovely palaces in the old town, the **Casa de los Golfines de Abajo**, just around the corner from Santa María at Cuesta de la Compañia, has the best façade, dating back even before the *conquistadores* to the 15th century. It was here that Franco declared himself Generalísimo in 1936. The lane in front of the palace descends through the last Roman gate that remains substantially intact, the **Arco Cristo**.

Cáceres' other major architectural ensemble, **Plaza de San Mateo**, was the Moorish centre of town. Tall, Gothic **San Mateo** stands on the site of the old mosque; the **Casa de las Veletas**, decorated with peculiar bright-coloured gargoyles, incorporates part of the Moorish Alcázar and its pretty cistern, or *algibe*, shaded by horseshoe arches. The building now contains the historical and ethnographic artefacts of the **Museo de Cáceres**. On the same plaza, the 1477 **Casa de las Cigüeñas** ('storks' house') is pointed out as the only one in town to retain the battlements on its tower; originally there were some 30 similar towers in Cáceres, but the nobles were so prone to fighting that Isabel la Católica ordered them cut down to size. The tower still serves as a barracks and you can't enter. Nor can you get into the Gothic **Convento de San Pablo**, which also shares the square, though in the doorway beneath the Arabic inscription you may purchase the best biscuits in town from the nuns, who use a turntable under a wooden hatch to preserve their privacy. The WOMAD international music festival is held in Cáceres every May.

Trujillo

An hour east, Cáceres' quieter twin-sister, Trujillo, is nicknamed the 'Cradle of the Conquistadores'—the birthplace of the remorseless Francisco Pizarro (1476–1541), who, suckled by a sow, began his career here as a swineherd before he almost singlehandedly destroyed the Inca civilization, as well as of Francisco Orellana, first European explorer of the Amazon. In the same epoch the town produced another extreme character in Diego García de Paredes (1466–1530), 'the Samson of Extremadura', a giant of a man who was the companion-in-arms of the Gran Capitán Gonzalo de Córdoba, known for holding off entire armies by himself with a 1.8m sword.

Trujillo has an especially fine **Plaza Mayor**, dominated by an equestrian **statue of Francisco Pizarro**, man and horse wearing *conquistador* helmets; if it looks familiar, you've seen its double in Lima, Peru. Diagonally opposite across the plaza stands the grandiose **Palacio de la Conquista**, built by Hernando Pizarro. Of the five Pizarros who led the expedition to Peru, Hernando was the only legitimate son and also the cleverest; while his brothers' bloody intrigues caused their untimely deaths, Hernando stayed out of the way, married his brother Francisco's half-Inca daughter Francisca and settled here, where his descendants received the honorary title of Marqués de la Conquista. Behind this palace, the **Palacio Orellana-Pizarro**, now a school (*open 9.30–2 and 4–6.30*), contains an elegant Renaissance courtyard and doorway. From here, enter the old walled town through the **Puerta de San Andrés**, and take the Calle de las Palomas up to **Santa María** (*open 10.30–2 and 4.30–7*), a fine Gothic church housing a *retablo* by the Flemish-inspired Fernando Gallego, and the tombs of numerous Pizarros and Diego García de Paredes. Further up, the restored Roman-Moorish-Castilian **castle** nowadays defends only vegetable gardens; from its commanding height there are views over Trujillo and its environs. The landscape is so bleak and comfortless that you can understand how the Pizarros could leave it all behind and sail into the unknown in search of the main chance, even if history will always condemn their cruelty and avarice, shocking even by the standards of the Age of Rapacity.

Guadalupe

One thing the *conquistadores* took to, rather than from, the New World was the cult of their Extremaduran goddess, the Virgin of Guadalupe. The little dark image, said to have been carved by St Luke, was discovered by a shepherd in the 13th century in the pretty verdant oasis of the Sierra de Guadalupe, but the statue had to wait until 1340 for a proper shrine in a Hieronymite monastery founded expressly to house her. Soon Guadalupe became a pilgrimage destination, so popular that a big city in Mexico and a Caribbean island were named after her. Deserted in the 19th century, the monastery (now Franciscan) has been reopened; its fortress-like bulk, its pinnacles, towers and domes dominate the tiny, medieval town that over the centuries has grown up around the central plaza. The setting is as superb as it is difficult to attain—Guadalupe is one of the most out of the way destinations in Spain.

The most intriguing thing in the **Monastery** (*open daily 9.30–1 and 3.30–7; adm*) is the *mudéjar* **Cloister**, its two storeys of horseshoe arches enclosing Extremadura's most singular and provocative piece of architecture, the 1405 **Templete**, a *mudéjar* pavilion topped by an octagonal spire consisting of three tiers of blind, gabled arches, built over a Moorish fountain. The **Sacristía** is also unique: its eight Zurbaráns still hang in places designed for them in the 17th century. Few paintings are as fortunate as these, to be seen as they were meant to be seen, in a sumptuous décor far removed from the sterile white walls of the museums. There's also a **museum** crammed full of more treasures: illuminated manuscripts and embroidered vestments, reliquaries and paintings.

The **Church** (*open 8.30–8.30 summer, 9–6 winter*) has attractive lacy stonework over its bronze doors, all dating from the 15th century. In the gloom you can just make out the glittering statue of the Virgin of Guadalupe high above the altar; for the climactic, close-up view you must take the stairs up to the **Camarín**, where the Virgin slowly turns on her enamelled gyrating throne to receive the homage of the faithful and the scrutiny of the merely curious. She is certainly old and wise, her mysterious, dark, Byzantine face peering out from her rich and gaudy jewelled attire. The enamels in the Camarín depict the glory of the Virgin before Santa Teresa and San Juan de Díos. After the Civil War two scenes were added here: one depicting a Guardia Civil killed on the monastery ramparts during 'the siege' and in the next panel, the triumphant entry of the Nationalists into Guadalupe, welcomed by a friar raising his arm in a fascist salute. The scenes may have been a backhanded slap at Mexico, whose patron saint is the Virgin of Guadalupe. It was also the one country in Latin America never to recognize the Franco government.

Where to Stay and Eating Out

For the most comfort at the best prices, stay at one of the many *paradores* in the area.

Las Hurdes

Up in Las Hurdes, Pinofranqueado has two *pensiones*; **★El Puente**, Pso. de Extremadura 38, ✆ 927 10 40 28 (*inexpensive*), with rooms at *4000 pts,* is the better of the two. Nuñomoral's *hostal*, **★El Hurdano**, La Fuente, ✆ 927 43 30 12 (*cheap*) has basic bathless rooms for *2500 pts* and a good restaurant serving generous portions for around *2000 pts* for a meal. Near Caminomorisco, the **★Riomalo** is in Riomalo de Abajo on C/ Larga, ✆ 927 43 30 20 (*cheap*), and has ten simple rooms at *3500 pts*. The **★Montesol** in Casares de Las Hurdes, Lindón 7, ✆ 927 43 30 25, has cheap rooms at *3500 pts*. The cheapest option in Jarandilla is the **★Marbella**, Calvo Sotelo 103, ✆ 927 56 02 18, with doubles at *4500 pts.*

Plasencia ✉ 22810

A friendly and central choice is the ★**Rincón Extremeño**, Vidrieras 6, ✆ 927 41 11 50 (*moderate*), for around *5000 pts*.

Yuste

Visitors heading to Yuste can rent rooms in the castle Charles V stayed in while waiting for his apartments at the monastery, at Jarandilla de la Vera's ★★★★**Parador**, Avda. García Prieto 1, ✆ 927 56 01 17, ✆ 927 56 00 88 (*expensive*), in a lovely location and complete with turrets and a drawbridge. The beamed restaurant serves *cuchifrito*, a delicious kid stew.

Losar de Vera ✉ 04620

The ★★**Hostería Fontivieja**, C/Mártires 8 (*inexpensive*) is an ideal base for walking or cycling trips throughout Valle de la Vera. For eating, the **Antigua Casa del Heno**, Finca Valdepimienta, ✆ 908 70 61 19 (*inexpensive*) offers homecooking in an atmosphere and with views that make a memorable meal. Worth checking out for the name alone in Jarandilla de la Vera, is the bar restaurant, **Puta Parió**, which means 'the whore spawned', in Calle Vicaría. The food is cheap, plentiful and hearty.

Coria ✉ 10800

★**Los Kekes**, Avda. Sierra de Gata 49, ✆ 927 50 09 00, is cheap at *5000 pts*, and fine for an overnight stop.

Cáceres ✉ 10000

The ★★★★**Parador de Cáceres** in the old town, C/ Ancha 6, ✆ 927 21 17 59, ✆ 927 21 17 29 (*expensive*) is in the Renaissance palace of El Comendador, with an excellent restaurant featuring *extremeño* dishes for *4000 pts*. ★★★★**Hotel Meliá** occupies a magnificent *palacio* in the lovely, quiet Pza. San Juan, ✆ 927 21 58 00, ✆ 927 21 40 70; discreet and tasteful luxury at *20,000 pts*. ★★**Goya**, Pza. Gral. Mola 33, ✆ 927 24 99 50 (*moderate*) has good value, modern rooms with bath and TV for about *6000 pts*. Probably the cheapest deal in Cáceres is family-run **Pensión Soraya**, Pza. Mayor 25, ✆ 927 24 43 10, at the top of plant-lined stairs and packing in more character than most; *3000 pts* rooms are basic and without bath, but decent and comfortable. Another cheap option is the ★**Castilla**, C/ Ríos Verdes 3, ✆ 927 24 44 04 (*inexpensive*), with bathless rooms for *3500 pts*.

The best restaurant, serving mostly game dishes in season (*perdiz en escabeche*), is the elegant **Atrio**, Avda. de España 30, ✆ 927 24 29 28; try also the *lenguado al vino* (*4500 pts*). Another very good restaurant with regional food is **El Figón de Eustaquio**, Pza. San Juan 12–14, ✆ 927 24 81 94; try the *jamón ibérico*, Extremadura's justly famous ham, reputedly made of swine fed on rattlesnakes (*3000–4000 pts*). Cheaper choices are clustered about the Pza. Mayor: try **El Gran Mesón**, Gral. Ezponda 7, ✆ 927 24 77 26, with an *1500 pts* set menu and good artichokes, *closed Tues*, or **El Pato Blanco** in the plaza itself, ✆ 927 24 87 36, where you can dine outside on fried trout or partridge (*3000 pts*). The restaurant **Álvarez**, 3km out of Cáceres on the road to Salamanca, ✆ 927 23 06 50, is a quiet and well run place serving interesting regional dishes; there is a terrace where you can dine when the nights are warm (*3500–5000 pts*). **El Puchero**, on the main plaza, has a good set menu for *850 pts*. There's a lively bar scene at the **Beriberi Blues Bar**, C/ Donoso Cortés, where pictures of blues legends cover the bar counter and dot the walls. Good music and a laid-back atmosphere make it popular with the town's students.

Trujillo ✉ 10200

The 16th-century convent of Santa Clara in Trujillo is now the **★★★★Parador de Trujillo**, C/ Santa Beatriz de Silva 1, ✆ 927 32 13 50, ✆ 927 32 13 66 (*expensive*), with attractive, air-conditioned rooms, a calm air and a pretty garden; the restaurant serves local specialities such as *cochinillo montanera* (roast sucking pig) for *5000 pts*. **★Hostal Nuria**, Pza. Mayor 27, ✆ 927 32 09 07, has very clean rooms with bath at *5000 pts* and its restaurant serves a decent *menú del día* for *1100 pts*. **★Hostal La Cadena**, Pza. Mayor 8, ✆ 927 32 14 63, is in an old *palacio*, boasting vast stone corridors and atmospheric rooms with bath at *5000 pts*. The beds, though, can be lumpy. Try **Pensión Emilia**, Gral. Mola 28, ✆ 927 32 00 83 (*inexpensive*), for basic rooms at around *4000 pts*, and for tasty home cooking in its restaurant (*3000 pts*).

Trujillo has a number of good places to eat. The restaurant **Pizarro**, on the main square, is a favourite with locals and visitors alike, serving delicious meals for around *3000 pts*; get there early to be sure of a table. If they're out of space, try the **Mesón La Troya** opposite. The portions defy description. For a drink in Trujillo, try **Cafetería Berlin**, C/ Tiendas 4, ✆ 927 32 26 93, just off the Pza. Mayor. It's popular with the town's young people and serves some good tapas, including soya sausages.

Guadalupe ✉ 10140

In Guadalupe, the **★★★★Parador de Guadalupe**, C/ Marqués de la Romana 10, ✆ 927 36 70 75, ✆ 927 36 70 76 (*expensive*), is located in a 16th-century palace with a lovely garden, pool and walls adorned with reproductions by *extremeño* artists; it's only a short walk to the church. The restaurant features excellent regional dishes for around *5000 pts*. **★★Hospedería del Real Monasterio**, Pza. Juan Carlos I, ✆ 927 36 70 00, ✆ 927 36 71 77 (*moderate*) is a much better bet, and is part of the monastery housing the Virgin of Guadalupe: excellent value for almost identical accommodation and setting. It has a good restaurant as well (*5000 pts*), where you can top off a meal with a glass of the home-brewed *licor de Guadalupe*.

Good meals—*perdiz escabechada, verduras guadalupanas*—can be had at the **Mesón El Cordero**, Alfonso Onceno 27, ✆ 927 36 71 31, for around *2500 pts*. *Closed Mon.* For a post-dinner coffee and cake, go to the **Atrium**, No.6 of the same street.

Lower Extremadura

Getting Around

By train: Extremadura's train timetable is subject to constant change, so it is always best to check with the tourist office first. At the time of writing, Badajoz and Mérida are linked to Madrid and Barcelona by two Talgos daily; Mérida has four trains daily to Cáceres and five to Badajoz; the Madrid trains to Badajoz (three a day) pass through

Mérida and Medellin. From Sevilla there's one train (at 9.58am) that connects Llerena and Zafra on its way to Mérida and Cáceres. From Huelva there's one train to Zafra, and two to Fregenal de la Sierra. For Portugal there are three trains from Mérida and Badajoz. In all of the above cities the train stations are within easy walking distance from the centre, except Badajoz, where the station is across the river, 1.5km from the centre, ℂ 924 23 71 70; ticket office at Avda. de Celada 3, ℂ 924 22 45 62. Badajoz also has a daily air service to Madrid, twice weekly to Barcelona.

By bus: On the whole you may find it more convenient to take the bus, as RENFE is doing its best to close the local trains of Extremadura (going so far as to put its most uncomfortable carriages on the route). Again Badajoz and Mérida are the hubs; there are three RENFE bus connections daily to Córdoba and Málaga; another route twice a day to Salamanca and points north. There is a new bus station in Mérida on the other side of the river near the Puente Romano (ℂ 924 30 04 04). In Badajoz buses leave from several locations, the main one being on Ctra. de Valverde, ℂ 924 25 86 61. Most of the destinations described in the text are served from the station south of town on Ctra. de Valverde. Buses between Badajoz and Sevilla (four a day) go by way of Jerez or Zafra.

Tourist Information

Mérida: Next to Teatro Romano, ℂ 924 31 53 53.
Badajoz: Pza. de la Libertade 3, ℂ 924 22 27 63.
Zafra: Pza. de España, ℂ 924 55 10 36.
Jerez de los Caballeros: information from the Ayuntamiento, ℂ 924 73 03 84.

Mérida

Many cities in Spain were founded by the Romans to settle their legions after the peninsula had been won. León and Zaragoza leap to mind, but in its day Mérida (founded in 23 BC as Augusta Emerita) outshone them all, growing to become the capital of the vast province of Lusitania, compared with some exaggeration to Athens. The Visigoths retained it as the capital of their western marches, but since the time of the Moors its monuments have been quarried (many of its stones going to build the Mezquita in Córdoba). Although modern Mérida is only half the size of Augusta Emerita, no place in Spain can offer more in the way of surviving monuments, scattered as they are all over the city.

Mérida has a rare and magnificent front entrance: a 60-arched, 1km-long **Roman bridge** over the Río Guadiana—the longest built in Spain and repaired by the Visigoths and Felipe III. The Guadiana is a wide, shallow river with numerous islands, and the bridge, with sleek cattle grazing beneath its arches, forms a delightful rustic scene. Just to the right of the bridge is the large **Alcazaba**, a confusing bulwark that has served every ruler from the Romans to the Templars and Knights of Santiago; what stands now was built mainly by the Moors, using stones from the Roman theatre. Within its walls (*open daily 9–1.45 and 5–7.15, Sun 9–2*) you can visit the conventual, or residence of the Knights of Santiago, a number of Roman houses with mosaics and, best of all, the *aljibe*, or cistern, its entrance adorned with lovely, carved Visigothic door-frames, from where twin corridors descend to a pool of cool water. The rest of the Alcazaba resembles a construction site.

Before tackling the rest of Roman Mérida, you can fortify yourself in one of the many cafés in nearby **Plaza de España**. The so-called **Temple of Diana** was probably a Nymphaeum before a local grandee in the 16th century used its tall Corinthian columns to frame his palace, much of which has since been cut away to reveal the Roman structure. Just off the Plaza de España, in Calle Santa Julia 1, in the Palacio de Burmay is a new **Museum of Visigothic Art** (*open Tues–Sat 10–2 and 4–6, Sun 10–2, closed Mon*) with Visigothic masonry and floral reliefs.

The Roman Museum and Theatre

Calle Romero Leal leads up to the **Museo Nacional de Arte Romano** (*open daily 9–1.45 and 5–7.15*), housed in an grand 1986 brick building by Rafael Mones Valles that looks as if the Romans themselves had a hand in it; it even incorporates a Roman road discovered when the foundation was dug. Roman artefacts from all over Spain are housed on its three large floors. Among the huge mosaics, there's a curiously primitive 4th-century AD banquet scene, a tall column from the Temple of Diana, busts, glass, statues and items from Augusta Emerita's religious shrines, most interestingly a statue from the Mithraeum, which portrays the god Chronos entwined in a snake. Guided tours leave from the lower ground floor into the basement crypt where you can see the Roman road and part of the town that was inhabited by the Visigoths.

Across from the museum lies the ancient entertainment complex: the **Theatre** and **Amphitheatre** (*adm covers both, and Roman villas*). The theatre, the best preserved in Spain, was built by Augustus' son-in-law Agrippa in 24 BC, the year after the founding of Augusta Emerita and, in forthright Roman confidence that the colony would succeed, was laboriously built in dry stone granite and designed to seat 6000. The magnificent two-storey colonnaded stage added under Hadrian in the 2nd century AD remains intact, as do the vaulted passageways leading to the orchestra and seats in the *cavea*. The theatre is still used for a classical drama festival in July. The adjacent amphitheatre (1 BC) has better-preserved seats and *vomitoria*, or entrance tunnels, through which as many as 15,000 spectators could come to watch gladiators kill wild animals or each other, or sea battles when the arena was flooded (*open 8am–10pm*).On the other side of the car park you can also visit the **Casa del Anfiteatro** (*open daily 9–1.45 and 5–7.15*), a patrician villa of the 1st century AD with a peristyle and atrium, and fine mosaics, including a beautiful one on wine-making; you can also see the pipes that fed the villa's private baths from the aqueduct. The first road left after the villa joins Avenida Extremadura near the scanty remains of this, the **Aqueduct San Lázaro** and the overgrown **Roman Circus**, where the Lusitanians watched their local hero Diocles chalk up some of his record 1462 victories on the chariot-race circuits of the Roman Empire. In the centre you can make out where the obelisks and turning-posts once stood, as well as parts of the stands that once seated 30,000 people.

Following Avenida Extremadura back to the centre, you'll pass Mérida's best-loved shrine, the church of **Santa Eulalia**, dedicated to the child martyr who, according to legend, was baked in an oven here for spitting in the eye of a pagan priest. Whatever the real story, here is as tidy an example of syncretism as you'll find in Spain, for in front of the church is a well-preserved **Temple of Mars**, which has suffered a name change as the *Hornito* (little oven) *de Santa Eulalia*, closed off by a grille, through which little girls traditionally dedicate locks of their hair to the saint. A bit further down towards the Guadiana stands the impressive triple-tiered **Acueducto de Los Milagros**, a lovely work of engineering that greets visitors who arrive by train. The **Roman bridge** next to it spans a tributary of the Guadiana.

The Mithraeum

The most beautiful art in Mérida, however, is across town next to the Plaza de Toros, in the **Mithraeum** (*open daily 9–1.45 and 5–7.15*). For the Roman soldiers, the cult of Mithras filled the same need as the Eleusinian Mysteries did for the ancient Greeks—the real religion, as opposed to official state rites performed in the Temples of Diana and Mars. Coincidentally (seeing the bullring next door) the sacrifice of bulls played an important part in Mithraic rites—rites to which the veteran legionaries of Augusta Emerita were especially devoted. Signs of frescoes remain on the walls of the underground *taurobolium* (where the bulls were killed), near a rectangular pool where the bulls' blood once flowed, now the home of turtles. In the enclosed **Casa del Mitreo** there is a brilliant-coloured mosaic floor devoted to river gods that come vividly to life when the caretaker moistens them with the mop he keeps in the corner; be sure to ask.

Badajoz

Downstream from Mérida, on the Portuguese border, sits the provincial capital of Badajoz, its name deriving from its Roman appellation *Pax Augusta*. Few places have ever been so misnamed; instead of Augustan peace Badajoz's story is essentially one of sanguinary sieges and warfare—between Moor and Moor when *Bataljoz* was an independent kingdom, then between Moor and Christian until Alfonso IX finally captured it for good in 1229, and then, as the 'key to Portugal' between Christians of several nationalities, most terribly in 1812, when Wellington lost a third of his 15,000 troops storming the French-held walls. Yet the nightmare that still haunts Badajoz is one that occurred after the siege in the Civil War, when the city was captured by foreign legionaries under Colonel Juan Yagüe, and the defenders, or any would-be refugees turned away from the Portuguese border (by order of the dictator Salazar), were corralled in the bullring and machine-gunned. Widely reported to a horrified world, this first atrocity of the Civil War tragically set the stage for countless others on both sides.

Unless you're continuing on to Portugal, there's little reason to visit Badajoz; in an effort to forget its bloodstained past, it has bulldozed most of itself and covered it over with bland *urbanizaciones*. The most elegant thing in the city is a bridge, the **Puente de Palmas**, built by Herrera in 1596, leading to a monumental gateway with round towers surviving from the old walls. **Plaza de España** is the unlovely heart of the city and home of its more-or-less **Gothic Cathedral**, begun by Alfonso the Wise. It has pretty Plateresque windows in the tower, a finely carved Renaissance choir, and paintings in the chapels and Sala Capitular by Ribera, Badajoz native Luis ('El Divino') Morales and his fellow *extremeño* Zurbarán—although none did their best work at home. Nearby is Badajoz's 'Giralda'—a bijou copy of the famous tower of Sevilla, stuck over a commercial block, while Calle Gabriel Hernán leads to the **Museo Provincial de Bellas Artes** (*open Mon–Fri 8.30–2.30, Sat 9–1*), which contain contemporary works and a handful of paintings by Morales and Zurbarán. The biggest sight in town is the rambling Moorish **Alcazaba** (1100) overlooking both the city and the Guadiana (*open 9–1 and 3–6*); from its walls you can look out over the irrigated Vegas Bajas, a happy result of the 'Badajoz Plan' that has brought new growth to the city. Below the fortress stands an octagonal Almohad tower, the **Torre del Apendiz**, better known as the 'Torre Espantaperros', or 'dog-scarer'. An **Archaeology Museum** housing Moorish finds from Badajoz's golden days, has been lodged near here in the Palacio de los Duques de Feria.

Small Towns Where No One Ever Goes

From Badajoz you can take a side-trip north to the picturesque frontier town of **Albuquerque**, in the centre of a cork-producing region; its 14th-century **castle** saw plenty of action, and through its namesake in New Mexico it has gained immortal fame as the town where Bugs Bunny knew he 'shoulda made a left'. **Valencia de Alcántara** to the north is the centre of an area rich in **dolmens**, while **Olivenza**, to the south was Portuguese until 1801, when Godoy wrote a treaty that moved the border a bit to the west. This act gained Spain its finest example of Manueline Gothic, in Olivenza's church **Santa María Magdalena**, decorated with graceful spiralling pillars and an altar crowned with the genealogical tree of the Virgin. Up the hill from the church stands the **castle**, built in 1488; an *extremeño* **Ethnographic Museum** has been installed in the old Royal Bakery (*open Sat and Sun am only*). Exiting through the Puerta de los Angeles you'll find the **Santa Casa de Misericordia**, with one chapel sumptuously decorated in Portuguese *azulejos* in 1723. From Mérida you can head out east along the Guadiana to tiny, whitewashed **Medellín**, the innocent birthplace of the ruthless *conquistador* Cortés and namesake of Colombia's notorious cocaine capital. After the castle, the biggest thing in town is the **monument to Cortés**; in Mexico, the land he won for Spain, such a memorial would be illegal. Southeast of here is a forbidding land known as the 'Siberia of Extremadura'. South of Mérida on the route to Zafra, **Almendralejo** is the capital of the **Tierra de Barros**–the land of clay which produces, besides ceramics, a tasty wine.

Zafra

Zafra is the belle of Lower Extremadura. Known as Zafar under the Moors, it was the seat of the Dukes of Feria, the first of whom in 1437 built the **Alcázar** with its great round towers and pyramidical merlons. Towering over the centre of town, this is Zafra's landmark and situation of one of Spain's finest *paradores*—even if you're not a guest, you can duck inside to see the marble patio attributed to Herrera, the Sala Dorada and the chapel. The nearby Plaza Mayor with its whitewashed arcades is split into the 18th-century **Plaza Grande** and the sweet 16th-century **Plaza Chica**, separated by an archway and with Zafra's finest streets on either side. Of its churches, the Gothic-Renaissance **Colegiata** (*open 10.30–1 and 7–8.30, winter 6–7.30*) built by the Dukes of Feria in 1546, is the most notable with a recently cleaned 1644 *retablo* by Zurbarán. The first duke and his wife lie in their fine alabaster tombs in the **Convento de Santa Clara** near the Plaza de España; in here and around town see if you can find the duke's fig-leaf symbol, a play on his name, Figueroa.

Jerez de los Caballeros

Although named after the Knights ('Caballeros'—both Templars and those of Santiago were here in the 13th century), Jerez de los Caballeros likes to point out that it's far older, having in its environs a number of megalithic monuments, especially the **Dolmen del Toriñuelo**, decorated with carvings of sun symbols, 5km northwest of town in the *dehesa* (pasture) of La Granja. Jerez produced its share of *conquistadores*: Balboa, discoverer of the Pacific, was born here, and Hernando de Soto, first to explore the Mississippi River, came from Barcarrota just to the north. Jerez went two better than Sevilla with its 'Giralda' towers and their silhouettes form the city's distinctive skyline. In the heart of town, in the **Plaza de España**, towers the brick **Torre de San Miguel** (1749), carved and intricately decorated. A few blocks away, the even more lavish **Torre de San Bartolomé** (1759) is embellished with polychrome *azulejos* to match the blue and gold façade of the church below. Across Plaza España stands a **Castle of the Templars**, where in 1307, the dark year of their dissolution, a number of them held out against the royal troops and were cut down in the **Torre Sangrienta** ('Bloody Tower'). The castle has recently been restored, revealing many traces of the Moorish alcazaba that preceded it. Next to the castle, the church of **Santa María** was consecrated in 556, although the Visigothic elements have been swamped by the Baroque. Jerez's third Giralda tower, **Santa Catalina** (1772), can be seen off to the left; its church has an impressive Baroque interior.

South of Jerez, **Fregenal de la Sierra** is a pretty village in the mountains near Andalucía, full of hermitages and traditional holy places; it was the birthplace of Felipe II's great librarian and reviser of the Polyglot Bible, Benito Arias Montano, who gathered the great collection of heterodox books in the library at El Escorial. Another town near Andalucía—and indeed, far more Andalucian and 'white' than an *extremeño* town—is **Llerena**, with a beautiful **Plaza Mayor** and its idiosyncratic church of **Nuestra Señora de Granada**, with a huge 'Giralda' tower and a façade crossed by a double-arcaded gallery.

Where to Stay and Eating Out

Mérida ✉ 06800

Mérida is endowed with the charming ★★★★**Parador Vía de la Plata**, Pza. de la Constitución 3, ✆ 924 31 38 00, ✉ 924 31 92 08 (*expensive*), in a former convent on a quiet square in the centre of town. Centrally placed on a quiet street near the Roman theatre is the modern ★★★**Nova Roma**, C/ Suárez Somonte 42, ✆ 924 31 12 61, ✉ 924 30 01 60 (*11,000 pts*). A former 14th-century palace on the main Pza. España is now the ★★★**Hotel Emperatriz**, ✆ 924 31 31 11, ✉ 924 31 33 05 (*moderate*), with a terrace in the front where you can take your morning coffee. Mérida's little ★**Hostal Nueva España**, Avda. Extremadura 6, ✆ 924 31 33 56 (*inexpensive*) is near the train station, has simple, modern rooms for *5000 pts* and the best showers in Extremadura.

Mérida has a number of *inexpensive* restaurants, and an excellent one serving *extremeño* dishes is the *parador* for around *5000 pts*. The **Rafael-2** on the pedestrian C/ Sta. Eulalia just off the Pza. de España has a set menu for *1800 pts*, including wine. Also just off the Pza. de España, on Pza. St Clara, the **Mesón el Emperador** offers local and Asturian dishes for around *2000 pts*. Near the bus station is the **Restaurant Hong Kong**, which serves a good oriental *menú del día* for around *2000 pts*. For tapas, try **Rufino** in Pza. St. Clara 2, ✆ 924 31 20 01, popular with the locals.

Badajoz ✉ 06000

In Badajoz, the ★★★**Hotel Río**, Avda. Adolfo Díaz Ambrona, ✆ 924 27 26 00, ✉ 924 27 38 74 (*expensive*) offers fine views, modern, air-conditioned rooms, a pool and an excellent restaurant. The ★★**Cervantes**, C/ Trinidad 2, ✆ 924 22 37 10 (*moderate*) is a good deal at *4500 pts*. If you're just passing through Badajoz, a good bargain choice is the ★**Hostal Menacho**, Abril 12, ✆ 924 22 14 46, with clean, air-conditioned but bathless rooms.

The best place to eat in Badajoz is the elegant **Aldebarán**, Avda. de Elvas, ✆ 924 27 42 61, whose dishes include ravioli stuffed with minced kid and wild mushrooms, and a supreme cheese and walnut tart. It'll set you back around *5000 pts*. *Closed Sun*. For some good Gallego cooking try **La Toja**, C/ Sánchez de la Rocha 22, © 924 23 74 77, where you can fill yourself for around *3000 pts* and when it's warm you can dine in the garden. For more pizzazz, try the popular **El Tronco**, C/ Muñoz Torrero 16, © 924 22 20 76, with a pleasant atmosphere and even better food (*3500 pts*); for something cheaper, dine off the tapas at El Tronco's amiable bar.

Zafra ✉ 06300

In Zafra, the Dukes' 15th-century castle has been carefully converted into a ★★★★**Parador Hernán Cortés**, Pza. Corazón de María 7, © 924 55 45 40, 🖂 924 55 10 18 (*expensive*); Hernán Cortés slept here as a guest of the Dukes of Feria. The décor may be Renaissance, but the comforts (pool, garden and good *extremeño* cuisine served in a magnificent setting) are up-to-date and first-class. A lovely second choice, ★★**Huerta Honda** on Avda. López Asme, © 924 55 41 00 (*expensive*) has fine rooms (*12,500 pts*) and views of the castle, a pretty patio and pool and an excellent restaurant (*5000 pts*), specializing in such regional delights as *ajo blanco* (white garlic) soup. ★★**Hotel Don Quijote**, C/ Huelva 3, © 924 55 47 71 (*moderate*) is a friendly place with nice rooms at a bargain *5000 pts*. Ask for a third floor room—attic rooms with beamed, sloping ceilings and a balcony. There are not many restaurants in Zafra—the ones attached to the hotels are the best bet.

Jerez ✉ 11400

In Jerez, ★**Los Torres**, Ctra. Jerez a Oliva 49, © 924 73 11 68 (*cheap*) has 12 simple rooms near the centre for *3000 pts*. Even cheaper is **El Gordito**, Avda. Portugal 104, © 924 73 14 52, but don't expect much for *1500 pts*.

La Mancha

We've been unfair to Nueva Castilla, chopping off its most interesting sections (Toledo, Cuenca, and Sigüenza) and including them in the section around Madrid (*see* pp.478–498). What's left is the Spanish Nebraska, a moderately fertile but astoundingly empty corner of the nation, covering about 160 by 320km between the capital and Andalucía. Iberians, Romans and Moors trod these lonely plains, all no doubt wondering why they were doing it. The centuries have left this land utterly devoid of notable towns and monuments, and the lack of interest nicely complements the monotonous scenery.

It isn't so oppressive in the spring, when red carpets of poppies fill the gaps between endless fields of young wheat and budding vines, but even then you're likely to find that a quick trip through on your way to the south is more than enough.

Getting Around

The region is well served by RENFE: all the southbound routes from Madrid must pass through it. Madrid–Badajoz trains pass through Ciudad Real, and there are two a day that stop at Almagro. Trains to Andalucía pass through Valdepeñas and the big, dull towns of Manzanares and Alcázar de San Juan, and all lines from Madrid to Murcia and Alicante stop at Albacete. For the other towns, you'll have to depend on bus services from the two provincial capitals, Ciudad Real and Albacete.

Ciudad Real: Avda. Alarcos 21, ✆ 926 21 20 03.
Almagro: C/ Mayor Carnicería 5, ✆ 926 86 07 17.
Albacete: C/ Mayor 46, ✆ 967 21 56 11.
Valdepeñas: Tourist booth on Pza. de España.

South of Madrid: Almagro and Valdepeñas

If you pass down the main road from Madrid, there are a few diversions en route. After **Tembleque**, near Toledo (*see* p.497) the first landmark is the decaying castle on the hill over **Consuegra**; one of the characteristic white conical-roofed windmills stands near it to remind us we are on the western borders of La Mancha. Near Daimiel, north of Ciudad Real, is one of the region's curiosities, the **Ojos de Guadiana**, a marshy area where the river Guadiana disappears underground, and pops back up a few miles to the west. Numerous species of migratory birds—especially various species of duck and purple herons—favour the area as a stopover, and it is included in the designated **Parque Nacional de las Tablas de Daimiel**. Sadly, though it has been a protected park since 1973, offences such as pollution of the water still persist and, in the early Eighties, the millions of gallons of water used to irrigate the huge commercial farms in this area caused the Guadiana to dry up for the first time in its history; consequently fewer waterfowl migrate through here. However, if you take the N430 or the N310 in the other direction, you will wind up in **Las Lagunas de Ruidera**, La Mancha's other surprisingly wet spot. The lagoons are formed by the serpentine meanderings of the upper Guadiana and are an ideal picnic and swimming spot for those not in a hurry to pass through La Mancha.

Ciudad Real, capital of the province, is a small and somewhat dismal town, with only a lone Moorish gateway from its old fortifications to show visitors. A better stop would be **Almagro**, changed little since its period of prosperity in the 16th century. Among its monuments are a lovely, arcaded **Plaza Mayor**, a convent of the Knights of Calatrava, and the oldest theatre in Spain, the **Corral de Comedias**. This relic of the golden age of Spanish theatre makes an interesting comparison with its northern contemporaries—like Shakespeare's Globe, it has a row of balconies all around for the gentlemen and ladies, and a small floor in the centre for the 'pitlings' below the stage (only it's square instead of round). Every year, during the month of July, Almagro is turned over to theatre, with a festival based on Spain's Golden Age in the 16th and 17th century. More recent works are also performed. The Corral is the centrepiece of the festival. The theatre is open to those visiting the theatre **museum** (*open Tues–Fri 10–2 and 4–7, Sat 10–2 and 4–6, Sun 11–2, closed Mon and holidays; adm, free on Sat pm and Sun*). Almost everything you see in Almagro was built by Jakob Fugger of Germany and his descendants, who started Europe's first great banking-house and at times controlled most of the continent's cloth trade. The Fuggers prospered greatly from Charles V's imperialist extravagance, and Almagro was their Spanish headquarters. They also introduced the art of making bobbin lace to this area, and beautiful designs are still worked on by the local women; if you can, buy your lace directly from them.

The back road south from Almagro passes through the **Campo de Calatrava**, scene of many battles of the Reconquista. The religious knightly Order of Calatrava, right arm of the Castilian kings in these wars, was founded here, and the ruins of their monastery headquarters at

Calatrava La Nueva, including the rough, fortress-like church with its rose window, are evocative of that grim age of the Church Militant. An excursion from here into the bleak **Sierra de Alandía** to the southwest would be a novelty—this is undoubtedly the least visited part of Spain; and not without reason. Villages like Tirteafuera and Gargantiel, Cabeza del Buey ('ox-head') and Pueblonuevo del Terrible are more interesting on the map than in person. Much mining goes on here, coal and zinc, and the famous mercury mine at **Almadén** that supplied the alchemists of Toledo. The main road is a better bet, passing through the country's biggest wine region, around **Valdepeñas**. Several *bodegas* in the town centre and off the highway would welcome your visit. Much of Spain's dependable 70-peseta-a-bottle brew comes from here, but also some of its finest vintages. The highway and railroad pass into Andalucía through the **Desfiladero de Despeñaperros**, 'hurling down the dogs', a wild rocky chute long the haunt of bandits.

Don Quixote's La Mancha

There's little evidence that Miguel de Cervantes ever cared to spend much time here. Certainly he would have had a big laugh at the expense of the Manchegans and literary critics who drone on about the 'poetic, essentially Spanish' landscape. Nothing could be less poetic than the bleak expanses of the region called 'the blot', and Cervantes found its empty spaces the perfect setting for his hopeless knight errant and his parable of a burnt-out, disillusioned Spain. Scholars have spent their careers tracing out the knight's imagined itinerary, and schools contend endlessly over which blank-faced, anonymous Manchegan village was the scene of the Encounter with the Windmills, the Adventures of the Inn, or Camacho's Marriage. But unless you can tell one Manchegan village from another, such scholarship may seem extravagant.

El Toboso, home of the peerless Dulcinea, and one of the very few villages Cervantes ever actually names, might be a good stopover for determined Quixotic pilgrims. Of course they'll show you Dulcinea's house, now restored and turned into a humble **Quixote museum**. Two of the nicer villages are **San Clemente** and **Campo de Criptana**, around which several much-honoured windmills can be seen. There's a grandly exotic 15th-century castle outside **Belmonte**. **Alcaraz** nearby is a town of some distinction; with its ensemble of interesting 16th-century buildings it seems a minor version of Úbeda. And not surprisingly Úbeda's architect, Andrés de Vandelvira, was a native and built many of them. Alcaraz has a riotous *romería* between September 4th and 8th to the Virgen de Cortes sanctuary nearby.

Albacete, the Manchegan metropolis, makes its living from artichokes and saffron from the country around it; it leads Spain in both these products, and has grown into a city of 100,000 people with dull, straight streets and little to see, other than the **museum** in Parque de Abelardo Sánchez, with finds from local prehistoric sights—particularly from the Alpera caves—and a collection of tiny articulated 'dolls' made from ivory and amber, discovered at the Roman necropolis of Ontur (*open Tues–Sat 10–2 and 4–7, Sun 9–2, closed Mon; adm*). Albacete was a ferociously Republican town during the Civil War, the training-ground of the International Brigades, and few of its old churches survived. From here you can choose between highways for Valencia, Murcia or Alicante, the last passing a 15th-century castle over the town of **Almansa**. The surrounding area contains the **Alpera caves**, a series of archaeological sites. The best one is **La Vieja** which has stone-age paintings of male and female figures and the usual hunting scenes. There are even some mysterious hand-prints. If you want to visit, get permission from Almansa's Ayuntamiento.

Almagro ✉ 13270

The ★★★★**Parador de Almagro**, is one of the finer *paradores*, set in the restored 16th-century Convento de San Francisco, Ronda de San Francisco 31, ✆ 926 86 01 00, 🖷 926 86 01 50 (*expensive*). Or try the new, ★★★**Almagro**, Bolaños 34, ✆ 926 86 00 11 (*moderate*). If you're thinking of staying during July, book months ahead.

Albacete ✉ 02000

The ★★★**Parador de Albacete**, C.N.301, ✆ 967 50 93 43, 🖷 967 22 60 92 (*expensive*) is a colourless place but the most comfortable in town. Or try ★★★**Albacete**, C/ Carcelén 8, ✆ (967) 21 81 11, 🖷 926 21 87 25, (*6000 pts for room, 3000 pts for food*).

Daimiel ✉ 13250

A bargain in Daimiel is ★★**Las Tablas**, C/ Virgen de Las Cruces 5, ✆ 926 85 21 07 (*moderate*); modest air-conditioned rooms with TV.

Ciudad Real ✉ 13000

The extremely comfortable ★★★**Santa Cecilia**, Tinte 3, ✆ 926 22 85 45, 🖷 924 22 86 18, has rooms at around *9000 pts* and a good restaurant, **El Real**, which does partridge for *3500 pts*. A cheaper option is ★★**Hostal Capri**, Pza. del Pilar 8, ✆ 926 21 40 44, with pleasant budget rooms at *3500 pts*.

Manzanares ✉ 13200

★★★**Parador de Manzanares,** on the NIV Madrid road, ✆ 926 61 04 00, 🖷 924 61 09 35, is a nice spot with a welcome swimming pool, though it's not as grand as some.

Campo de Criptana

The ★**Sancho** is on Pza. Mayor, ✆ 926 56 00 12 (*inexpensive*). Modest lodgings can be found in **Alcázar de San Juan** and at **Ruidera** near the lagoons, although most close from October to May.

Eating Out

Pisto is La Mancha's major contribution to Spanish cuisine: the classic is simply tomato and red pepper, with garlic. Game dishes are the speciality of most Manchegan restaurants, as at **Mesón Las Rejas** in Albacete, C/ Dionisio Guardiola 9, ✆ 926 22 72 42 (*3000 pts*), *closed Sun in summer*, the **Miami Park** in Ciudad Real, C/ Ciruelo 48, ✆ 926 22 20 43 (4500 pts), *closed Sun eve*, and **El Cruce** in Manzanares, Ctra. Madrid km 173, ✆ 926 61 19 00 (*3500–4000 pts*). Almagro's best restaurant is **Mesón El Corregidor**, Pza. Fray Fernando Fernández de Córdoba 2, ✆ 926 86 06 48, in an old house (*3500 pts*). *Closed Mon*. There are some good tapas bars in Ciudad Real: try **Casa Lucio**, C/ Gato, or **Mesón El Venetro** on Pza. Mayor. In El Toboso, **Hermanos Martínez,** on C/Clavileño 1, has a fine selection of regional dishes. In the centre of Puerto Lapice is an 18th-century inn called the **Venta del Quijote**. The food is splendid, and the atmosphere, give or take a century or two, the most authentic you'll find.

Andalucía

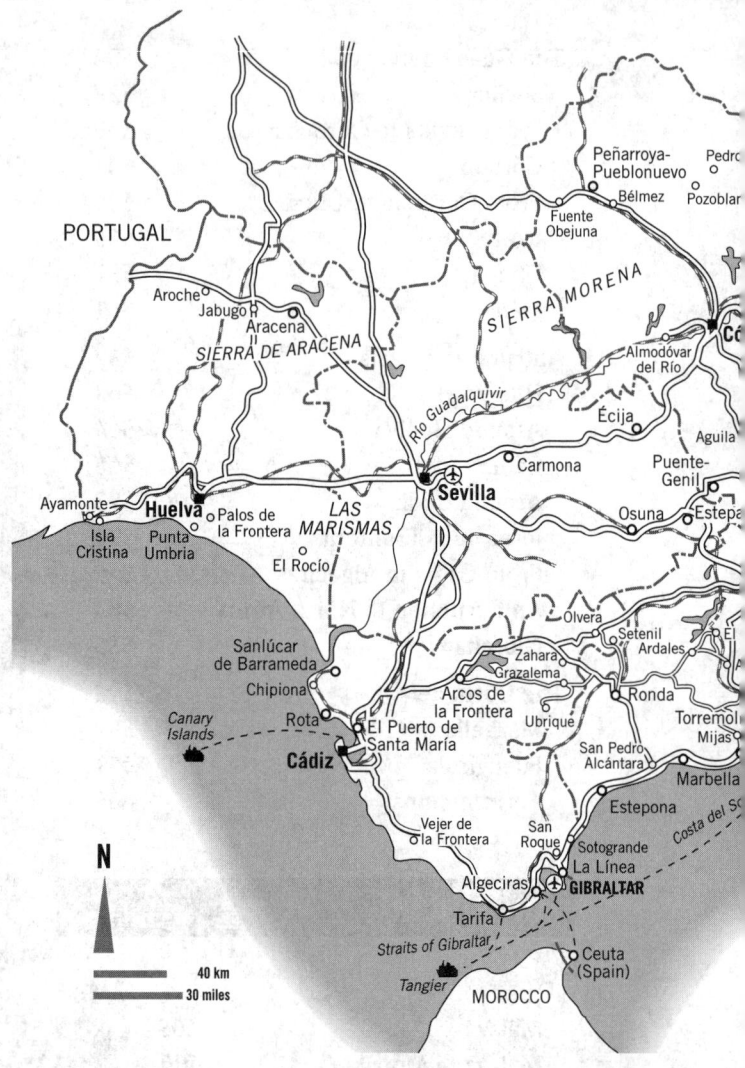

A vision of the lost Islamic civilization of Al-Andalus may come upon you where you least expect it. In the cities—Sevilla, Córdoba and Granada most of all—it is obvious, a separate reality that shines through centuries of Spanish veneer. In the whitewashed villages, still so like their counterparts across the Straits of Gibraltar, it is still present in spirit. But it is the country-side where the Moorish heritage shows up most surprisingly. One of Andalucía's most beautiful views unfolds from the *mirador* at the eastern end of Úbeda; the rolling hills recede towards the distant mountains, covered with olive trees planted in neat, varying patterns, and down below near the stream a small farm has its rows of carrots and beans arranged in patterns even more intricate and maze-like.

Think of that picture when you visit. Al-Andalus was a culture totally unlike any Europe has known, and it requires an effort of the imagination to appreciate its subtlety and delicacy. Its destruction was a tragedy, not just for Spain, but for the world. The ill-fortune that put Al-Andalus in the hands of Castile was like someone giving a complicated music-box to a small child; unable even to comprehend, let alone use it, the Castilians pounded it until it broke. Many of the bits and pieces survive to this day, but it would take a greater talent than a magician's from the Arabian Nights to put them back together.

In the long dark night of its conquerors, Andalucía fell under the hand of one of the most useless and predatory aristocracies Europe has ever known, heirs of the warriors of the Reconquista. As a result, its impoverished peasants became the most radicalized population in Spain, as manifested in frequent local revolts throughout the 19th and 20th centuries. Only now is Andalucía emerging from this situation—former Prime Minister Felipe González is an

Andalucían and so was his vice president. A big land-reform programme is under way, and the growth of tourism along the southern coasts has pumped plenty of money into Andalucía's economy. A hundred years ago travellers in this region never failed to note the wretchedness of the villages and the glaring contrasts of wealth and poverty. You'll see little of that now.

Today, with its new green and white flag flying proudly on every public building, autonomous, Socialist-run Andalucía may have the chance to rediscover itself. With a fifth of Spain's population, its biggest tourist industry, and potentially its richest agriculture, it has great promise for the future. And as the part of Spain with the longest and most brilliant artistic heritage—not only from the Moors, but from the troubled, creative, post-Reconquista Andalucía that has given Spain flamenco and bullfighting, Velázquez, García Lorca and Manuel de Falla—the region may find it still has the resources once more to become the leader, and not a follower, in Spain's cultural life.

For convenience, we have divided Andalucía's complicated geography into four parts: Sevilla, Córdoba, and the valley of the Guadalquivir; then the coasts, of which the famous Costa del Sol is only a small part; next come the inimitable white villages of the mountains, between the Guadalquivir and the sea; and finally, Granada and the Sierra Nevada. For its size, Andalucía contains a remarkable diversity of landscapes—from Spain's highest mountains to endless rolling hills covered with olive trees, Europe's biggest marshland preserve and even some patches of desert. And no other part of Spain can offer so many interesting large cities. Andalucía, like Catalunya, is a world unto itself; it has as many delights to offer as you have time to spend on it.

Andalucía: The Guadalquivir Valley

Much of essential Andaluz lies within the lush confines of the Guadalquivir Valley: flamboyant Sevilla, and hooded-eyed Córdoba. Upriver, the silver hills of the Sierra Morena watch over two Renaissance time-capsules: Baeza and Úbeda, and the Roman ruins at Italica and Carmona.

Sevilla

Apart from the Alhambra in Granada, the place where the lushness and sensuality of Al-Andalus survives best is Andalucía's capital. Sevilla may be Spain's fourth-largest city, but it is a place where you can pick oranges from the trees, and see open countryside from the centre of town. Come in spring if you can, when the gardens are drowned in birdsong and the air becomes intoxicating with the scent of jasmine and a hundred other blooms. If you come in summer, you may melt; the lower valley of the Guadalquivir is one of the hottest places in Europe. The pageant of Sevilla unfolds in the shadow of La Giralda, still the loftiest tower in Spain. Its size and the ostentatious play of its arches and arabesques make it the perfect symbol for this city, full of the romance of the south and the perfume of excess.

At times Sevilla has been a capital, and it remains Spain's eternal city; neither past reverses nor modern industry have been able to shake it from its dreams. That its past glories should return and place it alongside Venice and Florence as one of the jewels in the crown of Europe, a true metropolis with full international recognition, is the first dream of every *sevillano*. Sevilla is still a city very much in love with itself. Even the big celebration during Holy Week—although enjoyable to the foreigner (anyone from outside the city), with revelry in every café and on every street corner—is essentially a private one; the *sevillanos* celebrate in their own *casitas* with friends, all the time aware that they are being observed by the general public, who can peek but may not enter, at least not without an *enchufe* ('the right connection'). Sevilla is much like a beautiful, flirtatious woman; she'll tempt you to her doorstep and allow you a peck on the cheek—whether you get over the threshold depends entirely on your charm.

History: from Hispalis to Isbiliya to Sevilla

One of Sevilla's distinctions is its long historical continuity. Few cities in western Europe can claim never to have suffered a dark age, but Sevilla flourished after the fall of Rome—and even after the coming of the Castilians. Roman Hispalis was founded on an Iberian settlement, and soon became one of the leading cities of the province of Bætica. So was Itálica, the now ruined city just to the northwest; it is difficult to say which was the more important. During the Roman twilight, Sevilla seems to have been a thriving town. Its first famous citizen, St Isidore, was one of the Doctors of the Church and the most learned man of the age, famous for his great *Encyclopedia* and his *Seven Books Against the Pagans*, an attempt to prove that the coming of Christianity was not the cause of Rome's fall. Sevilla was an important town under the Visigoths, and after the Moorish conquest it was second only to Córdoba as a political power and a centre of learning. For a while after the demise of the western caliphate in 1023, it became an independent kingdom, paying tribute to the kings of Castile. Sevilla suffered under the Almoravids after 1091, but enjoyed a revival under their successors, the Almohads.

The disaster came for Muslim Isbiliya in 1248, 18 years after the union of Castile and León. Fernando III's conquest of the city is not a well-documented event, but it seems that more than half the population found exile in Granada or Africa preferable to Castilian rule; their property was divided among settlers from the north. Despite the dislocation, the city survived, and found a new prosperity as Castile's window on the Mediterranean and South Atlantic trade routes (the Río Guadalquivir is navigable as far as Sevilla). Everywhere in the city you will see its emblem, the word NODO (knot) with a double knot between the O and D. It recalls the civil wars of the 1270s, when Sevilla was one of the few cities in Spain to remain loyal to Alfonso the Wise. '*No m'a dejado*' ('She has not forsaken me'), Alfonso is recorded as saying; *madeja* is another word for knot, and placed between the syllables NO and DO it makes a clever rebus besides a tribute to Sevilla's loyalty to medieval Castile's greatest king.

From 1503 to 1680, Sevilla enjoyed a legal monopoly of trade with the Americas. The giddy prosperity this brought, in the years when the silver fleet ran full, contributed much to the festive, incautious atmosphere that is often revealed in Sevilla's character. Sevilla never found a way to hold on to much of the American wealth, and what little it managed to grab was soon dissipated in showy excess. It was in this period, of course, that Sevilla was perfecting its charm. Poets and composers have always favoured it as a setting. Bizet's Carmen rolled her cigars in the Royal Tobacco Factory, and for her male counterpart Sevilla contributed Don Juan Tenorio, who evolved through Spanish theatre in plays by Tirso de Molina and Zorrilla to become Mozart's Don Giovanni; the same composer also used the city as a setting for *The Marriage of Figaro*.

Getting There

By air: Sevilla has regular flights from Madrid, Málaga, and Barcelona, less regularly from Lisbon, the Canary Islands and Valencia. San Pablo airport is 12km (7½ miles) east of the city, and the airport bus leaves from Bar Iberia on Calle Almirante Lobos, near the southern end of Avenida de la Constitución. Airport information: © 95 467 29 81.

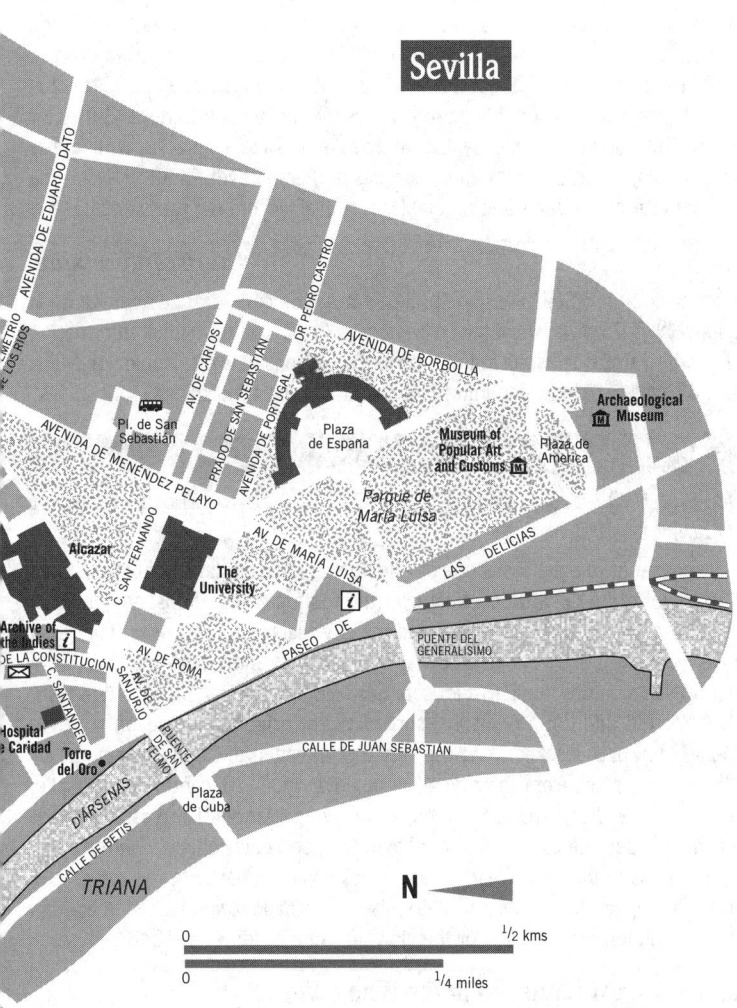

Sevilla

By train: Estación de Santa Justa, in the surreally named Avenida Kansas City in the northeast of town, is the modern Expo showpiece. There are train connections—to Madrid by AVE in a staggeringly quick 2 hours 15 minutes, a daily *Talgo* to Valencia and Barcelona, and to Córdoba, Jerez and Cádiz, among the other frequent regular services to these cities; for trains to Málaga, Ronda and Algeciras, you should watch out for possible train changes at Bobadilla Junction, the black hole of Andalucían railways where all lines cross. The central RENFE office is at Calle Zaragoza 29. **Information**, © 95 454 02 02; **reservations**, © 95 422 26 93.

By bus: Almost all lines for Madrid, the Levante, Andalucía and Portugal leave from the Estación de Autobuses, Plaza de Armas. Buses for Jerez and Cádiz run about every 1½ hours, and there are frequent connections to most other points in Andalucía (five daily to Granada, four to Málaga, three to Córdoba and Úbeda, at least two to the Costa del Sol, Aracena, Almería, La Línea, Tarifa and Algeciras, also three each to Madrid, Valencia and Barcelona). For destinations within the province (e.g. Carmona, Écija), buses depart from outside this station, across the Avenida de Carlos V. Buses for Matalascañas, Huelva, Badajoz and Ayamonte leave from Calle Segura 18, while those for Santiponce and the ruins leave from Marqués de Parada every hour or so during the day. **Information** on routes and timetables is available from the tourist office.

Tourist Information

The permanent tourist office is very helpful; it's near the cathedral at Avenida de la Constitución 21, ✆ 95 422 14 04 (*open weekdays 9–7*). The municipal information centre is near the Parque de María Luisa, next to the US consulate off Avenida de María Luisa, ✆ 95 423 44 65. There's an information centre at the airport, ✆ 95 444 91 28.

Around the Cathedral: La Giralda

Open Mon–Sat 10.30–5, Sun and hols 2–6; adm 200 pts, or 700 pts including entrance to the cathedral.

A good place to start your tour of Sevilla is at one of Andalucía's most famous monuments. You can catch the 319ft tower of **La Giralda** peeking over the rooftops from almost anywhere in Sevilla; it will be your best friend when you get lost in the city's labyrinthine streets. This great minaret, with its *ajimeces* and brickwork arabesques, was also built under the Almohads, from 1172 to 1195, just 50 years before the Christian conquest. The surprisingly harmonious spire stuck on top is a Christian addition. Whatever sort of turret originally stood on top was surmounted by four golden balls stacked up at the very top, designed to catch the sun and be visible to a traveller one day's ride from the city; all came down in a 13th-century earthquake. On the top of their spire, the Christians added a huge, revolving statue of Faith as a weathervane (many writers have noted the curious fancy of having a supposedly constant Faith turning with the four winds). La Giralda—the weathervane—has given its name to the tower as a whole. The climb to the top is easy; instead of stairs, there are shallow ramps—wide enough for Fernando III to have ridden his horse up for the view after the conquest in 1248.

The Cathedral: the Biggest Cathedral in the Whole World

The same opening hours as the Giralda—you visit both on one ticket.

For a while after the Reconquista, the Castilians who repopulated Sevilla were content to use the great Almohad mosque, built at the same time as La Giralda. At the turn of the 1400s, in a fit of pious excess, it was decided to build a new cathedral so grand that 'future ages shall call us mad for attempting it'. If they were mad, at least they were good organizers—they got it up in slightly over a century. The architects are unknown, though there has been speculation that the original master was either French or German.

The exterior, with its great rose window and double buttresses, is as fine as any of the Gothic cathedrals of northern Spain—if we could only see it. Especially on the west front, facing the

Avenida de la Constitución, the buildings close in; walking around its vast bulk, past the fence of Roman columns joined by thick chains, is like passing under a steep and ragged cliff. Some of the best original sculptural work is on the two portals flanking the main door: the **Puerta del Bautismo** (left), and the **Puerta del Nacimiento** (right). The groundplan of this monster, roughly 400ft by 600ft, probably covers the same area as did the mosque. On the northern side, the **Patio de los Naranjos** (Patio of the Orange Trees, and planted accordingly) preserves the outline of the mosque courtyard. The Muslim fountain survives, along with some of the walls and arches. In the left-hand corner, the Moorish 'Gate of the Lizard' has hanging from it a stuffed crocodile, said to have been a present from an Egyptian emir asking for the hand of a Spanish infanta. Along the eastern wall is the entrance of the **Biblioteca Colombina**, an archive of the explorer's life and letters.

The cavernous interior overpowers the faithful with its size more than its grace or beauty. The main altarpiece is the world's biggest *retablo*, almost 120ft high and entirely covered with carved figures and golden Gothic ornaments; it took 82 years to make, and takes about a minute to look at. Just behind the Capilla Mayor and the main altar, the **Capilla Real** contains the tombs of San Fernando, conqueror of Sevilla, and of Alfonso the Wise; Pedro the Cruel and his mistress, María de Padilla, are relegated to the crypt underneath. The art of the various chapels around the cathedral is lost in the gloom, but there are paintings by Murillo in the Capilla de San Antonio (in the north aisle), and an altarpiece by Zurbarán in the Capilla de San Pedro (to the left of the Capilla Real). In the southern aisle, four stern pallbearers on a high pedestal support the tomb of **Christopher Columbus**.

The Sacristy

Most of the cathedral's collections are housed in a few chambers near the turnstiles at the main entrance. In the **Sala Capitular**, which has an *Immaculate Conception* by Murillo, Sevilla's bishop can sit on his throne and pontificate under the unusual acoustics of an elliptical baroque ceiling. The adjacent **sacristy** contains paintings by Zurbarán, Murillo, Van Dyck and others, most in dire need of restoration. Spare a moment for the reliquaries. Juan de Arfe, maker of the world's biggest silver monstrances, is represented here with one that seems almost a small palace, complete with marble columns. Spain's most famous, and possibly most bizarre reliquary, is the **Alfonsine Tables**, filled with over 200 tiny bits of tooth and bone. They were said to have belonged to Alfonso the Wise and were made to provide extra-powerful juju for him to carry into battle.

The Archive of the Indies

Open weekdays, 10–1; research, by appointment, 8–3, © *95 421 12 34.*

In common with most of its contemporaries, parts of Sevilla's cathedral were public ground, and were used to transact all sorts of business. A 16th-century bishop put an end to this practice, but prevailed upon Felipe II to construct next to the cathedral an exchange, or **Lonja**, for the merchants. Felipe sent his favourite architect, Juan de Herrera, then still busy with El Escorial, to design it. The severe, elegant façades are typically Herreran, and the stone balls and pyramids on top are practically the architect's signature. By the 1780s, little commerce was still going on in Sevilla, and what was left of the American trade passed through Cádiz, so Carlos III converted the lonely old building to hold the **Archive of the Indies**, the repository of all the reports, maps, and documents the crown collected during the age of exploration.

The Alcázar

Open Tues–Sat 9.30–7, Sun and hols 9.30–5; adm 600 pts.

It's easy to be fooled into thinking this is simply a Moorish palace; some of its rooms and court-yards seem to come straight from the Alhambra. Most of them, however, were built by Moorish workmen for King Pedro the Cruel of Castile in the 1360s. The Alcázar and its king represent a fascinating cul-de-sac in Spanish history and culture, and allow the possibility that Al-Andalus might have assimilated its conquerors rather than been destroyed by them.

Pedro was an interesting character. In Froissart's *Chronicle*, we have him described as 'full of marveylous opinyons...rude and rebell agaynst the commandements of holy churche'. Certainly he didn't mind having his Moorish artists, lent by the kings of Granada, adorn his palace with sayings from the Koran in Kufic calligraphy. Pedro preferred Sevilla, still half-Moorish and more than half-decadent, to Old Castile, and he filled his court here with Moorish poets, dancers and bodyguards—the only ones he trusted. But he was not the man for the job of cultural synthesis. The evidence, in so far as it is reliable, suggests he richly deserved his honorific 'the Cruel'; although to *sevillanos* he was Pedro the Just. Long before Pedro, the Alcázar was the palace of the Moorish governors. Work on the Moorish features began in 712 after the capture of Sevilla. In the 9th century it was transformed into a palace for Abd ar-Rahman II. Important additions were made under the Almohads; the Alcázar was their capital in Al-Andalus. Almost all the decorative work you see now was done under Pedro, some by the Granadans and the rest by Muslim artists from Toledo; altogether it is the outstanding production of *mudéjar* art in Spain.

The Alcázar is entered through a little gate on the Plaza del Triunfo, on the south side of the cathedral. The first courtyard, the **Patio de la Montería**, has beautiful arabesques, with lions amid castles for Castile and León; this was the public court of the palace, where visitors were received, corresponding to the Mexuar at the Alhambra. At the far end of the Patio is the lovely **façade** of the interior palace, decorated with inscriptions in Gothic and Arabic scripts.

Much of the best *mudéjar* work can be seen in the adjacent halls and courts; their seemingly haphazard arrangement was in fact a principle of the art, to increase the surprise and delight in passing from one to the next. The **Patio de Yeso** (Court of Plaster) is largely a survival of the Almoravid palace of the 1170s, itself built on the site of a Roman *praetorium*. The **Patio de las Doncellas** (Court of the Maidens), entered through the gate of the palace façade, is the largest of the courtyards and leads to the **Salón de los Embajadores** (Hall of the Ambassadors), a small domed chamber that is the finest in the Alcázar despite jarring additions from the time of Charles V. In Moorish times this was the throne room. Another small court, the **Patio de la Muñecas** (Court of the Dolls), takes its name from two tiny faces on medallions at the base of one of the horseshoe arches—a little joke on the part of the Muslim stone-carvers. The columns here come from the ruins of Medinat az-Zahra.

Spanish kings after Pedro couldn't leave the Alcázar alone. Fernando and Isabel spoiled a large corner of it for their **Casa de Contratación**, a planning centre for the colonization of the Indies. There's little to see in it: a big conference table, Isabel's bedroom, a model of the *Santa María* in wood and a model of the royal family (Isabel's) in silver. Charles V added a **palace** of his own, as he did in the Alhambra. This contains a spectacular set of **Flemish tapestries** showing finely detailed scenes of Charles's campaigns in Tunisia. Within its walls, the Alcázar has extensive and lovely **gardens**, with reflecting pools, avenues of clipped hedges, and lemons and oranges everywhere. The park is deceptively large, but you can't get lost unless you find the little **labyrinth** near the pavilion built for Charles V in the lower gardens. Outside the walls, there is a formal promenade called the **Plaza Catalina de Ribera** with two monuments to Columbus, and the **Jardines de Murillo**, bordering the northern wall of the Alcázar.

West of the Cathedral

Avenida de la Constitución, passing the façade of the cathedral, is Sevilla's main street. Between it and the Guadalquivir are mostly quiet neighbourhoods, without the distinction of the Barrio Santa Cruz but still with a charm of their own.

Hospital de la Caridad

Built in 1647 behind a colourful façade on Calle Temprado is the Hospital de la Caridad. The Hospital's original benefactor was a certain Miguel de Mañara, a reformed rake who may have been a prototype for Tirso de Molina's Don Juan. Though it still serves its intended purpose as a charity home for the aged, visitors come to see the art in the hospital chapel. The best is gone, unfortunately—in the lobby they'll show you photographs of the Murillos stolen by Napoleon. Among what remains are three works of art, ghoulish even by Spanish standards. Juan de Valdés Leal (1622–90) was a competent enough painter, but warmed to the task only with such subjects as you see here: a bishop in full regalia decomposing in his coffin, and Death snuffing out your candle. Even better than these is the anonymous, polychrome bloody Jesus, surrounded by smiling baroque *putti*, who carry, instead of harps, whips and scourges.

Torre del Oro

The Moorish **tower of gold**, which takes its name from the gold and *azulejo* tiles that covered its 12-sided exterior in the days of the Moors, stands on the banks of the Guadalquivir. In the days of the explorers, ships were still small enough to make this the maritime centre of the city; picture the scene when the annual silver fleet came in. For over a century the fleet's arrival was the event of the year, the turning-point of an annual feast-or-famine cycle when debts would be made good, and long-deferred indulgences could be had. The Torre del Oro, built by the Almohads in 1220, was the southernmost point of the city's fortifications. In times of trouble a chain would be stretched from the tower and across the Guadalquivir. The interior now houses a small **Maritime Museum** (*open daily except Mon, 10–2, Sun 10–1*).

La Maestranza Bullring

On the river just north of the tower is another citadel of Sevillan *duende*. La Maestranza bullring, built in 1760, is not as big as Madrid's, but is still a lovely building, and perhaps the most prestigious of all *plazas de toros*. It also carries the third-busiest schedule, after Madrid and Barcelona; if you like to watch as your *cola de toro* is prepared, you may be fortunate enough to see a *corrida* while in town (*see* 'Bullfights', p.57). The bullring's name comes from the big **Maestranza** (naval dockyard) across the street.

Triana

Across the Guadalquivir from the bullring is the neighbourhood of Triana, an ancient suburb that takes its name from the Emperor Trajan. It has a reputation as the 'cradle of flamenco' and its workmen make all Sevilla's *azulejo* tiles. Queipo de Llano's troops wrecked a lot of it during the Civil War, but there are still picturesque white streets overlooking the Guadalquivir.

Back across the river, over the Puente de Triana, you'll approach the San Eloy district, full of raucous bars and hotels. On Calle San Pablo is **La Magdalena** (1704), with an eccentric baroque façade decorated with sundials. Among the art inside are two paintings of the *Life of St Dominic* by Zurbarán, and gilded reliefs by Leonardo de Figueroa.

Museo de Bellas Artes

Open daily except Wed, Mon–Sat 9–8, Sun 9–3; adm free to EU citizens, 250 pts for others.

This excellent collection is housed in the **Convento de la Merced** (1612), on Calle San Roque. There are some fine medieval works—sweetly naïve-looking virgins, and an especially expressive triptych by the 'Master of Burgos' from the 13th century. The Italian sculptor Pietro Torregiani (the fellow who broke Michelangelo's nose, and who died in a Sevilla prison) has left an uncanny barbaric wooden **St Jerome**. This saint, *Jerónimo* in Spanish, is a favourite in Sevilla, where he is pictured with a rock and a rugged cross instead of his usual lion. The museum has a roomful of Murillos (the painter was Sevillan and is buried in the Barrio Santa Cruz), including an *Immaculate Conception* and many other artful missal-pictures. Much more interesting are the works of Zurbarán, who could express spirituality without the simpering of Murillo or the hysteria of the others. His series of **female saints** is especially good, and the *Miracle of Saint Hugo* is perhaps his most acclaimed work. Occasionally even Zurbarán slips up; you may enjoy the *Eternal Father* with great fat toes and a triangle on his head, a *St Gregory* who looks like the scheming church executive he really was, and the wonderful *Apotheosis of St Thomas Aquinas*, where the great scholastic philosopher rises to his feet as if to say 'I've got it!'. Don't miss El Greco's portrait of his son Jorge. There are also more Valdés Leals and works by Jan Brueghel, Ribera, Caravaggio, and Mattia Preti.

Sevilla's business and shopping area has been since Moorish times the patch of narrow streets north of La Giralda. **Calle Sierpes** ('serpent street') is its heart, a sinuous pedestrian lane lined with every sort of old shop. Just to the north, **El Salvador** is a fine baroque church by Leonardo de Figueroa, picturesquely mouldering. On the **Plaza Nueva**, Sevilla's modern centre, you can see the grimy 1564 **Ayuntamiento**, with a fine, elaborate plateresque façade. From here, Avenida de la Constitución changes its name to Calle Tetuán. Sevilla has found a hundred ways to use its *azulejos*, but the best has to be in the **billboard** on this street for 1932 Studebaker cars; so pretty that no one's had the heart to take it down.

La Macarena

The north end of Sevilla contains few monuments; most of it is solid, working-class neighbourhoods clustered around baroque parish churches. The **Alameda de Hércules**, a once fashionable promenade adorned with copies of ancient statues, is in the middle of one of the shabbier parts. **Santa Clara** and **San Clemente** are two interesting monasteries in this area: Santa Clara includes a Gothic tower built by Don Fadrique, Pedro the Cruel's brother; its pretty chapel has one of Sevilla's best *artesonado* ceilings. North of Calle San Luis, some of the city's **Moorish walls** survive, near the **Basilica of La Macarena**, which gives the quarter its name. The Basilica is the home of the most-worshipped of Sevilla's idols, a delicate Virgin with glass tears on her cheeks who always steals the show in the Holy Week parades. Like a film star she makes her admirers gasp and swarm around her, crying '¡O la hermosa! ¡O la guapa!' ('O the beautiful! O the handsome!'). The small adjacent **museum** is divided between La Macarena's trinkets and costumes of famous bullfighters. South from here, along Calle San Luis, you'll pass another baroque extravaganza, Leonardo de Figueroa's **San Luis**, built for the Jesuits (1699–1731), with twisted columns and tons of encrusted ornament. **San Marcos**, down the street, has one of Sevilla's last surviving *mudéjar* towers.

East of the Cathedral

If Spain envies Sevilla, Sevilla envies **Barrio Santa Cruz**, a tiny, exceptionally lovely quarter of narrow streets and whitewashed houses. It is the true homeland of everything *sevillano*, with flower-bedecked patios and iron-bound windows. Before 1492, this was the Jewish quarter of Sevilla; today it's the most aristocratic corner of town. In the old days there was a wall around the barrio; today you may enter through the Jardines de Murillo, the Calle Mateos Gago behind the cathedral apse, or from the **Patio de las Banderas**, a pretty Plaza Mayor-style square next to the Alcázar. On the eastern edge of the Barrio, **Santa María la Blanca** (on the street of the same name) was a pre-Reconquista church; some details remain, but the whole was rebuilt in the 1660s, with spectacular rococo ornamentation inside and paintings by Murillo.

Casa de Pilatos

Open daily 9–7; adm 1000 pts.

On the eastern fringes of the old town, the Barrio Santa Cruz fades gently into other peaceful pretty areas—less ritzy, though their old streets contain more palaces. One of these, built by the Dukes of Medinaceli (1480–1571), is the **Casa de Pilatos** on Plaza Pilatos. It is a pleasant jumble of *mudéjar* and Renaissance work, with a lovely patio and lots of *azulejos* everywhere. The entrance, a mock-Roman triumphal arch done in Carrara marble by sculptors from Genoa, leads through a small court into the **Patio Principal**, with 13th-century Granadan decoration, beautiful coloured tiles, and rows of Roman statues and portrait busts—an introduction to the dukes' excellent collections of antique sculpture in the surrounding rooms, including a Roman copy of a Greek *herm* (boundary marker, with the head of the god Hermes), imperial portraits, and a bust of Hadrian's boyfriend, Antinous.

Behind the Casa de Pilatos, **San Esteban**, rebuilt from a former mosque, has an altarpiece by Zurbarán; around the corner on Calle Luis Montoto are remains of an Almoravid **aqueduct**. A few streets away to the north east, the **Palacio de la Condesa de Lebrija**, is worth a visit for its fine Roman mosaics brought from Itálica. On Calle Águilas, **San Ildefonso** has a pretty yellow and white 18th-century façade. Another post-1492 palace with *mudéjar* decoration, several streets north on Calle Bustos Tavera, is the huge **Palacio de las Dueñas**.

South of the Cathedral

Sevilla has a building even larger than its cathedral—twice as large, in fact, and probably better known to the outside world. Since the 1950s it has housed parts of the city's **university** and it does have the presence of a college building, but it began its life in the 1750s as the state Fábrica de Tabacos (Tobacco Factory). In the 19th century, it employed as many as

12,000 women to roll cigars. (One of its workers, of course, was Bizet's Carmen.) These sturdy women, with 'carnations in their hair and daggers in their garters', hung their capes on the altars of the factory chapels each morning, rocked their babies in cradles while they rolled cigars, and took no nonsense from anybody. Next to the Fábrica, the Hotel Alfonso XIII, built in 1929, is believed to be the only hotel ever commissioned by a reigning monarch—Alfonso literally used it as an annexe to the Alcázar when friends and relations came to stay. This landmark is well worth a visit, if you're not put off by an icy doorman. To the west of the hotel lies the baroque **Palacio de San Telmo**, originally a naval academy.

Parque de María Luisa

For all its old-fashioned grace, Sevilla has been one of the most forward-looking and progressive cities of Spain in the 20th century. In the 1920s, while they were redirecting the Guadalquivir and building the new port and factories that are the foundation of the city's growth today, the *sevillanos* decided to put on an exhibition. In a tremendous burst of energy, they turned the entire southern end of the city into an expanse of gardens and grand boulevards. The centre of it is **Parque de María Luisa**, a paradisiacal half-mile of palms and orange trees, covered with flower beds and dotted with hidden bowers and pavilions, one of the loveliest parks in Europe. Two of the largest pavilions on the **Plaza de América** have been turned into museums. The **Archaeological Museum** (*open Tues 3–8; Wed–Sat 9–8; Sun 9–2.30; EU citizens free, others 250 pts*) has one of the best collections of pre-Roman jewellery and icons, and some tantalizing artefacts from mysterious Tartessos. The Romans are represented, as in every other Mediterranean archaeology museum, with copies of Greek sculpture and oversized statues of emperors, but also with a mosaic of the *Triumph of Bacchus*, another of Hercules, architectural fragments, some fine glass, and finds of all sorts from Itálica and other nearby towns. Across the plaza, the **Museum of Popular Art and Customs** (*open Tues 3–8; Wed–Sat 9–8; Sun 9–2.30; EU citizens free, others 250 pts*) is Andalucía's attic, with everything from ploughs and saucepans to flamenco dresses and exhibits for the city's two famous celebrations, Semana Santa and the April Feria.

The Plaza de España

In the 1920s at least, excess was still a way of life in Sevilla, and to call attention to the *Exposición Iberoamericana* they put up a building even bigger than the Tobacco Factory. With its grand baroque towers (stolen gracefully from Santiago de Compostela), fancy bridges, staircases and immense colonnade, the Plaza de España is World Fair architecture at its grandest and most outrageous. One of the things Sevilla is famous for is its painted *azulejo* tiles; they adorn nearly every building in town, but here on the colonnade a few million of them are devoted to maps and historical scenes from every province in Spain.

La Cartuja

The island, northwest across the Río Guadalquivir, is currently open Tues–Sun, 11–6.30. For more information, © 95 448 06 11.

The Isla de la Cartuja was part of the Expo 92 site during the World Fair: it has since been repackaged as the 'Park of Discoveries', and includes four of the original Expo pavilions (focusing on Nature, Discovery, Navigation and the Future), a planetarium, a giant Omnimax Cinema and a tacky 17th-century island theme park complete with roller coaster. Everything is overpriced and uninspiring; though it costs just *500 pts* to walk around, entry to any of the pavilions is *2000 pts*, and the amusement park costs *3500 pts*. More interesting is Santa Maria de las Cuevas (*Tues–Sat 10–9; Sun 10–3; adm 300 pts*), the restored Carthusian monastery where Columbus once stayed while he mulled over his ambitions and geographical theories. Since then, the building has suffered various indignities; the monks were driven out by Marshal Soult who used it as a garrison during the Napoleonic occupation of 1810–12 and is responsible for the damage to the artesonado ceiling in the refectory—his troops used it for target practice. As if this wasn't enough, the city sold it off to wealthy Liverpudlian, Charles Pickman, in the 1830s, who had the bright idea of turning it into a ceramics factory. The brick kilns have been lovingly restored at great expense, presumably as some kind of tribute to the Industrial Age, and stand bizarre and incongruous next to the monastery garden. Now the monastery is the temporary home for the Andalucían Centre of Contemporary Art.

Shopping

All the paraphernalia associated with Spanish fantasy, such as *mantillas*, castanets, wrought iron, gypsy dresses and Andalucían dandy suits, *azulejo* tiles and embroidery, is available in Sevilla. Most of it's made here, and if you're interested in tours or just shopping, ask the tourist information office what's currently available. There are two branches of El Corte Inglés, where the well-heeled *sevillanos* shop, a branch of C&A on Calle Sierpes and a sizeable Marks & Spencer—its food department is the only place we know where you can find Indian food in Sevilla—on Plaza Duque de la Victoria. Vértice is a bookshop on Mateos Gago near the cathedral, with a small selection of English-language literature and local guide-books and history books; but for a pleasant wander head for the pedestrianised Calle Sierpes.

Sevilla ✉ *41000* **Where to Stay**

Not many of Sevilla's hotels are distinctive in any way, but there are plenty of rooms all over the centre. High season is March and April. During *Semana Santa* and the April *Feria* you should book even for inexpensive *hostales*, preferably a year ahead.

expensive

The ★★★★★**Alfonso XIII**, C/ San Fernando 2, ✆ 95 422 28 50, ✆ 95 421 60 33, was built by King Alfonso for the Exposición Iberoamericana in 1929. The grandest hotel in southern Spain, it attracts heads of state, opera stars and tourists who want a unique experience, albeit at a price. Sevilla society still meets around its lobby fountain and somewhat dreary bar (*28,000 pts for a low season single, rising to 56,000 pts for a double during feria*). The ★★★★★★**Hotel Colón**, C/ Canalejas 1, ✆ 95 422 29 00, ✆ 95 422 09 38, is grand and extremely comfortable. It used to be a haunt of bullfighters and their hangers-on. (*20,000–38,000 pts*).

By the Macarena walls, the ★★★★**Sol Macarena**, San Juan de Rivera 2, ✆ 95 437 58 00, ✆ 95 438 18 03, is another classy establishment although it's not exactly central; there is a beautiful *azulejo*-tiled fountain, a swimming pool, and views over the city from the roof-top terrace. The service is excellent and rates are very reasonable for this category (*from 14,000 pts*).

The utterly charming ★★★★**Hotel Doña María**, C/ Don Remondo 19, ✆ 95 422 49 90, ✆ 95 421 95 46, is superbly located by the cathedral. Among the mostly antique furniture are some beautifully painted headboards (*13,000–26,000 pts*). The delicious **Los Seises**, Segovias s/n in the Barrio, ✆ 95 422 94 95, ✆ 95 422 43 34, offers urban chic on a small scale—only it's well-nigh impossible to find it on your own, so take a cab (*16,000–35,000 pts*). The **Hotel Taberna de Alabardero**, Zaragoza 20, ✆ 95 456 06 37, in a former nobleman's house, has intimate rooms, all charmingly decorated. Prices include breakfast in the award-winning restaurant (*18,000 pts*).

moderate

Las Casas de la Judería, Callejón de Dos Hermanos 7, ✆ 95 441 51 50, ✆ 95 422 2170, is a row of perfectly restored townhouses in the Barrio Santa Cruz, expertly run by the Medina family—well-known and very stylish Sevilla hoteliers (*10,000–13,000 pts*). The ★**Hotel Simón**, García de Vinuesa 14, ✆ 95 422 66 60, ✆ 95 456 22 41, in a fine position just off the Avenida de la Constitución by the cathedral, is in a restored 18th-century mansion, spoilt by a Coke machine in the entrance courtyard (*6000–9000 pts*). The **Hotel Alvarez Quintero**, Alvarez Quintero 12 ✆ 95 422 12 98, has fine views of the Cathedral, air-conditioned rooms *from 14,000 pts*, and a delightful patio. The ★★**Hostal Atenas**, C/ Caballerizas 1, ✆ 95 421 80 47, is quiet and very nice, in a good location between the Plaza Pilatos and the cathedral. Take a cab, it's hard to find (*8000–13,000 pts*). The ★**Hostal Plaza Sevilla**, Canalejas 2, ✆ 95 421 71 49, ✆ 95 421 07 73, has a beautiful neoclassical facade, the work of Aníbal González, architect of the 1929 Exposición, and is ideally placed near the restaurants and bars of St Eloy (*10,000–13,000 pts*). The ★**Pensión Toledo**, Santa Teresa 15, ✆ 95 421 53 35, is respectable and good value (*5000–7000 pts*).

inexpensive

For inexpensive *hostales*, the Barrio Santa Cruz is surprisingly the best place to look. Even in July and August, you'll be able to find a place on the quiet side streets off C/ Mateos Gago. The ★**Monreal**, C/ Rodrigo Caro 8, ✆ 95 421 41 66, is closest to the cathedral, a lively place with almost too much character and a good cheap restaurant when it's open (*4000–7000 for a double, singles available at an amazing 2500 pts*). The ★**Pensión Fabiola**, Fabiola 6, ✆ 95 421 83 46 (*6000–8000 pts*), and **Pension Archeros**, Archeros 23, ✆ 95 441 84 65 (*3500–6000 pts for a double, 2000 pts for a single*) are quiet, cooler than most in summer and have little patios. **Hostal Círdoba**, Farnesio 12, ✆ 95 422 74 98 (*3000–4500 pts*) and the ★**Hostal El Buen Dormir**, Farnesio 8, ✆ 95 421 74 92 (*3500–4500 pts*) both offer clean rooms with fans. Cheapest of the lot are **Huespedes La Montorena**, San Clemente 12, ✆ 95 441 24 07 (*singles for 1500 pts and doubles for 3000 pts*) and **Pension Cruces El Patio**, Plaza Cruces de las Cruces 10, ✆ 95 422 96 33 (*dormitory beds for 1200 pts, singles at 2500 pts and doubles from 4500 pts*). There are some other cheap options outside Barrio Santa Cruz. The family-run **Hostal La Francesa**, Juan Rabadan 28, ✆ 95 438 31 07, is in a quiet part of town, close to the river and San Lorenzo Church (*from 3000 pts)* and the **Hostal ñ** (*4000–6000 pts*), Dona Guiomar 1, near the Plaza Nueva, ✆ 95 421 68 40, is spacious, clean and run by a slightly paranoid old woman who behaves like she's still living under Franco.

Eating Out

Restaurants here are more expensive than in most of Spain, but even around the cathedral and the Barrio Santa Cruz, in contrast to Córdoba, there are few places that can simply be dismissed as tourist traps. Remember that in the evening the *sevillanos*, even more than most Andalucíans, enjoy bar-hopping for tapas, rather than sitting down to one meal; two *sevillanos* in a bar is a party, three is a fiesta.

expensive

A few places have attractions beyond the cuisine: **La Albahaca**, Pza. Santa Cruz 12, ✆ 95 422 07 14, is situated in Santa Cruz on one of Sevilla's most delightful small squares. Specialities include scorpion fish with fennel and peanuts, mushrooms with green asparagus, and partridge with endives. Prices start at around *5000 pts* per head. *Closed Sun*. Nearby is **Corral del Agua**, Callejón del Agua 6, ✆ 95 422 07 14; well-seasoned travellers usually steer clear of cutesy wishing-wells, but the garden in which this one stands is a haven of peace and shade, perfect for a lazy lunch or unashamedly romantic dinner. The Corral del Agua is next to Washington Irving's garden. Splendidly situated on the corner of the Jardines Alcázar, opposite the university, is one of Sevilla's best-loved restaurants, the **Egaña-Oriza**, San Fernando 41, ✆ 95 422 72 11. Among its tempting delights are clams on the half-shell, baked *hongos* mushrooms, and a kind of *sevillano* jugged hare (*6000 pts minimum with wine*). *Closed Sat lunch, Sun and Aug*. Attached to it, the restaurant's own tapas bar is chic, bright, cosmopolitan—and the Basque tapas are sensational.

Northwest of La Giralda, you can dine in one of Sevilla's most celebrated restaurants, the **Taberna del Alabardero**, Zaragoza 20, ✆ 95 456 06 37. It's Michelin-starred, formerly a nobleman's house, and serves such specialities as aubergine and shrimp in filo, and *urta* (a firm-fleshed, white fish caught locally around Rota) cooked in red wine. There are seven guest rooms available if you over-indulge and can't make it home. The taberna is open daily year-round; its basement café serves an excellent set lunch at *1500 pts*. By the cathedral, in the narrow Argote de Molina (at No.26), is **Mesón Don Raimundo**, ✆ 95 422 33 55, a restaurant in what was once a convent. No enforced abstinence here, though. You can pig out on the large selection of fish, shellfish, and game dishes amid an eclectic décor of religious artefacts and suits of armour (*3500–4500 pts*). *Closed Sun evening*. Along the Triana side of the Guadalquivir you can dine with a tremendous view of the Torre del Oro and La Giralda at the restaurant **Río Grande**, C/ Betis s/n, ✆ 95 427 39 56. The kitchen here specializes in regional cuisine (*3500 pts*). The place has a faded Edwardian elegance about it, but the food doesn't quite cut the mustard. Along from here is the unfortunately-named **Ox's**, C/ Betis 61, ✆ 95 427 95 85, with Basque novelties—cod-stuffed peppers, fish and steaks (*from 4000 pts*). *Closed Sun night and Aug*.

moderate

Don Raimundo also owns two other restaurants near his Mesón: **La Barca**, Placentines 25, ✆ 95 456 04 91, which specializes in fish and seafood; and **Las Meninas** on Calle Manara. Also serving excellent fish tapas is **Restaurante A Babor**,

C/ Teodosio 51. The **Bodegón Torre del Oro**, C/ Santander 15, ☎ 95 421 42 41, specializes in *urta*. There's a three-course set meal with wine (*1300 pts*) and the *raciones* are good.

In a country where meat and fish reign supreme, it's a nice surprise to find **La Mandrágora**, a very friendly vegetarian restaurant with an interesting menu (*2000 pts*). *Closed Sun*. A good place for lunch is the **Restaurante San Marco**, Cuna 6, ☎ 95 421 24 40, in the shopping district, no relation of the **Pizzeria San Marco**, Meson del Moro 6–10, ☎ 95 421 43 90.

inexpensive

One particular pleasure, in a city which pursues so many, is to set out on a bar crawl, trying different sherries and tapas. Some will appeal, others will not; you will soon discover a favourite. To start, the lively tapas bar **Bodega La Andana**, C/ Argote de Molina, is where hordes of Sevilla's *caballeros* and *señoritas* spill out onto the pavement, particularly at weekends, to misspend their youth.

Around the corner you can eat decently at the bar-restaurant **Gonzalo**, on the corner of Alemanes and Argote de Molina, with the Giralda looming overhead. There's a reasonably priced and varied menu (*around 1200 pts*), but the walls could do with a lick of paint. **Bar Giralda**, C/ Mateos Gago, as its name suggests, is closer still and has a good selection of sherries. **Bar Modesto** is a short walk away from the cathedral on Calle Cano y Cueta, serving breakfast, *raciones* and full meals.

Kiosko de las Flores, a little difficult to find but well worth the search, is the best tapas bar in Sevilla, and the most charming in all of Andalucía, serving light fish lunches of *boquerones*, among other things. The place is an informal café-bar, right by the Puente de Isabel II, and part of it looks over the water. Prices are a little high—a glorified fishy snack with a drink costs *1300 pts*.

North of the cathedral, between the church of San Pedro and the convent Espíritu Santo, is **El Rinconcillo**, at C/ Gerona 42, the oldest bar in Sevilla. The place dates back to 1670 and is decorated in moody brown *azulejos*; here lively *sevillano cognoscenti* gather to dabble at the tasty nibbles. The staff, oblivious, chalk up the bill on the bar.

cheap

Sevilla's cheapest restaurants lurk around Calle San Eloy. Some almost give meals away, and they're worth no more. It's better to stick with the tapas and *mariscos* bars here and in the little streets of Calle Tetuán and Calle Sierpes. The **Antigua Bodequita** is a find, a tiny bar opposite the church on Plaza del Salvador, but if you just fancy cakes, coffee or ice cream head for **La Campana** on Calle Sierpes. Established in 1885, it's probably the prettiest pâtisserie around.

There are a string of cheap restaurants at the Guadalquivir end of Calle San Jose Santa Maria La Blanca in Santa Cruz. Most offer a three-course set menu including a drink for *800 pts*. The **Il Garibaldi** has good options for breakfast and a delicious range of frozen yogurts.

There are scores of great tapas bars in Sevilla where you can while away the hours. The **Bar Manolo**, Plaza de Alfalfa, is the best of a number of tapas bars on the square, and is lively at breakfast time and in the evening. The **Bar Alicantina** nearby, on the Plaza del Salvador, has great *ensalada rusa* and is a favoured hangout of the young and fashionable. The **Becerrita Centro**, near the cathedral on C/Hernando Colon,1, serves some of Sevilla's most traditional and tastiest tapas whilst the **Bar Giralda**, Mateos Gago 1, in an old Moorish bath-house, has a great range to choose from and is popular with tourists and locals. Opposite is a more rustic and basic local haunt, the **Bodega de Juan Garcia Aviles**, Mateos Gago 20. In Barrio Santa Cruz, try **Hostaría del Laurel**, Plaza de los Venerables 5, which serves superb tapas in a room filled with hanging *jamon* and beautiful Triana tiles. The **Casa Roman**, next door at Plaza de los Venerables 1, is famous for its ham tapas. In Triana, across the river, the moorish-looking **Bar Anslema**, Pages del Corro 49, has occasional impromptu flamenco. Opposite is **Las Golondrinas**, Antillano Campos 26, which serves great **alcauciles** (artichokes) and tortilla in a charming tiled two-floor bar.

If you've been longing to experience **flamenco**, Sevilla is a good place to do it, though not the best—shows in Granada and Córdoba are more authentic. The most touristy flamenco factories will hit you for *1500 pts* and up per drink. Bars in Triana and other areas do it better for less; Calle Salado and environs in Triana, for example, has some good bars like **La Caseta**, C/Febo 36, which, though a long way from either Sevillana dance or pure flamenco, is young, vibrant and popular with locals. The equally youthful and occasionally impromptu **El Simpecao**, Paseo de la O, near the Iglesia de O in Triana, is closer to the real thing. There are more venues across the river in Barrio Santa Cruz. The king of modern flamenco, the late El Camaron de la Isla, used to play at **La Carboneria**, C/Levies 18, and the bar is still one of the best venues in the city for extemporaneous performances of all styles. Thursday is best for flamenco. If you're looking for Sevillano dancing (very similar to flamenco though slightly less tortured and frenetic) head for **El Tamboril** on Plaza Santa Cruz, which is as popular with Sevillanos as it is with tourists. **Los Gallos,** a few doors away, is less spontaneous, with a *3000 pts* entrance charge and Sevillano and flamenco dancing lit by the flashes of tourist cameras. Even more formal is **El Palacio Andaluz**, Av. Maria Auxiliadora, 18B, a 1½-hour staged show for tourists in an expensive Sevilla restaurant.

They do play other kinds of music in Sevilla, and two publications, *El Giraldillo* and *Ocio*, available around town, have listings. For mainstream **drama**, the best-known theatre is the **Teatro Lope de Vega**, Avda. María Luisa, ✆ 95 423 45 46, built for the 1929 exhibition. The **Teatro de Maestranza**, Pso. de Cristóbal Colín, ✆ 95 422 33 44, has quickly established itself as one of the top **opera** houses in Europe.

Take a **river cruise** along the Guadalquivir. Three companies do it daily (3.45 and 4.30), all from around the Torre del Oro: Cruceros Turisticos Torre del Oro S.L, ✆ 95 421 13 96, Cruceros del Sur, ✆ 95 456 16 72, and Buque El Patio, Paseo de Colon, 11 (✆ 95 421 38 36). See a **bullfight** in the famous Maestranza if you can, but don't just turn up! Get tickets as far ahead as possible; prices at the ring office, ✆ 95 422 45 77, will be cheaper than at the little stands on Calle Sierpes.

Getting Around

There is no train service for the towns around Sevilla, but plenty of buses. Itálica is on the Ctra. Menda, with local buses leaving every half-hour from the Plaza de Armas, near the Puerto del Cachorro; the main highway east and south is the NIV.

If you're travelling south on your way to Jerez or Cádiz, stops at a few towns on the way will make an interesting alternative to the big four-lane highway. **Alcalá de Guadaira**, off the N334, is jocularly known in Sevilla as Alcalá de los Panaderos ('of the bakers'), as it used to supply the city with its daily bread. Its **castle** is the best-preserved Almohad fortress in Andalucía. Just outside Utrera, the tiny village of **Palmar de Troya** received a visit in 1968 from the Virgin Mary (to little girls, as usual) that has led to the founding of a new church, the 'Orden de la Santa Faz'. In **Lebrija**, the church of **Santa María de la Oliva** is really a 12th-century Almohad mosque, with a typical Middle Eastern roof of small domes and a tower that is a miniature version of La Giralda—but Lebrija is better-known for its wine.

Itálica

Open Tues–Sat 9–8; Sun 10–3; adm free for EU citizens, others 250 pts.

Eight kilometres (5 miles) north of the city, in the direction of Mérida, the only significant Roman ruins in Andalucía are at **Itálica**, a city founded in the 3rd century BC by Scipio Africanus as a home for his veterans. Itálica thrived in the imperial age. The Guadalquivir had a reputation for constantly changing its course in the old days, and this may explain the presence of two important cities so close together. Three great emperors, Trajan, Hadrian and Theodosius, were born here. The biggest ruins are an **amphitheatre**, with seating for 40,000, some remains of temples, and a street of villa foundations. The village of Santiponce, near the ruins, has a fine Gothic-*mudéjar* monastery built for the Cistercians in 1301: **San Isidoro del Campo**, with another gruesome Saint Jerome, carved in the 1600s by Juan Martínez Montañés (1566–1649), on the altarpiece.

From Sevilla to Córdoba

Getting There

There are two ways to go, both of approximately equal length. The **train**, and most of the **buses**, unfortunately take the duller route through the flat lands along the Guadalquivir. The only landmark here is the Spanish-Moorish castle of **Almodóvar del Río**, perched romantically on a height planted with olive trees. The southern route (the NIV) also follows the Guadalquivir valley, but the scenery is a more varied, and the road passes through two fine towns, Carmona and Écija. There are regular buses from Sevilla to these towns, from where you can find buses for Córdoba.

Tourist Information

Carmona: Oficina Municipal de Turismo, Arco de la Puerta de Sevilla, © 95 419 09 55, *carmona@andal.es. Open Mon–Fri 9–2, Sat and Sun 10.30–1.30.*

Écija: Ayuntamiento, Pza. de España, © 95 590 02 40. *Open Mon–Fri 9–1.*

Carmona and Marchena

The first town along the NIV, Carmona, seems a miniature Sevilla. It is probably much older. Remains of a Neolithic settlement have been found around town; the Phoenician colony that replaced it grew into a city and prospered throughout Roman and Moorish times. Pedro the Cruel favoured it and rebuilt most of its **Alcázar**. Sitting proudly on top of the town, with views over the valley, this fortress is now a national *parador*. Carmona is well worth a day's exploration. Its walls, mostly Moorish fortifications built over Roman foundations, are still standing, including a grand gateway on the road from Sevilla, the **Puerta de Sevilla**. Continue through the arch and up to the palm-decked Plaza de San Fernando; the Ayuntamiento here has a Roman mosaic of Medusa in its courtyard. Next, take Calle Martín López up to the lofty 15th-century church of **Santa María**, built on the site of an old mosque (*open daily 9–12 and 6–9*). The old quarters of town have an ensemble of fine palaces, and *mudéjar* and Renaissance churches. On one of these, **San Pedro** (1466), you'll see another imitation of La Giralda, *La Giraldilla*. Carmona's prime attraction is the **Roman necropolis**, a series of rock-cut tombs off the Avenida Jorge Bonsor. Some, like the 'Tomb of Servilia', are elaborate creations with subterranean chambers and vestibules, pillars, domed ceilings and carved reliefs (*open June–Sept, Tues–Fri 9–2; Oct–May, Tues–Fri 10–2; Sat and Sun all year round 10–2; adm free to EU citizens, 250 pts for others; © 95 414 08 11*). Near the entrance to the site are remains of the Roman amphitheatre, forlorn and unexcavated.

Twenty-eight kilometres south of Carmona on the C339, **Marchena** still retains many of its wall defences dating from Roman times, with later Moorish and Christian additions. The Gothic church of **San Juan Bautista** has a *retablo* by Alejo Fernández and a sculpture by Pedro Roldán. There's also a small museum with a collection of paintings by Zurbarán. Nearby **El Arahal** is a bleached white town well worth visiting for its baroque monuments, notably the church of **La Victoria** of *mudéjar* origin.

Écija

Écija makes much of one of its nicknames, the 'city of towers' and tries to play down the other—the 'frying pan of Andalucía', which isn't exactly fair. Any Andalucían town can overheat you thoroughly on a typical summer's day and, if Écija is a degree hotter and a little less breezy than most, only a born Andalucían could tell the difference. Ask one and you'll soon learn that the Andalucíans are the only people yet discovered who talk about the weather more than the English. Don't be put off by the clinical outskirts of the town; all is forgiven when you reach the **Plaza de España**, one of the loveliest in Andalucía, charmingly framed by tall palms with an exquisite fountain at its centre. The façade of the 18th-century **Santa María** wouldn't look out of place in a Sergio Leone movie. Most of the **towers** are sumptuously ornate, rebuilt after the great earthquake of 1755—the one that flattened Lisbon. Santa María has one, along with **San Juan Bautista**, gaily decorated in coloured tiles, and **San Gil**. This last is the highest of the towers, and within are paintings by Alejo Fernández and Villegas Marmolejo. Écija also has a set of Renaissance and baroque palaces second in Andalucía only to those in Úbeda; most of these showy façades can be seen on or near the **Calle de los Caballeros**. Worth visiting is the **Mudéjar Palace**, dating from the 14th century, where you can find some interesting archaeological remains, part *mudéjar*, part baroque, some Roman mosaics, and various reliefs, coins and glass. There's a museum in the

Peñaflor Palace on Calle de Castellar, with exhibits of 18th-century art and sculpture, contemporary art and local traditional costumes. The palace itself (1728), with its grandiose façade and lovely patio, is one of the outstanding works of Andalucían baroque. In the evening the town buzzes. After the big-city crush of Sevilla, you might find that this is the perfect place to spend a couple of days—busy enough to be interesting, but not too frantic.

Where to Stay and Eating Out

Carmona ✉ 39554

The ★★★★**Parador Alcázar del Rey Don Pedro**, C/ Los Alcázares, ✆ 95 414 10 10, ✉ 95 414 17 12, occupying a section of Cruel Pete's summer palace, is the finest in Andalucía for style and comfort. It has superlative views, a garden and pool and is good value for 18,500–20,000 pts. It used to be *the* place to stay, until along came ★★★★★**Casa de Carmona**, Pza. de Lasso 7, ✆ 95 414 33 00, ✉ 95 414 37 52. Lovingly restored by Marta Medina and her artist son Felipe, this 16th-century palace is the last word in refined good taste (*from 15,000 pts*). Among the town's attractive little *pensiones* and *hostales* are the ★**Casa Carmelo**, C/ San Pedro 15, ✆ 95 414 05 72, and the ★**Pensión Comercio**, C/ Torre del Oro, ✆ 95 414 00 18 (*both for 4000–5000 pts*). The restaurant **San Fernando**, Pza. San Fernando, has the best reputation in town. The five-course set menu is *5000 pts. Closed Sun eve, Mon and Aug.* Fish features largely on the menu at the **Parador**, where prices are more reasonable, and at **El Ancla**, Bonifacio 4, ✆ 95 414 15 18, where a full fish meal with wine will set you back a moderate *3000–3500 pts. Closed Mon and Sun nights.* **Mesón de la Reja** is on the main street as you enter from Sevilla. With a cool *azulejo* interior, it's a good place to try *cola de toro* and down a beer (*about 1000 pts*), while keeping an eye on the bus departures opposite.

Marchena ✉ 39554

The ★★**Ponce**, Pza. de Alvarado 2, ✆ 95 584 60 88, a hostal, has rooms for *5000 pts.* The ★★**Hostal Los Ángeles** is on the Ctra. Sevilla–Granada, Km 67, ✆ 95 484 70 88; it's basic but quite lively (*4500 pts*). Try local specialities at **Los Muleros**, ✆ 95 484 31 99, and **El Fogón**, both on Travesía de San Ignacio (*around 1500 pts*).

Écija ✉ 41400

The hotels are mostly motels on the outskirts, serving traffic on the Madrid–Cádiz highway. The ★★**Hotel Platería**, C/ Garcilópez 7, ✆ 95 483 50 10, just off the main square with a lovely marble courtyard is the best in town (*7000 pts*). The friendly ★★**Ciudad del Sol**, C/ Cervantes 42, ✆ 95 483 03 00, ✉ 95 483 58 79, is also good, with air-conditioned rooms (*6000 pts*). If that's full, try the ★★**Astigi**, ✆ 95 483 01 62, ✉ 95 483 57 01, on the same road (*7500 pts*). The delightful little **Fonda Santa Cruz**, Romero Gordillo 8, ✆ 95 483 02 22, has the simple rooms open out to the tiled courtyard (*3500 pts*). The best place to eat in town is the stylish **Bodegón del Gallego**, C/ A. Aparicio 3, ✆ 95 483 26 18, which concentrates on *andaluz* dishes (*3500 pts*). Also in the heart of town, the **Pasareli**, Pasaje Virgen del Rocío, ✆ 95 483 20 24, is a surprisingly efficient little restaurant (*under 2000 pts*).

Córdoba

There are a few spots around the Mediterranean where the presence of past glories becomes almost tangible, a mixture of mythic antiquity, lost power and dissipated energy that broods over a place like a ghost. In Istanbul you can find it, in Rome, or among the monuments of Egypt, and also here on the banks of the Guadalquivir at Córdoba's southern gate. Looking around, you can see reminders of three defunct empires: a Roman bridge, a triumphal arch built for Felipe II and Córdoba's Great Mosque, more than a thousand years old. The first reminds us of the city's beginnings, the second of its decline; the last one scarcely seems credible, as it speaks of an age when Córdoba was one of the most brilliant metropolises of all Europe. Córdoba's recent growth has allowed it a chance to renovate its sparkling old quarters and monuments. With the new prosperity has come a contentment the city probably hasn't known since the Reconquista. Everyone who visits Córdoba comes for the Great Mosque, but you should spare some time to explore the city itself. Old Córdoba is one of the largest medieval quarters of any European city and retains its Moorish character in a maze of whitewashed alleys opening into the loveliest patios in all Andalucía.

History

Roman *Corduba*, built on a prehistoric site, was almost from the start the leading city of interior Spain, capital of the province of *Hispania Ulterior*, and later of the reorganized province of Bætica. Córdoba had a reputation as the garden spot of Hispania; it gave Roman letters Lucan and both Senecas among others, testimony to its prominence as a city of learning. Córdoba became Christianized at an early date. Ironically, the True Faith got its comeuppance here in 572, when the Arian Visigoths under Leovigild captured the city from Byzantine rule. When the Arabs conquered, they found it an important town still, and it became the capital of Al-Andalus when Abd ar-Rahman established the Umayyad emirate in 756. For 300 years, Córdoba enjoyed the position of unqualified leader of Al-Andalus, and a city without equal in the West as a centre of learning. It would be enough to mention two 12th-century contemporaries, **Averroës**, the Muslim scientist and Aristotelian philosopher who contributed so much to the rebirth of classical learning in Europe, and **Moses Maimonides**, the Jewish philosopher whose reconciliation of faith and reason were assumed into Christianity by Thomas Aquinas. Medieval Córdoba was a great trading centre, and its luxury goods were coveted throughout western Europe. At its height, picture Córdoba as a city of bustling international markets, great palaces, schools, baths and mosques, with 28 suburbs and the first street lighting in Europe. In it Muslims, Christians, and Jews lived in harmony, at least until the coming of the fanatical Almoravids and Almohads. We can sense a certain decadence; street riots in Córdoba were an immediate cause of the break-up of the caliphate in 1031, but here, as in Sevilla, the coming of the Reconquista was an unparalleled catastrophe.

When Fernando III 'the Saint' captured the city in 1236, much of the population chose flight over putting themselves at the mercy of the priests, although history records that he was unusually tolerant of the Jews. It did not last. Three centuries of Castilian rule sufficed to rob Córdoba of all its glories and turn it into a depressed backwater. Only in the last hundred years has it begun to recover; today Córdoba has also become an industrial city, though you wouldn't guess it from its sympathetically restored centre. It is the third city of Andalucía, and the first and only big town since Franco's death to have elected a communist mayor and council.

By train: Córdoba is on the major Madrid–Sevilla rail line, so there are about 12 trains a day in both directions by AVE, with a journey time of 43 minutes from Sevilla and 1hour 40 mins from Madrid. There are also frequent AVE/Talgo services to Málaga (about 2 hours 15 mins). There is also one Talgo daily to Cádiz, Valencia and Barcelona, and regular trains to Huelva, Algeciras and Alicante. Trains for Granada and Algeciras pass through Bobadilla Junction, and may require a change. Córdoba's station is off the Avenida de América, 1.6km north of La Mezquita, © 95 749 02 02; ticket office at Ronda de los Tejares 10.

AV. MEDINA AZAHARA

ANTONIO MAURA

AV. REPÚBLICA ARGENTINA

PASEO DE LA VICTORIA

CONCEPCIÓN

San Nicolás

Almodovar Gate

F. RUANO

BUEN PASTOR

C. SEVILLA

C. BARROSA

BLANC

Casa del Indiano

ALMANZOR

Synagogue (ruin)

Municipal Museum

Plaza Juda Levi

CALLE DE LAS FLORES

Plaza Benavente

C. REY HERE

AV. CONDE VELLELLANO

AV. DR. FLEMING

C. TORRIJOS

La Mezquita

AMADORDE LOS RIOS

CARDENAL GONZALEZ

Alcazar de los Reyes Christianos

Triunfo

Puerta del Puente

AV. CORREGIOR

Moorish Walls (ruins)

Waterwheel

AVENIDA DEL ALCÁZAR

PUENTE ROMANO

Zoo

PUENTE DE SAN RAFAEL

Calahorra Tower

AVENIDA CONFEDERACIÓN

N

By bus: Buses for Sevilla (at least three daily), Granada, Cádiz and Málaga and most nearby towns leave from the Alsina Graells terminal on Avenida Medina Azahara 29, ✆ 95 723 64 74. Buses for Madrid (one daily), Valencia (three daily) and Barcelona (two a day), leave from the Ureña office on Avenida de Cervantes 22, ✆ 95 747 23 52. Other firms do go to Sevilla—but the train's a better bet for that city and for Málaga.

The Córdoba bus network is complicated and it's always best to check with tourist information as to times and departure points. If you want to go to Medinat az-Zahra, take bus no.01 for Villarubia or Veredón (from Republica Argentina at Azahara); it will drop you off about 2km (1.3 miles) from the site.

Tourist Information

The very helpful regional tourist office is on C/ Torrijos 10 next to the Mezquita, ✆ 95 747 12 35. The municipal office is in the Judería on Plaza Judá Levi, ✆ 95 720 05 22: both have detailed maps. To arrange personal guides to the mosque and other sights, ✆ 95 748 69 97, ask at the tourist offices, or turn up at the mosque itself.

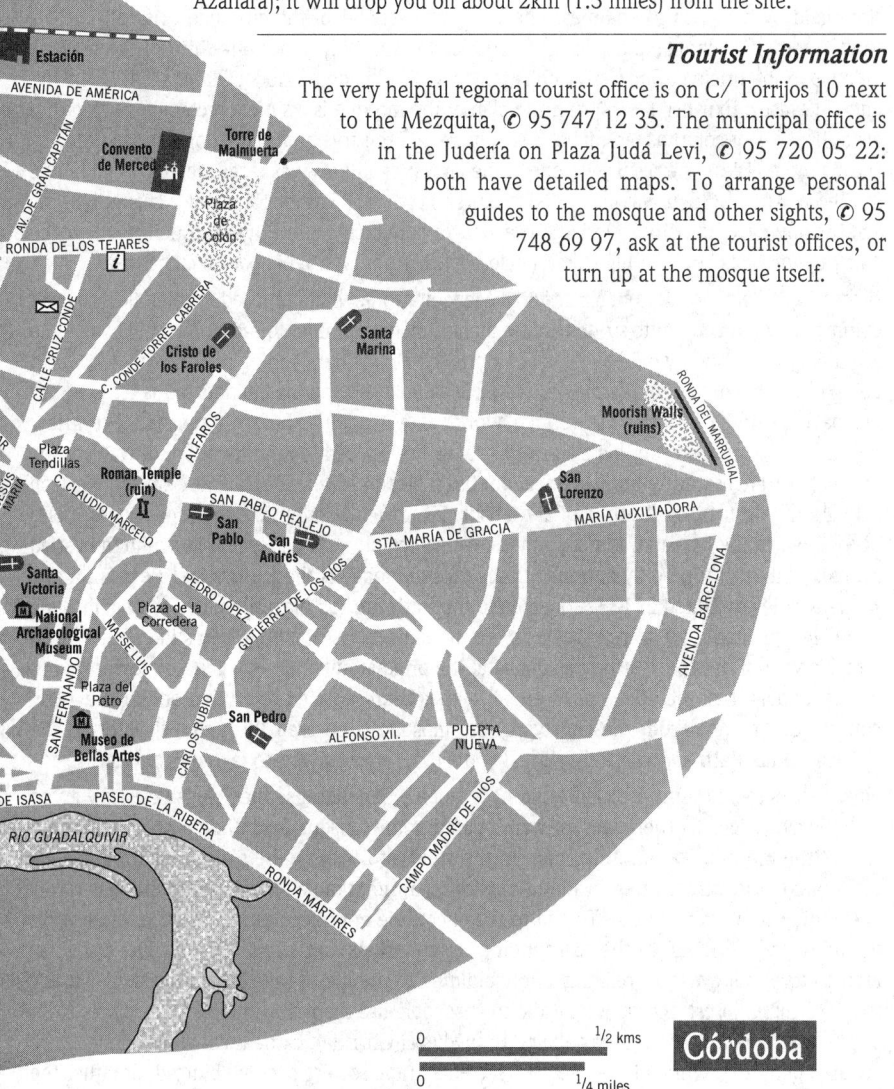

Córdoba

La Mezquita

Open Mon—Sat 10–7, Sun 1.30–7 in summer; 10–5.30 in winter; adm 750 pts.

La Mezquita is the local name for Abd ar-Rahman's Great Mosque. Mezquita means 'mosque' and even though the building has officially been a cathedral for more than 750 years, no one could ever mistake its origins. Abd ar-Rahman I, founder of a new state, felt it necessary to construct a great religious monument for his capital. As part of his plan, he also wished to make it a centre of pilgrimage to increase the sense of divorce from eastern Islam; Mecca was at the time held by his Abbasid enemies. The site, at the centre of the city, had originally held a Roman temple of Janus, and later a Visigothic church. Only about one-third of the mosque belongs to the original. Successive enlargements were made by Abd ar-Rahman II, al-Hakim, and al-Mansur. Expansion was easy; the plan of the mosque is a simple rectangle divided into aisles by rows of columns, and its size was increased to serve a growing population simply by adding more aisles. The result was one of the largest of all mosques, exceeded only by the one in Mecca. After 1236, it was converted to use as a cathedral without any major changes. In the 1520s, however, the city's clerics succeeded in convincing the Royal Council to allow the construction of a choir and high altar, enclosed structures typical of Spanish cathedrals.

Most people come away from a visit to La Mezquita somewhat confused. The endless rows of columns and red and white striped arches make a picture familiar to most of us, but actually to see them in this gloomy old hall does not increase one's understanding of the work. It's worth going into some detail, for learning to see La Mezquita the way its builders did is the best key we have to understanding the refined world of Al-Andalus. Before entering, take a few minutes to circumnavigate this massive pile of bricks. Spaced around its 685m of wall are the original entrances and windows, excellent examples of Moorish art. Those on the western side are the best, from the time of al-Mansur: interlaced Visigothic horseshoe arches, floral decorations in the Roman tradition, and Islamic calligraphy and patterns, a lesson in the varied sources of this art. The only entrance to the mosque today is the **Puerta del Perdón**, a fine *mudéjar* gateway added in 1377, opening to the **Patio de los Naranjos**, the original mosque courtyard, planted with orange trees, where the old Moorish fountain can still be seen. Built into the wall of the courtyard, over the gate, the original minaret—a legendary tower said to be the model for all the others in Al-Andalus—has been replaced by an ill-proportioned 16th-century bell tower. From the courtyard, the mosque is entered through a little door, the **Puerta de las Palmas**, where they'll sell you a ticket and tell you to take off your hat.

Now here is the first surprise. The building is gloomy only because the Spanish clerics wanted it that way. Originally there was no wall separating the mosque from the courtyard, and that side of the mosque was entirely open. In the courtyard, trees were planted to continue the rows of columns, translating inside to outside in a remarkable tour-de-force that has rarely been equalled in architecture. To add to the effect, the entrances along the other three walls would have been open to the surrounding busy markets and streets. It isn't just a trick of architecture, but a way of relating a holy building to the life of the city around it. In Turkey they call them 'forest' mosques, and the townspeople use them like indoor parks, places to sit and reflect or talk over everyday affairs. In medieval Christian cathedrals, whose doors were always open, it was much the same. The sacred and the secular become blurred, or rather the latter is elevated to a higher plane. In Córdoba, this principle is perfected.

In the aesthetics of this mosque, too, there is more than meets the eye. Many European writers have seen it as devoid of spirituality, a plain prayer-hall with pretty arches. To the Christian mind it is difficult to comprehend. Christian churches are modelled after the Roman basilica, a government hall, a seat of authority with a long central aisle designed to humble the suppliant as he approaches the praetor's throne (altar). Mosques are designed with great care to free the mind from such behaviour patterns. In this one, the guiding principle is a rarefied abstraction—the same kind of abstraction that governs Islamic geometric decoration. The repetition of columns is like a meditation in stone, a mirror of Creation where unity and harmony radiate from innumerable centres. Another contrast with Christian churches can be found in an obscure matter—the distribution of weight. The Gothic masters of the Middle Ages learned to pile stone upwards from great piers and buttresses to amazing heights, to build an edifice that aspires upwards to heaven. Córdoba's architects amplified the height of their mosque only modestly by a daring invention—adding a second tier of arches on top of the first. They had to, constrained as they were by the short columns they were recycling from Roman buildings, but the result was to make an 'upside-down' building, where weight increases the higher it goes, a play of balance and equilibrium that adds much to the mosque's effect. There are about 580 of these columns, mostly from Roman ruins and Visigothic churches the Muslims pulled down; originally, legend credits La Mezquita with a thousand. Some came from as far as Constantinople, a present from the emperors. The same variety can be seen in the capitals—Roman, Visigothic, Moorish and a few mysteries.

The surviving jewel of the mosque is its *mihrab*, added in the 10th century under al-Hakim II, an octagonal chamber set into the wall and covered by a beautiful dome of interlocking arches. A Byzantine emperor, Nikephoras Phokas, sent artists to help with its mosaic decoration, and a few tons of enamel chips and coloured glass cubes for them to work with. Though the *mihrab* is no longer at the centre of La Mezquita, it was at the time of al-Hakim II; the aisle extending from it was the axis of the original mosque. Looking back from the *mihrab*, you will see what once was the exterior wall, built in Abd ar-Rahman II's extension, from the year 848. Its gates, protected indoors, are as good as those on the west façade, and better preserved. Near the *mihrab* is the **Capilla de Villaviciosa**, a Christian addition of 1377 with fancy convoluted *mudéjar* arches that almost succeed in upstaging the Moorish work. Behind it is a small chapel, usually closed off. Fortunately, you can see most of the **Capilla Real** above the barriers; its exuberant stucco and *azulejo* decoration are among the greatest works of *mudéjar* art. Built in the 14th century as a funeral chapel for Fernando IV and Alfonso XI of Castile, it is contemporary with the Alhambra and shows some influence of the styles developing in Granada. Far more serious intrusions are the 16th-century **Coro** (choir) and **Capilla Mayor** (high altar). Not unlovely in themselves, they would not offend anywhere but here. Fortunately, La Mezquita is so large that from many parts of it you won't even notice them. Begun in 1523, the Plateresque Coro was substantially altered in the 18th century, with additional stucco decoration, as well as a set of baroque choir stalls by Pedro Duque Cornejo. Between the Coro and Capilla Mayor is the tomb of Leopold of Austria, Bishop of Córdoba at the time the works were completed (and, interestingly, Charles V's uncle). For the rest of the Christian contribution, dozens of locked, mouldering chapels line the outer walls of the mosque. Never comfortable as a Christian building, today the cathedral seems to be hardly used at all, and regular Sunday masses are generally relegated to a small corner of the building.

Around La Mezquita

The masses of tatty souvenir stands and third-rate cafés that surround La Mezquita on its busiest days unwittingly do their best to re-create the atmosphere of the Moorish *souks* that once thrived here, but walk a block in any direction and you'll enter the essential Córdoba—brilliant whitewashed lanes with glimpses into dreamily beautiful patios, each one a floral extravaganza. One of the best is a famous little alley called **Calle de las Flores** ('street of the flowers') just a block northeast of La Mezquita, although sadly its charms are diminished by the hordes of tourists who flock to see it.

Below La Mezquita, along the Guadalquivir, the melancholic plaza called **Puerta del Puente** marks the site of Córdoba's southern gate with a decorative **arch** put up in 1571, celebrating the reign of Felipe II. The very curious Churrigueresque monument next to it, with a statue of San Rafael (the Archangel Raphael), is called the **Triunfo** (1651). Wild baroque confections such as this are common in Naples and southern Italy (under Spanish rule at the time); there they are called *guglie*. Behind the plaza, standing across from La Mezquita, is the **Archbishop's Palace**, built on the site of the original Alcázar, the palace of Abd ar-Rahman. The **Roman bridge** over the Guadalquivir probably isn't Roman at all any more; it has been patched and repaired so often that practically nothing remains of the Roman work. Another statue of Raphael can be seen in the middle—probably replacing an old Roman image of Jupiter or Mercury. The stern-looking **Calahorra Tower**, built in 1369 over Moorish foundations, once guarded the southern approaches of the bridge and now contains a small **museum** (*open daily 10.30–6*) of Córdoba's history.

Just to the west, along the river, Córdoba's **Alcázar de los Reyes Cristianos**, © 95 747 20 00 ext. 210, was rebuilt in the 14th century and used for 300 years by the officers of the Inquisition. There's little to see, but a good view of La Mezquita and the town from the belvedere atop the walls. The **gardens** (*open daily 9.30–7*) are peaceful and lovely, an Andalucían amenity much like those in Sevilla's Alcázar. The gigantic stone figures of Columbus and the Catholic Kings are impressive. On the river's edge you'll see an ancient **waterwheel**—at least some of the Moors' talent for putting water to good use was retained for a while after the Reconquista. If you continue walking along the Guadalquivir, you'll come to Parque Cruz Conde and the **Córdoba zoo**, currently being renovated.

The Judería

As in Sevilla, Córdoba's ancient Jewish quarter has recently become a fashionable area, a nest of tiny streets between La Mezquita and Avenida Dr Fleming. Part of the Moorish walls can be seen along this street, and the northern entrance of the Judería is the old **Almodóvar gate**. The streets are tricky, and it will take some effort to find Calle Maimonides and the 14th-century **synagogue** (*open daily except Mon, 10–2; 3.30–5.30; adm free for EU citizens, others 1000 pts*), after which you will find yourself repeatedly back at this spot, whether or not you want to be there.

The diminutive Córdoban synagogue is one of the two oldest and most interesting Jewish monuments in Spain (the other is the Tránsito in Toledo). Set back from the street in a tiny courtyard, it was built in the Granadine style of the early 14th century and, according to Amador de los Rios, dates from 1315. There is an interesting plasterwork frieze of Alhambra-style arabesques and Hebrew inscriptions. The recess for the Ark (which contained the holy scrolls) is clearly visible, and the ladies' gallery still intact. Despite few obvious signs of the synagogue's original function, its atmosphere is still charged. While modern Córdoba has no active Jewish community, several *marrano* families live in the city and can trace their ancestry to the pre-expulsion age.

On Calle Ruano Torres, the 15th-century **Casa del Indiano** is a palace with an eccentric façade. On Plaza Maimonides is the **Museo Municipal de Arte Cordobés y Taurino** (*open Tues–Sat 10–2 and 6–8, Sun 9.30–3; adm 450 pts, free on Tues*) with its beautiful court-yard—not surprisingly it's a museum dedicated to the bullfights. Manolete and El Cordobés are the city's two recent contributions to Spanish culture; here you can see a replica of Manolete's sarcophagus, the furniture from his home and the hide of Islero, the bull that did him in, along with more bullfight memorabilia than you ever thought existed.

White Neighbourhoods

From the mosque you can walk eastwards through well over a mile of twisting white alleys, a place where the best map in the world wouldn't keep you from getting lost and staying lost. Every little square, fountain or church stands out boldly, and forces you to look at it in a way different from how you would look at a modern city—another lesson in the Moorish aesthetic. These streets have probably changed little since 1236, but their best buildings are a series of **Gothic churches** built soon after the Reconquista. Though small and plain, most are exquisite in a quiet way. Few have any of the usual Gothic sculptural work on their façades, to avoid offending a people accustomed to Islam's prohibition of images. **San Lorenzo**, on Calle María Auxiliadora, is perhaps the best, with a rose window designed in a common Moorish motif of interlocking circles. Some 15th-century frescoes survive around the altar and on the apse. **San Pablo** (1241), on the street of the same name, is early Gothic (5 years after the Christian conquest) but contains a fine *mudéjar* dome and ceiling. **San Andrés**, on Calle Varela, two streets east of San Pablo, **Santa Marina** on Calle Morales, and the **Cristo de los Faroles** on Calle Alfaros are some of the others. Have a look inside any you find open; most have some Moorish decoration or sculptural work in their interiors, and many of their towers (like San Lorenzo's) were originally minarets. **San Pedro**, off Calle Alfonso XII, was the Christian cathe-dral under Moorish rule, though largely rebuilt in the 1500s.

The neighbourhoods have other surprises, if you have the persistence to find them. **Santa Victoria** is a huge austere baroque church on Calle Juan Valera, modelled after the Roman Pantheon. Nearby, on Plaza Jerónimo Páez, a fine 16th-century palace houses the **National Archaeological Museum**, © 95 747 10 76 (*open Tues–Sun 10–1.30 and 6–8; adm 500 pts, free for EU citizens*), the largest in Andalucía, with Roman mosaics, a two-faced idol of Janus that probably came from the temple under La Mezquita, and an unusual icon of the Persian *torero*-god Mithras; also some Moorish-looking early Christian art, and early funeral steles with odd hieroglyphs. East of the Calle San Fernando, the wide street that bisects the old quarter, the houses are not as pristinely whitewashed as those around La Mezquita. Many parts are a bit run down, which does not detract from their charm.

In the approximate centre of the city is the **Plaza de la Corredera**, which is an enclosed 'Plaza Mayor', like the famous ones in Madrid and Salamanca. This ambitious project, surrounded by uniform blank façades (an echo of the *estilo desornamentado*) was never completed. Now neglected and a bit eerie, the city is apparently being rehabilitated a little at a time.Continuing south, the **Museo de Bellas Artes**, © 95 747 33 45 (*open Tues–Sat 10–2 and 5–7; Sun 10–1.30; adm 250 pts, free for EU citizens*) is on the lovely Plaza del Potro (mentioned by Cervantes, along with the little *posada* that still survives on it); its collections include works of Valdés Leal, Ribera, Murillo and Zurbarán, two royal portraits by Goya, and works by Córdoban artists of the 15th and 16th centuries. Beware the 'museum' across the plaza, dedicated exclusively to the works of a local named Julio Romero de Torres, the Spanish Bouguereau. Much prized by the Córdobans, this turn-of-the-century artist's *œuvre* consists almost entirely of naked ladies. Eastwards from here, the crooked whitewashed alleys continue as far as the surviving stretch of **Moorish walls** along Ronda del Marrubial.

Plaza de las Tendillas

The centre of Roman Corduba has, by chance, become the centre of the modern city. Córdoba is probably the slickest and most up-to-date city in Andalucía (Sevilla would beg to differ), and it shows in this busy district of crowded pavements, modern shops, cafés and wayward youth. The contrast with the old neighbourhoods is startling, but just a block off the plaza on Calle Gondomar the beautiful 15th-century **Church of San Nicolás** will remind you that you're still in Córdoba. In the other direction, well-preserved remains of a collapsed **Roman temple**, one of the most complete Roman monuments in Spain, have been discovered on the Calle Nueva near the Ayuntamiento. Next to the **Plaza de Colón**, a park a few blocks north of the Plaza de las Tendillas, the **Torre de Malmuerta** ('Bad Death') takes its name from a commander of this part of the old fortifications who murdered his wife in a fit of passion.

Across the plaza is a real surprise, the rococo **Convento de Merced** (1745), an enormous building that has recently been restored to house the provincial government and often hosts cultural exhibitions on various subjects. Don't miss it. The façade has been redone in its original painted *esgrafiado*, almost decadently colourful in pink and green, and the courtyards and grand staircases inside are incredible—more a palace than a monastery.

Medinat az-Zahra

Open Tues–Sat 10–1.30 and 6–8.30, Sun 10–1.30, © 95 723 4025. (Check winter hours with the tourist office.)

Eight kilometres (5 miles) northwest of the centre of Córdoba, Caliph Abd ar-Rahman III began to build a palace in the year 936. The undertaking soon got out of hand and, with the almost infinite resources of the caliphate to play with, he and his successors turned Medinat az-Zahra ('city of the Flower', so named after one of Abd ar-Rahman's wives) into a city in itself, with a market, mosques, schools and gardens, a place where the last caliphs could live in isolation from the world. The scale of it is pure Arabian Nights. Stories were told of the palace's African menageries, its interior pillars and domes of crystal, and curtains of falling water for walls; another fountain was filled with flowing mercury. Such carrying-on must have aroused a good deal of resentment; in the disturbances that put an end to the caliphate, Medinat az-Zahra was sacked and razed by Berber troops in 1013. After having served as a quarry for 900 years it's surprising anything is left; even under Muslim rule, columns from the palace were being carted away as far as Marrakesh. But in 1944 the royal apartments were discovered, with enough fragments to permit a restoration of a few arches with floral decorations. One hall has a roof on, and more work is under way, but as yet the rest is only foundations.

Shopping

Córdoba is famous for its silverwork—try the shops in C/ José Cruz Grande, where you'll get better quality than in the old quarter round the mosque. Handmade **crafts** are made on the premises at Meryan, C/ de las Flores 2, ℗ 95 747 59 02, where they specialize in embossed wood and leather furniture. For **antiques**, there's one shop with a very good selection of Spanish art and furniture in Plaza San Nicolás, and they'll arrange packing and shipment. High-quality ladies' and gents' suede and **leather goods** are sold at Sera, on the corner of Rondo de los Teares and Cruz Conde. The mainstream shopping areas are along Calle Conde de Gondomar and Calle Claudio Marcelo on either side of the Plaza de las Tendillas.

Córdoba ✉ 14000 — *Where to Stay*

Near La Mezquita, of course. Even during big tourist assaults the advantages outweigh the liabilities. However, if this area is full, or if you have a car and do not care to brave the old town's narrow streets and lack of parking, there are a few hotels in the new town and on the periphery worth trying.

moderate

The best bet is the newly opened ★★★★**NH Amistad Córdoba**, Pza. de Maimónides 3, ℗ 95 742 03 35, ✆ 95 742 03 65. It has been sensitively converted from an old *palacio*, the main entrance fronting the Plaza de Maimónides, with a back entrance neatly built into the old wall of the Judería. The double-room price of *15,000 pts* includes an excellent breakfast buffet. Underground parking is available for a small supplement. The ★★★★**Meliá Córdoba**, ℗ 95 729 80 66, ✆ 95 729 81 47, is a big modern hotel right in the middle of the Jardines de la Victoria, on the edge of the Judería. It has every conceivable luxury the chain is known for, including a pool and TV. A double room will set you back *15,600 pts*—worth it for the car park alone, some would consider. The recently refurbished ★★★★**El Conqistador**, C/ Magistral González Francés 15, ℗ 95 748 11 02, has rooms that look out onto the floodlit walls of La Mezquita, literally just a few metres from your balcony. Service is old-fashioned in the worst sense; but there is an underground car park (*13,500 pts*).

Five minutes north of the train station is ★★★★**Las Adelfas**, Avda. de la Arruzafa s/n, ℗ 95 727 74 20, ✆ 95 727 27 94, a modern hotel set in spacious gardens with a pool and beautiful views over Córdoba, definitely worth considering if you visit in summer, and a bargain at present for its rates in this category at *16,000 pts*. On the outskirts of town, service at the ★★★★**Parador de la Arruzafa**, Avda. de la Arruzafa, ℗ 95 727 59 00, ✆ 95 728 04 09, in common with much of the chain, seems to be improving. It isn't in an historic building (it was built in the 1960s), but offers a pool, tennis courts and air-conditioned rooms and a view (*15,500 pts*).

inexpensive

A bargain in this category is the **Al-Mihrab**, Avda. del Brillante, Km 5, ℗ 95 727 21 98. Situated just 5km from the centre of town, this agreeable hotel, which is a listed building, offers peace and a view of the Sierra Morena (*7500 pts*). In the Judería, near

La Mezquita, is the attractive, affordable and immaculate ★★**Albucasis**, C/ Buen Pastor 11, ✆/● 95 747 86 25, a former silversmith's with a charming flower-filled courtyard; it's one of the prettiest hotels in Córdoba (*8500 pts*). *Closed Jan–mid-Feb.* The ★★**Marisa**, C/ Cardinal Herrero 6, ✆ 95 747 31 42, is a simple but well-run establishment opposite the Patio de los Naranjos. The location is the only real amenity, but it will just do for the price (*9000 pts*). The ★★**Hotel González** is on the edge of the Judería, ✆ 95 747 98 19, ● 95 748 61 87 (*10,000 pts*). Rooms contain family antiques and the arabesque patio houses a popular restaurant.

cheap

The ★**Hostal Seneca**, C/ Conde y Luque 5, ✆ 95 747 32 34, just north of La Mezquita, is the real find among the inexpensive *hostales*, with a beautiful patio full of flowers, nice rooms and sympathetic management. Not surprisingly, it's hard to get a room (*5500 pts with breakfast included*). Plenty of other inexpensive *fondas* can be found in the area east of La Mezquita, especially on and around Calle Rey Heredia— which is also known as the street with five names so don't be thrown by the number of different signs. The **Fonda Agustina** on nearby Calle Zapatería Vieja, ✆ 95 747 08 72, is clean and central (*2500 pts*). Off the Plaza de las Tendillas, the ★**Boston**, C/ Málaga 2, ✆ 95 747 41 76, has modern clean rooms that are air-conditioned at night and popular with a young American crowd (*4900 pts*).

The ★★**Hostal Las Tendillas**, C/ Jesús y María 1, ✆ 95 722 30 29, has simple and unpretentious doubles for 2900 pts while the **Hostal La Magdalena**, ✆ 95 748 37 53, is good for those who don't mind a 10-minute walk through the picturesque backstreets into town. It's in a quiet location, there's no trouble parking (*doubles around 3600 pts*). **The Hostal Maestre**, C/ Romero Barros 16 & 18, ✆ 95 747 53 95, is popular with backpackers (so make a reservation), and has a range of rooms from doubles for *6000 pts* to small apartments for *6500 pts*; all have private bathrooms and those in the hotel have a/c. Next door is **Hostal Los Arcos**, C/ Romero Barros 14, ✆ 95 748 56 43, ● 95 748 60 11 (3500–4500 pts). The cheapest place in town is the **Hostal Martínez Rücker**, C/ Martínez Rücker 14, ✆ 95 47 25 62, which has tiny box-like rooms around a pleasant Moorish courtyard (*1500–3500 pts*).

Eating Out

Don't forget that Córdoba is the heart of a wine-growing region; there are a few *bodegas* in town that appreciate visitors, including **Bodega Campos**, C/ Colonel Cascajo; and **Bodega Doña Antonia**, Avda. Virgen Milagrosa 5, really a small restaurant serving its own wines.

expensive

Sitting in the heart of the old Jewish quarter, **El Churrasco**, C/ Romero 16, ✆ 95 729 08 19, is Córdoba's best-loved restaurant, located in an old town house. For food and atmosphere it is perhaps the finest restaurant in southern Spain—but it's not a grand restaurant, actually rather small, very intimate, and just a little bit cliquey. It specializes in grilled meats—*churrasco* is the name of the grill the meat is cooked on, and by extension the piece of grilled meat itself—and unless you're vegetarian or a mad fish-lover, a *churrasco* is your obvious choice here. In winter braziers are put under tables making it possible to dine on the patio all year round, and there's even valet parking if you need it. Additionally, El Churrasco has the best cellar in Andalucía, now so large it is housed in a separate building along the street—ask at the restaurant if you would like to visit. Relatively speaking, El Churrasco is not expensive—count on *4000–5000 pts. Closed Aug.* Another of Córdoba's best-known restaurants is **El Caballo Rojo**, Cardenal Herrero 28, ✆ 95 747 53 75. Its menu is supposed to be based on traditional *andaluz* cooking and old Arab recipes—*salmorejo* with cured ham, artichokes in Montilla wine, Mozarabic angler fish—but it has rather lost its way. Dreary-looking tourists sporting bumbags have hardly a word to say to each other and the restaurant is ugly and modern (*2500–4000 pts*).

The **Almudaina**, Jardines de los Santos Mártires 1, ✆ 95 747 43 42, is in an attractive old house dating from the 16th century, and would be a sophisticated spot to eat, but it has sold out to coachloads of Japanese. Its menu varies from day to day, depending on market availability, and special attention is paid to local produce. Look out for *ensalada de pimientos, alcachofas a la Cordobés*, and *lomo relleno a la Pedrocheña*, which are above average (*menú del día 3350–4050 pts, à la carte 4000 pts and up*). *Closed Sun from Jun to Sept, and Sun evening the rest of the year.* More easygoing than the above is **Oscar's**, Pza. de Chirinos 6, ✆ 95 747 75 17, where the emphasis is on fish—*ensalada de salmón marinado, lubina al vino oloroso de Montilla, lomos de merluza con langostinos en salsa de ajo* (*3500–4500 pts*). *Closed Sun and Aug.*

moderate

Adjoining El Caballo Rojo is **El Burlaero**, C/ La Hoguera 5, ✆ 95 747 27 19, inevitably trippery but with the advantage of a courtyard. Specialities include run-of-the-mill *rabo de toro, Paloma Torcaz, perdiz, jabalí* (*3500 pts with wine*). **Rincón de Carmen**, C/ Romero 4, ✆ 95 729 10 55, is family-run, noisy and full of atmosphere. The local dishes are prepared as well as at any establishment in the city, and the prices are low (*3000 pts*).

cheap

Just around the corner from La Mezquita, **El Tablón**, Cardenal González 75, ✆ 95 747 60 61, is a restaurant with character, offering one of the best bargains in the city, with a choice of *menús del día* (*1350 pts*) or *platos combinados* at *around 1500 pts*, glass of wine included. On Calle Cardenal Herrero, there are some good options, the best of which is the above-average **Los Patios** at No.18.

On the corner of Calle Deanes and Buen Pastor is the take-it-or-leave-it **Bodegón Rafaé**, with true *bodega* atmosphere and food. Sausages drape from barrels, religious figurines hang next to fake bulls' heads, the radio and TV are on simultaneously; *cola de toro* with a glass of wine at one of the vinyl-topped tables will cost you an exorbitant *700 pts*.

For the young, or young at heart, a lively spot is **El Campeón**, C/ Munda 8, ✆ 95 747 02 07, near Plaza de las Tendillas in one of those narrow streets. Here students gather amid the dotty décor to order enormous glass tankards of beer and *sangría*, and enjoy the loud music and snack food in one of the half-dozen tiny rooms with wooden benches. **Bar Sociedad de Plateros**, C/ San Francisco 6, is another popular place with good tapas and cheap wine.

Entertainment

Córdoba is the birthplace of Paco Peña—one of Spain's most famous modern flamenco maestros. His flamenco academy is still based in Córdoba and offers a range of guitar and dance courses; contact them at Compania de Paco Peña, Plaza del Potro 15, Córdoba 14002. Paco Peña is part of a long tradition of Córdoba flamenco and the city is a good place to catch some great players and dancers in more authentic venues than, say, Sevilla. If you love flamenco, June is the best time to visit the city, during the guitar festival, when flourishes and trills drift out of every other room in Córdoba's White Neighbourhood and there are several concerts every night (check with the Spanish tourist office for details). At other times, wait until midnight and then head for one of the secluded little flamenco bars tucked away throughout the city. These include the Peña Flamenca Fostorito on C/Ocaña 4, near the Plaza de San Agustín or the Peña Flamenca Las Orejas Negras, on Av. Carlos III 18, in Fatima Barrio, in the Córdoba suburbs. You could also try the shows at Tablao Cardenal, C/Torrijos 10, strategically positioned next to the tourist office, or La Buleria, on C/Pedro Lopez 3, though don't be deluded into thinking that either is much more than a tourist spectacle.

Though flamenco may be more authentic in Córdoba than in Sevilla, the bar nightlife is less lively. The most popular bars with locals are the street bars (*terrazas*) in Barrio Jardín, northwest of the Jardínes de la Vitoria, on the Avenida de Republica end of Camino de los Sastrés. **El Loro Verde** and the **Albaicín** are two of the busiest. **Barrio El Brillante**, northwest of the Plaza Colon is full of upper-middle class Spanish in the summer, particularly the nightclubs and bars around Plaza El Tablero.

North of Córdoba

Getting Around

Although **buses** do run from Córdoba up into the Sierra and villages of Los Pedroches, they are infrequent and very time-consuming. To really explore, you need a **car**.

The N432 out of Córdoba leads north to the Sierra Morena, the string of hills that curtain the western part of Andalucía from Extremadura, Castilla and La Mancha. This area is the **Valle de los Pedroches**, fertile grazing lands for the pigs, sheep and goats and an important hunting area for deer and wild boar. Thousands of these animals are stalked and shot in the numerous annual hunts, or *monterías*. It's also healthy hiking territory, but keep yourself visible at all times—you don't want to be mistaken for someone's supper.

A road winds 73km (46 miles) up to **Belmez**, with its Moorish castle perilously perched on a rock, from which there are panoramic views over the surrounding arid countryside. **Peñarroya-Pueblonuevo** is a dull industrial town that has fallen into decline, but is useful here as a reference point. Sixteen kilometres (10 miles) west on the N432, the village of **Fuente Ovejuna** is best remembered for the 1476 uprising of its villagers, who dragged their tyrannical lord from his palace and treated him to a spectacularly brutal and bloody end. Forty-four kilometres (27½ miles) east of Peñarroya (take the C421, then the C420) is the village of **Pozoblanco**, famous for the last *corrida* of the renowned bullfighter Francisco Rivera, better known as Paquirri. Gored, he died in the ambulance on the way to Córdoba; presumably, bouncing around on those roads didn't help. Paquirri's widow, the singer Isabel Pantoja, soared to even greater heights of popularity on his death, with the Spanish public obsessed as ever by the drama of life and mortality. **Pedroche**, 10km (6 miles) away, is a sleepy little village with a fine 16th-century Gothic church with a proud, lofty spire, and a Roman bridge. This place too has had its fair share of drama—in 1936 Communist forces shot nearly a hundred of the menfolk. Beyond the villages of **Villanueva de Córdoba** and **Cardeña** to the east is the **Parque Natural de Sierra Cardeña**—rolling hills forested in oak, more stag-hunting grounds and ideal rambling terrain.

Where to Stay and Eating Out

North of Córdoba there's nothing in the way of deluxe accommodation, but the area has a small selection of one- and two-star hotels. Two and a half kilometres (1½ miles) out of Pozoblanco (Ctra. Villanueva de la Serena–Andújar, Km 129), in a listed historic building, is the quiet **★★San Francisco**, ✆ 95 710 14 35, with tennis courts (*8000 pts*). Villanueva de Córdoba has the **★Demetrius**, Ctra. de Cardeña s/n, ✆ 95 712 02 94, a place that offers no frills for its *3500 pts* rooms. Though there's no reason to stay in Peñarroya-Pueblonuevo, you may like to use it as a base for your day trip. The **★Sevilla**, C/ Miguel Vigara 15, ✆ 95 756 01 00, ✆ 95 56 23 07, is the most comfortable place to stay, rooms with bath go for *6500 pts*; while **★El Sol**, C/ El Sol 24, ✆ 95 756 20 50, has basic rooms for around *4500 pts*.

This area is famed throughout Andalucía for its supreme quality *jamón ibérico* (locally cured ham) and sucking pig, the excellent *salchichón* from Pozoblanco, and the strong, spicy cheese made from ewes' milk. Sadly it is often difficult for visitors to the region to sample them. There are no outstanding restaurants around, and even indifferent ones are pretty thin on the ground, so finding a good roadside *venta* such as the **Huerta de San Rafael** at Luque, Ctra. Badajoz–Granada, ✆ 95 766 74 97, is a real boon. Driving off into the countryside in search of gastronomic delight can be a risky business. And, though it's true that it occasionally pays rich dividends, to be sure of eating really well you should head for the tapas bars in the villages or, better still, grab some goodies from a supermarket and have a picnic out on the slopes.

From Córdoba to Úbeda

In this section of the Guadalquivir valley the river rises into the heights of the Sierra Morena; endless rolling hills covered with neat rows of olive trees and small farms make a memorable Andalucían landscape. The three large towns along the way, **Andújar, Bailén** and **Linares**, are much alike, amiable industrial towns still painted a gleaming white.

The Gateway to Andalucía

This area is Andalucía's front door. The roads and railways from Madrid branch off here for Sevilla and Granada. Many important battles were fought nearby, including Las Navas de Tolosa near La Carolina, in 1212, which opened the way for the conquest of Al-Andalus; and Bailén, in 1808, where a Spanish-English force gave Napoleon's boys a sound thrashing and built up Spanish morale for what they call their War of Independence.

The NIV snakes along the Guadalquivir valley, and 42km (26 miles) east of Córdoba it brings you to the delightfully placed town of **Montoro**, sitting on a bend in the river. The facetious-looking tower that rises above the whitewashed houses belongs to the Gothic church of **San Bartolomé** in Plaza de España. Also in the square is the 16th-century **Ducal Palace**, with a plateresque façade. The beautiful 15th-century bridge that connects Montoro to its suburb, Retamar, is known as the Puente de Las Doñadas, a tribute to the women of the village who sacrificed their jewellery to help finance its construction. Seek out the kitsch **Casa de las Conchas**, a house and courtyard done out in sea shells.

Approaching **Andújar**, a further 35km (22 miles) down the NIV, you'll find the countryside dominated by huge, blue sunflower-oil refineries like fallen space stations. Sunflowers, like olives, are a big crop in the region and much in evidence in late summer. Nothing remains of Andújar's Moorish castle, but there are a couple of surprises in this town which might tempt you to linger a while. The church of **Santa María**, in the plaza of the same name, has in one chapel the *Immaculate Conception* by Pacheco, Velázquez's teacher, and in another the magnificent *Christ in the Garden of Olives*, by El Greco. A possible diversion, 30km (19 miles) north of Andújar on the J501, is the **Santuario de la Virgen de la Cabeza**. Although very little is left of the 13th-century sanctuary, and the present one is disappointing, it's worth packing a picnic and enjoying the drive; when you get there you'll be rewarded with panoramic views. One of southern Spain's biggest fiestas is the annual *romería* to the sanctuary on the last Sunday in April, when a quarter of a million pilgrims trek up on foot, horseback, carts and donkeys. The day before there's a competition for the best-decorated carriage.

Twenty-seven kilometres (17 miles) further east on the NIV is the modern, unprepossessing town of **Bailén**. The tomb of the Spanish general Francisco Javier Castaños (1756–1852), who so cleverly whipped the French troops and sent Napoleon back to the drawing board, is in the Gothic parish church of the **Encarnación**, which also has a sculpture by Alonso Cano. But don't dally here—the real treat is to be found 11km (7 miles) to the north on the NIV at **Baños de la Encina**, where the 10th-century oval Moorish castle is one of the best preserved in all Andalucía. Dominating the town, the castle has 14 sturdy, square towers and a double-horse-shoe gateway, scarcely touched by time, and from the walls you get a sweeping vista of the olive groves and distant peaks beyond Úbeda. An hour's trek from Baños, through difficult, hilly terrain, lies the natural refuge of **Canforos de Peñarrubia**, with its remarkably preserved Bronze Age paintings of deer and scenes of animal-taming. Serious hikers should ask for a guide at the Ayuntamiento in the town, © 95 361 30 04.

Twenty kilometres (12½ miles) north of here on the NIV is **La Carolina**, a model of 18th-century grid planning. The village owes its existence to forward-thinking Carlos III, who imported German artisans in the late 1700s and set them to work excavating the lead and copper mines, tilling the fields and herding sheep. But within two generations almost all the Germans had died off or fled. The town and surrounding area are best known now as a big game-hunting reserve, particularly for partridge—that is to say, not *big game*, but a big reserve.

From Bailén the N322 heads eastward to the mining town of **Linares**, birthplace of the guitarist Andrés Segovia, who later moved on; others weren't so lucky—in 1947 the great bullfighter Manolete had an off day and met his end on the horns of a bull in the ring here.If things had gone well for him, he might have gone to view the finds from the Roman settlement of nearby Castulo, housed in the town's **archaeology museum**, but unfortunately the last thing he probably saw was the ornate baroque portal of the hospital **San Juan de Dios**. From Linares it's a 27km (17 mile) run to Úbeda; a little more than halfway you'll pass an elegant castle at **Canena**.

Where to Stay and Eating Out

On the main Madrid–Cádiz road is the **★★Montoro**, at Km 358, ☎ 95 316 07 92 (*3700 pts*). Andújar has a bigger selection, but less reason to stay. The best here is the **★★Don Pedro**, C/ Gabriel Zamora 5, ☎ 95 350 12 74, @ 95 350 47 85, in the centre of town, with pleasant rooms for 5500 pts, and a tavern-style restaurant that specializes in game dishes; a meal with wine is about *3300 pts*. Ten kilometres outside Andújar at Marmolejo, the **★★★Gran Hotel Balneario**, Calvario 101, ☎ 95 354 00 00, @ 95 354 06 50, is probably the area's best hotel, with its swimming pool and adjoining health spa. There's a modern **★★★Parador**, Ctra. NIV, Km 296, ☎ 95 367 01 00, @ 95 367 25 30, just outside Bailén, with pleasant gardens, air-conditioning and pool—rates are a reasonable *7000 pts*. It also houses a restaurant and tapas bar.

In Linares the **★★★Aníbal**, C/ Cid Campeador 11, ☎ 95 365 04 00, @ 95 365 22 04, is the jumbo in town (*7000–10,000 pts*); and for dining **Mesón Castellano**, C/ Puente 5, ☎ 95 369 00 09, is the place to go (*3500 pts*). *Closed Sun, July and Aug.* In La Carolina the hotel **★★★★Perdiz**, Ctra. NIV, Km 268, ☎ 95 366 03 00, @ 95 368 13 62, is a classic stopover for travellers between Andalucía and northern Spain and has an appealing, coaching-inn ambience. It's got a pretty good restaurant too and, as its name ('partridge') implies, it has seasonal game dishes (*3000 pts*). Rates for the hotel, which has a pool, are a bold *12,500 pts* for a double. Baños de la Encina has a reliable restaurant, the **Mesón Buenos Aires**, Cateyana, ☎ 95 361 32 11, with good country cooking, including wild boar and venison in season.

Baeza

> Campo de Baeza, soñaré contigo cuando no te vea
> (Fields of Baeza, I will dream of you when I can no longer see you)
> Antonio Machado (1875–1939)

Sometimes history offers its recompense. The 13th-century Reconquista was especially brutal here; nearly the entire population fled, many of them moving to Granada, where they settled the Albaicín. The 16th century, however, when the wool trade was booming in this corner of Andalucía, was good to Baeza, leaving it a distinguished little town of neatly clipped trees and tan stone buildings. It seems a happy place, serene as the olive groves that surround it.

Getting Around

Come to Baeza by **train** at your own risk. The nearest station, officially named Linares-Baeza, is far off in the open countryside, 14km away. A bus to Baeza usually meets the train, but if you turn up at night or on a Sunday you may be stranded. Baeza's **bus** station, ☎ 95 74 04 68, is a little way from the centre on Av. Alcalde Puche Pardo. Baeza is a stop on the Úbeda–Córdoba bus route, with 12 a day running to Jaen (1¼ hrs); 8 to Granada (2 hrs); 2 to Cazorla and 1 to Málaga (4–5 hrs).

Pza. del Pópulo (also known as the Plaza de los Leones), ☎ 95 374 04 44. *Open Mon–Fri 9–2, Sat 10–12.30.*

The prettiest corner of the town is the small square, the **Plaza del Pópulo**, which houses the tourist office. It is enclosed by decorative pointed arches and Renaissance buildings, and contains a fountain with four half-effaced lions. In Plaza Cardinal Benavides, the façade of the **Ayuntamiento** (1599) is a classic example of Andalucían plateresque, and one of the last.

Heading north on the Cuesta de San Felipe, which can be reached by the steps leading off the Plaza del Pópulo, you pass the 15th-century **Palacio de Jabalquinto**, with an eccentric façade covered with coats of arms and pyramidal stone studs (a Spanish fancy of that age; you can see others like it in Guadalajara and Salamanca). The *palacio* was built in the 15th century by the Benavides family, and is now a seminary. Its patio is open to the public (*open Mon–Fri 9–2*) and boasts a beautiful two-tiered arcade around a central fountain, as well as a fine carved baroque staircase. Adjoining the *palacio*, the 16th-century **Antigua Universidad** was a renowned centre of learning for three hundred years, until its charter was withdrawn during the reign of Fernando VII. It has since been used as a school; its indoor patio, like that of the Jabalquinto, is open to the public (*officially open Mon–Fri 9–2, but times vary according to the school timetable*).

A right turn at the next corner leads to the 16th-century **cathedral** on Plaza Santa María, a work of Andrés de Vandelvira. For the best show in town, drop a coin in the box marked *custodia* in one of the side chapels; this will reveal, with a noisy dose of mechanical *duende*, a rich and ornate 18th-century silver tabernacle. The fountain in front of the cathedral, the **Fuente de Santa María**, with a little triumphal arch at its centre (1564), is Baeza's landmark and symbol. Behind it is the Isabelline Gothic **Casas Consistoriales**, formerly the town hall, while opposite stands the 16th-century seminary of **San Felipe Neri**, its walls adorned with student graffiti—recording their names and dates in bull's blood.

The Paseo de la Constitución, at the bottom of the hill, is Baeza's main, albeit quiet, thoroughfare, an elegant rectangle lined with crumbling shops and bars. Two buildings are especially worthy of note: **La Alhóndiga**, the 16th-century, porticoed Corn Exchange and, almost opposite, on the west side of the Paseo, the **Casa Consistorial**, the 18th-century town hall. At the end northern end of the Paseo, the inelegant Plaza de España marks the northern boundary of historic Baeza and houses yet more bars.

Baeza ✉ *23440*　　　　　　　　　　　　**Where to Stay and Eating Out**

The best place to stay is the **★★★Hotel Baeza**, C/ Concepción 3, ☎ 95 374 81 30, @ 95 374 25 19, which lies behind the Iglesia del Hospital de la Purísima Concepción, near the Plaza de España. This monasterial building, once part of the hospital, used to be a religious school, and rooms open on to a peaceful arched quadrangle (*from 9500 pts*). The **★★★Juanito**, Avda. Arca del Agua s/n, ☎ 95 374 00 40, @ 95 374 23 24, on the road leaving Baeza in the direction of Úbeda, has rooms with bath from *4800 pts*, plus its own pool, but the hotel is rather run down. A good cheaper bet is the **Adriano**, C/ Conde Romanones 13, ☎ 95 374 02 00, a Renaissance mansion set around a courtyard (*4000 pts*). The *pensión* **★★Comercio**, C/ San Pablo 21, ✆ 95 374 01 00, is a comfortable lodging with quite a good atmosphere where Machado stayed and perhaps even penned a few poems (*3600 pts*). The restaurant of the **Juanito** is in the Michelin guide. You can also try regional specialities at **Andrés de Vandelvira**, C/ San Francisco 14, ✆ 95 374 43 61. The restaurant is inside the San Francisco convent with tables filling the arched quadrangle; for more intimacy, dine upstairs (*around 5000 pts*). *Closed Sun afternoons.*

Úbeda

Even with Baeza for an introduction, the presence of this nearly perfect little city comes as a surprise. If the 16th century did well by Baeza, it was a golden age here, leaving Úbeda a 'town built for gentlemen' as the Spanish used to say, endowed with one of the finest collections of Renaissance architecture in all of Spain. Two men can take much of the credit: Andrés de Vandelvira, an Andalucían architect who created most of Úbeda's best buildings, and Francisco de los Cobos, imperial secretary to Charles V, who paid for them. Cobos is a forgotten hero of Spanish history. While Charles was off campaigning in Germany, Cobos had the job of running Castile. By the most delicate management, he kept the kingdom afloat while meeting Charles's ever more exorbitant demands for money and men. He could postpone the inevitable disaster, but not prevent it. Like most public officials in the Spanish Age of Rapacity, though, he also managed to salt away a few hundred thousand ducats for himself, and he spent most of them embellishing his hometown. Like Baeza, Úbeda is a peaceful and happy place; it wears its Renaissance heritage gracefully, and is always glad to have visitors. Slowly, it's gearing up for them. But it's still easy to understand the Spanish expression '*irse por los cerros de Úbeda*' ('take the Úbeda hill routes'). It equates to getting off the subject or wasting time and arose years ago after Úbeda gradually lost traffic to more commercial routes. Legend has it that a Christian knight fell in love with a Moorish girl and was reproached for his absence by King Fernando III. When questioned about his whereabouts during the battle the knight idly replied, 'Lost in those hills, sire'.

Getting Around

Úbeda's **bus** station, C/ San José, ✆ 95 375 21 57, is at the western end of town, and various lines connect the city directly to Madrid, Valencia and Barcelona, at least once daily, and more frequently to Baeza, (16 daily, 20mins), Córdoba (3 daily, 2½hrs), Sevilla (3 daily, Jaén (8 daily, 1½hrs) and Granada (2 daily, 2½hrs). Cazorla and other villages in the region can easily be reached from Úbeda.

Tourist Information

The office is currently in Hospital de Santiago, ✆ 95 3 75 08 97, and is due to move in late 1999 to the Palacio Marques de Contadero in C/ Baja de Marques. *Open Mon–Fri 9–2.30; Sat 11–1.30.*

Úbeda today leaves no doubt how its local politics are going. In the **Plaza de Andalucía**, joining the old and new districts, there is an old metal statue of a fascist civil war general named Sero glaring down from his pedestal. The townspeople have put so many bullets into it, it looks like a Swiss cheese. They've left it here as a joke, and have merrily renamed another square, from Plaza del Generallísimo to Plaza 1 de Mayo.

The **Torre de Reloj**, in the Plaza de Andalucía, is a 14th-century defensive tower now adorned with a clock. From here, Calle Real takes you into the heart of the old town. Nearly every corner has at least one lovely palace or church on it. Two of the best can be seen on this street: the early 17th-century **Palacio de Condé Guadiana** has an ornate tower and distinctive windows cut out of the corners of the building, a common conceit in Úbeda's palaces. Two blocks down, the **Palacio Vela de los Cobos** (*open 10–2 and 6–8*) is in the same style, with a loggia on the top storey. Northeast of here, on C/Cervantes, lies a small museum (*open Tues–Sun 11–12.45; 5–6.30*) with the tiny monastic cell where San Juan de la Cruz (St John of the Cross) died of cancer and ulceration of the flesh in 1591. The home of Francisco de los Cobos's nephew, another royal counsellor, was the great **Palacio de las Cadenas**, now serving as Úbeda's Ayuntamiento, on a quiet plaza at the end of Calle Real. The main façade, facing the **Plaza Vázquez de Molina**, is a stately Renaissance creation, the work of Vandelvira.

Plaza Vázquez de Molina

This is the only place in Andalucía where you can look around and not regret the passing of the Moors, for it is the only truly beautiful thing in all this great region that was not built either by the Moors or under their influence. The Renaissance buildings around the Palacio de las Cadenas make a wonderful ensemble, and the austere landscaping, old cobbles and plain six-sided fountain create the same effect of contemplative serendipity as any chamber of the Alhambra. Buildings on the plaza include the church of **Santa María de los Reales Alcázares**; a Renaissance façade on an older building with a fine Gothic cloister around the back; the *parador*; two sedate palaces, both from the 16th century; and Vandelvira's **Sacra Capilla del Salvador**, begun in 1540, the finest of Úbeda's churches, where Cobos is buried.

All the sculpture on the façades of Úbeda is first-class, especially the west front of the Salvador. This is a monument of the time when Spain was in the mainstream of Renaissance ideas, and humanist classicism was still respectable. Note the mythological subjects on the west front and inside the church, and be sure to look under the arch of the main door. Instead of Biblical scenes, it has carved panels of the ancient gods representing the five planets; Phoebus and Diana with the sun and moon; and Hercules, Aeolus, Vulcan and Neptune to represent the four elements. The interior, with its great dome, is worth a look despite a thorough sacking in 1936 (the sacristan lives on the first door on the left of Calle Francisco Cobos, on the north side of the church). Behind El Salvador, the **Hospital de los Honrados** has a delightful open patio—but only because the other half of the building was never completed. South of the plaza, the end of town is only a few blocks away, encompassed by a street called the **Redonda de Miradores**, a quiet spot favoured by small children and goats, with remnants of Úbeda's wall and exceptional views over the Sierra de Cazorla to the east.

Beyond Plaza Vázquez de Molina

Calle Montiel, north of El Salvador, has a few more fine palaces. At the foot of the street, on Plaza 1 de Mayo, is the 13th-century **San Pablo** church, much renovated in the 16th century; inside is an elegant chapel of 1536, the Capilla del Camarero Vago. **San Nicolás de Bari**, further north, was originally a synagogue, though nothing now bears witness to this. On the western outskirts of town, near the bus station on Calle Nueva is Vandelvira's most remarkable building, the **Hospital de Santiago** (*open 9–3 and 4–9*). This huge edifice, recently restored, has been called the 'Escorial of Andalucía'. Both have the same plan, a grid of quadrangles with a church inside. Oddly, both were begun at about the same time, though this one seems to have been started a year earlier, in 1568. Both are supreme examples of the *estilo desornamentado*. The façade here is not as plain as Herrera's; its quirky decoration and clean, angular lines are unique, more like a product of the 20th century than the 16th.

Úbeda's Pottery

Traditional dark green pottery, fired in kilns over wood and olive stones, is literally Úbeda's trademark. **Tito**, on the Plaza Ayuntamiento, is a class establishment that produces and fires pieces on the premises. The designs are exquisite and are packed and shipped all over the world. Highly recommended is a visit to the potters' quarter around the **Calle Valencia**, a 15-minute stroll northeast of the Plaza Ayuntamiento. Nearly every house is a potter's workshop; all are open to the public and you will soon find your own favourite. Ours is at no. 36, where **Juan José Almarza** runs his family business, handed down through several generations. Juan spent two years in Edinburgh, and is possibly the only potter in the province of Jaén with a Scottish accent.

Around Úbeda: the Sierra de Cazorla

If you go east out of Úbeda, you'll be entering a zone few visitors ever reach. Your first stop might be the village of Torreperogil, where the **Misericordia** growers' co-operative in the Calle España produces first-class red and white wines. The Sierra de Cazorla offers some memorable mountain scenery, especially around **Cazorla**, a lovely, undiscovered white village of narrow alleys hung at alarming angles down the hillsides. Cazorla's landmarks are a ruined Renaissance church (again, by Vandelvira) half-open to the sky, and its castle. But there's an even better castle, possibly built by the Templars, just east of town. **La Iruela** is a romantic ruin even by Spanish standards, with a Homage tower on a dizzying height behind. Beyond La Iruela is the pass into the Sierra, the wild territory of hiking, hunting and fishing.

The mountain ranges of Cazorla and Segura make up one of the 10 national parks in Spain. The Cazorla National Park covers over half a million acres, and teems with wild boar, deer, mountain goat, buck and mouflon, while rainbow trout do their best to outwit the patient anglers. The park abounds with mountain streams and is the source of the mighty Guadalquivir, nothing more than a trickle over a couple of stones at this point. A hike in search of the source of Andalucía's greatest river is desperately romantic (a good map will direct you). Visitors interested in flora and fauna find the area one of the richest in Europe, with a variety of small birdlife that's hard to match, as well as larger species such as eagles, ospreys and vultures.

Where to Stay and Eating Out

Úbeda ✉ 23400

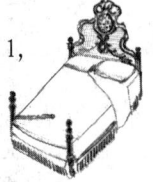

The ★★★★**Parador Condestable Dávalos**, Pza. Vázquez de Molina 1, ✆ 95 375 03 45, 🖷 95 375 12 59, in a 16th-century palace with a glassed-in courtyard, is one of the loveliest and most popular of the chain (*16,000 pts for a big double room*). All the beamed ceilings and fireplaces have been preserved and the restaurant is the best in town (which isn't saying a lot), featuring local specialities for around *3500 pts* for a full dinner. A romantic and slightly less expensive choice would be the **Palacio de la Rambla**, Pza. del Marqués 1, ✆ 95 375 01 96, a magnificent ivy-clad Renaissance mansion with beautiful double rooms (ask for 106) for *14,000 pts*. The rest of Úbeda's hotels are all good bargains; you'll find a large selection on Calle Ramón y Cajal in the modern town, just east of the bus station. The **★Hostal Los Cerros**, Peñarroya 1, ✆ 95 375 16 21, is spotless (*4500 pts*) and at the *pensión* **★★Sevilla**, C/ Ramón y Cajal 9, ✆ 95 375 06 12, you can get a clean and pleasant double with bath from *3800 pts*—air-conditioning is extra. The **★San Miguel**, Avda. Libertad 69, ✆ 95 375 20 49, is another cheapie, *4500 pts* without bath; while at the **★★Hotel Consuelo**, C/ Ramón y Cajal 12, ✆ 95 375 08 40, the rooms are a bit fancier for *5000 pts*.

Apart from the Parador, there are few good restaurants in Úbeda. The best is **Cuzco**, Parque Vandelvira 8, ✆ 95 375 34 13, which has local dishes and a *750 pts* menu of the day which includes two courses and wine. Near the Plaza Ayuntamiento, **El Seco**, C/ Corazón de Jesús 8, ✆ 95 379 14 52, is a small dining-room with reasonable food if little atmosphere. There are plenty of characters at the bar in **El Gallorojo**, C/ Estrella, at the top of Calle Trinidad, during the day and it's a lively place in the evening with excellent tapas and restaurant (*1000–2000 pts*). Also good for tapas and light meals is **Mesón Gabino**, Fuente Seca s/n, ✆ 95 375 42 07. A smattering of unremarkable places are around Calle Ramón y Cajal. **El Olivo**, Avda. Ramón y Cajal 6, ✆ 95 375 20 92, has average fare at average prices (*1500–2000 pts*). The restaurant at the **Hostal Sevilla**, Avda. Ramón y Cajal 20, ✆ 95 375 0612, is good value, and for pre-dinner drinks try the **Bar Palacio** in the courtyard of the Palacio de los Bussianos on Calle Trinidad. The bar scene is fairly advanced in Úbeda. Try **Lupo**, in Plaza de San Pedro with its state-of-the-art interior, or the Gothic **Siglo XV**, which used to be a brothel, on Calle de Muñoz García, Úbeda's liveliest street after dark.

Cazorla ✉ 23470

Cazorla has a surprising number of hotels, both in town and up in the mountains on the road to the dam and reservoir at El Tranco, 20km (12½ miles) north in a beautiful mountain setting. One of these is the **★Mirasierra**, Santiago de la Espada, Ctra. del Tranco, Km 20, ✆ 95 372 15 44, with a restaurant (*3200 pts*). The **★Don Diego**, C/ Hilario Marco 163, ✆ 95 372 05 45, is a comfortable little hotel (*doubles 4000 pts*). The **★★★Peña de las Halcones**, Travesía del Camino de La Iruela, s/n, ✆ 95 372 02 11, ✆ 95 372 13 35, is a relatively sophisticated place by La Iruela with wonderful views and minibars in the room (*5500 pts*).

A little further down the La Iruela road, the homely **★★La Finca**, Ctra. de la Sierra, ✆ 95 372 10 87, offers modest rooms, some with tremendous views. Its small dining room has the best kitchen in the area (*3500 pts*). The husband of the owner of La Finca is a ranger in the National Park, and occasionally mans the reception desk at the **★★★Parador El Adelantado**, ✆ 95 372 10 75, ✆ 95 372 13 03. Tucked about five miles inside the park, the Parador is a mountain chalet with 20 rooms. It is agreeably remote and has an appealing, if slightly institutional, feel to it. Its setting, however, is without equal; if budget allows, this is the obvious choice as a base for exploring the National Park (*10,500 pts*). The restaurant is lacklustre but there is nowhere else!

In the middle of the vast tracts of olive groves upon which its precarious economy depends is Jaén, the most provincial of all the Andalucían capitals. Jaén lacks the Renaissance charms of Úbeda or Baeza, but it is a decent, modern town, not as unattractive as many guidebooks claim; easily explored on foot in one day, along pleasant pedestrian walkways.

Getting Around

Jaén has direct **rail** links only with Córdoba (three trains daily) and Madrid (about six). The RENFE station is on the Paseo de la Estación, the main street, at the northern edge of town, by the Plaza de la Concordia. **Buses** are the best bet—Jaén is a real transport hub. The bus station is on the Avenida de Madrid, near the tourist office. Buses run to Úbeda via Baeza (12 daily); Granada (14 daily); Malaga (4 daily); Córdoba (8 daily); Almeria (2 daily).

Tourist Information

Arquitecto Bergés 1, ✆ 95 322 27 37. *Open Mon–Fri 10–1.30.*

Jaén was the first capital of the kingdom of Granada and the old Arab quarter is a part of the town well worth a visit. Its weaving, narrow, paved lanes are at the foot of the hill crowned by the 13th-century Moorish castle of **Santa Catalina**, built by ibn-Nasr (*open Mon–Sun 10.30–1.30, closed Wed*). The city's pride is its monumental **cathedral** on Plaza Santa María, begun in 1548 by Andrés de Vandelvira. His work inside has suffered many changes, and the façade isn't his at all; not begun until 1667, Eufrasio López de Rojas's design was the first genuine attempt at baroque in Andalucía, decorated with extravagant statuary by Pedro Roldán (*open 8.30–1 and 5–8*). Adjacent to the cathedral is the **Iglesia del Sagrario**, with a neoclassical interior designed by Ventura Rodríguez. On Calle Martínez Molina, west of the cathedral, an old hospital has been restored to hold the **Museum of Arts and Popular Customs**, but the real attraction is the **Baños Árabes**, well-preserved ruins of 11th-century Moorish baths, complete with cold rooms, hot rooms and a tepidarium, discovered underneath (✆ 953 23 62 92, *open Tues–Fri 9–8, 9.30–2.30 weekends; free adm for EU citizens*). Jaén's modern quarters can be a bit dreary, and peculiar at the same time. The centre, Plaza de las Batallas, has an extremely silly winged statue atop a pedestal, commemorating past victories over the Moors. Nearby, on the broad Plaza de la Estación, there is a good archaeological collection in the **Museo Provincial**, ✆ 95 325 03 20 (*open Wed–Sat 9–8; Sun 9–3; Tues 3–8; closed Mon*).

If you're on the way to Granada, a possible detour is to **Alcalá La Real**, with an unusual town square and picturesque castle, the **Castillo de la Mota**l. The **Castillo de Solera**, in that tiny village just east of Huelma, is an even finer sight; the castle seems to grow out of its crag.

Jaén ✉ *23000*   ### Where to Stay

The **★★★★Parador Castillo de Santa Catalina** is in the castle overlooking Jaén, ✆ 95 323 00 00, ✉ 95 323 09 30 (*17,000 pts*); General de Gaulle spent time here working on his memoirs. The management could do with an overhaul but the view is unsurpassable. If you are suffering from writer's block (or indeed vertigo), you might do better at the

***Condestable Iranzo**, Pso. de la Estación 32, © 95 322 28 00, ✆ 95 326 38 07, near the tourist office. It doesn't have the view, but you get more luxuries at a better price (*10,300–12,000 pts*). Another conveniently placed major hotel is the ***Xauen**, Pza. Deán Mazas 3, © 95 326 40 11, ✆ 95 319 03 12, further down the Paseo near Plaza Constitución (*7000 pts*). A couple of acceptable budget hotels are *La Española**, Bernardo López 9, © 95 325 02 54 (*around 4000–5000 pts*) and the *Carlos V**, Avda. de Madrid 4, © 95 322 20 91 (*around 3500 pts*).

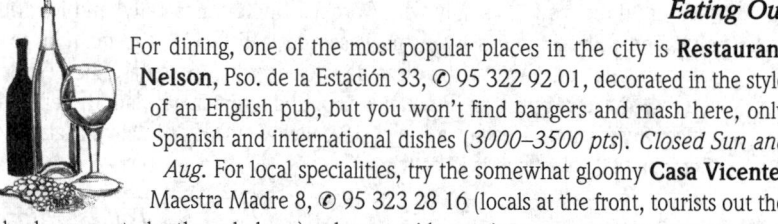

Eating Out

For dining, one of the most popular places in the city is **Restaurant Nelson**, Pso. de la Estación 33, © 95 322 92 01, decorated in the style of an English pub, but you won't find bangers and mash here, only Spanish and international dishes (*3000–3500 pts*). *Closed Sun and Aug*. For local specialities, try the somewhat gloomy **Casa Vicente**, Maestra Madre 8, © 95 323 28 16 (locals at the front, tourists out the back, seems to be the rule here), where a wide-ranging menu concentrates on meat and fish (*3000 pts*). *Closed Sun*. During the summer, get a table in the courtyard. The *parador's* restaurant has a good reputation, and wonderful views towards the Sierra Morena (*3000–4000 pts*). For less formal dining, check out the numerous excellent tapas bars around the Plaza de la Constitución and along the narrow alley, Calle Nueva, which leads off it.

Andalucían Coasts

Everyone has heard of the Costa del Sol, but there is a good deal more to Andalucía's coasts than just that narrow strip of salty Babylon—about 640km (400 miles) of it, from the empty spaces of Huelva to the empty spaces of Almería.

Andalucía's Atlantic coast, from Portugal to the Straits of Gibraltar, is not at all scenic, but it has plenty of long golden beaches that haven't yet become too crowded. The image-makers of the Spanish Tourism Ministry have bestowed upon it the name **Costa de la Luz**. The piquant, sea-washed town of **Cádiz** is its major attraction. After Cádiz the mountains close in, until **Algeciras**, a port town with the promise of a side-trip to Morocco, or to **Ceuta**, a tiny remnant of Spain's colonial empire in Africa. Next we stop for pie and two veg in **Gibraltar**; east of **La Línea**, the *urbanizaciones* of the **Costa del Sol** begin, stretching along the main resorts of **Estepona**, **Marbella**, **Fuengirola** and **Torremolinos**. **Málaga** comes next, a busy city not without charm, and after it the only section of the coast with any pretensions to scenery, around **Nerja**. After **Motril**, and the road to Granada, there's more solitude on the **Costa de Almería**, which is in parts pretty, in others nearly a desert. Altogether, these coasts have only one real purpose as far as the visitor is concerned—for planting yourself on a beach and dozing off. There are the inevitable peripheral attractions (mini-golf, seafood dinners, funfairs, English beer on tap, etc.), but little else. Pack a potent sunscreen and have a good time. For the thousands of Northern Europeans who have come to settle here, the story is different: a wonderful year-round climate, a relatively stress-free environment, enhanced quality of life along with a reduced cost of living, and easy access to the great cities and cultural centres of Andalucía.

A Huelva una vez y nunca vuelvas.
(One trip to Huelva and you don't go back.)

This Andalucían saying does seem a little unkind, but the provincial capital *is* full of factories and freshly laid cement; from the outskirts it looks like a sad Slovak town. Hit the centre however and, small as it is, it boasts an incongruously large number of fur shops and amusement arcades—history will probably prove that Las Vegas was actually founded by a Huelvan.

Getting Around

The **railway** station, ✆ 959 24 66 66 is on the Avenida de Italia, a 5-minute walk from the centre of Huelva; daily *Talgo* to Sevilla and Madrid (change at Linares for Granada and Almería), apart from the regular services to Sevilla, from where there are connections to Cádiz, Jerez, Córdoba, other points in Andalucía and Barcelona; also regular trains to Ayamonte, on the Portuguese border. The Damas **bus** company, ✆ 959 25 69 00, has its station at Avenida de Portugal 9, with services to Sevilla, Granada, Cádiz and Algeciras, and other destinations within the province: Ayamonte, Isla Cristina, Punta Umbria, Mazagón and Matalascañas on the coast, less frequently to Nerva and the mountain villages to the north. The nearest **airport** is Sevilla.

Tourist Information

Avda. de Alemania 14, ✆/🖨, 95 525 74 03. *Open weekdays 10–2 and 4.30–7.30, Sat 9–1.*

The town's tourist brochure, in a unique and disarmingly modest display of candour, states that Huelva 'has no particular historic interest'. The town was severely damaged by the earthquake of 1755, explaining the near-absence of anything older than that; exceptions include the 16th-century baroque church of **San Pedro**, built on the site of an old mosque, and the **Museo Provincial**, Alameda Sundheim 13 (*open Mon–Fri, 9–2*). The town's theatre is an Art Deco aberration that resembles an Italian ice cream parlour, but the real curiosity of Huelva is the **Barrio Reina Victoria**, a neighbourhood constructed by and for the employees of the English Río Tinto mining company in the 19th century. The houses, now in a state of disrepair, sport gable ends and chimney pots in true English suburban style. Just out of town, where the Odiel and Tinto rivers meet, is the 36m-high hooded statue of Christopher Columbus, sculpted by Gertrude Whitney and presented to Spain by the USA in 1929. Huelvans are an isolated bunch, flanked and maybe intimidated by the presence of haughty Sevilla on one side and the expanse of Portugal on the other. They are nonetheless friendly and welcoming and, hoping to put aside centuries of stagnation, are optimistic and fervent in their desire to play a more important role in the future of the new Spain and Europe.

Huelva ✉ *21000*

Where to Stay

There's little to detain you in Huelva for longer than one night, but there's a reasonable selection of accommodation. The ★★★★**Luz Huelva**, ✆ 95 925 00 11, 🖨 95 925 81 10, is at Alameda Sundheim 26, near the Columbus monument, with pool, tennis courts and air-conditioned rooms (*17,000* *pts*). The ★★★**Tartessos**, C/ Martín Alonso Pinzón 13, ✆ 95 928 27 11, 📠 95 925 06 17, is comfortable and central (*11,500 pts*). The solicitous ★★**San Miguel**, Santa María 6, ✆ 95 924 52 03, has decent rooms for around *4000 pts*, and at the bottom of the scale the ★**París**, C/ Rico 6, ✆ 95 924 88 16, and **La Vega**, Pza. Independencia 15, ✆ 95 924 15 63, both have basic rooms for *3000 pts*.

Eating Out

Huelva packs some surprises in the culinary department; its markets keep the restaurants well supplied with gleaming fresh seafood and Huelvans like to eat out. For perfectly prepared seafood at affordable prices, head 7km out of town to **Las Candelas**, Ctra. Punta Umbría at the Aljaraque crossing, ✆ 95 931 83 01 (*2700 pts*). *Closed Sun*. Traditionally the best place in town is still **Los Gordos**, Carmen 14, ✆ 95 924 62 66, where they concentrate on simple dishes such as shellfish soup and grilled red mullet, but there's also a good selection of meats (*2000 pts*). *Closed Sat eve and Sun*). In the busy pedestrian heart of the town **El Timón**, Arquitecto Peréz Carasa 18, ✆ 95 924 66 28, may be a bit shabby on the outside but inside it's as a good little Spanish restaurant should be, typical both in its décor and menu. A full dinner with starter, mixed fried fish and wine costs *2500 pts* and there's a set menu for *1500 pts*. The real find in Huelva has to be the plain, family-run bar **Los Gallegos** on the same street, where delicious tapas cost a measly *200 pts*, *raciones* from *450 pts*; *pinchitos, gambas ajillo, merluza frita* or *a la plancha, pulpo a la gallega, calamares*—they're all scrumptious.

Around Huelva

Twenty-seven kilometres (17 miles) east of Huelva on the N431 you may visit the once-important town of **Niebla**, now forgotten behind its decayed Romano-Moorish walls. There's a Roman bridge and some interesting old churches and Moorish buildings. Christopher Columbus set out on his epic voyage from **Palos de la Frontera**, 5km (3 miles) southeast of Huelva. Some 4km (2½ miles) to the west, the **Monasterio de la Rábida** was Columbus's home while he planned the trip, and the rooms he used are maintained much as they were then. (*Visits by guided tour only; Tues–Sun 10–1, 4–6, tours hourly*.) The **Muelle de las Carabelas** (*open Tues–Fri 10–2 and 5–9, Sat and Sun 11–8; adm 500 pts*), also at La Rabida, between the monastery and the river, features three full-size models of the original ships that made the voyage. Buses run to La Rábida hourly from Huelva's bus station.

Coming from Huelva by bus to **Ayamonte**, you'll be deposited next to the pretty square behind the harbour filled with small boats. If you're on your way to Portugal, walk through the square and follow the signs for about 500m, where a flat-bottomed boat will be waiting to take you and 40 cars across the narrow stretch of the Guadiana river to the Portuguese town of Vila Real de Santo António. Just across the water, the beaches of **Isla Cristina** are more popular with Spaniards than with foreigners. If you find yourself here around Easter, Isla Cristina's Holy Week processions rival those of Sevilla—it would be worth planning a visit for these alone. Heading back east to Huelva, along the N431, you'll pass the sleepy town of **Lepe**; the butt of Andalucían jokes, in the same way as the Irish, Poles and Newfoundlanders are elsewhere, though rather sportingly every May the *leperos* hold a festival of humour. This stretch of road between Huelva and Ayamonte has no real attraction for the tourist—orange groves interspersed with derelict buildings, scrapyards and mudflats. South of Lepe on the coast are two spots worth a visit—**La Antilla**, with its fine white sandy beach, and **El Rompido**, a pleasant little place being developed for tourism. Further east, the peninsula of **Punta Umbría** is one of the main tourist resorts of the area; its long sandy beaches offer all types of water sports.

Where to Stay and Eating Out

Ayamonte ✉ 21400

The **★★★★Parador Costa de la Luz**, El Castillito, ℰ 95 932 07 00, ☎ 95 932 07 00, may not be on the beach but is situated on the edge of the Guadiana river, with fine views over the sea and across the river to Portugal—and a big swimming pool. Although it occupies the site of a long-gone Moorish castle, the *parador* was built more recently, in 1966 (*11,500 pts*). Ayamonte has a number of inexpensive hotels, such as the **★Europa**, Avda. de la Playa 45, ℰ 95 932 01 91 (*3000 pts*). There's a line of fine little restaurants behind the plaza, on the Paseo de la Ribera, all offering the day's special for around *800 pts*; a seafood meal will cost around *2000 pts*. For shellfish and *paella*, try the **Casino España** with its cool arches and terrace. At the **Casa Barberi**, Pso. de la Ribera 13, ℰ 95 947 02 89, you can peep through the palm trees at Portugal. You'll also find excellent seafood and fish stews at **Casa Luciano**, La Palma del Condado 1, ℰ 95 947 10 71, where many of the dishes are Portuguese-influenced and a good-value *menú del día* is offered at *2200 pts*.

Isla Cristina ✉ 21410

On the beach you have a choice between **★★Los Geranios**, Ctra. Isla Cristina–Playa, ℰ 95 933 18 00 (*4000–5500 pts*) and **★El Paraíso**, Camino de la Playa, ℰ 95 933 18 73 (*3600–6000 pts*).The best food in Isla Cristina is to be found at **Casa Rufino**, Ctra. de la Playa, ℰ 95 933 08 10, where a *menú-degustación* for four people consists of eight dishes and will set you back a modest *8750 pts* for the lot. *Lunch only, closed Weds, except in summer*. A local favourite is the restaurant **Acosta**, Pza. Caudillo 13, ℰ 95 933 14 20, for traditional Andalucían stews (*1500 pts*). *Closed Mon in winter*. The restaurant of the hotel **Paraíso Playa**, Avda. de la Playa, ℰ 95 933 18 73, serves a reasonable lunch for *1500 pts* on its terrace, between Holy Week and September.

La Rábida ✉ 21810

Next to the monastery is a small and comfortable inn, **★★★Hostería de La Rábida**, ℰ 95 935 03 12, where doubles go for *7000 pts*. There are only a few rooms, and the place is very popular, so be sure to book ahead for high season.

Punta Umbría ✉ 21100

The choice is wider at Punta Umbría. **★★El Ayamontino**, Avda. Andalucía, ℰ 95 531 14 50, ☎ 95 531 03 16, has the advantage of a good restaurant although it's a fair walk from the beach (*6000–7500 pts*). Its sister hotel, the **Ayamontino Ría**, is better located on Plaza Pérez Pastor 25, ℰ 95 531 14 58. **Hostal La Playa**, Avda. Océano 95, ℰ 95 531 01 12, is one of the cheapest hotels on the beach (*5500–6000 pts*), though those on a tight budget should head for the **Youth Hostel**, Avenida del

Océano 13, ✆ 95 935 16 50 (*1500pts a bed*). All these little resorts have cheaper hotels within reasonable distance of the beaches. In the busy season, phone ahead.

You'll raise a few eyebrows if you don't order fish at **El Paraíso**, Ctra. de Huelva–Punta Umbría, Km 11, ✆ 95 931 27 56, which has two dining-rooms, one beachy and informal, the other quite elegant, serving wonderfully fresh local seafood such as *coquinas* —wedge-shell clams (*3500–4500 pts*). Long popular is **La Esperanza**, Pza. Pérez Pastor 7, ✆ 95 931 10 45, with satisfying well-cooked dishes at reasonable prices—dogfish with tomato costs *1500 pts;* the rest are under *1000 pts.* The **El Ayamontino**, Avda. Andalucía 35, ✆ 95 931 1450, serves tasty fish soup, oven-cooked bream and rather tough sirloin steaks (*2000 pts*).

North of Huelva to the Sierra de Aracena

If you have a car you can comfortably explore the little-visited mountain villages in the Sierra de Aracena, less than a 2-hour drive from the capital. The N435, passing through beautiful forests of holm oaks and cork trees, takes you to the heart of this area; the countryside gets more mountainous and the views more scenic.

Tourist Information

Aracena: Pza. San Pedro, ✆ 95 912 82 06. *Open Mon–Sat 10–2.30 and 3.30–6.*

Aracena has the big attraction, the **Gruta de las Maravillas**, cavernous natural chambers with underground lakes and a spectacular cave of stalagmites and stalactites. On the hill above the cave stand the ruins of a **Moorish castle**, once occupied by the Knights Templar, and the church of **Nuestra Señora de los Dolores**, a fine medieval church with a *mudéjar* tower. Twelve kilometres (7½ miles) away to the west on the bumpy H521 is the extremely pretty village of **Alájar**, worth a visit for its natural caves, the *Sillita del Rey* and the *Salón de los Machos*; and also for the **Ermita de Nuestra Señora de los Ángeles**, with a 13th-century Gothic carving, and wonderful views. Perhaps the best of these villages is the white village of **Almonaster la Real**, in an attractive rural setting, with the remains of a 1000-year-old **mosque**. Nearby **Cortegana** has the 16th-century church of **Divino Salvador**, with its three handsome wrought-iron pulpits, and the inevitable ruins of a medieval castle.

In **Aroche**, further west, the white houses bask in the sun under the remains of an Almoravid fortress, containing a bullring. There's a small municipal **archaeological museum** and the tiny, unbelievable **Museo del Rosario**—yes, a rosary bead museum. On your way back to Huelva from here, you can stop in **Jabugo** to try the best-known and best-tasting cured ham in Spain, and don't dare say otherwise. Heading back to Huelva on the N435, **Valverde del Camino** is notable only for its furniture and shoe industries.

Where to Stay and Eating Out

In the middle of the Sierra Morena on the road to Portugal, 6km (3½ miles) from Aracena, is the **★Finca Buenvino**, Los Marines, Huelva, ✆/🖷 95 912 40 34, a grand guest house run by a locally well-known English family, the Chestertons. Lunch is served beside the pool; dinner is taken with the family (*12,000 pts per person including dinner; book in advance*). Otherwise, accommodation north of Huelva is limited to simple *hostales*.

Aracena ✉ 21200

Aracena has the most comfortable rooms at the modern **Sierra de Aracena**, Gran Vía 21, ☎ 95 912 60 19 (*5500 pts*) and the **Sierpes**, C/ Mesones 19, ☎ 95 911 01 47 (*3600 pts*). In Aracena, at the entrance to the caves, **Restaurante Casas**, C/ Pozo de la Nieve 39, ☎ 95 911 00 44, styled after a traditional *venta*, serves Sierra pork every which way you can think of (*2000 pts and upwards*).

Almonaster la Real ✉ 21290

The **Casa García**, Avda. San Martín 2, ☎ 95 913 04 09 (*3500–5000 pts*), has the advantage of a reasonable restaurant attached to it, while **La Cruz**, C/ Los Llanos 8, ☎ 95 914 3135, has doubles for *3500 pts*. **Casa García**, Avda. de San Martín 2, ☎ 95 913 04 09, provides okayish country cooking at rock-bottom prices.

Jabugo ✉ 21290

Jabugo has a very friendly small hotel: **La Aurora**, C/ Barco 9, ☎ 95 912 11 46 (*3000 pts for a small double room with bath*). In a wonderful location in the heart of the Sierra de Aracena y Picos de Aroche Park, the **Galaroza Sierra**, Ctra. Sevilla-Lisboa, Km 69.5, Galaroza, ☎ 95 912 32 37, ✉ 95 911 72 36 offers rooms with a view (*from 4000 pts*). Try the delicious **Mesón Jabugo** in Jabugo, Ctra. de San Juan del Puerto s/n, ☎ 95 912 15 15. Here they smoke their own hams and export them to every corner of Spain, and beyond.

The Coast South of Huelva

Tourist Information

Mazagón: Edificio Mancomunidad Moguer–Palos, ☎ 95 937 60 44 (in the same building as the police station).

Matalascañas: Urbanización Playa de Matalascañas, ☎ 95 943 00 86.

Twenty-three kilometres (14½ miles) south of Huelva, along the coastal route, is **Mazagón**, a get-away-from-it-all family resort, surrounded by pine trees and lovely beaches. From here it's a straight shot to Torre de la Higuera, and the big hotel developments around the endless **Matalascañas Beach**, the most international of Huelva's resorts. This is the dead end of the coastal highway; the only place you can go is the tiny inland village of **El Rocío**, which would not even be on the map were it not for the annual *romería* at Pentecost, the biggest and perhaps the oldest in Spain. It is traditional to arrive in a horse-drawn, covered wagon. Campfires burn all night, and the atmosphere is pure electricity.

Las Marismas

Add the water of the broad Guadalquivir to this flat coastal plain, and the result is southern Europe's greatest marshland wildlife preserve. Las Marismas is another world, a bit of the Everglades in a country better known for hot dry mountains. Hundreds of species of migratory birds pass through in the spring and autumn—storks among them—but Las Marismas has a fantastically varied population of its own: rare golden eagles, snowy egrets, flamingos, griffin vultures, tortoises, red deer, foxes and European lynx.

As in the Everglades, wildlife congregates around 'islands' among the wetlands; here they're called *corrales*, built of patches of dune anchored by surrounding shrubs and stands of low pines. Also like the Everglades, Las Marismas is threatened by development from the growing resorts like Matalascañas. This has become Spain's top environmental concern, and the government has limited coastal development and also set aside a large slice of the area as the **Parque Nacional del Coto Doñana**. Doñana was closed to visitors in 1998; a chemical factory spilt thousands of tons of toxic mud into the Río Guadalquivir, and hence the park, causing an ecological disaster. Check with the tourist offices in Huelva or Sevilla before you go, then head for the Centro de Recepción de Acebuche about half-way between El Rocío and Matalascañas which runs Land Rover tours around the park. Keep in mind that the wetlands are largely dried up in the summer. Whenever you come, bring a few gallons of mosquito repellent and watch out for quicksand.

Where to Stay and Eating Out

In an attractive pine-tree setting, looking down onto Mazagón beach, the modern ★★★★**Parador Cristóbal Colón**, Ctra. Huelva– Matalascañas, © 95 953 63 00, ◉ 95 953 62 28, is the best option, with pleasant gardens, pool and air-conditioned rooms (*13,000 pts*). Mazagón has a number of restaurants and cafés around Avenida Fuente Piña. There's not much to distinguish between them but at least they're lively. Many people eat in their hotels down on Matalascañas Beach.

There are a number of resort hotels at Matalascañas, predictably packed in high season. ★★**El Cortijo**, Sector E–P 15/49, © 95 943 02 59, ◉ 95 944 85 70, is a pleasant alternative next to Coto Doñana; it's a 5-minute walk from the beach and there are facilities for horse-riding (*9000–10,500 pts*). In the unlikely setting of El Rocío, the resort hotel ★★★**Puente del Rey**, Avda. de Canaliega s/n, © 95 947 71 24, offers all kinds of amenities such as accompanied riding in the Coto Doñana National Park, language courses and even guitar lessons (*from 8500 pts*). **Da Pino,** Avda. Adelfas 1, © 95 943 02 03, is a pricey Italian restaurant but the food is good, with pastas, excellent salads and good steaks (*3500 pts*). *Closed Mon and Christmas.* **Los Galanes**, in the Edificio Las Begoñas, has a lovely terrace where you can enjoy your seafood at leisure (*1500 pts*).

Cádiz

If Cádiz were a tiny village, the government would immediately declare it a national monument and put up a sign. It's a big, busy seaport, though, and the tourist business generally leaves it alone. It's a pity, for Cádiz (if you pronounce it any other way but 'Caddy' with a long 'a', no one will understand you) is one of the most distinctive Spanish cities, worth spending a few days in even if there are few 'sights'. The city comes in colours—a hundred shades of off-white—bleached and faded by sun and spray into a soft patina, broken only by the golden dome of a rambling baroque cathedral.

History

Cádiz modestly claims to be the oldest city in western Europe. It's hard to argue; the Phoenician city of *Gadir* has a documented foundation date of 1100 BC and, while other cities

The Best Carnival in Spain

This took its present form in the 19th century; some claim there is a strong Cuban influence behind its masquerades and crazy music. It says something about Cádiz that under the dictatorship, this was the only carnival Franco failed to suppress, and if you ever experience it you'll know why. In the second week of February, if there were an instrument to measure atmosphere, it would glow red here; everyone, young or old, native or stranger, is roaming the streets, singing and dancing. Small food stalls spring up on every corner, and the bars, cafés and restaurants have a hard time keeping up with the constant flow of revellers.

---

have traces of older settlements, it would be difficult to find another city west of Greece with a continuous urban life of 3000 years. *Gadir* served as the port for shipping Spanish copper and tin, and was undoubtedly the base for the now-forgotten Phoenician trade routes with west Africa and England—and possibly even for explorations to America. Cádiz, however, prefers to consider Hercules its founder, and he appears on the arms of the city between his famous pillars. Under Roman rule *Gades*, as it was called, was a favoured city, especially under Julius Caesar who held his first public office here. The city was out of the spotlight until the 16th century, when the American trade and Spain's growth as a naval power made a major port of it once again. Sir Francis Drake came here in 1587 and, as every schoolboy knows—or used to know—'singed the king of Spain's beard'. Later, British admirals followed the custom for a century, calling every decade or so for a fish supper and an afternoon's sacking and burning. The years after 1720, when Cádiz controlled the American market, shaped its present character. Its shining hour came in 1812, when the constitution was declared here, and the city became the capital of free Spain.

Getting Around

By ferry: Cádiz isn't the big passenger port it used to be, but you can still take the weekly ferries to Tenerife–Las Palmas–Arrecife in the Canary Islands. They run a little more frequently in the summer. There's also a regular ferry ride from the port to El Puerto de Santa María. **Tickets: Transmediterránea** office, Avda. Ramón de Carranza 26, ✆ 95 628 43 11/95 628 43 50.

By train: You can go only to Jerez (20 daily, stopping at El Puerto de Santa María) and Sevilla (8 daily) directly. The station is at the narrow landward end of the old city, just a few blocks from the Plaza San Juan de Dios, ✆ 95 625 43 02.

By bus: Cádiz is served by two bus companies: Los Amarillos, Avda. Ramón de Carranza 31 (by the port), ✆ 95 622 42 71, takes the route west to Rota and Sanlúcar de Barrameda; Comes, Pza. de España, ✆ 95 621 17 63, takes the route east to Tarifa and Algeciras. City bus no.1, which leaves from in front of Comes, will take you from the Plaza de España to Cádiz's suburban beaches and to new Cádiz.

Tourist Information

On the corner of Plaza de Mina and Calle Calderón de la Barca 1, ✆ 95 621 13 13. *Open Mon and Sat 9–2, Tues–Fri 9–7, closed Sunday.*

The approach to Cádiz is a dismal one, through marshes, saltpans and modern suburbs before arriving at the **Puerta de Tierra**, entrance to the old city on the peninsula. Almost everything about warfare in the 18th century had a certain decorum, and Cádiz's gates and formidable **land walls** (1757), all well preserved, are among the most aesthetically pleasing structures in town. The old city is a maze of lanes bathed in soft lamplight after dusk, when the numerous cafés fill up with young, exuberant *gaditanos*. A walk through the myriad cobbled streets, past solid doors carved from the trees of South American forests, and balconies spilling over with flowers, will take you back in history to the time when mighty Cádiz bustled with industry as the gateway to the Americas. Keep an eye out for the little plaques—marking the birthplaces of, amongst others, Manuel de Falla, and Miranda, the first president of Venezuela— reminders of what an important role this small city has often played. In an hour or so you can walk entirely around Cádiz on the coast road, past parks like the pretty **Alameda de Apodaca**, and forts and bastions of the 18th century.

Plaza San Juan de Dios and Around

From the Puerta de Tierra, the Cuesta de las Calesas leads down to the port and rail station, then around the corner to **Plaza San Juan de Dios**, the lively, palm-shaded centre of Cádiz, with most of the restaurants and hotels on the surrounding streets. Two blocks away is the **cathedral**, on a small plaza. Of the paintings within, Zurbarán's *Santa Úrsula* stands out. The composer Manuel de Falla has his tomb in the cathedral crypt (*open weekdays 10–1*). The **Museo de la Catedral** has a lot of ecclesiastical gold and silverware, paintings by Murillo, Zurbarán and Alejo Fernández, and painted panels and an ivory crucifix by Alonso Cano (*open daily except Sun and Mon, 10–1; adm 500 pts, free for EU nationals*).

Continuing eastwards, the Plaza Topete was named after a *tophet*, the Phoenician temple dedicated to that nasty habit of theirs—sacrificing first-born babies; remains of one were found here. Now this is Cádiz's almost excessively colourful **market district**, spread around a wonderful, dilapidated old market building. A few more blocks east, the little church of **San Felipe Neri** on Calle Sacramento is an unprepossessing shrine to the beginnings of Spanish liberty. On 29 March 1812 an assembly of refugees from Napoleon's occupation of the rest of Spain gathered here and declared Spain an independent republic, guaranteeing full political and religious freedom. Though their **constitution**, and their revolution, proved stillborn, it was a notable beginning for Spain's struggle towards democracy. Inside is a beautiful *Immaculate Conception* by Murillo (*open Tues–Fri 8.30–10 and 5–7; Sat, Sun and hols 9–1*).

Around the corner, Cádiz's very good **Municipal Museum** has a huge Romantic-era mural depicting the 1812 event. In front of it, in the main hall, is the museum's star exhibit, a 15.4m (50ft) **scale model of Cádiz**, made entirely of mahogany and ivory by an unknown obsessive in 1779. Among a collection of portraits of Spanish heroes is the Duke of Wellington, who carried the title of Duke of Ciudad Rodrigo. The best picture shows Hercules about to give Napoleon a good bashing with his club (*open daily except Mon, 9–1 and 5–8, Sat and Sun 9–1*).

Plaza de Mina and Around

On this lovely square, in the northwestern corner of the peninsula, you'll find the tourist information office and the Museum of Fine Arts and Archaeology (*open Wed–Sat, 9–8; Tues 2.30–8; Sun 9.30–2.30; adm 250 pts, free for EU nationals*). Best in the museum are the

The Founding Father

Andalucía for itself, for Spain and for Humanity

So reads the proud device on the regional escutcheon, hurriedly cooked up by the Andalucíans after the regional autonomy laws of the 1970s made them masters in their own house once again. Above the motto we see a strong fellow, mythologically under-dressed and accompanied by two lions. Though perhaps more familiar to us for his career among the Hellenes, he is also the first Andalucían—HERCULES DOMINATOR FUNDATOR.

The Greeks themselves admit that Hercules found time for two extended journeys to the distant and little-known West. In the eleventh of his Twelve Labours, the Apples of the Hesperides caper, he made it as far as the environs of Tangier, where he dispatched the giant Antaeus. The tenth Labour brought Hercules into Spain, sailing in the golden goblet of Helios and using his lion skin for a sail. In the fabled land of Tartessos, on the 'red island' of Erytheia, he slew the three-headed titan Geryon and stole his cattle. Before heading back to Greece, he founded the city of Gades, or Cádiz, on the island (Cádiz, surrounded by marshes is almost an island). He also erected his well-known Pillars, Gibraltar and Mount Abyle, across the way in Africa. His return was one of the all-time bad trips; whenever you're crazed and dying on some five-hour 'semi-direct' Andalucían bus ride (say, Granada to Córdoba via Rute), think of Hercules, marching Geryon's cows through Spain and over the Pyrenees, then making a wrong turn that took him halfway down the Italian peninsula before he noticed the mistake. After mortal combats with several other giants and monsters, he finally made it to Greece— but then his nemesis, Hera, sent a stinging blue-tail fly to stampede the cattle. They didn't stop until they reached the Scythian Desert.

To most people, Hercules is little more than mythology's most redoubtable Dog Warden, rounding up not only Cerberus, the Hound of Hell, but most of the other stray monsters that dug up the roses and soiled the footpaths of the Heroic Age. But there is infinitely more than this to the character of the most-travelled, hardest-working hero of them all. In antiquity, wherever Hercules had set foot the people credited him with founding nations and cities, building roads and canals, excavating lakes and draining swamps. And there is the intellectual Hercules, the master of astronomy and lord of the zodiac, the god of prophecy and eloquence who taught both the Latins and the Spaniards their letters. One version has it that the original Pillars of Hercules were not mountains at all, but columns, like those of the Temple of Jerusalem, and connected with some alphabetical mysticism. Ancient mythographers had their hands full, sorting out the endless number of deities and heroes known to the peoples of Europe, Africa and the Middle East, trying to decide whether the same figure was hiding behind different names and rites. Varro recorded no fewer than 44 Hercules, and modern scholars have found the essential Herculean form in myths from Celtic Ireland to Mesopotamia. Melkarth, the Phoenician Hercules, would have had his temples in southern Spain long before the first Greek ever saw Gibraltar. Not a bad fellow to have for a founding father—and a reminder that in Andalucía the roots of culture are as as deep as in any corner of Europe.

paintings: some Murillos and very good portraits of the *Four Evangelists* and *John the Baptist* by Zurbarán. On the top floor are unaffectedly charming puppets and stage sets from a Cádiz genre of marionette show called *Tía Norica*, still performed in these parts. Around the corner, on Calle Rosario Ponce, the **Oratorio de la Santa Cueva**, with its three Goya frescoes (the only ones in Andalucía), is currently closed for renovation.

Cádiz ✉ *11000*

Where to Stay

moderate

There is a good *parador* in Cádiz—the ★★★★**Atlántico**, Avda. Duque de Nájera 9, ✆ 95 622 69 05, ✉ 95 621 45 82. It is a modern building with wonderful views over the Atlantic and a large outdoor swimming pool (*15,000–19,000 pts*).

inexpensive

The ★★★**Francia y París**, Pza. San Francisco 2, ✆ 95 622 23 48, ✉ 95 622 24 31, around the corner from Plaza Mina, is a quiet, well-run hotel (9500 pts). Nearby, the ★**Imares**, San Francisco 9, ✆ 95 621 22 57, has comfortable rooms (*4000–5500 pts*), prices depending on the plumbing. The **Hostal Bahia**, Plocia 5, off Plaza San Juan de Dios, ✆ 95 625 90 61, has air-conditioned rooms with TV (*6500 pts*). On the other side of the Puerta de Tierra, in the new part of Cádiz, there's just as much choice. The Paseo Marítimo is lively, so don't feel you're missing out if you stay here. The ★★**San Remo**, Pso. Marítimo 3, ✆ 95 625 22 02, ✉ 95 625 22 03, has comfortable rooms overlooking the beach (*7000–8500 pts*).

cheap

There will be no problem finding cheaper—lots of sailors pass through here. Some of the cheapest places are near the Plaza San Juan de Dios in the old town. Try the **Hostal Fantoni**, Flamenco 5, ✆ 95 628 27 04, full of tiles and cool marble with a breezy roof terrace (*3500–5000 pts*). The **Hostal España**, ✆ 95 628 55 00, nearby at Marques de Cadiz 9, has doubles from *4000–5000 pts*. The ★**Hostal Manolita**, Benjumeda 2, ✆ 95 621 15 77, is clean and family-run (*around 2800 pts*). For even cheaper establishments just look for the *camas* signs and take your pick. Don't hesitate to turn down anything that appears too run down; some places appear as if they haven't had visitors for decades. In a side street off the Paseo Marítimo is the reasonable and welcoming ★**La Playa**, Dr Herrera Quevedo 1, ✆ 95 625 84 00, with rooms going (*4000 pts with bath*).

Eating Out

expensive

Dining, of course, means more fish. **El Faro**, C/ San Félix 15, ✆ 95 621 10 68, is a place where you can get to know all of the amazingly wide range of seafood—things that we don't even have names for in English such as *mojarras* and *urtas*—that come out of this part of the Atlantic; but apart from these outlandish creatures you'll have no problem ordering the more recognizable varieties—steamed hake with asparagus, clams with spinach, fried fish *a la Gaditana*, as well as a selection of meat dishes (*dinner 3000–4500 pts and a menú del día at 2500 pts*). **El Balandro**, Alameda Apodaca 22, ✆ 95 622 09 92, is by the Alameda Apodaca walls, and its rustically decorated upstairs dining-room looks over to Puerto de Santa María. The menu is a mix of seafood and Spanish specialities like *Carne de Avila*. If you feel like you really can't look at another fish, try **El Candil**, Javier de Burgos s/n, in the heart of town. Its garlic chicken with paprika is sensational.

moderate

El Sardinero, Pza. San Juan de Dios 4, ✆ 95 628 25 05, is one of the oldest restaurants in the city, with a variety of Basque and *andaluz* dishes, which you can enjoy at the outside tables (*about 2500 pts*). Older still is the rustic **Ventorillo del Chato**, Vía Augusta Julia, Cortadura, ✆ 95 625 00 25, on the road to San Fernando. It claims to have been around for 200 years and is still going strong (*3500 pts*).

In newer Cádiz, along the Paseo Marítimo, there's a wide choice of restaurants, nearly all with terraces or outside seating. **Curro el Cojo**, Pso. Marítimo 2, ✆ 95 625 31 86, specializes in meats from the Sierra, pork and game in particular (*full dinner from 2500 pts*). **La Costera**, further along on Calle Dr Fleming 8, ✆ 95 627 34 88, specializes in Basque and Galician cuisine and also has a good wine list, and dining on the terrace (*around 3000 pts*). Behind the sea front, opposite the football stadium at Avda. José León de Carranza 4, **El Brocal**, ✆ 95 625 77 59, is a small restaurant serving meat with a North African and Greek bias (*2500–3500 pts*). *Closed Sun.*

inexpensive

A little further along, on the corner of Honduras and San Germán, the family-run **La Piconera**, C/ San Germán 5, ✆ 95 622 18 84, is a less expensive choice with a simpler, yet nonetheless wholesome menu (*around 2000 pts*)—but you don't get the view. Two smaller restaurants near La Costera in new Cádiz are **El Noray** and **Baro**, both predictably specializing in shellfish (*2000 pts*).

Around Cádiz

Like those to the east, the beaches around Cádiz are popular mostly with Spaniards—more crowded, though, at least in July and August. Just the same, the beaches are lovely and huge, the towns behind them relatively unspoiled; there may be few better places in Spain to baste yourself, with plenty of opportunities for exploring *bodegas*.

Tourist Information

Sanlúcar de Barrameda: Calzada del Ejército s/n, ✆ 95 636 61 10.
Rota: Pza. Andalucía 3, ✆ 95 681 01 05.
El Puerto de Santa María: C/ Guadalete, ✆ 95 654 24 75.

Sanlúcar and Rota

Sanlúcar de Barrameda makes *manzanilla*, most ethereal of sherries. It is known as the port that launched Magellan on his way around the world, and Columbus on his second voyage to the Indies; it is also the birthplace of the artist-writer Francisco Pacheco, Velázquez's teacher. The town has a certain crumbling colonial charm and an exceptionally pretty main plaza.

Worth a visit are the church of **Nuestra Señora de la O** with its fine *mudéjar* portal and 16th-century coffered ceiling (*open 9–1.30*), and the 19th-century **Montpensier Palace**, with its extensive library and paintings by Murillo, El Greco, Rubens and Goya (*open 8–2.30*). Although its beaches are not major-league, this town has always been a popular summer destination with Spanish holidaymakers for its excellent cheap seafood. The Bajo de Guía is a particularly charming fishing district, and from here you can take the motor boat over to Coto Doñana. If you have an afternoon to spare, amuse yourself by visiting the public fish auction in **Bonanza**, 4km away. **Chipiona** is a family resort, full of small *pensiones* and *hostales*, with a good beach at **Playa de Regla** near the lighthouse.

Next, on the edge of the bay of Cádiz, comes **Rota**, a bigger, flashier resort taking advantage of the best and longest beach on the coast; the town is pretty, though it's a bit overbuilt. It's also full of unpicturesque Americans from the largest naval base in the region, just outside town. This was the key base Franco gave up in the 1953 deal with President Eisenhower; in the dealings over the future of Spain's role in NATO, the Americans made it unpleasantly clear this base is not a subject for negotiation, although in the 1986 NATO referendum this region turned out the highest 'yes' vote in Spain. However, despite a fair amount of posturing on both sides, the numbers at the base have fallen by about a third in recent years.

El Puerto de Santa María and Puerto Sherry

Across the bay from Cádiz lies **El Puerto de Santa María**, the traditional port of the sherry houses in Jerez, which has quite a few *bodegas* of its own—Osborne, Terry and Duff Gordon among other famous names. The town has some interesting churches, some mansions of the Anglo-Spanish sherry aristocracy, and the fine, restored 13th-century *mudéjar* **Castillo de San Marcos**. The century-old **bullring** ranks with those of Sevilla and Ronda in prestige. El Puerto itself isn't a big resort, but it's a typical town of Cádiz province, with bright bustling streets, excellent restaurants and some good beaches (**Puntilla** especially) on the edges of town. **Puerto Sherry** is a modern marina, built in the late 1980s, and a pleasant place to spend an afternoon or evening. It has yet to reach its potential (or occupancy) so it's a little lacking in character.

Where to Stay and Eating Out

It's no problem finding a place to stay in any of the coastal resorts; especially in the high season, little old ladies meet the buses to drag you off to their *hostales*. But many of the restaurants in this area, informal cafés where you can pick out the fish that catches your fancy, are open only during the summer.

Sanlúcar ✉ 11540, **Chipiona** ✉ 11550, **and Rota** ✉ 11520

The resorts around Cádiz are seasonal and many hotels close during the winter months. In Sanlúcar, the most delightful hotel by far is **Los Helechos**, Pza. de Madre de Dios 9, ☎ 95 636 13 49, situated in the old part of town and built around two beautiful courtyards (*5500–7500 pts*). Or, in contrast, you could try unglamorous **Hostal La Blanca Paloma**, ☎ 95 36 36 44, Plaza San Roque 15, the only place in town suitable for those on a tight budget (*4500 pts*), or the neoclassical ★★★**Tartaneros**, Tartaneros 8, ☎ 95 636 20 44, ✆ 95 636 00 45 (*8000–10,000 pts*).

In Chipiona, the ***Paquita**, Francisco Lara 26, ✆ 95 637 02 06, or the **San Miguel**, Avenida de la Regla 79, ✆ 95 637 29 76, are decent *hostales* near the beach—and really typical of what you'll find in these modest resorts (*4500–5500 pts*). The ****Del Sur**, Avda. Sevilla 2, ✆ 95 637 03 50, is fancier, with a pool and garden, and still a bargain at the price (*7500 pts*). There's a campsite, **Pinar de Chipiona**, ✆ 95 637 23 21, 3km outside of Chipiona towards Rota.

Rota offers more of the same, including the **Hostal Macavi**, ✆ 95 681 33 36, Ecija 11, near the beach off Sevilla (*4000 pts*) and a campsite, **Camping Puntador**, ✆ 95 681 33 03 nearby, just out of the town. The place also has a few classy modern resort hotels including the *****Playa de la Luz**, on the beach at Arroyo Hondo, ✆ 95 681 05 00, 🖅 95 81 06 06, a sports-orientated hotel with a lovely pool and gardens (*14,500 pts*).

Casa Bigote, Bajo de Guía, ✆ 95 636 26 96, is a restaurant famous throughout Andalucía for its delicious appetizers, classic dishes of the region, and the best and freshest of seafood in all its varieties; the crayfish are a must, and you can try the local *manzanilla* with the day's catch. You may find you'll need more than one visit, though, as the tapas selection in the bar opposite is extensive and truly excellent. Get there early or you won't find a table (*3000–4000 pts*). *Closed Sun.*

Down on the beach front, Casa Bigote's main rival is the attractive **Mirador de Doñana**, Bajo de Guía, ✆ 95 636 42 05, another popular bar and restaurant on three levels with a panoramic view across to the bird reserve. Particularly delicious are: *cigalas* (crayfish), *angulas* (baby eels) and *nido de rapé a la Sanluqueña*, a nest of straw potato chips, deep-fried with monkfish and parsley (*3000 pts*). In Rota the cuisine is heavily influenced by the presence of the naval base—pizza and Chinese restaurants alongside the usual seafood.

El Puerto de Santa María ✉ 11500

The loveliest place to stay in El Puerto de Santa María is the ******Hotel Monasterio San Miguel**, C/ Larga 27, ✆ 95 654 04 40, 🖅 95 654 26 04, a 16th-century former monastery. It's marvellously soothing with tranquil cloisters, religious artefacts and a swimming pool discreetly placed where the vegetable garden used to be. The games room (once the refectory) and the restaurant are particularly interesting (*22,000 pts*). A less expensive alternative is the **Santa María**, Avda. Bajamar s/n, ✆ 95 687 32 11, a 17th-century palace with the modern addition of a swimming pool (*6500–12,000 pts*). Another place many people like is the *****Puertobahía**, Avda. de La Paz 38, Urbanización Valdelagrana, ✆ 95 686 27 21, 🖅 95 686 27 21, also on the beach (*7500–10,500 pts*). At the other end of the scale there's the **Pensión Piña Larga** 130, ✆ 95 685 35 32, near the centre (*2500 pts*) or another **Santa María**, Muñoz Seco 35, ✆ 95 685 36 31, a *pensión* far more basic than its namesake.

Apart from the excellent *bodegas* and simple beach cafés, El Puerto has some deservedly popular restaurants. The most successful is **La Goleta**, Ctra. de Rota, ✆ 95 685 42 32, with simple but well-prepared seafood dishes, especially the fish cooked in salt, the *tosta de salmón* and the *porgy* in brandy (*3000 pts*). *Closed Mon except in July and Aug.* **El Faro**, ✆ 95 687 09 52, near the roundabout on Ctra. de Roma, Km 0.5, just outside town, also has an excellent reputation for its regional cuisine (3000 pts). Down on the riverside quay, the **Guadalete**, Avda. de la Bajamar 14, ✆ 95 687

02 98, attracts crowds for its shrimps, sole and clams (*2500 pts*). *Closed Mon and 15–29 Nov*—a thoroughly professional joint that's been getting it right for decades. The liveliest place to dine is **Romerijo's** on the Ribera del Marisco, ℗ 95 654 33 53; you can eat the freshest of fish and seafood as you sit at the tables outside or enjoy a take-away wrapped in a paper funnel. Everyone throws discarded shells or crab claws into one of the red buckets on each table. A kilo of shellfish is enough for four people. The place is noisy and fantastic value; you can be fully sated for *around 1200 pts*). If you're in Puerto Sherry, try **Curro del Cojo**, Pza. Marqués Real Tesoro 7, ℗ 95 654 16 91. It's small and intimate and resembles the inside of a ship's cabin (*2000–2500 pts*).

Jerez de la Frontera

The name is synonymous with wine—by the English corruption of Jerez into sherry—but besides the *finos*, *amontillados*, *olorosos* and other varieties of that noble sauce, Jerez also ships out much of Spain's equally good brandy. Most of the well-known companies, whose advertising is plastered all over Spain, have their headquarters here, and they're quite accustomed to taking visitors through the *bodegas*. Don't be shy. Most are open to visitors between 9am and 1pm on Mondays to Fridays, though not in August, or when they're busy with the *vendimia* (harvest) in September. Admission prices are around 500 pts upwards and usually include tasting sessions. However, booking is strongly advised—numbers are restricted on guided tours and many people who have failed to reserve places have been turned away.

One of the most interesting *bodegas* to visit is that belonging to **González Byass**, C/ Manuel María González 12, ℗ 95 634 00 00. The tour includes the old sawdust-strewn *bodegas* that have held the sherry *soleras* for two centuries; the casks have been signed by many famous visitors over the years from Orson Welles to the Hollywood swimming star Esther Williams. The tour ends at the *degustacíon*, where the motto is, 'If you don't have a *copa* at eleven o'clock, you should have eleven at one', and cellarmen demonstrate their skill at pouring sherry from distances of a metre or more into the small *copitas*, in order to aerate the wine. There is a very classy gift shop. The *bodega* of **John Harvey** is another well worth a visit—watch out for the alligator at the end of the tour. The *Semana Santa* festival in Jerez is more intimate than, but in its way just as splendid as, that in Sevilla. The nightly processions escorting the Saint and Madonna images create a city-wide pageant. Late in the night, as they return home through the backstreets, they are serenaded by impromptu solo voices; for the finest singers, the whole procession halts in appreciation.

Getting Around

Cádiz is the base for visiting Jerez and the coasts. The Amarillo company provides a regular **bus** service from Cádiz to all the coastal towns, and at least five daily to Jerez. Infrequent buses connect Jerez with Rota, Sanlúcar and El Puerto. Almost all the Sevilla–Cádiz buses stop in Jerez and El Puerto as do the trains. There are frequent connections for Arcos de la Frontera and Ronda and one bus a day to Córdoba and Granada. Jerez stations for buses and **trains** are together on the eastern edge of town, ℗ 95 633 66 82.

There's a regular **ferry** service from El Puerto to Cádiz (*200 pts*)—more fun than the bus. Parking can be hard to find if you're in a **car** but it is sometimes best to be based in Jerez for the surrounding area to avoid the queues on the roads into Cádiz.

Tourist Information

Alameda Cristina s/n, ✆ 95 633 11 50 (offer information on visiting sherry *bodegas*).

Business is not as good as it was, for sherry sales are falling worldwide, but Jerez is growing. It's a fairly attractive town, at least in the centre, and it has a few lovely buildings for you to squint at after you've done the rounds of the *bodegas*. Its landmark is **La Colegiata** (also called San Salvador), a curious pseudo-Gothic church with a separate bell tower and baroque staircase. Works inside include a *Madonna* by Zurbarán and sculptures by Juan de Mesa. Nearby, on the central Plaza de los Reyes Católicos, **San Miguel** (begun in 1482) changes the scene to Isabelline Gothic—a fine example of that style, with a florid *retablo* inside (*open daily 8–9.45 and 7–9; Sun 9–1*). There is a Moorish **Alcázar** at the end of Calle Pérez Galdós, with a tower and some remains of the baths. **La Atalaya**, at Calle Cervantes, ✆ 95 618 21 00, is an interesting clock museum. Go before midday to hear them all chime (*open Mon–Fri 10.30–1*).

A new **archaeology museum** has opened opposite San Mateo on Plaza del Mercado (*open Tues–Sat 10–2.30 and Tues–Fri 4–7; adm 250 pts*). Outside town, on the road to Medina Sidonia, is the **Cartuja de la Defensión**, a 15th-century monastery with the best baroque façade (added in 1667) in Andalucía—a sort of giant *retablo* with sculptures by Alonso Cano and others. This is still a working monastery, and you'll need special permission to go inside. There is little reason to; what was the main attraction, a great altarpiece by Zurbarán, is scattered to the four winds—you can see panels in the museums of Sevilla and Cádiz. Do, however, visit the gardens and patio (*open Tues, Thurs and Sat 5–6.30*).

Horses and Flamenco

While in Jerez, look out for exhibitions scheduled at the **Escuela Andaluz del Arte Ecuestre** (School of Equestrian Art, Avda. Duque de Abrantes, ✆ 95 631 11 11). Jerez's snooty wine aristocracy takes horsemanship very seriously; they have some of the finest horses you're likely to see anywhere, and they know how to use them. You can see them, proud as Tío Pepe bottles, at the annual **Horse Fair** during the first half of May.

The origin of this fair can be traced back to the 13th century, and its events include jumping, classical riding, harness riding and Andalucían country riding. Being an Andalucían fair, it is also the best excuse for attending the *corrida*, drinking plenty of sherry and of course joining in the flamenco extravaganza. Every Thursday there is a spectacular 'horse ballet' at 12 noon (*adm from 2000 pts*). The show runs for about 1½ hours with a short interval (there's a bar which serves sherry), and afterwards you are free to wander through the stables meeting the delightful stars of the show. Additionally, there are tours between 11am and 1pm weekdays except Thursdays (*adm 500 pts*). Check with the tourist information for details of any special shows. Oh, and wear something warm during the winter months—the unheated arena can get very chilly.

Housed in one of the most beautiful buildings of the old part of the city is the **Flamenco Centre**, Palacio Penmartín, Pza. de San Juan, ✆ 95 634 92 65, which presents different activities throughout the year—concerts, exhibitions, seminars and video shows—in an effort to promote and prolong the art (*open Mon–Fri 9.30–1.30; closed for two weeks during Aug*).

In Jerez, there are many unremarkable hotels. The two top hotels are close to the centre of town, convenient for the fair and the Spanish Riding School.

expensive–moderate

The luxury ★★★★**Jerez**, Avda. Alcalde Álvaro Domecq 35, ✆ 95 633 06 00, ✉ 95 630 50 01, with a pool and tennis courts, is set in lovely tropical gardens, but is no bargain (*16,000–19,000 pts*). At no.11 of the same avenue, closer to town, the modern ★★★★**Royal Sherry Park**, ✆ 95 630 30 11, ✉ 95 631 13 00, has a pool and is set in a park (*16,500–18,000 pts*). Almost opposite is the ★★★**Avenida Jerez**, Avda. Álvaro Domecq 10, ✆ 95 634 74 11, ✉ 95 633 72 96, a characterless modern place (*overpriced at 14,000–28,000 pts*).

inexpensive–cheap

In the centre of town, with underground parking, the ★★**Serit**, Higueras 7, ✆ 95 634 07 00, ✉ 95 634 07 16, has comfy rooms for *6000 pts*. There's a decent selection down the lower end of the price scale. The ★★**Virt**, Higueras 20, ✆ 95 632 28 11, is a middle-range bargain with decent air-conditioned rooms from *3500 pts*. The ★**Las Palomas**, Higueras 17, ✆ 95 634 37 73, is good value at *3500 pts*; and the ★**San Andrés**, Morenos 12, ✆ 95 634 09 83, and the ★**Sanvi**, Morenos 10, ✆ 95 634 56 24, both offer basic rooms for about *3000 pts*. There's a Youth Hostel on Avenida Carrero Blanco 30, ✆ 95 634 28 90, 2km south of the centre (take bus nos.1 or 3 from Plaza del Arenal or no.9 from Plaza de las Angustias) with beds for *1500 pts*.

Eating Out

expensive

Even in a region of Spain known for the late hours it keeps, Jerez seems to go a step further. It's not at all unusual here to sit down to lunch at 3.30pm. Don't even think about dinner until after 10pm. The well-known **El Bosque**, Avda. Álvaro Domecq 26, ✆ 95 630 33 33/630 70 30, beautifully situated in the woods near the Parque de González Montoria, yet only a short distance from the centre of town, is formal, elegant and slightly dull. The seafood is good; try *langostinos de Sanlúcar, gambas de Huelva*, hake cooked in salt, or angler fish in shellfish sauce (*4000–5000 pts*). *Closed Sun.*

moderate

Closer to town, by the bullring, the **Tendido 6**, Circo 10, ✆ 95 634 48 35, has a covered patio with adjoining dining room, decorated on a *feria* theme, with bullfight memorabilia on the walls. Here the emphasis is on robust helpings of traditional food, and you can gorge to the full (*4000 pts*). *Closed Sun.* A couple of streets behind the tourist office is one of the favourite dining places in town, **Gaitán**, Gaitán 3, ✆ 95 634 58 59, proud bearer of a gastronomy award in the 1980s (*3500 pts*). *Closed Sun eve.* Near the Avenida Jerez hotel, **La Mesa Redonda**, Manuel de la Quintana 3, ✆ 95 634 00 69, is beautifully decorated with antique furniture and paintings, giving the impression of an old aristocratic Jerez home. It has a first-class kitchen serving excellent game and seasonal specialities, and takes its food seriously. For our money it's the best restaurant in Jerez (*3000–4000 pts*). *Closed Sun and Aug; reservations essential.*

inexpensive

Close by Gaitán, there's a great tapas bar in a passage off the Plaza del Arenal: **Bar Juanito** is the best among a clutch of tiny places on Pescadería Vieja. Try the *alcachofas en salsa* or the *costillas en adobo* (marinaded grilled pork chops). It is a crush at lunchtime; arrive early in the evening (*opens at 8pm*) if you want a table. Enjoy two or three tapas plus wine (*around 1000 pts*).

There are many street *bodegas* where you can try the whole spectrum of the area's produce. Try the **Alcazaba**, Medina 19, or **La Tasca**, C/ Matadero s/n, both near the centre.

From Cádiz to Algeciras

The green, hilly countryside of this region looks a lot like the parts of Morocco just across the straits. The hills force the main road away from the sea, leaving a few villages with fine beaches relatively unspoilt. These make good places to take time out from your overactive holiday; the problem is they're hard to reach unless you have a car.

Getting Around

By train: Trains go to Ronda, and from there to all points in eastern Andalucía; there is a daily *Talgo* to Madrid and points north. The station is across from the bus station.

By bus: Buses to Algeciras from the Comes station in Cádiz are frequent enough, but services to costal resorts like Conil, Barbate and Zahara are less so (two per day). Algeciras's bus station is in the Hotel Octavio complex, C/ San Bernardo; there are buses to La Línea (for Gibraltar) about every half-hour, and connections to the Costa del Sol.

Tourist Information

Algeciras: Juan de la Cierva s/n, by the port, ✆ 95 657 26 36.

Tarifa: Northern end of Paseo Alameda, outside the western wall of the old town, ✆ 95 668 09 93, *tarifa@mx3.redestb.es*. *Open Mon–Fri 10–2 and 6–8; 8–3 in winter.*

Beyond the marshland around Cádiz, you'll see the turn-offs first for **Sancti Petri**, a deserted town with a castle by the beach, then **Conil**. The main attraction of this stretch of road is **Vejer de la Frontera**, whitest of the 'white villages' of Andalucía, strangely moulded around its hilltop site like a Greek island town. The village was probably a Carthaginian citadel before becoming the Roman town of Besipo. Now it couldn't be more Moorish in its feel; a Moorish castle dominates the village and the 13th-century Gothic church built over the site of a mosque, lies deep within the town's sparkling clean, narrow whitewashed streets. There's a seldom-visited beach 9km away at El Palmar and, nearby, a Roman aqueduct in the beautiful village of **Santa Lucia**. From Vejer the C343 goes down to the modern town of **Barbate**, whose income comes not from tourists but tuna. Twice a year large shoals of tuna pass here, to be slaughtered in a bloody ambush similar to the *mattanza* (slaughter) off the coast of Sicily.

A small road leads west out of Barbate to the summer resort of **Los Caños de Meca**, traditionally busy in the height of summer with tourists from Sevilla and Cádiz. In recent years, hordes of Germans have adopted the place as their haven. Half an hour's walk west of here takes you to **Cape Trafalgar**, where Nelson breathed his last in 1805. Spaniards remember this well; it was mostly their ships that were getting smashed, under incompetent French leadership. Every Spaniard did his duty, though, and with their unflappable sense of personal honour the Spanish have always looked on Trafalgar as a sort of victory.

Ten kilometres (6 miles) south of here is another developing resort, **Zahara de los Atunes** ('of the tunas'). This is one of the most unspoilt coastlines in southern Spain, with miles of fine sandy beach that will be all yours in spring and autumn. The town was the birthplace of Francisco Rivera, or Paquirri, the famous bullfighter. Today it is fairly tranquil, with a few small hotels and restaurants. There's little to see or do other than laze around on the beach and watch the sun sinking into the sea whilst sipping a beer—but with the Costa del Sol for competition this could be a real attraction.

Tarifa

Tarifa, at the tip of Spain and of Europe, looks either exotic and evocative, or merely dusty and dreary, depending on the hour of the day and the mood you're in. You might even think you've arrived in Africa, it's so bleached by sun and salt. The town is one of the top destinations in Europe for the masters of the art of windsurfing and there are miles of beaches around to choose from. The town has a 10th-century Moorish **castle**, much rebuilt. As every Spanish schoolboy knows, or used to know, this is the site of the legend of Guzmán el Bueno. In 1292, this Spanish knight was defending Tarifa against a force of Moors. Among them was the renegade Infante Don Juan, brother of King Sancho IV, who had Guzmán's young son as a prisoner, and threatened to kill him if Guzmán did not surrender. Guzmán's response was to toss him a dagger. His son was killed, but Tarifa did not fall. Fascist propaganda recycled this legend for the 1936 siege of the Alcázar in Toledo, with the Republicans in the villain's role. Outside Tarifa, along the beaches east of the town, there are **ruins** of a once-sizeable Roman town, Bolonia, parts of which are currently undergoing restoration (*visit by guided tour*).

Algeciras

Ask at the tourist office what there is to see and you'll be told, 'Nothing. Nobody ever stays here'. Once you've seen the town you'll understand why: it's a dump. Nevertheless, Algeciras has an interesting history, and an attractive setting opposite the Rock of Gibraltar if you can see through the pollution. It played a significant role in the colonization of the eastern Mediterranean, becoming an important port in the Roman era. From AD 713 on, it was occupied by the Moors, and its name derives from the Arabic *Al-Jazira al-Khadra* (Green Island). Today, apart from its importance as a port , Algeciras is a sizeable industrial and fishing centre.

The bustling, seedy port area has little attraction for the visitor, although the small bazaars in the side streets, selling Moroccan leather goods, may whet your appetite for a trip across the straits—you can see Morocco's jagged, surreal peaks all along the coastal highway.

Inland, lying in a pleasantly wooded area, is **Los Barrios**, settled by refugees when Gibraltar was lost to the British; archaeological finds indicate that it was inhabited from earliest times. The parish church of **San Isidro** dates from the 18th century. There are two fairly decent beaches nearby—Guadarranque and Palmones.

On the N340 heading north, the road passes **San Roque,** with exceptional views over the bay of Algeciras and Gibraltar. Here are the ruins of *Carteya*, the first Roman settlement in the south of the peninsula. The 18th-century parish church of **Santa María Coronada** was built above the ancient hermitage of San Roque, and is worth a visit. This pretty little town is a welcome relief after the more sordid quarters of Algeciras, and a bonus are the nearby clean beaches of Puente Mayorga, Los Portichuelos and Carteya.

Where to Stay and Eating Out

Tarifa ✉ 11380

Rooms are surprisingly and unnecessarily expensive in the 'recently discovered' resort of Tarifa; the same is true of Conil. The Dutch-owned ★★★**Balcín de España**, Ctra. Cádiz–Málaga, Km 77, ✆ 95 668 43 26, ✆ 95 668 04 72, is one of the better options, situated in a pretty spot by the Playa de los Lances between Tarifa and Punta Palomas to the west of town. It has two pools, a gym, tennis courts and horse-riding facilities (*7500–11,000 pts*). *Closed Nov–Mar*. Further along the coast, windsurfers stay (where else?) at the English-owned ★★**Hurricane**, Ctra. N340, Km 94, ✆ 95 668 49 19; it's unimaginably trendy but they pay for the privilege (*12,000–17,000 pts*). *Closed Jan*. There are cheaper options in town—try the **Hostal Alameda**, Paseo Alameda 4, in the old town ✆ 95 668 11 81, some of whose pleasant rooms have sea views (*6000 pts*). Cheaper still are the characterless hostels like **Tarik**, San Sebastian 32-36, ✆ 95 668 85 36 (*3000–4500 pts*), outside the old city walls, off the main street Batalla del Salado.

One of the best restaurants in the area, **Mesín de Sancho,** Ctra. N340, Km 94, ✆ 95 668 49 00, ✆ 95 668 47 21, is near the Hurricane Hotel. Especially pleasing in winter with its roaring fire, it specializes in home-cooked dishes—favourites are the garlic soup, *urta* in cream sauce and *rabo de toro* (*3500 pts*). There's also a set menu for *1700 pts*, which includes wine or water. The town itself has few outstanding restaurants (though there is no shortage of cheap places and pizzerias catering to the surfing crowd). The best is **Restaurant Guzman**, Cervantes 4 which specializes in fried sea anemone and swordfish. Go there and try to persuade the owner not to sell up and leave—he's fed up with budget travellers asking him for egg and chips. Those seeking nightlife should wander around the old town where the crowds congregate in the numerous bars from about 11pm before heading down to the beach front disco, El Balneario.

Zahara and Los Caños de Meca ✉ 11393

The big resort complex the ★★★**Sol Atlanterra**, Urbanización Cabo de Plata, ✆ 95 643 90 00, ✆ 95 643 90 51, at the Bahía de la Plata is German-owned and rather soulless; it offers a variety of sports and recreational activities (*11,500–19,000 pts, depending on the season*). *Closed Nov–April*. The **Gran Sol**, on the beach at the end of Sanchez Rodriguez, ✆ 956 439 358, in Zahara itself is a better option, with comfortable air-conditioned rooms with TV, a fairly good restaurant and a pool (*10,000–15,000 pts*). Alternatively, you could try the the ★★**Nicholas**, María Luisa

13, ✆ 95 643 11 74 (*5000–6000 pts*), or the cavernous and gloomy Miramar, Trafalgar 100 (on the sea front), ✆ 95 643 70 24 (*3000 pts*), but both are packed throughout August. Campers should head for **Camping Bahia de la Plata**, ✆ 95 643 90 40, at the south end of the village. Tourists flock to the beach restaurant **Antonio**, Ctra. Atlanterra, Km 1, ✆ 95 643 12 41, for high-quality fish and seafood (*2000 pts*). During the season, the **Bar Marisquería Porfirio** on Plaza Tamrín serves excellent seafood. Vegetarians won't be disappointed with the sumptuous pizza at **Patio la Plazoleta**, next door, baked on the spot in Italian ovens. Inevitably, in Los Caños de Meca there had to be a **Trafalgar**; on the seafront with a pleasant terrace, the menu concentrates on international fare (*1800–2500 pts*). *Closed in winter.*

Algeciras ✉ 11200

The hotel of the town's bygone elegance is the ★★★★**Reina Cristina**, on Pso. de la Conferencia, ✆ 95 660 26 22, ✉ 95 660 33 23 (*all the luxuries for 13,500–17,500 pts*), scene of the Algeciras Conference of 1906, which carved up Morocco, and a hotbed of spies during the Second World War W.B. Yeats spent a winter here.

The convenient ★★★★**Octavio**, C/ San Bernardo 1, ✆ 95 665 27 00, borders the bus station and is within a few metres of the train station (*11,500–14,000 pts*). Right on the seafront, above the busy arcades filled with cafés and ticket offices, and looking out over the port area is ★★★**Al Mar**, Avda. de la Marina 2, ✆ 95 665 46 61, ✉ 95 665 45 01 (*9000–10,000 pts*). Very atmospheric and keenly priced is the **Alborán**, Álamo s/n (colonia San Miguel), ✆ 95 663 28 70, a wonderful building in classical Andalucían style, with an indoor patio and porticoed terrace (*8000–10,000 pts*). Clustered in the back streets of the area behind the Avenida de la Marina are a host of convenient little *hostales* in the *3000–4000 pts* range.

There are plenty of places to eat in Algeciras. Just back from the Avenida Virgen del Carmen (on the corner of Gómez Ortega and Trafalgar) is the **Marea Baja**, Trafalgar 2, ✆ 95 666 36 54, a fashionable restaurant specializing in seafood; try their *lubina* (*3500 pts for a full meal with wine*). For a break from salty marine life, you may care to drive out on to the N340 and try some of the grilled meats on offer at **El Bosque**, charmingly situated in the woods at Pelayo 5, Bulevar Pelayo, ✆ 95 667 91 13 (*2000–2500 pts*). *Closed Mon.*

Back in town, a popular place with working people is **Casa Montes**, San Juan 16, where *urta* surfaces again, along with roast kid and poultry (*1200 pts*). If you want to splash out a bit, **El Copo**, Trasmayo 2 (near Los Barrios), ✆ 95 667 77 10, is a good place for it. The restaurant is draped with fishermen's nets and takes pride in its enormous tanks of lobsters, sea urchins, spider crabs and mussels so that any fish or seafood dishes are supremely fresh. It serves a wide range of dishes, from fried sea nettles to *rabo de toro* and *solomillo* (*3500–4500 pts; reservations essential*). *Closed Sun.* If you get a chance take a look upstairs at the bullfighters' room and the room with a painted panorama of views from Palmones several hundred years ago. The most famous restaurant in the area is the long-established, Michelin-rosetted **Los Remos**, ✆ 95 669 84 12, at Villa Victoria, on the road out of San Roque to La Línea (it has only recently moved to this old house surrounded by lovely gardens), but carnivores beware—it serves mostly fish (*4000–6000 pts*).

The main reason for making the crossing will be to take a look at the limited attractions of Tangier. Unfortunately, the real treasures are all far to the south, in Fez, Marrakech and the Kasbahs of the Draa and Ziz valleys. But even an admittedly international city like Tangier will give you the chance to explore a fascinating society—and perhaps see a little reflection of the lost culture of Al-Andalus. On the other hand, you could shop at Ceuta, one of Spain's last remaining *presidios* on the North African coast.

Getting There

Algeciras's *raison d'être* is its port, and there's no trouble getting a **ferry** either to Ceuta (at least six boats a day, nine in the summer) or to Tangier (two at least, as many as seven daily in summer). Ceuta is 1½ hours away by ferry (*2000 pts each way*) and Tangier is 2 hours away (*3000 pts each way*). The **hydrofoil** is the faster, slightly more expensive option, but takes passengers only. Ceuta is half an hour away by hydrofoil (*every hour; 3000 pts each way*) and Tangier an hour away (*every half-hour; 3500 pts each way*).

There are plenty of official Transmediterránea agents at the port, and unofficial ticket booths along the N340 as far away as Estepona, all of which look extremely dodgy but actually sell legitimate tickets. You'll need your passport, and you are advised not to do anything foolish on these well-policed borders. There's also a summer hydrofoil service from Tarifa to Tangier (*1 hour, 3000 pts each way*) and to Gibraltar (*runs on Tues, Fri, and Sun*).

Tourist Information

Alcalde J. Victori Goñalons, ✆ 95 651 40 92.

Ceuta

Every time the Spanish make self-righteous noises about getting Gibraltar back, someone reminds them about their two colonial leftovers on the North African coast, Melilla and Ceuta. Ceuta has a mainly Spanish population; that is why it was excluded from the 1955 withdrawal from the Spanish-Moroccan protectorate. They are the stumbling block, and some way will have to be found to accommodate them before the inevitable transfer of sovereignty. Ceuta is a pleasant enough town, but there's little reason to go there, perhaps only the impressive 16th-century **walls** and moat. Like Andorra at the other end of Spain, Ceuta is a big duty-free supermarket. You can easily cross into Morocco from here, though it's better to take the ferry to Tangier.

Where to Stay and Eating Out

Finding a place to sleep can be a problem as there are only a few hotels. Within the walls, ★★★★**La Muralla**, Pza. de Nuestra Señora de África 15, ✆ 95 651 49 40, offers the most comfort and luxury, with a pool and gardens (*15,000 pts*). The **Puerta de Africa**, Gran Via 2, ✆ 95 651 71 91, ✉ 95 651 04 30 has a heated pool and not much else for an expensive *10,000–12,000 pts*. The best Moroccan restaurant in Ceuta is **La Kasba**, General Yagüe 12,

℡ 95 652 10 13, serving the requisite North African speciality, couscous, besides Spanish dishes (*3000 pts*). Ceuta's prettiest restaurant is **Méson de Serafín**, Monte Hacho, 4 Km, ℡ 95 651 40 03, with its wonderful view of the sea, Gibraltar and the Spanish and Moroccan coasts. A good place to meet the locals (and a strange bunch they are) is the **Restaurante Mar Chica**, Pso. Colón 9, ℡ 95 651 39 57, with decent fish dinners from *800 pts* up.

Trips to Morocco

Getting There

The most direct way of getting to Morocco is by **ferry** or **hydrofoil** from Algeciras. If you're travelling from Ceuta, you'll have to take a **cab** or **city bus** (the one marked '*frontera*') to the border; after some cacophonous border confusion, you wait for the infrequent bus or carefully negotiate a taxi trip to **Tetuán**, 30km (18.8 miles) away. There's no train from Tetuán to Tangier, but **buses** are cheap and run regularly from the central bus station. They'll take you right to Tangier's port.

Tourist Information

Tetuán: 30 Avenue Mohammed V, ℡ (9) 96 44 07 or (9) 96 70 09.
Tangier: 29 Boulevard Pasteur, ℡ (9) 93 82 39/40.

Some Moroccan Practicalities

money

Wait until you get into Morocco to change money. Spanish travel agents will do it, often at a dishonestly low rate, and the rates at the border crossings aren't much better. The currency is the *dirham*, lately about 14 to the pound, 9 to the dollar.

dealers and dealing

This corner of Morocco, being the fullest of tourists, is also full of English-speaking hustlers and creeps. We do not exaggerate; around the bus stations and ports they're thick as flies and ten times as persistent, sometimes weaselling, sometimes menacing. Entertain no offers, especially of drugs or guided tours, and do your best to totally ignore the scum. The Moroccans don't like them either. Beyond that, you'll need your wits to bargain with merchants, taxi drivers and even hotel-keepers. There's no reason why you can't do this firmly and gracefully, but the whole process is extremely tiring. Also, crime is a problem after dark in Tetuán and Tangier.

Tetuán and Tangier

Aside from its heavily polluted river and contraband appeal Tetuán is a decent town, full of gleaming white, Spanish colonial architecture; it has a famous market in its *medina*, a historical museum, and it's a good place to purchase Moroccan crafts. On the way into **Tangier**, note how the Moroccans have turned the old *plaza de toros* into flats. Once in the big square outside the port entrance, you may take your chances with the inexpensive hotels in the surrounding streets, or take a cab to fancier spots in the newer, Europeanized districts.The wares in the markets of the *medina* are fun to look at, but the quarter itself is down-at-heel and dusty. You may not enter mosques in Morocco, but in the old governor's palace are two fine

museums of archaeology and Moroccan art. Hotels, restaurants, and everything else will be almost half as expensive as in Spain. The food has an international reputation; national dishes like couscous and *harira* can be superb but seldom are. Don't judge Morocco by Tangier and Tetuán, and don't even judge these places by first impressions. A side-trip to Morocco may not be an epiphany, but think how much you'll regret it if you pass up the chance.

Gibraltar

> *... a cosy smell of provincial groceries. I'd forgotten how much the atmosphere of home depended on white bread, soap and soup squares.*

Laurie Lee, *As I Walked Out One Midsummer Morning*

In under two hours, you can experience the ultimate culture shock: sailing from the smoky souks of Tangier to Algeciras, Spain, with time for *churros* and chocolate before the bus takes you off to a mysterious enclave of red phone booths, warm beer and policemen in silly hats. The Spanish bus will take you only as far as **La Línea**. It's just a short walk through the **neutral zone** into Gibraltar, where immediately you'll be confronted with one of the Rock's curiosities: as you enter British territory you find yourself looking down the noses of 737s. Where else does a busy street cross an airport runway? The airport, built on landfill at right angles to the narrow peninsula (this area was included in the land ceded to Britain under the Treaty of Utrecht), symbolizes British determination to hold on during the years Franco was putting the squeeze on Gibraltar, and also points up the enclave's biggest problem—lack of space.

You'll soon find that Gibraltar has a unique mixture of people—mostly Genoese (who have been around for centuries), along with Maltese, Indians, Spaniards, Jews and Moroccans, all as British as Trafalgar Square; when a referendum on joining Spain was held in the 1960s, they voted it down by 99.6 per cent. With English as their official language, most Gibraltarians are, however, bilingual. For many Gibraltarians, Spanish is used in everyday situations and particularly in moments of high emotion and anger; English is reserved for more formal situations.

History

Gibraltar has been occupied for a long time: bones of Neanderthal man have been found here from 50,000 years ago. *Calpe*, as the Greeks knew the Rock, was of course one of the Pillars of Hercules, beyond which the jealous Phoenicians would permit no other nation's ships to trade. The other, less dramatic pillar is Mount Abyla in Morocco (visible across the straits on most days). The rock is full of caves, and can claim to be the oldest known inhabited spot in Spain—50,000-year-old bones of Neanderthal man were found here even before their discovery at Neanderthal in Germany, but no one on the Rock knew what they were. The Rock's name, *Jebel Tarik*, or 'mountain of Tarik', comes from its Moorish conqueror, Tariq ibn-Ziyad. Guzmán el Bueno seized it for Castile in 1309, and in the centuries that followed it was one of the battlegrounds of the Mediterranean. The Moors had it back for a while, and in 1540 Barbarossa's Turkish pirates briefly held the town.

The British arrived in 1704, taking Gibraltar in the name of Archduke Charles during the War of the Spanish Succession; after Charles' defeat they found the Rock such a convenient stepping-stone for their Mediterranean ambitions that they decided to keep it. It was a crucial

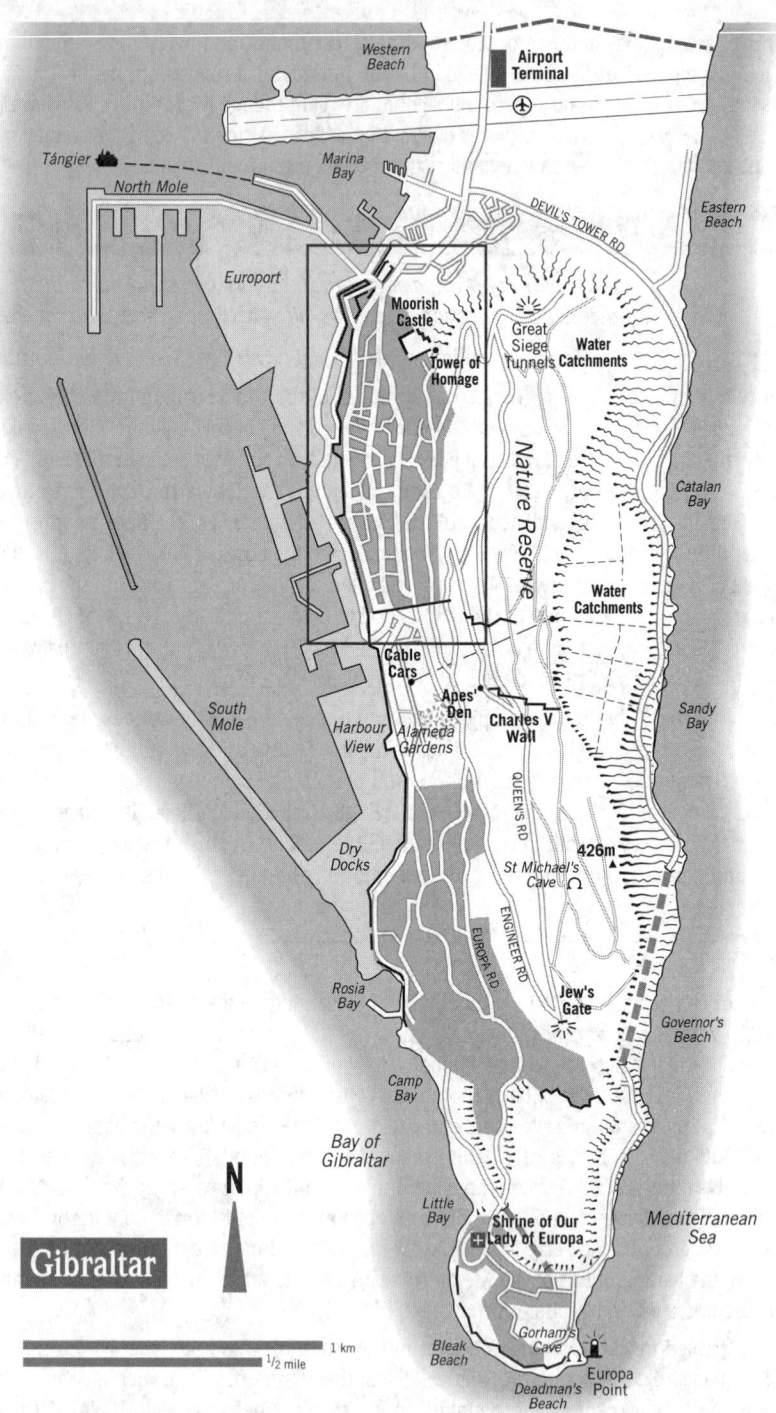

Western Beach

Airport Terminal

Tángier

North Mole

Marina Bay

DEVIL'S TOWER RD

Eastern Beach

Europort

Moorish Castle

Tower of Homage

Great Siege Tunnels

Water Catchments

Water Catchments

Catalan Bay

South Mole

Nature Reserve

Cable Cars

Apes' Den

Charles V Wall

Harbour View

Alameda Gardens

Sandy Bay

QUEEN'S RD

Dry Docks

426m

St Michael's Cave

ENGINEER RD

Rosia Bay

EUROPA RD

Jew's Gate

Governor's Beach

Camp Bay

Bay of Gibraltar

N

Little Bay

Mediterranean Sea

Gibraltar

Shrine of Our Lady of Europa

Gorham's Cave

Bleak Beach

Deadman's Beach

Europa Point

1 km

½ mile

acquisition; Britain's imperial expansion across the Mediterranean and Middle East would have been almost inconceivable without it. From 1779 to 1783 Gibraltar suffered its Great Siege, by a combined French and Spanish force, and the enclave survived only by the tenacity of its defenders, and their presence of mind in tunnelling up into the Rock to plant their guns on the commanding heights. That was the beginning of modern Gibraltar's series of tunnels and galleries. Now there are about 34 miles of them; Gibraltar is still very well defended.

Getting Around

By air: There are at least three daily flights to London (Heathrow and Gatwick, run by British Airways in partnership with GB Airways); twice-weekly flights to Manchester and regular flights to Casablanca and Tangier. British Airways has check-in facilities at Victoria, meaning you don't see your luggage again till you arrive. **Information:** British Airways, ✆ 79 300.

By sea: There are three ferries a week from Gibraltar to Tangier (Mon, Wed and Fri); three ferries a week from Tangier to Gibraltar (Mon, Fri and Sun). The fares are expensive, like everything else in Gibraltar. You'd be slightly better off doing it from Algeciras. **Information:** TourAfrica, ✆ 79 140.

By road: There is a direct **bus** service between Gibraltar and the Costa del Sol. Gibraltar's tiny buses and **taxis** serve the frontier, which is only 800m (½ mile) from the town centre. If you are coming by **car** leave it in La Línea, as there are frequently long delays as customs check the day-trippers' stash of goodies *in both directions.* There is a **taxi tour** of the Rock, taking in all the sites and lasting about 1½ hours. The charge is about £20, plus additional costs per passenger to include compulsory admission to the Nature Reserve. It's part of a scheme by the taxi drivers' cartel and should be resisted: you can always take the cable car and walk! **Information:** Gibraltar Taxi Association, 12 Waterport, ✆ 70 052; Gibraltar mini-cab, ✆ 79 999.

Tourist Information

Gibraltar Information Bureau: Duke of Kent House, Cathedral Square, ✆ 42 400/74 950.

Local information bureaux: Market Place, ✆ 74 982; Gibraltar Museum, 18–20 Bomb House Lane, ✆ 74 805 (*all open weekdays 10–6 and Sat 10–2*). There are booths within the airport terminal and at Waterport coach park.

The Gibraltar National Tourist Board has introduced the **Privilege Key Card**, which allows unlimited free entry to the tourist sights plus various discounts about town. The card is available only to visitors staying overnight in Gibraltar, and is designed to encourage would-be day-trippers to stop over on the Rock rather than cross back into La Línea, where the accommodation is a great deal cheaper.

Currency

The enclave has its own currency (the Gibraltar pound which is tied in value to the pound sterling) and stamps—don't be stuck with any currency when you leave, as it's hard to get rid of anywhere else, especially Britain! These days, most shops and restaurants in Gibraltar are perfectly happy to take British, Spanish or Gibraltarian money.

The international calling code from Spain to Gibraltar is ℡ (9567), and ℡ (350) if you are calling the Rock from elsewhere.

The Town

Despite a certain amount of bad press, Gibraltar is still much more than just a perfect replica of an English seaside town. The town is long and narrow, strung out along **Main Street**, which has most of the shops and pubs. The harbour is never more than a couple of blocks away, and the old gates, bastions and walls are fun to explore.

The short tunnel at **Landport Gate** will probably be your entry point if on foot; dating from the 18th century, it was for a long time the only entrance by land. It leads to **Casemates Square**, one-time parade ground and site of public executions, and now a bustling trading centre. **Grand Casemates** itself, part of the town's defences and barracks, provides seedy accommodation for Gibraltar's 4000-strong Moroccan labour force, but there are plans to revamp the whole area. **King's Bastion** is now used as an electricity generating station, but probably started out as an ancient Arab Gate, added to by the Spanish in 1575 and further extended in the 18th century by the British under General Boyd. It played an important defensive role at the time of the Great Siege, and it was from this spot that General Elliott commanded during the fierce fighting in 1782. **Ragged Staff Wharf** takes its name not from the sartorial deficiency of its troops, but either from the flagstaff that marked safe passage into the harbour or from an emblem on the arms of the House of Burgundy, to which Charles V belonged.

Near the centre of town, off Line Wall Road, you should spare a few minutes for the small but excellent **Gibraltar Museum**, 18–20 Bomb House Lane, (*open Mon–Fri 10–6, Sat 10–2; closed Sun*) which offers a painstakingly detailed room-sized model of the Rock as it was in the mid-1800s, and a thorough schooling in its complicated history. The museum is built over the remains of **Moorish baths**, with Roman and Visigothic capitals on its columns. It also

Gibraltar Town

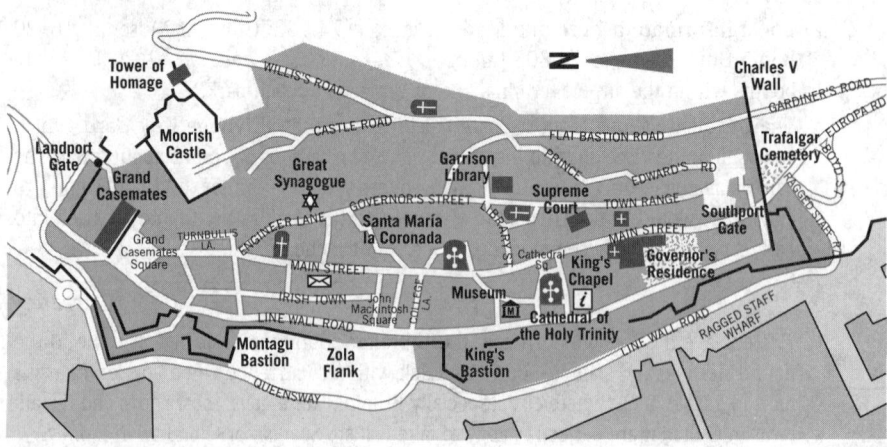

contains a replica of the female skull found in Forbes Quarry in 1848, a find that predates the Neanderthal skull found in Germany by 8 years. (Perhaps Neanderthal Man should be known as Gibraltar Woman.) Nearby, the **Supreme Court** looks diagonally across the street to the 16th-century former Franciscan convent, now the **Governor's Residence**, where the changing of the guard takes place (*check with tourist office for times*). **Southport Gate**, at the top of Main Street, was built in 1552, during the reign of Charles V and has additions from the 19th century; the wall stretching east from the gate is **Charles V's Wall**, which ends just short of the water catchments at **Philip II's Arch**. Beyond the gate you can wander through the small, shady **Trafalgar Cemetery**, where sad little inscriptions tell of children killed by disease, and of young men who met their bloody end at sea. The **Alameda Gardens**, a few yards away, are more cheerful; you can stop in to see the exotic flora before taking the **cable car** up the Rock to the Apes' Den (*leaves every 15 mins 9.30–6; £4.90 inc adm to nature reserve; children half-price. Closed Sundays*).

The cathedral of **St Mary the Crowned** (between Main Street and Cannon Lane) stands on the site of the chief mosque of Gibraltar, of which some remains can still be seen. The Anglican cathedral of the **Holy Trinity** (off Main Street, near the museum) was consecrated in 1838, and in Engineer Lane the **Great Synagogue**, rebuilt in 1768, is attended by Gibraltar's 700-strong Jewish community. **King's Chapel**, part of the Franciscan convent, was one of the few buildings left standing at the end of the Great Siege, and was an earlier sanctuary for those sheltering from the attack by Barbarossa and his pirates, although the place itself was looted.

The Rock

The famous silhouette, surprisingly, does not hang over the seaward edge, but faces backwards towards La Línea. From 500 yards up, the views from the upper part of the Rock are magnificent: the Costa del Sol curves away to the east, the mountains of Morocco sit in a purple haze across the narrow straits to the south; and way below, where the Mediterranean opens out into the wide and wild Atlantic, tiny toy-like craft plough through the waters in full sail. The Rock's entire eastern face is covered by the **water catchment system** that supplies Gibraltar's water—an engineering marvel to equal the tunnels. The upper part of the Rock has been turned into a nature reserve, which can be reached by cable car or through the entrance at Jews' Gate, on the hairpin bend where Engineer and Queen's Roads meet (*open daily except Sun, 9.30 to sunset; adm £4.50, children under 12 half-price, children under 5 free; cars £2.50*). Apart from views of a panoramic variety, admission to the reserve will get you a look at Gibraltar's best-known citizens. The **Apes' Den** is halfway up the Rock where you can see Barbary apes, a species of tailless macaque. These gregarious monkeys are much more common on the African side of the straits and in Europe are unique to Gibraltar. There is an old saying that, as long as they're here, the British will never leave. Understandably, they're well cared for, and have been since the days of their great benefactor, Winston Churchill. The Gibraltarians are fond of them, even though (as a local guidebook solemnly notes) they 'fail to share the same respect for private property' as the rest of us.

Nearby are remains of a **Moorish wall** and, a short walk to the south, **St Michael's Cave**, a huge cavern of delicate stalactites, now sometimes used as an auditorium (*son et lumière shows can be pre-arranged*). In the 19th century wealthy merchants would rent it out for extravagant parties; it was also a favourite venue for illegal duels, away from the censorious eye of the authorities. At the northern end of the Rock, facing Spain, are the Upper Galleries, now called the **Great Siege Tunnels**, an extensive section of the original British tunnels, which were hacked and blown out of the rock during the Great Siege. From here it's a short walk down to the **Moorish castle** probably founded in the 8th century by Tariq ibn Ziyad, but its best-known feature, the **Tower of Homage**, dates from the 14th century when Abd Hassan recaptured Gibraltar from the Spanish. At present Gibraltar's **prison** is housed (and occupied) in the keep.

Away from the nature reserve, to the south of the promontory, is the **Shrine of Our Lady of Europa**, adopted as a Catholic chapel in 1462, after which a flame was kept continuously alight—a predecessor to the present lighthouse at Europa Point. If you want to sit on a beach, Gibraltar has a few, but they're all on the eastern side, opposite the town, and accessible by bus. **Catalan Bay** and **Sandy Bay** are both a little built-up and crowded, the former slated for even greater development in the near future. **Eastern Beach** (dubbed 'Margate' in the 19th century) is better, though unfortunately it's next to the airport.

Shopping

Expats residing in Spain flock across the border to pick up familiar brand-name groceries and household items at British prices; the real bargains are to be had in the top range of luxury goods. Remember that Gibraltar is VAT-free, and savings can be considerable. Here is a selection—but shop around.

Antiques:	Bensaquen Antiques, 290 Main Street.
Cashmere:	Carruana, 181 Main Street (jerseys, suits and fabrics).
Cuban cigars and perfume:	S. M. Seruya, 165 Main Street, and Stagnetto's, 56 Main Street.
Gifts:	Marrache, 201 Main Street (jewellery, *objets*, silver).
Jewellery:	Sakata, 92 Main Street and The Red House, 66 Main Street (cultured pearls, Cartier, Rolex).
Menswear:	García, 190 Main St (Dax, Burberry, etc.).
Porcelain:	Omni, 3 Main Street.

Where to Stay

expensive

For the businessman the **Eliot Hotel (White's)**, Governor's Parade, ✆ 70 500, ✉ 70 243, offers sterile anonymity, along with air-conditioning, sauna and jacuzzi (*£110*). The **Rock Hotel**, 3 Europa Road, ✆ 73 000, ✉ 73 513, a resort hotel of long standing, is up on the heights—about halfway up, under the cable car and near Gibraltar's casino. Considering its position and its history, this should be one of the world's great 'colonial' hotels; sadly it isn't. Visiting dignitaries and the occasional celebrity stay here. There's a pool, landscaped gardens and rooms with sea view and balconies (*£110 for a double with balcony, £80 without, depending on land or sea view*).

moderate

The **Bristol**, 8–10 Cathedral Square, ✆ 76 800, ✉ 77 613, is in the heart of town, with swimming pool, and TV in all rooms (*£65 for double with bath, £60 with shower*). In the same price range, though not quite as comfortable, the **Continental**,

1 Engineer Lane, ✆ 76 900, ✉ 41 702, is just off Main Street (£55), with a tacky fast-food restaurant on the ground floor. The **Queen's Hotel**, just outside the old city walls at 17 Boyd Street, ✆ 74 000, ✉ 40 030, is crumbling and pretty characterless but has less expensive accommodation and there are good views of the Rock and Bay (£45 for a double). If you need a beach, the other resort hotel is the very modern **Caleta Palace**, Sir Herbert Miles Road, on Catalan Bay, ✆ 76 501, ✉ 71 050 (£55–65 for a double, depending on the view).

inexpensive

Stay in La Línea, if you're on a budget. Prices in Gibraltar are two to four times what they would be for comparable hotels in Spain. There is one opportunity for a cheap room in Gibraltar, the **Toc H Hostel**, Line Wall Road near the harbour, ✆ 73 431, which will put you up for £5 a person a day. Understandably, it is usually full.

Eating Out

This can be a problem. Main Street is lined with pubs, fish shops, and cafés; they are mostly horrible. The little places around Catalan Bay and the other beaches are no better. Nearly all the hotels have restaurants; none of them, with the possible exception of White's and the Rock, is very good.

expensive

The **Rock Hotel** is arguably the most pleasant place for lunch; its colonial-style décor and discreet waiters set the scene for Gibraltar's answer to Raffles in Singapore. The steaks are flown in fresh from the UK daily. Popular among the locals is the restaurant in the **International Casino Club**, 7 Europa Road, ✆ 76 666, and you won't find a better place for five-star service; concerned with maintaining high standards, the management has a strict ruling on dress—even local celebrities have been turned away for inappropriate attire. There's a wide range of international dishes on offer, and the terrace has great views overlooking the Bay and Algeciras—a perfect place to watch the sun go down on the Atlantic, if not the Empire (full meal with wine £25–35). In a lane off Main Street is the quaint **Country Cottage**, 13–15 Giros Passage, ✆ 70 084, complete with antique furnishings and Olde Worlde atmosphere. The menu includes sole mornay, shrimp, and meat dishes from brochettes to Angus steaks (£20–30).

moderate

El Patio, 54 Irish Town, ✆ 70 822, is a reasonably pleasant spot, if overpriced; it offers Basque cuisine and Mediterranean fish specialities—rare delights considering the British culinary traditions around here. Particularly popular with the business community, which jokingly refers to it as the 'Canteen', this place fills up at lunchtime (about £25–30 per head). Closed Sat lunchtime and Sun. **La Bayuca**, 21 Turnbulls Lane, ✆ 75 119, is a long-time favourite, not least for owners Tita and Johnnie; the walls are lined with photos of its more famous customers, and the décor is pleasantly rustic. The menu is lacklustre: steaks, chicken, fish, and some Mediterranean dishes (£15–25). Closed Tues and Sun lunch. **Strings**, 44 Cornwalls Lane, ✆ 78 800, a small and intimate restaurant, serves a selection of international dishes: smoked salmon, gravadlax, shrimp in wine sauce (£15–25). Closed Mon. **Sax** piano bar and restaurant, International Commercial Centre, attracts a young crowd; expect queues at weekends; the fare is mixed—English, Mexican, Italian—and the lunchtime menu particularly recommended; light snacks are also available, and there's live music two evenings a week (*around £20 for full meal*). *closed Sun lunch*). A little off the beaten track, **Jim's Den**, 25 Prince Edward's Road, ☏ 71 289, has a simple English menu, with simple whitewashed walls; it's popular with expats, and a friendly place to drop in for a chat and a bite to eat (*£15–20 for a full meal*).

There is a handful of Indian restaurants around; the **Maharaja**, 5 Tuckey's Lane, ☏ 75 233, with the simplest furnishings of the lot, offers some of the best food. The service is efficient and friendly, and all the old Indian favourites can be found on the menu (*£15–20*).

In Marina Bay, you can sit out and watch the yachts or plane-spot at **Bianca's**, ☏ 73 379, which has reasonably priced fish, meat and pizza (*around £15–20 for a full meal*). Next door, **Da Paolo**, our favourite place to eat in Gib, ☏ 76 799, has well-prepared fish specialities, such as fillet of John Dory in dill sauce, a particularly good Spanish wine list, a fine view and some interesting characters passing through (*a little more expensive at about £20*).

Danish business interests in the area contributed to the opening of **The Little Mermaid**, Marina Bay, ☏ 77 660, a refreshing addition to the ethnic culinary scene. The interior is sleek and modern, and all the usual Scandinavian specialities appear including marinated herring, salmon and prawns; help your open sandwiches down with an Aalborg Akvazit and Tuborg chaser, instead of wine (*£20*).

inexpensive

Cheers Brasserie, G1 Cornwall Centre, ☏ 79 699, fills up with tourists at lunchtime and is a popular meeting place, where you can enjoy the large terrace and soak up the sun. The tired snacks include club sandwiches, a variety of salads, and chilli, as well as full English breakfasts (*snacks £3–5, full meals £8–10*). There are around 360 pubs in Gibraltar, many serving food in one form or another.

The best are **The Clipper**, 78B Irish Town, popular with Gibraltarians and visitors alike for its roast beef and lasagna; and **The Royal Calpe**, 176 Main Street, where the grub is authentically English and served piping hot. And for a parting memory of Gibraltar before you cross back into Spain, drop into the patriotic **Old Bull and Bush**, complete with portrait of Queen Elizabeth II; drinks are chalked up on a slate as in days of yore. Pictures of England and English pubs cover the walls; and there are no tapas in sight, just crisps and hard-boiled eggs.

Entertainment and Nightlife

Many companies offer **guided tours** of Gibraltar and its sights; Bland Travel, Cloister Building, Irish Town, ☏ 77 012, also runs a 'Trafalgar Tour' from Rosia Bay to Tarifa in Algeciras during the summer months. There are large populations of whales and dolphins within the Bay and the Straits of Gibraltar, which makes it an excellent place to see these mammals. Mike Lawrence's **Dolphin Safari** from Sheppard's Marina, ☏ 71 914, is particularly good (*£25 June–Sept*). Gibraltar's late-nightlife happens up at the **Casino**, 7 Europa Road, ☏ 76 666—dress well and take lots of cash.

The Costa del Sol

At first glance, it doesn't seem the speculators and developers could have picked a more unlikely place to conjure up the Mediterranean's biggest holiday playground. The stretch of coast between Gibraltar and Málaga is devoid of beautiful or even attractive scenery. Spain's low prices are one explanation, and the greatest number of guaranteed sunny days in Europe another. The reason it happened here, though, is breathtakingly simple—cheap land. Forty years ago, this coast was one of the forgotten backwaters of Spain. After a few decades of holiday intensity, though, this unlikely strip, all concrete and garish signboards, is beginning to develop a personality of its own.

Any hype you hear or read about the Costa, anything that employs flowery prose and superlatives, is utter nonsense; on the other hand, it has become almost fashionable to mock the Costa for its brash *turismo* exuberance, and that is uncalled for. The Costa does attract people who don't expect much from their holiday (or retirement) except good weather, like-minded companions, and places to play. Their presence, in such large numbers and from so many nations, has created a unique international community of everyday folks. It's easy to forget you're in Spain, but if you ever get homesick you can always take a break from Andalucía and have a noisy good time by the beach.

La Línea to Málaga

La Línea is a modern town with little to detain you, though staying here is an alternative to the high prices on the Rock. Thirty years ago Gibraltarians who had money bought villas in Algeciras or San Roque. Nowadays they prefer **Sotogrande**, a relatively old-established British enclave 10 minutes along the Costa from Gib. Apart from some big houses and a couple of polo fields, this glorified *urbanización* isn't nearly as interesting as the rather forbidding barriers at the entrance would suggest.

The recently built **Puerto Sotogrande**, 10km east along the coast, is an up-and-coming marina complex with restaurants, shops and apartments. It could be worth a stop for lunch to break the drive along the Costa.

Getting Around

The Portillo **bus** company has the franchise for this stretch of coast; and with the growth of tourism its service has become almost like a city bus-line, stopping every few hundred yards in the developed areas between Algeciras and Málaga, so be sure to check how long your bus will take to arrive if you're planning an intercity journey and change to an express service. There's never too long a wait in either direction.

San Pedro is where the buses branch off for Ronda, an easy destination from any town on the coast. You can also go directly to Sevilla or Madrid at least once daily from the bus station in Marbella, Avda. Ricardo Soriano 21, ✆ 95 277 21 92.

The N340 connects all the towns and villages along the coast, and at Fuengirola you can pick up a suburban **train**, which runs a regular service to Málaga. It stops at Torremolinos and most other points in between.

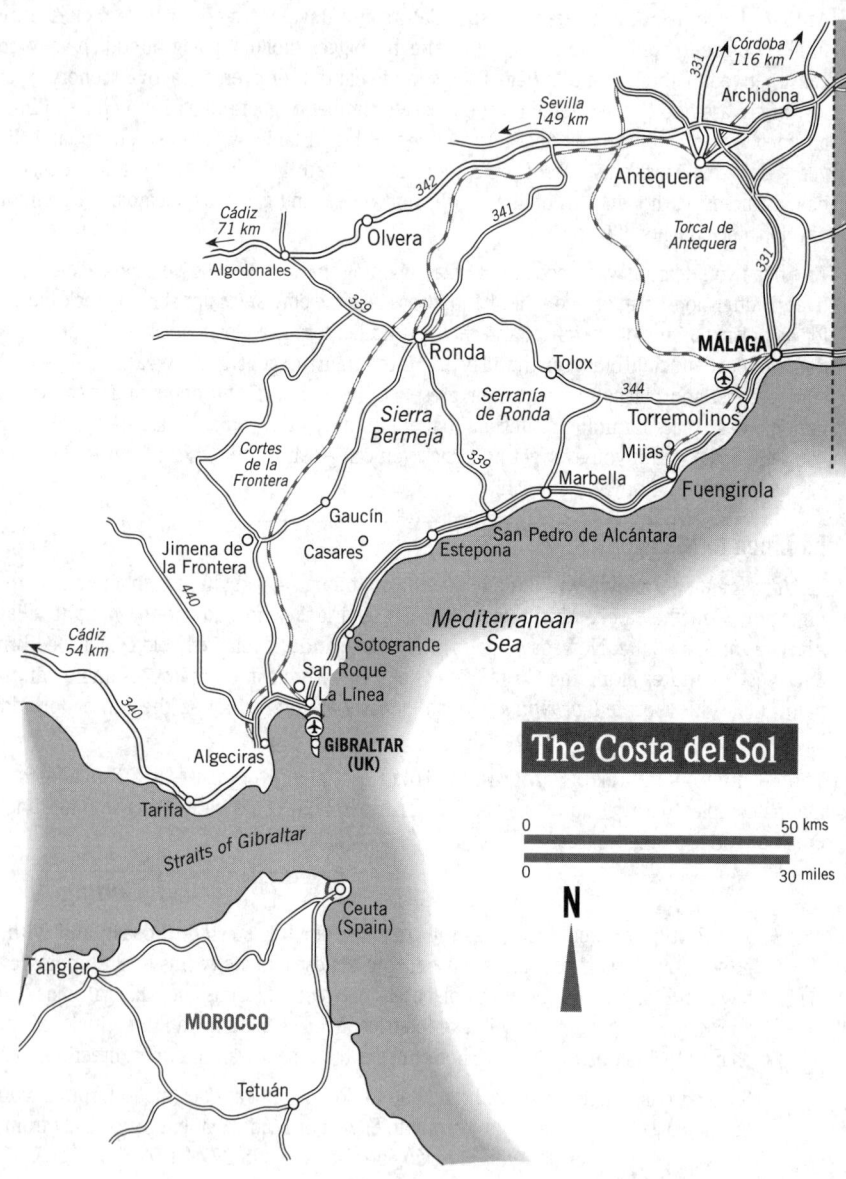

The Costa del Sol

0   50 kms

0   30 miles

N

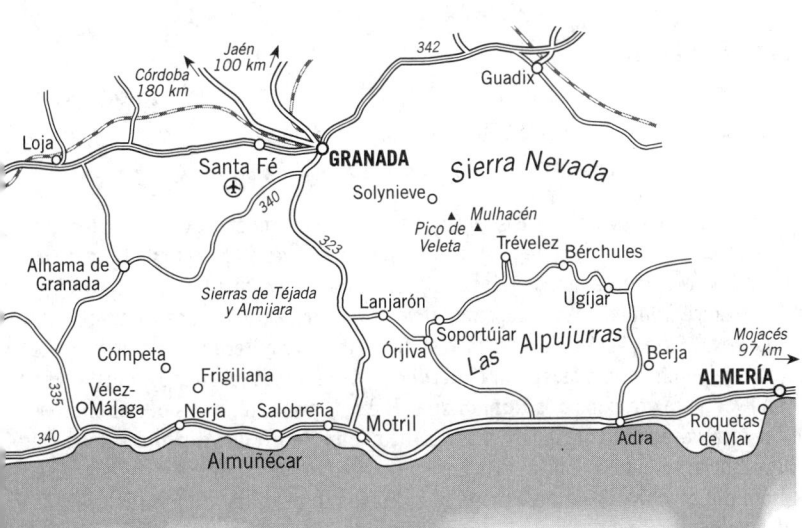

Activities

To discover what's on, take a quick look through the local publications—*Lookout*, a slick monthly magazine for the British on the Costa; a weekly English edition of Málaga's newspaper, *Sur*, which appears every Friday; and various local entertainment guides will show you all sorts of chances.

There are bullrings in Marbella, Fuengirola, Estepona, Mijas (a square one!) and Benalmádena Costa, though *corridas* are infrequent and the really serious action occurs in the big ring in Málaga. There are **concerts** at the Casa de Cultura and Salon Varietés in Fuengirola and the Mijas Arts Centre, and at the Nueva Andalucía bullring near Marbella, among others; many also offer art exhibitions and guitar and dance courses.

For sports, there are over 50 **golf courses** on the Costa, though green fees are a little dear (*3000 pts and up*); **tennis** at many of the hotels, most open to the public; even **snooker clubs** (in Fuengirola). All the **water sports** are popular; you can always make arrangements for equipment or instruction through your hotel. There are **casinos** at Benalmádena Costa (the Torrequebrada, on the coastal highway), and at Puerto Banús (the Casino de Marbella, at Torre del Duque), where the stakes are higher.

For kids there's a Disneyland-style amusement park at Benalmádena Costa called **Tivoli World** with a Wild West area, Chinese pagodas, Cinerama, flamenco and can-can shows as well as the **Sea Life Park**, where you can take a journey to the bottom of the sea. Also, a small **zoo** in Fuengirola, Super Bonanza cruise boats for leisurely excursions between Torremolinos and Puerto Banús, and horse-riding from the El Castillo Salvador stables outside Fuengirola (*1000 pts per hour*). The **Aquapark** in Fuengirola has slides and rides to keep the little ones amused for an afternoon. For something out of the ordinary, get in touch with the Viajes CHAT travel agency in Torremolinos, ☎ 95 238 71 86, and they'll make arrangements for a hot-air balloon ride over the Costa, champagne included.

Estepona and San Pedro

Estepona: Pso. Marítimo, ℃ 95 280 09 13. *Open 9.30–1.30 and 5–7, closed Sun.*

San Pedro de Alcántara: Arco de San Pedro, ℃ 95 278 52 52.

Estepona, the first of the resort towns east of Gibraltar, is also the quietest. Unfortunately the big developers have moved in, concrete blocks are sprouting all over and the town is losing its appeal. The old town remains a pleasant, quiet place, with narrow streets and whitewashed houses, an inheritance from its Arab occupation. If you're staying here, a worthwhile side-trip would be **Casares**, 20km (12½ miles) northwest, up in the Sierra Bermeja, a typical white Andalucían village perched on a steep hill under the ruins of its castle. Nearby, outside the village of Manilva, there are ruins of a **Roman spa**. The old spring still pours out sulphurous water, and the locals drop in to bathe for what ails them. **San Pedro de Alcántara** along the coast, is a little fancier, though still pleasingly unsophisticated to look at. Most of the town is a good walk from the beaches. From here the only good road through the mountains will take you to Ronda and its surrounding villages—the best excursion you can make from the Costa.

Where to Stay and Eating Out

La Línea ✉ 11300

The only reason to stay in La Línea is that it is cheaper than staying in Gibraltar. The hotels here are mostly as dull as the town. The ★★★Aparthotel Rocamar, Avda. de España 170, ℃ 95 610 66 50, ✆ 95 610 30 19, has the most comforts (*8500 pts*). The Almadraba, Los Caireles 2, ℃ 95 610 55 66, stands out with its yellow façade and has a first-class view of the Rock and the Bay of Algeciras. The bullfighter El Cordobés used to stay here (*10,500–13,500 pts*). The best bargain in town is the pensión ★La Campana, C/ Carboneros 3, ℃ 95 610 30 59, just off the main plaza. In the high season doubles with bath are *4500 pts*, low season *3500 pts*, and there's a good little restaurant downstairs with a menú del día for *850 pts*. There are cheaper hostales, recommended only if you are on a budget. Heading the list is the ★**Sevilla**, Duque de Tetuán 4, ℃ 95 676 47 96, for no reason other than its flamboyant, crumbling glass and stone building, and the cranky old folks who run it (*2500 pts, no bath*).

Eating out in La Línea is a lot cheaper than in Gibraltar, particularly if you want to spoil yourself on fish. At **La Marina** on the Paseo Marítimo the speciality is the favourite of the southern coast: grilled sardines on a spit (*2500 pts*). In an unfortunate position opposite the cemetery, **Casa Manuel** is nevertheless thriving. The menu is varied, but best are the *solomillo* and *entrecôte* steaks (*2000–2500 pts*). On the central pedestrian thoroughfare, the **Jerez** is a bar more than a restaurant, serving simple, cheap *raciones* for *700 pts*.

Estepona ✉ 29680

There are more real bargains to be found here than elsewhere on the coast. For a modicum of concrete splendour near the beach, the ★★**Buenavista**, Pso. Marítimo, ℃ 95 280 0137, is the best bet (*3900 pts*).

Estepona isn't a place to spend money, though; there are plenty of inexpensive *hostales* (such as **El Pilar**, Pza. de las Flores 22, ✆ 95 280 0018; 3000 pts, in a pretty setting), both in the town and on the beach. The best bet when you're tired of seafood is to try the Moroccan couscous at the **Restaurante del Paseo** on the coastal highway (*1500–2000 pts*). **El Vagabundo**, Urbanización Monte Biarritz, Ctra. Cádiz, Km 168.5, ✆ 95 278 66 98, a converted outpost tower on the N340, offers a choice of international dishes, including seafood pancakes and roast duck (*2500 pts*).

San Pedro de Alcántara ✉ 29670

San Pedro doesn't have a wide choice. **El Pueblo Andaluz**, on the coastal highway, Km 172, ✆ 95 272 06 39, is one of the outstanding bargains on the coast, a pretty place near the beach built around an old Andalucían home with a pool, playground, restaurant and garden (*6000 pts*). There are some *hostales* in the town such as the *Marta, Lagasca 24, ✆ 95 278 33 36, and the *Casa Armando*, 19 de Octubre 53, ✆ 95 278 11 90; all have rooms for around *3000 pts*.

There is, however, a wide variety of bars and restaurants in San Pedro itself and also on the 'Ronda Road' as you leave towards the Sierras, and in **Nueva Andalucía**, a vast area of beautiful country between San Pedro and Marbella which boasts a great deal of high-quality residential development. At **Alfredo**, Avda. Andalucía, Local 8, ✆ 95 278 61 65, the selection of grilled fish and meats is very choice, and the atmosphere buzzy (*2000–3000 pts*). Six kilometres above the town on the road to Ronda (you'll need a car or taxi) try **Méson El Coto**, a handsome Andalucían house with magnificent views over sea and mountains and a top-class kitchen specializing in delicious grills and seasonal game (*3500–4500 pts*). Not far away, tucked inside Nueva Andalucía near La Quinta, **El Gamonal**, Ctra. Ronda–Camino La Quinta, ✆ 95 278 99 21, a very pretty Spanish restaurant, cosy inside, with a flowering terrace, which specializes in roasts (*2500 pts*). And on a charming site by Los Naranjos Country Club, the stylish **Ogilvy & Mailer**, ✆ 95 281 07 42, without claiming to be particularly Spanish, serve some of the finest and most innovative Mediterranean food on the coast, accompanied by Carol Mailer's carefully selected wines. A memorable and delicious evening here is surprisingly reasonable for this kind of quality (*3500–4000 pts*). *Closed Sun.*

Marbella

Tourist Information

Marbella: C/ Miguel Cano 1, ✆ 95 277 14 42. *Open weekdays 9.30–8.30 (9.30–9.30 in summer) and Sat 10–4 (10–2 in summer)*. There's also an office on Pza. Los Naranjos, ✆ 95 282 35 50.

Puerto Banús: Avda. Principal, ✆ 95 281 74 74.

Marbella is the the smartest, probably most expensive and certainly most complex resort in Spain. When you arrive, you might find yourself asking why—its appeal is not obvious. The place has been much maligned and, it's true, over-developed, but the old quarter of town is still a delight, as whitewashed and charming as Andalucía at its most typical, and without ever being cutesy or tripperish.

Nonetheless, for the earnest tourist there is not a great deal of point in spending time in the town. You'll pay high-ish prices without getting in on the action, which takes place in a score of private clubs, private villas and private yachts. Besides, few foreigners actually live in old Marbella itself; self-styled artists and flashy bachelors take studios in **Puerto Banús**, English and Scandinavian golfers head for 'Golf Valley' in **Nueva Andalucía**, and well-heeled, well-dressed French, Italians and Germans heave-ho at the **Marbella Club** and **Puente Romano**, both situated a few miles west of town. **Puerto Banús** is the brilliantly designed, ancient-looking but actually modern development (it was opened in 1971) 6km (4 miles) to the west, with a marina full of outsize gin palaces; don't pass up the chance of spending an afternoon or evening here in one of the many waterside cafés, ogling all the yachts and some of the people.

Marbella ✉ *29600* **Where to Stay**

There are fewer hotels than you might imagine in the Marbella area, where villa life is very much the form. Don't count on finding a room at any price during the season; package tours have taken over here just as they have in the resorts to the east, and most places are booked pretty solid.

expensive

One of the oldest hotels in these parts, and for many the best-loved, is ★★★★★**Los Monteros**, Ctra. Cádiz, Km 187, ✆ 95 277 17 00, 🖷 95 282 58 46, situated 6km east of Marbella. With new ownership and policy changes, it has recently lowered its prices considerably, apparently without any drop in standards (*off-season doubles from 21,000 pts*). Its beach club is the height of restrained luxury and room prices include green fees at the hotel's own Río Real golf course. The ★★★★★**Meliá Don Pepe**, C/ José Meliá, ✆ 95 277 03 00, is another luxury, family-orientated hotel, facing out over the sea. It has a large tourist and sports complex, including an 18-hole golf course, 11 tennis courts, 5 squash courts, a riding school, heated pool, gym and sauna (*40,000–44,000 pts*).

The ★★★★★**Puente Romano**, Ctra. Cádiz, Km 178, ✆ 95 277 01 00, 🖷 95 277 57 66, is one of the most beautiful, if not the most expensive, and its name comes from the genuine Roman bridge incorporated into its lovely surroundings (*20,000–37,000 pts*). The ★★★★★**Marbella Club Hotel**, Ctra. de Cádiz 181, ✆ 95 282 22 11, 🖷 95 282 98 84, Alfonso Hohenlohe's jet-set retreat, which put Marbella on the map in the late 50s, is still going strong and is Marbella's most sophisticated hotel. A week with full board would have cost you less than £4 per person in 1959; in July 1999 you'll pay around *43,000 pts* per night, room only.

moderate

Ideally placed next to the Marbella shopping centre, at the end of the promenade over-looking the sea, is ★★★★**El Fuerte**, Avda. El Fuerte s/n, ✆ 95 277 15 00, 🖷 95 282 44 11, at a more affordable but still overly expensive *16,000 pts* for a double. If you do want to splurge here, the best buys among the luxury hotels will be found on the less-crowded beaches outside the town, like ★★★**Las Chapas**, Ctra. Cádiz, Km 192, ✆ 95 283 13 75, a nearly self-sufficient holiday complex with opportunities for tennis, golf and water sports—it's right on the beach on the coastal highway, 8km (5 miles) to the east (*10,000 pts*).

Or, if screaming infants and a round-the-clock disco beat are your thing, you could do worse than try **Don Miguel Club Med**, ✆ 95 277 28 00. Situated in the hills above Marbella—you won't need the address—Club Med does everything for you, from meeting you at the airport and minding your children to escorting you to the bullfight. Too regimented perhaps for some but the food is sensational, at least in quantity (*16,000 pts per person per day, full board and all entertainment included*). It helps if you speak French!

inexpensive

Surprisingly, there is a wide selection of *hostales* in the *3000–5000 pts* range, most of them in the old town, like the pleasant ★★**Hotel Paco**, C/ Peral 16, ✆ 95 277 1200 (*doubles 4500 pts with bath*), and a dozen other places in the *5000 pts* range around Calle Peral, Calle San Francisco and other streets nearby. The ★★**Hostal Enriqueta**, Los Caballeros 18, ✆ 95 282 7552, is particularly well placed near the Plaza Los Naranjos (*4000–5000 pts*). British-run **Hostal de Pilar** Mesconcillo 4, ✆ 95 282 99 36, is popular with young budget travellers (*2000 pts per bed*), and there's also a Youth Hostel—**Albergue Juvenil Marbella**, Trapiche 2, ✆ 95 277 14 91, which has small dormitories and some rooms (*from 1500 pts*).

Eating Out
expensive

There's a wealth of places to choose from to suit all tastes and pockets. **Hostería del Mar**, Avda. Cánovas del Castillo 1A, ✆ 95 277 02 18, has summer dining on the patio looking onto the swimming pool, and in winter is cosy inside. Specialities include chicken and shrimp Catalan style, stuffed quail, roast duck in a sauce of *cassis* and candied figs (*4000 pts*). *Open evenings only, closed Sun*. The Marbella Hill Club has now been transformed into the restaurant **LaCamargue**, Ctra. Cádiz, Km 178.5, ✆ 95 282 40 85, but still attracts the same select clientele. Its setting in beautiful gardens with lovely views and a flexible, interesting menu assure its continued popularity. The menu includes a medley of shrimp and lobster in a delicate sauce, poached salmon with fresh basil sauce, *solomillo* with two pepper sauces, and a selection of desserts, mostly based on fresh fruit (*4000–5000 pts*). *Open every evening in summer*.

Next to the Marbella Club, **Villa Tiberio**, ✆ 95 277 17 99, is a well-appointed restaurant with affordable prices, soft music and luxurious surroundings. Your Italian host will kiss you (women) on both cheeks, whether or not he has ever clapped eyes on you before. Some find this off-putting. Good *antipasto* dishes include the *bresola con aguacate* (thinly sliced cured beef with avocado), and delicious pasta. Main courses are good too, although less adventurous (*4000–5000 pts for dinner with wine*).

Marbella's most expensive and glamorous restaurant, **La Meridiana**, situated just behind the mosque, on Camino de la Cruz s/n, ✆ 95 277 61 90, offers international cuisine and designer dishes such as salad of angler fish marinated in dill, or braised veal sweetbreads with grapefruit (*6000–7000 pts; open evenings only in summer*). For something different go to **Francis Butler's Rustic Farmhouse**, Finca Besaya, Río Verde Alto, ✆ 95 286 13 86. Butler is usually a charming host and the baroque farmhouse interior is a magnificently tasteful testament to his background as a former West End theatre designer. There's a terrace overlooking the avocado trees and several rooms indoors warmed by open fires during the winter and littered with antiques. He serves an international cuisine which includes duck breast in mango sauce and an exquisite chocolate sorbet, and if the mood takes him he will do a couple of party pieces for you; high camp is the order of the day (*4000 pts*). *Open evenings Wed–Sat, reservations essential—if only to ask for directions!* Another special outing in Marbella is to the restaurant **Toni Dalli**, The Oasis Club, Ctra. Cádiz, Km 176, ✆ 95 277 00 35, housed in a Moorish mansion with a central courtyard and a magnificent view of the beach. Dalli, a retired Italian opera singer, often entertains his customers personally with the odd aria; otherwise there's the regular lively showbiz band to tap your toes to. Italian food is obviously the order of the day (*4000 pts*).

East of Marbella on the N340 in Las Chapas, the *Relais et Châteaux* **La Hacienda**, Ctra Cádiz, Km 193, Urbanización Las Chapas, ✆ 95 283 11 16, is frequently described as the best restaurant on the Costa del Sol. It prides itself on its super-fresh ingredients, but the service can be surly and the atmosphere strained. Try the hake in wine sauce, river crab and mushroom salad, fresh pasta, home-made ice cream. Dining out on the terrace, among the statues and stone arches, will set you back around *7000 pts* (*closed Mon and Tues, Sept–June and 14 Nov–21 Dec*).

Club Miraflores, on the Urbanización Miraflores, Ctra. Cádiz, Km 199, ✆ 95 283 01 02, serves consistently good food: spinach with onions and cream, *croquettes de crevettes*, grilled salmon with hollandaise sauce, beef stroganoff, or baby chicken casseroled in white wine (*3500 pts*); it would be hard to imagine a more agreeable spot to spend an evening, complete with live music and dancing. In town, by the picturesque Plaza de Los Naranjos, there are plenty of places to eat, most of them serving mediocre food but all wonderfully romantic on a warm evening outside, with the magical scent of orange blossom from the trees in the square. **Restaurante Mena**, ✆ 95 277 15 97, has a good reputation, serving superb *paella*, fish and seafood plus roast leg of yearling lamb and Châteaubriand (*3000 pts upwards*).

moderate

Toni Dalli seems to be building an empire around Marbella and no one begrudges him and his three charming sons their well-deserved success. The **Dalli Pasta Factory**, in the centre of Marbella, ✆ 95 277 67 76, serves fresh pasta, delicious *antipasto* and a spicy *tagliolini rabiaha* (pasta with prawns and chillis). You can eat well with wine for *under 2000 pts*. In Puerto Banús the Dalli brothers' Pasta and Pizza factories stand next door on Calle Rivera (*2500 pts*). For the best *paella* in Marbella, sucking pig, or white beans with clams—in fact some of the best Spanish cooking on the Coast—try the long-established **Santiago**, Pso. Maritímo, ✆ 95 277 43 39 (*about 3500 pts*).

inexpensive

The tapas bars of Marbella are excellent, both in the old town and in the streets behind the Alameda, such as Calle Carlos Mackintosh. Plenty of inexpensive places, mostly specializing in seafood, can be found in the area around Calle Aduar. **Casa La Vieja** at number 18, ✆ 95 282 13 12, does a good plate of mixed fish (*1000 pts*).

Many of the inexpensive beach restaurants that run the length of the coast, known as *chiringuitos,* are open year-round. You won't go far wrong anywhere with a plate of grilled sardines, but some places are inevitably better than others.

West of Marbella, **Victor's Beach**, Urbanización El Ancón, attracts a young and trendy crowd in summer. Four miles east of Marbella, between Los Monteros and Las Chapas, **Los Cano**, Playa Alicate, Ctra. de Cádiz, Km 187 (El Rosario exit off the Autovía, then follow signs), was once acknowledged to be the best *chiringuito* in the area, but recent reports suggest that standards are slipping (*2500 pts*).

Entertainment and Nightlife

Most action will be found in Puerto Banús, with its late bars, discos and piano bars. **Sinatra's**, at the main entrance to the port, is the classic hang-out of the see-and-be-seen set. **Crescendo**, behind *Da Paolo* in Puerto Banús, ✆ 95 281 55 15, is a very lively piano bar which slogs through nightly until 5am.

At **La Notte**, Camino de la Cruz, ✆ 95 282 60 24, run by fiery Marbella hostess Menchu, the crowd is more decorous and, dare we say it, slightly more interesting. It's situated in an elegant setting above the mosque, opposite Puente Romano hotel. In Marbella itself, try the clubs around Plaza Puente de Ronda or the street bars and discotecas along Avenida Ramon y Cajal, in the old town.

Fuengirola

You really should come on a package tour if you find Fuengirola and Torremolinos to your taste. That's what these places are for, and you would get a better deal. If you're just passing through and want to rest in anonymity by the beach, there are some possibilities.

Tourist Information

Avda. Jesús Santos Rein 6, in an old railway station, ✆ 95 246 74 57. *Open daily 9.30–1.30 and 4–8, Sat mornings only.*

Thirty years ago, Fuengirola was a typical whitewashed Spanish fishing village. It's still white, but hardly typical, and even less Spanish. With the miles of speculative *urbanizaciones* that surround it, it would be easy to be unkind to Fuengirola except that everyone there seems to be having such a good time. The town, and its adjacent community of **Los Boliches,** may be the only place in Spain where you'll see a sign in a shop-window reading '*Se habla español*'; the laid-back international community appreciates a good joke. Today the Spaniards live mostly in town, picnicking and sunbathing on their flat roofs or balconies; the foreigners drive in from the *urbanizaciones* for pub-hopping or to shop in the vast hypermarkets. The centre is becoming ever more determinedly multinational and multilingual, while upwardly mobile Spaniards are buying their way into the *urbanizaciones*. Fuengirola's weekly event is the Tuesday outdoor **market**, the best place to observe this curious community. Unlike other resorts on the Costa, there are some things to see—the Moorish **Castillo de Sohail** above town, a bullring, even the brand new façade of a **Roman temple**. In Roman times there were important marble quarries in the mountains here, and divers recently discovered a wreck off the coast with these stones, bound for somewhere else; they've been assembled near the beach.

Mijas

Visitors from Fuengirola totally overwhelm the village of Mijas, 3km (2 miles) up in the hills above town but at dusk it returns to the hands of the foreign residents, who count for 90% of the village's population. To escape the coastal sprawl, visitors drive up here by the coachload to find *real* Spain, and a typical Andalucían village, which it obviously is not, nor has been for 30 years. Yet it's still a pretty place with a promenade offering a view out to sea, a votive shrine to the Virgin, lots of pine woods, dozens of photogenic souvenir shops and 'officially licensed burro taxis' to take you around. The munchkin-sized whitewashed **bullring** sees its fair share of action throughout the year, but the town's museum of miniature curiosities is hard to take, even as a joke.

Fuengirola ✉ *29640*

Where to Stay

expensive

Only 5km from the centre of Fuengirola, the ★★★★★**Byblos Andaluz**, Urbanización Mijas Golf, ✆ 95 246 0250, 📠 95 247 67 83, is a haven of peace and tranquillity, with every imaginable luxury and a glamorous clientele; the Princess of Wales stayed here in 1994 (*30,000–35,000 pts*).

moderate

It's difficult to tell one new holiday hotel from the next, but for the best deals two places do stand out. The ★★★**Florida**, Pso. Marítimo, ✆ 95 247 61 00, 📠 95 258 15 29, has a pool and gardens, and though not luxurious is still a comfortable enough place (*6500–9500 pts*). The ★★**Cendrillon**, Ctra. Cádiz, Km 213 (just before El Rosario exit off the *autovía*), ✆ 95 247 53 16, is much the same as the Florida, only with tennis courts (*5000–8000 pts*). Both are on the beach and popular with families.

inexpensive

There are plenty of inexpensive *hostales* around the centre of Fuengirola, and especially in its suburb of Los Boliches on the northern end.

Eating Out

Dining in Fuengirola is an experience; you can choose from any sort of restaurant from Indonesian to Belgian without going broke. There are plenty to choose from along Calle del Hambre, which means 'hungry street', and Calle Moncayo, known as 'fish alley'.

expensive

Portofino, Edificio Perla 1, Pso. Marítimo, ✆ 95 247 06 42, is a popular restaurant where Italian specialities head the list (*3000 pts*). *Closed Mon, Jun–Aug dinner only*. Just outside Fuengirola, on the mountain road to Mijas, **Valparaíso**, Ctra. de Mijas, Km 4, ✆ 95 248 59 75, is one of the most attractive and popular restaurants in the area, with bars, terrace, swimming pool and an extensive international menu. Starters are labelled 'temptations' and women are given menus without the prices, but it's a favourite haunt, of the foreign communities in particular (*3000 pts*). *Closed Sun except July–Oct*.

If you are bursting at the seams with superfluous cash and want to lighten the load, head a few kilometres north to Hotel Torrequebrada, with its casino, nightclub and **Café Royal** restaurant, Ctra. Cádiz, Km 220, Benalmádena Costa, ✆ 95 244 60 00. In attractive surroundings, and with a fine view over the curve of the coastline, it offers international cuisine: pheasant with sour oranges, sea scallops in cider, smoked salmon between veal escalopes with truffles. Once you've paid around *5000 pts* for the meal, you can join the high rollers and spend some real money. If all this sounds wonderfully glamorous, believe us—it ain't! This isn't the Côte d'Azur and it shows.

moderate

The **Raj**, C/ Asturias 3, ✆ 95 246 94 70, is an attractive Indian restaurant and a welcome addition to Fuengirola's already cosmopolitan culinary scene. Decorated with charming *objets d'art* brought back from India, the cuisine is from the north of the subcontinent (*2500 pts*). If you've ever tried an Indonesian *rijstafel* in the Netherlands, you'll be glad to know there are plenty of places to sample such delights on the Costa; the Dutch wouldn't live without it. Long famous for these delectable dishes is **Bali Mas**, Sol Playa, C/ Martínez Catena, ✆ 95 247 19 94 (*2500 pts*). *Closed Wed*. **Mesón El Castellano**, Camino de Coín 5, ✆ 95 246 27 36, serves authentic Castilian food: roast meats, especially pork and lamb, and the service is fast and friendly (*2500 pts*). **Don Pé**, C/ de la Cruz, is also worth a visit (*2000 pts*).

Near Valparaíso on the road to Mijas **Casa Navarra**, Ctra. de Mijas, Km 4, ✆ 95 258 04 39, serves Spanish cuisine, unsurprisingly, from Navarra, including huge steaks and delicious fish that you can choose yourself. Try the *merluza* in shrimp and parsley sauce (*2000 pts*). *Closed Tues*. In Mijas itself there's a fair selection of eating places, **Blanco**, Pza. de la Constitución 13, ✆ 95 248 57 00, is a family-run restaurant with reasonably priced Basque fish specialities (*2500 pts*).

inexpensive

If you miss pub grub then drop into **La Cepa**, the English bar on Plaza Constitución in Fuengirola, run by Diane and her brother-in-law, Manolo. It's a good place to observe the plaza if you like chili con carne or steak and kidney pie tapas. If you don't, you'll find it unbearably depressing.

Torremolinos

Tourist Information

In the Ayuntamiento on Rafael Quintana, ✆ 95 237 95 12. *Open Mon–Fri 9.30–1.30.*

All sources agree about Torremolinos, the 'fishing village' immortalized in James Michener's *The Drifters*. The oldest and biggest resort town on the Costa, it is a ghastly, hyperactive, unsightly holiday inferno. In other words, it has character. Torremolinos isn't at all interested in our opinion, though, or in yours either; it's doing quite well with its endless screaming blocks of bars, shopping centres and concrete hotels. The predominant language is English, but a dozen others can be heard in the space of a few steps. To escape this horde step down to one of the beach cafés, popular day and night; if your luck is in, you'll be treated to some of the local street performers sharing their talents: an anís-soaked troubadour mangling an aria, cigarette dangling from his lower lip, or a transvestite flamenco dancer, whirling between the passing cars, his grim-looking mother handing round the hat. This is all received with good humour by the Spaniards, even if some of the tourists look a bit nonplussed. Part of Torremolinos' character arises from its status as capital of what the newspapers like to call the 'Costa del Crime'; crooks are only the surface, though; the most noticeable segment of an enormous permanent and transient population is made up of gawking sun-seekers from every corner of Europe. The welcome signs on the outskirts of town proclaim 'City of Tourists'.

Torremolinos ✉ *29620* — **Where to Stay**

In Torremolinos and its neighbouring stretch of tourist sprawl at Benalmádena Costa, the possibilities are endless, though these, too, will probably be packed with package tours. They come in all price ranges, from about *10,000 pts* to rock-bottom *hostales*.

expensive

There are a number of swanky four-star hotels in Torremolinos all offering much the same—swimming pool, air-conditioned rooms and dull hotel food. Try the **Melia Torremolinos**, Avda Carlota Alessandri 109, ✆ 95 238 05 00.

moderate

Perhaps Torremolinos's last secret is the hotel **★★Miami**, C/ Aladino 14, in Carihuela, ✆ 95 238 52 55. The house was built by Picasso's cousin Manolo Blasco as a holiday villa, and is quite charming despite its shabbiness (*from 7000 pts*). In a quiet corner of the Playamar area, 2km from the centre, the **★★★Príncipe Sol**, Pso. Colorado 26, ✆ 95 238 46 88, is a comfortable hotel with three pools and a good restaurant (*9000 pts*).

inexpensive

Some of the good bargains can be found out towards Carihuela, along Avenida Carlota Alessandri. Whether staying a few days or just passing through, the *hostal* **Victoria**, Los Naranjos 103 (opposite the bus station), ✆ 95 238 10 47, is pleasant, conveniently placed and reasonably priced (*6000 pts*). Carihuela is a good place to look for inexpensive accommodation, such as the spartan but acceptable **★★Hostal Pedro**, C/ Bulto 1, ✆ 95 238 05 36 (*3000–4000 pts*).

Eating Out

expensive

Dining in Torremolinos is much like Fuengirola—a lot of choice. There are more than 250 restaurants in town. **Dana's**, Avda. Carlota Alessandri 25, ✆ 95 238 22 88, on the main Fuengirola road, has long been one of the best restaurants, both for international cuisine and some classy Spanish dishes (*4000 pts*). On the main *carretera*, next to Los Álamos petrol station, **Frutos**, Ctra. Cádiz, Km 235, ✆ 95 238 14 50, is a popular restaurant, with high-quality food at reasonable prices, and the portions are generous: leg of lamb, sucking pig, Málaga fry, *tocino de cielo*—not a hint of *nouvelle cuisine* (*3000 pts*).

moderate

Highly recommended is the **Mar de Alborán**, Hotel Alay, Avda. de Alay 5, Benalmádena Costa, ✆ 95 244 64 27, for excellent Basque and Andalucían cuisine, this is a restaurant where the food gets better and better (*4000 pts*). The best seafood restaurants are in Carihuela, along the beach from Torremolinos, and the **Casa Guaquín**, C/ Carmen 37, ✆ 95 238 45 30, is very good indeed; try such specialities of the Costa as 'fish baked in salt'—it's a bit of an acquired taste (*2500 pts*). Another good place on the beach here is **La Jabega**, Mar 15, ✆ 95 238 63 75, with fish, of course, and a wide variety of starters and shellfish (*2500 pts*). In Torremolinos's Eurosol complex the **María de Valladolid**, ✆ 95 238 95 25, presents an alternative to *andaluz* cuisine. Its dishes are mainly Castilian; especially good are the stews, rabbit with rice, sucking lamb and tripe with chickpeas (*2500 pts*) *Closed Sun*.

If you want to escape the bedlam of Torremolinos, head up into the hills to the rambling, ranch-type restaurant run by a Hispano-German couple, **Venta los Pinos del Coto**, Cañada de Ceuta s/n, Churriana, ✆ 95 243 58 00, a 10-minute drive from town behind the airport. The spacious, attractive interior has stained-wood ceilings and a log fire for cold winter evenings. The menu is devoted to meat in large quantities (*3000 pts*). *Closed Sun evenings and Mon.*

inexpensive

A short walk from the Torremolinos bus station, and on the main road, **Mesón Gallego Antoxo** is a typical Spanish restaurant with a beautiful interior and charming little courtyard. There's a wide choice of fish, many dishes cooked to Galician recipes. Your wine will be served in the traditional Galician ceramic jug, and the drinking vessels resemble large finger bowls (*2500 pts*). If you've never had the Vietnamese variations on Chinese cuisine so popular in France, try **El Vietnam del Sur**, Pso. del Colorado, Urbanización Playamar, Bloque 9, ✆ 95 238 67 37, where they serve delicious food at affordable prices (*2500 pts*). *Closed Jan and Feb.*

Back in town, for a cheap aperitif, sit out at the **Bodega Quitapeñas** on the central steps down to the beach—everybody passes this way. One of the most interesting dining experiences to be had in the area is at the **Escuela de Hostelería de Málaga**, Finca La Cónsula, Churriana, ✆ 95 262 24 24, located in an old stately home near Hemingway's house. The hotel school's students prepare and serve delectable lunches featuring traditional and innovative Andalucían recipes (*5000 pts—booking essential*).

Málaga

Much-maligned Málaga, capital not only of the Costa del Sol, but also of crime and sleaze in southern Spain, is making a determined effort to improve its reputation and attract more tourists. In the past, a visit to the swish department store El Corte Inglés, may have been the only reason a tourist considered spending any time here at all. To miss Málaga, however, means to miss the most Spanish of cities, certainly on the Costa del Sol.

Whatever you may think of the place, it is alive and real: ungainly cranes and elegant palm trees compete for dominance of the skyline; police helicopters roar over the Plaza de la

Constitución as pretty Spanish girls toss their skirts and stamp their heels to flamenco music, to a private audience in a public square; elegant old Spanish ladies, scented with *Maja* soap, sit and reminisce, and dark-eyed tattooed gypsy boys flash their double-edged smiles to lure you into a shoeshine. From its tattered billboards and walls splashed with political slogans to its public gardens overflowing with exotic fauna, Málaga is a jamboree bag of colours, aromas and sounds. Admittedly Málaga cannot compete with Sevilla or Granada for sheer wealth of cultural distractions, but the *malagueños* are proud of their fun-loving metropolis. To experience a real local *juerga* (spree), treat yourself to an afternoon ramble through her many and famous tapas bars, where you will encounter more Spaniards in one afternoon than in a week in Torremolinos. Unfortunately, the old quarters of Málaga have been treated ruthlessly by town planners, and *El Perchel*, once the heart of Málaga's flamenco district, has lost a lot of its personality and charm. The Avenida de Andalucía cuts through this old district and then becomes the Alameda Principal and the Paseo del Parque. The essence of Málaga is within this limited area, from the elegant Avenida de Andalucía to the seedy, teeming neo-Moorish market on the Calle Atarazanas.

You will find it difficult to decide whether you love or loathe this city—will you notice the two snarling drivers impatient for the green light; or the two old gentlemen sipping sherry in the doorway of a cool, dark *bodega*, hung with Serrano hams and lined with wine casks?

Getting Around

As the main port of entry to the Costa del Sol and southern Andalucía, you'll probably pass through Málaga either coming or going.

By air: Málaga's often frenetic airport connects the city to Madrid, Valencia, Almería, Sevilla, Melilla and Tangier, besides being the charter-flight gateway to the Costa. A new terminal, aptly called **Pablo Ruiz Picasso**, has also relieved some of the summer congestion and baggage delays. The easiest way to get into the city, or to Torremolinos or Fuengirola, is the suburban railway line (separate stops at the airport for the regular and charter terminals). These trains and local buses stop running before midnight. After that you'll have to get a taxi (about *2500 pts* to Málaga centre or Torremolinos). **Airport information,** ✆ 95 204 88 04.

By train: There are five or more daily *ATV's* to Madrid (4 hours 10 minutes), plus four normal trains (7½ hours), and two trains a day to Valencia and Barcelona. Direct connections also to Sevilla and Córdoba; for all other destinations in Andalucía you'll have to make a change at the almost inescapable Bobadilla Junction. The attractive little station is on Calle Cuarteles. **Information:** C/ Strachen 2, ✆ 95 236 02 02.

By bus: The main bus station is by the train station at Pso. de los Tilos, south of the Avenida de Andalucía, ✆ 95 235 00 61. Connections for local destinations run hourly; for provincial destinations, generally every 1–2 hours. Portillo, ✆ 95 222 73 00, operate buses for the Costa, Sevilla, Ronda, Algeciras and towns and villages in the interior; Bacoma, ✆ 95 232 13 66, buses to Alora and Ronda; Los Amarillos, ✆ 95 441 93 62, for Antequera, Carratraca; Alsina Graells, ✆ 95 231 04 00 for Granada, Nerja and Almería, and also for Alicante and Barcelona.

Málaga: The Costa del Sol tourist board headquarters are at Compositor Lehmberg Ruiz 3, ✆ 95 228 83 54, 🖷 95 228 60 42. *Open Mon–Fri 9–1.30 and 5–7.* Tourist information offices are located at Pasaje Chinitas 4, just north of the Alameda, ✆ 95 221 34 45, and also at the airport, ✆ 95 224 00 00, ext. 2096. *Open 9–2 except Sun.* There is also a small booth in the bus station.

Melilla: Edificio Correos, Pablo Vallesca, ✆ 95 268 43 05.

The Heart of Málaga

As the Avenida de Andalucía, the main road from the west, crosses the dry rocky bed of the Guadalmedina river, it becomes the **Alameda Principal**, a majestic 19th-century boulevard. North of the Alameda is the **Plaza de la Constitución**, in the heart of the commercial centre, and the Pasaje Chinitas, an all-and-sundry shopping arcade. One of the clothes shops bears a commemorative plaque—it's the original site of the Café Chinitas, where bullfighters and flamenco singers would gather in the old days; the spirit of it was captured by García Lorca. The Alameda continues into the Paseo del Parque, a tree-lined promenade that runs along the port area, and leads to the city's **bullring**, built in 1874 with a capacity for 14,000, and very much in use today. Nearby is the **English cemetery**: Hans Christian Andersen declared he could 'well understand how a splenetic Englishman might take his own life in order to be buried in this place'. Its sea views, however, have long since been blocked by concrete buildings.

Just off the Paseo del Parque, steps lead up to the Moorish **Alcazaba**. Under the Moors, Málaga was the most important port of Al-Andalus, and from contemporary references it seems also to have been one of its most beautiful cities. Little remains of the Alcazaba, except a few Moorish gates, but the site has been restored to a lovely series of terraced gardens (*open Mon–Sat 10–1 and 6–8*). At the top is an **Archaeological Museum**, containing relics from the Phoenician necropolis found on the site and lists of Moorish architectural decoration salvaged from the ruins. The top of the Alcazaba also affords fine views over Málaga (*open 9.30–1.30 and 5–8 in summer, 10–1 and 4–7 in winter, Sat and Sun, mornings only*). There is a half-ruined **Roman theatre**, recently excavated, on the lower slopes of the hill, and from the Alcazaba you may climb a little more to the **Gibralfaro**, the ruined Moorish castle that dominates the city (*open 9–9*). But be careful—there have been reports of robberies on the path (*open 9.30–8*).

Back on the Paseo, note the chunky Art-Nouveau **Ayuntamiento**, one of the more unusual buildings in Málaga (*same hours as the Alcazaba*). On the opposite side of the Alcazaba is the **Museo de Bellas Artes**, C/ San Agustín 8, in a restored 16th-century palace. It is currently being turned into the city's Picasso museum. Picasso was a native of Málaga, though once he left it at the age of 14, he never returned. The artist's birthplace, **Casa Natal Picasso**, which now incorporates the **Municipal Picasso Foundation**, Pza. de la Merced, ✆ 95 221 50 05, is open for visits and holds occasional exhibitions (*open Mon–Sat 10–2 and 6–9; Sun 10–2*).

Málaga's **cathedral** is a few blocks away on Calle Molina Lario. It's an ugly, unfinished 16th-century work, immense and mouldering. Known as *La Manquita* (the one-armed lady), the only interesting feature is the faded, gaudy façade of the **sacristy**, left over from the earlier Isabelline Gothic church that once stood here (*open Mon–Sat 10–12.45 and 4–6.45; adm*

200 pts). The **Museo de Arte Sacro** is open daily except Sundays, *10–6.45*. Next to the dry river bed, the **Museo de Artes Populares,** Pasillo de Santa Isabel 10, occupies a restored 17th-century inn with a collection of household bric-à-brac (*open 10–1.30 and 5–8 in summer, 10–1.30 and 4–7 in winter; closed Sat afternoon and Sun; adm 200 pts*). An old farm, the **Finca de la Concepción**, ✆ 95 225 21 48, 7km (4½ miles) north of Málaga on the new road to Granada, is now owned by the municipality and has been turned into botanical gardens, with occasional summer shows of folklore and Andalucían dance; there are also some Roman remains on the site (*enquire at tourist office for details*).

Málaga ✉ *29000*   **Where to Stay**

moderate

****Parador de Gibralfaro**, Apartado de Correos 274, ✆ 95 222 19 02, ✇ 95 222 19 04, up in the old Moorish castle above the city, offers the best view of Málaga, and is one of the nicest places to stay following its 370 million peseta facelift (*15,000 pts*). Lunching on its terrace is unforgettable. Málaga's newest hotel, the ****Larios**, Marqués de Larios 2, ✆ 95 222 22 00, ✇ 95 222 24 07, is well appointed, extremely comfortable and good value at *16,000 pts* (cheaper rates at weekends).

Slightly dearer, a much-loved favourite, and our preferred choice, is the **Málaga Palacio**, Avda. Cortina del Muelle 1, ✆ 95 221 51 85, with its wonderful 50s atmosphere, excellent location at the top of the Alameda, and sweeping views over the port. Try to get a room on an upper floor (*18,500 pts*).

inexpensive

Try the *****Avenida**, Alameda Principal 5, ✆ 95 221 77 29 (*3300 pts*). South of here is the small ****Alameda**, Casa de Campos 3, ✆ 95 222 20 99 (*4500 pts*). Also south, the *****Castilla** and the *****Guerrero**, both C/ Córdoba 5, ✆ 95 221 86 35, are well-run establishments in the same building. The **Casa Huéspedes Bolivia**, Casa de Campos 24, ✆ 95 221 88 26, is spotlessly clean, central and inexpensive (*2000–3000 pts, shared bath*). Any place on or around the Alameda will be decent, but avoid the cheap dives around the train station.

Eating Out

Start your day with breakfast at the **Café Cosmopolita** on Marqués de Larios. Tables spill onto the pavement and surround the wooden horseshoe bar inside. Service is outrageously slow but at least this allows you to relax over an international paper from the kiosk next door, or watch the shoeshine boys at work on the customers' footwear.

If you've exhausted yourself shopping at the department store **El Corte Inglés**, Avda. de Andalucía, ✆ 95 230 00 00, stroll up to the top floor for a choice of three restaurants and two bars—the eat-all-you-can buffet lunch of meat and fish dishes, pastas and salads is a good bet (*2500 pts*). Also up here you'll find **El Club de Gourmets**, where you could put together some luxurious ingredients for a very special picnic, and **El Bar Inglés**, confusingly decked out in fine Scottish tartan.

Next door, the **Cafetería Horizonte**, ✆ 95 222 56 23, serves good tapas, cakes and ice creams. Popular with young people and reasonably priced is **La Taberna del Pintor**, Maestranza 6, ✆ 95 221 53 15, by the bullring, deserving its reputation as one of the best places to eat meat in Málaga; soups, salads and steaks done to your liking (*2000–3000 pts*). For sherry, shrimps and a marvellous atmosphere go to **Antigua Casa de Guardia**, Alameda 18; choose a drink from one of the 20 or so barrels lining the bar with names like *Pajarete 1908* and *Guinda*; a glass of sherry and a dozen mussels costs around *400 pts*. And for a really atmospheric *malagueño* restaurant that's on the up and up, enjoy a long, late lunch at **Méson Astorga**, C/ Gerona 11, ✆ 95 234 68 32 (*3000 pts*).

For tapas head for the **Bar Lo Güeno**, Marín García 9; it's literally a hole in the wall serving imaginative *raciones* and a decent selection of wines. Or try **Orellana**, C/ Moreno Monroy, one of the city's oldest and most classic tapas bars (they still offer a free *tapa*—or 'lid'—with your first glass of sherry). *Malagueños* flock to the Paseo Marítimo and the El Palo district east of town on Sunday especially, to fill up the many restaurants that line the beaches in what was once a simple fishing community. A favourite is **Antonio Martín**, out on the Paseo Marítimo, ✆ 95 222 21 13, right next to the sea; fish and rice dishes are the basis of the menu; try scrambled eggs with baby eel and salmon, or gilthead cooked in salt (*3000 pts*). *Open 1–4 and 8–12; closed in winter*. Other restaurants in the area include **El Cabra**, C/ Copo 21, Pedregalejo, ✆ 95 229 15 95, which has a more expensive range of seafood; and **Casa Pedro**, Quitapenas 4, El Palo, ✆ 95 229 00 13, where you may well be deafened by the din while you tuck into skewered sardines or Sierra-style angler fish (*2500 pts*). *Closed Mon evenings*. If heading south from Málaga, pop into **Casa Pepe** on the Carretera de Cádiz, an honest-to-goodness family-run place with local goodies (*2000 pts*).

Nightlife

Málaga has a buzzing summer club scene. On Friday or Saturday nights, it's hard to move through the streets between Plaza de la Constitucion and Plaza de Siglo. Hundreds of trendy Spaniards spill out of a bewildering variety of street bars and clubs. It's worth wandering down around midnight to Ir de Copas to while the night away. Make sure you look fashionable if you want anyone to give you a second glance.

Málaga to Motril

For some reason the tourist industry has neglected the areas east of the city. There are a few resorts strung out along the coastal highway, notably **Torre del Mar**, but they are all grim-looking places: little bits of Málaga that escaped to the beach. Nearby are some scanty remains of a Graeco-Phoenician settlement called **Mainake**.

Getting Around

The Portillo and Alsina Graells **buses** from Málaga or Motril serve Nerja, Almuñécar and Salobreña, and connections can be made from these towns to the interior villages. Note that long-distance buses along the coast do not usually stop at these towns.

Nerja: Puerto de Mar 1, © 95 252 15 31. *Open weekdays 10–2 and 5–7, Sat 10–1.*
Almuñécar: Avda. de Europa (in the small Moorish palace), © 95 863 11 25.
Salobreña: Pza. Goya, © 95 882 83 45.

Vélez-Málaga and Alhama de Granada

From Torre del Mar you can make a short detour inland to **Vélez-Málaga**, lying in a fertile valley at the foot of the Axarquía mountain area. Above the town, the castle (of which a restored tower remains) was one of the last Moorish outposts to fall to Christian forces during the purge by Isabel and Fernando. Below it, the church of **Nuestra Señora de la Encarnación** has had a chequered career—first as a Visigothic church, then a mosque, then a church again when the town was recaptured by Christian forces in 1487.

For a further detour into the mountains, you can tackle the 50km (31 mile) drive up on the C335 (becoming the C340 at Ventas) over the Sierra to **Alhama de Granada** which balances precariously on a rocky lip and looks down to the deep grassy-banked gorge. Up here you're away from it all. 'Oh for my Alhama' was the lament of Boabdil el Chico, who had to abandon this beauty spot to the Christians in 1482. The town's 17th- to18th-century church of **El Carmen** has a terrace from which you can enjoy the panorama. No prizes for guessing the town's other attractions—the remains of a Moorish castle, in the main square, and a 15th-century parish church, a gift to the town from Fernando and Isabel. Alhama has been famous since Roman times for its spa waters; ask at the modern spa, the Hotel Balneario, to see the **Roman and Moorish baths** below.

Another detour, which will eventually bring you back to the coast, is to take the twisting MA117 to Archez and continue on to **Cómpeta**, a truly lovely old village known principally for its sweet wines; its big wine fiesta is held on 15 August in the main square. Beyond Cómpeta begin the wilds of the **Reserva Nacional de Sierra de Tejeda**; you'll have to leave your car to explore it, though, and strong comfortable shoes are recommended. To get back to the coast, take the MA137 through beautiful vine-clad slopes to **Torrox**, another Nordic enclave, and continue down to **Torrox-Costa**, an expanding resort, 8km (5 miles) from Nerja.

Nerja

Approaching this town, the scenery becomes impressive as the mountains grow closer to the sea. Sitting at the base of the Sierra de Tejeda, Nerja itself is pleasant and quiet for a Costa resort. In Moorish times the town was a major producer of silk and sugar, an industry that fell into rapid decline after their departure. An earthquake in 1884 partially destroyed Nerja, and from then to the early 1960s it had to eke a living out of fishing and farming.

Its attractions are the **Balcón de Europa**, a promenade with a fountain overlooking the sea, and a series of secluded beaches under the cliffs—the best are a good walk away on either side of the town. A few kilometres east, the **Cueva de Nerja** is one of Spain's fabled grottoes, full of Gaudiesque formations and needle-thin stalactites. They have been fitted out with lights and music, with photographers lurking in the shadows who'll try to sell you a picture of yourself when you leave. The caves were popular with Cro-Magnon man (first found in a cave of that name in France), and there are some Palaeolithic artworks. Occasionally, this perfect setting is used for ballets and concerts.

A scenic 7km (4½-mile) drive north of Nerja on the MA105 finds pretty **Frigiliana**, a pristine whitewashed village of neat houses, cobbled streets and a large expat population. There are splendid views down to the eastern coast, especially from the ruins of the Moorish fort. This was the site of one of the last battles between Christians and Moriscos in 1569; the story of the battle is retold on ceramic plates around the village's old quarter. Nowadays, Frigiliana is like an English colony rather than an inland Andalucían village.

Almuñécar and Salobreña

The coastal road east of Nerja, bobbing in and out of the hills and cliffs, is the best part of the Costa, where avocado pears and sugar cane keep the farming community busy; the next resort, however, **Almuñécar**, is better left alone; a nest of dreary high-rises around a beleaguered village. Its only interesting feature is the **Moorish castle**, which houses the local cemetery. Outside the town are the remains of a Roman aqueduct. **Salobreña** is much better, though it may not stay that way. The village's dramatic setting, slung down a steep, lone peak overlooking the sea, is the most stunning on the coast, and helps to insulate it just a little from the tourist industry. The beaches, just starting to become built up, are about 2km (1¼ miles) away.

From here, the next town is **Motril**, a large settlement set back from the sea with little to attract visitors; it's the centre of the coastal sugar-cane production, thanks to the gin family, Larios. There isn't much Costa left further east, and the only real choice for a destination is the spectacular mountain road that runs through the Sierra Nevada and on towards Granada.

Where to Stay

Nerja ✉ 29780

Nerja has two fine hotels: the ★★★★**Parador de Nerja**, Playa de Burriana, Almuñécar 8, ✆ 95 252 00 50, ✆ 95 252 19 97, just outside town at El Tablazo (*14,000 pts*), and the ★★★**Balcón de Europa 1**, Pso. Balcón de Europa, ✆ 95 252 08 00, ✆ 95 252 44 90 (*10,000 pts, doubles with sitting room 13,500 pts*). The latter is probably the better bet, though not quite as luxurious as the *parador*; the beautiful location on the 'balcony of Europe' in the town centre and the reasonable rates make the difference. Both hotels have lifts down to the beaches under Nerja's cliffs. Another good bargain on the beach is the ★**Portofino**, Puerta del Mar 4, ✆ 95 252 01 50 (*around 6500 pts*). The **Alhambra Antonio Milon** at Chaparil is friendly with attractive rooms with sea-facing balconies (*5500 pts*).There are a few more inexpensive places about town, notably the ★**Florida**, C/ San Miguel 35, ✆ 95 252 07 43 (*3500 pts*), but Nerja is notoriously tight during the high season; you will have serious trouble finding a place without a reservation.

A popular restaurant in Nerja is the **Rey Alfonso**: there is nothing special about the cuisine but the view is superb, on cliffs directly under the Balcón de Europa (*3500 pts*). You can dine in genuine old Spanish surroundings in the restaurant at the hotel **Cala Bella**, C/ Puerta del Mar 10, ✆ 95 252 07 00, complete with wrought ironwork, ceramics and cool tiled floors, and views of Calahonda Bay and the Balcón; *salmón con salsa de anchoa* (salmon in anchovy sauce), *perdiz a la almijara* (partridge with local herbs), plus a selection of meats (*3500 pts*). Reservations are essential at **De Miguel**, C/ Pintada 2, ✆ 95 252 29 96, celebrated for its international meat and fish dishes, not least for the flambéd strawberries (*closed Mon and Feb*). **Jiménez** on the Plaza de la Marina serves a wide range of fish and seafood tapas for *under 1000 pts*.

Almuñécar ✉ 18690, **Salobreña** ✉ 18680

There are plenty of hotels to be found in Almuñécar along the narrow tiled streets of the old town, with cheaper ones around the Plaza de la Rosa. Try the **Casablanca**, Plaza San Cristobal 4, ✆ 95 86 55 75, a family-run pseudo-Moorish affair with rooms looking out to sea from *5000 pts*. In Salobreña, you have a choice between the **★★★Salobreña**, outside the town on the coastal highway, ✆ 95 261 02 61, ✆ 95 261 01 01, with pool, garden and close to the beach (*7500 pts*) and a number of *hostales* on the beach and in the alleys. Of these, the **★Mari Tere**, Ctra. de la Playa 7, ✆ 95 261 01 26, has doubles with bath for *3500–4500 pts*. **Camping El Peñón**, ✆ 95 61 02 07, near the beach, is closed between November and March.

Los Geranios, Pza. Rosa 4a, ✆ 95 263 07 24, is a cheerful restaurant in Almuñécar, full of geraniums and owned by a Hispano-Belgian couple; the menu is international with a Spanish bias (*about 3000 pts*). *Closed Sun and Nov.* The **Bodega Francisco**, C/ Real 15, ✆ 95 263 01 68, is a wonderful watering-hole serving inexpensive tapas and the usual *andaluz* staples (*1000–1500 pts*). Salobreña has one good restaurant: the Mesón Durán, N340, Km 323, specializing in meat and some *andaluz* dishes (*2500 pts*). *Closed Mon.* If you're in the Motril area, head for Gualchos, 17km (10½ miles) to the east. There you'll find **La Posada**, Pza. de la Constitución 9, ✆ 95 264 60 34, a delightful old coaching inn where you can stay as well as eat. They serve spinach with fish mousse, red mullet with *andaluz* mayonnaise, swordfish with garlic, cream and wine, and duck in Jerez vinegar and raisins (*2000–3000 pts*). *Closed Mon.*

Motril to Mojácar

The coastal road cuts between the sea and the plastic—not coastal development, but agricultural plastic, covering a good percentage of Europe's winter vegetables. At **Adra** you enter the province of Almería, the sunniest, driest and hottest little corner of all Europe. Until the 1970s the **Costa de Almería**, difficult of access and bereft of utilities and water, was untouched by tourism. Now, charter flights drop in from northern Europe, and hotels are sprouting up here and there—but compared to the region further west, it's pleasantly underwhelming.

Adra was an ancient Phoenician town, and the last spot in Spain surrendered by the Moors, at the moment Boabdil sailed from here to Africa. Though it's still basically a fishing and agricultural village, it has spawned **Almerimar**, a large new development of mostly villas and flats, with a new marina and one of Spain's best golf courses. The resorts at **Roquetas de Mar** (more golfing) and **Aguadulce** (oldest and biggest course on the Almería coast) are easily reached from Almería by bus.

Almería

Getting Around

By air: Almería's airport is 8km (5 miles) from the city on the road to Níjar, ✆ 95 033 31 11. Besides charters from London, Iberia has regular connections with Madrid, Barcelona and Melilla.

By boat: Transmediterránea runs car ferries from Almería to Melilla on the North African coast at 2pm every Tuesday, Thursday and Saturday; the voyage takes 6½ hours. The ticket office is at Parque Nicolás Salmerón 19, ✆ 95 023 61 56.

By train: Almería's RENFE station is a block from the bus station, on Ctra. Ronda, easy walking distance from the centre, ✆ 95 025 11 35. The city office is at Calle Alcalde Muñoz 1, ✆ 95 023 12 07. There are daily trains and *Talgos* to Madrid, Barcelona and Valencia; for Granada three times a day; or make an all-night journey across Andalucía, departures daily around 11pm, arriving in Córdoba at 7am, or Sevilla at 8am.

By bus: The bus station, in the new part of town on the Plaza Barcelona, ✆ 95 021 00 29, has a daily service to the major cities of the Levante up to Barcelona; also to Madrid, Granada, Sevilla, Cádiz, Málaga and Algeciras. There are two buses daily to Adra; hourly connections to Aguadulce and Roquetas; five buses daily to Berja; at least three to Cabo de Gata, four to Mojácar, two each to Níjar and Tabernas and weekday connections to Jaén and Guadix.

Tourist Information

Parque de Nicolás Salmerón at Martínez Campos, on the sea front, ✆ 95 027 43 55. *Open Mon–Fri 9–2 and 4–7.*

Almería has been a genial, dusty little port since its founding by the Phoenicians, though for a short time in the 11th century, after the fall of the caliphate, it dominated this end of Al-Andalus, rivalling Córdoba and Sevilla. The upper city, with its narrow streets, tiny pastel houses and whitewashed cave dwellings hugging the looming walls of the **Alcazaba** (*open 10–2 and 4–9*), has retained a fine Moorish feel to this day. Built by Caliph Abd ar-Rahman II in the 10th century, the Alcazaba was the most powerful Moorish fortress in Spain; today its great curtain walls and towers defend mostly market- and flower-gardens—nothing remains of the once-splendid palace. Behind the fortress, by the wall of Jayrán, you can visit the **Centre for the Rescue of Animals of the Sahara**: before going up, get permission from the centre's headquarters near the tourist office—they'll give you a note letting you wander through the cages and enclosures of a wide variety of endangered animals, in an environment that must feel just like home. Almería's **cathedral**, begun in 1524, was seemingly built for defence with its four mighty towers. Prettier, and boasting a fine carving of St James (Santiago) Matamoros and a minaret-like tower, is **Santiago El Viejo**, just off the Puerta de Purchena near the top of the Paseo de Almería.

Almería has a small **archaeological museum** on Calle Javier Sanz, with remains from the remarkable Neolithic culture of Los Millares that flourished here about 3500–3000 BC (*adm free with an EU passport*). You'll learn more about it here than at the sites themselves, but determined Neolithic fans will want to see Los Millares itself, in stark, barren mountains about 25km (15½ miles) north on the N324 at Santa Fe de Mondújar. Five thousand years ago this was rich farmland, and the people who lived here had the leisure to create one of the most advanced prehistoric civilizations in Spain. The burial mounds here are almost true temples, with interior passages and surrounding concentric stone circles, broken by concave semicircular entrances. Five millennia of erosion have made these difficult to discern, and you'll have an even harder time distinguishing the remains of the walled town that once stood nearby.

East of Almería

The **Sierra Alhamilla**—one of the driest, most rugged and lunar of Spanish sierras—occupies this most southeastern corner of Spain. The coastal road struggles out to the **Cabo de Gata**, with a pretty beach, solitary lighthouse and crystal-clear waters, popular with divers. Inland, the white village of **Níjar** is a charming oasis in an arid setting where potters actively carry on a craft introduced by the Phoenicians. In **Tabernas** there are a couple of spaghetti-western sets. At **Mini Hollywood,** the town built by Sergio Leone for such classics as Clint Eastwood's first vehicle, *A Fistful of Dollars*, cowboy shoot-ups and bank robberies are staged at weekends for visitors (*open July–Sept; adm 850 pts*). **Sorbas**, with its hanging houses, is most impressive seen from the highway; between the two, the government has decided to exploit the province's greatest natural resource—sunlight—with the country's largest solar energy installation.

Mojácar

Isolated amidst the rugged mountains, on a hill 2km (1¼ miles) from the beach, trendy Mojácar has often been compared to a pile of sugar cubes. No town in Spain wears such a Moorish face—its little, flat-roofed, white houses stacked almost on top of one another. Most unusually, the old women in the village used to paint a symbol known as the *indalo* (a stick figure with outstretched arms, holding up an arc) on their doors as a charm against the evil eye and thunderbolts. No one knows when this practice originated, though in the nearby caves of Vélez-Blanco Neolithic drawings of *indalos* dating from 3000 BC have led anthropologists to the conclusion that this is one of the few cases of a prehistoric symbol being handed down in one place for thousands of years. Northeast of Mojácar, there's nothing but empty spaces as far as the Andalucía-Murcia border (and well beyond it, for that matter). The nondescript village of **Palomares** occupied all the world's headlines for a while in 1966, when an American B-52 crashed nearby and littered the countryside and sea with live hydrogen bombs.

Where to Stay and Eating Out

El Ejido and Níjar ✉ 04700

In El Ejido you can splurge in the ★★★★**Golf Hotel Almerimar,** ✆ 95 049 70 50, ● 95 040 70 19, a plush 38-room refuge, with tennis courts, pool and recreational activities in an attractive setting (*13,500 pts*). If you'd prefer peace and quiet to comfort and facilities, try the little ★**Isleta del Moro,** ✆ 95 036 63 13, a *hostal* near Níjar, with a simple restaurant (*3000 pts*).

Almería ✉ 04000

When on location in Almería, Hollywood denizens have traditionally checked into the ★★★★**Gran Hotel Almería,** in town on the Avenida Reina Regente 8, ✆ 95 023 80 11, ● 95 027 06 91. Rooms are plush and air-conditioned, and among the available diversions are a pool and bingo hall (*16,000–18,000 pts; breakfast only*). On the beach similar smart lodgings are available at the ★★★★**Playaluz,** Playa del Palmer, ✆ 95 034 0 04, located in a lovely setting, and offering golf, tennis, sauna, indoor and outdooor pools, and children's facilities (*9500–15,000 pts*).

Another comfortable and air-conditioned choice in town is the ★★★**Torreluz** hotel complex, Pza. de Flores 1, ✆ 95 023 47 99, offering one-, two- and three-star accommodation (*5000–8000 pts*). There are a number of inexpensive *hostales*. The ★**Maribel**, Avda. F.G. Lorca 153, ✆ 95 023 51 73, is within easy walking distance of the bus and train stations, offering simple but adequate rooms (*around 3000 pts*). Seven kilometres from Almería at Pechina, check out the **Baños Sierra de Alhamilla**, ✆ 95 031 74 13, a beautifully restored 18th-century palace next to the thermal springs (*7000–8000 pts*).

The best restaurant is probably **El Bello Rincón**, Ctra. Nacional 340, Km 436, ✆ 95 023 84 27, with a beautiful vista over the sea and wonderfully fresh seafood (*2500–3500 pts*). *Closed Mon, July and Aug.* **La Gruta**, beside the Bello Rincón in a natural grotto, is equally good with meat dishes and grills. *Closed Sun and Nov.* The popular **Ánfora**, C/ G. Garbín 25 (off Pza. San Sebastián), ✆ 95 023 13 74, specializes in the freshest of local ingredients—vegetables and seafood (*3000 pts*). *Closed Sun.* Nearby is another good seafood restaurant, the **Imperial**, Puerta de Purchena 13, ✆ 95 023 17 40, with a decent three-course house menu for *1500 pts*, and good seafood soups and mixed fish platters for *2000 pts* . *Closed Wed.* On the seafront, facing the gardens, are a couple of inexpensive choices, **La Cartuja** and the **Canoe**, the latter with a *850 pts* set menu.

Mojácar ✉ 04638

The modern beach-side ★★★★**Parador Reyes Católicos**, ✆ 95 047 82 50, ✆ 95 047 81 83, has a pool and air-conditioning (*9000–10,500 pts*). In the village there are a couple of new, trendy hotels at lovely Mirador de la Puntica; ★★★**El Moresco**, Avda. Horizón; ✆ 95 047 80 25, ✆ 95 047 81 76, has the advantage of being open all year, with indoor, outdoor and children's swimming pools (*7500 pts*). There's little in the budget category; but we like **Mamabel's**, C/ Embajadores 3, ✆ 95 047 24 48, a beach house owned by Belgian poet Jean-Marie Raths. Ask for Room 1—you'll like the view (*4000–6000 pts*). You'll spend less at **El Puntazo** on the beach, ✆ 95 047 82 29, where a nondescript double will set you back *3800–4250 pts*. Seafood and couscous to order on Fridays are served at **Mamabel's** on Embajadores 3, along with onion tart and chicory salad with Roquefort and nuts (2500 pts); less expensive and overlooking the sea, **Mediterráneo** at Cueva del Lobo has more seafood for *1500–2000 pts*. **Palacio** in the Plaza del Caño is the best restaurant in town, with excellent chocolate truffles (*2500 pts*).

Turre ✉ 04638

At the **Finca Listonero**, Cortijo Grande, ✆ 95 047 90 94, the management is English and so are most of the guests. If you don't mind that, this restored farmhouse on an estate in the Turre mountains is a peaceful place, just a few kilometres away from Mojácar itself (*from 8000 pts*).

Garrucha ✉ 04630

A few kilometres north of Mojácar, **El Almejero**, Explanada del Puerto, ✆ 95 046 04 05, is a restaurant serving super-fresh and delicious seafood, with a view of the fishing port where the catch is landed.

The Andalucian Interior

For some, the mountainous area between the Guadalquivir and the coast will be the best of Andalucía. It doesn't have beaches, and it doesn't have famous buildings or museums. Tourists are in short supply too—mostly young Germans and Britons with backpacks, along with day-trippers from the Costa and a few examples of that beloved but endangered species, the serious British traveller, with his nose in a Latin chronicle or a bird-watcher's guide. What this region does have is a chain of peaceful white villages, draped along hillsides under their castles, their steep streets lined with pots of geraniums. Some are prosperous, some quite poor; some have a reputation for friendliness, others can seem silent and introverted. It is a region of rolling hills broken by patches of grey mountains, well-tended lands devoted to the traditional Mediterranean staples of wheat, vines and olives, coloured in the spring by orange and almond blossom in the lower areas.

Arcos de la Frontera to Ronda

Getting Around

In this region, without a car, you'll be depending on **buses**. Arcos de la Frontera has regular connections to Jerez, Cádiz and Ronda; less frequently to Sevilla. From Ronda you can go directly to Jerez, Cádiz, Málaga, and most of the towns along the Costa del Sol; there are also four daily buses to and from Sevilla. Arcos and Ronda have connections to the villages in their hinterlands—usually only once a day, so if you're day-tripping, make sure there's a return. Ronda's bus station is in the new town, on the Paseo de Andalucía. Ronda has **trains**, too; there are at least three a day for Algeciras and Málaga, with connections at Bobadilla Junction for Madrid and the other cities of Andalucía. Some trains stop at Gaucín and Setenil. The station is just a few blocks down Paseo de Andalucía, © 95 287 16 73. When you are travelling by **car**, be warned that some streets of the Sierra towns and villages are very narrow.

Tourist Information

Ronda: Plaza de España, by the bridge, © 95 287 12 72. *Open weekdays 10–2.*

Arcos de la Frontera

Starting from the west, near Jerez, **Arcos de la Frontera** is the first and one of the most spectacular of the towns, hanging on a steep rock with wonderful views over the valley of the Guadalete from the *mirador* near the Plaza del Ayuntamiento. The narrow streets twist and turn like an oriental maze, an inheritance from its Moorish past. The older sections of town under the castle contain some ancient palaces and the Isabelline Gothic **Santa María de la Asunción**, next to which is a rectangular esplanade hanging over the cliff above the Guadalete. Arcos was an important fortress for the Moors, a seemingly impregnable eyrie that Alfonso the Wise was smart enough to take in 1264.

Further east, **Grazalema** is a lovely village, full of flowers and surrounded by pine woods. It has been famous for hand-woven blankets since Moorish times, and they are still made here on big, old, wooden looms. It also claims—incredibly, if you visit on a sunny day—to be the rainiest village in Spain. The surrounding area is a national park; details of walks, horse-trekking, etc., can be found at the campsite office just above the village. To the south is **Benaocaz**, which has a small museum of local archaeology. Nearby, **Ubrique** hangs dramatically over the Río Majaceite; though a growing industrial town, best known for its leather-work, it still manages to retain some of its medieval charm. **Zahara** and **Olvera** have memorable silhouettes, their castles and churches sticking bravely up over the whitewashed houses. Zahara ('flower' in Arabic) is a quiet town, perfumed by orange groves, clinging to the slopes of a hill crowned by a medieval castle which the Christians captured from the Moors towards the end of the 15th century. Once a famous bandits' hideout, Olvera has the ruins of a 12th-century Moorish castle, from which there is a heady view down to the village and a very dignified 17th-century church, **La Encarnación**. Halfway between Olvera and Ronda is **Setenil**, a peculiar village with some of its few streets lining the walls of a gorge. The houses are tucked under the overhanging rock, and their front doors overlook a stream.

Ronda

The Serranía de Ronda is a region of difficult topography, and it made life difficult for most would-be conquerors. A band of southern Celts gave the Romans fits in these mountains; various Christian chieftains held out for centuries against the Moors, and to return the favour the Moors kept Castile at bay here until 1485, just seven years before the conquest of Granada.

Ronda, the only city in the Serranía, is a beautiful place, blessed with a perfect postcard shot of its lofty bridge over the steep gorge that divides the old and new towns. Because of its proximity to the Costa del Sol, it has lately become the only really tourist-ridden corner of the interior. Don't be discouraged from a visit; the views from the top of the city alone are worth the trip. One of the best places from which to enjoy them is the **Alameda del Tajo**, a park on the edge of the **Mercadillo**, as the new town is called. Next to it, Ronda has one of Spain's oldest and most picturesque bullrings. The 1785 **Plaza de Toros**, the 'cathedral of bullfighting', stages only about three *corridas* a year, but it still has great prestige: the art of bullfighting was developed here; there's also a small museum. The **Puente Nuevo** was built at the second try in 1740—the first one immediately collapsed. The bridge's two thick piers descend almost 92m (300ft) to the bottom of the narrow gorge. Crossing the bridge into the **Ciudad** (old town), a steep path heads downwards to two 18th-century palaces: the **Palacio de Salvatierra** and the **Casa del Rey Moro**, built over Moorish foundations. From its garden there is a stairway—365 steps cut out of the rock, called the **Mina**—that takes you down to the bottom of the gorge. Here there's a Moorish bridge and well-preserved remains of a **Moorish bath**. Back on top, if you survive the climb back up, there is the town's main church, **Santa María La Mayor**, still retaining the mihrab and minaret of the mosque it replaced, and the ruins of the **Alcázar**, blown up by the French.

Around Ronda

Besides the opportunities for walks in and around the valleys under Ronda, an interesting excursion can be made to an area of curiosities 15–20km (9–12 miles) west of town. The hills around the hamlet of **Montejaque** are full of caves. Two, the Cueva del Gato and Cueva del Hundidero, both full of stalactites and odd formations, are connected. The little stream called the Gaduares disappears in one and comes out in the other. Five kilometres south, past the village of Benaoján, the **Cueva de la Pileta** has some 25,000-year-old art—simple drawings in black of animals and magic symbols (*open 9–1, 4–6*; the caretaker lives in the farmhouse near the entrance). Twelve kilometres west of Ronda, off the road to Grazalema, are the Roman ruins of **Acinipo** known locally as 'Ronda la Vieja', with a theatre and stage building like Mérida's. And finally, if you have a car or even a bicycle, take the 40km 'scenic route' along the spectacular C341, which leaves Ronda to the southwest. It's a breathless roller-coaster ride through the heart of the Serranía. You'll pass by the villages of Ajatate, Benadalid and Algatocín before reaching the ancient, no longer so isolated, village of **Gaucín**.

Where to Stay and Eating Out

Arcos ✉ 11630

The ★★★★**Parador Nacional Casa del Corregidor**, Pza. de España, ✆ 95 670 05 00, ✉ 95 670 11 16, is a lovely and quite popular place so book ahead (*15,500 pts*). ★★★**Cortijo Faín**, Ctra. de Algar, Km 3, ✆ 95 670 11 67, offers 10 rooms and suites in a 17th-century country house (*10,000–16,000 pts*). Another excellent choice, the ★★★**Marqués de Torresoto**, Marqués de Torresoto 4, ✆ 95 670 07 17, is an aristocratic, 17th-century mansion, situated in the historic quarter of Arcos near the Ayuntamiento (*9000 and 10,000 pts*). More reasonable is ★★★**Los Olivos**, San Miguel 2, ✆ 95 670 08 11, ✉ 95 670 20 18, where rooms go for *7150–9000 pts*. **Pension Calle de las Monjas**, Calle Deán Espinosa 4, next to the Iglesia de Santa Maria, ✆ 95 70 23 02, has doubles from *3500 pts*, and a barber's shop in reception. The best place to eat in Arcos is **El Convento**, Marqués de Torresoto 7, ✆ 95 670 32 32, which offers typical cuisine of the Sierras in a 16th-century nobleman's house (*4000 pts*). The **Mesón del Brigadier**, Presa de Arcos, ✆ 95 670 10 03, serves mostly pork and game dishes (*3000 pts*).

Ronda ✉ 29400

Ronda has a wide choice. The recently opened ★★★★**Parador de Ronda**, Pza. de España, ✆ 95 287 75 00, ✉ 95 287 81 88, preserves the façade of the old town hall, but is painfully modern inside. It is the flagship of the Parador chain; comfort and service are excellent, and the views from the duplex suites are matchless. The ★★★★**Reina Victoria**, C/ Jerez 25, ✆ 95 287 12 40, ✉ 95 287 10 75, is a fine and handsome old hotel, which can no longer afford to rest on its laurels (*13,500–17,000 pts*). In the centre of town, the **Polo**, C/ Mariano Souvirón 8, ✆ 95 287 24 47, ✉ 95 287 43 78, is a busy little place with old-fashioned comfort at a modest price (*6500–9000 pts*). Less expensive, near the old town, is ★★**Royal**, C/ Virgen de la Paz 42, ✆ 95 287 11 41, near the bullring (*5000 pts for doubles*). A stylish small hotel, situated in an old inn at the foot of the cliffs, is **Posada Real**, C/ Real 42, ✆ 95 287 71 76. You'll pay a big *12,500–15,000 pts* for a not very big room. There are dozens of small *hostales* and *camas* over bars—most of them quite agreeable—on all the side streets of Calle Jerez in the Mercadillo.

The best meals Ronda can offer, with a view to match, are at the **Don Miguel**, Villanueva 4, ✆ 95 287 10 90, overlooking the gorge next to the famous bridge; they also have a bar built into the bridge itself (*3000–4000 pts for a dinner*). Otherwise, stick to the restaurants in the Mercadillo like the **Mesón Santiago**, C/ Marina 3, ✆ 95 287 15 59, or the **Doña Pepa** overlooking the square on Plaza del Socorro, ✆ 95 287 47 77 (*2000–3000 pts*), with its quail sautéed in garlic, and partridge.

Benaoján ✉ 29370

The British-owned ★★★**Molino del Santo**, Bulevar de la Estación, ✆ 95 216 71 51, is a converted water mill beside a mountain stream, close to the Pileta caves with a spring-fed swimming pool. The kitchen serves *andaluz* cuisine. It's friendly and intimate and offers excursions each week—hiking, cycling and mini-bus nature tours in the Grazalema National Park (*8000–10,000 pts*). The **Casitas de la Sierra**, ✆ 95 216 73 92, ☎ 95 216 72 99, offers fully-furnished village houses with all mod cons; a cheaper and more rustic option (*between 3500 and 5000 pts*).

Gaucín ✉ 29400

Below the village, on an exclusive residential estate set within a 50-hectare farm, **Cortijo El Puerto del Negro**, Ctra. a El Colmenar, ✆/☎ 95 215 12 39, has a country house hotel atmosphere and is beautifully run by Tony and Christine Martin. (*14,500 pts*). A real workman's *comedor*, but with a nobleman's view from the terrace on a sunny day, **El Pilar**, opposite the petrol station, ✆ 95 215 13 47, offers an excellent-value, three-course lunch with a quarter-bottle of wine for *950 pts*.

Antequera and Around

Getting Around

Antequera is on the **rail** line from Algeciras to Granada, and there are easy connections to all points from nearby Bobadilla Junction. The station is on Avenida de la Estación, ✆ 95 284 23 30. Lots of **buses** go to Málaga and Sevilla, less frequently to Granada and Córdoba, as well as to Olvera, Osuna and the other villages of the region. The bus station is on Calle Alameda.

Tourist Information

Antequera: C/ Infante Don Fernando, Edificio San Luis, ✆ 95 270 04 05. *Open 10–2 and 5–8.*
Archidona: in the Ayuntamiento, ✆ 95 271 63 21. *Open Mon–Fri 9–2.*

Antequera

Known in Roman times as *Antiquaria*, it was the first of the Granadan border fortresses to fall to the Reconquista, in 1410, although subsequently it was retaken by the Moors and lost again. It is not an especially interesting city, though it's as large as Ronda. There is, however, quite an impressive ensemble of 16th- to 18th-century buildings. The 17th-century Nerja Palace houses the **Municipal Museum** (*open Mon–Fri 10–1.30; Sat 10–1*), with many religious works including a wonderful *St Francis* by Alonso Cano and a Roman bronze of a boy. Up the Cuesta Zapateros, at the top of the hill, is the 16th-century **Arco de los Gigantes**, meant as a sort of triumphal arch for the seldom-victorious Felipe II, and incorporating ancient fragments; next to it, the ruins of a Moorish fortress offer views over the town. Nearby is the plateresque church of **Santa María La Mayor**, attached to which is an art restoration centre.

East of Antequera

The Romans may have given Antequera its name, 'old town', and there was probably a settlement here some centuries before the arrival of the Phoenicians. Another possibility is that the name is related to *anta*, the local word for dolmen. Just out of town are the Neolithic monuments known as the **Cuevas de Menga,** the 'first real architecture in Spain'. They are hardly as impressive as the *talayots* and *taulas* of the island of Menorca, but there's nothing like them in mainland Spain. Le Corbusier came here in the 1950s, as he said, 'to pay homage to my predecessors'. There are three, dating from anything between 4500 BC and 2500 BC. The two largest, the Menga and Viera dolmens (*open 10–1.30 and 5–7, 5–8 in summer*) are covered chambers about 21.5m (70ft) long, roughly elliptical and lined with huge, flat stones; other monoliths support the roof-like pillars. At El Romeral nearby, under a mound and in the grounds of a sugar factory, the third of these temples has two chambers with domed ceilings. Originally the mound would have been about 100 yards in diameter, as big as Newgrange in County Meath, Ireland. All three have etchings of figures and symbols around their walls.

Fifteen kilometres (9 miles) east of Antequera on the N342 is **Archidona.** The town overlooks acres of olive trees, but its main feature is the unique, octagonal Plaza Mayor, the **Ochavada.** Built between 1780 and 1786 by Francisco Astorga and Antonio González, it is one of the loveliest plazas in Andalucía. Nearby **Loja** had a 9th-century **alcazaba** and the 16th-century church of **San Gabriel** has a cupola attributed to Diego de Siloé.

South of Antequera

The sierras between Antequera and Málaga contain some of the remote villages of the region and offer some spectacular scenery—almond trees, cacti, olive groves and mountains that drop steeply away to the silver ribbon of a stream down below. A natural park has been laid out around the rock formations at **El Torcal,** a tall but hikeable mountain with unusual eroded red limestone crags around it. Several paths are marked out. The nearest town is **Villanueva de la Concepción.** Here you should take the MA424 and travel south for about 17km. You will be rewarded with **Almogía,** presenting a dramatic spectacle overlooking a high ridge. From 15 to 18 August this place comes to life with dancing in the streets in celebration of San Roque and San Sebastián. The best views are from the ruined tower.

A more roundabout route south from Antequera will take you to the town of **Alora,** where you should turn northwest towards one of Andalucía's natural wonders. **El Chorro Gorge,** in the deep rugged canyon of the Río Guadalhorce, has sheer walls of limestone tossed about at crazy angles. The very agile can circumnavigate it on an old concrete catwalk called **El Camino del Rey,** which is steadily crumbling into a ruin. If you have time to explore this region, seek out the church of **Bobastro.** Just west of El Chorro, it's a twisty drive for a couple of kilometres after turning off the little Alora–Ardales road. Bobastro is a 9th-century basilica cut out of bare rock that supposedly contains the tomb of ibn Hafsun, the (possibly) Christian emir who founded a short-lived independent state in the mountains around 880. From Bobastro follow the road to **Ardales** and **Carratraca.** Carratraca has been a spa town from Greek and Roman times, and can be visited by would-be cure-seekers from June to October. From here the road twists and turns its way back to Alora.

Where to Stay and Eating Out

Archidona ✉ 29200

Archidona has only small one-star *hostales.* Of them, **★Las Palomas,** Ctra. Jerez–Granada, Km 177, ✆ 95 271 43 26, is the best bet (*3000 pts without bath*). If you're not on a budget, then *the* hotel in the area is

★★★★★La Bobadilla, Finca La Bobadilla, ✆ 95 832 18 61, 🖷 95 832 18 10, along the same road, you turn off at the sign for Villanueva de Tapia, halfway to Loja. It's an honest attempt at reconstructing the typical Andalucían *pueblo*, complete with Moorish touches, and covers a large area of land on a hilltop (*35,000 pts*). *Andaluz* and international dishes are on the menu of **La Finca**, the hotel's restaurant (*6000–7000 pts for a full dinner*).

Antequera ✉ 29200

The **★★★Parador de Antequera**, Pso. García del Olmo s/n, ✆ 95 284 02 61, 🖷 95 284 13 12, is a plain, modern building but has the most comforts here, and is reasonably priced at *11,500 pts* for air-conditioned doubles. In the town centre, the best choice is the **★Manzanito**, Pza. San Sebastián, ✆ 95 284 10 23 (*4000 pts*). The management also runs a good restaurant underneath (*1500 pts*). **Bar Madrona**, C/ Calzada 25, ✆ 95 284 00 14, is clean and basic (*3700 pts*) and does good *churros* and breakfasts. For the most interesting setting in Antequera, your choice has to be **La Espuela**, Pso. Maria Cristina s/n, Pza. de Toros, ✆ 95 270 26 33, the only restaurant in Spain actually located inside a bullring—*rabo de toro* is usually the dish of the day, if you can stomach it! (*3000 pts,* menú del día *1300 pts*).

Alora and Carratraca ✉ 29200

Alora has a new *parador* with a pool, **Paseo Garcia del Olmo**, ✆ 95 284 09 01, 🖷 95 284 13 12 (*11,000 pts*), and a few of other hotels such as the **★Durán**, C/ La Parra 9, ✆ 95 249 66 42 (*4000 pts*), and the **Colón**, Infante Don Fernando 3, ✆ 95 284 00 10, 🖷 95 284 11 64 (*4000 pts*). The place to stay in Carratraca is **★El Príncipe**, C/ Antonio Riobo 9, ✆ 95 245 80 20, but in season it's advisable to book beforehand (*3000—5000 pts*). Away from the hotels, the roadside *ventas* are best for eating out.

North of Antequera

This is the heart of Andalucía, a vast tract of bountiful hills covered in olive groves and vines. The area is more densely populated and a bit more prosperous than most of the region's rural districts. The towns are closer together, all white, and all punctuated by the warm sandstone of their palaces and towers. Along the way, on what we hope will be a properly Spanish picaresque journey through a region few tourists enter, there will be flamingos, dolmens, rococo frippery, memorabilia of Julius Caesar, a cask of *amontillado*, and 139 gargoyles.

Tourist Information

Osuna: Casa de la Cultura, near Pza. Mayor, ✆ 95 481 22 11.
Estepa: Ayuntamiento, Pza. del Carmen 1, ✆ 95 591 27 17.
Priego de Círdoba: Rio 33, ✆ 95 770 06 25.
Cabra: Pza. de España 11, ✆ 95 752 21 11.

Heading northwest out of Antequera into the gentler hills flanking the southern slopes of the Guadalquivir valley, you'll discover a few towns worth seeing. But before you reach the first of these, turn off the A92 at Fuente de Piedra and you'll come to the **Laguna de Fuente de Piedra**, one of Europe's largest breeding grounds for flamingos. They're here from March to September; the rest of the year you'll have to look them up in Senegal.

Back on the N334 you'll come to **Estepa**, known for its Christmas biscuits (*polverones* and *mantecado*), and the mass suicide of its inhabitants who preferred not to surrender to the Roman enemy in 208 BC. Further west, **Osuna** is a larger, neater version of Estepa. Founded by a busy, go-ahead governor named Julius Caesar, it was an important Roman military centre for the south of Spain, and survives as an attractive little city of white houses with characteristic *rejas* over every window. Osuna was an aristocratic town after the Reconquista, home of the objectionable Dukes of Osuna who lorded it over much of Andalucía. Their 'pantheon' of tombs may be seen in the fine Renaissance **Colegiata** church (*open 10.30–1.30 and 3.30–6.30; adm 300 pts*) on a hill on the west side of town. Inside is a memorable *Crucifixion* by José Ribera, and four other works of his in the high altar *retablo*.

The Cordobés Subbética and La Campiña

Here in the heartland of Andalucía lies the **Parque Natural de las Sierras Subbéticas de Córdoba**—a succession of wooded hills that dip into the valleys of the rivers Zagrillo, Salado and Caicena. The landscape of oak trees, olive groves and much shrubland is home to eagles, vultures, partridge, bats and badgers; the rivers and small lakes dotted around brim with perch and trout. Most tourists miss these untouched corners of Andalucía, where the people are God-fearing and industrious, and where the visitor is welcomed but watched carefully.

Twenty kilometres north of Estepa at **Puente Genil,** an old Moorish-style mill still turns in a pretty setting along the Río Genil. Further east, **Lucena** is one of the centres of a great wine-growing region. The town is not known for its beauty, but for making the biggest wine barrels in Andalucía. Nearby are the remains of the **Tower of Moral**, where Granada's last king, Boabdil el Chico was imprisoned by Ferdinand in 1483. Twenty kilometres south of here, the town of **Rute** produces the potent *anís*. Right at the centre of Andalucía, fittingly set in a sea of vineyards, is **Cabra**, 10km north of Lucena on the C327. From here you get a sweeping view of the Sierra Nevada to the southeast and the Guadalquivir valley to the north. **Priego de Córdoba** lies at the foot of the highest mountain in the province, **La Tiñosa**, and has a famous ensemble of baroque churches and monasteries; the best is the **Asunción** church with a beautiful dome over its *sagrario* chapel and a sumptuous stucco interior. The town's other pride is the baroque **Fuente del Rey**: three connecting fountain pools lined with 139 gargoyles, and a centrepiece of Neptune and Aphrodite on a horse-drawn carriage—it wouldn't look out of place in a *piazza* in Rome.

From Cabra the C327 heads northeast to **Baena**, a town of major importance in Moorish times, now squeezing out olive oil in remarkable quantities. A clean, tightly packed town with the ruins of a Moorish castle, Baena sees most of its visitors arrive for the Holy Week celebrations, when a deafening drum-rolling competition is held to see who can play the longest and the loudest; it lasts *two days*. Twenty-two kilometres northwest from Cabra is **Aguilar de la Frontera**, another attractive wine town (producing *solera fina*, mostly). From Aguilar it's a short hop up the road to the prince of the wine-producing towns, **Montilla**, sitting on a rise amidst endless acres of vines. Although pale dry sherry, *amontillado*, takes its name from this town, the wine produced here is not a sherry, in that no extra alcohol is added to fortify it, unlike in Jerez. The town is refreshingly short of baroque churches, but its *bodegas* can be visited to sample the good stuff. The 1512 Gothic convent of **Santa Clara** is worth a visit for its *mudéjar* roof and baroque altarpiece.

Cabra ✉ 14940, **Baena** ✉ 14850, **and Luque** ✉ 14940

Cabra has a good restaurant, **Mesón del Vizconde**, C/ Martín Belda 16, ✆ 95 752 17 02, with modern interpretations of classic Andalucían dishes, such as stuffed oxtail (*3000–4000 pts*). In Luque, the ★★**Hostal Villa de Luque**, Pza. de España, ✆ 95 766 71 36, is a useful place which shares its premises with the town hall (*4000 pts*). While in Baena, you can stay and eat at the *hostal* ★★**Rincón,** Llano de Rincón 13, ✆ 95 767 02 23, near the town centre. There's a popular *venta* on the N432 Baena–Luque road, Km 340, **Huerta San Rafael**, ✆ 95 366 74 97, serving regional specialities at giveaway prices (*1500 pts*).

Osuna and Estepa ✉ 416400

In Osuna, try the ★**Cinco Puertas** (*3000 pts*)—there's nowhere else. In Estepa, ★★**Los Angeles**, Avda. Andalucía 35, ✆ 95 591 28 32, is adequate (*4500 pts*).

The Sierra Subbética

Puente Genil has only one *hostal*, the ★★**Xenil**, C/ García Lorca 3, ✆ 95 760 02 00, ✆ 95 760 04 43 (*doubles with bath 4500 pts*). In Priego de Córdoba, the ★★**Río-Piscina**, Ctra. Monturque–Alcalá la Real, Km 44, ✆ 95 770 01 86, ✆ 95 754 09 77, has a small pool and tennis court, and reasonable rates (*5500 pts*). There are cheaper options in the town itself. Try the basic **Andalucía**, Calle del Rio 13, in the centre ✆ 95 754 01 74 (*2500 pts*). Aguilar has a number of places, but none offering any luxury; the **San José**, C/ Pescadería 6, ✆ 95 766 02 22, is the best (*2500 pts for basic room*). Montilla is the only place with sophisticated accommodation: the ★★★**Don Gonzalo**, Ctra. Madrid–Málaga, Km 447, ✆ 95 765 06 66, on the main road outside Montilla, has gardens, swimming pool and tennis court (*7500–8500 pts*). Montilla also has a decent restaurant, **Las Camachas**, again on the main road, with no phone, where you can wash down the tasty fish dishes with a glass or two of the local brew (*2000 pts*).

Granada

> *Dale limosna mujer, que no hay en la vida nada*
> *Como la pena de ser ciego y en Granada.*
>
> (Give him alms, woman, for there is nothing in life so cruel as being blind in Granada.)
>
> Francisco de Icaza

The first thing to do upon arrival is to pick up a copy of Washington Irving's *Tales of the Alhambra*. Every bookshop in town can sell you one in just about any language. It was Irving who put Granada on the map, and established the Alhambra as the necessary romantic pilgrimage of Spain. Granada, in fact, might seem a disappointment without Irving. The modern city underneath the Alhambra is a stolid, remarkably unmagical place, with little to show for the 500 years since the Catholic kings put an end to its ancient glory.

As the Moors were expelled, the Spanish Crown replaced them with Castilians and Galicians from up north, and even today *granadinos* are thought of as a bit foreign by other Andalucíans. Their Granada has never been a happy place. Particularly in the last hundred years it has been full of political troubles.

Around the turn of the century even the Holy Week processions had to be called off for a few years because of disruptions from the leftists, and at the start of the civil war the reactionaries who always controlled Granada made one of the first big massacres of Republicans.

One of their victims was Federico García Lorca, the *granadino* who, in the decades since his death, has come to be recognized as one of the greatest Spanish dramatists and poets since the 'Golden Age'. If Irving's fairy tales aren't to your taste, consider the works of Lorca, in which Granada and its sweet melancholy are recurring themes. Lorca once wrote that he remembered Granada 'as one should remember a sweetheart who has died'.

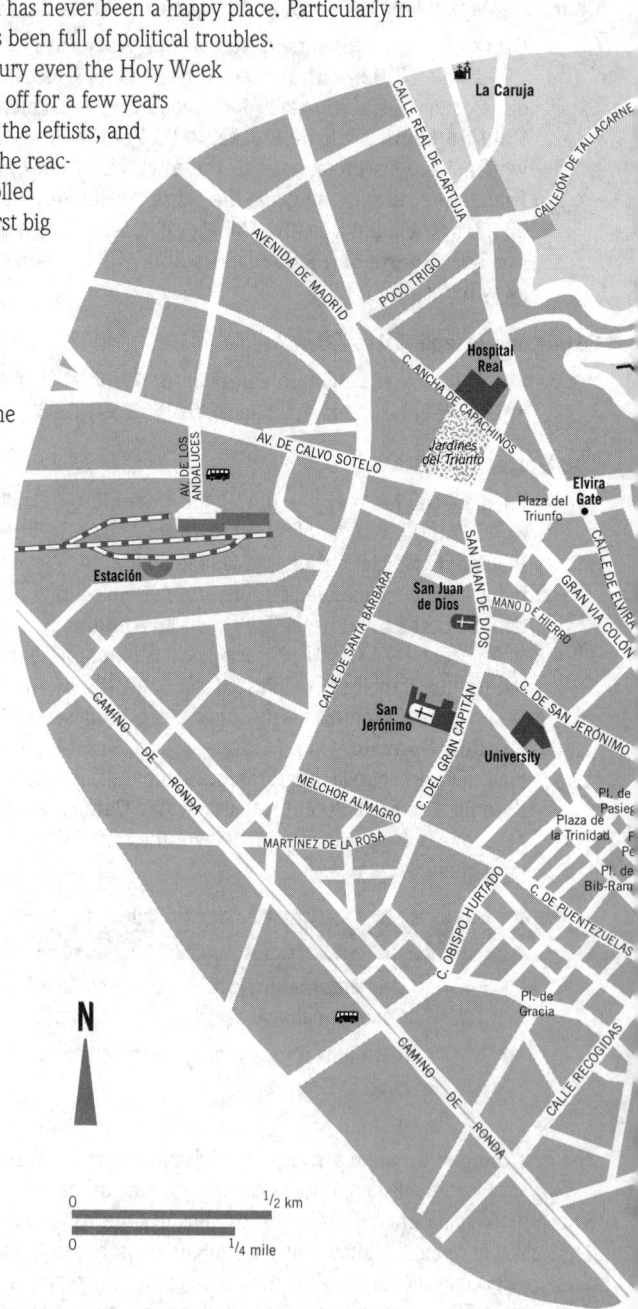

History: the Nasrid Kingdom of Qarnatah

First Iberian *Elibyrge*, then Roman *Illiberis*, the town did not make a name for itself until the era of the *taifas* in the early 11th century, when it emerged as the centre of a very minor state. In the 1230s, while the Castilians were seizing Córdoba and preparing to polish off the rest of the Almoravid states of Al-Andalus, an Arab chieftain named Mohammed ibn-Yusuf ibn-Nasr established himself around Jaén. When that town fell to the Castilians in 1235, he moved his capital to the town the Moors called *Qarnatah*. Ibn Nasr (or Mohammed I, as he is generally known) and his descendants enjoyed great success at first in extending their domains. By 1300 this last Moorish state of Spain extended from Gibraltar to Almería, but this accomplishment came entirely at the expense of other Moors. Mohammed and his successors were in fact vassals of the kings of Castile, and aided them in campaigns more often than they fought them.

Granada

Qarnatah at this time is said to have had a population of some 200,000—almost as many as it has now—and both its arts and industries were strengthened by refugees from the fallen towns of Al-Andalus. Thousands came from Córdoba, especially, and the Albaicín quarter was largely settled by the former inhabitants of Baeza. Although a significant Jewish population remained, there were very few Christians. In the comparatively peaceful 14th century, Granada's conservative, introspective civilization reached its height, with the last flowering of Arabic-Andaluz lyric poetry and the architecture and decorative arts of the Alhambra.

This state of affairs lasted until the coming of the Catholic kings. Isabel's religious fanaticism made the completion of the Reconquista the supreme goal of her reign; she sent Ferdinand out in 1484 to do the job, which he accomplished in eight years by a breathtakingly brilliant combination of force and diplomacy. Qarnatah at the time was suffering the usual curse of Al-Andalus states—disunity founded on the egotism of princes. In this fatal feud, the main actors were Abu al-Hasan Ali (Mulay Hassan in Irving's tales), king of Qarnatah, his brother El Zagal ('the valiant') and the king's rebellious son, Abu abd-Allah, better known to posterity as Boabdil el Chico. His seizure of the throne in 1482 started a period of civil war at the worst possible time. Fernando was clever enough to take advantage of the divisions; he captured Boabdil twice, and turned him into a tool of Castilian designs. Playing one side against the other, Fernando snatched away one Nasrid province after another with few losses. When the unfortunate Boabdil, after renouncing his kingship in favour of the Castilians, finally changed his mind and decided to fight for the remnants of Qarnatah (by then little more than the city itself and the Sierra Nevada), Fernando had the excuse he needed to mount his final attack. Qarnatah was besieged and, after two years, Boabdil agreed to surrender under terms that guaranteed his people the use of their religion and customs. When the keys of the city were handed over on 2 January 1492, the Reconquista was complete.

Under a gentlemanly military governor, the Conde de Tendilla, the agreement was kept until the arrival in 1499 of Cardinal Ximénez de Cisneros, the most influential cleric in Spain and a man who made it his personal business to destroy the last vestiges of Islam and Moorish culture. The new Spanish policy—planned, gradual genocide (*see* **History**, p.42)—was as successful in the former lands of Granada as it was among those other troublesome heathens of the same period, the Indians of Central and South America. The famous revolt in Las Alpujarras (1568) was followed by a rising in the city itself, in the Albaicín. Between 1609 and 1614, the last of the Muslims were expelled, including most of those who had converted to Christianity, and their property confiscated. It is said that, even today, there are old families in Morocco who sentimentally keep the keys to their long-lost homes in Granada.

Such a history does not easily wear away, even after so many centuries. The Castilians corrupted Qarnatah to *Granada*; just by coincidence that means 'pomegranate' in Spanish, and the pomegranate has come to be the symbol of the city. With its associations with the myth of Persephone, with the mysteries of death and loss, no symbol could be more suitable for this capital of melancholy.

Getting Around

By air: There are two flights daily to Madrid (Mon–Sat), two daily to Barcelona (Mon–Fri) and flights three times a week to the Balearics and Canaries. The airport is 16km west of Granada, near Santa Fé. **Information**: ✆ 95 822 75 92.

By train: Granada has connections to Guadix and Almería (three daily), to Algeciras, Sevilla, and Córdoba by way of Bobadilla Junction (they are sometimes complicated) and two daily to Madrid and Barcelona; three daily to Alicante, one a day to Valencia. The station is at the northern end of town, about a mile from the centre, on Avenida de los Andaluces; the city ticket office is on Calle Reyes Católicos, off Plaza Nueva. **Information:** ✆ 95 822 34 97.

By bus: Nearly all intercity buses leave from the main bus station, on the outskirts of town on the Carretera de Jaén. **Information:** ✆ 95 818 50 10. Bus no.3 runs between the bus station and the city centre. Buses to the ski resorts and the Alpujarras leave from the corner of Paseo de los Basilios and Prof Tierno Golvan. The '*Alhambra*' bus from the Plaza Nueva will save you the trouble of climbing up to the Alhambra.

By car: Parking is a problem, so if you plan staying overnight make sure that your hotel has parking facilities and check whether there is a charge or not—it can cost as much as the accommodation in some places. Traffic police are extremely vigilant. Fines of up to 20,000 pts are payable on the spot if you are a tourist. Ignore people at the bottom of the Alhambra trying to persuade you to park before you reach the top; there's plenty of parking space by the entrance and it's a steep walk to get there.

Tourist Information

Provincial tourist office, Pza. Mariana Pineda 10, ✆ 95 822 66 88. *Open Mon–Fri 9.30–7 and Sat 10–2.*

There's a smaller office inside the Corral del Carbón, C/ Liberos 2, ✆ 95 822 59 90. *Open Mon–Sat 9–7 and Sun 10–2.*

A Sentimental Orientation

In spite of everything, more of the lost world of Al-Andalus can be seen in Granada than even in Córdoba. Granada stands where the foothills of the Sierra Nevada meet the fertile Vega de Granada, the greenest and best stretch of farmland in Andalucía. Two of those hills extend into the city itself. One bears the **Alhambra**, the fortified palace of the Nasrid kings, and the other the **Albaicín**, the most evocative of the 'Moorish' neighbourhoods of Andalucían cities. How much you enjoy Granada will depend largely on how successful you are in ignoring the new districts, in particular three barbarically ugly streets that form the main automobile route through Granada: the **Gran Vía Colón** chopped through the centre of town in the 19th century, the **Calle Reyes Católicos,** and the **Acera del Darro.**

The last two are paved over the course of the Río Darro, the little stream that ran picturesquely through the city until the 1880s. Before these streets were built, the centre of Granada was the **Plaza Nueva**, a square that is also partly built over the Darro. The handsome building that defines its character is the **Audiencia** (1584), built by Felipe II for the royal officials and judges. **Santa Ana** church, across the plaza, was built in 1537 by Diego de Siloé, one of the architects of Granada's cathedral. From this plaza the ascent to the Alhambra begins, winding up a narrow street called the **Cuesta de Gomérez**, past guitar-makers' shops and gypsies with vast displays of tourist trinkets, and ending abruptly at the **Puerta de las Granadas**, a monumental gateway erected by Charles V.

Open daily 9–7.45, Sun 9–5.45, also open Tues, Thurs and Sat evenings 10–midnight (summer), 8–10pm (mid season); adm 750pts. Admission times constantly change, so always check beforehand with the ticket office, © 95 822 09 12.

The grounds of the Alhambra begin here with a bit of the unexpected. Instead of the walls and towers, not yet even in view, there is a lovely grove of great elms, the **Alameda**; even more unexpectedly, they are the contribution of the Duke of Wellington, who took time off from chasing the French to plant them during the Peninsular War. Take the path to the left—it's a stiff climb—and in a few minutes you'll arrive at the **Puerta de Justicia**, entrance of the Alhambra. The orange tint of the fortress walls explains the name *al-hamra* (the red), and the

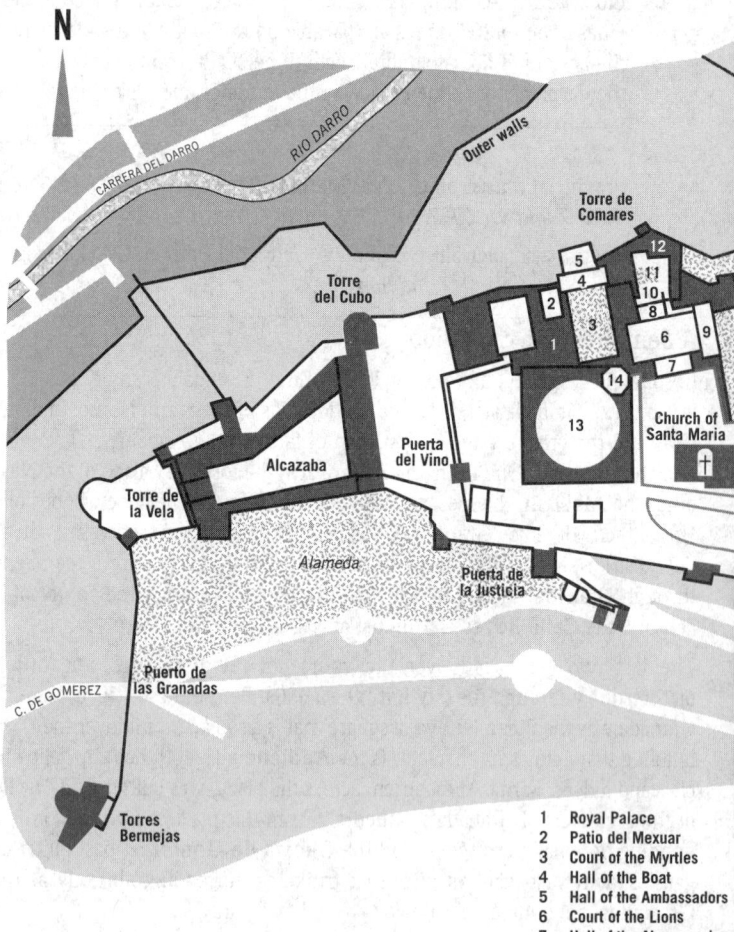

1	Royal Palace
2	Patio del Mexuar
3	Court of the Myrtles
4	Hall of the Boat
5	Hall of the Ambassadors
6	Court of the Lions
7	Hall of the Abencerrajes
8	Hall of the Two Sisters

unusual style of the carving on the gate is the first clue that here is something very different. The two devices, a hand and a key, carved on the inner and outer arches, are famous. According to one of Irving's tales, the hand will one day reach down and grasp the key; then the Alhambra will fall into ruins, the earth will open, and the hidden treasures of the Moors will be revealed. From the gate, a path leads up to a broad square. Here are the ticket booth, and the **Puerta del Vino**, so called from a long-ago Spanish custom of doling out free wine from this spot to the inhabitants of the Alhambra. To the left you'll see the walls of the **Alcazaba**, the fort at the tip of the Alhambra's narrow promontory, and to the right the huge **Palacio de Carlos V**; signs point your way to the entrance of the **Casa Real** (Royal Palace), with its splendidly decorated rooms that are the Alhambra's main attraction. Visit again after dark; seeing it under the stars is the treat of a lifetime.

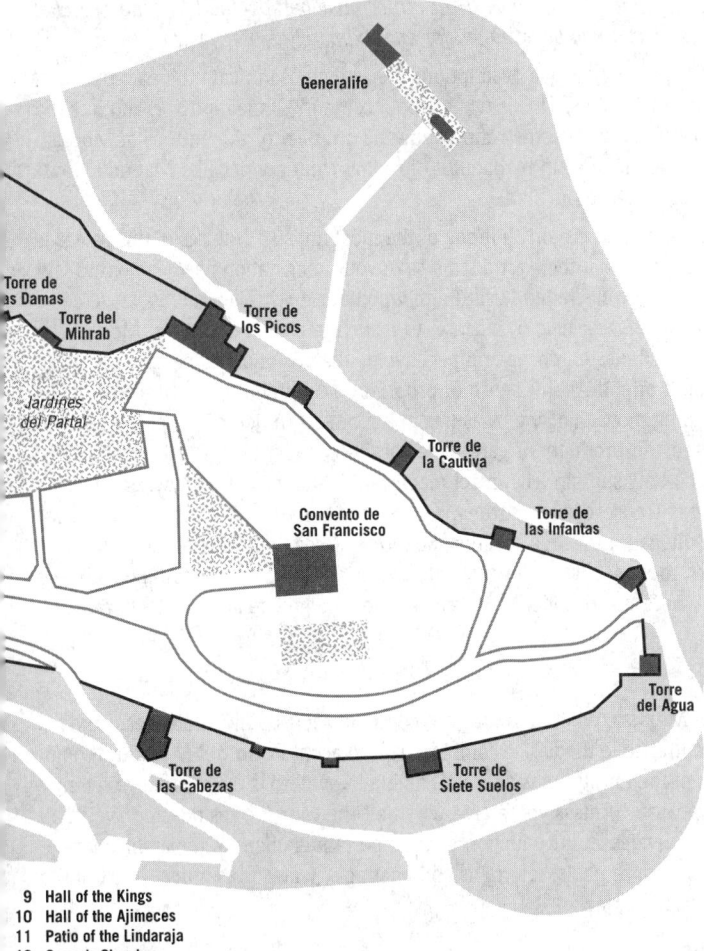

Generalife

Torre de as Damas

Torre del Mihrab

Torre de los Picos

Jardines del Partal

Torre de la Cautiva

Convento de San Francisco

Torre de las Infantas

Torre del Agua

Torre de las Cabezas

Torre de Siete Suelos

9 Hall of the Kings
10 Hall of the Ajimeces
11 Patio of the Lindaraja
12 Queen's Chamber
13 Palace of Charles V / Museo de Bellas Artes
   / Museo Nacional de Art Hispano - Musulman
14 Chapel and Crypt

The Alcazaba

Not much remains of the oldest part of the Alhambra. This citadel probably dates back to the first of the Nasrid kings. Its walls and towers are still intact, but only the foundations of the buildings that once stood within it have survived. The **Torre de la Vela** at the tip of the promontory has the best views over Granada and the Vega. Its big bell was rung in the old days to signal the daily opening and closing of the water gates of the Vega's irrigation system; the Moors also used the tower as a signal post for sending messages. The Albaicín, visible on the opposite hill, is a revelation; its rows of white, flat-roofed houses on the hillside, punctuated by palm trees and cypresses, provide one of Europe's most exotic urban landscapes.

Casa Real (Royal Palace)

Palace visits are limited to ½hr and the time must be specified at time of ticket purchase, otherwise it will be arranged for approximately 1½hrs later.

Words will not do, nor will exhaustive descriptions help, to communicate the experience of this greatest treasure of Al-Andalus. This is what people come to Granada to see, and it is the surest, most accessible window into the refinement and subtlety of the culture of Moorish Spain—a building that can achieve in its handful of rooms what a work like Madrid's Royal Palace cannot even approach with its 2800.

It probably never occurs to most visitors, but one of the most unusual features of this palace is its modesty. What you see is what the Nasrid kings saw; your imagination need add only a few carpets and tapestries, some well-crafted furniture of wood inlaid with ivory, wooden screens, and big round braziers of brass for heat or incense, to make the picture complete. Most of the actual building is wood and plaster, cheap and perishable, like a World Fair pavilion; no good Muslim monarch would offend Allah's sense of propriety by pretending that these worldly splendours were anything more than the pleasures of a moment (much of the plaster, wood, and all of the tiles, are the products of careful restorations over the last 100 years). The Alhambra, in fact, is the only substantially intact medieval Muslim palace—anywhere. Like so many old royal palaces (those of the Hittites, the Byzantines or the Ottoman Turks, for example), this one is divided into three sections: one for everyday business of the palace and government; the next, more secluded, for the state rooms and official entertainments of the kings; and the third, where few outsiders ever reached, for the private apartments of the king and his household.

The Mexuar

Of the first, the small Mexuar, where the kings would hold their public audiences, survives near the present-day entrance to the palace complex. The adjacent **Patio del Mexuar**, though much restored, is one of the finest rooms of the Alhambra. Nowhere is the meditative serenity of the palace more apparent (unless you arrive when all the tour groups do) and the small fountain in the centre provides an introduction to an important element of the architecture—water. Present everywhere, in pools, fountains and channels, water is as much a part of the design as the wood, tile and stone.

Patio de los Arrayanes

If you have trouble finding your way around, remember the elaborately decorated portals never really lead anywhere; the door you want will always be tucked unobtrusively to the side; here, as in Sevilla's Alcázar, the principle is to heighten the sense of surprise. The entrance to the grand Patio de los Arrayanes (Court of the Myrtles), with its long goldfish pond and lovely arcades, was the centre of the second, state section of the palace; directly off it, you pass through the **Sala de la Barca** (Hall of the Boat), so called from its hull-shaped wooden ceiling, and into the **Salón de Embajadores** (Hall of Ambassadors), where the kings presided over all important state business. The views and the decoration are some of the Alhambra's best, with a cedarwood ceiling and plaster panels (many were originally painted) carved with floral arabesques or Arabic calligraphy. These inscriptions, some Koranic scripture (often the phrase 'Allah alone conquers', the motto of the Nasrids), some eulogies of the kings, and some poetry, recur throughout the palace. The more conspicuous are in a flowing script developed by the Granadan artists; look closely and you will see others, in the angular Kufic script, forming frames for the floral designs.

In some of the chambers off the Patio de los Arrayanes, you can peek out over the domed roofs of the baths below; opposite the Salón de Embajadores is a small entrance (often closed) into the dark, empty **crypt** of the Palace of Charles V, with curious echo effects.

Patio de los Leones

Another half-hidden doorway leads you into the third and most spectacular section, the king's residence, built around the Patio de los Leones (Court of the Lions). Here the plaster and stucco work is at its most ornate, the columns and arches at their most delicate, with little pretence of any structural purpose; balanced on their slender shafts, the façades of the court seem to hang in the air. As in much of Moorish architecture, the overripe arabesques of this patio conceal a subtle symbolism. The 'enclosed garden' that can stand for the attainment of truth, or paradise, or for the cosmos, is a recurring theme in Islamic mystical poetry. Here you may take the 12 endearingly preposterous lions who support the fountain in the centre as the months, or signs of the zodiac, and the four channels that flow out from the fountains as the four corners of the cosmos, the cardinal points, or, on a different level, the four rivers of paradise.

The rooms around the patio have exquisite decorations: to the right, from the entrance, the **Sala de los Abencerrajes**, named after the legend of the noble family that Boabdil supposedly had massacred at a banquet here during the civil wars just before the fall of Granada; to the left, the **Sala de las dos Hermanas** (Hall of the Two Sisters). Both of these have extravagant domed *muqarnas* ceilings. The latter chamber is also ornamented with a wooden window grille, another speciality of the Granadan artists; this is the only one surviving in the Alhambra. Adjacent to the Sala de las dos Hermanas is the **Sala de los Ajimeces**, so called for its doubled windows. The **Sala de los Reyes** (Hall of the Kings), opposite the court's entrance, is unique for the paintings on its ceiling, works that would not be out of place in any Christian palace of medieval Europe. The central panel may represent six of Granada's 14th-century kings; those on the side are scenes of a chivalric court. The artist is believed to have been a visiting Spanish Christian painter, possibly from Sevilla. From the Sala de las dos Hermanas, steps lead down to the **Patio de Lindaraja** (or Mirador de Daraxa), with its fountain and flowers, Washington Irving's favourite spot in the Alhambra. Originally the inner garden of the palace, it was remodelled for the royal visits of Charles V and Felipe V. Irving actually lived in the **Queen's Chamber**, decorated with frescoes of Charles V's expedition to Tunis—in 1829, apartments in the Alhambra could be had for the asking! Just off this chamber, at ground-floor level, is the beautifully decorated **hammam**, the palace baths.

Follow the arrows, out of the palace and into the outer gardens, the **Jardines del Partal**, a broad expanse of rose terraces and flowing water. The northern walls of the Alhambra border the gardens, including a number of well-preserved towers: from the west, the **Torre de las Damas**, entered by a small porch, the **Torre del Mihrab**, near which is a small mosque, now a chapel; the **Torre de los Picos**; the **Torre de la Cautiva** (Tower of the Imprisoned Lady), one of the most elaborately decorated; and the **Torre de las Infantas**, one of the last projects in the Alhambra (*c.* 1400).

Palacio de Carlos V

Anywhere else this elegant Renaissance building would be an attraction in itself. Here it seems only pompous and oversized, and our appreciation of it is lessened by the mind-numbing thought of this emperor, with a good half of Europe to build palaces in, having to plop it down here—ruining much of the Alhambra in the process. Once Charles had smashed up the place, he lost interest, and most of the palace, still unfinished, was not built until 1616. The original architect, Pedro Machuco, had studied in Italy, and he took the opportunity to introduce into Spain the chilly, Olympian High Renaissance style of Rome. At the entrances are intricately detailed sculptural **reliefs** showing scenes from Charles's campaigns and military 'triumphs' in the antique manner: armoured torsos on sticks amidst heaps of weapons. This is a very particular sort of art, arrogant and weird, and wherever it appears around the Mediterranean, it will usually be associated with the grisly reign of the man who dreamt of being Emperor of the World. Inside, Machuco added a pristinely classical circular courtyard, based perhaps on a design by Raphael. For all its Doric gravity, the patio was used almost from its completion for bullfights and mock tournaments.

The Museums

> *Museo de Bellas Artes, © 95 822 48 43; Museo Nacional de Arte Hispano-Musulmán, © 95 822 62 79. Opening times are the same as the Alhambra, but the museums are closed at night.*

On the top floor of the Palace is the **Museo de Bellas Artes**, a largely forgettable collection of religious paintings from Granada churches. Downstairs, the **Museo Nacional de Arte Hispano-Musulmán** contains perhaps Spain's best collection of Moorish art, including some paintings, similar to those in the Moorish palace's Sala de los Reyes. Also present are original *azulejo* tiles and plaster arabesques from the palace, and some exceedingly fine wooden panels and screens. There is a collection of ceramic ware with fanciful figurative decoration—elephants and lady musicians—and some lovely astronomical instruments. Tucked in a corner of the museum are four big copper balls stacked on a pole, an ornament that once stood atop a Granada minaret. These were a typical feature of Andalucían minarets (as on La Giralda in Sevilla) and similar examples can be seen in Morocco today. Behind Charles's palace a street leads into the remnants of the town that once filled much of the space within the Alhambra's walls, now reduced to a small collection of restaurants and souvenir stands. In Moorish times the Alhambra held a large permanent population, and even under the Spaniards it long retained the status of a separate municipality. At one end of the street, the church of **Santa María** (1581), designed by Juan de Herrera, architect of El Escorial, occupies the site of the Alhambra's mosque; at the other, the first Christian building on the Alhambra, the **Convento de San Francisco** (1495) has been converted into a *parador*.

The Generalife

Opening hours are the same as for the Alhambra; adm included in Alhambra ticket.

The Generalife (*Djinat al-Arif*: high garden) was the summer palace of the Nasrid kings, built on the height the Moors called the Mountain of the Sun. Many of the trillions of visitors the Alhambra receives each year have never heard of it, and pass up a chance to see the finest garden in Spain. To get there, it's about a five-minute walk from the Alhambra along a lovely avenue of tall cypresses. The buildings here hold few surprises if you've just come from the Alhambra. They are older than most of the Casa Real, which was probably begun around 1260. The gardens are built on terraces on several levels along the hillside, and the views over the Alhambra and Albaicín are transcendent. The centrepiece is a long pool with many water sprays that passes through beds of roses. A lower level, with a promenade on the hill's edge, is broken up into secluded bowers by cypress bushes cut into angular shapes of walls and gateways. There is no evidence that the original Moorish gardens looked anything like this; everything here has been done in the last 200 years.

If you're walking down from the Alhambra, you might consider a different route, across the Alameda and down through the picturesque streets below the **Torres Bermejas**, an outwork of the Alhambra's fortifications built on foundations that date back to the Romans. The winding lanes and stairways around Calle del Aire and Calle Niño del Rollo, one of the most beautiful quarters of Granada, will eventually lead you back down near the Plaza Nueva.

Albaicín

Even more than the old quarters of Córdoba, this hillside neighbourhood of whitewashed houses and tall cypresses has successfully preserved some of the atmosphere of . Its difficult site and the fact that it was long the district of Granada's poor explain the lack of change, but today the Albaicín looks as if it is becoming fashionable again.

From the Plaza Nueva, a narrow street called the **Carrera del Darro** leads up the valley of the Darro between the Alhambra and Albaicín hills; here the little stream has not been covered over, and you can get an idea of how the centre of Granada looked in the old days. On the Alhambra side, old stone bridges lead up to a few half-forgotten streets hidden among the forested slopes; here you'll see some 17th-century Spanish houses with curious painted *esgrafiado* façades. Nearby, traces of a horseshoe arch can be seen where a Moorish wall once crossed the river; in the corner of Calle Baruelo there are well-preserved **Moorish baths** (*open Tues–Sat 10–2*). Even more curious is the façade of the **Casa Castril** on the Darro, a flamboyant 16th-century mansion with a portal carved with a phoenix, winged scallop shells and other odd devices that have been interpreted as elements in a complex mystical symbolism. Over the big corner window is an inscription 'Waiting for her from the heavens'.

Casa Castril has been restored as Granada's **archaeological museum** (*open Tues 3–8, Wed–Sat 9–8, Sun 9–2.30*) with a small collection of artefacts from the huge number of caves in Granada province, many inhabited since Palaeolithic times, and a few Iberian settlements. There is a Moorish room, with some lovely works of art, and finally, an even greater oddity than Casa Castril itself. One room of the museum holds a collection of beautiful alabaster burial urns, made in Egypt, but found in a Phoenician-style necropolis near Almuñécar. Nothing else like them has ever been discovered in Spain, and the Egyptian hieroglyphic inscriptions on them are provocative in the extreme (translations given in Spanish), telling how the deceased travelled here in search of some mysterious primordial deity.

Farther up the Darro, there's a small park with a view up to the Alhambra; after that you'll have to do some climbing, but the higher you go the prettier the Albaicín is. Among the white houses are some of the oldest Christian churches in Granada. As in Córdoba, they are tidy and extremely plain, built to avoid alienating a recently converted population unused to religious imagery. **San Juan de los Reyes** (1520) on Calle Zafra and **San José** (1525) are the oldest; both retain the plain minarets of the mosques they replaced. Quite a few Moorish houses survive in the Albaicín, and some can be seen on **Calle Horno de Oro**, just off the Darro; on **Calle Daralhorra,** at the top of the Albaicín, are the remains of a Nasrid palace that was largely destroyed to make way for Isabel's **Convento de Santa Isabel la Real** (1501).

Here, running parallel to Cuesta de la Alhacaba, is a long-surviving stretch of Moorish wall. There are probably a few miles of walls left, visible around the hillsides over Granada; the location of the city made a very complex set of fortifications necessary. In this one, about halfway up, you may pass through **Puerta de las Pesas**, with its horseshoe arches. The heart of the Albaicín is here, around the pretty, animated **Plaza Larga**; only a few blocks away the **mirador de San Nicolás**, in front of the church of that name, offers the most romantic view imaginable of the Alhambra with the snow-capped peaks of the Sierra Nevada behind it. Granada today has a small but growing Muslim community, and they are beginning to build a mosque just off the mirador. On your way back from the Albaicín you might take a different route, down a maze of streets to the **Puerta de Elvira**; one of the most picturesque corners of the neighbourhood.

Sacromonte

For something completely different, you might strike out beyond the Albaicín hill to the **gypsy caves of Sacromonte**. Granada has had a substantial gypsy population for several centuries now. Some have become settled and respectable, others live in trailers on vacant land around town. The most visible are those who prey on the tourists around the Alhambra and the Capilla Real, handing out carnations with a smile and then attempting to extort huge sums out of anyone dumb enough to take one (of course, they'll tell your fortune, too). The biggest part of the gypsy community, however, still lives around Sacromonte in streets of some quite well-appointed cave homes, where they wait to lure you in for a little display of flamenco. For a hundred years or so, the consensus of opinion has been that the music and dancing are usually indifferent, and the gypsies' eventually successful attempts to shake out your last peseta can make it an unpleasantly unforgettable affair. Hotels sell tours for around 2000 pts. Nevertheless, if you care to match wits with the experts, proceed up the Cuesta del Chapiz from the Río Darro, turn right at the **Casa del Chapiz**, a big 16th-century palace that now houses a school of Arab studies, and keep going until some gypsy child drags you home with him. The bad reputation has been keeping tourists away lately so it's now much safer and friendlier as the gypsies are worried about the loss of income. Serious flamenco fans will probably not fare better elsewhere in Granada except during the festivals, though there are some touristy flamenco nightspots—the **Reina Mora** by Mirador San Cristóbal is the best of them. On the third Sunday of each month, though, you can hear a **flamenco mass** performed in the San Pedro Church on the Carrera del Darro at 9am.

The old city wall swung in a broad arc from Puerta de Elvira to Puerta Real, now a small plaza full of traffic where Calle Reyes Católicos meets the Acera del Darro. Just a few blocks north of here, in a web of narrow pedestrian streets that make up modern Granada's shopping district, is the pretty **Plaza de Bib-Rambla**, full of flower stands and toy shops, with an unusual fountain supported by leering giants at its centre. This was an important square in Moorish times, used for public gatherings and tournaments of arms. The narrow streets leading off to the east are the **Alcaicería**. This was the Moorish silk exchange, but the buildings you see now, full of tourist souvenir shops, are not original; the Alcaicería burned down in the 1840s and was rebuilt in more or less the same fashion with Moorish arches and columns.

The Cathedral

Pza. de Pasiegas, © 95 822 29 59. Open Mon–Sat 10.30–1.30 and 4–7, Sun 4–7.

The best way to see Granada's **cathedral** is to approach it from Calle Marqués, just north of the Plaza Bib-Rambla. The unique façade, with its three tall, recessed arches, is a striking sight, designed by the painter Alonso Cano (1667). On the central arch, the big plaque bearing the words 'Ave María' commemorates the exploit of the Spanish captain who sneaked into the city one night in 1490 and nailed up this message up on the door of the great mosque this cathedral has replaced. The other conspicuous feature is the name 'José Antonio Primo de Rivera' carved on the façade. Son of the 1920s dictator, Miguel Primo de Rivera, José Antonio was a mystic fascist who founded the Phalangist Party. His thugs provoked many of the disorders that started the civil war, and at the beginning of the conflict he was captured by the loyalists and executed. Afterwards his followers treated him as a sort of holy martyr, and chiselled his name on every cathedral in Spain.

The rest of the cathedral isn't up to the standard of its façade, and there is little reason to go in and explore its cavernous interior or dreary museum. Work was begun in 1521, after the Spaniards broke their promise not to harm the great mosque. As in many Spanish cathedrals, the failure of this one stems from artistic indecision. Two very talented architects were in charge: Enrique de Egas, who wanted it Gothic, like his adjacent Capilla Real, and (five years later) Diego de Siloé, who decided Renaissance would look much nicer. A score of other architects got their fingers in the pie before its completion in 1703. Some features of the interior: the grandiose **Capilla Mayor**, with statues of the apostles, and of Fernando and Isabel, by Alonso de Mena, and enormous heads of Adam and Eve by Alonso Cano, whose sculptures and paintings can be seen all over the cathedral; the **Retablo de Jesús Nazareno** in the right aisle, with paintings by Cano and Ribera, and a *St Francis* by El Greco; the Gothic **portal** leading into the Capilla Real (now closed) by de Egas.

Capilla Real

Gran Vía de Colón, © 95 822 92 39; open daily 10.30–1 and 4–7, Sun 11–1; adm.

Leaving the cathedral and turning left, you pass the outsized **sacristy**, begun in 1705 and incorporated in the cathedral façade. Turn left again at the first street, Calle de los Oficios, a narrow lane paved in charming patterns of coloured pebbles—a Granada speciality; on the left, you can pay your respects to *Los Reyes Católicos*, in the Capilla Real. The royal couple had already built a mausoleum in Toledo, but after the capture of Granada they decided to plant themselves here. Even in the shadow of the bulky cathedral, Enrique de Egas's chapel (1507) reveals itself as the outstanding work of the Isabelline Gothic style, with its delicate roofline of traceries and pinnacles. Charles V thought it not nearly monumental enough for his grandparents, and only the distraction of his foreign wars kept him from wrecking it in favour of some elephantine replacement. Inside, the Catholic Kings are buried in a pair of Carrara marble sarcophagi, decorated with their recumbent figures, elegantly carved though not necessarily flattering to either of them. The little staircase behind them leads down to the crypt, where you can peek in at their plain lead coffins and those of their unfortunate daughter, Juana the Mad, and her husband, Felipe the Handsome, whose effigies lie next to the older couple above. Juana was Charles V's mother, and the rightful heir to the Spanish throne. There is considerable doubt as to whether she was mad at all; when Charles arrived from Flanders in 1517, he forced her to sign papers of abdication, and then locked her up in a windowless cell for the last 40 years of her life, never permitting any visitors. The interior of the chapel is sumptuously decorated—it should be, considering the huge proportion of the crown revenues that were expended on it. The iron *reja* by Master Bartolomé de Jaén and the *retablo* are especially fine; the latter is largely the work of a French artist, Philippe de Bourgogne. In the chapel's sacristy you can see some of Isabel's personal art collection—works by Van der Weyden, Memling, Pedro Berruguete, Botticelli (attributed), Perugino and others, mostly in need of some restoration—as well as her crown and sceptre, her illuminated missal, some captured Moorish banners, and Fernando's sword.

Across the narrow street from the Capilla Real, an endearingly garish, painted baroque façade hides **La Madraza**, a domed hall of the Moorish *madrasa* (Islamic seminary); though one of the best Moorish works surviving in Granada, it is hardly ever open to visitors (just walk in if the building is open). The Christians converted it into a town hall, whence its other name, the Casa del Cabildo.

Across Calle Reyes Católicos

Even though this part of the city centre is as old as the Albaicín, most of it was rebuilt after 1492, and its age doesn't show. The only Moorish building remaining is also the only example left in Spain of a *khan* or *caravanserai*, the type of merchants' hotel common throughout the Muslim world. The 14th-century **Corral del Carbón**, just off Reyes Católicos, takes its name from the time, a century ago, when it was used as a coal warehouse. Today it houses a government handicrafts outlet, and much of the building is under restoration. The neighbourhood of quiet streets and squares behind it is the best part of Spanish Granada and worth a walk if you have the time. Here you'll see the *mudéjar* **Casa de los Tiros**, a restored mansion built in 1505 on Calle Pavaneras, with strange figures carved on its façade; it houses a **museum** of the city's history. **Santo Domingo** (1512), the finest of Granada's early churches, is just a few blocks to the south. Fernando and Isabel endowed it, and their monograms figure prominently on the lovely façade. This neighbourhood is bounded on the west by the Acera del Darro, the noisy heart of modern Granada, with most of the big hotels. It's a little discouraging but, as compensation, just a block away the city has adorned itself with a beautiful string of wide boulevards very like the Ramblas of Barcelona, a wonderful spot for a stroll. The **Carretera del Genil** usually has some sort of open-air market on it, and further down, the **Paseo del Salón** and **Paseo de la Bomba** are quieter and more park-like, joining the pretty banks of the Río Genil.

From the little street on the north side of the cathedral, the Calle de la Cárcel, Calle San Jerónimo skirts the edge of Granada's markets and leads you towards the old **university** district. Even though much of the university has relocated to a new campus half a mile to the north, this is still one of the livelier spots of town, and the colleges themselves occupy some fine, well-restored baroque structures. The long yellow College of Law is one of the best, occupying a building put up in 1769 for the Jesuits; a small botanical garden is adjacent. Calle San Jerónimo ends at the Calle del Gran Capitán, where the landmark is the church of **San Juan de Dios**, with a baroque façade and a big green and white tiled dome. **San Jerónimo**, a block west, is another of the oldest and largest Granada churches (1520); it contains the tomb of Gonzalo de Córdoba, the 'Gran Capitán' who won so many victories in Italy for the Catholic Kings; adjacent are two Gothic cloisters.

Here you're not far from the Puerta de Elvira, in an area where old Granada fades into anonymous suburbs to the north. The big park at the end of the Gran Vía is the **Jardines del Triunfo**, with coloured, illuminated fountains the city hardly ever turns on. Behind them is the Renaissance **Hospital Real** (1504–22), designed by Enrique de Egas. A few blocks southwest, climbing up towards the Albaicín, your senses will be assaulted by the gaudiest baroque chapel in Spain, in the **Cartuja**, or Carthusian monastery, on Calle Real de Cartuja (*open daily except Mon, 10–1 and 4–8, © 95 816 19 32*). Gonzalo de Córdoba endowed this Charterhouse, though little of the original works remain. The 18th-century chapel and its sacristy, done in the richest marble, gold and silver, and painted plaster, fairly oozes with a froth of twisted spiral columns, rosettes and curlicues. It has often been described as a Christian attempt to upstage the Alhambra, but the inspiration more likely comes from the Aztecs, via the extravagant Mexican baroque.

Granada ✉ *18000*

Where to Stay

The city centre, around the Acera del Darro, is full of hotels, and there are lots of inexpensive *hostales* around the Gran Vía—but the less you see of these areas the better. Fortunately, you can choose from a wide range around the Alhambra and in the older parts of town if you take the time to look.

expensive

Right in the Alhambra itself, the ★★★★**Parador Nacional San Francisco**, © 95 822 14 40, ✆ 95 822 22 64, is perhaps the most famous of all *paradores*, housed in a convent where Queen Isabel was originally interred. It's beautiful, expensive, and small; you'll always need to book well in advance—a year would not be unreasonable (*33,000 pts*).

Alternative choices very near the Alhambra would be the outrageously florid, neo-Moorish ★★★★**Alhambra Palace**, C/ Peña Portida 2, © 95 822 14 68, ✆ 95 822 64 04, where most rooms have terrific views over the city (*20,500 pts*).

The ★★★★**Hotel Triunfo–Granada**, Pza. del Triunfo 19, © 95 820 74 44, ✆ 95 827 90 17, stands by the Moorish Puerta de Elvira at the foot of the Albaicín. It's a quiet place with a restaurant that's popular with locals (*16,800 pts*).

The old ★★★**Washington Irving**, Pso. del Generalife 2, ✆ 95 822 75 50, ✉ 95 22 88 40, is a little faded but still classy (*10,500 pts*). On the slopes below the Alhambra you can get a pool and air-conditioning at ★★★**Los Ángeles**, Cuesta Escoriaza 17, ✆ 95 822 14 24, ✉ 95 822 21 25 (*10,500 pts*). There's one other hotel in the Alhambra, the ★**Hotel América**, Real de la Alhambra 53, ✆ 95 822 74 71, ✉ 95 822 74 70, with simple, pretty rooms for *11,500 pts* and a delightful garden and patio but, as for the *parador*, book well in advance. The **Casa del Aljarife**, Placeta de la Cruz Verde 2, ✆ and ✉ 95 822 24 25, *most @mx3.redestb.es*, a 17th-century Moorish house with tastefully refurbished rooms, is the only hotel in the Albaicín, and one of the most delightful places to stay in the city, with a view of the Alhambra that you won't better elsewhere. There are only three rooms so be sure to book in advance (*8500 pts*). The friendly owners can arrange parking and will even collect you from the train station or airport.

inexpensive

For inexpensive *hostales*, the first place to look is the Cuesta de Gomérez, the street leading up to the Alhambra from Plaza Nueva. Besides the ★★**Britz**, at No.1, ✆ 95 822 36 52 (*4000 pts with bath, 3000 pts without*) and the ★**Gomérez**, at No.10, ✆ 95 822 44 37 (*2300 pts, no bath*), both nice, there are plenty of other spots nearby. Off Calle San Juan de Dios, in the university area, there are dozens of small *hostales* used to accommodating students. The ★**San Joaquín**, C/ Mano de Hierro, ✆ 95 828 28 79, is one, with a pretty patio (*4000 pts*). Centrally placed is the immaculate *hostal* ★★**Lisboa**, Pza. del Carmen 29, ✆ 95 822 14 13 (*5200 pts*).

Eating Out

Granada isn't known for its cuisine. There are too many touristy places around the Plaza Nueva, with very little to distinguish between them.

expensive

Best known and best loved is the famous **Sevilla**, C/ Oficios 12, ✆ 95 822 12 23, where Lorca often met fellow poets and intellectuals. The character of the restaurant has been preserved and the specialities are still the local dishes of Granada and Andalucía (*3500–4500 pts*). *Closed Sun eve.* Both are near the cathedral. Some of the finest cooking in Granada can be found at the **Ruta del Veleta** on the Ctra. de la Sierra, Km 50, ✆ 95 848 61 34, 5km away from the city towards the Sierra Nevada. Dishes include partridge with onion ragôut and salad of angler fish with vegetable stuffing (*5000 pts*).

moderate

The *granadinos* trust dining out at **Cunini**, Pza. de Pescadería 14, ✆ 95 825 07 77, where the menu depends on availability (*2500–3500 pts*). *Closed Mon.* For agreeable dining in an intimate family-run restaurant, there is no better in Granada than **Mesón Antonio**, Ecce Homo 6, ✆ 95 822 95 99, which serves international dishes of meat and fish (*2700 pts*). *Closed Sun, July and Aug.* You should try to get up to the Albaicín for dinner on at least one night.

The **Mirador de Morayma**, Pianista García Carrillo 2, Albaicín, ✆ 95 822 82 90, is in a charming 16th-century house with views over the Alhambra from the top-floor dining room; *la sopa de espárragos verdes de Huétor* (asparagus soup) is particularly good, and be sure to leave room for an *andaluz* pudding (*3200 pts*). *Closed Sun eve.* A place popular with *granadinos* is **Chikito**, Pza. de Campillo 9, ✆ 95 822 33 64, serving classic Granada dishes in an intimate atmosphere (*3500 pts*).

inexpensive

Everyone's favourite rock-bottom, filling 750 pts menu is served up at the tiny **Cepillo** on Calle Pescadería. It's a few doors away from the Cunini and is one of the few places where you can get paella for one—order fish or squid.

For *bocadillos* (hot and cold sandwiches) try **Bar Aliatar** in a small street between Plaza de Bib-Rambla and Calle Reyes Católicos. If you like ice creams, head for **Los Italianos** at Gran Vía 4. Delicious.

Nightlife

Granada is one of the best places in Andalucia to catch flamenco. Though there are touristy shows in the caves of Sacromonte, there are also some more spontaneous venues, and it's well worth heading up to Sacromonte to wander around—try **Los Faroles**, one of the last and best of the atmospheric cave flamenco bars, or the popular **El Niño de los Almendras**, in Calle Muladar de Dona Sancha, near Plaza San Miguel Bajo in the Albaicín.

There are a number of discos popular with the locals in Sacromonte, the most famous of which is El Camborio, which is packed on Friday and Saturday nights.

The Sierra Nevada and Las Alpujarras

From everywhere in Granada, the mountains peer over the tops of buildings. Fortunately, Spain's loftiest peaks are also its most accessible; from the city centre you can be riding on Europe's highest mountain road in a little more than an hour. Even if you're without a car, there's a daily bus from town that makes the Sierra Nevada an easy day trip. Dress warmly, though. As the name implies, the Sierra Nevada is snowcapped nearly all year, and even in late July and August, when the road is clear and you can travel right over the mountains to the valley of Las Alpujarras, it's as chilly and windy as you would expect it to be, some 3300m above sea level. These mountains, a geological curiosity of sorts, are just an oversized chunk of the Penibetic System, the chain that stretches from Arcos de la Frontera almost to Murcia. Their highest peak, **Mulhacén** (3481m), is less than 40km from the coast. Mulhacén and especially its sister peak **Veleta** (3392m) can be climbed without too much exertion; the road goes right by Veleta, and in August you can even drive to the top.

Getting Around

For the Sierra Nevada, there is a daily **bus** from the Bar El Ventorrillo, in Granada's Paseo del Violón, to the Albergue Universitario some 12km from the peak of Veleta. Departures are at 9am, returning at 5.30. Bus **tours** are run by Autocares Bonal, ✆ 95 827 31 00; check at the Granada tourist office for other companies. Most of them cost around *3000 pts* and run only at weekends, provided there are enough passengers.

If you're going by **car**, the road is open in August; it's a rough trip but worth it for the views. For **road snow reports** in English and Spanish, call © 95 824 91 19. Some 20km before you reach Veleta, you'll enter the **Solynieve** ski area, beginning at its main resort **Pradollano**, and continuing up to Veleta. From Pradollano there are cable cars up to the peak itself.

For Las Alpujarras: some **buses** on the Granada–Motril route stop in Lanjarón, but to penetrate the more isolated sections of the valley, you'll have to take a bus from Granada to Orjiva, the base for connecting buses to the other villages. With the area growing in popularity, routes are constantly being extended and increased, so it's always worth checking with the bus companies. For destinations further east, the Bacoma line (from Avenida de los Andaluces in front of Granada's train station) runs daily **buses** to Murcia and Alicante which stop in Guadix.

Tourist Information

For skiing information contact the tourist office in Granada or the Federación Andaluza de Montaña, Pso. de Ronda 101, © 95 829 13 40. *Open Mon–Fri 8.30–10.30pm.*

If you're adventurous and the road is clear, you can continue onwards from Veleta down into **Las Alpujarras**, a string of white villages along the valley of the Río Guadalfeo, between the Sierra Nevada and the little Contraviesa chain along the sea coast. In Moorish times this was a densely populated region, full of vines and orchards. Much of its population was made up of refugees from the Reconquista, coming mainly from Sevilla. Under the conditions for Granada's surrender in 1492, the region was granted as a fief to Boabdil el Chico but, with forced Christianization and the resulting revolts, the entire population was expelled and replaced by settlers from the north.

Most visitors don't chance the Sierra Nevada route to Capileira, but use the front door to Las Alpujarras, off the main road from Granada to Motril. On the way, just outside the city, you'll pass the spot called **Suspiro de Moro**, where poor Boabdil sighed as he took his last look back over Granada. His mother was less than sympathetic—'Weep like a woman for what you were incapable of defending like a man,' she told him. It gave Salman Rushdie the title for his novel *The Moor's Last Sigh* (1995). The last 33km (20½ miles) of this route, where the road joins the Guadalfeo valley down to Motril, is one of the most scenic in Spain, but if you want to see Las Alpujarras, you'll have to take the turn-off for **Lanjarón**, the principal tourist centre in the region. Lanjarón has been attracting visitors to its spas since Roman times and now markets its bottled water all across Spain. The ruined Moorish castle on the hill saw the Moors' last stand against the Imperial troops on March 8th 1500. Well and truly Catholic today, Lanjaran's *Semana Santa* celebrations are the most famous in the province.

Orjiva was made the regional capital by Isabel II in 1839 and it remains the biggest town of Las Alpujarras today. There are few remains of its Moorish past; the castle of the Counts of Sástago may look the part but it dates from the 17th century. Orjiva springs to life on Thursdays, when everyone congregates for the weekly market. From here you'll have a choice of keeping to the main road for **Ugíjar** or heading north through the highest and loveliest part of the region, with typical white villages climbing the hillsides under terraced fields. **Soportújar**, the first, has one of Las Alpujarras' surviving primeval oak groves behind it. Next comes **Pampaneira**, a pretty little town of cobbled streets and flowers. **Bubión** is a Berber-style village in a spectacular setting with a textile mill and tourist shops. All these villages are within sight of each other on a short detour along the edge of the beautiful (and walkable) ravine called **Barranco de Poqueira**. **Capileira**, the last village on the mountain-pass route over Mulhacén and Veleta, sees more tourists than most. Its treasure, in the church of Nuestra Señora de la Cabeza, is a statue of the Virgin donated to the village by Fernando and Isabella. North from here a tremendously scenic road takes you up across the Sierra Nevada and eventually to Granada. In winter this pass is snowbound, and even in summer you need to take extra care—it's steep and dangerous with precipitous drops down the ravines.

The road carries on through the villages of **Pórtugos**, a pilgrimage centre for Our Lady of Sorrows, and **Busquistar**, before arriving in **Trevélez**, on the slopes of Mulhacén. Trevélez likes to claim it's the highest village in Europe. It's also famous in Andalucía for its snow-cured hams—Henry Ford and Rossini were fans—and a ham feast is held in their honour every August. This is the main starting point for climbers heading for the summit of Mulhacén and the other peaks in the Sierra Nevada, but, despite the tacky tourist shops, there's little to detain other visitors.

From there the road slopes back downwards to **Juviles** and **Bérchules**, one of the villages where the tradition of carpet-weaving has been maintained since Moorish times. **Yegen**, some 10km further, became famous as the long-time home of British writer Gerald Brenan. After that come more intensively farmed areas on the lower slopes, with oranges, vineyards and almonds; you can either hit Ugíjar and the main roads to the coast and Almería, or detour to the seldom-visited villages of **Laroles** and **Mairena** on the slopes of **La Ragua**, one of the last high peaks of the Sierra Nevada.

Around the Sierra Nevada

It's a better road entering Granada from the west than that leaving it to the east. Between the city and Murcia are some of the emptiest, bleakest landscapes in Spain. The first village you pass through is **Purullena**, long famous for its pretty ceramic ware; the entire stretch of highway through it is lined with enormous stands and displays.

The poverty of this region has long forced many of its inhabitants to live in caves, and nowhere more so than in **Guadix**. Several thousand of this city's population, most of them gypsies, have homes, complete with whitewashed façades, chimneys and television aerials sticking out of the top, built into the hillsides. The centre of Guadix is dominated by a Moorish **Alcazaba**, largely rebuilt in the 16th century; near the arcaded central **Plaza Mayor** stands the huge **cathedral**, begun by Diego de Siloé, builder of Granada's cathedral, and given its magnificent façade in the 1700s by Andalucía's great rococo eccentric, Vicente Acero.

There's not much else to distract you in this corner of Spain. If you're headed for Almería and the coast (N324), you'll pass near **La Calahorra**, with an unusual Renaissance castle with domed turrets, and **Gérgal**, whose equally singular, perfectly preserved castle was built by the Moors. They claim you can see the stars more clearly here than anywhere in Europe, and Spain has built its national observatory outside the town. The N342 from Guadix west to Murcia is even lonelier; here the surprisingly elegant little whitewashed villages of **Vélez Blanco** and **Vélez Rubio** will provide a pleasant break in your travels. There are several caves in the neighbourhood where a wealth of 4000-year-old rock paintings of abstract patterns and symbols have been found.

Sierra Nevada ✉ 18196

Most of the ski hotels close from June to December. Ask at the tourist office in Granada for what's available, or contact the Cetursa Reservation Centre in Pradollano, ✆ 95 824 91 11. An exception, staying open all year round, is the ★★★ **Hotel Parador**, on the main highway, ✆ 95 848 06 61, ✉ 95 848 02 12 (*from 9500 pts low season, room only*), one of the smaller and newer *paradores*. Among the five modern hotels in the ski resort of Pradollano, none particularly stands out; in the skiing season accommodation at these places means a week's stay on half board for *90,000–120,000 pts per person* (*instruction extra*). In summer months the pleasant ★**Telecabina**, Pza. de Pradollano, ✆ 95 824 91 20, ✉ 95 824 91 22, has doubles for *9000 pts*.

The alpine-style ★★★**Kenia Nevada**, ✆ 95 848 09 11, ✉ 95 848 08 07, has a jacuzzi, pool, gym and sauna for those stiff days on the slopes (*high season doubles go from 19,500 pts*). Cheaper accommodation can be had at Peñones de San Francisco, where the **Albergue Universitario**, ✆ 95 848 01 22, has rooms for *3500 pts* for half board. Most restaurants are open only in the skiing season, and most are a little pretentious—but that's ski resorts for you. **Rincón de Pepe Reyes** in Pradollano has good Andaluz cooking (*2000–3000 pts*). You can take the cable car up to the frenetic and none-too-clean **Borreguiles** café/restaurant, ✆ 95 848 00 79, halfway up Veleta, and sit out on the terrace to take in the view. In Edificio Bulgaria, try the **Ruta de Veleta**, ✆ 95 848 12 28 (*4000 pts*).

Las Alpujarras

Lanjarón has most of the rooms; a score of good bargains in the *3000–4000 pts* range are to be found on or near the central Calle Generalísimo Franco. Elsewhere, you'll find minimal though acceptable accommodation and food in Orjiva, Pampaneira, Capileira and Ugíjar. In Pórtugos is the ★**Mirador de Pórtugos**, ✆ 95 876 60 14 (*7900 pts*) and the ★★**Nuevo Malagueño**, Ctra. Orgiva–Trevélez, ✆ 95 876 60 98, with comfortable rooms and views over the Alpujarras (*7200 pts*). The **Hostal Mulhacén**, Ctra. Ugíjar, ✆ 95 885 85 87, in Trevélez is well situated for hill walks and the annual all-night pilgrimage up Spain's highest mountain at midnight on August 4th. The *hostal* is also beside the river, where locals swim during the summer (*5000 pts*).

In Trevélez, **Mesón Haraiçel**, ✆ 95 885 85 30, serves delicious Arabic-influenced food with plenty of almond sauces and meat dishes. Try a *soplillo* for dessert (honey and almond meringue, *80 pts*). A three-course meal will cost around *1500 pts*. **La Fragua**, Barro del Medio, ✆ 95 885 85 73, concentrates on Alpujarras specialities, with several dishes featuring mountain-cured ham (*2000–3000 pts*). The **Alpujarras Grill** in Orgiva, Ctra. de Trevélez, ✆ 95 878 55 49, does a wonderful roast kid, while the **Finca Los Llanos**, Ctra. de Sierra Nevada, ✆ 95 876 30 71, in Capileira, is known for its speciality: aubergines in honey.

In Ugíjar, the **Hostal Vidaña**, Ctra. de Almería, ✆ 95 876 70 10 serves up humungous portions of delicious mountain fare, such as partridge, goat and rabbit.

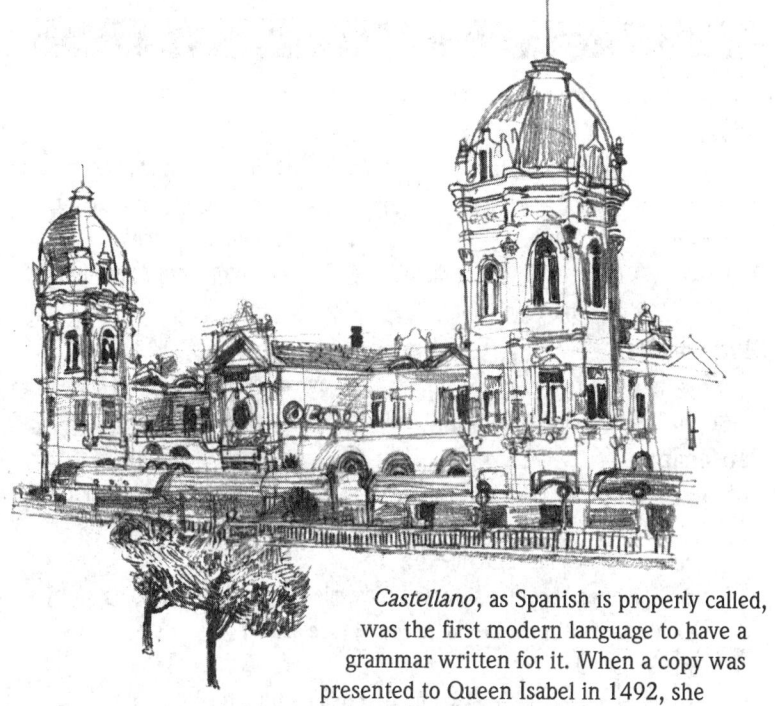

Castellano, as Spanish is properly called, was the first modern language to have a grammar written for it. When a copy was presented to Queen Isabel in 1492, she understandably asked what it was for. 'Your majesty', replied a perceptive bishop, 'language is the perfect instrument of empire'. In the centuries to come, this concise, flexible and expressive language would prove just that: an instrument that would contribute more to Spanish unity than any laws or institutions, while spreading itself effortlessly over much of the New World.

Among other European languages, Spanish is closest to Portuguese and Italian—and of course, Catalan and Gallego. Spanish, however, may have the simplest grammar of any Romance language, and if you know a little of any one of these, you will find much of the vocabulary looks familiar. It's quite easy to pick up a working knowledge of Spanish; but Spaniards speak colloquially and fast, and in Andalucía they do it with a pronounced accent, leaving out half the consonants and adding some strange sounds all their own. Expressing yourself may prove a little easier than understanding the replies. Spaniards will appreciate your efforts, and when they correct you, they aren't being snooty; they simply feel it's their duty to help you learn. There are dozens of language books and tapes on the market; one particularly good one is *Teach Yourself Spanish*, by Juan Kattán-Ibarra (Hodder & Stoughton, 1984). If you already speak Spanish, note

Language

that the Spaniards increasingly use the familiar *tú* instead of *usted* when addressing even complete strangers.

Pronunciation

Pronunciation is phonetic but somewhat difficult for English speakers.

Vowels

a	short *a* as in 'pat'	u	silent after *q* and gue- and gui-;
e	short *e* as in 'set'		otherwise long *u* as in 'flute'
i	as *e* in 'be'	ü	*w* sound, as in 'dwell'
o	between long *o* of 'note'	y	at end of word or meaning *and*, as **i**
	and short *o* of 'hot'		

Dipthongs

ai, ay	as *i* in 'side'	**ei, ey**	as *ey* in 'they'
au	as *ou* in 'sound'	**oi, oy**	as *oy* of 'boy'

Consonants

c	before the vowels *i* and *e*, it's a *castellano* tradition to pronounce it as *th*; many Spaniards and all Latin Americans pronounce it in this case as an *s*
ch	like *ch* in 'church'
d	often becomes *th*, or is almost silent, at end of word
g	before *i* or *e*, pronounced as **j** (*see below*)
h	silent
j	the *ch* in loch—a guttural, throat-clearing *h*
ll	*y* or *ly* as in million
ñ	*ny* as in canyon (the ~ is called a tilde)
q	*k*
r	usually rolled, which takes practice
v	often pronounced as *b*
z	*th*, but *s* in parts of Andalucía

Stress is on the penultimate syllable if the word ends in a vowel, an *n* or an *s*, and on the last syllable if the word ends in any other consonant; exceptions are marked with an accent.

If all this seems difficult, consider that English pronunciation is even worse for Spaniards. Young people in Spain seem to be all madly learning English these days; if your Spanish friends giggle at your pronunciation, get them to try to say *squirrel*.

Practise on some of the place names:

Madrid	ma-DREED	**Trujillo**	troo-HEE-oh
León	lay-OHN	**Jerez**	her-ETH
Sevilla	se-BEE-ah	**Badajóz**	ba-da-HOTH
Cáceres	CAH-ther-es	**Málaga**	MAHL-ah-gah
Cuenca	KWAYN-ka	**Alcázar**	ahl-CATH-ar
Jaén	ha-AIN	**Valladolid**	ba-yah-dol-EED
Sigüenza	sig-WAYN-thah	**Arévalo**	ahr-EB-bah-lo

Time

What time is it?	*¿Qué hora es?*	morning	*mañana*
It is 2 o'clock	*Son las dos*	afternoon	*tarde*
… half past 2	*… las dos y media*	evening	*noche*
… a quarter past 2	*… las dos y cuarto*	today	*hoy*
… a quarter to 3	*… las tres menos cuarto*	yesterday	*ayer*
		soon	*pronto*
month	*mes*	tomorrow	*mañana*
week	*semana*	it is early	*está temprano*
day	*día*	it is late	*está tarde*

Days

Monday	*lunes*	Friday	*viernes*
Tuesday	*martes*	Saturday	*sábado*
Wednesday	*miércoles*	Sunday	*domingo*
Thursday	*jueves*		

Shopping and Sightseeing

I would like…	*Quisiera…*	pharmacy	*farmacía*
Where is/are…?	*¿Dónde está/están…?*	post office	*correos*
How much is it?	*¿Cuánto vale eso?*	postage stamp	*sello*
open	*abierto*	sea	*mar*
closed	*cerrado*	shop	*tienda*
cheap/expensive	*barato/caro*	Do you have any change?	*¿Tiene cambio?*
bank	*banco*		
beach	*playa*	telephone	*teléfono*
booking/box office	*taquilla*	toilet/toilets	*servicios/aseos*
church	*iglesia*	men	*señores/ hombres/caballeros*
museum	*museo*		
theatre	*teatro*	women	*señoras/damas*

Accommodation

Where is the hotel?	*¿Dónde está el hotel?*	week?	*semana?*
		… with 2 beds	*con dos camas*
Do you have a room?	*¿Tiene usted una habitación?*	… with double bed	*con una cama grande*
Can I look at the room?	*¿Podría ver la habitación?*	… with a shower/ bath	*con ducha/baño*
How much is the room per day/	*¿Cuánto cuesta la habitación por día/*	… for one night/ one week	*una noche/ una semana*

Driving

rent	*alquiler*	driver	*conductor, chófer*
car	*coche*		
motorbike/moped	*moto/ciclomotor*	exit	*salida*
bicycle	*bicicleta*	entrance	*entrada*
petrol	*gasolina*	danger	*peligro*
This doesn't work	*Este no funciona*	dangerous	*peligroso*
road	*carretera*	no parking	*estacionamento prohibido*
Is the road good?	*¿Es buena la carretera?*	give way/yield	*ceda el paso*
breakdown	*avería*	road works	*obras*
(international) driving licence	*carnet de conducir (internacional)*	Note: Most road signs will be in international pictographs	

Transport

aeroplane	*avión*	platform	*andén*
airport	*aeropuerto*	port	*puerto*
bus/coach	*autobús/autocar*	seat	*asiento*
bus/railway station	*estación*	ship	*buque/barco/ embarcadero*
bus stop	*parada*		
car/automobile	*coche*	ticket	*billete*
customs	*aduana*	train	*tren*

Directions

I want to go to...	*Deseo ir a...*	Have a good trip!	*¡Buen viaje!*
How can I get to...?	*¿Cómo puedo llegar a...?*	here	*aquí*
		there	*allí*
Where is...?	*¿Dónde está...?*	close	*cerca*
When is the next...?	*¿Cuándo sale el próximo...?*	far	*lejos*
		left	*izquierda*
What time does it leave (arrive)?	*¿Parte (llega) a qué hora?*	right	*derecha*
		straight on	*todo recto*
From where does it leave?	*¿De dónde sale?*	forwards	*adelante*
		backwards	*hacia atrás*
Do you stop at ...?	*¿Para en...?*	up	*arriba*
How long does the trip take?	*¿Cuánto tiempo dura el viaje?*	down	*abajo*
		corner	*esquina*
I want a (return) ticket to...	*Quiero un billete (de ida y vuelta) a*	square	*plaza*
How much is the fare?	*¿Cuánto cuesta el billete?*	street	*calle*

Fish (*Pescados*)

acedías	small plaice	*langosta*	lobster
adobo	fish marinated in white wine	*langostinos*	giant prawns
		mariscos	shellfish
almejas	clams	*mejillones*	mussels
anchoas	anchovies	*merluza*	hake
anguilas	eels	*mero*	grouper
ástaco	crayfish	*navajas*	razor-shell clams
bacalao	codfish (usually dried)	*ostras*	oysters
bogavante	lobster	*percebes*	barnacles
calamares	squid	*pescadilla*	whiting
cangrejo	crab	*pez espada*	swordfish
chanquetes	whitebait	*platija*	plaice
chipirones	cuttlefish	*pulpo*	octopus
... en su tinta	...in its own ink	*rape*	anglerfish
dorado, lubina	sea bass,	*trucha*	trout
escabeche	pickled or marinated fish	*veneras*	scallops
gambas	prawns	*zarzuela*	fish stew

Meat and Fowl (*Carnes y Aves*)

albóndigas	meatballs	*morcilla*	blood sausage
asado	roast	*pato*	duck
buey	ox	*pavo*	turkey
callos	tripe	*perdiz*	partridge
cerdo	pork	*pinchitos*	spicy mini kebabs
chorizo	spiced sausage		
chuletas	chops	*pollo*	chicken
cochinillo	sucking pig	*rabo/cola de toro*	bull's tail with onions and tomatoes
conejo	rabbit		
corazón	heart		
cordero	lamb	*salchicha*	sausage
faisán	pheasant	*salchichón*	salami
fiambres	cold meats	*sesos*	brains
hígado	liver	*solomillo*	sirloin steak
jabalí	wild boar	*ternera*	veal
jamón de York	raw cured ham		
jamón serrano	baked ham		
lomo	pork loin		

Note: *potajes, cocidos, guisados, estofados, fabadas* and *cazuelas* are various kinds of stew.

Vegetables (*Verduras y Legumbres*)

alcachofas	artichokes	*espinacas*	spinach
apio	celery	*garbanzos*	chickpeas
arroz	rice	*judías (verdes)*	French beans
arroz marinera	rice with saffron and seafood	*lechuga*	lettuce
		lentejas	lentils
berenjena	aubergine (eggplant)	*patatas (fritas/salteadas)*	potatoes (fried/sautéed)
cebolla	onion	*(al horno)*	(baked)
champiñones	mushrooms	*puerros*	leeks
col, repollo	cabbage	*remolachas*	beetroots (beets)
coliflor	cauliflower	*setas*	Spanish mushrooms
endibias	endives		
espárragos	asparagus	*zanahorias*	carrots

Desserts (*Postres*)

arroz con leche	rice pudding	*pajama*	flan with ice cream
bizcocho/pastel/torta	cake		
blanco y negro	ice cream and coffee float	*pasteles*	pastries
		queso	cheese
flan	crème caramel	*requesón*	cottage cheese
galletas	biscuits (cookies)	*tarta de frutas*	fruit pie
helados	ice creams	*turrón*	nougat

Restaurant Vocabulary

menu	*carta/menú*	**Can I see the menu, please?**	*Déme el menú, por favor*
bill/check	*cuenta*		
change	*cambio*	**Do you have a wine list?**	*¿Hay una lista de vinos?*
set meal	*menú del día*		
waiter/waitress	*camarero/a*	**Can I have the bill (check), please?**	*La cuenta, por favor*
Do you have a table?	*¿Tiene una mesa?*		
... for one/two?	*¿... para uno/dos?*	**Can I pay by credit card?**	*¿Puedo pagar con tarjeta de crédito?*

Historical, Architectural, Geographical Terms

ajimez	in Moorish architecture, an arched double window
Aaameda	park or promenade
ayuntamiento	city hall
azulejo	painted glazed tiles, popular in Moorish and *mudéjar* work and later architecture
baldachin	canopy on posts over an altar or throne
barrio	city quarter or neighbourhood
calvario	calvary, or outdoor Stations of the Cross
castizo	anything purely Spanish (from the Castilian point of view)
castrum	Roman military camp
churrigueresque	florid Baroque style of the late 17th and early 18th centuries in the style of José Churriguera (1650–1725), Spanish architect and sculptor
converso	Jew who converted to Christianity
coro	walled-in choir in the centre of a Spanish cathedral
corregidor	royal magistrate
cortes	Spanish Parliament
fueros	exemptions, or privileges of a region under medieval Spanish law
hidalgo	literally 'son of somebody'—the lowest level of the nobility, just good enough for a coat-of-arms
homage tower	the tallest tower of a fortification, sometimes detached from the wall
hórreo	Asturian or Galician granary or corn crib
Isabelline Gothic	late 15th-century style, roughly corresponding to the English Perpendicular
judería	Jewish quarter
mirador	a scenic overlook or belvedere
modernista	Catalan Art Nouveau
morisco	Muslims who submitted to Christianization to remain in Spain after the Reconquista
mozarabic	referring to Christians under Muslim rule in Moorish Spain
mudéjar	Moorish-influenced architecture; Spain's 'National style' in the 12th–16th centuries
ogival	pointed (arches)
pallazo	circular, conical-roofed shepherd's hut in Asturias and Galicia
pazo	Galician manor house
Plateresque	16th-century style; heavily ornamented Gothic
plaza de toros	bullring
pronunciamiento	a military coup
reja	iron grilles, either decorative ones in churches or those covering the exterior windows of buildings
retablo	carved or painted altarpiece
transitional	in northern Spanish churches, referring to the transition between Romanesque and Gothic

Borrow, George, *The Bible in Spain* (various editions, first written in 1843). A jolly travel account by a preposterous Protestant Bible salesman in 19th-century Spain.

Boyle, Christine and Chris Nawrat, *The Traveller's Food and Wine Guide: Spain and Portugal* (Carberry). Pocket guide deciphering menus in Castilian and Catalan.

Brenan, Gerald, *Spanish Labyrinth* (Cambridge, 1943), *The Literature of the Spanish People* (Cambridge, 1951), *South from Granada*, a classic on living in a remote Andalucian village in the 1920s (Penguin).

Burckhardt, Titus, *Moorish Culture in Spain* (out of print). Vital for understanding the world of Al-Andalus.

Calderon de la Barca, Pedro, *Life is a Dream* (Nick Hern). The Catholic Hamlet.

Casas, Penelope, *The Foods and Wines of Spain* (Penguin). The best Spanish cookbook in English.

Castro, Américo, *The Structure of Spanish History* (E. L. King, 1954).

Cervantes, Miguel de, *Don Quixote* (Penguin and other editions). As great as its reputation.

Elliot, J. H., *Imperial Spain 1469–1714* (Pelican, 1983). Elegant proof that much of the best writing these days is in the field of history.

Epton, Nina, *Navarre: the Flea between Two Monkeys*, and *Grapes and Granite* (on Galicia); good reads.

Ford, Richard, *Gatherings from Spain* (Everyman). A boiled-down version of the all-time classic travel-book *A Handbook for Travellers in Spain*, written in 1845. Hard to find but worth the trouble.

Gibson, Ian, *Fire in the Blood* (Faber). Fascinating introduction and analysis of the New Spain and its spirit of *desfase*—happily unresolvable paradoxes; also *The Assassination of Federico García Lorca* (Penguin).

Harrison, Richard J., *Spain at the Dawn of History* (Thames and Hudson). Spain before the Romans.

Harvey, L.P., *Islamic Spain, 1250–1500* (Chicago University Press). A thorough account.

Harnilton, R. and Janet Perry, translators, *The Poem of the Cid*, (Penguin).

Hemingway, Ernest, *The Sun Also Rises*, (*Fiesta* in the UK) and *Death in the Afternoon* (various editions).

Hooper, John, *The Spaniards* (Viking, 1993). A comprehensive account of modern Spanish life and politics.

Hughes, Robert, *Barcelona* (Harvill, Vintage). Fat, erudite and witty: not only the best book on Barcelona and the Catalans, but one of the best tales of a city, full stop.

Irving, Washington, *Tales of the Alhambra* (various editions).

Keay, S.J., *Roman Spain* (British Museum/University of California). Lively new account of the period.

Lee, Laurie, *As I Walked Out One Midsummer Morning* and *A Rose for Winter*. Very well-written adventures of a young man in Spain in 1936, walking from Vigo to Málaga and his return 20 years later.

Lojendio, Louis, *Navarre Romaine,* one of the excellent illustrated volumes in the French Zodiaque series on medieval art; other pertinent volumes for nothern Spain are *Le Pre-Romaine Hispanique* (on the Visigoths and Asturian churches) and *Le Mozarabe*.

Lorca, Federico García, *Three Tragedies and Five Plays* (Penguin). Good translation of his best works.

Morris, Jan, *Spain* (Penguin, 1982). A little disappointing; dubious ideas sustained by crystalline prose.

Mitchell, David, *The Spanish Civil War* (Granada, 1982). Anecdotal; wonderful photographs.

Mullins, Edwin, *The Pilgrimage to Santiago* (Secker & Warburg/Taplinger). Perhaps the most colourful and wide-ranging account of the journey.

Orwell, George, *Homage to Catalonia* (Penguin). Fascinating first-hand account of the Civil War in and around Barcelona.

Pritchett, V.S., *The Spanish Temper* (Hogarth Press). Evocative account of Spain in the 1950s—another country altogether.

Thomas, Hugh, *The Spanish Civil War* (Penguin, 1977). The best general work.

Zabalbeascoa, Anatxu, *The New Spanish Architecure* (Rizzoli). Well-illustrated account of the fruits of Spain's edifice complex in the 1980s to the present.

Main page references are in **bold**; page references to maps are in *italics*

Index